The Wiley-Blackwell Handbook of
Childhood Social Development

Wiley-Blackwell Handbooks of Developmental Psychology

This outstanding series of handbooks provides a cutting-edge overview of classic research, current research, and future trends in developmental psychology.

- Each handbook draws together 25–30 newly commissioned chapters to provide a comprehensive overview of a sub-discipline of developmental psychology.
- The international team of contributors to each handbook has been specially chosen for its expertise and knowledge of each field.
- Each handbook is introduced and contextualized by leading figures in the field, lending coherence and authority to each volume.

The *Blackwell Handbooks of Developmental Psychology* will provide an invaluable overview for advanced students of developmental psychology and for researchers as an authoritative definition of their chosen field.

Published

The Wiley-Blackwell Handbook of Infant Development, 2nd edition
Edited by Gavin Bremner and Theodore D. Wachs

The Wiley-Blackwell Handbook of Childhood Social Development, 2nd edition
Edited by Peter K. Smith and Craig H. Hart

The Wiley-Blackwell Handbook of Childhood Cognitive Development, 2nd edition
Edited by Usha Goswami

Blackwell Handbook of Adolescence
Edited by Gerald R. Adams and Michael D. Berzonsky

The Science of Reading: A Handbook
Edited by Margaret J. Snowling and Charles Hulme

The Blackwell Handbook of Early Childhood Development
Edited by Kathleen McCartney and Deborah A. Phillips

The Blackwell Handbook of Language Development
Edited by Erika Hoff and Marilyn Shatz

Not yet published

The Blackwell Handbook of Developmental Psychology in Action
Rudolph Schaffer and Kevin Durkin

The Wiley-Blackwell Handbook of Adulthood and Aging
Susan Krauss Whitbourne and Martin Sliwinski

The Wiley-Blackwell Handbook of Childhood Social Development

Second Edition

Edited by

Peter K. Smith and Craig H. Hart

⟨W⟩WILEY-BLACKWELL

A John Wiley & Sons, Ltd., Publication

This second edition first published 2011
© 2011 Blackwell Publishing Ltd

Edition history: Blackwell Publishing Ltd (1e, 2002).

Blackwell Publishing was acquired by John Wiley & Sons in February 2007. Blackwell's publishing program has been merged with Wiley's global Scientific, Technical, and Medical business to form Wiley-Blackwell.

Registered Office
John Wiley & Sons Ltd, The Atrium, Southern Gate, Chichester, West Sussex, PO19 8SQ, UK

Editorial Offices
350 Main Street, Malden, MA 02148-5020, USA
9600 Garsington Road, Oxford, OX4 2DQ, UK
The Atrium, Southern Gate, Chichester, West Sussex, PO19 8SQ, UK

For details of our global editorial offices, for customer services, and for information about how to apply for permission to reuse the copyright material in this book please see our website at www.wiley.com/wiley-blackwell.

The right of Peter K. Smith and Craig H. Hart to be identified as the authors of the editorial material in this work has been asserted in accordance with the UK Copyright, Designs and Patents Act 1988.

Wiley also publishes its books in a variety of electronic formats. Some content that appears in print may not be available in electronic books.

Designations used by companies to distinguish their products are often claimed as trademarks. All brand names and product names used in this book are trade names, service marks, trademarks or registered trademarks of their respective owners. The publisher is not associated with any product or vendor mentioned in this book. This publication is designed to provide accurate and authoritative information in regard to the subject matter covered. It is sold on the understanding that the publisher is not engaged in rendering professional services. If professional advice or other expert assistance is required, the services of a competent professional should be sought.

Library of Congress Cataloging-in-Publication Data

The Wiley-Blackwell handbook of childhood social development / [edited by] Peter K. Smith, Craig H. Hart. – 2nd ed.
        p. cm. – (Wiley-Blackwell handbooks of developmental psychology)
    Originally published under title: The Blackwell handbook of childhood social development
    Includes bibliographical references and index.
    ISBN 978-1-4051-9679-6 (hardback)
    1. Developmental psychology–Social aspects.   2. Child psychology–Social
aspects.   I. Smith, Peter K.   II. Hart, Craig H., 1957-   III. Blackwell handbook of
childhood social development.   IV. Title: Handbook of childhood social development.
    BF713.B565 2011
    155.4'13–dc22

                        2010021920

A catalogue record for this book is available from the British Library.

Set in 10.5 on 12.5 pt Adobe Garamond by Toppan Best-set Premedia Limited
Printed and bound in Singapore by Markono Print Media Pte Ltd

1   2010

Contents

List of Contributors

Alisa Almas, University of Toronto, Toronto, Canada

Harriet A. Ball, King's College, University of London, London, England

Martyn Barrett, University of Surrey, Guildford, England

Amy D. Bellmore, University of Wisconsin, Madison, WI, USA

Joyce Benenson, Emmanuel College, Boston, MA, USA

Oana Benga, Babeş-Bolyai University, Cluj-Napoca, Romania

Mihaly Berkics, Hungarian Academy of Sciences, Budapest, Hungary

David F. Bjorklund, Florida Atlantic University, Boca Raton, FL, USA

Julie C. Bowker, University at Buffalo, Buffalo, NY, USA

Laura E. Brumariu, Kent State University, Kent, OH, USA

Eithne Buchanan-Barrow, University of Surrey, Guildford, England

Tanya M. M. Button, University of Colorado at Boulder, Boulder, CO, USA

Simona C. S. Caravita, Catholic University of the Sacred Heart, Brescia, Italy

Jeremy Carpendale, Simon Fraser University, Burnaby, Canada

Charissa S. L. Cheah, University of Maryland, Baltimore, MD, USA

Xinyin Chen, University of Pennsylvania, Philadelphia, PA, USA

Jui-Chih Chin, Taipei Municipal University of Education, Taipei City, Taiwan

Janet Chung, University of Western Ontario, London, Canada

Antonius H. N. Cillessen, Radboud Universiteit Nijmegen, Nijmegen, The Netherlands and University of Connecticut, Storrs, CT, USA

Leanna M. Closson, University of British Columbia, Vancouver, Canada

W. Andrew Collins, University of Minnesota ,Twin Cities, MN, USA

Robert J. Coplan, Carleton University, Ottawa, Canada

Sarah M. Coyne, Brigham Young University, Provo, UT, USA

Susanne Denham, George Mason University, Fairfax, VA, USA

Karen E. Diamond, Purdue University, West Lafayette, IN, USA

Doran French, Purdue University, West Lafayette, IN, USA

Márta Fülöp, Hungarian Academy of Sciences, Budapest, Hungary

Heidi Fung, Academia Sinica, Taipei, Taiwan

Elena Geangu, Durham University, Durham, England

Kate Gee, University of Sheffield, Sheffield, England

Susan Golombok, University of Cambridge, Cambridge, England

Alice M. Gregory, Goldsmiths, University of London, London, England

Joan E. Grusec, University of Toronto, Toronto, Canada

Gerald Handel, The City College and The Graduate Center, City University of New York, New York, USA

Craig H. Hart, Brigham Young University, Provo, UT, USA

Paul Hastings, Concordia University, West Montreal, Canada

Charles C. Helwig, University of Toronto, Toronto, Canada

Sheryl A. Hemphill, Murdoch Children's Research Institute, Parkville, Australia

Melissa Hines, University of Cambridge, Cambridge, England

Ernest V. E. Hodges, University of Turku, Turku, Finland and St. John's University, New York, USA

Nina Howe, Concordia University, West Montreal, Canada

Carollee Howes, University of California, Los Angeles, Los Angeles, CA, USA

Hsin-Hui Huang, National Taipei University of Nursing and Health Science, Taipei, Taiwan

Shelley Hymel, University of British Columbia, Vancouver, Canada

Kathryn A. Kerns, Kent State University, Kent, OH, USA

Becky Kochenderfer-Ladd, Arizona State University, Tempe, AZ, USA

Rajani Konantambigi, Tata Institute of Social Sciences, Mumbai, India

Willem Koops, Utrecht University, Utrecht, The Netherlands

Janis B. Kupersmidt, University of North Carolina at Chapel Hill and Innovation Research and Training, Chapel Hill, NC, USA

Gary W. Ladd, Arizona State University, Tempe, AZ, USA

Rachel Lechcier-Kimel, University of Western Ontario, London, Canada

Christy Y. Y. Leung, University of Maryland, Baltimore, MD, USA

Charlie Lewis, University of Lancaster, Lancaster, England

Marc D. Lewis, University of Toronto, Toronto, Canada

Sandee McClowry, New York University, New York, USA

Melissa Menzer, University of Maryland, College Park, MD, USA

David A. Nelson, Brigham Young University, Provo, UT, USA

Vickie Pasterski, University of Warwick, Coventry, England

Kätlin Peets, University of Turku, Turku, Finland

Anthony D. Pellegrini, University of Minnesota, Minnesota, MN, USA

Thomas G. Power, Washington State University, Pullman, WA, USA

Stephen M. Quintana, University of Wisconsin, Madison, WI, USA

Holly Recchia, University of Utah, Salt Lake City, UT, USA

Stephanie M. Reich, University of California, Irvine, CA, USA

Hildy S. Ross, University of Waterloo, Waterloo, Canada

Kenneth H. Rubin, University of Maryland, College Park, MD, USA

Alan Russell, The Flinders University of South Australia, Adelaide, Australia

Ann-Margret Rydell, University of Uppsala, Uppsala, Sweden

Christina Salmivalli, University of Turku, Turku, Finland and University of Stavanger, Stavanger, Norway

Mónika Sándor, Eötvös Loránd University, Budapest, Hungary

Ann Sanson, University of Melbourne, Melbourne, Australia

Barry H. Schneider, University of Ottawa, Ottawa, Canada

Peter K. Smith, Goldsmiths, University of London, London, England

Christopher Spencer, University of Sheffield, Sheffield, England

Elizabeth A. Steed, Georgia State University, Atlanta, GA, USA

Elliot Turiel, University of California, Berkeley, CA, USA

Marion Underwood, University of Texas at Dallas, Dallas, TX, USA

Tracy Vaillancourt, University of Ottawa, Ottawa, Canada

Deborah Lowe Vandell, University of California, Irvine, CA, USA

Suman Verma, Panjab University, Chandigarh, India

Mary Ellen Voegler-Lee, University of North Carolina at Chapel Hill, Chapel Hill, NC, USA

Maria von Salisch, Freie Universitat Berlin, Berlin, Germany

Heather Warren, George Mason University, Fairfax, VA, USA

Steven Woltering, University of Toronto, Toronto, Canada

Bilge Yagmurlu, Koç University, Istanbul, Turkey

Introduction by the Editors

Peter K. Smith and Craig H. Hart

This is the second edition of this handbook, which has proved to be a successful volume in a successful series. In editing this second edition, we have sought to maintain the strengths of the first edition, update and further strengthen the breadth of coverage, and provide an advanced text that will be useful to many individual researchers, as well as an indispensable library resource. Many features are in common with the first edition, but there are some distinctive new features that we mention below.

This volume is part of a series, and there are companion volumes on infancy, cognitive development in childhood, and adolescence. Thus, the age range covered in this volume is broadly from postinfancy (around 3 years) up to adolescence. It does not include material on infancy, or adolescence and beyond, except in so far as it might be necessary for understanding or contextualizing the theories, methods, and findings of the research in childhood. Of course, a wide age range remains, from preschool (3 to 5 years), to early school (5 to 7 years), through to later elementary or middle school (8 to 11 years). Also, the chapters focus on social development. This includes several chapters in the social cognition area, which is covered in Part VIII.

We asked for chapters at a certain level. Thus this handbook is not meant for beginners in the area. Those who have not studied child development previously will be better served by one of the many introductory texts available. The brief we gave to authors was to give a clear and succinct account of work in their area, which would be suitable for anyone wishing to go beyond basic textbook coverage. This would include advanced undergraduates in psychology and behavioral sciences, and postgraduates taking taught master's degrees or pursuing independent research. It will also include teaching staff and researchers who wish for an authoritative update outside their immediate teaching or research area. The book should also be useful for those professionals outside academic life – for example, educators, social workers, counselors, and probation officers – who have had training in the behavioral sciences and retain an active interest in the implications of research for their professional practice.

As in the first edition, we attempted to get – and feel we have succeeded in getting – a good geographical coverage of contributors. Much of the work in our domain does come from North America, and it is appropriate that about half our contributors come from the United States. However, it is also appropriate that we have contributors from Canada, the United Kingdom, the Netherlands, Sweden, Finland, Germany, Hungary, Italy, Romania, Turkey, Taiwan, India, and Australia. This reflects the increasingly international community of child development researchers. As we forecast in the introduction to the first edition, it is a broader spread than we had then, in 2001.

Regardless of their origin, we asked our contributors to be not only clear and succinct but also interesting and, where appropriate, challenging. In our letters of invitation we asked authors to "provide authoritative reviews of focused areas in social development, which both summarize existing knowledge, and highlight areas of debate and growing points in the discipline." We worked with authors, sometimes intensively, to try to ensure that this was achieved.

For this new edition, although we retained some contributors from the first edition, over half are new contributors. In all cases we pointed out that this new edition was being designed to capture emerging trends in the study of childhood social development as well as to provide updated insights on traditional topics covered in the first edition. We have some extra chapters: 34 compared to 30 in the first edition. We have broadened Part II on different disciplinary views, including the history of childhood and new perspectives from neuroscience. There is also a new chapter on culture and acculturation, and two new chapters on intervening in social development, including one from the perspective of developing countries. Part III includes a new chapter on environmental psychology in relation to social development. There are also other changes (e.g., we decided that rather than have separate chapters on pretend play and rough-and-tumble play, one integrated chapter was sufficient and perhaps preferable).

We have nine parts in this new handbook. The first part is a single chapter, providing a historical overview of psychological research in social development. The second part (six chapters) covers different disciplinary perspectives. The third part (four chapters) is on ecological contexts for social development. The fourth part (five chapters) is on contextual factors such as temperament, child care experience, parental and peer influences compared, sex, and ethnicity. The fifth part (three chapters) is on the family context. The sixth part (four chapters) is on the peer group context. The seventh part (four chapters) covers play, cooperation and competition, aggression, and bullying. Part VIII (four chapters) covers areas broadly in social cognition. Finally, Part IX (three chapters) covers interventions, and children with disabilities, in relation to social development. In short part introductions, we highlight particular areas of debate or contrasting perspectives among the chapters.

We have enjoyed working with the authors, and with our publishers, now transmuted from Blackwell to Wiley-Blackwell. We hope that you will also enjoy the end product, and find it a useful and rewarding resource, whether for study, teaching, research, or professional practice.

PART I

Historical Overview

This part of the handbook has only one chapter, but it is a chapter that sets the scene for the rest of the book. W. Andrew Collins is in an excellent position to do this. He has worked for many years at the Institute of Child Development at the University of Minnesota, which was one of the pioneering sites of study of young children in North America. Much valuable work was done from the 1920s onward, including Mildred Parten's famous work on social participation in preschool children (Parten, 1932), which was based on her doctoral thesis at the institute.

Collins outlines what are now seen as three main eras in the study of childhood development. The emergent era (around 1890–1919) marks the beginning of systematic interest in children's social development, including baby diaries and some empirical studies. The middle period (around 1920–1946) saw a great increase in research, including the founding of child study centers and institutes (as at Minnesota, discussed above); normative descriptions of child behaviors; the development of observational, experimental, and questionnaire methodologies; and theoretical influences from behaviorism, psychoanalysis, and symbolic interactionism. The modern era (from around 1947 to the present) has seen the more structuralist approaches of Jean Piaget and Kohlberg, and a general consensus around the scientific nature of child development, moving beyond descriptive studies to testing various theoretical approaches in different domains.

The "modern era" is now over 60 years in duration, and it is likely that future historians of the period will, looking back, subdivide it into further periods. Many of the changes in approaches and methodologies are summarized by Collins in this chapter. Researchers in recent decades have developed more sophisticated quantitative approaches (such as multilevel analyses and structural equation modeling). In other areas, there has been increased interest in qualitative methodologies, and more participation or involvement of young people in research. And in recent years, it is clear that advances in behavior

---

The Wiley-Blackwell Handbook of Childhood Social Development, Second Edition, edited by Peter K. Smith and Craig H. Hart
© 2011 by Blackwell Publishing Ltd.

genetics (see Chapter 2) and neuropsychology (Chapter 3) are impacting our understanding of social development. These will take forward our discipline in new and potentially exciting ways; and it is easy to ignore the past and how we got to where we are. But the past may still exert a strong influence on the parameters of our present thinking, and we may learn something too from the successes and failures of our predecessors.

Reference

Parten, M. B. (1932). Social participation among preschool children. *Journal of Abnormal and Social Psychology, 27*, 243–269.

CHAPTER ONE

Historical Perspectives on Contemporary Research in Social Development

W. Andrew Collins

Research in social development began more than a century ago. Its roots are much older, springing from enduring philosophical traditions, as well as from theory and research in other sciences such as biology and pedagogical studies (e.g., Dewey, 1899; Hall, 1904). Only in the most general way, however, can these distal influences be discerned in the directions and concerns of social development research today. Much more visible are the intellectual currents within the social sciences themselves and themes arising from pressing social problems. The goal of this chapter is to detect those currents in this vital and increasingly diverse research enterprise.

The traditional purview of research in social development is "changes over time in the child's understanding of, attitudes toward, and actions with others" (Hartup & Laursen, 1991, p. 253). Although interest in these phenomena was apparent from the earliest research on psychological development, no history of social development as a coherent field of inquiry has previously appeared. Rather, existing historical accounts have addressed particular research topics (e.g., Eisenberg, 2002; Hartup & Laursen, 1999; Maccoby, 1992a, 1992b; Modell & Elder, 2002), the contributions of influential researchers (e.g., Arnett & Cravens, 2006; Cahan, 2003; Cairns, 1992; Emde, 1992; Grusec, 1992; Horowitz, 1992; White, 1992), and institutions and organizations that have shaped social development research (e.g., Hartup, Johnson, & Weinberg, 2002; Sears, 1975; Senn, 1975). This chapter aims to distill from these disparate efforts a historical perspective on contemporary research in the field. The chapter is divided into three sections: (a) a brief overview of historical trends, identifying significant shifts and transitions; (b) a description of major historical transformations in the field during the past century; and (c) an

The Wiley-Blackwell Handbook of Childhood Social Development, Second Edition, edited by Peter K. Smith and Craig H. Hart
© 2011 by Blackwell Publishing Ltd.

attempt to show how methodological issues have been interwoven with the substantive concerns of social development researchers.

Three Eras of Social Development Research

Few scholarly fields yield easily to simple chronological accounts. Social development is no exception. Cairns and Cairns's (2006) division of the first century of developmental psychology into three periods provides useful markers, with slight adjustments for social development: emergence (roughly 1890–1919), the middle period of institutionalization and expansion (1920–1946), and the modern era (from 1947 to the present). These broad divisions reveal striking variations in the degree to which systematic theoretical perspectives influenced the dominant questions and methods of social development research.

Emergence

Interest in the phenomena of social development suffuses early accounts of childhood, from the writings of philosophers to the writings of diarists and social historians (e.g., Darwin, 1877; Shinn, 1893–1899). Systematic scientific study began only in the final decade of the nineteenth century (White, 1992). Among the early efforts were Hall's questionnaire studies focusing on "(a) simple automatisms, instincts, and attitudes, (b) the small child's activities and feelings, (c) control of emotions and will," and the like (White, 1992, p. 29). In the same decade, studies of peer collaboration (Triplett, 1897) and similarity between friends' attitudes and values (Barnes, 1896–1897, 1902–1903; Monroe, 1899) appeared. The interests of these early researchers, if not their methods and interpretations, thus are strikingly like the topics that preoccupy researchers at the beginning of the 21st century.

Middle period

Initially, concern with theory in social development research was slight, at best. Researchers generally shared the view that "nascent social competences were … among the child's endowments, and the work of the scientist was to chart their unfolding" (Hartup, 1992, p. 107). This situation changed as views of psychological research shifted and as strong formal theories from other fields penetrated the study of social development. These converging forces asserted that experience, not merely the unfolding of natural endowments, was an essential element in development. The most commanding figure in American psychology at this time, Watson (1913), declared that learning alone accounted for development, effectively challenging the suppositions underlying most work in the field up to that point.

   The orientation to environmental forces in behavior and development intensified as psychoanalytic propositions permeated the literature. Although of greatest interest to clinical and personality psychologists, Freud's ideas further pressed social researchers to consider the nature and substance of socialization, or "the processes through which the child is assimilated into society" (Hartup, 1992, p. 107; Maccoby, 1992a, 1992b). Similar pressures emanated from sociological theories, such as symbolic interactionism (Cooley, 1909; Mead, 1934), that were concerned with how developmentally advanced individuals contribute to child growth and development. The interest in socialization born in this period dominated social development research from the 1930s until the 1960s and remains a salient theme today. Among its early ramifications were an emphasis on parental influences and a relative neglect of interactions with peers, who were thought to lack the experience and authority to serve as socializing agents (Hartup, 1992).

The modern era

The most recent sea change occurred in the 1960s with the renascence of structuralist ideas. Piaget's theory emphasized the significance of social processes and the role of the child as an active agent in development (Flavell, 1963). Without denying the role of authority figures in early development, Piaget (1932/1965) took the view that children most readily experienced the cognitive conflict necessary for developmental change when interacting with peers. Kohlberg (1969), in a germinal chapter on stage and sequence in social development, further developed the notion of cognitive conflict as a necessary ingredient of movement from one stage to another and peers as ideal social resources for this process. Kohlberg's essay remains the major marker of a shift to theory encompassing both social environments and a child actively operating on those elements.

Piaget's and Kohlberg's writings gave rise to a new interest among social developmentalists in a normative descriptive account of social cognitive functioning (e.g., Selman, 1980). For many researchers, however, issues of socialization and the prediction of social behavior remained salient (e.g., Dunn, 1992; Harris, 1992), raising the possibility that cognitive activity was central to other aspects of social development. Three current directions in the field have resulted from this impetus: (a) increasing interest in the ways in which children regulate their own behavior and emotions, (b) attention to biological processes in control and regulation, and (c) a conviction that the dyad is an essential unit of analysis in social development.

What Is Social Development the Development Of?
Historical Determinants

Over the first century of social development research, the answer to the question "What is social development the development of?" changed in concert not only with shifting theoretical emphases but also with changing societal views of optimal behavior (Beatty, Cahan, & Grant, 2006; Kagan, 1992; Sears, 1975). Early studies of children focused on the qualities of independence, intelligence, honesty, and sociability largely because "wise commentators in America were certain" that these qualities represented the ideal culmination of development (Kagan, 1992, p. 992). In an era with little theoretical commitment, social values determined the typical set of outcome variables of interest in psychological research.

As psychoanalytic theory and its offshoots became more dominant, other variables become more salient. The classic longitudinal studies of the 1920s and 1930s, for example, focused on social and mastery variables. Among these were dependence, independence, aggression to peers and parents, achievement, anxiety, and sociability. All have demonstrable connections to Freudian theory and the related shift to primary interest in parental socialization and children's social dispositions and control of emotions. An interesting corollary is the significance of these assumptions for the salience of particular parenting variables. Before World War II, when most mothers stayed at home, concerns about child-rearing problems tended toward fears about overprotectiveness, encouragement of dependency, and discouragement of age-appropriate independence. In this case, the psychodynamically influenced concerns with independence and emotional control accorded with typical rearing circumstances for middle-class American children (Kagan, 1992).

By the 1960s, a driving vision of the active child further redirected scientific attention. Interest increased in children's concepts of self, others, and the interrelation of the two (Kohlberg, 1969; Selman, 1980) and in constructs such as intentions and causal attributions (e.g., Dodge, 1986; Dweck, 1986). Growing attention to biological processes and related constructs (e.g., temperament) led to greater focus on regulation of behavior, including coping, inhibition, and attention (Eisenberg, 2002; Rothbart & Bates, 2006). Research on social behavior gradually shifted attention to dyadic interactions as regulatory contexts, and constructs of relationship became more central. Rather than focusing on issues of dependence and anxiety alone, researchers also attended to parents' sensitive responding, signs of emotional security, and measures of relationship quality (Hartup & Laursen, 1999; Thompson, 2006).

Changes in economic and social patterns relevant to development and child rearing exerted further pressures on research questions. The preoccupation with assuring independence and emotional control seemed less relevant when more than half of the mothers in the United States were in the labor force. Public concerns shifted toward the prospect that increasing numbers of children might experience insufficient parental affection and sensitivity toward the child, thus giving issues of attachment, the quality of out-of-home care, and the emotional life of the child considerable currency in the public arena as well as in social development research. Concerns about the greater likelihood of parental inattention also extended to fears of less supervision and monitoring of children, which in turn focused widespread attention to developmental problems of poor regulation and psychopathology (Beatty et al., 2006; Kagan, 1992).

Transformations in Social Development Research

The breadth of social development research today cannot be subsumed easily by a few common themes. Yet most of the activity in the field reflects four intellectual and empirical transformations during its first century. These include increasing interest in specifying developmental processes and intraindividual processes, understanding the nature and significance of interpersonal contexts in development, identifying the dynamics of interpersonal experience, and recognizing the significance of variations in extrafamilial social contexts.

Specifying developmental processes

The maturationist assumptions of researchers stemmed both from a naïve psychology of natural endowments and from an interest in the practical ramifications of "child study" (Hartup et al., 2002). Hall, for example, emphasized that the study of children was valuable for gaining insights that might eventually inform efforts to enhance their development (Cairns & Cairns, 2006; White, 1992). Careful description was a useful first step, and the descriptive work of the middle period was generally more rigorous than in the early period. This later work was facilitated by substantial investment in research by funding agencies like the Laura Spelman Rockefeller Memorial and the Payne Fund, which shared the goal of improving the lives of children (e.g., Senn, 1975). Diverse scientists contributed to the advances of this period. Bühler (1927, 1930) conducted compelling observational studies demonstrating the truly social nature of infants' behavior; Goodenough (1929, 1931) studied children's emotional upset during testing and fears by children of different ages; and Shirley (1931, 1933) published a three-volume report of a pioneering short-term longitudinal study of motor, intellectual, and personality development in the first 2 years of life. In perhaps the most striking empirical advance of the period, two scholars of religion, Hartshorne and May (1928–1930), produced a series of experimental observational studies showing that moral behavior was highly situation specific.

The search for developmental processes   The essential work of developing sound research methods preempted the energies needed for developing and testing theories during the middle period (Cairns & Cairns, 2006; White, 2002). Bühler's (1931) review of studies of children's social behavior, barely 35 years after the first published work on social development, culminated in her judgment that these early studies failed because of "the lack of a systematic point of view" (p. 392). In neglecting theoretical development, social development researchers fell behind other developmental psychologists of the middle period. With the challenges to naïve maturationist views from behaviorism and psychoanalytic concepts, researchers finally shifted focus to rigorous testing of hypotheses regarding the nature and processes of changes in social behaviors, attitudes, and values.

The most theoretically innovative researchers in this period were Watson and Gesell. Watson's (1913) conviction that conditioning accounted for the acquisition of all behaviors had inspired many social developmentalists to grapple with mechanisms of growth and change. Other able psychologists tested key implications of Watson's ideas with respect to infant behavior (e.g., Jones's [1931] rigorous demonstration of the counterconditioning of learned fear).

Gesell, best known for normative descriptive studies of physical and mental growth (Cairns & Cairns, 2006; Thelen & Adolph, 1992), also advanced the view that human infants were endowed with a "pre-eminent sociality" or impulse to seek connection with others. He regarded development as a transactional process: "Growth ... is a historical complex which reflects at every stage the past which it incorporates ... a continuous self conditioning process, rather than a drama controlled" (Gesell, 1928, p. 357). Gesell's speculations about his findings implied a developmental theory much like that of Baldwin (1897) before him and many more recent theorists.

Not until the 1930s and 1940s, however, did compelling theory-testing research appear in the literature. Of particular note were the efforts of a group of young psychologists at Yale University to reinterpret psychoanalytic predictions in terms of Hullian theory learning mechanisms. Soon organized as the Institute of Human Relations, they first reconstrued Freud's view of aggression by treating aggressive behavior as a learned response to being thwarted in efforts to reach a goal (frustration; Dollard et al., 1939). Two members of the group then reexplained identification as imitation reinforced by the experience of similarity to a valued other (secondary reinforcement; Miller & Dollard, 1941). The best known among the few longitudinal studies of the middle period incorporated similar constructs to these pioneering process-oriented efforts (Baldwin, 1949; Kagan & Moss, 1962), as did other large-scale studies (e.g., Sears, Maccoby, & Levin, 1957; Sears, Rau, & Alpert, 1965; Sears, Whiting, Nowlis, & Sears, 1953) and laboratory experiments (e.g., Hartup, 1958; Hartup & Coates, 1967). The empirical fallout lasted for more than 2 decades.

The theoretical hybridizing of the Yale group proceeded in parallel to tests of predictions from other formulations, such as operant learning (e.g., Gewirtz & Baer, 1958). An extensive body of findings accumulated around these behaviorist conceptions of social processes, evident in Stevenson's (1965) influential analysis of social reinforcement. By testing the theories that then occupied others in psychology, social developmental researchers finally moved into the mainstream of the discipline (Cairns & Cairns, 2006; White, 2002).

The mechanistic core processes of social-learning theory, however, eventually quailed under accumulating evidence from infant studies, showing that abilities commonly thought to require conditioning were present very early and that children did not react identically to the same stimuli or the same reinforcers (Kagan, 1992; Maccoby, 1992a). Responses to such findings stimulated a search for intraindividual factors in behavioral and conceptual change. Following Bandura and Walters's (1963) classic volume on social learning and personality development, Mischel (1973) and Bandura (1986) proposed cognitive social-learning formulations, in which such basic processes as reinforcement were reinterpreted as having informational, as well as emotional, significance (Grusec, 1992).

Mediational processes in social development   Buttressed by the "cognitive revolution" in psychology, with its focus on such processes as memory, attention, and inferential thought, and in particular by the influx of Piagetian concepts (Flavell, 1963; Maccoby, 1992a), social development researchers moved toward change processes based on notions of structural reorganization of thought and action. Baldwin (1897) had proposed similar dynamic structural processes in his writing at the turn of the twentieth century, and his ideas were echoed in the thought of Dewey and Gesell, among others (Cahan, 2003). Piaget's formulation fell on more fertile ground than the previous views had.

Advanced primarily to account for intellectual development, Piaget's theory depicted the child as trying to reconcile an expectation, or cognitive schema, and incompatible information from the environment. The resulting intrapsychic conflict motivated the child to adapt the schema to the new experience, thus enlarging his or her capacity to grasp new instances. Development occurred as the child inevitably confronted and adapted to a wide range of experiences.

A social dimension was implicit in this formulation, because many of these conflict-inducing instances inevitably involved other persons. In contrast to the emphasis of learning theorists on parental socialization, Piaget gave special credence to interactions with peers. He reasoned that children encountering a discrepancy between their own schemata and the views of a parent would simply adopt the parent's view, a change that would not necessarily require cognitive change. With persons of equal power, children would be more likely to engage fully in grappling with discrepant viewpoints and inconsistent events; this effort to adapt to more socially challenging circumstances in turn would foster cognitive growth. Piaget's explicit description of how and why children's actions were essential to growth and especially his linking of this process to peer social interactions concretized the notion for researchers accustomed to the "social molding" accounts of social-learning theorists (Hartup et al., 2002; Hsueh, 2004). Kohlberg's (1969) classic essay elaborated the social ramifications of cognitive change, identifying equilibration following cognitive conflict as a fundamental process of social development.

The Piagetian Kohlbergian account received most direct research attention in connection with stage-related hypotheses. However, researchers working on a wide range of developmental problems today, some of them drawn from alternative theoretical models (e.g., information processing), invoke transactional accounts of social development. An example is formulations identifying cognitive biases, such as the tendency to misattribute the causes of behavior in instances of provocation or failure, accounts of aggression (e.g., Dodge, 1986), or lack of persistence in difficult tasks (e.g., Dweck, 1986). Such cognitive biases result when children form schemata of events from repeated experiences interpretable as confirming existing social scripts. Moreover, homeostatic notions such as equilibration following conflict and transactional accounts of behavioral development suffuse the literature in fields such as parent–child relations, peer relations, stress and coping, and the development of prosocial behavior (e.g., Collins, 1995; Furman & Wehner, 1994; Gunnar, 1994).

Expanded views of regulatory processes

Socialization, the dominant concern of social development research throughout the middle period (Hartup et al., 2002), implies that individuals are "induced in some measure to conform to the ways of [their] society or of the particular groups to which [they] belong" (Clausen, 1968, p. 4). In social-learning formulations, regulation processes almost uniformly implied "other" regulation, whereas theories like Piaget's implied that children were collaborators in socialization. Moreover, research on language development and attachment implied that many developmental outcomes could not be explained by top-down influences; and studies of reinforcement and observational learning pointed to the likely variability in children's cognitive processing of, and inferences about, events, learning history, and other subjective intrusions into supposedly fixed, externally controlled processes (e.g., Maccoby, 1992a).

In the era of the active child, efforts to understand self-regulation have commonly focused on children's capacities for balancing internal and external demands to minimize disruptions of optimal functioning. Studies of regulation subsume diverse contexts, processes, and aspects of behavior and emotion. Among the salient topics have been attentional control and cognitive structuring of control tasks in delay of gratification (e.g., Eisenberg & Fabes, 2006), coping strategies in stressful or anxiety-arousing conditions (Compas, 1987), and the relation between behavioral strategies and physiological "dampening" processes in response to stressors (Gunnar, 1994).

The interest in responses to stress, like numerous topics before it, reflects the widespread assumption – and considerable empirical evidence – that technological advances, social changes, and economic and political pressures well beyond the immediate sphere of child and family make coping with multiple stressors an essential competence in modern life (Compas, 1987). Integral to research on this topic is the psychological task of regulating emotions. Evidence of emotional self-regulation is abundant. For example, children "manage" their emotional displays in accord with societal expectations and the demands of their parents (Saarni, 1990); and hormonal reactivity spikes under conditions of fear or novelty for some children, but typically returns to ambient levels following self-soothing activities of various kinds (Gunnar, 1994). Moreover, children vary in their typical emotion regulation, partly as a function of the socialization of emotion in families (Dunn, 1992; Eisenberg, 2002).

Interest in emotion regulation significantly influenced a renascence of research on temperament. The construct of temperament had languished for 3 decades. Contributing to this neglect were political and popular resistance to implications of fixed qualities in individuals (Kagan, 1992), few convergent definitions of key constructs, and the inadequacy of measures of temperamental differences (Rothbart & Bates, 2006). With advanced instrumentation and sophisticated biological indicators, combined with behavioral profiles (Kagan, 1992), it is now more feasible to examine the regulatory patterns of infants and children who differ along common dimensions of temperament (e.g., Kagan, 1994). Moreover, evidence is growing of interactions between temperament and socialization (e.g., Kochanska, Aksan, Knaack, & Rhines, 2004).

Interest in self-regulatory processes also contributed to a resurgence of research on personality development. Personality development had quavered under attacks from behaviorists (e.g., Mischel, 1968), but recent evidence from longitudinal studies and new techniques of combining research results across studies have provided stronger evidence of long-term continuity and change than previously was available (for reviews, see Caspi & Shiner, 2006; Roberts & DelVecchio, 2000).

Expanded units of social experience

The concept of an active child also fed a growing conviction that many of the most significant socializing experiences took place in interactions with others in which the child was an active partner. Sears (1951), in his presidential address to the American Psychological Association, had contended, "A diadic unit is essential if there is to be any conceptualization of the relationships between people" (p. 479). Two decades later, Bell's (1968) article, "A Reinterpretation of the Direction of Effects in Studies of Socialization," and Rheingold's (1969) elegant essay, "The Social and Socializing Infant," again set forth the argument for child as well as parental effects. Another decade passed, however, before proposals for a science of relationships began to take hold in developmental and social psychology (Hinde, 1979; Kelley et al., 1983; Maccoby & Martin, 1983). New lines of research both bolstered the earlier argument for dyadic formulations and expanded research in the area.

The dominant line of research stemmed from Bowlby's (1958) theory of attachment. Writing in reaction to earlier secondary-drive formulations (e.g., Freud, 1910/1957; Sears et al., 1957), Bowlby argued that initial bonds between infants and their caregivers result from evolved tendencies to maintain proximity to assure the infant's safety and survival. Such themes converged nicely with the interest in security as a social motive suggested by the discovery that young rhesus monkeys deprived of social interaction sought contact comfort, rather than gravitating toward a source of food (Harlow & Zimmerman, 1959). Bowlby's (1969, 1973, 1980) theoretical works spurred systematic empirical studies of childhood attachment and numerous theoretical elaborations and refinements that continue unabated today.

Among the historically most important empirical sequelae of these activities are the following. First, the emergence of a bond between child and caregiver in the second half of the first year of life appears to be normative and universal (Ainsworth, 1967; Schaffer & Emerson, 1964). Second, both members of the caregiver–child dyad contribute to these attachments (for reviews, see Marvin & Britner, 2008; Thompson, 2006). Third, the functional significance of attachment is underscored by evidence from nonhuman species that even minor deprivation of contact with responsive others results in abnormal neuroanatomical structures and impaired endocrinological sensitivity related to stress and coping (e.g., Ginsberg, Hof, McKinney, & Morrison, 1993). Studies of human children adopted from orphanages, some having impoverished opportunities for human interaction, also reveal neurohormonal sequelae of restricted social contact (Chisholm, 1998; Gunnar, Morison, Chisholm, & Schuder, 2001; Rutter and English and Romanian Adoptees [ERA] Study Team, 1998). Fourth, research on the long-term significance of early attachments has yielded some compelling findings of continuity with relationships in childhood, adolescence, and adulthood, but many instances of null findings as well (for a review, see Thompson, 2008). Fifth, the process by which relationships are linked to behavior patterns at a much later time is thought to be one instance of the more general process of expectancies being applied to new situations. Few researchers now espouse a simple "early determinism" model, embracing instead multivariate accounts that acknowledge the sometimes overlapping contributions of multiple kinds of dyads and that also attempt to explain discontinuities (e.g., Belsky, Campbell, Cohn, & Moore, 1996; Weinfield, Sroufe, Egeland, & Carlson, 1999).

Studies of peer relations also rest heavily on assumptions of bidirectional influence and the dyad as a unit of analysis (Hartup & Laursen, 1999). A compelling example comes from findings that, when two toddlers or school-aged children interact, the qualities of their interactions are a joint function of their respective early relationships (Pastor, 1981). Thus, "[I]t is not simply that children behave differently depending on the relationship histories of their partners, but that relationships with different partners themselves vary in quality" (Sroufe & Fleeson, 1986, p. 59).

Developmentalists face several unique challenges in research with dyadic units of analysis. One is that both developmental and power differentials contribute to the unique functioning of a dyad composed of individuals of different ages. Moreover, different rates of change in two partners of different ages make it difficult to determine which partner is contributing more to the ongoing adaptations between the two persons (Hartup & Laursen, 1991). A second challenge is the need to shift from viewing developmental outcomes in terms of only individual traits or habit patterns toward thinking of outcomes as competences for participating in social life (e.g., security, effective conflict resolution, commitment, involvement, and hostility; see Furman, Brown, & Feiring, 1999; Maccoby, 1992a). Although contemporary researchers have devised more compelling ways of specifying and analyzing relationships than were available before 1980, scholars continue to grapple with questions regarding the methods and statistical strategies appropriate for research with dyads (Reis, Collins, & Berscheid, 2000).

Incorporating contextual variations into social processes

The fourth and final transformation in social development concerns the significance of aspects of the contexts in which relationships and interactions occur. Until the 1970s, the term *environment* implied varied sources of stimulation, from the proximal social models or social reinforcers encountered by a child to other, unspecified sources of influence. Psychological researchers were bent toward demonstrating generality in the effects of certain environmental influences, not appreciating the distinctions among them (Bronfenbrenner & Morris, 2006; Modell & Elder, 2002).

An early challenge to this environment-neutral stance came from Lewin (1931), who argued that the individual's psychological environment, as opposed to the physical or objectively determined environment, was composed of both intraindividual forces and external ones. Children's perceptions of the stimuli specified by the researcher had to be assessed and included in both design and statistical analyses. Both Lewin's conceptual prediction and his empirical findings (e.g., Lewin, Lippitt, & White, 1938) have influenced generations of research on the effects of parenting behavior (Baldwin, 1949; Baumrind, 1973; Maccoby, 1992b) and teachers' classroom behavior (e.g., Arnold, McWilliams, & Arnold, 1998), and the dynamics of peer groups (Hartup, 1992).

Lewin's emphasis on context has reappeared in a variety of formulations in the ensuing decades. Bronfenbrenner's (1979) germinal volume, *The Ecology of Human Development*, provided an organizing framework for diverse potential environmental influences, including those of historical period and cohort. In his now famous concentric levels diagram, aspects of the environment that the child did not experience directly were pictured as distal, but possibilities for indirect influences were clearly apparent. Research examples of these indirect influences are increasingly familiar (e.g., Elder, 1974; McLoyd, 1998). Another post-Lewinian manifestation came from developmental anthropologists, many of whom provided reminders of the potency of the experienced, not the presumed, environment (e.g., Super & Harkness, 1986).

The impact of contextual variables is felt today not only in social development but also in other subfields of developmental psychology and psychology generally. Many psychologists now believe that constructs and reports of empirical findings should be labeled to specify the contexts to which they apply (Kagan, 1992). An example in social development is peer gender segregation (Maccoby, 1990), which refers specifically to the tendency for children to affiliate with same-gender peers in mixed-gender settings. Nevertheless, social developmentalists, like other psychologists, face continuing challenges in fully incorporating contexts into studies of development and the developmental process (for critiques, see Bronfenbrenner & Morris, 2006; Elder, Modell, & Parke, 1993; Modell & Elder, 2002).

The Search for Method

The earliest methods in social development research were observation and survey questionnaires. Studies reported between 1890 and 1920 rarely reported more than frequency counts of behaviors, attitudes, or values. Although description is an essential phase of any natural science, early samples were too restricted and the administration of measures too error ridden to serve this purpose for the emerging field of social development (Cairns & Cairns, 2006; White, 1992). Early studies of children's social judgments (Schallenberger, 1894) and peer relations (Barnes, 1896–1897, 1902–1903; Monroe, 1899) were similarly descriptive and drawn from questionnaire responses. Observational and experimental methods were few. One notable exception was Triplett's (1897) landmark experiment showing that children wound fishing reels faster when working with other children than when working alone. Not until more rigorous descriptive studies became the standard in the 1930s did compelling observational work appear. Methodological improvements increased relatively quickly. Innovations came less rapidly, however, in studies of very early social development. Leading the way on controlled experimental observations of infants, Charlotte Bühler observed the babies of poor families at a milk station in Berlin and documented simple social coordinations in the exchanges of 6-month-old infants. Similar advances in the study of infant social behavior did not appear for another 30 years.

Careful observational studies of nursery school children in the United States, though, showed age-related patterns during early childhood. For example, coordinated interactions of many different kinds increased with age (e.g., Parten, 1932–1933); physical aggression increased and subsequently declined across ages (Goodenough, 1931); and verbal aggression initially increased with age, but then stabilized (Jersild & Markey, 1935). Similar methods also revealed that children's relationships with one another moderated conflict instigation and management (Green, 1933).

The social behavior of older children demanded still more creative techniques. Group behavior, both normative and antisocial, was studied through participant observation (e.g., Thrasher, 1927). Field experiments, such as Lewin et al.'s (1938) classic work on group atmospheres, anticipated later equally classic studies of groups like the Robbers Cave experiment (Sherif, Harvey, White, Hood, & Sherif, 1961). Still later, ethnographic studies expanded the study of individuals and groups in context (e.g., Bryant, 1985). The most influential strategy to date has been comparing the behavior of children who vary in peer group status. Sociometric methods, derived from Moreno's (1934) method for studying institutionalized adults, has undergone important refinements and has yielded significant clues to meaningful variations in social skills and behavior (e.g., Coie, Dodge, & Copotelli, 1982).

Despite the relatively greater rigor of later studies, studies of peer relations in the middle period were scarcely more theoretically motivated (Cairns & Cairns, 2006). Only after 1960 were theoretically driven studies of behavior with peers conducted extensively. Contemporary studies draw from a range of theoretical formulations, such as those of exchange theory, Sullivan's (1953) theory of interpersonal relations, attachment theory, and an array of newer formulations (Hartup & Laursen, 1999).

Work on parenting generally has trailed these efforts in sophistication, despite the longer history of sustained interest in, and the larger number of, studies of parental effects and child outcomes. Questionnaire studies and self-report inventories dominate research on parenting behavior even today. Observational studies (e.g., Forgatch & DeGarmo, 1999; Patterson, 1982) and laboratory analogs (e.g., Kochanska et al., 2004; Kuczynski, 1984) are relatively rare. Reliance on self-report methods and correlational statistics has weakened the contributions of these studies. Collins, Maccoby, Steinberg, Hetherington, and Bornstein (2000) identified several more rigorous types of designs that have been used to specify parental contributions to social development. Among these are behavior–genetics designs augmented by specific measures of environment; studies distinguishing among children varying in genetically influenced predispositions in terms of their responses to different environmental conditions; experimental and quasi-experimental studies of change in children's behavior as a result of their exposure to parents' behavior, after controlling for children's initial characteristics; and research on interactions between parenting and nonfamilial environmental influences and contexts.

Many methodological innovations of the modern era followed changes in relevant technologies. Video recorders greatly facilitated progress in early studies of infant affect and mother–infant interaction (e.g., Cohn & Tronick, 1987). Digital and computer technologies, combined with video, have enhanced specificity in observational and laboratory studies of social interaction in families and peers. Techniques to measure brain electrical activity, heart rate, blood pressure, muscle tension, cortisol, and blood chemistry have contributed to studies of temperament and are likely to be even more widely applied in the decade ahead (Kagan, 1992, 1994; Rothbart & Bates, 2006).

Longitudinal studies, though more numerous in social development than in other subfields of developmental psychology, were understandably rare in the first 6 decades of the history of social development. The exceptions were noteworthy for their scope and impact. The Berkeley and Oakland surveys (e.g., Clausen, 1993), Baldwin's study of parenting styles (1949), and the Fels longitudinal study (e.g., Kagan & Moss, 1962) all provided significant descriptive data on key constructs. The same can be said of pioneering short-term follow-ups of infants (e.g., Shirley, 1933). Today, the relatively numerous longitudinal efforts in the United States and Europe are all the more remarkable because of their size and scope. These efforts permit researchers to address heretofore intractable issues, such as the duration of the impact of significant social experiences, trajectories of change, the significance of timing of social experiences, and so forth (e.g., Grossmann, Grossmann, & Waters, 2005; Pulkkinen & Caspi, 2002).

Conclusion

The first century of research on social development is a story of evolution, rather than revolution. Shifts of strategy and method are more apparent than shifts of interest or focal questions. The interests underlying the canonical work in the field are present today in more theoretically and methodologically sophisticated forms. For example, the best work on parental influences today takes account of the nature of the child and the possibility of bidirectionality, as well as the strong likelihood of other socializing influences such as peers, schools, and the mass media (Collins et al., 2000). Research on peer relations acknowledges contextual effects and qualitative variations among peer companions, as well as child temperament, familial relationship history, and quantitative differences in the nature of the relationship. Studies of individual differences in behaviors (e.g., aggression) and behavioral orientations (e.g., gender) draw broadly on knowledge of social, biobehavioral, cognitive, and emotional processes to formulate hypotheses and interpret research results. The first century has been a promising start on the next one.

Acknowledgments

Preparation of the chapter was supported partly by a grant from the National Institute of Child Health and Human Development to W. Andrew Collins, a grant from the National Institute of Mental Health to Byron Egeland, and the Rodney S. Wallace Professorship for the Advancement of Teaching and Learning, University of Minnesota. The author gratefully acknowledges helpful information and comments from Willard W. Hartup, Brett Laursen, Ross D. Parke, Richard A. Weinberg, and Sheldon H. White.

References

Ainsworth, M. D. S. (1967). *Infancy in Uganda: Infant care and the growth of love*. Baltimore: Johns Hopkins University Press.

Arnett, J. J., & Cravens, H. (2006). G. Stanley Hall's *Adolescence*: A centennial reappraisal. *History of Psychology, 9*, 165–171.

Arnold, D. H., McWilliams, L., & Arnold, E. H. (1998). Teacher discipline and child misbehavior in day care: Untangling causality with correlational data. *Developmental Psychology, 34*, 267–287.

Baldwin, A. (1949). The effect of home environment on nursery school behavior. *Child Development, 20*, 49–62.

Baldwin, J. M. (1897). *Social and ethical interpretations in mental development: A study in social psychology*. New York: Macmillan.

Bandura, A. (1986). *Social foundations of thought and action: A social cognitive theory*. Englewood Cliffs, NJ: Prentice Hall.

Bandura, A., & Walters, R. H. (1963). *Social learning and personality development*. New York: Holt, Rinehart and Winston.

Barnes, E. (1896–1897, 1902–1903). *Studies in education* (2 vols.). Philadelphia: Author.

Baumrind, D. (1973). The development of instrumental competence through socialization. In A. D. Pick (Ed.), *Minnesota symposium on child psychology* (Vol. 7, pp. 3–46). Minneapolis: University of Minnesota Press.

Beatty, B., Cahan, E. D., & Grant, J. (Eds.). (2006). *When science encounters the child: Education, parenting, and child welfare in 20th century America*. New York: Teachers College Press.

Bell, R. Q. (1968). A reinterpretation of the direction of effects in studies of socialization. *Psychological Review, 75*, 81–95.

Belsky, J., Campbell, S. B., Cohn, J. F., & Moore, G. (1996). Instability of infant-parent attachment security. *Developmental Psychology, 32*, 921–924.

Bowlby, J. (1958). The nature of the child's tie to his mother. *International Journal of Psycho-Analysis, 39*, 350–373.

Bowlby, J. (1969). *Attachment and loss: Vol. 1. Attachment*. New York: Basic Books.

Bowlby, J. (1973). *Attachment and loss: Vol. 2. Separation: Anxiety and anger*. New York: Basic Books.

Bowlby, J. (1980). *Attachment and loss: Vol. 3. Loss: Sadness and depression*. New York: Basic Books.

Bronfenbrenner, U. (1979). *The ecology of human development: Experiments by nature and design*. Cambridge, MA: Harvard University Press.

Bronfenbrenner, U., & Morris, P. A. (2006). The bioecological model of human development. In R. Lerner & W. Damon (Eds.), *Handbook of child psychology: Vol. 1. Theoretical models of human development* (pp. 793–828). New York: Wiley.

Bryant, B. (1985). The neighborhood walk: Sources of support in middle childhood. *Monographs of the Society for Research in Child Development, 50*(3, Serial No. 210).

Bühler, C. (1927). *Die ersten soziale Verhaltungsweisen des Kindes. In Soziologische und psychologische Studien Uber das erste Lebensjahr*. Jena, Germany: Fischer.

Bühler, C. (1930). *The first year of life*. New York: John Day.

Bühler, C. (1931). The social behavior of the child. In C. Murchison (Ed.), *A handbook of child psychology* (pp. 374–416). Worcester, MA: Clark University Press.

Cahan, E. D. (2003). James Mark Baldwin: The natural and the good. *Developmental Review, 23*, 9–28.

Cairns, R. B. (1992). The making of developmental science: The contribution and intellectual heritage of James Mark Baldwin. *Developmental Psychology, 28*, 17–24.

Cairns, R. B., & Cairns, B. D. (2006). The making of developmental psychology. In W. Damon (Series Ed.) & R. M. Lerner (Vol. Ed.), *Handbook of child psychology. Vol. 1: History and systems of developmental psychology* (pp. 25–105). New York: Wiley.

Caspi, A., & Shiner, R. (2006). Personality development across the life course. In W. Damon (Series Ed.) & N. Eisenberg (Vol. Ed.), *Handbook of child psychology. Vol. 3: Social, emotional, and personality development* (pp. 25–105). New York: Wiley.

Chisholm, K. (1998). A three-year follow-up of attachment and indiscriminate friendliness in children adopted from Romanian orphanages. *Child Development, 69*, 1092–1106.

Clausen, J. A. (1968). Socialization as a concept and as a field of study. In J. A. Clausen (Ed.), *Socialization and society* (pp. 1–17). Boston: Little, Brown.

Clausen, J. A. (1993). *American lives: Looking back at the children of the Great Depression*. New York: Free Press.

Cohn, J. F., & Tronick, E. Z. (1987). Mother-infant face-to-face interaction: The sequence of dyadic states at 3, 6, and 9 months. *Developmental Psychology, 23*, 68–77.

Coie, J. D., Dodge, K. A., & Coppotelli, H. (1982). Dimensions and types of social status: A cross-age perspective. *Developmental Psychology, 18*, 557–570.

Collins, W. A. (1995). Relationships and development: Family adaptation to individual change (pp. 128–154). In S. Shulman (Ed.), *Close relationships and socioemotional development*. New York: Ablex.

Collins, W. A., Maccoby, E. E., Steinberg, L., Hetherington, E. M., & Bornstein, M. H. (2000). Contemporary research on parenting: The case for nature and nurture. *American Psychologist, 55*, 218–232.

Compas, B. (1987). Coping with stress during childhood and adolescence. *Psychological Bulletin, 101*, 393–403.

Cooley, C. H. (1909). *Social organization*. New York: Scribner.

Darwin, C. (1877). Biographical sketch of an infant. *Mind, 2*, 285–294.

Dewey, J. (1899). *The school and society*. Chicago: University of Chicago Press.

Dodge, K. A. (1986). A social information processing model of social competence in children. In M. Perlmutter (Ed.), *Minnesota symposia on child psychology* (Vol. *18*, pp. 77–125). Hillsdale, NJ: Erlbaum.

Dollard, J., Miller, N. E., Doob, L. W., Mowrer, O. H., & Sears, R. R., with Ford, C. S., et al. (1939). *Frustration and aggression*. New Haven, CT: Yale University Press.

Dunn, J. (1992). Mindreading and social relationships. In M. Bennett (Ed.), *Developmental psychology: Achievements and prospects* (pp. 72–88). Philadelphia: Psychology Press.

Dweck, C. (1986). Motivational processes affecting learning. *American Psychologist, 41*(10), 1040–1048.

Eisenberg, N. (2002). Emotion-related regulation and its relation to quality of social functioning. In W. W. Hartup & R. A. Weinberg (Eds.), *Child psychology in retrospect and prospect: The Minnesota symposia on child psychology* (Vol. 32, pp. 127–164). Mahwah, NJ: Erlbaum.

Elder, G. H., Jr. (1974). *Children of the Great Depression: Social change and life experience*. Chicago: University of Chicago Press.

Elder, G. H., Jr., Modell, J., & Parke, R. D. (Eds.). (1993). *Children in time and place: Developmental and historical insights*. New York: Cambridge University Press.

Emde, R. N. (1992). Individual meaning and increasing complexity: Contributions of Sigmund Freud and Rene Spitz to developmental psychology. *Developmental Psychology, 28*, 347–359.

Flavell, J. H. (1963). *The developmental psychology of Jean Piaget*. Princeton, NJ: Van Nostrand.

Forgatch, M. S., & DeGarmo, D. S. (1999). Parenting through change: An effective prevention program for single mothers. *Journal of Consulting and Clinical Psychology, 67*, 711–724.

Freud, S. (1910/1957). The origin and development of psychoanalysis. *American Journal of Psychology, 21*, 181–218.

Furman, W., Brown, B. B., & Feiring, C. (Eds.). (1999). *The development of romantic relationships in adolescence*. New York: Cambridge University Press.

Furman, W., & Wehner, E. (1994). Romantic views: Toward a theory of adolescent romantic relationships. In R. Montemayor, G. R. Adams, & T. P. Gullotta (Eds.), *Personal relationships during adolescence* (pp. 168–195). Thousand Oaks, CA: Sage.

Gesell, A. (1928). *Infancy and human growth*. New York: Macmillan.

Gewirtz, J. L., & Baer, D. (1958). The effect of brief social deprivation on behaviors for a social reinforcer. *Journal of Abnormal and Social Psychology, 56*, 49–56.

Ginsberg, S. D., Hof, P. R., McKinney, W. T., & Morrison, J. H. (1993). Quantitative analysis of tuberoinfundibular tyrosine hydroxylase- and corticotropin-releasing-factor-immunoreactive neurons in monkeys raised with differential rearing conditions. *Experimental Neurology, 120,* 95–105.

Goodenough, F. L. (1929). The emotional behavior of young children during mental tests. *Journal of Juvenile Research, 13,* 204–219.

Goodenough, F. L. (1931). *Anger in young children.* Minneapolis: University of Minnesota Press.

Green, E. H. (1933). Friendships and quarrels among preschool children. *Child Development, 4,* 237–252.

Grossmann, K. E., Grossmann, K., & Waters, E. (Eds). (2005). *The power of longitudinal attachment research: From infancy and childhood to adulthood* (pp. 48–70). New York: Guilford Press.

Grusec, J. E. (1992). Social learning theory and developmental psychology: The legacies of Robert Sears and Albert Bandura. *Developmental Psychology, 28,* 776–786.

Gunnar, M. (1994). Psychoendocrine studies of temperament and stress in early childhood: Expanding current models. In J. E. Bates & T. D. Wachs (Eds.), *Temperament: Individual differences at the interface of biology and behavior* (pp. 387–410). Hillsdale, NJ: Erlbaum.

Gunnar, M., Morison, S. J., Chisholm, K., & Schuder, M. (2001). Salivary cortisol levels in children adopted from Romanian orphanages. *Development and Psychopathology, 13,* 611–628.

Hall, G. S. (1904). *Adolescence: Its psychology and its relations to physiology, anthropology, sociology, sex, crime, religion, and education* (2 vols.). New York: Appleton.

Harlow, H. F., & Zimmerman, R. (1959). Affectional responses in the infant monkey. *Science, 130,* 421–432.

Harris, P. L. (1992). Acquiring the art of conversation: Children's developing conception of their conversation partner. In M. Bennett (Ed.), *Developmental psychology: Achievements and prospects* (pp. 89–105). Philadelphia: Psychology Press.

Hartshorne, H., & May, M. S. (1928–1930). *Studies in the nature of character* (3 vols.). New York: Macmillan.

Hartup, W. W. (1958). Nurturance and nurturance-withdrawal in relation to the dependency behavior of preschool children. *Child Development, 29,* 191–201.

Hartup, W. W. (1992). Peer experience and its developmental significance. In M. Bennett (Ed.), *Developmental psychology: Achievements and prospects* (pp. 106–125). Philadelphia: Psychology Press.

Hartup, W. W., & Coates, B. (1967). Imitation of a peer as a function of reinforcement from the peer group and rewardingness of the model. *Child Development, 38,* 1003–1016.

Hartup, W. W., Johnson, A., & Weinberg, R. A. (2002). The Institute of Child Development: Pioneering in science and application. In W. W. Hartup & R. A. Weinberg (Eds.), *Child psychology in retrospect and prospect: The Minnesota symposia on child psychology* (Vol. *32,* pp. 217–248). Mahwah, NJ: Erlbaum.

Hartup, W. W., & Laursen, B. (1991). Relationships as developmental contexts. In R. Cohen & A. W. Siegel (Eds.), *Context and development* (pp. 253–279). Hillsdale, NJ: Erlbaum.

Hartup, W. W., & Laursen, B. (1999). Relationships as developmental contexts: Retrospective themes and contemporary issues. In W. A. Collins & B. Laursen (Eds.), *Relationships as developmental contexts: The Minnesota symposia on child psychology* (Vol. 30, pp. 13–35). Mahwah, NJ: Erlbaum.

Hinde, R. A. (1979). *Towards understanding relationships.* London: Academic Press.

Horowitz, F. D. (1992). John B. Watson's legacy: Learning and environment. *Developmental Psychology, 28,* 360–367.

Hsueh, Y. (2004). "He sees the development of children's concepts upon a background of sociology": Jean Piaget's honorary degree at Harvard University in 1936. *History of Psychology, 7,* 20–44.

Jersild, A. T., & Markey, F. U. (1935). *Conflicts between preschool children (Child Development Monographs No. 21)*. New York: Columbia University Press.

Jones, M. C. (1931). The conditioning of children's emotions. In C. Murchison (Eds.), *A handbook of child psychology* (pp. 71–93). Worcester, MA: Clark University Press.

Kagan, J. (1992). Yesterday's premises, tomorrow's promises. *Developmental Psychology, 28*, 990–997.

Kagan, J. (1994). *Galen's prophecy: Temperament in human nature*. Cambridge, MA: Harvard University Press.

Kagan, J., & Moss, H. A. (1962). *Birth to maturity: A study in psychological development*. New York: Wiley.

Kelley, H. H., Berscheid, E., Christensen, A., Harvey, J. H., Huston, T. L., Levinger, G., et al. (Eds.). (1983). *Close relationships*. New York: Freeman.

Kochanska, G., Aksan, N., Knaack, A., & Rhines, H. M. (2004). Maternal parenting and children's conscience: Early security as a moderator. *Child Development, 75*, 1229–1242.

Kohlberg, L. (1969). Stage and sequence: The cognitive-developmental approach to socialization. In D. A. Goslin (Ed.), *Handbook of socialization theory and research* (pp. 347–480). Chicago: Rand McNally.

Kuczynski, L. (1984). Socialization goals and mother-child interaction: Strategies for long-term and short-term compliance. *Developmental Psychology, 20*, 1061–1073.

Lewin, K. (1931). Environmental forces in child behavior and development. In C. Murchison (Ed.), *A handbook of child psychology* (2nd ed., pp. 590–625). Worcester, MA: Clark University Press.

Lewin, K., Lippitt, R., & White, R. K. (1938). Patterns of aggressive behavior in experimentally created "social climates." *Journal of Social Psychology, 10*, 271–299.

Maccoby, E. E. (1990). Gender and relationships. *American Psychologist, 45*, 513–520.

Maccoby, E. E. (1992a). The role of parents in the socialization of children: An historical overview. *Developmental Psychology, 28*, 1006–1017.

Maccoby, E. E. (1992b). Trends in the study of socialization: Is there a Lewinian heritage? *Journal of Social Issues, 48*, 171–185.

Maccoby, E. E., & Martin, J. A. (1983). Socialization in the context of the family: Parent–child interaction. In E. M. Hetherington (Ed.), *Handbook of child psychology: Socialization, personality, and social development* (Vol. 4, pp. 1–101). New York: Wiley.

Marvin, R., & Britner, P. (2008). Normative development: The ontogeny of attachment. In J. Cassidy & P. R. Shaver (Eds.), *Handbook of attachment: Theory, research, and clinical applications* (2nd ed., pp. 269–294). New York: Guilford Press.

McLoyd, V. C. (1998). Socioeconomic disadvantage and child development. *American Psychologist, 53*, 185–204.

Mead, G. H. (1934). *Mind, self, and society*. Chicago: University of Chicago Press.

Miller, N. E., & Dollard, J. (1941). *Social learning and imitation*. New York: McGraw-Hill.

Mischel, W. (1968). *Personality and assessment*. New York: Wiley.

Mischel, W. (1973). Toward a cognitive social learning reconceptualization of personality. *Psychological Review, 80*, 252–283.

Modell, J., & Elder, G. H., Jr. (2002). Children develop in history: So what's new? In W. W. Hartup & R. A. Weinberg (Eds.), *Child psychology in retrospect and prospect: The Minnesota symposia on child psychology* (Vol. 32). Mahwah, NJ: Erlbaum.

Monroe, W. S. (1899). *Die Entwicklung des sozialen Bewusstseins der Kinder*. Berlin: Reuther & Reichard.

Moreno, J. L. (1934). *Who shall survive?* Washington, DC: Nervous and Mental Disease Publishing.

Parten, M. B. (1932–1933). Social participation among preschool children. *Journal of Abnormal and Social Psychology, 27*, 243–269.

Pastor, D. (1981). The quality of mother-infant attachment and its relationship to toddlers' initial sociability with peers. *Developmental Psychology, 17*, 326–335.

Patterson, G. R. (1982). *Coercive family process.* Eugene, OR: Castalia.

Piaget, J. (1932/1965). *The moral judgment of the child.* New York: Free Press.

Pulkkinen, L., & Caspi, A. (Eds.). (2002). *Paths to successful development: Personality in the life course.* New York: Cambridge University Press.

Reis, H. T., Collins, W. A., & Berscheid, E. (2000). The relationship context of human behavior and development. *Psychological Bulletin, 126*, 844–872.

Rheingold, H. (1969). The social and socializing infant. In D. A. Goslin (Ed.), *Handbook of socialization theory and research* (pp. 779–790). Chicago: Rand McNally.

Roberts, B. W., & DelVecchio, W. F. (2000). The rank-order consistency of personality traits from childhood to old age: A quantitative review of longitudinal studies. *American Psychologist, 126*, 3–25.

Rothbart, M. K., & Bates, J. E. (2006). Temperament. In W. Damon (Series Ed.) & N. Eisenberg (Vol. Ed.), *Handbook of child psychology: Vol. 3. Social, emotional, and personality development* (pp. 105–176). New York: Wiley.

Rutter, M., & English and Romanian Adoptees (ERA) Study Team. (1998). Developmental catch-up, and deficit, following adoption after severe global early privation. *Journal of Child Psychology and Psychiatry, 39*, 465–476.

Saarni, C. (1990). Emotional competence: How emotions and relationships become integrated. In R. A. Thompson (Ed.), *Socioemotional development. Nebraska symposia on motivation* (Vol. 36, pp. 115–181). Lincoln: University of Nebraska Press.

Schaffer, H. R., & Emerson, P. E. (1964). The development of social attachments in infancy. *Monographs of the Society for Research in Child Development, 29*(3, Serial No. 94).

Schallenberger, M. E. (1894). A study of children's rights, as seen by themselves. *Pedagogical Seminary, 3*, 87–96.

Sears, R. R. (1951). A theoretical framework for personality and social behavior. *American Psychologist, 6*, 476–483.

Sears, R. R. (1975). Your ancients revisited: A history of child development. In E. M. Hetherington (Ed.), *Review of child development research* (Vol. 5, pp. 1–73). Chicago: University of Chicago Press.

Sears, R. R., Maccoby, E. E., & Levin, H. (1957). *Patterns of child rearing.* Evanston, IL: Row Peterson.

Sears, R. R., Rau, L., & Alpert, R. (1965). *Identification and child rearing.* Stanford, CA: Stanford University Press.

Sears, R. R., Whiting, J. W. M., Nowlis, V., & Sears, P. S. (1953). Some child-rearing antecedents of aggression and dependency in young children. *Genetic Psychology Monographs, 47*, 135–234.

Selman, R. (1980). *The growth of interpersonal understanding.* New York: Academic Press.

Senn, M. J. E. (1975). Insights on the child development movement in the United States. *Monographs of the Society for Research in Child Development, 40*(3–4, Serial No. 161).

Sherif, M., Harvey, O. J., White, B. J., Hood, W. R., & Sherif, C. W. (1961). *Intergroup conflict and cooperation: The Robbers Cave experiment.* Norman, OK: University Book Exchange.

Shinn, M. (1893–1899). *Notes on the development of a child* (University of California Publications No. 1). Berkeley: University of California Press.

Shirley, M. (1931). *The first two years. A study of twenty-five babies: Vol. 1. Postural and locomotor development.* Minneapolis: University of Minnesota Press.

Shirley, M. (1933). *The first two years. A study of twenty-five babies: Vol. 3. Personality manifestations.* Minneapolis: University of Minnesota Press.

Sroufe, A., & Fleeson, J. (1986). Attachment and the construction of relationships. In W. W. Hartup & Z. Rubin (Eds.), *Relationships and development* (pp. 57–71). Mahwah, NJ: Erlbaum.

Stevenson, H. W. (1965). Social reinforcement with children. In L. P. Lipsitt & C. C. Spiker (Eds.), *Advances in child development and behavior* (Vol. 2, pp. 97–126). New York: Academic Press.

Sullivan, H. S. (1953). *The interpersonal theory of psychiatry*. New York: Norton.

Super, C., & Harkness, S. (1986). The developmental niche: A conceptualization at the interface of the child and culture. *International Journal of Behavioral Development, 9*, 545–570.

Thelen, E., & Adolph, K. E. (1992). Arnold L. Gesell: The paradox of nature and nurture. *Developmental Psychology, 28*, 368–380.

Thompson, R. A. (2006). The development of the person: Social understanding, relationships, conscience, self. In W. Damon & N. Eisenberg (Eds.), *Handbook of child psychology: Vol. 3. Social, emotional, and personality development* (pp. 24–98). New York: Wiley.

Thompson, R. A. (2008). Early attachment and later development: Familiar questions, new answers. In J. Cassidy & P. R. Shaver (Eds.), *Handbook of attachment: Theory, research, and clinical applications* (2nd ed., pp. 348–365). New York: Guilford Press.

Thrasher, F. M. (1927). *The gang*. Chicago: University of Chicago Press.

Triplett, N. (1897). The dynamogenic factors in peacemaking and competition. *American Journal of Psychology, 9*, 507–533.

Watson, J. B. (1913). Psychology as the behaviorist views it. *Psychological Review, 20*, 158–177.

Weinfield, N., Sroufe, L. A., Egeland, B., & Carlson, E. A. (1999). The nature of individual differences in infant-caregiver attachment. In J. Cassidy & P. R. Shaver (Eds.), *Handbook of attachment: Theory, research, and clinical applications* (pp. 68–88). New York: Guilford Press.

White, S. H. (1992). G. Stanley Hall: From philosophy to developmental psychology. *Developmental Psychology, 28*, 25–34.

White, S. H. (2002). Notes toward a philosophy of science for developmental science. In W. W. Hartup & R. A. Weinberg (Eds.), *Child psychology in retrospect and prospect: The Minnesota symposia on child psychology* (Vol. 32, pp. 197–216). Mahwah, NJ: Erlbaum.

PART II

Disciplinary Perspectives on Social Development

Psychology forms a recognized discipline, and most of the contributors to this volume are developmental psychologists. This disciplinary perspective predominates through most of this handbook. However, child development is an interdisciplinary area. The Society for Research in Child Development, based in the United States, has an explicitly interdisciplinary membership base. Traditional disciplines (such as psychology) are, after all, no more than convenient labels or packages for organizing study and research, which run a danger of becoming ossified rather than reflecting the dynamic nature of evolving knowledge. The historical context of how child development as a discipline has evolved was summarized in Chapter 1. In this part, we examine six different disciplinary perspectives in the area, ranging from the very biological to the very social. These perspectives enrich the area and provide vital theoretical perspectives and methodological inputs.

In Chapter 2, Alice Gregory, Harriet Ball, and Tanya Button introduce the approach of behavioral genetics to understanding social development in childhood. Besides twin and adoption studies, newer techniques of linkage and association studies are helping us understand the relative importance of genes, and shared and nonshared environments, on development. It is also beginning to be possible to link specific genes or gene complexes to specific behaviors (not in a narrow deterministic sense, but in terms of possible developmental pathways). The authors give detail in the areas of antisocial behavior (see also Chapter 26), bullying (Chapter 27), and prosocial behavior (Chapter 29) to illustrate the potential of such approaches.

Steven Woltering and Marc Lewis provide a neuropsychological perspective in Chapter 3. However, they do this in an unusual and interesting way. They first discuss conceptual development and the role of desire and emotion in this, as well as more cognitive elements such as executive function. They then move on to consider neuropsychological correlates, and the areas of the brain found to be particularly important in these respects,

The Wiley-Blackwell Handbook of Childhood Social Development, Second Edition, edited by Peter K. Smith and Craig H. Hart.
© 2011 by Blackwell Publishing Ltd.

introducing their concept of the motivated action loop. Further progress in this and related areas of neuropsychology is likely to have an important impact in the near future, as more connections are made both to genetic factors in brain development (cf. Chapter 2) and to better studied psychological phenomena such as motivation and learning.

In Chapter 4, David Bjorklund and Anthony Pellegrini provide a perspective on social development from evolutionary developmental psychology. Evolutionary psychology generally has been seen as controversial in some quarters, but it is now increasingly accepted that our evolutionary history, and the selection pressures that worked on our development as hominids to modern humans, provides a vital part of our understanding of who we are and how we function. Evolutionary psychology has emphasized domain-specific aspects of human cognition and behavior, selected especially during some hundreds of thousands of years during which our ancestors had a hunter–gatherer lifestyle sometimes referred to as the *environment of evolutionary adaptedness*. However, evolutionary developmental psychology puts more emphasis on plasticity within the developmental process. Bjorklund and Pellegrini expound this viewpoint, with particular reference to aspects of social cognition (such as theory of mind; cf. Chapter 30) and of peer interaction (such as social dominance, aggression, and prosocial behavior; see Chapters 26 and 29).

Evolutionary processes operate over thousands of years. Historical processes operate over a shorter time span. In Chapter 5, Willem Koops illustrates how societies have viewed children and childhood in modern Europe and Western thinking, from Rousseau onward. This is reflected in the work of philosophers and educators. In the second half of his chapter, Koops especially considers the perspectives of historians of childhood, such as Philip Ariès. Ariès argued that childhood was a modern invention. Although many psychologists have dismissed Ariès' approach, Koops argues that it cannot be totally discarded; and he debates too the arguments about how the advent of the mass media has changed childhood so that it is perhaps "disappearing." Certainly, the Internet is radically changing the experiences of children and young people in ways that we cannot fully foresee.

Anthropologists have long studied childhood, including the work of pioneers such as Margaret Mead (who did in fact have a master's degree in child psychology before developing a career as an anthropologist; see also Chapter 25 for more on Mead's work in different cultures). As Heidi Fung shows in Chapter 6, cultural psychologists have taken from such researchers the importance of the cultural context, and social development has been an especially important arena in this respect, because it is the context of what is traditionally referred to as *socialization*. Fung points out how cultural contexts are all too often neglected by developmental psychologists. Nevertheless, aspects such as the nature of parent–child interaction, language acquisition, the management of emotions, and categorizations of people (cf. also Chapter 32) are greatly influenced by the culture of upbringing. Issues around culture, and acculturation, are also taken up (from a psychological perspective) in Chapters 8 and 9.

Sociologists have also studied children, and one can talk of a sociology of child development, as Gerald Handel's chapter on this topic (Chapter 7) makes clear. Handel gives a clear but critical account of the functionalist approach of Parsons and the symbolic interactionist approach of George Herbert Mead. He is especially critical of some recent sociological theorizing that rejects the concept of "socialization" completely. The latter part of his chapter illuminates the various agencies and contexts of socialization that sociologists often consider. Sociologists see the child's development more naturally in terms of larger societal influences and structures (the more outer circles of Bronfenbrenner's ecological model, perhaps) rather than the dynamics of individual interactions. Nevertheless, they have not totally neglected the latter, just as psychologists have not totally neglected the wider context.

CHAPTER TWO

Behavioral Genetics

Alice M. Gregory, Harriet A. Ball, and Tanya M. M. Button

Some children seemingly effortlessly enter into supportive peer relationships, are healthily attached to their parents, and appear to be sensitive to the thoughts and needs of others. Of course, others do not display such behaviors, and the extent to which children develop socially can heavily impact all aspects of their lives. It is therefore important to understand risk and resilience factors influencing social development. Behavioral genetics is one area of research that can inform this issue (see Plomin, DeFries, McClearn, & McGuffin, 2008). Amongst other things, this type of research can provide estimates of the extent to which individual differences with regard to a behavior are heritable, help to *specify* genetic and environmental influences on social behaviors, and explain the interactions between these influences. This chapter will begin with a discussion of the basic techniques commonly used by behavioral geneticists in order to understand genetic and environmental influences on behavior. Next, some empirical data from genetic studies shall be presented. As social development is such a broad construct, three key aspects of social behavior will be focused on: antisocial behavior, bullying, and prosocial behavior.

Behavioral Genetic Techniques

Phenotypic variance

One of the primary goals of behavior genetics is to partition the variance of a given trait or phenotype (V_P) into its constituent components, namely, genetic variance (V_{Gen}) and

The Wiley-Blackwell Handbook of Childhood Social Development, Second Edition, edited by Peter K. Smith and Craig H. Hart
© 2011 by Blackwell Publishing Ltd.

environmental variance (V_{Env}), as well as the interaction ($V_{G\times E}$) and correlation (R_{GE}) of genetic and environmental influences, such that $V_P = V_{Gen} + V_{Env} + V_{G\times E} + R_{GE}$.

The genetic variance can be further partitioned into additive genetic variance (V_A) and nonadditive genetic variance (V_D). Additive genetic effects occur when the effects of alleles (different forms of genetic sequences – such as different versions of a gene) influencing a phenotype act in a cumulative manner when contributing to that phenotype. Nonadditive genetic variance results from two phenomena: (a) dominance deviation, which refers to the interaction of alleles at *a single locus* (position on a chromosome); and (b) epistasis, which is the result of the interactions of genes at *different loci*.

Similarly, the environmental variance can be further partitioned into common, or shared, environmental variance (V_C) and nonshared environmental variance (V_E). *Shared environment* is defined as any environment that is correlated among family members and acts to make family members more similar, and might include factors such as prenatal environment and certain family factors (e.g., socioeconomic status could act so as to make young siblings more alike with regard to certain traits). *Nonshared environment* is defined as any environmental influence that is uncorrelated between family members and acts to make people different from one another, and might include peer relationships and school environments. It is important to note, however, that some environments that might intuitively seem to be shared might in fact be nonshared according to the definitions used in behavior genetic research. One example of this is parenting. Because two siblings within the same family share their parents, it is intuitive to believe that the parents would provide the same environment for one sibling as for the other, and this environment would therefore influence both children similarly. However, it is well established amongst geneticists that parenting can act as a nonshared environmental influence, making siblings dissimilar (e.g., see Plomin et al., 2008). Parents may treat one sibling in a different way from another, or a behavior displayed by parents to both children may have a different impact on different children. Adding complexity to the situation, it is also known that certain "environmental" influences may be influenced by genes (e.g., parenting has been shown to be genetically influenced; Pike, McGuire, Hetherington, Reiss, & Plomin, 1996). These points are important to note as those who are unfamiliar with behavior genetic research can sometimes misinterpret small shared environmental influence as suggesting that parenting is of little importance.

As represented in the equation above, there are other contributors to the variance of a phenotype. One is gene–environment interactions ($V_{G\times E}$). These occur when environments affect only the phenotypic variance in the presence of certain genotypic risks, and certain genotypic risks affect only the phenotypic variance in the presence of certain environments. For example, a study of criminality in adopted adult males showed that males had a greater chance of becoming criminal if they had *both* a genetic risk, as indicated by having a biological parent with antisocial behavior, *and* an adverse upbringing (Cadoret, Yates, Troughton, Woodworth, & Stewart, 1995). Having either the genetic risk or the environmental risk alone did not increase the risk of becoming criminal.

Another contributor to phenotypic variance is gene–environment correlation (rGE), whereby genes and environment correlate. One example of this was given above, where it was noted that genetic predisposition may affect the way you are treated by your parents. Three types of rGE have been described: passive, active, and evocative. Passive rGE arises because parents pass on both genes and environment to their children; for example, a parent may both pass on genes for higher IQ and provide an environment that is conducive to learning. Active rGE arises because people seek out or modify their environment to suit their genetic predispositions. For example, a person of high IQ might be more inclined to seek out books that enhance knowledge. Evocative rGE arises as a result of other peoples' reactions to a person's genetically influenced behaviors. An example could be parenting styles changing from one sibling to another, based on the children's own behavior.

Based on the information provided thus far, it is possible to see that the partitioning of the phenotypic variance can be more fully explained as $V_P = V_A + V_D + V_C + V_E + V_{G \times E} + V_{rGE}$. Behavior geneticists have employed a number of techniques to estimate these variance components from the phenotypic variance, V_P, which can be directly observed and measured. Two methods are primarily utilized: twin studies and adoption studies.

Twin studies

Twin studies utilize the genetic relatedness of two different twin types to estimate the magnitude of each of the variance components discussed above. Identical or monozygotic (MZ) twin pairs are the result of fertilization of a single egg that splits into two during development. Consequently, MZ twin pairs are genetically identical. Fraternal or dizygotic (DZ) twin pairs, similar to nontwin full siblings, are the result of fertilization of two separate eggs, and consequently share, on average, 50% of their segregating genes (those genes that differ between individuals).

The correlation between MZ twin pairs (rMZ) is due to the additive genetic variance they share in common (V_A), the nonadditive genetic effects (V_D), and the shared environment (V_C) (for simplicity, we will not discuss $V_{G \times E}$ or V_{rGE} in this section). The nonshared environment (V_E), by definition, acts to make twins different from one another and as such does not contribute to their correlation on a trait. Therefore, rMZ $= V_A + V_D + V_C$. By contrast, DZ twin pairs share 50% of their additive genes ($0.5V_A$), 25% of the dominant genes ($0.25\ V_D$), and the shared environment (V_C). Therefore, the correlation between DZ twin pairs (rDZ) equals $0.5V_A + 0.25V_D + V_C$ (for more details, see Plomin et al., 2008). Information about the relatedness between twins is most commonly used to estimate the values of V_A, V_C, and V_E. The influences of V_D, rGE, or $V_{G \times E}$ can also be estimated from this information, but this is complex and requires a more sophisticated approach, which is beyond the scope of the current chapter. Therefore, from here onward we will consider rMZ $= V_A + V_C$ and rDZ $= 0.5V_A + V_C$ (i.e., we shall ignore nonadditive genetic effects as well as gene–environment interplay).

If a phenotype is genetically influenced, MZ twin pair correlations for that phenotype will be higher than for DZ twin pairs, because the former type of twin pair will possess more genes in common. However, we can take this a step further and estimate the proportion of the phenotypic variance that is due to additive genetic effects, also referred to as the *heritability*. Because here we consider rMZ $= V_A + V_C$ and rDZ $= 0.5V_A + V_C$, to

estimate the V_A, first we subtract the DZ twin correlation from the MZ twin correlation:
rMZ − rDZ = $(V_A + V_C) - (0.5V_A + V_C) = 0.5V_A$. This estimates the value for $0.5V_A$,
because this is what accounts for the difference between MZ and DZ correlations. We
therefore multiply this value by 2, such that

$$V_A = 2(\text{rMZ} - \text{rDZ})$$

As here the rMZ consists of V_A and V_C, once we know V_A, we can estimate V_C as being
the remaining variance after V_A has been accounted for (i.e., subtracting the V_A estimate
from the rMZ) such that

$$V_C = \text{rMZ} - V_A$$

Finally, we know that of the three variance components, V_A, V_C, and V_E, only V_E makes
MZ twins differ from one another (as opposed to DZ twins, in which V_E and the 50%
of their genes they do not share in common make them differ from one another).
Therefore, V_E must account for all the difference between MZ twin pairs such that

$$V_E = 1 - \text{rMZ}$$

In order to find out more about how the nonshared environment influences behavioral
traits (e.g., aggression), researchers have focused on the *MZ differences approach*, whereby
they study pairs of MZ twins exclusively and examine which environmental factors can
account for differences between MZs.

There are certain assumptions of twin studies that might affect their validity. For
example, there is the *equal environments assumption*, which proposes that MZ and DZ
twin environments are equally similar. However, some researchers have suggested that
MZ twins might share a more similar environment as compared to DZ twin pairs. For
example, MZ twin pairs may be treated more similarly by friends and family members
because they look more alike. Research has examined the degree to which this issue
impacts estimates from twin studies, finding that such differences do not tend to influence
twin resemblance for various traits (e.g., Kendler, Neale, Kessler, Heath, & Eaves, 1993,
1994). On a similar note, MZ twins are more likely to share a chorion (the outermost
of the fetal membranes) as compared to DZ twins, who almost always have separate
chorions, and it has been suggested that this increase in environmental similarity may
account for the increased behavioral similarity of MZ as compared to DZ twins. There
has been some support for this hypothesis with regard to certain traits (e.g., monochori-
onic as compared to dichorionic twins were found in one study to have more similar
scores with regard to certain IQ subscales; see Jacobs et al., 2001) – although, overall,
evidence is mixed (see Plomin et al., 2008).

Another assumption of twin studies is that there is random mating between the parents
of the twins. In fact, there is some evidence that some people attract and have children
with people who are very similar to themselves, and therefore are likely to have more
similar genetic propensities. If parents of twins are more similar than would occur by
chance, this might influence the genetic similarities between DZ twins, thereby affecting

the estimated heritability. Although the classical twin design discussed here assumes that all mating is random, it is possible to test the role of nonrandom mating using a twin design (Maes et al., 1998).

Other potential limitations of the twin study design include the possibility that being a twin (as compared to a singleton) has an impact on social development, and as such, results from twin studies may not be applicable to nontwin populations. Finally, MZ twins are also more likely to experience birth defects as compared to DZ twins, which can also contribute to the difference in correlations between them. Despite the limitations discussed here, the twin design has proved highly informative in estimating the general magnitude of the variance components for many behavioral phenotypes.

Adoption studies

Adoption studies utilize the relationships between adoptees and family members of differing genetic and environmental relatedness. For example, an adoptee may have biological parents, with whom the adoptee shares 50% of his or her genes but no postnatal environment, and adoptive parents and adoptive siblings, with whom they share their environment but no genes. In contrast, nonadopted children may live with their biological parents and biological siblings, with whom they share genes and environment. Two types of adoption studies are generally employed for genetic analyses.

The first compares the similarity of the adoptee with both the adoptive parent(s) and the biological parent(s). If the child is more like his or her biological parent for a certain phenotype, then genes likely contribute to this similarity (because they have not shared a common environment), and if they are more like their adoptive parents, then shared environment is a likely explanation. The second type of adoption study is similar to the twin method described previously, only instead of comparing MZ and DZ twin correlations, biological sibling and adoptive sibling correlations are compared. In this scenario, biological sibling correlations (rBS) are due to $0.5V_A + V_C$, whereas adoptive sibling correlations (rAS) are due to V_C only. Therefore, we can estimate V_A using the equations $0.5V_A = rBS - rAS = (0.5V_A + V_C) - V_C$; therefore,

$$V_A = 2 \times (rBS - rAS)$$

Because the only contributor to the adopted sibling correlation is V_C, this correlation is a direct estimate of V_C, such that

$$V_C = rAS$$

Finally, we can estimate V_E as

$$V_E = 1 - (V_A + V_C)$$

As with twin studies, adoption studies have a number of limitations. These include the issue of selective placement, whereby adoptive children are placed in families that most resemble their biological family. Adoption studies may also be limited by a paucity of information with regard to biological parents. Finally, adoption studies are now less prevalent than twin studies, partly due to decreasing rates of adoption.

Specifying Genetic Influences on Traits

Once research has demonstrated genetic influence on a trait, the next logical step is to specify the genes involved in that trait. Two commonly employed techniques are linkage and association studies.

Linkage studies are based on the finding that different *alleles* (defined previously as different forms of genetic sequences – such as different versions of a gene) that are physically close to one another on a *chromosome* (which refers to a structure found in cells containing DNA) are more likely to be inherited together as compared to those alleles that are further apart. If an allele is found more frequently in individuals with a certain trait as compared to people without that trait, we can infer that there must be at least one gene influencing the trait on the chromosome in the region of the allele under investigation. The allele actually influencing the trait is said to be *functional*. Linkage allows researchers to identify measured alleles associated with traits even when that allele is not having any effect on the trait (i.e., is not "functional"). Instead, the measured allele that is associated with the trait of interest can be quite far away from the functional allele. One way of examining linkage is to look at large family pedigrees to investigate whether those who show a certain trait are more likely to have a certain allele as compared to family members who do not show that trait. Linkage is typically used to identify genes that have a large effect on the trait under investigation.

Association studies are used to examine whether an allele at a particular position on a chromosome is more likely to occur when a trait is present. One way of examining association is to compare groups who score high and low on a trait and to see whether there are differences in the frequency of a certain allele between these two groups. The association technique can be used to examine associations between genes of small effect sizes and traits, although it is important that the allele being investigated is close to the functional allele (defined previously as that which is actually affecting the trait).

In addition to examining DNA sequence variation in association with traits, there has recently been a growing interest in epigenetic processes. These processes focus on heritable, but reversible, regulation of gene expression without change in DNA sequence (see Jirtle & Skinner, 2007). Epigenetic processes may be able to explain some of the behavioral differences between identical twins. For example, although MZ twins may be genetic clones of one another, certain genes may be expressed in one twin to a greater extent than the other – and this may partly explain why one twin behaves differently from the other (e.g., is more aggressive). Little is currently known about epigenetic processes and social behavior, but it is possible that examining epigenetic differences between MZ twins in association with such behavioral differences will prove informative.

Social Behavior: Lessons From Behavioral Genetic Studies

Antisocial behavior

Rates of antisocial behavior are generally lower in young children, increasing throughout adolescence before decreasing again in early adulthood. It is important to understand what differentiates children who choose to participate in such behaviors from those who do not.

It has been suggested that antisocial behavior that begins in childhood may have an underlying neurological basis (Moffitt, 1993), is genetically influenced, and is likely to persist throughout the life of the individual. Most studies of antisocial behavior in children support the hypothesis of a genetic basis to antisocial behavior, and moderate to substantial heritability estimates have been reported (e.g., Arseneault et al., 2003; Baker, Jacobson, Raine, Lozano, & Bezdjian, 2007; Burt, Krueger, McGue, & Iacono, 2001; Hudziak, Rudiger, Neale, Heath, & Todd, 2000; van Beijsterveldt, Bartels, Hudziak, & Boomsma, 2003; van der Valk, van den Oord, Verhulst, & Boomsma, 2003). Interestingly, antisocial behavior that persists across different situations appears to be under stronger genetic influence as compared to behavior that is situation specific, and the heritability of situation-specific behavior is moderated by both the person rating the behavior and the measure used (Arseneault et al., 2003; Baker et al., 2007). Arseneault and colleagues (2003) used scores from a combination of raters and measures and found that antisocial behavior in 5-year-olds was moderately to highly heritable. Nonshared environment contributed to the remaining variance. There was no evidence of shared environmental effects on antisocial behavior for any of the scores ascertained in this study. Heritabilities (V_A) were estimated to be .42 based on child report, .61 for examiner report, .69 for maternal report, and .76 for teachers' report. The factor common to all four raters, referred to as *pervasive antisocial behavior*, was also genetically influenced.

Throughout childhood, the heritability of antisocial behavior, although influenced by definition, measure, rater, and other components of the environment, does not usually differ according to age or sex (although a minority of studies do find a sex difference). For example, van Beijsterveldt and colleagues estimated the heritability of aggression, examined using the aggression subscale of the Child Behavior Checklist (Achenbach, 1991) at ages 3, 7, 10, and 12 years (van Beijsterveldt et al., 2003). Heritability estimates varied only slightly across age and sex, ranging from .56 to .67 in males and from .50 to .64 in females. This report also found that shared environmental effects contributed significantly to the variance of parental-rated aggression, something that is found less often in older samples. Much of the genetic and shared environmental influences for aggression were transmitted across age, meaning that some of the same genetic and shared environmental influences on aggression at one time point also influenced aggression at another time point. The nonshared environmental factors were largely age specific.

The first evidence for an interaction between a latent (estimated rather than measured) genotype and measured environment in the development of antisocial behavior came from an adult adoption study (Cadoret et al., 1995). The authors demonstrated that having an adverse environment and a genotypic risk (indexed by having a biological parent showing criminality) increased the risk for antisocial outcomes more than would be expected as an additive effect of both. Jaffee et al. (2005) reported a similar finding based on data from 5-year-old twins. It was found that maltreatment was only a significant risk for childhood antisocial behavior in the presence of a high genetic risk, as indicated by having a MZ twin with conduct disorder (Jaffee et al., 2005).

A second form of interplay between latent genotype and measured environment occurs when environmental background moderates the heritability of a phenotype. Unlike the interaction described above, in which the interaction influences the mean of the trait, the effect here is on the variance, such that the genetic and environmental variances vary as a function of the level of the environmental risk. The majority of studies that have looked at the moderation of heritability of antisocial behavior by different environments have focused on adolescents and adults. Environmental factors explored include the family environment (Button, Scourfield, Martin, Purcell, & McGuffin, 2005), peer groups (Button et al., 2007), and parenting (Button, Lau, Maughan, & Eley, 2008; Feinberg, Button, Neiderhiser, Reiss, & Hetherington, 2007). With regard to family environment, it was found that family dysfunction moderates genetic risk of antisocial behavior in children and adolescents (Button et al., 2005). There are currently no studies of this type that focus exclusively on children within the postinfancy to adolescence age range.

As with most behavioral studies, research into specific genes that contribute to anti-social phenotypes has largely focused on the serotonin and dopamine neurotransmitter systems. Many studies of adolescent and adult antisocial behavior have shown evidence that genes influencing catechol-O-methyl-transferase (COMT; Rujescu, Giegling, Gietl, Hartmann, & Moller, 2003; Strous, Bark, Parsia, Volavka, & Lachman, 1997), monoamine oxidase A (MAOA; Manuck, Flory, Ferrell, Mann, & Muldoon, 2000), serotonin transporter (Bellivier et al., 2000), and tryptophan hydroxylase (TPH; Manuck et al., 1999) may be involved, although positive replications of these findings are typically scarce. There are far fewer studies of this type focusing on antisocial behavior in childhood. However, the twin study by van Beijsterveldt et al. (2003), which pointed to genetic continuity across age, suggests some of these specific genes may also be involved at younger ages.

There is a paucity of research specifying polymorphisms (i.e., versions of genes or other sections of DNA) in association with antisocial behavior in childhood, but some studies have demonstrated links. For instance, Schmidt and colleagues (Schmidt, Fox, Rubin, Hu, & Hamer, 2002) demonstrated an association between a polymorphism of the dopamine D4 receptor gene (DRD4) and maternal report of problems with aggression in 4-year-olds. Evidence of an association between the serotonin transporter gene and aggression has also been reported (Beitchman et al., 2003), although results are not consistent (Schmidt et al., 2002). Differences may be due to population and polymorphism differences across studies.

Some studies have started to provide evidence that interactions between specific genetic polymorphisms and specific environmental factors increase the risk for antisocial behavior. The majority of these have focused on polymorphisms within the MAOA gene, which moderated the association between maltreatment and antisocial behavior, as demonstrated in a seminal paper by Caspi and colleagues (2002). Results are somewhat inconsistent, with some finding in favor of an interaction (Foley et al., 2004), and others failing to replicate these findings (Haberstick et al., 2005; Huizinga et al., 2006; Young et al., 2006). This same interaction has been replicated in children, where it was found that 7-year-old boys with a high-risk allele were at significantly greater risk for antisocial behavior than those with the low-risk allele, but only in those who had been exposed to physical abuse (Kim-Cohen et al., 2006). In those who were not exposed to abuse, there was no significant difference in antisocial behavior in those with a high-risk MAOA allele as compared to those without this allele. Despite this study of 7-year-olds, the majority of studies of this type have focused on antisocial behavior in adolescents and adults.

Other interactions have been found between different genes and environmental risks in children. For example, one study reported an interaction between a 7-repeat polymorphism of the DRD4 and maternal insensitivity in predicting externalizing behavior (Bakermans-Kranenburg & van IJzendoorn, 2006). The authors found significantly more externalizing behavior in preschoolers exposed to maternal insensitivity, but only in the presence of the DRD4 7-repeat polymorphism, thereby concluding that the presence of the 7-repeat DRD4 allele confers susceptibility to insensitive parenting.

Bullying

One specific form of antisocial behavior is bullying (see also Chapter 27). *Bullying* is defined as deliberate interpersonal aggression that involves a power imbalance (i.e., the bully is physically or psychologically stronger than the victim, who is thus unable to retaliate effectively) and is repeated over time (Rigby, 2002). Much previous research has described the association between bullying or victimization and environmental factors (Griffin & Gross, 2004). However, little research has considered the role of genetic susceptibility, or the interplay between genetic vulnerabilities and environments. There are increased rates of emotional and behavioral problems in bullies and victims, but the worst outcomes are seen in bully-victims, who both bully others and experience being the victim (Arseneault et al., 2006).

As bullying is a subset of antisocial or aggressive behavior, the etiology of bullying might be expected to be similar to that of antisocial behavior. In a sample of 87 twin pairs (average age 7.6 years), the correlation for bullying behavior among MZ twins was estimated at .72, compared to .42 among DZ same-sex twins (O'Connor, Foch, Sherry, & Plomin, 1980). The sample size was too small for model fitting, but we can infer a genetic effect because the MZ correlation was significantly greater than the DZ correlation.

This finding was corroborated by results from the Environmental Risk (E-Risk) Study, which was designed to examine specific environmental risks on the development of disruptive behavior in over 1,000 twin pairs from families in England and Wales. Items specifically indexing bullying were assessed when the twins were 10 years old. Model fitting was used to estimate that over half of the variance in bullying behavior was influenced by genetic factors, with the remainder due to nonshared environmental effects (Ball et al., 2008). This suggests that when several children in a family are bullies, it is more likely to be due to shared genetic inheritance than the family environment (such as parenting style). The genetic influences are unlikely to come in the form of a "gene for bullying"; instead, genes may influence physical characteristics or psychological factors such as social cognition or emotional regulation, which are associated with bullying behavior (Sutton, Smith, & Swettenham, 1999). The nonshared environmental influences could include the influence of peer groups, in so far as these differ within the twin pairs (Harris, 1998), as well as measurement error. These results are largely similar to findings for antisocial behavior, except for the lack of any influence from the shared environment.

In addition to focusing on bullying behavior, behavioral genetic research has also focused on the victims of bullying. In the aforementioned E-Risk study, mother reports of children's experiences as victims of bullying (aged 9 or 10) revealed that over two thirds of individual differences in this victimization were influenced by genetics (MZ twins had much more similar victimization experiences than did DZ twins). Moreover, as well as item checklists, mothers were asked to describe the specific victimization experience. This ensured that only descriptions of bullying were included (rather than a falling out between children who were both equally abusive to the other), and also confirmed that within-pair bullying (i.e., one twin bullying the co-twin, a situation that cannot be generalized to nontwins) was virtually nonexistent.

Because victimization is an exposure rather than a behavior, the genetic influences on victimization probably act to make children more likely to be targeted by bullies (i.e., some of children's heritable characteristics act to evoke bullying). For example, there are genetic influences on personality and coping strategies in response to difficult situations (Bouchard & Loehlin, 2001; Kozak, Strelau, & Miles, 2005), and these characteristics may lead to initiation or perpetuation of victimization by bullies. Such situations, in which genes are associated with the particular environment to which a child is exposed, are examples of gene–environment correlations. Molecular studies of victimization in young children are scarce, but one study examined the role of the dopamine D2 receptor gene in adolescent and young adult victims of violent criminal behavior (although not necessarily victimization by a bully). White males with more risk alleles were more likely to be victimized, but only if they also had few delinquent peers (Beaver et al., 2007). This association was not found for Black participants or females.

Strong genetic influences were not found in the Quebec Newborn Twin Study (QNTS), which assessed peer nominations of twins' victimization just after they began kindergarten at 6 years of age (Brendgen et al., 2008). The etiology of young children's victimization experiences was found to be entirely environmental, mainly through nonshared environmental factors but to a lesser degree through twins' shared environmental factors. This etiology is similar to that relating to young twins' experiences of maltreatment by adults (as described by mothers when the twins were 5 years old; Jaffee, Caspi, Moffitt, & Taylor, 2004). This suggests that children's genetic propensities largely do not evoke their victimization or maltreatment experiences when they are very young. The environmental experiences that might precipitate the victimization could include characteristics of parents, or even bad luck (being in the wrong place at the wrong time). At older ages, there do appear to be strong influences of heritable characteristics on children's victimization status.

Clearly, twin studies can provide novel information about bullying and being a victim of bullying. Going further, these studies have also examined links between early victimization experiences and later psychological and behavioral problems. In the E-Risk study, problems associated with victimization included the internalization of problems, reduced happiness at school, and lower prosocial behavior, and persisted even when controlling for these characteristics before the children started school (Arseneault et al., 2006). This is important to note because the children who later became victims had higher levels of these characteristics at school entry (age 5), but the experience of being victimized was associated with even higher levels at age 7 years. In addition, girls who were victimized displayed more externalizing problems at age 7 than those who were not involved in bullying (as bullies, victims, or bully-victims). A later analysis of this sample focused on just the MZ twins to reveal that the victimization the children experienced between ages 7 and 9 acted as an environmental influence on internalizing problems at age 10 (Arseneault et al., 2008). This was deduced by examining differences within pairs of MZ twins: To the extent that victimization experiences differed within each pair of twins, the victimized twin was more likely to have subsequent internalizing problems. This association cannot be down to genes or shared family influences (because these are, by definition, shared within MZ pairs). This environmental effect supports interventions that aim to reduce bullying involvement in order to improve later mental health, because it suggests that internalizing problems are in part caused by victimization, rather than entirely pre-existing and leading to victimization. This finding also illustrates the importance of environmental influences on victimization, even though there are also substantial genetic influences.

The Montreal-based QNTS study (Brendgen et al., 2008) examined the relationship between victimization and later aggression: Some but by no means all children who are victimized were more aggressive later on (i.e., the association was relatively modest). The authors tested a variant of the diathesis–stress hypothesis, which acknowledges that the levels of stress required to produce a negative outcome depend on the extent of one's genetic vulnerability for that outcome. Specifically, it was proposed that a genetic propensity to aggression (diathesis), in combination with exposure to victimization (stress), would lead to heightened levels of aggression. Genetic propensity to aggression was assessed as a function of the co-twin's aggression and the zygosity of the pair. Children have the greatest genetic propensity if they have an aggressive MZ co-twin, the next greatest propensity if they have an aggressive DZ co-twin, lower propensity if they have a nonaggressive DZ co-twin, and the lowest genetic propensity if they have a nonaggressive MZ co-twin. Victimized girls showed elevated aggression only if they had a high genetic propensity to aggression, but this diathesis–stress effect was not seen in boys. This may be due to different normative aggression across the sexes: Aggression is more unusual in girls and so may only be elicited in response to the stress of victimization if the girl is genetically predisposed to such behavior (Brendgen et al., 2008).

The etiology leading to bully-victims was also examined in the E-Risk study. A bivariate model decomposed the co-occurrence of bullying and victimization. It was found that genes were the main driver behind the overlap (Ball et al., 2008). The genetic effects may operate through (a) heritable characteristics (e.g., introverted personality) eliciting victimization, the experience of which leads the child to become a bully; (b) heritable characteristics (e.g., physical strength) influencing bully perpetration, which leads the child to become a victim; or (c) certain heritable characteristics leading to both bullying and victimization within the same individual (i.e., the same genes predispose the child to both social roles). One possible pathway could be through poor emotional regulation, which is substantially heritable (Goldsmith, Lemery, Buss, & Campos, 1999) and is associated with both bullying and victimization, but especially with bully-victims (Schwartz, Proctor, & Chien, 2001).

In order to interpret the results of twin studies of bullying, it is important to assess the extent to which these results can be generalized from twins to nontwin children (e.g., to assess whether the same type of bullying occurs in both sorts of children). Some research suggests that having a best friend to some degree protects children from victimization, and a co-twin may act like a friend in this respect (Lamarche et al., 2006). However, generalizability is largely supported by the finding that the prevalence of bullying among twins is within the range found in nontwins, and prevalence does not differ significantly according to zygosity (Ball et al., 2008).

Prosocial behavior

Behavioral genetic studies have also provided information about *prosocial behavior*, which can be generally defined as voluntary behavior intended to benefit another. The main theories of prosocial behavior provide little information as to the role of genetic and environmental influences. For example, certain theories highlight the important role of parenting in children's development of prosocial behavior. It has been shown that parental use of induction (explanations for requests that children amend their behavior) is associated with prosocial behavior in children (e.g., Krevans & Gibbs, 1996). As parenting is influenced by both genetic and environmental factors, parenting research tells us little about the role of genetic and environmental factors in influencing prosocial behavior. Furthermore, although evolutionary theories of empathy and prosocial behavior such as reciprocal altruism (Trivers, 1971) highlight the importance of genetics in these behaviors, these approaches tend to focus on species-level behavior and typically do not explain individual differences, which is the focus of behavioral genetic research.

A study of mother reports of instigating cooperation in twins aged 3–8 years found that environmental influences alone explained reports of cooperative behavior, with shared environmental influences accounting for 61% of the variance and nonshared environmental influences accounting for the remaining 39% (Lemery & Goldsmith, 2002).

As well as providing basic information about the heritability of prosocial behavior, twin studies have also investigated other aspects of prosocial behavior such as commonly reported sex differences, as well as developmental changes. One twin study examined parent and teacher reports of prosocial behavior in children (5–11 years) and adolescents (11–17 years) (Scourfield, John, Martin, & McGuffin, 2004). Girls were more prosocial than boys; but despite sex differences in the amount of prosocial behavior reported, the magnitude of genetic and environmental influences on prosocial behavior did not differ between the sexes. This study also highlighted the importance of considering who is rating a behavior; for adolescents, the heritability estimates were greater when based on teacher as compared to parental data.

Developmental questions can also be addressed by assessing samples prospectively. One such study examined reports of prosocial behavior in twins who were initially aged

2 years. The families were followed up when the twins were 3, 4, and 7 years of age (Knafo & Plomin, 2006b). The results suggest that whereas genetic influences become more important over time, shared environmental influences become less important.

Observations of prosocial behavior provide a complementary way of assessing this phenotype. Such data were obtained in a twin study of prosocial behavior in infancy (Zahn-Waxler, Schiro, Robinson, Emde, & Schmitz, 2001). Differences in patterns of heritability were found for mother report as compared to observations of prosocial behavior. For example, shared environment accounted for continuity in mother-reported prosocial behavior, whereas genetic factors were more important for continuity in observational data. This could suggest that maternal perception is confounded with environmental effects and highlights the significance of the way in which prosocial behavior is assessed in genetic studies. Experiments using tasks such as the prisoner's dilemma have examined cooperation in twins and could also be useful in increasing our understanding of factors influencing prosocial behavior (Segal & Hershberger, 1999).

One feature of most of the studies reviewed is that the data come from a limited number of locations (Europe and the United States). Heritability is a population statistic, meaning that conclusions are relevant to the specific group of people being investigated and do not necessarily apply to other populations. It is therefore important to examine whether genes and environmental factors influencing prosocial behavior in one geographical location are the same as those having an influence in another. Toward this aim, researchers have begun to investigate twin samples in other locations. One study focused on South Korean twins aged 2–9 years (Hur & Rushton, 2007). Based on maternal ratings, heritability was estimated at 55%, with the rest of the variance due to nonshared environmental influences. The authors concluded that these results are similar to those found in Western samples.

Although twin studies have provided important information about genetic and environmental influences on prosocial behavior, it is useful to keep in mind challenges that have been raised. One relevant issue – namely, the importance of chorionicity – was addressed with regard to prosocial behavior in a sample of twins (mean age 4 years; Hur, 2007). There was little difference between identical twins who had shared a chorion and those who had not in terms of similarity for prosocial behavior. This led the researchers to conclude that chorionicity appears to have no effect on prosocial behavior. Instead, variance in prosocial behavior was largely explained by genetic and nonshared environmental influences. A further issue relevant to twin studies concerns the representativeness of the data. For example, it is possible that twins may differ from nontwins with regard to their prosocial behavior, although a study in adolescents did not find such differences between twins and nontwins (Gregory, Light-Haeusermann, Rijsdijk, & Eley, 2009).

Having established from twin studies that both genes and environmental factors influence prosocial behavior, researchers have attempted to identify the specific genes and environmental factors involved. With regard to the former, a genetic polymorphism in DRD4 has been associated with prosocial behavior (Bachner-Melman et al., 2005). Further consideration of what is actually being inherited may be useful when searching for these genes. For example, it is possible that the genetic component of prosocial behavior is partly mediated by its effects on associated heritable traits such as temperament, for which specific genes have been implicated (e.g., see Lakatos et al., 2003).

Environmental influences on prosocial behavior have also begun to be specified, and one successful approach to identifying nonshared environmental influences has been the MZ differences approach. One study of this type focused on 62 pairs of identical twins aged 3 1/2 years. There was an association between high levels of supportive parenting/ low levels of punitive parenting and prosocial behavior (Deater-Deckard et al., 2001). Consistent results come from a further study of 2,353 identical twins aged 4 years (Asbury, Dunn, Pike, & Plomin, 2003). Here it was found that twins who were subject to harsher parental discipline and more negative emotions were less likely than their co-twin to be reported to behave prosocially. Genetic and environmental influences on the links between parental discipline and affection and prosocial behavior have also been studied, with data suggesting that children's genes could play a role in eliciting parental behaviors that are then associated with their prosocial behavior (Knafo & Plomin, 2006a).

Conclusions

Behavioral genetic research has told us a great deal about social behavior. Moving beyond whether genes and environments influence social behaviors, researchers are now interested in more complex questions, such as how the magnitude and types of genetic and environmental influences differ with development and across the sexes. Furthermore, although researchers often consider genetic influences in isolation from environmental ones (and vice versa), associations between genetic and environmental influences are undeniable. In reflection of this, research into gene–environment correlations and interactions has provided an important addition to our knowledge. Such issues have been addressed for antisocial behavior, although as yet this research is less developed for specific examples of antisocial behavior such as bullying, and other areas of social behavior such as prosocial acts. New questions continue to emerge, and sophisticated techniques to address these questions are being developed. Understanding more about the pathways by which genes and the environment influence certain behaviors remains an important issue, and increased knowledge in this area will hopefully aid the identification of those at risk for developing socially undesirable behaviors. Such information may eventually lead to successful interventions to help children reduce their socially undesirable behaviors and promote those that are desirable, which could benefit society as a whole.

Acknowledgments

Alice M. Gregory is supported by a research fellowship from the Leverhulme Trust. Please note that all authors have written separate sections of this chapter, and therefore all should be considered first authors.

References

Achenbach, T. M. (1991). *Manual for the Child Behaviour Checklist and 1991 profile*. Burlington: University of Vermont, Department of Psychiatry.

Arseneault, L., Milne, B. J., Taylor, A., Adams, F., Delgado, K., Caspi, A., et al. (2008). Being bullied as an environmentally mediated contributing factor to children's internalizing problems. *Archives of Pediatrics & Adolescent Medicine, 162*, 145–150.

Arseneault, L., Moffitt, T. E., Caspi, A., Taylor, A., Rijsdijk, F. V., Jaffee, S. R., et al. (2003). Strong genetic effects on cross-situational antisocial behaviour among 5-year-old children according to mothers, teachers, examiner-observers, and twins' self-reports. *Journal of Child Psychology and Psychiatry, 44*, 832–848.

Arseneault, L., Walsh, E., Trzesniewski, K., Newcombe, R., Caspi, A., & Moffitt, T. E. (2006). Bullying victimization uniquely contributes to adjustment problems in young children: A nationally representative cohort study. *Pediatrics, 118*, 130–138.

Asbury, K., Dunn, J. F., Pike, A., & Plomin, R. (2003). Nonshared environmental influences on individual differences in early behavioral development: A monozygotic twin differences study. *Child Development, 74*, 933–943.

Bachner-Melman, R., Gritsenko, I., Nemanov, L., Zohar, A. H., Dina, C., & Ebstein, R. P. (2005). Dopaminergic polymorphisms associated with self-report measures of human altruism: A fresh phenotype for the dopamine D4 receptor. *Molecular Psychiatry, 10*, 333–335.

Baker, L. A., Jacobson, K. C., Raine, A., Lozano, D. I., & Bezdjian, S. (2007). Genetic and environmental bases of childhood antisocial behavior: A multi-informant twin study. *Journal of Abnormal Psychology, 116*, 219–235.

Bakermans-Kranenburg, M. J., & van IJzendoorn, M. H. (2006). Gene-environment interaction of the dopamine D4 receptor (DRD4) and observed maternal insensitivity predicting externalizing behavior in preschoolers. *Developmental Psychobiology, 48*, 406–409.

Ball, H. A., Arseneault, L., Taylor, A., Maughan, B., Caspi, A., & Moffitt, T. E. (2008). Genetic and environmental influences on victims, bullies and bully-victims in childhood. *Journal of Child Psychology and Psychiatry, 49*, 104–112.

Beaver, K. M., Wright, J. P., DeLisi, M., Daigle, L. E., Swatt, M. L., & Gibson, C. L. (2007). Evidence of a gene x environment interaction in the creation of victimization: Results from a longitudinal sample of adolescents. *International Journal of Offender Therapy and Comparative Criminology, 51*, 620–645.

Beitchman, J. H., Davidge, K. M., Kennedy, J. L., Atkinson, L., Lee, V., Shapiro, S., et al. (2003). The serotonin transporter gene in aggressive children with and without ADHD and nonaggressive matched controls. *Roots of Mental Illness in Children, 1008*, 248–251.

Bellivier, F., Szoke, A., Henry, C., Lacoste, J., Bottos, C., Nosten-Bertrand, M., et al. (2000). Possible association between serotonin transporter gene polymorphism and violent suicidal behavior in mood disorders. *Biological Psychiatry, 48*, 319–322.

Bouchard, T. J., & Loehlin, J. C. (2001). Genes, evolution, and personality. *Behavior Genetics, 31*, 243–273.

Brendgen, M., Boivin, M., Vitaro, F., Girard, A., Dionne, G., & Perusse, D. (2008). Gene-environment interaction between peer victimisation and child aggression. *Development & Psychopathology, 20*, 455–471.

Burt, S. A., Krueger, R. F., McGue, M., & Iacono, W. G. (2001). Sources of covariation among attention-deficit hyperactivity disorder, oppositional defiant disorder, and conduct disorder: The importance of shared environment. *Journal of Abnormal Psychology, 110*, 516–525.

Button, T. M. M., Corley, R. P., Rhee, S. H., Hewitt, J. K., Young, S. E., & Stallings, M. C. (2007). Delinquent peer affiliation and conduct problems: A twin study. *Journal of Abnormal Psychology, 116*, 554–564.

Button, T. M. M., Lau, J. Y. F., Maughan, B., & Eley, T. C. (2008). Parental punitive discipline, negative life events and gene-environment interplay in the development of externalizing behavior. *Psychological Medicine, 38*, 29–39.

Button, T. M. M., Scourfield, J., Martin, N., Purcell, S., & McGuffin, P. (2005). Family dysfunction interacts with genes in the causation of antisocial symptoms. *Behavior Genetics, 35*, 115–120.

Cadoret, R. J., Yates, W. R., Troughton, E., Woodworth, G., & Stewart, M. A. (1995). Genetic-environmental interaction in the genesis of aggressivity and conduct disorders. *Archives of General Psychiatry, 52*, 916–924.

Caspi, A., McClay, J., Moffitt, T. E., Mill, J., Martin, J., Craig, I. W., et al. (2002). Role of genotype in the cycle of violence in maltreated children. *Science, 297*, 851–854.

Deater-Deckard, K., Pike, A., Petrill, S. A., Cutting, A. L., Hughes, C., & O'Connor, T. G. (2001). Nonshared environmental processes in social-emotional development: An observational study of identical twin differences in the preschool period. *Developmental Science, 4*, F1–F6.

Feinberg, M. E., Button, T. M. M., Neiderhiser, J. M., Reiss, D., & Hetherington, E. M. (2007). Parenting and adolescent antisocial behavior and depression: Evidence of genotype × parenting environment interaction. *Archives of General Psychiatry, 64*, 457–465.

Foley, D. L., Eaves, L. J., Wormley, B., Silberg, J. L., Maes, H. H., Kuhn, J., et al. (2004). Childhood adversity, monoamine oxidase A genotype, and risk for conduct disorder. *Archives of General Psychiatry, 61*, 738–744.

Goldsmith, H. H., Lemery, K. S., Buss, K. A., & Campos, J. J. (1999). Genetic analyses of focal aspects of infant temperament. *Developmental Psychology, 35*, 972–985.

Gregory, A. M., Light-Haeusermann, J., Rijsdijk, F. V., & Eley, T. C. (2009). Behavioural genetic analyses of prosocial behaviour in adolescents. *Developmental Science, 12*, 165–174.

Griffin, R. S., & Gross, A. M. (2004). Childhood bullying: Current empirical findings and future directions for research. *Aggression and Violent Behavior, 9*, 379–400.

Haberstick, B. C., Lessem, J. M., Hopfer, C. J., Smolen, A., Ehringer, M. A., Timberlake, D., et al. (2005). Monoamine oxidase A (MAOA) and antisocial behaviors in the presence of childhood and adolescent maltreatment. *American Journal of Medical Genetics Part B: Neuropsychiatric Genetics, 135B*, 59–64.

Harris, J. R. (1998). *The nurture assumption: Why children turn out the way they do*. New York: Free Press.

Hudziak, J. J., Rudiger, L. P., Neale, M. C., Heath, A. C., & Todd, R. D. (2000). A twin study of inattentive, aggressive, and anxious/depressed behaviors. *Journal of the American Academy of Child & Adolescent Psychiatry, 39*, 469–476.

Huizinga, D., Haberstick, B. C., Smolen, A., Menard, S., Young, S. E., Corley, R. P., et al. (2006). Childhood maltreatment, subsequent antisocial behavior, and the role of monoamine oxidase A genotype. *Biological Psychiatry, 60*, 677–683.

Hur, Y. M. (2007). Effects of the chorion type on prosocial behavior in young South Korean twins. *Twin Research and Human Genetics, 10*, 773–777.

Hur, Y. M., & Rushton, J. P. (2007). Genetic and environmental contributions to prosocial behaviour in 2-to 9-year-old South Korean twins. *Biology Letters, 3*, 664–666.

Jacobs, N., Gestel, S. V., Derom, C., Thiery, E., Vernon, P. A., Derom, R., et al. (2001). Heritability estimates of intelligence in twins: Effect of chorion type. *Behavior Genetics, 31*, 209–217.

Jaffee, S. R., Caspi, A., Moffitt, T. E., Dodge, K. A., Rutter, M., Taylor, A., et al. (2005). Nature X nurture: Genetic vulnerabilities interact with physical maltreatment to promote conduct problems. *Development and Psychopathology, 17*, 67–84.

Jaffee, S. R., Caspi, A., Moffitt, T. E., & Taylor, A. (2004). Physical maltreatment victim to antisocial child: Evidence of an environmentally mediated process. *Journal of Abnormal Psychology, 113,* 44–55.

Jirtle, R. L., & Skinner, M. K. (2007). Environmental epigenomics and disease susceptibility. *Nature Reviews Genetics, 8,* 253–262.

Kendler, K. S., Neale, M. C., Kessler, R. C., Heath, A. C., & Eaves, L. J. (1993). A test of the equal-environment assumption in twin studies of psychiatric illness. *Behavior Genetics, 23,* 21–27.

Kendler, K. S., Neale, M. C., Kessler, R. C., Heath, A. C., & Eaves, L. J. (1994). Parental treatment and the equal environment assumption in twin studies of psychiatric-illness. *Psychological Medicine, 24,* 579–590.

Kim-Cohen, J., Caspi, A., Taylor, A., Williams, B., Newcombe, R., Craig, I. W., et al. (2006). MAOA, maltreatment, and gene-environment interaction predicting children's mental health: New evidence and a meta-analysis. *Molecular Psychiatry, 11,* 903–913.

Knafo, A., & Plomin, R. (2006a). Parental discipline and affection and children's prosocial behavior: Genetic and environmental links. *Journal of Personality and Social Psychology, 90,* 147–164.

Knafo, A., & Plomin, R. (2006b). Prosocial behavior from early to middle childhood: Genetic and environmental influences on stability and change. *Developmental Psychology, 42,* 771–786.

Kozak, B., Strelau, J., & Miles, J. N. V. (2005). Genetic determinants of individual differences in coping styles. *Anxiety Stress and Coping, 18,* 1–15.

Krevans, J., & Gibbs, J. C. (1996). Parent's use of inductive discipline: Relations to children's empathy and prosocial behavior. *Child Development, 67,* 3263–3277.

Lakatos, K., Nemoda, Z., Birkas, E., Ronai, Z., Kovacs, E., Ney, K., et al. (2003). Association of D4 dopamine receptor gene and serotonin transporter promoter polymorphisms with infants' response to novelty. *Molecular Psychiatry, 8,* 90–97.

Lamarche, V., Brendgen, M., Boivin, M., Vitaro, F., Perusse, D., & Dionne, G. (2006). Do friendships and sibling relationships provide protection against peer victimization in a similar way? *Social Development, 15,* 373–393.

Lemery, K. S., & Goldsmith, H. H. (2002). Genetic and environmental influences on preschool sibling cooperation and conflict: Associations with difficult temperament and parenting style. *Marriage and Family Review, 33,* 77–99.

Maes, H. H., Neale, M. C., Kendler, K. S., Hewitt, J. K., Silberg, J. L., Foley, D. L., et al. (1998). Assortative mating for major psychiatric diagnoses in two population-based samples. *Psychological Medicine, 28,* 1389–1401.

Manuck, S. B., Flory, J. D., Ferrell, R. E., Dent, K. M., Mann, J. J., & Muldoon, M. F. (1999). Aggression and anger-related traits associated with a polymorphism of the tryptophan hydroxylase gene. *Biological Psychiatry, 45,* 603–614.

Manuck, S. B., Flory, J. D., Ferrell, R. E., Mann, J. J., & Muldoon, M. F. (2000). A regulatory polymorphism of the monoamine oxidase: A gene may be associated with variability in aggression, impulsivity, and central nervous system serotonergic responsivity. *Psychiatry Research, 95,* 9–23.

Moffitt, T. E. (1993). Adolescence-limited and life-course-persistent antisocial behavior: A developmental taxonomy. *Psychological Review, 100,* 674–701.

O'Connor, M., Foch, T. T., Sherry, T., & Plomin, R. (1980). A twin study of specific behavioral problems of socialization as viewed by parents. *Journal of Abnormal Child Psychology, 8,* 189–199.

Pike, A., McGuire, S., Hetherington, E. M., Reiss, D., & Plomin, R. (1996). Family environment and adolescent depressive symptoms and antisocial behavior: A multivariate genetic analysis. *Developmental Psychology, 32,* 590–603.

Plomin, R., DeFries, J. C., McClearn, G. E., & McGuffin, P. (2008). *Behavioral genetics* (5th ed.). New York: Worth.

Rigby, K. (2002). *New perspectives on bullying*. London: Jessica Kingsley.

Rujescu, D., Giegling, I., Gietl, A., Hartmann, A. M., & Moller, H. J. (2003). A functional single nucleotide polymorphism (V158M) in the COMT gene is associated with aggressive personality traits. *Biological Psychiatry, 54*, 34–39.

Schmidt, L. A., Fox, N. A., Rubin, K. H., Hu, S., & Hamer, D. H. (2002). Molecular genetics of shyness and aggression in preschoolers. *Personality and Individual Differences, 33*, 227–238.

Schwartz, D., Proctor, L. J., & Chien, D. H. (2001). The aggressive victim of bullying: Emotional and behavioural dysregulation as a pathway to victimisation by peers. In J. Juvonen & S. Graham (Eds.), *Peer harassment in school: The plight of the vulnerable and victimized* (pp. 147–174). New York: Guilford Press.

Scourfield, J., John, B., Martin, N., & McGuffin, P. (2004). The development of prosocial behaviour in children and adolescents: A twin study. *Journal of Child Psychology and Psychiatry, 45*, 927–935.

Segal, N. L., & Hershberger, S. L. (1999). Cooperation and competition between twins: Findings from a prisoner's dilemma game. *Evolution and Human Behavior, 20*, 29–51.

Strous, R. D., Bark, N., Parsia, S. S., Volavka, J., & Lachman, H. M. (1997). Analysis of a functional catechol-O-methyltransferase gene polymorphism in schizophrenia: Evidence for association with aggressive and antisocial behavior. *Psychiatry Research, 69*, 71–77.

Sutton, J., Smith, P. K., & Swettenham, J. (1999). Social cognition and bullying: Social inadequacy or skilled manipulation? *British Journal of Developmental Psychology, 17*, 435–450.

Trivers, R. L. (1971). Evolution of reciprocal altruism. *Quarterly Review of Biology, 46*, 35–57.

van Beijsterveldt, C. E. M., Bartels, M., Hudziak, J. J., & Boomsma, D. I. (2003). Causes of stability of aggression from early childhood to adolescence: A longitudinal genetic analysis in Dutch twins. *Behavior Genetics, 33*, 591–605.

van der Valk, J. C., van den Oord, E. J. C. G., Verhulst, F. C., & Boomsma, D. I. (2003). Using shared and unique parental views to study the etiology of 7-year-old twins' internalizing and externalizing problems. *Behavior Genetics, 33*, 409–420.

Young, S. E., Smolen, A., Hewitt, J. K., Haberstick, B. C., Stallings, M. C., Corley, R. P., et al. (2006). Interaction between MAO-A genotype and maltreatment in the risk for conduct disorder: Failure to confirm in adolescent patients. *American Journal of Psychiatry, 163*, 1019–1025.

Zahn-Waxler, C., Schiro, K., Robinson, J. L., Emde, R. N., & Schmitz, S. (2001). Empathy and prosocial patterns in young MZ and DZ twins: Development and genetic and environmental influences. In R. N. Emde & J. K. Hewitt (Eds.), *Infancy to early childhood: Genetic and environmental influences on developmental change* (pp. 141–162). New York: Oxford University Press.

CHAPTER THREE

Conceptual Development and Emotion: A Neuropsychological Perspective

Steven Woltering and Marc D. Lewis

For a long time, philosophers and psychologists have viewed cognition and emotion as phenomena with different underlying mechanisms. Recently, neuropsychological research shows that emotion strongly interacts with cognition in several areas like attention (Armony & Dolan, 2002), perception (Anderson & Phelps, 2001), decision making (Bechara, Tranel, & Damasio, 2000), and learning (Hamann, Ely, Grafton, & Kilts, 1999). Based on such findings, theoretical models have emerged that integrate cognition and emotion into one system (Lewis, 2005; Pessoa, 2008). We propose that models viewing emotions as an integral part of our cognitive functioning, present in every aspect of our thoughts, could also lead us to a new understanding of how the mind acquires concepts.

Unfortunately, little is known about the formation of concepts, especially from a neuropsychological perspective. Furthermore, psychological and neuropsychological accounts of conceptual development focus on purely cognitive factors and/or language, often ignoring socioemotional factors (e.g., Mahon & Caramazza, 2009; Neisser, 1987; Siegal, 2004). This chapter will offer an exploratory framework for conceptual development in children, highlighting the emotion of desire. We will ground this idea in a neuropsychological model of motivated cognitive activity, and we thus hope to provide a unique contribution to understanding conceptual development.

Concept Formation and Desire

Concepts and their origins

Connectionist models have helped us a great deal in understanding how it is possible for an intelligent system to form internal representations (Plunkett, Karmiloff-Smith, Bates, Elman, & Johnson, 1997; Smith & Gasser, 2005). From this perspective, our brain can be best described as a natural pattern recognizer that finds regularities and associations in the multitude of experiences and perceptual stimuli that we encounter every moment. By generalizing across sensory stimuli and their associations, our brain finds patterns of similarity that become predictable in time and space. Such generalizations become stable and form what are sometimes called *internal representations*. For example, babies automatically learn that human voices sound similar, and they categorize them separately from nonhuman sounds (e.g., a concept of human voice; Decasper & Fifer, 1980). Increasing complexity emerges as overarching regularities form second-order generalizations. Infants recognize that their mother's voice is a human voice, and that her voice is distinct from their father's voice. Colunga and Smith (2003) thought of such generalizations as conceptual abstractions. Note that in this view perceptual categorization and concept formation are seen as one process (Mandler, 2004).

However, we are not just passive pattern recognizers. Certain predispositions, some even present at birth, constrain and bias us toward linking certain configurations of sensory stimuli. For example, the perception of object boundaries is crucial to identify different categories of shapes, and this representational ability seems to be present at birth (Aguiar & Baillargeon, 1999). Spelke and Kinzler (2007) called these *core knowledge structures* and suggested they could form a primary foundation on which concepts can develop. More generally, existing concepts are thought to influence the acquisition of new ones. There is strong evidence showing that children and adults are actively processing information and modifying information on the basis of internal mental schemata. These conceptual structures create expectations that seek to confirm or reject the emergence of other concepts based on prior experience and assumptions (Gelman, 2009).

There are many definitions of *concept formation*, but we will simply define it as the acquisition of a general schema or category that refers to a subset of events or objects, such that those events or objects are viewed as similar (e.g., instantiations of a schema, or members of a category). These mental representations organize experience and can include events, objects, actions, and mental and affective states.

Concept formation is embodied: action is important

Unlike a computer, which gets its energy from an electrical power cord, living organisms need to seek out food, mate, and find safety to exist and continue existing. In other words, we are designed to act. As a consequence, mental computational processes have primarily evolved to serve the purpose of acting in a fashion that is in our best interest. Perception is therefore not a goal in itself. Rather, the goal of vision might be to seek out food and guide action toward it. The concepts that perception brings to mind are integrally linked to the purpose of acting in the world through our bodies.

That sensorimotor experience is necessary, for developing thought has been confirmed by a large body of research building on Piaget's insights into the role of active engagement with objects in cognitive development (Scholnick, Nelson, Miller, & Gelman, 1999; Wellman & Gelman, 1998). In this line of thought, the embodiment hypothesis (Smith & Gasser, 2005) proposes that representation emerges through the interaction of an agent with the environment, as initially mediated through sensorimotor experiences. Representations are structured, constrained, and formed according to the interactions between our actions and perceptual experiences.

The relation between the development of cognitive representation and action has been demonstrated in a classic experiment by Held and Hein (1963). Here, two kittens were raised in a carousel. One cat was hovering above the ground, strapped in a pouch that was pulled by another cat that could move around freely. Upon release, the cat that could move around freely behaved normally. By comparison, the other cat not only showed impaired movement, but also acted as if it was blind, despite being exposed to exactly the same visual stimuli (as a result of the movement of the carousel). This cat had apparently never learned to link its perceptions to its own action and could therefore not form any concepts from its sensory input. Its visual input was essentially meaningless. The cat had developed a form of visual agnosia – it was mentally blind.

Why is this important to our model of the role of *emotion* in concept formation? Similar to bodily experience, we will argue that emotional needs and drives are crucial for concepts to develop. Furthermore, acting is always subserved by goal seeking, and goals are understood to be driven or motivated. Here is where emotions, as motivators, come to play a role in the formation of concepts. We will argue that one such motivation, perhaps the most powerful approach motive, is desire.

Concept formation is motivated: the role of desire

Very few emotion theorists actually include desire as a basic emotion; Arnold (1960) and Frijda (1986) are the exceptions. Desire is generally not considered a basic emotion because it does not correspond to any facial expression and it is not short-lived, two criteria emphasized by Ekman (1984). Yet desire is nothing if not basic. It is subserved by a distinct neural mechanism (Berridge & Robinson, 1998; Depue & Collins, 1999; Panksepp, 1998) and evident early in the life span, a criterion emphasized by Izard (1993). It may be useful to subdivide this affective dimension into interest, at the less intense end, and craving, at the more intense end. Regardless of the terminology one uses, the feeling of "wanting" is fundamental.

In this chapter, we focus on the emotion of desire as an essential ingredient in the formation of concepts. We can see desire as being strongly linked to goal pursuit, which can be described as a natural and continuous "pull" between a goal state and a current state. Motivation in the moment, then, can come in two flavors: first, in the presence of the object while the goal is being achieved, which is wanting and getting; and, second, when the object is absent, which boils down to wanting and not getting (Lewis, 2009).

The first case is usually short-lived. All the signs of desire dissipate rapidly if the goal is in hand (or in the mouth, as with ice cream). But the second case may last for some time: This must be the period in which the memory of the goal supplies enough information to maintain the state of anticipation, attentional focus, motivation, and so forth. We propose that this state is required for conceptual development.

It is probably the case that there is not much concept formation going on *during* the event of acting itself. Rather, emerging concepts can be seen as bridges between a present goal and a future outcome – emotional bridges (Lewis, 2009). The concept is of an expected, rewarded event that is remembered when the ice cream, or the friendly compliment, is still some distance off. It is an event or object (i.e., a goal) that is desired. It then seems as if motivation and concept formation are each defined in terms of the other. A new concept cannot but be motivated, and a motive cannot help but bring forth a search for the concept that can satisfy it.

This notion of the importance of motivation could further refine accounts of conceptual development as driven by similarity and emerging generalizations. A major criticism has long been that such accounts are simply too unconstrained (Medin, 1989). The extent of definable regularities is overwhelming, and the world can be partitioned in limitless ways. Why is it, then, that only a subset of the multitude of possible associations becomes meaningful, and from that subset only a few become stable and recurrent? One answer to this question, provided by our framework, could lie in the nature of the organism and its goals. What an organism determines to be meaningful is largely dictated by its needs and drives, and these could supply the constraining influence that seems theoretically indispensable.

How do concepts develop over time?

We will now propose a psychological framework that will integrate desire and action as embedded in the development of concepts. The idea is that the influence of emotion on concepts takes the form of a feedback loop (Lewis, 2009). The brain is constantly changing, and concepts form and develop continuously. Each time a thought or image crystallizes in working memory, it must leave a change in the psychological apparatus generally speaking, a stronger association or memory trace. The increased strength of the memory trace increases the probability of the same thought or image becoming activated the next time around. Hence, concepts relevant to the *goal* to which desire points, or to the subgoal that brings one closer to that goal, tend to become more elaborated, articulated, or refined each time they are brought to mind. Thus, on each successive occasion, the real-time process of iteration (the cycle shown in Figure 3.1) can now get underway more rapidly, with more predictability. Developmentalists with a dynamic systems orientation refer to this as the deepening of an attractor on the behavioral state space (Lewis, 1995; Thelen & Smith, 1994). This real-time "advantage" once again contributes to the consolidation of the image in memory, fashioning a larger feedback loop between one occasion and the next – a developmental feedback relation.

A classical, and perhaps more intuitive, perspective views concepts as fixed mental representations with essential features. Properties may be added or subtracted, but, overall, there are fundamental and stable characteristics to the concept that can be

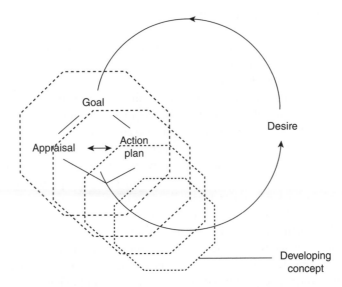

Figure 3.1 A sketch of the feedback loop that entrains desire with goals that embed cognitive events (appraisals and action plans), each augmenting the other. This feedback loop is proposed to drive conceptual development over the life span.
Source: Lewis (2009). Copyright © 2009 by the American Psychological Association. Reproduced with permission.

retrieved unspoiled, like a file stored in one's computer. The framework we propose implies that concepts do not resemble fixed entities. Instead, the content of a representation varies dynamically with context and emotional state and is subject to constant revision (Nader, 2003; Roth & Shoben, 1983). In our view, the emotional state of desire constitutes a primary influence on the content and form of the concept during the process of acquisition. We view desire (or other emotions) as a factor that mediates the variability imposed by context on conceptual development. This sometimes subtle influence accumulates throughout the life span and becomes embedded in the formation and manipulation of concepts.

We have suggested that the role of emotion in concept formation is ubiquitous. Desire may be a special case of particular relevance to concept formation. In the remainder of this chapter, we will look exclusively at this emotion.

Conceptual Development in Childhood

This section discusses concept formation in infancy, after which we focus on early and middle childhood. We describe conceptual development as influenced by increases in executive function skills, which allow for more complexity in thought in general and emotion regulation in particular. With these advances come more sophisticated goals and more refined desires, which further shape the progression and elaboration of conceptual development.

Concept formation from infancy to childhood

It is hard to imagine what type of concepts and memories newborns bring to mind, and because infants don't have language, we can only infer their concepts by observing their behavioral orientation toward particular sets of events or objects. The breast, for example, can be seen as one of the earliest concepts. In the first few days of life, babies have to be encouraged to nurse, but after several weeks the breast, or nursing-at-the-breast, can become a concept. This new concept is accessible even in the absence of the breast: That is, it becomes a memory, an association, triggered by other stimuli or capable of being recalled when hunger arises. Importantly, the concept applies not to the present moment, but to a future moment, to what is about to occur: It is an expectation. The concept expresses, "I will be sucking on this breast!" or "I want to grasp this fascinating object." We assume not only a strong sensory and motor component in these early concepts but also a motivational component – the emotion of desire.

In childhood, it is likely that the emotional component of concepts becomes more specific or more refined, as concepts become increasingly abstract, and their content less tied to appetitive states and perceptual salience. Malatesta and Haviland (1985) wrote of a desomatization during the life course. However, our model assumes that action, including verbal action, remains rooted in desires, and that these elements are essential to the development and refinement of concepts throughout the life span. People are always in the process of formulating actions geared toward the attainment of goals, even when at rest, and even when merely anticipating outcomes that are not presently available. And acting is always motivated, because goal attainment is the point of acting.

Before going into more detail on how desire shapes the formation of concepts in development, we first discuss how concepts and their use change across the years of childhood.

Conceptual development in early and middle childhood: increasing sophistication and control of concepts

Compared to in infancy, desired goals and actions become increasingly abstract in early and middle childhood as children get better at representing objects and events without any perceptual cues present. Furthermore, because concepts can be held in mind for a longer period, due to increased control of working memory, they also become increasingly manipulable. The processes required to control and manipulate cognitive entities such as concepts are known as *executive functions*.

Executive functions include a set of cognitive abilities like inhibitory control, goal setting, and working memory. These abilities allow for logical operations, which Piaget thought to be characteristic of childhood (Piaget & Inhelder, 1969). Research indicates that the development of such skills takes place gradually throughout childhood and early adolescence (Zelazo & Muller, 2002). Working memory, for example, improves steadily; infants are able to represent about three objects at a time (Feigenson & Carey, 2003), whereas this number steadily increases in early and middle childhood to about seven (Cowan, 1997). Case (1991) contended that working memory constrains the maximum number of representations a child can control at a given time.

With the rise of executive function skills, not only are children able to manipulate more mental elements at a time, but also they become more flexible in combining conceptual elements and thereby create new and more sophisticated concepts. In early childhood, most cognitive structures are quite concrete and specific, in that they are directly tied to perceptions or feeling states. For example, the concept of *a lot* may only pertain to wanting desired objects, or the concept of *parent* may be tied to one's own parents. Later, concepts become more contextualized. The concept of *parent* is different when your brother refers to mothers and fathers, compared to the meaning of *parent* used by a teacher referring to the parents of children in your class. It is implied that later acquired concepts will build on earlier, more rudimentary concepts.

Related to the rise in executive function, and with implications for the role of emotions in concept formation, is the development of emotion regulation (Cole, Martin, & Dennis, 2004). *Emotion regulation* refers to the control of emotions, including desire, through the application of a variety of executive functions, such as response inhibition, self-monitoring, and reinterpretation or reappraisal. Emotion regulation is a relatively automatic process in infancy. For example, infants regulate emotions of anxiety or distress by averting their gaze from people or objects that become overstimulating. By comparison, from early childhood on, desires come under more control, something that has been reliably indexed by delay-of-gratification tasks (Metcalfe & Mischel, 1999). Furthermore, children become increasingly aware that the content of their thoughts and emotions is partly under their own conscious control. For example, they develop *metacognition*, which means "thinking about thinking," and are able to utilize this reflective knowledge to control their emotions and behavior (Flavell, Green, & Flavell, 1995).

How does the rise of executive function and emotion regulation skills allow for more sophisticated concepts to form? First, the control of emotions, like desire, may allow for concept formation to become more guided and intentional. Children can increasingly direct and regulate their attention to internally and externally generated desires, and they can do this for longer periods of time. This skill allows children to be less limited to the "here and now" and to demonstrate an interest in events or objects because they believe them to be of benefit in the long run. For example, children in North American schools are able to pay attention to a lecture on the capital cities of Europe, even though this knowledge doesn't have much direct practical use to them. Second, an implication of more sophisticated cognitive and regulatory abilities is that they allow for more complex goals to co-emerge with desire. In tandem with changing biological drives (Fiske, 2004), new and more complex goals will lead to the acquisition of more complex and better contextualized concepts. We will look at the role of desire in the acquisition of social concepts in order to illustrate this point.

Desire and social concepts in middle childhood

In infancy, desires are simple and predictable, being strongly connected to basic needs such as hunger, safety, and comfort. Later, with the rise of more complex thought and the sense of social agency, children's desires become more diverse and sophisticated. A lot of concerns that older children have, for example, are related to social situations. Fear of rejection, disapproval, and ridicule by friends or parents is common. These fears in turn generate desires for safety in relation to goals concerning inclusion and affiliation. Later childhood is also a time when children begin to compare themselves to others, and the desire for popularity and group membership becomes a powerful motivating force. Indeed, studies show that much thought is dedicated to making friends, and a more sophisticated theory of mind is utilized to maneuver oneself in an increasingly complex social world (Astington, 1994; Hardy, Bukowski, & Sippola, 2002).

Social concepts will also become more complex and rich when desires change and become more specific. Let's take the already existing social concept of *friendship* as an example. Before, the concept of *friendship* could simply mean doing-things-together. The representation of friendship was built around cumulative experiences of simply wanting to play together with this particular someone. However, the concept becomes more elaborate as desires for mutual trust and reliance become more explicit and important. For example, the desire to rely on each other and stick to a social "pact" drives more complex conceptualizations of friendship. In fact, the desire for interpersonal support may lead to the establishment of new concepts of friendship, based on loyalty, trust, and sharing of worldviews. With these desires driving conceptual development, events like gossiping and breaking promises become important violations of friendship. Thus, the concept of friendship continues to be elaborated and refined, based on more specific desires both growing from and contributing to normative advances in cognitive development.

The pressures of peer influence are ubiquitous throughout middle childhood and adolescence. Being able to find your place in the group becomes increasingly important (Minuchin & Shapiro, 1983). Children are focused on social interactions and attuned to how they themselves, and others, are being categorized in the group. More advanced expectancies and social categorizations of behavior make the world more predictable and easier to maneuver in (e.g., being rude to a "cool kid" is not so smart, as you'll get into trouble with him and his friends). Naturally, social concepts that are referred to by labels such as *cool, nerd,* or even *redhead* begin to play an important role in children's lives. The desire for social mastery focuses attention, highlights certain events, and labels those as significant among a huge set of alternatives. This allows children to form mental categorizations that are more precise and differentiated, a progression that is fundamental to conceptual development. So can the desire for autonomy drive the concepts related to one's identity (like heroism) and the desire for social status drive conceptualization of the very objects and processes that grant this popularity, like iPods or acquisitions in online multiplayer games.

To conclude, concept formation may become a drier affair by the age of 4 or 5 years, but it is not free of motivation. Desired goals consolidate thought and give rise to the formation of concepts throughout the life span. So, as the feedback loop cycles forward in time, from the motivation for appetitive acts to social and linguistic goals and appraisals, the complexity of concepts will increase with cognitive development and accompanying changes in social context. Increasingly sophisticated emotion regulation will allow for a more directed attentional focus, especially in the presence of desire. Holding goals and their motivations in mind for longer periods of time benefits the elaboration and refinement of existing concepts. Furthermore, this focus allows concepts to be manipulated with greater flexibility, thus facilitating the emergence of new, more complex concepts.

The Neurobiology of Concepts and Desire

Is it possible to ground ideas of concept acquisition and its relation to desire in neuroscience? Demonstrating that the neurobiology of motivation mediates brain processes involved in concept formation can lend support to the proposed model. It can also point to an integrated neuropsychological model with more precision than would be available through psychological constructs alone. We will now discuss the brain areas and brain chemistry thought to underpin the emotion of desire and, according to recent perspectives in neuroscience, to participate in cognitive processes necessary for concept acquisition. First, however, we look at the neural correlates of concepts from a more traditional standpoint.

The neuropsychological correlates of concepts

Where in the brain are concepts located? Cognitive science theories long assumed that concepts arise as distinct, higher order abstractions. Such representations were thought to be derived from sensory input but ultimately end up as abstract symbols, detached from the original modality-specific (e.g., visual) processes that are active when the representation is called to mind (Smith, 1978). Recent neuroscientific findings, however, indicate that regions in the brain involved in perceiving are also involved in representing – they are overlapping systems (Barsalou, 2008). So the concept of *your friend* will be represented in various modality-specialized regions of the brain. The visual cortex will aid in representing how she looks, the auditory cortex will be involved in representing the sound of her voice, the limbic regions will convey your affective associations, and the hypothalamic and brainstem regions will mediate your current feelings toward her. These activations are influenced by ongoing experiences and are, as we argued before, subject to constant revision through variations in context and emotional state.

Case studies with semantic category-specific deficits and neuroimaging studies support this view. In an exhaustive literature review, Capitani, Laiacona, Mahon, and Caramazza (2003) confirmed that lesions to patients' sensory systems created some impairments in their concepts. For example, lesions to visual areas of the brain impaired category knowledge of more visually dependent concepts (e.g., horse) compared to functional ones (e.g., screwdriver). Furthermore, Buxbaum, Schwartz, and Carew (1997) described a patient who, after a stroke, lost the ability to use tools. The patient was able to name a tool, but not describe it by function. The patient was even unable to point at a tool when a function was described. Due to the lesion, the patient wasn't able to call the practical aspects of this tool to mind because these weren't linked to the concept of *tool* anymore. This suggests that the many aspects of a concept are mediated in a distributed fashion across many brain regions. Neuroimaging studies, in turn, confirm that different regions of the brain's perceptual and associative areas correspond to different types of concepts. Martin and Chao (2001) found different, though overlapping, activations in the fusiform gyrus (an occipital-temporal region involved in processing complex stimuli such as faces) for each of the categories *animals, tools, houses,* and *faces.* Furthermore, Martin (2007) found that activation in unique modality-specific regions changed when different concepts were imagined. For example, areas for animate motion and visual form were activated when thinking about animals, whereas processing concepts of tools activated areas in the brain associated with inanimate motion and action.

There is no single region in the brain that "does" concepts. Instead, a highly distributed and interconnected system integrates various perceptual and associative regions of the brain into meaningful representations. Most important to our discussion, it is likely that ventral prefrontal cortical regions (e.g., the orbitofrontal cortex, which mediates emotional value or reward) represent an integrated sense of the meaning of a concept in terms of its relevance to current goals.

The neurobiology of desire

Our understanding of desire can be aided by an investigation of the neural systems that mediate it. Our brains are well crafted to attend to and pursue goals – potential future states that are rewarding or simply important. For our argument, motivation is central, so we will focus on the structures and chemistry involved with goal-seeking motivation.

The motivated action loop

Lewis (2005) described three macroscopic systems of reciprocally connected structures in a model of neural self-organization: an object evaluation loop, a self-monitoring loop, and a motivated action loop. We will take the last of these loops as a starting point and describe it in more detail. What is unique about the motivated action loop is that motivation and action fashion a *directional* stream of neurocognitive activity and, ultimately, behavior. That is, a sequence of neural events continues to cycle while the focus of cognitive activity changes in real time and action unfolds continuously. The connections linking the structures in this loop – the striatum, thalamus, motor cortex, and prefrontal cortex – are the actual nodes that mediate this ongoing sequence. These four structures, and their connections, will form the core of our model of goal seeking, concept formation, and desire. We will highlight the role of the striatum, which is central to this loop.

The striatum

The striatum, a subset of the basal ganglia, is a neural assembly consisting of several structures, including the nucleus accumbens (NAS), caudate, globus pallidum, and putamen. Due to its central location in the brain, the striatum is well suited as a major communication center between the thalamus and the phylogenetically younger cortex. It is involved in directing behavior toward acquiring rewards by motivating the selection of actions and arranging them in a goal-directed sequence.

Neuroscientists who study motivation often focus on the NAS. This ventral striatal structure has been referred to as the *motivation-to-action interface* (Goto & O'Donnell, 2001) and is known to be activated in affective states related to the *anticipation* of reward (Burgdorf & Panksepp, 2006), especially immediate reward. What it motivates is the selection of actions leading to an expected reward. This motivation–action interface is supported by cooperation between the NAS and other regions of the striatum that are specifically involved in motor control, such as the caudate nucleus. Whereas the ventral striatum may be more involved in immediate reward, the dorsal striatum may also be activated by static or long-term rewards (see Graybiel, 2005, for a review). Streams of activity from both regions are integrated in an ongoing cycle that includes the thalamus and several areas of the cortex.

The prefrontal cortex

Pathways emanating from the prefrontal cortex (PFC) generally travel through the striatum and modulate the expression of cognition and emotion (Chow & Cummings, 2007). These pathways consist of bundles of fibers that connect many cortical circuits to the striatum (see Alexander, DeLong, & Strick, 1986, for a review). The PFC is important to our argument as, through its connections, the striatum is attuned to reinforcement contingencies and goals. Through its efferents to the PFC, the striatum organizes effortful control and working memory, both of which involve the sequencing of steps. These are both crucial elements of executive function, particularly the organization of information in working memory, which is processed through the dorsolateral PFC, as well as the reappraisal and regulation of emotional situations, mediated through the lateral and medial orbitofrontal cortex.

The NAS receives inputs from many regions of the PFC, but especially the orbitofrontal cortex (OFC), which it recruits for evaluating specific goals and rewards (Rolls, 1999). The OFC can be thought of as having its own appraisal system and/or working memory, by which potential rewards (or punishments) can be represented for some period of time (Depue & Collins, 1999; Rolls, 2004).

Motor cortex and thalamus

Outputs from the striatum travel back to the PFC to help organize cognitive and motor activity. Some of these outputs are routed through the thalamus, where they are integrated with cortical activities supporting motor articulation as well as attention to goals (Depue & Collins, 1999; Rolls, 1999). Meanwhile, dorsal striatal structures feed specific motor information through the thalamus to the supplementary motor area, where action routines are orchestrated.

Dopamine: the fuel of the motivated action loop

Dopamine can be seen as the critical fuel for the motivated action loop. Activation of dopaminergic corticostriatal circuits was initially thought to be the basis of organized motor activity, but it is now also considered critical for the organization of thinking, goal pursuit, and learning.

Dopamine is necessary for synaptic activation within the striatum and between the striatum and other structures such as the prefrontal cortex. The ventral tegmental area (VTA), located on the floor of the midbrain, is the home of the dopaminergic cell bodies and the source of dopamine. Outputs from the NAS and PFC also target the VTA in a reciprocal fashion to keep the dopamine pump going (Depue & Collins, 1999).

The relation between dopamine and incentive motivation is epitomized by the self-administration of stimulating drugs (such as cocaine) that are thought to increase dopamine activity in corticostriatal circuits. However, dopamine activation isn't necessarily "happy" activation. High levels of incentive salience, mediated by the striatum, are probably experienced as desire or craving rather than the euphoria produced by psychostimulant drugs. This critical distinction between wanting and liking is now accepted by many neuroscientists, based mostly on the work of Berridge and Robinson (1998). These authors demonstrated that dopamine is critical for wanting something, but liking something may depend more on opioid systems (see also Panksepp, 1981).

The incentive properties of dopamine are further demonstrated by the fact that dopamine projections to the NAS are triggered by anticipated rewards, *not* by already available rewards. In a study of self-initiated brain stimulation, dopamine surges corresponded with enhanced firing rates in striatal cells whose activation *precedes* delivery of the reward (Cheer et al., 2007).

Dopamine is also thought to enhance associations between stimuli and responses, thus facilitating learning, in the presence of potential rewards (Depue & Collins, 1999). Dopamine-enhanced learning results from the modification of synapses within striatal and corticostriatal circuits (see Wickens, Horvitz, Costa, & Killcross, 2007, for a review). Dopamine increases the sensitivity of striatal synapses to excitatory inputs (mediated by the neurotransmitter glutamate). It may boost strong concurrent glutamate inputs while minimizing weak inputs (Horvitz, 2002). These inputs arrive primarily from the PFC (e.g., the OFC) and also from the hippocampus, amygdala, midbrain, and thalamus. Over several occasions, dopamine-induced augmentation in the plasticity of striatal and corticostriatal neurons may facilitate learning via long-term potentiation (LTP), a chief candidate for synaptic change based on glutamate uptake (Kelley, Smith-Roe, & Holahan, 1997; Kerr & Wickens, 2001). Dopamine–glutamate interactions may thus be the principal means by which new skills and motor responses are acquired (see Graybiel, 2005, for a review).

In sum, dopamine can enhance incentive motivation and facilitate the learning of strings of activities that eventually lead to reinforcement. Whatever the precise mechanism, converging evidence suggests that striatal neurons become enlisted both in the anticipation of reward and in feedback-based learning due to synaptic changes that are supported by dopamine activation.

How do desire and concept formation fit in the motivated action loop?

The motivated action loop, central to anticipated reward processing, must be influenced by other loops and structures. Emotional salience is intrinsic to this loop, due principally to the activation of the NAS and ventral pallidum, whose synapses are rich in both dopaminergic and opioid receptors (Berridge, 2007; Smith & Berridge, 2007). But emotional associations and the feeling states they induce can also arrive through inputs from the amygdala. The NAS has been shown to receive input from the amygdala based on emotional salience (Cardinal, Parkinson, Hall, & Everitt, 2002), and supported by the hippocampus (Kelley & Domesick, 1982), which is involved in contextualizing present events within known routines or plans. It is likely that this context is also mediated by cortical structures implicated in representing the abstract meaning of concepts. The study of concepts has placed a strong emphasis on sensory systems, as reviewed above, and the conventional assumption has been that neural networks interconnecting these sensory sites are the actual locus of concepts in the brain. Our suggestion is to include orbitostriatal circuits – involved in the goal-oriented activities from which new concepts evolve and in the affective states that motivate these activities – as central players in the neurobiology of concepts. Activity in these orbitostriatal circuits, as influenced by dopamine, is associated with feelings of desire and goal seeking (Berridge, 2007). We suggest that synaptic alterations in orbitostriatal circuits, influenced by dopamine, are part of the mechanism by which concepts are learned in the context of current goals. We also postulate a key role for connections between the OFC and posterior sensory regions that represent the perceptual attributes of these concepts. There is good evidence for two-way connections between the ventral PFC and temporal and occipital cortices that mediate the visual and auditory attributes of stimuli and events. For example, dense fiber bundles send messages from the sensory cortices to the orbitofrontal cortex for processing. Moreover, the inferotemporal and posterior parietal cortical regions have been shown to have reciprocal connections to striatal circuits (Chow & Cummings, 2007).

The Neuropsychology of Motivated Concept Formation

We started with a psychological account of how concept formation is not only embodied but also inherently motivated. Next, we set out a neurobiological framework for motivated concept formation. With these neural parts and processes mapped out in some detail, the psychological model of desire and concept formation set out earlier can be translated into precise biological terms. The precision afforded by a biological analysis can then be taken as the occasion for clarifying and further elaborating the psychological account, with the eventual goal of fully integrating the biological and psychological perspectives into a neuropsychological model.

As discussed earlier, the motivated action loop cycles from (OFC-mediated) goal processing, to (striatally mediated) motivational gating and action selection, to (thalamo-cortically mediated) motor generation and output, and then back to goal processing, in a sequence by which action is continually generated, shaped, and refined. Despite reciprocal connections between many elements in this loop, and despite the supporting roles played by the amygdala, hippocampus, and other areas contributing emotional meaning and contextual relevance to the stream of processing, the loop has a unidirectional flow that keeps motivated action moving forward in time. This process provides a basis for the integration of emotion into the formation of concepts.

Synaptic modification is thought to underlie all learning. In terms of the time-honored Hebbian rule "What fires together, wires together," frequently coactivated networks of neurons strengthen their connections (Hebb, 1949). These synaptic changes very likely extend to the learning of new concepts. More specifically, in terms of our model, a concept is acquired by the iteration of feedback loops involving cortical and subcortical structures. These recurring and self-reinforcing patterns of activation result in synaptic changes across the regions that mediate emotions like desire as well as those underlying cognitive operations. We conclude that the conceptual representation, the desire, the motor program, and the contextual associations, all of which are mediated by neural assemblies coactivated almost simultaneously, will become integrated psychologically just as their neural substrates are integrated physically. It is these processes, at both the psychological and neuropsychological levels, that contribute to the development of conceptual systems.

Because synaptic plasticity, resulting from neuromodulator action, is a necessary precursor to synaptic modification (Centonze, Picconi, Gubellini, Bernardi, & Calabresi, 2001; Izquierdo, 1997), it makes sense that the synaptic changes underlying concept formation are partly supported by dopaminergic activity involving the structures in the motivated action loop. Research indicates that the learning of instrumental behaviors in animals indeed depends on dopamine activity and the interaction of dopamine and other neurotransmitters (especially glutamate) in the striatum (e.g., the nucleus accumbens) (Kelley et al., 1997; Kerr & Wickens, 2001). Furthermore, in humans, dopamine activation in corticostriatal circuits corresponded with the anticipation of rewards (e.g., desire), not their presence, and a sudden increase in the probability of reward acquisition results in increased dopamine release (Burgdorf & Panksepp, 2006; Graybiel, 2005). More evidence comes from a functional magnetic resonance imaging (fMRI) study by Adcock, Thangavel, Whitfield-Gabrieli, Knutson, and Gabrieli (2006), showing that mesolimbic dopamine release, associated with levels of desire, *precedes* the forming of representations. In a monetary incentive–encoding task, high-value reward cues activated the VTA, NAS, and hippocampus (including the parahippocampal cortex). These cues were also better remembered in a subsequent test. All of these findings suggest that dopamine activity is a critical contributor to the consolidation of learning, especially learning about valued goals. At the psychological level, we suggest that the feeling of wanting, which corresponds to dopamine activity in the striatum and orbitostriatal regions, precedes the strengthening and consolidation of new concepts and the elaboration of already present concepts.

Implications

We have argued that concept formation may depend on a very specific emotional state, experienced in the context of goal seeking. From this perspective, there is nothing dry about conceptual development, and we can only hope to model it accurately if we consider the role of emotion as well as that of cognition. This work can therefore contribute to the scientific study of conceptual development, which has generally excluded emotion. Furthermore, the model can lead to a better understanding of how we develop, socially and cognitively, through the acquisition and elaboration of motivated concepts.

An obvious implication for education is that academic advancement – especially that which relies on concept acquisition – cannot solely be related to intellectual understanding, but must rely on motivational factors as well. Schools fostering the motivational aspect of learning, for example by engaging students before starting each lesson, may do more than just make the lesson more enjoyable and increase attention span. The intensity of the interest or desire generated by such an approach may be a critical variable determining the success of the educational process itself.

Our model is consistent with the merits of a process-learning approach. Instead of providing children with answers, it may be more important to provide questions or situations that elicit a sense of desire to explore and seek out answers. The anticipated state of knowing may be a superordinate goal that motivates learning across subjects, contexts, and individuals. This higher order anticipation may help to elaborate and systematize knowledge systems by driving the acquisition of needed concepts. *Wanting* to know something, then, not only is a motivator but also may constitute a crucial aspect of concept formation. Indeed, educational approaches whereby students are actively searching for answers to questions have been associated with improved learning outcomes (Bruner, 1991; Olson, 1964).

Individual differences in the intensity of desire for specific goals could explain differences in the learning of concepts. High- versus low-intensity motivational states could lead to slower versus more rigid styles of learning, respectively. However, seldom do children show a consistently low or high level of motivation. Rather, motivational intensity usually varies with topics of interest and domains of knowledge. For example, one child can have trouble following narratives on how to cook spaghetti, but demonstrate no trouble with an equally complex account of how to grow plants. In both cases representations are linked to task performance, but the value and attractiveness of those representations differ with experience. When children are learning academic knowledge, they are often relating the abstract algorithms to their own intuitive understandings. These understandings are based on previous experiences and on goal appraisals that make the current task more or less appealing. Small differences in prior experiences and emotional preferences may accumulate and produce major impacts on the conceptual acquisitions that distinguish one person from another.

The intensity of the tension that exists between a goal state and a current state of anticipation can also be mediated by motivational factors that are social in nature, for example the approval of a teacher or of parents when succeeding in intellectual tasks. Underlying social desires may drive the emergence of inherently social concepts, like those involving others' identity, personality, or social rank (Silk, Brosnan, Vonk, Henrich, & Povinelli, 2005). Humans are constantly categorizing social entities and events, drawing social inferences, and planning and remembering social interactions. Because we are a highly social species, the desire to be heard and to understand others is crucial to our well-being (Baldwin, 2000; House, 2001). As a consequence, variations in the intensity and type of motivational factors that guide learning can have major implications for developing social competencies.

The implications of this model are not new to educators, parents, or anyone else working with children. We know that motivation is important for learning (Dweck, 1986; Ormrod, 2003). However, we do not understand the kinds of emotions and motivations most relevant to concept learning or the means by which motivation and conceptual processes become connected. The proposed model of motivated conceptual development may provide a useful step toward understanding these mechanisms in detail. The main message of the model is that concept development is embedded in feelings related to goal pursuit – interest, desire, and attraction. As every teacher and parent can confirm, these feelings are a major attribute of childhood, and they only grudgingly give way to the more arid motivational terrain of adulthood.

References

Adcock, R. A., Thangavel, A., Whitfield-Gabrieli, S., Knutson, B., & Gabrieli, J. D. E. (2006). Reward-motivated learning: Mesolimbic activation precedes memory formation. *Neuron, 50,* 507–517.

Aguiar, A., & Baillargeon, R. (1999). 2.5-month-old infants' reasoning about when objects should and should not be occluded. *Cognitive Psychology, 39,* 116–157.

Alexander, G. E., DeLong, M. R., & Strick, P. L. (1986). Parallel organization of functionally segregated circuits linking basal ganglia and cortex. *Annual Review of Neuroscience, 9,* 357–381.

Anderson, A. K., & Phelps, E. A. (2001). Lesions of the human amygdala impair enhanced perception of emotionally salient events. *Nature, 411,* 305–309.

Armony, J. L., & Dolan, R. J. (2002). Modulation of spatial attention by fear-conditioned stimuli: An event-related fMRI study. *Neuropsychologia, 40,* 817–826.

Arnold, M. B. (1960). *Emotion and personality.* New York: Columbia University Press.

Astington, J. W. (1994). *The child's discovery of the mind.* London: Fontana.

Baldwin, D. A. (2000). Interpersonal understanding fuels knowledge acquisition. *Current Directions in Psychological Science, 9,* 40–45.

Barsalou, L. W. (2008). Cognitive and neural contributions to understanding the conceptual system. *Current Directions in Psychological Science, 17,* 91–95.

Bechara, A., Tranel, D., & Damasio, H. (2000). Characterization of the decision-making deficit of patients with ventromedial prefrontal cortex lesions. *Brain, 123,* 2189–2202.

Berridge, K. C. (2007). The debate over dopamine's role in reward: the case for incentive salience. *Psychopharmacology, 191,* 391–431.

Berridge, K. C., & Robinson, T. E. (1998). What is the role of dopamine in reward: Hedonic impact, reward learning, or incentive salience? *Brain Research Reviews, 28,* 309–369.

Bruner, J. S. (1991). *Beyond the information given.* New York: Norton.

Burgdorf, J., & Panksepp, J. (2006). The neurobiology of positive emotions. *Neuroscience and Biobehavioral Reviews, 30,* 173–187.

Buxbaum, L. J., Schwartz, M. F., & Carew, T. G. (1997). The role of semantic memory in object use. *Cognitive Neuropsychology, 14,* 219–254.

Capitani, E., Laiacona, M., Mahon, B., & Caramazza, A. (2003). What are the facts of category-specific deficits? A critical review of the clinical evidence. *Cognitive Neuropsychology, 20,* 213–261.

Cardinal, R. N., Parkinson, J. A., Hall, J., & Everitt, B. J. (2002). Emotion and motivation: The role of the amygdala, ventral striatum, and prefrontal cortex. *Neuroscience and Biobehavioral Reviews, 26,* 321–352.

Case, R. (1991). General and specific views of the mind, its structure, and its development. In R. Case (Ed.), *The mind's staircase* (pp. 3–16). Hillsdale, NJ: Erlbaum.

Centonze, D., Picconi, B., Gubellini, P., Bernardi, G., & Calabresi, P. (2001). Dopaminergic control of synaptic plasticity in the dorsal striatum. *European Journal of Neuroscience, 13,* 1071–1077.

Cheer, J. F., Aragona, B. J., Heien, M. L. A. V., Seipel, A. T., Carelli, R. M., & Wightman, R. M. (2007). Coordinated accumbal dopamine release and neural activity drive goal-directed behavior. *Neuron, 54,* 237–244.

Chow, T. W., & Cummings, J. L. (2007). Frontal-subcortical circuits. In B. L. Miller & J. L. Cummings (Eds.), *The human frontal lobes, functions and disorders* (pp. 25–43). New York: Guilford Press.

Cole, P., Martin, S., & Dennis, T. (2004). Emotion regulation as a scientific construct: Methodological challenges and directions for child development research. *Child Development, 75,* 317–333.

Colunga, E., & Smith, L. B. (2003). The emergence of abstract ideas: Evidence from networks and babies. *Philosophical Transactions of the Royal Society of London: Biological Sciences, 358,* 1205–1214.

Cowan, N. (1997). The development of working memory. In N. Cowan (Ed.), *The development of memory in childhood* (pp. 163–199). East Sussex, UK: Psychology Press.

Decasper, A. J., & Fifer, W. (1980). Of human bonding: Newborns prefer their mothers' voices. *Science, 208,* 1174–1176.

Depue, R. A., & Collins, P. F. (1999). Neurobiology of the structure of personality: Dopamine, facilitation of incentive motivation and extraversion. *Behavioral and Brain Sciences, 22,* 491–569.

Dweck, C. S. (1986). Motivational processes affecting learning. *American Psychologist, 41,* 1040–1048.

Ekman, P. (1984). Expression and the nature of emotion. In K. Scherer & P. Ekman (Eds.), *Approaches to emotion* (pp. 319–344). Hillsdale, NJ: Erlbaum.

Feigenson, L., & Carey, S. (2003). Tracking individuals via object-files: Evidence from infants' manual search. *Developmental Science, 6,* 568–584.

Fiske, S. T. (2004). *Social beings: A core motives approach to social psychology.* New York: Wiley.

Flavell, J. H., Green, F. L., & Flavell, E. R. (1995). Young children's knowledge about thinking. *Monographs of the Society for Research in Child Development, 60*(1, Serial No. 243).

Frijda, N. H. (1986). *The emotions.* Cambridge: Cambridge University Press.

Gelman, S. A. (2009). Learning from others: Children's construction of concepts. *Annual Review of Psychology, 60,* 115–140.

Goto, Y., & O'Donnell, P. (2001). Network synchrony in the nucleus accumbens in vivo. *Journal of Neuroscience, 21,* 4498–4504.

Graybiel, A. M. (2005). The basal ganglia: Learning new tricks and loving it. *Current Opinion in Neurobiology, 15,* 638–644.

Hamann, S. B., Ely, T. D., Grafton, S. T., & Kilts, C. D. (1999). Amygdala activity related to enhanced memory for pleasant and aversive stimuli. *Nature Neuroscience, 2,* 289–293.

Hardy, C. L., Bukowski, W. M., & Sippola, L. K. (2002). Stability and change in peer relationships during the transition to middle-level school. *Journal of Early Adolescence, 22,* 117–142.

Hebb, D. O. (1949). *The organization of behavior.* New York: Wiley.

Held, R., & Hein, A. (1963). Movement-produced stimulation in the development of visually guided behavior. *Journal of Comparative and Physiological Psychology, 56,* 872–876.

Horvitz, J. C. (2002). Dopamine, Parkinson's disease, and volition. *Behavioral and Brain Sciences, 25,* 586.

House, J. S. (2001). Social isolation kills, but how and why? *Psychosomatic Medicine, 63,* 273–274.

Izard, C. E. (1993). Four systems for emotion activation: Cognitive and noncognitive processes. *Psychological Review, 100,* 68–90.

Izquierdo, I. (1997). The biochemistry of memory formation and its regulation by hormones and neuromodulators. *Psychobiology, 25,* 1–9.

Kelley, A. E., & Domesick, V. B. (1982). The distribution of the projection from the hippocampal formation to the nucleus accumbens in the rat: An anterograde- and retrograde-horseradish peroxidase study. *Neuroscience, 7,* 2321–2335.

Kelley, A. E., Smith-Roe, S. L., & Holahan, M. R. (1997). Response-reinforcement learning is dependent on N-methyl-D-aspartate receptor activation in the nucleus accumbens core. *Proceedings of the National Academy of Sciences, 94,* 12174–12179.

Kerr, J. N. D., & Wickens, J. R. (2001). Dopamine D-1/D-5 receptor activation is required for long-term potentiation in the rat neostriatum in vitro. *Journal of Neurophysiology, 85,* 117–124.

Lewis, M. D. (1995). Cognition-emotion feedback and the self-organization of developmental paths. *Human Development, 38,* 71–102.

Lewis, M. D. (2005). Bridging emotion theory and neurobiology through dynamic systems modeling (target article). *Behavioral and Brain Sciences, 28,* 169–194.

Lewis, M. D. (2009). Desire, dopamine, and conceptual development. In M. A. Bell & S. D. Calkins (Eds.), *Development at the intersection of cognition and emotion* (pp. 175–199). Washington, DC: American Psychological Association.

Mahon, B. Z., & Caramazza, A. (2009). Concepts and categories: A cognitive neuropsychological perspective. *Annual Review of Psychology, 58,* 27–51.

Malatesta, C. Z., & Haviland, J. M. (1985). Signals, symbols and socialization: The modification of emotional expression in human development. In M. Lewis & C. Saarni (Eds.), *The socialization of emotions* (pp. 89–116). New York: Plenum Press.

Mandler, J. M. (2004). Thought before language. *Trends in Cognitive Sciences, 8,* 508–513.

Martin, A. (2007). The representation of object concepts in the brain. *Annual Review of Psychology, 58,* 25–45.

Martin, A., & Chao, L. L. (2001). Semantic memory and the brain: Structure and processes. *Current Opinion in Neurobiology, 11,* 194–201.

Medin, D. M. (1989). Concepts and conceptual structure. *American Psychologist, 44,* 1469–1481.

Metcalfe, J., & Mischel, W. (1999). A hot/cool system analysis of delay of gratification: Dynamics of willpower. *Psychological Review, 106,* 3–19.

Minuchin, P. P., & Shapiro, E. K. (1983). The school as a context for social development. In P. H. Mussen (Ed.), *Handbook of child psychology: Vol. 3. Social development* (pp. 230–238). New York: Wiley.

Nader, K. (2003). Memory traces unbound. *Trends in Neurosciences, 26,* 65–72.

Neisser, U. (1987). From direct perception to conceptual structure. In U. Neisser (Ed.), *Concepts and conceptual development: Ecological and intellectual factors in categorization* (pp. 11–24). Cambridge: Cambridge University Press.

Olson, D. R. (1964). *Cognitive development: The child's acquisition of diagonality.* New York: Academic Press.

Ormrod, J. (2003). *Educational psychology: Developing the learners* (4th ed.). Upper Saddle River, NJ: Prentice Hall.

Panksepp, J. (1981). The ontogeny of play in rats. *Developmental Psychobiology, 14,* 327–332.

Panksepp, J. (1998). *Affective neuroscience: The foundations of human and animal emotions.* New York: Oxford University Press.

Pessoa, L. (2008). On the relationship between emotion and cognition. *Nature Reviews Neuroscience, 9,* 148–158.

Piaget, J., & Inhelder, B. (1969). *The psychology of the child.* New York: Basic Books.

Plunkett, K., Karmiloff-Smith, A., Bates, E., Elman, J. L. & Johnson, M. (1997). Connectionism and developmental psychology. *Journal of Child Psychology and Psychiatry, 38,* 53–80.

Rolls, E. T. (1999). *The brain and emotion.* Oxford: Oxford University Press.

Rolls, E. T. (2004). The functions of the orbitofrontal cortex. *Brain and Cognition, 55,* 11–29.

Roth, E. M., & Shoben, E. J. (1983). The effect of context on the structure of categories. *Cognitive Psychology, 15*, 346–378.

Scholnick, E., Nelson, K., Miller, P. & Gelman, S. A. (Eds). (1999). *Conceptual development: Piaget's legacy.* Mahwah, NJ: Erlbaum.

Siegal, M. (2004). Language and conceptual development. *Trends in Cognitive Sciences, 8*, 287.

Silk, J. B., Brosnan, S. F., Vonk, J., Henrich, J., & Povinelli, D. (2005). Chimpanzees are indifferent to the welfare of unrelated group members. *Nature, 437*, 1357–1359.

Smith, E. E. (1978). Theories of semantic memory. In W. K. Estes (Ed.), *Handbook of learning and cognitive processes* (Vol. 6). Hillsdale, NJ: Erlbaum.

Smith, K. S., & Berridge, K. C. (2007). Nucleus accumbens and ventral pallidum interact as opioid hotspots to amplify "liking" and "wanting" for food reward. *Journal of Neuroscience, 27*, 1594–1605.

Smith, L. B., & Gasser, M. (2005). The development of embodied cognition: Six lessons from babies. *Artificial Life, 11*, 13–30.

Spelke, E. S., & Kinzler, K. D. (2007). Core knowledge. *Developmental Science, 10*, 89–96.

Thelen, E., & Smith, L. B. (1994). *A dynamic systems approach to the development of cognition and action.* Cambridge, MA: MIT Press/Bradford.

Wellman, H. M., & Gelman, S. A. (1998). Knowledge acquisition in foundational domains. In D. Kuhn & R. S. Siegler (Eds.), *Handbook of child psychology: Vol. 2. Cognition, perception, and language* (pp. 523–573). Hoboken, NJ: Wiley.

Wickens, J. R., Horvitz, J. C., Costa, R. M., & Killcross, S. (2007). Dopaminergic mechanisms in actions and habits. *Journal of Neuroscience, 27*, 8181–8183.

Zelazo, P. D., & Muller, U. (2002). Executive function in typical and atypical development. In U. Goswami (Ed.), *Handbook of childhood cognitive development* (pp. 445–469). Oxford: Blackwell.

CHAPTER FOUR

Evolutionary Perspectives on Social Development

David F. Bjorklund and Anthony D. Pellegrini

Evolutionary psychology has slowly achieved mainstream respectability among academic psychologists (see Barkow, Cosmides, & Tooby, 1992; Buss, 2005). Although many developmentalists, particularly those concerned with social development, have implicitly or explicitly incorporated concepts of evolution into their theories (e.g., Bowlby, 1969; Hinde, 1980), many others have been slow to take up the evolutionary banner, based on the belief that evolutionary psychology implies a form of genetic determinism (e.g., Lickliter & Honeycutt, 2003). In the past decade, a number of theorists have addressed this issue (e.g., Bjorklund & Pellegrini, 2000; Geary, 2005), and developmental research and theory from an evolutionary perspective have blossomed. This has particularly been the case for topics in social development.

In the sections that follow, we introduce the basic concepts of evolutionary psychology and evolutionary developmental psychology, taking our examples from the arena of social development. We then examine several aspects of social development from an evolutionary perspective. In the final section, we discuss briefly the benefits of an evolutionary perspective for social development.

Evolutionary Psychology

Evolutionary psychology takes the basic ideas developed by Charles Darwin (1859) and updated through the 20th century, and applies them to human behavior. The central

The Wiley-Blackwell Handbook of Childhood Social Development, Second Edition, edited by Peter K. Smith and Craig H. Hart
© 2011 by Blackwell Publishing Ltd.

concept of Darwin's theory is *natural selection.* Darwin proposed that, in any generation, more offspring are born than will survive. Individuals vary in a host of features, and these features are heritable. Some of these features afford a better fit with local environments than others, and individuals possessing these characteristics are more apt to survive, reproduce, and pass on these same features to their offspring than individuals not possessing these features. In other words, heritable variations in the physical or psychological characteristics of an individual interact with the environment and, over many generations, change in frequency, resulting, eventually, in species-wide traits in the population. Thus, through the process of natural selection, adaptive changes in individuals, and eventually species, are brought about.

Evolutionary psychologists use natural selection to explain complex psychological functioning (Buss, 1995; Daly & Wilson, 1988; Tooby & Cosmides, 1992). However, evolutionary psychologists have focused mainly on adults, individuals who do the reproducing, the sine qua non of Darwinian success. Yet, individuals must first survive infancy and childhood before they can reproduce, and we believe that psychological characteristics favorable to survival during the juvenile period are as, or more, important to an organism as are characteristics of the adult. Along these lines, several researchers have applied an explicitly developmental perspective to evolutionary thinking and formulated the subfield of *evolutionary developmental psychology.*

Evolutionary Developmental Psychology

Evolutionary developmental psychology (see Bjorklund & Hernández Blasi, 2005; Bjorklund & Pellegrini, 2000, 2002; Burgess & MacDonald, 2005; Ellis & Bjorklund, 2005; Geary & Bjorklund, 2000; Hernández Blasi & Bjorklund, 2003) is defined as "the study of the genetic and ecological mechanisms that govern the development of social and cognitive competencies common to all human beings and the epigenetic (gene–environment interactions) processes that adapt these competencies to local conditions" (Geary & Bjorklund, 2000, p. 57). Evolutionary developmental psychology assumes not only that behaviors and cognitions that characterize adults are the product of selection pressures operating over the course of evolution, but also that they are characteristic of children's behaviors and minds. In fact, natural selection has operated as much, if not more, on the early stages of life as it has on adults. A central concern of evolutionary developmental psychology is how these mechanisms develop and come to be expressed in the phenotypes of adults through interaction between individuals and their environments. Below we articulate what we see as some of the concepts central to evolutionary developmental psychology, particularly as they are applied to social development.

Basic principles of evolutionary developmental psychology

1. *All evolved characteristics develop via continuous and bidirectional gene–environment interactions that emerge dynamically over time.*

Taking an evolutionary psychological approach requires that one make explicit one's stance on the nature–nurture issue. Most developmentalists, we believe, would concur that the issue is not "how much" of any trait is due to nature and "how much" is due to nurture, but rather "How do nature and nurture interact to produce a particular pattern of development?" But stating that biology and environment, broadly defined, interact in and of itself advances the argument very little. We must specify *how* biological and environmental factors interact. We posit that a *developmental contextual approach* (e.g., Gottlieb, 1991, 2002) provides the most appropriate model for describing the nature of this interaction.

Central to this approach is the concept of *epigenesis*, which Gottlieb (1991) defined as "the emergence of new structures and functions during the course of development" (p. 7). New structures do not arise fully formed, but are the result of the bidirectional relationship between all levels of biological and experiential factors, from the genetic to the cultural. *Experience*, from this perspective, involves not only events exogenous to the individual such as perceptual stimulation and social interaction (*macroenvironments*), but also events internal to the individual, such as hormones, the presence of neurotransmitters, and even the firing of one neuron as it affects its neighbors and itself (*microenvironments*). Functioning at one level influences functioning at adjacent levels, with constant feedback between levels. This relationship can be expressed as follows:

genetic activity (DNA $\leftrightarrow$ RNA $\leftrightarrow$ proteins) $\leftrightarrow$ structural maturation
$\leftrightarrow$ function, activity

From this viewpoint, all development is the product of epigenesis, with complex interactions occurring among multiple levels.

Evolved psychological mechanisms can be thought of as genetically coded "messages" that, following epigenetic rules, interact with the environment over time to produce behavior (see Bjorklund, Ellis, & Rosenberg, 2007). Because the experiences of each individual are unique, this suggests that there should be substantial plasticity in development. Yet, there is much that is universal about the form and function of members of a species, despite this plasticity. The reason for this is that individuals inherit not only a species-typical genome but also a species-typical environment, beginning with the prenatal environment. To the extent that individuals grow up in environments similar to those of their ancestors, development should follow a species-typical pattern.

2.   *Development is constrained by both genetic and environmental factors.*

Infants are not born as blank slates; natural selection has prepared them to "expect" certain types of environments and to process some information more readily than others. From this perspective, one can talk of infants and children inheriting biases that increase the likelihood of their developing adaptive responses to their environment. Such biases and constraints *enable* learning.

For example, neonates show decided preferences in what they like to attend to (faces and voices, among them). There are some things that infants and children learn easily (such as language) and other things that are very difficult for them to learn. Some of these biases are the result of prenatal experiences and not "just genes." For instance, babies at birth prefer to listen to the language that their mothers speak rather than to other languages (Mehler et al., 1988), a bias that surely is the result of prenatal auditory experiences. One should not think of such biases as "innate," but see them as nearly inevitable outcomes that are constrained by the ways genes and experience interact in a species-typical way during early development. With respect to social development, evolutionarily oriented psychologists have proposed that infants and children have evolved domain-specific mechanisms that bias their learning and processing of information in the areas of attachment, hierarchical power (social dominance), coalition groups, reciprocity, and mating (Bugental, 2000), as well as for theory of mind and other forms of social cognition (Geary, 2005).

3. *There is need for an extended childhood to learn the complexities of human social communities.*

Central to the application of evolutionary thinking to human development is the recognition that members of *Homo sapiens* have a life history in which they spend a disproportionate amount of time as prereproductives. Clearly there are costs to postponing reproduction. From an evolutionary perspective, the benefits associated with an extended period of immaturity must have outweighed the costs. Those benefits can be seen in mastering the complexities of a human social community. A number of theorists have proposed that the single most potent pressure on human intellectual evolution was the need to cooperate and compete with conspecifics (e.g., Dunbar, 1995; Humphrey, 1976). As hominid social groups became more complex, individuals who could better understand their social world gained more of the benefits in terms of available mates and resources and passed those characteristics along to their offspring. The greater social complexity of hominid groups required a greater awareness of ourselves and the needs and motivations of others so that we could better understand, and perhaps manipulate, others. But there is much variability in human social life, necessitating a flexible intelligence to master the vagaries of group living. This requires not only a large brain but also a long time to accomplishment. According to this view, it was the confluence of a large brain, social complexity, and an extended juvenile period that set the stage for the modern human mind (e.g., Bjorklund & Bering, 2003).

4. *Many aspects of childhood serve to prepare the way for adulthood and were selected over the course of evolution (deferred adaptations).*

Some adaptations of childhood result in children gaining experience that will provide them with skills or knowledge that will be useful in adulthood. Children's play provides a good example. During play, children acquire the social skills needed to cooperate and compete with conspecifics both as children and as adults. Moreover, in traditional cultures today and certainly for our ancestors, children's playmates will likely become their adult peers, with the result that children acquire not only general social skills that will be useful in adulthood but also information about the very people they will interact with as adults.

Although play probably serves as a deferred adaptation for both sexes, there are differences in how boys and girls play. Sex differences in play, and perhaps other aspects of childhood, prepare boys and girls for the different roles they will likely play (or would have played in ancestral environments) as adults. The reproductive goals of men and women are similar (i.e., to get their genes into the next generation), but they are approached in different ways. According to *parental investment theory* (Trivers, 1972), this is because males and females invest differently in their offspring. The amount of time and resources individuals devote to mating versus parenting influences their behavior. In most mammals, including humans, females invest substantially more in parenting than males. For example, the potential consequence of any copulation is substantially greater for women than for men. For women, conception can result in 9 months of pregnancy and, until the recent advent of baby formula, in 3 to 4 years of nursing. Men, unlike the majority of males of other mammalian species, do spend significant time caring for and interacting with their offspring, but still, in all cultures observed, spend significantly less time in such endeavors than women (see Geary, 2000). These basic differences in reproductive and parenting effort should have served as selective pressures for the evolution of different mating and child-rearing strategies in men and women. Although one's culture, a proximal mechanism, surely has a profound impact on such sex differences, evolved "strategies" are the distal mechanisms that interact with these differences in all societies. But importantly, these differences do not arise fully formed at adolescence, but develop gradually over childhood, with children adapting their gender-specific behavior to the local norm, based on evolved predispositions, and much of these behaviors are learned during play.

Children's sexually segregated groups and sex differences in play styles provide good examples of precursors to (and thus preparations for) adult sex differences (Pellegrini, Long, Roseth, Bohn, & Van Ryzin, 2007). Boys and girls in all cultures, and indeed in many nonhuman mammalian species (e.g., Smith, 1982), segregate themselves by sex when there are enough children in the peer group to do so (Maccoby, 1998). One reason for this sex segregation is the way in which boys and girls play. For example, as early as 3 years of age, boys engage in more active and rough play than girls (see Pellegrini et al., 2007), a pattern that is also found in many nonhuman primates (Pellegrini, 2004; Smith, 1982, 2010). One function proposed for the vigorous social behavior characteristic of male groups is to develop skeletal and muscle systems associated with sexual dimorphism in size and subsequent adult reproductive roles (Pellegrini, 2004). Most girls, on the other hand, engage in less vigorous behavior (Pellegrini et al., 2007), and their social play involves more play parenting (i.e., doll play) than boys' play, a sex difference that is even found in some primates (Pryce, 1995).

Another robust sex difference that is found in early childhood is an interest in infants, with girls across the world showing more interest in nurturing babies than boys (see Maestripieri & Pelka, 2002). A similar sex difference is seen in many primates (Maestripieri & Roney, 2006). Females of nearly all mammal species are the primary caretakers for young offspring, and this was certainly true for our hunter–gatherer foremothers and is true for most women today, even in developed societies (Geary, 2000). Experience with taking care of infants provides girls with the skills they will need as mothers in the future, or certainly would have needed in traditional environments.

The proposal that sex differences in children's social behaviors serve as preparations for adulthood (or did for our ancestors) and are based upon evolved epigenetic rules does not minimize the role of culture. These evolved "strategies" develop in interaction with children's physical and social environment and can be viewed as biases that will lead children in the "right" direction (i.e., a form of adult behavior that has, over many generations, been associated with reproductive success). The strategies for complicated social behaviors that humans have evolved possess a substantial degree of plasticity. But the universality of these behaviors, and the fact that many are also observed in nonhuman primates, suggests that they share a common evolved mechanism that requires a prolonged developmental period for their eventual expression.

5. *There have been different selection pressures on organisms at different times in ontogeny, and some characteristics of infants and children were selected in evolution to serve an adaptive function at that time in development and not to prepare them for later adulthood (ontogenetic adaptations).*

Development is understandably thought of as being progressive, with earlier, immature forms of acting and thinking being replaced with later, more mature forms. Coupled with this idea is the notion that childhood is a preparation for adulthood in a similar niche. Early experience serves to organize the personality or the mind, setting the stage for later functioning, an argument we advocated for aspects of children's play. However, we believe that many features of infancy and childhood have been selected in evolution to serve an adaptive function at that time in development only and not to prepare the child for later life (Bjorklund, 2007; Bjorklund, Periss, & Causey, 2009). These have been referred to as *ontogenetic adaptations* (Bjorklund, 1997; Oppenheim, 1981). Moreover, most deferred adaptations likely also provide infants and children some immediate benefits. For example, play not only serves to prepare children for dealing with others in adulthood, but also helps children navigate the social world of childhood (Bjorklund & Pellegrini, 2002).

One area of social cognitive development that may be a candidate for an ontogenetic adaptation is young children's abilities to estimate their competence on a wide range of tasks. Young children are notorious overestimators of their own skills. Preschool and early school-aged children think they are smarter, stronger, and generally more skilled than they really are (e.g., Stipek, 1984). More specific to the social domain, preschoolers overestimate their own toughness, or dominance, in relation to the estimates of their peers (e.g., Boulton & Smith, 1994; Sluckin & Smith, 1977). Bandura (1989) postulated that the confidence people have in their competence in a particular domain affects which tasks they choose to perform and how long they persist at those tasks. Thus, children who think they are skilled in a domain are likely to attempt more challenging tasks and stick at them longer than less optimistic children, and this, in turn, will influence how much they learn (see Lopez, Little, Oettingen, & Baltes, 1998; Shin, Bjorklund, & Beck, 2007).

6. *Children show a high degree of plasticity, or flexibility, and the ability to adapt to different contexts (conditional adaptations).*

Human beings are the most cognitively flexible species on the planet, and infants and young children are sensitive to early environmental conditions and can alter their path of development, based on current conditions, in anticipation of future conditions. Along these lines, Boyce and Ellis (2005) proposed the concept of *conditional adaptations*:

> [E]volved mechanisms that detect and respond to specific features of childhood environments – features that have proven reliable over evolutionary time in predicting the nature of the social and physical world into which children will mature – and entrain developmental pathways that reliably matched those features during a species' natural selective history. (p. 290)

Children living in different environments (e.g., low versus high stress, plentiful versus scarce resources, and stable versus unstable relationships) develop different cognitive or behavioral strategies in anticipation of the environment they will likely inhabit as adults.

Such differential patterns have been predicted and observed for adolescent behavior as a function of the nature or degree of parental support over childhood. For example, in comparison to children from low-stress, father-present homes, children from homes characterized by high stress, marital discord or father absence, inadequate resources, and harsh and inconsistent child care attain puberty earlier (especially girls), form short-term and unstable pair bonds, invest relatively little in their own offspring, and tend to be noncompliant and aggressive (especially boys) (e.g., Belsky, Steinberg, & Draper, 1991; Quinlan, 2003; for reviews, see Belsky, 2007, Del Giudice, 2009; Ellis, 2004). Given the unpredictability of resources, this pattern of early maturation and adolescent promiscuity may lead to the greatest inclusive fitness and be a better strategy than delaying reproduction and investing more in fewer offspring. The latter strategy may be most adaptive for children growing up in low-stress and stable environments. Thus, depending on the availability of resources, which is related to parental investment and spousal harmony, different patterns of socialization occur that result in differential investment in the next generation.

Consistent with this interpretation, several studies have reported a significant relationship between father absence and accelerated pubertal development in girls (e.g., Quinlan, 2003; Tither & Ellis, 2008; and see Mustanski, Viken, Kaprio, Pulkkinen, & Rose, 2004, who also reported an effect in boys), and increased sexual activity and adolescent pregnancy (e.g., Ellis et al., 2003). Other research has shown that the earlier a father leaves the family, the earlier his daughters reach puberty (e.g., Moffitt, Caspi, Belsky, & Silva, 1992; Surbey, 1990). In one study, father absence was associated not only with an earlier menarche but also with greater interest in infants, suggesting that such girls are becoming "prepared" for early reproduction and parenting (Maestripieri, Roney, DeBias, Durante, & Spaepen, 2004). Other research in father-intact homes has shown that the quality of the father–daughter relationship impacts age of puberty: The better the father–daughter relationship, the later girls reach puberty (Ellis, McFadyen-Ketchum, Dodge, Pettit, & Bates, 1999).

Topics in Social Development From an Evolutionary Perspective

Evolutionary psychologists believe that all aspects of human functioning can be (and perhaps *should be*) explained from the perspective of natural selection. There are some domains within social development, however, that have been analyzed extensively in terms of evolutionary theory, and we will describe briefly research for several of these topics.

Social cognition: developing a theory of mind

Perhaps the single most basic ability underlying human social interaction is the understanding that other people behave intentionally and have knowledge and desires that may be different from one's own. *Theory of mind* has been used to reflect this knowledge. As noted earlier, the most potent pressure on human intellectual evolution was the need to cooperate and compete with conspecifics, putting social intelligence at the core of what makes our species unique. Human social intelligence is based on the abilities to take the mental perspective of another and to realize that the actions people take are based on their *intentions* (Bandura, 2006; Tomasello, 1999). They come to realize that their behavior and the behavior of others are directed to achieving some goal. That is, children learn that what they do is based on what they know or believe to be true, plus what they want to achieve or desire, termed *belief–desire reasoning*. They also learn that other people's behavior is so motivated.

Infants show the first signs of understanding others as intentional agents at about 9 months of age through *shared attention* (Carpenter, Nagell, & Tomasello, 1998; Tomasello & Carpenter, 2007). Shared, or joint, attention is a form of *triadic interaction*, in which two people attend to a common third object, each one being aware of what the other is seeing. This is something that parents of infants do readily, pointing to or gazing at objects while catching their infant's attention, drawing the baby into a social relationship that extends beyond the dyad. These abilities improve over the next year. For instance, 12-month-olds will point to let others know about events they don't know – such as a toy that fell off a table and onto the floor (Liszkowski, Carpenter, Striano, & Tomasello, 2006), and by 18 months children can tell the difference between intentional actions by an adult (e.g., throwing a marker on the floor) and unintentional actions (e.g., dropping a marker on the floor) (Warneken & Tomasello, 2006).

These social cognitive abilities permit learning by imitation (recognizing the intentions of a model and then duplicating important portions of the model's behavior to achieve a goal) and learning from instruction (Tomasello, 1999). However, social cognition develops further over early childhood, as reflected by children 4 years of age and older passing *false-belief tasks* (Perner, Leekam, & Wimmer, 1987; Wellman, Cross, & Watson, 2001), understanding that other people can possess a false belief (e.g., that someone who saw a cookie placed in a jar continues to believe it is in the jar despite the cookie being removed to another container; for a similar example, see Chapter 28 by Lewis and Carpenter).

As we mentioned earlier, many evolutionary psychologists believe that humans evolved domain-specific mechanisms, or modules, to deal with recurrent problems faced by our ancestors. Consistent with this domain-specific perspective of evolutionary psychology, several researchers have proposed that theory of mind consists of a series of highly specialized modules that develop over the preschool years (Baron-Cohen, 1995, 2005; Leslie, 1994). For example, Baron-Cohen (1995) proposed that four separate interacting modules are involved in theory of mind. The *intentionality detector* (ID) module permits one to infer that a moving object may have some intent toward him or her (e.g., it may bite me or groom me). The *eye direction detector* (EDD) module serves to interpret eye gazes (if an organism's eyes are looking at something, that organism then *sees* that thing). These modules develop in infancy (by 9 months of age). The *shared attention mechanism* (SAM) involves three-way interactions between the child, another person, and a third object (i.e., shared attention). This develops by about 18 months. The *theory-of-mind module* (TOMM) reflects "adult" understanding (i.e., belief–desire reasoning) and develops around 4 years of age.

Although other social primates display impressive social-learning abilities (see, e.g., Bjorklund, Causey, & Periss, 2010; Whiten et al., 1999), none display theory of mind comparable to humans, and the last two modules in Baron-Cohen's theory may be unique to humans. For example, although chimpanzees will point out things to other individuals (Leavens, Hopkins, & Bard, 2005), there is no evidence that they engage in shared attention (e.g., Herrmann, Call, Hernández-Lloreda, Hare, & Tomasello, 2007; Krachun, Carpenter, Call, & Tomasello, 2009; Tomasello & Carpenter, 2005). Moreover, when nonverbal false-belief tasks have been constructed for use with chimpanzees, there is no evidence that they can pass them (e.g., Call & Tomasello, 1999; Herrmann et al., 2007). There is also evidence that the principal deficit in high-functioning autistic people is an inability to read minds, or *mindblindness* (see Baron-Cohen, 2005, for a review). What these individuals lack, presumably, are the SAM and TOMM modules, making the social lives of these people very different from those of others.

Although theory of mind develops at about the same time in most children around the world (e.g., Liu, Wellman, Tardif, & Sabbagh, 2008; Wellman, Fang, Liu, Zhu, & Liu, 2006), the rate of its development is related to aspects of children's social environment, including quality of attachment, parenting styles, parent–child communication (Carpendale & Lewis, 2004), maternal warmth, mothers' use of mental state talk (Ruffman, Slade, Devitt, & Crowe, 2006), and both the number of adults and older siblings and/or peers that a preschool child interacts with daily (Lewis, Freeman, Kyriakidou, Maridaki-Kassotaki, & Berridge, 1996; Ruffman, Perner, Naito, Parkin, & Clements, 1998). There may be many reasons for the importance of interacting with older siblings, peers, and adults for theory-of-mind development, such as greater opportunities for discussions of mental states, managing social conflict, pretend play, and reasoning about social issues (e.g., Lewis et al., 1996; Ruffman et al., 1998). For example, Ruffman et al. (1998) argued that having older siblings stimulates fantasy play, which helps children represent "counterfactual states of affairs," a skill necessary for solving false-belief tasks. Cummins (1998) suggested an explanation based on dominance theory. Siblings are always competing for resources, with older sibs typically having the advantage because of their greater size and mental abilities. Younger children would be motivated to develop whatever latent talents they have to aid them in their social competition with their older sibs, and developing an understanding of the mind of his or her chief competitor sooner rather than later would certainly be to the younger sib's advantage. A similar argument can be made for interacting with older peers.

Human children are clearly prepared to develop a theory of mind, and at this point in our evolutionary history, it seems that any "normal" human social environment will suffice. However, individual differences in children's social experiences, particularly over the infancy and early childhood years, may lead not only to differential rates of theory-of-mind development but also perhaps to different *types* of theory of mind, conducive to the type of social environment (e.g., supportive or nonsupportive) in which children develop.

Interacting with peers

Much research in social development has focused on peer interactions, and rightfully so, given the significant role that peers play in children's lives and in shaping their development. Harris (1995) proposed that humans, and other primates, have inherited four evolutionary adaptations that underlie much of our social interactions with peers: (a) group affiliation and in-group favoritism; (b) fear of, and/or hostility toward, strangers; (c) within-group status seeking; and (d) the seeking and establishment of close dyadic relationships. Although these adaptations are found early in life, they nonetheless develop over childhood. Harris (1995), in her *group socialization theory*, further proposes that the peer group plays *the* critical role in socialization, with the effects of parents and teachers being filtered through the peer group. Although we do not mean to minimize the role that parents play in children's development (see Collins, Maccoby, Steinberg, Hetherington, & Bornstein, 2000), research has consistently documented the waning influence of the home environment on personality and intellectual development over the course of childhood (e.g., McCartney, Harris, & Bernieri, 1990). This makes good evolutionary sense, as Harris proposes, in that as they grow older, children will operate outside the home and compete and cooperate with agemates of their group. Becoming too well adapted to the home and too agreeable to the demands of one's parents is not (usually) conducive to one's inclusive fitness by adolescence.

A thorough examination of peer relations from an evolutionary perspective is beyond the scope of this chapter. We will discuss briefly several important topics: the role of *social dominance* in children's groups, and *aggressive and prosocial behaviors*.

Social dominance   Dominant individuals within a group have greater access to resources (be they food, mates, or toys in the case of children) and will use a variety of techniques to attain and maintain their preferred status (see Hawley, 1999; Pellegrini et al., 2007). Dominance is expressed at two levels (Hinde, 1978). First, at the dyadic level, individuals compete for resources and the winner gets preferred access to the resource. These dyadic relationships, in turn, are used to order individuals in a group hierarchically. Dominance in children's groups is often expressed in terms of both aggressive and cooperative behaviors (e.g., Hawley, 2003; Pellegrini et al., 2007). In both children (e.g., Pellegrini et al., 2007) and chimpanzees (e.g., de Waal, 1982), cooperative and reconciliatory strategies are used in situations where the dominant individual needs his or her subordinates and the subordinates are free to leave the group. That dominance includes both affiliation and agonistic behaviors is consistent with findings from the periods of both early childhood and early adolescence, where dominance is positively and significantly correlated with popularity (e.g., Hawley, Card, & Little, 2008; Pellegrini et al., 2007).

Dominance relationships serve to reduce antagonism within the group, distribute scarce resources, and focus division of labor. They are found at all ages in which children interact in groups, beginning during the toddler years (see Hawley, 1999). In the initial stages of group formation, children (particularly boys) attempt to establish leadership and gain access to resources via aggression (Strayer & Noel, 1986). Once dominance hierarchies are established, rates of aggression in children and adolescents decrease and leaders use more cooperative and reconciliatory strategies (Pellegrini & Long, 2002; Roseth, Pellegrini, Bohn, Van Ryzin, & Vance, 2007). In this way, "defeated" individuals can be integrated into the alpha individual's group of possible allies (Hawley, 2003; Pellegrini et al., 2007).

Cummins (1998) has argued that social reasoning grew out of the need to negotiate dominance hierarchies. The realities of life in a complex social group make dominance hierarchies necessary (at least in the absence of codified laws and police enforcement). The tendency to affiliate is strong and emerges early in childhood, and patterns of social dominance seem to be a necessary dimension of such affiliations. Children are well prepared for social relations, based on both inherited evolutionary adaptations and their species-typical experiences as infants. They require no formal instruction from adults to form groups and seem intuitively to understand and to learn quickly the reality of dominance hierarchies and how to live within them.

Aggressive and prosocial behaviors   Although social developmentalists are concerned with a wide range of behaviors, most can be divided into two broad categories: prosocial and antagonistic, the latter including aggression and overt competition. Evolutionary psychologists have similarly been concerned with these two broad classes of social behavior, attempting to determine how these behaviors serve to benefit the reproductive success of those who engage in them.

Any behavior has both costs and benefits to an individual, and if a behavior is associated with greater benefits relative to costs within a population, over many generations, it will be favored by natural selection. From this perspective, it is easy to see why aggression would be adaptive, especially when it is associated with low risks (see Hawley, Little, & Rodkin, 2007). When aggression "works" to secure mates or other resources more often than it fails, natural selection will favor those individuals who use it effectively. This does not make aggression inevitable; natural selection would not favor cases where costs associated with aggression outweighed benefits – for example, incurring a debilitating injury for the sake of securing a mate. But it does help us understand why aggression is so difficult to eliminate, especially in environments where resources go to the bold rather than the meek.

There are substantial sex differences in children's expression of aggression. Males engage in more physical aggression than females in all cultures and at all ages, but the greatest consequence of this sex difference is seen in adolescence and young adulthood (Daly & Wilson, 1988). According to parental investment theory (Trivers, 1972), the sex that invests more in offspring (in humans, females) is more selective in choosing a mate, and the sex that invests less in offspring (in humans, males) competes for access to the higher investing sex. In humans, as in other mammalian species, there is substantial fitness variance between the sexes. Most mammalian females will find a mate, even if not a highly desirable one; in contrast, many mammalian males will be totally excluded from mating (Trivers, 1972). As a result, selection favored a male psychology that emphasized competitive risk (Daly & Wilson, 1988). Such risk taking, and the violence that can accompany it, peaks in adolescence and young adulthood when males are entering the reproductive market. This is seen in deaths and injuries from automobile accidents (Evans, 2006) as well as being victims and perpetrators of homicide (Daly & Wilson, 1988; National Center for Health Statistics, 1999).

Females engage in aggression as well, but are more apt to use indirect, or relational, aggression (see Crick & Gropeter, 1995), defined as "noxious behavior in which the target person is attacked not physically or directly through verbal intimidation but in a more circuitous way, through social manipulation" (Kaukiainen et al., 1998, p. 83). Females' avoidance of physical aggression may be related to their role as primary caregivers. In ancient environments, the death of a mother almost certainly resulted in the death of her young offspring, making a cautious competitive strategy a better bet for females (Campbell, 1999). Consistent with this, the difference between male and female longevity among primates is related to the amount of parental care that males provide (Allman, 1999). In species where males provide no care for offspring (e.g., chimpanzees), females have a substantially longer life span than males. This is actually reversed in the few species in which males provide a greater amount of the child care (owl and titi monkeys).

Prosocial behavior is more difficult to explain from an evolutionary perspective. Individuals who help others incur an immediate cost and no obvious immediate benefit. The evolutionary explanations for prosocial behavior are complicated and contentious, and we will not address them here, other than to mention that current research points to children developing social cognition as the origin of prosocial behavior. As we mentioned previously, *Homo sapiens* evolved a form of social cognition more advanced than that of any other species. For instance, in an extensive battery of cognitive and social cognitive tests, chimpanzees (*Pan troglodytes*) were shown to have an understanding of the physical world comparable to that of 2.5-year-old human children; however, the children significantly outperformed the chimps on tests of social cognition (Herrmann et al., 2007). Although primates and other mammals may display some forms of empathy toward others (see Preston & de Waal, 2002), only humans display *cognitive empathy*, which involves the ability to take the emotional perspective of another (see Bjorklund et al., 2010). Such empathy is the foundation for prosocial behavior. As noted by Sarah Hrdy (1999), "What makes us humans rather than just apes is the capacity to combine intelligence with articulate empathy" (p. 392). Such "articulate empathy" is an outgrowth of human's social nature and children's developing social cognition.

Infants, of course, are highly attentive to their social partners and develop close social relationships with their primary caregivers (see Thompson, 2006, for a review of the attachment literature). However, by 18 months they also display spontaneously helping behavior to unfamiliar adults. This was demonstrated in a study in which 18- and 24-month-old children helped an adult when he or she, for example, misplaced a book on a stack or accidentally dropped a marker on the floor. They failed to help (e.g., retrieve the fallen book or marker) when the adult intentionally threw the marker on the floor or placed the book beside the stack (Warneken & Tomasello, 2006). Human-reared chimpanzees also helped the adults in some, but not all, situations. It is interesting that human-reared (enculturated) chimpanzees also display more human-like forms of social learning than mother-reared chimpanzees (e.g., Bjorklund, Yunger, Bering, & Ragan, 2002; Buttelmann, Carpenter, Call, & Tomasello, 2007; Tomasello, Savage-Rumbaugh, & Kruger, 1993), suggesting that the common ancestor of chimpanzees and humans likely possessed the roots of a human-like prosociality.

Evolution and Social Development

One cannot consider "human nature" independent of the social world in which people live and develop. Evolutionary psychology assumes that the human mind has been prepared by natural selection, operating over geological time, for life in a human group. But social complexity is not limited to adult interactions; it also characterizes the interactions of children. Moreover, because of the diversity of environments in which humans live, the complicated and often shifting nature of social alliances, and the need to both compete and cooperate with kin, familiar nonkin, and strangers, humans need a long apprenticeship to master the ways of their social world. Children, as well as adults, have been prepared by evolution to navigate these often stormy social waters. An evolutionary developmental psychological perspective provides a broader framework (a "metatheory") for understanding children's social behaviors and permits us to ask new questions and to see development from a different vantage point. It also may provide insights to some contemporary social issues not directly addressed in this chapter, such as teenage pregnancy (Ellis, 2004), bullying in schools (Pellegrini & Bartini, 2000), sibling rivalry (Michalski & Euler, 2007), child abuse (Daly & Wilson, 1988), and parent–child conflict (Salmon, 2007), among others. Adopting evolutionary theory does not "reduce" humans to being "mere animals," but rather allows us to view our kind from a broader perspective and to gain a better appreciation for what it means to be human.

References

Allman, J. M. (1999). *Evolving brains.* New York: Scientific American Library.

Bandura, A. (1989). Social cognitive theory. In R. Vasta (Ed.), *Annals of child development* (pp. 1–60). Greenwich, CT: JAI Press.

Bandura, A. (2006). Toward a psychology of human agency. *Perspectives on Psychological Science, 1,* 164–180.

Barkow, J. H., Cosmides, L., & Tooby, J. (Eds.). (1992). *The adapted mind: Evolutionary psychology and the generation of culture.* New York: Oxford University Press.

Baron-Cohen, S. (1995). *Mindblindness: An essay on autism and theory of mind.* Cambridge, MA: MIT Press.

Baron-Cohen, S. (2005). The empathizing system: A revision of the 1994 model of the mindreading system. In B. J. Ellis & D. F. Bjorklund (Eds.), *Origins of the social mind: Evolutionary psychology and child development* (pp. 468–492). New York: Guilford Press.

Belsky, J. (2007). Experience in childhood and the development of reproductive strategies. *Acta Psychologica Sinica, 39,* 454–468.

Belsky, J., Steinberg, L., & Draper, P. (1991). Childhood experience, interpersonal development, and reproductive strategy: An evolutionary theory of socialization. *Child Development, 62,* 647–670.

Bjorklund, D. F. (1997). The role of immaturity in human development. *Psychological Bulletin, 122,* 153–169.

Bjorklund, D. F. (2007). *Why youth is not wasted on the young: Immaturity in human development.* Oxford: Blackwell.

Bjorklund, D. F., & Bering, J. M. (2003). Big brains, slow development, and social complexity: The developmental and evolutionary origins of social cognition. In M. Brüne, H. Ribbert, & W. Schiefenhövel (Eds.), *The social brain: Evolutionary aspects of development and pathology* (pp. 133–151). New York: Wiley.

Bjorklund, D. F., Causey, K., & Periss, V. (2010). The evolution and development of human social cognition. In P. Kappeler & J. Silk (Eds.), *Mind the gap: Tracing the origins of human universals.* Berlin: Springer Verlag.

Bjorklund, D. F., Ellis, B. J., & Rosenberg, J. S. (2007). Evolved probabilistic cognitive mechanisms: An evolutionary approach to gene × environment × development. In R. V. Kail (Ed.), *Advances in child development and behavior* (Vol. 35, pp. 1–39). Oxford: Elsevier.

Bjorklund, D. F., & Hernández Blasi, C. (2005). Evolutionary developmental psychology. In D. Buss (Ed.), *Evolutionary psychology handbook* (pp. 828–850). New York: Wiley.

Bjorklund, D. F., & Pellegrini, A. D. (2000). Child development and evolutionary psychology. *Child Development, 71,* 1687–1708.

Bjorklund, D. F., & Pellegrini, A. D. (2002). *The origins of human nature: Evolutionary developmental psychology.* Washington, DC: American Psychological Association.

Bjorklund, D. F., Periss, V., & Causey, K. (2009). The benefits of youth. *European Journal of Developmental Psychology, 6,* 120–137.

Bjorklund, D. F., Yunger, J. L., Bering, J. M., & Ragan, P. (2002). The generalization of deferred imitation in enculturated chimpanzees (*Pan troglodytes*). *Animal Cognition, 5,* 49–58.

Boulton, M. J., & Smith, P. K. (1994). Affective bias in children's perception of dominance relations. *Child Development, 61,* 221–229.

Bowlby, J. (1969). *Attachment and loss: Vol. 1. Attachment.* London: Hogarth.

Boyce, W. T., & Ellis, B. J. (2005). Biological sensitivity to context: I. An evolutionary-developmental theory of the origins and functions of stress reactivity. *Development & Psychopathology, 17,* 271–301.

Bugental, D. B. (2000). Acquisition of the algorithms of social life: A domain-based approach. *Psychological Bulletin, 126,* 187–219.

Burgess, R., & MacDonald, K. (Eds.). (2005). *Evolutionary perspectives on human development.* Thousand Oaks, CA: Sage.

Buss, D. M. (1995). Evolutionary psychology: A new paradigm for psychological science. *Psychological Inquiry, 6,* 1–30.

Buss, D. M. (Ed.). (2005). *Evolutionary psychology handbook.* New York: Wiley.

Buttelmann, D., Carpenter, M., Call, J., & Tomasello, M. (2007). Enculturated chimpanzees imitate rationally. *Developmental Science, 10,* F31–F38.

Call, J., & Tomasello, M. (1999). A nonverbal false belief task: The performance of children and great apes. *Child Development, 70,* 381–395.

Campbell, A. (1999). Staying alive: Evolution, culture, and women's intrasexual aggression. *Behavioral and Brain Sciences, 22,* 203–252.

Carpendale, J. I. M., & Lewis, C. (2004). Constructing an understanding of mind: The development of children's social understanding within social interaction. *Behavioral and Brain Sciences, 27,* 79–151.

Carpenter, M., Nagell, K., & Tomasello, M. (1998). Social cognition, joint attention, and communicative competence from 9 to 15 months of age. *Monographs of the Society for Research in Child Development, 63*(4, Serial No. 255).

Collins, W. A., Maccoby, E. E., Steinberg, L., Hetherington, E. M., & Bornstein, M. H. (2000). Contemporary research on parenting: The case for nature and nurture. *American Psychologist, 55*, 218–232.

Crick, N. R., & Grotpeter, J. K. (1995). Relational aggression, gender, and social psychological adjustment. *Child Development, 66*, 710–722.

Cummins, D. D. (1998). Social norms and other minds: The evolutionary roots of higher cognition. In D. D. Cummins & C. Allen (Eds.), *The evolution of mind* (pp. 28–50). New York: Oxford University Press.

Daly, M., & Wilson, M. (1988). *Homicide.* New York: Aldine.

Darwin, C. (1859). *The origin of species.* New York: Modern Library.

Del Giudice, M. (2009). Sex, attachment, and the development of reproductive strategies. *Behavioral and Brain Sciences, 32*, 1–21.

de Waal, F. B. M. (1982). The integration of dominance and social bonding in primates. *Quarterly Review of Biology, 61*, 459–479.

Dunbar, R. I. M. (1995). Neocortex size and group size in primates: A test of the hypothesis. *Journal of Human Evolution, 28*, 287–296.

Ellis, B. J. (2004). Timing of pubertal maturation in girls: An integrated life history approach. *Psychological Bulletin, 130*, 920–958.

Ellis, B. J., Bates, J. E., Dodge, K. A., Fergusson, D. M., Horwood, L. J., Pettit, G. S., et al. (2003). Does father absence place daughters at special risk for early sexual activity and teenage pregnancy? *Child Development, 74*, 801–821.

Ellis, B. J., & Bjorklund, D. F. (Eds.). (2005). *Origins of the social mind: Evolutionary psychology and child development.* New York: Guilford Press.

Ellis, B. J., McFadyen-Ketchum, S., Dodge, K. A., Pettit, G. S., & Bates, J. E. (1999). Quality of early family relationships and individual differences in the timing of pubertal maturation in girls: A longitudinal test of an evolutionary model. *Journal of Personality and Social Psychology, 77*, 387–401.

Evans, L. (2006, Winter). Innate sex differences supported by untypical traffic fatalities. *Chance, 19*, 10–16.

Geary, D. C. (2000). Evolution and proximate expression of human parental investment. *Psychological Bulletin, 126*, 55–77.

Geary, D. C. (2005). *The origin of mind: Evolution of brain, cognition, and general intelligence.* Washington, DC: American Psychological Association.

Geary, D. C., & Bjorklund, D. F. (2000). Evolutionary developmental psychology. *Child Development, 71*, 57–65.

Gottlieb, G. (1991). Experiential canalization of behavioral development: Theory. *Developmental Psychology, 27*, 4–13.

Gottlieb, G. (2002). Developmental-behavioral initiation of evolutionary change. *Psychological Review, 109*, 211–218.

Harris, J. R. (1995). Where is the child's environment? A group socialization theory of development. *Psychological Review, 102*, 458–489.

Hawley, P. A. (1999). The ontogenesis of social dominance: A strategy-based evolutionary perspective. *Developmental Review, 19*, 97–132.

Hawley, P. A. (2003). Strategies of control, aggression and morality in preschoolers: An evolutionary perspective. *Journal of Experimental Child Psychology, 85*, 213–235.

Hawley, P. A., Card, N. A., & Little, T. D. (2008). The myth of the alpha male: A new look at dominance related beliefs and behaviors among adolescent males and females. *International Journal of Behavioral Development, 32,* 76–88.

Hawley, P. A., Little, T. D., & Rodkin, P. C. (Eds.). (2007). *Aggression and adaptation: The bright side to bad behavior.* Mahwah, NJ: Erlbaum.

Hernández Blasi, C., & Bjorklund, D. F. (2003). Evolutionary developmental psychology: A new tool for better understanding human ontogeny. *Human Development, 46,* 259–281.

Herrmann, E., Call, J., Hernández-Lloreda, M. V., Hare, B., & Tomasello, M. (2007). Humans have evolved specialized skills of social cognition: The cultural intelligence hypothesis. *Science, 317,* 1360–1365.

Hinde, R. A. (1978). Dominance and role: Two concepts with two meanings. *Journal of Social Biology Structure, 1,* 27–38.

Hinde, R. A. (1980). *Ethology.* London: Fontana.

Hrdy, S. B. (1999). *Mother nature: A history of mothers, infants, and natural selection.* New York: Pantheon.

Humphrey, N. K. (1976). The social function of intellect. In P. P. G. Bateson & R. A. Hinde (Eds.), *Growing points in ethology* (pp. 303–317). Cambridge: Cambridge University Press.

Kaukiainen, A., Björkqvist, K., Lagerspertz, K., Österman, K., Salmivalli, C., Rothberg, S., et al. (1999). The relationship between social intelligence, empathy, and three types of aggression. *Aggressive Behavior, 25,* 81–89.

Krachun, C., Carpenter, M., Call, J., & Tomasello, M. (2009). A competitive nonverbal false belief task for children and apes. *Developmental Science, 12,* 521–535.

Leavens, D. A., Hopkins, W. D., & Bard, K. A. (2005). Understanding the point of chimpanzee pointing: Epigenesis and ecological validity. *Current Directions in Psychological Science, 14,* 185–189.

Leslie, A. (1994). ToMM, ToBY, and agency: Core architecture and domain specificity. In L. Hirschfeld & S. Gelman (Eds.), *Mapping the mind: Domain specificity in cognition and culture* (pp. 119–148). Cambridge: Cambridge University Press.

Lewis, C., Freeman, N. H., Kyriakidou, C., Maridaki-Kassotaki, K., & Berridge, D. M. (1996). Social influence on false belief access: Specific sibling influences or general apprenticeship? *Child Development, 67,* 2930–2947.

Lickliter, R., & Honeycutt, H. (2003). Developmental dynamics: Towards a biologically plausible evolutionary psychology. *Psychological Bulletin, 129,* 819–835.

Liszkowski, U., Carpenter, M., Striano, T., & Tomasello, M. (2006). 12- and 18-month-olds point to provide information for others. *Journal of Cognition and Development, 7,* 173–187.

Liu, D., Wellman, H. M., Tardif, T., & Sabbagh, M. A. (2008). Theory of mind development in Chinese children: A meta-analysis of false-belief understanding across cultures and languages. *Developmental Psychology, 44,* 523–531.

Lopez, D. F., Little, T. D., Oettingen, G., & Baltes, P. B. (1998). Self-regulation and school performance: Is there optimal level of action-control? *Journal of Experimental Child Psychology, 70,* 54–74.

Maccoby, E. E. (1998). *The two sexes: Growing up apart, coming together.* Cambridge, MA: Harvard University Press.

Maestripieri, D., & Pelka, S. (2002). Sex differences in interest in infants across the lifespan: A biological adaptation for parenting? *Human Nature, 13,* 327–344.

Maestripieri, D., & Roney, J. R. (2006). Evolutionary developmental psychology: Contributions from comparative research with nonhuman primates. *Developmental Review, 26,* 120–137.

Maestripieri, D., Roney, J. R., DeBias, N., Durante, K. M., & Spaepen, G. M. (2004). Father absence, menarche and interest in infants among adolescent girls. *Developmental Science, 7*, 560–566.

McCartney, K., Harris, M. J., & Bernieri, F. (1990). Growing up and growing apart: A development meta-analysis of twin studies. *Psychological Bulletin, 97*, 226–237.

Mehler, J., Jusczyk, P., Lambertz, G., Halsted, N., Bertoncini, J., & Amiel-Tison, C. (1988). A precursor of language acquisition in young infants. *Cognition, 29*, 143–178.

Michalski, R. L., & Euler, H. A. (2007). Evolutionary perspectives on sibling relationships. In C. A. Salmon & T. K. Shackelford (Eds.), *Family relationships: An evolutionary perspective* (pp. 185–204). New York: Oxford University Press.

Moffitt, T. E., Caspi, A., Belsky, J., & Silva, P. A. (1992). Childhood experience and the onset of menarche: A test of a sociobiological hypothesis. *Child Development, 63*, 47–58.

Mustanski, B. S., Viken, R. J., Kaprio, J., Pulkkinen, L., & Rose, R. J. (2004). Genetic and environmental influences on pubertal development: Longitudinal data from Finnish twins at ages 11 and 14. *Developmental Psychology, 40*, 1188–1198.

National Center for Health Statistics. (1999). *Health: United States*. Hyattsville, MD: Author.

Oppenheim, R. W. (1981). Ontogenetic adaptations and retrogressive processes in the development of the nervous system and behavior. In K. J. Connolly & H. F. R. Prechtl (Eds.), *Maturation and development: Biological and psychological perspectives* (pp. 73–108). Philadelphia: International Medical.

Pellegrini, A. D. (2004). Sexual segregation in childhood: A review of evidence for two hypotheses. *Animal Behaviour, 68*, 435–443.

Pellegrini, A. D., & Bartini, M. (2000). A longitudinal study of bullying, victimization, and peer affiliation during the transition from primary to middle school. *American Educational Research Journal, 37*, 699–726.

Pellegrini, A. D., & Long, J. D. (2002). A longitudinal study of bullying, dominance, and victimization during the transition from primary to secondary school. *British Journal of Developmental Psychology, 20*, 259–280.

Pellegrini, A. D., Long, J. D., Roseth, C., Bohn, K., & Van Ryzin, M. (2007). A short-term longitudinal study of preschool children's sex segregation: The role of physical activity, sex, and time. *Journal of Comparative Psychology, 121*, 282–289.

Perner, J., Leekam, S. R., & Wimmer, H. (1987). Three-year-olds' difficulty with false belief: The case for a conceptual deficit. *British Journal of Developmental Psychology, 5*, 125–137.

Preston, S. D., & de Waal, F. B. M. (2002). Empathy: Its ultimate and proximate bases. *Behavioral and Brain Science, 25*, 1–72.

Pryce, C. R. (1995). Determinants of motherhood in human and nonhuman primates: A biosocial model. In C. R. Pryce, R. D. Martin, & D. Skuse (Eds.), *Motherhood in human and nonhuman primates: Biosocial determinants* (pp. 1–15). Basel, Switzerland: Karger.

Quinlan, R. J. (2003). Father absence, parental care, and female reproductive development. *Evolution and Human Behavior, 24*, 376–390.

Roseth, C. J., Pellegrini, A. D., Bohn, C. M., Van Ryzin, M., & Vance, N. (2007). Preschoolers' aggression, affiliation, and social dominance relationships: An observational, longitudinal study *Journal of School Psychology, 45*, 479–497.

Ruffman, T., Perner, J., Naito, M., Parkin, L., & Clements, W. A. (1998). Older (but not younger) siblings facilitate false belief understanding. *Developmental Psychology, 34*, 161–174.

Ruffman, T., Slade, L., Devitt, K. & Crowe, E. (2006). What mothers say and what they do: The relation between parenting, theory of mind, language and conflict/cooperation. *British Journal of Developmental Psychology, 24*, 105–124.

Salmon, C. A. (2007). Parent-offspring conflict. In C. A. Salmon & T. K. Shackelford (Eds.), *Family relationships: An evolutionary perspective* (pp. 145–161). New York: Oxford University Press.

Shin, H.-E., Bjorklund, D. F., & Beck, E. F. (2007). The adaptive nature of children's overestimation in a strategic memory task. *Cognitive Development, 22,* 197–212.

Sluckin, A., & Smith, P. K. (1977). Two approaches to the concept of dominance in preschool children. *Child Development, 4,* 917–923.

Smith, P. K. (1982). Does play matter? Functional and evolutionary aspects of animal and human play. *Behavioral and Brain Sciences, 5,* 139–184.

Smith, P. K. (2010). *Understanding children's worlds: Children and play.* Hoboken, NJ: Wiley-Blackwell.

Stipek, D. (1984). Young children's performance expectations: Logical analysis or wishful thinking? In J. G. Nicholls (Ed.), *Advances in motivation and achievement: Vol. 3. The development of achievement motivation* (pp. 33–56). Greenwich, CT: JAI Press.

Strayer, F. F., & Noel, J. M. (1986). The prosocial and antisocial functions of aggression. In C. Zahn-Waxler, E. M. Cummings, & R. Iannoti (Eds.), *Altruism and aggression* (pp. 107–131). New York: Cambridge University Press.

Surbey, M. K. (1990). Family composition, stress, and the timing of human menarche. In T. E. Ziegler & F. B. Bercovitvch (Eds.), *Socioendocrinology of primate reproduction* (pp. 11–32). New York: Wiley-Liss.

Thompson, R. A. (2006). The development of the person: Social understanding, relationships, conscience, self. In N. Eisenberg (Vol. Ed.), *Social, emotional, and personality development: Vol. 3. Handbook of child psychology* (Gen. Ed. W. Damon & R. M. Lerner, 6th ed., pp. 24–98). New York: Wiley.

Tither, J. M., & Ellis, B. J. (2008). Impact of fathers on daughters' age at menarche: A genetically and environmentally controlled sibling study. *Developmental Psychology, 44,* 1409–1420.

Tomasello, M. (1999). *The cultural origins of human cognition.* Cambridge, MA: Harvard University Press.

Tomasello, M., & Carpenter, M. (2005). The emergence of social cognition in three young chimpanzees. *Monographs of the Society for Research in Child Development, 70*(1, Serial No. 279).

Tomasello, M., & Carpenter, M. (2007). Shared intentionality. *Developmental Science, 10,* 121–125.

Tomasello, M., Savage-Rumbaugh, S., & Kruger, A. C. (1993). Imitative learning of actions on objects by children, chimpanzees, and enculturated chimpanzees. *Child Development, 64,* 1688–1705.

Tooby, J., & Cosmides, L. (1992). The psychological foundations of culture. In J. H. Barkow, L. Cosmides, & J. Tooby (Eds.), *The adapted mind: Evolutionary psychology and the generation of culture* (pp. 19–139). New York: Oxford University Press.

Trivers, R. L. (1972). Parental investment and sexual selection. In B. Campbell (Ed.), *Sexual selection and the descent of man* (pp. 136–179). New York: Aldine.

Warneken, F., & Tomasello, M. (2006). Altruistic helping in human infants and young chimpanzees. *Science, 311,* 1301–1303.

Wellman, H. M., Cross, D., & Watson, J. (2001). Meta-analysis of theory-of-mind development: The truth about false belief. *Child Development, 72,* 655–684.

Wellman, H. M., Fang, F., Liu, D., Zhu, L., & Liu, G. (2006). Scaling theory-of-mind understanding in Chinese children. *Psychological Science, 17,* 1075–1081.

Whiten, A., Goodall, J., McGrew, W. C., Nishida, T., Reynolds, V., Sugiyama, Y., et al. (1999, June). Cultures in chimpanzees. *Nature, 399,* 682–685.

CHAPTER FIVE

Historical Reframing of Childhood

Willem Koops

Introduction

To understand and develop ideas on childhood, child development, and education, empirical studies of children's behavior cannot suffice. Apart from "normal" empirical analytical knowledge – or, better, data sets – it is very important to study the cultural historical context of this "normal science" and its predecessors.

In this chapter, we first revisit the philosophical foundation of developmental thinking and its application to understanding children. This brings the reader to the great German philosopher Immanuel Kant (1724–1804) and to the founder of child development and education: Jean-Jacques Rousseau (1712–1778). In particular, Rousseau's book on the boy Émile will be presented as the core publication of modern thoughts on childhood and education, followed by the reception of this book by historical founders of developmental psychology and pedagogy in Germany, Switzerland, and the Netherlands.

After the explanation of the role of Enlightenment thinking in terms of "progress" and development, it will be made clear that one essential feature of the Enlightenment philosophy is disputable: the unjustified belief in "progress." This idea of "progress" is fully present in the original developmental ideas of Rousseau, and also in those of his later follower Jean Piaget (1896–1980). It will be explained in this chapter that neo- and post-neo-Piagetian research essentially leads us back to the insight that children are serious interlocutors at a much younger age than we have been inclined to think since the Rousseau–Piaget tradition.

Research on the tenability of Philip Ariès's (1914–1984) hypothesis on infantilization will be presented to demonstrate that he was right in claiming that infantilization was

The Wiley-Blackwell Handbook of Childhood Social Development, Second Edition, edited by Peter K. Smith and Craig H. Hart
© 2011 by Blackwell Publishing Ltd.

increasing over the last few centuries. On the other hand, it will be demonstrated that since the 1950s infantilization came to an end. This discussion will be connected to Neil Postman's ideas on the disappearance of childhood.

Finally, it will be concluded that the study of the cultural history of childhood and child development makes clear that child development is less (biologically) continuous than has been the assumption since Rousseau. Post-neo-Piagetian research (e.g., about the child's *theory of mind*), makes clear that children are much more serious, if not adult, interlocutors. We may speak of a historical reframing of childhood, with numerous new possibilities for pedagogy and education.

Enlightenment

A scholar who wants to think, speak, and write about children has no choice but to come to terms with the Enlightenment. This call takes us to the greatest Enlightenment philosopher of all, Kant, who said that "autonomous thinking is finding the ultimate test of truth in oneself (i.e. in one's own reason); and the fundamental principle of continuously autonomous thinking is Enlightenment" (Kant, 1799). It is highly recommendable to read his pamphlet "Beantwortung der Frage: Was ist Aufklärung" ("An Answer to the Question: What Is Enlightenment?") from 1784 (see Kant, 1799), containing the appeals "Habe Mut, dich deines eigenen Verstandes zu bedienen!" ("Have the Courage to Use

Figure 5.1 Immanuel Kant (1724–1804).

Your Own Understanding!") and "Sapere aude!" ("Dare to Discern!" – even, to make a contemporary addition, when reading claims in "peer-reviewed" "top" journals).

Modern scholars should open up their minds to the relevant Enlightenment literature. When their scientific work is mainly concerned with children, they can learn a lot about child development and upbringing by following the course of history from the 18th century onward. Here, Kant's admiration for Rousseau will serve as the basis of the description of this Western history. Rousseau's *Émile, ou de l'éducation* (1762/1763) was called "the birth certificate of pedagogy" by Kant (see Prins, 1963, p. 139) and was later received with at least equal enthusiasm by Johann Goethe (1749–1832) as "the natural gospel of education," and by Johann Herder (1744–1803) and Gotthold Lessing (1729–1781) as a "divine work" (see Soëtard, 1989, p. 144). It is good to note that hardly any philosopher has been written about as much as Rousseau, including voluminous literature on the reception of Rousseau's thinking as such (e.g., L'Aminot, 1992). Classical works on Rousseau include Cassirer (1932, 1955), Burgelin (1952), and Rang (1959). An accessible and abundantly illustrated biography is Soëtard (1989). Many works of Rousseau were originally printed and published in Amsterdam; in the Netherlands, there has always been a profound and scholarly interest in Rousseau's (pedagogical) ideas, as, for example, Roland Holst (1918), Brugmans (1951), and Van der Velde (1967). Furthermore, there is a continuing series entitled *Annales de la Société Jean-Jacques Rousseau* from Geneva (since 1905).

Figure 5.2 Jean-Jacques Rousseau (1712–1778). *Source*: Allan Ramsay, *Jean-Jacques Rousseau*, National Gallery of Scotland.

I have a strong conviction that no educationalist or developmental psychologist can bear this professional title with honor without having determined his or her own standpoint in relation to Rousseau's *Émile*. Until some 50 years ago, many colleagues would have endorsed this without a doubt. I am afraid that now they may ironically shrug their shoulders, for what importance does history have to modern empirical researchers? This chapter is meant as an answer to this question.

Rousseau's *Émile*

What message did Rousseau wish to convey? He claimed that pedagogy should be child oriented; and that there are age-related stages, to which approaches toward the child, including the pedagogical and educational approaches, must be tailored; and that children must be offered knowledge only when they display a need for it. Moreover, knowledge must spring from a child's own explorations, from hands-on experience, preferably not from books. A child should certainly not be exposed to wisdom from books before the age of 12! Despite much enthusiasm, from Kant among others, Rousseau's book should in the first place be regarded as a revolutionary Enlightenment text, *not* as a pedagogical handbook. His book stemmed from the tradition that Israel (2001, 2005) named "radical Enlightenment."

According to Israel, the key figure of this radical Enlightenment is Baruch Spinoza (1632–1677), the great Dutch philosopher. The "Epilogue" of Israel's book (2001, 2005) is entitled "Rousseau, Radicalism, Revolution." Spinoza, by way of Denis Diderot (1713–1784), led to Rousseau and the French Revolution. *Émile* was indeed radical. In *Émile* the author pointed out that he rebelled not only against French society, but also and foremost against its *reproduction* (Soëtard, 1989, p. 97). Rousseau thought that children should be taken "back to nature" (however, this expression did not appear in his writings, but in those of his commentators). By "back to nature," Rousseau meant as far away as possible from Parisian decadence. Children should learn to think autonomously, without being led astray by French culture, without following other people's wisdom from books. This Enlightenment idea is the radical expression of the primacy of the autonomously thinking individual, which had great appeal to Kant. And this is the reason that Rousseau's *Émile* is a book for philosophers, *not* for educationalists, fathers, and mothers, as Rousseau emphasized (Bloom, 1979, p. 28). However, to no avail!

The first four books (parts) of *Émile* describe the stages of a child's cognitive and moral development, and also how the upbringer must respect and be in keeping with these stages. Its correspondence with the theory of the future founder of developmental psychology, Piaget, the lifetime director of L'Institut J.-J. Rousseau in Geneva, is striking. Thanks to Piaget's research on cognitive development, the institute became the most prestigious center for pedagogical and developmental psychological research worldwide for the largest part of the 20th century. Piaget's and Rousseau's stage theories are like two peas in a pod. At first glance, this may not seem odd. After all, Rousseau was from Geneva, and the Genevan Institute must have been named after him for some good reason. That, however, is *too* simple a line of reasoning. It should be realized that Piaget's stage theory is deemed to be the result of unprecedented large-scale and worldwide, albeit mainly Western, empirical research. Particularly, observing his own three children was a rich source of scientific ideas to Piaget. Contrastingly, Rousseau abandoned his five children immediately after birth; he did not like children of flesh and blood at all. The boy Émile is a mere literary concoction. So how can it be that Piaget discovered in empirical research what Rousseau had made up in the process of writing? I think there is a simple answer: European education, particularly in public schools, was shaped according to Rousseau's ideas, despite Rousseau's warnings. Below, this process is described in a nutshell.

Émile and Schooling

The most important source of Rousseauian education was located in Dessau, Germany, home to the Philanthropinum, a model school, and a teacher-training school, founded by the educationalist Johann Basedow (1724–1790). The fact that these educationalists called themselves *philanthropists* displayed a pedagogical enthusiasm, very much in accordance with the Rousseauian belief in a benign human nature. They were dedicated to "natural education" and aimed at "developing a child's possibilities as freely as possible, creating a cheerful development and learning atmosphere, stimulating autonomous thinking, and facilitating a world orientation and practical attitude to life which are focused on the present" (Reble, 1977, p. 62).

Johann Pestalozzi (1746–1827), an educationalist who was inspired by these Philanthropines, implemented Rousseau's educational ideas in Switzerland. He and his wife, Anna, read and commented on *Émile* and preferred to call their son Jacob by the name of Jean-Jacques (after Rousseau). Although Pestalozzi rejected *Émile* as an "unpractical dream book" (quoted in Noordam, 1975, p. 227), he was greatly influenced by it. Like Rousseau, he emphasized a child's self-motivation, spontaneity, and natural development. The pedagogy influenced by Pestalozzi is generally referred to with the slogan "Vom Kinde aus" (Gläser, 1920) and is very succinctly expressed in his following quote: "Alles was du bist, alles was du willst, alles was du sollst, geht von dir selber aus" ("Everything you are, everything you want, everything you should be, originates from yourself": quoted in Van der Velde, 1967, p. 39).

The ideas of the Philanthropines and Pestalozzi not only influenced each other, but also reached the homes of modern upper-middle-class citizens. A fine example is the upbringing of Otto van Eck, which Baggerman and Dekker (2005, 2006) have reported on. The enlightened environment in which Otto was raised in The Hague, the Netherlands, around 1780 had been introduced to modern educational methods. This boy's everyday life, which has remained accessible through his diaries, is much like Émile's life. He has his own garden, in which he seeds and plants and harvests. He walks around carrying his weeder, hammer, and chisel, accompanied by a goat. Clearly, his father, a patriot and Batavian revolutionary, had learned a lot from Rousseau. His son Otto had to be raised on the land, in close contact with nature, far away from what Rousseau had called "the sewers of the human race" (see Baggerman & Dekker, 2006, p. 39).

The Philanthropines adopted these principles from Rousseau, although they did make them more bourgeois. Being a radical Enlightener, Rousseau in *Émile* made it clear how much he rejected the decadence of prevailing French culture, and in doing so he paved the way for the French Revolution. The Philanthropines, however, did not take their children to the depths of the woods, as far away as possible from urban life, like Rousseau did with Émile. Rather, they built school gardens in the urban areas in which their schools were located. Rousseau deemed simple craftsman work much more important than what he condescendingly called armchair learning. The Philanthropines agreed, but very much unlike Rousseau they did not let their pupils work autonomously. They organized trips to workshops, farms, and factories. It is true to say that Rousseau's radical enlightened educational ideas were turned into bourgeois variations by the Philanthropines, who practiced urbanized variations and reflections based on books. These refined variations of Rousseau are encountered when one has the opportunity, thanks to Baggerman and Dekker, to browse through Otto van Eck's diaries. Otto's example also shows how the middle class slowly developed a breeding ground for organizing community schooling.

The second half of the 18th century marked the beginning of the establishment of primary schools (De Swaan, 2004) in Prussia. They were inspired by both the Philanthropines in Dessau and Pestalozzi in Switzerland. In the Netherlands, the initiative was mainly taken by the Maatschappij tot Nut van 't Algemeen (Society for the Benefit of the Public; Het Nut for short). This organization was founded in Edam in 1784 (see Mijnhardt & Wichers, 1984) by Jan Nieuwenhuyzen (1724–1806), a Mennonite preacher in Monnikendam. Wildens (1745–1809), a fervent patriot and professor in Franeker, most likely was the *auctor intellectualis* (instigator). His ideas can be recognized in Het Nut: striving for general public schooling, educating children to become democratic citizens, and child-rearing in a general Christian spirit of tolerance and love for one's home country. Het Nut founded many primary schools and a number of teacher-training schools, published numerous educational books, and took to translating and editing foreign pedagogical works (mainly from Dessau and Pestalozzi's Switzerland). Also, it established public libraries and savings banks, and held courses for adults, providing systematic information on vital questions and general knowledge. In 1796, Het Nut submitted a proposal to the National Assembly to centrally organize education and to found a general national school. It is in this spirit that the first Dutch School Acts for primary education of 1801, 1803, and 1806 were adopted. The Seminary for Pedagogy in Amsterdam, founded in 1918 at the instigation of Abraham Kohnstamm (1875–1951), must be mentioned separately. Kohnstamm, a physicist, became Extraordinary Professor of Pedagogy on account of Het Nut, and is generally considered the father of Dutch pedagogy.

This nutshell description of the history of education and upbringing so far can be summarized as follows. German, Swiss, and Dutch modern pedagogy of the 19th century can be traced back to Rousseau and, by way of a Rousseauian organization of the primary school (originally a Prussian initiative), institutionalized and in a culturally historical way realized the ideas on child development Rousseau devised at his writing table – so much so that in the 20th century, Piaget's empirical research reveals a developmental course that is very similar to the prototypical development of Rousseau's *Émile.*

Progress in Enlightenment and Romanticism

About one thing the Enlightenment critics – including the French postmodernists (see Koops, 2008) – were right: The Enlightenment was riddled with an unjustified belief in progress. The monumental work from the Enlightenment, the *Encyclopedia* by Diderot, d'Alembert, and others, intended "to further develop our descendants and at the same time make them more virtuous and fortunate" ("Knowledge *is* virtue" was the motto of Het Nut). Both history and Rousseau's *Émile* were thought to be characterized by a spontaneous, natural development for the better. However, there are two objections to this. First, learning does not automatically lead to a higher morality; and, second, there is no reason to assume that reality develops into something better and more beautiful by a law of nature. By now these objections have been generally accepted, so much so that many contemporary intellectuals consider the Enlightenment superseded. Drawing on an acute and rapturous essay by the philosopher Alain Finkielkraut, I would like to forcefully object to this notion to prevent the baby from being thrown out with the bathwater.

In "La défaite de la pensée" ("The Undoing of Thought"), Finkielkraut (1987, 1988) displayed the sad consequences of the introduction of the term *Volksgeist* by Herder in 1774. Before exploring the fatal thinking of Herder and German Romanticism in more detail, it should be realized that German Romanticism was motivated by the Prussian defeat at the Battle of Jena (Germany) in 1806. In Jena, the Prussians (joined by allied forces) suffered a crushing and unexpected defeat against Napoleon. It was not without reason that Georg Hegel (1770–1831) spoke of "the end of history" (see Fukuyama, 1989, 1992), implying that history had been completed with the permanent establishment of the principles of the French Revolution, of the liberal democratic state. In Prussia, the intellectuals responded by withdrawing into a Romanticism that was primarily based on Herder, thereby creating a countermovement to the French Enlightenment, a countermovement in honor of the unique German *Volksgeist* that contradictorily was also founded on Rousseau's sentimentalism. This intensified post-Jena Romanticism centered on the romanticized child personifying the hope for a better future. The finest abstract of this new creature is a lost drawing by Philipp Runge (1777–1810) from 1809. According to the art historian Rosenblum (1988), this drawing is *the* symbol of the Romantic Child, just like Leonardo da Vinci's drawing of a naked man in a circle and square has become the symbol of the Renaissance man:

> This drawing of 1809 can also be seen to evoke a state of natural innocence and religious purity so primal that the vision of a sacred beginning to a radiantly new and magical world can hover in our imagination above the baby's fixed gaze. (Rosenblum, 1988, p. 9)

Notwithstanding the beautiful wordings of German Romanticism, in the wake of Finkielkraut we must be extraordinarily fearful of its ideological core. As his name reveals, Finkielkraut, a French philosopher with a German name, was born in Alsace-Lorraine. The area of Alsace-Lorraine in the northeast of France (or, depending on the point of view, the southwest of Germany), rich with its large coal resources, fell prey to a series of wars between France and Germany in the 19th century, changing nationality each

Figure 5.3   The Romantic child. *Source*: Philipp Otto Runge, *The Child* (1809).

time, a situation that ended only after the Second World War, when the area was allocated to France. Finkelkraut, born in this area, alleges to have, like no other philosopher, access to the unique cultural history of this particular area, representing the clash between German Romanticism and French Enlightenment. After Herder, says Finkelkraut, the term *culture* is no longer associated with science, no longer refers to diminishing prejudice and ignorance, but expresses the irreducible individuality of the unique soul of the people (Finkielkraut, 1987, p. 13ff.). Herder's Germanic Romanticism provided what Finkielkraut expressively called "the maternal warmth of prejudice" (Finkielkraut, 1987, p. 27). The *Volksgeist* proved to be "the most dangerous explosive of modern times" and resulted in two world wars. This expression originates from the French historian Ernest Renan (1823–1892), in response to the German conquest of Alsace-Lorraine in 1870 (see Finkielkraut, 1988, p. 133).

After World War II, the United Nations created a special division that was to devote itself to science and culture, UNESCO. The UN intended to create an organization that would protect against abuse of power "and which would arm people with knowledge and understanding permanently against demagogical attempts at leading their thinking astray" (Finkielkraut, 1988, p. 54). This implies, says Finkielkraut, that the government officials and intellectual authorities invited by the UN intuitively endorsed the spirit of the Enlightenment. However, in one respect they did not, and this still has an impact today. The universal subject of man from the "Déclaration des droits de l'homme et du citoyen" has been replaced by actual people, in all their diverse modes of existence.

This replacement was prompted by a text, *Race et histoire*, written in 1950 by the cultural anthropologist Claude Lévi-Strauss (1908–2009), upon the request of UNESCO (Lévi-Strauss, 1951/1987). First, Lévi-Strauss stated that the term *race* has zero scientific value. Differences between human groups stem from "geographical, historical, and social circumstances," not from "anatomical or physiological conditions." Second, he told us to resist value hierarchy:

> The many shapes adopted by mankind in time and space cannot be categorised in an order of increasing perfection: they are no beacons lighting the road to triumph, no stages on the way to the highest form of civilisation: Western. (Based on the translation by Finkielkraut, 1988, p. 56)

This is the very temptation the enlightened philosophers succumbed to: placing human communities on a scale of values, and occupying the highest level themselves. This repugnant conviction laid the foundations for colonialism, and formed the basis of the closely connected 19th-century ethnological science. However, when ethnologists discovered the complexity of traditions and modes of living in so-called primitive societies, they did not take part in it anymore, as Lévi-Strauss made clear. Ethnology became *cultural anthropology*, and the general enlightened notion of man was replaced by a nonhierarchical diversity of culturally specific characters (Finkielkraut, 1988, p. 65).

The essence of Finkielkraut's essay is that it makes clear that Lévi-Strauss strikes out at hierarchizing so strongly that in doing so he also abolishes the universality of Enlightenment thinking. And Lévi-Strauss has gathered a following. Following structural anthropology, all life sciences have opened the hunt for ethnocentrism, leading to what Finkielkraut (1988) dramatizingly called "the second death of mankind" (the first being that of Romanticism) (p. 59). Contemporary fanatics of cultural identity have continued to glorify the collective soul, a glorification stemming from the term *Volksgeist* and culminating in racial theory and Hitlerism (Finkielkraut, 1988, pp. 76–79). And, I am inclined to add, in the current multicultural debate in the Netherlands and many other European countries, it has taken the form of anti-Muslim activism.

Child Development in Enlightenment and Romanticism

The described course of history from Herder to Lévi-Strauss is also applicable to thinking about children. The developmental psychologist Kessen made clear that the modern child and the mere concept of child development to a large extent are cultural constructions. Developmental psychology itself can be characterized as "a peculiar invention that moves with the tidal sweeps of the larger culture" (Kessen, 1993, p. 227; see also Kessen, 1979).

Enlightenment and its notion of progress (Rousseau) are explicitly based on the assumption that the child itself, through natural education and development, would work its way to the highest level: that of adult Western cultural man. Rousseau's adoration of the "noble savage" (see Rousseau, 1755, 1762) formed the basis for a hierarchical organization of peoples and of child development stages. Piaget endorsed this line of thinking. This is illustrated by the influence exerted on him by the cultural anthropologist he frequently quoted, Lucien Lévy-Bruhl (1857–1939), who wrote the classic works *Les fonctions mentales dans les sociétés inférieures* (Lévy-Bruhl, 1910) and *La mentalité primitive* (Lévy-Bruhl, 1922). In this last book, Lévy-Bruhl described the thinking of "primitive" man as being "pre-logic." This was a characterization that Piaget applied to young children; in its development, a child passes through different phases, from primitive to developed.

At the end of the 19th century, this concept was biologized (Morss, 1990). The biogenetic law of Ernst Haeckel (1834–1919) from Jena, which was as influential as it was controversial, stated that "ontogenesis is a recapitulation of phylogenesis." This fundamental law gave child development the status of a firm phylogenetically embedded structure and became the basis of Western developmental psychology (see Koops, 1990). William Preyer (1841–1897), a friend of Haeckel, is generally considered the author of the first thorough developmental psychological study (see Preyer, 1882/1989). It is justifiable to observe here that developmental psychology could not but originate from the battlefield of Jena. In the works of many key figures in the history of developmental psychology, a strong echo of Haeckel's biogenetic law can be discerned (Koops, 1990), very much so in the work of Piaget. This implies that the child in its individual development rises from the primitive level to the highest level, that of Western European cultural man, by a law of nature.

After the Second World War, the idea of hierarchical organized stages has been challenged little by little. Lévi-Strauss has done away with the reprehensible idea of the primitive state of natural peoples, which formed a justification of colonization. He has done so in such a radical way that modern cultural anthropologists feel shame because of the incomparability of prelogical thinking by so-called savages and by children. In a fine article on the question of "Why Don't Anthropologists Like Children?" Hirschfeld (2002) recalled an extract from the essay "The Anti-Semite" by the French philosopher Jean-Paul Sartre (1905–1980; see Sartre, 1954). Following an unpleasant experience with a Jewish furrier, Sartre's Anti-Semite started hating Jews, not furriers (Sartre, 1954, p. 14). Similarly, cultural anthropologists felt very awkward about comparing children with natural peoples and as a result gave up studying children, not peoples.

Hirschfeld did exaggerate a little. I would like to comment here that although there is no such thing as a well-established subdiscipline of the "cultural anthropology of the child," some interesting studies have been carried out. The most important are included in an excellent anthology (see LeVine & New, 2008).

Applying Lévi-Strauss's view to the stages of child development dismisses the idea that these stages are hierarchically interrelated (see Van der Veer, 1985, p. 108; Van IJzendoorn, Van der Veer, & Goossens, 1981, p. 66) and results in age groups being considered groups with an independent "culture." Ultimately, the concept of childhood loses its meaning. According to authors who will be discussed below, this has indeed happened since the 1970s. A fine example of this new *de*infantilizing thinking is a book by the Dutch children's book author Kuijer (1980), who described a stage theory equivalent to Piaget's as "a series of locks ensuring that not a spark of 'childlikeness' accidentally passes into adulthood" (p. 15). In such a view, the classical idea of childlikeness primarily consists of contempt of childhood. Relinquishing this contempt would imply humane respect for children, resulting in the disappearance of the child. Has this indeed happened? The answer to this question will comprise two steps: First, the history of infantilization will be described; and, second, this will then serve as a background against which the relatively recent "disappearance of childhood" will be sketched.

Infantilization According to Ariès

No image is as pliable as that of the child. Since the beginning of the 1960s, there has been a separate subdiscipline within the domain of historical studies, which is directed particularly at the history of these pliable images, called the *history of childhood*. This new subdiscipline is primarily inspired by the work of Ariès (see Ariès, 1960, 1962). Here I must resist the temptation to expand on Ariès's work and provide only a brief summary with respect to what I consider his two main hypotheses: the discontinuity hypothesis and the change hypothesis (Koops, 1996, 1998, 2004).

The discontinuity hypothesis assumes that the child did not exist until after the Middle Ages. In medieval civilization, there was a negligible difference between the worlds of children and of adults; as soon as the child was weaned, it was seen as the natural companion of the adult. Other historians have found little or no evidence to support this hypothesis. Important research has been done by Hanawalt (1993) that shows that children in London in the 14th and 15th centuries, in many respects, did indeed inhabit a world that was specifically for children and not for adults: They played more than adults, and in separate, safe places; they were part of age groups and had their own, age-related social environment. Even Ariès himself admitted that his discontinuity hypothesis requires far-reaching modifications, so far reaching that I would simply conclude that the discontinuity hypothesis is not tenable (for more detailed documentation, see Koops, 1996, 1998).

The change hypothesis states that, from about the 13th century, there was a continuous increase in childishness in the cultural representations of children. For this continuous increase in childishness, I will use the term *infantilization*, which is an increasing duration of the childhood stage, which is necessarily accompanied by an increasing distance between the worlds of children and adults (Elias, 1939; Koops, 1998; Plessner, 1946). Much empirical historical support has been gathered for the change hypothesis. Instead of going into the abundant and complex literature, I will illustrate Ariès's notion of historical changes by referring to a series of paintings. Although Ariès used many types of historical material to support his change hypothesis, it is his interpretation of the child in the world of art that is most controversial. I will briefly illustrate Ariès's interpretation of children in paintings and refute some of the most persistent academic arguments, which so persistently criticize him precisely on this point.

Ariès argued that up to the 14th century, there are no depictions of children characterized by a special artistic representation, but only images of men on a reduced scale. From around the 14th century onward, the Christ child is gradually portrayed as increasingly childish. In the 16th century, genre paintings arose in which the child was apparently depicted because of his or her graceful or picturesque qualities. In the 17th century, the modern child was, at last, fully represented in paintings, particularly in Dutch paintings: For the first time there are portraits of children on their own, an intense interest in typical childish scenes is shown, and even family portraits were completely planned around the child. Probably the most dramatic change in the attitude toward the portrayal of children occurred in the 18th century, and generally Rousseau is seen as the troubadour of the new stance – not by painting but through his book on the boy Émile. In the 19th century the romantic interest in children even extended to adolescence, which at that time began to take on dramatic forms for the first time in Western history (Koops & Zuckerman, 2003).

Several years ago I made the effort to study the empirical tenability of Ariès's assertions on children in paintings (Koops, 1996). This was primarily to investigate the most important argument *against* Ariès's interpretations, namely, that his discussion of some tens of paintings (out of a population of tens of millions of paintings: Koops, 1996; Van der Woude, 1997) certainly cannot be called representative for Western paintings in general. Thanks to a careful and time-consuming inventory of Dutch and Flemish paintings in which children are portrayed, we were able to draw random samples of paintings that were rated by adults. For the methodology of this research, see Koops (1996). In essence we compared the painted images of children with the characteristics of "childish" mammals, as once described by the ethologist Konrad Lorenz as the *Kindchenschema* (child scheme; Lorenz, 1971). As decisive features of juvenility that trigger the innate releasing mechanisms for affection and nurturing, he mentioned, among other things, a relatively large head, predominance of the brain capsule, large and low-lying eyes, a bulging cheek region, and short and thick extremities.

We operationalized Ariès's change hypothesis so that the infantilization intended by him would mean that images of children in paintings became increasingly childish from the 15th to 20th centuries. We predicted that the paintings of children across the centuries would demonstrate a kind of cultural historical neotony. We simply calculated the correlation between the historic dates and the childishness scores, based on ratings by adults according to the *Kindchenschema* criteria. The findings supported the change hypothesis: The correlation was .60, which indicates that paintings in the past emphasized less childishness than modern paintings. This is a surprising and important result, precisely because, contrary to what most historians and in particular art historians claim, it does support Ariès's interpretation of the paintings.

This research concerning the most controversial part of Ariès's influential original study shows that we certainly cannot discard Ariès's view on the infantilization of children as a fable. I therefore consider it important to study the history of pedagogy and developmental psychology, themselves cultural historical phenomena, from an Ariès-type perspective, rather than from a naïve progressive view, as has been the case for too long. The names of Montaigne, Locke, and Rousseau are often proposed as milestones in the progressive modernization of our approach to children. However, instead of a gradual progression in our attitude toward children, supported by science, from my perspective there are culturally and historically changing images of children, of which scientific study is rather the result than the cause (Koops, 1990, 1996, 1998, 2004).

A most important cultural historical change that in fact ended the process of infantilization is the influence of the modern electronic media, actually leading to what could be called the disappearance of childhood.

The Disappearance of Childhood

According to the culture critic and media specialist Neil Postman (1931–2003; see Postman, 1992), the Western child started to disappear in the early 1960s. Following the beliefs of Ariès, Postman observed that without education – or, better, without schools – there are no children in the modern sense of the word. After all,

> In an illiterate society (like that of the Middle Ages) there was no need to sharply distinguish
> between children and adults, such a society harbours few secrets, and civilization does not
> need to supply education in order to understand itself. (Postman, 1992, p. 22)

The notion of the "child" is redundant if everyone shares the same information environment and lives in the same social and intellectual world. In the wake of many media experts and historians, Postman believed that the art of printing created a new world of symbols, which in its turn required a new interpretation of the notion of "adulthood" (Postman, 1992, p. 28).

The invention of the printing press, most likely by Johannes Gutenberg (1394–1468) in 1440, resulted in "adulthood becoming a symbolic achievement, not a biological phenomenon. With the invention of the art of printing, children were required to develop, which would be effected by learning to read, by entering the world of typography" (Postman, 1992, p. 43). As a result, children needed education and were compelled to go to school. This made the notion of the "child" inevitable. We can join Postman in observing that this notion had its "finest hour" (or, more appropriately, its "finest century") between 1850 and 1950. Children had to work in factories as little as possible and were sent to school without relent. They were given their own clothes, furniture, literature, games, and social world. A process, usually called *infantilization*, took place, a historical lengthening of childhood (see Koops, 1998). In contrast, the person who according to Postman is responsible for the "childless era" starting after 1950 is Samuel Morse (1791–1872). Morse's invention of the telegraph (demonstrated in public for the first time in 1837) further denaturalized information from "personal possession to merchandise of global value." "Telegraphy marked the beginning of the process of information becoming uncontrollable" (Postman, 1992, p. 74). All this affected the notion of the child immensely.

The child originated from an environment in which the information in books was controlled by adults and was gradually supplied to children. However, anonymization as a result of telegraphy caused a development that would ultimately take away information from the authority of parents and the family. After the invention of telegraphy, this development was boosted by a continuous stream of inventions: the rotation press, the camera, the telephone, the gramophone, film, radio, and television (Postman, 1992, p. 76), culminating in what was not described by Postman: the launch of the Internet. Mainly because these modern means of communication primarily use image language, the typical characteristic of childlikeness, illiteracy, loses its meaning. Knowing the alphabet is not a requirement for understanding images (Postman, 1992, p. 81). Television, for example, removes the dividing lines between children and adults to a large extent: "Supported by other electronic media which do not rely on the written word, television re-creates communication conditions like those existing in the 14th and 15th centuries" (Postman, 1992, p. 82); and "in the new media climate everything is available to everyone at the same time: electronic media cannot keep secrets," and "without secrets the notion of the 'child' is void" (p. 83).

Postman (1992) thoroughly demonstrated the actual disappearance of the child by presenting a large amount of (anecdotal) information on the portrayal of young people as miniature adults in the media (p. 122), the disappearance of children's songs (p. 123), the fading of the Disney view of the child (p. 125), the disappearance of children's clothes while adults have begun to wear clothes that were previously intended for children (pp. 127ff.), the disappearance of children's games (p. 129) while top-class sport has become normal to children (p. 129), and the decline of good manners (p. 132). All this together points to the decline of the notion of the "child," said Postman, "and accordingly to a weakening of the nature of adulthood." Postman's book is concisely and powerfully summarized in the final sentence of the cover text: "The basic notion of this book – that our electronic information environment makes the 'child' disappear – can also be read as follows: an electronic information environment makes the adult disappear."

It is important to realize that many books had been published in the 1970s that intended to free the child from the chains of its immaturity. An example of these books is the book by Kuyer (1980). Other examples are Illich's book (1973) calling for a "deschooling" of society as it hinders children from participating in an adult society; Holt's book (1976) consistently pleading for freeing the child from the chains of a 300-year-old tradition of servitude; and, finally, Farson's book (1974) interpreting the rights of the child very literally and broadly, for example by demanding that children are given the right to vote, "because adults do not stand up for their interests and cannot vote on their behalf" (p. 179).

Interestingly, the period discussed by Postman in relation to the disappearance of childhood, the 1970s, also witnessed an unprecedented large global research effort centered on undermining Piaget's structural cognitive theory. In other words, the noninterconvertible developmental stages, referred to as *cognitive structures*, were gradually replaced by continuous domain-specific developmental processes. Neo-Piagetian research from that time undermined the presumptions of the Rousseau–Piaget tradition, which emphasized the *in*accessibility of childlike thinking, like never before. The fanaticism with which the origins of all kinds of childlike rationality were explored caused many a researcher to end up as an "infancy expert" (Koops, 1990, 2004). This post neo-Piagetian research, among other things, resulted in research on the child's *theory of mind* (see also Chapter 28), experimentally demonstrating how 2- to 3-year-old children already have a command of current lay psychology, based on a simple theory of desires and beliefs. Meanwhile, the search for the increasingly younger origins of generally human means of communication has not come to an end. Onishi and Baillargeon (2005), for example, demonstrated in an article in *Science* that 13-month-old babies basically have a command of generally human, ordinary communication principles ("beliefs" and "desires"). Remarkably, cultural historical developments – the disappearance of traditional childhood – go hand in hand with the experimental empirical scientific search for (and finding of!) generally human and age-independent means of communication. To put it briefly, developmental psychology moves with the tides of culture.

New Possibilities?

It will be clear that the modern Western child, construed in the 18th and 19th centuries – the Enlightened child – disappeared in the second half of the 20th century, marking the end of the historical process of infantilization. Traditional upbringing, which was based on this infantilization, was referred to as "Bringing up by keeping small" in a much quoted publication of Dasberg (1975). In essence, it boiled down to setting the child apart from the adult world and leading it step by step into that adult world by what was called *upbringing*. This style of upbringing has become outmoded: Infantilization is behind us in the sense that borders and border guards have become inoperative. Mainly through electronic media, today's children have access to the adult world from the beginning, including the world of violence and sex, areas in which children on the basis of the then current pedagogy were not allowed access for 2 and a half centuries. Given the child's access to the Internet, it is an improbable atavism that American parents as late as in 2006 pressed charges against teachers who persisted in marking schoolwork with red ink (Stearns, 2009). The parents feared that the feeble self-esteem of their vulnerable children would be damaged.

Raising children will have to be reinvented. We are assisted by a tremendous amount of sophisticated and splendid studies on child behavior and on that of their upbringers. However, I would like to point out that all this research will only prove advantageous *if we know what our objective is with regard to children*, and that is what we are in the dark about. Worse still, modern academic pedagogy is hardly occupied with it. People who, like me, are followers of Kant's much maligned successor, the educationalist Johann Herbart (1776–1841), are convinced that pedagogy as a science cannot do without ethics, on the one hand, and (developmental) psychology, on the other (Herbart, 1841). The first helps to formulate objectives; the latter offers the means to achieve them. An evolutionary view like Bjorklund's (2007; see also Chapter 4), however relevant, will not help out. Bjorklund explained why a lengthy human youth is necessary to be able to adapt to an ever-changing culture. This view only makes clear why we should cherish an extended explorative childhood, but not if and how it should be oriented.

Let us return for a final time to the example set by Rousseau. His incredibly effective book on education was a book on a new ethical person in a Utopian society. This very context turned his book into such a success. Of course, we are not in a position, nor do we wish, to write a book in which a successor of Napoleon in a contemporary Jena establishes a child image using armed forces. Nevertheless, we could develop a vision of an ideal society in the spirit of which we would like to raise our children. In doing so, I recommend restoring the Enlightenment principles of rationality and autonomous and critical thinking, high-grade ethical principles forming the basis of a modern *contrat social* (Rousseau, 1762), and commitment to a democratic society in which freedom of speech and interhuman respect are balanced. All this needs to be worked out. However, it is good and reassuring to know that we can fall back on enlightened classical literature. But only when we have clear normative notions will we be able to profit from the rich modern empirical developmental psychology that is today at our disposal.

This chapter hopefully demonstrates that understanding of childhood and child development is not fully and satisfyingly possible without studying the cultural historical context. Empirical analytical research is necessary but not sufficient. Historical framing and reframing are the keys to the contextual understanding of children.

Acknowledgments

This chapter builds on an address, given upon accepting the position of Distinguished Professor, entitled "Foundations and History of Developmental Psychology and Education," at Utrecht University, April 18, 2008.

References

Ariès, P. (1960). *L'enfant et la vie familiale sous l'ancien régime*. Paris: Libraire Plon.

Ariès, P. (1962). *Centuries of childhood: A social history of family life*. New York: Vintage Books.

Baggerman, A., & Dekker, R. (2005). *Kind van de toekomst: De wondere wereld van Otto van Eck (1780–1798)*. Amsterdam: Wereldbibliotheek.

Baggerman, A., & Dekker, R. (2006). Verlichte pedagogiek rond 1800: ideaal, praktijk en door-werking. De opvoeding van Otto van Eck (1780–1798). In N. Bakker, R. Dekker, & A. Janssens (Eds.), *Tot burgerschap en deugd: Volksopvoeding in de negentiende eeuw* (pp. 35–47). Hilversum, the Netherlands: Verloren.

Bjorklund, D. F. (2007). *Why youth is not wasted on the young: Immaturity in human development*. Oxford: Blackwell.

Bloom, A. (1979). Introduction. In J.-J. Rousseau, *Émile, or on education*. New York: Basic Books.

Brugmans, H. (1951). *De révolte van het gemoed. Rousseau en het sentimentalisme*. Arnhem, the Netherlands: Van Loghum Slaterus.

Burgelin, P. (1952). *La philosophie de l'existence de J.-J. Rousseau*. Paris: Plon.

Cassirer, E. (1932). Das Problem Jean-Jacques Rousseau. *Archiv für Geschichte der Philosophie, 41*, 177–213, 479–513.

Cassirer, E. (1955). *The philosophy of the Enlightenment*. Boston: Beacon Press.

Dasberg, L. (1975). *Grootbrengen door kleinhouden als historisch verschijnsel*. Meppel, the Netherlands: Boom.

De Swaan, A. (2004). *Zorg en staat. Welzijn, onderwijs en gezondheidszorg in Europa en de Verenigde Staten in de nieuwe tijd*. Amsterdam: Bert Bakker.

Elias, N. (1939). *Uber den Prozess der Zivilisation. Soziogenetische und psychogenetische Untersuchungen*. Basel, Switzerland: Haus zum Falken.

Farson, R. (1974). *Birthrights*. New York: Vintage Books.

Finkielkraut, A. (1987). *La défaite de la pensée*. Paris: Gallimard.

Finkielkraut, A. (1988). *De ondergang van het denken*. Amsterdam: Contact.

Fukuyama, F. (1989, Summer). The end of history? *National Interest*, 16.

Fukuyama, F. (1992). *The end of history and the last man*. New York: Free Press.

Gläser, J. (1920). *Vom Kinde aus*. Hamburg: Westermann.

Hanawalt, B. (1993). *Growing up in medieval London*. New York: Oxford University Press.

Herbart, J. F. (1841). *Umriss Pädagogischer Vorlesungen* (2nd ed.). Göttingen, Germany: Dieterich.

Hirschfeld, L. A. (2002). Why don't anthropologists like children? *American Anthropologist, 104*, 611–627.

Holt, J. (1976). *Escape from childhood*. New York: Vintage Books.

Illich, I. (1973). *Deschooling society*. Harmondsworth, UK: Penguin.

Israel, J. I. (2001). *Radical enlightenment: Philosophy and the making of modernity*. Oxford: Oxford University Press.

Israel, J. I. (2005). *Radicale Verlichting. Hoe radicale Nederlandse denkers het gezicht van onze cultuur voorgoed veranderen*. Franeker, the Netherlands: Uitgeverij Van Wijnen.

Kant, I. (1799). Beantwortung der Frage: Was ist Aufklärung. In *Imanuel Kant's vermischte Schriften*. Halle, Belgium: Johann Heinrich Tieftrunk.

Kessen, W. (1979). The American child and other cultural inventions. *American Psychologist, 34,* 815–820.

Kessen, W. (1993). A developmentalist's reflections. In G. H. Elder Jr., J. Modell, & R. Parke (Eds.), *Children in time and place: Developmental and historical insights* (pp. 226–230). Cambridge: Cambridge University Press.

Koops, W. (1990). A viable developmental psychology in the nineties by way of renewed respect for tradition. In P. J. P. Drenth, J. A. Sergeant, & R. J. Takens (Eds.), *European perspectives in psychology* (Vol. 1, pp. 171–194). New York: Wiley.

Koops, W. (1996). Historical developmental psychology: The sample case of paintings. *International Journal of Behavioral Development, 19,* 393–413.

Koops, W. (1998). Infantilisatie bij kinderen, jeugdigen en volwassenen. In N. Verloop (Ed.), *75 jaar onderwijs en opvoeding: 75 Pedagogische Studiën* (pp. 131–161). Groningen, the Netherlands: Wolters-Noordhoff.

Koops, W. (2004). Imaging childhood in European history and developmental psychology. *European Journal of Developmental Psychology, 1,* 1–18.

Koops, W. (2008). *Historical reframing of childhood*. Utrecht: University of Utrecht Press.

Koops, W., & Zuckerman, M. (2003). A historical developmental approach to adolescence [Special issue]. *History of the Family, 8,* 345–421.

Kuijer, G. (1980). *Het geminachte kind*. Zwolle, the Netherlands: Tulp.

L'Aminot, T. (1992). *Images de Jean-Jacques Rousseau*. Oxford: Voltaire Foundation.

Lévi-Strauss, C. (1987). *Race et histoire*. Paris: Denoël. (Originally published in 1951)

LeVine, R. A., & New, R. S. (2008). *Anthropology and child development. A cross-cultural reader*. Oxford: Blackwell.

Lévy-Bruhl, L. (1910). *Les functions mentales dans les sociétés inférieures*. Paris: Retz.

Lévy-Bruhl, L. (1922). *La Mentalité primitive*. Paris: PUF.

Lorenz, K. (1971). *Studies in animal and human behaviors* (Vol. 2). London: Methuen.

Mijnhardt, W. W., & Wichers, A. J. (1984). *Om het algemeen volksgeluk: Twee eeuwen particulier initiatief 1784–1984*. Edam, the Netherlands: Maatschappij tot Nut van 't Algemeen.

Morss, J. R. (1990). *The biologising of the child*. Hillsdale, NJ: Erlbaum.

Noordam, N. F. (1975). Pestalozzi. In I. Van der Velde (Ed.), *Grote denkers over opvoeding* (pp. 225–251). Amsterdam: Meulenhoff Educatief.

Onishi, K. H., & Baillargeon, R. (2005). Do 15-month-old infants understand false beliefs? *Science, 308,* 255–258.

Plessner, H. (1946). Over de infantiliserende invloed van de moderne maatschappij op op de jeugd. *Pedagogisce Studiën, 23,* 193–202.

Postman, N. (1992). *The disappearance of childhood*. New York: Dell. (Originally published in 1982)

Preyer, W. T. (1989). *Die Seele des Kindes (Eingeleitet und mit Materialien zur Rezeptionsgeschichte versehen von Georg Eckardt)*. Berlin: Springer Verlag. (Originally published in 1882)

Prins, F. W. (1963). *Verleden en heden. Beknopte geschiedenis van opvoeding en onderwijs*. Groningen, the Netherlands: Wolters.

Rang, M. (1959). *Rousseaus Lehre vom Menschen*. Göttingen, Germany: Vandenhoek & Ruprecht.

Reble, A. (1977). Filantropisme. In A. de Block (Ed.), *Standaard Encyclopedie voor opvoeding en onderwijs* (pp. 62–63). Antwerp: Standaard Uitgeverij.

Roland Holst, H. (1918). *Jean Jacques Rousseau. Een beeld van zijn leven en werken*. Amsterdam: Wereld Bibliotheek.

Rosenblum, R. (1988). _The Romantic child_. London: Thames and Hudson.

Rousseau, J.-J. (1755). _Discours sur l'origine et les fondements de l'inégalité parmi les hommes_. Amsterdam: Rey.

Rousseau, J.-J. (1762). _Du contrat social: ou principes du droit politique_. Amsterdam: Rey.

Rousseau, J.-J. (1763). _Émile, or on Education_. London: Nourse and Vaillant. (Originally published as Émile ou de l'Éducation in 1762)

Sartre, J.-P. (1954). The Anti-Semite [in French]. In _Réflexions sur la question juive_. Paris: Editions Paul Morihien.

Soëtard, M. (1989). _Jean-Jacques Rousseau. Philosoph-Pädagoge. Zerstörer der alten Ordnung. Eine Bildbiographie_. Zürich: Schweizer Verlagshaus.

Stearns, P. (2009). Culture and function in childhood: A modern American case. _European Journal of Developmental Psychology, 6_, 34–52.

Van der Veer, R. (1985). _Cultuur en Cognitie_. Groningen, the Netherlands: Wolters-Noordhoff.

Van der Velde, I. (1967). _Jean-Jacques Rousseau, pedagoog_. Amsterdam/Brussels: Agon Elsevier.

Van der Woude, A. (1997). De schilderijenproductie in Holland tijdens de Republiek [The production of paintings in Holland during Republican times]. In A. Schuurman, J. De Vries, & A. Van der Woude (Eds.), _Aards Geluk_ [Earthly happiness] (pp. 223–258). Amsterdam: Uitgeverij Balans.

Van IJzendoorn, R., Van der Veer, R., & Goossens, F. (1981). _Kritische Psychologie. Drie Stromingen_. Baarn, the Netherlands: Ambo.

CHAPTER SIX

Cultural Psychological Perspectives on Social Development in Childhood

Heidi Fung

In the previous edition of this handbook (Smith & Hart, 2002), Harkness (2002) illustrated how culture shapes children's social development in her thorough review of the changing paradigms in social anthropology (with a briefer discussion on approaches to culture in psychology). This chapter also addresses issues regarding culture and social development, but from the perspective of cultural psychology – the study of how culture and psyche make each other up. In the *Handbook of Cultural Psychology* (Kitayama & Cohen, 2007), Shweder (2007), a leading cultural psychologist, commented on how he was struck by "the breadth of the collection [in the volume] and how the expression of 'cultural psychology' has come to encompass so many very different types of intellectual traditions" (p. 827). This chapter examines a "narrow" intellectual tradition of cultural psychology that emerged at the interface of psychology and anthropology in the 1980s. This tradition was heavily influenced by the subfields of *culture and personality* (which had been most active from 1925 to the 1950s) and *ethnopsychology* (prominent during the 1970s and 1980s) in social anthropology (LeVine, 2001, 2007a, 2007b). It makes cultural psychology distinguishable from cross-cultural psychology epistemologically, theoretically, and methodologically. Cross-cultural psychology is another approach to culture in psychology that emerged from mainstream social psychology (Berry, 2000; Triandis, 2000).

For a comprehensive review of the cultural psychology of child development, see Shweder et al. (2006). This chapter seeks to highlight the stances and major concerns in cultural psychology in the realm of social development during childhood, illustrating these by reference to particular studies. I shall pay particular attention to why culture

The Wiley-Blackwell Handbook of Childhood Social Development, Second Edition, edited by Peter K. Smith and Craig H. Hart
© 2011 by Blackwell Publishing Ltd.

matters and how taking culture seriously might further our understanding of the developing child. I then close by pointing to the challenges and directions for cultural psychological studies in an increasingly transnational era.

Cultural Psychology: The Co-Creation of Culture and Person

The marginal state of culture in mainstream psychology can be reflected in leading professional journals. According to Arnett (2008), for over 90% of all papers ever published in the *Journal of Personality and Social Psychology*, or over 70% in the flagship APA journals in all areas in the past 5 years, their authors originated in North America. The keyword *culture* appeared in less than 5% of articles in all major psychological journals from 1994 to 2002 (Norenzayan & Heine, 2005). Although Americans comprise less than 5% of the world's population, nearly 70% of the participant samples in these studies were Americans, among which 80% (for papers published in 2007) were of European descent (Arnett, 2008). All samples (in the United States or elsewhere) predominantly came from an educated and middle-class background, for example undergraduate students in psychology courses or children from middle-class families (Miller, 2005; Norenzayan & Heine, 2005). In other words, despite a growing effort to promote international cooperation at an institutional level (Cole, 2006), the United States has played a continuously dominant role in psychological journals since World War II. Furthermore, most sociocultural groups in the world, including those in the United States, are underrepresented or unrepresented in contemporary psychological research. If the objective of such research is to make universal claims and apply identified fundamental principles and mental attributes to the whole of humankind, then there are serious concerns about the generalizability and applicability of their findings. This is perhaps most problematic when diagnoses and even treatments are intended, for instance to determine what is considered mentally healthy as opposed to pathological, and what the ideal developmental outcomes of parenting should be.

Whereas contemporary mainstream psychology tends to pay little attention to culture and is content with constant appeals to discover genuine psychological universals guided by the epistemological model of natural sciences, cultural psychology counters this trend and pleads not only "to bring culture in" – with more inclusion of diverse sociocultural groups and developmental pathways – but also "to take culture seriously," with more tolerance for particularism and a wider variety of research methods that are based on the epistemological model of interpretive social science. The motto "One mind, many mentalities" (Shweder, 2000; Shweder et al., 2006) stresses that cultural psychology aims to reassess the uniformitarian principle of inner mental unity and to develop a credible theory of psychological pluralism. Although cultural psychology alone may not disentangle complex issues involved in the long-standing nature versus nurture debate, it does not negate the role of heredity, neural systems, and the innate organization of the brain in human development. Nor does it dismiss the species-wide mechanisms caused by gene duplication, adaptation, selection, and modularity in evolutionary history (Suplizio, 2006), because "random events can divert the trajectories of growth, but the trajectories are confined within an envelope of functioning designs for the species" (Pinker, 2004, p. 12). After all, if it were not for the commonalities that we share, it would be impossible to comprehend and appreciate cultural categories and human life in other sociocultural groups. Cultural psychology, nevertheless, is particularly concerned with the following question:

> [H]ow can we create categories that will illuminate rather than obscure the unique patterns of different cultural meaning systems, and that will appreciate the primacy and power of culture to shape human experience, rather than attempt to subsume cultural variation within a set of universal categories? (Harwood, 2006, p. 127)

Instead of treating culture as an antecedent, independent, or intervening variable that affects or determines attitudes and behavior; group means to be compared with; or onion skins to be peeled off (Poortinga, van de Vijver, Joe, & van de Koppel, 1987), cultural psychology sees culture as simultaneously symbolic and behavioral. *Symbolic inheritance* refers to "the beliefs and doctrines that make it possible for a people to rationalize and make sense of the life they lead," whereas *behavioral inheritance* refers to "patterns of behavior that are learned and passed on from generation to generation" (Shweder et al., 2006, p. 719). Culture consists not only of cognitive models that guide thoughts and behavior, but also of practices and activities within which human action is lived out (Weisner, 1998). Cultural psychologists tend to avoid resorting to simplistic bipolar dichotomies at both the cultural level (e.g., West versus East, individualism versus collectivism, or modern versus primitive) and the individual level (e.g., mind versus body, cognition versus emotion, or autonomy versus relatedness) (Mascolo & Li, 2004; Much, 1997). They also tend to deemphasize the contrasts between person and culture, and between meaning and context. Person and culture cannot be understood in isolation from each other, and both context and meaning are theoretically represented as part of the psychological system. Moreover, culture cannot be reduced to bounded and fixed categories such as ethnicity, race, religion, or class. Compiling or controlling any of these freestanding variables does not help capture the dynamic nature of the cultural configurations and transactions of human life (Rogoff & Angelillo, 2002).

In order to illuminate the unique and dynamic patterns of cultural meaning systems, cultural psychologists devotedly "think through cultures" (Shweder, 1991) from "the native's point of view" (Malinowski, 1922; see also Geertz, 1984). The inner mental processes are seen as instantiated in "the custom complex" (Whiting & Child, 1953), the customary discourses and practices guided by the symbolic and behavioral inheritances of the sociocultural group that one belongs to. By entering into other peoples' conceptions of what is right, normal, beautiful, and true, and what makes them happy, proud, angry, and sad, the goal is to render them intelligible within their own collectively shared interpretive frameworks.

Although the "natives" are the true experts of their own group, cultural beliefs and practices passed down from earlier generations might have become too natural, habitual, and taken for granted to them. They tend to know more than they can tell. Hence, it is the researcher's task and responsibility to discover and articulate the culturally and historically situated meanings embedded in their research participants' customary discourses and practices. Methodologically, cultural psychologists tend to favor field research methods, such as participant observations, in-depth interviews, and ethnographic field-work, over experimental designs and use of measurement scales (Jessor, Colby, & Shweder, 1996; Miller, Hengst, & Wang, 2003). To generate *experience-near* (as opposed to *experience-distant*) categories and constructs that validly and closely reflect the lived experi-ences and true feelings of laypeople's daily life, *thick description* – full account of the context that gives rise to a particular discursive practice (Geertz, 1973, 1984) – is required. Indeed, "from the particularist's point of view, the devil is in the details" (Harwood, 2006, p. 123).

Instead of addressing generalities, cultural psychology advocates the greater need to "focus on finding regularities in patterns of cultural variation and similarity" (Rogoff & Angelillo, 2002, p. 223). However, this is not to argue that cultures vary infinitely with no basis for comparison. What really matters is how and what to compare. Comparisons within and across cultures make sense only when they are grounded in descriptions of the local meanings of the people being studied (Greenfield, 1997). Namely, cross-cultural comparative studies should be conducted in the manner of *contextualized comparisons* (as opposed to *decontextualized comparisons*), which scrutinize a specific case in great detail on its own terms and then compare it with other cases studied in equally great detail on their own terms (Gaskins, Miller, & Corsaro, 1992). Particularly valuable are negative cases and evidence counter to identified regularities in each comparative group, because they shed light on the limitations of initial interpretations and lead to necessary revisions and modifications. As asserted by Gaskins et al. (1992), "[W]hen similarities are found by taking individual variation into account, they are likely to be more robust than those that result from aggregating data and comparing group means" (p. 13).

Cultural Psychology and Child Development: The Integration of Context and Development

According to LeVine (1989), there are three blind spots in mainstream developmental psychology:

1. *The optimality assumption:* All the arrangements and resources available to chil-dren who grow up in a middle-class environment in Western societies provide the optimal conditions for development. Any deviation from those conditions is seen as deficiency.
2. *The assumption of endogenous development:* The normative ontogenetic trends found in children who grow up in Western societies reveal universal capacities triggered by biological maturational process.
3. *The assumption of methodological rigor:* Only studies that adopt standardized tests or strict experimental controls earn credibility.

Damon (1996) added a fourth blind spot: the assumption that treats variations in sociocultural contexts as exerting extraneous effects on the formation of an individual's mind, emotion, and behavior. Such an assumption "separates social influences from personal meaning, reduces complex experiences like culture or class to unidimensional 'marker' variables, and removes the key process of interpersonal communication from the development mix entirely" (Damon, 1996, p. 460).

To redress these blind spots, cultural psychology demands a holistic treatment of context that incorporates multiple layers ranging from immediate interactional situations to broad institutional processes, and evolves from time frames ranging from proximate to remote historical circumstances (Fung, 2003; Gaskins et al., 1992; Holland & Lave, 2001; Super & Harkness, 1986; Watson-Gegeo, 1992; Wortham, 2005). These concurrent multilayered contexts should not be viewed as a static and homogeneous given, but rather as ongoing accomplishments negotiated among the "multiple agencies" and "multiple perspectives" of all participants, including the novice. The developmental model in cultural psychology slights neither culture nor development. Indeed, "[C]ulture is not a shopping cart that comes to us already loaded with a set of historical cultural goods. Rather we construct culture by picking and choosing items from the shelves of the past and the present" (Nagel, 1994, p. 162). These choices are never unburdened but are weighted by emotion-laden experiences and a hierarchy of values and beliefs, and preferences and constraints, which may or may not support one another. In the process of becoming, the young child's subjectivity is exemplified at least in the manner of an active participant and meaning maker.

Developing selves as active cultural participants

Influenced by prominent social constructivist theorists such as Piaget, Vygotsky, and Bruner, cultural psychologists often portray children as active participants in their communities. Adopting theoretical frameworks such as "the practice approach" (Goodnow, Miller, & Kessel, 1995), "the activity setting" (Gallimore, Goldenberg, & Weisner, 1993), and "the developmental niche" (Super & Harkness, 1986, 2002), and learning models like "legitimate peripheral participation" (Lave & Wenger, 1991), "intent participation" (Rogoff, 2003; Rogoff, Paradise, Mejía Arauz, Correa-Chávez, & Angelillo, 2003), and "apprenticeship" (Rogoff, 1991), these theories more or less share the following basic premises:

1. Development does not occur in a social vacuum, but rather takes place in networks of interpersonal relationships and materializes through interacting with more mature and expert cultural members, each of whom has a personal historical past.
2. Although teaching is not confined to preaching or direct instruction, children may learn and acquire knowledge through keenly observing, listening, or eavesdropping during participation in events and activities at home and in the community.
3. Although most events and activities are mundane, they are no less significant than salient and bizarre ones. These mundane routine activities also inevitably involve redundancy. Not only do children repeatedly engage in situationally specific instantiations of cultural values in recurrent settings, but also similar socializing messages

can be repeatedly relayed to them through various channels with or without intent (Harwood, Schölmerich, & Schulze, 2000; Miller & Goodnow, 1995).

4.   As maintained by Weisner (1998),

> Daily routines and activities children routinely participate in are the most important influence shaping a child's cultural developmental pathway ... [because] they are organized by cultural models. ... [T]hrough repetitive, redundantly patterned participation in these activities they guide the cultural developmental pathways of children. (p. 75)

These theories hence place greater emphasis on the process of becoming than on developmental outcomes.

Developing selves as active meaning-making agents

When engaging in events and activities and participating in social interactions, the young child not only observes and learns the necessary skills and competence; she also actively makes sense of the world around her. Indeed, to cultural psychologists, the fundamental developmental problem should be "How do children come to invest cultural resources with meaning?" (Gaskins et al., 1992; Miller & Mangelsdorf, 2005; Miller et al., 2003). Culture provides affordances as well as constraints, which both enable and limit the individual's development. Power, capital, and resources are not equally distributed among all participants. Nevertheless, exactly because of the child's immaturity and lack of full-fledged membership in the adult world, she may be allowed to perform a unique role or be entitled to certain privileges. According to Gaskins et al., "[M]eaning creation through participation in collective cultural routines and practices is anything but passive, especially for children" (1992, p. 11). Children do not simply parrot adult words, nor do they appropriate cultural resources in unaltered forms. Instead, they flexibly and creatively use collective resources to contribute meanings to experience in order to accomplish their own particularity. Due to the child's in-born well-defined predispositions and the natural capacities to learn and make sense of the world, "[I]t is as accurate to say that [the child] shapes culture as it is to say that culture shapes the child" (Damon, 1996, p. 462). The meaning creation process is at once collective and individual.

Situating Developing Selves in Cultural Contexts

With its methodological, theoretical, and epistemological underpinnings, cultural psychology approaches issues regarding social development with special concerns for how to situate the developing child in the sociocultural and historical contexts in which she and her world are embedded, without slighting either the child or the context. Cultural psychologists' efforts to bring culture in and take culture seriously often lead their works to go beyond the conventional disciplinary boundaries. The selected studies in the following sections demonstrate how their efforts might further our understanding of children's diverse developmental pathways.

From language acquisition to language socialization

Although human beings might be genetically predisposed to learn languages and become linguistically competent speakers, they are not genetically predisposed to acquire a particular language. The first language that a child learns depends on the linguistic environment that the child is exposed to. Nevertheless, language acquisition is far beyond cognitive code learning. Combining insights from psycholinguistics and linguistic anthropology, Ochs and Schieffelin (1984; see also Ochs, 1988; Schieffelin & Ochs, 1986) expanded the focus of syntax in language acquisition to pragmatics and discourse in language socialization, which emphasizes the inseparable process of language learning and the learning of cultural norms and values. Their comprehensive fieldwork in Upolu, Western Samoa (a hierarchical society), and Kaluli, Papua New Guinea (an egalitarian society), revealed that characteristically Euro-American middle-class child-centered interactional routines, such as using baby talk lexicon (simplified speech) and immersing the child with highly attentive and "stimulating" dyadic face-to-face interactions, are not developmentally universal. At both locations, children are immersed from an early age in multiparty environments where people converse and perform tasks. Instead of treating the young child as a conversational partner, adults demonstrate a situation-centered manner by engaging the child in ongoing practical activities, directing her attention to other participants' words, and cultivating her sensitivity to others' needs.

As Ochs and Schieffelin (2008) suggested,

> A language is more than a formal code, more than a medium of communication, and more than a repository of meanings. Language is a powerful semiotic tool for evoking social and moral sentiments, collective and personal identities tied to place and situation, and bodies of knowledge and belief. (p. 8)

By adopting ethnographic and longitudinal approaches, the language socialization paradigm analyzes naturally occurring talk and discursive practices and demonstrates the acquisition of particular linguistic and cultural resources over time and across contexts. Both the caregivers' and children's speech behaviors and skills reflect culturally preferred ways of communication and personhood. In other words, pervasive and orderly everyday talk provides a window to the actual mechanisms of how culture and psyche create each other (Goodwin, 1990; Heath, 1983; Kulick & Schieffelin, 2004; Miller, Fung, & Koven, 2007; Ochs, 1988; Schieffelin, 1990; Sperry & Sperry, 1995, 1996).

Extensive comparisons of how narratives of personal experience are practiced at home in Taipei, Taiwan, and Longwood, Illinois (a middle-class neighborhood near Chicago), uncovered children's diverse meaning-making trajectories (Miller, Fung, & Mintz, 1996; Miller, Mintz, Hoogstra, Fung, & Potts, 1992; Miller, Potts, Fung, Hoogstra, & Mintz, 1990; Miller, Wiley, Fung, & Liang, 1997). In storytelling events, the understanding of self is subject to revision and reconstruction at both the narration level in the present as a narrator, and the narrated level in the past as a protagonist (Miller & Mangelsdorf, 2005). In both groups, spontaneous co-narration of the child's past experiences is part of everyday family life, which occurs at a similar rate and shares similar participant structures. However, compared to their American counterparts, Taiwanese families are much more likely to use storytelling to impart moral and social standards and to treat children's past transgressions as a didactic resource. Euro-American families, on the other hand, tend to downplay the child's misdeeds and to treat stories as a medium of entertainment and affirmation. By contrast, in another storytelling context – the caregiver's narration of his or her own past to the child – such a pattern is somehow reversed (Miller, Sandel, Liang, & Fung, 2001). Although American caregivers consider invocation of the child's misdeeds as potentially damaging to her well-being, they frequently report their own misdeeds for fun and for strengthening the connection between them and their children. To Taiwanese caregivers, in contrast, the adults' past transgressions are seen as potentially undermining parental authority and diverting the child from the narrow right path, and therefore should not be divulged to the young child.

The self-favorability bias encouraged by Euro-American parents among their children resonates with discourses that valorize self-esteem in the American society, whereas the interpretive framework of self-improvement held by Taiwanese families reflects Confucian values that still prevail in most contemporary Chinese societies. Indeed, the Confucian values are also manifested in the Taiwanese tendency to valorize the listener's role in storytelling events (Fung, Miller, & Lin, 2004). Caregivers hold young children to high standards of moral conduct and offer them numerous opportunities to reflect upon their actions by structuring children's participation as a listener and competent learner. Children's responses range from silent attentiveness to verbal and nonverbal gestures of assent, repetition of the adult's words, novel inputs, as well as corrections or critiques of the adult's behavior. These observations lead us to question the implicit assumption in mainstream studies that only the narrator plays an active and productive role in storytelling, and to rethink the contribution that a wider range of participant roles, including attentive listening, makes to language development. In sum, everyday conversations and discursive practices, including narratives, should not be analyzed only at their representational level as disembodied text, but as embedded in broad multiple sociocultural contexts and relational networks.

From emotion as social cognition to emotion as cultural constructs

All humans come equipped at birth with primitive means for expressing emotions. Nevertheless, the emotional experience in the adult world is much more elaborate and complex. It encompasses components of antecedent events, event coding, appraisal, physiological reaction patterns, action readiness, emotional behavior, and regulation (Mesquita & Frijda, 1992). According to Lewis and Michalson (1983), there are at least five feeling rules that a child needs to learn: how to appropriately express emotions, when to express emotions, how emotions are managed, how emotions are labeled, and how they are interpreted. Indeed,

> [Y]oung children cannot suppress the signal of an emotional state; they cannot feel but not express. Moreover, they do not easily express an emotion they do not feel, nor do they understand the social function of expressing but not feeling…. They cry when it hurts. The major capacity that they have to acquire, hence, is to 'decouple' elicitors from reactions and reactions from expressive signals. (Shweder, 1991, p. 260)

The fundamental developmental questions, then, are "How are these rules and meanings brought to bear, socialized, or otherwise acquired?" And "What is the role of everyday discourse and social interpretation in the activation of these rules and meanings?" (Lutz & White, 1986; Shweder, Haidt, Horton, & Joseph, 2008).

In a White working-class community in South Baltimore, children's interactions with their family members were found to elicit anger (Miller, 1986; Miller & Sperry, 1987, 1988). Young girls routinely participate in multiple socializing contexts in which their caregivers direct their attention to anger. They are often exposed to their mothers' personal storytelling, which sometimes involves violence and aggression. Although the incidents in the narrated past are described in detail, the narrators seldom express fear, vulnerability, or pain during the storytelling. Whereas they may threaten or fantasize retaliatory acts, they seldom portray themselves as committing any physical aggression. When interacting with their children, in addition to tacitly accepting, controlling, or suppressing the child's anger, they may also actively provoke, encourage, and intensify the child's anger toward themselves through playful teasing, insults, or threats. From these working-class mothers' point of view, anger and aggression are closely related to issues regarding strength versus weakness and self-protection versus self-indulgence. By 2 years old, girls who grow up in this community have started to learn not only how and when to suppress their anger and aggression when feeling angry, but also how and when to create a display of anger when not necessarily feeling so in order to be able to stand up for themselves and get their needs met. In other words, they have to acquire the ability to distinguish justifiable anger (e.g., being tough for self-defense) from unjustifiable anger (e.g., being self-indulgent as a sissy).

In another longitudinal study that observed spontaneous interactions in Taiwanese preschoolers' families, the invocation of shame was found to occur regularly (Fung, 1999, 2009a, 2009b; Fung & Chen, 2001). Caregivers apply a variety of communicative resources – verbal, vocal, paralinguistic, as well as nonverbal – to cast the child in an unfavorable light and attempt to arouse shame feelings within her. Most of these "events of shame" are occasioned by the child's precipitating transgression in the here and now, whereas one third of these events contain multiple transgressions committed by the child in multiple spatiotemporal worlds in the past and the present. These practices exemplify the notion of *opportunity education*, a term coined by the caregivers. According to them, it is more effective to situate a moral lesson in the child's concrete experience than to preach in the abstract, and, as responsible parents, they should take every opportunity to provide such concrete lessons. Moreover, they also report that their 2-year-olds have already acquired *xiu*, the affective aspect of shame (shame-as-disgrace), but not yet *chi*, the moral aspect of shame (shame-as-discretion). Rooted in the Confucian tenets, propriety, justice, honesty, and knowing shame (*zhi chi*) constitute the four cardinal virtues. Charged with affective stress by manipulating the child's rudimentary sense of shame, the caregiver alerts the child to tune into the moral messages that are induced from closely and patiently reviewing her misdeeds in the past and present.

When teaching the child *discretion shame*, the parent expects a better self in the future in order to prevent the child from being condemned by others and hence experiencing *disgrace shame*. These seemingly harmful and risky practices, in fact, aim to include the child in the group instead of setting her apart. Shame in Taiwanese families serves similar functions – motivational, prosocial, and moral – as empathy, the precursor of guilt, found in routine moral socializing practices of Euro-American families, as illustrated in Hoffman's affect primacy theory (see Fung, 2006). In sum, emotions should not be seen as merely pure or intrinsic cognitive processes, but rather as content-laden experiences that are contingent on implicit meanings, conceptual schemes, as well as interpretations that give them life (Shweder, 2003; Shweder et al., 2008). Their meanings and interpretations are subject to socioculturally patterned norms and assumptions and require socialization.

From ethnic categories to cultural beings

Rogoff and Morelli (1989) noted that, given the ethnic diversity in the United States,

> [R]esearch on minorities in the United States has [historically] followed a different course than the cross-cultural investigation.... For many years researchers were intent on comparing the behavior and skills of minority children with mainstream children without taking into consideration the cultural contexts in which minority and mainstream children develop. (p. 346)

They went on to suggest that

> research on minorities must move beyond reiterating the value of cultural diversity and begin more seriously to examine the source and functioning of the diversity represented in the United States to increase our understanding of the processes underlying development in cultural context. (p. 346)

Suárez-Orozco and Carhill (2008) also similarly criticized psychological studies of immigrant children, which tend to conceptualize immigrants as "aggregated pan-ethnic categories" (e.g., Asians, Latinos, and Blacks). In so doing, they often lose sight of the wide variation within each ethnic group and ignore the sociocultural contexts of their origins as well as destinations. As a result, their works run the risk of "stereotyping immigrants as 'problem' and 'model' minorities, and overlooking the complexity of race, gender, documentation, and language in the lives of immigrant families and youth" (p. 89).

From cultural psychological perspectives, minorities and immigrants should be seen as cultural beings instead of ethnic categories, and the development of minority and immigrant children should be situated in the contexts of their cultural heritage and social and linguistic environments. For example, Chao's works (1994, 1995, 2000, 2001) on the parenting style of Taiwanese and Chinese immigrant parents in southern California demonstrate efforts to appreciate Chinese parenting on its own terms. Although Chinese parents tend to score higher than their Euro-American counterparts on almost every standard measure of the authoritarian parenting style, characterizing their parenting as authoritarian can be misleading. The concept of the authoritarian parenting style, which is rooted in evangelical and Puritan religious traditions, implies a notion of hostility, dominance, aggression, and rejection. In contrast, the Chinese parenting style, characterized as "training (*guan*)," takes place in the context of a supportive, devoted, and physically close mother–child relationship. As a way to show love and caring, "[Caregivers] are responsible for early training by exposing the child to explicit examples of proper behavior and restricting exposure to examples of undesirable behaviors" (Chao, 1994, p. 1112). Due to this culturally and historically rooted concept of *guan*, Chinese mothers are more demanding regarding their children's diligence, self-discipline, and obedience. On the other hand, they are also more likely than their Euro-American counterparts to involve themselves in helping the child to succeed, perceiving themselves as the primary moral educator for the child, and keeping the child in close proximity, including co-sleeping. Such a parenting style is more in line with the socialization goal of fostering prolonged interdependence and filial obligations than that of enhancing the child's own self-development (Chao, 2000).

Likewise, instead of merely comparing group means at the behavioral level (e.g., academic performance) and searching for freestanding explanatory variables (e.g., spending more time on homework, and the drive for social mobility), Li (in press) pointed out that "what may be amiss [in the current literature] is a cultural framework that can link all of these and other factors to explain Chinese children's learning beliefs and achievement." Works by Li and her colleagues (Cheah & Li, 2010; Li, 2001, 2002a, 2002b, 2004a, 2004b; Li, Holloway, Bempechat, & Loh, 2008) systematically investigated the cultural meaning of learning held by Chinese and Chinese immigrant families. Chinese parents and children see learning as a virtue rather than a task, as expressed in the popular term "Heart and mind for wanting to learn (*haoxuexin*)." Rooted in Confucian fundamental teaching philosophies, the highest purpose of learning is to engage in a lifelong striving for self-perfection and moral advancement, which entails the notions of diligence, perseverance, concentration, and humility. Their analyses of storytelling showed that by 4 years of age, children in China have already demonstrated concern for self-improvement, mastery of knowledge, contributions to society, as well as earning social respect and economic reward. In contrast, their Euro-American counterparts talk more about mental processes and creative strategies in learning and reflect a tendency to socially isolate and reject high achievers.

Chinese Americans continue to endorse their own cultural beliefs and values in their adopted country. In a community near Boston, low-income Chinese immigrant parents are unable to help with their children's schoolwork due to their struggle for economic survival and the lack of cultural capital and linguistic proficiency. Nevertheless, these families can resort to various support networks including designated anchor helpers (e.g., an older sibling or other relatives who are high achievers) or members of the extended family, and strategies like appealing to role models for the child (e.g., high-achieving students in the community, who help set clear standards and benchmarks that children can easily identify with). In other words, despite the parents' inability to be directly involved, *guan* can extend across families, towns, states, or even continents (e.g., the child's grandparents in China or uncle and aunt in Australia). Because of shared cultural values and beliefs, home support comes in different forms and styles as a collective effort in nurturing and guiding the next generation. Children growing up in this community, who speak to their parents in Chinese, also overwhelmingly report that education is the highest value in their families and the only path to successful learning is to work hard. Even without parental involvement, they do relatively well in school (with an average grade of 3.27 or about B+). Indeed, in the process of adaptation and acculturation to mainstream values and norms, immigrants may still choose to maintain their cultural and ethnic identities (a point that will be further discussed later). Only by adopting a cultural lens can we avoid the pitfall of simplistically equating deviations from the mainstream with deficits, or becoming blind to our own color-blindness, oblivious of the significance of cultural and ethnic identity to immigrants (Markus, 2008; Markus, Steele, & Steele, 2002).

Concluding Remarks and Future Directions

As explained above, cultural psychology emerged at the interface of psychology and anthropology, and aims to explore the dynamic process of the co-creation of person and culture across the individual life span and across societies. Cultural psychologists attempt to identify ethnic and cultural sources of human diversities and raise the questions of whether culture-specific selves can be readily translated into dominating Western psychological concepts and whether lived experiences can be adequately understood in terms of indigenous categories without reference to other cultural groups. In search of "thick description" of cultural meaning from "the native's point of view," cultural psychologists tend to favor field research methods over experimental designs and use of measurement scales. When studying children's social development, the cultural psychological perspective treats children and their behaviors as inseparable from the sociocultural world that they inhabit. In addition to folk beliefs, cultural psychologists are also interested in customary practices of how children interact with others in their daily life and "natural" ecological environments. These practices do not come value free, but are packaged with affect-laden evaluations and agentic choices regarding what is morally acceptable or aesthetically pleasing. Developmental change is seen as an ongoing process in which new forms emerge from interactions and negotiations between individual characteristics and multilayered contexts of daily routines and activities. Informed by ethnographic accounts of childhood in non-Western societies and nonmainstream communities (see Lancy, 2008; LeVine & New, 2008), cultural psychologists are fully aware of alternate developmental pathways.

Cultures have never been homogeneous or static. They not only evolve over time from within but also constantly encounter influxes and impacts from other cultural currents. Migration in today's increasingly transnational and globalized world has made this process even more dramatic and remarkable than ever before. Recent advancements in communication, transportation, and computer technologies have effectively compressed time and distance, and brought quantitative changes to global migration trends as well as qualitative changes in the daily lives of ordinary people. Unlike the earlier waves of immigrants, today's immigrants traverse national borders and geographic barriers easily and frequently. The back-and-forth flows involve not only people but also information, knowledge, remittances, goods, symbols, and affective ties. In other words, today's immigrants, literally and virtually, live lives that straddle two worlds and incorporate daily routines and activities in different countries. Adapting and assimilating to a host society and maintaining enduring ties with the home culture are not necessarily contradictory (Levitt, 2001, 2004; Levitt & Schiller, 2004; Parreñas, 2005a; Schiller, Basch, & Blanc, 1992, 1995; Suárez-Orozco, 2002; Vertovec, 2001, 2004).

Transnational migration affects not simply immigrants themselves but also their families and children, folks who are left behind in the native country and those who reside in their adopted country (Fadiman, 1997; Hondagneu-Sotelo & Avila, 1997; Levitt & Waters, 2002; Parreñas, 2005b; Suárez-Orozco & Suárez-Orozco, 2001). The increasing recognition and acceptance of ethnic, cultural, religious, and linguistic diversity present both challenges and opportunities to parents and children, and generate tension between equality and differences or between a pluralism agenda and an inclusion agenda for educators and policy makers (Minow, Shweder, & Markus, 2008; Shweder, Minow, & Markus, 2002; Suárez-Orozco & Qin-Hilliard, 2004). Cultural psychologists, who try to capture the dynamic nature of cultural configurations and transactions of human life, inevitably must respond to current issues in the transnational era (Fung & Liang, 2008, 2009; Mahalingam, 2006; Suárez-Orozco, Suárez-Orozco, & Todorova, 2008). Methodologically, they may have to consider moving beyond the pitfalls of a narrowly bounded "methodological nationalism" (Wimmer & Schiller, 2002a, 2002b) and engage in "multi-sited fieldwork" (Marcus, 1995) in order to follow their research participants' footsteps, even as they cross national borders. It may also be important and necessary to learn their research participants' native language in order to fully decode and grasp the hidden cultural messages embedded in the words and thoughts of the interlocutor. Conceptually, they may need to discover what exactly transnational ties and practices and bilingual and bicultural competence mean to parents and their children in terms of identity formation and self-construction. They may need to establish a cultural theory of human development that accounts for how individual agency is instantiated in concrete life events when people are confronted with competing or conflicting meaning systems and customary practices within and outside the family. The motto "One mind, many mentalities" will carry new significance amidst the complex dimensions of an increasingly transnational and transcultural world.

References

Arnett, J. J. (2008). The neglected 95%: Why American psychology needs to become less American. *American Psychologist, 63*, 602–614.

Berry, J. W. (2000). Cross-cultural psychology: A symbiosis of cultural and comparative approaches. *Asian Journal of Social Psychology, 3*, 197–205.

Chao, R. K. (1994). Beyond parental control and authoritarian parenting style: Understanding Chinese parenting through the cultural notion of training. *Child Development, 65*, 1111–1119.

Chao, R. K. (1995). Chinese and European American cultural models of the self reflected in mothers' childrearing beliefs. *Ethos, 23*, 328–354.

Chao, R. K. (2000). The parenting of immigrant Chinese and European American mothers: Relations between parenting styles, socialization goals, and parental practices. *Journal of Applied Developmental Psychology, 21*, 233–248.

Chao, R. K. (2001). Extending research on the consequences of parenting style for Chinese Americans and European Americans. *Child Development, 72*, 1832–1843.

Cheah, C. S. L., & Li, J. (2010). Parenting of young immigrant Chinese children: Challenges facing their social emotional and intellectual development. In E. L. Grigorenko & R. Takanishi (Eds.), *Immigration, diversity, and education* (pp. 225–241). New York: Routledge.

Cole, M. (2006). Internationalism in psychology: We need it now more than ever. *American Psychologist, 61*, 904–917.

Damon, W. (1996). Nature, second nature, and individual development: An ethnographic opportunity. In R. Jessor, A. Colby, & R. A. Shweder (Eds.), *Ethnography and human development: Context and meaning in social inquiry* (pp. 459–475). Chicago: University of Chicago Press.

Fadiman, A. (1997). *The spirit catches you and you fall down: A Hmong child, her American doctors, and the collision of two cultures.* New York: Farrar, Straus & Giroux.

Fung, H. (1999). Becoming a moral child: The socialization of shame among young Chinese children. *Ethos, 27*, 180–209.

Fung H. (2003). When culture meets psyche: Understanding the contextualized self through the life and dreams of an elderly Taiwanese woman. *Taiwan Journal of Anthropology, 1*, 149–175.

Fung H. (2006). Affect and early moral socialization: Some insights and contributions from indigenous psychological studies in Taiwan. In U. Kim, K. S. Yang, & K. K. Hwang (Eds.), *Indigenous and cultural psychology: Understanding people in context* (pp. 175–196). New York: Springer.

Fung, H. (2009a). To know shame is to be near courage: Moral socialization in Taipei. In R. A. Shweder, T. R. Bidell, A. C. Dailey, S. D. Dixon, P. J. Miller, & J. Modell (Eds.), *The child: An encyclopedic companion* (pp. 900–901). Chicago: University of Chicago Press.

Fung, H. (2009b). Shame and guilt. In R. A. Shweder, T. R. Bidell, A. C. Dailey, S. D. Dixon, P. J. Miller, & J. Modell (Eds.), *The child: An encyclopedic companion* (pp. 900–902). Chicago: University of Chicago Press.

Fung, H., & Chen, E. C. H. (2001). Across time and beyond skin: Self and transgression in the everyday socialization of shame among Taiwanese preschool children. *Social Development, 10*, 419–436.

Fung, H., & Liang, C. H. (2008). Vietnamese mothers, Taiwanese children: Socializing practices with young children in Sino-Vietnamese cross-border marriage families in Taipei, Taiwan [in Chinese]. *Taiwan Journal of Anthropology, 6*, 47–88.

Fung, H., & Liang, C. H. (2009). Transnational practices in the private domain: How Vietnamese mothers socialize their Taiwanese children [in Chinese]. In H. Z. Wang & P. Y. Guo (Eds.), *To cross or not to cross: Transnational Taiwan, Taiwan's transnationality* (pp. 161–197). Taipei, Taiwan: Academia Sinica.

Fung, H., Miller, P. J., & Lin, L. C. (2004). Listening is active: Lessons from the narrative practices of Taiwanese families. In M. W. Pratt & B. E. Fiese (Eds.), *Family stories and the life course: Across time and generations* (pp. 303–323). Mahwah, NJ: Erlbaum.

Gallimore, R., Goldenberg, C. N., & Weisner, T. S. (1993). The social construction and subjective reality of activity settings: Implications for community psychology. *American Journal of Community Psychology, 21*, 537–559.

Gaskins, S., Miller, P. J., & Corsaro, W. A. (1992). Theoretical and methodological perspectives in the interpretive study of children. In W. A. Corsaro & P. J. Miller (Eds.), *Interpretive approaches to children's socialization* (pp. 5–23). San Francisco: Jossey-Bass.

Geertz, C. (1973). *The interpretation of cultures.* New York: Basic Books.

Geertz, C. (1984). From the natives' point of view. In R. A. Shweder & R. A. LeVine (Eds.), *Culture theory: Essays on mind, self and emotion* (pp. 123–136). New York: Cambridge University Press.

Goodnow, J. J., Miller, P. J., & Kessel, F. (Eds.). (1995). *Cultural practices as contexts for development.* San Francisco: Jossey-Bass.

Goodwin, M. H. (1990). *He-said-she-said: Talk as social organization among black children.* Bloomington: Indiana University Press.

Greenfield, P. (1997). Culture as process: Empirical methods for cultural psychology. In. J. W. Berry, Y. Poortinga, & J. Pandey (Eds.), *Handbook of cross-cultural psychology* (Vol. 1, pp. 301–346). Boston: Allyn & Bacon.

Harkness, S. (2002). Cultural and social development: Explanations and evidence. In P. K. Smith & C. H. Hart (Eds.), *Blackwell handbook of childhood social development* (pp. 60–77). Malden, MA: Blackwell.

Harwood, R. L. (2006). Multidimensional culture and the search for universals. *Human Development, 49,* 122–128.

Harwood, R. L., Schölmerich, A., & Schulze, P. A. (2000). Homogeneity and heterogeneity in cultural belief systems. *New Directions for Child and Adolescent Development, 87,* 41–57.

Heath, S. B. (1983). *Ways with words: Language, life and work in communities and classrooms.* Cambridge: Cambridge University Press.

Holland, D., & Lave, J. (2001). *History in person:* An introduction. In D. Holland & J. Lave (Eds.), *History in person: Enduring struggles, contentious practice, intimate identities* (pp. 3–33). Santa Fe, NM: School of American Research Press.

Hondagneu-Sotelo, P., & Avila, E. (1997). I'm here, but I'm there: The meaning of Latina transnational motherhood. *Gender and Society, 11,* 548–571.

Jessor, R., Colby, A., & Shweder, R. A. (1996). *Ethnography and human development: Context and meaning in social inquiry.* Chicago: University of Chicago Press.

Kitayama, S., & Cohen, D. (2007). *Handbook of cultural psychology.* New York: Guilford Press.

Kulick, D., & Schieffelin, B. B. (2004). Language socialization. In A. Duranti (Ed.), *A companion to linguistic anthropology* (pp. 349–368). Malden, MA: Blackwell.

Lancy, D. F. (2008). *The anthropology of childhood: Cherubs, chattel, changelings.* Cambridge: Cambridge University Press.

Lave, J., & Wenger, E. (1991). *Situated learning: Legitimate peripheral participation.* Cambridge: Cambridge University Press.

LeVine, R. A. (1989). Cultural environments in child development. In W. Damon (Ed.), *Child development today and tomorrow* (pp. 52–68). San Francisco: Jossey-Bass.

LeVine, R. A. (2001). Culture and personality studies, 1918–1960: Myth and history. *Journal of Personality, 69,* 803–818.

LeVine, R. A. (2007a). Anthropological foundations of cultural psychology. In S. Kitayama & D. Cohen (Eds.), *Handbook of cultural psychology* (pp. 40–58). New York: Guilford Press.

LeVine, R. A. (2007b). Ethnographic studies of childhood: A historical review. *American Anthropologist, 109,* 247–260.

LeVine, R. A., & New, R. S. (Eds.). (2008). *Anthropology and child development: A cross-cultural reader.* Hoboken, NJ: Wiley-Blackwell.

Levitt, P. (2001). *The transnational villagers.* Berkeley: University of California Press.

Levitt, P. (2004). Conceptualizing simultaneity: A transnational social field perspective on society. *International Migration Review, 3*, 1002–1039.

Levitt, P., & Schiller, N. G. (2004). Transnational perspectives on migration: Conceptualizing simultaneity. *International Migration Review, 38*, 595–629.

Levitt, P., & Waters, M. C. (Eds.). (2002). *The changing face of home: The transnational lives of the second generation.* New York: Russell Sage Foundation.

Lewis, M., & Michalson, L. (1983). *Children's emotions and moods: Developmental theory and measurement.* New York: Plenum Press.

Li, J. (2001). Chinese conceptualization of learning. *Ethos, 29*, 111–137.

Li, J. (2002a). A cultural model of learning: Chinese "heart and mind for wanting to learn." *Journal of Cross-Cultural Psychology, 33*, 248–269.

Li, J. (2002b). Models of learning in different cultures. *New Directions for Child and adolescent Development, 96*, 45–63.

Li, J. (2004a). Learning as a task or virtue: U.S. and Chinese children explain learning. *Developmental Psychology, 40*, 595–605.

Li, J. (2004b). "I learn and I grow big": Chinese preschoolers' purposes for learning. *International Journal of Behavioral Development, 28*, 116–128.

Li, J. (in press). How culture influences the learning beliefs of Chinese, Chinese-American, and European-American children. In U. Kim & Y-S. Park (Eds.), *Asia's educational miracle: Psychological, social, and cultural perspectives.* New York: Springer.

Li, J., Holloway, S. D., Bempechat, J., & Loh, E. (2008). Building and using a social network: Nurture for low-income Chinese American adolescents' learning. *New Directions for Child and Adolescent Development, 121*, 9–25.

Lutz, C., & White, G. M. (1986). The anthropology of emotions. *Annual Review of Anthropology, 15*, 405–436.

Mahalingam, R. (Ed.). (2006). *Cultural psychology of immigrants.* Mahwah, NJ: Erlbaum.

Malinowski, B. (1922). *Argonauts of the western Pacific.* New York: Dutton.

Marcus, G. E. (1995). Ethnography in/of the world system: The emergence of multi-sited ethnography. *Annual Review of Anthropology, 24*, 95–117.

Markus, H. R. (2008). Identity matters: Ethnicity, race, and the American dream. In M. Minow, R. A. Shweder, & H. R. Markus (Eds.), *Just schools: Pursuing equality in societies of difference* (pp. 63–98). New York: Russell Sage Foundation.

Markus, H. R., Steele, C. M., & Steele, D. M. (2002). Color blindness as barrier to inclusion: Assimilation and nonimmigrant minorities. In R. A. Shweder, M. Minow, & H. R. Markus (Eds.), *Engaging cultural differences: The multicultural challenge in liberal democracies* (pp. 453–472). New York: Russell Sage Foundation.

Mascolo, M. F., & Li, J. (Eds.). (2004). Culture and developing selves: Beyond dichotomization. *New Directions for Child and Adolescent Development, 104*, 1–100.

Mesquita, B., & Frijda, N. H. (1992). Cultural variations in emotions: A review. *Psychological Bulletin, 112*, 179–204.

Miller, J. G. (2005). Essential role of culture in developmental psychology. *New Directions for Child and Adolescent Development, 109*, 33–41.

Miller, P. J. (1986). Teasing as language socialization and verbal play in a white working-class community. In B. B. Schieffelin & E. Ochs (Eds.), *Language socialization across cultures* (pp. 199–212). Cambridge: Cambridge University Press.

Miller, P. J., Fung, H., & Koven, M. (2007). Narrative reverberations: How participation in narrative practices co-creates persons and cultures. In S. Kitayama & D. Cohen (Eds.), *Handbook of cultural psychology* (pp. 595–614). New York: Guilford Press.

Miller, P. J., Fung, H., & Mintz, J. (1996). Self-construction through narratives practices: A Chinese and American comparison of early socialization. *Ethos, 24*, 1–44.

Miller, P. J., & Goodnow, J. J. (1995). Cultural practices: Toward an integration of culture and development. In J. J. Goodnow, P. J. Miller, & F. Kessel (Eds.), *Cultural practices as contexts for development* (pp. 5–16). San Francisco: Jossey-Bass.

Miller, P. J., Hengst, J. A., & Wang, S.-H. (2003). Ethnographic methods: Applications from developmental cultural psychology. In P. M. Camic, J. E. Rhodes, & L. Yardley (Eds.), *Qualitative research in psychology: Expanding perspectives in methodology and design* (pp. 219–242). Washington, DC: American Psychological Association.

Miller, P. J., & Mangelsdorf, S. (2005). Developing selves are meaning-making selves: Recouping the social in self development. *New Directions for Child and Adolescent Development, 109*, 51–59.

Miller, P. J., Mintz, J., Hoogstra, L., Fung, H., & Potts, R. (1992). The narrated self: Young children's construction if self in relation to others in conversational stories of personal experience. *Merrill-Palmer Quarterly, 38*, 45–67.

Miller, P. J., Potts, R., Fung, H., Hoogstra, L., & Mintz, J. (1990). Narrative practices and the social construction of self in childhood. *American Ethnologist, 17*, 292–311.

Miller, P. J., Sandel, T. L., Liang, C. H., & Fung, H. (2001). Narrating transgressions in Longwood: The discourses, meanings, and paradoxes of an American socializing practice. *Ethos, 29*, 159–186.

Miller, P. J., & Sperry, L. L. (1987). The socialization of anger and aggression. *Merrill-Palmer Quarterly, 33*, 1–31.

Miller, P. J., & Sperry, L. L. (1988). The socialization and acquisition of emotional meanings, with special reference to language: A reply to Saarni. *Merrill-Palmer Quarterly, 34*, 217–222.

Miller, P. J., Wiley, A. R., Fung, H., & Liang, C. H. (1997). Personal storytelling as a medium of socialization in Chinese and American families. *Child Development, 68*, 557–568.

Minow, M., Shweder, R. A., & Markus, H. R. (Eds.). (2008). *Just schools: Pursuing equality in societies of difference*. New York: Russell Sage Foundation.

Much, N. C. (1997). A semiotic view of socialization, lifespan development and cultural psychology: With vignettes from the moral culture of traditional Hindu households. *Psychology and Developing Societies, 9*, 65–106.

Nagel, J. (1994). Constructing ethnicity: Creating and recreating ethnic identity and culture. *Social Problems, 41*, 152–176.

Norenzayan, A., & Heine, S. J. (2005). Psychological universals: What are they and how can we know? *Psychological Bulletin, 131*, 763–784.

Ochs, E. (1988). *Culture and language development: Language acquisition and language socialization in a Samoan village*. Cambridge: Cambridge University Press.

Ochs, E., & Schieffelin, B. (1984). Language acquisition and socialization: Three developmental stories and their implications. In R. A. Shweder & R. A. LeVine (Eds.), *Culture theory: Essays on mind, self, and emotion* (pp. 276–320). Cambridge: Cambridge University Press.

Ochs, E., & Schieffelin, B. (2008). Language socialization: An historical overview. In P. A. Duff & N. H. Hornberger (*Eds.*), *Encyclopedia of language and education* (Vol. 8, pp. 3–15). New York: Springer.

Parreñas, R. S. (2005a). *Children of global migration: Transnational families and gendered woes*. Stanford, CA: Stanford University Press.

Parreñas, R. S. (2005b). Long distance intimacy: Gender and intergenerational relations in transnational families. *Global Networks, 5*, 317–336.

Pinker, S. (2004). Why nature and nurture won't go away. *Dædalus, 133*, 5–17.

Poortinga, Y. H., van de Vijver, F. J. R., Joe, R. C., & van de Koppel, J. M. H. (1987). Peeling the onion called culture: A synopsis. In Ç. Kagitçibasi (Ed.), *Growth and progress in cross-cultural psychology* (pp. 22–34). Lisse, the Netherlands: Swets & Zeitlinger.

Rogoff, B. (1991). *Apprenticeship in thinking: Cognitive development in social context*. New York: Oxford University Press.

Rogoff, B. (2003). *The cultural nature of human development*. New York: Oxford University Press.

Rogoff, B., & Angelillo, C. (2002). Investigating the coordinated functioning of multifaceted cultural practices in human development. *Human Development, 45*, 211–225.

Rogoff, B., & Morelli, G. (1989). Perspectives on children's development from cultural psychology. *American Psychologist, 44*, 343–348.

Rogoff, B., Paradise, R., Mejía Arauz, R., Correa-Chávez, M., & Angelillo, C. (2003). Firsthand learning through intent participation. *Annual Review of Psychology, 54*, 175–203.

Schieffelin, B. B. (1990). *The give and take of everyday life: Language socialization of Kaluli children*. Cambridge: Cambridge University Press.

Schieffelin, B. B., & Ochs, E. (1986). *Language socialization across cultures*. New York: Cambridge University Press.

Schiller, N. G., Basch, L., & Blanc, C. S. (1992). Transnationalism: A new analytic framework for understanding migration. In N. G. Schiller, L. Basch, & C. Blanc (Eds.), *Towards a transnational perspective on migration: Race, class, ethnicity, and nationalism reconsidered* (pp. 1–24). New York: New York Academy of Sciences.

Schiller, N. G., Basch, L., & Blanc, C. S. (1995). From immigrant to transmigrant: Theorizing transnational migration. *Anthropological Quarterly, 68*, 48–63.

Shweder, R. A. (1991). *Thinking through cultures: Expeditions in cultural psychology*. Cambridge, MA: Harvard University Press.

Shweder, R. A. (2000). The psychology of practice and the practice of the three psychologies. *Asian Journal of Social Psychology, 3*, 207–222.

Shweder, R. A. (2003). Toward a deep cultural psychology of shame. *Social Research, 70*, 1109–1130.

Shweder, R. A. (2007). An anthropological perspective: The revival of cultural psychology – some premonitions and reflections. In S. Kitayama & D. Cohen (Eds.), *Handbook of cultural psychology* (pp. 821–836). New York: Guilford Press.

Shweder, R. A., Goodnow, J. J., Hatano, G., LeVine, R. A., Markus, H. R., & Miller, P. J. (2006). The cultural psychology of development: One mind, many mentalities. In R. M. Lerner (Ed.), *Handbook of child psychology* (Vol. 1, pp. 716–792). Hoboken, NJ: Wiley.

Shweder, R. A., Haidt, J., Horton, R., & Joseph, C. (2008). The cultural psychology of the emotions: Ancient and renewed. In M. Lewis, J. M. Haviland-Jones, & L. F. Barrett (Eds.), *Handbook of emotions* (pp. 409–427). New York: Guilford Press.

Shweder, R. A., Minow, M., & Markus, H. R. (Eds.). (2002). *Engaging cultural differences: The multicultural challenge in liberal democracies*. New York: Russell Sage Foundation.

Smith, P. K., & Hart, C. H. (2002). *Blackwell handbook of childhood social development*. Malden, MA: Blackwell.

Sperry, L. L., & Sperry, D. E. (1995). Young children's presentation of self in conversational narration. *New Directions for Child Development, 69*, 47–60.

Sperry, L. L., & Sperry, D. E. (1996). The development of narrative skills. *Cognitive Development, 11*, 443–465.

Suárez-Orozco, C., & Carhill, A. (2008). Afterword: New directions in research with immigrant families and their children. *New Directions for Child and Adolescent Development, 121*, 87–104.

Suárez-Orozco, C., & Suárez-Orozco, M. M. (2001). *Children of immigration*. Cambridge, MA: Harvard University Press.

Suárez-Orozco, C., Suárez-Orozco, M. M., & Todorova, I. (2008). *Learning a new land: Immigrant students in American society.* Cambridge, MA: Belknap Press.

Suárez-Orozco, M. M. (2002). Everything you ever wanted to know about assimilation but were afraid to ask. In R. A. Shweder, M. Minow, & H. R. Markus (Eds.), *Engaging cultural differences: The multicultural challenge in liberal democracies* (pp. 19–42). New York: Russell Sage Foundation.

Suárez-Orozco, M. M., & Qin-Hilliard, D. B. (2004). *Globalization: Culture and education in the new millennium.* Berkeley: University of California Press.

Super, C. M., & Harkness, S. (1986). The developmental niche: A conceptualization at the interface of child and culture. *International Journal of Behavioral Development, 9,* 545–569.

Super, C. M., & Harkness, S. (2002). Culture structures the environment for development. *Human Development, 45,* 270–274.

Suplizio, J. (2006). Evolutionary psychology: The academic debate. *Science in Context, 19,* 269–293.

Triandis, H. C. (2000). Dialectics between cultural and cross-cultural psychology. *Asian Journal of Social Psychology, 3,* 185–195.

Vertovec, S. (2001). Transnationalism and identity. *Journal of Ethnic and Migration Studies, 27,* 573–582.

Vertovec, S. (2004). Migrant transnationalism and modes of transformation. *International Migration Review, 3,* 970–999.

Watson-Gegeo, K. A. (1992). Thick explanation in the ethnographic study of child socialization: A longitudinal study of the problem of schooling for Kwara'ae (Solomon Islands) children. In W. A. Corsaro & P. J. Miller (Eds.), *Interpretive approaches to children's socialization* (pp. 51–66). San Francisco: Jossey-Bass.

Weisner, T. S. (1998). Human development, child well-being, and the cultural project of development. *New Directions for Child and Adolescent Development, 80,* 69–85.

Whiting, J. W. M., & Child, I. (1953). *Child training and personality.* New Haven, CT: Yale University Press.

Wimmer, A., & Schiller, N. G. (2002a). Methodological nationalism and beyond: Nation-state building, migration, and the social sciences. *Global Networks, 2,* 1470–2266.

Wimmer, A., & Schiller, N. G. (2002b). Methodological nationalism and the study of migration. *European Journal of Sociology, 43,* 217–240.

Wortham, S. S. (2005). Socialization beyond the speech event. *Journal of Linguistic Anthropology, 15,* 95–112.

CHAPTER SEVEN

Sociological Perspectives on Social Development

Gerald Handel

The distinctive characteristic of sociological approaches to the study of children and child development is the focus on three basic concepts: social interaction, social structure, and socialization as a bridge between them. The elaboration and interweaving of these concepts and their components form the basis for sociological research and theorizing about children. These concepts will be explained here.

The perspective taken is primarily an American one, although there is not a universally shared American outlook. Empirical studies to be discussed will be qualitative American studies of children within the age range of 3 to 11, but we begin with a quick sketch of children's birth circumstances in order to understand a basic sociological perspective. Also, the entire subject of how sociology should conceptualize and study childhood is currently the focus of a deep dispute, with a challenge to the concept of socialization at its center, which must be described to present contemporary perspectives.

Terms like *child development* and *social development* are not part of sociology's conceptual and theoretical vocabulary, but until about 20 years ago sociologists unselfconsciously used the word *development* in a commonsense way when referring to an accepted reality in discussions of socialization. Clausen (1968) wrote, "Most simply, the study of socialization focuses upon the development of the individual as a social being and participant in society" (p. 3). Adler and Adler, a wife–husband team, inaugurated an annual research series entitled *Sociological Studies of Child Development* (Adler & Adler, 1986), but after five volumes a new editor changed the title to *Sociological Studies of Children*. Most American sociologists would accept the notion of child development as a commonsense, observable, and experiential reality. Contemporary sociologists think of the development concept as connoting rigid, invariant stage theories such as Freud's

The Wiley-Blackwell Handbook of Childhood Social Development, Second Edition, edited by Peter K. Smith and Craig H. Hart
© 2011 by Blackwell Publishing Ltd.

(psychosexual development), Piaget's (cognitive development), or Kohlberg's (moral development), which do not consider the social variety of children's lives as the socialization concept does.

Social Interaction

Social interaction encompasses emotional and cognitive communication through language, gestures, and other types of signs and symbols (e.g., visual images, sounds, and touch) in groupings ranging in size from two people (dyads) to small groups, organizations of various sizes, large gatherings, and mass publics. Social interaction produces both momentary effects and longer lasting ones. Children participate in most of these kinds of interactions: mother–child, father–child, family group, peer groups, and school classrooms. By age 4, if not earlier, many children participate in large gatherings – in religious services, and as spectators at sporting events, circuses, street parades, movie theaters, and musical performances. They learn how to participate in such gatherings, including emotional expression. Laughter at circuses, cheering and screaming at sporting events, and subdued conduct at a religious service become parts of a child's accumulated knowledge and self-knowledge. Through watching television, children become part of a mass public, fellow consumers of stories and advertising, joint admirers of favorite characters and plots. What they see and hear often becomes transformed into content contributed to peer and family conversations.

Social Structure

Social structure consists of relatively enduring relationships, most importantly institutions and stratification. *Stratification* expresses inequality in the distribution of major social resources: power, wealth, and prestige. People who have a comparable amount of these resources can be thought of as being in the same social class. A child's position (status) in the class structure, at birth and in early childhood, is influential in determining what the sociologist Weber called *life chances* for access to opportunities to acquire those resources and the further benefits they make possible: standard of living, amount and quality of education, and possibilities for desired and desirable life experiences (see Gerth & Mills, 1946, pp. 180–184).

   Institutions are ongoing social formations that organize a society's handling of what it construes to be central social tasks. They include kinship institutions (regulating sexuality, population continuity, residence, child rearing, and property inheritance), educational institutions (continuity of and increase in the society's collective knowledge, and preparation of the young for adult life), economic institutions (production and distribution of goods, services, and incomes), legal institutions (regulating and adjudicating conflict, and defining delinquency and crime), religious institutions (expressing spiritual life, and establishing moral order), and political institutions (regulating the exercise of power and public decision making). Each institution exists through multiple organizations (e.g., families, schools, businesses and markets, police departments and courts, houses of worship, legislatures, and political executives). Social structure has intersocietal aspects as in the demarcation of nationality, which is also an institution.

Organizations assemble people whose interactions are governed by values, norms, customs, and habits of mind – the basic constituents of culture, created through interaction. Organization members occupy statuses, some of which are ascribed (assigned by society without any action by the person) and others achieved (gained by a person's own actions). Parenthood is an achieved status; grandparenthood is an ascribed status. At birth a child acquires several ascribed statuses: a nationality, membership in a family, membership in a sex category, a social class ranking, an ascribed residence location, perhaps membership in a religious denomination, a socially recognized racial or ethnic group, and possibly others. The child also has an ascribed status as a prospective speaker of an expected first language. In combination, these ascribed statuses give a newborn child a social identity that will influence subsequent interactions through early childhood and long thereafter. A girl born into the upper-middle-class Italian Catholic Gennaro family in Milan will have a somewhat different social experience than a boy born into the working-class Scottish Presbyterian MacIntosh family in Glasgow or a child of either sex born into an Amish farming family near Lancaster, Pennsylvania.

But these differences in children's structural location do not preclude some fundamental similarities in their interactional prospects. A newborn child has the ascribed status of son or daughter, but will almost immediately be drawn into social interactions that will conduce toward transforming the ascribed status into the achieved status of acceptable son or daughter. Thereafter, in ongoing interactions the child will be induced to achieve the qualifications of acceptable pupil in nursery school or kindergarten, acceptable playmate with other children in neighborhood and school, and so on to a succession of qualifications in diverse settings throughout the life course.

Acceptability means knowing the expectations of others and being able to conduct oneself within the limits of those expectations, but it can include actions that successfully induce modifications of their expectations. Acceptability can include innovation and creativity as well as conformity. Acceptability will be judged differently in different settings, notably the family, peer group, and school. Therefore, most children are likely to experience some inner conflict as they attempt to sort out conflicting expectations. Further, in all of those settings, expectations change with age, as children are socialized, by peers as well as adults, to increasingly more demanding standards of knowledge, understanding, emotion, and performance. *Socialization* may be defined as "the processes by which we learn and adapt to the ways of a given society or social group so as to adequately participate in it" (Handel, Cahill, & Elkin, 2007, p. 2). Socialization is the central concept in the sociological understanding of child development. It will be the main focus of this chapter.

Social Change

Social structure, although relatively enduring, also continually changes through changes in patterns of social interaction. Sometimes changes cumulate dramatically enough that we can demarcate distinctive historical periods. The overall nature of economic institutions in a particular historical period has a bearing on children's upbringing and the nature of interactions in which they will participate. In Europe, during the predominantly agricultural feudal period, children, whether of nobility or peasants, worked in status-appropriate ways alongside their parents on the manor where they lived. During the Industrial Revolution, beginning in the late eighteenth century, children as young as 5 worked in factories, often away from their parents. Social change does not affect all members of a society in the same way. Farming families continued in industrial society, as they do in contemporary postindustrial society.

When we talk of social change or changes in a society's economy, it is easy to forget that these terms are abstract summaries of human activities that created those changes. When industrial society replaced its predecessors, it became a new reality. Such change highlights a general principle: "human reality [is] socially constructed reality" (Berger & Luckmann, 1967, p. 189). This principle points to the further conclusion that childhood itself is, to some extent, socially constructed. This is nicely illustrated by Zelizer. In the 19th century, children, defined as economically useful, were valued for their economic contribution to their families. In keeping with the general cultural disapproval of idleness, the economically useful child represented a widespread cultural definition of childhood. By the early 20th century, reformers redefined children's economic contribution to family income as mercenary exploitation by parents indifferent to children's health and well-being (Zelizer, 1985, p. 71). Over the course of the 19th century, children had become sentimentalized or "sacralized." Child labor laws were enacted, and children were pushed out of the workplace. As the culture changed, child labor was defined as exploitation, and children were to be loved, protected, comforted, and educated (Synnott, 1983).

Families are consequential for child social development but are not isolated organizations. They are linked in complex ways to other institutions in the social structure. Changes in technology can result in changes in social structure. In our own era, the introduction of electronic media has been a significant social change that has had a bearing on how children's social participation develops. Meyerowitz (1985) has observed how the advent of television reduced parents' ability to control the information their children acquire. The subsequent advent of computers and the Internet further enhanced children's independent ability to gain information and knowledge. Children learn things about the adult world at much earlier ages than in the period preceding these inventions. Further, sending a child to his or her room as a form of punishment, "excommunication from social interaction," once not uncommon, is of questionable effectiveness if the child has in the room a television set, a computer link to the Internet, and now cell phones and text messaging. These technological inventions have changed society, including parent–child interactions at home. They have given children somewhat greater autonomy from parents.

Social movements are a significant source of social change. In the United States, the civil rights movement significantly enhanced the life chances of African American children. The women's movement and resurgent feminism significantly challenged prevailing stereotyped notions of sex and gender, resulting in expansion of life chances for girls.

The Socialization Concept and Its Critics

The concept of socialization is significant at both the societal and individual levels. It captures the idea that a society reproduces itself (approximately) through the various processes that inform the young of its ways. Newborns do not know how to participate in their families, much less in the society beyond. By 3, they have established a base of social knowledge that continues to grow. Learning how to participate in society with increasing knowledge and skill is as essential for the person as it is for the society. A newborn child becomes a person through the successive interactions in family, school, playground, and neighborhood streets that contribute to reproducing the society. A 7-year-old child who for the first time is sent alone by parents to the neighborhood store to buy a loaf of bread or a container of milk has gained a new level of responsibility that becomes a component of self-knowledge and an element of economic understanding.

There have been two major American theoretical approaches to socialization, each part of a larger theoretical effort. One, functionalism, constructs its argument beginning with social structure. The other, symbolic interactionism, constructs its argument beginning with social interaction.

The functionalist approach

Parsons, the leading proponent of the functionalist approach to childhood socialization, was one of the most influential sociologists between 1950 and 1980. He and his colleagues embarked on an ambitious project to explain society as a system analogous to such other systems as the human body. Just as each organ of the body has a specific function in maintaining the organism's equilibrium, so each institution plays a part in maintaining society's equilibrium. The concept of social structure carries no assumption that institutions are well integrated or that existing social stratification is a necessarily optimum distribution of social rewards. But Parsons transformed social structure into social system in which all the parts are integrated and each has a particular function in stabilizing the society. Further, each institution is a subsystem, and each is made up of its own subsystems (Parsons, 1955b, pp. 37, 53). Thus, the family has a husband–wife subsystem, a mother–child subsystem, a sibling subsystem, a male subsystem (father and sons), and a female subsystem (mother and daughters).

Using "the American family" as his case, he argued that the family has two important functions: (a) the socialization of children, and (b) the stabilization of adult personality. He argued that these two "functional imperatives" explain why it is necessary for every normal adult to be a member of a nuclear family (a family consisting of a male parent, a female parent, and their children) and why "every child must begin his process of socialization in a nuclear family" (Parsons, 1955a, p. 17). Because in "the normal family" the husband-father is the family's link to the economic system as breadwinner, whereas the wife-mother stays at home nurturing the children and managing household tensions, they have distinctly different roles. His is "instrumental," whereas hers is "expressive."

Parsons blended sociological ideas with psychoanalytic ideas to explain socialization. He states that the very young child is not a member of the whole family but of only the mother–child subsystem. Indeed, the neonate is not a member of any social system but is a possession of the mother. The child becomes a member once socialization begins. Socialization is presented as a series of predictable phases (Parsons, 1955b, pp. 37, 42–44, 63). The child proceeds from pure organism to oral dependency based on attachment to a social object, usually the mother, who offers gratification. The anal phase results in the imposition of a new level of autonomous self-control on the part of the child. This leads to the stage of love dependency, in which the child not only is loved but also actively loves. The "oedipal crisis" disturbs the love relationship with the mother and leads to the latency period, in which the child has a new level of integration in the family system and is able to act more autonomously toward each parent and toward siblings. The central focus of socialization (Parsons, 1955a, p. 17) is "the internalization of the culture of the society into which the child is born."

Parsons's analysis of socialization fell out of favor for several reasons. His image of the child was that a child either conformed or resisted. Although personality is an outcome of socialization and is defined as a system of action, the interactions that produce personality and the internalization of culture are semiautomatic. The social system requires certain socialization interactions, and therefore they mostly occur as required. This analysis fails to conceptualize the child as an actor, only as someone who is acted upon, unless the child resists socialization in a major way. Current sociological thinking (and even some thinking in Parsons's time) understands that children are active participants in their socialization, not systematically produced replicas of the preceding generation. A second problem is that within a few years of Parsons's publication, the standard family system that he posited had lost much of whatever validity it might have had. Thirty-three percent of babies born in the United States in recent years are born to unmarried parents, and a large percentage of the parents do not stay together to raise the child (England & Edin, 2007, pp. 3–4). Some are single women who choose to have a child by sperm donor or adoption (Hertz, 2006). Mothers of preschool-aged children increasingly entered the labor force, resulting in two-job and two-career families. Fathers' participation in early care of their children became increasingly socially acceptable, although not as rapidly as their spouses wished. In brief, Parsons's analysis was too exclusively adult centered and too inflexible to deal either with the diversity and complexity of socialization in his own time or with the social changes that came soon after. Further, with few exceptions (e.g., Chodorow, 1978) sociologists became increasingly skeptical about psychoanalysis.

The symbolic interactionist approach

The basic ideas comprising symbolic interactionism were developed by several scholars in the first third of the 20th century. Mead, a philosopher who taught a social psychology course, was the central figure. The term itself was coined in 1937 by Blumer (1969), a sociologist who was Mead's student and who became a major exponent of the sociological implications of Mead's thought.

Social interaction is fundamental. Human society consists of human beings acting in relation to each other. They align their actions in relation to each other. Each person interprets his or her own actions and interprets the actions of others.

> [T]he term "symbolic interaction" refers... to the peculiar and distinctive character of interaction as it takes place between human beings. The peculiarity consists in the fact that human beings interpret or "define" each other's action instead of merely reacting to each other's actions. Their "response" is not directly to one another but instead is based on the meaning which they attach to such actions. Thus, human action is mediated by the use of symbols, by interpretation, or by ascertaining the meaning of one another's interactions. (Blumer, 1969, pp. 78–79)

This fundamental character of human interaction is both possible and necessary because human beings have a *self*, which is a basic outcome of socialization. Mead described key steps in the development of the self.

Infants are born helpless, needing care, vocal but without speech, without interactive competence, but with a potential to become full participants in society. Socialization begins with the child being cared for by one or more persons committed to care, leading to the child's personal attachment to one or more caregivers (Bowlby, 1969). Being cared for is the child's first experience of social life. The child evokes response and thereby develops initial expectations and a rudimentary sense of social order. The child's attachment to the earliest caregiver is the first of many significant emotional relationships with *significant others*, those who play a part in the child's socialization.

Over time a child becomes increasingly self-regulating. This is made possible by the development of a self, which, Mead (1934, pp. 135–226) emphasized, is the fundamental outcome of socialization. The self consists of two "structures" or phases that Mead called the "I" and the "me." He considered the *I* to be biologically based and the source of impulses to act, the self as an acting *subject*. The *me* begins as the accumulation of attitudes toward the child expressed by diverse others (the *object* of others' actions). Taken over by the child, the *me* then also becomes the self as the object of one's own actions. All actions involve an inner dialogue, usually instantaneous, between the *I* and the *me*. It becomes slow and conscious only in uncertainty, as when a child (or adult) considers, "How will he react if I do such and such?" This ongoing reflexive activity of the self results in a somewhat stable product, the self-concept, and many self-activities (Gecas, 1982, 2003) such as self-confidence, self-doubt, self-esteem, self-criticism, self-reliance, and self-interest.

Two important processes are central in generating the self. One is the acquisition of language. A word becomes a significant symbol when a child becomes able to share its meaning with those who speak it to the child. A child then becomes able to transform something in his or her own mind (a mental representation) into a message to another person (a linguistic representation). The second process is role taking, which builds on the acquisition of language and occurs in two stages. In the play stage, the child plays at taking the role of parent or teacher or policeman or other interesting figure. "The child says something in one character and responds in another character, and then his responding in another character is a stimulus to himself in the first character, and so the conversation goes on" (Mead, 1934, p. 151). When the child moves beyond the play stage to the game stage, he must be able to take the roles of all the others in the game. Mead uses the example of a baseball game, in which there are pitchers, batters, runners, and fielders. In order to play his own role, the child must be able to present to himself the roles of all the others; he must understand how his actions relate to the possible actions of the others. Mead called this *taking the role of the generalized other*, or *taking the role of the organized group or community*. This illustrates his larger point that a fully developed self requires incorporating the attitude of the larger community into the self. "The immediate effect of such role-taking lies in the control which the individual is able to exercise over his own response" (Mead, 1934, p. 254).

The concept of the generalized other is abstract and elusive, and seems counterintuitive to people who have a conviction that the self is purely individual. To demonstrate its concreteness and its social nature, the author would engage in a typical colloquy with students in his course on the sociology of childhood:

Professor:	How many of you looked in the mirror before you left home today?
Student(s):	Some raise hands. Some say, "I did." Some do not respond.
Professor:	Why?
Student(s):	To see if I look OK.
Professor:	Look OK for whom?
Student(s):	For anybody who sees me.
Professor:	You have incorporated the generalized other, the attitude of the community, into your self (yourself).

Although Mead does not specify ages for the play and game stages, the rules that organize the game of baseball make it unlikely that children younger than 7 have the self-development to incorporate the degree of complexity that baseball rules entail, although they can acquire component skills of throwing, catching, and batting a ball at a younger age. A study of nursery school pupils by Corsaro (1986, pp. 254–270) justifies an inference that 3- to 5-year-olds have a beginning capacity to take the role of the generalized other. Corsaro noted that children distinguish their world from a grown-up world. Further, "Although membership and participation in the adult world is important to nursery school children, their developing sense of who they are is also strengthened through their active resistance of certain adult rules and expectations regarding their behavior." He described several resistance strategies children employ, most of which are collaborative. Thus, when the teacher announces clean-up time, a group of children may jointly employ a "relocation strategy." Upon hearing the announcement, they move from one area of the school to another. When asked to clean up the new area, they claim they had not been playing there and had already cleaned up elsewhere. Corsaro's explanation focuses on his central interest in peer culture as contributing to the acquisition of interactive skills and knowledge, but the explanation can be extended to include recognition that the children's resistance activities go beyond the play stage to the game stage. To do what they do, they have to take the roles of each other and of the teacher and teaching assistants, and understand the parts that each will play. They have begun to take the role of the generalized other.

The critics

In recent years, a number of sociologists have undertaken to initiate what they call a new field of children's studies or social studies of children. They focus on understanding children from the children's point of view. Although they cannot escape that adults (including themselves) interpret the meanings that children express, they emphasize listening to children more than they believe other scholars did and do. These initiatives reject the concept of socialization.

Thorne (1993), an American sociologist and author of a well-received study of gender relationships in childhood, asserts at the outset, "Children's interactions are not preparation for life; they are life itself" (p. 3). The first part of this statement is not correct. Childhood is both life itself and preparation for later life. She objects to the concept of socialization because she sees it as something that adults do to children. To her, the term implies, "The more powerful socialize, and the less powerful get socialized" (1993, p. 3). But although she rejects the concept, she occasionally refers to some socialization phenomena: "Of course, children are influenced by cultural beliefs and by parents, teachers, and other adults" (p. 4). And "By frequently using gender labels when they interact with kids, adults make being a girl or boy central to self-definition, and to the ongoing life of schools" (Thorne, 1993, p. 35). Thorne also observed, "There is much to be gained by seeing children not as the next generation's adults but as social actors in a range of institutions" (1993, p. 3). One can accept this statement without agreeing that it replaces the study of socialization.

Thorne is unhappy with the idea (and the fact) that adults have more power than children. But, she believes that adults are not as powerful as social scientists have thought because children not only socialize adults while they are being socialized but also have devised ways to resist adult efforts. Both of these observations are valid, but (a) the fact that children also socialize adults does not obviate adults' roles in socializing children, and (b) she does not distinguish between creative resistance that leads to accepted forms of autonomy or social change and resistance that results in delinquency and criminality. Another objection she raises is that the concepts of development and of socialization presume to know the outcomes of adult efforts, but she protests that in fact outcomes are uncertain. She is correct that outcomes are uncertain, but they more often fall within a range of social acceptability than outside it.

Thorne's two fundamental arguments are for (a) recognizing that children are more competent than she believes social scientists have given them credit for; and (b) learning from children by listening carefully to what they say and observing carefully their actions and interactions. She acknowledges that contemporary approaches to socialization recognize that children participate in their own socialization, but she dismisses these approaches as "tinkering." They still define children primarily as learners, people who are more acted upon than acting. Her view has the merit of challenging social scientists to examine their assumptions about children and attune more sharply to what children say and do. But it is inattentive to the fact that children begin life with ascribed statuses that specify their location in the social structure and that this will have a general influence on the types and qualities of their experiences. And it underestimates the extent to which the world is organized and administered by adults.

James, Jenks, and Prout (1998), a team of British sociologists, issued

> a call for children to be understood as social actors.... This represents a definitive move
> from the more or less inescapable implication of the concept of socialization: that children
> are to be seen as a defective form of adult, social only in their future potential but not in
> their present being. (p. 6)

Their implication of defect is not only a caricature of the socialization concept but also a complete rejection of the idea of human development. Their caricature means that they make no distinction between a 6-month-old child and a 6-year-old child. Indeed, they say (1998) that "childhood is less a fact of nature and more an interpretation of it" (p. 62). This statement takes a valid sociological idea concerning the social interpretation of reality and carries it to an unreasonable extreme. Childhood is socially constructed out of biological, as well as cultural, material.

James et al. (1998) contradicted their own position on socialization when they write, "In short, we argue that the particular cognitive, emotional, social and material relations of children's childhood – ... 'children's culture' – simply represent particular instances of the day-to-day process whereby children become socialized" (p. 83). But this is not, in fact, what they have been arguing. Throughout the book their argument is that (a) children's situation is to be understood primarily in terms of the spaces they occupy – school, neighborhood streets, and home; and (b) adults control those spaces, to the detriment of children. They write (1998),

> The central issue to be explored in relation to childhood space is ... that of control. Focusing
> on three spatial contexts – the school, the city, and the home – we explore here how each is
> dedicated to the control and regulation of the child's body and mind through regimes of
> discipline, learning, development, maturation, and skill. (p. 38)

Their use of the terms *development* and *maturation* in this sentence, and their one-time use of *socialization* as part of their own explanation of childhood, provide evidence that an effort to understand childhood without these concepts cannot succeed. They try to sustain two contradictory arguments: (a) Adults have power and use it to control children; and (b) children are social actors who have agency – the ability to take actions on their own – and therefore adults do not much influence them.

Corsaro (1997, pp. xiii–xiv) is the leading sociological student of preschool children in preschool settings, and he has conducted insightful and illuminating ethnographic studies in nursery schools and kindergartens in the United States and Italy (Corsaro, 1986; Corsaro & Rizzo, 1988). He expresses appreciation for socialization studies but also argues that a new sociology of childhood detached from socialization concerns is necessary in order to understand children's ongoing lives, needs, and desires from the children's point of view. Children need to be appreciated "in their own right." This view is also expressed by Qvortrup (1994), a Danish sociologist.

Corsaro (1997, p. xiii) writes, "I offer an interpretive perspective to the sociology of childhood, which I contrast with more traditional socialization or outcome approaches to children and child development." This statement represents a reversal of his previous view, when the title of his Italian study (Corsaro & Rizzo, 1988) expressly stated that it was a study of socialization. His current perspective does contrast with the obsolete functionalist view, but it does not contrast with the symbolic interactionist approach. It is, rather, an unrecognized partial continuation of symbolic interactionism.

Corsaro's most basic theoretical concept (1997) is "interpretive reproduction – the idea that children actively contribute to societal preservation (or reproduction) as well as societal change" (p. 5). This concept cannot be distinguished in any significant way from the symbolic interactionist concept of interpretation as set forth by Mead and Blumer. In seeking to understand children's perspective, Corsaro makes explicit what is implicit in Blumer, who did not study children. He also introduces (Corsaro, 1997, p. 41) three specific categories of children's interpretive activity. Further, the children's activities that Corsaro describes could not occur unless each child developed a self in the basic way that Mead explained. Finally, Corsaro could not escape using the idea of socialization, even though he avoided the term. He wrote (Corsaro, 1997) that

> children's interactions with grandparents occur often in multigenerational settings (for example, in the presence of grandparents, parents, aunts, uncles, and cousins). These occasions provide an ideal setting for priming activities in which children are prepared for transitions into a variety of social relations in their lives. (p. 33)

Here Corsaro offers a clear description of socialization activity, despite his disavowal of the concept. *Priming* and *preparation for transitions* are among the phenomena of socialization. Similarly, he declines to acknowledge socialization interaction when he writes (Corsaro, 1997, p. 99) that "children's early conception of 'friend' is primarily as a label for certain other children they know who have been designated as such by parents."

The effort to create a sociology of childhood based on the notion that the concept of socialization is obsolete or inappropriate cannot succeed. The claims of such a sociology depend either on trying to ignore the phenomena of socialization, which continue to occur despite the claimants' attempted avoidance, or on refusing to apply the concept to the described phenomena to which it clearly applies. Both tactics undermine clarity and produce obfuscation. The activities and associations that children create for themselves are made possible by earlier socialization, and they also produce social knowledge and skills that build toward a future. Thorne seems to argue that children of all ages are immersed in their own here and now, oblivious to any future, and therefore the only focus of children's studies should be to study them in that bubble. Both she and Corsaro acknowledge adult influence, but neither thinks it should be a significant component of the study of children. But restricting the study of children and childhood to "children in their own right" blocks out attention to the ways in which peers, families, schools, and media compete for influence in children's lives. Further, although Corsaro focuses on how children create their own peer cultures, he now declines to recognize that while doing so they are socializing each other. James et al. (1998) construe adult power as overwhelming, and they see the job of sociologists as discerning, describing, and facilitating children's efforts to get out from under it. This is a constricted view of sociology's task.

Agencies of Socialization

Socialization is carried out by organizations that function as agencies of socialization. Families and schools (including nursery schools) have legal responsibilities in this task. Peer groups and mass media do not have such legal obligations, but they are also important in shaping children's participation in society. A few selected studies will give the reader some idea of the range of work in this field.

Certain important socialization outcomes are not directly traceable to particular agencies but can be considered societal expectations that are communicated through a variety of channels. Children (and adults) are expected to be law abiding and loyal to their society. Every person is expected to develop some kind of competence.

Families

The study of families has largely been a split enterprise. Researchers mostly study either spouses (in marriage, divorce, remarriage, and/or cohabitation) or mother–child relationships, and sometimes father–child or sibling relationships. A pioneering article, "The Family as a Unity of Interacting Personalities" by Burgess (1926), a sociologist colleague of Mead's, opened a new vista with a symbolic interactionist idea. Burgess wrote that a family exists in the interaction (whether harmonious or otherwise) of its members. It exists as long as interaction takes place and dies when it ceases. Although this implies that the study of families requires knowledge of each member's participation, Burgess studied marriage, divorce, and related topics, but never included children in his studies. In 1952, a social science team (Handel, 1990; Handel & Hess, 1956; Hess & Handel, 1959/1995) embarked on the first attempt to study two-parent families with two or three children between the ages of 6 and 18 by interviewing each parent and each child. This methodological innovation– interviewing all the children and both parents in a family, and conceptualizing the family as a group– I later called "whole-family methodology" (Handel, 2002, p. 507). (It is also appropriate for any family or household composition of three or more members, e.g., a single parent and two children; or a grandparent, parent, and child.)

Building on Burgess's concept, we wrote,

> The members of a family– parents and their young children– inhabit a world of their own making, a community of feeling and fantasy, action, and precept. Even before their infant's birth, the expectant couple makes plans for his family membership, and they prepare not only a bassinet but a prospect of what he will be to them. He brings his own surprises, but in time there is acquaintance, then familiarity, as daily the family members compose their interconnection through the touch and tone by which they learn to know one another. ...
> In their mutual interaction, the family members develop more or less adequate understanding of one another. (Hess & Handel, 1959/1995, p. 1)

The contrast with Parsons's view of the newborn infant could not be more pronounced.

Families are not passive transmitters of culture to children. By action and communication, they establish boundaries to screen in cultural components they approve and screen out those they disapprove. Children as well as parents participate in this screening.

> Parents seek to shape their children in keeping with their own desire to achieve preferred experience. They stimulate the children in accordance with what they feel children should be, as a part of their activity in defining their own world. The nature of parental stimulation – its intensity, frequency, and diversity – expresses the aims of their care and authority. (Hess & Handel, 1959/1995, pp. 1–2, 17)

But this study includes not only the parents' views and feelings about family relationships but also the children's. Through the interaction of all its members, each family develops its own local culture (Hess & Handel, 1959/1995).

Social class Lareau (2003) studied 9- and 10-year-old children in 12 families, using participant observation (also called *ethnography*; her study is also an example of *whole-family methodology*). Six of the families were upper middle class, and six were either working class or poor. The scope of the data she collected is unprecedented. She or an assistant visited each family about 20 times in the course of a month, including one overnight stay with most. They took meals with the family, sat on the floor watching television with the children, and rode in the car on family errands. They played ball with the children or hung around while they played with their friends. They sat in on the children's school classes.

Lareau found three major ways in which social class makes a difference in children's lives: the organization of daily life, language use, and interactions between families and other institutions. Upper-middle-class children, encouraged by their parents, participate in a considerable number of after-school activities. With two or three children, parents have a hectic routine chauffeuring their multiply scheduled children to their activities. Working-class children mostly play with friends after school, and their parents believe they need such unscheduled free play after the school-day schedule. Unlike middle-class parents, who bring work briefcases home, working-class parents draw a sharp distinction between the work day and leisure time, and the two categories of children's after-school lives mirror their parents' patterning of the days. Middle-class children develop larger vocabularies and more complex reasoning abilities. Working-class children are polite and respectful, and do not badger their parents. In dealing with institutions, middle-class mothers teach their children "not to take 'no' for an answer" when seeking to have needs and desires met, for example in school matters. Working-class and poor parents are generally deferential to teachers and school administrators. Lareau concluded that middle-class and working-class parents operate with two different child-rearing philosophies. She called the middle-class view "the practice of concerted cultivation" and the working-class view "the accomplishment of natural growth."

Racial socialization Despite improvements in race relations in recent years, race remains a complicated problem in American society. Hill (1999, pp. 89–102) reviewed several studies and drew on her own observations and interviews with African American parents of young children to conclude that racial socialization is nearly universal in Black families. Its nature has changed in recent years. Formerly, African American children were instructed in "the customs and racial dissimulation required of Blacks for survival in a racial caste system." In the decades after the civil rights movement of the 1960s, Black children have more often become socialized to feel pride and self-acceptance. Parents teach their children not only about racism and to expect to encounter it, but also that it can be overcome by the children pursuing education, working hard, and knowing their racial heritage. Hill noted that Black children's self-esteem remains a controversial and contested issue among scholars.

In a study of parents in 10 African American families who reside in a predominantly White upper-middle-class community, Tatum (1997, pp. 214–231) found that they have two main strategies for socializing their children to deal with racism. Some parents use a "race-conscious" strategy. Because they want their children to have a positive Black identity – while also enjoying the educational and other advantages of their chosen community – they make active efforts to create Black peer groups for their children because there are not enough Black children in the community for such groups to form naturally. Parents who pursue a "race-neutral" strategy do not make such efforts, either because they believe the situation cannot be altered or because they believe that the situation will change naturally when the children get older.

Gender socialization   Although every society has prevailing cultural interpretations of gender, in Western societies, and probably others, multiple interpretations exist. Parents draw on the culture in various ways and define gender norms and expectations for their own children. Thus, in an interview study, the working-class father of an 8-year-old son and an early-adolescent daughter said that if the children fight, he would slap them, and he then added, "I don't mind Lucy slapping Jim, but I don't like men to slap women. I want Jim to grow up with the idea that a woman is a lady even if she isn't." Jim reveals that he often feels mistreated (Hess & Handel, 1959/1995, pp. 4, 40, 46). A lower-middle-class father of two daughters, ages 9 and 11, conveyed his interpretation of gender when he said, "They don't fight. If we had boys I'd teach them to stand up for themselves but try to have them understand that fighting is not the way to settle everything" (Hess & Handel, 1959/1995, p. 91).

Preschools

Corsaro's studies of 3- to 5-year-old children in preschools focus almost exclusively on how children create their peer culture, the first in what will become a sequence of peer cultures in childhood. He says little about the influence of teacher authority. Martin (1998) focused on teacher authority in shaping gendered bodies among 3- to 5-year-old nursery school pupils. From Jackson (1968), she adopted the concept that schools have a hidden curriculum, "covert lessons that schools teach, and are often a means of social control" (p. 495). The hidden curriculum she studied in five preschool classrooms involved teachers' differential instruction and sanctioning of boys and girls in how to manage their bodies. She began by noting that such differences begin in families. Children come to school wearing clothes color coded by gender. On average, 61% of 89 girls wore pink clothing on each day that she observed (three times a week) over an 8-month observation period. Boys never did.

Martin found that not only are children's bodies disciplined by schools but also boys and girls tend to be disciplined differently. She used a distinction between formal behavior and relaxed behavior. Formal behavior includes sitting up straight and raising one's hand. Relaxed behavior includes crawling on the floor, yelling, and lying down during teacher's presentation. Teachers were much more likely to reprimand girls than boys for relaxed behavior. Teachers encouraged girls to do table activities. Generally, Martin found that "boys come to take up more room with their bodies, to sit in more open positions, and to feel freer to do what they wish with their bodies" (p. 503). Also, although boys' play tended to be noisier than girls', girls were told to be quiet or ask in a "nicer" voice about three times as often as boys. Her most general conclusion is that, along with family influence and others, preschool teachers play an identifiable role in gendering children's bodies. Children whose bodily comportment is similar when they enter nursery school are transformed into boys and girls whose body movements differ by gender in ways that come to be considered "natural." (See also Handel, 2006, pp. 113–153.)

Schools

Brint (1998), an educational sociologist, observed that schools are secondary to families in socializing children because families typically have a mix of emotional intimacy and consistent attentiveness that is not replicated in the more impersonal school setting. But schools prepare children to work in an impersonal work environment. He proposed that three types of socialization occur in schools. (a) Behavioral conformity is sought by requiring children to manage their bodies according to rules, such as sitting up straight, raising hands to be called on, and having pencils sharpened at all times. (b) Moral conformity is promoted by teachers talking about honesty, fairness, hard work, and other virtues. Reading assignments may be made to illustrate their importance. (c) Cultural conformity is "a matter of learning approved styles and outlooks." These requirements are incorporated in school rules and routine practices, and embodied in the teacher's authority.

Brint cites Jackson's (1968) observation that schools try to have children develop "good work habits," a goal that carries an implication of preparation for later work life. Anyon (1980) portrayed the different meanings that this concept has for children of different social class levels. She observed fifth-grade classes (10-year-old children) in five elementary schools for ten 3-hour periods each over a school year. The schools differed by the social class (parental occupations) of the pupils attending, and the work habits cultivated varied dramatically. In two working-class schools, in the classroom the children were largely engaged in rote behavior. Rules were prominent, mostly concerning steps to follow. Teachers wrote the steps on the board, and pupils were to copy them. Evaluation was often based on whether children followed the steps rather than on whether their work product was right or wrong. Teachers gave few explanations of why children were to do what was asked. Adherence to procedure rather than developing understanding was the teaching focus.

In the middle-class school, classroom instruction focused on teaching children how to get the right answers. This included some choice and decision making as they were expected to figure out for themselves how to solve a math problem or show understanding of a social studies assignment.

In a school she calls Affluent Professional, work is defined as creative activity carried out independently. Teachers expect pupils to express and apply ideas and concepts. In a school she calls Executive Elite, instruction is geared to having the children develop their intellectual and analytical powers. They are encouraged to reason through a problem, and show the logic of their thinking.

Peer groups

In and out of school, in playgrounds, parks, neighborhood streets, and dwellings, children form their own associations on their own terms. These peer groups are organized for the pleasures of association, but experiences in them may have longer term meanings. In several ways peer groups increase awareness of gender identity (Handel et al., 2007, pp. 305–311). Children tend to prefer to play with others of their own gender, and this has led to the notion of separate boys' and girls' cultures. However, Thorne (1993) conducted extensive observations in two schools (classrooms, lunchrooms, and playgrounds) that produced a more complex picture. In one school, she focused on kindergarten and second-grade children (ages 5 and 7); in the other, children in the fourth and fifth grades (ages 9 and 10). Her research question (1993, p. 4) was "How do children actively come together to help create, and sometimes challenge, gender structures and meanings?"

She found that the importance of gender fluctuates in children's lives. Sometimes boys and girls are intent on keeping apart from those of the other gender. But there is "a choreography of gender separation and integration among children (and adults)" (p. 61). There are times when gender separation is central and times when children neutralize gender as a sense of opposition. The widely accepted idea of separate boys' and girls' cultures is obsolete, she argued. School situations foster gender separation to a greater extent than is found in neighborhoods, where groups are more mixed by gender. Although Thorne drew no socialization implications, her observations justify the conclusion that the children she observed are learning how to form both within-gender and cross-gender affiliations, knowledge that not only serves them in the moment but will serve in the future as well.

Drawing on other studies as well as their own, Adler and Adler (1994) found a growing trend of adult organizing of children's after-school activities. The two main reasons for the trend appear to be (a) an increase in dual-job families, resulting in a perceived need for nonparental supervision; and (b) growing concern about dangers to unsupervised children in public places.

Television

One of the long-running debates concerning the impact of television on children is about the effects of advertising. There is wide agreement among those who study it that television advertising socializes children to the consumer role but not whether that is desirable or undesirable. Giroux (1999) argues that consumer culture has replaced public culture and that the language of the market has replaced the language of citizenship and democracy. Consumerism has become central to children's lives, at the expense of civic awareness. Seiter (1993) argues that contemporary society is a consumer society, that advertising is a necessary part of it, and that it is a delusion to believe that children can be shielded from it. Toys and other advertised products provide a basis for children to interact and form relationships, as they compare and discuss each other's possessions and preferences. "Consumer culture provides children with a shared repository of images, characters, plots, and themes; it provides the basis for small talk and play" (Seiter, 1993, p. 7).

Videogames

Videogames have begun to be studied by sociologists. Turkle (1995) interviewed 300 children and observed many playing games on their computers. She concluded that children and adults are becoming more comfortable with substituting representations of reality for the real and that they are being socialized into a culture of simulation. Gottschalk (1995) observed children and teenagers playing videogames in arcades segregated from gambling areas and freely open to children in casino-hotels in Las Vegas. He concluded that the games are organized on the basis of ideological assumptions that he called "videology." The major one is violence. The games often feature a hero fighting an enemy whose skin is browner or yellower than the hero's. Girls are portrayed as objects of temptation and in need of rescue by violent male action. The players are in a fantasy world that borrows sights and sounds from the real world. Gottschalk regards the games as having a socializing effect because they reproduce a dominant cultural reality.

Childhood and Adult Life: Continuity or Discontinuity?

When children are born, they receive several ascribed statuses that place them in the social structure. Through interactions in family, peer groups, school classes, and media involvement, they develop selves that enable them to interpret their social memberships, resulting in various forms of satisfaction and dissatisfaction with them. Interpretations mostly have immediate, situational meanings – how to act now. But some have longer horizons in such forms as fantasies, wishes, plans, and decisions. The human life course can be understood as an open-ended sequence of interpretations. As a person moves through childhood and adolescence into adulthood, his or her interpretation of childhood experience contributes to shaping the life course. This can be illustrated in the life course narrative of a 47-year-old construction worker who said of his childhood, "I always hung out with fellows like three or four years older than me. I was always the youngest one in the crowd. I believe it gave me the smarts – the experience, how to handle different situations, you know" (Handel, 2003, p. 35).

Contentment or discontentment with childhood leads to efforts to shape the ongoing life course (Handel, 2003, pp. 104–107). Ascribed statuses can be reinterpreted: A new nationality can be achieved by migration, a new religion by conversion, a new sex through surgical and hormonal intervention. General satisfaction with one's childhood will likely result in seeking later experiences that are harmonious with or elaborations of it, in what may be called an *elaborative* life course (e.g., following in one's father's or mother's footsteps). A person who interprets his or her childhood experience as bad or harmful will seek a life course that is *dissociative* from childhood. An interpretation that regards childhood as generally satisfactory but blotted or disfigured by some major damage will likely lead to efforts at major repair, a *restitutive* life course. Finally, childhood experience can be interpreted as benign but outgrown, leading to an *innovative* life course. A person may try to construct a life course that emphasizes one of these directions or may construct blended or sequential directional strands. The fact that childhood socialization does not stamp people as precise copies of their predecessors does not mean that it has no significance for adult life.

Acknowledgment

For helpful suggestions, I thank Professor Michael J. Handel of Northeastern University, Boston.

References

Adler, P., & Adler, P. (Eds.). (1986). *Sociological studies of child development* (Vol. *1*). Greenwich, CT: JAI Press.

Adler, P., & Adler, P. (1994). Social reproduction and the corporate other: The institutionalization of after-school activities. *Sociological Quarterly, 35*, 309–328.

Anyon, J. (1980). Social class and the hidden curriculum of work. *Journal of Education, 162,* 67–92.

Berger, P., & Luckmann, T. (1967). *The social construction of reality.* Garden City, NY: Anchor Books.

Blumer, H. (1969). *Symbolic interactionism.* Englewood Cliffs, NJ: Prentice Hall.

Bowlby, J. (1969). *Attachment.* New York: Basic Books.

Brint, S. (1998). *Schools and societies.* Thousand Oaks, CA: Pine Forge Press.

Burgess, E. (1926). The family as a unity of interacting personalities. *The Family, 7,* 3–9.

Chodorow, N. (1978). *The reproduction of mothering.* Berkeley: University of California Press.

Clausen, J. (1968). Introduction. In J. Clausen (Ed.), *Socialization and society.* Boston: Little, Brown.

Corsaro, W. (1986). *Friendship and peer culture in the early years.* Westport, CT: Greenwood.

Corsaro, W. (1997). *The sociology of childhood.* Thousand Oaks, CA: Pine Forge Press.

Corsaro, W., & Rizzo, T. (1988). *Discussione* and friendship: Socialization processes in the peer culture of Italian nursery school children. *American Sociological Review, 33*, 879–894.

England, P., & Edin, K. (2007). Unmarried couples with children: Hoping for love and the white picket fence. In P. England & K. Edin (Eds.), *Unmarried couples with children* (pp. 3–21). New York: Russell Sage Foundation.

Gecas, V. (1982). The self-concept. In R. Turner & J. Short (Eds.), *Annual Review of Sociology* (Vol. 8, pp. 1–31). Palo Alto, CA: Annual Reviews.

Gecas, V. (2003). Self-agency and the life course. In J. Mortimer & M. Shanahan (Eds.), *Handbook of the life course* (pp. 369–388). New York: Kluwer Academic/Plenum.

Gerth, H. H., & Mills, C. W. (Eds.). (1946). *From Max Weber: Essays in sociology.* New York: Oxford University Press.

Giroux, H. (1999). *The mouse that roared.* Lanham, MD: Rowman & Littlefield.

Gottschalk, S. (1995). Videology: Video games as postmodern sites/sights of ideological reproduction. *Symbolic Interaction, 18*, 1–18.

Handel, G. (1990). Revising socialization theory. *American Sociological Review, 55*, 463–465.

Handel, G. (2002). Toward understanding families as groups. In S. Steinmetz & G. Peterson (Eds.), *Pioneering paths in the study of families* (pp. 489–510). New York: Haworth Press.

Handel, G. (2003). *Making a life in Yorkville: Experience and meaning in the life-course narrative of an urban working-class man.* New York: Aldine de Gruyter.

Handel, G. (Ed.). (2006). *Childhood socialization* (2nd ed.). New Brunswick, NJ: Transaction.

Handel, G., Cahill, S., & Elkin, F. (2007). *Children and society: The sociology of children and childhood socialization.* New York: Oxford University Press.

Handel, G., & Hess, R. (1956). The family as an emotional organization. *Marriage and Family Living, 18*, 99–101.

Hertz, R. (2006). *Single by chance, mothers by choice.* New York: Oxford University Press.

Hess, R. D., & Handel, G. (1995). *Family worlds.* Lanham, MD: University Press of America. (Originally published in 1959 by University of Chicago Press)

Hill, S. A. (1999). *African American children.* Thousand Oaks, CA: Sage.

Jackson, P. (1968). *Life in classrooms.* New York: Holt, Rinehart & Winston.

James, A., Jenks, C., & Prout, A. (1998). *Theorizing childhood.* New York: Teachers College Press.

Lareau, A. (2003). *Unequal childhoods.* Berkeley: University of California Press.

Martin, K. A. (1998). Becoming a gendered body: Practices of preschools. *American Sociological Review, 63*, 494–511.

Mead, G. H. (1934). *Mind, self, and society.* Chicago: University of Chicago Press.

Meyerowitz, J. (1985). *No sense of place: The impact of electronic media on social behavior.* New York: Oxford University Press.

Parsons, T. (1955a). The American family: Its relations to personality and to the social structure. In T. Parsons & R. F. Bales (Eds.), *Family, socialization and interaction process* (pp. 3–33). Glencoe, IL: Free Press.

Parsons, T. (1955b). Family structure and the socialization of the child. In T. Parsons & R. F. Bales (Eds.), *Family, socialization, and interaction process* (pp. 35–131). Glencoe, IL: Free Press.

Qvortrup, J. (1994). Childhood matters: An introduction. In J. Qvortrup, M. Bardy, H. Wintersberger, & G. Sgritta (Eds.), *Childhood matters: Social theory, practice, and politics* (pp. 1–23). Brookfield, VT: Avebury.

Seiter, E. (1993). *Sold separately: Children and parents in consumer culture.* New Brunswick, NJ: Rutgers University Press.

Synnott, A. (1983). Little angels, little devils: A sociology of children. *Canadian Review of Sociology and Anthropology, 20*, 79–95.

Tatum, B. (1997). Out there stranded? Black families in white communities. In H. P. McAdoo (Ed.), *Black families* (3rd ed., pp. 214–231). Thousand Oaks, CA: Sage.

Thorne, B. (1993). *Gender play: Girls and boys in school.* New Brunswick, NJ: Rutgers University Press.

Turkle, S. (1995). *Life on the screen: Identity in the age of the Internet.* New York: Simon & Schuster.

Zelizer, V. (1985). *Pricing the priceless child: The changing social value of children.* New York: Basic Books.

PART III

Ecological Contexts for Social Development

It has long been recognized that children's social development does not occur in a vacuum. Children grow up in a complex system of relationships that are affected by influences found in different levels of the surrounding environment. As illuminated in other parts of this handbook, social developmental characteristics are molded as children's biologically influenced dispositions join with environmental forces in ways that affect how children perceive their immediate social environment and respond to it (cf. Bronfenbrenner & Morris, 2006). This part focuses more on the environmental side of the equation, emphasizing mesosystem (e.g., schools) and macrosystem (e.g., culture or ethnicity) levels of influence. Insights are also provided concerning dynamic nature–nurture interactions that are moderated by forces within these larger levels of environmental influence.

In Chapter 8, Xinyin Chen, Janet Chung, Rachel Lechcier-Kimel, and Doran French begin this part of the handbook by discussing how cultural norms and values may enhance or diminish various aspects of socioemotional functioning. Drawing from socioecological and sociocultural theories, the authors review recent cross-cultural studies that describe how children in different societies display socioemotional characteristics that vary in accordance with culturally defined socialization practices reflected in parenting attitudes and practices. They also discuss how cultural values impact children's play and self-expression in peer group interactions, as well as how different cultural norms and values impact prosocial and cooperative behavior, aggressive behavior, and shyness–sensitivity. Cultural variations on the structure and function of friendship and peer group affiliation are also examined with an eye toward explaining how adjustment in different societies is explained by adherence to indigenous values.

Charissa Cheah and Christy Leung, in Chapter 9, narrow the focus on cultural influence by highlighting the need for better understanding of how increased global migration impacts children's social development in different countries. What has been learned from the more developed research literature on Asian and Hispanic immigrant children in the United States is explained in a manner that can inform needed research on immigrant

The Wiley-Blackwell Handbook of Childhood Social Development, Second Edition, edited by Peter K. Smith and Craig H. Hart
© 2011 by Blackwell Publishing Ltd.

populations in other cultural settings. Overviewed are immigrant-related issues that are important to children's social and emotional development. The authors discuss how Asian and Hispanic family structure and cultural values have important implications for the socialization process, which subsequently is reflected in how well children adjust to their new cultural milieu. They describe how differential adaptation to loss of homeland and significant individuals, learning a new language, adjusting to new cultural norms and expectations, cultural and language brokering, racial discrimination and prejudice, and socioeconomic status impact acculturation processes and child socioemotional adjustment. The chapter concludes with an insightful presentation of conceptual and methodological strengths and limitations to current approaches of studying immigrant children's social development.

In Chapter 10, Gary Ladd, Becky Kochenderfer-Ladd, and Ann-Margret Rydell bring the focus of this part of the handbook down to the mesosystem level by discussing how the interpersonal challenges of schooling impact social development as reflected in a variety of school adjustment outcomes. The authors discuss child-level factors that predict school adjustment, namely, aggressive behavior and social withdrawal. They also illuminate environment-level factors comprising the social ecology of classrooms that impact school adjustment as children are exposed to processes stemming from how classmates and teachers respond to them in ways that affect their ability to adapt to school challenges. Differential contributions of peers and teachers are examined, along with ways that these factors operate in concert to impact school adjustment. The chapter concludes with a critical analysis of child and environment models of school adjustment, with an eye toward enhancing empirical knowledge that can inform prevention and intervention programs in school settings.

Christopher Spencer and Kate Gee round out this part with Chapter 11, an informative chapter describing how the sociophysical environment, in terms of space, facilities, and other features, impacts children's social development. They discuss how physical and social elements of environments have powerful influences on children's behavior. For example, small schools afford more opportunities for involvement in clubs and other activities than larger schools. Children spend time differently according to varying features of their neighborhoods and larger communities. The authors examine how urban versus rural living affords children different types of social experiences and opportunities. Research examining the influence of designed spaces on social experiences is overviewed, as well as how children use these places in ways unexpected by their designers. How cultural norms and expectations moderate ways that children utilize these spaces is also considered, along with how children's attachment to different types of physical space affects their personal and social identity. The chapter wraps up with a discussion of how children can participate in planning their physical environments and how this can help them develop an appreciation for democracy and a sense of competence.

Reference

Bronfenbrenner, U., & Morris, P. S. (2006). The bioecological model of human development. In R. M. Lerner (Ed.), *Handbook of child psychology: Vol. 1. Theoretical models of human development* (6th ed., pp. 297–342). Hoboken, NJ: Wiley.

CHAPTER EIGHT

Culture and Social Development

Xinyin Chen, Janet Chung, Rachel Lechcier-Kimel, and Doran French

Developmental theorists have long argued that culture plays an important role in children's social development (e.g., Hinde, 1987). Culture may promote or constrain the exhibition of specific aspects of socioemotional functioning through facilitation or suppression processes (e.g., Weisz et al., 1988). Cultural norms and values may provide guidance for interpreting and evaluating social behaviors and thus impart meanings to the behaviors (Benedict, 1934; Chen & French, 2008). Moreover, culture may direct social interactions and affect the nature, structure, and function of social relationships.

In this chapter, we review recent studies focused on understanding the impact of culture on multiple levels of social development. We first discuss theoretical issues and provide a conceptual framework concerning culture and social development (Chen & French, 2008). Next, we review cross-cultural work on children's dispositional characteristics and socialization in the early years and their contributions to social development. Next, we review the research on children's social behaviors and interactions including play, prosocial-cooperative behavior, aggression, and shyness–inhibition in different cultures. We then focus on cultural influence on peer relationships including friendships and groups, and conclude with a discussion of future directions in the study of culture and social development.

Culture, Social Interactions and Relationships, and Development: Theoretical Perspectives

Two of the most prominent theories developed to explain culture and human development are the socioecological theory (Bronfenbrenner & Morris, 2006; Super & Harkness,

The Wiley-Blackwell Handbook of Childhood Social Development, Second Edition, edited by Peter K. Smith and Craig H. Hart
© 2011 by Blackwell Publishing Ltd.

1986) and the sociocultural theory (Rogoff, 2003; Vygotsky, 1978). According to socio-ecological theory, the beliefs and practices that are endorsed within a cultural group play an important role as a part of the socioecological environment in shaping children's social and cognitive functions. In addition to its direct effects, culture may regulate development through organizing various social settings such as community services and school and day care conditions. The sociocultural theory focuses primarily on the internalization of external symbolic systems such as language and symbols, along with their cultural meanings, from the interpersonal level to the intrapersonal level. An important mechanism of internalization is collaborative or guided learning in which more experienced peers or adults act as skilled tutors and representatives of the culture and assist the child in understanding and solving problems. Thus, participation in social and cultural activities is believed to facilitate the development of social and cognitive abilities (e.g., Rogoff, 2003).

Chen and his colleagues (e.g., Chen & French, 2008) have recently proposed a contextual-developmental perspective focused on the links between cultural values and social functioning and the role of social interactions and relationships in mediating the links. This perspective, which incorporates features of the socioecological and sociocultural theories, posits that social initiative and self-control, as two fundamental dimensions of socioemotional functioning, may be valued differently across cultures. *Social initiative* refers to the tendency to initiate and maintain social interactions, which is most easily evidenced by reactions to challenging social situations. Whereas some children may readily engage in potentially challenging interactions, others may experience internal anxiety, leading to exhibition of low levels of social initiative (Asendorpf, 1990). *Self-control* represents the regulatory ability to modulate behavioral and emotional reactivity, a dimension necessary for maintaining appropriate behavior during social interactions. Different societies emphasize social initiative and norm-based behavioral control in children to different extents. In Western individualistic cultures, where acquiring autonomy and assertive social skills is an important socialization goal, social initiative is viewed as a major index of social maturity and the display of anxious and inhibited behavior is often considered to reflect social incompetence. Although self-regulation and control are perceived as necessary for positive social interactions, individuals are encouraged to maintain a balance between the needs of the self and those of others. Consequently, behavioral control is regarded as less important, especially when it conflicts with the attainment of individual goals (Triandis, 1995). In group-oriented cultures, social initiative may not be highly appreciated or valued because it may interfere with the harmony and cohesiveness of the group. To maintain interpersonal and group harmony, individuals need to restrain personal desires in an effort to address the needs and interests of others, and thus self-control is more strongly and consistently emphasized. Cultural values of social initiative and self-control may influence specific aspects of social functioning, including aggression–disruption (high social initiative and low control), shyness–sensitivity (low social initiative and adequate control to constrain behavioral and emotional reactivity), and sociable and prosocial behaviors (active social initiative with effective control).

The contextual-developmental perspective emphasizes the role of social evaluation and response processes in facilitating the links between culture and development. Specifically, during interactions, adults and peers may evaluate socioemotional characteristics in manners that are consistent with cultural belief systems, and may thus respond differently to particular behaviors and express different attitudes (e.g., acceptance and rejection) toward children who display the behaviors. Social evaluations and responses, in turn, may serve to regulate children's behaviors and ultimately their developmental patterns (Chen, Chung, & Hsiao, 2008). At the same time, children actively engage in social interactions through expressing their reactions to social influence and through participating in constructing cultural norms for social evaluations and other group activities (Corsaro & Nelson, 2003). Thus, the social processes that mediate the links between culture and individual development are bidirectional and transactional in nature.

Early Socioemotional Characteristics, Socialization, and Cultural Context

Children in different societies may differ in their display of socioemotional characteristics in the early years. Researchers have found, for example, that Asian children are less expressive in positive emotions (e.g., smiling and laughing) than their Western counterparts (e.g., Camras et al., 1998; Gartstein et al., 2006; Knyazev, Zupancic, & Slobodskaya, 2008). Asian children also tend to display more negative emotions such as crying in the early years than Western children, although the results are not consistent (e.g., Fogel, Toda, & Kawai, 1988; Porter et al., 2005).

Early characteristics may elicit different reactions from socialization agents in different cultures. For example, Wang (2003) found that, compared with Euro-American mothers, Chinese mothers engaged in fewer conversations about emotions with their children and were less likely to assist children to understand their feelings. Researchers have also found cross-cultural differences in parental attitudes toward sociability and impulsivity (e.g., Ho, 1986; Porter et al., 2005). According to Chen and French (2008), the cross-cultural differences may reflect largely the relations between culture and child reactivity and regulation (or control) in social situations.

Reactivity and regulation

Child reactivity to stressful challenging situations is a fundamental socioemotional characteristic that has pervasive and enduring effects on social development (Kagan, 1997; Rothbart & Bates, 2006). Researchers have found cross-cultural differences in reactivity in the early years. Hsu, Soong, Stigler, Hong, and Liang (1981), for example, found that Taiwanese parents rated infants as displaying greater reactivity than did American parents; Taiwanese infants were more intense and irritable, more negative in mood, and less likely to approach an unfamiliar situation. Similarly, Japanese, Vietnamese, and Haitian mothers reported high levels of reactivity in their infants (e.g., Pomerleau, Sabatier, & Malcuit, 1998; Prior, Garino, Sanson, & Oberklaid, 1987).

Asian and Western children have also been observed to differ in their reactivity to stressful situations. Rubin et al. (2006) found that Korean and Chinese toddlers exhibited higher fearful and anxious reactions than Italian and Australian toddlers in novel laboratory situations. In a comprehensive analysis of children's inhibited behavior in laboratory situations, Chen et al. (1998) found that, compared with Canadian toddlers, Chinese toddlers were more vigilant and reactive in novel situations. Specifically, Chinese toddlers stayed closer to their mothers and were less likely to explore the environment. When interacting with a stranger, Chinese toddlers displayed more anxious behaviors, as reflected in their higher scores on the latency to approach the stranger and to touch the toys when they were invited to do so.

Reactivity in challenging situations is considered to be biologically rooted (Kagan, 1997). Some evidence has indicated that Chinese and Japanese people differ from European Americans in serotonin transporter genetic polymorphisms (5HTTLPR), cortisol reactivity, and the function of the autonomic nervous system such as heart rate and heart rate variability in stressful settings (e.g., Kagan, Kearsley, & Zelazo, 1978; Tsai, Hong, & Cheng, 2002). These biological measures are associated with anxiety and reactivity in Western children (e.g., Kagan, 1997). Future work is needed to examine whether similar associations exist in Asian children to understand the extent to which biological factors contribute to cross-cultural differences in reactivity.

There is cultural variation in levels of self-regulation and control in early childhood (e.g., Ho, 1986). Gartstein et al. (2006) found that Chinese infants were rated by their mothers as more persistent in orienting than U.S. and Spanish infants, and these differences increased substantially with age from 3 to 9 months. Chen et al. (2003) found that Chinese children maintained their compliant behaviors without adult intervention during a clean-up session, indicating committed and internalized control, more often than Canadian children. Moreover, during a delay task in which the experimenter told the child to wait to play with a packet of attractive crayons until she returned to the room, Chinese toddlers waited for a significantly longer time than Canadian toddlers. Sabbagh, Xu, Carlson, Moses, and Lee (2006) and Oh and Lewis (2008) also found that Chinese and Korean preschoolers performed more competently than their U.S. counterparts on executive function tasks assessing self-control abilities that are associated with the prefrontal cortex of the brain. Although open to various alternative interpretations, most researchers tend to emphasize the role of culture, including values emphasizing group harmony and individual behavioral restraint, in the early socialization of self-control (e.g., Ho, 1986).

Parental attitudes and socialization practices

The impact of child early temperament characteristics on development may be moderated by cultural context. The mechanism for the moderation involves the socialization process, which includes social judgments of, and responses to, specific child behaviors.

Chen and colleagues (1998) examined relations between parental attitudes and children's reactive and inhibited behavior in Chinese and Canadian children. Whereas this behavior was associated with parental punishment orientation and rejection in Canada, it was associated with warm and accepting parental attitudes in China. Parents in Canada and China also appear to react differently to self-control. Compared with Canadian parents, Chinese parents tend to expect their children to maintain a higher level of control (Chen et al., 2003; Ho, 1986). The greater emphasis of Chinese parents on behavioral control may be attributable in part to the influence of traditional values in the culture in which children are required to learn the dictates of *li* (propriety) – a set of rules for actions – to cultivate and strengthen innate virtues (Ho, 1986).

Keller et al. (2004) also found cross-cultural differences in parental attitudes toward children's self-regulation. Rural Cameroonian Nso mothers were higher than Costa Rican mothers, who in turn were higher than middle-class Greek mothers, on a proximal parenting style (body contact and body stimulation), which was believed to facilitate child obedience and regulation. Accordingly, Cameroonian Nso toddlers displayed more regulated behaviors, as indicated by their compliance with maternal requests and prohibitions, than their counterparts in the other two groups. Costa Rican toddlers also had higher regulation scores than Greek toddlers. Keller et al. argued that whereas behavioral training and control may be viewed as interfering and infringing on the child's freedom in individualistic cultures, self-regulation and compliance are viewed as a duty, expressing social maturity and competence in group-oriented cultural contexts.

Cole, Tamang, and Shrestha (2006) compared caregivers' attitudes and reactions to children's anger and undercontrolled behavior in two different villages in Nepal: Brahmans and Tamangs. Brahmans are high-caste Hindus who value hierarchy and dominance. In contrast, Tamangs, with a background of Tibetan Buddhism, value social equality, compassion, modesty, and nonviolence. Brahman and Tamang adults responded to young children's anger differently; the majority (70%) of active responses by Tamang caregivers (i.e., not ignoring) involve rebuking the angry youngster, whereas 85% of active responses by Brahman caregivers involve supporting and coaxing the angry child to feel better. Thus, the attitudes in Tamang households seem to indicate that the children's anger is unjustified and does not warrant any positive attention. In contrast, Brahman parents tend to send the message to the child that anger is acceptable and can be addressed.

In sum, cultural beliefs and values may be reflected directly in parental socialization attitudes and practices. Through organizing the socialization environment, culture may shape the ways in which dispositional characteristics are expressed in social development.

Play, Peer Interaction, and Self-Expression Across Cultures

Developmental researchers have attempted to understand children's behavior through observing peer interaction in play. Research findings from different societies indicate that cultural and social conditions are related to levels of social participation. Moreover, cultural values may impact the quality of peer interactions, such as playfulness and self-expression.

Play and playfulness in peer interaction

Although play seems to be a cross-culturally universal activity in children (Larson & Verma, 1999), there are nevertheless substantial variations across cultures in the amount of time that children spend in play. In general, children in preindustrialized societies tend to spend less time playing with peers than their counterparts in Western postindustrialized societies. For example, Whiting and Edwards (1988) reported that, because of household responsibilities, children in rural Kenya and India played less than children in the United States and Japan. Children in some East Asian countries such as China and Korea also spend less time playing than North American children partly because Asian children spend a large amount of time doing schoolwork (Larson & Verma, 1999). It has been suggested that the amount of time that children spend in play is related to socialization beliefs about the role of play in development; parents in many African, Asian, and Latin American societies have traditionally seen little developmental value in children's play (Parmar, Harkness, & Super, 2004; Rogoff, Mistry, Goncu, & Mosier, 1993).

Social and cultural context may also influence the quality of children's play. Little, Brendgen, Wanner, and Krappmann (1999) found that children in the former East Berlin reported less fun and enjoyment within their peer relationships than did children in West Berlin largely due to the adult control of children's peer interactions. With the changes in the education system after the German reunification, peer interactions among children in East Berlin became more directed by children and less controlled by adults. Consequently, children in the former East Berlin seem to engage in more playful and intimate interactions with friends, express more personal likings, and experience higher enjoyment in their peer interactions.

Self-expression in peer interaction: sociodramatic behavior

Another qualitative aspect of peer interaction that varies across cultures is sociodramatic activity in children's play. From a cognitive developmental perspective, the ability to engage in sociodramatic play reflects the understanding of the symbolic or substitutive function of the object (e.g., a toy or person is given new identity) and mental representations of others (Howes, 1992). According to Farver, Kim, and Lee (1995) and Edwards (2000), sociodramatic behavior and pretense require children to control their social evaluative anxiety and to express their inner interests and personal styles. Cultural values of assertiveness and self-expression may affect the display of sociodramatic behavior in social interaction.

In Western societies, children are socialized to behave in a self-directive manner and are encouraged to develop and exhibit personal styles (e.g., Triandis, 1995). Accordingly, the social and ecological environment (e.g., the structuring of activities, and physical settings) is constructed to facilitate the development of self-directive and expressive skills. As a result, Western children tend to engage in more sociodramatic behaviors than children in many other, particularly group-oriented, cultures. Little sociodramatic activity has been exhibited by Mayan children (Gaskins, 2000), Bedouin Arab children (Ariel & Sever, 1980), and Kenyan, Mexican, and Indian children (Edwards, 2000). Farver et al. (1995) also found that Korean American preschool children displayed less social and pretend play than Anglo-American children. Moreover, when Korean children engaged in pretend play, it contained more everyday and family role activities and less fantastic themes (e.g., actions related to legend or fairy tale characters that do not exist) (Farver & Shin, 1997). Similar results were found in studies conducted with preschool children in Korea and China (Parmar et al., 2004; Tieszen, 1979).

Cultural differences in children's sociodramatic behaviors may reflect the extent to which the community or village has been urbanized or exposed to Western values. Gosso, Lima, Morais, and Otta (2007), for example, examined the play behaviors of children from three different places in Brazil: an Indian village (Paranowaona), a small coastal town (Seashore in São Paulo state), and urban São Paulo. The researchers found that during peer free play activities, the urban children, especially those from high–socioeconomic status (SES) families, displayed more pretend or sociodramatic behaviors than others. Moreover, the sociodramatic activities involved more fantastic characters or themes in urban children than in the other two groups. Interestingly, relatively frequent prevalent characters in the pretend play of the coastal village were domestic animals (dogs and horses), which, according to Gosso et al. (2007), was due to the close contact of the children with them in daily life. Therefore, the extent to which children engage in socio-dramatic activities and their content are constrained by social and cultural conditions.

Children's Social Functioning Across Cultures

Researchers who study children's social functioning often focus on prosocial-cooperative, aggressive, and shy-sensitive behaviors (e.g., Rubin, Bukowski, & Parker, 2006). From the contextual-developmental perspective, the cultural values that different societies place on social initiative and self-control may affect the exhibition and the meaning of these social behaviors.

Prosocial-cooperative behavior

Cross-cultural researchers have been interested in children's prosocial-cooperative behavior (e.g., Whiting & Edwards, 1988). Children in traditional societies where extended families live together and where children are required to assume family responsibilities tend to display more prosocial-cooperative behaviors than children in economically complex societies with class structures and occupational division of labor (Edwards, 2000). Moreover, as a society changes toward urbanization, there seems to be a decline in children's cooperative behavior. Graves and Graves (1983) found that Aituaki (Cook Islands) children from rural and extended families displayed more cooperative and compliant behavior than their urban counterparts in both family and peer interactions. Kagan and Knight (1981) found that acculturation of Mexican American children in the United States was associated with a decrease in cooperation displayed on cooperative and competitive tasks. There is also evidence that children in China, India, Korea, and some other Asian countries were more cooperative in social interactions than children in the West (e.g., Farver et al., 1995; Orlick, Zhou, & Partington, 1990).

The display of prosocial-cooperative behavior may be related to self-regulatory abilities (Eisenberg, Fabes, & Spinrad, 2006), which in turn may be related to cultural values of responsibility in socialization. According to Miller (1994), individuals in sociocentric societies view responsiveness to the needs of others as a fundamental commitment, whereas individuals in Western societies attempt to maintain a balance between prosocial concerns and individual freedom of choice. Thus, prosocial-cooperative behavior is seen in Western cultures as a personal decision based on such factors as how much one likes the target person(s). In societies that value group harmony, however, there is considerable pressure on children to view prosocial-cooperative behavior as obligatory (e.g., Miller, 1994). In these societies, socialization of responsibility and cooperation often emerges in the early years. Consistent with this argument, Fung (2006) found that parents in Taiwan often used shaming practices to help children develop prosocial behavior. Similarly, Nelson et al. (2007) and Wu et al. (2002) found that Chinese parents were more likely than American parents to emphasize shaming in parenting and that shaming was perceived more positively by Chinese than American parents. Fung (2006) argued that shaming practices are based on a strong group concern because the experience of shame may lead to self-examination, which may promote the internalization of rules and social responsibility.

Prosocial-cooperative behavior is robustly associated with indices of adjustment such as peer acceptance and school achievement in a variety of cultures (e.g., Casiglia, Lo Coco, & Zappulla, 1998; Chen, Li, Li, Li, & Liu, 2000; Eisenberg, Pidada, & Liew, 2001). Children who display prosocial-cooperative behaviors are generally liked by peers and perform competently in school. Nevertheless, it has been argued that prosocial-cooperative behavior may have a more extensive impact on children's adjustment, including emotional well-being, in group-oriented than self-oriented cultures. Chen et al. (2000), for example, found that prosocial behavior served as a protective factor for Chinese children who experienced difficulties in emotional adjustment such as loneliness and depression. It will be interesting to investigate whether the protective function of prosocial behavior in psychological adjustment is specific to Chinese or group-oriented cultures.

Aggressive behavior

Cultures that value competitiveness and the pursuit of personal goals seem to allow for more coercive and aggressive behavior, whereas cultures that emphasize group harmony and personal control tend to inhibit aggressive behavior. Relative to their North American counterparts, children in some Asian countries such as China, Korea, and Thailand; Australia; and some European nations such as Sweden and the Netherlands tend to exhibit lower levels of aggressive and externalizing behavior (e.g., Bergeron & Schneider, 2005; Russell, Hart, Robinson, & Olsen, 2003; Weisz et al., 1988). Cultural norms and values may affect aggressive behavior through shaping individual beliefs and attitudes about aggression and views about appropriate reactions to provocations. Zahn-Waxler, Friedman, Cole, Mizuta, and Hiruma (1996) found that Japanese children showed less anger and less aggressive behavior than U.S. children in their responses to hypothetical situations involving conflict and distress. Cole et al. (2006) found that Brahman children are more likely to endorse anger and aggressive behaviors than Tamang children in Nepal. Brahman children react to difficult social situations such as peer conflict with anger and other negative emotions more often than Tamang children.

Children's aggressive behavior is generally associated with adjustment problems because it may threaten the well-being of individuals and the group. However, different consequences of aggressive behavior have been found across cultures. In cultures such as that of the Yanoamo Indians, where aggressive and violent behaviors are considered socially acceptable or even desirable, aggressive children, especially boys, may be regarded as "stars" and "heroes" by their peers (Chagnon, 1983). In some central and southern Italian communities, due to social and historical circumstances, aggressive and defiant behaviors may be perceived by children as reflecting social assertiveness and competence (Casiglia et al., 1998; Schneider & Fonzi, 1996). As a result, it seems reasonable to expect that aggressive children in these communities experience less social problems such as peer rejection than their counterparts in cultures that strictly prohibit aggression.

In North America, although aggression is generally discouraged, aggressive children may receive social support from their peers (e.g., Rodkin, Farmer, Pearl, & van Acker, 2000). This peer support and approval in turn may lead to the development of biased self-perceptions of social competence in aggressive children (Asher, Parkhurst, Hymel, & Williams, 1990). In China, children regularly engage in public evaluations in school in which they are required to evaluate themselves in relation to their conformity with school standards; peers and teachers provide feedback on these self-evaluations. This social interactive process makes it difficult for aggressive children to develop inflated or biased self-perceptions of their competence. Consequently, aggressive children in China experience pervasive social and psychological difficulties including low social status, negative self-perceptions, and feelings of loneliness and depression (Chen, Rubin, & Li, 1995).

Shyness–sensitivity

Shyness–sensitivity is a wary, restrained, and anxious reaction to novel social situations or social evaluations (Rubin, Coplan, & Bowker, 2009). In Western, particularly North American, societies, children who display shy and sensitive behavior are likely to be rejected or isolated by peers and perceived by adults as socially incompetent (e.g., Coplan, Prakash, O'Neil, & Armer, 2004). When they realize their difficulties in social situations, shy-sensitive children may develop negative self-perceptions of their competence and other psychological problems such as loneliness, social dissatisfaction, and depression (e.g., Coplan et al., 2004). Shyness–sensitivity in childhood may contribute to later problems in various areas such as educational attainment, career stability, and emotional disorder (e.g., Asendorpf, Denissen, & van Aken, 2008; Caspi, Elder, & Bem, 1988).

The maladaptive outcomes of shy-inhibited behavior in Western children may be related to the cultural emphasis on individual assertiveness and autonomy. In societies where assertiveness and autonomy are not valued or encouraged, shy and restrained behavior is likely to be viewed as less deviant and maladaptive. Although the research findings in this area are somewhat inconsistent, most findings suggest that shyness seems to be less problematic for children in some Asian countries than in North America. Eisenberg et al. (2001) found, for example, that shyness in Indonesian children was negatively associated with peer nominations of dislike and behavioral problems and teacher-rated negative emotionality. Farver et al. (1995) noted that shy and reticent behaviors in Korean children were consistent with the school expectation of "proper" behavior and cultural values that emphasize group harmony. Cross-cultural variations in the relations between shyness and adjustment were found in a series of studies in urban Chinese and Canadian children in the early 1990s (e.g., Chen, Rubin, & Li, 1995). These studies showed that unlike their North American counterparts, shy Chinese children tended to be accepted by peers and viewed as competent by teachers, and perform well in social, academic, and psychological areas. Similar results were found recently in rural Chinese children (Chen & Wang, in press; Chen, Wang, & Wang, 2009).

Developmentally, shyness appears to be related to less negative outcomes in less self-oriented and competitive societies. Kerr, Lambert, and Bem (1996) examined the long-term outcomes of shyness in a sample of children born in a suburb of Stockholm in the mid-1950s. Although shyness predicted later marriage and parenthood, it did not affect adulthood careers, including occupational stability (as indicated by frequency of job changes), education, or income among Swedish men. According to Kerr et al., the social welfare and support systems that evolved from the egalitarian values in Sweden assured that people did not need to be assertive or competitive to achieve career success. Perhaps because similar social support systems were not yet available for girls during the period in which the study was conducted, Swedish shy girls appeared to attain lower levels of education than nonshy girls. Kerr et al. expected that shy and nonshy girls would not differ in Sweden today. The positive contribution of shyness–inhibition to later social, school, and psychological adjustment has also been found in Chinese children. Shyness in childhood positively predicts adolescent adjustment, including teacher-assessed competence, leadership, academic achievement, and self-perceptions of competence in China (Chen, Rubin, Li, & Li, 1999). Taken together, the findings from various projects suggest that shyness–sensitivity in some cultures such as China and Sweden does not necessarily lead to maladaptive development. In these cultures, shy children may not experience obstacles in social interactions, and they may receive social support from others, both of which help them perform socially and psychologically.

It should be noted that shyness–sensitivity differs from social withdrawal, social disinterest, and unsociability (e.g., "kids who would rather be alone"). Social disinterest or unsociability is inconsistent with the group orientation. Children who prefer solitude and intentionally stay away from the group may be regarded as selfish or anticollective, which may elicit negative reactions from others in group-oriented cultures. Indeed, children who are socially solitary or withdrawn are clearly rejected by peers and experience socioemotional problems in China, which is similar to the results in Western cultures (Chang et al., 2005; Chen, 2008; Chen & Wang, in press).

Finally, Chen and his colleagues (e.g., Chen & Chen, 2010) have recently explored how the large-scale social transformation in China affects the significance of shyness–sensitivity for adjustment. China has evolved rapidly toward a market-oriented society since the early 1980s, particularly in the past 15 years. As a result, parents, especially those in urban areas with a relatively high education, increasingly realize that independence, expression of personal opinions, and self-confidence are required for adaptation to the new environment and that it is important to help children develop these qualities. Many schools in China have also changed their education goals and practices to facilitate the development of assertive social skills. Relative to some other aspects of socioemotional functioning, shyness may be particularly susceptible to the influence of the macrolevel changes. Shy, anxious, and wary behavior that impedes exploration and self-expression in stressful situations may no longer be regarded as adaptive and competent in social and psychological adjustment in the new environment (Hart et al., 2000; Xu, Farver, Chang, Zhang, & Yu, 2007).

In a cohort design study based on elementary school children in urban China, Chen, Cen, Li, and He (2005) found that whereas shyness was positively associated with peer acceptance, leadership, and academic achievement in 1990, it was negatively associated with peer acceptance and teacher-rated social competence and positively associated with peer rejection and depression in 2002. Shy-sensitive children today, unlike their counterparts in the early 1990s, are perceived as incompetent and problematic by teachers, rejected by peers, displayed school problems, and reported high levels of depression. An interesting finding of Chen, Cen, et al.'s study (2005) was that shyness was positively associated with both peer acceptance and rejection in 1998, perhaps reflecting an ambivalent attitude of peers toward shy children, which, to some extent, may reflect the cultural conflict between the new values of assertiveness and traditional Chinese values of self-control. Another interesting finding was that social evaluations and relationships such as peer rejection and teacher-rated competence were more sensitive than other aspects of adjustment such as academic achievement and depression to the change in social and cultural norms. Thus, social and historical changes may affect different aspects of socioemotional functioning and adjustment gradually and cumulatively. The finding supports the argument that social attitudes and relationships serve as a major mediator of contextual influence on individual development (Chen, Chung, et al., 2008).

Friendship and Peer Group Affiliation: Cultural Variations on the Structure and Function of Peer Relationships

A major developmental outcome of social behaviors is children's success in developing and maintaining relationships with peers. The indices of success with peer relationships include establishing specific friendships with others and being integrated into group networks (Rubin, Bukowski, et al., 2006). Cultures seem to differ in the extent to which group integration or formation of specific relationships is encouraged. Moreover, cultural beliefs and values may have a direct impact on the structural and functional aspects of peer relationships.

Friendship across cultures

With the exception of a few societies such as that of the Yucatán Mayan (Gaskins, 2006), where children interact with age mates mainly within extended family networks of siblings and cousins, the majority of children, ranging from 70% to over 90%, in the world today have reciprocal friends who are nonkin same-age peers (e.g., French, Jansen, Riansari, & Setiono, 2003). Children's friendships are formed primarily in school contexts. Across cultures, more girls than boys form mutual friendships, and girls' friendships tend to be more stable over time (e.g., Schneider, Fonzi, & Tani, 1997).

The functions of friendship that are identified and accepted by children appear to differ across cultures. In Western cultures, friendship is considered critical for developing positive views of self-worth (Rubin, Bukowski, et al., 2006; Sullivan, 1953). This function may be less salient in some non-Western cultures where the development of the self is not considered an important developmental task. It has been found that whereas one of the major reasons for friendship among North American children is that friends make them feel good about themselves, Chinese (e.g., Chen, Kaspar, Zhang, Wang, & Zheng, 2004; Cho, Sandel, Miller, & Wang, 2005) and Indonesian (French, Pidada, & Victor, 2005) children and children with an Arab and Caribbean background (Dayan, Doyle, & Markiewicz, 2001) often do not report the enhancement of self-worth to be an important function of friendship.

Instrumental assistance appears to be important for friendships of children in many group-oriented cultures. Researchers have found that children tend to highly value the instrumental assistance of friends in some Asian nations such as China (Chen et al., 2004), Indonesia (French et al., 2005), South Korea (French, Lee, & Pidada, 2006), and the Philippines (Hollnsteiner, 1979); Latino societies such as Cuba (Gonzalez, Moreno, & Schneider, 2004) and Costa Rica (DeRosier & Kupersmidt, 1991); and low-income Black and Hispanic groups in the United States (Way, 2006). Instrumental assistance in those societies and groups may be reflected in broad areas ranging from sharing money and protecting friends from harm to helping others solve problems and learn social skills (Chen et al., 2004; Way, 2006).

There exists some controversy regarding intimacy in friendship across cultures. Triandis, Bontempo, Villareal, Asai, and Lucca (1988) argued that friendships in collectivistic cultures tend to be more intimate than those in individualistic cultures. Sharabany (2006), however, suggested that in certain collectivistic societies, friendships are characterized as low in intimacy because of the availability of other sources of emotional support, the reduced privacy inherent in collectivistic lifestyles, and the potential threat of exclusive dyadic friendships to the cohesiveness of the larger group. There is empirical evidence supporting each of these arguments. For example, youth in South Korea, Japan, and central and southern Italy report highly intimate friendships (French et al., 2006; Schneider et al., 1997). On the other hand, relatively low intimacy has been found in children's friendships in some other group-oriented societies such as Indonesia, rural Arab societies, and Israeli kibbutzim (e.g., French et al., 2005, 2006; Sharabany, 2006). Despite the cultural differences, there appear to be similarities in many of the functions of friendship. Friendship may be a social resource for fulfilling common needs of children and serve as a context for them to achieve common tasks in development.

The peer group across cultures

Much of school-aged children's social interaction in both Western and non-Western societies occurs in the context of a peer group (e.g., Cairns & Cairns, 1994; Chen, Chang,

He, & Liu, 2005; Salmivalli, Huttunen, & Lagerspetz, 1997). Peer groups are often composed of same-sex members, with more mixed-sex groups appearing in late adolescence. The size of groups tends to increase with age. Boys appear to be more likely to belong to groups and more susceptible to peer pressure than girls, and boys' groups tend to be larger than girls' groups (e.g., Dekovic, Engels, Shirai, De Kort, & Anker, 2002; Salmivalli et al., 1997), although no gender differences have been reported in several studies (e.g., Chen, Chang, et al., 2005).

Peer group involvement in Western cultures is considered to be derived mainly from the desire of youth to become autonomous from the family (Rubin, Bukowski, et al., 2006). Once they enter the peer group, youth need to learn independence while maintaining positive relationships with others, and eventually to acquire a sense of self-identity (Brown, 1990; Sullivan, 1953). Individual independence may be less of a concern to youth in group-oriented cultures that emphasize conformity to others and commitment to social relationships. In these cultures, children are expected and encouraged to maintain strong social affiliations and to identify with the group (Sharabany, 2006).

In North American youth, intensive interaction within the small clique appears to be the major form of peer activity in childhood, but this tends to decline from middle childhood, when affiliation with multiple groups and larger crowds becomes more salient (e.g., Brown, 1990). As children increasingly seek independence and attempt to avoid group restrictions, there is a general loosening of group ties, and children's sense of belongingness declines steadily with age (see Rubin, Bukowski, et al., 2006). Peer groups, particularly deviant groups, may contribute significantly to individual social and psychological adjustment factors such as academic motivation and antisocial behavior in Western cultures (e.g., Cairns & Cairns, 1994; Kinderman, 1993). In general, however, the role of peer groups is often highlighted in the formation of self-identity and the development of positive self-perceptions and self-feelings (e.g., Rubin, Bukowski, et al., 2006).

Children in group-oriented societies may maintain strong group affiliation across different developmental periods because the tension between the pursuit of independence and personal identity and the commitment to group undertaking in these societies is lower than in Western societies. In group-oriented cultures, there is often great pressure on group members to conform to group norms (Sharabany, 2006). Peer groups tend to be valued according to their socialization functions in helping children learn social standards and develop socially acceptable behaviors (Chen et al., 2004; Sharabany, 2006). In these cultures, particular attention is paid to the *nature* of peer groups in terms of whether group activities are guided by the "right" social goals. Children in China, for example, describe group activities mainly in terms of how they are in accord with adults' social requirements and standards in social and academic achievement (Chen et al., 2004). Indeed, Chen, Chang, Liu, and He (2008) found that group academic context made significant contributions to individual development in Chinese children. Whether peer groups have similar significance for individual development in other cultures such as Latino cultures, which highly endorse peer group affiliation (Azmitia & Cooper, 2004), will be an interesting question.

Conclusions and Future Directions

Cross-cultural research has identified some of the ways in which cultural factors are involved in social development. Culture may affect how disposition and socialization interact in their contributions to later social behaviors and relationships. Moreover, cultural beliefs and values may determine, in part, the display and significance of social behaviors, and the structure, function, and organization of social relationships.

In this chapter, we focused mainly on how cultural values may affect two fundamental dimensions of social functioning, social initiative and control, and the social behaviors and relationships that are formed based upon these dimensions. There are other important areas, such as self-perceptions and interpersonal understanding, in which cross-cultural differences have been found (e.g., Kwok, 1995). Culture may influence social development in a comprehensive manner.

Cross-cultural researchers are often interested in comparing children in Western, self-oriented societies with those in collectivistic or group-oriented societies. It is important to note that cultural exchanges and interactions may lead to the merging, coexistence, and integration of diverse value systems (Tamis-LeMonda et al., 2008). During globalization, for example, individualistic ideologies and values have been introduced into many non-Western societies and exerted influence on the social attitudes and behaviors of children and adults in these societies. However, Western values are unlikely to be adopted completely in their original forms, but instead may be integrated with the cultural traditions. It will be interesting to investigate how children develop their social competence in the culturally integrated and sophisticated settings.

Researchers have started to explore the processes in which culture affects social development through socialization and social interaction (e.g., Chen, DeSouza, Chen, & Wang, 2006). Nevertheless, cultural influence on children's behaviors and relationships is a complex phenomenon, involving personal and contextual factors at multiple levels. For example, children may play increasingly active roles in socialization and development through participating in social interaction in which they construct cultural norms for their activities and mutual evaluations (Chen, Chung, et al., 2008; Corsaro & Nelson, 2003). However, the active role of children has received relatively little attention in cross-cultural research. Therefore, it is crucial to engage in continuous exploration of the issues in the area in order to achieve a more thorough understanding of social development in cultural context.

References

Ariel, S., & Sever, I. (1980). Play in the desert and play in the town: On play activities of Bedouin Arab children. In H. B. Schwartzman (Ed.), *Play and culture* (pp. 164–175). West Point, NY: Leisure Press.

Asendorpf, J. (1990). Beyond social withdrawal: Shyness, unsociability, and peer avoidance. *Human Development, 33,* 250–259.

Asendorpf, J. B., Denissen, J. J. A., & van Aken, M. A. G. (2008). Inhibited and aggressive pre-school children at 23 years of age: Personality and social transition into adulthood. *Developmental Psychology, 44*, 997–1011.

Asher, S., Parkhurst, J. T., Hymel, S., & Williams, G. A. (1990). Peer rejection and loneliness in childhood. In S. R. Asher & J. D. Coie (Eds.), *Peer rejection in childhood* (pp. 253–273). New York: Cambridge University Press.

Azmitia, M., & Cooper, C. R. (2004). Good or bad? Peer influences on Latino and European American adolescents' pathways through school. *Journal of Education for Students Placed at Risk, 6*, 45–71.

Benedict, R. (1934). Anthropology and the abnormal. *Journal of General Psychology, 10*, 59–82.

Bergeron, N., & Schneider, B. H. (2005). Explaining cross-national differences in peer-directed aggression: A quantitative synthesis. *Aggressive Behavior, 31*, 116–137.

Bronfenbrenner, U., & Morris, P. A. (2006). The bioecological model of human development. In W. Damon (Series Ed.) & R. M. Lerner (Vol. Ed.), *Handbook of child psychology: Vol. 1. Theoretical models of human development* (pp. 793–828). New York: Wiley.

Brown, B. B. (1990). Peer groups and peer cultures. In S. S. Feldman & G. R. Elliott (Eds.), *At the threshold: The developing adolescent* (pp. 171–196). Cambridge, MA: Harvard University Press.

Cairns, R. B., & Cairns, B. D. (1994). *Lifelines and risks: Pathways of youth in our time*. New York: Cambridge University Press.

Camras, L. A., Oster, H., Campos, J., Campos, R., Ujiie, T., Miyake, K., et al. (1998). Production of emotional facial expressions in European American, Japanese, and Chinese infants. *Developmental Psychology, 34*, 616–628.

Casiglia, A. C., Lo Coco, A., & Zappulla, C. (1998). Aspects of social reputation and peer relationships in Italian children: A cross-cultural perspective. *Developmental Psychology, 34*, 723–730.

Caspi, A., Elder, G. H., Jr., & Bem, D. J. (1988). Moving away from the world: Life-course patterns of shy children. *Developmental Psychology, 24*, 824–831.

Chagnon, N. A. (1983). *Yanomamo: The fierce people*. New York: Holt, Rinehart and Winston.

Chang, L., Lei, L., Li, K. K., Liu, H., Guo, B., Wang, Y. et al. (2005). Peer acceptance and self-perceptions of verbal and behavioural aggression and withdrawal. *International Journal of Behavioral Development, 29*, 49–57.

Chen, X. (2008). Shyness and unsociability in cultural context. In A. S. Lo Coco, K. H. Rubin, & C. Zappulla (Eds.), *L'isolamento sociale durante l'infanzia* [Social withdrawal in childhood] (pp. 143–160). Milan: Unicopli.

Chen, X., Cen, G., Li, D., & He, Y. (2005). Social functioning and adjustment in Chinese children: The imprint of historical time. *Child Development, 76*, 182–195.

Chen, X., Chang, L., He, Y., & Liu, H. (2005). The peer group as a context: Moderating effects on relations between maternal parenting and social and school adjustment in Chinese children. *Child Development, 76*, 417–434.

Chen, X., Chang, L., Liu, H., & He, Y. (2008). Effects of the peer group on the development of social functioning and academic achievement: A longitudinal study in Chinese children. *Child Development, 79*, 235–251.

Chen, X., & Chen, H. (2010). Children's social functioning and adjustment in the changing Chinese society. In R. K. Silbereisen & X. Chen (Eds.), *Social change and human development: Concepts and results* (pp. 209–226). London: Sage.

Chen, X., Chung, J., & Hsiao, C. (2008). Peer interactions, relationships and groups from a cross-cultural perspective. In K. H. Rubin, W. Bukowski, & B. Laursen (Eds.), *Handbook of peer interactions, relationships, and groups*. New York: Guilford Press.

Chen, X., DeSouza, A., Chen, H., & Wang, L. (2006). Reticent behavior and experiences in peer interactions in Canadian and Chinese children. *Developmental Psychology, 42*, 656–665.

Chen, X., & French, D. (2008). Children's social competence in cultural context. *Annual Review of Psychology, 59*, 591–616.

Chen, X., Hastings, P., Rubin, K. H., Chen, H., Cen, G., & Stewart, S. L. (1998). Childrearing attitudes and behavioral inhibition in Chinese and Canadian toddlers: A cross-cultural study. *Developmental Psychology, 34*, 677–686.

Chen, X., Kaspar, V., Zhang, Y., Wang. L., & Zheng, S. (2004). Peer relationships among Chinese and North American boys: A cross-cultural perspective. In N. Way & J. Chu (Eds.), *Adolescent boys in context* (pp. 197–218). New York: New York University Press.

Chen, X., Li, D., Li, Z., Li, B., & Liu, M. (2000). Sociable and prosocial dimensions of social competence in Chinese children: Common and unique contributions to social, academic and psychological adjustment. *Developmental Psychology, 36*, 302–314.

Chen, X., Rubin, K. H., & Li, B. (1995). Depressed mood in Chinese children: Relations with school performance and family environment. *Journal of Consulting and Clinical Psychology, 63*, 938–947.

Chen, X., Rubin, K. H., Li, B., & Li. Z. (1999). Adolescent outcomes of social functioning in Chinese children. *International Journal of Behavioural Development, 23*, 199–223.

Chen, X., Rubin, K. H., & Li, Z. (1995). Social functioning and adjustment in Chinese children: A longitudinal study. *Developmental Psychology, 31*, 531–539.

Chen, X., Rubin, K. H., Liu, M., Chen, H., Wang, L., Li, D., et al. (2003). Compliance in Chinese and Canadian toddlers. *International Journal of Behavioral Development, 27*, 428–436.

Chen, X., & Wang, L. (in press). Shyness-sensitivity and unsociability in rural Chinese children: Relations with social, school, and psychological adjustment. *Child Development.*

Chen, X., Wang, L., & Wang, Z. (2009). Shyness-sensitivity and social, school, and psychological adjustment in rural migrant and urban children in China. *Child Development, 80*, 1499–1513.

Cho, G. E., Sandel, T. L., Miller, P. J., & Wang, S. (2005). What do grandmothers think about self-esteem? American and Taiwanese folk theories revisited. *Social Development, 14*, 701–721.

Cole, P. M., Tamang, B. L., & Shrestha, S. (2006). Cultural variations in the socialization of young children's anger and shame. *Child Development, 77*, 1237–1251.

Coplan, R. J., Prakash, K., O'Neil, K., & Armer, M. (2004). Do you "want" to play? Distinguishing between conflicted-shyness and social disinterest in early childhood. *Developmental Psychology, 40*, 244–258.

Corsaro, W. A., & Nelson, E. (2003). Children's collective activities and peer culture in early literacy in American and Italian preschools. *Sociology of Education, 76*, 209–227.

Dayan, J., Doyle, A. B., & Markiewicz, D. (2001). Social support networks and self-esteem of idiocentric and allocentric children and adolescents. *Journal of Social and Personal Relations, 18*, 767–784.

Dekovic, M., Engels, R. C. M. E., Shirai, T., De Kort, G., & Anker, A. L. (2002). The role of peer relations in adolescent development in two cultures: The Netherlands and Japan. *Journal of Cross-Cultural Psychology, 33*, 577–595.

DeRosier, M. E., & Kupersmidt, J. B. (1991). Costa Rican children's perceptions of their social networks. *Developmental Psychology, 27*, 656–662.

Edwards, C. P. (2000). Children's play in cross-cultural perspective: A new look at the Six Culture Study. *Cross-Cultural Research, 34*, 318–338.

Eisenberg, N., Fabes, R. A., & Spinrad, T. L. (2006). Prosocial development. In N. Eisenberg (Ed.), *Handbook of child psychology: Vol. 3. Social, emotional, and personality development* (pp. 646–718). New York: Wiley.

Eisenberg, N., Pidada, S., & Liew, J. (2001). The relations of regulation and negative emotionality to Indonesian children's social functioning. *Child Development, 72*, 1747–1763.

Farver, J. M., Kim, Y. K., & Lee, Y. (1995). Cultural differences in Korean- and Anglo-American preschoolers' social interaction and play behaviors. *Child Development, 66*, 1088–1099.

Farver, J. M., & Shin, Y. L. (1997). Social pretend play in Korea- and Anglo-American preschoolers. *Child Development, 68*, 544–556.

Fogel, A., Toda, S., & Kawai, M. (1988). Mother-infant face-to-face interactions in Japan and the United States: A laboratory comparison using 3-month-old infants. *Developmental Psychology, 24*, 398–406.

French, D. C., Jansen, E. A., Riansari, M., & Setiono, K. (2003). Friendships of Indonesian children: Adjustment of children who differ in friendship presence and similarity between mutual friends. *Social Development, 12*, 605–621.

French, D. C., Lee, O., & Pidada, S. (2006). Friendships of Indonesian, South Korean and United States youth: Exclusivity, intimacy, enhancement of worth, and conflict. In X. Chen, D. French, & B. Schneider (Eds.), *Peer relationships in cultural context* (pp. 379–402). New York: Cambridge University Press.

French, D. C., Pidada, S., & Victor, A. (2005). Friendships of Indonesian and United States youth. *International Journal of Behavioral Development, 29*, 304–313.

Fung, H. (2006). Affect and early moral socialization: Some insights and contributions from indigenous psychological studies in Taiwan. In U. Kim, K. S. Yang, & K. K. Hwang (Eds.). *Indigenous and cultural psychology: Understanding people in context* (pp. 175–196). New York: Springer.

Gartstein, M. A., Gonzalez, C., Carranza, J. A., Ahadi, S. A., Ye, R., Rothbart, M. K., et al. (2006). Studying cross-cultural differences in the development of infant temperament: People's Republic of China, the United States of America, and Spain. *Child Psychiatry and Human Development, 37*, 145–161.

Gaskins, S. (2000). Children's daily activities in a Mayan village: A culturally grounded description. *Cross-Cultural Research, 34*, 375–389.

Gaskins, S. (2006). The cultural organization of Yucatec Mayan children's social interactions. In X. Chen, D. French, & B. Schneider (Eds.), *Peer relationships in cultural context* (pp. 283–309). New York: Cambridge University Press.

Gonzalez, Y., Moreno, D. S., & Schneider, B. H. (2004). Friendship expectations of early adolescents in Cuba and Canada. *Journal of Cross-Cultural Psychology, 35*, 436–445.

Gosso, Y., Lima, M. D., Morais, S. E., & Otta, E. (2007). Pretend play of Brazilian children: A window into different cultural worlds. *Journal of Cross-Cultural Psychology, 38*, 539–558.

Graves, N. B., & Graves, T. D. (1983). The cultural context of prosocial development: An ecological model. In D. L. Bridgeman (Ed.), *The nature of prosocial development* (pp. 795–824). San Diego, CA: Academic Press.

Hart, C. H., Yang, C., Nelson, L. J., Robinson, C. C., Olson, J. A., Nelson, D. A., et al. (2000). Peer acceptance in early childhood and subtypes of socially withdrawn behaviour in China, Russia and the United States. *International Journal of Behavioral Development, 24*, 73–81.

Hinde, R. A. (1987). *Individuals, relationships and culture.* Cambridge: Cambridge University Press.

Ho, D. Y. F. (1986). Chinese pattern of socialization: A critical review. In M. H. Bond (Ed.), *The psychology of the Chinese people* (pp. 1–37). Hong Kong: Oxford University Press.

Hollnsteiner, M. R. (1979). Reciprocity as a Filipino in value. In M. R. Hollnsteiner (Ed.), *Culture and the Filipino* (pp. 38–43). Quezon City, Philippines: Atteneo de Manila University.

Howes, C. (1992). *The collaborative construction of pretend.* Albany: State University of New York Press.

Hsu, C., Soong, W., Stigler, J. W., Hong, C., & Liang, C. (1981). The temperamental characteristics of Chinese babies. *Child Development, 52,* 1337–1340.

Kagan, J. (1997). Temperament and the reactions to unfamiliarity. *Child Development, 68,* 139–143.

Kagan, J., Kearsley, R. B., & Zelazo, P. R. (1978). *Infancy: Its place in human development.* Cambridge, MA: Harvard University Press.

Kagan, S., & Knight, G. P. (1981). Social motives among Anglo-American and Mexican-American children: Experimental and projective measures. *Journal of Research in Personality, 15,* 93–106.

Keller, H., Yovsi, R., Borke, J., Kartner, J., Jensen, H., & Papaligoura, Z. (2004). Developmental consequences of early parenting experiences: Self-recognition and self-regulation in three cultural communities. *Child Development, 75,* 1745–1760.

Kerr, M., Lambert, W. W., & Bem, D. J. (1996). Life course sequelae of childhood shyness in Sweden: Comparison with the United States. *Developmental Psychology, 32,* 1100–1105.

Kinderman, T. A. (1993). Natural peer groups as contexts for individual development: The case of children's motivation in school. *Developmental Psychology, 29,* 970–977.

Knyazev, G. G., Zupancic, G. G., & Slobodskaya, H. R. (2008). Child personality in Slovenia and Russia: Structure and mean level of traits in parent and self-ratings. *Journal of Cross-Cultural Psychology, 39,* 317–334.

Kwok, D. C. (1995). The self-perception of competence by Canadian and Chinese children. *Psychologia, 38,* 9–16.

Larson, R. W., & Verma, S. (1999). How children and adolescents spend time across the world: Work, play, and developmental opportunities. *Psychological Bulletin, 125,* 701–736.

Little, T. D., Brendgen, M., Wanner, B., & Krappmann, L. (1999). Children's reciprocal perceptions of friendship quality in the sociocultural contexts of East and West Berlin. *International Journal of Behavioral Development, 23,* 63–89.

Miller, J. G. (1994). Cultural diversity in the morality of caring: Individually oriented versus duty-based interpersonal moral codes. *Cross-Cultural Research, 28,* 3–39.

Nelson, L. J., Hart, C. H., Wu, B., Yang, C., Roper, S. O., & Jin, S. (2007). Relations between Chinese mothers' parenting practices and social withdrawal in early childhood. *International Journal of Behavioral Development, 30,* 261–271.

Oh, S., & Lewis, C. (2008). Korean preschoolers' advanced inhibitory control and its relation to other executive skills and mental state understanding. *Child Development, 79,* 80–99.

Orlick, T., Zhou, Q. Y., & Partington, J. (1990). Co-operation and conflict within Chinese and Canadian kindergarten settings. *Canadian Journal of Behavioral Science, 22,* 20–25.

Parmar, P., Harkness, S., & Super, C. M. (2004). Asian and Euro-American parents' ethnotheories of play and learning: Effects on preschool children's home routine and school behaviour. *International Journal of Behavioral Development, 28,* 97–104.

Pomerleau, A., Sabatier, C., & Malcuit, G. (1998). Quebecois, Haitian, and Vietnamese mothers' report of infant temperament. *International Journal of Psychology, 33,* 337–344.

Porter, C. L., Hart, C. H., Yang, C., Robinson, C. C., Olsen, S. F., Zeng, Q. et al., (2005). A comparative study of child temperament and parenting in Beijing, China and the western United States. *International Journal of Behavioral Development, 29,* 541–551.

Prior, M., Garino, E., Sanson, A., & Oberklaid, F. (1987). Ethnic influences on "difficult'" temperament and behavioural problems in infants. *Australian Journal of Psychology, 39,* 163–171.

Rodkin, P. C., Farmer, T. W., Pearl, R., & van Acker, R. (2000). Heterogeneity of popular boys: Antisocial and prosocial configurations. *Developmental Psychology, 36,* 14–24.

Rogoff, B. (2003). *The cultural nature of human development.* New York: Oxford University Press.

Rogoff, B., Mistry, J., Goncu, A., & Mosier, C. (1993). Guided participation in cultural activity by toddlers and caregivers. *Monographs of the Society for Research in Child Development, 58*(8, Serial No. 236).

Rothbart, M. K., & Bates, J. E. (2006). Temperament. In N. Eisenberg (Ed.), *Handbook of child psychology: Vol. 3. Social, emotional, and personality development* (pp. 99–166). New York: Wiley.

Rubin, K. H., Bukowski, W., & Parker, J. G. (2006). Peer interactions, relationships, and groups. In N. Eisenberg (Ed.), *Handbook of child psychology: Vol. 3. Social, emotional, and personality development* (pp. 571–645). New York: Wiley.

Rubin, K. H., Coplan, R., & Bowker, J. (2009). Social withdrawal in childhood. *Annual Review of Psychology, 60*, 141–171.

Rubin, K. H., Hemphill, S. A., Chen, X., Hastings, P., Sanson, A., Lo Coco, A., et al. (2006). A cross-cultural study of behavioral inhibition in toddlers: East-west-north-south. *International Journal of Behavioral Development, 30*, 219–226.

Russell, A., Hart, C. H., Robinson, C. C., & Olsen, S. F. (2003). Children's sociable and aggressive behavior with peers: A comparison of the US and Australia, and contributions of temperament and parenting styles. *International Journal of Behavioral Development, 27*, 74–86.

Sabbagh, M. A., Xu, F., Carlson, S. M., Moses, L. J., & Lee, K. (2006). The development of executive functioning and theory of mind: A comparison of Chinese and U.S. preschoolers. *Psychological Science, 17*, 74–81.

Salmivalli, C., Huttunen, A., & Lagerspetz, K. (1997). Peer networks and bullying in schools. *Scandinavian Journal of Psychology, 38*, 305–312.

Schneider, B. H., & Fonzi, A. (1996). La stabilita dell'amicizia: Unostudio cross-culturale Italia-Canada [Friendship stability: A cross-cultural study in Italy-Canada]. *Eta Evolutiva, 3*, 73–79.

Schneider, B. H., Fonzi, A., & Tani, F. (1997). A cross-cultural exploration of the stability of children's friendships and the predictors of their continuation. *Social Development, 6*, 322–333.

Sharabany, R. (2006). The cultural context of children and adolescents: Peer relationships and intimate friendships among Arab and Jewish children in Israel. In X. Chen, D. French, & B. Schneider (Eds.), *Peer relationships in cultural context* (pp. 452–478). New York: Cambridge University Press.

Sullivan, H. S. (1953). *The interpersonal theory of psychiatry*. New York: Norton.

Super, C. M., & Harkness, S. (1986). The developmental niche: A conceptualization at the interface of child and culture. *International Journal of Behavioral Development, 9*, 545–569.

Tamis-LeMonda, C. S., Way, N., Hughes, D., Yoshikawa, H., Kalman, R. K., & Niwa, E. (2008). Parents' goals for children: The dynamic co-existence of collectivism and individualism in cultures and individuals. *Social Development, 17*, 183–209.

Tieszen, H. R. (1979). Children's social behavior in a Korean preschool. *Journal of Korean Home Economics Association, 17*, 71–84.

Triandis, H. C. (1995). *Individualism and collectivism*. Boulder, CO: Westview Press.

Triandis, H. C., Bontempo, R., Villareal, M. J., Asai, M., & Lucca, N. (1988). Individualism and collectivism: Cross-cultural perspectives on self-ingroup relationships. *Journal of Personality and Social Psychology, 54*, 323–333.

Tsai, S. J., Hong, C. J., & Cheng, C. Y. (2002). Serotonin transporter genetic polymorphisms and harm avoidance in the Chinese. *Psychiatric Genetics 12*, 165–168.

Vygotsky, L. S. (1978). *Mind in society: The development of higher psychological processes* (Ed. M. Cole, V. John-Steiner, S. Scribner, & E. Souberman). Cambridge, MA: Harvard University Press.

Wang, Q. (2003). *Emotion* situation knowledge in American and Chinese preschool children and adults. *Cognition and Emotion, 17*(5), 725–746.

Way, N. (2006). The cultural practice of close friendships among urban adolescents in the United States. In X. Chen, D. French, & B. Schneider (Eds.), *Peer relationships in cultural context* (pp. 403–425). New York: Cambridge University Press.

Weisz, J. R., Suwanlert, S., Chaiyasit, W., Weiss, B., Walter, B. R., & Anderson, W. W. (1988). Thai and American perspectives on over-and undercontrolled child behavior problems: Exploring the threshold model among parents, teachers, and psychologists. *Journal of Consulting and Clinical Psychology, 56,* 601–609.

Whiting, B. B., & Edwards, C. P. (1988). *Children of different worlds.* Cambridge, MA: Harvard University Press.

Wu, P., Robinson, C. C., Yang, C., Hart, C. H., Olsen, S. F., Porter, C. L., et al. (2002). Similarities and differences in mothers' parenting of preschoolers in China and the United States. *International Journal of Behavioral Development, 26,* 481–491.

Xu, Y., Farver, J. M., Chang, L., Zhang, Z., & Yu, L. (2007). Moving away or fitting in? Understanding shyness in Chinese children. *Merrill-Palmer Quarterly, 53,* 527–556.

Zahn-Waxler, C., Friedman, R. J., Cole, P. M., Mizuta, I., & Hiruma, N. (1996). Japanese and United States preschool children's responses to conflict and distress. *Child Development, 67,* 2462–2477.

CHAPTER NINE

The Social Development of Immigrant Children: A Focus on Asian and Hispanic Children in the United States

Charissa S. L. Cheah and Christy Y. Y. Leung

Although the United States is the prototypical "nation of immigrants" and the focus of this chapter, it is important to note that increased migration is a global trend. Immigrants comprise more than 15% of the population in more than 50 counties (Greenberg, Haskins, & Fremstad, 2004; United Nations, 2004). According to the *International Migration 2006* report, 3% (191 million) of the 6.5 billion world population lived outside their country of birth in 2005 (United Nations, 2006). About 60% of the migrant population resided in more developed countries, most of them in Europe (64 million), followed by Asia (53 million) and North America (45 million). As reviewed throughout this chapter, context plays an important role in the social development of immigrant children.

The field is ripe for more research to be conducted on immigrant children in different countries to enhance our understanding of their social development. Although some research on this topic is being conducted around the world, inconsistencies in methods and findings across studies make it difficult to compile a cohesive picture of factors that impact immigrant children's social development from a multicultural perspective. Illustrative of this point are studies that have been conducted on immigrant Asian and Hispanic children and their families in the United States, where more data are currently available to draw from. Accordingly, our chapter will focus on these two groups. As seen in this chapter, general conceptual and methodological issues pertaining to research focusing on social development in these two populations have broader implications for research

The Wiley-Blackwell Handbook of Childhood Social Development, Second Edition, edited by Peter K. Smith and Craig H. Hart
© 2011 by Blackwell Publishing Ltd.

on a variety of immigrant groups. As this area of scholarship matures, it is our hope that future chapters of this nature can address the broader global view.

Growing Population of Asian and Hispanic Immigrant Children in the United States

There has been a major demographic shift in the U.S. population over recent decades (U.S. Census Bureau, 2004). The minority population is predicted to account for half of the U.S. population by the year 2050 (Council of Economic Advisors, 1998), largely due to immigration. In 2000, about 11% of the U.S. population– 32 million people– were foreign born, and Asians and Hispanics were the two fastest growing ethnic groups (U.S. Census Bureau, 2004). Importantly, children today are more likely to be a member of an ethnic minority than of a majority group (Hernandez, 2004); 35.0% of Hispanics and 27.1% of Asians are under the age of 18, compared with 23.0% of European Americans (U.S. Census Bureau, 2004). As of 2005, nearly one in four children lived in immigrant families, with 84% of these children being of Asian or Hispanic origin (Hernandez, Denton, & Macartney, 2007).

Despite this quickly advancing demographic shift in the U.S. population, commensurate research on these immigrant populations has yet to occur. Most of the existing research on immigrant children targets their academic development, and focuses on older children and adolescents. Research on *young immigrant children's social and emotional development* from a developmental perspective is very limited (Chase-Lansdale, D'Angelo, & Palacios, 2007; García Coll & Magnuson, 1997; Marks, Patton, & García Coll, 2010; Sam, 2006). As noted earlier, the available research focuses primarily on immigrant Asian and Hispanic children, which will be used to illustrate the major themes of this chapter that might inform the examination of other immigrant groups in future studies.

In this chapter, we first discuss the family structure and cultural values of Asian and Hispanic immigrants as may be pertinent to these children's social and emotional development. Then, we highlight immigrant-related issues that are important to children's social and emotional development that are illustrated by research from Asian and Hispanic immigrant populations. Finally, we discuss the implications of these issues and directions for future research. Our desire is to provide readers with a sense of where the major gaps are in the current literature that need to be filled. Following the lead of other researchers in this field, the term *immigrant children* will be used to refer to children who have themselves immigrated to the United States, as well as children who were born in the United States of immigrant parents.

A brief overview of the extant research comparing the social, emotional, and behavioral outcomes of immigrant versus nonimmigrant children and adolescents reveals the difficulties in reconciling inconsistent findings that have been obtained thus far. For example, some research on Asian American adolescents indicates that they may experience greater psychological and social emotional difficulties, including depression, suicidal risk, and anxiety, than their European American counterparts (e.g., Bae & Brekke 2003; Okazaki, 1997; Rhee, Chang, & Rhee, 2003; Stewart, Rao, & Bond, 1998; Sue, Mak

& Sue, 1998; Zhou, Peverly, Xin, Huang, & Wang, 2003). Farver, Kwak, and Lee (1995) reported that although Korean American children scored higher on cognitive measures than Anglo-American children, they were less socially skilled than their Anglo-American peers. However, other studies report no significant differences between these groups. For example, Huntsinger, Jose, and Larson (1998) found that second-generation middle-class Chinese American school-aged children did not differ from their European American peers on teacher-rated peer acceptance, and withdrawn and social behavioral problems. Moreover, Chinese American children were rated by teachers as being lower on anxious and depressive symptoms than their European American counterparts, although Chinese American parents rated their children as higher on social problems than European American parents.

Similar inconsistencies have been reported for Hispanic children. For example, immigrant Mexican American youth reported significantly higher social anxiety and loneliness than their U.S.-born Mexican American peers (Polo & López, 2009). When comparing English- and Spanish-speaking preschoolers enrolled in Head Start on emotional understanding, Downs, Strand, and Cerna (2009) found that growth in the ability to recognize and understand others' emotions likely follows a similar developmental trajectory in both groups of children, but Spanish-speaking children lagged behind their English-speaking peers. Emotion understanding in both groups was consistently positively related to teacher ratings of the children's prosocial behavior and emotion recognition ability.

In contrast, other studies report better behavioral outcomes among non-U.S.-born compared to U.S.-born Hispanic youth (Dawson & Williams, 2008; Ortega, Rosenheck, Alegría, & Desai, 2000). Although first- and second-generation Hispanic immigrants performed more poorly than in nonimmigrant families in cognitive and language skills, they excelled by comparison in socioemotional skills and behavior. First-generation immigrant children even showed more advanced development than second-generation in many cases, providing some evidence for an immigrant advantage in the early years (De Feyter & Winsler, 2009).

These inconsistent findings highlight the need for more research regarding the social development of immigrant children. In order to understand variations within these two cultural groups with regard to immigrant children's social development, it is important to review general cultural values that guide the socialization of these children, and to recognize the immigrant-related issues that are pertinent to their social and emotional development.

Family Structure and Cultural Values of Asian and Hispanic Immigrants

Asian immigrants

The U.S. Census Bureau does not restrict its definition of the term *Asian* to national origin, but also includes racial identification. According to Census 2000, the term *Asian* refers to people who have their origins in East Asia, Southeast Asia, or the Indian subcontinent, for example Chinese, Korean, Japanese, Vietnamese, Filipino, Thai, Asian Indian, Pakistani, Burmese, Hmong, and other Asians (Barnes & Bennett, 2002; Grieco & Cassidy, 2001).

Asian Americans represent a diverse group of people who have considerable within-group heterogeneities in terms of traditions, religions, and reasons for migration, educational attainment, and socioeconomic status (Shields & Behrman, 2004; Zhou & Xiong, 2005). Specifically, immigrants from China, India, Japan, Korea, and the Philippines, who are often perceived as the "model minority," tend to achieve high levels of educational attainment and occupational success in the United States (Shields & Behrman, 2004). On the other hand, a large portion of immigrants from Southeast Asian countries such as Cambodia, Laos, Thailand, and Vietnam have entered the United States as refugees, or under conditions of duress. They tend to have low levels of education and work as low-skilled laborers in the United States (Shields & Behrman, 2004).

Despite the within-group heterogeneity, Asian Americans share some similarities in their collectivistic orientation, family structure, and cultural values. Children of Asian American families are more likely than their non-Hispanic European American counterparts to live in a two-parent and multigenerational household with a larger family size on average (Zhou & Xiong, 2005). They endorse a value of "family as center," indicating the importance of family and a strong emphasis on interdependence among family members (Chao & Tseng, 2002). Within the Asian American family, the interdependent construct of the self emphasizes people's relations with others within harmonious relationships (Suizzo et al., 2008), even among young children (Chao, 1995). There tends to be a strong focus on hierarchy in the family (favoring males). Moreover, solemnity, self-control, and behavioral restraint are valued (Baptiste, 2005; Cheah & Rubin, 2004; Park & Cheah, 2005).

Hispanic immigrants

Hispanic origin and race are considered by the U.S. Census Bureau as two separate and distinct concepts in order to better reflect the diversity in country of origin. According to Census 2000, the term *Hispanic* refers to people who originate from Cuba, Mexico, Puerto Rico, South or Central America, or other Spanish cultures regardless of race (Grieco & Cassidy, 2001). This term represents a group of Spanish-speaking people sharing a history of colonization by Spain. These various groups of Hispanics have entered the United States for widely different reasons, such as political and economic unrest, family reunion, employment opportunities, and educational purposes (Guzmán, 2001; Harwood, Leyendecker, Carlson, Asencio, & Miller, 2002). Thus, Hispanic Americans represent a diverse group of people who have considerable within-group heterogeneity in terms of their educational level and socioeconomic status (Grieco & Cassidy, 2001; Guzmán, 2001). Specifically, immigrants from Cuba, Puerto Rico, the Dominican Republic, and Central America tend to attain comparatively high levels of education, whereas those from Mexico generally have lower levels. In terms of socioeconomic status, immigrants from Cuba have the lowest poverty rate, whereas immigrants from Puerto Rico have the highest.

Nonetheless, Hispanic Americans share some within-group commonalities in their collectivistic orientation, family structure, and cultural values relevant to children's social development. Compared with their European American counterparts, Hispanic American families are composed of a larger proportion of extended family members. Hispanic families in the United States have been said to endorse two core cultural values relevant to socialization within the family and children's development, specifically, *respeto* and *familismo*. *Respeto* refers to respectfulness, whereas *familismo* refers to a sense of loyalty, reciprocity, and solidarity toward family members and a belief that the family is an extension of the self (Harwood et al., 2002). Consistent with the Hispanic cultural value of *familismo*, the primary parenting socialization goal of Hispanic parents was found to be fostering positive family relationships with their children (Harwood et al., 2002).

Immigrant socialization processes

The culture-specific commonalities in the interdependent orientation, family structure, and cultural values among immigrant Asian as well as immigrant Hispanic families have important implications for their socialization processes, and in turn their children's social, emotional, and behavioral development (Chao & Tseng, 2002; Harwood et al., 2002). In their integrative model of the development of minority children, García Coll et al. (1996) presented several important reasons for why parenting may function differently for families from different ethnic groups.

First, cultural influences in family structure and co-parenting expectations likely result in differences in parenting roles. For example, immigrant communal social resources are characterized by shared norms and values, reciprocal trust, mutual benefit, and connectedness with others (Fuligni & Yoshikawa, 2003; Grim-Feinberg, 2007; Michael et al., 2008). These social resources can serve as a source of familial and extrafamilial support that assists in the socialization efforts of parents, as well as the monitoring of children's conduct and reporting of children's transgressions by non–family members within the community (Short & Johnston, 1997; Zhou, 1997).

Second, cultural influences on parenting beliefs, attitudes, and values may have direct implications on the use of various parenting strategies, as well as the consequences of these parenting strategies for children's social outcomes (Whiteside-Mansell, Bradley, & McKelvey, 2009). Fung and Lau (2009) found that although Chinese immigrant parent-reported punitive discipline was associated with more child internalizing and externalizing problems overall, the negative effects of physical and verbal punitive discipline were buffered when parents subscribed strongly to an indigenous training ideology. The motivation of nurturing the child toward a cultural ideal of social responsibility may lead children to perceive punitive discipline as reflective of parental concern and involvement rather than acts of hostility and rejection. Importantly, the authors emphasized that neither physical nor punitive verbal discipline was adaptive in the context of indigenous training beliefs; rather, they were less harmful. Importantly, middle-class Chinese immigrant mothers were found to strongly endorse warmth, reasoning, and autonomy granting with their preschoolers (Cheah, Leung, Tahseen, & Schultz, 2009).

Moreover, these practices predicted greater behavioral and attention regulation abilities in these young children, which in turn predicted decreased teacher-rated child socioe-motional and behavioral difficulties. In Chinese society, the preschool child is treated with leniency and indulgence. Young children are considered to be incapable of under-standing things and therefore not punished for misbehavior (Ho, 1989). Instead, a lot of direction and guidance is given regarding the appropriate behavior (Cheah & Rubin, 2003, 2004).

Third, culture influences the parents' views of the child, and expectations for the development of different skills. A qualitative examination of Mexican immigrant and Mexican American families reported that these families helped their young children develop the social skills and concepts required in school, including friendship, sharing (cooperating), and respect. Parents talked about using modeling during family gatherings, and storytelling and other oral traditions (Riojas-Cortex & Flores, 2009). Farver and colleagues (Farver, Kim, & Lee, 1995; Farver, & Lee-Shin, 2000) found that Korean American preschool children tended to engage in lower frequencies of pretend play and shared positive affect during play compared with their Anglo-American counterparts. The authors attributed these findings to Korean values deemphasizing individuality and self-expression, leading to less abandonment of self-consciousness and fewer expressions of inner creativity, both of which are required for pretend play. Moreover, in the Korean context, neutral affect may support emotional restraint, which is encouraged in social contexts. Interestingly, children whose mothers encouraged pretend play in the home because such play is valued in that culture were also more likely to engage in such play with their peers in the preschool setting.

Children's social experiences in the peer group can be both a major source of stress and a developmental asset for immigrant children, including discrepancies in the cultural norms regarding appropriate social behaviors, as described below. However, this research has focused predominantly on adolescents (e.g., García Coll et al., 1996; Zhou et al., 2003). In understanding the role of family and peers in immigrant children's social development and variations within these two overarching cultural groups, it is particularly important to recognize the immigrant-related issues that are pertinent to these children's social and emotional development.

Challenges to Immigrant Children's Social, Emotional, and Behavioral Development

Loss of homeland and significant individuals

The literature suggests that immigrant children are particularly vulnerable to emotional distress when they experience a sudden loss of beloved relatives, close friends, or signifi-cant individuals, as well as homeland and familiar surroundings (Ashworth, 1982; García Coll & Magnuson, 1997). The feeling of loss may be experienced after an extended period of postmigration time, even if not initially (Baptiste, 1993). Moreover, as migration pat-terns change, the issues of separation and reunion also become more complex. Serial migration is practiced by many ethnic groups leaving their home countries in search of economic opportunity (Orellana, Thorne, Chee, & Lam, 2001; Smith, Lalonde, & Johnson, 2004; Suârez-Orozco, Todorova, & Louie, 2002), and is characterized by a staggered pattern of immigration in which parents migrate to the new country first with the children following later. Serial migration typically involves two stages: *separation* as parents migrate to the host country, leaving children behind; and later *reunification* as children join their parents in the host country (Smith et al., 2004).

Another form of serial migration is practiced by some immigrant families, in which they return American-born children to reside in the parents' native country while they work to establish themselves in the new country (Sengupta, 1999). Although not exclusively practiced among Chinese immigrants, recent news and anecdotal reports have raised awareness of this issue among U.S.-born Chinese children who are cared for in China by grandparents, other extended family, or even a foster home setting until the children reach school age, around kindergarten or first grade (Borh & Tse, 2009; Sengupta, 1999). This phenomenon has been termed *reverse migration separation* (Kwong, Chung, Sun, Chou, & Taylor-Shih, 2009) or described as the experiences of *satellite babies in transnational situations* (Borh & Tse, 2009).

Children who are separated from their primary caregivers for a period of time upon migration may show withdrawn behaviors and have problems with trusting their caregivers at reunion. They also report a higher level of depressive symptoms than their counterparts who did not experience separation at migration (Suárez-Orozco et al., 2002). Separation from the primary caregivers is stressful for children, due to the formation of selective attachments during this developmental period (Suárez-Orozco et al., 2002). The added issue with reverse migration is that attachment bonds may be disrupted at least twice, first with the biological parent, and then again with the caregiver in China. Importantly, children's ability to cope with the loss of significant individuals during migration may be shaped by their temperament, cognitive appraisal of the separation, attribution style, and locus of control (García Coll & Magnuson, 1997). However, there is little systematic study that has assessed the psychological and socioemotional impact of migration-related separation on children, although many social and medical service providers anecdotally report increased adjustment, depression, and attentional disorders seen in the children upon reunification with their parents (Kwong et al., 2009).

Learning a new language

Learning to communicate in English is one of the immediate challenges for immigrants emigrating from non-English-speaking countries to the United States. Studies show that children of Southeast Asian, Chinese, Mexican, and Central American immigrant families are disadvantaged with regard to learning English (Shields & Behrman, 2004; Zhou & Xiong, 2005). These children are likely to have parents who are non–English speakers and to live in linguistically isolated households where no one over the age of 13 speaks English very well (Hernandez, Denton, & Macartney, 2010). Importantly, these immigrant children have to learn to communicate in English to adapt well and make new friends at school. Language proficiency is, therefore, expected to be associated with the social and emotional adjustment of these immigrant children (García Coll & Magnuson, 1997; Zhou & Xiong, 2005).

Consistent with this expectation, English proficiency has been found to be associated with higher self-esteem and fewer depressive symptoms among Latino immigrants (Rumbaut, 1994) and lower internalizing distress among Mexican American youth (Polo & López, 2009). Having difficulties communicating in English outside the home significantly interferes with these children's school adjustment and minimizes their social opportunities with others, putting them at risk for psychological distress (Polo & López, 2009). Thus, being able to master English fluently is associated with immigrant children's adaptation to mainstream society and their socioemotional adjustment. In examining language status as an acculturative stressor throughout the early elementary school years among Latino children, Dawson and Williams (2008) found that students who were not English proficient at the end of the first grade had significantly higher rates of externalizing symptoms than their English-proficient counterparts by the end of the third grade.

Furthermore, bilingual skills are shown to be strongly associated with better adjustment and lower psychopathology among immigrant children (e.g., Toppelberg, Medrano, Pena Morgens, & Nieto-Castanon, 2002), suggesting that these children are at an advantage if they are able to communicate in both English and their language of origin. Nevertheless, because the language barrier is one of the most immediate and obvious challenges faced by immigrant families, it is often examined as a stressor in the acculturation process. It is essential to further examine the unique role of multiple languages in the course of acculturation among immigrant children to fully understand its implication for social and emotional development.

Adjusting to new cultural norms and expectations

An important factor associated with the social and psychological adjustment of immigrant children is acculturation (e.g., Kang, 2006). *Acculturation* generally refers to the process of change in the attitudes and behaviors of immigrant and ethnic minority adults and children due to contact with the new culture (Berry & Kim, 1988). The extent to which cultural beliefs play a role is related to the degree of acculturation of the family. Parents' acculturation may impact their parenting, and consequently children's social and behavioral outcomes. For instance, higher maternal acculturation to the host culture among low-income Mexican immigrant and Mexican American families was related to decreased maternal inconsistent discipline and to reduced levels of child conduct disorder and depression in fourth-grade children (Dumka, Roosa, & Jackson, 1997). Among Korean immigrant mothers, mothers who had an integrated acculturation style engaged in more warmth, reasoning, and encouragement of autonomy compared to mothers who were separated or marginalized from the American culture, and the former were positively associated with child prosocial behaviors (Shin, Bayram Özdemir, Lee, & Cheah, in press). However, the acculturation process may not be uniform across cultural groups or aspects of parenting and socialization goals. For example, Latino American families' acculturation has been shown to have little effect on their feelings of *familismo* (Sabogal et al., 1987). Thus, whereas some culturally valued social behaviors may change over time in the United States, others may maintain their importance.

Immigrant children may also encounter discrepancies between their parents' culture and the mainstream culture (García Coll & Magnuson, 1997). Children are often caught "between two worlds," struggling between two sets of norms. The bicultural conflicts experienced by these immigrant children become more pronounced if their parents strongly maintain aspects of their heritage culture that contradict mainstream cultural norms (Sung, 1985). For example, adolescent children of Chinese immigrants reported difficulty understanding their parents' love because their traditionally distant and formal parent–child relationships contrasted the Western image of affectionate parent–child interactions (Cheah & Jin, 2010; Qin, 2006). Xiong et al.'s (2005) examination of Southeast Asian immigrant families revealed that parents believed "a good parent" was someone who provided food, clothing, and cultural education for their children. Adolescents' perceptions of good parents, however, were those who understood their children and verbally expressed their love.

Immigrant children usually become more familiar with mainstream cultural norms than their parents because of their attendance in school, one of the most significant socializing agents in any culture (García Coll & Magnuson, 1997; Sam, 2006). Differences in the parent–child acculturation level may contribute to conflict between the two generations in both Asian American and Hispanic American families (Quintana et al., 2006). Family conflicts become more pronounced over time when immigrant children increasingly endorse mainstream cultural values, whereas their parents continue to maintain heritage cultural values (Johnson, 2007). Family conflicts have also been shown to be a strong negative predictor of immigrant children's psychological, social, and emotional adjustment (Pawliuk et al., 1996; Sam, 2006). Interestingly, Schofield, Parke, Kim, and Coltrane (2008) found that first- and second-generation Mexican father–child acculturation gaps were associated with negative outcomes only when children reported a poor relationship with their fathers, illustrating the protective role of a good parent–child relationship.

Moreover, because immigrant children engage in social interactions with adults and other children from mainstream society most often in the school setting, they are likely to encounter novel, unforeseen social and cultural challenges posed by their majority-culture peers and teachers (Marks et al., 2010). In order to promote the psychological and social aspects of school adjustment of immigrant children, it is essential for parents to socialize their children to understand their ethnic heritages as well as to prepare their children to appropriately interact with peers of other races (Hughes, Rodrigues, Smith, Johnson, & Stevenson, 2006; Marks et al., 2010). Illustrating the effects of teacher–family cultural mismatch, Sirin, Ryce, and Mir (2009) examined the role of first-grade teachers' views of Muslim *immigrant* parents and children. When teachers perceived parents as having discrepant value differences, they rated students more negatively in terms of both academic competence and behavioral problems, even after controlling for student gender and ethnicity, parental education, and school involvement. Thus, the role of family cultural socialization, and the cultural match between parents, peers, and teachers in expectations of social behaviors in predicting immigrant children's social emotional adjustment and development, should also be considered further in future research.

Culture and language brokering

As with other aspects of acculturation, immigrant children usually become more fluent in English than their parents because of their formal language training at school (García Coll & Magnuson, 1997; Sam, 2006). It is quite common for Chinese, Korean, Vietnamese, and Hispanic immigrant children to serve as culture and language brokers for their parents, especially for those parents with limited English proficiency, with lower education levels, and who migrated to the United States at older ages (Chao, 2006; Morales & Hanson, 2005; Tse, 1995; 1996; Weisskirch & Alva, 2002; Zhou, 1997). Culture and language brokers serve as cross-cultural mediators and translators between parents and the mainstream society (McQuillan & Tse, 1995; Morales & Hanson, 2005; Weisskirch & Alva, 2002). Many Chinese American and Hispanic American adolescents feel obligated to serve as culture and language brokers to help their parents because of the value placed on familial relationships and obligation in their cultures (Chao, 2006; García Coll & Magnuson, 1997; Wu & Kim, 2009).

The experience of language brokering appeared to enhance these adolescents' sense of responsibility, maturity, efficacy, and self-esteem as well as fostered positive parent–child relationships (Chao, 2006; McQuillan & Tse, 1995). On the other hand, parents have to rely on their children to communicate with the mainstream society in important contexts (e.g., school and medical settings), undermining their roles as authority figures (Menjívar, 2000). Children are consequently involved in adult business that is usually otherwise restricted from them (Baptiste, 1993). The changes in the roles of parent and child can be very stressful for immigrant families, especially for those who are accustomed to parental authority and rigid and distinct generational boundaries in their heritage culture (García Coll & Magnuson, 1997). In fact, previous studies also found that some Asian American and Hispanic American adolescents perceived their role as a culture and language broker as embarrassing and burdening (McQuillan & Tse, 1995; Tse, 1996; Wu & Kim, 2009). Such dissonance and role reversal that undercut parental authority may also generate family conflicts (Trickett & Jones, 2007). The experience of language brokering has been shown to be positively associated with internalizing symptoms among Chinese American and Korean American adolescents (Chao, 2006). However, the research on language brokering has been conducted exclusively on immigrant adolescents, and this is a topic in need of further examination in younger children.

Racial discrimination and prejudice

For immigrant children, the added stress resulting from racial discrimination and prejudice from peers and teachers needs to be considered. Studies have found that Chinese American adolescents report being discriminated against by teachers or other adults at schools (Qin, Way, & Rana, 2008), and racial discrimination is positively associated with behavior problems among Latino American adolescents (Vega, Khoury, Zimmerman, & Gil, 1995). Importantly, immigrant children from different ethnic backgrounds may have varying types of racial discrimination experiences. For example, compared with other ethnic minorities, Asian American adolescents face the highest level of peer racial discrimination, teasing, and harassment related to the "model minority" stereotype, which was associated with more depressive symptoms and lower self-esteem (Alvarez, Juang, & Liang, 2006; Kohatsu et al., 2000; Qin et al., 2008; Rivas-Drake, Hughes, & Way, 2009).

Rumbaut (1994) suggested that Asian and Latino immigrant children who experience racial discrimination and prejudice from peers are less likely to identify with the dominant group or interact with the mainstream culture than those who do not experience racial discrimination and prejudice. Unfortunately, the majority of research examining these processes in immigrant children has focused on adolescents to the neglect of younger children, despite research showing that ethnic minority children as young as 6 years of age report strong ethnic identity and in-group social preferences (Marks, Szalacha, Lamarre, Boyd, & García Coll, 2007).

Thus, the role of racial discrimination, prejudice, teasing, and harassment on immigrant children's coping mechanisms and associated socioemotional outcomes is complex. Immigrant children who live in ethnically diverse areas may have different experiences than those who live in areas with limited ethnic minorities. Thus, more research is needed to further examine the multiple pathways in which immigrant children learn to cope with such potentially negative experiences in mainstream society, and the associated effects on their social and emotional development.

Socioeconomic and other migratory circumstances

According to Census 2000, children in immigrant families are at a substantially higher risk for poverty than children in U.S.-born families (Hernandez, 2004; Shields & Behrman, 2004). Based on recent reports from the National Academy of Sciences, a majority (88.5%) of first-generation Hispanic Americans face multiple socioeconomic challenges, and more than 42% of the children of these first-generation Hispanic American families live in poverty (Tienda & Mitchell, 2006). The high poverty rate of children in immigrant families is a direct consequence of the fact that immigrant parents of certain ethnic groups often have to suffer from low-wage work, limited access to benefits, and a lack of full-time year-round work because of their low educational attainments and English language proficiency (Hernandez et al., 2007, 2010).

Although these parents may have high expectations and strong aspirations for their children to succeed, they face additional challenges in helping their children because of their low education levels and unfamiliarity with the mainstream society (Shields & Behrman, 2004). For example, a recent study found that acculturative stress from these migratory-related experiences was associated with feelings of loneliness, social anxiety, and depressive symptoms among Mexican American middle school children (Polo & López, 2009). Immigrant Mexican parents reported a lack of confidence in their parenting ability due to their language barriers and unfamiliarity with the mainstream society. Importantly, social support promoted the use of warmth and minimized the use of control in parenting among these parents, partly because they reported a stronger sense of parenting efficacy when they received more social support. In turn, the use of parental warmth and control was positively associated with children's socioemotional adjustment (Izzo, Weiss, Shanahan, & Rodriguez-Brown, 2000).

Moreover, the prekindergarten and nursery school enrollment rate of young children in immigrant families from Mexico, Central America, the Dominican Republic, Cambodia, Laos, Thailand, and Vietnam is generally low, often due to their parents' limited financial ability, lack of awareness regarding the benefits of early education experience, and language barriers (Hernandez et al., 2007, 2010). Because quality center-based child care has been shown to benefit preschool-aged children and help prepare them for school, both academically and socially, less use of center-based child care among children in immigrant families compared to children in nonimmigrant families is potentially troubling (Brandon, 2004). Moreover, disproportionately high numbers of Mexican American immigrant children attend low-achieving schools in kindergarten, which places these students at significant risk for problems in academic achievement as well as social and emotional development in the classroom (Crosnoe, 2005).

Many immigrant families from Southeast Asia such as Cambodia, Laos, Thailand, and Vietnam entered the United States as refugees (Shields & Behrman, 2004). Due to the sudden, often involuntary departure from their homeland, these immigrant families often have little preparation and few resources when they enter the United States. Refugee parents may also suffer from posttrauma-related illness, remain isolated from mainstream society, and fail to help their children adapt to mainstream society. Thus, children in refugee families may face additional challenges obtaining adequate support in meeting these expectations and adjusting to the new environment. These children likely also feel additional pressure to succeed at school in order to repay their parents, and encounter racism and discrimination in mainstream society as well as low expectations from teachers about their abilities to achieve at school (Shields & Behrman, 2004; Zhou, 1997). Without adequate help and support during their adaptation process, children of refugees may experience high levels of acculturative stress, feel helpless in meeting their family expectations, and develop feelings of alienation as well as negative attitudes toward mainstream society. Thus, important demographic variables and the specific circumstances of the migration must also be considered when examining these children's social and emotional outcomes.

Limitations and Future Directions

Given the inconsistent findings regarding the social outcomes of immigrant children found in the literature, we outline some existing gaps in the research and offer suggestions for future directions.

Methodological limitations

For most of the studies reviewed, the immigration status of immigrant children (i.e., first generation or second generation) is not provided or directly assessed as an independent variable. Assessments of acculturation and ethnic identity are also often not administered due to the young age of the child, making it difficult to ascertain the role of cultural stability and change in immigrant children's social development and skills (Marks et al., 2010). Furthermore, longitudinal studies are rare in this area of research but are greatly needed to examine how the social development of immigrant children varies across time, as children acculturate and develop (Sam, 2006).

Regarding the social, emotional, and behavioral outcomes examined, criticisms have been raised regarding the use of standardized measures in immigrant populations without empirical support for cross-cultural equivalence (Leung & Barnett, 2008). The majority of standardized measures have been developed using Western, middle-class populations; these measures are culturally specific to the European American culture (Padilla & Borsato, 2008) but are assumed to be applicable to diverse immigrant populations (Pernice, 1994). However, this assumption may be invalid or should at least be empirically assessed. Thus, researchers need to empirically validate the cross-cultural equivalence of the measures (Prediger, 1994; van de Vijver, 2003), ensuring that the meaning and subjective experiences of the construct measured and the scales utilized are interpreted similarly across cultures (Gil & Bob, 1999).

Moreover, given that the primary languages of immigrant families may not be English, the use of translated measures in this research is common. To address potential translation issues, Brislin (1980) suggested the emic-etic method where some items are described using concepts indigenous to specific cultures when necessary (emic), whereas other items are described by imposing external criteria when appropriate (etic). Moreover, all translations should be completed with an established, comprehensive, multistep translation and validation process such as the translation and back-translation method in order to ensure the quality and accuracy of the translation (Harkness, 2003; Pena, 2007). The original and translated versions of the measures should demonstrate linguistic, functional, cultural, and metric equivalences to guard against validity threat (Pena, 2007; Pernice, 1994).

A strengths approach

The current review has mainly examined migration as a stressful experience, focusing on the associated negative impacts and immigrant children's adjustment and adaptation. This bias reflects the approach taken by a majority of the existing research. According to the assimilation or culturally deficient models (e.g., Gordon, 1964; Senn, 1975), the ethnic and cultural background of immigrant children may impede their assimilation process into the mainstream culture and thus result in difficulties in their interactions with others. Additionally, the different or conflictual expectations and standards that adults and peers hold in the home and the school place additional stress on these children, which may lead to confusion, frustration, and distress (Chen & Tse, 2008). However, immigration may be a positive, growth-enhancing experience for immigrant children including building strong, positive cultural and ethnic identities and traditions; inspirations for achievement; close and cohesive family functioning; and bilingualism (Chase-Lansdale et al., 2007; García Coll & Magnuson, 1997).

From the pluralist-constructivist perspective (Conzen et al., 1992; García Coll et al., 1996; Zhou, 1997), ethnicity and mixed cultural backgrounds can serve as resources for adaptive development. Children can learn diverse and complementary values such as interpersonal cooperation, responsibility, and independent skills (e.g., Fuligni, 2001), and additional coping strategies and behaviors from various experiences and interactions with culturally different others. Thus, cultural strengths may also be displayed, and children also acquire social skills and coping mechanisms and learn adaptive skills in these interaction contexts. Chen and Tse (2008) argued that the integration of these different values and norms may be particularly beneficial for the development of social competence in children because of the importance of maintaining a balance between pursuing one's own goals and establishing group harmony during peer interactions in most cultures. Thus, when adequately supported, bicultural children might engage in a process of construction, incorporate different social behavioral attributes, and construct new strategies to function flexibly and effectively in different settings. Consequently, these children might even have an advantage over others in learning various skills that are necessary for the attainment of peer acceptance and approval. This perspective has received increasing attention (Chen & Tse, 2008; Hong, Morris, Chiu, & Benet-Martinez, 2000).

Moreover, social capital appears to serve as a protective factor providing essential socioeconomic resources and minimizing the negative effect of poverty for immigrant families. Studies have shown that despite their low socioeconomic status, immigrant Hispanic and Asian children living in immigrant communities or neighborhoods have fewer emotional behavioral problems and better school performance (Fuligni & Yoshikawa, 2003; Georgiades, Boyle, & Duku, 2007). Cultural knowledge helps children develop social skills needed to succeed in school (Moreno & Perez-Granado, 2002). Social emotional competencies are part of a child's fund of knowledge, cultural knowledge acquired through the daily interactions within the home and community (Riojas-Cortex & Flores, 2009). Knight, Bernal, and Carlo (1995) examined young Latino children's cooperative, competitive, and individualistic behaviors and found that cooperative behavior, such as sharing and working together, is valued within Latino families. However, second- and third-generation Latino children demonstrate a preference toward competitive and individualistic behaviors. For both Asian and Hispanic children, politeness and consideration are valued prosocial behaviors that demonstrate social understanding, which is the child's ability to ascertain other's feelings and intentions within a social context (Chao, 1995; Riojas-Cortex & Flores, 2009). Also, the form of social control within the immigrant community may help enforce the endorsement of traditional family values and parenting practices, as well as children's conformity and obedience (Fuligni & Yoshikawa, 2003; Zhou, 1997).

Therefore, future study should incorporate a developmental strengths-based approach to examine how children's individual characteristics, relationships, and social contexts may lead to enhanced coping skills, life experiences, psychological benefits, and social competence (Chase-Lansdale et al., 2007; García Coll & Magnuson, 1997; Sam, 2006). Further examinations of the interactions among specific characteristics of children and families, their social and physical contexts, and public policies that affect them in predicting immigrant children's social development are essential. Findings regarding both risk and protective factors can be applied to educate policy makers about the importance of providing services and interventions to enhance the social and emotional adjustment of immigrant children. These findings can also be used to guide community, regional, and national planning of policy development, welfare reform, and advocacy regarding the adaptation and healthy social development of immigrant children and their families around the world.

References

Alvarez, A. N., Juang, L., & Liang, C. T. (2006). Asian Americans and racism: When bad things happen to "model minorities." *Cultural and Diversity and Ethnic Minority Psychology*, *12*, 477–492.

Ashworth, M. (1982). The cultural adjustment of immigrant children in English Canada. In R. C. Nann (Ed.), *Uprooting and surviving* (pp. 77–83). Boston: Reidel.

Bae, S.-W., & Brekke, J. (2003). The measurement of self-esteem among Korean Americans: A cross-ethnic study. *Cultural Diversity & Ethnic Minority Psychology*, *9*(1), 16–33.

Baptiste, D. A. (1993). Immigrant families, adolescents, and acculturation: Insights for therapists. *Marriage and Family Review*, *19*, 341–363.

Baptiste, D. A. (2005). Family therapy with East Indian immigrant parents rearing children in the United States: Parental concerns, therapeutic issues, and recommendations. *Contemporary Family Therapy: An International Journal*, *27*(3), 345–366.

Barnes, J. S., & Bennett, C. E. (2002). The Asian population: 2000. *Census 2000 brief.* Retrieved from http://www.census.gov/prod/2002pubs/c2kbr01-16.pdf

Berry, J. W., & Kim, U. (1988). Acculturation and mental health. In P. R. Dasen, J. W. Berry, & N. Sartorius (Eds.), *Health and cross-cultural psychology: Toward applications* (pp. 207–236). Newbury Park, CA: Sage.

Bohr, Y., & Tse, C. (2009). Satellite babies in transnational families: A study of parents' decision to separate from their infants. *Infant Mental Health Journal*, *30*(3), 265–286.

Brandon, P. D. (2004). The child care arrangements of preschool-age children in immigrant families in the United States. *International Migration*, *42*(1), 65–87.

Brislin, R. (1980). Translation and content analysis of oral and written materials. In H. C. Triandis & J. W. Berry (Eds.), *Handbook of cross-cultural psychology: Vol. 2. Methodology* (pp. 389–444). Boston: Allyn & Bacon.

Chao, R. K. (1995). Chinese and European American cultural models of the self reflected in mothers' childrearing beliefs. *Ethos*, *23*(3), 328–354.

Chao, R. K. (2006). The prevalence and consequences of adolescents' language brokering for their immigrant parents. In M. H. Bornstein & L. R. Cote (Eds.), *Acculturation and parent-child relationships: Measurement and development* (pp. 271–296). Mahwah, NJ: Erlbaum.

Chao, R. K., & Tseng, V. (2002). Parenting of Asians. In M. H. Bornstein (Ed.), *Handbook of parenting* (2nd ed., Vol. *4*, pp. 59–93). Hillsdale, NJ: Erlbaum.

Chase-Lansdale, P., D'Angelo, A., & Palacios, N. (2007). A multidisciplinary perspective on the development of young children in immigrant families. In J. E. Lansford, K. Deater-Deckard, & M. H. Bornstein (Eds.), *Immigrant families in contemporary society* (pp. 137–156). New York: Guilford Press.

Cheah, C. S. L., Leung, C. Y. Y., Tahseen, M., & Schultz, D. (2009). Authoritative parenting among immigrant Chinese mothers of preschoolers. *Journal of Family Psychology*, *23*(3), 311–320.

Cheah, C. S. L., & Li, J. (2010). Parenting of young immigrant Chinese children: Challenges facing their social-emotional and intellectual development. In E. L. Grigorenko & R. Takanishi (Eds.), *Immigration, diversity, and education* (pp. 225–241). New York: Routledge.

Cheah, C. S. L., & Rubin, K. H. (2004). European American and Mainland Chinese mothers' responses to aggression and social withdrawal in preschoolers. *International Journal of Behavioral Development, 28*(1), 83–94.

Cheah, C. S. L., & Rubin, K. H. (2003). European American and Mainland Chinese mothers' socialization beliefs regarding preschoolers' social skills. *Parenting: Science and Practice, 3*(1), 1–21.

Chen, X., & Tse, H. (2008). Social functioning and adjustment in Canadian-born children with Chinese and European backgrounds. *Developmental Psychology, 44*(4), 1184–1189.

Conzen, K. N., Gerber, D. A., Morawska, E., Pozzetta, G. E., & Vecoli, R. J. (1992). The invention of ethnicity: A perspective from the U.S.A. *Journal of American Ethnic History, 11*, 3–41.

Council of Economic Advisors. (1998). Changing America: Indicators of social and economic well-being by race and Hispanic origin. Retrieved from http://www.gpoaccess.gov/eop/ca/pdfs/ca.pdf

Crosnoe, R. (2005). Double disadvantage or signs of resilience? The elementary school contexts of children from Mexican immigrant families. *American Educational Research Journal, 42*(2), 269–303.

Dawson, B. A., & Williams, S. A. (2008). The impact of language status as an acculturative stressor on internalizing and externalizing behaviors among Latino/a children: A longitudinal analysis from school entry through third grade. *Journal of Youth and Adolescence, 37*(4), 399–411.

De Feyter, J. J., & Winsler, A. (2009). The early developmental competencies and school readiness of low-income, immigrant children: Influences of generation, race/ethnicity, and national origins. *Early Childhood Research Quarterly, 24*(4), 411–431.

Downs, A., Strand, P., & Cerna, S. (2007). Emotion understanding in English- and Spanish-speaking preschoolers enrolled in Head Start. *Social Development, 16*(3), 410–439.

Dumka, L. E., Roosa, M. W., & Jackson, K. M. (1997). Risk, conflict, mothers' parenting, and children's adjustment in low-income, Mexican immigrant, and Mexican American families. *Journal of Marriage and the Family, 59*(2), 309–323.

Farver, J. A. M., Kim, Y. K., & Lee, Y. (1995). Cultural differences in Korean- and Anglo-American preschoolers' social interaction and play behaviors. *Child Development, 66*(4), 1088–1099.

Farver, J. A. M., & Lee-Shin, Y. (2000). Acculturation and Korean-American children's social and play behavior. *Social Development, 93*, 316–336.

Fuligni, A. (2001). Family obligation and the academic motivation of adolescents from Asian, Latin American, and European backgrounds. In Fuligni, A. J. (Ed.), *Family obligation and assistance during adolescence: Contextual variations and developmental implications* (pp. 61–75). San Francisco, CA: Jossey-Bass.

Fuligni, A., & Yoshikawa, H. (2003). Socioeconomic resources, parenting, and child development among immigrant families. In M. H. Bornstein & R. H. Bradley (Eds.), *Socioeconomic status, parenting, and child development* (pp. 107–124). Mahwah, NJ: Erlbaum.

Fung, K. J., & Lau, A. S. (2009). Punitive discipline and child behavior problems in Chinese-American immigrant families: The moderating effects of indigenous child-rearing ideologies. *International Journal of Behavioral Development, 33*(6), 520–530.

García Coll, C., Crnic, K., Lamberty, G., Wasik, B. H., Jenkins, R., García, H. V., et al. (1996). An integrative model for the study of development competencies in minority children. *Child Development, 67*, 1891–1914.

García Coll, C., & Magnuson, K. (1997). The psychological experience of immigration: A developmental perspective. In A. Booth, A. C. Crouter, & N. Landale (Eds.), *Immigration and the family: Research and policy on U.S. immigrants* (pp. 91–131). Mahwah, NJ: Erlbaum.

Georgiades, K., Boyle, M., & Duku, E. (2007). Contextual influences on children's mental health and school performance: The moderating effects of family immigrant status. *Child Development, 78*(5), 1572–1591.

Gil, E. F., & Bob, S. (1999). Culturally competent research: An ethical perspective. *Clinical Psychological Review, 19*(1), 45–55.

Gordon, M. M. (1964). *Assimilating in American life: The role of race, religion, and national origins.* Now York: Oxford University Press.

Grieco, E. M., & Cassidy, R. C. (2001). Overview of race and Hispanic origin 2000. *Census 2000 brief.* Retrieved from http://www.census.gov/population/ www/cen2000/briefs.html

Grim-Feinberg, K. (2007). Strengthening social capital through bilingual competence in a transnational migrant community: Mexicans in upstate New York. *International Migration, 45*(1), 177–208.

Guzmán, B. (2001). The Hispanic population. *Census 2000 brief.* Retrieved from http://www.census.gov/prod/2001pubs/c2kbr01-3.pdf

Harkness, J. A. (2003). Questionnaire translation. In J. A. Harkness, F. J. R. van de Vijver, & P. P. Mohler (Eds.), *Cross-cultural survey methods* (pp. 35–56). Hoboken, NJ: Wiley.

Harwood, R., Leyendecker, B., Carlson, V., Asencio, M., & Miller, A. (2002). Parenting among Latino families in the U.S. In M. H. Bornstein (Ed.), *Handbook of parenting* (2nd ed., Vol. 4, pp. 21–46). Hillsdale, NJ: Erlbaum.

Haskins, R., Greenberg, M., & Fremstad, S. (2004). Federal policy for immigrant children: Room for common ground? *The Future of Children, 14*(2), 1–6.

Hernandez, D. (2004). Demographic change and the life circumstances of immigrant families. *Future of Children, 14*(2), 17–47.

Hernandez, D. J., Denton, N. A., & Macartney, S. E. (2007). Family circumstances of children in immigrant families: Looking to the future of America. In J. E. Lansford, K. Deater-Deckard, & M. H. Bornstein (Eds.), *Immigrant families in contemporary society* (pp. 9–29). New York: Guilford Press.

Hernandez, D. J., Denton, N. A., & Macartney, S. E. (2010). Children of immigrants and the future of America. In E. L. Grigorenko & R. Takanishi (Eds.), *Immigration, diversity, and education* (pp. 7–25). New York: Routledge.

Ho, D. Y. F. (1989). Continuity and variation in Chinese patterns of socialization. *Journal of Marriage and the Family, 51*, 149–163.

Hong, Y., Morris, M., Chiu, C., & Benet-Martínez, V. (2000). Multicultural minds: A dynamic constructivist approach to culture and cognition. *American Psychologist, 55*(7), 709–720.

Hughes, D., Rodrigues, J., Smith, E., Johnson, D., & Stevenson, H. (2006). Parents' ethnic-racial socialization practices: A review of research and directions for future study. *Developmental Psychology, 42*(5), 747–770.

Huntsinger, C. S., Jose, P. E., & Larson, S. L. (1998). Do parent practices to encourage academic competence influence the social adjustment of young European American and Chinese American children? *Developmental Psychological, 34*(4), 747–756.

Izzo, C., Weiss, L., Shanahan, T., & Rodriguez-Brown, F. (2000). Parental self-efficacy and social support as predictors of parenting practices and children's socioemotional adjustment in Mexican immigrant families. *Journal of Prevention & Intervention in the Community, 20*(1–2), 197–213.

Johnson, M. (2007). The social ecology of acculturation: Implications for child welfare services to children of immigrants. *Children and Youth Services Review, 29*(11), 1426–1438.

Kang, S. M. (2006). Measurement of acculturation, scale formats, and language competence: Their implications for adjustment. *Journal of Cross-Cultural Psychology, 37*, 669–693.

Knight, B., & Hughes, D. (1995). Developing social competence in the preschool years. *Australian Journal of Early Childhood, 20*(2), 13–19.

Kohatsu, E. L., Dulay, M., Lam, C., Concepcion, W., Perez, P., Lopez, C., et al. (2000). Using racial identity theory to explore racial mistrust and interracial contact among Asian Americans. *Journal of Counseling and Development, 14*, 421–439.

Kwong, K., Chung, H., Sun, L., Chou, J., & Taylor-Shih, A. (2009). Factors associated with reverse-migration separation among a cohort of low-income Chinese immigrant families in New York city. *Social Work in Health Care, 48*(3), 348–359.

Leung, C. Y. Y., & Barnett, J. E. (2008). Multicultural assessment and ethical practice. *Independent Practitioner, 28*(3), 139–143.

Marks, A. K., Patton, F., & García Coll, C. (2010). More than the A-B-Cs and 1-2-3s: The importance of family cultural socialization and ethnic identity development for children of immigrants' early school success. In E. L. Grigorenko & R. Takanishi (Eds.), *Immigration, diversity, and education* (pp. 242–258). New York: Routledge.

Marks, A. K., Szalacha, L. A., Lamarre, M., Boyd, M. J., & García Coll, C. (2007). Emerging ethnic identity and interethnic group social preferences in middle childhood: Findings from the Children of Immigrants Development in Context (CIDC) study. *International Journal of Behavioral Development, 31*(5), 501–513.

McQuillan, J., & Tse, L. (1995). Child language brokering in linguistic minority communities: Effects on cultural interaction, cognition, and literacy. *Language and Education, 9*, 195–215.

Menjivar, C. (2000). *Fragmented ties: Salvadorian immigrant networks in American.* Berkeley: University of California Press.

Michael, Y., Farquhar, S., Wiggins, N., & Green, M. (2008). Findings from a community-based participatory prevention research intervention designed to increase social capital in Latino and African American communities. *Journal of Immigrant & Minority Health, 10*(3), 281–289.

Morales, A., & Hanson, W. (2005). Language brokering: An integrative review of the literature. *Hispanic Journal of Behavioral Sciences, 27*(4), 471–503.

Moreno, F., & Neto, F. (2002). Gender stereotypes among gypsy children. *Psicologia Educação Cultura, 6*(1), 203–223.

Okazaki, S. (1997). Sources of ethnic difference between Asian American and White American college students on measures of depression and social anxiety. *Journal of Abnormal Psychology, 106*, 52–60.

Orellana, M., Thorne, B., Chee, A., & Lam, W. (2001). Transnational childhoods: The participation of children in processes of family migration. *Social Problems, 48*(4), 572–591.

Ortega, A., Rosenheck, R., Alegría, M., & Desai, R. (2000). Acculturation and the lifetime risk of psychiatric and substance use disorders among Hispanics. *Journal of Nervous and Mental Disease, 188*(11), 728–735.

Padilla, A. M., & Borsato, G. N. (2008). Issues in culturally appropriate assessment. In L. A. Suzuki, J. G. Ponterotto, & P. J. Meller (Eds.), *Handbook of multicultural assessment: Clinical, psychological, and educational applications* (3rd ed., pp. 5–21). San Francisco: Jossey-Bass.

Park, S., & Cheah, C. (2005). Korean mothers' proactive socialization beliefs regarding preschoolers' social skills. *International Journal of Behavioral Development, 29*(1), 24–34.

Pawliuk, N., Grizenko, N., Chan-Yip, A., Gantous, P., Mathew, J., & Nguyen, D. (1996). Acculturation style and psychological functioning in children of immigrants. *American Journal of Orthopsychiatry, 66*(1), 111–121.

Pena, E. D. (2007). Lost in translation: Methodological considerations in cross-cultural research. *Child Development, 78*(4), 1255–1264.

Pernice, R. (1994). Methodological issues in research with refugees and immigrants. *Professional Psychology: Research and Practice, 25*(3), 207–213.

Polo, A., & López, S. (2009). Culture, context, and the internalizing distress of Mexican American youth. *Journal of Clinical Child & Adolescent Psychology, 38*(2), 273–285.

Qin, D. (2006). "Our child doesn't talk to us anymore": Alienation in immigrant Chinese families. *Anthropology & Education Quarterly, 37*(2), 162–179.

Qin, D. B., Way, N., & Rana, M. (2008). The "model minority" and their discontent: Examining peer discrimination and harassment of Chinese American immigrant youth. In H. Yoshikawa & N. Way (Eds.), *Beyond the family: Contexts of immigrant children's development: New directions for child and adolescent development* (pp. 27–42). Danvers, MA: Wiley Periodicals.

Quintana, S., Aboud, F., Chao, R., Contreras-Grau, J., Cross, W., Hudley, C., et al. (2006). Race, ethnicity, and culture in child development: Contemporary research and future directions. *Child Development, 77*(5), 1129–1141.

Rhee, S., Chang, J., & Rhee, J. (2003). Acculturation, communication patterns, and self-esteem among Asian and Caucasian American adolescents. *Adolescence, 38*, 749–768.

Riojas-Cortez, M., & Flores, B. (2009). *Sin olvidar a los padres*: Families collaborating within school and university partnerships. *Journal of Latinos & Education, 8*(3), 231–239.

Rivas-Drake, D., Hughes, D., & Way, N. (2009). A preliminary analysis of associations among ethnic racial socialization, ethnic discrimination, and ethnic identity among urban sixth graders. *Journal of Research on Adolescence, 19*(3), 558–584.

Rumbaut, R. G. (1994). The crucible within: Ethnic identity, self-esteem, and the segmented assimilation among children of immigrants. *International Migration Review, 28*, 748–794.

Sabogal, F., Marín, G., Otero-Sabogal, R., & Marín, B. (1987). Hispanic familism and acculturation: What changes and what doesn't? *Hispanic Journal of Behavioral Sciences, 9*(4), 397–412.

Sam, D. (2006). Adaptation of children and adolescents with immigrant background: Acculturation or development? In M. H. Bornstein & L. R. Cote (Eds.), *Acculturation and parent-child relationships: Measurement and development* (pp. 97–111). Mahwah, NJ: Erlbaum.

Schofield, T. J., Parke, R. D., Kim, Y., & Coltrane, S. (2008). Bridging the acculturation gap: Parent-child relationship quality as a moderator in Mexican American families. *Developmental Psychology, 44*(4), 1190–1194.

Sengupta, S. (1999, September 15). Women keep garment jobs by sending babies to China. *New York Times*. Retrieved from http://www.nytimes.com

Senn, M. (1975). Insights on the child development movement. *Monographs of the Society for Research in Child Development, 40*(3–4, Serial No. 161), 1–107.

Shields, M. K., & Behrman, R. E. (2004). *Children* of immigrant families: Analysis and recommendations. *Future of Children, 14*(2), 4–15.

Shin, J., Bayram Özdemir, S., Lee, J., & Cheah, C. S. L. (In press). The parenting practices and child social-emotional outcomes of Korean immigrant mothers with different acculturation strategies. *Korean Child Study Journal.*

Short, K. H., & Johnston, C. (1997). Stress, maternal distress, and children's adjustment following immigration: The buffering role of social support. *Journal of Consulting and Clinical Psychology, 65*(3), 494–503.

Sirin, S., Ryce, P., & Mir, M. (2009). How teachers' values affect their evaluation of children of immigrants: Findings from Islamic and public schools. *Early Childhood Research Quarterly, 24*(4), 463–473.

Smith, A., Lalonde, R., & Johnson, S. (2004). Serial migration and its implications for the parent-child relationship: A retrospective analysis of the experiences of the children of Caribbean immigrants. *Cultural Diversity and Ethnic Minority Psychology, 10*(2), 107–122.

Stewart, S. M., Rao, N., & Bond, M. H. (1998). Chinese dimensions of parenting: Broadening Western predictors and outcomes. *International Journal of Psychology, 33*(5), 345–358.

Suârez-Orozco, C., Todorova, I., & Louie, J. (2002). Making up for lost time: The experience of separation and reunification among immigrant families. *Family Process, 41*(4), 625–643.

Sue, D., Mak, W. S., & Sue, D. W. (1998). Ethnic identity. In L. C. Lee & N. W. S. Zane (Eds.), *Handbook of Asian American psychology* (pp. 289–323). Thousand Oaks, CA: Sage.

Suizzo, M., Chen, W., Cheng, C., Liang, A., Contreras, H., Zanger, D., et al. (2008). Parental beliefs about young children's socialization across US ethnic groups: Coexistence of independence and interdependence. *Early Child Development and Care, 178*(5), 467–486.

Sung, B. L. (1985). Bicultural conflicts in Chinese immigrant children. *Journal of Comparative Family Studies, 16*(2), 255–269.

Tienda, M., & Mitchell, F. (Eds.). (2006). *Hispanics and the future of America*. Washington, DC: National Academy Press.

Toppelberg, C. O., Medrano, L., Pena Morgens, L., & Nieto-Castanon, A. (2002). Bilingual children referred for psychiatric services: Associations of language disorders, language skills, and psychopathology. *Journal of the American Academy of Child & Adolescent Psychiatry, 41*, 712–722.

Trickett, E., & Jones, C. (2007). Adolescent culture brokering and family functioning: A study of families from Vietnam. *Cultural Diversity and Ethnic Minority Psychology, 13*(2), 143–150.

Tse, L. (1995). Language brokering among Latino adolescents: Prevalence, attitudes, and school performance. *Hispanic Journal of Behavioral Sciences, 17*, 180–193.

Tse, L. (1996). Language brokering in linguistic minority communities: The case of Chinese- and Vietnamese-American students. *Bilingual Research Journal, 20*, 485–498.

United Nations. (2004). World economic and social survey 2004: International migration. Retrieved from http://www.un.org/esa/policy/wess/wess2004files/part2web/part2web.pdf

United Nations. (2006). International migration 2006 (E.06.XIII.6). Retrieved from http://www.un.org/esa/population/publications/2006Migration_Chart/Migration2006.pdf

U.S. Census Bureau. (2004). Hispanic and Asian Americans increasing faster than overall population. *U.S. Census Bureau News*. Retrieved from http://www.census.gov/Press-Release/www/releases/archives/race/001839.html

van de Vijver, F. J. R. (2003). Bias and equivalence: Cross-cultural perspectives. In J. A. Harkness, F. J. R. van de Vijver, & P. P. Mohler (Eds.), *Cross-cultural survey methods* (pp. 143–155). Hoboken, NJ: Wiley.

Vega, W. A., Khoury, E. L., Zimmerman, R. S., & Gil, A. G. (1995). Cultural conflicts and problem behaviors of Latino adolescents in home and school environments. *Journal of Community Psychology, 23*, 167–179.

Weisskirch, R., & Alva, S. (2002). Language brokering and the acculturation of Latino children. *Hispanic Journal of Behavioral Sciences, 24*(3), 369–378.

Whiteside-Mansell, L., Bradley, R. H., & McKelvey, L. (2009). Parenting and preschool child development: Examination of three low-income U.S. cultural groups. *Journal of Child and Family Studies, 18*(1), 48–60.

Wu, N., & Kim, S. (2009). Chinese American adolescents' perceptions of the language brokering experience as a sense of burden and sense of efficacy. *Journal of Youth and Adolescence, 38*(5), 703–718.

Xiong, Z. B., Eliason, P. A., Detzner, D. F., & Cleveland, M. J. (2005). Southeast Asian immigrants' perceptions of good adolescents and good parents. *Journal of Psychology, 139*, 159–175.

Zhao, Z. (2002). Fertility control in China's past. *Population & Development Review, 28*(4), 751–757.

Zhou, M. (1997). Growing up American: The challenge confronting immigrant children and children of immigrants. *Annual Review of Sociology, 23*, 63–95.

Zhou, M., & Xiong, Y. S. (2005). The multifaceted American experiences of the children of Asian immigrants: Lessons for segmented assimilation. *Ethnic and Racial Studies, 28*(6), 1119–1152.

Zhou, Z., Peverly, S. T., Xin, T., Huang, A. S., & Wang, W. (2003). School adjustment of first-generation Chinese-American adolescents. *Psychology in the Schools, 40*, 71–84.

CHAPTER TEN

Children's Interpersonal Skills and School-Based Relationships

Gary W. Ladd, Becky Kochenderfer-Ladd, and Ann-Margret Rydell

Attending school, adjusting to classroom demands, and making academic progress each school year are among the most challenging tasks that children encounter during childhood. This is because schools and classroom practices (e.g., didactic, small-group, and large-group instruction; teacher- and peer-mediated learning activities; and programmatic curriculum sequences) are designed to challenge children and, in the process, promote their intellectual and interpersonal development.

Only recently have researchers begun to consider the interpersonal challenges of schooling and the possible impact that these factors may have on children's educational adjustment, performance, and progress. For example, as children enter school, they are typically faced with shifting social ecologies, relationships, and social and emotional resources (see Ladd, 1996; Perry & Weinstein, 1998). Beyond basic tasks such as relating with classmates and forming ties with teachers, children find that they are under increasing pressure to compare and evaluate themselves, their abilities, and their achievements to those of age mates. Many of these interpersonal challenges are repeated as children progress through the grades because, as they enter new classrooms, they must reestablish relationships with classmates and teachers. Moreover, it is likely that these challenges are intensified when children change schools or cope with school transitions (see Eccles, Wigfield, & Schiefele, 1998; Ladd, 1996).

Because researchers have focused on children's cognitive and linguistic skills as precursors of school adjustment, they have typically relied on measures of scholastic achievement (language and verbal, math, etc.) rather than indicators of interpersonal success as evidence of how well children have adjusted to school. In this chapter, we take the position

The Wiley-Blackwell Handbook of Childhood Social Development, Second Edition, edited by Peter K. Smith and Craig H. Hart
© 2011 by Blackwell Publishing Ltd.

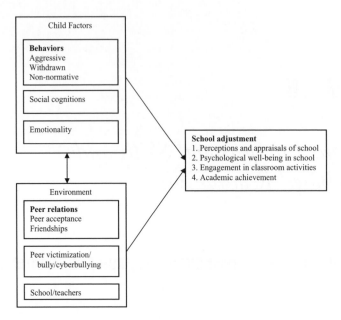

Figure 10.1   Child by environment model: links to school adjustment.

that children's success at classroom interpersonal tasks, as well as the cognitive and linguistic challenges of schooling, is an important precursor of their school adjustment (see Ladd, Herald, & Kochel, 2006). Moreover, it is our contention (see Ladd & Burgess, 2001; Ladd, Kochenderfer, & Coleman, 1997) that a more holistic view of school adjustment is needed – one that includes indicators of children's (a) perceptions and appraisals of school and the classroom environment, (b) psychological and emotional well-being while in school, (c) involvement in and disengagement from classroom activities, and (d) achievement and academic progress (see Figure 10.1).

Thus, to more fully understand the process by which children adjust to school, researchers need to investigate the role of children's classroom interpersonal skills and relationships. Thus far, researchers have tended to focus on features of the child (e.g., behavioral, cognitive, and emotional) and facets of the child's relational environment (e.g., peer and teacher relationships). Although evidence produced by these two investigative agendas implies that children's attributes as well as features of their relational environments are important determinants of school adjustment, much remains to be learned about conjoint influences – that is, how these factors combine to influence school adaptation. For this reason, researchers have begun to utilize child *and* environment models (which are sometimes termed *child by environment models*) as frameworks for guiding research on school adjustment.

Briefly, child and environment models posit that characteristics of the child and the child's environment operate conjointly to affect children's adjustment (see Coie et al., 1993; Ladd, 1989, 2003). Inherent in such models are assumptions about (a) the locus of these factors (e.g., within the child, within the child's the environment, or both), (b) the observable manifestations of such characteristics (e.g., a child's behavioral tendencies, or the supportiveness of peers and teachers), and (c) the way these factors combine or interact to determine children's risk for victimization (see Ladd, 2003, p. 86).

We are of the view that child and environment perspectives constitute valuable tools for (a) generating hypotheses, (b) organizing what is known about the interpersonal (child and school) antecedents of school adjustment, and (c) identifying implications for school-based intervention and prevention programs. Accordingly, our aim for this chapter is to articulate and assess extant evidence that pertains to (a) features of children's interpersonal skills and behaviors that predict their school adjustment; (b) features of children's relationships with classmates or teachers that may facilitate or impede their school adjustment, depending upon the processes (e.g., affirmation or conflict) or instrumental or psychological properties (e.g., stress or support) that children are exposed to in these relationships; and (c) how attributes of the child and his or her relational environment may combine to predict their school adjustment. Last, we consider the implications of these findings for intervention and prevention programs.

Child-Level Factors

Two behavioral propensities – acting in an aggressive or withdrawn manner among classmates – have received considerable investigative attention as child-level predictors of school adjustment. Of these two behavioral styles, aggression more than withdrawal has been a focal point for theory and research on children's social and school adjustment (see Ladd, 2005), and, consequently, more is known about the role of aggressive than withdrawn behavior as an antecedent of children's school adjustment. In the sections that follow, we assess what has been learned empirically about each of these child-level factors.

Aggressive behavior

Initially, studies were undertaken to determine whether preadolescent and adolescents' aggressive acts correlated with certain indicators of their school adjustment, including dropping out of high school, absences and truancy, and remedial instruction and grade retentions (Feldhusen, Thurston, & Benning, 1973; Havighurst, Bowman, Liddle, Matthews, & Pierce, 1962; Kupersmidt & Coie, 1990; Lambert, 1972). Havighurst et al. (1962), for example, found that aggressive preadolescents were less likely to complete high school as compared to their nonaggressive schoolmates. Likewise, Cairns and Cairns (1994) reported that not only did aggressive adolescents drop out of school at a higher rate than did nonaggressive youth, but also their dropout rates exceed those of low–socioeconomic status (SES) youth.

In recent years, concerns about school readiness have motivated investigators to consider whether aggressive behavior affects early adaptation to school, particularly as children enter school or progress from kindergarten through the primary grades. Discoveries indicate that aggression is common during preschool and kindergarten, and is a significant predictor of both early and later school maladjustment (Ladd & Mars, 1986; Ladd &

Price, 1987). Ladd and Price (1987), for example, found that preschoolers who aggressed against many, rather than few, of their classmates were more likely to develop social and learning difficulties during kindergarten. Studies of kindergartners showed that aggressive children were more likely than their nonaggressive counterparts to develop interpersonal problems with classmates and teachers, and maintain these difficulties throughout the primary grades (Ladd & Burgess, 1999). In another study, aggressive children who were identified early in kindergarten and followed over a 2-year period exhibited increases in thought problems, misconduct, and classroom disengagement, and were prone toward underachievement and negative school attitudes. Of these children, those who were chronically aggressive (i.e., remained aggressive over multiple school years) evidenced extreme forms of these and other school adjustment problems.

In sum, these findings and others (see Coie & Dodge, 1998; Parker & Asher, 1987; Parker, Rubin, Price, & DeRosier, 1995; Tolan & Gorman-Smith, 1998) have led many scholars to conclude that aggressive children are at risk for school maladjustment. Importantly, it appears that many children exhibit this risk factor at very early stages in their school careers.

Withdrawn behavior

Less is known about the risks posed by withdrawn as opposed to aggressive behavior for children's school adjustment. It has been hypothesized, however, that social withdrawal prevents children from participating in peer interaction where social abilities are learned and refined (e.g., Parker et al., 1995; Rubin, LeMare, & Lollis, 1990). This lack of engagement, in turn, is seen as inhibiting children's interpersonal maturity and preventing them from mastering social skills that would enable them to adapt to school. Indeed, withdrawn children, as compared to their nonwithdrawn counterparts, tend to have lower mental age scores, underdeveloped problem-solving skills, and egocentric speech. They also make fewer requests of peers, comply during interactions, and are often ignored by peers (Rubin, 1982; Rubin & Borwick, 1984; Rubin, Daniels-Bierness, & Bream, 1984).

Findings from longitudinal studies suggest that withdrawn children are likely to develop school adjustment problems. Data from a long-term follow-up study of Swedish children (Kerr, Lambert, & Bem, 1996) showed that girls who were rated as shy by their mothers at ages 8 to 10, as compared to nonshy girls, developed lower levels of educational attainment. Findings from a 5-year longitudinal study (Ollendick, Greene, Weist, & Oswald, 1990) showed that social withdrawal, assessed at age 10, was associated with dropping out of high school.

Recently, investigators have begun to identify and study subtypes of withdrawn children. Rubin and colleagues, for example, have proposed the subtypes "solitary-passive," "solitary-active," and "reticent" (see Rubin & Coplan, 2004). Other researchers have classified withdrawn children into subtypes termed *passive-anxious*, *active-isolated*, *depressed*, and *unsociable* (see Harrist, Zaia, Bates, Dodge, & Pettit, 1997; Ladd & Burgess, 1999), or *asocial-withdrawn* and *aggressive-withdrawn* (see Ladd & Burgess, 1999; Ledingham & Schwartzman, 1984). What has been discovered is that, among preschoolers, withdrawn behavior coupled with anxiety (e.g., anxious withdrawal or reticence) predicts internalizing problems (Coplan, 2000; Coplan & Rubin, 1998; Coplan, Rubin, Fox, Calkins, & Stewart, 1994). Similarly, grade-school children who are both withdrawn and sad or anxious (e.g., the depressed-withdrawn and anxious-withdrawn subtypes) appear to be at risk for maladjustment. Harrist et al. (1997) found that kindergartners who fit a depressed-withdrawn profile were more likely to have social problems as they moved through the elementary grades. Using growth-curve analyses, Gazelle and Ladd (2003) found that children who manifested stable patterns of anxious-withdrawal during early grade school (from kindergarten to the second grade) tended to have elevated trajectories toward depression by middle childhood. Thus, there is some evidence to suggest that withdrawn behavior coupled with sad or anxious affect is associated with the development of psychological and school adjustment problems.

Other findings imply that the combination of withdrawn and aggressive behavior poses a risk for school adjustment problems. Ledingham and colleagues (Ledingham, 1981; Ledingham & Schwartzman, 1984) found that aggressive-withdrawn children not only were disliked by peers but also tended to suffer academic difficulties. Ladd and Burgess (1999) followed asocial-aggressive children from kindergarten to the second grade and compared them to samples of aggressive children and normative, matched controls. Across all grades, children in the aggressive-withdrawn group were more likely to form and maintain teacher–child relationships that were high in conflict and dependency and low in closeness. The relationship difficulties of asocial-withdrawn children, in contrast, were found to be more transient. These children exhibited more dependent relationships with their teachers as they began kindergarten, but not thereafter.

In sum, support for the premise that withdrawn behavior is a risk factor for school maladjustment is not as strong as that obtained for aggressive behavior. Withdrawn behavior may be less of a risk factor than aggressive behavior because the forms of maladjustment that it portends are less obvious, less harmful to others, or more difficult to measure (e.g., internalizing rather than externalizing problems). From what is known thus far, anxious- and sad-withdrawn children would appear to be at greater risk for developing internalizing problems and debilitating self-perceptions. Extant findings also suggest that children with aggressive-withdrawn behavioral styles, much like their aggressive counterparts, are likely to develop externalizing difficulties and school adjustment problems. It is less clear that shy-, passive-, asocial-, or unsociable-withdrawn children are likely to manifest long-term adjustment problems. These inferences are preliminary and subject to revision based on new evidence.

Environment-Level Factors

Next, we consider the proposition that classrooms are social ecologies, and many features of these environments impinge on children and have the potential to impact their school adjustment. Here, researchers tend to work from the premise that children's relationships with classmates and teachers immerse them in processes (e.g., participation versus exclusion, or receiving assistance versus being ignored) that affect their ability to adapt to school challenges, which, ultimately, affects their adjustment in this context.

To address questions about the nature and functions of classroom relationships, researchers have differentiated among the types of relationships that children form with peers and teachers, and attempted to identify processes that occur in these relationships. In the following sections, we review theory and research that have been formulated to understand how children's relations with classmates and teachers might affect their school adjustment. Specifically, three types of classroom peer relationships (i.e., peer group acceptance or rejection, friendships, and peer victimization) and three forms of teacher–student relations (i.e., close, dependent, and conflictual) are considered.

Classroom peer relations

Conceptually, arguments have been made for distinguishing among three types of peer relationships as precursors of adjustment on both structural and psychological grounds (see Bukowski & Hoza, 1989; Ladd, 1988; Perry, Kusel, & Perry, 1988). Whereas peer acceptance or rejection has been defined as a child's relational "status" in peer *groups*, as indicated by the degree to which he or she is liked or disliked by group members, friendships are viewed as voluntary, *dyadic* forms of relationship that often embody a positive affective tie. In comparison, peer victimization has been defined as a form of relationship in which a subset of the peer group (e.g., one or several peers) frequently aggresses against specific children.

In classrooms, children typically engage in more than one form of relationship (e.g., they may be rejected, but have a friend; they may be rejected and victimized; etc.; see Ladd et al., 1997; Perry et al., 1988) and, thus, are exposed to different relational processes or experiences (Furman & Robbins, 1985). Thus, it is important to consider how multiple forms of peer relations may be intertwined within classrooms, and how participation in different types of relationships may contribute to school adjustment (Ladd et al., 1997). Accordingly, in the sections that follow, we first review evidence about the role of individual relationships in children's school adjustment and, then, consider what is known about conjoint relationship influences.

Peer group acceptance   Evidence from a number of studies suggests that classroom peer acceptance and rejection is a precursor of children's school adjustment. Initial findings indicated that low peer acceptance was a significant correlate of later school adjustment, such as dropping out of high school (Parker & Asher, 1987). More recent studies show that peer acceptance and rejection predict school adjustment at much earlier stages of children's school careers (Ladd, Herald-Brown, & Reiser, 2008).

At school entry, for example, peer rejection has been linked with negative school attitudes, school avoidance, and underachievement (Buhs & Ladd, 2001; Ladd, 1990; Ladd, Birch, & Buhs, 1999). Buhs and Ladd (2001), for example, found that children's peer acceptance at school entry predicted changes in classroom participation that, in turn, predicted later academic and emotional adjustment.

During the elementary years, peer acceptance has been linked with loneliness (Parker & Asher, 1993), peer interaction difficulties, lower emotional well-being, and academic deficits (Flook, Repetti, & Ullman, 2005; Ladd, Kochenderfer, & Coleman, 1997;

Vandell & Hembree, 1994). Also linked with peer rejection are problems such as absenteeism during the grade school years (e.g., DeRosier, Kupersmidt, & Patterson, 1994; Hymel, Rubin, Rowden, & LeMare, 1990), grade retention, and adjustment difficulties during the transition to middle school (Coie, Lochman, Terry, & Hyman, 1992).

The reasons why peer rejection adversely affects children's school adjustment appear to be diverse. Evidence shows that rejected children often are excluded from peer activities (Buhs, Ladd, & Herald, 2006; Ladd, Price, & Hart, 1990), develop lower academic self-concepts (Flook et al., 2005), and disengage from classroom activities (Buhs & Ladd, 2001; Casillas, 2009). Perhaps the most compelling evidence of rejection's association with school disengagement is found in a study conducted by Ladd et al. (2008). These investigators traced children's movement in and out of classroom peer rejection across grades K–6 and found that regardless of whether children were rejected during the early or later years of grade school, longer periods of rejection were accompanied by lesser growth in classroom participation. The most serious patterns of disengagement were found for children who were chronically rejected throughout grade school. In contrast, children who moved out of rejection and toward acceptance by their classmates were more likely to show gains in classroom participation.

Other data imply that peer rejection's effects on children's school engagement may be fairly pervasive within the school context. Not only do rejected children tend to be more disengaged during structured activities (e.g., classroom cooperative-learning groups; see Furman & Gavin, 1989; Johnson & Johnson, 1991), but also they appear more excluded during unstructured activities (e.g., recess and playground periods; see Asher, Rose, & Gabriel, 2001; Ladd et al., 1990). For example, in the classroom, disliked children are often the last to be chosen by peers for group work, even when assigned to learning activities by teachers (Johnson & Johnson, 1991).

In general, these results provide support for the premise that classroom peer rejection has adverse consequences for school adjustment, and may be particularly detrimental to children's motivation and school engagement. Conversely, this evidence also implies that classroom peer acceptance promotes inclusion in school activities, which, in turn, yields resources (e.g., sense of belongingness, and involvement in learning activities) that enhance children's interpersonal and scholastic adjustment.

Friendship To learn about school friendships, researchers have studied children's participation in a close friendship, the number of mutual friends they have in their classrooms, the duration of these relationships, and positive and negative features of classroom friendships (see Berndt, 1996; Ladd, Kochenderfer, & Coleman, 1996; Parker & Asher, 1993). Studies conducted with young children lend support to the hypothesis that one or more of these forms of friendship are instrumental in school adjustment. At school entry, kindergartners appear better adjusted if they have a preestablished friend in their classroom (Ladd, 1990). Also, during this period, children who make new friends tend to like school and perform better academically than peers who do not form new friendships (Ladd, 1990). Interactions with friends matter as well; young children – particularly boys – who have conflicts with their friends appear more at risk for school adjustment difficulties, including lower levels of classroom engagement and participation (Ladd et al., 1996). Conversely, children who had friendships that offered higher levels of support and assistance were more likely to perceive their classrooms as supportive environments.

Links between friendship and school adjustment have also been found with older children. Findings show that friendship participation and quality are important predictors of children's adjustment during early- and middle-grade school (Bukowski & Hoza, 1989; Ladd et al., 1996; Parker & Asher, 1993). Children appear to benefit from having friends that affirm their positive attributes and downplay their shortcomings (Buhrmester & Furman, 1986; Furman & Robbins, 1985). For example, children who have friends tend to see themselves more positively (Berndt & Burgy, 1996; Keefe & Berndt, 1996; Savin-Williams & Berndt, 1990) and experience greater perceived social support and less loneliness (Ladd et al., 1996; Parker & Asher, 1993). Conversely, friendships that lack supportive features appear to be of little benefit; children with these kinds of friends were found to be lonelier in school (Parker & Asher, 1993).

It should also be noted that friendships may not always contribute positively to school adjustment. Berndt and Keefe (1995), for example, found that fighting and disruptiveness tended to increase if adolescents had stable friendships with peers who exhibited the same problems.

In sum, less is known about friendship than peer group relations as predictors of children's school adjustment. However, existing evidence largely is consistent with the hypothesis that friendships, and particularly participation in supportive friendships, aid children's adaptation to school.

Peer victimization   Peer victimization has garnered considerable research attention as bullying is a pervasive problem in schools worldwide that has serious consequences for children's school adjustment (Iyer, Kochenderfer-Ladd, Eisenberg, & Thompson, 2010; Juvonen & Graham, 2001; Kochenderfer-Ladd & Wardrop, 2001; Ladd, 2005). Further, as new technologies such as cell phones have emerged, *cyberbullying* (e.g., harming others through e-mail, instant messaging, chat rooms, websites, and video images) has proliferated both inside and outside the school context (Kowalski, Limber, & Agatston, 2007; Smith et al., 2008). Moreover, because cyberbullying can occur 24 hours a day, 7 days a week, it may affect children's school adjustment as much as or more than traditional forms of bullying (see Smith et al., 2008).

This aspect of children's peer relations consistently has been linked with multiple forms of school maladjustment, including absenteeism, low GPA, poor academic achievement, and school avoidance (e.g., Iyer et al., 2010; Juvonen, Nishina, & Graham, 2000; Kochenderfer & Ladd, 1996a, 1996b; Ladd et al., 1997; Lopez & DuBois, 2005; Schwartz, Gorman, Nakamoto, & Toblin, 2005). In addition, evidence shows that peer victimization predicts children psychosocial stress that they experience while in school, including loneliness, depression, anxiety, low self-esteem, and social problems (e.g., Alsaker, 1993; Björkqvist, Ekman, & Lagerspetz, 1982; Boivin, Hymel, & Bukowski, 1995; Boulton & Underwood, 1992; Egan & Perry, 1998; Graham & Juvonen, 1998; Kochenderfer & Ladd, 1996a, 1996b; Olweus, 1993). For example, Kochenderfer and Ladd (1996a, 1996b) found that greater exposure to victimization in kindergarten forecasted significant increases in loneliness during children's first year in school. These increases in adjustment difficulties co-occurred with the onset of victimization, and children who had been victimized for longer periods of time had more severe adjustment difficulties than those who had been abused for brief periods. Similarly, Ladd et al. (1997) found that young children who were exposed to high levels of peer victimization displayed increases in school avoidance and loneliness.

A key hypothesis underlying the victimization–school adjustment link is that involvement in bully–victim interactions at school interferes with children's motivation, thinking, and ability to participate effectively in classroom learning activities. For example, it has been posited that harassment causes children to become so preoccupied with fears, feelings of social alienation, and safety concerns that they are unable to attend to school tasks and, eventually, come to dislike and avoid school (Hoover & Hazler, 1991; Kochenderfer & Ladd, 1996a, 1996b; Slee, 1994). Support for such arguments was recently obtained in a longitudinal study that we (Iyer et al., 2010) conducted following first and third graders into second and fourth grades, respectively. Specifically, we found that peer victimization predicted disruptions in children's effortful control skills (i.e., attention shifting and focusing, and inhibitory control), which, in turn, reduced their classroom participation and academic achievement.

Additionally, in research conducted with third and fourth graders, Schwartz et al. (2005) found that victimization predicted increases in depression, which, in turn, forecasted increasing academic difficulties (i.e., GPA and achievement test scores) over a one-year period. Consistent with these findings, evidence from studies of middle school children showed that the link between victimization and school adjustment (i.e., GPA level and absenteeism) was mediated by psychological symptoms (e.g., self-worth, loneliness, and depression; Juvonen et al., 2000; Lopez & DuBois, 2005). Findings from other studies show that victims are more likely than nonvictims to report negative feelings and attitudes toward school and classroom tasks (Boivin & Hymel, 1997; Boulton & Underwood, 1992). Taken together, these studies suggest that victims of peer harassment are at high risk for school maladjustment and that psychological difficulties represent one mechanism underlying the relation between peer victimization and school maladjustment.

Evidence also indicates that, for many children, peer abuse persists from one school year to the next, and that school adjustment problems worsen if peer abuse remains chronic. Further, it appears that children's school adjustment problems do not always abate when victimization ceases (Kochenderfer-Ladd & Wardrop, 2001).

Thus, evidence clearly indicates that many children encounter peer abuse in school, some consistently over many years. Although further investigation is needed, especially across age groups and gender, the bulk of extant evidence conforms to the hypothesis that victimization is a determinant of school-related difficulties. Unfortunately, the effects of victimization appear not only serious but also wide ranging. Victimization has been implicated as a risk factor for numerous types of school adjustment problems.

Classroom teacher–child relations

Because teachers are an integral part of the classroom social ecology, the nature of children's relationships with teachers and the role of teacher–child relations in children's school adjustment have become important areas of research (Howes & Hamilton, 1992; Howes, Hamilton, & Matheson, 1994; Kochenderfer-Ladd & Pelletier, 2008; Pianta & Steinberg, 1992; Valiente, Lemery-Chalfant, Swanson, & Reiser, 2008). The most commonly investigated properties of the teacher–child relationship are closeness, conflict, and dependency (see Pianta & Steinberg, 1992). With some exceptions, researchers find that teacher–child relationships are linked with aspects of children's school adjustment.

Close teacher–student relationships appear beneficial to children's school adjustment. In studies of young children, investigators have found that teacher closeness in kindergarten was associated with concurrent academic readiness (Birch & Ladd, 1997) and with greater progress in math and reading as well as in socially appropriate and attentive classroom behavior by second grade (Peisner-Feinberg et al., 2001). In a study conducted with school-aged children, Valiente et al. (2008) reported that positive teacher–child relationships predicted gains in GPA from fall to spring, and decreases in absences.

Conversely, conflictual teacher–child relationships have been linked with school maladjustment. In one study, kindergarten children high in dependency evidenced lower academic readiness (Birch & Ladd, 1997), and in another investigation children with conflictual teacher–child relationships in kindergarten were more prone to dislike school and act uncooperatively by the end of first grade (Ladd & Burgess, 2001). Likewise, Pianta and Steinberg (1992) found that poor teacher–child relations in kindergarten forecasted in-grade retentions. In research conducted over a longer period of schooling, Hamre and Pianta (2001) found that, after controlling for IQ and behavior problems, negative teacher–child relationships in kindergarten forecasted poor academic performance and disciplinary infractions and suspensions in eighth grade. The relations observed for disciplinary infractions and suspensions were especially strong for children who had initially high levels of behavior problems, supporting the hypothesis that teacher–child relationships often serve to moderate school adjustment outcomes.

Researchers have also begun to study the processes that account for the associations between the teacher–child relationship and achievement, such as classroom engagement and participation (Casillas, 2009; Ladd et al., 1999; Valiente et al., 2008) and positive work habits (Baker, 2006; Baker, Grant, & Morlock, 2008). For example, O'Connor and McCartney (2007) found that children whose relationships with their teachers deteriorated between preschool to third grade had lower academic achievement than their counterparts whose relationships had improved. Moreover, this association was partially mediated through lower classroom engagement in third grade, even after controlling for preschool behavior problems and early cognitive ability. Ladd et al. (1999) also found that the impact of the teacher–child relationship on academic achievement was mediated by classroom participation.

Exceptions to this general pattern of findings have also been reported. For example, after controlling for children's learning problems, Baker (2006) did not find that positive teacher–child relationships predicted children's reading grades across a school year. Likewise, Ladd and Burgess (2001) and Henricsson and Rydell (2006) failed to find that teacher–student relationships predicted achievement when they controlled for baseline achievement and/or behavior problems.

Thus, there is growing evidence to suggest that teacher–child relationships, particularly positive features of this relationship, are influential in children's school adjustment. Support for this premise has been somewhat stronger and more consistent in relation to children's interpersonal growth as opposed to their academic growth. Further, the teacher–child relationship appears to moderate school adjustment for children with behavior problems. It should be noted, however, that most of the evidence obtained to date comes from studies conducted with young children. Thus, very little is known about connections between the teacher–child relationship and school adjustment for older children, such as preadolescents and adolescents.

Differential contributions of classroom relationships to children's school adjustment

The movement to study individual classroom relationships (with peers and teachers) as contributors to children's school adjustment has been supplemented by investigations in which researchers have examined multiple forms of relationship and the relative (differential) "contributions" of these relationships to specific adjustment outcomes (e.g., see Parker & Asher, 1993; Vandell & Hembree, 1994). It has been more common for researchers to study classroom peer rather than teacher–child relationships simply because children spend more time interacting with peers while in school. Further, few researchers have examined the relative or combined contributions of peer and teacher–child relationships within the same investigation.

The functional distinctions that researchers have drawn among classroom peer relationships have, to some extent, been supported by evidence indicating that different peer relationships contribute distinctly to children's school adjustment. For example, Ladd and colleagues (Ladd et al., 1997, 1999) found that, even after controlling for other forms of peer and teacher–child relationships, peer rejection predicted children's participation in the classroom, and that this form of engagement forecasted later achievement. In addition, evidence suggests that the effects of different forms of relationships on children's development are unique relative to one another – suggesting that the relationships differ in their adaptive value for specific adjustment outcomes. For instance, research with adolescents indicates that loneliness is more closely linked with friendship than peer acceptance, and feelings of isolation are more closely tied to peer acceptance than friendship (see Bukowski & Hoza, 1989). Among grade-school children, friendship and peer acceptance make separate contributions to the prediction of both socioemotional adjustment and academic competence (Parker & Asher, 1993; Vandell & Hembree, 1994). With young children, Ladd (1990) found that friendship and peer acceptance uniquely predicted changes in kindergartner's school perceptions, avoidance, and performance.

Even broader ranges of children's classroom peer relationships have been researched in recent years. In one investigation (Ladd, Kochenderfer, & Coleman, 1997), four forms of peer relationships were examined simultaneously as predictors of changes in multiple indices of children's school adjustment. These investigators found that several types of peer relationships were linked with most of the examined psychological and school adjustment criteria, but that the adaptive significance of particular forms of relationship (i.e., the presence of unique versus shared predictive linkages) varied across adjustment domains. To illustrate, when the four forms of peer relationship (i.e., two forms of friendship, peer group acceptance, and peer victimization) were examined individually rather than jointly as predictors of children's affect in school (e.g., loneliness), significant associations were found for number of friends, peer group acceptance, and peer victimization. However, when the contributions of these relationships were examined after adjusting for shared predictive linkages, some relationships were found to be better predictors than others. Peer victimization, for example, predicted gains in children's loneliness above and beyond associations that were attributable to the other three forms of peer relationship, and peer group acceptance uniquely predicted improvements in children's achievement. Overall, these findings were consistent with the view that peer relationships are not only special-ized in the types of resources or constraints they create for children, but also diverse in the sense that some resources may be found in more than one form of relationship.

Thus, although far from being conclusive or exhaustive, there is evidence to suggest that children's participation in several types of peer relationships are associated with school maladjustment. In addition to peer group acceptance, children's participation in friendships and the features of children's friendships have been linked with concurrent and subsequent school adjustment indicators across a wide range of ages. Peer victimiza-tion, a form of relationship most closely resembling child abuse, appears to antecede several forms of maladjustment including school avoidance, loneliness, and negative attitudes toward classmates, school tasks, and the larger school environment.

Child and Environment Models

As illustrated in prior sections, two rather distinct literatures have grown up around main effects perspectives – one of which has been a response to the hypothesis that children's behavioral dispositions contribute to later adjustment, and the other of which has been guided by the premise that children's classroom relationships foreshadow their school adjustment. Previously, many investigators – depending on their theoretical orientations – have regarded the explanatory power of one of these two "main effects" perspectives as dominant over the other.

For example, when considering how relationship difficulties contribute to adjustment, relative to children's behavioral dispositions, the former have been often been construed as "marker variables" or links ultimately attributable to children's underlying behavioral propensities (see MacDougall, Hymel, Vaillancourt, & Mercer, 2001; Parker & Asher, 1987). However, many researchers have subsequently begun to reexamine these "main effects" perspectives by conducting investigations guided by "child and environment" models. In such models, characteristics of the child and the child's environment are viewed as operating in concert to effect subsequent adjustment (see Coie et al., 1993; Ladd, 1989, 2003). In the following sections, we describe the premises inherent within three types of child and environment models, each of which has been used to guide research in this area: (a) additive models, (b) moderator models, and (c) mediator models.

Additive models

In an additive model, the social environment's contribution to children's adjustment is seen as distinct from that made by their behavioral styles. It is assumed that children's experiences in the peer environment can have positive or negative effects on adjustment, but such effects are "additive" when they occur together with other risk factors, such as the child's behavioral style.

Thus far, most of the research conducted on the interface between behavioral and relational risk factors as predictors of school adjustment has been designed to explicate the relative contributions of children's aggressive behavior and their participation in constructive versus adversarial classroom relationships (e.g., acceptance versus rejection by classmates, or close versus conflictual relations with teachers; see Ladd, 1999; MacDougall et al., 2001). For example, in a study of aggressive children across 2 years of elementary school, a warm and supportive teacher relationship was associated with concurrent lower aggression, taking prior aggression levels into account (Meehan, Hughes, & Cavell, 2003). In contrast, conflicted teacher–child relationships exacerbated children's antisocial and externalizing behavior from kindergarten through third grade, above the effect of their aggressive behavior in kindergarten and preschool respectively (Birch & Ladd, 1998; Silver, Measelle, Armstrong, & Essex, 2005). Further, Ladd and Burgess (2001) gathered data on children's aggressive dispositions as well as their relationship risks (i.e., classroom peer rejection, peer victimization, and conflicted teacher–child relationships) and protective factors (i.e., classroom peer acceptance, mutual friendships, and close teacher–child relationships) over a 2-year period from kindergarten through the first grade. Of the findings obtained, one pattern of results showed that each of the investigated risk factors – that is, child aggression, peer rejection, and conflictual teacher–child relationships – were associated with *increases* in children's school maladjustment, after accounting for the influence of the other risk factors. Conversely, when evaluated with aggression, relational resources such as peer group acceptance predicted *decreases* in attention problems and misconduct, and *increases* in cooperative participation and school liking, independently of this behavioral risk. These findings were consistent with the premise that supportive peer relations inhibited the development of maladjustment, regardless of children's risk status for aggression.

Researchers have also examined the relative contributions of withdrawn behavior and peer group rejection to the prediction of children's school adjustment. Renshaw and Brown (1993) assessed grade-school children's withdrawn behavior and low peer acceptance over a one-year interval and found that both predictors were additively associated (both concurrently and predictively) with loneliness in the school context. A similar pattern of concurrent linkages was reported by Boivin and Hymel (1997).

Thus, findings from these studies support the view that certain child and environmental risks and resources *additively* combine to forecast children's school adjustment. From the perspective of this model, the effects of one risk factor (e.g., the child's aggressive or withdrawn behavior style) are relatively independent of the effects of a second risk factor (i.e., participation in adverse, stressful peer relationships). When multiple risk factors are operative, the effects of one may compound or exacerbate that of others. Conversely, relational resources that are present in children's repertoires or school environments may have the effect of mitigating or offsetting risk factors.

Moderator models

Moderator models are founded on the premise that the extent to which children's behavior determines whether they become healthy or maladjusted in school is *contingent* upon the types of peer or teacher–child relations they are afforded. In this model, the joint effects of the child's disposition and peer experience may create more extreme adjustment consequences than would the additive effects of the individual components.

In one application of this model, Gazelle and Ladd (2003) used growth-curve analyses to examine how a particular subclass of solitary behavior (i.e., anxious-solitary behavior) and specific form of peer rejection (i.e., exclusion by peers) were linked with children's depressive trajectories, as reported by classroom teachers. They found evidence of a *moderated* association between these behavioral and relational risk factors and children's adjustment in that the joint influence of anxious solitude and exclusion predicted the most elevated depressive symptom trajectories. Children who were prone toward anxious-solitary behavior during the early school years were more likely to manifest and maintain depressive symptoms if they had been subjected to higher rather than lower levels of peer exclusion. Further, as illustrated by the trajectories found for two high exclusion groups (i.e., solitary anxious–high excluded and solitary anxious–high excluded externalizing groups), the propensity for solitary-anxious excluded children to exhibit depressive symptoms apparently was not attributable to the co-occurrence of other risk factors, such as externalizing problems. In contrast, children whose risk status was defined by anxious-solitary behavior and low levels of peer exclusion had adjustment trajectories that originated near the mean of the sample and declined over time. A similar but even greater decline in depressive symptoms was found for children whose tendency to engage in anxious-solitary behavior decreased over the first few grade levels (i.e., the solitary offset group).

In addition, evidence of moderated relations has been reported in research conducted on children's aggressive behavior and peer victimization in school contexts. In one such study (Ladd & Burgess, 2001), it was discovered that chronic peer victimization predicted greater gains in school dysfunction (i.e., thought problems) for aggressive than for nonaggressive children. Similar relations were found for adverse teacher–child relations; chronically aggressive children who also had conflictual relationships with their teachers were more likely to develop thought problems and be disruptive in classrooms. A buffering effect of positive aspects of the teacher–child relationship has also been reported, insofar as decelerations of externalizing behavior over time were reported for highly aggressive children who were high in closeness (Silver et al., 2005). Thus, these findings suggest that one risk-related factor's ability to predict children's adjustment problems was *contingent* upon the presence of other risk – or buffering – factors. Of the three child and environment models, this one is most likely to be construed as a child *by* environment model because the assumption is that neither child nor environmental factors alone are responsible for adjustment outcomes, but rather it is the interaction that determines the risk.

Mediator models

In this class of models, the links from children's behavioral dispositions to peer relationships, and from their peer experiences to adjustment, are conceptualized as a series of cause–effect linkages. An illustration of this model can be found in research where it has been hypothesized that the effects of risky child behaviors on school maladjustment are mediated through adverse peer or teacher–child relationships.

Research by Boivin and colleagues is exemplary. Boivin et al. (1995) found that the association between children's withdrawn behavior (assessed in year 1) and two types of internalizing problems (assessed in year 2) was mediated by adverse peer experiences (e.g., peer rejection and victimization) that were measured concurrently with social withdrawal in year 1. Further, in a cross-sectional study, Boivin and Hymel (1997) found that the association between children's behaviors (aggression and withdrawal) and feelings of loneliness in school was partially mediated by adverse peer experiences (rejection and victimization), but not by positive peer affiliations.

Likewise, Ladd et al. (1999) found that both classroom peer rejection and conflictual teacher–child relationships mediated the effects of aggressive behavior on children's scholastic maladjustment. Specifically, these investigators found that children's aggressiveness at the start of kindergarten predicted rejection by peers, and, once children were rejected, they were less likely to engage in classroom activities. A similar but not as powerful path was found through teacher–child conflict, suggesting that both of these forms of relational adversity (e.g., problems with peers and teachers) interfered with classroom participation. Conversely, children whose interactions were more prosocial during the first weeks of kindergarten tended to develop mutual friends and higher levels of peer acceptance. Furthermore, consistent with past research on the antecedents of scholastic progress (see Finn, 1989, 1993; Wentzel, 1991), Ladd et al. (1999) found direct, positive pathways from classroom participation to achievement.

In sum, although models of this form could, conceivably, provide a foundation for many novel avenues of investigation, only a few have been explored. The findings obtained thus far suggest that children's behavioral dispositions operate as the proximal cause of their classroom relationships, and, once formed, these relationships – rather than children's behaviors – create the conditions (i.e., social resources or constraints) that benefit or detract from their school adjustment.

Child and Environment Models of School Adjustment: Provisions and Prospects

Though still emergent and underutilized, child and environment models have become one of the main conceptual tools that researchers have for testing hypotheses about the role of multiple child and relational variables in the development of school adjustment. Thus far, researchers have concentrated their efforts on testing the premise that children's classroom behaviors (a child's behavioral attributes, or propensities) and the experiences they have with classmates and teachers (processes within the relational environment) conjointly influence school adaptation.

Empirical accomplishments

Recent findings strengthen the credibility of child and environment models – that is, frameworks in which it is assumed that both behavioral risks and relational experiences affect early-emerging patterns of maladjustment. Importantly, this evidence contradicts the view that relational factors have little or no adaptive significance beyond that attributable to manifest behavioral risks (see Parker & Asher, 1987). This is because, although various features of children's behavior and classroom relationships have been shown to predict their adjustment, the predictive power of either factor alone appears to be less than their additive, contingent, or mediated contributions. One of the most convincing illustrations of this point comes from results showing that children' early behavioral dispositions – especially those prone to make them aggressive with peers – affect their relational ecologies, which, in turn, appear to influence their participation in learning activities and achievement (e.g., Ladd et al., 1999).

Current findings also underscore the importance of children's relationships in the school context. Along with children's behavioral styles, exposure to relationship adversity (e.g., peer rejection), deprivation (e.g., friendlessness), or support (e.g., peer acceptance) consistently emerges as a predictor of children's adjustment trajectories. In this sense, extant findings not only illustrate the adaptive significance of children's peer and teacher–child relationships but also suggest that relational adversity operates as a stressor in the school environment (e.g., see Ladd et al., 1999).

Considerable support has been obtained for the hypothesis that chronic risks are a greater threat to children's school adjustment than are transient risks. For example, stable relational status in classrooms (e.g., chronic rejection) appears to be a more powerful predictor of school adjustment than brief relational experiences. These findings are consistent with chronic stress models in which it is assumed that persistent or enduring stressors take a greater toll on adjustment than do acute or transient stressors (e.g., see DeRosier, Cillessen, Coie, & Dodge, 1994; Johnson, 1988). Also substantiated is the premise that children's behavioral dispositions may be exacerbated by *enduring* relationship adversity (e.g., chronic victimization: Kochenderfer & Wardrop, 2001; and sustained peer rejection: Ladd et al., 2008), and buffered by stable relationship advantage (e.g., a history of peer acceptance).

Heuristic value of multiple child and environment models

The validity of the different child and environment models, and their utility as paradigms that are likely to produce new discoveries, may be debated in light of extant evidence. Clearly, much of the data obtained thus far appear consistent with the premises of additive models in which it is assumed that both child and environment factors make distinct and independent contributions to children's adjustment. The findings reported by Ladd and Burgess (2001), for example, suggest that aggressive children may develop peer relationships that, depending on their form, exposed them to higher levels of interpersonal stress or support. When exposed to adverse peer relations (e.g., rejection and victimization), aggressive children may have experienced a level of stress that further increased the likelihood of school maladjustment. Conversely, when exposed to support (acceptance by peers), aggressive children may have experienced a sense of inclusion that decreased their risk for school maladjustment. Thus, in terms of predictive contributions, adverse peer relationships "added" to the effects of risky behavioral dispositions (i.e., exacerbated an existing risk), whereas supportive peer relations "subtracted" from the risks posed by aggressive behaviors (e.g., compensated for an existing risk). Stated at a broader level of analysis, these findings suggest that the likelihood that children will develop school adjustment problems is equal to the sum of the risk factors minus the sum of the resources that are operative in the child and within the child's school environment.

Support has also been found for moderator models. This evidence implies that classroom relationships have the capacity to alter (i.e., amplify or modulate) children's behavioral styles, thereby increasing or decreasing risk for maladjustment. Gazelle and Ladd (2003), for example, argued that many anxious-withdrawn children tend to have social fears that make them reserved among peers, and especially vulnerable to the effects of peer exclusion. Should these children be excluded by peers, the experience is likely to confirm or intensify their social fears, and increase rather than maintain the stability of their solitary tendencies – placing them at greater risk for maladjustment. Alternatively, if these children do not experience peer exclusion, their social fears are less likely to be confirmed and they will be less prone to isolate themselves or develop more severe forms of dysfunction. This logic is similar to that found in diathesis–stress frameworks in which it is argued that individuals with certain vulnerabilities are particularly susceptible to the effects of stress.

Accordingly, the application of moderator models has made it possible for researchers to differentiate between those relational conditions that have little effect on children's adjustment beyond their behavioral styles and those that tend to activate children's vulnerabilities in ways that exaggerate their behavioral dispositions and risk for maladjustment. Although research of this type is off to a good start, much remains to be learned about whether certain behavioral propensities make children especially vulnerable to particular forms of peer influence.

Mediator models have also been corroborated, and relevant findings imply that the link between one predictor (i.e., either child- or environment-level factors) and school adjustment is mediated through another. Considerable evidence in the peer relations literature substantiates the first assumption of mediator models – that children's behavioral styles are closely associated with the types of relationships they develop with classmates and teachers. Yet, it is also clear that not all aggressive children are rejected by their classmates or destined to form conflictual relationships with their teachers. Neither is it the case that all withdrawn children become friendless or victimized by peers. Coie, Dodge, Terry, and Wright (1991), for example, estimated that no more than half of aggressive children are rejected by their peers. Thus, although some association has been documented between children's behavioral styles and their peer relations, the magnitude of this linkage appears to be modest rather than robust. These findings, although somewhat equivocal, would appear to elevate the status of mediator and moderator models as potential paradigms for future research. However, when the logic of these models is also weighed against evidence pertinent to the second assumption – that is, findings from studies in which both child and environmental predictors have been examined – all these perspectives appear to receive some degree of empirical support.

Directions for further investigation and applications

A number of important matters remain to be investigated. It is likely that a better understanding of the precursors of school adjustment could be obtained if investigators examined the validity and generalizability of additive, moderator, and mediator models (and other competing perspectives) within model-comparison analyses rather than by assessing the predictive efficacy of each model separately with different samples, studies, and analytic tools (as has been typical in past research). The process of comparing models, and their implications for the study of children's school adjustment, would encourage social scientists to argue the merits of differing theoretical positions and, in this process, generate controversies that will raise novel questions and stimulate new research. For example, a comparison of how the social environment is viewed within continuity models (see Caspi et al., 1987, 1988) and moderator models raises an underresearched question: Is it that the social environment acts to maintain behavior styles over time and it is the continuity of children's behavioral styles that continues to create adjustment problems, or is it that children's dispositions make them vulnerable to the effects of *certain kinds* of peer experience, and the interaction of these factors is what causes maladjustment? In the former case, one would expect to find that children's behavioral styles consistently predict dysfunction across development and that, once this factor had been accounted for, measures of children's peer experiences would have little or no predictive power. Conversely, the former perspective could be interpreted as suggesting that children's behavioral dispositions are but one facet of a larger syndrome or array of child characteristics (e.g., associated cognitive, affective propensities), and that some peer experiences tend to accentuate these vulnerabilities more than others.

Also at issue is the question of whether the children's behavior and the relational experiences in classrooms have lasting or temporary effects on their school adjustment. For example, there is some evidence to suggest that the nature of peer experience that children encounter in classrooms changes dramatically across developmental transitions (e.g. from preschool to grade school, or from late childhood into adolescence; see Berndt & Keefe, 1995; Cairns & Cairns, 1994; Ladd, 1990; Ladd & Price, 1987). Such findings might lead us to expect that children's peer experiences differ qualitatively across transitions and, thus, have effects on adjustment that are limited to particular developmental periods. Evidence of this type would argue against the idea that children's peer experiences remain aligned with their behavioral dispositions across the life cycle and, instead, lead us to suspect that there may be developmental discontinuities or "turning points" (Rutter, 1996), where children's peer experiences no longer support their dispositions and, therefore, permit or promote changes in their behavior.

If the nature and form of children's peer experiences shift over time, then it may be important to conceptualize the role of the social environment as a dynamic force in shaping children's adjustment. Development and socialization regularly expose children to challenges and periods of vulnerability, and during these transitions (see Ladd, 1996) the adaptive significance of the child's attributes and ecological-environmental systems may vary. Similarly, early-emerging forms of maladjustment may not be static, but rather evolve into other (and possibly multiple) forms of dysfunction over the life cycle (see Coie et al., 1993). If this is the case, then the adaptive value of the child's characteristics or environmental inputs may not be enduring; rather, their effects may change with age and experience (see Parker et al., 1995). Alternatively, some behavioral or environmental influences that appear transient may actually be enduring because the modes through which these forces are expressed may change as children grow older.

Thus, a fundamental question is whether children's peer experiences, in combination with their behavior, have effects on adjustment that endure across development, or are limited to particular life stages. On the one hand, as some have suggested (Bowlby, 1973; Freud & Dann, 1951; Rutter, 1979), early childhood may be a sensitive period for social development, and certain types of peer experiences during this stage have lasting effects on children's behavior or adjustment. Early behavioral styles and peer experiences may crystallize into enduring patterns that promote stable or even escalating maladjustment trajectories. On the other hand, as children's peer experiences change, the effects of these experiences on their behavioral dispositions and adjustment may change as well. Transitions across developmental periods may destabilize established maladaptive behavioral tendencies and relationships, allowing for a progression toward more or less adaptive developmental outcomes. Thus, although we need to focus on delineating mechanisms that underlie continuity over time, we also must identify predictors of changes in developmental trajectories as children move from childhood through adolescence.

Implications for prevention and intervention   Unfortunately, little effort has been made to consider the implications of evidence from research on child and environment models for prevention and intervention research. Such an assessment is worth undertaking because it has the potential to sharpen the distinctions between competing frameworks, distill existing knowledge, and guide program development, testing, and implementation. For example, on one hand, individualized prevention and intervention efforts aimed at promoting school adjustment typically focus on child behavior, such as reducing antisocial behaviors (Gresham, 1985; Hudley & Grahm, 1993; Ladd & Mize, 1983; Lochman, White, & Wayland, 1991) while increasing prosocial behaviors (Asher, Renshaw, & Hymel, 1982), social knowledge, and problem-solving abilities (e.g., Gesten et al., 1982; Spivak & Shure, 1974). However, although changes in social skills and behaviors may be observed, they don't necessarily translate into better relationships or school outcomes (see Ladd, Buhs, & Troop, 2002). On the other hand, environment-level programs are typically designed to alter the classroom context through means such as creating more positive social interactions, acceptance, inclusion, tolerance, and so on between classmates or among students, teachers, and other school personnel (i.e., lunch and recess monitors, principals, and so forth). Again, even though such efforts may result in improved relationships, there is little evidence that they lead to improvements in school adjustment (for a brief review, see Ladd et al., 2002).

Findings consistent with child by environment perspectives suggest that both individual and relational factors need to be addressed in programs designed to increase classroom engagement and to prevent school adjustment problems such as loneliness, anxiety, and poor academic progress. Attempts to devise and apply programs of this type have begun to appear in areas such as bullying prevention and intervention research, where it has been argued that programs must address multiple factors to be effective (see Frey, Hirschstein, Edstrom, & Snell, 2009). Frey et al.'s (2009) Steps to Respect program, for example, targets both individual and environment factors to reduce school bullying.

Unfortunately, few researchers have utilized child by environment models to create classroom- or school-based programs that are designed to improve children's school adjustment. Thus, little or no evidence exists that attests to the utility of this theoretical perspective. However, recommendations from research aimed at reducing classroom bullying and victimization illustrate potential directions for the design of such programs. For instance, Pepler and Craig (2008) suggested that teachers should play a more active role in teaching children how to form healthy peer relationships, such as through direct instruction on how students should relate positively and constructively with one another. They further suggest that teachers may be more active in promoting positive peer relationships by controlling how working groups are organized and conducted, such as by not allowing children of similar behavioral propensities, such as aggressiveness, to work together as they tend to reinforce each others' deviance. Similarly, they argue against allowing children to group themselves together in both academic and social tasks to ensure that groups are balanced in the skills they bring to bear on the activities as well as to avoid the social embarrassment and humiliation that come from being excluded or not willingly chosen by peers. Although such recommendations have not been directly evaluated via an intervention study, they serve as simple examples of how child (e.g., social skills and aggressive behaviors) and environment (e.g., teacher and peer relations) factors may be conjointly addressed to influence children's adjustment to school.

In summary, it is the intention of this chapter, and the hope of the authors, that the child and environment perspectives offered will provide a solid foundation for planning prevention and intervention school programs to promote the healthy development of children. Evidence clearly suggests that we can no longer focus our attention on only one aspect of the equation (child or environment) at the expense of the other if we want to make a difference in children's school lives.

References

Alsaker, F. (1993, March). Bully/victim problems in day-care centers: Measurement issues and associations with children's psychosocial health. Paper presented at the biennial meeting of the Society for Research in Child Development, New Orleans, LA.

Asher, S. R., Renshaw, P. D., & Hymel, S. (1982). Peer relations and the development of social skills. In S. G. Moore & C. R. Cooper (Eds.), *The young child: Reviews of research* (pp. 137–158). Washington, DC: National Association for the Education of Young Children.

Asher, S. R., Rose, A. J., & Gabriel, S. W. (2001). Peer rejection in everyday life. In M. R. Leary (Ed.), *Interpersonal rejection* (pp. 105–142). Oxford: Oxford University Press.

Baker, J. A. (2006). Contributions of teacher–child relationship to positive school adjustment during elementary school. *Journal of School Psychology, 44*, 211–229.

Baker, J. A., Grant, S., & Morlock, L. (2008). The teacher–student relationship as a developmental context for children with internalizing or externalizing behavior problems. *School Psychology Quarterly, 23*(1), 3–15.

Berndt, T. J. (1996). Exploring the effects of friendship quality on social development. In W. M. Bukowski, A. F. Newcomb, & W. W. Hartup (Eds.), *The company they keep: Friendship in childhood and adolescence* (pp. 346–365). New York: Cambridge University Press.

Berndt, T. J., & Burgy, L. (1996). Social self-concept. In B. A. Bracken (Ed.), *Handbook of self-concept: Developmental, social, and clinical considerations* (pp. 171–209). New York: John Wiley.

Berndt, T. J., & Keefe, K. (1995). Friends' influence on adolescent's adjustment to school. *Child Development, 66*, 1312–1319.

Birch, S., & Ladd, G. W. (1997). The teacher–child relationship and children's early school adjustment. *Journal of School Psychology, 35,* 61–79.

Birch, S., & Ladd, G. W. (1998). Children's interpersonal behaviors and the teacher–child relationship. *Developmental Psychology, 34,* 934–946.

Björkqvist, K., Ekman, K., & Lagerspetz, K. (1982). Bullies and victims: Their ego picture, ideal ego picture and normative ego picture. *Scandinavian Journal of Psychiatry, 23,* 307–313.

Boivin, M., & Hymel, S. (1997). Peer experiences and social self-perceptions: A sequential model. *Developmental Psychology, 33,* 135–145.

Boivin, M., Hymel, S., & Bukowski, W. M. (1995). The roles of social withdrawal, peer rejection, and victimization by peers in predicting loneliness and depressed mood in childhood. *Development and Psychopathology, 7,* 765–785.

Boulton, M. J., & Underwood, K. (1992). Bully/victim problems among middle school children. *British Journal of Educational Psychology, 62,* 73–87.

Buhrmester, D., & Furman, W. (1986). The changing functions of friends in childhood: A Neo-Sullivanian perspective. In V. J. Derlega & B. A. Winstead (Eds.), *Friendship and social interaction* (pp. 41–61). New York: Springer-Verlag.

Buhs, E., & Ladd, G. W. (2001). Peer rejection in kindergarten: Relational processes mediating academic and emotional outcomes. *Developmental Psychology, 37,* 550–560.

Buhs, E. S., Ladd, G. W., & Herald, S. (2006). Peer exclusion and victimization: Processes that mediate the relation between peer group rejection and children's classroom engagement and achievement? *Journal of Educational Psychology, 98,* 1–13.

Bukowski, W. M., & Hoza, B. (1989). Popularity and friendship: Issues in theory, measurement, and outcome. In T. J. Berndt & G. W. Ladd (Eds.), *Peer relationships in child development* (pp. 15–45). New York: John Wiley.

Cairns, R. B., & Cairns, B. D. (1994). *Lifelines and risks: Pathways of youth in our time.* New York: Cambridge University Press.

Casillas, R. S. (2009). *Sense of belonging: Implication for Latino students' academic achievement in U.S. schools* (Unpublished doctoral dissertation). Arizona State University, Tempe.

Caspi, A., Elder, G. H., & Bem, D. J. (1987). Moving against the world: Life-course patterns of explosive children. *Developmental Psychology, 23,* 308–313.

Caspi, A., Elder, G. H., & Bem, D. J. (1988). Moving away from the world: Life-course patterns of shy children. *Developmental Psychology, 24,* 824–831.

Coie, J. D., & Dodge, K. A. (1998). Aggression and antisocial behavior. In W. Damon (Series Ed.) & N. Eisenberg (Vol. Ed.), *Handbook of child psychology* (Vol. 3, pp. 779–862). New York: John Wiley.

Coie, J. D., Dodge, K. A., Terry, R., & Wright, V. (1991). The role of aggression in peer relations: An analysis of aggression episodes in boys' play groups. *Child Development, 62,* 812–826.

Coie, J. D., Lochman, J. E., Terry, R., & Hyman, C. (1992). Predicting adolescent disorder from childhood rejection and peer rejection. *Journal of Consulting and Clinical Psychology, 60,* 783–792.

Coie, J. D., Watt, N. F., West, S., Hawkins, J. D., Asarnow, J. R., Markman, H. J., et al. (1993). The science of prevention: A conceptual framework and some directions for a national research program. *American Psychologist, 48,* 1013–1022.

Coplan, R. J. (2000). Assessing nonsocial play in early childhood: Conceptual and methodological approaches. In K. Gitlin-Weiner, A. Sandgrund, & C. Schaefer (Eds.), *Play diagnosis and assessment* (2nd ed., pp. 563–598). New York: Wiley.

Coplan, R. J., & Rubin, K. H. (1998). Exploring and assessing nonsocial play in the preschool: The development and validation of the Preschool Play Behavior Scale. *Social Development, 7,* 73–91.

Coplan, R. J., Rubin, K. H., Fox, N. A., Calkins, S. A., & Stewart, S. L. (1994). Being alone, playing alone, and acting alone: Distinguishing among reticence, and passive- and active-solitude in young children. *Child Development, 65*, 129–137.

DeRosier, M. E., Cillessen, T., Coie, J. D., & Dodge, K. A. (1994). Group social context and children's aggressive behavior. *Child Development, 65*, 1068–1079.

DeRosier, M. E., Kupersmidt, J. B., & Patterson, C. J. (1994). Children's academic and behavioral adjustment as a function of the chronicity and proximity of peer rejection. *Child Development, 65*, 1799–1813.

Eccles, J. S., Wigfield, A., & Schiefele, U. (1998). Motivation to succeed. In W. Damon & N. Eisenberg (Eds.), *Handbook of child psychology* (Vol. 5, 5th ed., pp. 1017–1095). New York: Wiley.

Egan, S. E., & Perry, D. G. (1998). Does low self-regard invite victimization? *Developmental Psychology, 34*, 299–309.

Feldhusen, J. F., Thurston, J. R., & Benning, J. J. (1973). Aggressive classroom behavior and school achievement. *Journal of Special Education, 4*, 431–439.

Finn, J. D. (1989). Withdrawing from school. *Review of Educational Research, 59*, 117–142.

Finn, J. D. (1993). *School engagement and students at risk* (ERIC Document Reproduction Service No. ED362322). Washington, DC: Department of Education, National Center for Educational Statistics.

Flook, L., Repetti, R. L., & Ullman, J. B. (2005). Classroom social experiences as predictors of academic performance. *Developmental Psychology, 41*, 319–327.

Freud, A., & Dann, S. (1951). An experiment in group upbringing. In R. Eisler, A. Freud, H. Hartmann, & E. Kris (Eds.), *Psychoanalytic study of the child* (Vol. 6, pp. 127–168). New York: International University Press.

Frey, K. S., Hirschstein, M., Edstrom, L., & Snell, J. (2009). Observed reductions in school bullying, nonbullying aggression, and destructive bystander behavior: A longitudinal evaluation. *Journal of Educational Psychology, 101*(2), 466–481.

Furman, W., & Gavin, L. A. (1989). Peer's influence on adjustment and development: A view from the intervention literature. In T. J. Berndt & G. W. Ladd (Eds.), *Peer relationships in child development* (pp. 319–340). New York: John Wiley.

Furman, W., & Robbins, P. (1985). What's the point? Issues in the selection of treatment objectives. In B. Schneider, K. H. Rubin, & J. E. Ledingham (Eds.), *Children's peer relations: Issues in assessment and intervention* (pp. 41–54). New York: Springer-Verlag.

Gazelle, H., & Ladd, G. W. (2003). Anxious solitude and peer exclusion: A diathesis–stress model of internalizing trajectories in childhood. *Child Development, 74*, 257–278.

Graham, S., & Juvonen, J. (1998). Self-blame and peer victimization in middle school: An attributional analysis. *Developmental Psychology, 34*, 587–599.

Hamre, B. K., & Pianta, R. C. (2001). Early teacher–child relationships and the trajectory of children's school outcomes through eighth grade. *Child Development, 72*, 625–638.

Harrist, A. W., Zaia, A. F., Bates, J. E., Dodge, K. A., & Pettit, G. S. (1997). Subtypes of social withdrawal in early childhood: Sociometric status and social-cognitive differences across four years. *Child Development, 68*, 278–294.

Havighurst, R. J., Bowman, P. H., Liddle, G. P., Mathews, C. V., & Pierce, J. V. (1962). *Growing up in River City*. New York: John Wiley.

Henricsson, L., & Rydell, A-M. (2006). Children with behavior problems: Development during the first six years of school. *Infant and Child Development, 15*, 347–366.

Hoover, J. H., & Hazler, R. J. (1991). Bullies and victims. *Elementary School Guidance & Counseling, 25*, 212–219.

Howes, C., & Hamilton, C. E. (1992). Children's relationships with caregivers: Mothers and child care teachers. *Child Development, 63*, 859–866.

Howes, C., Hamilton, C. E., & Matheson, C. C. (1994). Children's relationships with peers: Differential associations with aspects of the teacher–child relationship. *Child Development, 65,* 253–263.

Hymel, S., Rubin, K. H., Rowden, L., & LeMare, L. (1990). Children's peer relationships: Longitudinal prediction of internalizing and externalizing problems from middle to late childhood. *Child Development, 61,* 2004–2021.

Iyer, R., Kochenderfer-Ladd, B., Eisenberg, N., & Thompson, M. (2010). Peer victimization, effortful control and school engagement: Relations to academic achievement. *Merrill-Palmer Quarterly, 56,* 361–387.

Johnson, D., & Johnson, F. (1991). *Joining together: Group theory and group skills* (4th ed.). Englewood Cliffs, NJ: Prentice Hall.

Johnson, J. H. (1988). *Life events as stressors in childhood and adolescence.* Newbury Park, CA: Sage.

Juvonen, J., & Graham, S. (2001). *Peer harassment in school: The plight of the vulnerable and victimized.* New York: Guilford Press.

Juvonen, J., Nishina, A., & Graham, S. (2000). Peer harassment, psychological adjustment, and school functioning in early adolescence. *Journal of Educational Psychology, 92,* 349–359.

Keefe, K., & Berndt, T. J. (1996). Relations of friendship quality to self-esteem in early adolescence. *Journal of Early Adolescence, 16,* 110–129.

Kerr, M., Lambert, W. W., & Bem, D. (1996). Life course sequelae of childhood shyness in Sweden: Comparison with the United States. *Developmental Psychology, 32,* 1100–1105.

Kochenderfer, B. J., & Ladd, G. W. (1996a). Peer victimization: Cause or consequence of children's school adjustment difficulties? *Child Development, 67,* 1305–1317.

Kochenderfer, B. J., & Ladd, G. W. (1996b). Peer victimization: Manifestations and relations to school adjustment in kindergarten. *Journal of School Psychology, 34,* 267–283.

Kochenderfer-Ladd, B., & Pelletier, M. E. (2008). Teachers' views and beliefs about bullying: Influences on classroom management strategies and students' coping with peer victimization. *Journal of School Psychology, 46,* 431–453.

Kochenderfer-Ladd, B., & Wardrop, J. (2001). Chronicity and instability in children's peer victimization experiences as predictors of loneliness and social satisfaction trajectories. *Child Development, 72,* 134–151.

Kowalski, R. M., Limber, S. P., & Agatston, P.W. (2007). *Cyber bullying: Bullying in the digital age.* Malden, MA: Blackwell.

Kupersmidt, J. B., & Coie, J. D. (1990). Preadolescent peer status, aggression, and school adjustment as predictors of externalizing problems in adolescence. *Child Development, 61,* 1350–1362.

Ladd, G. W. (1988). Friendship patterns and peer status during early and middle childhood. *Journal of Developmental and Behavioral Pediatrics, 9,* 229–238.

Ladd, G. W. (1989). Children's social competence and social supports: Precursors of early school adjustment? In B. Schneider, G. Attili, J. Nadel, & R. Weissberg (Eds.), *Social competence in developmental perspective* (pp. 277–292). Amsterdam: Kluwer Academic.

Ladd, G. W. (1990). Having friends, keeping friends, making friends, and being liked by peers in the classroom: Predictors of children's early school adjustment? *Child Development, 61,* 1081–1100.

Ladd, G. W. (1996). Shifting ecologies during the 5–7 year period: Predicting children's adjustment to grade school. In A. Sameroff & M. Haith (Eds.), *The five to seven year shift* (pp. 363–386). Chicago: University of Chicago Press.

Ladd, G. W. (1999). Peer relationships and social competence during early and middle childhood. In *Annual Review of Psychology* (Vol. 50, pp. 333–359), Palo Alto, CA: Annual Reviews.

Ladd, G. W. (2003). Probing the adaptive significance of children's behavior and relationships in the school context: A child by environment perspective. In R. Kail (Ed.), *Advances in child behavior and development* (pp. 43–104). New York: John Wiley.

Ladd, G. W. (2005). *Children's peer relationships and social competence: A century of progress.* New Haven: CT: Yale University Press.

Ladd, G. W., Birch, S. H., & Buhs, E. (1999). Children's social and scholastic lives in kindergarten: Related spheres of influence? *Child Development, 70,* 1373–1400.

Ladd, G. W., Buhs, E., & Troop, W. (2002). Children's interpersonal skills and relationships in school settings: Adaptive significance and implications for school-based prevention and intervention programs. In P. K. Smith & C. H. Hart (Eds.), *Blackwell's handbook of childhood social development* (pp. 394–415). London: Blackwell.

Ladd, G. W., & Burgess, K. B. (1999). Charting the relationship trajectories of aggressive, withdrawn, and aggressive/withdrawn children during early grade school. *Child Development, 70,* 910–929.

Ladd, G. W., & Burgess, K. B. (2001). Do relational risks and protective factors moderate the linkages between childhood aggression and early psychological and school adjustment? *Child Development, 72,* 1579–1601.

Ladd, G. W., Herald, S. L., & Kochel, K. P. (2006). School readiness: Are there social prerequisites? *Early Education and Development, 17,* 115–150.

Ladd, G. W., Herald-Brown, S. L., & Reiser, M. (2008). Does chronic classroom peer rejection predict the development of children's classroom participation during the grade school years? *Child Development, 79*(4), 1001–1015.

Ladd, G. W., Kochenderfer, B. J., & Coleman, C. (1996). Friendship quality as a predictor of young children's early school adjustment. *Child Development, 67,* 1103–1118.

Ladd, G. W., Kochenderfer, B. J., & Coleman, C. C. (1997). Classroom peer acceptance, friendship, and victimization: Distinct relational systems that contribute uniquely to children's school adjustment? *Child Development, 68,* 1181–1197.

Ladd, G. W., & Mars, K. T. (1986). Reliability and validity of preschoolers' perceptions of peer behavior. *Journal of Clinical Child Psychology, 15,* 16–25.

Ladd, G. W., & Mize, J. (1983). A cognitive-social learning model of social-skill training. *Psychological Review, 90,* 127–157.

Ladd, G. W., & Price, J. M. (1987). Predicting children's social and school adjustment following the transition from preschool to kindergarten. *Child Development, 58,* 1168–1189.

Ladd, G. W., Price, J. M., & Hart, C. H. (1990). Preschoolers' behavioral orientations and patterns of peer contact: Predictive of peer status? In S. R. Asher & J. D. Coie (Eds.), *Peer rejection in childhood* (pp. 90–115). New York: Cambridge University Press.

Lambert, N. A. (1972). Intellectual and nonintellectual predictors of high school status. *Journal of Scholastic Psychology, 6,* 247–259.

Ledingham, J. E. (1981). Developmental patterns of aggressive and withdrawn behavior in childhood: A possible method for identifying preschizophrenics. *Journal of Abnormal Child Psychology, 9,* 1–22.

Ledingham, J. E., & Schwartzman, A. E. (1984). A 3-year follow-up of aggressive and withdrawn behavior in childhood: Preliminary findings. *Journal of Abnormal Child Psychology, 12,* 157–168.

Lopez, C., & DuBois, D. L. (2005). Peer victimization and rejection: Investigation of an integrative model of effects on emotional, behavioral, and academic adjustment in early adolescence. *Journal of Clinical Child and Adolescent Psychology, 34,* 25–36.

MacDougall, P., Hymel, S., Vaillancourt, T., & Mercer, L. (2001). The consequences of childhood peer rejection. In M. R. Leary (Ed.), *Interpersonal rejection* (pp. 213–247). Oxford: Oxford University Press.

Meehan, B. T., Hughes, J. N., & Cavell, T. A. (2003). Teacher–student relationships as compensatory resources for aggressive children. *Child Development, 74,* 1145–1157.

O'Connor, E., & McCartney, K. (2007). Examining teacher–child relationships and achievement as part of an ecological model of development. *American Educational Research Journal, 44*(2), 340–369.

Ollendick, T. H., Green, R. W., Weist, M. D., & Oswald, D. P. (1990). The predictive validity of teacher nominations: A five-year follow-up of at risk youth. *Journal of Abnormal Child Psychology, 18*, 699–713.

Olweus, D. (1993). Victimization by peers: Antecedents and long-term outcomes. In K. H. Rubin & J. B. Asendorf (Eds.), *Social withdrawal, inhibition, and shyness in childhood* (pp. 315–342). Hillsdale, NJ: Erlbaum.

Parker, J. G., & Asher, S. R. (1987). Peer acceptance and later interpersonal adjustment: Are low-accepted children at risk? *Psychological Bulletin, 102*, 357–389.

Parker, J. G., & Asher, S. R. (1993). Friendship and friendship quality in middle childhood: Links with peer group acceptance and feelings of loneliness and social dissatisfaction. *Developmental Psychology, 29*, 611–621.

Parker, J. G., Rubin, K. H., Price, J. M., & DeRosier, M. (1995). Peer relationships, child development, and adjustment: A developmental psychopathology perspective. In D. Cicchetti & D. Cohen, (Eds.), *Developmental psychopathology: Vol. 2. Risk, disorder and adaptation* (pp. 96–161). New York: John Wiley.

Peisner-Feinberg, E. S., Burchinal, M., Clifford, R. M., Culkin, M. L., Howes, C., Kagan, S. L., et al. (2001). The relation of preschool child-care quality to children's cognitive and social developmental trajectories through second grade. *Child Development, 72*, 1534–1553.

Pepler, D., & Craig, W. M. (2008). Bullying, interventions and the role of adults. Retrieved from http://www.education.com

Perry, D. G., Kusel, S. J., & Perry, L. C. (1988). Victims of peer aggression. *Developmental Psychology, 24*, 807–814.

Perry, K. E., & Weinstein, R. S. (1998). The social context of early schooling and children's school adjustment. *Educational Psychologist, 33*, 177–194.

Pianta, R. C., & Steinberg, M. (1992). Teacher-child relationships and the process of adjusting to school. *New Directions for Child Development, 57*, 61–80.

Renshaw, P. D., & Brown, P. J. (1993). Loneliness in middle childhood: Concurrent and longitudinal predictors. *Child Development, 64*, 1271–1284.

Rubin, K. H. (1982). Nonsocial play in preschoolers: Necessary evil? *Child Development, 53*, 651–657.

Rubin, K. H., & Borwick, D. (1984). The communication skills of children who vary with regard to sociability. In H. Sypher & J. Applegate (Eds.), *Social cognition and communication* (pp. 152–170). Hillsdale, NJ: Erlbaum.

Rubin, K. H., & Coplan, R. (2004). Paying attention to and not neglecting social withdrawal and social isolation, *Merrill-Palmer Quarterly, 50*, 506–534.

Rubin, K. H., Daniels-Bierness, T., & Bream, L. (1984). Social isolation and social problem-solving: A longitudinal study. *Journal of Consulting and Clinical Psychology, 52*, 17–25.

Rubin, K. H., LeMare, L., & Lollis, S. (1990). Social withdrawal in childhood: Developmental pathways to peer rejection. In S. R. Asher & J. D. Coie (Eds.), *Peer rejection in childhood* (pp. 217–249). New York: Cambridge University Press.

Rutter, M. (1979). Maternal deprivation, 1972–1978: New findings, new concepts, new approaches. *Child Development, 50*, 283–305.

Rutter, M. (1996). Transitions and turning points in developmental psychopathology: As applied to the age span between childhood and mid-adulthood. *International Journal of Behavioral Development, 19*, 603–626.

Savin-Williams, R. C., & Berndt, T. J. (1990). Friendship and peer relations. In S. S. Feldman & G. R. Elliott (Eds.), *At the threshold: The developing adolescent* (pp. 277–307). Cambridge, MA: Harvard University Press.

Schwartz, D., Gorman, A., Nakamoto, J., & Toblin, R. L. (2005). Victimization in the peer group and children's academic functioning. *Journal of Educational Psychology, 97*, 425–435.

Silver, R. B., Measelle, J. R., Armstrong, J. M., & Essex, M. J. (2005). Trajectories of classroom externalizing behavior: Contributions of child characteristics, family characteristics, and the teacher–child relationship during the school transition. *Journal of School Psychology, 43*, 39–60.

Slee, P. T. (1994). Situational and interpersonal correlates of anxiety associated with peer victimization. *Child Psychiatry and Human Development, 25*(2), 97–107.

Smith, P. K., Mahdavi, J., Carvalho, M., Fisher, S., Russell, S., & Trippett, N. (2008). Cyberbullying: Its forms and impact in secondary school pupils. *Journal of Child Psychology and Psychiatry, 49*(4), 376–385.

Tolan, P. H., & Gorman-Smith, D. (1998). Development of serious and violent offending careers. In R. Loeber & D. P. Farrington (Eds.), *Serious and violent juvenile offenders: Risk factors and successful interventions* (pp. 68–85). Thousand Oaks, CA: Sage.

Valiente, C., Lemery-Chalfant, K., Swanson, J., & Reiser, M. (2008). Prediction of children's academic competence from their effortful control, relationships and classroom participation. *Journal of Educational Psychology, 100*, 67–77.

Vandell, D. L., & Hembree, S. E. (1994). Peer social status and friendship: Independent contributors to children's social and academic adjustment. *Merrill-Palmer Quarterly, 40*, 461–477.

Wentzel, K. R. (1991). Social competence at school: Relation between social responsibility and academic achievement. *Review of Educational Research, 61*, 1–24.

CHAPTER ELEVEN

Environmental Psychology

Christopher Spencer and Kate Gee

The Place of the Environment Within Psychology, and Developmental Psychology

Environmental psychologists believe that perceptions, attitudes, and actions are always situated in an environment that is both social *and* physical (Gifford, 2007); at its heart is understanding the transactions between people and their sociophysical environment as a two-way process. An oft-quoted statement of Churchill (1943) is "We shape our buildings, and afterwards our buildings shape us." Topics studied in environmental psychology (EP) include the cognition of places: cognitive maps and their role in navigating places, environmental preferences and thus location of a person's activities, and environments that are stressful or restorative. Implications for public policy and for the design of habitats for humans are often drawn from such research. Most of EP's topics have focused on adult populations, but there is now a substantial body of research concerning the developing child (Evans, 2006).

Sadly, psychology as a whole has largely ignored the sociophysical environment of the behaviors it studies; and this applies to much of developmental psychology, including social development. For much of developmental psychology, it seemed the only setting researchers considered was the purely social: the family, the school, the peer group. Just a few articulate pioneers stood out: for example, Hart (1979) and R. C. Moore (1986). Matthews and Limb (1999) reminded us that a young person's day differs in rhythm, scale, and content from that of adults. Similarly, in their use of space and facilities, children are often more restricted by caretaking conventions, physical constraints, and lack of access to transport and resources.

The Wiley-Blackwell Handbook of Childhood Social Development, Second Edition, edited by Peter K. Smith and Craig H. Hart
© 2011 by Blackwell Publishing Ltd.

Ecological Psychology as a Predecessor for EP

EP owes much of its thinking about the transactions between people and places to its predecessor, *ecological psychology*, created by the developmental psychologist, Barker (1968; see also Wicker, 1984). Barker felt that the child's behavior as conventionally studied in the psychology laboratory in the 1950s failed to notice how the physical and social setting determined behavior. He set up field stations in Oskaloosa (United States) and Leyburn (England) to study the ecology of childhood, using anthropological techniques of recording (Barker & Wright, 1971). He felt that none of the techniques then employed in psychology captured the essence of what was "causing" the child's behavior. Barker gave this example:

> Eight year old Margaret's behaviour at the drug store was not explained by either Margaret's personality or her family's social inputs to the girl. It became clear that the *behaviour setting* was the predominant factor influencing her behaviour: when Margaret was in the drug store "she behaved drug store." (1968, p. 24)

The stream of an individual's behavior could be empirically studied, but could be best understood not by studying either the individual or the stream of behavior but rather by studying the environment (Barker, 1968). Behavior-setting theory proposes that the environment contains specific, identifiable units. By combining both physical and social elements of the environment within these units, they are shown to have powerful influences on human behavior. A *behavior setting* is "a naturally occurring unit of the environment at the molar level, recognized by its inhabitants, regular people going about their everyday lives" (Barker, 1968; Gump, 1975).

How is a behavior setting identified? Let us take the example of a school class. It is a natural phenomenon, and it has a space–time locus. A self-generated boundary surrounds the meeting of a school class, which changes as the class changes in size and the nature of its activity. The coming together of the class is objective, existing independently of anyone's perception. It has two sets of components: behaviors such as sitting, discussing, and doing maths; and nonpsychological objects with which behavior is conducted, such as the chairs, walls, and equipment. The people who inhabit the class are interchangeable: Pupils come and go, and even the teacher may be replaced. But the behavior of the entity cannot be greatly changed without destroying it, as there must always be teaching and study (Gump, 1987).

Not all physical settings are equally suited to the activities therein. *Synomorphy* was the ecological psychologists' term for the goodness of fit between the physical setting and a particular activity taking place within it. They were also concerned with the size and population of a setting (the *staffing level*). For example, the child's experiences of a small school and a big one may differ considerably, not just because of the environmental stress but also because the smaller institution can offer more opportunities for engagement with school clubs and activities (Barker & Wright, 1951). What, however, might happen if there is understaffing? Here, children typically increase their effort and spend more time supporting the setting; they will participate in a greater variety of tasks and roles, and in more difficult and important tasks. This can affect their self-perception and perception of others, as they tend to assume more responsibility in the setting, perceiving self and others in terms of task-related characteristics, and paying less attention to personality and other non-task-related differences between individuals.

The Natural History of Childhood: What Do Children Do All Day?

The early ecological psychologists brought child studies out of the lab and recorded everyday behavior. *One Boy's Day* (Barker & Wright, 1951) is based on the minute-by-minute observations of the children of Oskaloosa from morning to night. Initially, few studies within mainstream psychology extended this research. Perhaps the most influential pioneer has been Hart (1979). He studied children's experience of place in a small New England town ("Inavale"). Hart chose a small ecological unit (a group of 86 children) and used an eclectic mix of observational, interview, and test techniques to both discover local places that held a consensus of meaning whilst being sensitive to unique, personal meanings. In this way, children become "experts," showing a stranger around the home patch. Hart (1979) frequently found, "Children seem to find as much enjoyment in getting to places as they do in being there. In fact, there often is no 'there': they are just exploring" (p. 145).

Parents defined the allowable range for such exploration and play, with boys not only having a larger permitted range than girls of the same age but also being more likely to admit to the researcher as having gone beyond these limits. Parents' anxieties about perceived dangers, related to their estimate of the child's competence, were often given as reasons. Boys were given, on average, twice the free range of girls, which made for a powerful socialization tool within sex-stereotyped roles (see Torrell & Biel, 1985, for comparable European data).

R. C. Moore (1986) was another pioneer in studying children's everyday interactions. In three contrasting urban sites in the United Kingdom, children completed maps and drawings of their favorite places, followed by interviews on their activities and perceived boundaries. One quarter of the children then took Moore on field trips around their territories. Moore analyzed the data by group (producing "turf maps") and by individual: "Each child wove a pattern of personal playtraces through the neighbourhood, laced together with the traces of other known and unknown players" (p. 56). As each child responded to new opportunities, the pattern extended geographically. It was guided by the child's developing capacity, whose environmental competence was, in turn, enhanced by his or her continuing interaction with the surroundings.

Since these pioneer field studies, there have been many successors throughout the world; from rural Nepal to the slums of South America; from settled prosperous communities in Sweden to refugee camps in Africa and Asia (e.g., Chawla, 2002; Corbishley, 1995; Derr, 2006; Fjortoft, 2004; G. T. Moore, 1986). Much of this research has focused on young people's access to resources, the opportunities that these places afford, and the quality of places frequented by children. They have also been concerned with how landscapes are arranged, consciously or not, in relation to people's different conceptions of childhood (see the Children's Environments Research Group [CERG] website; CERG, 2006).

In the decades since the early studies, the free range allowed to children has noticeably diminished, especially in the more industrialized countries, with profound implications for their sense of belonging to a local community. Children now spend less time playing outdoors than had their parents at the same age, as, for example, Clements's (2004) survey of 800 mothers in the United States documents. A study by Karsten (2005) confirms that children's use of space has changed from being primarily outdoors and free to indoors and supervised. Karsten took a detailed look at three different streets in Amsterdam to investigate children's use of a space in 2003, compared with the 1950s and early 1960s. She made numerous observations of three streets and conducted over 90 interviews with children and parents, and with adults who lived there in the 1950s and 1960s. These were validated by archival and statistical analyses of historical data. In the 1950s and early 1960s, "playing meant playing outside," a matter of necessity (due to small living spaces) and pleasure. She found that children had considerable freedom to move around on their own, through a large territory. They played with children from diverse backgrounds and used urban public space for many of their activities. In contrast, children in 2003 did not play outside as much or for great lengths of time. They were restricted in their range, had fewer playmates from less diverse backgrounds, and were more home centered.

Other recent studies have documented this change in the pattern of daily activities. Hofferth (2009) looked at changes in how American children spent their time between 1981 and 1997, and between 1997 and 2002–2003. By collecting 24-hour time diaries from thousands of participants, she investigated time spent in 18 different activities and analyzed the impact of various demographics on children's time. Children's discretionary time (i.e., time not spent in school, etc.) declined by 12% (7.4 hours a week) from 1981 to 1997 and by an additional 4% (2 hours) from 1997 to 2002–2003. The way children spent their discretionary time had changed – less time spent in unstructured activities (e.g., free play) and more time in structured activities (e.g., sports and youth programs). Other changes of interest included a doubling of computer use.

Roberts, Foehr, and Rideout (2005) have documented how children now spend considerable time with electronic media rather than playing outdoors. Children whose parents have lower incomes or less formal education tend to watch more TV and play more video games than children whose parents have higher incomes and more formal education.

The Settings of Childhood: Town and Country Compared

Often discussed, but less often researched, are the implications for children's social life and social identity of a rural versus an urban upbringing.

Towns have been portrayed both as positive and as negative (Spencer & Woolley, 2000). Lennard and Crowhurst Lennard (1992) described the positive features of those European towns that "work" best for children. These include a network of safe, traffic-reduced places, allowing children to explore their neighborhoods whilst promoting social interaction; and periodic access during the day to parents, made possible by bringing living and working places closer together.

Such towns afford the opportunity to observe adults and children engaged in a variety of work activities and social relationships. They will have social and physical arrangements that promote trust, such as public places where the presence of unknown adults guarantees protection and safety for children, and where the design of public settings enhances contact among people of different ages and backgrounds. They will have visually interesting characteristics of the built environment (e.g., varied textures, colors, materials, shapes, and forms), and will afford exposure to a variety of public events that generate surprise and delight, including street entertainment.

But many researchers have seen a decline in the quality of the city for children (e.g., Bjorklid, 1994; Noschis, 1992). Blinkert (2004) criticized developmental psychology's many studies of changes in childhood for focusing solely on the social experiences of children:

> Very little has been done to show how spatial conditions of childhood have changed and have thus produced what is arguably an entirely new type of childhood. This concentration on the "social paradigm" has severe consequences on policies for children. Development of these policies is strictly dominated by *social* experts: psychologists, teachers, educational experts, therapists, social workers and sociologists. (p. 99)

How do children see it? In a large-scale study across Britain, Woolley, Spencer, Dunn, and Rowley (1999) talked to 10–12-year-old British children about their town centers. Children of this age proved to be articulate and in possession of their own attitudes, rather than repeating stereotypical views copied from parents. Perhaps the most striking finding was that children of this age held powerful civic values: They were strongly against litter, dirt and smells, pollution, disorder, and incivilities. They were generally supportive of the agents of order, endorsing closed-circuit television on the street (because it made them feel safer) and generally approving of security guards. Their aesthetic appreciation coincided with management programs, generally liking street furniture, some street art, fountains, or places to sit (but they were careful to reject some places as more suited to the elderly!).

Many EPs have begun collecting children's views of their towns worldwide (see Chawla, 2002). Derr (2002) compared the lives of 9–11-year-olds in three towns in New Mexico, exploring children's sense of place by asking the children to create maps and essays, and to talk about their use of place. She developed four themes showing how children interact with and learn from their environment: exploration allows a sense of freedom, control, and self-sufficiency; special places provide opportunities for creativity, imagination, and getting away from others; activities can help develop a sense of responsibility, respect, and empathy; and family and community interactions help children see place experiences within their broader culture. Derr's research shows how place experiences lead to place attachments and thus help shape a child's social and personal identity.

In contrast to town life, popular writing often portrays rural childhoods as idyllic:

> For many onlookers, rural places are conceived as safe, risk-free, community-rich spaces where parents can bring up their children in trouble-free ways, away from the turmoil and social tumours that comprise the canker of urban living today. (Matthews & Tucker, 2006, p. 161)

Shoard (1980) typified this view. She described five conditions that make rural places enriching spaces for children's play: the number of environmental props that are freely available (e.g., grass, slopes, and trees); freedom of movement; the availability of play spaces away from the home; animals and wildlife that provide a source of fun; and the unknown – that is, the surprises that are around every rustic corner. The countryside presented here is typically well organized and pastoral, and not remote, wild, and desolate (Ward, 1988). In their surveys in the English countryside, Matthews and Tucker (2006) heard from older children and adolescents, who felt their needs and decision-making views were neglected, ignored, or tokenized. Feelings of powerlessness, exclusion, and frustration were commonplace. Rather than being part of an ideal community, many children, especially the least affluent and teenagers, felt dislocated and detached from village life.

If the rural environment is less than idyllic, how then is this image maintained? Valentine (1996, 2004) described rural parents' glowing accounts of the opportunities for children in village life, whilst simultaneously challenging this with negative accounts of their children's safety, thereby contradicting popular ideas of the rural as a safe place. In order to justify their claims about the relative safety of the village as a place to grow up, parents further mobilize another ingredient of the "rural idyll" – "community."

Affordances: Children Discovering That Places Have Social Possibilities

Gibson's concept of affordances has proved to be a powerful way of describing the way children use places in ways unexpected by their designers. Gibson (1977) defined *affordances* as all "action possibilities" latent in the environment. His position in perceptual psychology may be controversial, but what environmental psychology draws from the concept is that places, features, and situations offer a range of possibilities for physical and social action. Think, for example, of the way skateboarding children can use the city furniture in novel ways. Woolley and Johns (2001) gave us a vivid child's-eye view of the city as a playground:

> Young people, and skateboarders especially, are very good at finding "affordances" in the environment, that is objects and places that allow certain things to happen, but not necessarily with the use that the space or object was designed for. For example they will turn a handrail, an object of safety, into a challenging, dangerous element down which to slide a board, or a shallow flight of steps into an obstacle to be jumped in one move. (p. 212)

Heft (1988) has suggested that we can use affordances to assess the environments of children from a functional point of view. He demonstrated the utility of this approach by reworking the example of *One Boy's Day*, Barker and Wright's (1951) classic ecological account. Hart (1979) and others showed how whole cohorts of children share common perceptions of the affordances of each neighborhood setting. Using this approach, we can think about and describe environments in psychological terms rather than just physical ones, offering us a way of establishing a taxonomy of places that will be predictive of behavior.

Children of all ages are adept at seeing the play possibilities of everyday environments. Lennard and Crowhurst Lennard's (1992) photo essay shows how they convert the non-social aspects of the city into resources for sociability: Areas of the neighborhood abandoned by adults can become informal clubhouses for children, and much play takes place in undesigned and undesignated areas. Ward (1978) documented children's unusual use of spaces, such as playing on the front steps of their house, these marking the boundary between private and public spheres, affording both safety and vistas beyond the home.

There are some basic environmental needs of shelter, safety, and support that will hold true of all ages. Beyond these, differences occur due to age, gender, culture, and social and economic context. Evans and McCoy (1988) reviewed stress-inducing environmental features: spaces that are incoherent, confusing, or overloaded with information or stimulation. They reduce our sense of control and do not offer spaces for withdrawal or solitude when desired. Several studies have produced evidence that emotions and opportunity for self-regulation are predictive of favorite places – children and adolescent's attachment to favorite places for restorative experiences (Korpela & Hartig, 1996; Korpela, Kyttä, & Hartig, 2002). With increasing age (especially as adolescence is approached), place preferences reflect the possibilities for social interaction and a growing social competence with peers (Clark & Uzzell, 2002; Malinowski & Thurber, 1996).

Cultural Similarities and Differences

Culturally sensitive field studies within developmental environmental psychology had their earliest landmark study with the UNESCO study *Growing Up in Cities* (Lynch, 1977). A generation later (Chawla, 2002), UNESCO relaunched its comparative study of children in some of the world's cities. The study covered a diversity of places and a diversity of settings, including old working-class neighborhoods, suburbs, a self-build settlement, and a squatter camp. Viewed from space, it is dramatically clear that most of Earth's population now lives in urban settings; viewed at ground level, many of these settings appear bleak, an awful place in which to grow up. Yet, as many studies in the 2002 volume indicate, children are resilient and energetic: Their considerable abilities and maturity should not be underestimated.

One might expect the greatest feelings of alienation in the poorest areas, but this is not so. The communities where children expressed the most happiness were one of the poorest districts of Buenos Aires, the self-build settlement in Bangalore, an old working-class district of Warsaw, as well as two relatively more affluent locations in Trondheim. Greatest alienation was found amongst American, British, and Australian children, as well as among the children of the South African squatter camp. Thus, there is not a simple relationship between material well-being and happiness. The quality of the culture that surrounds the children is key: It is possible to discern characteristics that facilitate a supportive culture, and then to suggest how such a culture could be developed.

Evans (2004) offered a major review on the environment of childhood poverty: residential crowding may affect children's psychological health (Evans, Seagert, & Harris, 2001) and can increase tension between family members. Crowding is connected with unwanted social interaction, which in children can lead to a loss of control and learned helplessness. Poverty per se was not necessarily associated with poor child-rearing environments; not all poor neighborhoods were physically disordered (Kohen, Brooks-Gunn, Leventhal, & Hertzman, 2002). As studies of built form in China indicate (Wang, 2008), well-defined spaces allow smaller groups such as the family to retain a sense of identity within larger populations (e.g., the community). Wang described the traditional Chinese courtyard as embodying social and emotional relationships, contributing to a sense of place.

Children's Place Attachment and Their Personal and Social Identity

A fundamental claim made by EP is that the individual's early and continuing transactions with places contribute importantly to their developing personal, social, and cultural identity (Altman & Low, 1992; Heft & Chawla, 2006; Twigger-Ross & Uzzell, 1996).

This area had been previously characterized by autobiographical accounts, literary exemplars, and case studies of particular places and their shaping of children: rich and intuitively convincing, but unsystematic and without unifying theory. Altman and Low (1992); Golledge, Smith, Pellegrino, Doherty, and Marshall (1995); and Groat (1995) went some way to applying developmental theory to EP. Clark and Uzzell (2002, 2006) offered us a theoretical base from within EP, showing how adults interrelate place and identity: Four principles of identity guide an adult's action – continuity, self-esteem, self-efficacy, and distinctiveness – all of which should emerge in the child as identity develops.

As competence and confidence grow through childhood, the area of travel and exploration increases: from the rooms of home, to the immediate surroundings, to the local neighborhood, through to familiarity with a wider region. As the child's cognitive map extends, facilitating travel and location of resources, the child's sense of place attachment and identification with place widens (Altman & Low, 1992). Personal identity derives in part from the child's social environment and also from the familiar physical environment. The child claims the freedom to travel as an assertion of independence, and may be met by an acknowledgment of the child's increasing competence and individuality. This has always been judged against adult estimates of potential hazards "out there" and, recently, by vastly increased adult worries about "stranger danger" (Valentine, 2004).

Some writers are confident in their assertions of the importance of place attachment for a full personal or social identity. Corbishley (1995) argued that a sense of rootedness is important for our ability to participate in social networks as adults. Cooper Marcus (1992) presented adults' memories of childhood places and concluded that gaining control over space is important in order to feel a positive sense of self-identity. Fuhrer,

Kaiser, and Hartig (1993) reviewed the literature on place attachment and its role in the self-concept, showing how measured levels of attachment can predict the way individuals will use places for restorative reasons. There are many reasons why this area can be seen as of practical as well as theoretical importance: What implications would frequent relocation have for children's well-being? What are the minimal conditions for a place to have those qualities that allow attachment to occur? What are the implications of being a minority group member within the city (Woolley & Amin, 1995)?

During preadolescent and early adolescent phases, the shift toward greater independence in activities and choices marks an important development in the child's personal, social, and civic identity: moving beyond parental protection, and becoming a full member of society. This involves exploring the diversity of society through active interaction with some members (and avoidance of others!). In this way social competences are learned, and personal and social identities are tried out with a wider range of peers and adults. Learning the social and environmental grammar of one's community is facilitated by some patterns of town, and hindered by others (Lennard & Crowhurst Lennard, 1992; Lynch, 1977).

Children's Well-Being and Designing the "Child-Friendly Town"

"Child-friendly cities" have developed over the past 15–20 years, signifying a movement bringing together research on children's needs, social concerns, and local and national commitments to action. A child-friendly city promotes the active participation of children, ensuring children's freedom to express their views and ensuring that their views are given due weight in all matters affecting them.

There is now the International Child Friendly Cities Secretariat at the UNICEF Innocenti Research Centre in Florence (www.childfriendlycities.org). This builds on the Convention of the Rights of the Child, four principles of which are used to assess the friendliness of a particular city: nondiscrimination (Article 2), the best interests of the child (Article 3), the right to life and maximum development (Article 6), and respecting children's views (Article 12) (see CERG, 1996).

Kyttä (2006) has contributed a hypothetical model of what it is to be child friendly, based on the opportunities for independent mobility and the actualization of affordances. Kyttä called it the "Bullerby model," suggesting the ideal circumstances for independent movement in an environment full of affordances. *Bullerby* can be literally translated as a noisy village. Kyttä used this interpretative model to assist in comparing data from four Finnish and five Belarussian neighborhoods of various levels of urbanization.

How much freedom (actual or licensed) does the child have to move independently round town? Mobility restrictions affect younger children and girls most often (Hillman, Adams, & Whitelegg, 1990; Prezza et al., 2001); and the size and the density of a city are connected to opportunities for independent mobility. A consistent finding is that children who live in rural or lower-density environments enjoy more freedom to move around than do children in high-density city environments (Kyttä, 2006). But some studies on territorial range and mobility (Matthews & Tucker, 2006) have not supported the suggestion that rural children have more independence. The neighborhood may also have an impact on independent mobility: The quality of traffic management is connected to children's mobility (Björklid, 2002). Prezza et al. (2001) found that the most independent children living in Rome were those who lived in apartment buildings with courtyards, near the parks, and in new neighborhoods. Peers can also stimulate a child to move around independently (Berg & Medrich, 1980), as can the community as a whole, if the responsibility of children's supervision is collective (Hillman et al., 1990).

Green Environments

In the early days of EP, the positive effects of contact with nature were asserted, but with little supporting evidence. Now, however, there is strong empirical data (Kaplan, 1995, 2001; Kaplan & Kaplan, 1989; Ulrich, 1983, 1992) and at least two theoretical accounts of the benefits.

Psychoevolutionary theory (PET; Ulrich, 1983) suggested that natural surroundings reduce stress reactions to any situation that threatens well-being, by reducing negative emotions and various physiological indicators of increased autonomic arousal. Recovery from stress can occur in settings that evoke moderate levels of interest, pleasantness, and calm, such as greenery and water. Natural settings tend to abound in the features thought to promote recovery from stress. Support for PET has come from a number of studies comparing emotional and physiological responses to natural and urban settings experienced after stress induction (e.g., Korpela, Hartig, Kaiser, & Fuhrer, 2001; Ulrich et al., 1991).

Attention restoration theory (ART; Kaplan & Kaplan, 1989) focuses on directed attention requiring mental effort, which can be fatigued from overuse. Settings that enable recovery from directed attention fatigue are known as *restorative settings*, and should (a) have fascination that effortlessly engages attention, allowing fatigued directed attention to rest; (b) have a sense of being different from the usual environment; (c) be sufficiently rich and coherent to engage the mind and promote exploration; and (d) be a good fit between one's intentions and the activities supported by the setting. Many studies have supported ART, typically by inducing attentional fatigue and then offering either urban or natural scenes for recuperation, with typically better performance on attention-demanding tasks by people exposed to natural settings (Berto, Massaccesi, & Pasini, 2008; Faber Taylor, Kuo, & Sullivan, 2001, 2002; Kaplan, 2001).

Many factors may covary with greenery levels. Thus, children in leafy suburbs and in inner-city districts experience different levels of particle pollutants, quality of housing stock, traffic noise and dangers, social pressures, and parental income and education levels, among others. Faber Taylor and Kuo (2006) have reviewed the recent literature as it relates to children, concluding that the many positive findings linking green space to positive childhood development provide "pervasive and generalizable" evidence as to their applicability to different populations and environments. They argued that there is compelling evidence for a link between green space and enhanced attentional capacity in children: home views of nature and the components of self-discipline – concentration, impulse inhibition, and the ability to delay gratification. Levels of greenery can be related to behavioral conduct disorders, anxiety, and depression.

Having discussed positive aspects of the green environment, it must be noted that some children see it negatively. Bixler and Floyd (1997) found that, when shown images of wild areas, children in their study reported feeling that nature is "scary, disgusting and uncomfortable"!

City as Danger: Social Dangers to Children

Having earlier discussed some positive aspects of towns and cities for children's social development, we need to explore why such places may worry children, often due to traffic, pollution, fear of crime, or experiences of bullying. In research on the social dangers that parents of 9–11-year-olds in New York saw threatening their children, Blakely (1994) showed how the fears of kidnapping, assault, and so on may be transmitted by word of mouth, amplifying reportage from the media. This is a study that could be replicated in virtually every city as the world is perceived as becoming more dangerous. Surveys such as Lyons and Breakwell (1994) and Woolley, Spencer, et al. (1999) provide evidence for children having environmental awareness and concerns, often characterized by anger and frustration about the apparent indifference and poor stewardship of adults.

Woolley, Dunn, Spencer, Short, and Rowley's (1999) study of British 10–12-year-olds focused on children's perceptions of their local urban centers, particularly on their concerns and fears regarding using the centers. Children were generally very positive about what town and city centers can offer now and in the future. Nonetheless, they gave vivid accounts of perceived threats from some adults on the street, from older adolescents, and from out-of-town groups. In general, the areas studied that scored higher on the number of reports of negative experiences were the ones where the overall level of stimulation and excitement given by the place was reported to be higher. Quieter, less threatening places were perceived as the more dull areas. Poor standards of maintenance may signal social indifference and danger (Pitner & Astor, 2008). Agents of order (police, security guards, and the presence of older people on the streets) are welcomed, as is CCTV.

Björklid (1994) argued that the anxiety that parents and children now share about the dangers from traffic are such that we should consider them victims of "traffic environmental stress," which in its turn is leading to social isolation. And the deleterious effect of ambient noise upon children is well documented (Evans, 2001; Evans & Lepore, 1993). Woolley, Dunn, et al. (1999) found that in some of the smaller towns, frequent responses by children to "dislikes and dangers" questions were to do with traffic, problems crossing the roads, crowded pavements, and getting separated from friends or family in the crush. In the larger towns, issues such as these tended to be replaced by altogether darker worries and fears, generally about one's personal safety and the presence of threatening or dangerous groups of people. Although traffic and crowds are probably in fact more of a hassle in the larger towns than in the smaller ones, their significance pales alongside these latter personal threats. Certain stereotypical groups of adults were most mentioned and feared – drunks and drug users, for example. Many children also mentioned threats to themselves from potential abductors and rapists: The general public and parental concerns about "mucky men" had in some cases been given credence for the children by their knowledge of specific local incidents, their locations, and the victims. Perkins, Wandersman, Rich, and Taylor (1993) have shown that researchers can construct almost a predictive *place–grammar* of likely street crime and incivilities. Woolley, Dunn, et al. (1999) showed children to be very aware indeed of danger spots in their locale, and to shape their use and movement accordingly. The general tenor in children's discussions was that one had to learn how to minimize risk by avoiding particular areas and particular times of day. Safety in town centers is perceived to come not only from the presence of agencies such as the police and CCTV, but also from the fact that in many areas there are "people around," which is reassuring to the children. Shopping malls may be sanitized and commercial, but in many children's opinion they are sanitary and safe. Many of the negative issues raised by the children should concern us all: poor maintenance of streets and buildings, the unpleasantness of smelly places (and the lack of care for the town center that this signals), and incivilities experienced or imagined, shading into actual dangers to oneself.

Children's Participation in Planning: Can "the Outsiders" Contribute?

Hart (1997) has suggested that only through direct participation can children develop a genuine appreciation of democracy and a sense of their own competence and responsibility to participate. "The planning, design, monitoring and management of the physical environment is an ideal domain for the practice of children's participation; it seems to be clearer for children to see and understand than many social problems" (Hart, 1997, p. 147). Yet in practice children remain "outsiders" as far as the world of planning is concerned, a section of society with little or no power or influence on decision making. As a result, most environmental planning effectively reflects only adult values and patterns of activity.

> Despite a burgeoning body of research which highlights the singular environmental needs of older children, most large-scale environments are designed to reflect only adult values and usages. The visions of environmental planners and landscape architects implicitly reflect the dominant perceptions of a society, such that groups already on the edge become further marginalized by policy making. (Matthews, 1995, p. 456)

There is now a considerable research literature on children's participation in planning (see worldwide reviews in the journal *Child and Youth Environments*, 2007–2008). But what *participation* means in practice can vary considerably. Hart (1997) noted that much work that terms itself *children's participation* is, in fact, not authentic participation at all but "manipulation, decoration or tokenism" (p. 155). Participation is authentic when children understand clearly what they are doing and voluntarily choose to contribute. At the lowest level, children may be mobilized to help with short-term actions, such as cleaning up litter or carrying health messages home to their families, if they agree with these goals. Genuine democratic processes do not begin, however, until children are consulted about their own ideas, and their views are taken seriously.

Francis and Lorenz (2002) presented a historical and critical review of children's participation in city planning and design. They traced 30 years and seven styles of participation, from an early romantic phase, where children were idealized as "the best designers"; through phases stressing advocacy and children's particular needs and rights; and through to recent proactive planning with children as full participants.

Perhaps the best documented series of studies of participation are given in the UNESCO study (Chawla, 2002). Some come from the least advantaged settings: For example, in the South African squatter camp of Canaansland, Swart-Kruger (2002) found that the Growing Up in Cities research process met with the enthusiasm of a severely underprivileged group of children, unaccustomed to involvement but readily taking to expressing their critique of their settlement and its lack of facilities.

From the UNESCO studies in these diverse settings of childhood, can we indicate the qualities that make communities good places to grow up in, or frustrating and alienating? Chawla (2002) concluded that safety and freedom of movement would seem fundamental to those districts most positively experienced; so too is the friendliness of the community, and the existence of places to gather. A place with a good variety of interesting activity settings seems important to satisfaction and well-being: either within the immediate neighborhood or, as in South Africa, India, and Poland, in the easily accessible city center. Greenery, where it was available, was much prized, and was often at the top of children's most wanted local improvements.

What characterized the least appreciated of the study sites (including some of the more affluent cities) were stigma and social exclusion; the boredom of overdesigned play areas; traffic, trash, and litter; and experiences of harassment, crime, and racial bullying. A sense of political powerlessness, and a disbelief that their voices would be heard, was commonplace amongst children in all study sites; and it required the skill of the various research teams to begin to dispel this learned helplessness in the action phases of the research. It seems universally true that participation not only is a social good but also, for the individual, fosters an intrinsic sense of self-esteem and self-efficacy that is a basic preparation for citizenship, and in turn this benefits the whole community.

Conclusion

There is now a huge body of research evidence on the significance of children's transactions with their local sociophysical environment. It is an important literature that developmental psychology ignores at the risk of remaining out of touch with the context of children's social development, and the child's developing personal, social, and cultural identity. As the early ecological psychologists convincingly demonstrated, the setting of a behavior is generally a better predictor of a child's actual behavior than are any measures of their personality, upbringing, parental style, or "theory of mind."

References

Altman, I., & Low, S. M. (1992). *Place attachment*. New York: Plenum Press.

Barker, R. G. (1968). *Ecological psychology*. Stanford, CA: Stanford University Press.

Barker, R. G., & Wright, H. F. (1951). *One boy's day*. New York: Harper.

Barker, R. G., & Wright, H. F. (1971). *Midwest and its children*. Hamden, CT: Archon.

Berg, M., & Medrich, E. (1980). Children in four neighborhoods. *Environment and Behavior*, *12*, 320–348.

Berto, R., Massaccesi, S., & Pasini, M. (2008). Do eye movements measured across high and low fascination photographs differ? Addressing Kaplan's fascination hypothesis. *Journal of Environmental Psychology*, *28*, 185–191.

Bixler, R. D., & Floyd, M. F. (1997). Nature is scary, disgusting, and uncomfortable. *Environment and Behavior*, *29*, 443–467.

Björklid, P. (1994). Children – traffic – environment. *Architecture et Comportement*, *10*, 399–406.

Björklid, P. (2002). *Out and play – but where?* Stockholm: Stockholm Institute of Education.

Blakely, K. S. (1994). Parents' conceptions of social dangers to children in the urban environment. *Children's Environments*, *11*, 20–35.

Blinkert, B. (2004). Quality of the city for children: Chaos and order. *Children, Youth and Environments*, *14*, 99–112.

Chawla, L. (Ed.). (2002). *Growing up in an urbanizing world*. Paris: UNESCO and London: Earthscan.

Chawla, L. (2006). Learning to love the natural world enough to protect it. *Barn*, *2*, 57–78. Trondheim, Norway: Norsk senter for barneforskning.

Children's Environments Research Group (CERG). (2006). About CERG. Retrieved from "http://web.gc.cuny.edu/che/cerg/about_cerg/index.htm.

Children's Environments Research Group (CERG) and UNICEF. (1996). *Children's rights and habitat: Report of the expert seminar for Habitat II*. New York: Authors.

Churchill, W. S. (1943, October 28). *[Speech to the House of Commons]*. London: House of Lords.

Clark, C., & Uzzell, D. L. (2002). The affordances of the home, neighbourhood, school and town centre. *Journal of Environmental Psychology*, *22*, 95–108.

Clark, C., & Uzzell D. L. (2006). The socio-environmental affordances of adolescents' environments. In C. Spencer & M. Blades (Eds.), *Children and their environments: Learning, using and designing spaces* (pp. 176–195). Cambridge: Cambridge University Press.

Clements, R. (2004). An investigation of the state of outdoor play. *Contemporary Issues in Early Childhood*, *5*, 68–80.

Cooper Marcus, C. (1992). Environmental memories. In I. Altman & S. M. Low (Eds.), *Place attachment* (pp. 87–112). New York: Plenum Press.

Corbishley, P. (1995). A parish listens to its children. *Children's Environments*, *12*, 18–37.

Derr, V. (2002). Children's sense of place in northern New Mexico. *Journal of Environmental Psychology*, *22*, 125–137.

Derr, T. (2006). "Sometimes birds sound like fish": Perspectives on children's place experience. In C. Spencer & M. Blades (Eds.), *Children and their environments: Learning, using and designing spaces* (pp. 108–123). Cambridge: Cambridge University Press.

Evans, G. W. (2001). Environmental stress and health. In A. Baum, T. Revenson, & J. E. Singer (Eds.), *Handbook of health psychology* (pp. 365–385). Mahwah, NJ: Erlbaum.

Evans, G. W. (2004). The environment of childhood poverty. *American Psychologist*, *59*, 77–92.

Evans, G. W. (2006). Child development and the physical environment. *Annual Review of Psychology*, *57*, 423–451.

Evans G. W., & Lepore, S. J. (1993). Nonauditory effects of noise on children: A critical review. *Children's Environments, 10*, 31–51.

Evans, G. W., & McCoy, J. M. (1988). When buildings don't work: The role of architecture in human health. *Journal of Environmental Psychology, 18*, 85–94.

Evans, G. W., Seagert, S., & Harris, R. (2001). Residential density and psychological health among children in low-income families. *Environment and Behavior, 33*, 165–180.

Faber Taylor, A., & Kuo, F. (2006). Is contact with nature important for healthy child development? In C. Spencer & M. Blades (Eds.), *Children and their environments: Learning, using and designing spaces* (pp. 124–140). Cambridge: Cambridge University Press.

Faber Taylor, A., Kuo, F. E., & Sullivan, W. C. (2001). Coping with ADD: The surprising connection to green play settings. *Environment and Behavior, 33*, 54–77.

Faber Taylor, A., Kuo, F. E., & Sullivan, W. C. (2002). Views of nature and self-discipline: Evidence from inner city children. *Journal of Environmental Psychology, 22*, 49–63.

Fjortoft, I. (2004). Landscape as playscape. *Children and Youth Environments, 14*, 21–44.

Francis, M., & Lorenz, R. (2002). Seven realms of children's participation. *Journal of Environmental Psychology, 22*, 157–169.

Fuhrer, U., Kaiser, F. G., & Hartig, T. (1993). Place attachment and mobility during leisure time. *Journal of Environmental Psychology, 13*, 309–321.

Gibson, J. J. (1977). The theory of affordances. In R. Shaw & J. Bransford (Eds.), *Perceiving, acting, and knowing: Toward an ecological psychology* (pp. 67–82). Hillsdale, NJ: Erlbaum.

Gifford, R. (2007). *Environmental psychology: Principles and practice* (4th ed.). Colville, WA: Optimal.

Golledge, R. G., Smith, T. R., Pellegrino, J. W., Doherty, S., & Marshall, S. P. (1995). A conceptual model and empirical analysis of children's acquisition of spatial knowledge. In C. Spencer (Ed.), *The child's environment* (pp. 39–66). San Diego, CA: Academic Press.

Groat, L. (Ed.). (1995). *Giving places meaning*. London: Academic Press.

Gump, P. V. (1975). *Ecological psychology and children*. Chicago: University of Chicago Press.

Gump, P. V. (1987). School and classroom environments. In D. Stokols & I. Altman (Eds.), *Handbook of environmental psychology* (pp. 691–732). New York: Wiley.

Hart, R. (1979). *Children's experience of place*. New York: Irvington.

Hart, R. (1997). *Children's participation: The theory and practice of involving young citizens in community development and environmental care*. Paris and London: UNESCO Earthscan.

Heft, H. (1988). Affordances of children's environments. *Children's Environments, 5*, 29–37.

Heft, H., & Chawla, L. (2006). Children as agents in sustainable development: The ecology of competence. In C. Spencer & M. Blades (Eds.), *Children and their environments: Learning, using and designing spaces* (pp. 199–216). Cambridge: Cambridge University Press.

Hillman, M., Adams, J., & Whitelegg, J. (1990). *One false move: A study of children's independent mobility*. London: PSI.

Hofferth, S. L. (2009). Media use vs work and play in middle childhood. *Social Indicators Research, 93*, 127–129.

Kaplan, R., & Kaplan, S. (1989). *The experience of nature*. New York: Cambridge University Press.

Kaplan, S. (1995). The restorative effects of nature: Toward an integrative framework. *Journal of Environmental Psychology, 15*, 169–182.

Kaplan, S. (2001). Meditation, restoration and the management of mental fatigue. *Environment and Behavior, 33*, 480–506.

Karsten, L. (2005). It all used to be better? Different generations on continuity and change in urban children's daily use of space. *Children's Geographies, 3*, 275–290.

Kohen, D. E., Brooks-Gunn, J., Leventhal, T., & Hertzman, C. (2002). Neighborhood income and physical and social disorder in Canada: Associations with young children's competencies. *Child Development, 73*, 1845–1860.

Korpela, K., & Hartig, T. (1996). Restorative qualities of favorite places. *Journal of Environmental Psychology*, *16*, 221–233.

Korpela, K. M., Hartig, T., Kaiser, F. G., & Fuhrer, U. (2001). Restorative experience and self regulation in favorite places. *Environment and Behavior*, *33*, 572–589.

Korpela, K., Kyttä, M., & Hartig, T. (2002). Restorative experience, self-regulation, and children's place preferences. *Journal of Environmental Psychology*, *22*, 387–398.

Kyttä, M. (2006). Environmental child friendliness in the light of the Bullerby model. In C. Spencer & M. Blades (Eds.), *Children and their environments: Learning, using and designing spaces* (pp 141–158). Cambridge: Cambridge University Press.

Lennard, H. L., & Crowhurst Lennard, S. H. (1992). Children in public places: Some lessons from European cities. *Children's Environments*, *9*, 37–47.

Lyons, E., & Breakwell, G. M. (1994). Factors predicting environmental concern and indifference in 13- to 16-year-olds. *Environment and Behavior*, *26*, 223–238.

Lynch, K. (Ed.). (1977). *Growing up in cities*. London: MIT Press and UNESCO.

Malinowski, J. C., & Thurber, C. A. (1996). Developmental shifts in the place preferences of boys aged 8–16 years. *Journal of Environmental Psychology*, *16*, 45–54.

Matthews, H., & Limb, M. (1999). Defining an agenda for the geography of children: Review and prospect. *Progress in Human Geography*, *23*, 61–90.

Matthews, H., & Tucker, F. (2006). On the other side of the tracks: The psychogeographies and everyday lives of rural teenagers in the UK. In C. Spencer & M. Blades (Eds.), *Children and their environments: Learning, using and designing spaces* (pp. 161–175). Cambridge: Cambridge University Press.

Matthews, M. H. (1995). Living on the edge: Children as "outsiders." *Tijdschrift voor Economische en Sociale Geografie*, *86*, 456–466.

Moore, G. T. (1986). Effects of the spatial definition of behavior settings on children's behavior: A quasi-experimental field study. *Journal of Environmental Psychology*, *6*, 205–231.

Moore, R. C. (1986). *Childhood's domain: Play and place in child development*. London: Croom Helm.

Noschis, K. (1992). Child development theory and planning for neighborhood play, *Children's Environments*, *9*, 3–10.

Perkins, D. D., Wandersman, A., Rich, R., & Taylor, R. (1993). The physical environment of street crime: Defensible space, territoriality and incivilities. *Journal of Environmental Psychology*, *13*, 29–49.

Pitner, R. O., & Astor, R. A. (2008). Children's reasoning about poverty, physical deterioration, danger, and retribution in neighborhood contexts. *Journal of Environmental Psychology*, *28*, 327–338.

Prezza, M., Pilloni, S., Morabito, C., Sersante, C., Alparone, F. R., & Giuliani, M. V. (2001). The influence of psychosocial and environmental factors on children's independent mobility and relationship to peer frequentation. *Journal of Community & Applied Social Psychology*, *11*, 435–450.

Roberts, D. F., Foehr, U., & Rideout, V. (2005). *Generation M: Media in the lives of 8 to 18 year olds*. New York: Kaiser Family Foundation.

Shoard, M. (1980). *The theft of the countryside*. London: Temple-Smith.

Spencer, C. P., & Woolley, H. (2000). Children and the city: a summary of recent environmental psychology research. *Child: Care, Health and Development*, *26*, 181–198.

Swart-Kruger, J. (2002). Children in a South African squatter camp gain and lose a voice. In L. Chawla (Ed.), *Growing up in an urbanizing world* (pp. 111–133). Paris and London: UNESCO and Earthscan.

Torrell, G., & Biel, A. (1985). Parents' influence on children's cognitive maps and of activity ranges in residential neighborhoods. In T. Gärling & J. Valsiner (Eds.), *Children in environments* (pp. 107–118). New York: Plenum Press.

Twigger-Ross, C. L., & Uzzell, D. L. (1996). Place and identity processes. *Journal of Environmental Psychology, 16*, 205–220.

Ulrich, R. S. (1983). Aesthetic and affective response to natural environments. In I. Altman & J. F. Wohlwill (Eds.), *Human behavior and environment* (pp. 241–267). New York: Plenum Press.

Ulrich, R. S. (1992). How design impacts wellness. *Healthcare Forum Journal, 20*, 20–25.

Ulrich, R. S., Simons, R. F., Losito, B. D., Fiorito, E., Miles, M. A., & Zelson, M. (1991). Stress recovery during exposure to natural and urban environments. *Journal of Environmental Psychology, 11*, 201–230.

Valentine, G. (1996). Children should be seen and not heard? The role of children in public space. *Urban Geography, 17*, 205–220.

Valentine, G. (2004). *Public space and the culture of childhood.* London: Ashgate.

Wang, D. (2008). A form of affection: Sense of place and social structure in the Chinese courtyard residence. *Journal of Interior Design, 32*, 28–39.

Ward, C. (1978). *The child in the city.* London: Architectural Press.

Ward, C. (1988). *The child in the country.* London: Robert Hale.

Wicker, A. W. (1984). *An introduction to ecological psychology.* Cambridge: Cambridge University Press.

Woolley, H., & Amin, N. (1995). Pakistani children in Sheffield and their perception and use of public open spaces. *Children's Environments, 12*, 479–488.

Woolley, H., Dunn, J., Spencer, C., Short, T., & Rowley, G. (1999). Children describe their experiences of the city centre: A qualitative study of the fears and concerns which may limit their full participation. *Landscape Research, 24*, 287–301.

Woolley, H., & Johns, R. (2001). Skateboarding: The city as a playground. *Journal of Urban Design, 6*, 211–230.

Woolley, H., Spencer, C., Dunn, J., & Rowley, G. (1999). The child as citizen: Experiences of British town and city centres. *Journal of Urban Design, 4*, 255–282.

PART IV

Child and Contextual Factors in Social Development

Building on the ecological context theme briefly described in the introduction for Part III, chapters in this part emphasize what children bring to their social environments. This includes temperament, sex differences, ethnicity, race, communicative abilities, and other developmental capabilities and characteristics. Contextual factors in which these characteristics are expressed and the dynamic nature–nurture interchange that occurs are illustrated in this part. Child contributions to the socialization context are further illustrated in a chapter on child care and early education, and in another chapter focusing on children's social development in the context of parents and peers.

With Chapter 12, Ann Sanson, Sheryl Hemphill, Bilge Yagmurlu, and Sandee McClowry provide a carefully constructed foundational chapter for this part of the handbook that focuses on children's temperament. Theoretical perspectives on temperament and how it influences social development are discussed. The authors then synthesize the research literature describing how temperament and observed social behaviors and competence are related. Further addressing the theme of this part, embedded in this review are discussions of how gender differences, social class, and cultural factors moderate temperament–social behavior associations. Temperament-focused intervention programs to enhance social development are overviewed, with the final portion of the chapter focusing on future directions for research.

The temperament chapter is followed by an insightful discussion of children's social development in the context of child care and early childhood education. In Chapter 13, Carollee Howes reviews recent research findings that illuminate how features of these programs (e.g., emotional climate) provide the context for social interactions and relationships with nonrelative adults and peers, as well as how they impact children's social development. Of particular interest is the literature review on the social adjustment of

The Wiley-Blackwell Handbook of Childhood Social Development, Second Edition, edited by Peter K. Smith and Craig H. Hart
© 2011 by Blackwell Publishing Ltd.

children from different racial and non–English language heritage cultures, based in part on other personal characteristics that they bring to these settings. Beyond cultural and ethnic backgrounds, these characteristics include prior relationship histories, prior child care experiences, dispositions and communicative abilities, and gender-based influences. All of this is carefully set in a theoretical framework that explicates the developmental and cultural interface for understanding processes of socialization within non-home care and early education environments.

Stephanie Reich and Deborah Lowe Vandell, in Chapter 14, shift our focus in this part from child care to the interplay between parents and peers in the socialization process. Beyond considering research findings that illuminate the influence of parents and peers on children's social development, these authors conduct a careful synthesis of the literature that also reveals additive and synergistic effects of parents and peers in this arena. What children bring to this dynamic interchange in terms of underlying genetic predispositions are addressed, along with a discussion of methodologies and statistical methods that are currently being used to disentangle gene–environment correlations. The moderating effects of neighborhood and culture on the interplay between parents and peers are also considered, as well as the complementary contributions of mothers and fathers to children's social development.

Vicki Pasterski, Susan Golombok, and Melissa Hines address sex differences in social behavior in Chapter 15. This is an insightful discussion of differences in social behavior that are displayed by boys and girls and how these differences develop, starting very early in life. Research findings on gender identity, toy preferences, same-sex playmate preferences, and play styles during early and middle childhood are reviewed. Biological and psychological theoretical explanations for these sex differences are described. The authors conclude that sex differences that are present at birth and prior in the womb can be enhanced or diminished by environmental influences. Parents and others not only respond to sex-differentiated behavior that already exists but also help create these differences according to how they treat their children.

Stephen Quintana rounds out this part of the handbook with Chapter 16 on ethnicity, race, and children's social development. He reviews interesting research suggesting that children are born with a predisposition to organize their world into social groups. Race and ethnicity are two of many categories that children use. Infants and young children show sensitivity to different race faces and have notions about ethnicity and race early in life, oftentimes prior to exposure to other racial and ethnic groups. The adaptive significance of these predispositions are discussed, as well as how their expression evolves and changes over the course of development across early and middle childhood due to important social cognitive advances. He also explains the formation of racial bias and skills that help children detect discrimination. This is discussed in the context of increasing globalization that has resulted in more interracial social interactions for children, including web-based social exchanges.

CHAPTER TWELVE

Temperament and Social Development

Ann Sanson, Sheryl A. Hemphill, Bilge Yagmurlu, and Sandee McClowry

This chapter reviews the ways in which child temperament impacts aspects of social development in the periods from preschool to late elementary school. We start by providing some theoretical background on temperament and how it influences social development. After noting some methodological issues, we review research on the connections between temperament and social relations, social competence, and problematic social behaviors. Where evidence is available, we discuss the roles of gender differences, social class, and cultural factors. We then review temperament-focused intervention programs, which are designed to promote positive social development. In the concluding section, we link current evidence with various theoretical propositions regarding temperament and social development and highlight some areas where future research is likely to be particularly illuminating.

What Is Temperament?

Temperament refers to constitutionally based individual differences in behavioral style relating to affect, activity, and attention that are visible from early childhood (Rothbart & Bates, 2006; Sanson, Hemphill, & Smart, 2004). Ideas about temperament go back to ancient times, but modern interest in child temperament dates particularly to the work of Thomas and Chess (Thomas, Chess, Birch, Hertzig, & Korn, 1963). Drawing from clinical insights, they identified nine dimensions of temperament on which infants and young children differed, and that impacted upon their psychosocial development.

The Wiley-Blackwell Handbook of Childhood Social Development, Second Edition, edited by Peter K. Smith and Craig H. Hart
© 2011 by Blackwell Publishing Ltd.

Despite wide acceptance of Thomas and Chess's model, especially in clinical settings, consensus is emerging that two broader dimensions underlie temperament: negative emotionality or reactivity, and self-regulation (Rothbart & Bates, 2006). *Reactivity* refers to irritability, negative mood, and high-intensity negative reactions, including distress to both limitations (irritability, or anger) and novelty (fearfulness). *Self-regulation* refers to the effortful control of attentional processes (e.g., persistence and nondistractibility), as well as self-regulation of emotions and behavior. Self-regulatory aspects of temperament mature over early childhood (Calkins & Degnan, 2006). A bimodal factor, labeled *approach-withdrawal, inhibition,* or *sociability,* describes the tendency to approach novel situations and people, or conversely to withdraw and be wary. Other narrower-band factors such as adaptability, activity level, and rhythmicity are examined in some studies (see Rothbart & Bates, 2006, for fuller discussion).

Thomas et al. (1963) categorized children as "easy," "difficult," and "slow to warm up." "Difficult" children tend to be negative in mood, withdrawing, unadaptable, highly intense, and arrhythmic, and tend to have more troubled development. Later research has questioned the utility of these constructs, showing that their constituent dimensions do not cluster together. The *difficult* term is value laden, whereas any temperament characteristic can be adaptive or nonadaptive, dependent on the situation. These global categories also obscure the roles of particular temperament dimensions (Putnam, Sanson, & Rothbart, 2002). However, in the research reviewed below, a range of temperament constructs, from "micro" aspects such as soothability or anger to global conceptualizations such as "difficult" or "easy," have been examined.

It is accepted that temperament is biologically based, but influenced over time by maturation and experience. Burgeoning research in neuroscience and psychobiology is starting to elucidate the nature of its biological foundations. Space precludes a comprehensive review of this literature (see Rothbart & Bates, 2006), but in brief: Behavioral genetics studies document not only moderate heritability of temperament but also the importance of (shared and nonshared) environmental influences. Relationships between effortful control (the ability to inhibit a dominant response) and neural networks underlying executive attention have been identified. Links between some aspects of temperament (particularly emotionality and fear) and variants of specific genes (in particular, the dopamine receptor DRD4 and the serotonin transporter 5-HTTLRR) are emerging, along with evidence of gene–environment interactions. Other areas of investigation include autonomic reactivity (e.g., vagal tone), the hypothalamic-pituitary-adrenal axis as indicated by cortisol levels, and differences in cerebral hemispheric activation. Despite remarkable progress in recent years, current findings reinforce the complexity of the interacting systems involved, and much more research is needed to fully specify the biological underpinnings of temperament.

A meta-analysis by Roberts and DelVecchio (2000) found modest stability for temperament in the first 3 years of life (around 0.35), but higher stability in later childhood (0.50 on average), perhaps reflecting the development of self-regulation and effortful control in early life. Because the behavioral manifestations of temperament vary with age, it is difficult to ensure that identical constructs are assessed across age. Measurement error hence reduces estimates of stability (Pedlow, Sanson, Prior, & Oberklaid, 1993). Nevertheless, some change in children's temperament is common, and understanding the processes underlying these changes is an important current research question.

Links between temperament and personality, and differences in temperament by gender, socioeconomic status (SES), and culture, have been identified. Temperament is typically seen as the early "core" of later-developing personality (Sanson et al., 2004). Positive affect and approach dimensions of temperament appear to be related to the Big 5 personality factor of extraversion, negative reactivity relates to neuroticism, and regulatory dimensions map onto conscientiousness (Rothbart & Bates, 2006). Where gender differences have been identified, they tend to be relatively small in magnitude. A recent meta-analysis found that effortful control tended to be higher in girls, whereas positive affect or "surgency" was higher in boys (Else-Quest, Hyde, Goldsmith, & Van Hulle, 2006). Although some studies report no or only small differences in temperament across socioeconomic backgrounds (Mednick, Hocevar, Schulsinger, & Baker, 1996), others suggest that children in lower-SES groups are more likely to be "difficult" (e.g., Prior, Sanson, Smart, & Oberklaid, 2000), perhaps due to exposure to more environmental risks. However, SES differences are usually small in size. Studies examining the link between culture and temperament typically find that infants in "Western" countries (e.g., the United States, Canada, and Australia) are more intense (in both positive and negative emotions) and more outgoing than infants in "Eastern" countries (e.g., China and Korea), with only minor differences amongst infants in Western countries (Prior, Kyrios, & Oberklaid, 1986; Rubin et al., 2006).

In sum, understanding of the nature of temperament is growing. It is now established as a critical component of individuality that needs to be taken into account in the study of developmental processes.

Theoretical Perspectives on the Role of Temperament in Social Development

In order to provide a conceptual context for the review of empirical literature, here we briefly review current ideas about the processes by which temperament affects social development (see Bates & Pettit, 2007; Rothbart & Bates, 2006; and Sanson et al., 2004, for further discussion).

First, temperament may have *direct linear* effects on social development. For example, an extreme temperamental characteristic (such as extreme inhibition) may be synonymous with, or create a vulnerability or predisposition toward, a particular outcome (such as social withdrawal). Further, two or more temperament dimensions may contribute additively to social development (e.g., high reactivity and poor regulation both contribute to the development of aggressive behavior).

Indirect or *mediated* effects refer to when a child's temperament affects the environment, which then impacts social adjustment. Children with different temperaments elicit different responses from others – a cheerful sociable child is likely to experience more positive responses than a moody withdrawing one; and a highly negative and reactive child might elicit more punitive discipline, which in turn may increase risk for aggression.

Studies investigating *interactional* effects are often framed around the concept of "goodness of fit" proposed by Chess and Thomas (1986): Particular temperament characteristics may "fit" well or poorly with a particular environment. Thus an active child in a cramped environment might do less well than a less active child, or an active child in a spacious environment. Although goodness of fit is difficult to operationalize (Paterson & Sanson, 1999), it remains a popular theoretical model and is often used to frame clinical interventions (see later in this chapter). Temperament-by-temperament interactions can also occur – for example, self-regulatory aspects of temperament might modify the expression of other aspects (such as high activity level), promoting competent outcomes.

A more elaborated, *transactional* model posits that development is the outcome of a continuous interaction among intrinsic child characteristics (such as genetics, health, and cognitive characteristics as well as temperament) and the environment (e.g., parent and family circumstances and the prevailing sociocultural context) (see, e.g., Sameroff, 2009). Hence, temperament is often seen as one of several interacting risk or protective factors.

The last decade has seen increasing research on *moderational* effects. The influence of temperament may be moderated by environmental factors (e.g., poor child self-regulation may lead to behavior problems, particularly when children receive hostile parenting; see below in this chapter). Temperament may also moderate other influences (e.g., gentle discipline promotes conscience, particularly in fearful children; Kochanska, Aksan, & Joy, 2007; and see below in this chapter). Such findings have given rise to propositions such as Belsky, Bakermans-Kranenburg, and IJzendoorn's (2007) "differential susceptibility" hypothesis. This suggests that children with more extreme temperament characteristics are more susceptible to socialization experiences such as parenting, for better or for worse. For example, negatively emotional children may be more adversely affected by poor parenting than those with less negative affect, but they may also benefit more from positive parenting. Hence a "difficult" temperament in itself may not predict poor outcomes, but may even promote optimal development in the context of positive socialization.

In the review sections below, it will be seen that there is some support for each of these conceptualizations of developmental processes.

Methodological Issues

There has been considerable debate about the measurement of temperament. Because *temperament* refers to the overall behavioral style of a child, rather than moment-by-moment behavior, parents who observe the child across time and contexts have been considered appropriate informants. However, parents may lack a normative basis for rating their child. Findings that maternal depression and stress affect temperament ratings (e.g., Mednick et al., 1996) suggest a subjective element to maternal reports, leading some to doubt their value (Kagan & Fox, 2006). However, there is also evidence of reasonable validity of maternal reports (see Rothbart & Bates, 2006). Observations and laboratory manipulations can be useful but also have limitations, being restricted in both the time period and contexts of assessment, and usually lack normative data. Observational settings may also alter the behavior of children and caregivers. Parent reports and observations tend to be only moderately associated. Rothbart and Bates provided a useful summary of the relative strengths and weaknesses of each method, and recommend careful use of parent reports, with or without observations, but caution against reliance on only observations. The optimal solution is to use multiple measures of temperament, but few studies currently do so.

In this area of research, a recurring difficulty is separating, conceptually and methodologically, the predictive temperament factors from the outcomes. For example, wariness and fearful affect in the face of novelty not only are common measures of temperamental inhibition, but also form part of the definition of social withdrawal and anxiety. Further, if the same source (e.g., a parent or teacher report) provides information on both the temperamental precursor and the social developmental outcome, shared method variance is likely. Hence, statistical associations between temperament and social development may be inflated through contamination of measures or shared method variance and do not necessarily reflect causal relationships (Sanson, Prior, & Kyrios, 1990). Although longitudinal associations do not in themselves imply causation, they do allow more confident interpretations. We therefore focus our review on studies that meet at least one of two requirements: a longitudinal design, and more than one informant or method of data collection.

The next three sections focus on the social development of children aged from 3 to 11 years. However, many studies follow children longitudinally over time, and therefore division into narrower age ranges (e.g., preschool or late elementary school) is not feasible. Further, in some studies, temperament was assessed earlier than 3 years, or social developmental outcomes were assessed later than 11 years. Throughout the review we draw attention to the influence of gender, social class, and culture, although as will be seen the research base is often sparse.

Temperament Influences on Social Relations

Here we review research on the influence of temperament on children's social relations, including relations with teachers, parents, and siblings, but with the majority of current work being on relations with peers (tendencies to withdraw and to be shy or sociable with peers, and peer group status).

Most research has focused on the role of temperamental inhibition in the development of peer social withdrawal (solitary, onlooking, and unoccupied behaviors). As noted above, a challenge here is that indicators of inhibition can overlap with those of social withdrawal. Because this research is reviewed by Rubin, Coplan, Bowker, and Menzer (Chapter 23, this volume), we provide only a brief overview.

Many longitudinal studies indicate that inhibition in infancy and toddlerhood is associated with social withdrawal or lack of peer interaction in preschool and middle childhood (Burgess, Rubin, Cheah, & Nelson, 2005; Eisenberg, Shepard, Fabes, Murphy, & Guthrie, 1998). However, this is not always a simple or invariant relationship. Consistent with a transactional model, there is a growing body of evidence of temperament-by-parenting interactions. As examples, Early et al. (2002) showed that children who were fearful at age 15 months displayed more active peer engagement and less withdrawal in kindergarten if they received sensitive mothering. Similarly, inhibited toddlers were socially reticent at 4 years only if they had an overcontrolling mother (Rubin, Burgess, & Hastings, 2002).

Temperamental dimensions other than inhibition have received less research attention, but some direct and moderated relationships have been found. For example, task orientation (attentional self-regulation) and flexibility (positive mood, adaptability, and approach) have been associated with more peer interaction (Keogh & Burstein, 1988). David and Murphy (2007) found that effortful control moderated the relationship between interparental conflict and peer relations: Interparental conflict was positively related to problematic peer relations for preschoolers low in effortful control but negatively related to problems for children high in effortful control, who may avoid overarousal and also develop compensatory positive peer relations.

There is suggestive evidence that temperament may have different implications for boys' and girls' peer relations, perhaps due to cultural expectations about gender roles, although no clear-cut picture has yet emerged. Shyness appears more strongly associated with peer exclusion and rejection for boys than for girls (Coplan, Closson, & Arbeau, 2007). In the Australian Temperament Project (ATP), which has followed a representative sample of over 2,000 children from infancy into adulthood (Prior et al., 2000), temperament was found to be a stronger predictor for boys than girls of peer relations at 11–12 years. Low attention regulation, assessed from 1–3 years on, distinguished boys but not girls with problem peer relations, and higher reactivity in early and middle childhood predicted problem relations more strongly for boys than girls. Family factors appeared more important for girls' peer relations.

Investigations of cultural differences in this area are scant. Chen, Rubin, and Li (1995) found that 8–10-year-old inhibited Chinese children were more accepted by peers, and rated higher on "honorship" and leadership, than children identified as aggressive or average. The mediating role of culturally based parenting beliefs and behaviors was suggested by findings that for Chinese children, inhibition was positively correlated with maternal acceptance and encouragement, but in Canadian children the correlations were negative (Chen et al., 1998). The authors argued that in China, unlike North America, inhibition is seen to reflect social maturity and is viewed positively. These findings are somewhat inconsistent with findings that teacher-reported reticence was associated with lower peer sociometric ratings amongst American, Russian, and Chinese children (Hart et al., 2000). Further, these differences appear to be diminishing amongst urban Chinese children, suggesting the influence of the adoption of more "Western" values in modern China (Chen, Cen, Li, & He, 2005).

Few studies have examined associations between temperament and children's relations with siblings, parents, and teachers. In an early study, Stocker and Dunn (1990) found that temperament was concurrently related to the quality of relations with friends and peers but not siblings. Studying grade 1 children, Arbeau, Coplan, and Weeks (2010) suggested that strong teacher–child relations may lessen the relationship between shyness and later poor adjustment, playing a protective role.

To summarize, although there are many research gaps, there is clear evidence of associations between early temperament (particularly inhibition, but also attentional self-regulation and reactivity) and later social relations. There is suggestive evidence of sex differences in these links. Increasing evidence of temperament-by-parenting interactions suggests transactional processes involving parenting and cultural expectations.

Temperamental Influences on Social Competence

The recognition that individual differences in positive social behaviors stem from early childhood has fueled interest in the role of temperament, and there is increasing evidence for its link with socially competent behaviors. Included here is a review of research on socially skilled behavior, prosocial behavior, and conscience.

Some direct links with specific temperament dimensions have been found. First, negative emotionality appears to be associated with socially competent behavior in distinct and complex ways. Rothbart, Ahadi, and Hershey (1994) found that temperamental fear (unease, worry) and sadness (lowered mood or energy) were related to empathy, guilt, and shame; whereas aspects of negative affectivity reflecting irritability (anger or discomfort) were related to antisocial, but not prosocial, behaviors. Similarly, Eisenberg et al. (1996) found that low levels of negative emotionality (reactivity, fear, and sadness) were related to constructive social skills in middle childhood.

Second, research has indicated the importance of effortful control and attentional, behavioral, and emotional self-regulation (Rothbart & Bates, 2006). Attentional regulation (persistence) predicted prosocial behaviors in preschool children (Yagmurlu & Sanson, 2009), and was also a powerful predictor of social skills in 5–6-year-old children in Australia, accounting for 24% of the variance (Paterson & Sanson, 1999). Regulatory capacities may help children attend to and respond appropriately to social cues. However, associations with effortful control may vary by gender and context. For instance, using naturalistic observation, Fabes et al. (1999) reported that socially competent responding was associated with effortful control only in high-intensity (energetic or stressful) peer interactions, and Blair, Denham, Kochanoff, and Whipple (2004) found that effortful control predicted socially competent behavior only for preschool-aged boys, but not for girls.

Other temperament dimensions also impact social competence. Using naturalistic observations of American preschoolers from homeless families, Youngblade and Mulvihill (1998) found that children who were soothable or persistent displayed more positive behaviors than emotional or shy children. Norwegian children who displayed good social skills and adaptive functioning in middle childhood had low emotionality and high sociability as infants (Mathiesen & Prior, 2006). In the ATP sample, temperament in earlier years explained 16–20% of the variance in 11–12-year-olds' social skills (by parent, teacher, and child reports). Attentional self-regulation, reactivity, flexibility, and sociability were the most important predictors (Prior et al., 2000).

Interactions amongst temperament characteristics also appear to influence social competence, shown particularly by the work of Eisenberg and colleagues. Eisenberg et al. (1993) found that low social skills (assessed by parent, teacher, and observer reports) were strongly predicted by low self-regulation capacities and high emotionality. In a later study (Eisenberg, Fabes, Guthrie, & Reiser, 2002), moderate to high self-regulation appeared optimal for successful social functioning, and it was even more important amongst children high in negative emotionality. Eisenberg, Pidada, and Liew (2001) found that similar relations among negative emotions, emotion regulation, and social competence held for children in a non-Western country (Indonesia) (see Eisenberg et al., 2002, for further review).

The interaction between temperament and parenting has been the focus of studies by Kochanska and colleagues, who posit that affective and self-regulatory aspects of temperament contribute to conscience development, through evolving interactions with parenting. Kochanska (1995) showed that for fearful toddlers, gentle maternal discipline facilitated conscience development by preschool age. For fearless children, higher attachment security and higher maternal responsiveness predicted later conscience. Subsequent work (e.g., Kochanska et al., 2007) indicated that for relatively fearful children, parents' power assertion, even at low levels, predicted very low levels of prosocial behavior, supporting Belsky et al.'s (2007) differential susceptibility hypothesis (see above).

Studies have also identified complex interactions amongst gender, context, parenting, and temperament. For example, Hastings, Rubin, and Meilcarek (2005) found that maternal protectiveness was most strongly related to children's prosocial behavior in highly inhibited girls, but was related to less prosocial behavior in less inhibited girls. No relationships were found for inhibited boys. Less attentive children displayed lower social competence, particularly when their parents were under high levels of stress (Coplan, Bowker, & Cooper, 2003). Spinrad et al. (2007) showed that effortful control mediated the relation between early supportive parenting (emotion socialization, warmth, and sensitivity) and social competence at both 18 months and 30 months of age. These results emphasize the importance of family and environmental factors, in conjunction with intrinsic child characteristics, in the development of social competence.

The moderating role of temperament was recently demonstrated by Stright, Gallagher, and Kelley (2008), who showed that the link between high-quality parenting during infancy and early childhood (providing emotional support and encouraging autonomy) and teacher-rated social competence (social skills, and peer and teacher interactions) in first grade was moderated by child temperament. When parenting quality was low, children who were "difficult" as infants had poorer social competence, but when it was high, difficult infants had higher social competence than less difficult children, consistent with Belsky et al.'s (2007) hypothesis (see above).

Temperamental Influences on Emotional and Behavioral Problems

The contribution of temperament to the development of emotional and behavioral problems has been extensively researched, particularly regarding externalizing behavior problems (EBPs) such as aggression, hyperactivity, and oppositional behavior, and internalizing problems (IPs) such as anxiety and depression.

Externalizing behavior problems

Given the large number of studies in this area and several comprehensive reviews (e.g., Calkins & Degnan, 2006; Rothbart & Bates, 2006; Sanson et al., 2004), only highlights of this research are presented, focusing particularly on longitudinal studies.

Negative emotionality or reactivity consistently emerges as a risk factor for EBPs. As examples, parent-reported negative emotionality at 5 years was a substantial predictor of teacher-reported EBPs at 8 years (Nelson, Martin, Hodge, Havill, & Kamphaus, 1999), and amongst Norwegian children, emotionality/self-control at 18 months was associated with more behavior problems at 8–9 years (Mathiesen & Prior, 2006). Similarly, emotion regulation plays an important role in EBPs. Cole, Zahn-Waxler, Fox, Usher, and Welsh (1996) found that children with poor emotion regulation had more EBP symptoms (by parent and teacher reports) at preschool age and 2 years later than did children with "modulated" expressiveness.

Commonly, studies find that two or more aspects of temperament contribute to EBPs. Rubin, Coplan, Fox, and Calkins (1995) found that children with poor emotional regulation and high levels of sociability had more EBPs than high regulation–high sociability and average groups, whereas the low regulation–low sociability group had more IPs. Thus, emotional dysregulation appeared to be a generalized risk factor for adjustment difficulties, the expression of which was affected by the presence of other factors. In an ATP study, Sanson, Smart, Prior, and Oberklaid (1993) showed that aggressive and hyperactive-aggressive 7–8-year-old children had been less manageable and more reactive, irritable, inflexible, and nonpersistent from infancy to early childhood than those with only hyperactivity or neither problem. Other factors, including poorer mother–child relationships, larger family size, and more family stresses, also differentiated the groups, indicating transactional processes. Similarly, Miller-Lewis et al. (2006) found that parent-reported EBPs at 6 years were predicted by higher temperamental inflexibility and nonpersistence at 4 years. A study of 11-year-old Dutch children found that low effortful control and high frustration concurrently predicted EBPs (Veenstra, Oldehinkel, De Winter, Lindenberg, & Ormel, 2006). This study is one of few to report the influence of social class, with high SES being protective against EBPs for children low in effortful control and high in frustration. Surprisingly, it also found that parental rejection predicted EBPs for children *low* in frustration.

The moderating role of parenting in temperament–EBP associations was demonstrated by Rubin, Burgess, Dwyer, and Hastings (2003), who followed a Canadian sample from 2 to 4 years and found that low regulation (undercontrol) more strongly predicted EBPs when mothering was hostile and intrusive at age 2. Hemphill and Sanson (2001) followed an Australian sample over the same age range, and similarly found that high-reactive children who showed higher EBPs at 4 years had experienced poorer parenting (low warmth, high punishment, or low induction) at 2 years than similarly reactive children who did not show later EBPs. In an example of both additive and transactional effects in a large sample, Lahey et al. (2008) showed that infant fussiness, activity, predictability, and positive affect contributed additively to the prediction of EBPs (conduct problems) at 4–13 years (both by mother report). The temperament-by-temperament interaction of low fussiness and high predictability was protective against EBPs. Low maternal cognitive stimulation was also a direct contributor to EBPs, whereas maternal responsiveness was predictive only for low-fearful infants, and the effect of spanking was moderated by fussiness and positive affect.

Surprisingly few studies have explicitly investigated sex differences in temperament–EBP connections, but there are a few relevant reports. Lahey et al. (2008; and see above) reported gender differences with fussiness more strongly predicting boys' EBPs and fearfulness predicting girls' EBPs. Fabes, Shepard, Guthrie, and Martin (1997) found that problem behavior during peer play increased in boys with high arousal levels but decreased for high-arousal girls (see also Bates, Bayles, Bennet, Ridge, & Brown, 1991).

Similarly, there are few studies examining cultural differences in these connections. In one study comparing predictors of relational and physical aggression in Australian and North American preschoolers (Russell, Hart, Robinson, & Olsen, 2003), no country differences were found. Overall, the similarity in findings from studies conducted in the United States, Canada, Norway, Sweden, the Netherlands, and Australia suggests little cultural variability in the role of temperament across these Western countries, but there is a dearth of studies from non-Western countries.

Internalizing problems

Most studies investigating connections between temperament and IPs have focused on inhibition, where associations are frequently reported. To some extent, this research overlaps with that reviewed earlier in this chapter, because social withdrawal and social anxiety are at the same time aspects of relationships and symptoms of IPs. In an Australian study, Bayer, Sanson, and Hemphill (2009) found that inhibited temperament in toddlers predicted IPs (anxious and depressive behaviors) at 4 years. Kagan and Snidman (1999) followed infants to 7 years and reported that infant negative reactivity predicted toddler and preschool inhibition, which subsequently predicted childhood IPs. Schwartz, Snidman, and Kagan (1999) followed the same sample into adolescence and found that 61% of adolescents who had been extremely inhibited toddlers displayed social anxiety symptoms, compared to only 27% of uninhibited toddlers. However, in their recent review, Degnan and Fox (2007) noted that between a third and a half of inhibited children are not inhibited by adolescence, and, across studies, between 39% and 83% do not develop anxiety disorders.

Relatively few studies have investigated links between temperament and depression, another aspect of IPs. In a study of the Dutch sample reported above, Oldehinkel, Veenstra, Ormel, de Winter, and Verhulst (2006) found concurrent links between depressive problems and temperamental fearfulness and frustration, and temperament-by-parenting interactions, with high frustration combined with overprotective parenting or low warmth predicting more depressive problems. In a rare demonstration of gender differences, the effects of frustration were stronger for boys, and fearful girls but not boys who experienced parental rejection showed more depressive problems. Using the ATP sample, Letcher, Smart, Sanson, and Toumbourou (2009) identified a number of different trajectories in IPs from ages 3 to 15 (low, high, decreasing, and increasing) for both girls and boys, and showed that temperamental reactivity and shyness, along with less optimal parenting and peer difficulties, were more prominent predictors of increasing trajectories for girls, whereas EBPs were more predictive for boys on increasing trajectories. Such studies are starting to shed light on why some but not all reactive and/or inhibited children go on to show difficulties in adolescence, an essential guide to early intervention.

Several studies examine temperament connections with both EBPs and IPs. In a sample of grade 1–2 students (60% African American, and 35% White), Morris et al. (2002) collected parent questionnaires on children's temperament, teacher reports on children's EBPs and IPs, and children's reports on parenting. Irritable distress (anger and frustration) positively related to EBPs and IPs, and effortful control negatively correlated with EBPs. Further, for children high in irritable distress and those low in effortful control, maternal hostility predicted EBPs, and for children high in irritable distress, maternal psychological control predicted IPs. Although small and cross-sectional, this study demonstrates multiple data collection methods and analysis of interaction effects in an ethnically diverse sample. Finally, Mathiesen, Sanson, Stoolmiller, and Karevold (2009) identified trajectories of both EBPs (undercontrol) and IPs over three waves from 18 months to 4 years in a large Norwegian sample, and examined the prediction of both their initial status (intercept) and change (slope) from temperament and family factors. Interestingly, they also investigated the impact of *change* in these factors over time. Negative emotionality, along with family stress, maternal depressive symptoms, and partner support, predicted both outcomes, whereas shyness and low sociability also predicted IPs, and high activity predicted EBPs. Further, increases over time in emotionality, shyness, and family stress predicted escalating IPs, and increases in activity, shyness, and emotionality and decreases in partner support predicted escalating EBPs. This study demonstrates the value of taking a dynamic view not only of social development outcomes but also of risk and protective factors, including temperament.

In summary, a large body of research indicates that negative emotionality, reactivity, and low attention regulation are strongly implicated in the development of EBPs, whereas inhibition and negative emotionality appear to be important predictors of IPs. Few studies specifically examine cultural or social class differences in the role of temperament in this age range. Gender differences are underexplored, but some suggestive findings are emerging for both EBPs and IPs. Although most research has concentrated on linear and additive relationships, there has been a recent upsurge in findings of interesting moderational effects.

Temperament-Based Intervention

The body of literature reviewed above demonstrates that temperament is closely implicated in children's social development and provides a foundation for temperament-based interventions. These aim to promote social competence, prevent behavior problems, or treat disorders by enhancing the responsiveness and effectiveness of parents and teachers, and help children to apply temperament-based strategies to enhance their own self-regulation. Temperament-based interventions are informed by the goodness-of-fit model of Chess and Thomas (1986; and see above). When there is consonance between the child's temperament and the expectations, demands, and opportunities of their environment, optimal development is possible. If there is a mismatch or poor fit, maladaptive functioning is likely to occur. In general, the goal of temperament-based intervention is to improve the "fit" between children and their environment.

Especially as children get older, it is often difficult to achieve a good "fit" (McClowry, Rodriguez, & Koslowitz, 2008). Schools and community settings may not accommodate children's individual needs, and even in a responsive environment, children can encounter challenges because of their temperament. Achieving a better "fit" entails two strategies: scaffolding and stretching. Responsive caregivers scaffold children when they recognize that a situation may be uncomfortable for them and, if it is likely to overwhelm them, act to either remove or reduce the challenge. Stretching involves helping children to develop internal regulation over the aspects of their temperament that undermine their competence. With repeated practice, children can learn to self-administer such strategies to enhance their own self-regulation.

Despite considerable interest in applying temperament principles to enhance children's competence, the development and empirical testing of interventions have been slow (McClowry et al., 2008). Although still limited in number, temperament-based interventions have adopted universal prevention, targeted prevention, and treatment approaches. Examples of these three approaches are reviewed below.

Temperament-based universal prevention approaches

For more than 20 years, temperament-based anticipatory guidance has been offered to members of a large U.S. health maintenance organization (HMO; Cameron & Neville, 2008). As part of their children's routine health care, parents are offered individualized written feedback about their child's temperament, alerting them to behavior management issues that may occur. Significantly fewer health care visits for attention deficit with hyperactivity disorder (ADHD), obesity, and general anxiety were found among the school-aged children whose parents took advantage of the guidance compared to those who did not.

In an Australian program aiming to prevent anxiety and behavior problems called REACH for RESILIENCE, participants were parents of preschool children (Dadds & Roth, 2001). In six sessions, they were taught cognitive behavioral strategies to use when children encountered anxiety-provoking social situations. Teachers reported that the program, compared to a no-treatment condition, was effective in reducing children's anxiety and anger-aggression. Parents did not report changes, which may have been due to few children initially having IPs.

Temperament-based targeted interventions

Children at risk for behavior problems due to poverty have been the focus of two U.S. temperament-based preventive programs. The curriculum of Tools for the Mind is intended to help preschool children to enhance their inhibitory control, working memory, and cognitive flexibility (Diamond, Barnett, Thomas, & Munro, 2007). Children were randomly allocated to Tools for the Mind or a literacy program. After 1–2 years, the children in Tools, compared to those in the literacy program, demonstrated higher memory scores and attention skills.

The second preventive intervention for disadvantaged children is INSIGHTS into Children's Temperament, a 10-week program for primary school children, parents, and teachers (McClowry, 2003). In parallel workshops, parents and teachers learn how to match management strategies to a child's specific temperament. Children learn related content in classroom sessions (McClowry, Snow, & Tamis-LeMonda, 2005). INSIGHTS was more effective than an attention control read-aloud program in reducing children's EBPs, with greater efficacy among children initially at diagnostic levels of disruptive disorders.

Two other studies focused on children at risk for behavior problems due to their temperaments. Sheeber and Johnson (1994) provided a 9-week program for U.S. mothers who reported that their 3–5-year-old children had difficult temperaments. The intervention was designed to help parents adopt more effective disciplinary strategies. Mothers in the program, compared to a wait-list control group, reported increased satisfaction in their parent–child relationships, enhanced parental competence, and improved affect. They also reported reduced IPs and EBPs and fewer disruptions in family life. The effects were maintained at a 2-month follow-up.

An early intervention program in Australia targeted inhibited children identified through screening at preschools (Rapee, Kennedy, Ingram, Edwards, & Sweeney, 2005). Their parents were randomly assigned to a no-treatment group or a six-session program in which they learned about the development of anxiety, parent management techniques to reduce children's symptoms, and cognitive restructuring of their own worries. Anxiety was significantly reduced in children whose mothers were in the intervention condition.

Temperament-based treatment

Another temperament-based intervention offered through an HMO in a suburban U.S. community involved treatment for preschoolers exhibiting serious EBPs (Pade, Taube, Aalborg, & Reiser, 2006). In a 10-week program called TOTS, parents learned play and discipline strategies. Following the intervention, parents reported a reduction in child behavior problems and less difficulty managing the children, and treatment effects were maintained 5–6 years later for those children available for follow-up.

In summary, there is accumulating evidence that temperament-based interventions can assist parents and teachers to enhance child competence. It is clear, however, that the potential for such approaches is not fully realized. The continued development of temperament-based interventions whose efficacy is tested in rigorous randomized control studies is recommended.

Comments and Conclusions

Temperament is now a well-established construct. Understanding of its structure and developmental course is increasing, and burgeoning research is shedding light on its biological foundations, although these are far from fully understood. And it clearly impacts many aspects of social development. However, this does not mean that its influence on social development is straightforward. In fact, research conducted since the first edition of this handbook reinforces the complexity of its effects.

The progress over a mere 7 years has been impressive. Early research focused predominantly on linear relations between temperament and social development, and many researchers still look for, and find, such relationships. These provide some evidence for what Rothbart and Bates (2006) described as "differentiated linkages" – for example, inhibition has a strong link to social withdrawal and internalizing problems, and the combination of low self-regulation and reactivity is a potent predictor of EBPs. There is no doubt that such direct effects of temperament account for a significant portion of its impact.

However, developmental theory has long proposed more complex interactional and transactional processes involving temperament (see Sanson et al., 2004). Until recently, these ideas were largely speculative, but the adoption of more complex designs and sophisticated analytic tools in the last decade is now providing empirical evidence to support them. There has been remarkable growth in evidence of moderational effects, mostly involving temperament and parenting but sometimes other aspects of the social environment. These may be conceptualized as temperament moderating the impact of the environment, or vice versa – as Rothbart and Bates (2006) noted, the choice is largely a matter of interpretation. Many moderational findings support Chess and Thomas's original "goodness-of-fit" model, elucidating the nature of an optimal "fit" between temperament and environment. Intriguingly, these seem to have considerable specificity – for example, gentleness promotes conscience development in fearful children, but overprotectiveness contributes to anxiety in these same children. A number of findings are also concordant with Belsky's differential susceptibility model, suggesting that children with more extreme temperaments are more susceptible to socialization, either positively or negatively (e.g., Kochanska et al., 2007). Such moderational findings will provide increasingly specific guidance to interventions, whether universal, targeted, or treatment oriented. However, a note of caution is that many of these interactional effects account for little variance and have not been replicated. Although some authors reported failure to find interaction effects, there are probably also unpublished "failures." There is a critical need for further replication efforts, including reporting of the absence of interactions.

In keeping with a transactional model of development, there is a trend for a number of other influences on social development to be included in studies besides temperament. In such studies it is notable that the contribution of temperament is not "washed out" by parent, family, and broader social environments such as child care and school. Future development of transactional models may elaborate the influence of multiple temperament dimensions on children's social development in interaction with multiple environmental factors and socializing agents, although obtaining sufficient power in such work will require large samples.

In contrast to these areas of progress, there have been few notable advances in our understanding of the roles of sociocultural factors. Although there are more studies with non-English-speaking children, it is important to recognize that current knowledge is mostly derived from middle-class "Western" samples, and may be therefore mostly generalizable to them. Cultures may attribute different values to the same child characteristics, eliciting different responses from others, thus impacting social development. Therefore, sociocultural background may mediate the relation between parental socialization, temperament, and social development. Much more work is needed on the roles of temperament in social development in different social and cultural settings in order to increase our understanding of how temperament "works" in context.

Remarkably little attention has been given to gender effects in the association of temperament to social development, and it is difficult to discern a clear pattern amongst current findings. This is clearly an area in need of further exploration. In terms of age, although there is evidence of important changes in the operation of temperament in the very early years, associations of temperament with social development appear very similar across the age range studied here. In impressive demonstrations of the importance of the early years, temperament in infancy and toddlerhood is predictive of social adjustment throughout childhood and adolescence (e.g., Lahey et al., 2008; Mathiesen et al., 2009; Prior et al., 2000).

Overall, this review indicates that more flesh is now being put on the bones of previously theoretical conceptualizations of the processes by which temperament impacts social development. However, recent research also underlines the complexities in these processes. After a period of "lumping" temperament into broad categories, it is now becoming clear that we also need to attend to finer differentiations, such as distinct components of negative affect (anger, fear, irritability, distress to novelty, and frustration). The increasing body of intriguing findings of moderational effects is also a story of complexity, and we are far from a coherent overall model of how specific temperament factors interact with aspects of the environment to predict social developmental outcomes. Moreover, these phenomena need to be explored across a much broader range of sociocultural contexts. Luckily, we now have the methodological and statistical tools available to address these complexities. Hence, these are exciting times for temperament research.

References

Arbeau, K., Coplan, R., & Weeks, M. (2010). Shyness, teacher-child relationships, and socio-emotional adjustment in grade 1. *International Journal of Behavioral Development, 34*(3), 259–269.

Bates, J., Bayles, K., Bennet, D., Ridge, B., & Brown, M. (1991). Origins of externalising behavior problems at eight years of age. In D. Pepler & K. Rubin (Eds.), *The development and treatment of childhood aggression* (pp. 93–121). Hillsdale, NJ: Erlbaum.

Bates, J., & Pettit, G. (2007). Temperament, parenting, and socialisation. In J. Grusec & P. Hastings (Eds.), *Handbook of socialisation: Theory and research* (pp. 153–180). New York: Guilford Press.

Bayer, J., Sanson, A., & Hemphill, S. (2009). Early childhood aetiology of internalising difficulties: A longitudinal community study. *International Journal of Mental Health Promotion, 11*, 22–32.

Belsky, J., Bakermans-Kranenburg, M., & IJzendoorn, M. (2007). For better and for worse: Differential susceptibility to environmental influences. *Current Directions in Psychological Science, 16*, 300–304.

Blair, K. A., Denham, S. A., Kochanoff, A., & Whipple, B. (2004). Playing it cool: Temperament, emotion regulation, and social behavior in preschoolers. *Journal of School Psychology, 42*, 419–443.

Burgess, K. B., Rubin, K. H., Cheah, C. S. L., & Nelson, L. J. (2005). Behavioral inhibition, social withdrawal, and parenting. In W. R. Crozier & L. E. Alden (Eds.), *The essential handbook of social anxiety for clinicians* (pp. 99–120). New York: Wiley.

Calkins, S., & Degnan, K. (2006). Temperament in early development. In R. Ammerman (Ed.), *Comprehensive handbook of personality and psychopathology*. New York: Wiley.

Cameron, J., & Neville, H. (2008, October). In a health maintenance organization, can early temperament-based anticipatory guidance reduce subsequent medical visits over the next decade? Paper presented at the 17th Occasional Temperament Conference, San Rafael, CA.

Chen, X., Cen, G., Li, D., & He, Y. (2005). Social functioning and adjustment in Chinese children: The imprint of historical time. *Child Development, 76*, 182–195.

Chen, X., Hastings, P., Rubin, K., Chen, H., Cen, G., & Stewart, S. (1998). Childrearing attitudes and behavioral inhibition in Chinese and Canadian toddlers: A cross-cultural study. *Developmental Psychology, 34*, 677–686.

Chen, X., Rubin, K., & Li, D. (1995). Social and school adjustment of shy and aggressive children in China. *Development and Psychopathology, 7*, 337–349.

Chess, S., & Thomas, A. (1986). *Temperament in clinical practice.* New York: Guilford Press.

Cole, P., Zahn-Waxler, C., Fox, N., Usher, B., & Welsh, J. (1996). Individual differences in emotion regulation and behavior problems in preschool children. *Journal of Abnormal Psychology, 105*, 515–532.

Coplan, R., Bowker, J., & Cooper, S. (2003). Parenting daily hassles, child temperament, and social adjustment in preschool. *Early Childhood Research Quarterly, 18*, 376–395.

Coplan, R. J., Closson, L., & Arbeau, K. (2007). Gender differences in the behavioral associates of loneliness and social dissatisfaction in kindergarten. *Journal of Child Psychology and Psychiatry, 48*, 988–995.

Dadds, M. R., & Roth, J. (2001). Family processes in the development of anxiety problems. In M. Vasey & M. Dadds (Eds.), *The developmental psychopathology of anxiety* (pp. 278–303). New York: Oxford University Press.

David, K. M., & Murphy, B. (2007). Interparental conflict and preschoolers' peer relations: The moderating roles of temperament and gender. *Social Development, 16*, 1–23.

Degnan, K. A., & Fox, N. (2007). Behavioral inhibition and anxiety disorders: Multiple levels of a resilience process. *Development and Psychopathology, 19*, 729–746.

Diamond, A., Barnett, W. S., Thomas, J., & Munro, S. (2007). Preschool program improves cognitive control. *Science, 318*, 1387–1388.

Early, D. M., Rimm-Kaufman, S. E., Cox, M. J., Saluja, G., Pianta, R. C., Bradley, R. H., & Payne, C. C. (2002). Maternal sensitivity and child wariness in the transition to kindergarten. *Parenting: Science and Practice, 2*, 355–377.

Eisenberg, N., Fabes, R., Bernweig, J., Karbon, M., Poulin, R., & Hanish, L. (1993). The relations of emotionality and regulation to preschoolers' social skills and sociometric status. *Child Development, 64*, 1418–1438.

Eisenberg, N., Fabes, R. A., Guthrie, I. K., & Reiser, M. (2002). The role of emotionality and regulation in children's social competence and adjustment. In L. Pulkkinen & A. Caspi (Eds.), *Paths to successful development: Personality in the life course* (pp. 46–70). New York: Cambridge University Press.

Eisenberg, N., Fabes, R., Karbon, R., Murphy, B., Wosinski, M., Polazzi, L., et al. (1996). The relations of children's dispositional prosocial behavior to emotionality, regulation, and social functioning. *Child Development, 67*, 974–992.

Eisenberg, N., Pidada, S., & Liew, J. (2001). The relations of regulation and negative emotionality to Indonesian children's social functioning. *Child Development, 72*, 1747–1763.

Eisenberg, N., Shepard, S., Fabes, R., Murphy, B., & Guthrie, I. (1998). Shyness and children's emotionality, regulation, and coping: Contemporaneous, longitudinal, and across-context relations. *Child Development, 69,* 767–790.

Else-Quest, N., Hyde, J., Goldsmith, H., & Van Hulle, C. (2006). Gender differences in temperament: A meta-analysis. *Psychological Bulletin, 132,* 33–72.

Fabes, R., Eisenberg, N., Jones, S., Smith, M., Guthrie, I., Poulin, R., et al. (1999). Regulation, emotionality, and preschoolers' socially competent peer interactions. *Child Development, 70,* 432–442.

Fabes, R. A., Shepard, S. A., Guthrie, I. K., & Martin, C. L. (1997). Roles of temperamental arousal and gender-segregated play in young children's social adjustment. *Developmental Psychology, 33,* 693–702.

Hart, C., Yang, S., Nelson, L., Robinson, C., Olsen, J., Nelson, D., et al. (2000). Peer acceptance in early childhood and subtypes of socially withdrawn behaviour in China, Russia, and the United States. *International Journal of Behavioral Development, 24,* 73–81.

Hastings, P., Rubin, K., & Meilcarek, L. (2005). Helping anxious boys and girls to be good: The links between inhibition, parental socialization, and development of concern for others. *Merrill-Palmer Quarterly, 51,* 501–527.

Hemphill, S., & Sanson, A. (2001). Matching parenting with child temperament. *Family Matters, 59,* 42–77.

Kagan, J., & Fox, N. A. (2006). Biology, culture, and temperamental biases. In N. Eisenberg, W. Damon, & R. M. Lerner (Eds.), *Handbook of child psychology: Vol. 3. Social, emotional, and personality development* (6th ed., pp. 167–225). Hoboken, NJ: Wiley.

Kagan, J., & Snidman, N. (1999). Early childhood predictors of adult anxiety disorders. *Biological Psychiatry, 46,* 1536–1541.

Keogh, N., & Burstein, N. (1988). Relationship of temperament to preschoolers' interactions with peers and teachers. *Exceptional Children, 54,* 456–461.

Kochanska, G. (1995). Children's temperament, mothers' discipline, and security of attachment: Multiple pathways to emerging internalization. *Child Development, 66,* 597–615.

Kochanska, G., Aksan, N., & Joy, M. E. (2007). Children's fearfulness as a moderator of parenting in early socialization: Two longitudinal studies. *Developmental Psychology, 43,* 222–237.

Lahey, B. B., Van Hulle, C., Keenan, K., Rathous, P., D'Onofrio, B., Rodgers, J., et al. (2008). Temperament and parenting during the first year of life predict future child conduct problems. *Journal of Abnormal Child Psychology, 36,* 1139–1158.

Letcher, P., Smart, D., Sanson, A., & Toumbourou, J. (2009). Psychosocial precursors and correlates of differing internalizing trajectories from 3 to 15 years. *Social Development, 18,* 618–646.

Mathiesen, K. S., & Prior, M. (2006). The impact of temperament factors and family functioning on resilience processes from infancy to school age. *European Journal of Developmental Psychology, 3,* 357–387.

Mathiesen, K., Sanson, A., Stoolmiller, M., & Karevold, E. (2009). The nature of predictors of undercontrolled and internalizing problem trajectories across early childhood. *Journal of Abnormal Child Psychology, 37,* 209–222.

McClowry, S. G. (2003). *Your child's unique temperament: Insights and strategies for responsive parenting.* Champaign, IL: Research Press.

McClowry, S. G., Rodriguez, E. T., & Koslowitz, R. (2008). Temperament-based intervention: Re-examining goodness of fit. *European Journal of Developmental Science, 2,* 120–135.

McClowry, S., Snow, D. L., & Tamis-LeMonda, C. S. (2005). An evaluation of the effects of "INSIGHTS" on the behavior of inner city primary school children. *Journal of Primary Prevention, 26,* 567–584.

Mednick, B., Hocevar, D., Schulsinger, C., & Baker, R. (1996). Personality and demographic characteristics of mothers and their ratings of their 3- to 10-year-old children's temperament. *Merrill-Palmer Quarterly, 42*, 397–417.

Miller-Lewis, L., Baghurst, P., Sawyer, M., Prior, M., Clark, J., Arney, F., et al. (2006). Early childhood externalising behaviour problems: Child, parenting, and family-related predictors over time. *Journal of Abnormal Child Psychology, 34*, 891–906.

Morris, A. S., Silk, J. S., Steinberg, L., Sessa, F. M., Avenevoli, S., & Essex, M. J. (2002). Temperamental vulnerability and negative parenting as interacting of child adjustment. *Journal of Marriage and Family, 64*, 461–471.

Nelson, B., Martin, R. P., Hodge, S., Havill, V., & Kamphaus, R. (1999). Modeling the prediction of elementary school adjustment from preschool temperament. *Personality and Individual Differences, 26*, 687–700.

Oldehinkel, A. J., Veenstra, R., Ormel, J., de Winter, A. F., & Verhulst, F. C. (2006). Temperament, parenting, and depressive symptoms in a population sample of preadolescents. *Journal of Child Psychology and Psychiatry, 47*, 684–695.

Pade, H., Taube, D. O., Aalborg, A. E., & Reiser, P. J. (2006). An immediate and long-term study of a temperament and parent-child interaction therapy based community program for preschoolers with behavior problems. *Child Family Behavior Therapy, 28*, 1–28.

Paterson, G., & Sanson, A. (1999). The association of behavioural adjustment to temperament, parenting and family characteristics among 5-year-old children. *Social Development, 8*, 293–309.

Pedlow, R., Sanson, A., Prior, M., & Oberklaid, F. (1993). The stability of temperament from infancy to eight years. *Developmental Psychology, 29*, 998–1007.

Prior, M., Kyrios, M., & Oberklaid, F. (1986). Temperament in Australian, American, Chinese and Greek infants: Some issues and directions for future research. *Journal of Cross Cultural Psychology, 17*, 455–474.

Prior, M., Sanson, A., Smart, D., & Oberklaid, F. (2000). *Pathways from infancy to adolescence: Australian Temperament Project 1983–2000*. Melbourne: Australian Institute of Family Studies.

Putnam, S., Sanson, A., & Rothbart, M. (2002). Child temperament and parenting. In M. Bornstein (Ed.), *Handbook of parenting* (2nd ed., pp. 255–278). Mahwah, NJ: Erlbaum.

Rapee, R. M., Kennedy, S., Ingram, M., Edwards, S., & Sweeney, L. (2005). Prevention and early intervention of anxiety disorders in inhibited preschool children. *Journal of Consulting and Clinical Psychology, 73*, 488–497.

Roberts, B., & DelVecchio, W. (2000). The rank-order consistency of personality traits from childhood to old age: A quantitative review of longitudinal studies. *Psychological Bulletin, 126*, 3–25.

Rothbart, M., Ahadi, S., & Hershey, K. (1994). Temperament and social behaviour in childhood. *Merrill-Palmer Quarterly, 40*, 21–39.

Rothbart, M. K., & Bates, J. E. (2006). Temperament. In N. Eisenberg, W. Damon, & R. M. Lerner (Eds.), *Handbook of child psychology: Vol. 3. Social, emotional, and personality development* (6th ed., pp. 99–166). Hoboken, NJ: Wiley.

Rubin, K. H., Burgess, K. B., Dwyer, K. M., & Hastings, P. D. (2003). Predicting preschoolers' externalizing behaviors from toddler temperament, conflict, and maternal negativity. *Developmental Psychology, 39*, 164–176.

Rubin, K. H., Burgess, K. B., & Hastings, P. D. (2002). Stability and social-behavioral consequences of toddlers' inhibited temperament and parenting behaviors. *Child Development, 73*, 483–495.

Rubin, K., Coplan, R., Fox, N., & Calkins, S. (1995). Emotionality, emotion regulation, and prechoolers' social adaptation. *Development and Psychopathology, 7*, 49–62.

Rubin, K., Hemphill, S., Chen, X., Hastings, P., Sanson, A., Lo Coco, A., et al. (2006). A cross-cultural study of the behavioral inhibition in toddlers: East-west-north-south. *International Journal of Behavioral Development, 30*, 219–226.

Russell, A., Hart, C., Robinson, C., & Olsen, S. (2003). Children's sociable and aggressive behavior with peers: A comparison of the US and Australia, and contributions of temperament and parenting styles. *International Journal of Behavioral Development, 27*, 74–86.

Sameroff, A. (2009). *The transactional model of development: How children and contexts shape each other*. Washington, DC: American Psychological Association.

Sanson, A., Hemphill, S. A., & Smart, D. (2004). Connections between temperament and social development: A review. *Social Development, 13*, 142–170.

Sanson, A., Prior, M., & Kyrios, K. (1990). Contamination of measures in temperament research. *Merrill-Palmer Quarterly, 36*, 179–192.

Sanson, A., Smart, D., Prior, M., & Oberklaid, F. (1993). Precursors of hyperactivity and aggression. *Journal of the American Academy of Child and Adolescent Psychiatry, 32*, 1207–1216.

Schwartz, C., Snidman, N., & Kagan, J. (1999). Adolescent social anxiety as an outcome of inhibited temperament in childhood. *Journal of the American Academy of Child and Adolescent Psychiatry, 38*, 1008–1015.

Sheeber, L., & Johnson, J. (1994). Evaluation of a temperament-focused parent training program. *Journal of Clinical Child Psychology, 23*, 249–259.

Spinrad, T. L., Eisenberg, N., Gaertner, B., Popp, T., Smith, C. L., Kupfer, A., et al. (2007). Relations of maternal socialization and toddlers' effortful control to children's adjustment and social competence. *Developmental Psychology, 43*, 1170–1186.

Stocker, C., & Dunn, J. (1990). Sibling relationships in childhood: Links with friendships and peer relationships. *British Journal of Developmental Psychology, 8*, 227–244.

Stright, A. D., Gallagher, K. C., & Kelley, K. (2008). Infant temperament moderates relations between maternal parenting in early childhood and children's adjustment in first grade. *Child Development, 79*, 186–200.

Thomas, A., Chess, S., Birch, H., Hertzig, M., & Korn, S. (1963). *Behavioral individuality in early childhood*. New York: New York University Press.

Veenstra, R., Oldehinkel, A. J., De Winter, A. F., Lindenberg, S., & Ormel, J. (2006). Temperament, environment, and antisocial behavior in a population sample of preadolescent boys and girls. *International Journal of Behavioral Development, 30*, 422–432.

Yagmurlu, B., & Sanson, A. (2009). Parenting and temperament as predictors of prosocial behaviour in Australian and Turkish Australian children. *Australian Journal of Psychology, 61*, 77–88.

Youngblade, L. M., & Mulvihill, B. (1998). Individual differences in homeless preschoolers' behavior. *Journal of Applied Developmental Psychology, 19*, 595–616.

CHAPTER THIRTEEN

Children's Social Development Within the Socialization Context of Child Care and Early Childhood Education

Carollee Howes

For many children, experiences within formal or informal child care, nursery school, preschool, or another form of early childhood education (CC/ECE)[1] are significant for their social development because these programs are the context for interactions and relationships with nonrelative adults and peers. Social trends and some new reports of research released since the first edition of this handbook highlight the importance of these socializing contexts. Over the past several decades, the proportion of nonmajority children in the United States and Europe has been increasing. As a result, large numbers of immigrant children and children whose racial and language heritage cultures are other-than-White and English are enrolled in CC/ECE programs. This demographic shift means that children and their adult caregivers and teachers are interacting and forming relationships with persons who come from communities with different patterns of interaction and engagement than their own. A landmark review paper by Johnson and colleagues (2003) called attention to experiences of children of color in CC/ECE. For these children, moving between home and CC/ECE requires adaptive social skills not only because of differences in social style but also because of unconscious bias and racism. The authors argued that research attention is needed to understand the influences of CC/ECE as a socialization experience for these children, and we speculate that children's social development is facilitated by caregiving adults who are sensitive to the children's transitions between socialization environments.

A second social trend is in the number of CC/ECE programs that are oriented toward preacademic learning, preparing children for schooling that is increasingly driven by issues

The Wiley-Blackwell Handbook of Childhood Social Development, Second Edition, edited by Peter K. Smith and Craig H. Hart

of accountability for children's academic achievement. These programs include new pre-K programs positioned as transitional programs between traditional child care and preschool and kindergarten (Clifford et al., 2005). In the United States, Head Start programs are under public pressure to teach school readiness skills. Children's social skills in this paradigm often are redefined away from positive relationships with adults and peers toward skills like sitting quietly while listening to the teacher. Although some developmentalists have argued that to learn preacademic skills, children need to form positive relationships with teachers in order to use them to learn, this is not always the prevailing view (Hamre & Pianta, 2005; Howes, Burchinal, et al., 2008; Pianta et al., 2005).

Finally, a widely disseminated finding from the United States' large and representative National Institute of Child Health and Human Development (NICHD) study of early child care suggests a link between *quantity* of CC/ECE and children's externalizing behaviors and conflict with adults in kindergarten and the first grade (NICHD Early Child Care Research Network [ECCRN], 2003a, 2003b). Although the effect sizes were small, the levels of problem behaviors were in the normal range, and more of the variance in problematic behaviors was explained by family influences (Campbell, Spieker, Burchinal, Poe, & NICHD ECCRN, 2006), the report has generated renewed interest in understanding dynamics within CC/ECE that can explain children's social development (e.g., Fabes, Hanish, & Martin, 2003).

Theoretical Underpinnings

Given these changes in social and historical contexts, examining CC/ECE as a socialization context requires a theoretical framework that integrates theories of development with theories of development within context, as well as with theories of cultural community. Furthermore, to discuss social development within CC/ECE requires attention to individuals, dyads, peer and classroom groupings, and cultural communities. There also must be concern for both concurrent and long-term effects – that is, we hope children are enjoying and learning within their CC/ECE setting, and we want to know the long-term consequences of these experiences.

To account for these intervening changes in this second edition of the *Handbook of Childhood Social Development*, I have elaborated the explanatory model from the first edition (Howes & James, 2002). Figure 13.1 is a graphic representation of this model of developmental and cultural interface, which guides our understandings of children's social development within CC/ECE. In order to explain children's development of social skills and relationships, we must first account for dispositions and histories that the child brings to the CC/ECE setting. By the time children enter a particular CC/ECE program, they have had varying experiences with interaction and relationships, both with parents (Howes & Spieker, 2008) and with CC/ECE programs (Cryer, Hurwitz, & Wolery, 2001; Cryer et al., 2006). The meanings and understandings that children have derived from these experiences and bring to their CC/ECE program are formed against the background of the children's home cultural community, depicted in the left-hand column of Figure 13.1.

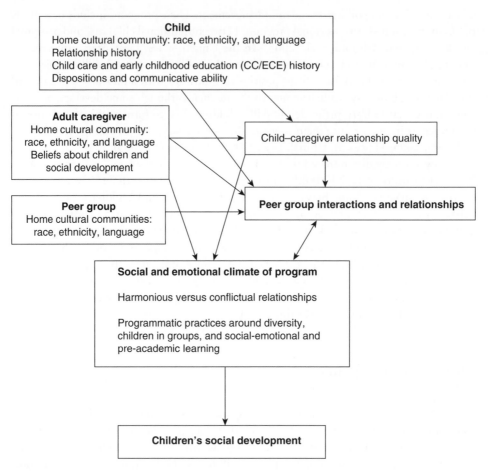

Figure 13.1 A theory of developmental and cultural interface for understanding processes of socialization within child care.

A *cultural community* is defined as a grouping of people who share goals, beliefs, and everyday practices, and often a racial or ethnic identity (Rogoff, 2003). Children and adults who participate in the same cultural community develop social interaction forms and styles through common activities and practices. For example, in some (but not all) cultural communities, dinner table conversations and bedtime stories are times when children and their parents co-create narratives of the day's experiences. By participation in everyday activities like these, children develop styles of social interaction that are particular to their cultural community. In one cultural community, the "way things are done" is to interrupt the speaker to elaborate a fantasy story, such as "And then the little girl found a really big elephant just sitting in the back yard," and in another it would be rude to interrupt and even worse to make up an untruth. Children and adults may find it relatively easy to identify practices and interactive styles that are different from their own, and almost impossible to identify their way of doing things as particular to themselves. Differences in practices and interactive styles may be in even sharper contrast when the home language of the cultural community is different (e.g., Spanish at home and English at CC/ECE).

It is important to understand that cultural communities are dynamic; the experiences of each of the members of the cultural community influence their participation with other members, and as a result activities and practices – and ways of thinking about activities and practices – change. Therefore, home cultural community activities, practices, and beliefs may change as a result of parents and children participating in social interaction and relationship construction with adults and children in CC/ECE. For example, children in Spanish monolingual households often bring pretend play themes and English home from CC/ECE and share them with their younger siblings.

The adult caregivers in CC/ECE also participate in cultural communities. Their home cultural communities function in much the same way as the children's home cultural communities, providing the adults with understandings, ways of doing things, interactive styles, and a home language to use when engaging with others. This home cultural community may be the same as or different from those of the children in the CC/ECE. These similarities and differences may influence the relationships and interactions co-constructed by children and adults in the program (Howes & Shivers, 2006). Adult caregivers in CC/ECE also participate in a cultural community of the program, carrying out activities and practices that are consistent with their beliefs around caring for children and helping them develop (Wishard, Shivers, Howes, & Ritchie, 2003). These practices (e.g., what teachers do and say when children are excluded from play, as well as their interactions and relationships with children) shape the social development of children in CC/ECE.

Finally, it is rare that all the children in a given program group are the same, or even similar, in home cultural communities, and therefore the peer group cultural community is important to consider when understanding socialization in CC/ECE. Children in the program may not all speak the same home language and may come from homes with different ideas and expectations about how to engage with others (e.g., to share materials or not to share). Construction of interactions and relationships among children from different home cultural communities may require different skills or different adult support than when all children are similar (Howes & Lee, 2007).

The right-hand column of Figure 13.1 probably looks quite familiar to developmental psychologists. Children bring dispositions and skills, sociability and wariness, emotional regulation, and communicative skills, which influence their construction of an attachment relationship with the adult caregiver (Howes & Spieker, 2008) and their interactions and friendships with peers (Howes, in press; Howes & Lee, 2006). Positive attachment relationships with caregivers influence children's formation of positive relationships with peers (Howes, in press), and children who are in less conflict with peers are more likely to form positive relationships with caregivers (Howes & Shivers, 2006).

Because CC/ECE classrooms contain individuals, dyads (child–caregiver, peer friendships, and playmates), and at least one peer group, these interactions between children and caregivers and among peers, as well as the tone the caregivers set for the entire group, all contribute to the social and emotional climate of the classroom or program. Imagine a CC/ECE setting in which most of the interactions are harmonious and respectful, in which children and adults work together on projects, in which a child who is distressed or frustrated is comforted and helped, and in which laughter and other expressions of positive affect predominate. Contrast this with a CC/ECE setting in which children are ridiculed for being different; are spoken to and touched in a harsh, rejecting manner; and compete with each other rather than help each other, and where the general tone includes mistrust and anger. We can imagine that the social development of children would take different paths in these two extremes. Because for the child the CC/ECE program is ultimately an experience of "living" within a group, it is impossible to understand the social development of a child as isolated from the group.

Methodology and Analytic Issues

Recognizing that social development within CC/ECE includes attending to individual child behaviors, to dyadic interactions and relationship quality, and to peer groups necessitates particular methodological strategies. Descriptions of children's socialization experiences must be at each level – individual, dyad, and group. Often CC/ECE setting descriptions as well as peer group descriptions (e.g., number of children in the group, or quality of the classroom social and emotional climate) are at the group level. In order to fully understand the complexity of socialization within CC/ECE programs, interactions between levels must be considered. For example, a shy child may find engaging with peers more difficult in a hostile versus a harmonious classroom climate (Gazelle, 2006). And having one peer who speaks a child's home language is a different socialization experience from having the child's home language spoken by the entire group (Howes & Lee, 2007; Howes, Sanders, & Lee, 2008). Analysis strategies must include attention to how individuals and dyads are nested within groups, how groups are nested within settings, and how settings are nested within and across cultural communities. Fortunately, advances in hierarchical linear modeling have made these multilevel analyses possible.

Most, if not all, of the research on socialization within CC/ECE requires time-consuming observing and interviewing within the programs. As I will discuss below, dimensions of settings rather than general qualities of settings are more predictive of children's social development. Although there are valid and reliable measures of general setting characteristics, for example the Early Childhood Environmental Rating Scales (Harms, Clifford, & Cryer, 1998) and the Classroom Assessment Scoring System (CLASS; Pianta, La Paro, & Hamre, 2004), these more targeted observations of setting dimensions usually require a time-sampling procedure such as the Peer Play Scale (Howes & Matheson, 1992) or Q-sort procedures as in the Attachment Q-Set (Waters, 1987). Including measures of the cultural community requires intensive open-ended interviews with adults by interviewers who are culturally as well as linguistically bilingual (see, e.g., Howes, Wishard Guerra, & Zucker, 2007).

Beyond observing dimensions and socialization encounters within the CC/ECE, careful observation and inference are necessary to describe children's social behaviors, interactions, and relationships within the program. For example, when a 2-year-old starts to join two other children playing at a water table and then quickly leaves, the observer must attend carefully to body language, eye gaze, and the affect of all three children to determine if the reason she left was because the other children excluded her from play, or a peer accidentally splashed her and she doesn't like being wet, or she was distracted by a child riding by on a bike. Children who are this young are very limited in their ability to reflect and to report on their own perceptions of interactions and relationships. Training and establishing reliability on observational coding schemes are extremely important in this area of research. By age 3, children begin to reliably report on their social relationships with peers using sociometric methodology, and their social and emotion regulation skills can be individually assessed (Raver, 2004; Rubin, Bukowski, & Parker, 2006).

In the remaining sections of this chapter, I provide elaborated descriptions of the processes within and between each component of the theoretical model.

What Does the Child Bring to the CC/ECE Setting?

Social interactive style from a home cultural community

All children come to CC/ECE with a social interactive style particular to their own cultural community. For example, in certain cultural communities, titles are important when children address adults. Adults are addressed as *Mr.*, *Mrs.*, *Miss*, *Auntie*, *Uncle*, or the like, followed by their family name or first name. It is not uncommon to hear a child call a caregiver by her first name but preface it with *Miss*. "Miss Helen, can I play with this?" In other communities, however, it is quite appropriate for children to address an adult by her first name only. In the African American community, tone and eye expression are especially important in understanding social interactions. For example, Mrs. Pettaway, a favorite among her 4-year-olds, is helping the children to needlepoint. Deondre is clearly frustrated and communicates this with his face as he continues to work on his project. Mrs. Pettaway calls to him, but he continues to fumble with his artwork. She then says, "Boy, get over here," in a sassy but humorous manner. Deondre immediately breaks out in a smile and approaches her. Although we do not want to imply that this is typical of all African American caregivers, the tone and language of the interaction could be misunderstood outside of the African American community. The caregiver plays with a harsh statement, but softens it to an endearment.

Another example lies in the Latino community's use of terms of endearment. It is not uncommon to hear a caregiver say to a Spanish-speaking toddler, "¿Papi, que quieres?" ("Little father, what do you want?") or "Mami, ven acá" ("Little mother, come here"). The language used in these social interactions connotes feelings of warmth and nurturance for the participants.

Social interactive styles can be socially competent or maladaptive, and the same behavior can be considered socially competent in one context and socially maladaptive in another. For example, we observe Jesse taunting his peer Lucia as he attempts to take her truck. In a loud, assertive voice, Lucia says, "No, Jesse!" instead of hitting him. Lucia, in a "use-your-words" child care program, is exhibiting socially competent behavior. Now, if Lucia were responding to her caregiver and was supposed to have put the truck away 5 minutes ago, her loud voice would be socially maladaptive. Or if Lucia were a teen parent admonishing her one-year-old child, her loud voice would be extreme and would be considered inappropriate. The interpretation of all these interactions depends on the context. As stated above, children must learn when and where to employ one style over another.

Relationship history

All children come to CC/ECE programs with prior experience with caregiving relationships. From an attachment theory perspective these prior relationships, usually with parents, orient children toward the adults and children they encounter in the program (Cassidy & Shaver, 2008; Howes & Spieker, 2008). From the first day in a new classroom setting, children are assessing which adults can be trusted. If their prior experience suggests that there will be someone they can trust, then they act in a sociable, friendly manner to at least one adult caregiver (Howes & Oldham, 2001). If they have not had prior experiences with trusting adults and secure base behaviors, they are less likely to look for adults who can be trusted and more likely to antagonize teachers and peers as they enter the classroom (Howes & Ritchie, 2002).

Prior experience in child care or early childhood education

Most children experience changes in nonrelative caregivers and/or CC/ECE settings. The NICHD Study of Early Child Care found that almost half (39–40%) of children experienced at least one change before their second birthdays (NICHD ECCRN, 1997; Tran & Weinraub, 2006). Therefore, many children's approach to the adults and peers in CC/ECE may be influenced by their prior relationships and social interaction patterns in programs.

Change in CC/ECE per se does not necessarily have negative influences on children's development (Tran & Weinraub, 2006). For example, a child may "outgrow" family child care and move to a preschool setting with more children and activities, or a family may realize that the interactive style of adults and peers in a current program is not consistent with their values for their child's socialization.

However, a child may enter a new social setting with social behaviors that were adaptive in prior settings but are not in the current setting. Most worrisome is when children adapt by withdrawing from or aggressing toward peers. In a new CC/ECE setting, these social behaviors can keep children from opportunities to learn how to play well with peers. Only with multiple opportunities to engage with peers do young children begin to understand how to engage in prosocial and complex play with peers (Rubin, Burgess, Dwyer, & Hastings, 2003) and to resolve conflicts (Bakeman & Brownlee, 1982; Chen, Fein, Killen, & Tam, 2001; Fonzi, Schneider, Tani, & Tomada, 1997; Hay, 1982). Young children who do not play with others are at risk for not learning how to play and not learning how to resolve conflicts. A particular concern about children who do not play with others or only play with others in an aggressive manner within CC/ECE is that they may develop patterns of aggression and conflict with peers (Howes & Phillipsen, 1998).

Dispositions and communicative ability

Some children run, wiggle, and shout their way into a CC/ECE program. They can't wait to climb, run, and explore the block corner. Others are slow to find their place, sad to leave the side of the parent, and slow to find playmates and activities pleasurable. Children who are able to strike a balance between their own desires and interests and those of the other children and caregivers are those who are able to regulate and control their emotions and impulses (Eisenberg, Fabes, & Losoya, 1997; Fabes et al., 1999; Rothbart, Ahadi, & Hershey, 1994). If children have these dispositions or are helped to develop them within CC/ECE, they are more likely to engage in harmonious interactions with others and to develop positive relationships with others (Howes & Ritchie, 2002). Children who are shy or slow to warm fare better when caregivers provide support for their interactions with others (Coplan & Prakash, 2003).

In addition to dispositions, children more skillful in verbal, nonverbal, and emotional decoding are more able to communicate with peers and caregivers (Dunn, 2004; Spinrad et al., 2004). Communicative skills may interact with dispositions; for example, in one study, shy preschool-aged children who had larger expressive vocabularies seemed to have more confidence in their interactions with peers than shy children with smaller expressive vocabularies (Coplan & Armer, 2005).

Child–Caregiver Relationship Quality

The theoretical model highlights the importance of children's attachments to their careivers in CC/ECE. Through multiple and recursive interactions with these caregivers, children develop internal working models of their child–caregiver relationships (Bowlby, 1969). Recursive interactions are well-scripted social exchanges that are repeated many times with only slight variation. Examples include child–adult interaction around naptime or morning greetings. From these recursive interactions, the infant or young child internalizes a set of fundamental social expectations about the behavioral dispositions of the caregiver or partner (Bowlby, 1969). It is important to note that both the structure and content of experiences of interacting with a partner are part of the child's representation of the partner. Children who engage in more complex interactions are more likely to recognize the partner as a social other and construct a relationship. Furthermore, the content and context of the interaction are likely to influence the quality of the resulting relationship.

Attachment relationships with caregivers in CC/ECE are independent of children's familial attachment relationships (Ahnert, Pinquart, & Lamb, 2006), although the process of relationship formation for familial and nonrelative caregivers is similar (Howes & Spieker, 2008). Thus, warm, sensitive, and responsive caregivers are associated with secure child–caregiver relationships (Howes & Ritchie, 2002). Secure attachment relationships between children and their caregivers are in turn associated with children's positive interactions with peers and with children's willingness to use the caregiver as a teacher (Howes & Ritchie, 2002; Pianta, Hamre, & Stuhlman, 2003).

Peer Group Interactions and Relationships

Children in CC/ECE programs co-construct their peer group. Whereas, as we have discussed, adults influence the quality of the social interaction within the peer group, it is the children who form friendships and play groups, and construct hierarchies of popular, rejected, and neglected social status.

A boys' peer group and a girls' peer group, or one peer group?

In their response to the NICHD Early Child Care Study's findings regarding child care and social development (NICHD ECCRN, 2003a, 2003b). Fabes and colleagues (2003) suggested that sex-segregated peer groups, particularly boys' peer groups with disproportionate numbers of dysregulated group members, may contributed to maladaptive socialization in CC/ECE. Maccoby (1998) argued that the peer group has a more powerful socializing effect on gender than do adults, whether parents or caregivers. She analyzed large bodies of biological, psychological, anthropological, and sociological evidence to conclude that children, by age 3, separate into gender-segregated peer groups. Within these peer groups, children develop the social behaviors and interaction styles specific to their gender. This suggests that children's experiences in child care may be gender specific, and that because children are spending their daytime hours in child care they have multiple opportunities for socialization by same-gender peers in gender-segregated groups.

Gender segregation appears to influence the style rather than the competence of peer play. There are well-established differences in the content of the play of boys and girls (Maccoby, 1984). However, there appear to be few gender differences in the competence of children's peer play (Howes, 1980, 1988; Howes & Matheson, 1992). Girls and boys of the same age engage in structurally similar play, although the social interaction style and content may differ. For example, both a game of Mother, Sister, and Baby among girls and a game of The Day the Tigers Ate the Village among boys are very likely to be rated as competent social pretend play.

Gender socialization within segregated peer groups does not entirely negate the role of the adult values in the organization of experiences in child care. If the adults in the CC/ECE setting encourage the girls to use the tool bench, make airplanes, and run frantically around the yard being women pilots, they are acknowledging that girls are active, powerful, and able to do anything. If, instead, caregivers ignore the boys ruling the play yard and block corner, or covertly encourage it, the girls' group will have a different repertoire of self-images. Thus, caregivers can support or actively disconfirm traditional gender socialization.

Aggression, boys' peer groups, and behavior problems

Boys' peer groups do tend to play as far away from the supervising eye of the caregiver as possible, and boys' play more often than girls' involves physical contact, fighting, and taunting (Fabes et al., 2003). Although examining the child and environmental influences on aggression is a topic beyond the scope of this chapter, there are some recent studies of peer interaction in preschool that raise concerns about very young children's experiences with conflict and aggression in peer groups. Preschool children classified as aggressive in one study of a Head Start classroom played with only a few children, and in general had difficulty establishing play contacts and friendships (Snyder, Horsch, & Childs, 1997). Aggressive and nonaggressive children tended to form friendships with children similar to themselves in aggression, and as the school year progressed, aggressive dyads increased in aggressive play.

A second recent study found that when preschoolers were in conflict – for example, over who was going to play the mother and who was going to play the baby, or whose turn it was to have the swing – they tended to engage in nonaggressive conflict strategies unless one of the children involved in the conflict engaged in physical aggression (Thornberg, 2006). In other words, turn taking without hitting or pulling usually happened more or less smoothly. If physical aggression was introduced into the conflict, then the partner tended to be aggressive as well. To continue the swing example, if a child who wanted a turn on the swing yanked on the feet of the swinger, the swinger would be more likely to hit than if the same child yelled, "I really want the swing, and you have had it for too long." This research suggests that everyday conflicts between very young children can become aggressive with peers all too quickly. Finally, a 3-year longitudinal study, beginning in toddlerhood, found that early aggressive behavior reduced children's likelihood of being the target of prosocial behavior (Persson, 2005). Thus, children who began their peer group experiences with many experiences of being aggressive toward others became less likely to be the recipients of positive overtures that could have resulted in more productive play. In other words, if young children figure out that they are likely to be hit or pinched by a peer, they tend to exclude this child from further play opportunities.

Playmates and friendships within peer groups

The development of children's peer relations may be semi-independent of their relationships with adults (Hay, 1985). This argument is based in part on the premise that the construction of social interaction with a peer is different than with an adult. Peers, unlike adults, are not particularly more knowledgeable or skillful in social interaction than the infant or toddler. But, to their advantage, peers share interests in activities that adults generally do not. Most adults quickly tire of games like Run-Chase or Jumping off a Step. There is evidence that with more time in a particular peer group, children do become more socially skillful at interactions and friendships (Howes, 1988).

The perspective that peer relations are primarily constructed within peer groups is not necessarily at odds with an attachment theory perspective. It is possible that early adult–child attachment relationships serve to orient children toward or away from the peer group. Children with secure adult–child attachment relationships may perceive peers as potentially fun and interesting social partners, enter into peer play, and, with experience, become socially skilled. Children with insecure adult–child attachments may perceive peers as hostile or threatening and withdraw from or aggress toward peers. Once a child has withdrawn from peers or has constructed antagonistic patterns of interaction and relationships, it may be especially difficult to develop alternative behaviors with peers

(Howes & Phillipsen, 1998). Unlike some sensitive adults who can understand that what appear to be maladaptive behaviors are instead based on mistrust, peers may perceive the potential peer partner as unpleasant and to be avoided. A skillful adult can work to disconfirm a child's hostile or withdrawing behavior. A peer is more likely to react in ways that maintain the maladaptive sequences.

All children have friends, but not every peer interaction results in friendship. Some children are able to "hit it off" and become friends, whereas others never pass the stage of acquaintanceship. Friendship is more than just interpersonal attraction; beginning in infancy, friendships are relationships based on mutual support, affection, and companionship. It is important to note that peer interaction is conceptually different from friendship formation. Relationships with friends are more intense and intimate than ones with playmates. Young children behave differently toward friends than nonfriends; for example, they engage in more complex play with friends and are more likely to stay close with one another after conflicts (Hartup, Laursen, Stewart, & Eastenson, 1988; Howes, 1996). In essence, friendship formation entails moving beyond peer interaction and becoming more involved and invested in one another.

The Care Setting: Moving the Focus From Forms and Quality to Social and Emotional Climate

The function of a CC/ECE arrangement includes keeping children safe from physical harm and, when optimal, providing a context for enhancing social and/or cognitive development for the children in care. The adults who provide care in these settings may be grandmothers, neighbors, nannies, or teachers, and the setting may be called Grandma's house, family child care, or center-based care. Because the parents directly or indirectly communicate to their children that these other-than-mother adults are to keep them safe, these adults function (well or not so well) as attachment figures (Howes & Spieker, 2008). Most, but not all, of the children in child care are cared for in the presence of peers. In some settings, peers tend to be same-age nonrelatives, and in other less formal arrangements, peers may be of mixed ages and may be siblings or cousins. Thus, in terms of opportunities for experiences with adults and peers, any of these forms of CC/ECE can be considered a context for social development.

In the first edition of this handbook, we concluded, based on the evidence available, that the form of the CC/ECE was not a significant predictor of children's social development. However, the preponderance of the evidence available at the time suggested that the quality of the program did influence concurrent and long-term social development.

> There is general agreement among researchers that child care quality can be defined and reliably measured. ... The positive effects of child care quality on virtually every facet of children's development is one of the most consistent findings in developmental science. The effects of child care quality on children's development are only about half as large as those associated with family environments, but emerge repeatedly in study after study and are consistent across children of every ethnicity and every language group. (Howes & James, 2002, p. 146)

The findings of the NICHD ECCRN (2003a, 2003b) that quantity of child care rather than quality of child care predicted long-term social development led researchers to reconsider this conclusion (Crockenberg, 2003; Fabes et al., 2003; Maccoby & Lewis, 2003). The theoretical model introduced in the first edition of this handbook and elaborated in this chapter is intended to provide a more nuanced description of the interactions between child and family characteristics, CC/ECE settings, cultural communities, and children's social development. Research published since 2003 suggests that the social and emotional climate of the CC/ECE program as opposed to general quality are predictive of children's social development (Hamre & Pianta, 2001, 2005; Howes, Burchinal, et al., 2008; Pianta et al., 2005). There are two dimensions to the social and emotional climate of the program. The affective dimension of the climate is based on harmonious versus conflictual relationships among adults and peers within the group. The programmatic practices dimension includes practices around children in groups, as well as social emotional and preacademic learning.

The affective dimension of the social and emotional climate of a program

The social and emotional climate of the classroom can enhance or impede the social development of children. Although there is an extensive literature describing the interactions of teachers and children and classroom management strategies (see Pianta, Hamre, & Stuhlman, 2002, for a review of this literature), only recently has attention turned to the general climate that is created within the classroom from the interactions of participants.

Several recent large-scale observational studies of classrooms for young children identified two dimensions of classroom climate: instructional support and social emotional support (Hamre & Pianta, 2005; La Paro, Pianta, Hamre, & Stuhlman, 2002; NICHD ECCRN, 2002; Pianta et al., 2005). Classrooms that score high on the measure of social-emotional support are pleasant places where there are conversations, spontaneous laughter, and enjoyment expressed as children and teachers engage in various activities and interactions. Teachers are warm and sensitive to all of the children; they are emotionally and physically involved with the children's activities, and they rarely are intrusive, angry, or annoyed. In these classrooms there are clear but flexible rules and expectations for classroom routines. Children tend to follow these rules so that teachers rarely have to employ control techniques. In contrast, classrooms with negative climates are characteristically filled with relational as well as physical aggression among children and hostile conflictual interactions between children and teachers. Children in these classrooms have few options for activities. Interactions and activities are adult driven and most often based on behavioral management of out-of-control children.

Classrooms with positive emotional climates are associated with positive teacher–child relationships (Howes, 2000; Howes & Ritchie, 2002); children in classrooms with high scores for positive emotional climate are likely to construct positive relationships with teachers. But beyond the secure base that positive teacher–child relationships provide, a positive emotional climate appears to facilitate peer relationship development by providing rules for engagement that promote prosocial rather than hostile peer interactions. If it is difficult for young children to construct play sequences when they are just developing the capacity to do so, it is even more difficult to do so when they are interrupted by conflict occurring around them. In one longitudinal study, children who experienced positive emotional climates as 3-year-olds were also likely to have positive peer relationships as second graders (Howes, 2000).

Positive social and emotional climates also can facilitate positive peer relationships in newly formed peer groups. In most large-scale studies of preschool classrooms, climate scores are on the average fairly positive, above the median of the scale (see, e.g., Pianta et al., 2005). However, in our recent study of children entering preschool, the average social emotional climate scores were near the negative end of the scale (Howes & Shivers, 2006). As such, it was a challenge for children in these classrooms to create relationships and complex play within these newly formed peer groups (Howes, Sanders, et al., 2008).

The programmatic practices dimension of the social and emotional climate of a program

Understanding how CC/ECE program practices influence children's social development is a new and not very well-developed area of research. Practices are "ways of doing things," or ingrained habits rooted in participants' beliefs, expectations, traditions, and relations – in particular, what CC/ECE programs, their directors, and teachers intend to and actually do to enhance children's social development and to manage and sustain their program (Wishard et al., 2003). Practices within programs are developed by program directors and caregivers based on their shared beliefs and understandings of children. Because practices are the "way things are done," they could be intentional and articulated, but more often they are unintentional and unarticulated. For example, programs have practices around their focus on individual and groups. If the program places more importance on children gaining individual skills than in building a peer group community, its staff may be less likely to teach conflict resolution skills or talk with children about including everyone in their play games, and more likely to exclude children with behavior problems. If the program is more focused on children's academic skills and less on social emotional development, children may spend less time playing in the "dress-up" corner and more time in teacher-directed activities. There may be an emergent literacy curriculum but not a social skills curriculum. There is not yet a literature that links practices within CC/ECE programs to children's social development. Extrapolating from literature on parenting practices, it is logical to expect these linkages (Rogoff, 2003). Future generations of research on social development within CC/ECE may fill this gap.

Closing Thoughts

For most children, social interactions and relationships with adults and peers outside of their families occur within their CC/ECE program. Research to examine CC/ECE as a socialization context requires a theoretical framework that integrates theories of development with theories of development within context, and with theories of cultural community. Furthermore, to discuss social development within CC/ECE requires attention to individuals, dyads, peer and classroom groupings, and cultural communities. For many children CC/ECE programs are places where they encounter interactive styles and practices of engaging with others that are different than those they experience at home. These can be challenging experiences for young children, who are just beginning to develop social skills and relationships. Recent research suggests that rather than focusing on the influence of general CC/ECE quality, it is important to refocus on the social and emotional climate of the program.

Note

1. The appropriate nomenclature for a program and for an adult in a program tends to be difficult to determine. For the purposes of this chapter, any setting outside of the child's home and with one or more nonrelative adults will be called *CC/ECE*, and the adult taking care of the child in that setting will be called the *caregiver*.

References

Ahnert, L., Pinquart, M., & Lamb, M. E. (2006). Security of children's relationships with non-parental care providers: A meta analysis. *Child Development, 74,* 664–679.

Bakeman, R., & Brownlee, J. (1982). Social rules governing object conflicts in toddlers and pre-schoolers. In K. Rubin & H. Ross (Eds.), *Peer relationships and social skills in childhood*. New York: Springer-Verlag.

Bowlby, J. (1969). *Attachment and loss: Vol. 1. Attachment*. London: Hogarth.

Campbell, S., Spieker, S., Burchinal, M., Poe, M., & National Institute of Child Health and Human Development Early Child Care Research Network (NICHD ECCRN). (2006). Trajectories of aggression from toddlerhood to age 9 predict academic and social functioning through age 12. *Journal of Child Psychology and Psychiatry, 47,* 791–800.

Cassidy, J., & Shaver, P. R. (Eds.). (2008). *Handbook of attachment theory and research* (2nd ed.). New York: Guilford Press.

Chen, D. W., Fein, G. G., Killen, M., & Tam, H-P. (2001). Peer conflicts of preschool children: Issues, resolution, incidence, and age-related patterns. *Early Education and Development, 12,* 523–544.

Clifford, R. M., Barbarin, O., Chang, F., Early, D., Bryant, D., Howes, C., et al. (2005). What is prekindergarten? Characteristics of public pre-kindergarten programs. *Applied Developmental Science, 9*(3), 126–134.

Coplan, R. J., & Armer, M. (2005). Talking yourself out of being shy: Shyness, expressive vocabulary, and socioemotional adjustment in preschool. *Merrill Palmer Quarterly, 52,* 20–41.

Coplan, R. J., & Prakash, K. (2003). Spending time with teacher: Characteristics of preschoolers who frequently elicit versus initiate interactions with teachers. *Early Childhood Research Quarterly, 19,* 1–6.

Crockenberg, S. (2003). Rescuing the baby from the bathwater: How gender and temperament (may) influence how child care influences child development. *Child Development, 74,* 1034–1038.

Cryer, D., Hurwitz, S., & Wolery, M. (2001). Continuity of caregiver for infants and toddlers in center-based child-care: Report on a survey of center practices. *Early Childhood Research Quarterly, 15,* 497–514.

Cryer, D., Wagner-Moore, L., Burchinal, M., Yazejian, N., Hurwitz, S., & Wolery, M. (2006). Effects of transitions to new child care classes on infant/toddler distress and behavior. *Early Childhood Research Quarterly, 20*, 37–56.

Dunn, J. (2004). *Children's friendships*. Malden, MA: Blackwell.

Eisenberg, N., Fabes, R. A., & Losoya, S. (1997). Emotional responding: Regulation, social correlates, and socialization. In E. P. Salovey, E. David, & J. Sluyter (Eds.), *Emotional development and emotional intelligence: Educational implications* (pp. 129–167). New York: Routledge.

Fabes, R. A., Eisenberg, N., Jones, S., Smith, M., Guthrie, I., Poulin, R., et al. (1999). Regulation emotionality and preschoolers' socially competent peer interactions. *Child Development, 70*, 432–442.

Fabes, R. A., Hanish, L. D., & Martin, C. L. (2003). Children at play: The role of peers in understanding the effects of child care. *Child Development, 74*, 1039–1043.

Fonzi, A., Schneider, B. H., Tani, F., & Tomada, G. (1997). Predicting children's friendship status from their dyadic interaction in structured situations of potential conflict. *Child Development, 68*, 496–506.

Gazelle, H. (2006). Class climate moderates peer relations and emotional adjustment in children with an early history of anxious solitude: A child X environment model. *Developmental Psychology, 43*, 1179–1192.

Hamre, B., & Pianta, R. C. (2001). Early teacher-child relationships and trajectory of school outcomes through eighth grade. *Child Development, 72*, 625–638.

Hamre, B., & Pianta, R. C. (2005). Can instructional and emotional support in the first grade classroom make a difference for children at risk for school failure? *Child Development, 76*, 949–967.

Harms, T., Clifford, R. M., & Cryer, D. (1998). *Early Childhood Environment Rating Scale* (Rev. ed.). New York: Teachers College Press.

Hartup, W., Laursen, B., Stewart, M. I., & Eastenson, A. (1988). Conflict and the friendship relations of young children. *Child Development, 59*, 1590–1600.

Hay, D. (1982). The social nature of early conflict. *Child Development, 53*, 105–113.

Hay, D. (1985). Learning to form relationships in infancy: Parallel attainments with parents and peers. *Developmental Review, 5*, 122–161.

Howes, C. (1980). Peer play scale as an index of complexity of peer interaction. *Developmental Psychology, 16*, 371–372.

Howes, C. (1988). Peer interaction in young children. *Monograph of the Society for Research in Child Development, 53*(1, Series No. 217).

Howes, C. (1996). The earliest friendships. In W. M. Bukowski, A. F. Newcomb, & W. W. Hartup (Eds.), *The company they keep: Friendships in childhood and adolescence* (pp. 66–86). New York: Cambridge.

Howes, C. (2000). Social-emotional classroom climate in child care, child-teacher relationships, and children's second grade peer relations. *Social Development, 9*, 191–204.

Howes, C. (in press). Peer relationships in early childhood: Friendship. In K. Rubin, W. Bukowski, & B. Laursen (Eds.), *Handbook of peer interaction, relationships, and groups*. New York: Guilford Press.

Howes, C., Burchinal, M., Pianta, R. C., Bryant, D., Early, D., Clifford, R., et al. (2008). Ready to learn? Children's pre-academic achievement in prekindergarten. *Early Childhood Research Quarterly, 23*, 27–50.

Howes, C., & James, J. (2002). Children's social development within the socialization context of child care and early childhood education. In C. Hart & P. Smith (Eds.), *Handbook of childhood social development*. London: Blackwell.

Howes, C., & Lee, L. (2006). Peer relations in young children. In L. Balter & C. S. Tamis-Le Monda (Eds.), *Child psychology: A handbook of contemporary issues* (pp. 135–152). New York: Taylor & Francis.

Howes, C., & Lee, L. (2007). If you are not like me, can we play? Peer groups in preschool. In B. Spodek & O. Saracho (Eds.), *Contemporary perspectives on research in social learning in early childhood education*. Durham, NC: Information Age.

Howes, C., & Matheson, C. C. (1992). Sequences in the development of competent play with peers: Social and social pretend play. *Developmental Psychology, 28*, 961–974.

Howes, C., & Oldham, E. (2001). Processes in the formation of attachment relationships with new caregivers. In A. Goncu & E. Klein (Eds.), *Children in play, story and school*. New York: Greenwood.

Howes, C., & Phillipsen, L. C. (1998). Continuity in children's relations with peers. *Social Development, 7*, 340–349.

Howes, C., & Ritchie, S. (2002). *A matter of trust: Connecting teachers and learners in the early childhood classroom*. New York: Teachers College Press.

Howes, C., Sanders, K., & Lee, L. (2008). Entering a new peer group in ethnically and linguistically diverse child care classrooms. *Social Development, 17*(4), 922–940.

Howes, C., & Shivers, E. M. (2006). New child-caregiver attachment relationships: Entering child care when the caregiver is and is not an ethnic match. *Social Development, 15*, 343–360.

Howes, C., & Spieker, S. (2008). Attachment relationships in the context of multiple caregivers. In J. Cassidy & P. R. Shaver (Eds.), *Handbook of attachment theory and research* (2nd ed.). New York: Guilford Press.

Howes, C., Wishard Guerra, A. G., & Zucker, E. (2007). Cultural communities and parenting in Mexican-heritage families. *Parenting: Science and Practice, 7*, 1–36.

Johnson, D. J., Jaeger, E., Randolph, S. M., Cauce, A. M., Ward, J., & National Institute of Child Health and Human Development Early Child Care Research Network (NICHD ECCRN) (2003). Studying the effects of early child care experiences on the development of children of color in the United States: Towards a more inclusive research agenda. *Child Development, 74*, 1227–1244.

La Paro, K. M., Pianta, R. C., Hamre, B., & Stuhlman, M. (2002). *Classroom Assessment Scoring System (CLASS): Pre-K version*. Charlottesville: University of Virginia.

Maccoby, E. E. (1984). Socialization and developmental change. *Developmental Psychology, 55*, 317–328.

Maccoby, E. E. (1998). *The two sexes: Growing up apart, coming together*. Cambridge, MA: Harvard University Press.

Maccoby, E., & Lewis, C. (2003). Less day care or different day care? *Child Development, 74*, 1069–1075.

National Institute of Child Health and Human Development Early Child Care Research Network (NICHD ECCRN). (1997). Child care in the first year of life. *Merrill Palmer Quarterly, 43*, 340–361.

National Institute of Child Health and Human Development Early Child Care Research Network (NICHD ECCRN). (2002). The relation of global first grade environment to structural classroom features, teacher, and student behaviors. *Early Elementary School Journal, 102*, 367–387.

National Institute of Child Health and Human Development Early Child Care Research Network (NICHD ECCRN). (2003a). Does amount of time in child care predict socioemotional adjustment during the transition to kindergarten? *Child Development, 74*, 976–1005.

National Institute of Child Health and Human Development Early Child Care Research Network (NICHD ECCRN). (2003b). Social functioning in first grade: Associations with earlier home and child care predictors and with current classroom experiences. *Child Development, 74,* 1639–1662.

Persson, G. E. B. (2005). Young children's prosocial and aggressive behaviors and their experiences of being targeted for similar behaviors by peers. *Social Development, 14,* 206–228.

Pianta, R. C., Hamre, B., & Stuhlman, M. (Eds.). (2002). *Relationships between teachers and children* (Vol. 7). New York: Wiley.

Pianta, R., Hamre, B., & Stuhlman, M. (2003). Relationships between teachers and children. In W. M. Reynolds & G. Miller (Eds.), *Handbook of psychology: Educational psychology* (Vol. 7, pp. 199–234). New York: Wiley.

Pianta, R., Howes, C., Burchinal, M., Bryant, D., Clifford, R., Early, D., et al. (2005). Features of pre-kindergarten programs, classrooms, and teachers: Do they predict observed classroom quality and child-teacher interactions? *Applied Developmental Science, 9,* 144–159.

Pianta, R. C., La Paro, K. M., & Hamre, B. (2004). *Classroom assessment scoring system.* Charlottesville: University of Virginia.

Raver, C. C. (2004). Placing emotional self-regulation in sociocultural and socioeconomic contexts. *Child Development, 75,* 346–353.

Rogoff, B. (2003). *The cultural nature of human development.* New York: Oxford University Press.

Rothbart, M. K., Ahadi, S. A., & Hershey, K. L. (1994). Temperament and social behavior in childhood. *Merrill Palmer Quarterly, 40,* 21–39.

Rubin, K. H., Bukowski, W., & Parker, J. (2006). Peer interactions, relationships, and groups. In N. Eisenberg, W. Damon, & R. Lerner (Eds.), *Handbook of child psychology: Vol. 3. Social, emotional, and personality development* (pp. 571–645). Hoboken, NJ: Wiley.

Rubin, K. H., Burgess, K. B., Dwyer, K. M., & Hastings, P. P. (2003). Predicting preschoolers' externalizing behaviors from toddler temperament, conflict, and maternal negativity. *Developmental Psychology, 39,* 164–176.

Snyder, J., Horsch, E., & Childs, J. (1997). Peer relationships of young children: Affiliative choices and the shaping of aggressive behavior. *Journal of Clinical Child Psychology, 26,* 145–156.

Spinrad, T. L., Eisenberg, N., Harris, E., Hanish, L., Fabes, R. A., Kupanoff, K., et al. (2004). The relation of children's everyday nonsocial peer play behavior to their emotionality, regulation, and social functioning. *Developmental Psychology, 40,* 67–80.

Thornberg, R. (2006). The situated nature of preschool children's conflict strategies. *Educational Psychology, 26,* 109–112.

Tran, H., & Weinraub, M. (2006). Child care effects in context: Quality, stability, and multiplicity in nonmaternal child care arrangements during the first 15 months of life. *Developmental Psychology, 42,* 566–582.

Waters, E. (1987). *Attachment Behavior Q-Set (Revision 3.0)* [Unpublished instrument]. Stony Brook: State University of New York at Stony Brook, Department of Psychology.

Wishard, A., Shivers, E., Howes, C., & Ritchie, S. (2003). Child care program and teacher practices: Associations with quality and children's experiences. *Early Childhood Research Quarterly, 18,* 65–103.

CHAPTER FOURTEEN

The Interplay Between Parents and Peers as Socializing Influences in Children's Development

Stephanie M. Reich and Deborah Lowe Vandell

For the most part, separate research traditions have developed to study children's relationships with parents and peers. The organization and format of this handbook reflect these separate and distinct literatures. Studies of children's interactions with their parents have focused on attachment security (see Chapter 17), parenting practices (see Chapter 18), and variations associated with demographic and cultural factors (see Chapters 8 and 9). As a quick perusal of these chapters reveals, a central issue for many researchers is identifying the effects of children's experiences with their parents on a host of social and emotional outcomes including mental health, adjustment, empathy, and prosocial behaviors. Other researchers have focused on children's relationships with their peers and studied areas such as peer acceptance and rejection (see Chapter 21), friendship (see Chapter 25), and peer group interaction (see Chapter 23) as socializing influences on child developmental outcomes. As a review of the four chapters in the "Peer Group" part of this handbook clearly illustrates, this corpus of work is also large.

The purpose of the current chapter is to consider the smaller but important body of literature that examines the role of both parents *and* peers on child development. We consider five interrelated issues: (a) the influence of parent–child relationships on children's interactions and relationships with their peers, (b) the influence of peer experiences on children's interactions and relationships with their parents, (c) additive or cumulative effects of parents and peers on social and cognitive outcomes, (d) interactive or synergistic effects of parents and peers on child developmental outcomes, and finally

The Wiley-Blackwell Handbook of Childhood Social Development, Second Edition, edited by Peter K. Smith and Craig H. Hart
© 2011 by Blackwell Publishing Ltd.

(e) the moderating effects of neighborhood and culture on the interplay between parents and peers. Our particular focus is on the developmental period between 3 and 12 years, although we also include findings from longitudinal studies that considered longer term consequences of parenting and peer experiences into adolescence and beyond. Research findings pertaining to children's experiences with both their mothers and fathers are examined, wherever possible, due to evidence that mothers and fathers contribute to social development differently.

Some Words of Caution

Before turning to these studies of parent and peer influences, limitations that are inherent in much of the literature should be acknowledged. As noted by Scarr and McCartney (1983) almost 30 years ago, gene–environment correlations introduce serious questions about causality and the direction of influences in typical or traditional studies of the effects of parenting (or of peers). (See Chapter 2 for a more extensive discussion of this issue.)

Gene–environment correlations may be manifested in both passive and active ways. As an example, sociable parents may arrange more play dates for their preschoolers, whereas less sociable parents arrange fewer such activities for their children. Sociable children may also seek out their parents and peers for play and interaction. Children who regularly interact with others may be more socially skilled because of these experiences. Such a pattern makes it difficult to determine if the association between participation in parent-organized playgroups and social competencies is simply the result of a parenting practice and more peer exposure, or whether it reflects underlying differences in genetic predispositions. Although research has shown that there are clear genetic contributions to behavior, emerging evidence supports the strong influence of environments as well (e.g., Moffitt & Caspi, 2007).

Because genes and environments are correlated and because children live in a rich social world composed of many potential social figures (siblings, teachers, and grandparents, to name a few), efforts to identify and understand ways in which experiences with parents and peers influence children's development require ingenuity and an expanded toolbox of research methods and analytic strategies. This toolbox includes longitudinal studies that examine changes in child developmental outcomes associated with changes in parenting and/or peer experiences. Longitudinal studies have the advantage of examining temporal sequences, a key component for inferring causality. However, temporal order alone is not sufficient. Studies over time that lack experimental control are susceptible to many rival hypotheses. Both experimental and nonexperimental studies that hope to approximate directional relationships need to include multiple measures over time (to assess both stability and change) and ideally involve multiple methods as well. When exploring associations (rather than causation), the use of cross-lagged correlations provides useful ways of looking at the relationships between parents and peers over time. Furthermore, efforts to disentangle gene–environment correlations also have used genetically informed designs that involve participants with shared genes (e.g., twins or nontwin siblings) or different genetic makeup (e.g., adoption studies). More recently, molecular genetic research is also appearing. Natural experiments or studies in nature, such as the research involving Romanian orphans (Chisholm, 1998), also are informative. Last, statistical methods are becoming more sophisticated, and studies are using a more extensive set of covariates to reduce the likelihood that obtained relations between parent and peer relations can be explained by other factors (i.e., third or omitted variables).

The research discussed in this chapter utilizes a variety of these research methods. However, few are true experiments. For heuristic purposes, we will use terms such as *influence* and *effect*, although we recognize that few studies have tested either parent or peer influences experimentally.

Affordances of Parents and Peers

Children's interactions with their parents and their peers afford different social opportunities. Although parent–child relationships in early and middle childhood are clearly transactional with parents and children exerting influences on one another, parents and children are not equals in terms of their underlying power, control of resources, cognitive competencies, or social skills. By virtue of their greater knowledge and expertise, parents are able to provide children with social and emotional support and scaffold interactions and experiences, enabling children to appear more competent than they may be. Young preschoolers' pretend play with their parents, for example, is more complex than their solitary pretend play or their social pretend play with peers (Bretherton, 1984; Howes, 1992). During play, parents help their children develop more sophisticated thinking and skills necessary for social interactions by assessing their child's current level, supporting his or her interest, and proposing new and more complex ways to play (e.g., Damast, Tamis-LeMonda, & Bornstein, 1996). In middle childhood, parents continue to have greater power and control over resources than children, although their interactions increasingly reflect a dynamic and transactional give-and-take.

Interactions with peers are, by definition, exchanges between individuals who are more equivalent in skill and interests. The opportunity to interact with equals in more horizontal relationships may afford different developmental opportunities and supports for development. For instance, in the 1970s, Harlow, Suomi, and colleagues tested the impact of rhesus macaque monkeys' peer relationships on social and physical development. They found that not only were peers essential for healthy development (e.g., Champoux, Metz, & Suomi, 1991; Suomi, Collins, Harlow, & Ruppenthal, 1976), but also interactions with peers could help rehabilitate monkeys who were reared in isolation. When these previously isolated monkeys were given opportunities to interact with a younger peer, they developed skills that increased their social functioning more than occurred with adult monkeys or older juveniles (Suomi & Harlow, 1972).

Although these relationships may differ, we do not want to draw too firm a line between the qualities of parent–child and peer interactions. Russell, Pettit, and Mize (1998) have theorized that even though parent–child interactions are typically characterized by vertical power dynamics, many parents provide opportunities for children to engage in horizontal power displays that are more typical in peer interactions. They proposed that these horizontal exchanges help children to transition from vertical patterns with parents to the more common horizontal power exchanges with peers. Some empirical support for this proposition has been found (e.g., Gerrits, Goudena, & van Aken, 2005). Although peer–child interactions have more horizontal power displays than mother–child or father–child interactions, interactions with parents include horizontal qualities such as mutual responsiveness, shared positive emotions, and balance of control. Furthermore, peer interactions do include some vertical power displays.

In the sections that follow, we examine the research evidence pertaining to the contributions of experiences with parents and peers to children's development. We also note some gaps in our understanding of how these important agents influence one another during the course of childhood.

Links From Parent–Child Relationships to Children's Interactions With Peers

By far, the bulk of the research examining the intersection between parents *and* peers has focused on the ways in which parents (or parent–child interactions) influence children's peer relationships. In considering this *parent-to-peer pathway*, three theoretical perspectives – attachment theory, social learning theory, and social information processing theory – have guided much of the research. Within each of these theories, interactions with their parents are viewed as preparing children for interactions or relationships with their peers. Although having this similarity, the theories differ in their emphases on particular underlying mechanisms believed to account for the link to subsequent relationships with peers.

Attachment theory

Attachment theory (Ainsworth, 1973; Bowlby, 1969) posits that the quality of children's early attachment relationships with their primary caregivers influences their feelings of security, sense of freedom to explore, and development of mental representations of themselves and others. On the basis of these internal working models, children come to predict the behavior of others and make attributional assumptions about these behaviors. According to the theory, children with secure attachment relationships come to expect interactions with their parents and others to be caring, reciprocal, and safe, whereas children with insecure attachments have less positive and more inconsistent expectations (Elicker, Englund, & Sroufe, 1992). As such, attachment researchers have hypothesized that the parent–child attachment relationship, due to its primacy, is the core around which other social relationships, including relationships with peers, are framed (LaFreniere & Sroufe, 1985; Sroufe, 2005).

Support for a link between attachment security and peer relationships has been tested in a number of studies, including a meta-analysis conducted by Schneider, Atkinson, and

Tardif (2001). Using studies published between 1970 and 1998, Schneider et al. quantitatively synthesized 63 eligible studies with a combined sample of 3,510 children. They reported evidence of a parent–child attachment link to peer relationships, with an average effect size of .20, suggesting a moderate association. The authors found that the effect size associated with child–mother attachment and close friendship was higher (mean ES = .24) than that associated with other, less intimate types of peer relationships (mean ES = .14), indicating that close friendships involve features such as closeness, security, and trust that are more similar to parent–child attachment. At the time of this analysis, only seven studies of child–father attachment were eligible for inclusion. From these few studies, Schneider and colleagues were not able to detect a significant difference between the influence of attachment to mothers or fathers.

Studies published since this meta-analysis have extended the investigations of parent–child attachment to the peer relations pathway. For example, Verschueren and Marcoen's (1999) study of kindergarteners found that children who were securely attached to both mother and father were more popular and accepted by their peers than children who were securely attached to only one parent. The children were also less anxious and withdrawn than children with insecure attachments to both parents. Recent research by Michiels, Grietens, Onghena, and Kuppens (2008) found that attachment security was linked to relational aggression as well as physical aggression, with some evidence that same-sex attachments (sons with fathers, daughters with mothers) are more predictive of outcomes than mixed-sex attachments. Along these lines, Casas and colleagues (2006) found that insecure attachment with mothers was associated with relational and physical aggression for girls, but not boys, whereas insecure attachment with fathers was correlated with relational aggression for boys, but not girls. Attachment research and its role in subsequent peer relationships continue to be a vibrant research area, especially in conjunction with other theoretical frameworks.

Social learning theory

Other investigators working from a social learning perspective view early relationships with parents as a developmental pathway in which children are learning how to interact with peers (Parke & Ladd, 1992). Based on Rotter's (1954) theory that "the basic modes of behaving are learned in social situations" (p. 84), and because children spend the bulk of their time in the first few years with parents, these adults must help shape their ways of interacting with others.

Working within the general social learning framework, Parke and colleagues proposed a tripartite model in which parents influence their children's relations through their child-rearing practices and roles as instructor and social manager (O'Neil & Parke, 2000; Parke, Burks, Carson, Neville, & Boyum, 1994). Specifically, parents provide early experiences in social interactions, help develop their children's language and communication skills, and facilitate and/or hinder children's opportunities for peer interaction (e.g., arrange play dates, enroll children in sports, restrict after-school activities, and even select the neighborhoods in which children will play and meet peers; Parke & Ladd, 1992). As McDowell and Parke (2009) noted, "[P]arents influence their children's peer relationships through the quality of the parent–child interaction, by offering explicit advice concerning ways of successfully negotiating peer relationship issues and by the provision of opportunities for social contact with peers" (p. 224). Studies of the role of parents in the development of peer interactions have found that parents tend to mentor young children during play, facilitate peer activities (Ladd & Hart, 1992; Profilet & Ladd, 1994), mediate when conflict arises, and model cooperative behaviors (Lollis, Ross, & Tate, 1992).

Although parents seem to play a key role in the development of peer interactions, the impact of parenting behaviors may change as children age. McDowell and Parke's (2009) study of 159 children from fourth to fifth grade tested separate models of maternal and paternal behaviors on peer relations. The authors found evidence that parent–child interactions (warmth and positive responses) and parental provisions for peer interactions were positively related to both teacher- and peer-reported social competences with peers (less aggressive and more prosocial behavior) and peer acceptance. For younger children, parental advice was positively related to social competence, whereas for older ages, more parental advice was related to less social competence.

There is also considerable evidence that children's experiences with their mothers and fathers may serve different socializing functions in children's learning of social skills for interacting with peers (e.g., Hart, DeWolf, Wozniak, & Burts, 1992). In one frequently cited study, MacDonald and Parke (1984) observed that fathers who were involved in physical play (but low in directiveness) had preschoolers who experienced higher peer acceptance. Similarly, Pettit, Brown, Mize, and Lindsey (1998) reported that mothers' and fathers' behaviors were largely independent, both within and across contexts. Father–child play was associated with boys', but not girls', peer competence, and mothers' coaching was associated with girls', but not boys', competence. Mothers' involvement in child–peer play predicted lower levels of child competence, whereas fathers' involvement predicted higher levels of competence. Research by Davidov and Grusec (2006) also found some differential parenting effects. In their study of 6- to 8-year-olds, maternal (but not paternal) warmth was related to greater emotional regulation and greater peer acceptance for boys (but not girls). Examining somewhat older children (first, third, and fifth graders), Wong, Diener, and Isabella (2008) found mothers' (but not fathers') encouragement of negative emotional expression to be linked to children's greater peer competence. Together, these studies suggest that mothers and fathers play unique roles in children's learning of social information.

Studies conducted outside of the United States have also examined effects of children's experiences with their mothers and fathers in relation to peer relationships. Hart and colleagues' (Hart, Nelson, Robinson, Olsen, & McNeilly-Choque, 1998; Hart et al., 2000; Hart, Yang, et al., 1998) studies of parenting styles and overt and relational aggression in Russian preschoolers have found that maternal and paternal coercion, lack of responsiveness, and psychological control (for mothers only) were significantly associated with children's overt aggression with peers. Less responsiveness (for mothers and fathers) and maternal coercion also were associated with relational aggression. Paternal playfulness and patience were related to less aggressive behavior with peers. These paternal effects were present even after controlling for maternal effects. Furthermore, these authors found that fathers were more likely to function as a playmate and mothers performed more as a manager and advisor. As such, they proposed that fathers may influence children's peer competencies through emotional regulatory processes and excitability, whereas mothers may influence children through explicit teaching strategies and verbalizations.

Other international work suggests that parenting behaviors might contribute to children's behavior with peers (Chen, French, & Schneider, 2006; Hart, 2007). For instance, a study of parenting and peer relations in China by Nelson and colleagues (Nelson, Hart, Yang, Olsen, & Jin, 2006) found that mother and fathers' coercive and psychologically controlling behaviors were related to children's physical and relational aggression. For girls, psychological control predicted more aggressive behavior, whereas for boys coercion was more predictive of aggression. In Greece, Georgiou's (2008) study of fourth to sixth graders found that children whose mothers were responsive were less likely to bully peers or be disruptive in school. However, children whose mothers were overprotective were more likely to experience victimization by peers.

Social information processing

An intriguing issue that has begun to receive attention is the determination of *why* these parenting behaviors are linked to peer-related outcomes. In exploring the mechanisms or processes through which parenting influences peer interactions, some have found that children's cognitive and temperamental qualities mediate the relationships between parenting and peers. Oftentimes this mediation occurs through children's ability to read social cues, process social information, and inhibit impulsive responses (see Hart, Newell, & Olsen, 2003).

In looking at the ways in which children's processing of social information could influence these parent–peer connections, Rah and Parke (2008) found that fourth graders' negative interactions with parents predicted their negative cognitions with parents. These negative cognitions with parents led to negative cognitions with peers, which in turn led to being less liked by peers one year later (but not disliked). This relationship was strongest for interactions with fathers and was most predictive when looking at same-sex dyads (e.g., fathers with sons).

The National Institute of Child Health and Human Development Early Child Care Research Network (NICHD ECCRN, 2009) also has studied familial antecedents of the quality of peer relationships by examining direct and indirect pathways between the family and peer systems. The investigators observed mother–child and father–child interactions at 54 months and the first grade. They found that the quality of mother–child and father–child interactions predicted children's ability to sustain attention as well as ratings of attentional problems. These attentional processes served as mediators of children's skilled interactions with peers in the first and third grades. Maternal and paternal interactions accounted for unique variance in these outcomes.

In an earlier paper by the NICHD ECCRN (2003), attention errors due to errors of commission (i.e., a failure to inhibit such as impulsive responding) and errors of omission (failures due to lack of sustained attention) were related to lower peer social competence at 4½ years of age. This finding supported earlier evidence that early parenting is related to the development of sustained attention and lower attentional impulsivity.

In considering attachment, social learning, and social information processing theories in conjunction, McElwain, Booth-LaForce, Lansford, Wu, and Dyer's (2008) recent study of over 1,000 children found that secure attachment at 36 months predicted social competence in the first grade and friendship quality in the third grade. Moreover, these relationships were mediated through children's social information processing (hostile attributions), language ability, and affective mutuality. Thus, early attachment may contribute to mental representations of relationships, and through interactions with the attachment object, children may learn the skills (e.g., communicating and processing social cues) and behaviors that are necessary for the development of high-quality relationships with peers.

Links From Peer Relationships to Children's Interactions and Relations With Their Parents

It is not surprising that the vast majority of studies have examined a pathway from parent–child relations to peer relations. The focus on a *parent-to-peer* pathway makes sense given that young children spend most of their time in the company of adult caregivers. However, more and more young children are spending much of their day with peers. In the United States, over half of children under the age of 6 years are in child care settings with other children (Childstats.gov, 2005). For children 5 to 12 years, a substantial portion of their school day, after-school hours, and weekends are spent with peers. As such, it seems reasonable to posit that these early experiences with peers may be influencing children's interactions and relationships with their parents. Surprisingly, much less attention has been directed toward examining ways in which interactions and relationships with peers may influence interactions and relationship with parents, with some notable exceptions (e.g., Harris, 1998; Suomi et al., 1976; Vandell, 1979, 2000).

In this section, we consider a pathway in which early peer experiences are posited to influence parent–child relations. The work of Repetti (1996) is one example consistent with this *peer-to-parent* pathway. In this work, children completed questionnaires several times a day about school events, moods, and parent–child interactions. Children who reported experiencing problems with peers at school were more likely to describe themselves as difficult and demanding with their parents later in the evening. Using a similar procedure, Lehman and Repetti (2007) also found that following a problematic day with peers at school, children reported having more aversive interactions with parents at home. Although assessing only a relatively immediate period of time, these studies suggest a clear influence of peer relationships on parent–child interactions.

Although studies of the direct impacts of peers on parent–child interactions are uncommon with young children, there is mounting evidence of the importance of peer influences on parent–adolescent relationships. Studies have shown that for adolescents, being liked and having high-quality peer relationships may contribute to better parent–child interactions, whereas poor peer interactions, especially when coupled with delinquent behaviors, may reduce parental monitoring and parent–child interaction quality (Mounts, 2001). Furthermore, parent–child–peer relationships may be reciprocal in nature. For example, in a study of seventh and eighth graders, Allen, Porter, McFarland, Marsh, and McElhaney (2005) found that popularity with peers (being liked and not disliked) was related to positive relationships with parents and that positivity in these parent–child relationships, especially when coupled with parental support and guidance, was associated with youth being more well liked by their peers. As of yet, less is known about how peer interactions before adolescence influence parent–child interactions. Given that so many children are spending large portions of their time with peers, this is an area that clearly warrants more attention.

Additive or Cumulative Effects of Parents and Peers on Child Developmental Outcomes

Given that ample research has demonstrated the importance of parents and peers on children's social development (see Chapters 17, 18, 21, 23, and 24), it seems likely that these two sets of experiences may represent additive effects. A third body of research has sought to identify possible additive or main effects of parents and peers on child developmental outcomes.

In one such effort, Kan and McHale (2007) used a person-centered approach to study the combined influence of parents and peers on social functioning (self-worth, depression, and risk taking) from middle childhood to adolescence. Three groups of children with different parent–peer relationship patterns were identified. One group, with high parental acceptance *and* high perceived peer competence, was associated with less depression and higher self-worth. Another group, with low parental acceptance and high peer competence, reported fewer depressive symptoms but engaged in more risk-taking behaviors. The third group, with low parental acceptance and low perceived peer competence, reported feeling more depressed and a lower sense of self-worth. However, this group had the smallest increase in risk-taking behavior over time. Interestingly, for those children experiencing low parental acceptance, females were more likely to have low peer competence, whereas boys reported more peer competence.

In considering the effects of neighborhoods, parents, and peers on child behaviors, Criss, Shaw, Moilanen, Hitchings, and Ingoldsby's (2009) study of males from toddlerhood to early adolescence found additive effects of neighborhood dangerousness, supportive parenting, maternal depression, and peer group acceptance on children's antisocial behavior and social skills. Specifically, "[P]ositive family and neighborhood experiences [maternal-report] in early childhood and supportive peer relationships [sociometric friendship and acceptance] in middle childhood were significantly related to low levels of antisocial behavior and high levels of social skills in early adolescence" (Criss et al., 2009, p. 19).

Also looking at combined effects, Brendgen and colleagues (Brendgen, Wanner, Morin, & Vitaro, 2005) conducted a longitudinal study of 414 children from middle childhood to early adolescence to identify predictors of depressive symptoms in early adolescence. From this, four depression trajectories were identified, and both additive (i.e., main) effects and interactive effects (consistent with the diathesis–stress model) were tested with an index of family adversity (a composite of parental demographic and family structure variables) used as a control variable. Although girls were more likely than boys to evince consistently moderate, consistently high, and sharply increasing depressive symptoms, children with difficult temperaments (high reactivity and negative emotionality) were more likely to show sharply increasing or consistently high depressive trajectories. Children with more family adversity were more likely to show consistently high depressive trajectories, whereas those with higher parental support experienced decreased likelihood for depressive symptoms. No main effects (or additive effects) were found for peer relations. However, increasing depression was predicted for girls who were temperamentally vulnerable and experienced rejection from same-gender peers, showing the potential additive risk of poor peer and parent relationships.

Taken together, these studies suggest some of the ways that parental and peer influences may be additive. Unfortunately, the role these important agents play in conjunction is not often explored, and when it is, most of the research has focused on early to later adolescence rather than younger ages (Brown & Mounts, 2007).

Synergistic Effects of Parents and Peers on Child Developmental Outcomes

In addition to studying additive effects of children's experiences with parents and peers, investigators have identified interactive or synergistic effects. These synergistic effects can occur in several forms. Positive (or negative) influences can be amplified over and above additive influences and negative effects can be buffered or ameliorated.

Primate studies conducted in the 1960s and 1970s reported evidence that peer relationships can ameliorate the detrimental influences of absent or negative parent–child interactions (e.g., Suomi & Harlow, 1972). In looking at children, researchers have also found that peers can moderate the harmful effects of poor parenting, disruptive home life, and parental marital discord. For instance, in a study of the impact of family adversity at age 5 on behavior in the second grade, Criss, Pettit, Bates, Dodge, and Lapp (2002) found that positive peer relationships in early elementary school could attenuate the association between negative family experiences and later externalizing behavior. Specifically, peer acceptance and friendship were shown to buffer the effects of violent marital conflict and harsh discipline. Along these lines, Wasserstein and La Greca's (1996) longitudinal study of fourth to sixth graders found that social support from close friends moderated the relationship between perceived parental discord and children's teacher-reported behavior problems. Numerous studies have also found moderating effects of peer relationships for turbulent family experiences in adolescence (e.g., Lansford, Criss, Pettit, Dodge, & Bates, 2003; Larsen, Branje, van der Valk, & Meeus, 2007).

In addition to buffering the effects of negative family experiences, there is evidence that peer relationships can strengthen the influence of positive parent–child interactions as well. For instance, in a study of Chinese third and sixth graders, Chen and colleagues (Chen, Chang, He, & Liu, 2005) found that peer group characteristics moderated the influence of supportive parenting on social and school adjustment. Peer groups that were cooperative and prosocial strengthened the association between maternal supportive parenting and children's social and school competence, whereas antisocial and destructive peer groups undermined the beneficial role of positive parenting. Similarly, Criss and colleagues' (2009) longitudinal study of boys from 18 months to 12 years found that the effects of supportive parenting on social skills and antisocial behavior were facilitated by peer group acceptance. Specifically, being liked by peers in middle childhood mediated the relationship between early parental supportiveness and increased adolescent social skills and decreased externalizing behavior. The authors also found support for an additive model in which both childhood parenting and peer acceptance individually contributed to adolescent behaviors.

Although peers may moderate the impact of parenting on child development, research suggests that parenting may also influence the impact of peers on child outcomes. Collins, Maccoby, Steinberg, Hetherington, and Bornstein (2000) concluded that peers are more likely to influence superficial aspects of behavior (e.g., hair, clothing styles, and slang) whereas involved parents carry more weight in the development of long-lasting core values. And it is the quality of the parent–child relationship that often helps determine whether teenagers choose peers who share similar values.

Although similar research has yet to be done with younger children, high-quality parent–child interactions have been found to help protect children from the consequences of being disliked and/or victimized by peers. In a short-term longitudinal study of first graders, Patterson, Cohn, and Kao (1989) observed maternal warmth in a laboratory playroom in the summer before children began first grade. In the fall, they assessed children's sociometric status, and in the spring, the children's teacher reported on the first graders' behavior problems and school competencies. This multimethod study found a significant interaction between maternal warmth and peer rejection and children's behavior problems at the end of the school year. Children who experienced peer rejection in conjunction with low maternal warmth were significantly more likely to act out, have learning problems, and be shy or anxious according to their teachers. Children who were rejected by their peers but experienced high levels of maternal warmth had fewer teacher-reported behavior problems.

In looking at parent–child interactions and peer influences on 567 boys from 6 to 12 years old, Vitaro, Brendgen, and Tremblay (2000) found that 10-year-olds' self-reported emotional attachment to parents reduced the influence of deviant friends on their anti-social behavior at age 12 years. Surprisingly, high levels of parental monitoring did not moderate the positive influence of having a deviant best friend on one's own delinquent behavior. However, this influence was present when earlier delinquency was not controlled for, leading the authors to conclude, "Although not reported, this result clearly suggests that age 10 parental monitoring has an indirect effect on delinquency at ages 13–14 through the mediating role of the association with deviant friends" (p. 321).

Others have examined family adversity as an exacerbating factor to the negative influence of peers. In a 12-year longitudinal study of 1,037 boys from low–socioeconomic status (SES) neighborhoods, Lacourse and colleagues' (2006) study of temperamental risk in kindergarten (hyperactive, fearless, and low on prosocial behaviors) found it to be a significant predictor of an early adolescent trajectory of deviant peer group affiliation (odds ratio of 6.68). This risk was substantially increased when coupled with family adversity, even after controlling for aggression in kindergarten (odds ratio of 4.18). Most boys (55%) who displayed the temperamental risk profile and lived in family adversity (e.g., an index of family and parental characteristics) followed an early starter trajectory, versus 26% of boys who displayed the temperament profile but lived in low family adversity, and the 5% of the boys with a low risk profile and either type of family.

Other studies of the ways in which parenting behaviors could influence the impact of peer relationships on child development have focused on adolescence. These studies of middle and high school students have found that parental monitoring (Mounts, 2001; Soenens, Vansteenkiste, & Luyckx, 2006), warmth (Dorius, Bahr, Hoffmann, & Harmon, 2004), involvement (Goldstein, Davis-Kean, & Eccles, 2005), discipline (Marshal & Chassin, 2000), and expectations (Simon-Morton, 2004) moderate the negative influences of peers on substance use and delinquency. Unfortunately, although the influence of parenting on children's relationships with peers has been a frequent focus of research, the ways in which parents may alter the impact of peers on children's social development have rarely been studied. The few studies in childhood and the growing body of work in adolescence suggest that such a research endeavor is worthwhile.

Parent and Peer Relations Within the Broader Social Context

Children's interactions with their parents and peers occur within a broader social context, and research has demonstrated that neighborhood conditions and cultural norms can influence how parents and peers affect children and their development (Leventhal & Brooks-Gunn, 2000). For instance, research has found that parental monitoring matters more in high-risk environments than low-risk ones (Schonberg & Shaw, 2007), that parental monitoring decreases as children age (McDowell & Parke, 2009), and that parental monitoring has varying influences on peer relationships (Mounts, 2001). Thus, the impact of parenting practices on peer interactions may be accentuated or attenuated by environmental risk at different developmental ages.

In a study of Anglo-American and Mexican American families, Roosa and colleagues (2005) assessed the impact of neighborhood risk (maternal-perceived neighborhood crime and quality) on life stressors (child reported), parent–child conflict (child and maternal reported), and association with delinquent peers (child reported) on fourth, fifth, and sixth graders' externalizing behaviors (maternal reported). They found support for a model in which neighborhood risk led to increased life stressors, more parent–child conflict, and increased association with deviant peers. These parent, peer, and life stressors contributed to children's increased externalizing behavior. This structural model accounted for over 25% of the variance in children's externalizing behavior for the whole sample. When looking at the effects for the children of Mexican- versus U.S.-born mothers, the influence of neighborhood risk on the mediators was comparable, but the effect of life stress, deviant peers, and parent–child conflict on externalizing behavior differed. Specifically, the mediators were less predictive of Mexican American children's externalizing behavior, suggesting that cultural influences may moderate this relationship.

In considering the effects of neighborhoods, parents, and peers on child behaviors, Ingoldsby, Shaw, Winslow, and Schonberg (2006) explored the influence of neighborhood disadvantage and early starting antisocial behavior for 218 boys measured at least five times between 5 and 11 years of age. Using census and maternal reports of neighborhood quality, the authors tested whether neighborhood disadvantage contributed to parent–child conflict in early childhood (assessed in the lab and at home), association with deviant peers in middle childhood, and subsequent antisocial behavior. Using a person-oriented group trajectory analysis, four patterns were identified with only a small group showing an early starter trajectory of antisocial behavior. Given the direct and mediational effects, Ingoldsby et al. concluded that "in early childhood, neighborhood disadvantage and family conflict place children at risk for early-starting trajectories, and that involvement with deviant peers in the neighborhood takes on an increasingly important role in patterns of antisocial behavior over middle childhood" (p. 303). Although the authors did explore the influence of ethnicity, no differences were found.

Research with adolescents has found that environmental conditions impact parenting and the types of peers with which children interact. These parenting and peer interactions then influence such things as substance use (Crawford & Novak, 2008), antisocial and delinquent behavior (Cantillon, 2006), and sexual activity (Fasula & Miller, 2006). Although this is a growing area of research on adolescents, fewer investigations have been directed toward younger children and their parents and peers in context.

Parent–Peer Transactions

Another area in which there is little research is the ways in which parents and peers directly interact (i.e., Bronfenbrenner's (1979) mesosystem) and how these interactions may affect children's social development. This neglected area of research is surprising given that many children have regular contact with the parents of their classmates and friends. Parents serve as coaches of youth sports. They attend musical and sporting events. They host birthday parties and sleepovers, and some drive carpools. Put simply, children often interact with parents other than their own, yet the role of direct parent–peer relations has not often been researched.

Only a handful of studies have explored the link between parents and their children's friends and classmates. These studies illustrate, however, the potential value of further research. In a study of adolescents and their parents, Updegraff, McHale, Crouter, and Kupanoff (2001) found that although mothers were likely to know more about their teen's friendships than fathers, both parents spent similar amounts of time with their children's friends. This time with adolescents' friends was associated with children's improved peer relationships (e.g., having emotional intimacy and a best friend), even after controlling for indirect parenting effects such as warmth and acceptance.

Other research has found that when parents viewed a peer as a negative influence on their child, they were more likely to share their preference, such as recommending limiting time with that friend or advocating for spending time with a different, more preferred friend (Tilton-Weaver & Galambos, 2003). These adolescent studies of direct parent–peer relationships support the importance of these connections and the need for exploring these ties for younger children.

Summary and Conclusions

This brief overview illustrates five approaches to the study of parents *and* peers and some of the ways these relationships have been explored. Research on the influence of parents and peers on children's social development has become more sophisticated in its design and analytic procedures. Longitudinal designs are being used, multiple methods are being employed, and analyses are exploring bidirectional relationships as well as mediating and moderating influences. By far, the most research has examined ways in which parent–child relationships may impact or influence children's interactions and relationships with their peers. Less is known about how interactions with peers influence children's relations with their parents. Although this *peer-to-parent* pathway is being investigated with adolescents, studies with younger children are needed. Additional research exploring additive and synergistic effects of these two sets of social relationships is also warranted, as is further study of parents' direct connections with their children's peers.

Although it is clear that both parents and peers are essential components to children's healthy social development, we hope this chapter helps to convey the importance of looking at the interplay between parents and peers as socializing agents.

References

Ainsworth, M. (1973). The development of infant-mother attachments. In B. M. Caldwell & H. R. Ricciuti (Eds.), *Review of child development research* (Vol. 3, pp. 1–94). Chicago: University of Chicago Press.

Allen, J., Porter, M., McFarland, C., Marsh, P., & McElhaney, K. (2005). The two faces of adolescents' success with peers: Adolescent popularity, social adaptation, and deviant behavior. *Child Development, 76*(3), 747–760.

Bowlby, J. (1969). *Attachment and loss.* Middlesex, UK: Penguin.

Brendgen, M., Wanner, B., Morin, A. J. S., & Vitaro, F. (2005). Relations with parents and peers, temperament, and trajectories of depressed mood during early adolescence. *Journal of Abnormal Child Psychology, 33*, 579–594.

Bretherton, I. (1984). *Symbolic play: The development of social understanding.* New York: Academic Press.

Bronfenbrenner, U. (1979). *The ecology of human development.* Cambridge, MA: Harvard University Press.

Brown, B. B., & Mounts, N. (2007). The cultural context of family-peer linkages in adolescence. *New Directions in Child and Adolescent Development, 116,* 1–15.

Cantillon, D. (2006). Community social organization, parents, and peers as mediators of perceived neighborhood block characteristics on delinquent and prosocial behavior. *American Journal of Community Psychology, 37*(1/2), 111–127.

Casas, J., Weigel, J., Crick, N., Ostrov, J., Woods, K., Jansen Yeh, E., et al. (2006). Early parenting and children's relational and physical aggression in the preschool and home contexts. *Applied Developmental Psychology, 27*, 209–227.

Champoux, M., Metz, B., & Suomi, S. J. (1991). Behavior of nursery/peer-reared and mother-reared rhesus monkeys from birth through 2 years of age. *Primates, 32*(4), 509–514.

Chen, X., Chang, L., He, Y., & Liu, H. (2005). The peer group as a context: Moderating effects on relations between maternal parenting and social and school adjustment in Chinese children. *Child Development, 76*(2), 417–434.

Chen, X., French, D., & Schneider, B. (Eds.). (2006). *Peer relations in cultural context.* Cambridge: Cambridge University Press.

ChildStats.gov: Forum on Children and Family Statistics. (2005). Percentage of children ages 0–6 not yet in kindergarten by type of care arrangement, 2005. Retrieved from http://www.childstats.gov/americaschildren/famsoc3.asp

Chisholm, K. (1998). A three year follow-up of attachment and indiscriminate friendliness in children adopted from Romanian orphanages. *Child Development, 69*(4), 1092–1106.

Collins, W. A., Maccoby, E. E., Steinberg, L., Hetherington, E. M., & Bornstein, M. H. (2000). Contemporary research on parenting: The case for nature and nurture. *American Psychologist, 55*, 218–232.

Crawford, L., & Novak, K. (2008). Parent–child relations and peer associations as mediators of the family structure–substance use relationship. *Journal of Family Issues, 29*(2), 155–184.

Criss, M. M., Pettit, G. S., Bates, J. E., Dodge, K., & Lapp, A. (2002). Family adversity, positive peer relationships, and children's externalizing behavior: A longitudinal perspective on risk and resilience. *Child Development, 73*(4), 1220–1237.

Criss, M. M., Shaw, D., Moilanen, K., Hitchings, J., & Ingoldsby, E. (2009). Family, neighborhood, and peer characteristics as predictors of child adjustment: A longitudinal analysis of additive and mediation models. *Social Development, 18*(3), 511–535.

Damast, A., Tamis-LeMonda, C., & Bornstein, M. (1996). Mother-child play: Sequential interactions and the relation between maternal beliefs and behavior. *Child Development, 67*(4), 1752–1766.

Davidov, M., & Grusec, J. (2006). The links of parental responsiveness to distress and warmth to child outcomes. *Child Development, 77*(1), 44–58.

Dorius, C. J., Bahr, S. J., Hoffmann, H. P., & Harmon, E. L. (2004). Parenting practices as moderators of the relationship between peers and adolescent marijuana use. *Journal of Marriage and Family, 66*(1), 163–178.

Elicker, J., Englund, M., & Sroufe, A. (1992). Predicting peer competence and peer relationships in childhood and early parent-child relationships. In R. D. Parke & G. Ladd (Eds.), *Family-peer relationships: Modes of linkage* (pp. 77–106). Hillsdale, NJ: Erlbaum.

Fasula, A., & Miller, K. (2006). African-American and Hispanic adolescents' intentions to delay first intercourse: Parental communication as a buffer for sexually active peers. *Journal of Adolescent Health, 38*(3), 193–200.

Georgiou, S. N. (2008). Bullying and victimization at school: The role of mothers. *British Journal of Educational Psychology, 78*(1), 109–125.

Gerrits, M., Goudena, P., & van Aken, M. (2005). Child-parent and child-peer interaction: Observational similarities and differences at age seven. *Infant and Child Development, 14*, 229–241.

Goldstein, S., Davis-Kean, P., & Eccles, J. (2005). Parent, peers, and problem behavior: A longitudinal investigation of the impact of relationship perceptions and characteristics on the development of adolescent problem behavior. *Developmental Psychology, 41*(2), 401–413.

Harris, J. R. (1998). *The nurture assumption: Why children turn out the way they do.* New York: Free Press.

Hart, C. H. (2007). Why are parents important? Linking parenting to childhood social skills in Australia, China, Japan, Russia and the United States. In A. S. Loveless & T. B. Holman (Eds.), *The family in the third millennium* (Vol. 1, pp. 227–247). London: Praeger.

Hart, C. H., DeWolf, M., Wozniak, P., & Burts, D. C. (1992). Maternal and paternal disciplinary styles: Relations with preschoolers' playground behavioral orientations and peer status. *Child Development, 63*, 879–892.

Hart, C. H., Nelson, D. A., Robinson, C. C., Olsen, S. F., & McNeilly-Choque, M. K. (1998). Overt and relational aggression in Russian nursery-school-age children: Parenting style and marital linkages. *Developmental Psychology, 34*, 687–697.

Hart, C. H., Nelson, D. A., Robinson, C. C., Olsen, S. F., McNeilly-Choque, M. K., Porter, C. L., et al. (2000). Russian parenting styles and family processes: Linkages with subtypes of victimization and aggression. In K. A. Kerns, J. M. Contreras, & A. M. Neal-Barnett (Eds.), *Family and peers: Linking two social worlds* (pp. 47–84). Westport, CT: Praeger.

Hart, C. H., Newell, L. D., & Olsen, S. F. (2003). Parenting skills and social/communicative competence in childhood. In J. O. Greene & B. R. Burleson (Eds.), *Handbook of communication and social interaction skills* (pp. 753–797). Mahwah, NJ: Erlbaum.

Hart, C. H., Yang, C., Nelson, D. A., Jin, S., Bazarskaya, N., Nelson, L., et al. (1998). Peer contact patterns, parenting practices and preschoolers' social competence in China, Russia and the United States. In P. T. Slee & K. Rigby (Eds.), *Children's peer relations* (pp. 3–30). London: Routledge.

Howes, C. (1992). *The collaborative construction of pretend: Social pretend play functions.* Albany: State University of New York Press.

Ingoldsby, E. M., Shaw, D. S., Winslow, E., & Schonberg, M. (2006). Neighborhood disadvantage, parent–child conflict, neighborhood peer relationships, and early antisocial behavior problem trajectories. *Journal of Abnormal Child Psychology, 34*(3), 303–319.

Kan, M., & McHale, S. (2007). Clusters and correlates of experiences with parents and peers in early adolescence. *Journal of Research on Adolescence, 17*(3), 565–586.

Lacourse, E., Nagin, D. S., Vitaro, F., Cote, S., Arsenault, L., & Tremblay, R. E. (2006). Prediction of early-onset deviant peer affiliation. *Archives of General Psychiatry, 63*, 562–568.

Ladd, G. W., & Hart, C. H. (1992). Creating informal play opportunities: Are parents' and preschoolers' initiations related to children's competence with peers? *Developmental Psychology, 28*, 1179–1187.

LaFreniere, P. J., & Sroufe, L. A. (1985). Profiles of peer competence in the preschool: Interrelations between measures, influence of social ecology, and relation to attachment history. *Developmental Psychology, 21*(1), 56–69.

Lansford, J. E., Criss, M. M., Pettit, G. S., Dodge, K. A., & Bates, J. E. (2003). Friendship quality, peer group affiliation, and peer antisocial behavior as moderators of the link between negative parenting and adolescent externalizing behavior. *Journal of Research on Adolescence, 13*(2), 161–184.

Larsen, H., Branje, S., van der Valk, I., & Meeus, W. (2007). Friendship quality as a moderator between perception and interparental conflicts and maladjustment in adolescence. *International Journal of Behavioral Development, 31*, 549–558.

Lehman, B., & Repetti, R. (2007). Bad days don't end when the school bell rings: The lingering effects of negative school events on children's mood, self-esteem, and perceptions of parent–child interaction. *Social Development, 16*(3), 596–618.

Leventhal, T., & Brooks-Gunn, J. (2000). The neighborhoods they live in: The effects of neighborhood residence on child and adolescent outcomes. *Psychological Bulletin, 126*, 309–337.

Lollis, S., Ross, H., & Tate, E. (1992). Parents' regulation of children's peer interactions: Direct influences. In R. D. Parke & G. Ladd (Eds.), *Family-peer relationships: Modes of linkage* (pp. 255–281). Hillsdale, NJ: Erlbaum.

MacDonald, K., & Parke, R. D. (1984). Bridging the gap: Parent-child play interaction and peer interactive competence. *Child Development, 55,* 1265–1277.

Marshal, M. P., & Chassin, L. (2000). Peer influence on adolescent alcohol use: The moderating role of parental support and discipline. *Applied Developmental Science, 4,* 80–88.

McDowell, D. J., & Parke, R. D. (2009). Parental correlates of children's peer relations: An empirical test of a tripartite model. *Developmental Psychology, 45*(1), 224–235.

McElwain, N., Booth-LaForce, C., Lansford, J. E., Wu, X., & Dyer, J. (2008). A process model of attachment–friend linkages: Hostile attribution biases, language ability, and mother–child affective mutuality as intervening mechanisms. *Child Development, 79*(6), 1891–1906.

Michiels, D., Grietens, H., Onghena, P., & Kuppens, S. (2008). Parent-child interactions and relational aggression in peer relationships. *Developmental Review, 28,* 522–540.

Moffitt, T., & Caspi, A. (2007). Evidence from behavioral genetics for environmental contributions to antisocial conduct. In J. Grusec & P. Hastings (Eds.), *Handbook of socialization: Theory and research* (pp. 96–123). New York: Guilford Press.

Mounts, N. (2001). Young adolescents' perceptions of parental management of peer relationships. *Journal of Early Adolescence, 21,* 92–122.

Nelson, D., Hart, C., Yang, C., Olsen, J., & Jin, S. (2006). Aversive parenting in China: Association with child physical and relational aggression. *Child Development, 77*(3), 554–572.

National Institute of Child Health and Human Development Early Child Care Research Network (NICHD ECCRN). (2003). Do children's attention processes mediate the link between family predictors and school readiness? *Developmental Psychology, 39,* 581–593.

National Institute of Child Health and Human Development Early Child Care Research Network (NICHD ECCRN). (2009). Family-peer linkages: The mediational role of attentional processes. *Social Development, 18,* 875–895.

O'Neil, R., & Parke, R. D. (2000). Family-peer relationships: The role of emotion regulation, cognitive understanding, and attentional processes as mediating processes. In K. A. Kerns, J. M. Contreras, & A. M. Neal-Barnett (Eds.), *Family and peers: Linking two social worlds* (pp. 195–225). Westport, CT: Praeger.

Parke, R. D., Burks, V. M., Carson, J. L., Neville, B., & Boyum, L. A. (1994). Family-peer relationships: A tripartite model. In R. D. Parke & S. G. Kellam (Eds.), *Exploring family relationships with other social contexts* (pp. 115–145). Hillsdale, NJ: Erlbaum.

Parke, R. D., & Ladd, G. (1992). *Family-peer relationships: Modes of linkage.* Hillsdale, NJ: Erlbaum.

Patterson, C., Cohn, D., & Kao, B. (1989). Maternal warmth as a protective factor against risks associated with peer rejection among children. *Development and Psychopathology, 1,* 21–38.

Pettit, G. S., Brown, E. G., Mize, J., & Lindsey, E. (1998). Mothers' and fathers' socializing behaviors in three contexts: Links with children's peer competence, *Merrill-Palmer Quarterly, 44,* 173–193.

Profilet, S. M., & Ladd, G. (1994). Do mothers' perceptions and concerns about preschoolers' peer competence predict their peer management practices? *Social Development, 3*(3), 206–221.

Rah, Y., & Parke, R. (2008). Pathways between parent–child interactions and peer acceptance: The role of children's social information processing. *Social Development, 17*(2), 341–357.

Repetti, R. (1996). The effects of perceived daily social and academic failure experiences on school-age children's subsequent interactions with parents. *Child Development, 67,* 1467–1482.

Roosa, M., Deng, S., Ryu, E., Burell, G. L., Tin, J., Jones, S., et al. (2005). Family and child characteristics linking neighborhood context and child externalizing behavior. *Journal of Marriage and Family, 67,* 515–529.

Rotter, J. B. (1954). *Social learning and clinical psychology.* New York: Prentice Hall.

Russell, A., Pettit, G. S., & Mize, J. (1998). Horizontal qualities in parent–child relationships: Parallels with and possible consequences for children's peer relationships. *Developmental Review, 18,* 313–352.

Scarr, S., & McCartney, K. (1983). How people make their own environments: A theory of genotype → environment effects. *Child Development, 54*(2), 424–435.

Schneider, B., Atkinson, L., & Tardif, C. (2001). Child-parent attachment and children's peer
relations: A quantitative review. *Developmental Psychology, 37*(1), 86–100.

Schonberg, M., & Shaw, D. (2007). Do the predictors of child conduct problems vary by high-
and low-levels of socioeconomic and neighborhood risk? *Clinical Child and Family Psychology,
10*(2), 101–136.

Simon-Morton, B. G. (2004). The protective effect of parental expectations against early adolescent
smoking initiation, *Health Education Research, 19*, 561–569.

Soenens, B., Vansteenkiste, K., & Luyckx, K. (2006). Parenting and adolescent problem behavior:
An integrated model with adolescent self-disclosure and perceived parental knowledge as intervening variables. *Developmental Psychology, 42*, 305–318.

Sroufe, L. A. (2005). Attachment and development: A prospective, longitudinal study from birth
to adulthood. *Attachment and Human Development, 7*(4), 349–367.

Suomi, S. J., Collins, M. L., Harlow, H. F., & Ruppenthal, G. C. (1976). Effects of maternal and
peer separation on young monkeys. *Journal of Child Psychology and Psychiatry, 17*, 101–112.

Suomi, S. J., & Harlow, H. F. (1972). Social rehabilitation of isolate-reared monkeys. *Development
Psychology, 6*(3), 487–496.

Tilton-Weaver, L. C., & Galambos, N. L. (2003). Adolescent' characteristics and parents' beliefs
as predictors of parents' peer management behaviors. *Journal of Research on Adolescence, 13*(3),
269–300.

Updegraff, K., McHale, S. M., Crouter, A., & Kupanoff, K. (2001). Parents' involvement in
adolescents' peer relationships: A comparison of mothers' and fathers' roles. *Journal of Marriage
and the Family, 63*(3), 655–668.

Vandell, D. L. (1979). Effects of a playgroup experience on mother-son and father-son interaction.
Developmental Psychology, 15(4), 379–385.

Vandell, D. L. (2000). Parents, peer groups, and other socializing influences. *Developmental
Psychology, 36*, 699–710.

Verschueren, K., & Marcoen, A. (1999). Representation of self and socioemotional competence
in kindergartners: Differential and combined effects of attachment to mother and to father.
Child Development, 70(1), 183–201.

Vitaro, F., Brendgen, M., & Tremblay, R. (2000). Influence of deviant friends on delinquency:
Searching for moderator variables. *Journal of Abnormal Child Psychology, 28*(4), 313–325.

Wasserstein, S. B., & La Greca, A. M. (1996). Can peer support buffer against behavioral consequences of parental discord? *Journal of Clinical Child & Adolescent Psychology, 25*(2), 177–182.

Wong, M., Diener, M., & Isabella, R. (2008). Parents' emotion related beliefs and behaviors and
child grade: Associations with children's perceptions of peer competence. *Journal of Applied
Developmental Psychology, 29*, 175–186.

CHAPTER FIFTEEN

Sex Differences in Social Behavior

Vickie Pasterski, Susan Golombok, and Melissa Hines

From an early age, boys and girls can be easily distinguished according to sex. Although this is partly due to appearance and the way in which their parents dress them and cut their hair, it is also because of the things that children do. Boys and girls like to play with different toys, prefer different games, and engage in different activities. Long before they reach school age, it is possible to tell with a reasonable degree of accuracy whether a child is a boy or a girl simply on the basis of his or her behavior. This does not mean that all boys engage in male-typical activities, or that all girls engage in female-typical activities, all of the time. There is a great deal of overlap between the sexes, with some girls seeming quite "boyish" and some boys seeming quite "girlish." Although there is considerable variation in the behavior of children within each sex, it is generally more acceptable for girls to behave like boys than it is for boys to behave like girls. This may explain why the term *tomboy* used to describe masculine girls is often used endearingly, whereas *sissy* is a much more derogatory term when applied to feminine boys.

What exactly are the differences in behavior shown by boys and girls? And how do these differences develop? These are the questions that will be addressed in this chapter. First, sex differences in social behavior will be described from the preschool to the elementary school years. This will be followed by a consideration of the various theories that have been put forward to explain this phenomenon. The sections on biological theories draw from Collaer and Hines (1995) and Hines (2004, 2009), whereas those on psychological theories draw from Golombok and Fivush (1994). As will be seen, some theories have greater empirical support than others. Following Maccoby (1988), the terms *sex* and *gender* will be used interchangeably throughout the chapter without any assumption that *sex* implies biological causes or that *gender* results from socialization.

The Wiley-Blackwell Handbook of Childhood Social Development, Second Edition, edited by Peter K. Smith and Craig H. Hart
© 2011 by Blackwell Publishing Ltd.

Behavioral Sex Differences

Preschool (3–4 years)

Gender identity   By their third birthday, children have generally developed a rudimentary sense of gender identity (Slaby & Frey, 1975). When asked, "Are you a boy or a girl?" they usually respond correctly. They can also correctly identify other people as male or female. But children of this age base judgments on physical appearance. A person with long hair and wearing a skirt will be deemed female, and a short-haired person with a necktie will be seen as male. If these same people change their clothes and hairstyle to look like the other sex, children will report that their gender has also changed.

At around 3 to 4 years of age, children develop gender stability, that is, they begin to recognize that gender does not change over time (Slaby & Frey, 1975). They realize that if they are a girl or a boy now, then they used to be a girl baby or a boy baby, and they will grow up to be a woman or a man. However, they still believe that children can change gender by changing their behavior; if a boy wears a dress, he can become a girl, and if a girl plays with guns, she can become a boy.

Toy preference   One of the most striking differences between boys and girls is their preference for different types of toys. This can be detected in the visual preferences of infants (Alexander, Wilcox, & Woods, 2009; Campbell, Shirley, Heywood, & Crook, 2000; Jadva, Golombok, & Hines, in press; Serbin, Poulin-Dubois, Colburne, Sen, & Eichstedt, 2001), and by the age of 3 years, girls are much more likely than boys to play with dolls and domestic toys, whereas boys are more often found with weapons and vehicles (De Lucia, 1963; Golombok et al., 2008; O'Brien & Huston, 1985; Sutton-Smith & Rosenberg, 1971).

Playmate preference   From as early as 2 years old, children prefer same-sex playmates (Maccoby & Jacklin, 1987; Pellegrini et al., 2007). This phenomenon, known as *gender segregation*, is not specific to particular nationalities or cultures and can be seen in play groups around the world (Whiting & Edwards, 1988). Furthermore, gender segregation is most likely to occur when children are left to their own devices, which suggests that it is children, not adults, who are driving this process. In an observational study of children in a day care setting, LaFreniere, Strayor, and Gauthier (1984) found that the tendency for girls to play together became apparent at age 2, and for boys by age 3. Howes (1988) reported similar findings. She observed children in day care, and showed that 3-year-olds were more likely to form new friendships with same-sex children.

Play style   Differences in the play styles of boys and girls can also be seen from age 3 (Maccoby, 1998; Maccoby & Jacklin, 1987; Pitcher & Shultz, 1983). Boys tend to play in a more active, rough-and-tumble, and sometimes physically aggressive fashion than girls, who tend to talk more to each other and to be more nurturant. Boys also like to play outdoors in large groups, whereas girls are more often to be found in twos or threes indoors. Differences in the way in which boys and girls resolve conflict are also apparent from age 3. Whereas girls incline toward reaching a compromise, it is more common for boys to use physical force (Sheldon, 1990). Pretend play also differentiates the sexes with boys acting out heroic roles involving fighting and adventure, and girls preferring to be family characters or dressing up in female-typical clothes.

Early school (5–7 years)

Gender identity   It is not until the early school years that children attain gender constancy, the final stage of gender identity development (Slaby & Frey, 1975). They now realize that gender is constant across time and all situations, and that however much someone wants to be the other sex, behaves like the other sex, and wears other-sex clothes, this simply cannot happen. The attainment of gender constancy is closely related to the conservation stage of cognitive development (Piaget, 1968). When Marcus and Overton (1978) administered both a conservation task and a gender constancy task to early school-aged children, they found that children who could successfully complete the conservation task were more likely to pass the gender constancy task as well. There has been some controversy over the age at which children reach gender constancy, with different studies producing different findings depending on the assessment methods used (Emmerich, Goldman, Kirsh, & Sharabany, 1977; Martin & Halverson, 1981; Ruble et al., 2007; Zucker et al., 1999). Many children, it seems, do not reach the stage of gender constancy until the end of the early school years. It used to be thought that it was necessary for children to develop a full understanding of the gender concept before they would consistently engage in sex-typed behavior (Kohlberg, 1966), but sex differences in toy, playmate, and activity preference shown by children younger than 3 years old clearly demonstrate that this is not the case. Indeed, Ruble et al. (2007) have worked to revise Kohlberg's theory based on evidence that an earlier stage of gender constancy, gender stability, mediates relationships between gender knowledge and other sex-typed preferences.

Toy preference   The sex difference in toy preference that is apparent among preschool children continues to characterize the early school years. In a study of 3–5-year-olds, Martin, Wood, and Little (1990) demonstrated a greater preference among boys for vehicles and tools over domestic toys and a greater preference among girls for domestic toys over vehicles and tools. Children in this study were also more likely to report that they preferred unfamiliar neutral items such as a pizza cutter and a hole puncher if presented to them as something that children of their sex really like.

Playmate preference   Gender segregation is an important feature of the early school years. Maccoby and Jacklin (1987) examined the playmate preferences of 100 children at 4½ years old and again at 6½ years. When first observed, the children were spending nearly three times as much time playing with same-sex peers than other-sex peers. Two years later, the amount of time spent playing with same-sex peers was more than 10 times greater than that spent with other-sex peers. A similar increase in the preference for same-sex peers was demonstrated by Serbin, Powlishta, and Gulko (1993) when they compared children in kindergarten with children in the early school years.

Play style   As children move from preschool to the early school years, the play styles of boys and girls continue to diverge. Achieving dominance appears to be of particular importance to boys. In order to have status, boys need to be seen as "tough" (Maccoby, 1998). The way in which girls and boys communicate is also different. Girls talk to each other to form and strengthen relationships. Boys use language to give information, assert themselves, and command attention (Lever, 1976; Maccoby & Jacklin, 1987). Additionally, boys of this age like to play in large groups, whereas girls prefer the company of one or two female friends. The nature of these relationships also differs between the sexes. Whereas girls' friendships are characterized by emotional and physical closeness, the friendships of boys are founded on shared activities and interests (Maccoby, 1998). A longitudinal study of 2,726 boys and 2,775 girls showed that behavior at age 2.5 predicted behavior at age 5 (Golombok et al., 2008). The children who showed the strongest preference for sex-typed play style before starting preschool continued to show strong preferences 2.5 years later.

Late elementary school (8–11 years)

Toy preference   The preference for sex-typed toys appears to continue right through childhood. In fact, Golombok et al.'s (2008) longitudinal study of over 5,000 children showed that not only did sex-typed toy preferences persist, but also they increased to some extent up until age 8. It seems that right until the end of elementary school, boys and girls have a strong preference for sex-typed toys.

Playmate preference   The preference for same-sex peers is strongest among elementary school children. In reviewing the literature on relationships within the school environment, Maccoby (1998) reported that children's best friends are almost always same sex. Furthermore, when observed during free time, boys and girls are even more likely to be found interacting with same-sex friends. Maccoby (1998) illustrated this with a description of behavior in the lunchroom:

> In school lunchrooms, the children usually have a shared understanding that certain tables are "girls' tables" and other tables are for boys. Very few instances are seen in which a child sits down next to an opposite-sex child after emerging from the cafeteria line. (p. 24)

A study of 8- to 11-year-olds by Gray and Feldman (1997) was particularly revealing. When they investigated peer group interaction at an ungraded school where boys and girls of all ages had the opportunity to mix, more than half of children spent no time at all with opposite-sex children.

Play styles   In the elementary school years, much of boys' free time is spent in large groups of other boys playing competitive games. When Crombie and Desjardins (1993) observed boys and girls at play, they found that boys in large groups were involved in competition with other boys 50% of the time, whereas this was true for girls in their smaller groups only 1% of the time. Girls spend most of their free time conversing with a female best friend, often sharing secrets or talking about mutual interests (Lever, 1976). Tannen (1990) examined the content of girls' and boys' conversations in a laboratory setting. The girls had long, intimate conversations. Boys, in contrast, found little to say and resorted to talking about finding something to do.

Explanatory Theories

Theories attempting to explain the development of sex differences in childhood behavior have been classified as biological or psychological. This distinction is somewhat misleading, because psychological processes have biological counterparts and because biology and psychology influence one another. In addition, the theories discussed under these headings are not mutually exclusive. Nevertheless, to date, so-called biological and psychological research approaches have proceeded largely separately, and so each will be discussed in turn.

Biological explanations

Biological mechanisms underlying sexual development have been studied extensively in nonhuman mammals, and have been found to be similar for the genitalia, the brain, and behavior. These processes are summarized below, and discussed more fully in Goy and McEwen (1980); Wilson, George, and Griffin (1981); and Hines (2004, 2009).

The primary and immediate biological determinants of sex differences are gonadal hormones. At conception, both genetically male (XY) and female (XX) mammals have the capacity to differentiate phenotypically as either males or females. In XY individuals, a region on the Y chromosome directs the primordial gonads (originally identical in males and females) to become testes. Without this direction, the gonads differentiate as ovaries. The human testes then begin to produce hormones by about week 8 of gestation. These testicular hormones direct male-typical sexual differentiation of the internal and external genitalia, where receptors for these hormones are located. In the absence of testicular hormones, these tissues differentiate in the female-typical pattern.

Similar processes occur within the brain, certainly in nonhuman mammals and apparently in humans as well. Like the genitalia, some brain regions have receptors for testicular hormones. The same brain regions that contain these receptors show structural sex differences and regulate reproductive behaviors or other behaviors that show sex differences. Treating female animals with the testicular hormone, testosterone (T), during early development masculinizes their brain structure and behavior, and removing T from developing males produces the opposite effects. For example, treating pregnant rhesus monkeys with T produces female offspring who show increased rough-and-tumble (male-typical) play as juveniles, and increased male-typical sexual behavior, and decreased female-typical sexual behavior, as adults.

These hormonal influences are graded and linear; smaller doses have smaller effects than larger doses. Therefore, small or moderate changes in hormones during development can move an organism along a male–female continuum. Thus, gradations in hormone levels during development could contribute to individual differences in sex-typical behavior within each sex as well as between the sexes. Also, the effects occur during critical or sensitive periods of early development that correspond to times when testicular hormones are higher in males than in females. In humans, such periods appear to occur from about weeks 8 to 24 of gestation, as well as from the first to the third, or even sixth, month of postnatal life, although the prenatal surge in testicular hormones has received more research attention than the postnatal surge (see Hines, 2009, for more details).

Knowledge of the basic mechanisms underlying sexual differentiation of the mammalian brain and behavior has come from experimental studies in species such as rats and rhesus monkeys, where hormones can be manipulated. Similar experiments are impossible in humans because of ethical considerations. Therefore, information on the applicability of these animal models to human development has come from other sources. These include endocrine disorders of prenatal onset, situations where women have been prescribed hormones during pregnancy, and cases where information about prenatal hormone levels is available for individuals with no hormone abnormalities. As might be expected, these sources are limited, and generally it is not possible to discuss the evidence in the age frames specified at the beginning of this chapter. However, where possible, data will be described in terms of the age groups for which they were gathered. In addition, because many studies have involved small numbers of subjects, sample sizes will be specified.

Toy preferences   Girls exposed prenatally to high levels of androgens (the major type of testicular hormone), because of the genetic disorder congenital adrenal hyperplasia (CAH), have been a major source of evidence regarding prenatal hormonal influences on human gender development. CAH causes deficiency in an enzyme needed to produce cortisol, and, consequently, substances that would normally be used to produce cortisol are shunted into a pathway that produces androgens. Genetic females with CAH almost always are born with ambiguous (partially masculinized) genitalia caused by the elevated androgen prenatally. The degree of virilization varies, ranging from essentially female-appearing genitalia, to some degree of labial fusion and clitoral hypertrophy, to male-appearing genitalia. In the great majority of cases, diagnosis is made shortly after birth, hormones are prescribed to regulate the postnatal hormonal environment, the genitalia may be surgically feminized, and the child is assigned and reared as a girl.

Despite these procedures, girls with CAH show masculinized toy preferences (Berenbaum & Hines, 1992; Dittman et al., 1990; Ehrhardt & Baker, 1974; Ehrhardt, Epstein, & Money, 1968; Pasterski et al., 2005; Slijper, 1984). Studies have obtained information from questionnaires and interviews with the girls and their mothers, and from direct observation of toy choices in a playroom. Questionnaire and interview studies often combine information on toy choices with other behaviors, such as playmate and activity preferences. However, observational studies indicate that toy choices are altered when considered alone. In two such studies, a total of 64 girls with CAH (ages 3 to 10 years) spent more time with toys typically preferred by boys and less time with toys typically preferred by girls than did unaffected female relatives (Berenbaum & Hines, 1992; Pasterski et al., 2005). Similar findings have been reported by a separate research group, who also found that the severity of the CAH disorder, and associated androgen exposure, correlated with the degree of male-typical toy play (Servin, Nordenstrom, Larsson, & Bohlin, 2001).

The interpretation of data from CAH girls has been questioned because of their virilization at birth, and because their parents might treat them differently based on the knowledge that they were exposed to "masculinizing" hormones (Fausto-Sterling, 1992). However, a recent investigation of parental responses to children's sex-typed toy preferences showed that this is not the case. In an observational study, Pasterski et al. (2005) compared parents' responses to 34 girls with CAH and 27 unaffected sisters playing with girls' and boys' toys. What they found was remarkable. Not only did parents reward their daughters for girl-typical play, but they did so more for daughters with CAH than for unaffected daughters. A significant but negative correlation suggested that the more the CAH daughters played with male-typical toys, the more parents encouraged play with female-typical toys. It appears that parents are encouraging CAH daughters to play with girl-typical toys, but this encouragement is insufficient to override a predisposition to male-typical toy play. Changes in toy play are not typically found between boys with and without CAH.

Evidence for the role of androgens in the development of sex differences in toy preferences of normally developing children comes from studies linking T in maternal blood during pregnancy and in amniotic fluid (aT) to subsequent behavior in the offspring. As part of a large-scale population study, Hines and colleagues (Hines, Golombok, Rust, Johnston, & Golding, 2002) measured T in blood samples from pregnant women and subsequent sex-typed behavior in their children (342 males, 337 females) at 3.5 years using the Pre-School Activities Inventory (PSAI), a measure designed to be sensitive to both between- and within-sex variation in involvement with sex-typed toys, activities, and interests. They found a linear relationship between maternal T and PSAI scores in girls. That is, higher levels of maternal T were linked to more masculine PSAI scores in daughters at 3.5 years. Conversely, lower levels of maternal T were linked to more feminine scores, and midrange levels of T were linked to midrange PSAI scores.

T measured in amniotic fluid during fetal development shows variability in both sexes and is typically higher in male fetuses, making it a plausible measure of prenatal androgen exposure. Although two studies reported no relationship between aT and sex-typical play (Knickmeyer et al., 2005; van de Beek, van Goozen, Buitelaar, & Cohen-Kettenis, 2009), these studies may have lacked sufficient experimental power to detect effects. The first study assessed childhood behavior by maternal report in 22 girls and 31 boys, and the second by observed toy choice in 63 girls and 63 boys. To apply a more rigorous test, Auyeung and colleagues (2009) assessed sex-typed behavior in a larger sample of 212 children using the PSAI. They found a significant correlation between aT and childhood sex-typed behavior in both boys and girls. Like the findings of Hines et al. (2002), these findings support a contribution of prenatal T exposure to the development of sex-typed toy, activity, and interest preferences in normally developing children.

Gender identity   Though several studies of girls with CAH have noted reduced female-typical gender identity or reduced satisfaction with the female gender role, the majority identify as female. Dessens, Slijper, and Drop (2005) reviewed the literature dating from 1950 and reported on gender identity in a total of 250 women with CAH. They found that 94.8% of the girls and women did not feel gender dysphoric, whereas 5.2% exhibited serious problems with their gender identity. However, a closer look at other studies might elucidate nuanced effects of prenatal T. For example, in a sample of 16 women with CAH, Hines, Brook, and Conway (2004) found reduced satisfaction with the female sex of assignment compared with 15 unaffected women, which is consistent with several other studies (Ehrhardt & Baker, 1974; Ehrhardt et al., 1968; Hurtig & Rosenthal, 1987; Slijper, 1984). Although the girls and women in these studies identified as female, the reduced satisfaction suggests that prenatal hormones may contribute to the differentiation of gender identity.

Playmate preferences   Playmate preferences also are altered in girls exposed to androgens prenatally. Three studies have reported that girls with CAH show reduced preferences for female playmates (Ehrhardt & Baker, 1974; Ehrhardt et al., 1968; Hines & Kaufman, 1994). The studies included a total of 58 CAH girls (ages 3 to 20 years) from three different regions of the United States who were compared to matched or sibling controls. The first two studies used interviews to assess playmate preferences along with other sex-typical behaviors. The third asked children to name their three favorite playmates and calculated the percentage of males. The 10 girls exposed to androgens reported increased preferences for male playmates (Money & Ehrhardt, 1972). Boys with CAH do not show alterations in preferences for male playmates (Ehrhardt & Baker, 1974; Hines & Kaufman, 1994), again consistent with research in other species.

Play styles   Studies of hormone-exposed children have not looked at play styles as extensively as have studies of normal children. However, there is some information concerning aggression and rough-and-tumble play.

Until recently, reports on aggression following prenatal exposure to androgenic hormones have produced confusing results. For example, one study found that 22 women with CAH scored higher than matched controls on a questionnaire measure of "indirect aggression" (Helleday, Edman, Ritzen, & Siwers, 1993). A second study, also using questionnaires, presented a more complicated picture (Berenbaum & Resnick, 1997): Six groups of CAH individuals (three female and three male) were compared to siblings of the same sex, with only one of them showing an effect. The different outcomes across the groups could relate to the age of participants, the specific questionnaire used to measure aggression, or the sample size. A more recent study used a larger sample (38 girls with CAH and 25 unaffected sisters) and a more direct method of assessment. To avoid biases in girls' reporting of their own aggressive behavior, Pasterski et al. (2007) asked mothers to rate how aggressive their 3- to 10-year-old CAH and non-CAH daughters were, as well as how often they got into fights with other children. They found that girls with CAH were rated as more aggressive and as having more fights than their unaffected sisters, suggesting a link between prenatal androgen exposure and aggression. A 2008 study of adolescents and adults also found that females with CAH recalled increased physical aggression in early adolescence (Mathews, Fane, Conway, Brook, & Hines, 2009). Similarly, a study of girls and boys exposed to progestins, particularly those with androgenic properties, because their mothers were prescribed these hormone during pregnancy found increased propensities to physical aggression compared to offspring from untreated pregnancies (Reinisch, 1981).

CAH girls also have been reported to show high energy expenditure and preferences for rough, active play, particularly in the context of "tomboyish" behavior (Ehrhardt & Baker, 1974; Ehrhardt et al., 1968). These studies included a total of 32 CAH girls (4 to 20 years) compared to matched or sibling controls. Similar findings were reported for the 10 girls (3 to 14 years) exposed to androgenic progestins prenatally (Ehrhardt & Money, 1967). A third study of 34 CAH girls (11 to 41 years) found no differences from unaffected sisters in energy expenditure based on interview responses (Dittman et al., 1990). This study also found no differences in dominance or assertiveness in CAH versus control girls. A fourth study, however, supports previous findings that prenatal androgens influence activity levels. Pasterski et al. (2007) found that, according to mothers' reports, their daughters with CAH ($n = 38$) were more active than their unaffected daughters ($n = 25$). Again, no difference was found between boys with and without CAH.

In terms of rough-and-tumble play, one study observed the behavior of 20 girls with CAH (ages 3 to 8 years) and their unaffected relatives. Children played with a partner in a room containing toys selected to elicit rough-and-tumble play (e.g., a "Bobo" punching doll). Control boys showed more rough-and-tumble play than did control girls (e.g., hitting the Bobo doll, playfully hitting one another, and wrestling), as found in prior studies using similar procedures (DiPietro, 1981; Maccoby, 1988). However, girls with CAH did not differ from control girls (Hines & Kaufman, 1994). These results contrast with data from female rats and rhesus monkeys, where androgen exposure during early development increases rough-and-tumble behavior (e.g., Goy & McEwen, 1980). Perhaps similar processes do not occur in humans. Alternatively, the testing situation might not have been adequate to detect effects. Most girls do not like rough-and-tumble play, and most boys will not play rough with girls. Consequently, girls with CAH may have found that neither male nor female partners were interested in joining them in rough-and-tumble interactions (see Hines & Kaufman, 1994, for additional discussion).

Summary   Studies of girls exposed to high levels of androgen prenatally, because of genetic disorders such as CAH, suggest that prenatal androgen influences the development of male-typical toy choices, gender identity, and playmate preferences. Some convergent evidence of hormonal influences on these behaviors has come from studies linking normative within-sex variation to T in maternal blood as well as in aT. Alterations in play styles, including rough-and-tumble play and aggressive play, are less well established. Variability in the early hormone environment has generally not been found to influence gender development in boys. However, the recent study by Auyeung et al. (2009) demonstrated a correlation between aT and sex-typed behavior in a large sample of normally developing boys. Clearly, although findings from girls with CAH, together with the normative studies, suggest that hormones can influence the development of children's gender-related behavior, further research is needed to fully understand the role of hormonal factors in the full range of behaviors that show sex differences and to understand their importance in the development of healthy boys as well as girls.

Psychological explanations

The psychological explanations discussed below have been organized according to theoretical approach as each theory has been applied to more than one aspect of gender development of interest in this chapter (gender identity, toy preference, playmate preference, and play style). The particular focus of each theoretical perspective will be highlighted where appropriate.

Social-learning theory   The idea, founded in psychoanalytic theory, that children's gender development results from identification with the same-sex parent is a cornerstone of social-learning theory. According to classic social-learning theory, two mechanisms are at play: (a) the differential reinforcement of boys and girls, and (b) children's modeling of individuals of the same sex as themselves (Bandura, 1977; Mischel, 1966, 1970). Classic social-learning theory posits that parents play a key role in the gender development of children, both by differentially reinforcing daughters and sons and by acting as models of sex-typed behavior. However, it is acknowledged that others such as teachers and peers, as well as images presented by the media, are also influential.

The role of differential reinforcement in children's acquisition of sex-typed behavior has been widely investigated in an attempt to establish whether parents really treat sons and daughters differently. In an influential review of the early studies, Maccoby and Jacklin (1974) concluded that there was little evidence that they do. In terms of the extent to which they allowed sons and daughters to be independent, and the way in which they responded to children's aggressive behavior, there was little evidence for differential reinforcement of boys and girls. Nevertheless, there were some differences. Parents reinforced their children for specifically sex-typed activities and interests such as doll play for girls and more active play for boys, and discouraged play that was associated with the other sex. A more recent review (Lytton & Romney, 1991) found a similar result. The only consistent differences to emerge in parental treatment of boys and girls once again involved sex-typed behaviors relating to toys, games, and activities.

Although Maccoby and Jacklin (1974) thought these differences were of little significance, other researchers believe that the differential reinforcement of children's toy, game, and activity preferences plays a part in the acquisition of sex-typed behavior (Block, 1983; Lytton & Romney, 1991). From the moment of birth, parents treat sons and daughters differently. They describe newborn girls as soft and newborn sons as strong (Rubin, Provenzano, & Luria, 1974), they give more physical stimulation to male infants and talk more to female infants (Moss, 1967; Parke & Sawin, 1980), they dress girls in pink and boys in blue (Shakin, Shakin, & Sternglanz, 1985), they give daughters dolls and sons cars and trucks (Rheingold & Cook, 1975), and they decorate children's bedrooms according to sex (Rheingold & Cook, 1975). The way in which parents interact with infants and children is also guided by the child's gender. From at least as early as 1 year old, parents encourage infants to play with sex-typed toys (Snow, Jacklin, & Maccoby, 1983), a phenomenon that becomes even more marked during the toddler years (Fagot, 1978; Langlois & Downs, 1980) but seems to wane by the time they reach 5 years old (Fagot & Hagan, 1991). In addition, mothers are more likely to discuss emotions with daughters than with sons (Dunn, Bretherton, & Munn, 1987; Fivush, 1989). Sex differences can also be found *between* mothers and fathers in the speech they use with their children. In a meta-analysis, an approach that looks at results across many studies to determine overall trends, Leaper and colleagues (Leaper, Anderson, & Sanders, 1998) found that mothers tended to talk more, use more supportive and negative speech, and use less directive and informing speech with their children than did fathers. Also, mothers tended to talk more and use more supportive speech with daughters than with sons. This report highlights the complexities of systematic differential gender typing by mothers and fathers toward their sons and daughters.

It seems, therefore, that parents do treat sons and daughters differently. But this does not mean that differential reinforcement by parents is responsible for the behavioral differences that are apparent between boys and girls. Might parents simply be reacting to the sex-typed behavior of their children rather than causing it? As already discussed, boys and girls may have a biologically based predisposition to behave in sex-typed ways. Most likely, differential reinforcement by parents not only produces sex-typed behavior in children but also increases preexisting behavioral differences between boys and girls.

Maccoby and Jacklin (1974) also examined the role of modeling in children's development of sex-typed behavior and concluded that the imitation of same-sex parents does not play a major part in this process. They argued that boys did not closely resemble their fathers, or girls their mothers, which would be expected if children imitated their same-sex parent more than their other-sex parent. Moreover, in observational studies, children did not necessarily imitate adults of the same sex as themselves. It is no longer thought that children learn sex-typed behavior simply by imitating individual same-sex models. Instead, it seems that children learn which behaviors are considered appropriate for their sex by observing large numbers of males and females and by noticing which behaviors are performed frequently by each sex. Children then model the behaviors that they consider appropriate for their sex (Perry & Bussey, 1979).

Children observe a wide variety of role models – not just their parents. Friends, in particular, appear to be important role models. As already discussed, school-aged boys and girls show a strong preference for same-sex peers (Maccoby, 1988). But it is gender stereotypes (widely held beliefs about the characteristics that are typical of males and females), rather than specific individuals, that seem to be most influential in the acquisition of sex-typed behavior. Gender stereotypes are pervasive in our society, and children are aware of these stereotypes from as early as 2 years of age (Martin, 1991; Signorella, Bigler, & Liben, 1993; Stern & Karraker, 1989).

Cognitive theory   For cognitive theorists, the role of parents is minor. A central tenet of this approach is that children play an active part in their own development; they seek out information about gender and socialize themselves as male or female. Parents are viewed as simply one source of gender-related information. Early studies of cognitive processes focused on children's developing understanding of the concept of gender (see above). More recently, gender schema theorists have examined the way in which children organize knowledge about gender (Bem, 1981; Martin, 1989, 1991; Martin & Halverson, 1981). *Gender schemata* refer to organized bodies of knowledge about gender, and are functionally similar to gender stereotypes. Gender schemata influence the way in which we perceive and remember information about the world around us so that we pay greater attention to, and are more likely to remember, information that is in line with our gender schemata than opposing information.

An important step in gender understanding occurs when children can categorize themselves as belonging to one gender or the other. From as early as 2 to 3 years, soon after they begin to consistently label themselves and others as male or female, children organize information according to gender. If told that a person is male or female, they will make gender-related inferences about that person's behavior (Martin, 1989; Martin et al., 1990). For example, preschool children will say that boys like to play with cars and trains. Older children have a more complex understanding of gender and become more flexible in their understanding of gender stereotypes (Martin, 1993; Martin et al., 1990). Although they may know that boys in general like football, cars, and trains, and that girls in general prefer dolls and dressing up, they also come to understand there are many exceptions to the rule (Signorella et al., 1993). Thus, it seems that gender stereotypes are more strongly held by younger than by older children.

Individual children differ in the extent to which they organize, attend to, and remember information according to gender (Carter & Levy, 1988; Levy & Carter, 1989). Interestingly, however, children who are highly gender schematized are not necessarily more sex typed in their behavior (Huston, 1985; Martin, 1991).

Social cognitive theory   Social cognitive theory draws upon both social-learning theory and cognitive theories (Bandura, 1986; Bussey & Bandura, 1984, 1999). Although same-sex modeling continues to be viewed as an important mechanism in the acquisition of sex-typed behavior, the processes involved are believed to involve complex cognitive skills rather than the direct incorporation of a model's characteristics and behavior. Social cognitive theorists stress the importance of cultural factors in influencing which behaviors are acquired.

Social cognitive theory and the cognitive approach differ in their view of the mechanisms involved in the development of sex-typed behavior (Bussey & Bandura, 1999). Whereas cognitive theorists have focused on children's acquisition of knowledge about gender, social cognitive theorists are interested in the translation of gender knowledge into gender-related behavior, and see that a number of cognitive mechanisms are at work. Self-regulatory mechanisms in the form of both social sanctions and sanctions that children impose on themselves are believed to operate; children do things that are valued and give them a sense of self-worth. Motivational mechanisms such as self-efficacy are also considered to be important. It is thought that children are most likely to model behavior that they believe they can master. Although social cognitive theory provides a framework for examining the relationship between gender knowledge and gender role behavior, existing research has failed to establish a consistent link between the two.

Gender segregation   Although psychological explanations of gender development have tended to focus on the individual, group processes may also be important. Gender segregation is a striking aspect of gender development that occurs at the group rather than the individual level. Although there is evidence that biological, socialization, and cognitive mechanisms each play a part in this phenomenon, the most parsimonious explanation – that children segregate by gender due to behavioral compatibility with same-sex others – incorporates all three approaches (Maccoby, 1988, 1990, 1998; Maccoby & Jacklin, 1987). Maccoby argued that children prefer to play with other children who have similar interaction styles, and that this both creates and serves to preserve gender segregation. It is believed that girls begin to avoid boys because of boys' higher levels of physical activity and aggression, and boys begin to avoid girls because they find girls too sedentary. Pellegrini et al. (2007) have extended this argument to suggest that a further factor, status, acts to keep the sexes segregated. In a study of 73 3- to 5-year-olds, they found that children segregated at first according to individual preferences, including activity level, but this segregation initially found highly active girls choosing male playmates. As time went on, highly active girls segregated into subgroups themselves. The authors could not say whether they chose to leave the boys' groups or if they were ejected. They suggest that the latter is likely and probably due to the reduced social status of being female.

Differences in communication style between the sexes may also play a part. As we have already seen, boys are more dominant than girls. Girls tend to be more cooperative and may find it difficult to have their say. Thus girls may not wish to interact with boys because they see boys as too assertive, and boys may not wish to interact with girls because they find girls too quiet. Once formed, same-sex groups become even more differentiated in their interaction styles. In this way, distinctive male and female cultures are established and maintained.

Summary

Gender development begins in the womb. Early in gestation, gonadal hormones mold the internal and external genitalia, as well as certain regions of the brain, contributing to such behaviors as sex-typical toy choices, playmate preferences, and gender identity. As a consequence, girls and boys are born with behavioral biases that can be enhanced or diminished by postnatal factors. From birth onward, children are treated differently according to sex. Although parents and others may simply be responding to differences in behavior that already exist, they may also be creating these differences. It seems likely that both processes are at work.

The extent to which the various aspects of gender development discussed in this chapter (gender identity, toy preference, playmate preference, and play style) are inter-related, or develop independently of each other, remains uncertain. Although cognitive theorists have argued that the ability to label gender, and knowledge of gender stereotypes, are essential for children to acquire sex-typed behavior, the sex differences in toy preference that are apparent from as early as 1 year old suggest that this is not the case. It does seem, however, that a child's knowledge of his or her own gender, but not necessarily of gender stereotypes, is associated with a greater preference for sex-typed behaviors. It is also important to remember that gender development does not occur in isolation from the child's social environment. Sex differences in social behavior are most apparent when children interact with each others.

Existing data suggest that components of children's sex-typed behavior are influenced by prenatal androgen exposure and postnatal socialization, particularly parental reinforcement. Thus, sex-typical toy choices, for example, appear to be multidetermined, promoted by the prenatal hormone environment as well as by several postnatal factors, including parental reinforcement, modeling, and gender labeling. A *biopsychosocial* model of gender development accounts for prenatal and postnatal factors. That is to say, it is very likely that sex differences in hormone exposure shape gendered behavior and that socialization, environment, and cognitive developments further modify these existing predispositions.

References

Alexander, G. M., Wilcox, T., & Woods, R. (2009). Sex differences in infants' visual interest in toys. *Archives of Sexual Behavior, 38*(3), 427–433.

Auyeung, B., Baron-Cohen, S., Ashwin, E., Knickmeyer, R., Taylor, K., Hackett, G., et al. (2009). Fetal testosterone predicts sexually differentiated childhood behavior in girls and boys. *Psychological Science, 20*(2), 144–148.

Bandura, A. (1977). *Social learning theory.* Englewood Cliffs, NJ: Prentice Hall.

Bandura, A. (1986). *Social foundations of thought and action: A social cognitive theory.* Englewood Cliffs, NJ: Prentice Hall.

Bem, S. (1981). Gender schema theory: A cognitive account of sex typing. *Psychological Review, 88*, 354–364.

Berenbaum, S. A., & Hines, M. (1992). Early androgens are related to childhood sex-typed toy preferences. *Psychological Science, 3*, 203–206.

Berenbaum, S. A., & Resnick, S. M. (1997). Early androgen effects on aggression in children and adults with congenital adrenal hyperplasia. *Psychoneuroendocrinology, 22*, 505–515.

Block, J. H. (1983). Differential premises arising from differential socialization of the sexes. *Child Development, 54*, 1335–1354.

Bussey, K., & Bandura, A. (1984). Influence of gender constancy and social power on sex-linked modeling. *Journal of Personality and Social Psychology, 47*, 1292–1302.

Bussey, K., & Bandura, A. (1999). Social cognitive theory of gender development and differentiation. *Psychological Review, 106*(4), 676–713.

Campbell, A., Shirley, L., Heywood, C., & Crook, C. (2000). Infants' visual preference for sex-congruent babies, children, toys and activities: A longitudinal study. *British Journal of Developmental Psychology, 18*, 479–498.

Carter, D. B., & Levy, G. D. (1988). Cognitive aspects of early sex-role development: The influence of gender schemas on preschoolers' memories and preferences for sex-typed toys and activities. *Child Development, 59*, 782–792.

Collaer, M. L., & Hines, M. (1995). Human behavioral sex differences: A role for gonadal hormones during early development? *Psychological Bulletin, 118*(1), 55–107.

Crombie, G., & Desjardins, M. J. (1993, March). Predictors of gender: The relative importance of children's play, games and personality characteristics? Paper presented at the biennial conference of the Society for Research in Child Development, New Orleans.

De Lucia, L. A. (1963). The toy preference test: A measure of sex role identification. *Child Development, 34*, 107–117.

Dessens, A. B., Slijper, F. M., & Drop, S. L. (2005). Gender dysphoria and gender change in chromosomal females with congenital adrenal hyperplasia. *Archives of Sexual Behavior, 34*(4), 389–397.

DiPietro, J. A. (1981). Rough and tumble play: A function of gender. *Developmental Psychology*, *17*, 50–58.

Dittman, R. W., Kappes, M. H., Kappes, M. E., Borger, D., Meyer-Bahlburg, H. F. L., Stegner, H., et al. (1990). Congenital adrenal hyperplasia II. Gender-related behavior and attitudes in female salt-wasting and simple-virilizing patients. *Psychoneuroendocrinology*, *15*, 401–420.

Dunn, J., Bretherton, I., & Munn, P. (1987). Conversations about feeling states between mothers and their young children. *Developmental Psychology*, *23*, 132–139.

Ehrhardt, A. A., & Baker, S. W. (1974). Fetal androgens, human central nervous system differentiation and behavioral sex differences. In R. C. Friedman, R. M. Richart, & R. L. Vande Wiele (Eds.), *Sex differences in behavior* (pp. 33–51). New York: Wiley.

Ehrhardt, A. A., Epstein, R., & Money, J. (1968). Fetal androgens and female gender identity in the early-treated adrenogenital syndrome. *Johns Hopkins Medical Journal*, *122*, 160–167.

Ehrhardt, A. A., & Money, J. (1967). Progestin-induced hermaphroditism: IQ and Psychosexual identity in a study of ten girls. *Journal of Sex Research*, *3*, 83–100.

Emmerich, W., Goldman, K. S., Kirsh, B., & Sharabany, R. (1977). Evidence for a transitional phase in the development of gender constancy. *Child Development*, *48*, 930–936.

Fagot, B. I. (1978). The influence of sex of child on parental reactions to toddler children. *Child Development*, *49*, 459–465.

Fagot, B. I., & Hagan, R. (1991). Observations of parent reactions to sex-stereotyped behaviors. *Child Development*, *62*, 617–628.

Fausto-Sterling, A. (1992). *Myths of gender*. New York: Basic Books.

Fivush, R. (1989). Exploring sex differences in the emotional content of mother-child conversations about the past. *Sex Roles*, *20*, 675–691.

Golombok, S., & Fivush, R. (1994). *Gender development*. New York: Cambridge University Press.

Golombok, S., Rust, J., Zervoulis, K., Croudace, T., Golding, J., & Hines, M. (2008). Developmental trajectories of sex-typed behavior in boys and girls: A longitudinal general population study of children aged 2.5 to 8 years. *Child Development*, *79*(5), 1583–1593.

Goy, R. W., & McEwen, B. S. (1980). *Sexual differentiation of the brain*. Cambridge, MA: MIT Press.

Gray, P., & Feldman, J. (1997). Patterns of age mixing and gender mixing among children and adolescents in at an ungraded school. *Merrill Palmer Quarterly*, *42*, 67–86.

Helleday, J., Edman, G., Ritzen, E. M., & Siwers, B. (1993). Personality characteristics and platelet MAO activity in women with congenital adrenal hyperplasia (CAH). *Psychoneuroendocrinology*, *18*, 343–354.

Hines, M. (2004). *Brain gender*. Oxford: Oxford University Press.

Hines, M. (2009). Gonadal hormones and sexual differentiation of human brain and behavior. In D. W. Pfaff, A. P. Arnold, A. M. Etgen, S. E. Fahrback, & R. T. Rubin (Eds.), *Hormones, brain and behavior* (2nd ed., Vol. 3). New York: Academic Press.

Hines, M., Brook, C., & Conway, G. (2004). Androgen and psychosexual development: Core gender identity, sexual orientation, and recalled childhood gender role behavior in women with congenital adrenal hyperplasia (CAH). *Journal of Sex Research*, *41*(1), 75–81.

Hines, M., Golombok, S., Rust, J., Johnston, K. J., & Golding, J. (2002). Testosterone during pregnancy and gender role behavior of preschool children: A longitudinal, population study. *Child Development*, *73*(6), 1678–1687.

Hines, M., & Kaufman, F. R. (1994). Androgen and the development of human sex-typical behavior: Rough-and-tumble play and sex of preferred playmates in children with congenital adrenal hyperplasia (CAH). *Child Development*, *65*, 1042–1053.

Howes, C. (1988). Peer interaction among children. *Monographs for the Society for Research in Child Development*, *53*(1, Serial No. 217).

Hurtig, A. L., & Rosenthal, I. M. (1987). Psychological findings in early treated cases of female pseudohermaphroditism caused by virilizing congenital adrenal hyperplasia. *Archives of Sexual Behavior, 16*, 209–223.

Huston, A. (1985). The development of sex-typing: Themes from recent research. *Developmental Review, 5*, 1–17.

Jadva, V., Golombok, S., & Hines, M. (in press). Infants' preferences for toys, colors and shapes: Sex differences and similarities. *Archives of Sexual Behavior.*

Knickmeyer, R. C., Wheelwright, S., Taylor, K., Raggatt, P., Hackett, G., & Baron-Cohen, S. (2005). Gender-typed play and amniotic testosterone. *Developmental Psychology, 41*(3), 517–528.

Kohlberg, L. (1966). A cognitive-developmental analysis of children's sex-role concepts and attitudes. In E. E. Maccoby (Ed.), *The development of sex differences.* Stanford, CA: Stanford University Press.

LaFreniere, P., Strayor, F., & Gauthier, R. (1984). The emergence of same-sex affiliative preference among preschool peers: A developmental/ethological perspective. *Child Development, 55,* 1958–1965.

Langlois, J. H., & Downs, A. C. (1980). Mothers, fathers, and peers as socialization agents of sex-typed play behaviors in young children. *Child Development, 51,* 1237–1247.

Leaper, C., Anderson, K. J., & Sanders, P. (1998). Moderators of gender effects on parents' talk to their children: A meta-analysis. *Developmental Psychology, 34*(1), 3–27.

Lever, J. (1976). Sex differences in the games children play. *Social Problems, 23,* 478–487.

Levy, G. D., & Carter, D. B. (1989). Gender schema, gender constancy and gender role knowledge: The roles of cognitive factors in preschoolers' gender-role stereotypic attitudes. *Developmental Review, 25,* 444–449.

Lytton, H., & Romney, D. M. (1991). Parents' differential socialization of boys and girls: A meta-analysis. *Psychological Bulletin, 109,* 267–296.

Maccoby, E. E. (1988). Gender as a social category. *Developmental Psychology, 24,* 755–765.

Maccoby, E. E. (1990). Gender and relationships: A developmental account. *American Psychologist, 45,* 513–520.

Maccoby, E. E. (1998). *The two sexes: Growing up apart, coming together.* Cambridge, MA: Harvard University Press.

Maccoby, E. E., & Jacklin, C. N. (1974). *The psychology of sex differences.* Stanford, CA: Stanford University Press.

Maccoby, E. E., & Jacklin, C. N. (1987). Gender segregation in children. In H. W. Reese (Ed.), *Advances in child development and behavior.* New York: Academic Press.

Marcus, D. E., & Overton, W. F. (1978). The development of cognitive gender constancy and sex role preferences. *Child Development, 49,* 434–444.

Martin, C. L. (1989). Children's use of gender-related information in making social judgements. *Developmental Psychology, 25,* 80–88.

Martin, C. L. (1991). The role of cognition in understanding gender effects. In H. W. Reese (Ed.), *Advances in child development and behavior* (pp. 113–164). New York: Academic Press. *23.*

Martin, C. L. (1993). New directions for assessing children's gender knowledge. *Developmental Review, 13,* 184–204.

Martin, C. L., & Halverson, C. (1981). A schematic processing model of sex typing and stereotyping in children. *Child Development, 52,* 1119–1134.

Martin, C. L., Wood, C. H., & Little, J. K. (1990). The development of gender stereotype components. *Child Development, 61,* 1891–1904.

Mathews, G. A., Fane, B. A., Conway, G. S., Brook, C. G., & Hines, M. (2009). Personality and congenital adrenal hyperplasia: Possible effects of prenatal androgen exposure. *Hormones and Behavior, 55,* 285–291.

Mischel, W. (1966). A social learning view of sex differences in behavior. In E. E. Maccoby (Ed.), *The development of sex differences*. Stanford, CA: Stanford University Press.

Mischel, W. (1970). Sex-typing and socialization. In P. Mussen (Ed.), *Carmichael's manual of child psychology* (Vol. 2, pp. 3–72). New York: Wiley.

Money, J., & Ehrhardt, A. A. (1972). Man and woman, boy and girl. *The differentiation and dimorphism of gender identity from conception to maturity*. Baltimore: Johns Hopkins University Press.

Moss, H. A. (1967). Sex, age, and the state as determinants of mother-infant interaction. *Merrill-Palmer Quarterly, 13*, 19–36.

O'Brien, M., & Huston, A. C. (1985). Development of sex-typed play behavior in toddlers. *Developmental Psychology, 21*(5), 866–871.

Parke, R. D., & Sawin, D. B. (1980). The family in early infancy: Social interactional and attitudinal analyses. In F. Pedersen (Ed.), *The father-infant relationship: Observational studies in a family context*. New York: Praeger.

Pasterski, V. L., Geffner, M. E., Brain, C., Hindmarsh, P., Brook, C., & Hines, M. (2005). Prenatal hormones and postnatal socialization by parents as determinants of male-typical toy play in girls with congenital adrenal hyperplasia. *Child Development, 76*(1), 264–278.

Pasterski, V. L., Geffner, M. E., Brain, C., Hindmarsh, P., Brook, C., & Hines, M. (2007). Increased aggression and activity level in 3- to 11-year-old girls with congenital adrenal hyperplasia (CAH). *Hormones and Behavior, 52*, 368–374.

Pellegrini, A. D., Long, J. D., Roseth, C. J., Bohn, C. M., & van Ryzin, M. (2007). A short-term longitudinal study of preschoolers' (*Homo sapiens*) sex segregation: The role of physical activity, sex, and time. *Journal of Comparative Psychology, 121*(3), 282–289.

Perry, D. G., & Bussey, K. (1979). The social learning theory of sex difference: Imitation is alive and well. *Journal of Personality & Social Psychology, 37*, 1699–1712.

Piaget, J. (1968). *On the development of memory and identity*. Worcester, MA: Clark University Press.

Pitcher, E. G., & Shultz, L. H. (1983). *Boys and girls at play: The development of sex roles*. South Hadley, MA: Bergin and Garvey.

Reinisch, J. M. (1981). Prenatal exposure to synthetic progestins increases potential for aggression in humans. *Science, 211*, 1171–1173.

Rheingold, H. L., & Cook, K. V. (1975). The content of boys' and girls' rooms as an index of parents' behavior. *Child Development, 46*, 459–463.

Rubin, J. Z., Provenzano, F. J., & Luria, Z. (1974). The eye of the beholder: Parents' views on sex of newborns. *American Journal of Orthopsychiatry, 44*, 512–519.

Ruble, D. N., Taylor, L. J., Cyphers, L., Greulich, F. K., Lurye, L., & Shrout, P. E. (2007). The role of gender constancy in early gender development. *Child Development, 78*(4), 1121–1136.

Serbin, L. A., Poulin-Dubois, D., Colburne, K. A., Sen, M. G., & Eichstedt, J. A. (2001). Gender stereotyping in infancy: Visual preferences for and knowledge of gender-stereotyped toys in the second year. *International Journal of Behavioral Development, 25*, 7–15.

Serbin, L. A., Powlishta, K. K., & Gulko, J. (1993). The development of sex typing in middle childhood. *Monographs of the Society for Research in Child Development, 58*(2), 1–74.

Servin, A., Nordenstrom, A., Larsson, A., & Bohlin, G. (2003). Prenatal androgens and gender-typed behavior: A study of girls with mild and severe forms of congenital adrenal hyperplasia. *Developmental Psychology, 39*, 440–450.

Shakin, M., Shakin, D., & Sternglanz, S. H. (1985). Infant clothing: Sex labelling for strangers. *Sex Roles, 12*, 955–963.

Sheldon, A. (1990). Pickle fights: Gendered talk in preschool disputes. *Discourse Processes, 13*, 5–31.

Signorella, M. L., Bigler, R. S., & Liben, L. S. (1993). Developmental differences in children's gender schemata about others: A meta-analytic review. *Developmental Review, 13,* 106–126.

Slaby, R. G., & Frey, K. S. (1975). Development of gender constancy and selective attention to same-sex models. *Child Development, 46,* 849–856.

Slijper, F. M. E. (1984). Androgens and gender role behavior in girls with congenital adrenal hyperplasia (CAH). *Progress in Brain Research, 61,* 417–422.

Snow, M. E., Jacklin, C. N., & Maccoby, E. E. (1983). Sex-of-child differences in father-child interaction at one year of age. *Child Development, 49,* 227–232.

Stern, M., & Karraker, K. H. (1989). Sex stereotyping of infants: A review of gender labelling studies. *Sex Roles, 20,* 501–522.

Sutton-Smith, B., & Rosenberg. B. G. (1971). Sixty years of historical change in the game preferences of American children. In R. E. Herron & D. Sutton-Smith (Eds.), *Child's play.* New York: Wiley.

Tannen, D. (1990). Gender differences in topical coherence: Creating involvement in best friend's talk. *Discourse Processes, 13,* 73–90.

van de Beek, C., van Goozen, S. H. M., Buitelaar, J. K., & Cohen-Kettenis, P. T. (2009). Prenatal sex hormones (maternal and amniotic fluid) and gender-related play behavior in 13-month-old infants. *Archives of Sexual Behavior, 38*(1), 6–15.

Whiting, B. B., & Edwards, C. P. (1988). *Children of different worlds: The formation of social behavior.* Cambridge, MA: Harvard University Press.

Wilson, J. D., George, F. W., & Griffin, J. E. (1981). The hormonal control of sexual development. *Science, 211,* 1278–1284.

Zucker, K. J., Bradley, S. J., Kulsis, M., Pecore, K., Birkenfeld, A., Doering, R. W., et al. (1999). Gender constancy judgements in children with gender identity disorder: Evidence for a developmental lag. *Archives of Sexual Behavior, 28*(6), 475–502.

CHAPTER SIXTEEN

Ethnicity, Race, and Children's Social Development

Stephen M. Quintana

Children's interracial interactions and attitudes have been the interest of researchers for nearly 6 decades. The increasing globalized nature of society, including ease of movement to new lands, ensures that many children will continue to function in interracial contexts. Children's social development in interracial contexts has been of considerable interest to researchers for many decades, and this research has uncovered important insights into children's social development. For example, children develop notions about ethnicity and race early in life, oftentimes even before they have interethnic or interracial contact. Children learn about other social categories, such as gender- or age-related groupings, through extensive interpersonal interactions, but young, preschool children often learn about those who are ethnically or racially different in the absence of personal contact. Despite this social distance, the precociousness of children's learning about race and ethnicity suggests that they have strong motivations or natural inclinations to learn about social categories involving race and ethnicity.

Research into how children learn about race and ethnicity is particularly interesting because several popular notions regarding race and ethnicity have been contradicted by psychological research. For example, many presume that children start life with neutral notions about sociocultural groups and later internalize the society's ethnic and racial hierarchy. Analogously, many believe that children first learned to differentiate among ethnic or racial groups and then develop attitudes toward those groups. In contrast, research suggests that children acquire racial attitudes prior to developing the ability to categorize by race and that the initial attitudes are not neutral but reflect society's biases against certain racial groups (Hirschfeld, 2008). In short, it appears as if children first

The Wiley-Blackwell Handbook of Childhood Social Development, Second Edition, edited by Peter K. Smith and Craig H. Hart
© 2011 by Blackwell Publishing Ltd.

acquire racial attitudes, then the ability to sort and classify others into racial categories (Hirschfeld, 2008), the opposite of popular notions about the development of children's racial cognitions.

In order to capture the complexity of race and ethnicity in children's social world, several theoretical perspectives have been applied, including evolutionary, developmental, and social psychological ones, to account for children's social functioning in these areas. These theoretical perspectives were proposed to explain the various interesting observations and findings that have emerged about children's ethnic or racial cognitions and interactions. This chapter begins by discussing the theory and research associated with the emergence of racial and ethnic cognitions, followed by reviews of the formation of children's racial attitudes and bias and then of the factors associated with children's detection, awareness, and consciousness of racial and ethnic bias.

Children's Early Conceptions of Race

Evolutionary perspectives

What are the origins of young children's cognitions and attitudes about race and ethnicity? Do children begin with a *tabula rasa* with respect to racial and ethnic groupings, or do they start with some innate tendencies? Do children develop racial attitudes from strictly personal and vicarious experiences, or do evolutionary principles drive children's early development? At what age do children begin to be sensitive to ethnic and racial socialization? The extant research and theories have some answers to these intriguing questions.

As mentioned above, historically and for many contemporary children, interracial or interethnic contact often did not occur until mid- or late childhood, with many having their first personal contact upon entering school; and for some children, contact with racially different persons does not occur until adolescence or adulthood. Those who live in racially homogeneous contexts and countries may not ever have much direct contact with persons who are racially different. Previously, many researchers reasoned that children's interracial or interethnic attitudes were a subset of the larger domain of social cognition, that is, how children reason about racial or ethnic groups is largely determined by social cognition. For example, Aboud (1988) suggested that children's racial and ethnic attitudes are predicated on the development of children's cognitive development. However, when presuming children's naïveté about racial and ethnic groups, researchers may have underestimated children's abilities.

In contrast to early expectations, young children do not appear to be naïve with respect to the racial and ethnic hierarchies in society (see Baron & Banaji, 2006). Research has contradicted popular notions that children first learn about the racial and ethnic categories and then develop attitudes in response to these categories (for review, see Hirschfeld, 2008). Instead, children appear to have nascent notions about race and ethnicity early in infancy. Young infants show sensitivity to different-race faces as evidenced by the amount of time they spend inspecting different-race versus same-race faces (Kelly et al., 2005), suggesting that young infants might have predispositions to recognize and respond favorably to same-race faces and react to the foreignness of different-race faces. Research on adults also suggests that different-race faces activate neural activity in the amygdala, the region of the brain associated with startle effects (Cunningham et al., 2004). Clearly, there may be some adaptive significance, from an evolutionary perspective, to having humans primed to react with caution, fear, or startle when contacting persons with a different racial or ethnic heritage.

Moreover, longitudinal research has found that variations in parental socialization as early as 18 months predict racial attitudes at 36 and 48 months (Katz, 2003). These findings suggest that children demonstrate sensitivity to race and ethnicity earlier than anticipated by popular notions and previous theoretical formulations. It is hard to account for the precociousness of children's reactions to ethnic and racial stimuli based simply on experiential factors, particularly given that exposure of many children to ethnic and racial differences does not occur until much later, if at all, in their development. For example, young Japanese children manifest racial bias against African origin persons early in life, even though they have not had any personal contact with them (Dunham, Baron, & Banaji, 2006). These findings may imply that evolutionary principles influence children's nascent racial and ethnic awareness (see Hirschfeld, 1994, 2008).

Application of Piagetian theories of egocentrism (Inhelder & Piaget, 1958) might lead to the prediction that children would consider their views of race to be centered on the notion that their own group would be normative and/or most desirable. Although that anticipation is consistent with the early racial cognitions of White children in, for example, North America, Western Europe, Australia, and South Africa, it is inconsistent with research on children in those same societies who have a minority racial background (e.g., Gregor & McPherson, 1966; and see Nesdale, 2008). Early research on children's racial attitudes in the United States, for example, suggested that both White and African American children had more favorable attitudes toward lighter skinned persons than darker complexioned persons. Specifically, findings from Clark and Clark's (1939, 1940) famous doll study was interpreted as suggesting that African American children favored dolls depicted as having white skin over those that had brown skin. In response to these findings and subsequent research, Williams, Best, and Boswell (1975) suggested evolutionary principles to explain this apparent White bias in both White and African American children. It is important to note that subsequent analyses suggested that Black children did not favor White over Black dolls, but merely favored Black dolls less strongly than White children favored White dolls (Banks, 1976). The same pattern of findings, in which children who are in the racial majority have stronger ethnocentrism than minority children, has been detected for children outside of the United States. In Spain, majority Spanish children manifest the same ethnocentrism as White children in the United States, and minority Latin American children in Spain evidence the same patterns as racial minority children in the United States (Enesco, Guerrero, Callejas, & Solbes, 2008). Clearly, simple application of notions of childhood egocentrism cannot fully account for the patterns of racial minority children's racial preferences.

The term *colorism* could be used to describe Williams et al.'s (1975) theory accounting for the difference in children's ethnocentrism young children's racial bias. Williams et al. suggested that young children's racial attitudes are influenced by their preference for lighter colors over darker colors. Williams and colleagues' research indicated that children from a variety of different countries tend to prefer light colors to dark colors. Moreover, they demonstrated a connection between individual children's color bias and their racial attitudes as reflected in scores on William et al.'s Preschool Racial Attitudes Measure (PRAM). Williams et al. reasoned that humans' and other primates' diurnal nature predisposes them to prefer light colors over darker ones, which is consistent with children's fearfulness of the dark and their association of positive affect with lighter colors. Williams et al. demonstrated further that it is possible to alter children's attitudes toward colors and that these changes were associated with more favorable racial attitudes on the PRAM. It is important to note a confound in Williams et al.'s research in that the PRAM, the measure used to reflect racial attitudes, signals race through the coloration of research stimuli (e.g., pictures or drawings). Theorists have questioned whether the PRAM is an accurate reflection of children's racial attitudes, rather than their chromatic attitudes (Hirschfeld, 1994; Quintana, 1999). Subsequent research investigations have clarified if children's attitudes about different colors and apparent racial bias based on preference of racial groups with lighter skin complexions are translated into their interracial social behavior.

Hirschfeld (2008) suggested that children appear to demonstrate a predisposition to organize their social world into social groups. He argued that there may not be an innate tendency to perceive racial groups, per se, but rather a tendency to organize into social groups, of which race and ethnicity are two of many different categories that children can use to organize their social worlds. This innate tendency to perceive and sort persons into groups may be malleable, in that Hirschfeld suggested that the particular groups to which children sort their social world will depend on the societal context. Hence, children's precocious sensitivity to racial and ethnic groupings is seen as reflecting the social salience of race and ethnicity in many societies, not only in modern societies but also historically. Hirschfeld noted that young children in some intergroup contexts may not use racial categories to sort social groups (e.g., children in Northern Ireland), but instead quickly acquire the social categories that are assigned importance in their society. He made an analogy between Chomsky's learning acquisition device to account for the precociousness of children's acquisition of language and the efficiency with which children learn the social groupings that are important in their societies.

Hirschfeld's (1995, 1996) research has supported his views and also challenged the popular notion that young children first learn about race and ethnicity based on their observations of different racial phenotypes. As mentioned above, popular and some scholarly notions suggested that children first learn about racial groups based on observable differences in phenotype. Some research suggests that children will classify stimuli into racial groups based on physical appearances, and if the appearances change then children believe the racial groups change, leading researchers to suggest that there is impermanence in racial constancy, analogous to young children lacking object permanence when an object is removed from their view (Aboud, 1977; Inhelder & Piaget, 1958). However, Hirschfeld (1994) showed that young children were aware of the permanence of racial status even when appearances change. Similarly, his other research demonstrated that children retained information better about racial groups when information was presented in a narrative format than in response to pictorial information – he suggested that if young children equate race with racial phenotype, then they would process visual stimuli more readily than information presented in the context of a narrative. Interestingly, he found that autistic children, who have impairments in processing social interactions, also processed racial information more readily using narrative information than visual information. Detecting these same patterns with autistic children suggests that even those children who evidence social impairments appear to have the capacity to process racial information, and that these capacities seem somewhat independent of actual social experiences. Hirschfeld (2008) concluded that these findings support his notion that humans have evolved an innate capacity to be sensitive to the human social groupings that are important in society.

To account for children's racial cognitions, Hirschfeld (1994) proposed that children's understanding is partly based on their folk theories of biology. That is, children appear to have some innate abilities to understand the biological properties of humans and animals. Children seem to integrate these early understandings of biological principles, such as the inheritance of physical characteristics, to help them understand the biological principles associated with the inheritance of racial phenotypes. For example, children recognize that offspring will share some of their parents' physical characteristics. Consequently, Hirschfeld suggested that young children use their innate folk theories of biology to understand the permanence of racial status that is a product of heritage and further challenges the popular belief that children begin learning about race and ethnicity from a blank slate or based strictly on Piagetian notions of object permanence.

Although Hirschfeld (2008) has compelling evidence suggesting that children have precocious notions of race that are not limited to their observations of the physical properties associated with race, there is significant evidence that children's verbal reasoning about race is focused on physical manifestations of race and ethnicity (for reviews, see Quintana, 1994, 1998). It seems important to differentiate between levels of understanding ranging from receptive skills and expressive skills. In this regard, I refer to *receptive skills* as those conceptions for which children may have an intuitive sense, but may not be able to explicitly articulate their understanding using oral reasoning; and to *expressive skills* as the level of understanding that allows the children to explicate their understanding using expressive verbal reasoning. Differentiating between receptive and expressive reasoning allows us to reconcile Hirshfeld's theory and research and others' empirical and theoretical research.

Specifically, Hirschfeld's research represents cleverly designed studies that appear to elicit children's receptive understanding of race and ethnicity that is more advanced than is represented by their verbal articulation of their reasoning regarding race that had been the focus of others' research (e.g., Aboud, 1993). My own research (Quintana, 1994, 1998) suggests that children's verbal reasoning regarding racial and ethnic group membership focuses heavily on references to physical manifestations of race. Young children may have a zone of proximal development in which their intuitive and implicit understanding exceeds their explicit and oral reasoning skills concerning race and ethnicity. This zone of proximal development helps explain why young children will appear not to have racial permanence when shown pictorial stimuli in which racial status appears to change, but demonstrate racial permanence when their intuitive sense of race is elicited in which they respond nonverbally, as they do in Hirschfeld's (1994, 1995) investigations.

Cognitive development and racial cognitions

One of the more prominent aspects of social development during middle childhood is that there appears to be an attenuation of the racial bias reflected earlier in childhood. Although early childhood is marked by racial bias that is explicitly expressed by many young children, there is a clear reduction in such expressions during middle childhood. This attenuation in prejudice is the result of an increase in more balanced attitudes toward their own group as children age, but not in a reduction of negative characteristics about the minority group (Doyle & Aboud, 1995). The reduction in prejudice seems to correspond to a reduction in ethnocentrism rather than reduction in negative attitudes toward outgroups. These shifts in racial attitudes appear to be due to growth in children's cognitive development and the application of cognitive skills to interracial contexts. These developmental patterns require theoretical explication.

Aboud (2008) reasoned that (a) children's racial cognitions represent a subset of their social cognitions, and (b) racial attitudes reflect children's racial cognitions. Hence, Aboud proposed that developmental changes in children's social cognitions would be associated with the evolution of their racial attitudes. Aboud mapped these changes in racial attitudes to different stages of cognitive development, using Piagetian theory; children's transition from preoperational to concrete operations appears to mirror the shift from young children's racial bias to a reduction in that racial bias. Aboud suggested that preoperational children focus their social cognitions on perceptions of physical appearances and, based on their verbal reasoning, will then make judgments based on skin color. Conversely, children's acquisition of concrete operations corresponds to the reduction in bias. With concrete operations, children are able to infer similarities associated with internal qualities about persons and, thus, can infer similarities based on internal qualities across racial differences despite superficial differences in appearance. Consequently, when judging someone from another racial group who has a different physical appearance, young children may respond verbally by making attributions based on the differences in appearance, but older children can infer internal characteristics and thereby identify similar characteristics shared by persons despite racial differences.

Aboud (2008) has also noted that children's ability to classify along multiple dimensions appears to correspond to a reduction in children's ethnocentrism. Aboud suggested that early ethnocentrism is fueled by simplistic cognitive abilities in which objects are either good or bad, but not mixed. Consequently, according to children's early cognitive abilities, if attributes associated with the self are good, then other characteristics would be considered not good. By extension, if a particular racial group is considered good, then different racial groups would be not good. This dichotomous logic early in childhood gives way during middle childhood to the ability to have a blended, mixed evaluation of a characteristic and to the realization that more than one kind of characteristic can be regarded as positive. This shift in cognitive abilities corresponds to a decrease in ethnocentric attitudes in young children. Other social cognitive advances, including role and perspective taking, are associated with developmental shifts in children's racial and ethnic cognitions. More generally, Aboud described this as a shift from perceptual to cognitive in that racial attitudes in middle childhood were based more on cognitive processes (e.g., considering multiple dimensions) and less on perceptual processes, such as focusing on skin color differences to make attributions about persons.

Quintana (1994, 1998) accounted for the general reduction in racial bias during middle childhood based on important social cognitive advances. Young children tend to reason about persons' characteristics and about implications of racial group membership based on physical features; consequently, differences in physical characteristics might be conflated with differences in behavior or moral character. On the other hand, older children reason about personalities based on inferring internal psychological characteristics (e.g., preferences), and, consequently, they define racial group membership based on ancestry or heritage. Hence, older children would be less likely to presume differences in racial groups based on differences in physical appearance, relative to younger children. Moreover, because older children disassociate personological from physical characteristics, they are more prone to view similarities in internal psychological characteristics across racial groups than younger children. These two developmental shifts were evident in children's verbal reasoning about race during interviews (Quintana, 1998).

Formation of Racial Bias

There has been considerable theoretical and empirical research into the development of children's racial attitudes, particularly when those attitudes reflect bias. Research has focused on identifying predictors of different forms of racial bias and different contextual features that correspond to high or low levels of racial bias. One of the strongest predictors of the focus for racial bias is associated with identification with an ethnic and racial group. Upon identifying with an ethnic or racial group, children and adults tend to develop positive attitudes toward ingroup members and negative attitudes toward outgroup members (Barrett & Davis, 2008; Nesdale, 2008). The formation of this ethnocentrism is accounted for by social identity theory (SIT; Tajfel & Turner, 1986), which is elaborated below. Additionally, investigations of adults have detected covert or implicit forms of racial bias separate from explicit forms of bias. Researchers are beginning to investigate different forms of the development of covert, implicit forms of bias in children (Dunham et al., 2006). Similarly, abstract notions of race elicit different responses than do situations in which race and racial differences are embedded into social situations. Although much antibias programming targets the more abstract notions of race, the reactions to racial differences that are embedded in social situations are likely to be more generalizable to real-world situations. There are other important contextual factors in which racial bias is manifest, including the relative composition of racial minority and racial majority groups. These influence the perceptions of race and of racially different peers. Theory and research associated with these influences on the formation of racial bias are described below.

Social identity theories

Social identity and self-categorization theories (SIT and SCT, respectively) articulate psychological consequences of identifying with a social group or categorizing oneself as a member of a group (Barrett & Davis, 2008). SIT assumes that persons are motivated to maintain self-esteem and do so through their identifications with groups. This assumption seems consistent with young children's ethnocentrism and their apparent bias against outgroups – children would enhance their esteem by viewing positively the social groups to which they belong. Relatedly, SCT (Turner, 1985) suggests that persons' views toward social groups change once they categorize themselves as a member of that group. Another variant of the SIT is the subjective group dynamics model (SGDM; Abrams & Rutland, 2008), which suggests that there are important social and psychological dynamics that unfold once a person identifies with a social group. Abrams and Rutland demonstrated that the characteristics of the intergroup context influence these dynamics with, for example, strong bias being elicited in contexts in which an outgroup is perceived to be in competition with or an enemy of the person's ingroup. Another important group dynamic is that members of a group often resent other group members who demonstrate disloyalties toward the group. For example, traitors to a group are often held in lower regard than are outgroup members (Abrams, Rutland, Ferrell, & Pelletier, 2008); although ingroup members tend to be viewed more favorably than outgroup members, ingroup members who are traitors are viewed more negatively than outgroup members.

Most of the social identity applications to children's intergroup attitudes have demonstrated that the context of the intergroup relations has important implications for the nature of attitudes (e.g., Barrett & Davis, 2008). For example, when the social group membership has personal significance and the outgroup is identified as being in competition with the child's social group, the group bias appears to be particularly strong. In certain intergroup contexts, children will not evidence the developmental attenuation in bias evident in middle childhood (for review, see Barrett, 2007). This suggests that Aboud's theory that social cognitive advances precipitate shifts in racial bias may only hold in certain contexts (e.g., when the racial outgroup is not seen as being in competition).

On the other hand, these social identity theorists and researchers have had limited success in accounting for developmental differences in the social and psychological sequelae of identification with or categorization as a member of a social group. Indeed, SIT and SCT appear not to assume developmental prerequisites for these social and psychological sequelae (Abrams & Rutland, 2008). However, Abrams and Rutland's subjective group dynamics theory acknowledges that a child perceiving him or herself as a member of a group and having a concept of a social group would seem to be an important prerequisite of social cognitive skill in order to manifest loyalty toward the group. Moreover, Abrams and Rutland demonstrated that some subjective group dynamics are stronger in older children who have more advanced social cognitive skills, relative to younger children. For example, older children demonstrated a better mastery of the dynamics of group loyalty by viewing members who violate group norms more negatively than (a) younger children viewed the atypical group members and (b) more negatively than they viewed some outgroup members (Abrams & Rutland, 2008).

Implicit versus explicit racial attitudes

As outlined above, there appears to be a developmental attenuation in racial bias in the shift from early to middle childhood. Other researchers and theoreticians demonstrate that children's intergroup attitudes are more complex. (Indeed, an intriguing factor in understanding developmental trends is that there appear to be different levels in children's racial attitudes.) Namely, there are different developmental trajectories between children's explicit and implicit manifestations of racial bias (Dunham et al., 2006). *Explicit* forms of racial bias are those that are expressed verbally and can be reported directly through self-report methods. *Implicit* racial bias reflects those attitudes that are not available through reflection or introspection (Greenwald & Banaji, 1995) but can still influence decisions and reactions in response to interracial situations.

Research on implicit racial attitudes demonstrates that there is not a concomitant attenuation in implicit racial bias relative to the attenuation of explicit racial bias. Rather, children are uniform in their manifestation of negative implicit attitudes toward outgroups, particularly racial outgroups (Dunham et al., 2006). Baron and Banaji (2006) found that implicit racial bias was evident in U.S. White children by 6 years of age and was stable into adulthood.

Dunham et al. (2006) also found that, like White children in the United States, young Japanese children held negative attitudes toward outgroups. It is interesting to note that Japanese children held negative attitudes toward outgroups toward which they had little, if any, personal contact, including children of Caucasian and African origin. As regards explicit attitudes, Japanese children evidenced reductions over age for both Caucasian and African origin children. However, although they detected an age-related decline in implicit forms of racial bias against Caucasians, they did not find a similar decline in implicit bias against African origin children. Hence, despite knowing that they should not be biased toward African origin groups (as evidenced by reduction in explicit forms of bias), Japanese children and adults still manifested implicit racial bias against a racial group with whom they have very few mundane interactions.

The cross-cultural consistency of implicit bias against racial outgroups supports an evolutionary foundation for the bias, but the finding that implicit bias is maintained toward some, but not all, outgroups also suggests that social and cultural experiences help to maintain or undermine some implicit racial bias. Children's exposure to the notion that some outgroups can be held in relatively high esteem may be responsible for why Japanese children's implicit bias against Caucasians attenuates before they reach adulthood.

Abstract versus socially embedded attributions

Much of the traditional research on children's racism has focused on abstract attributions of race in which racial differences are obvious. Research on adult cognition has differentiated *old-fashioned* from *modern* forms of racism (Henry & Sears, 2002). Old-fashioned racism is a categorical rejection of a racial group that is usually based on essentialistic views of race. That is, essentialism assumes that there are essential characteristics associated with, in this case, racial status, in which all racial group members share this essential nature and other racial groups share other essential natures. Civil rights movements in the United States, South Africa, and elsewhere have directly challenged old-fashioned racism and essentialistic attributions of race. These movements tend to replace these old-fashioned forms of bias with a "color-blind" orientation in which differences among racial groups are seen as superficial and there is the presumption of similarity despite differences in racial groups.

Modern manifestations of bias are more subtle and are based not on categorical rejection but on interpretations of behavior (Henry & Sears, 2002). Moreover, bias tends to be manifest in more subtle contexts in which the judgment is viewed as being focused on behavior rather than overtly based on racial group membership. Most children do not support racial exclusion and have more balanced social evaluations across race when race is a salient aspect of social comparisons, consistent with the tendency for adults to reject old-fashioned versions of racism. For example, when asked, most White American children will rate the inherent goodness of African Americans positively, but when asked to make judgments about socially embedded behaviors, on average White children will rate the behavior of African Americans more negatively than the same behavior of White Americans (Brown, 2008). White Americans reflect more racial bias when judging ambiguous social actions in which motivation or intent must be inferred, relative to actions in which intentions are manifest (McGlothlin et al., 2005; McGlothlin & Killen, 2006).

Social judgment, moral reasoning, and racial attitudes

Levy and colleagues (Levy, Karafantis, & Ramirez, 2008) have shown that a variety of lay theories about human nature influence children's racial attitudes. For example, those children in the United States who subscribe to the Protestant work ethic (PWE), the belief that those who work hard get ahead in U.S. society, tend to have more egalitarian attitudes toward racial groups. The children take from the PWE that anyone who tries and works hard can succeed, and they use this as a basis for endorsing egalitarianism. Interestingly, older adolescents and young adults who subscribe to PWE tend to have low levels of egalitarianism in that they use it as a justifier for why there is an unequal distribution of income – in the sense that those who worked hard have succeeded but those who have not succeeded did not work hard.

Levy and colleagues (2008) found this effect for those children who endorse those attitudes in an observational study, as well as in experimental studies in which one group was randomly primed with the PWE by reading a passage endorsing the PWE. They also found that the extent to which children endorsed belief in an incremental view toward human nature, which is that humans can change, versus entity theory, or the sense that peoples' basic character is fixed and unchanging, influenced their attitudes toward other social groups. When children are exposed to positive information about a group, those who held a stronger entity theory had more positive views, but when exposed to negative information about a group, they had more negative views toward the social group, relative to those who subscribed to a more incremental view (Levy et al., 2008).

Children's moral reasoning also influences children's view toward the social exclusion of members of a social, ethnic, or racial group. Killen and colleagues (Killen, Lee-Kim, McGlothlin, & Stangor, 2002) described how children use moral reasoning to justify the social exclusion of peers based solely on race, but the view of exclusion varied across the nature of the exclusion. In this U.S.-based study, nearly every child indicated that exclusion from school was inappropriate. Interestingly, some children believed that racial exclusion could be justified based on less formal peer groups, such as peer clubs or friendship, and the number of children justifying such exclusion increased with age (Killen et al., 2002). When asked to justify racial exclusion in social contexts, most children cited a nonracial rationale (e.g., lack of similarities or lower levels of ability for the club).

Subsequent research has indicated that Whites in racially homogeneous contexts were more likely to cite justification based on racial status and racial stereotypes than White children in racially heterogeneous contexts (Killen, Richardson, Kelly, Crystal, & Ruck, 2007). Minority children were more likely to view racial exclusion as wrong, even when nonracial justifications (e.g., personal choice) for the exclusion were provided (Killen et al., 2007).

Spanish researchers (Enesco et al., 2008) attempted to replicate Killen and colleagues' (2002) findings associated with reasoning about exclusion, borrowing the same vignettes and stimulus questions. In contrast to the U.S. research, Enesco et al. (2008) found no differences in reasoning in exclusion across school, peer group, or friendship when the stigmatized groups were outgroups within Spanish society (i.e., Gypsies and children from southern Africa); the Spanish children reasoned that all types of exclusion could not be justified.

Racial density and attitudes

Children's racial attitudes are influenced by the relative density of racial minority children. Guerra and Williams (2006) found that the development of Spanish children raised in a monoracial country evidenced delays in children's abilities to categorize according to race and apply racial labels, relative to children raised in multiethnic countries, such as the United States, the United Kingdom, or Canada, but no delays in their ability to identify their racial grouping or their social preferences based on pictorial stimuli.

Desegregation efforts in the United States have stimulated considerations about what constitutes a critical mass for a racial minority, where the critical mass represents the proportion of a racial minority sufficient for them to feel comfortable or may be based on sufficient numbers for the racial minority to have influence. In examining the density of African Americans relative to White children in classrooms, Jackson, Barth, Powell, and Lochman (2006) found that the sociometric ratings of peer status for African American children were lower than those for White children, except in school classrooms in which 66% or more of the students were African American. Peer ratings of leadership qualities were also lower for African American than White children in all classrooms except in those with 66% or more African American children, in which the leadership ratings of African Americans only matched, but did not exceed, the ratings of White children. In short, the trend is that the greater the representation of a minority group, the more positive their sociometric status, based on peer ratings. It is worth noting that ratings of White children did not decline as their proportion of the class composition decreased.

Interestingly, Jackson et al. (2006) found that the race of the teacher influenced ratings of leadership for Black children, but had little effect on peer perceptions of White children. White children were viewed positively as leaders when the teacher was White or African American, but the leadership ratings for African American children were considerably lower when their teacher was White than Black. Assuming a connection between the representation of African Americans and the culture of the classroom, with the race of the teacher also contributing to the culture, it appears that the more the culture of the classroom reflected African Americans, the closer the evaluation of African Americans was with that of White Americans.

Analogous research with Latino and White American children has produced similar findings. Specifically, Latino children were rated more favorably the more the classroom instruction was conducted in Spanish: White children rated Latino peers highest in bilingual classrooms, which were evenly mixed between Latinos and White Americans, and lowest in classrooms where the language of instruction was English and the class composition was predominately White American (Tropp & Prenovost, 2008). Interestingly, Latinos' ratings of their White peers were relatively unchanged across the language of instruction and ethnic mix of the classrooms.

In summary, across the studies by Jackson et al. (2006) and Tropp and Prenovost (2008), contextual factors had significant influence on the ratings of minority schoolchildren, but had minimal effects on White children's peer status.

Ethnic socialization

Ethnic socialization also influences the formation of children's racial attitudes. As mentioned above, parental socialization appears to have influence early in childhood; those parents in the United States who raise issues of race and racial differences in an open manner during early childhood tend to have children who express more openness, compared to those parents who avoided mentioning race (Katz, 2003). Hughes and colleagues' (2008) research in the United States has identified four main parental socialization strategies: egalitarianism, cultural socialization, preparation for bias, and promoting mistrust. Across several racial groups, the most common and frequently utilized parental socialization strategy was exposing children to egalitarian views toward racial groups. White parents attempt to promote children's sense of egalitarianism as a way of preventing racist attitudes in their children (Hughes et al., 2008). The least utilized strategy by parents was the promotion of mistrust, suggesting that explicit encouragement of racial bias occurs the most infrequently among parents.

Although many have suggested that parents socialize their children to adopt parents' racial attitudes, the findings have been mixed on the connection between parental and child racial attitudes (Fishbein, 2000). For example, although finding that children's racial attitudes were not associated with their parents' racial attitudes, Aboud and Doyle (1996) found that children's racial attitudes were associated with what attitude children believed their parents held. Somewhat similarly, Sinclair, Dunn, and Lowery (2005) found significant association between children's and parent's racial attitudes when children identified with their parents, but weak association for children who did not identify closely with parents. Given how influential parents can be in children's development, it is surprising that the connection between parents' and children's racial attitudes is not stronger.

Children's Detection of and Preparation for Bias

Given the prevalence of children's exposure to ethnic and racial bias, being prepared for this stigmatization is important in the development of ethnic and racial minority children. Following the decrease of old-fashioned racism in many societies and the probable increase in subtle expressions of racial bias, it becomes more challenging for persons to understand when they have been the target of racial and ethnic bias. In some instances, children who have been the victims of racism need to infer a racial attitude in the perpetrator of which the perpetrator is unaware, and, if confronted, the perpetrator is likely to deny the racist foundation of the action and also to justify the action in nonracial ways. Moreover, individual racism is not the only form that children and adolescents need to understand, given their exposure to institutional forms of discrimination. Importantly, children and youth need to also understand how indirect exposure to racism influences their lives, given that their lives have likely been affected by their parents being targets of racism and also by their vicarious exposure to racism when their peers or family members are the targets (Quintana & McKown, 2008).

Social perspective of ethnicity and race

Quintana (1998) described how children progress from an objective, literal perspective on race and ethnicity to a social perspective. This progression during mid- to late childhood corresponds to the children's understanding that there are social consequences associated with race and ethnicity. In early childhood, children understand race and ethnicity primarily based on heritage and implications of heritage on cultural patterns, such as language and customs. A social perspective of race and ethnicity facilitates children's understanding of the social components, such as the possibility of discrimination and that social interactions may be influenced by ethnic and racial group membership. They recognize that forming same-race friendships may be easier than cross-race friendships due to intrarace similarities and interracial differences in social behavior and manner. This social perspective allows children to understand how peers from other racial groups may view them – to see themselves through the eyes of others.

The perspective-taking abilities described by Quintana (1998) are part of the skills necessary for children to detect or perceive discrimination according to Brown and Bigler's (2005) model. Brown and Bigler formulated a developmental model describing the prerequisite skills and conditions for children to detect being the target of discrimination. Their model specifies three components: cognitive development, situational factors, and individual differences associated with perceiving discrimination. The cognitive abilities identified by Brown and Bigler divide the social perspective described by Quintana into subcomponents. Specifically, cognitive abilities include knowledge about attributes and perceptions of race and ethnicity, the ability to take others' perspectives, and the ability to make social comparisons.

Brown and Bigler (2005) reason that before children attribute a social action to discrimination, they must have some knowledge about the characteristics commonly ascribed to race and ethnicity; they are then able to recognize when someone is making a distorted characterization associated with race and ethnicity. Additionally, the ability to detect discrimination requires that the perpetrator be perceived as holding discriminatory beliefs or stereotypes and that these beliefs motivated the social action. Moreover, some social comparisons are required in order to understand if the person was treated differently from how members of other ethnic or racial groups are treated. Further, children perceiving racism or ethnic prejudice need to have the moral-reasoning skills necessary to understand issues of fairness and inequities in order to determine that some behavior was unfair or unequal treatment (Brown & Bigler, 2005).

With these requisite cognitive skills, children have the ability to perceive discrimination, but particular situational factors increase the likelihood that children will perceive discrimination (Brown & Bigler, 2005). Specifically, some knowledge of the perpetrator may be important to inferring his or her intentions and deciding if the intentions were based on discriminatory beliefs. Similarly, if the action is relevant to some stereotype associated with racial or ethnic bias, then it is more likely that discrimination will be inferred. Moreover, some comparison of how the target is treated with how others are usually treated may be necessary if a child is to attribute the action as discriminatory. Rude behavior, for example, will not be perceived as discriminatory if the person is rude to everyone. Others' support may also help a child perceive treatment as discriminatory, particularly if the others define the behavior as biased.

The third set of factors in Brown and Bigler's (2005) model is individual differences. There may be some children who are particularly sensitive to perceiving discrimination and others who avoid making such attributions unless the evidence is overwhelming. Brown and Bigler noted that children who belong to stigmatized ethnic or racial groups are more likely to react to hostile treatment as discriminatory than those who do not belong to a stigmatized group. Similarly, those children who are aware of discrimination are more likely to perceive it, as are those who believe their group should not be treated in an inferior manner. Finally, those whose racial or ethnic identity is a central and salient aspect of their identity may be more likely to attribute negative treatment to their race or ethnicity.

Racial and ethnic identity

Quintana (1998) described the emergence in early adolescence of the development of ethnic or racial group consciousness. This consciousness involves the integration of racial and ethnic group membership into an adolescent's identity. Until adolescence, interethnic or interracial interactions tend to be perceived as involving individuals. The group consciousness of adolescence allows youth to understand that social interactions are not only interactions between individuals but also interactions between ethnic or racial groups in which prior sociocultural history and events have a role. Developing an ethnic or racial identity that is central to an adolescent's sense of self helps that adolescent anticipate discrimination and also helps prepare the adolescent for coping with discrimination in ways that can help salvage or even enhance self-esteem, despite degrading treatment.

There is evidence that supports the notion that racial-ethnic identity exploration is normative during adolescence for the targets of racial or ethnic stigmatization (Quintana, 2008). Several longitudinal studies have demonstrated that African American, Latinos, and American Indians show increases or acceleration in racial-ethnic identity exploration during early adolescence (Pahl & Way, 2006; Whitesell, Mitchell, Kaufman, & Spicer, 2006) and a deceleration during mid- to late adolescence (French, Seidman, Allen, & Aber, 2000, 2006).

Research has examined relationships between ethnic identity and experience of discrimination prospectively. Longitudinal studies have demonstrated empirical links between perceptions of discrimination and later increases in racial and ethnic identity (Pahl & Way, 2006; Sellers & Shelton, 2003). These studies also indicate that some forms of racial identity increase persons' sensitivity to later bias, suggesting a reciprocal relationship between racial identity and perceptions of discrimination. Sellers and Shelton demonstrated that those for whom racial status was more central to their identity perceived more bias 6 to 9 months later. Pahl and Way also found that discrimination has a larger influence on later racial identity development than the influence of racial identity on later perceptions of racial discrimination.

Strong identifications with an adolescent's racial group can put the adolescent at some psychological risk, as anticipated by SIT; in particular, when youths' racial identity is central to their sense of self, they are more strongly affected by discrimination, compared to those for whom their racial identity was less central. Greene, Way, and Pahl (2006) found that strong connections to a racial group were associated negatively with well-being when the youths were in contexts involving moderate to high levels of discrimination. Conversely, those Latino, Asian, and African American youth who had low levels of connection to their ethnic or racial group had higher self-esteem than those who expressed high levels of pride in their ethnic or racial origin. On the other hand, the pattern was reversed in contexts involving low levels of discrimination: Those who felt strongly about their racial group membership were associated with higher self-esteem in conditions in which there were low levels of discrimination.

Summary

The processes by which children develop notions of race and racial group membership are intriguing. Children demonstrate precociousness early in life that is difficult to explain based solely on social experiences or parental socialization. The innate tendency to group their social world into major social categories allows children to be sensitive to interracial dynamics such as bias and prejudice. Much of the research has focused on how children acquire conceptions of racism associated with old-fashioned forms of racism, which were abstract notions regarding racial status. More contemporary research has focused on implicit forms as well as socially embedded expressions of attitudes. There are considerable skills involved in being able to detect discrimination, including cognitive abilities as well as situational and personological factors. Consciousness of race and ethnicity can be adaptive in preparing for discrimination but can also put the young person at some disadvantage in some contexts. Given the acceleration of globalization, the future of children's development will involve more personal as well as indirect interracial interactions for children and adolescents. Research will need to keep pace on how youth navigate social life in an increasing technological manner, including virtual realities and social-networking websites.

References

Aboud, F. (1977). Interest in ethnic information: A cross-cultural developmental study. *Canadian Journal of Behavioural Science/Revue canadienne des sciences du comportement*, 9(2), 134–146.

Aboud, F. (1988). *Children and prejudice*. Oxford: Blackwell.

Aboud, F. (1993). The developmental psychology of racial prejudice. *Transcultural Psychiatric Review*, 30, 229–242.

Aboud, F. (2008). A social-cognitive developmental theory of prejudice. In *Handbook of race, racism, and the developing child* (pp. 55–71). Hoboken, NJ: Wiley.

Aboud, F., & Doyle, A. (1996). Parental and peer influences on children's racial attitudes. *International Journal of Intercultural Relations*, 20, 371–383.

Abrams, D., & Rutland, A. (2008). The development of subjective group dynamics. In S. R. Levy & M. Killen (Eds.), *Intergroup attitudes and relations in childhood through adulthood* (pp. 47–65). New York: Oxford University Press.

Abrams, D., Rutland, A., Ferrell, J., & Pelletier, J. (2008). Children's judgments of disloyal and immoral peer behavior: Subjective group dynamics in minimal intergroup contexts. *Child Development*, 79, 444–461.

Banks, W. C. (1976). White preference in Blacks: A paradigm in search of a phenomenon. *Psychological Bulletin*, 83, 1179–1186.

Baron, A., & Banaji, M. (2006). The development of implicit attitudes: Evidence of race evaluations from ages 6 and 10 and adulthood. *Psychological Science*, 17, 53–58.

Barrett, M. (2007). *Children's knowledge, beliefs and feelings about nations and national groups*. New York: Psychology Press.

Barrett, M., & Davis, S. (2008). Applying social identity and self-categorization theories to children's racial, ethnic, national, and state identifications and attitudes. In S. M. Quintana & C. McKown (Eds.), *Handbook of race, racism, and the developing child* (pp. 72–110). Hoboken, NJ: John Wiley.

Brown, C. (2008). Children's perceptions of racial and ethnic discrimination: Differences across children and contexts. In S. M. Quintana & C. McKown (Eds.), *Handbook of race, racism, and the developing child* (pp. 133–153). Hoboken, NJ: John Wiley.

Brown, C. S., & Bigler, R. S. (2005). Children's perception of discrimination: A developmental model. *Child Development*, 76, 533–553.

Clark, K. B., & Clark, M. K. (1939). The development of consciousness of self and the emergence of racial identification in Negro preschool children. *Journal of Social Psychology*, 10, 591–599.

Clark, K. B., & Clark, M. K. (1940). Skin color as a factor in racial identification of Negro pre-school children. *Journal of Social Psychology, 11,* 159–169.

Cunningham, W., Johnson, M., Raye, C., Gatenby, J., Gore, J., & Banaji, M. (2004). Separable neural components in the processing of Black and White faces. *Psychological Science, 15,* 806–813.

Doyle, A., & Aboud, F. (1995). A longitudinal study of White children's racial prejudice as a social-cognitive development. *Merrill-Palmer Quarterly, 41,* 209–228.

Dunham, Y., Baron, A., & Banaji, M. (2006). From American city to Japanese village: A cross-cultural investigation of implicit race attitudes. *Child Development, 77,* 1268–1281

Enesco, I., Guerrero, I., Callejas, C., & Solbes, I. (2008). Intergroup attitudes and reasoning about social exclusion in majority and minority children in Spain. In S. R. Levy & M. Killen (Eds.), *Intergroup attitudes and relations in childhood through adulthood* (pp. 105–125). New York: Oxford University Press.

French, S., Seidman, E., Allen, L., & Aber, J. (2000). Racial/ethnic identity, congruence with the social context, and the transition to high school. *Journal of Adolescent Research, 15,* 587–602.

French, S., Seidman, E., Allen, L., & Aber, J. (2006). The development of ethnic identity during adolescence. *Developmental Psychology, 42,* 1–10.

Greene, M., Way, N., & Pahl, K. (2006). Trajectories of perceived adult and peer discrimination among Black, Latino, and Asian American adolescents: Patterns and psychological correlates. *Developmental Psychology, 42,* 218–238.

Gregor, A., & McPherson, D. (1966). Racial preference and ego identity among White and Bantu children in the Republic of South Africa. *Genetic Psychology Monographs, 73*(2), 217–253.

Guerra, N., & Williams, K. (2006). Ethnicity, youth violence, and the ecology of development. In *Preventing youth violence in a multicultural society* (pp. 17–45). Washington, DC: American Psychological Association.

Henry, P., & Sears, D. (2002). The Symbolic Racism 2000 Scale. *Political Psychology, 23,* 253–283.

Hirschfeld, L. A. (1994). The child's representation of human groups. *Psychology of Learning and Motivation, 31,* 133–185.

Hirschfeld, L. A. (2008). Children's developing conceptions of race. In S. M. Quintana & C. McKown (Eds.), *Handbook of race, racism, and the developing child* (pp. 37–54). Hoboken, NJ: John Wiley.

Hughes, D., Rivas, D., Foust, M., Hagelskamp, C., Gersick, S., & Way, N. (2008). How to catch a moonbeam: A mixed-methods approach to understanding ethnic socialization processes in ethnically diverse families. In S. M. Quintana & C. McKown (Eds.), *Handbook of race, racism, and the developing child* (pp. 226–277). Hoboken, NJ: John Wiley.

Inhelder, B., & Piaget, J. (1958). *The growth of logical thinking from childhood to adolescence.* New York: Basic Books.

Jackson, M., Barth, J., Powell, N., & Lochman, J. (2006). Classroom contextual effects of race on children's peer nominations. *Child Development, 77,* 1325–1337.

Katz, P. (2003). Racists or tolerant multiculturalists? How do they begin? *American Psychologist, 58*(11), 897–909.

Kelly, D., Quinn, P., Slater, A., Lee, K., Gibson, A., Smith, M., et al. (2005). Three-month-olds, but not newborns, prefer own-race faces. *Developmental Science, 8,* F31–F36.

Killen, M., Henning, A., Kelly, M., Crystal, D., & Ruck, M. (2007). Evaluations of interracial peer encounters by majority and minority US children and adolescents. *International Journal of Behavioral Development, 31,* 491–500.

Killen, M., Lee-Kim, J., McGlothlin, H., & Stangor, C. (2002). How children and adolescents evaluate gender and racial exclusion. *Monographs of the Society for Research in Child Development, 67*(4), i–vii, 1–119.

Levy, S., Karafantis, D., & Ramirez, L. (2008). A social-development perspective on lay theories and intergroup relations. In S. R. Levy & M. Killen (Eds.), *Intergroup attitudes and relations in childhood through adulthood* (pp. 146–156). New York: Oxford University Press.

McGlothlin, H., & Killen, M. (2006). Intergroup attitudes of European American children attending ethnically homogeneous schools. *Child Development, 77*(5), 1375–1386.

McGlothlin, H., Killen, M., & Edmonds, C. (2005). European-American children's intergroup attitudes about peer relationships. *British Journal of Developmental Psychology, 23*(2), 227–249.

Nesdale, D. (2008). Social identity development and children's ethnic attitudes in Australia. In S. M. Quintana & C. McKown (Eds.), *Handbook of race, racism, and the developing child* (pp. 313–338). Hoboken, NJ: John Wiley.

Pahl, K., & Way, N. (2006). Longitudinal trajectories of ethnic identity among urban Black and Latino adolescents. *Child Development, 77*, 1403–1415.

Quintana, S. M. (1994). A model of ethnic perspective taking ability applied to Mexican-American children and youth. *International Journal of Intercultural Relations, 18*, 419–448.

Quintana, S. M. (1998). Development of children's understanding of ethnicity and race. *Applied & Preventive Psychology: Current Scientific Perspectives, 7*, 27–45.

Quintana, S. (2008). Racial perspective taking ability: Developmental, theoretical, and empirical trends. In S. M. Quintana & C. McKown (Eds.), *Handbook of race, racism, and the developing child* (pp. 16–36). Hoboken, NJ: John Wiley.

Quintana, S., & McKown, C. (2008). Introduction: Race, racism, and the developing child. In S. M. Quintana & C. McKown (Eds.), *Handbook of race, racism, and the developing child* (pp. 1–15). Hoboken, NJ: John Wiley.

Sellers, R., & Shelton, J. (2003). The role of racial identity in perceived racial discrimination. *Journal of Personality and Social Psychology, 84*, 1079–1092.

Sinclair, S., Dunn, E., & Lowery, B. (2005). The relationship between parental racial attitudes and children's implicit prejudice. *Journal of Experimental Social Psychology, 41*, 283–289.

Tajfel, H., & Turner, J. (1986). The social identity theory of intergroup behavior. In S. Worchel & W. Austin (Eds.), *Psychology of intergroup relations* (pp. 7–24). Chicago: Nelson-Hall.

Tropp, L. R., & Prenovost, M. (2008). Role of intergroup contact in predicting children's interethnic attitudes: Evidence from meta-analytic and field studies. In S. R. Levy & M. Killen (Eds.), *Intergroup attitudes and relations in childhood through adulthood* (pp. 236–248). New York: Oxford University Press.

Whitesell, N., Mitchell, C., Kaufman, C., & Spicer, P. (2006). Developmental trajectories of personal and collective self-concept among American Indian adolescents. *Child Development, 77*, 1487–1503.

Williams, J., Best, D., & Boswell, D. (1975). The measurement of children's racial attitudes in the early school years. *Child Development, 46*(2), 494–500.

PART V

Family Context

Research suggests that a host of variables contribute to the social development of young children. As described in other parts of this volume, these include individual biologically based genetic and temperament factors as well as more distal extrafamilial influences, including the peer group, schools, media, and culture. Parenting and family interactions are factors proximal to children that combine with individual and extrafamilial influences in ways that are linked to childhood social competencies. Although peers and other extrafamilial influences become increasingly important across early and middle childhood, parents and siblings continue to constitute a major portion of a child's social milieu in many parts of the world. This part focuses specifically on their contributions to children's social development.

In Chapter 17, Laurie Brumariu and Kathryn Kerns begin this part of the handbook by considering recent theory and research on parent–child attachment in early and middle childhood. Key concepts of attachment theory are described. The authors then review how attachment is measured during early and middle childhood, as well as studies that shed light on the stability of attachment over time. How child temperament, caregiving history, parental sensitivity and insensitivity, and marital relationships play into the development of attachment security is also explained, with an eye toward explicating how the quality of attachment relationships is associated with children's social development. The discussion of social development centers on peer relationships, including peer acceptance and friendship. The authors conclude this chapter by considering the limitations of current research in this area, reflecting on unanswered questions, and pointing to directions for future studies.

In Chapter 18, Alan Russell follows the overview of attachment with a discussion of many other aspects of the parent–child relationship. This chapter is designed to help readers understand the multilayered, multidimensional, and transactional nature of

The Wiley-Blackwell Handbook of Childhood Social Development, Second Edition, edited by Peter K. Smith and Craig H. Hart
© 2011 by Blackwell Publishing Ltd.

parent–child relationships and how they are modular and specific in their influence on children's social development. He begins by discussing the implications of understanding the mutual influences that parents and children have on each other. A number of relationship processes that facilitate or diminish adaptive parent–child interactions are also considered. Hearkening back to Part IV of this volume, the wider environmental context that impinges on parent–child interactions is discussed from a systems perspective, along with various models that explicate the elements and specific processes of parent–child relationships. These include themes such as bidirectionality, child effects, styles versus processes, context-specific parenting, metaparenting, and gender and developmental differences in parent–child relationships. Attention is then turned to explicating biological, evolutionary, and behavioral genetic approaches in the analysis of parent–child relationships. Methodological issues and demographic and society-wide changes that impinge on the study of parent–child relationships are also overviewed. With all this as a backdrop, the chapter concludes with an overview of research findings on how parent–child relationships influence children's social development.

The final chapter in this part, Chapter 19, focuses on another aspect of family influence on children's social development. Nina Howe, Hildy Ross, and Holly Recchia walk readers through recent research findings that illuminate how this important aspect of family dynamics helps young children develop social understanding. First, the question of why sibling relationships are an important context for development is considered. Major characteristics of sibling relationships are described, and how these relationships help children create knowledge about their social world is explained. Second, specific ways that siblings teach each other through complementary interactions are explicated. How age differences play into the reciprocal teaching process is described. Third, the authors review the literature on sibling play with an eye toward explaining how pretend play is an important context for enhancing sibling relationships and promoting social understanding. Fourth, sibling conflict is a normal part of sibling interaction, occurring approximately eight times per hour during the early years. Different features of sibling conflict and their developmental significance for good and for ill are described. How parents can enhance or diminish potential for learning how to negotiate the social world in how they respond to children's disputes is also considered. The authors conclude with a discussion of linkages between children's sibling and peer relationships. How sibling relationships provide a training ground for learning how to get along with others outside of the home is an important theme of this chapter.

CHAPTER SEVENTEEN

Parent–Child Attachment in Early and Middle Childhood

Laura E. Brumariu and Kathryn A. Kerns

Attachment theory (Ainsworth, Blehar, Waters, & Wall, 1978; Bowlby, 1973) has provided one of the best developed theoretical frameworks for understanding parent–child relationships and children's social emotional development. This chapter focuses on parent–child attachment in early and middle childhood. We first discuss key concepts of attachment theory, including the definition, nature, and assessment of attachment in early childhood (3 to 7 years) and middle childhood (7 to 12 years). Next, we describe factors promoting individual differences in attachment. We also provide a theoretical perspective for the relations between parent–child attachment and children's social development, and summarize the main findings in this area. Finally, we identify unanswered questions and future directions.

Key Issues

Definition and patterns of attachment

Attachment (in children) is defined as an emotional long-lasting bond that a child forms with an attachment figure who is not interchangeable with another person (Ainsworth, 1989). The child wishes to maintain proximity to or contact with the attachment figure, although the type and extent of contact vary as a function of factors such as the child's

The Wiley-Blackwell Handbook of Childhood Social Development, Second Edition, edited by Peter K. Smith and Craig H. Hart
© 2011 by Blackwell Publishing Ltd.

age and the settings. An attachment relationship is also characterized by "distress upon inexplicable separation, pleasure or joy upon reunion, and grief at loss" (Ainsworth, 1989). The unique feature of attachment, compared to other affectional bonds, is that the child seeks comfort or security from the attachment figure.

All children are expected to form attachments as long as a parent figure is available, even if that figure provides care that is less than optimal (Bowlby, 1969). Attachment relationships do vary, however, in quality. Bowlby (1969, 1973) asserted that *securely attached* children use their attachment figures as a secure base for exploration and as a "safe haven" to return to in times of distress (type B). They also perceive their caregivers as responsive, sensitive to their needs, and available. Three forms of insecure attachment have been identified (Ainsworth et al., 1978; Main & Solomon, 1986). *Avoidantly attached* children (type A) do not seek out the caregiver when distressed, a behavioral strategy that allows them to maintain a connection to a caregiver who has been rejecting of the child, especially when the child is distressed (Cassidy, 1994). Children who form *ambivalent attachments* (type C) develop a heightening strategy in which they manifest high levels of attachment behavior to a caregiver whom they view as inconsistently responsive (Cassidy, 1994). Children with *disorganized attachments* (type D) have typically experienced a caregiver who has shown frightened or frightening behavior or disrupted affective communication (e.g., intrusive or contradictory behaviors; Lyons-Ruth & Jacobvitz, 2008). In infancy, these children often fail to show a consistent organization of attachment behavior (e.g., showing a mix of ambivalent and avoidant behaviors). After age 3, they may show disorganized behavior or may take control of the relationship by showing role reversal with the attachment figure, with the child directing caregiving or punitive behaviors to the caregiver (Lyons-Ruth & Jacobvitz, 2008).

Normative changes in attachment in early and middle childhood

The current data allow for a general outline of the normative course of attachment between 3 and 12 years (Kerns, 2008; Marvin & Britner, 2008). Some changes are reflected in children's attachment behaviors. In early childhood (the third and fourth years of life), children readily show attachment behaviors (e.g., seeking the caregiver and clinging). They may maintain close physical contact with caregivers or use language to communicate with caregivers across a distance. Four-year-olds may be mildly upset when they are briefly separated from the attachment figure in unfamiliar settings, but less upset than infants. If they and their mothers agree upon a shared plan regarding the mother's absence, 4-year-olds can handle such separations successfully and are to some extent comfortable spending time in the company of peers and adults (Marvin & Britner, 2008). This does not imply that preschoolers do not enjoy contact with the attachment figure, but that they have an understanding that their relationship with the attachment figure is a continuing relationship, regardless of close proximity. By middle childhood there is a decline in the frequency and intensity of attachment behaviors directed toward the attachment figures, such as clinging and following, with availability rather than proximity of the attachment figures becoming the goal of the attachment system (Bowlby, 1987, personal communication cited in Ainsworth, 1990). This decline reflects children's increased self-reliance, the need to rely on parents less often and in fewer situations, and their ability to successfully handle greater physical separations from their parents as long as they know that the parents can be reached if needed (e.g., by telephone; Kerns, 2008; Marvin & Britner, 2008). The decline in the frequency of attachment behavior also occurs due to parents' and children's expectations regarding greater child autonomy (Kerns, Tomich, & Kim, 2006). However, there is no decline in middle childhood in children's perceptions of the availability of attachment figures (Kerns et al., 2006; Lieberman, Doyle, & Markiewicz, 1999). Availability of the attachment figures is reflected in parents' physical accessibility and responsiveness to the children's needs.

A second area of change concerns the emerging partnership between the parent and the child. Bowlby (1969) proposed that the goal-corrected partnership is the last phase of attachment, emerging after the age of 3 years. Marvin and Britner (2008) suggested that young preschoolers show an "emergent partnership" characterized by children's ability to inhibit attachment behaviors and to include the caregiver's plans into their own plans for proximity. Older preschoolers are better able to understand parents' goals and interests, and to engage in negotiations regarding a shared plan for proximity. In the preschool years, however, parents still assume greater responsibility for maintaining contact than does the child. In middle childhood, there may be a shift to mutual co-regulation with the child taking more responsibility for initiating contact, monitoring, and maintaining the availability and accessibility of the attachment figure (Kerns, 2008). Thus, the change to a goal-corrected partnership may actually emerge in middle childhood, later than Bowlby initially thought (Waters, Kondo-Ikemura, Posada, & Richters, 1991).

Bowlby (1973) also elaborated the concept of "internal working models," or mental representations about the world. These representations have been conceptualized as schemata, scripts, or relationship rules that include complementary views of the self, the "other," and the nature of relationships, and act as interpretive filters that guide one's actions and beliefs about what to expect from the social world (Bretherton & Munholland, 2008). Models of self and others are likely to be mutually confirming. For example, a child with an internal representation of the self as worthy of care, arising from a history of sensitive and responsive parenting, may expect others to be sensitive and responsive. From infancy to middle childhood, representations of attachment become more elaborated, sophisticated, and organized with age (Mayseless, 2005). This shift also parallels the many changes in children's cognitive and social cognitive abilities that take place as children mature, and that affect their interpretation of their world. For example, changes in reasoning ability, improved capacity for self-reflection, and greater attention to psychological states and traits are likely to influence children's representations of attachment figures and the self (Raikes & Thompson, 2005). Preschoolers and school-aged children's attachment representations are assessed in relation to specific attachment figures (e.g., their mother and father). Children in middle childhood also have attachment representations of specific attachment figures, but there is a possibility that by the end of this age period they may develop an additional, general model of attachment relationships (Kerns, Schlegelmilch, Morgan, & Abraham, 2005).

With advances in children's social repertoire from infancy to middle childhood, a legitimate question is "Who functions as an attachment figure?" According to Bowlby (1969), "[R]esponsiveness to crying and readiness to interact socially" in the first year are the main variables influencing who is the attachment figure (p. 315). In most cultures the parents, particularly mothers, are the primary attachment figures in infancy and early and middle childhood. Children, however, encounter alternative attachment figures who change with time and circumstances. In some cases, other adults (e.g., day care providers and grandparents) or older siblings may also function as attachment figures (Howes & Spieker, 2008). Although by late middle childhood children spend considerable time with peers, peers do not yet serve as primary attachment figures. When interviewed about distressing situations that trigger attachment behaviors (e.g., being scared or sad), children 7 to 12 years of age prefer parents over peers (Kerns et al., 2006; Seibert & Kerns, 2009). Although parents are children's primary attachment figures, children in middle childhood may direct attachment behaviors to peers, particularly if parents are unavailable, as they "practice" their greater investment in peer relationships that is likely to occur in adolescence. Thus, children directing attachment-related behaviors to nonparental figures in middle childhood may serve an evolutionary function in that such behaviors prepare the children for mating (Mayseless, 2005). An intriguing question is whether children in middle childhood start utilizing different attachment figures in different situations rather than one attachment figure for all situations (Mayseless, 2005). For example, children may turn to one figure (e.g., a peer or grandparent) when facing one type of distress (e.g., problems with parents) and rely on another (e.g., a parent) when encountering another type of distress (e.g., being sick). The context-specific hypothesis has not been extensively investigated (but see Seibert & Kerns, 2009).

Measuring attachment in early and middle childhood

Several recent reviews extensively discuss measurement approaches and specific measures commonly used to assess attachment in early and middle childhood (Kerns et al., 2005; Kerns & Seibert, in press; Solomon & George, 2008). Although a detailed treatment of the topic is beyond the scope of this chapter, we briefly introduce the most commonly employed methods to illustrate how attachment has been conceptualized and assessed in early and middle childhood. The methods are all based on the secure base conceptualization of attachment. That is, the measurement approaches include either observations of secure base behavior or child reports of situations where secure base behavior is expected. The latter are designed to assess child representations or perceptions of attachment. Most measures assess a child's relationship with a specific attachment figure, although some measures for older children assess a child's general "state of mind" or stance in regard to attachment relationships.

The first measure of attachment was designed to assess the organization of an infant's attachment behavior in reference to a specific caregiver. The Strange Situation (Ainsworth et al., 1978) is a laboratory procedure designed to capture the balance between secure base and exploratory behavior under conditions of increasing and moderate stress. It consists of eight episodes of separations and reunions between the parent and infant and also involves the presence of a stranger. The attachment classifications are based primarily on the child's behavior toward the parent during reunions. These procedures and coding criteria were later modified to adjust for developmental transformations (e.g., increasing the lengths of separation episodes), and are now also used to assess attachment in pre-schoolers (Cassidy & Marvin, 1992) and early-elementary-aged children (Main & Cassidy, 1988). One other alternative to assess attachment behavior is the Attachment Q-Sort (AQS) method (Waters, 1995), which enables observers to describe 1- to 5-year-olds' secure base behavior (i.e., balance between proximity seeking and exploration) in the home.

Children develop not only patterns of secure base use but also representations of the attachment figure and their relationship. As noted earlier, across middle childhood attachment behavior declines in frequency and intensity, which makes it challenging to use behavioral observation to assess attachment in older children (Main & Cassidy, 1988). As an alternative approach, a number of techniques have been developed to assess children's attachment representations. These techniques are based on having children discuss attachment-related topics, and narratives are scored based on both the content of what children say and their ability to discuss attachment themes in a coherent and organized way. The three most common approaches are story stems, discussion of pictures of parent–child separations, and autobiographical interviews. Children's narrations are then used to classify children into attachment categories.

With the story stem technique (e.g., Bretherton, Ridgeway, & Cassidy, 1990; Granot & Mayseless, 2001), the interviewer begins to tell an attachment-evoking story (e.g., a child sees a monster in the bedroom), and the child uses dolls and props to complete the story. Several different story sets have been developed for use with 3- to 12-year-old children. In another approach, children are shown pictures of parent–child separation experiences, and are asked how the child in the picture feels, why the child feels that way, and what the child is going to do. Although the method has been used with 6- to 12-year-olds, the procedure appears to be most valid for children 6–8 years of age (Kerns & Seibert, in press). Autobiographical interviews (e.g., Ammaniti, van IJzendoorn, Speranza, & Tambelli, 2000; Shmueli-Goetz, Target, Fonagy, & Datta, 2008) are a newer approach that is based conceptually and procedurally on the Adult Attachment Interview. Children (8 to 12 years of age) are asked to describe and reflect on experiences with their caregivers, and to give specific examples as well as more general descriptions of their relationships. All of the representational measures require extensive training on administration and coding procedures. Questionnaires (e.g., Finnegan, Hodges, & Perry, 1996; Kerns, Aspelmeier, Gentzler, & Grabill, 2001) have been used to assess 8- to 12-year-old children's conscious representations of the mother–child and father–child relationships.

As this brief review indicates, there is no single measure that can be used to assess attachment in both early and middle childhood. This state of affairs greatly complicates the study of attachment, as different methods are used at different ages, and the different approaches have only modest conceptual and empirical overlap (i.e., some methods assess behavior, and some representations; and some assess specific relationships, whereas others assess a general state of mind). The reader should keep in mind that the following literature review is based on studies that used a variety of methods to assess attachment.

Stability and instability of attachment

Attachment theory predicts that, in the absence of disruptions in the quality of caregiving or loss of attachment figures, attachment quality should show some consistency over time. One reason is that stability in the quality of caregiving would contribute to stability in attachment. In addition, children carry forward an understanding of how to relate to others based on their previous experiences in attachment relationships (i.e., new experiences are framed through and in a way consistent with previous experiences); thus, the internal working models have also a self-perpetuating quality (Sroufe & Fleeson, 1986).

A meta-analysis of longitudinal attachment studies (Fraley, 2002) revealed that attachment quality shows moderate stability from infancy to any later point in time (average $r = .39$). Moderate to high stability also has been reported within the middle childhood years (Kerns, 2008). There is, however, also variability across studies. Among the studies that assessed the continuity of attachment from infancy to the preschool or kindergarten years (reviewed in Solomon & George, 2008), some studies reported low or no stability (e.g., National Institute of Child Health and Human Development Early Child Care Research Network [NICHD ECCRN], 2001), whereas others showed moderate and significant continuity (Main & Cassidy, 1988; Stevenson-Hinde & Shouldice, 1995). Secure attachment shows the highest consistency over time, whereas the insecure patterns show the most change from one study to another. Similarly, studies assessing attachment stability from infancy or early childhood to middle childhood (reviewed in Kerns, 2008) provided mixed evidence, with some studies showing no associations between attachment assessments (e.g., Bohlin, Hagekull, & Rydell, 2000), and others reporting significant associations (e.g., Madigan, Ladd, & Goldberg, 2003).

As a whole, then, there is a tendency for attachment quality to be stable over time, probably due to both environmental and intrapersonal sources of continuity. However, attachment can also change over time in response to changes in life circumstances (see Waters, Hamilton, & Weinfield, 2000), and shifts between secure and insecure classifications often coincide with changes in mother–child interaction or other key life changes (e.g., losses; Solomon & George, 2008). The issues of stability and change of attachment quality, especially over long periods of time, are further complicated by the fact that attachment at different ages is assessed with different measures, which, as previously discussed, capture different aspects of parent–child relationships.

What Factors Promote Individual Differences in Attachment?

Individual differences in attachment quality are hypothesized to be mainly products of caregiving history, with sensitive and responsive care thought to be one especially important determinant of attachment security (Bowlby, 1969, 1973). De Wolff and van IJzendoorn's (1997) meta-analysis has indeed documented an association between maternal sensitivity and an infant's secure attachment to mother, although this link is weaker for fathers (van IJzendoorn & de Wolff, 1997). Experimental studies have also shown that interventions that were effective in enhancing parental sensitivity also enhanced infant attachment security, which supports the notion of a causal role of sensitivity in shaping attachment (Bakermans-Kranenburg, van IJzendoorn, & Juffer, 2003). A similar conclusion was reached in a meta-analyses focusing on sensitivity and attachment disorganization in infancy (Bakermans-Kranenburg, van IJzendoorn, & Juffer, 2005). Further, studies have shown that parents who themselves have a secure state of mind in regard to attachment have infants who are securely attached to them (Hesse, 2008).

Maternal sensitivity is also a significant precursor of attachment security in early and middle childhood. Several studies show that parents, mainly mothers, of children classified as (more) secure in preschool or early school years show higher levels of sensitivity, warmth and acceptance, open communication, emotional openness, role balance, and mutual responsiveness and enjoyment of the child, and less controlling behaviors and negativity, than parents of children classified as insecure (Barnett, Kidwell, & Leung, 1998; Booth, Rose-Krasnor, McKinnon, & Rubin, 1994; Diener, Nievar, & Wright, 2003; Moss, Bureau, Cyr, Mongeau, & St.-Laurent, 2004; Moss, Cyr, & Dubois-Comtois, 2004; NICHD ECCRN, 2001; Stevenson-Hinde & Shouldice, 1995). Similarly, securely attached children in later middle childhood have parents who are more accepting (Kerns, Klepac, & Cole, 1996; Kerns, Tomich, Aspelmeier, & Contreras, 2000; Yunger, Corby, & Perry, 2005), and are more aware of their children's activities and whereabouts in the sixth grade, but not third grade (Kerns et al., 2001). These studies confirm the important but not exclusive role of maternal sensitivity or other related maternal behaviors in the development of attachment security.

A few studies examined the association between parenting and specific insecure patterns in early and middle childhood. Avoidant attachment has been related to low levels of task monitoring and planning, parental involvement, and support (Karavasilis, Doyle, & Markiewicz, 2003; Kerns et al., 2000; Stevenson-Hinde & Shouldice, 1995). Ambivalent attachment has been related to higher levels of maternal psychological control in one study of middle childhood (Yunger et al., 2005), but not another (Karavasilis et al., 2003). Disorganized attachment in childhood has been associated with mother–child interactions manifesting low coordination, more negative affect, disruptive affective communication, and role reversal (Humber & Moss, 2005; Moss, Cyr, et al., 2004; Moss, Rousseau, Parent, St.-Laurent, & Saintonge, 1998). Some studies also found concordance between maternal representations of attachment and children's attachments to their mothers (e.g., Ammaniti, Speranza, & Fedele, 2005; Shmueli-Goetz et al., 2008).

Parents' well-being and the family dynamic are also likely to influence the quality of attachment that their children form. Couple conflict has been negatively related to security (Davies, Cummings, & Winter, 2004; Harold, Shelton, Goeke-Morey, & Cummings, 2004). Regarding mothers' well-being, maternal depressive symptoms predict higher rates of insecure attachment (Campbell et al., 2004). Specifically, mothers who reported intermittent depression across their child's first 3 years had preschoolers who were more likely to be ambivalent or disorganized. Mothers with chronic depression were more likely to have children with disorganized attachments. In another study, mothers of ambivalent preschoolers rated themselves as the most depressed and anxious (Stevenson-Hinde & Shouldice, 1995). Their interaction with their preschoolers in home but not laboratory settings was characterized by friction, which is in accord with findings that mothers of ambivalently attached young children are intrusive and interfering (reviewed in Cassidy

& Berlin, 1994). Similarly, at school age, mothers of ambivalent children report high levels of stress related to their maternal function, feel more depressed and less competent, and experience more health problems than do mothers of children with other insecure attachments (Moss et al., 1998). Disorganized attachment in childhood is linked to maternal unresolved loss and trauma (Lyons-Ruth & Jacobvitz, 2008).

In summary, attachment in childhood is related to sensitive and accepting parenting, maternal state of mind and well-being, and couple conflicts. Presumably, parental characteristics and marital conflict affect children's security by undermining effective parenting, although these hypotheses have not yet been tested directly. In addition, parenting variables other than sensitivity (e.g., control) are important at older ages, and need to be investigated more thoroughly. Unlike at younger ages, experimental evidence does not exist as most intervention programs target the parent–child relationship at early ages.

One interesting topic debated over the last 3 decades is whether child temperament explains individual differences in the quality of attachment. Is a child forming an insecure relationship with his or her attachment figure because he or she is temperamentally prone to distress and irritability? Van IJzendoorn, Schuengel, and Bakermans-Kranenburg's (1999) meta-analysis found no association ($r = .0008$) between disorganized attachment in infancy and temperament variables. Vaughn and Bost's (1999) extensive review of the literature suggests that the answer depends on how attachment and temperament are conceptualized. When temperament is measured with reports of behavioral style, emerging personality, emotional and physiological regulation, or social construct (e.g., perceived temperament), it does not distinguish securely attached children from insecurely attached children. When temperament is conceptualized as irritability and it is assessed at very early ages, differences between secure and insecure children have been reported. Although acknowledging that children prone to distress and irritability are less likely to use their parents as a secure base and may be more challenging to parent, Vaughn and colleagues (Vaughn & Bost; 1999; Vaughn, Bost, & van IJzendoorn, 2008) recommended caution when interpreting difficult temperament as a risk factor for insecure attachment. Instead, they concluded that although attachment and temperament areas may overlap (i.e., both refer to affect expression to some extent), one construct cannot be reduced to the other, and the two domains are not consistently related to one another.

We would add one more note to this conclusion. Only a few studies assessing relations of attachment and temperament included assessments of attachment at or after 36 months (Contreras, Kerns, Weimer, Gentzler, & Tomich, 2000; Diener et al., 2003; Kochanska, 1995; Nair & Murray, 2005; Rydell, Bohlin, & Thorell, 2005; Shamir-Essakov, Ungerer, & Rapee, 2005; Szewczyk-Sokolowski, Bost, & Wainwright, 2005; Vaughn et al., 1992). Further, as Vaughn and Bost (1999) noted, most of the studies (of preschoolers or older children) that found a significant association between attachment and temperament (mainly the difficult temperament dimension) relied on data that came from a common source (e.g., mother report) and from assessments that emphasize the expression of affect (e.g., Attachment Q-Sort; Diener et al., 2003), which is likely to elevate the correlations. By contrast, studies that assessed temperament (fearfulness, shyness, or negative emotionality) and attachment with measures that do not involve the same report sources found small or no relations between the constructs (e.g., Contreras et al., 2000; Kochanska, 1995; Rydell et al., 2005). Thus, although associations are sometimes found between attachment quality and difficult temperament, temperament does not explain variations in attachment quality. Temperament is not irrelevant to attachment, as it may be more demanding to parent a difficult or irritable child.

Attachment in Early and Middle Childhood and Children's Social Development

Bowlby (1973) suggested that children's self-views are influenced by the quality of their attachment relationships. Specifically, children who experience sensitive and responsive care learn that they are loved and lovable, and thus are likely to hold positive views of self. Cassidy (1988) found that securely attached 6-year-olds describe themselves in positive terms, but that they are able to admit that they are not flawless, which suggests that these children develop positive but realistic views of themselves. Consistent with this line of reasoning, insecurely attached children in Cassidy's study either reported a more negative image of themselves or had difficulties acknowledging that they are not perfect. Other studies, reviewed in Thompson (2008), confirmed that securely attached preschoolers and early school-aged children show a positive implicit (i.e., inferred) and explicit (i.e., self-described) self-concept. By contrast, attachment and positive self-esteem have not been consistently related in middle childhood (Kerns, 2008), perhaps because global measures of self-esteem do not distinguish between unrealistic and realistic positive self-evaluations.

In early childhood, parental influences play a major role in the development of children's emotion regulation (Thompson, 2008). Through interactions with sensitive caregivers, securely attached children may internalize effective ways to manage negative emotions in stressful situations and are consequently resilient when coping with problems, even in the absence of the caregiver (Contreras & Kerns, 2000; Kerns, 2008; Sroufe, 1983). Studies of preschoolers have shown that securely attached children, compared to insecurely attached children, use more constructive strategies to manage negative emotions in a waiting paradigm (Gilliom, Shaw, Beck, Schonberg, & Lukon, 2002), show more positive affect with peers (Park & Waters, 1989; Sroufe, Schork, Motti, Lawroski, & LaFreniere, 1984), display emotions more openly with an adult (Lutkenhaus, Grossmann, & Grossmann, 1985), and are more advanced in emotion understanding (Laible & Thompson, 1998). Further, by middle childhood, more securely attached children exhibit more positive mood and less negative mood in daily interactions, use more constructive coping strategies, and show better frustration tolerance and emotional adaptation in classrooms (Contreras et al., 2000; Granot & Mayseless, 2001; Kerns, Abraham, Schlegelmilch, & Morgan, 2007; Sroufe, Egeland, & Carlson, 1999). Overall, previous findings are consistent with the conclusion that securely attached children show more adaptive emotion regulation.

Attachment theorists have proposed that peer competence is shaped by the quality of preceding parent–child dyadic regulation (Sroufe et al., 1999) and that children learn in the attachment relationship a set of specific expectations about relationships and interactive skills that will then guide their interactions with peers (Booth-LaForce & Kerns,

2008; Kerns, 1996). Moreover, through the parents' acceptance and willingness to discuss openly both positive and negative emotions, securely attached children may develop more adaptive emotion regulation capacities, which are particularly important when negotiating one's place in the peer world (Contreras & Kerns, 2000).

Studies show that attachment security is linked to children's peer relationships (for extensive evidence and discussions, see Booth-LaForce & Kerns, 2008; Kerns, 2008; Sroufe, Egeland, Carlson, & Collins, 2005). For example, children with more secure attachments are more socially competent with peers in preschool and middle childhood (Booth-LaForce & Kerns, 2008). Attachment is also related to friendship when the quality of friendship but not the number of friends is considered (Kerns, 2008). Regarding associations of attachment with peer acceptance (i.e., popularity), the findings are mixed, with some studies reporting significant relations (e.g., Bohlin et al., 2000), and others not finding meaningful associations (Lieberman et al., 1999). Schneider, Atkinson, and Tardif's (2001) meta-analysis quantitatively summarized the strength of the associations between attachment, measured at various ages between infancy and adolescence, and peer relations. Based on 63 studies, Schneider et al. reported a modest but significant effect size (.20) for the relation between attachment and children's peer relationships. Consistent with the reviews cited above, they also concluded that this association is stronger for studies of children's friendships than for studies of relationships with other peers. Their results also suggested that the attachment–peer relationship association is stronger in middle childhood than in early childhood. The latter conclusion is not surprising, given that by middle childhood, peers have greater salience in children's lives, with children developing and maintaining close friendships, functioning in stable groups of peers, and spending a considerable amount of time with peers (Sroufe et al., 2005).

Given the strong evidence that attachment and peer relationships in childhood are related, the next step to pursue is studies explaining these links. So far, a limited numbers of studies have tackled this issue, and they show that emotion competence, expectations of peers, and self-esteem may be good candidates for explaining how attachment influences peer relationships in early and middle childhood (Cassidy, Kirsh, Scolton, & Parke, 1996; Contreras et al., 2000; Verschueren & Marcoen, 2005). Children with more secure attachments are likely to develop better emotion regulation skills and a balanced self-view, which in turn would facilitate higher quality peer relationships.

One other important tenet of attachment theory is that the quality of parent–child attachment impacts later personality development (Bowlby, 1979). Bowlby postulated that whereas secure attachment relationships set the stage for healthy adaptation, insecure attachments are likely to be associated with difficulties in later functioning and possibly clinical symptoms. Research indeed suggests that children who form secure attachments with their attachment figures are less likely to experience clinical symptoms such as internalizing or externalizing problems (Brumariu & Kerns, 2010; DeKlyen & Greenberg, 2008).

Other attachment theorists further refined Bowlby's ideas and speculated that specific patterns of insecure attachment, rather than insecurity per se, are related to different types of problems. For example, Rubin and Mills (1991) suggested that ambivalently attached children, who tend to show "wariness" and fearful behavior in unfamiliar settings, are more likely to develop internalizing symptoms than are avoidantly attached children. In contrast, they predicted that avoidantly attached children would be more likely to develop externalizing aggressive behaviors. Perry and colleagues advanced similar hypotheses (Hodges, Finnegan, & Perry, 1999; Yunger et al., 2005). Their reasoning stems from the fact that ambivalent attachment is characterized by inhibition of autonomy and exploration and difficulty regulating emotions during minor stressors that promote fear responses and self-perceptions of weakness and helplessness, which in turn are often associated with internalizing symptoms. Avoidant coping may hamper children's emotional connectedness capacities and may promote inflated self-concepts, which ultimately may lead to little regard for others and a focus on satisfying only one's own needs. The outcome is externalizing problems, such as aggression. Carlson and Sroufe (1995) also suggested that avoidant attachment may be associated with anger, conduct problems, or antisocial personality styles. Currently, there is no clear evidence for these specific patterns, as both avoidant and ambivalent attachment patterns are linked with a variety of symptoms (Brumariu & Kerns, 2010; DeKlyen & Greenberg, 2008). In the few studies that included disorganization, this attachment pattern entailed a greater risk for clinical problems than the other insecure attachment patterns (Brumariu & Kerns, 2010; Lyons-Ruth & Jacobvitz, 2008).

In summary, secure attachment has been associated with several markers of social development, including self-concept, emotion regulation, peer relationships, and clinical symptoms. Regarding the latter, it is important to note that an insecure attachment is not equivalent with psychopathology, but is conceptualized as a risk factor along with others (DeKlyen & Greenberg, 2008). Also, although it has been shown that securely attached children are more competent in these areas than are insecurely attached children, less is known about whether specific insecure attachment patterns (i.e., avoidant, ambivalent, or disorganized attachment) are linked to specific adaptational difficulties. This represents an important area for future research.

New Directions or Unanswered Questions

Growing out of Bowlby's interest in clinical work with children, attachment research has burgeoned in the last decades and also captivated the social and developmental psychology fields. In short, attachment theory has its own, undeniable place among other insightful theories of close relationships. Important and interesting questions have been answered, confirming the salience and significance of the quality of parent–child relationships in children's lives and, particularly, in their social development. Now that we learned that several of the basic tenets of attachment theories are empirically supported, it is time to accelerate research on important new directions.

A limitation of the literature is that most research on attachment and parenting has focused on parental sensitivity and paid little attention to other parenting variables that might promote differences in attachment quality. Although there is evidence for a link between parental sensitivity and attachment, this association is modest in size ($r = .24$ in meta-analysis; De Wolff & van IJzendoorn, 1997), suggesting that other parenting variables need to be studied in relation to attachment. Caregivers have multiple parenting tasks other than being available and sensitive to their children's needs. For example, parents act as "filters" and make choices relative to the social contexts their children experience (e.g., type of school, type of TV programs, playmates, and extracurricular involvement; Saarni, 1999). Simultaneously, parents manage children's opportunities to learn about emotions, and their parental strategies for socialization of emotion may be influenced by their own beliefs and values regarding the emotion regulation process (Eisenberg, Spinrad, & Cumberland, 1998). Other important parenting tasks are encouraging children's increasing autonomy, individuation, and mastery with age, and using age-appropriate discipline. The implications of these aspects of parenting for attachment have been rarely studied. As a result, we lack an understanding of the broader parenting context that fosters the quality of attachment. It is also important to note that bidirectional effects are likely to take place: Parenting strategies influence the quality of attachment, but quality of attachment may also influence some parenting strategies.

Another limitation is that most studies have focused exclusively on mother–child attachment, without extensively considering the role of attachments to fathers or other attachment figures. Grossmann et al.'s (2002) work suggests that fathers foster secure attachment via "sensitive and challenging interactive play" and influence children's exploratory behavior. Given the playmate role of fathers, one would expect that father–child attachment may be particularly relevant for children's social development. Indeed, the fledging research in this area suggests that children securely attached to their fathers have better quality of peer relationships (Booth-LaForce & Kerns, 2008). Nevertheless, studies investigating the effects of father–child attachment on children's emotion regulation, self-concept, or adjustment are missing. Additional studies focusing on mechanisms explaining relations of parent–child attachment and different indices of children's social development, and embedding attachment in a broader developmental context, are also needed (see Sroufe et al., 2005).

There is also a need to understand how individual differences in the organization of attachment may change across childhood. For example, do children with disorganized attachments still show caregiving or punitive behaviors to the caregivers in middle childhood? If yes, how are these behaviors manifested? A related limitation is that researchers tend to study and follow over time specific age groups (either *within* 3 to 7 years or 8 to 12 years), and we lack studies that investigate attachment across age groups, thus making the task of understanding continuity and change more difficult. Studies incorporating multiple measures of attachment, spanning different developmental periods, are desirable.

Future research should also clarify whether there are gender and cultural differences in attachment. Del Giudice (2009) suggested that although preschoolers and early school-aged children do not show consistent gender differences in the distributions of attachment classifications, gender differences may emerge during the latter half of middle childhood. Although this view is controversial (e.g., see Bakermans-Kranenburg & van IJzendoorn, 2009), it requires further examination. Relatedly, although similar patterns of attachment are identified in cross-cultural studies, and a majority of children are classified as securely attached (van IJzendoorn & Sagi-Schwartz, 2008), the determinants of attachment security (including parental sensitivity) may vary based on ethnic or subcultural values (e.g., child-rearing norms and early child care). In conclusion, although progress has been made, there are still questions to be answered on the topic of attachment in childhood.

References

Ainsworth, M. D. S. (1989). Attachments beyond infancy. *American Psychologist, 44*, 709–716.

Ainsworth, M. D. S. (1990). Epilogue: Some considerations regarding theory and assessment relevant to attachments beyond infancy. In M. T. Greenberg, D. Cicchetti, & E. M. Cummings (Eds.), *Attachment in the preschool years: Theory, research, and intervention* (pp. 463–488). Chicago: University of Chicago Press.

Ainsworth, M. D. S., Blehar, M. C., Waters, E., & Wall, S. (1978). *Patterns of attachment*. Hillsdale, NJ: Erlbaum.

Ammaniti, M., Speranza, A. M., & Fedele, S. (2005). Attachment in infancy and in early and late childhood: A longitudinal study. In K. A. Kerns & R. A. Richardson (Eds.), *Attachment in middle childhood* (pp. 115–136). New York: Guilford Press.

Ammaniti, M., van IJzendoorn, M. H., Speranza, A. M., & Tambelli, R. (2000). Internal working models of attachment during late childhood and early adolescence: An exploration of stability and change. *Attachment & Human Development, 2*, 328–346.

Bakermans-Kranenburg, M. J., & Van IJzendoorn, M. H. (2009). No reliable gender differences in attachment across the lifespan. *Behavioral and Brain Sciences, 32*, 22–23.

Bakermans-Kranenburg, M. J., Van IJzendoorn, M. H., & Juffer, F. (2003). Less is more: Meta-analysis of sensitivity and attachment interventions in early childhood. *Psychological Bulletin, 129*, 195–215.

Bakermans-Kranenburg, M. J., Van IJzendoorn, M. H., & Juffer, F. (2005). Disorganized infant attachment and preventive interventions: A review and meta-analysis. *Infant Mental Health Journal, 26*, 191–216.

Barnett, D., Kidwell, S. L., & Leung, K., H. (1998). Parenting and preschooler attachment among low-income urban African American families. *Child Development, 69*, 1657–1671.

Bohlin, G., Hagekull, B., & Rydell, A. (2000). Attachment and social functioning: A longitudinal study from infancy to middle childhood. *Social Development, 9*, 24–39.

Booth, C. L., Rose-Krasnor, L., McKinnon, J., & Rubin, K. H. (1994). Predicting social adjustment in middle childhood: The role of preschool attachment security and maternal style. *Social Development, 3*, 189–204.

Booth-LaForce, C. L., & Kerns, K. A. (2008). Child-parent attachment relationships, peer relationships, and peer-group functioning. In K. H. Rubin, W. M. Bukowski, & B. Laursen (Eds.), *Handbook of peer interactions, relationships, and groups* (pp. 490–507). New York: Guilford Press.

Bowlby, J. (1969). *Attachment and loss: Vol. 1. Attachment*. New York: Basic Books.

Bowlby, J. (1973). *Attachment and loss: Vol. 2. Separation, anxiety and danger*. New York: Basic Books.

Bowlby, J. (1979). *The making and breaking of affectional bonds*. London: Tavistock.

Bretherton, I., & Munholland, K. A. (2008). Internal working models in attachment relationships: Elaborating a central construct in attachment theory. In J. Cassidy & P. R. Shaver (Eds.), *Handbook of attachment: Theory, research, and clinical applications* (2nd ed., pp. 102–130). New York: Guilford Press.

Bretherton, I., Ridgeway, D., & Cassidy, J. (1990). Assessing internal working models of the attachment relationship. In M. T. Greenberg, D. Cicchetti, & E. M. Cummings (Eds.),

Attachment in the preschool years: Theory, research, and intervention (pp. 273–308). Chicago: University of Chicago Press.

Brumariu, L. E., & Kerns, K. A. (2010). Parent-child attachment and internalizing symptoms in childhood and adolescence: A review of empirical findings and future directions. *Development and Psychopathology, 22,* 177–203.

Campbell, S. B., Brownell, C. A., Hungerford, A., Spieker, S. J., Mohan, R., & Blessing, J. S. (2004). The course of maternal depressive symptoms and maternal sensitivity as predictors of attachment security at 36 months. *Development and Psychopathology, 16,* 231–252.

Carlson, E. A., & Sroufe, L. A. (1995). Contribution of attachment theory to developmental psychopathology. In D. Cicchetti & D. J. Cohen (Eds.), *Developmental psychopathology: Vol. 1. Theory and method* (pp. 581–616). New York: Wiley.

Cassidy, J. (1988). Child-mother attachment and the self in six-year-olds. *Child Development, 59,* 121–134.

Cassidy, J. (1994). Emotion regulation: Influences on attachment relationships. *Monographs of the Society for Research in Child Development, 59*(2–3, Serial No. 240), 228–249.

Cassidy, J., & Berlin, L. J. (1994). The insecure/ambivalent pattern of attachment: Theory and research. *Child Development, 65,* 971–991.

Cassidy, J., Kirsh, S. J., Scolton, K. L., & Parke, R. D. (1996). Attachment and representations of peer relationships. *Developmental Psychology, 32,* 892–904.

Cassidy, J., & Marvin, R. S., with the MacArthur Attachment Working Group. (1992). Attachment organization in preschool children: Coding guidelines (4th ed.). Unpublished manuscript, University of Virginia.

Contreras, J. M., & Kerns, K. A. (2000). Emotion regulation processes: Explaining links between parent-child attachment and peer relationships. In K. A. Kerns, J. M. Contreras, & A. M. Neal-Barnett (Eds.), *Family and peers: Linking two social worlds* (pp. 1–25). Westport, CT: Praeger.

Contreras, J. M., Kerns, K. A., Weimer, B. L., Gentzler, A. L., & Tomich, P. L. (2000). Emotion regulation as a mediator of associations between mother-child attachment and peer relationships in middle childhood. *Journal of Family Psychology, 14,* 111–124.

Davies, P. T., Cummings, E. M., & Winter, M. A. (2004). Pathways between profiles of family functioning, child security in the interparental subsystem, and child psychological problems. *Development and Psychopathology, 16,* 525–550.

DeKlyen, M., & Greenberg, M. T. (2008). Attachment and psychopathology in childhood. In J. Cassidy & P. R. Shaver (Eds.), *Handbook of attachment: Theory, research and clinical applications* (2nd ed., pp. 637–666). New York: Guilford Press.

Del Giudice, M. (2009). Sex, attachment, and the development of reproductive strategies. *Behavioral and Brain Sciences, 32,* 1–21.

De Wolff, M. S., & Van IJzendoorn, M. H. (1997). Sensitivity and attachment: A metaanalysis on parental antecedents of infant attachment. *Child Development, 68,* 571–591.

Diener, M. L., Nievar, M. A., & Wright, C. (2003). Attachment security among mothers and their young children living in poverty: Associations with maternal, child, and contextual characteristics. *Merrill-Palmer Quarterly, 49,* 154–182.

Eisenberg, N., Spinrad, T. L., & Cumberland, A. (1998). The socialization of emotion: Rely to commentaries. *Psychological Inquiry, 9,* 317–333.

Finnegan, R. A., Hodges, E. V. E., & Perry, D. G. (1996). Preoccupied and avoidant coping during middle childhood. *Child Development, 67,* 1318–1328.

Fraley, R. C. (2002). Attachment stability from infancy to adulthood: Meta-analysis and dynamic modeling of developmental mechanisms. *Personality and Social Psychology Review, 6,* 123–151.

Gilliom, M., Shaw, D. S., Beck, J. E., Schonberg, M. A., & Lukon, J. L. (2002). Anger regulation in disadvantaged preschool boys: Strategies, antecedents, and the development of self-control. *Developmental Psychology, 38,* 222–235.

Granot, D., & Mayseless, O. (2001). Attachment security and adjustment to school in middle childhood. *International Journal of Behavioral Development, 25*, 530–541.

Grossmann, K., Grossmann, K. E., Fremmer-Bombik, E., Kindler, H., Scheuerer-Englisch, H., & Zimmermann, P. (2002). The uniqueness of the child-father attachment relationship: Father's sensitive and challenging play as a pivotal variable in a 16-year longitudinal study. *Social Development, 11*, 307–331.

Harold, G. T., Shelton, K. H., Goeke-Morey, M. C., & Cummings, E. M. (2004). Marital conflict, child emotional security about family relationships, and child adjustment. *Social Development, 13*, 350–376.

Hesse, E. (2008). The Adult Attachment Interview: Protocol, method of analysis, and empirical studies. In J. Cassidy & P. R. Shaver (Eds.), *Handbook of attachment: Theory, research, and clinical applications* (2nd ed., pp. 552–598). New York: Guilford Press.

Hodges, E. V. E., Finnegan, R. A., & Perry, D. G. (1999). Skewed autonomy-relatedness in preadolescents' conceptions of their relationships with mother, father, and best friend. *Developmental Psychology, 35*, 737–748.

Howes, C., & Spieker, S. (2008). Attachment relationships in the context of multiple caregivers. In J. Cassidy & P. R. Shaver (Eds.), *Handbook of attachment: Theory, research, and clinical applications* (2nd ed., pp. 317–332). New York: Guilford Press.

Humber, N., & Moss, E. (2005). The relationship of preschool and early school age attachment to mother-child interaction. *American Journal of Orthopsychiatry, 75*, 128–141.

Karavasilis, L., Doyle, A. B., & Markiewicz, D. (2003). Associations between parenting style and attachment to mother in middle childhood and adolescence. *International Journal of Behavioral Development, 27*, 153–164.

Kerns, K. A. (1996). Individual differences in friendship quality: Links to child-mother attachment. In W. M. Bukowski, A. F. Newcomb, & W. W. Hartup (Eds.), *The company they keep: Friendship in childhood and adolescence* (pp. 137–157). New York: Cambridge University Press.

Kerns, K. A. (2008). Attachment in middle childhood. In J. Cassidy & P. R. Shaver (Eds.), *Handbook of attachment: Theory, research, and clinical applications* (2nd ed., pp. 366–382). New York: Guilford Press.

Kerns, K. A., Abraham, M. M., Schlegelmilch, A., & Morgan, T. A. (2007). Mother-child attachment in later middle childhood: Assessment approaches and associations with mood and emotion regulation. *Attachment and Human Development, 9*, 33–53.

Kerns, K. A., Aspelmeier, J. E., Gentzler, A. L., & Grabill, C. M. (2001). Parent-child attachment and monitoring in middle childhood. *Journal of Family Psychology, 15*, 69–81.

Kerns, K. A., Klepac, L., & Cole, A. (1996). Peer relationships and preadolescents' perceptions of security in the child-mother relationship. *Developmental Psychology, 32*, 457–466.

Kerns, K. A., Schlegelmilch, A., Morgan, T. A., & Abraham, M. M. (2005). Assessing attachment in middle childhood. In K. A. Kerns & R. A. Richardson (Eds.), *Attachment in middle childhood* (pp. 46–70). New York: Guilford Press.

Kerns, K. A., & Seibert, A. C. (in press). Finding your way through the thicket: Promising approaches to assessing attachment in middle childhood. In E. Waters (Ed.), *Measuring attachment*. New York: Guilford Press.

Kerns, K. A., Tomich, P. L., Aspelmeier, J. E., & Contreras, J. M. (2000). Attachment-based assessments of parent-child relationships in middle childhood. *Developmental Psychology, 36*, 614–626.

Kerns, K. A., Tomich, P. L., & Kim, P. (2006). Normative trends in children's perceptions of availability and utilization of attachment figures in middle childhood. *Social Development, 15*, 1–22.

Kochanska, G. (1995). Children's temperament, mothers' discipline, and security of attachment: Multiple pathways to emerging internalization. *Child Development, 66*, 597–615.

334   *Laura E. Brumariu and Kathryn A. Kerns*

Laible, D. J., & Thompson, R. A. (1998). Attachment and emotional understanding in preschool children. *Developmental Psychology, 34*, 1038–1045.

Lieberman, M., Doyle, A. B., & Markiewicz, D. (1999). Developmental patterns in security of attachment to mother and father in late childhood and early adolescence: Associations with peer relations. *Child Development, 70*, 202–213.

Lutkenhaus, P., Grossmann, K. E., & Grossmann, K. (1985). Infant-mother attachment at 12 months and style of interaction with a stranger at 3 years. *Child Development, 56*, 1538–1542.

Lyons-Ruth, K., & Jacobvitz, D. (2008). Attachment disorganization: Genetic factors, parenting context, and developmental transformation from infancy to adulthood. In J. Cassidy & P. R. Shaver (Eds.), *Handbook of attachment: Theory, research, and clinical applications* (2nd ed., pp. 667–697). New York: Guilford Press.

Madigan, S., Ladd, M., & Goldberg, S. (2003). A picture is worth a thousand words: Children's representations of family as indicators of early attachment. *Attachment and Human Development, 5*, 19–37.

Main, M., & Cassidy, J. (1988). Categories of response to reunion with the parent at age 6: Predictable from infant attachment classifications and stable over a 1-month period. *Developmental Psychology, 24*, 415–426.

Main, M., & Solomon, J. (1986). Discovery of a new, insecure-disorganized/disoriented attachment pattern. In T. B. Brazelton & M. V. Yogman (Eds.), *Affective development in infancy* (pp. 95–124). Norwood: Ablex.

Marvin, R. S., & Britner, P. A. (2008). Normative development: The ontogeny of attachment. In J. Cassidy & P. R. Shaver (Eds.), *Handbook of attachment: Theory, research, and clinical applications* (2nd ed., pp. 269–294). New York: Guilford Press.

Mayseless, O. (2005). Ontogeny of attachment in middle childhood: Conceptualization of normative changes. In K. A. Kerns & R. A. Richardson (Eds.), *Attachment in middle childhood* (pp. 1–23). New York: Guilford Press.

Moss, E., Bureau, J. F., Cyr, C., Mongeau, C., & St.-Laurent, D. (2004). Correlates of attachment at age 3: Construct validity of the preschool attachment classification system. *Developmental Psychology, 40*, 323–334.

Moss, E., Cyr, C., & Dubois-Comtois, K. (2004). Attachment at early school age ad developmental risk: Examining family context and behavior problems or controlling-caregiving, controlling-punitive, and behaviorally disorganized children. *Developmental Psychology, 40*, 519–532.

Moss, E., Rousseau, D., Parent, S., St.-Laurent, D., & Saintonge, J. (1998). Correlates of attachment at school age: Maternal reported stress, mother-child interaction, and behavior problems. *Child Development, 69*, 1390–1405.

Nair, H., & Murray, A. D. (2005). Predictors of attachment security in preschool children from intact and divorced families. *Journal of Genetic Psychology, 166*, 245–263.

National Institute of Child Health and Human Development Early Child Care Research Network. (NICHD ECCRN). (2001). Child-care and family predictors of preschool attachment and stability from infancy. *Developmental Psychology, 28*, 584–592.

Park, K. A., & Waters, E. (1989). Security of attachment and preschool friendships. *Child Development, 60*, 1076–1081.

Raikes, H. A., & Thompson, R. A. (2005). Relationships past, present and future: Reflections on attachment in middle childhood. In K. A. Kerns & R. A. Richardson (Eds.), *Attachment in middle childhood* (pp. 255–282). New York: Guilford Press.

Rubin, K. H., & Mills, R. S. (1991). Conceptualizing developmental pathways to internalizing disorders in childhood. *Canadian Journal of Behavioural Science/Revue Canadienne des Sciences du Comportement, 23*, 300–317.

Rydell, A. M., Bohlin, G., & Thorell, L. B. (2005). Representations of attachment to parents and shyness as predictors of children's relationships with teachers and peer competence in preschool. *Attachment & Human Development, 7*, 187–204.

Saarni, C. (1999). *The development of emotional competence.* New York: Guilford Press.

Schneider, B. H., Atkinson, L., & Tardif, C. (2001). Child-parent attachment and children's peer relations: A quantitative review. *Developmental Psychology, 37*, 86–100.

Seibert, A. C., & Kerns, K. A. (2009). Attachment figures in middle childhood. *International Journal of Behavioral Development, 33*, 347–355.

Shamir-Essakow, G., Ungerer, J. A., & Rapee, R. M. (2005). Attachment, behavioral inhibition, and anxiety in preschool children. *Journal of Abnormal Child Psychology, 33*, 131–143.

Shmueli-Goetz, Y., Target, M., Fonagy, P., & Datta, A. (2008). The Child Attachment Interview: A psychometric study of reliability and discriminant validity. *Developmental Psychology, 44*, 939–956.

Solomon J., & George, C. (2008). The measurement of attachment security and related constructs in infancy and early childhood. In J. Cassidy & P. R. Shaver (Eds.), *Handbook of attachment: Theory, research, and clinical applications* (2nd ed., pp. 383–418). New York: Guilford Press.

Sroufe, L. A. (1983). Infant-caregiver attachment and patterns of adaptation in preschool: The roots of maladaptation and competence. In M. Perlmutter (Ed.), *Minnesota Symposium on Child Psychology* (Vol. 16, pp. 41–81). Hillsdale, NJ: Erlbaum.

Sroufe, L. A., Egeland, B., & Carlson, E. A. (1999). One social world: The integrated development of parent-child and peer relationships. In W. A. Collins & B. Laursen (Eds.), *Minnesota Symposia on Child Psychology: Vol. 30. Relationships as developmental contexts: Festschrift in honor of Willard W. Hartup* (pp. 241–261). Mahwah, NJ: Erlbaum.

Sroufe, L. A., Egeland, B., Carlson, E. A., & Collins, W. A. (2005). *The development of the person: The Minnesota study of risk and adaptation from birth to adulthood.* New York: Guilford Press.

Sroufe, L. A., & Fleeson, J. (1986). Attachment and the construction of relationships. In W. W. Hartup & Z. Rubin (Eds.), *Relationships and development* (pp. 57–71). Hillsdale, NJ: Erlbaum.

Sroufe, L. A., Schork, E., Motti, F., Lawroski, N., & LaFreniere, P. (1984). The role of affect in social competence. In C. Izard, J. Kagan, & R. Zajonc (Eds.), *Emotions, cognition, and behavior* (pp. 289–319). Oxford: Oxford University Press.

Stevenson-Hinde, J., & Shouldice, A. (1995). Maternal interactions and self-reports related to attachment classifications at 4.5 years. *Child Development, 66*, 583–596.

Szewczyk-Sokolowski, M., Bost, K. K., & Wainwright, A. B. (2005). Attachment, temperament, and preschool children's peer acceptance. *Social Development, 14*, 379–397.

Thompson, R. A. (2008). Early attachment and later development: Familiar questions, new answers. In J. Cassidy & P. R. Shaver (Eds.), *Handbook of attachment: Theory, research, and clinical applications* (2nd ed., pp. 348–365). New York: Guilford Press.

Van IJzendoorn, M. H., & De Wolff, M. S. (1997). In search of the absent father – meta-analyses of infant-father attachment: A rejoinder to our discussants. *Child Development, 68*, 604–609.

Van IJzendoorn, M. H., & Sagi-Schwartz, A. (2008). Cross-cultural patterns of attachment: Universal and contextual dimensions. In J. Cassidy & P. R. Shaver (Eds.), *Handbook of attachment: Theory, research, and clinical applications* (2nd ed., pp. 880–905). New York: Guilford Press.

Van IJzendoorn, M. H., Schuengel, C., & Bakermans-Kranenburg, M. J. (1999). Disorganized attachment in early childhood: Meta-analysis of precursors, concomitants, and sequelae. *Development and Psychopathology, 11*, 225–249.

Vaughn, B. E., & Bost, K. K. (1999). Attachment and temperament: Redundant, independent, or interacting influences on interpersonal adaptation and personality development? In J. Cassidy & P. R. Shaver (Eds.), *Handbook of attachment: Theory, research, and clinical applications* (pp. 198–225). New York: Guilford Press.

Vaughn, B. E., Bost, K. K., & van IJzendoorn, M. H. (2008). Attachment and temperament: Additive and interactive influences on behavior, affect, and cognition during infancy and childhood. In J. Cassidy & P. R. Shaver (Eds.), *Handbook of attachment: Theory, research, and clinical applications* (2nd ed., pp. 192–216). New York: Guilford Press.

Vaughn, B. E., Stevenson-Hinde, J., Waters, E., Kosaftis, A., Lefever, G. B., Shouldice, A., et al. (1992). Attachment security and temperament in infancy and early childhood: Some conceptual clarifications. *Developmental Psychology, 28,* 463–473.

Verschueren, K., & Marcoen, A. (2005). Perceived security of attachment to mother and father: Developmental differences and relations to self-worth and peer relationships at school. In K. A. Kerns & R. A. Richardson (Eds.), *Attachment in middle childhood* (pp. 212–230). New York: Guilford Press.

Waters, E. (1995). The attachment Q-set, version 3.0 (Appendix A). In E. Waters, B. Vaughn, G. Posada, & K. Kondo-Ikemura (Eds.), *Caregiving, cultural, and cognitive perspectives on secure-base behavior and working models: New growing points on attachment theory and research. Monographs of the Society for Research in Child Development, 60*(2–3, Serial No. 244), 234–245.

Waters, E., Hamilton, C. E., & Weinfield, N. S. (2000). The stability of attachment security from infancy to adolescence and early adulthood. General introduction. *Child Development, 71,* 678–683.

Waters, E., Kondo-Ikemura, K., Posada, G., & Richters, J. E. (1991). Learning to love: Mechanisms and milestones. In M. Gunnar (Ed.), *Minnesota Symposium on Child Psychology* (Vol. *24,* pp. 217–255). Hillsdale, NJ: Erlbaum.

Yunger, J. L., Corby, B. C., & Perry, D. G. (2005). Dimensions of attachment in middle childhood. In K. A. Kerns & R. A. Richardson (Eds.), *Attachment in middle childhood* (pp. 89–114). New York: Guilford Press.

CHAPTER EIGHTEEN

Parent–Child Relationships and Influences

Alan Russell

Parents and the home environment comprise one of a complex set of interrelated influences on children's development. The influences include genetic and biological factors, peers, siblings, media, and the school. Parent–child relationships, parenting, and the home environment, however, are probably the most prominent among influences on development (Bornstein, 2006; Collins, Maccoby, Steinberg, Hetherington, & Bornstein, 2000; Kochanska, Aksan, Prisco, & Adams, 2008; Maccoby, 2000).

In recent years there have been several conceptual and methodological advances in the study of parent–child relationships. There has been an increasing accent on the relationship context of human development (Kochanska et al., 2008; Kuczynski, 2003a, 2003b; Laible & Thompson, 2007; Reis, Collins, & Berscheid, 2000), a systems approach to family relationships (Cox & Paley, 1997; Lerner, Rothbaum, Boulos, & Castellino, 2002; Maccoby, 2007; Parke & Buriel, 2006; Reis et al., 2000), and an emphasis on dynamic processes in parent–child relationships (Kuczynski, 2003a, 2003b; Reis et al., 2000). Greater attention has been given to evolutionary, behavioral genetic, biological, and neuroscience approaches to socialization and parent–child relationships (Beaulieu & Bugental, 2007; Bornstein, 2006; Grusec & Hastings, 2007; Maccoby, 2007; Plomin, DeFries, McClearn, & McGuffin, 2008). There has been an increasing stress on the conceptualization and analysis of parent–child relationships as bidirectional. Finally, analyses of possible influences on social development have incorporated more complex models and research designs that acknowledge the role of both environmental and genetic influences.

Parent–child relationships can be considered as partly falling under a broader umbrella of family or parental socialization (Grusec & Hastings, 2007). Nevertheless, parent–child relationships are somewhat separate from the field of socialization, which has an emphasis on parental influences on child behavior and development. The overlap between *parenting*

The Wiley-Blackwell Handbook of Childhood Social Development, Second Edition, edited by Peter K. Smith and Craig H. Hart
© 2011 by Blackwell Publishing Ltd.

and *parent–child relationships* is also complex, and sometimes the two concepts are treated as almost interchangeable. In the present chapter, the literature on parenting and socialization will be drawn on when and as relevant to parent–child relationships.

Definitional Questions

Prominence in developmental psychology has often been given to the broad-based definitional efforts of Hinde (1987, 1997) and Kelley and colleagues (1983). These efforts include assumptions that relationships involve mutual influence on each other's behavior, and that interactions constitute the core of relationships. Relationships, therefore, are composed of interactions, and two-way processes link relationships and interactions, so that interactions are in turn influenced by relationships. As a consequence, relationships are more than the sum of the individual interactions. Relationships require attention to questions such as relationship satisfaction and expectations (Hinde, 1997), the security provided by the relationship (Laible & Thompson, 2007), and the implications of past history together with an orientation to the future (Kuczynski, 2003a, 2003b; Lollis, 2003). Relationships involve a past, present, and future. In contrast, interactions occur at specific points in time.

Reis et al. (2000) analyzed relationships to yield a number of "relationship processes." These processes assist in defining the elements or scope of parent–child relationships. Their first process is relationship cognition, with attention to how cognitions about the other person and one's connection with them are influential in the formation, development, and quality of the relationship. The second process covers emotion and relationships. Their final process is relationship development. The emphasis on cognitions and emotions is consistent with Laible and Thompson's (2007) description of a relationship as an "integrated network of enduring emotional ties, mental representations, and behaviors that connect one person to another over time and across space" (p. 181).

Hinde's (1997, p. xv) model of relationships underscores other matters that provide direction to theoretical and empirical scholarship on parent–child relationships, including the proposition that interactions and relationships arise out of characteristics and psychological processes within individuals, both the parent and the child. Further, relationships influence and are influenced by the groups and broader society in which the individuals participate. Finally, relationships are influenced by the sociocultural structure of beliefs, values, and institutions, and by characteristics of the physical environment.

Models of Parent–Child Relationships

Systems approaches to parent–child relationships

It is helpful to first examine models of parent–child relationships that incorporate a wider environmental context. These provide a systems perspective with an emphasis on the ecology of human development and relationships (Lerner et al., 2002). The systems perspective fuses parents and children "both structurally and functionally, in a multilevel system involving biological through sociocultural and historical tiers or organization" (Lerner et al., 2002, p. 317). Accordingly, parent–child relationships are assumed to be influenced by other levels of the system and in turn influence those other levels.

An early instance was Belsky's (1984) process model of the determinants of parenting. In this model, parenting is influenced by characteristics of the individual parent (such as his or her personality and own developmental history) and of the individual child (e.g., his or her temperament). In addition, the parent–child relationship is embedded in a broader social context (e.g., the marital relationship, and social support networks) that also influences those relationships.

Along similar lines, Patterson and Fisher (2002) developed a model linking context (cultural beliefs and values, socioeconomic status [SES], stress, parent antisocial behavior, parent biology, and child biology) to parenting and parent–child relationships, which in turn influence child outcomes. With comparable layers, Conger and Donnellan's (2007) "family stress model" links socioeconomic stress to within-family processes and parent–child relationships, with effects on child outcomes. The more recent biological approaches (see below) have shed increasing light on the contributions of parent and child characteristics to parenting and parent–child relationships.

Comprehensive examples of the systems perspective are provided by Bronfenbrenner's bioecological theory of human development (1979, 1999) and Lerner's developmental context model (Lerner et al., 2002). At the individual level of parent and child in the development context model, the individual is affected by characteristics such as age, biology, temperament, health, and others. The wider context includes peers, the school, the marriage, the workplace, the community, the society, and the culture. Parent–child relationships are embedded in the same contextual layers.

Culture is at the outer level of Lerner et al.'s (2002) model. Parke and Buriel (2006) have a parallel emphasis on context in their model of family subsystems and children's socialization outcomes. Cox and Paley (1997, 2003) and Cummings and Schermerhorn (2003) also outlined comparable family systems perspectives in placing individual functioning and the parent–child relationship in the context of the family as an organized whole. Bornstein (2006) included characteristics of parents, characteristics of children, and contextual characteristics as determinants of parenting.

Not only do the ecological and systems approaches draw attention to influences on parent–child relationships, but also they identify sets of conditions and influences that may contribute to developmental outcomes. This means that children's social development must be seen as influenced by the contextual elements inside and outside the family as well as by parenting and parent–child relationships.

Models conceptualizing elements and specific processes of parent–child relationships

A number of approaches have focused on different components or elements of interactions and relationships such as cognitions, behavior, practices, goals, values, domains, styles, qualities, as well as specific relationship processes.

The social relations model This model, developed for the analysis of social perceptions and dyadic interactions, conceptualizes and analyzes parent–child relationships and relationship processes (Cook, 2003; Cook & Kenny, 2004). Relationships between parents and children are partitioned into actor, partner, relationship, and family effects. This enables interdependence among family members to be examined. The emphasis in the model is on the actor (e.g., mother), the partner (e.g., child), and the relationship between the two. The model contributes to the examination of bidirectionality and behavioral reciprocity in dyads (Kenny, Mohr, & Levesque, 2001).

Bidirectionality Themes about the effects of children on parents (and parents on children) and bidirectionality in parent–child relationships have been evident since Bell's (1968) early reinterpretation of the direction of effect in socialization and Sameroff's (1975) proposal of a transactional model of parent–child relationships. Bidirectionality has received increasing attention in the conceptualization of parent–child relationships (Bornstein, 2006; Kuczynski, 2003a, 2003b; Laible & Thompson, 2007; Maccoby, 2007; Pardini, Fite, & Burke, 2008; Patterson & Fisher, 2002; Pettit & Arsiwalla, 2008). Kuczynski's (2003a, 2003b) emphasis on bidirectionality draws on and extends a common theme in the relationship literature (e.g., the social relations model) that in dyadic interactions or relationships, each affects the other. However, Kuczynski (2003b) argued that although progress has been made in conceptualizing bidirectionality in causality, empirical research has lagged in reflecting these models in research.

A number of conceptual approaches emphasize bidirectional processes. Synchrony, for example, has been claimed to capture mutuality and reciprocity in parent–child interactions (Harrist & Waugh, 2002; Skuban, Shaw, Gardner, Supplee, & Nichols, 2006). Mutual responsive orientation has been described as "a positive, mutually binding, and mutually cooperative relationship that evolves in some parent-child dyads" (Kochanska et al., 2008, p. 30). Horizontality in parent–child interactions and relationships (Russell, Pettit, & Mize, 1998) is another construct linked to bidirectionality.

Child effects The emphasis on bidirectionality continues to be reflected in research on child effects. Research on temperamental characteristics suggests that certain child behaviors might prompt parent behaviors and thereby shape the parent–child relationship. If hyperactive, aggressive, difficult, or irritable child behavior evokes parental hostility and lack of playfulness (Collins et al., 2000) or elicits harsh or coercive parenting (Bates, Pettit, & Dodge, 1995; Kent & Pepler, 2003; Patterson & Fisher, 2002), for example, this pattern of child behavior has a powerful influence on the parent–child relationship.

Styles versus processes An important distinction is made between relationship style or quality versus particular practices of parenting or particular parent–child relationship processes. The assumption is that quality of the relationship contributes to the effectiveness of the parenting practices (Darling & Steinberg, 1993; Eisenberg, Fabes, & Spinrad, 2006; Laible & Thompson, 2007; Pettit & Mize, 1993). Therefore, the overall quality of the relationship enhances or impedes the role in socialization of more specific aspects of the relationship. The quality of the relationship is generally considered to include elements such as warmth given and received, security and trust, and mutuality (Laible & Thompson, 2007), as well as warmth and positive interactions, meeting the needs of the child, responding appropriately and quickly to the child's signals, and negotiating conflict (Moreno, Klute, & Robinson, 2008).

Domains Parent–child relationships are likely to vary as a function of the domain of parenting, suggesting that parenting is situation or context specific (Bornstein, Tamis-LeMonda, Hahn, & Haynes, 2008; Grusec & Davidov, 2007; Maccoby, 2007). Beaulieu and Bugental (2007) identified a number of domains involving different types of parent–child interactions: (a) protective care (e.g., providing for the safety and security of offspring), (b) hierarchical power (e.g., interactions involving the management of control where the parent is more socially dominant and holds more resources), (c) coalition formation (e.g., interactions involving shared defense against threats from outsiders), and (d) reciprocity and mutuality (e.g., interactions between functional equals, designed to prepare children for these kinds of relationships outside of the family).

Metaparenting and metarelationships Hawk and Holden (2006) outlined a social cognitive construct they called *metaparenting*: "Meta-parenting refers to the thoughts parents have about their children or childrearing" (p. 322). Elements of metaparenting can be implicit, automatic cognitions, or more deliberate and based on awareness, such as attributions, goals, beliefs or expectations, and knowledge. It includes anticipating, assessing, problem solving, and reflecting. The metaparenting construct draws attention to important cognitive elements that contribute to the construction, development, and monitoring of their relationship by both parents and children.

Gender and developmental differences in parent–child relationships Research has focused especially on the uniqueness of and differences between mother–child versus father–child relationships in both content and outcomes for children (Bornstein, 2006; Parke, 2002). Differences in parent relationships with boys and girls have been examined (Bornstein, Putnick, et al., 2008; Leaper, 2002; Maccoby, 1998). At a more differentiated level, there is also the possibility of differences in father–son and father–daughter relationships as well as in mother–son and mother–daughter relationships (Butler & Shalit-Naggar, 2008; Russell & Saebel, 1997).

It has been recognized that core features of parent–child relationships change throughout childhood. Collins and Madsen (2003) and Collins, Madsen, and Susman-Stillman (2002) suggested that impacts on the parent–child relationship during middle childhood can arise from a reduction in the relative amount of time that children spend interacting with parents; the relationships being less likely to involve negative emotions; greater congruity in perceptions of each other; changing expectations of behavior; more independence; different methods of behavioral regulation because of the reduced face-to-face interaction, with increased emphasis on parents encouraging self-regulation; and parents developing different attributions for the causes of child behavior.

Biological Perspectives

Biological, evolutionary, and behavioral genetic approaches are becoming more prominent in the analysis of parent–child relationships. The role of social relationships in human survival suggests that innate social response systems have evolved, with these genetically determined systems providing the substratum for parent–child relationships (Reis et al., 2000). Beaulieu and Bugental (2007) used evolutionary psychology as well as evolutionary history and processes in analyzing the social domains that comprise human relationships and in turn parent–child relationships. In addition, these domains are considered to comprise distinctive developmental and neurohormonal processes (Bugental, 2000).

Aligned with the evolutionary perspective is what Bugental, Olster, and Martorell (2003) described as a developmental neuroscience approach. This highlights ways in which the central nervous system influences parent–child relationships and parenting, and how the developing organism's central nervous system is influenced by parenting and parent–child relationship experiences. They discuss biological systems, such as the stress response systems, involved as regulators of social interaction. They also identify biological costs to children of maladaptive relationships with parents. These costs could occur in terms of changes to brain development and/or impaired neurohormonal response systems. For instance, cortisol reactivity could be related to chronic stress from parent–child relationships (De Bellis & Putnam, 1994).

Differences in maternal caregiving behavior (sensitivity and intrusiveness) in infancy have been found to be related to stress reactivity in infants (Hane & Fox, 2006). Stress reactivity was revealed in terms of greater fearful reactions, less positive joint attention, more infant negative affect, and a pattern of right frontal electroencephalographic asymmetry. Ordinary variations in maternal caregiving may influence the expression of neural systems involved in stress reactivity in offspring. Therefore, the caregiving may contribute to "phenotypic changes that both alter the infants' behavior at that time and prime infants to respond in a similar fashion to similar environmental stressors in the future" (Hane & Fox, 2006, pp. 550, 555).

Hastings et al. (2008) examined the contention that child physiology in the form of lower vagal tone increases children's susceptibility to maladaptive socialization. Similarly, Hastings and De (2008) reported that children's parasympathetic regulation moderated the relationship between parenting and children's social adjustment.

Finally, genetic influences on parent–child relationships have been examined through the similarity in parenting and parent–child relationships of identical and nonidentical twins (Moffitt & Caspi, 2007). Genetic influences on parent–child relationships have also been found in child-based designs (e.g., Deater-Deckard & O'Connor, 2000).

Methodology

Research on parent–child relationships and their influence on social development confronts significant methodological challenges. These arise at all steps in the research enterprise: definition and measurement of relationship and outcome variables, research design, methods and data collection, data analysis, and interpretation of findings.

The starting point is specification of the dependent variable, the phenomenon to be examined or explained. For parent–child relationships conceived as bidirectional, the dependent variable could be a child outcome, a parent outcome, or a process occurring in the parent–child relationship (Cook, 2003). Most attention has been directed to child outcomes and to relationships processes, with each type of research associated with different research designs and issues. However, at a broad level, a researcher needs to consider first the appropriateness of quantitative (Cook, 2003) and/or qualitative (Kuczynski & Daly, 2003) methods. With the development of theoretical models and a foundation of prior findings in recent decades, research on parent–child relationships has moved increasingly toward theory-driven strategies and away from more exploratory approaches.

Early methodological challenges are associated with the meaning and measurement of relationship and interaction. For example, it is one thing to define and measure parental warmth, but another to define and measure warmth in the parent–child relationship. As Cook (2003) explained, questions arise as to whether this means child warmth to parent, parent warmth to child, or some quality of the dyad. Many have argued for the value of dyadic variables over the aggregation of individual variables (Hinde, 1987; Reis et al., 2000) or pointed to limitations of combining data from an individual to obtain dyadic or family-level variables (Heatherington & Lavner, 2008). Despite the obvious implication that parent–child relationships are dyadic, research often includes only parent behavior in the assessment of the relationship (Connor & Rueter, 2006) or uses self-report from parents to measure parent–child relationships (Jones et al., 2008; Overbeek, Stattin, Vermulst, Ha, & Engels, 2007). More researchers are turning to dyadic measures of relationships (Deater-Deckard & O'Connor, 2000; Kochanska et al., 2008; Lindsey, Mize, & Pettit, 1997). Consistent with this dyadic approach are dyadic measures of synchrony based on ratings of observed interactions (Criss, Shaw, & Ingoldsby, 2003; Mize & Pettit, 1997; Skuban et al., 2006). Nevertheless, Parke and Buriel (2006) argued that "even if such terms as reciprocal or synchronous hold promise, there remains little real advance in this regard" (p. 487).

Overlapping questions of individual versus dyadic measurement is the matter of the "level" that is being examined, or the unit of analysis (Heatherington & Lavner, 2008; Pettit & Arsiwalla, 2008). The emphasis could be at the relationship level, for example in terms of global attitudes; at an intervening level of self-report behaviors; or at a micro level of interactive behaviors. When self-reports or questionnaires are used, the unit of analysis includes who serves as informants. There are also questions about whether or to what degree measurement equivalence occurs between mother–child and father–child relationships (Adamsons & Buehler, 2007).

When the bidirectional emphasis is extended into a family systems perspective (Cook, 2003; Cox & Paley, 1997; Parke & Buriel, 2006), further methodological issues emerge. There is a need to design research that is capable of investigating circular causal processes that involve reciprocal influences among different levels of the system. This requires the collection of data at multiple levels: individuals, dyads, triads, and the whole family. It is straightforward to identify the kinds of research that are needed, but more difficult to provide concrete strategies or models. Parke and Buriel (2006) argued for a need to examine the connections between relationship-level/molar and interaction-level/molecular levels of analyses. Similarly, Cook and Kenny (2006) discussed the need for data at the level of individuals, dyads, and the family as a whole. Parke and Buriel noted, however, that only limited attention has been given to relationships between different levels of data using a family systems perspective. Cook and Kenny (2006) as well as Manders et al. (2007) acknowledged the need for data at different levels, but pointed out that more effort needs to be given to separating possible confounding effects and assessing validity across the levels.

Research linking parent–child relationships to child outcomes

When research efforts move to the effects of parent–child relationships on child outcomes, there is a new set of methodological challenges, with the need to take account of bidirectional influence processes as well as contemporaneous and overtime influences in both directions in a transactional and circular causal process (Bornstein, 2006; Collins et al., 2000; Cook, 2003; Hastings et al., 2008; Kuczynski, 2003a; Laible & Thompson, 2007; O'Connor, 2002; Patterson & Fisher, 2002; Pettit & Arsiwalla, 2008). There are also conceptual and methodological difficulties associated with the separation of correlation and causality (Cook, 2003; Cowan & Cowan, 2002; Howe, Reiss, & Yuh, 2002) as well as the specification and separation of the contributions of different environmental effects, including separating the contributions of parent–child relationships from other environmental effects (Bradley, 2002). The bidirectional or transactional nature of influence processes lends itself to twin, stepfamily, and adoption studies with an emphasis on quantitative behavior genetics and estimations of the strength of genetic effects, effects of the shared environment, and effects of nonshared environments for children in the family (Maccoby, 2000; Moffitt & Caspi, 2007; O'Connor, 2003; Plomin, Asbury, & Dunn, 2001; Plomin et al., 2008).

Children's genetic predispositions affect parenting and parent–child relationships, and genetic factors can account for environmental effects (Moffitt & Caspi, 2007; O'Connor, 2003). The field of behavioral genetics is contributing substantially to knowledge about parent–child relationships (Collins et al., 2000; Maccoby, 2000; Moffitt & Caspi, 2007). Longitudinal research designs have been increasingly used to untangle questions of causation, especially the direction of effect (Lacourse et al., 2002; Patterson & Fisher, 2002; Pettit & Arsiwalla, 2008). Although family research is not easily amenable to experimental manipulation, intervention strategies to improve parent–child and/or marital relationships provide powerful opportunities to examine causal effects (Cowan & Cowan, 2002; Howe et al., 2002; O'Connor, 2002; Patterson & Fisher, 2002).

Demographic and Society-Wide Changes

Diversity in parent–child relationships and parenting has been a theme in the literature. This diversity has been discussed and examined with respect to cultural differences (Bornstein, Putnick, et al., 2008; Nelson, Hart, Yang, Olsen, & Jin, 2006; Rothbaum & Trommsdorff, 2007; Rubin & Chung, 2006; Trommsdorff, 2006) and social class, socioeconomic status, and poverty or economic stress (Conger & Dogan, 2007; Conger & Donnellan, 2007; Wadsworth & Santiago, 2008). Demographic and other changes in recent decades have added to diversity (Patterson & Hastings, 2007; Trommsdorff & Nauck, 2006). Research on parent–child relationships has included attention to single parents (Weinraub, Horvath, & Gringlas, 2002); young mothers and teenage parents (Moore & Brooks-Gunn, 2002); gay and lesbian families (Patterson & Hastings, 2007); families with youth who are lesbian, gay, or bisexual (Heatherington & Lavner, 2008); families with a child conceived through embryo donation (MacCallum, Golombok, & Brinsden, 2007) or other reproductive technologies (Golombok, 2002); and families with internationally adopted children (Lee, Grotevant, Hellerstedt, & Gunnar, 2006).

There has been a continuation of research on father–child relationships (Hastings & De, 2008; Lamb, 2004; Parke, 2002; Summers, Boller, Schiffman, & Raikes, 2006; Vogel, Bradley, Raikes, Boller, & Shears, 2006), including unmarried and nonresident fathers, and fathers with adolescent mothers (Howard, Lefever, Borkowski, & Whitman, 2006); and parent–child relationships in stepfamilies or remarried families and in divorced families (Hetherington & Stanley-Hagan, 2002). Effects on parent–child relationships of recent demographic changes, such as declining fertility and family sizes in Western countries, and increased longevity have been identified (Trommsdorff & Nauck, 2006). As well, there has been a delay in the timing of the onset of parenthood for many mothers. Scholarship has been directed to the effects on parent–child relationships of shifting employment and unemployment patterns for mothers and fathers, including job loss (Gottfried, Gottfried, & Bathurst, 2002; Parke & Buriel, 2006), and to the effects of work quality on parent–child relationships (Parke & Buriel, 2006).

Influence of Parent–Child Relationships on Social Development

Social development includes internalizing and externalizing behaviors, prosocial behavior, and social competence (Sanson, Hemphill, & Smart, 2004). Laible and Thompson (2007) added values internalization, knowledge of relationship processes, conscience development, self-regulation, self-control, emotion understanding, and an orientation to the needs of others. Saarni, Campos, Camras, and Witherington (2006) extended social developmental outcomes to more individual components such as emotional regulation, emotional competence, awareness of own emotions, ability to understand emotions in others, capacity for empathic and sympathetic involvement, and so on.

It is no longer accepted that research can simply demonstrate that parent–child relationships predict child outcomes. Rather, research needs "to understand the processes and pathways that account for children's outcomes, including mediators and moderators of effects on children, in an effort to create more sophisticated explanatory models" (Cummings & Schermerhorn, 2003, p. 91).

Overall relationship quality

A prominent theme in scholarship about influences on social development has been the contribution and role of the overall quality of the parent–child relationship. Laible and Thompson (2007) argued that early relationships initiate the child into a system of reciprocity and mutuality that influences children's identification with their relational partners (primarily parents, but also peers and siblings) and their motivation to respond cooperatively and affectionately to them. Children are motivated to attend to parental messages, for example, because of the close emotional attachment they share with them. As a consequence, the general quality of the relationship enhances or diminishes young children's receptivity to the socialization initiatives of others and, in this manner, also affects the responsiveness of others to the child. (p. 183)

Their argument is consistent with the earlier proposition of Darling and Steinberg (1993) and other writers (Denham, Bassett, & Wyatt, 2007; Eisenberg et al., 2006; Kuczynski & Parkin, 2007). Bugental and Grusec (2006) similarly suggested, "The basis of successful socialization is the creation of a positive relationship with parents ... that fosters a willingness or desire to be receptive to their directives" (p. 394). Inherent here is the idea of mutual compliance (Maccoby, 2007), where parental compliance to the child is reciprocated by the child's compliance to the parent. This state of mutual responsiveness is seen as creating a foundation for socialization.

Specific relationship qualities and the question of specificity of influence

Beyond overall relationship quality, there is a need to understand how particular aspects of the relationship influence social development (Bornstein, Tamis-LeMonda, et al., 2008). This includes broad dimensions of parent–child relationships (such as positive and negative relationship qualities) and more specific features or processes. Laible and Thompson (2007) outlined a number of separate relationship qualities (e.g., warmth and security) and relationship processes (e.g., communication and modeling) and argued that the separate qualities and processes may play different roles and make distinct contributions to developmental outcomes. Bugental and Grusec (2006) argued that parent–child relationships in different domains might have different consequences for child development. Hastings, Utendale, and Sullivan (2007) included sensitivity, warmth, and attachment as separate elements, and Eisenberg et al. (2006) examined the separate effects of warmth and the attachment relationship. Some aspects of parent–child relationships (such as warmth) might be linked to multiple child outcomes, and some child outcomes (such as prosocial behavior or aggression) might be linked to many aspects of parenting and the parent–child relationship (Caron, Weiss, Harris, & Catron, 2006).

It has been suggested that children's experience of horizontal or synchronous relationship qualities with parents provides opportunities for them to participate in and practice interactions associated with these kinds of relationships (Harrist & Waugh, 2002; Lindsey et al., 1997; Russell et al., 1998), with consequences for the development of social competence. Mize and Pettit (1997) reported that preschool children's social competence was more closely related to measures of mother–child synchrony than to maternal warmth. Lindsey, Colwell, Frabutt, Chambers, and MacKinnon-Lewis (2008) found that synchrony in the form of shared positive affect was related to early adolescents' prosocial behavior with peers. There were some differences in results for European American and African American families, suggesting that processes linking parent–child relationships to child outcomes may differ across ethnic groups.

In research on the specificity of influences, Jones et al. (2008) investigated whether particular parenting behaviors (warmth and supervision) had a unique effect on specific child outcomes (aggression and depressive symptoms). Garner, Dunsmore, and Southam-Gerrow (2008) examined relationships between mother and child emotion discourse and the outcomes of child prosocial behavior, relational aggression, and physical aggression. There is a need for more research on the question of unique contributions of particular elements of parent–child relationships to specific child outcomes (Bornstein, Tamis-LeMonda, et al., 2008).

Specificity of influence can take the form of effects occurring under certain conditions but not under others. This is a question about moderators of the linkages between parent–child relationships and child outcomes (Jones et al., 2008; Pettit & Arsiwalla, 2008). The moderators could include the sex of the child and the sex of the parent (Cummings, Schermerhorn, & Keller, 2008; Hastings & De, 2008; Kochanska et al., 2008; McElwain, Halberstadt, & Volling, 2007; Mize & Pettit, 1997; Nelson, Hart, Wu, et al., 2006). There have also been continuing issues about the combined and separate contributions of mother–child and father–child relationships (Hastings et al., 2008; Lamb, 2004; Nelson, Hart, Yang, et al., 2006; Papp, Cummings, & Goeke-Morey, 2005; Ryan, Martin, & Brooks-Gunn, 2006). Culture is also a possible moderator of parental influences (Nelson, Hart, Yang, et al., 2006; Nelson, Hart, Wu, et al., 2006).

Influence mechanisms and processes

At a broad level, the issue about influence processes centers on the source of the influence as genetic and/or environmental (Brendgen et al., 2008; Collins et al., 2000; Moffitt & Caspi, 2007). The latter, in turn, must be divided into shared and nonshared environments, with research pointing to most of the effects being associated with nonshared environments. Children in the same family are different from each other partly because of their unique or differential environments and relationships with parents (Alexandra, McGue, Iacono, & Krueger, 2006; Plomin et al., 2001). Children to a degree create their own environments (Scarr & McCartney, 1983) through their own interests, personalities, and choices inside and outside the family. Continued effort needs to be directed to the separation and elucidation of different forms of genetic and environmental components of influences of parent–child relationships on children's social development.

Overlapping the problem of genetic and environmental influences is that of direction of effect and the role of parent and child in presumed influence processes that are transactional and bidirectional (Bornstein, 2006; Bugental & Grusec, 2006; Grusec & Davidov, 2007; Kuczynski, 2003a, 2003b; Maccoby, 2000, 2007; Pettit & Arsiwalla, 2008). When child effects are considered, possibilities include genetic variations in children's responses and reactivity to the environment as reflected in their temperament (Sanson et al., 2004), variations in children's responsiveness to socialization (Bugental & Grusec, 2006), and the possibility that children may elicit different responses and behaviors from parents (Collins et al., 2000; Patterson & Fisher, 2002).

Bugental and Grusec (2006) outlined a number of mechanisms that could lead to differential outcomes for children. These include the intervening effects of children's social cognitions (e.g., their representations of the social world). As well, they outlined two possible mechanisms of influence at the biological level: the effects of relationships and the socialization environment on child hormones (such as the stress regulation system) and on gene expression. Padilla-Walker (2008) developed a model where parenting practices are mediated through child perceptions of parental intent and perceptions of appropriateness that are then linked to adolescent emotions and the internalization of values. This suggests that effects of the parent–child relationship and parenting are mediated by child perceptions and interpretations (Cummings et al., 2008; Kuczynski & Parkin, 2007), or child self-presentations (Kochanska et al., 2008).

Children's temperament could make them differentially sensitive to parenting and thereby moderate the relationship between parenting and child outcomes (Stright, Gallagher, & Kelly, 2008). Or, children's dispositional capacity for self-regulation could moderate the relationships between parenting and socioemotional development (Hastings & De, 2008). Taken overall, child temperamental characteristics can directly affect child outcomes, and/or they can operate in transaction with the environment, for example by eliciting parent behavior (Bates & Pettit, 2007). Child temperament and parent–child relationships could have additive effects on child outcomes, or outcomes could be a product of parenting-by-child-temperament interactions (Bates & Pettit, 2007). In summary, any focus on mechanism of influence has to give attention to the broad question of "child effects" in a number of forms.

A body of scholarship has focused on processes and mediators for the effects of mutually responsive orientation, synchrony, and horizontality. For example, Harrist and Waugh (2002) argued that dyadic synchrony in parent–child relationships could be a crucial achievement that facilitates social and emotional development by enabling children to function as competent social partners. Mize and Pettit (1997) suggested that participation in synchronous relations with parents might help children learn the rules of effective social discourse. Russell et al. (1998) made similar claims about the possible effects of horizontal qualities in parent–child relationships, especially for the development of social and peer competence.

Although efforts have been made to identify the mechanisms or processes associated with the influence of parent–child relationships on social development, progress has been limited, arguably because of the overall complexity of the possibilities together with the associated design and conceptual issues.

Putting It Together

Parent–child relationships are multilayered, multidimensional, and bidirectional. They are also modular and specific in their influence (Bornstein, Tamis-LeMonda, et al., 2008). Influences of those relationships on social development are complex because of the over-time process, the role of moderators and mediators, the need to incorporate influences from other aspects of the environment, and genetic and biological contributions. In turn, interactions between environmental and genetic contributions need to be taken into account (Moffitt & Caspi, 2007; O'Connor, 2003).

The inherent complexity associated with understanding parent–child relationships and their influences is reflected in current theoretical models (Bornstein, 2006; Cummings & Schermerhorn, 2003; Denham et al., 2007; Eisenberg et al., 2006). These efforts (a) include parent–child relationships as part of an overall explanatory system for child development, (b) elucidate the contributions of environmental and genetic factors to child development, and (c) determine possible mechanisms of influence at biological, social, or individual levels.

Influences associated with parent–child relationships can also be examined in research that treats the relationship as a mediator or moderator rather than as an independent variable. For example, parent–child relationships have been investigated as mediators between maternal depression (Cummings et al., 2008; Lim, Wood, & Miller, 2008), child social risk factors (Burchinal, Roberts, Zeisel, Hennon, & Hooper, 2006), family SES (Conger & Donnellan, 2007), family stress (Crnic & Low, 2002), neighborhood characteristics (Kohen, Leventhal, Dahinten, & McIntosh, 2008), and parental psychological distress (Papp et al., 2005) and child outcomes. Parent–child relationships can also be examined as a moderator variable. Deater-Deckard, Ivy, and Petrill (2006) reported that physical punishment was more strongly connected to child externalizing problems when the mother–child relationship lacked warmth.

Overall, strong themes apparent in the recent theoretical and empirical literature are that (a) parent–child relationships are bidirectional, (b) there is a need to conceptualize and examine influences over time using a transactional framework, and (c) relationship quality should be central when conceptualizing influences of parent–child relationships on social development.

References

Adamsons, K., & Buehler, C. (2007). Mothering versus fathering versus parenting: Measurement equivalence in parenting measures. *Parenting, 7*, 271–303.

Alexandra, B. S., McGue, M., Iacono, W. G., & Krueger, R. F. (2006). Differential parent-child relationships and adolescent externalizing symptoms: Cross-lagged analyses within a monozygotic twin difference design. *Developmental Psychology, 42*, 1289–1298.

Bates, J. E., & Pettit, G. S. (2007). Temperament, parenting, and socialization. In J. E. Grusec & P. D. Hastings (Eds.), *Handbook of socialization: Theory and research* (pp. 153–177). New York: Guilford Press.

Bates, J. E., Pettit, G. S., & Dodge, K. A. (1995). Family and child factors in stability and change in children's aggressiveness in elementary school. In J. McCord (Ed.), *Coercion and punishment in long-term perspectives* (pp. 124–138). New York: Cambridge University Press.

Beaulieu, D. A., & Bugental, D. B. (2007). An evolutionary approach to socialization. In J. E. Grusec & P. D. Hastings (Eds.), *Handbook of socialization: Theory and research* (pp. 71–95). New York: Guilford Press.

Bell, R. Q. (1968). A reinterpretation of the direction of effects in studies of socialization. *Psychological Review, 75*, 81–95.

Belsky, J. (1984). The determinants of parenting. *Child Development, 55*, 83–96.

Bornstein, M. H. (2006). Parenting science and practice. In W. Damon & R. M. Lerner (Series Eds.) & I. E. Sigel & K. A. Renninger (Vol. Eds.), *Handbook of child psychology: Vol. 4. Child psychology in practice* (6th ed., pp. 893–949). New York: Wiley.

Bornstein, M. H., Putnick. D. L., Heslington, M., Gini, M., Suwalsky, J. T. D., Venuti, P. et al. (2008). Mother-child emotional availability in ecological perspective: Three countries, two regions, two genders. *Developmental Psychology, 44*, 666–680.

Bornstein, M. H., Tamis-LeMonda, C. S., Hahn, C., & Haynes, M. (2008). Maternal responsiveness to young children at three ages: Longitudinal analysis of a multidimensional, modular, and specific parenting construct. *Developmental Psychology, 44*, 867–874.

Bradley, R. H. (2002). Environment and parenting. In M. H. Bornstein (Ed.), *Handbook of parenting: Vol. 2. Biology and ecology of parenting* (pp. 281–314). Mahwah, NJ: Erlbaum.

Brendgen, M., Bolvin, M., Vitaro, F., Bukowski, W. M., Dionne, G., Tremblay, R. E., et al. (2008). Linkages between children's and their friends' social and physical aggression: Evidence for a gene-environment interaction? *Child Development, 79*, 13–29.

Bronfenbrenner, U. (1979). *The ecology of human development.* Cambridge, MA: Harvard University Press.

Bronfenbrenner, U. (1999). Environments in developmental perspective: Theoretical and operational models. In S. L. Friedman & T. D. Wachs (Eds.), *Measuring environment across the life span: Emerging methods and concepts* (pp. 3–28). Washington, DC: American Psychological Association.

Bugental, D. B. (2000). Acquisitions of the algorithms of social life: A domain-based approach. *Psychological Bulletin, 26*, 187–209.

Bugental, D. B., & Grusec, J. E. (2006). Socialization processes. In W. Damon & M. Lerner (Series Eds.) & N. Eisenberg (Vol. Ed.), *Handbook of child psychology. Social, emotional and personality development* (pp. 366–428). New York: Wiley.

Bugental, D. B., Olster, D. H., & Martorell, G. A. (2003). A developmental neuroscience perspective on the dynamics of parenting. In L. Kuczynski (Ed.), *Handbook of dynamics in parent-child relations* (pp. 25–48). Thousand Oaks, CA: Sage.

Burchinal, M., Roberts, J. E., Zeisel, S. A., Hennon, E. A., & Hooper, S. (2006). Social risk and protective child, parenting, and child care factors in early elementary school years. *Parenting, 6*, 79–113.

Butler, R., & Shalit-Naggar, R. (2008). Gender and patterns of concerned responsiveness in representations of mother-daughter and mother-son relationships. *Child Development, 79*, 836–851.

Caron, A., Weiss, B., Harris, V., & Catron, T. (2006). Parenting behavior dimensions and child psychopathology: Specificity, task dependency, and interactive relations. *Journal of Clinical Child and Adolescent Psychology, 35*, 34–45.

Collins, W. A., Maccoby, E. E., Steinberg, L., Hetherington, E. M., & Bornstein, M. H. (2000). Contemporary research on parenting: The case for nature and nurture. *American Psychologist, 55*, 218–232.

Collins, W. A., & Madsen, S. D. (2003). Developmental change in parenting interactions. In L. Kuczynski (Ed.), *Handbook of dynamics in parent-child relations* (pp. 49–66). Thousand Oaks, CA: Sage.

Collins, W. A., Madsen, S. D., & Susman-Stillman, A. (2002). Parenting during middle childhood. In M. H. Bornstein (Ed.), *Handbook of parenting: Vol. 1. Children and parenting* (pp. 73–101). Mahwah, NJ: Erlbaum.

Conger, R. D., & Dogan, S. J. (2007). Social class and socialization in families. In J. E. Grusec & P. D. Hastings (Eds.), *Handbook of socialization: Theory and research* (pp. 433–460). New York: Guilford Press.

Conger, R. D., & Donnellan, M. B. (2007). An interactionist perspective on the socioeconomic context of human development. *Annual Review of Psychology, 58*, 175–199.

Connor, J. J., & Rueter, M. A. (2006). Parent-child relationships as systems of support or risk for adolescent suicidality. *Journal of Family Psychology, 20*, 143–155.

Cook, W. L. (2003). Quantitative methods for deductive (theory-testing) research on parent-child dynamics. In L. Kuczynski (Ed.), *Handbook of dynamics in parent-child relations* (pp. 347–372). Thousand Oaks, CA: Sage.

Cook, W. L., & Kenny, D. A. (2004). Application of the social relations model to family assessment. *Journal of Family Psychology, 18,* 361–371.

Cook, W. L., & Kenny. D. A. (2006). Examining the validity of self-report assessments of family functioning: A question of the level of analysis. *Journal of Family Psychology, 20,* 209–216.

Cowan, P. A., & Cowan, C. P. (2002). Interventions as tests of family systems theories: Marital family relationships in children's development and psychopathology. *Development and Psychopathology, 14,* 731–759.

Cox, M., & Paley, B. (1997). Families as systems. *Annual Review of Psychology, 48,* 243–267.

Cox, M., & Paley, B. (2003). Understanding families as systems. *Current Directions in Psychological Science, 12,* 193–196.

Criss, M. M., Shaw, D. S., & Ingoldsby, E. (2003). Mother-son synchrony in middle childhood: Relations to child and peer antisocial behavior. *Social Development, 12,* 379–400.

Crnic, K., & Low, C. (2002). Everyday stresses and parenting. In M. H. Bornstein (Ed.), *Handbook of parenting: Vol. 5. Practical issues in parenting* (pp. 243–267). Mahwah, NJ: Erlbaum.

Cummings, E. M., & Schermerhorn, A. C. (2003). A developmental perspective on children as agents in the family. In L. Kuczynski (Ed.), *Handbook of dynamics in parent-child relations* (pp. 91–108). Thousand Oaks, CA: Sage.

Cummings, E. M., Schermerhorn, A. C., & Keller, P. S. (2008). Parental depressive symptoms, children's representations of family relationships, and children's adjustment. *Social Development, 17,* 278–305.

Darling, N., & Steinberg, L. (1993). Parenting style as context: An integrative model. *Psychological Bulletin, 113,* 487–496.

Deater-Deckard, K., Ivy, L., & Petrill, S. A. (2006). Maternal warmth moderates the link between physical punishment and child externalizing problems: A parent-offspring behavior genetic analysis. *Parenting, 6,* 59–78.

Deater-Deckard, K., & O'Connor, T. G. (2000). Parent-child mutuality in early childhood: Two behavioral genetic studies. *Developmental Psychology, 36,* 561–570.

De Bellis, M. D., & Putnam, F. W. (1994). The psychobiology of child maltreatment. *Child Abuse, 3,* 663–678.

Denham, S. A., Bassett, H. H., & Wyatt, T. (2007). The socialization of emotional competence. In J. E. Grusec & P. D. Hastings (Eds.), *Handbook of socialization: Theory and research* (pp. 614–637). New York: Guilford Press.

Eisenberg, N., Fabes, R. A., & Spinrad, T. L. (2006). Prosocial development. In W. Damon & R. M. Lerner (Series Eds.) & N. Eisenberg (Vol. Ed.), *Handbook of child psychology: Vol. 3. Social, emotional, and personality development* (6th ed., pp. 646–718). Hoboken, NJ: Wiley.

Garner, P. W., Dunsmore, J. C., & Southam-Gerrow, M. (2008). Mother-child conversations about emotions: Linkages to child aggression and prosocial behavior. *Social Development, 17,* 259–277.

Golombok, S. (2002). Parenting and contemporary reproductive technologies. In M. H. Bornstein (Ed.), *Handbook of parenting: Vol. 3. Being and becoming a parent* (pp. 339–360). Mahwah, NJ: Erlbaum.

Gottfried, A. E., Gottfried, A. W., & Bathurst, K. (2002). Maternal and dual-earner employment status and parenting. In M. H. Bornstein (Ed.), *Handbook of parenting: Vol. 2. Biology and ecology of parenting* (pp. 207–229). Mahwah, NJ: Erlbaum.

Grusec, J. E., & Davidov, M. (2007). Socialization in the family: The roles of parents. In J. E. Grusec & P. D. Hastings (Eds.), *Handbook of socialization: Theory and research* (pp. 284–308). New York: Guilford Press.

Grusec, J. E., & Hastings, P. D. (2007). Introduction. In J. E. Grusec & P. D. Hastings (Eds.), *Handbook of socialization: Theory and research* (pp. 1–9). New York: Guilford Press.

Hane, A. S., & Fox, N. A. (2006). Ordinary variations in maternal caregiving influence human infants' stress reactivity. *Psychological Science*, *17*, 550–556.

Harrist, A. W., & Waugh, R. M. (2002). Dyadic synchrony: Its structure and function in children's development. *Developmental Review*, *22*, 555–592.

Hastings, P. D., & De, I. (2008). Parasympathetic regulation and parental socialization of emotion: Biopsychosocial processes of adjustment in preschoolers. *Social Development*, *17*, 211–238.

Hastings, P. D., Sullivan, C., McShane, K. E., Coplan, R. J., Utendale, W. T., & Vyncke, J. D. (2008). Parental socialization, vagal regulation, and preschoolers' anxious difficulties: Direct mothers and moderated fathers. *Child Development*, *79*, 45–64.

Hastings, P. D., Utendale, W. T., & Sullivan, C. (2007). The socialization of prosocial development. In J. E. Grusec & P. D. Hastings (Eds.), *Handbook of socialization: Theory and research* (pp. 638–664). New York: Guilford Press.

Hawk, C. K., & Holden, G. W. (2006). Meta-parenting: An initial investigation into a new parental social cognition construct. *Parenting*, *6*, 321–342.

Heatherington, L., & Lavner, J. A. (2008). Coming to terms with coming out: Review and recommendations for family systems-focused research. *Journal of Family Psychology*, *22*, 329–343.

Hetherington, E. M., & Stanley-Hagen, M. (2002). Parenting in divorced and remarried families. In M. H. Bornstein (Ed.), *Handbook of parenting: Vol. 3. Being and becoming a parent* (pp. 287–315). Mahwah, NJ: Erlbaum.

Hinde, R. A. (1987). *Individuals, relationships and culture: Links between ethology and the social sciences*. Cambridge: Cambridge University Press.

Hinde, R. A. (1997). *Relationships: A dialectical perspective*. Hove, UK: Psychology Press.

Howard, K. S., Lefever, J. E. B., Borkowski, J. G., & Whitman, T. L. (2006). Fathers' influence in the lives of children with adolescent mothers. *Journal of Family Psychology*, *20*, 468–476.

Howe, G. W., Reiss, D., & Yuh, J. (2002). Can prevention trials test theories of etiology? *Development and Psychopathology*, *14*, 673–694.

Jones, D. J., Forehand, R., Rakow, A., Colletti, C. J. M., McKee, L., & Zalot, A. (2008). The specificity of maternal parenting behavior and child adjustment difficulties: A study of inner-city African American families. *Journal of Family Psychology*, *22*, 181–192.

Kelley, H. H., Berscheid, E., Christensen, A., Harvey, J. H., Huston, T. L., Levinger, G., et al. (1983). *Close relationships*. New York: Freeman.

Kenny, D. A., Mohr, C. D., & Levesque, M. J. (2001). A social relations variance partitioning of dyadic behavior. *Psychological Bulletin*, *127*, 128–141.

Kent, D., & Pepler, D. (2003). The aggressive child as agent in coercive family processes. In L. Kuczynski (Ed.), *Handbook of dynamics in parent-child relations* (pp. 131–144). Thousand Oaks, CA: Sage.

Kochanska. G., Aksan, N., Prisco, T. R., & Adams, E. E. (2008). Mother-child and father-child mutually responsive orientation in the first 2 years and children's outcomes at preschool age: Mechanisms of influence. *Child Development*, *79*, 30–44.

Kohen, D. E., Leventhal, T., Dahinten, V. S., & McIntosh, C. N. (2008). Neighborhood disadvantage: Pathways of effects for young children. *Child Development*, *79*, 156–169.

Kuczynski, L. (2003a). Introduction and overview. In L. Kuczynski (Ed.), *Handbook of dynamics in parent-child relations* (pp. ix–xv). Thousand Oaks, CA: Sage.

Kuczynski, L. (2003b). Beyond bidirectionality: Bilateral conceptual frameworks for understanding dynamics in parent-child relations. In L. Kuczynski (Ed.), *Handbook of dynamics in parent-child relations* (pp. 3–24). Thousand Oaks, CA: Sage.

Kuczynski, L., & Daly, K. (2003). Qualitative methods for inductive (theory-generating) research: Psychological and sociological approaches. In L. Kuczynski (Ed.), *Handbook of dynamics in parent-child relations* (pp. 373–392). Thousand Oaks, CA: Sage.

Kuczynski, L., & Parkin, C. M. (2007). Agency and bidirectionality in socialization: Interactions, transactions, and relational dialectics. In J. E. Grusec & P. D. Hastings (Eds.), *Handbook of socialization: Theory and research* (pp. 259–283). New York: Guilford Press.

Lacourse, E., Cote, S., Nagin, D. S., Vitaro, F., Brendgen, M., & Tremblay, R. E. (2002). A longitudinal-experimental approach to testing theories of antisocial behavior development. *Development and Psychopathology, 14*, 909–924.

Laible, D., & Thompson, R. A. (2007). Early socialization: A relationship perspective. In J. E. Grusec & P. D. Hastings (Eds.), *Handbook of socialization: Theory and research* (pp. 181–207). New York: Guilford Press.

Lamb, M. E. (Ed.). (2004). *The role of the father in child development* (4th ed.). New York: Wiley.

Leaper, C. (2002). Parenting girls and boys. In M. H. Bornstein (Ed.), *Handbook of parenting: Vol. 1. Children and parenting* (pp. 189–225). Mahwah, NJ: Erlbaum.

Lee, R. M., Grotevant, H. D., Hellerstedt, W. L., & Gunnar, M. R. (2006). Cultural socialization in families with internationally adopted children. *Journal of Family Psychology, 20*, 571–580.

Lerner, R. M., Rothbaum, F., Boulos, S., & Castellino, D. R. (2002). Developmental systems perspective on parenting. In M. H. Bornstein (Ed.), *Handbook of parenting: Vol. 2. Biology and ecology of parenting* (pp. 315–344). Mahwah, NJ: Erlbaum.

Lim, J., Wood, B. L., & Miller, B. D. (2008). Maternal depression and parenting in relation to child internalizing symptoms and asthma disease activity. *Journal of Family Psychology, 22*, 264–273.

Lindsey, E. W., Colwell, M. J., Frabutt, J. M., Chambers, J. C., & MacKinnon-Lewis, C. (2008). Mother-child dyadic synchrony in European American and African American families during early adolescence. *Merrill-Palmer Quarterly, 54*, 289–315.

Lindsey, E. W., Mize, J., & Pettit, G. S. (1997). Mutuality in parent-child play: Consequences for children's peer competence. *Journal of Social and Personal Relationships, 14*, 523–538.

Lollis, S. (2003). Conceptualizing the influence of the past and the future in parent parent-child relationships. In L. Kuczynski (Ed.), *Handbook of dynamics in parent-child relations* (pp. 67–87). Thousand Oaks, CA: Sage.

MacCallum, F., Golombok, S., & Brinsden, P. (2007). Parenting and child development in families with a child conceived through embryo donation. *Journal of Family Psychology, 21*, 278–287.

Maccoby, E. E. (1998). *The two sexes: Growing up apart, coming together*. Cambridge, MA: Harvard University Press.

Maccoby, E. E. (2000). Parenting and its effects on children: On reading and misreading behavior genetics. *Annual Review of Psychology, 51*, 1–27.

Maccoby, E. E. (2007). Historical overview of socialization research and theory. In J. E. Grusec & P. D. Hastings (Eds.), *Handbook of socialization: Theory and research* (pp. 13–41). New York: Guilford Press.

Manders, W. A., Cook, W. L., Oud, J. H. L., Scholte, R. H., Janssens, J. M. A., & De Bruyn, E. E. J. (2007). Level validity of self-report whole-family measures. *Journal of Family Psychology, 21*, 605–613.

McElwain, N. L., Halberstadt, A. G., & Volling, B. L. (2007). Mother- and father-reported reactions to children's negative emotions: Relations to young children's emotional understanding and friendship quality. *Child Development, 78*, 1407–1425.

Mize, J., & Pettit, G. S. (1997). Mothers' social coaching, mother-child relationship style, and children's peer competence: Is the medium the message? *Child Development, 68,* 312–332.

Moffitt, T. E., & Caspi, A. (2007). Evidence from behavioral genetics for environmental contributions to antisocial conduct. In J. E. Grusec & P. D. Hastings (Eds.), *Handbook of socialization: Theory and research* (pp. 96–123). New York: Guilford Press.

Moore, M. R., & Brooks-Gunn, J. (2002). Adolescent parenthood. In M. H. Bornstein (Ed.), *Handbook of parenting: Vol. 3. Being and becoming a parent* (pp. 173–214). Mahwah, NJ: Erlbaum.

Moreno, A. J., Klute, M. M., & Robinson, J. L. (2008). Relational and individual resources as predictors of empathy in early childhood. *Social Development, 17,* 613–637.

Nelson, D. A., Hart, C. H., Yang, C., Olsen, J. A., & Jin, S. (2006). Aversive parenting in China: Associations with child physical and relational aggression. *Child Development, 77,* 554–574.

Nelson, L. J., Hart, C. H., Wu, B., Yang, C., Roper, S. O., & Jin, S. (2006). Relations between Chinese mothers' parenting practices and social withdrawal in early childhood. *International Journal of Behavioral Development, 30,* 261–271.

O'Connor, T. G. (2002). The "effects" of parenting reconsidered: Findings, challenges, and applications. *Journal of Child Psychology and Psychiatry, 43,* 555–572.

O'Connor, T. G. (2003). Behavioral genetic contributions to understanding dynamic processes in parent-child relationships. In L. Kuczynski (Ed.), *Handbook of dynamics in parent-child relations* (pp. 145–163). Thousand Oaks, CA: Sage.

Overbeek, G., Stattin, H., Vermulst, A., Ha, T., & Engels, R. C. M. E. (2007). Parent-child relationships, partner relationships and emotional adjustment: A birth-to-maturity prospective study. *Developmental Psychology, 43,* 429–437.

Padilla-Walker, L. M. (2008). "My mom makes me so angry!" Adolescent perceptions of mother-child interactions as correlates of adolescent emotions. *Social Development, 17,* 306–325.

Papp, L. M., Cummings, E. M., & Goeke-Morey, M. C. (2005). Parental psychological distress, parent-child relationship qualities, and child adjustment: Direct, mediating, and reciprocal pathways. *Parenting, 5,* 259–283.

Pardini, D. A., Fite, F. J., & Burke, J. D. (2008). Bidirectional associations between parenting practices and conduct problems in boys from childhood to adolescence: The moderating effect of age and African-American ethnicity. *Journal of Abnormal Child Psychology, 36,* 647–662.

Parke, R. D. (2002). Fathers and families. In M. H. Bornstein (Ed.), *Handbook of parenting: Vol. 3. Being and becoming a parent* (pp. 27–73). Mahwah, NJ: Erlbaum.

Parke, R. D., & Buriel, R. (2006). Socialization in the family: Ethnic and ecological perspectives. In W. Damon & R. M. Lerner (Series Eds.) & N. Eisenberg (Vol. Ed.), *Handbook of child psychology: Vol. 3. Social, emotional, and personality development* (6th ed., pp. 429–504). Hoboken, NJ: Wiley.

Patterson, C. J., & Hastings, P. D. (2007). Socialization in the context of family diversity. In J. E. Grusec & P. D. Hastings (Eds.), *Handbook of socialization: Theory and research* (pp. 328–351). New York: Guilford Press.

Patterson, G. R., & Fisher, P. A. (2002). Recent developments in our understanding of parenting: Bidirectional effects, causal models, and the search for parsimony. In M. H. Bornstein (Ed.), *Handbook of parenting: Vol. 5. Practical issues in parenting* (pp. 59–88). Mahwah, NJ: Erlbaum.

Pettit, G. S., & Arsiwalla, D. D. (2008). Commentary on special section on "bidirectional parent-child relationships": The continuing evolution of dynamic, transactional models of parenting and youth behavior problems. *Journal of Abnormal Child Psychology, 36,* 711–718.

Pettit, G. S., & Mize, J. (1993). Substance and style: Understanding the ways in which parents teach children about social relationships. In S. Duck (Ed.), *Understanding relationship processes series: Volume 2: Learning about relationships* (pp. 118–151). Newbury Park, CA: Sage.

Plomin, R., Asbury, K., & Dunn, J. (2001). Why are children in the same family so different? Nonshared environment a decade later. *Canadian Journal of Psychiatry, 46,* 225–233.

Plomin, R., DeFries, J. C., McClearn, G. E., & McGuffin, P. (2008). *Behavioral genetics* (5th ed.). London: Worth.

Reis, H. G. T., Collins, W. A., & Berscheid, E. (2000). The relationship context of human behavior and development. *Psychological Bulletin, 126,* 844–872.

Rothbaum, F., & Trommsdorff, G. (2007). Do roots and wings complement or oppose one another? The socialization of relatedness and autonomy in cultural context. In J. E. Grusec & P. D. Hastings (Eds.), *Handbook of socialization: Theory and research* (pp. 461–489). New York: Guilford Press.

Rubin, K. H., & Chung, O. B. (Eds.). (2006). *Parenting beliefs, behaviors, and parent-child relations: A cross-cultural perspective.* New York: Psychology Press.

Russell, A., Pettit, G. S., & Mize, J. (1998). Horizontal qualities in parent-child relationships: Parallels with and possible consequences for children's peer relationships. *Developmental Review, 18,* 313–352.

Russell, A., & Saebel, J. (1997) Mother-son, mother-daughter, father-son, and father-daughter: Are they distinct relationships? *Developmental Review, 17,* 111–147.

Ryan, R. M., Martin, A., & Brooks-Gunn, J. (2006). Is one good parent good enough? Patterns of mother and father parenting and child cognitive outcomes at 24 and 36 months. *Parenting, 6,* 211–228.

Saarni, C., Campos, J. J., Camras, L. A., & Witherington, D. (2006). Emotional development: Action, communication, and understanding. In W. Damon & R. M. Lerner (Series Eds.) & N. Eisenberg (Vol. Ed.), *Handbook of child psychology: Vol. 3. Social, emotional, and personality development* (6th ed., pp. 226–299). Hoboken, NJ: Wiley.

Sameroff, A. (1975). Transactional models in early social relations. *Human Development, 18,* 65–79.

Sanson, A., Hemphill, S. A., & Smart, D. (2004). Connections between temperament and social development: A review. *Social Development, 13,* 142–170.

Scarr, S., & McCartney, K. (1983). How people make their own environments: A theory of genotype-environment effects. *Child Development, 54,* 424–435.

Skuban, E. M., Shaw, D. S., Gardner, F., Supplee, L. H., & Nichols, S. R. (2006). The correlates of dyadic synchrony in high-risk, low-income toddler boys. *Infant Behavior & Development, 29,* 423–434.

Stright, A. D., Gallagher, K. C., & Kelly, K. (2008). Infant temperament moderates relations between maternal parenting in early childhood and children's adjustment in first grade. *Child Development, 79,* 186–200.

Summers, J. A., Boller, K., Schiffman, R. F., & Raikes, H. H. (2006). The meaning of "good fatherhood": Low-income fathers' social constructions of their roles. *Parenting, 6,* 145–165.

Trommsdorff, G. (2006). Parent-child relations across the life-span: A cross-cultural perspective. In K. H. Rubin & O. B. Chung (Eds.), *Parenting beliefs, behaviors, and parent-child relations: A cross-cultural perspective* (pp. 143–183). New York: Psychology Press.

Trommsdorff, G., & Nauck, B. (2006). Demographic changes and parent-child relationships. *Parenting, 6,* 343–360.

Vogel, C. A., Bradley, R. H., Raikes, H. H., Boller, K., & Shears, J. K. (2006). Relation between father connectedness and child outcomes. *Parenting, 6,* 189–209.

Wadsworth, M. E., & Santiago, C. D. (2008). Risk and resiliency processes in ethnically diverse families in poverty. *Journal of Family Psychology, 22,* 399–410.

Weinraub, M., Horvath, D. L., & Gringlas, M. B. (2002). Single parenthood. In M. H. Bornstein (Ed.), *Handbook of parenting: Vol. 3. Being and becoming a parent* (pp. 109–140). Mahwah, NJ: Erlbaum.

CHAPTER NINETEEN

Sibling Relations in Early and Middle Childhood

Nina Howe, Hildy S. Ross, and Holly Recchia

Sibling relationships are among the most enduring connections that individuals experience over their lifetimes. Given that approximately 80% of Western children have brothers and sisters, it is clearly a significant relationship for young children. Yet, in the large theoretical and empirical literature on family relationships, siblings are frequently overlooked when explaining family dynamics. However, as we argue in this chapter, siblings play a critical role in family dynamics and are important developmental influences on one another. Earlier work (1950–1970s) on sibling relations typically focused on structural variables (e.g., gender, age, and birth order), whereas more recent work has investigated the role of process in explaining developmental influences. This shift is evident in the kinds of questions posed, for example investigating the roles of different types of sibling interactions in the development of social understanding. This chapter focuses on sibling relations in early and middle childhood, but it is apparent that children are acutely aware of their younger sibling's presence from the time of their arrival in the family, and early patterns of interaction influence later development (see Dunn, 2002; Dunn & Kendrick, 1982).

Sibling Relationships as a Context for Development

Relationships theory posits that children's development occurs in the context of intimate and close relationships such as with parents and siblings (Carpendale & Lewis, 2006;

The Wiley-Blackwell Handbook of Childhood Social Development, Second Edition, edited by Peter K. Smith and Craig H. Hart
© 2011 by Blackwell Publishing Ltd.

Dunn, 2002). In particular, research on the development of social understanding describes how children construct knowledge about their social worlds, namely, other's perspectives, feelings, thoughts, beliefs, and goals, and how this knowledge is linked to the behavior of individuals. Carpendale and Lewis argued that children develop this understanding in the context of close relationships and sometimes show precocious social knowledge in their daily interpersonal interactions (e.g., teasing, play, conversations, and internal state language) before demonstrating it on more formal assessments such as theory-of-mind measures (de Rosnay & Hughes, 2006). Some contexts, such as play and conflict, are conducive to promoting the use of internal state language, although wide individual differences have been noted (Howe, Rinaldi, Jennings, & Petrakos, 2002).

Hinde (1979) argued that relationships are defined by two main types of interactions. First, complementary or hierarchical interactions are characterized by unequal distributions of power and knowledge (i.e., parent–child relationships), which are also evident in teacher–learner, leader–follower, and caretaking exchanges. Second, reciprocal or mutually returned, equal interactions, typical of peer relations, are seen in play and conflict. Sibling interactions are defined by a unique combination of both complementary and reciprocal exchanges. Age, birth order, and knowledge differences between siblings are apparent in their complementary exchanges, yet siblings also engage in reciprocal interactions. Dunn (1983) argued that the long and shared history of reciprocity creates critical opportunities to promote social understanding, because as siblings co-construct shared meanings during mutual and returned exchanges an understanding of the other's perspective may be required. In fact, Dunn labeled reciprocal interactions as the "building blocks" of relationships, given the opportunities they afford for understanding the self and others. Nevertheless, the importance of complementary interactions in children's development should also be acknowledged, while keeping in mind that many exchanges contain elements of both types of interactions (Howe & Recchia, 2005).

Four major characteristics of the sibling relationship have been identified in early and middle childhood (Howe & Recchia, 2008). First, sibling relations are defined by strong positive, negative, and sometimes ambivalent affect, making it hard to overlook or ignore one's sibling. Unlike friendships, which are voluntary and will cease if children do not get along, siblings are siblings for life, and from the early years they must learn to live together and share both social and nonsocial resources (Laursen, Hartup, & Koplas, 1996). Increasingly, the psychological literature has regarded conflict as a normative feature of the sibling relationship. Second, particularly in early childhood, siblings spend a great deal of time together and come to know each other very well, thus potentially establishing an intimate bond. Constructing a common history translates into opportunities for engaging in play (particularly pretense), for emotional and instrumental support, and for disagreements. Third, there are wide individual differences in sibling relationship quality, which are in turn linked to the kinds of interactions observed between children. Moreover, age differences between siblings result in an asymmetry of power, which has implications for the dynamics of both cooperation and conflict. Finally, nonshared environmental effects on siblings' development are evident, and various processes lead to differences between siblings in the same family (Dunn & Plomin, 1990), including issues related to differential parental treatment.

There is fairly strong continuity in the quality of the sibling relationship from early to middle childhood and beyond (Volling, 2003), especially for the older sibling's feelings and behavior directed to the younger child (Dunn, Slomkowski, & Beardsall, 1994; Howe, Fiorentino, & Gariépy, 2003; McGuire, McHale, & Updegraff, 1996). Individual differences in aggression and positive behavior are quite stable, particularly for older siblings (Martin & Ross, 1995; Volling, 2003). By middle childhood, children can reliably rate the degree of warmth and hostility in their sibling relationship, and researchers have used these reports to identify four types of relationships: hostile (high conflict and low warmth) are the most negative, compared to affectively intense (high-warmth and high-conflict), harmonious (high-warmth and low-conflict), and uninvolved (low-warmth and low-conflict) relationships (McGuire et al., 1996). According to maternal and teacher reports in a Mexican American sample, a lack of warmth between preschool-aged siblings (but not conflict) predicted long-term maladjustment (Modry-Mandell, Gamble, & Taylor, 2007). In sum, large individual differences in relationship quality may have an impact on the nature and types of interactions between siblings.

The contexts that may be important in facilitating children's social development are now discussed with a view to considering how context is associated with individual differences in social understanding and relationship quality. Although there has been an emphasis on the negative aspects of sibling relations such as conflict, positive features of these relationships are also relevant to children's socioemotional and cognitive development. We now address three important contexts: teaching, play, and conflict.

Sibling teaching: a case of complementary interactions

The inherent imbalance of power, knowledge, and relative ability between siblings may be a key factor in facilitating social understanding. Consider the case of sibling teaching. The primary goal of teaching is to transfer information and knowledge from an informed to a less informed individual, which may be a tricky process for young children given that they need to both focus on instructional strategies and manage the situation. Rogoff's (1998) notion of guided participation provides a conceptual framework for understanding the dynamics of teaching. She argued that teaching is a bidirectional process, and emphasized the role of both children as the teacher builds bridges between the known and unknown information, supports and structures the learner's attempts to complete a task, and gives the learner responsibility for problem solving. This approach to teaching must depend on shared knowledge about teaching and learning roles and understanding each other's skills, as well perhaps on the quality of the siblings' relationship.

Most studies have employed seminaturalistic experimental paradigms in which one child (usually the older sibling) is taught a task (e.g., a categorization game, or how to construct a toy) and subsequently teaches the younger sibling. Large individual and developmental differences in teaching strategies (verbal instruction, physical demonstrations, control, and degree of learner involvement) are evident (Howe, Brody, & Recchia, 2006; Poris & Volling, 2001). School-aged teachers are more likely than younger teachers to employ detailed verbal instruction and scaffolding (i.e., hints and explanations), and to structure the task; these behaviors are associated with learner-centered strategies such as encouraging learner participation and allowing the learner to correct errors (Howe et al.,

2006; Poris & Volling, 2001; Recchia, Howe, & Alexander, 2009). In contrast, preschool teachers are more likely to demonstrate during teaching. Further, Recchia et al. reported that older firstborn teachers focused less on controlling the teaching process than younger firstborn teachers.

Age differences between siblings are also important. Teachers used more frequent and varied teaching strategies during a categorization game when the age gap between siblings was larger rather than smaller (Perez-Granados & Callanan, 1997), but Howe and Recchia (2008) reported more varied teaching strategies and negative feedback during a construction teaching task when the siblings' age gap was smaller. The learner's age was also important, namely, older school-aged (versus preschool-aged) learners asked more questions, perhaps because they had stronger cognitive skills and wanted to be active participants. However, in dyads with a larger age gap between siblings, learners asked fewer questions but responded positively to the instruction. Further, during a puzzle task of increasing difficulty, older school-aged teachers were more likely to employ scaffolding techniques, especially when the learner was quite young (Howe et al., 2006), indicating that teachers were skilled in adjusting their techniques according to task difficulty and the learner's developmental level. The ability to understand the other's perspective as well as knowledge of the learner's skills are likely to guide the adjustments that teachers make to ensure learners understand the task (Ziv & Frye, 2004).

In contrast to most studies in which the teaching role is assigned to the older sibling, Howe and Recchia (2005, 2009) and Recchia et al. (2009) switched roles and made the younger sibling the teacher. Thus, the natural balance of power between the siblings was reversed. Indeed, Recchia et al. found that secondborn teachers used more learner-centered strategies than firstborn teachers. They were more likely to involve the older learner in the task and to allow the learner to correct his or her own errors. However, birth order moderated age effects on children's teaching strategies. For example, with age, firstborn children increasingly involved the learner in the task and focused less on exerting strict control over the process. Despite being more involved in the task, the learner did not make more mistakes. In contrast, although older secondborns minimized the number of errors made by the learner, they did so by limiting their sibling's involvement in the task. These findings suggest that firstborn children's teaching strategies particularly benefited from the knowledge and experience gained with age. Thus, differential role experiences (teacher versus learner) and comfort with these roles, as well as age, appear to have an impact on the nature of sibling teaching. Clearly, secondborns can teach and may have co-constructed a shared understanding regarding teaching and learning roles and successful strategies. Yet, in dyads where a novice secondborn assumed the teaching role, exchanges reflected more collaborative or learner-centered interactions, in comparison with the teaching environment created by an expert older sibling teacher.

Findings regarding gender differences in sibling teaching are inconsistent; some authors reported no differences in brothers' and sisters' teaching (e.g., Recchia et al., 2009), whereas others did (Cicirelli, 1972). In early childhood, older boys (compared to older sisters) employed more highlighting techniques (pointing out key features) with younger brothers than with younger sisters (Klein, Feldman, & Zarur, 2002). In middle childhood, sisters engaged in more guidance and teaching than brothers (Poris & Volling, 2001), especially with younger sisters who were more active participants in learning than younger brothers (Stoneman, Brody, & MacKinnon, 1986).

Despite this recent research, there are a number of unanswered questions about the processes of sibling teaching. We know little about the frequency and skill of firstborn (or secondborn) teachers during naturalistic sibling exchanges at home and whether children learn procedural (e.g., how to build a construction toy) and/or conceptual (e.g., days of the week) knowledge from their siblings. Little is also known about the social-cognitive skills of more successful versus less successful sibling teachers and learners. Finally, beyond a very small longitudinal study suggesting that the friendly quality of earlier sibling relations predicted later teaching (Howe & Recchia, 2009), there is a lack of information about longitudinal predictors of teaching, although there is recent evidence that teaching is concurrently associated with relationship quality (Howe & Recchia, 2005). Finally, preliminary evidence suggests that culture may influence the form and content of sibling teaching; Maynard (2004) documented the skills of Mayan children during middle childhood while they taught younger siblings. Play was a key context for older children to teach younger ones about domestic tasks (e.g., making tortillas). Over time these teachers developed quite sophisticated strategies that incorporated observation, scaffolding, contextualized conversation, and physical closeness between teacher and learner, but they appeared to depend less on verbal instruction than might be apparent in Western cultures or the context of formal schooling.

Reciprocal features of sibling relations: play and prosocial behavior

Friendly sibling relationships in early childhood are associated with adaptive functioning in the later years (Volling, 2003). Play, specifically pretend play, is an important context for facilitating friendly interactions and promoting social understanding (Howe, Petrakos, & Rinaldi, 1998). Siblings growing up together in the same family develop intimate and shared knowledge of one another that may facilitate engagement in social pretense. Positive associations between the frequency of pretense and both observational and formal social cognitive measures have been documented (e.g., Hughes & Dunn, 1998). This literature provides evidence to suggest that pretend play is linked to children's social understanding.

To illustrate this point, we describe three of our studies that illuminate the processes of sibling pretense and associations with social understanding. Sibling dyads were given a wooden farm set (two barns, silo, fences, animals, people, and trees) to construct and play with as they wished. Children who frequently engaged in pretense also used sophisticated negotiation strategies designed to create joint understanding about the play scenario such as assigning roles, transforming objects, storytelling, scaffolding ideas such as "Let's pretend ...", and employing internal state language (Howe et al., 1998). In contrast, the dyads who engaged in little pretend play were more interested in the physical setup (constructing the barns) and props (arranging the animals and people) and employed less internal state language. These findings corroborate observations of children during ongoing home interactions (e.g., Dunn & Dale, 1984; Hughes & Dunn, 1998; Youngblade & Dunn, 1995). Moreover, children who engaged in sophisticated pretense negotiations argued more about the plans for their scenarios and used more internal state language during their conflicts compared to dyads who were less engaged in pretense

(Howe et al., 2002). Finally, a detailed investigation of how siblings co-construct shared meanings in play (Howe, Petrakos, Rinaldi, & LeFebvre, 2005) revealed that older siblings in frequent pretend dyads were adept at creating sophisticated scaffolds for their younger siblings to draw them into and sustain collaborative play. Younger siblings were also active in this process, but were likely to employ paralinguistic devices (e.g., play voices, and sounds) and simpler strategies such as imitating and calling for the attention of the older sibling. The strategies of both siblings were associated with more pretense and talk about internal states. In contrast, dyads who did not engage in frequent pretense were more controlling and agonistic. Overall, these findings suggest that children who understand others' internal states are effective play partners because they have knowledge regarding their partner's thoughts, emotions, and concepts about the social world, and they may like one another. These factors are all considered to be critical in creating a context conducive for joint pretend play.

Other prosocial aspects of the sibling relationship have also been investigated. In early childhood, older siblings, in particular sisters, initiate the majority of prosocial interactions at home, whereas younger siblings are more likely to imitate and respond positively to the older's initiations, and also engage in more teasing behavior (Dunn & Munn, 1985, 1986b; Pepler, Abramovich, & Corter, 1981). Over time, younger siblings become more active in initiating prosocial interactions, indicating that the exchanges are becoming increasingly reciprocal. Although teasing has a negative connotation, it also demonstrates playfulness and knowledge about what will irritate one's sibling and requires an understanding of the other's point of view.

A warm and friendly sibling relationship is linked to a variety of prosocial behaviors in both early and middle childhood, namely cooperation, sharing, and helping (Dunn & Munn, 1986b); emotional support, intimacy, and nurturance (Howe & Rinaldi, 2004); and understanding other's emotional and mental states (Howe, 1991; Youngblade & Dunn, 1995). Prosocial behaviors provide evidence of children's social and emotional understanding, moral sensibilities, and understanding of their sibling's abilities and points of view (Dunn, 2002). In support of this argument, Karos, Howe, and Aquan-Assee (2007) examined associations between grade 5–6 children's self-reports of daily reciprocal and complementary interactions, relationship quality, and socioemotional problem solving. Reciprocal interactions (e.g., play and companionship) were positively associated with problem-solving skills and a warm, happy relationship. Thus, sibling warmth may be a key factor associated with social cognitive understanding (Modry-Mandell et al., 2007), although studies addressing issues of causality remain to be conducted. In conclusion, these reciprocal, prosocial, and warm interactions may set the stage for children's later adaptive functioning, and as Dunn (1983) argued, they may be the "building blocks" of relationships.

Blending reciprocal and complementary interaction: sibling conflict

There is widespread agreement that conflict is a normal part of siblings' interaction. Indeed, sibling conflicts, in the early years, occur approximately eight times an hour. Although sibling conflicts can often be very brief skirmishes over the possession of a toy or attempts to control objectionable actions, physical and verbal aggression are also often present and sometimes quite severe. Older siblings are more often the initiators of conflict, as well as the winners when conflicts are resolved. They are at a decided advantage, especially when it comes to aggression. Depending upon the age difference between brothers and sisters, the typically greater strength of elder siblings allows them to hurt more than they are hurt. Perhaps for this reason older siblings are more likely to initiate aggressive actions against their younger counterparts, who in turn are less likely to respond with force to the elder's forcefulness (Dunn & Munn, 1986a; Martin & Ross, 1995; Perlman & Ross, 2005).

There are two viewpoints concerning the motivational underpinnings of sibling fights. Psychoanalytic theory holds strongly to the concept of siblings as rivals – specifically, that siblings fight because they are competitors for the love and attention of parents (Adler, 1924; Dreikurs, 1964). From this perspective, parents are advised to stay out of their children's conflicts because their intervention provides the children with the attention they seek by fighting with one another. Children's rivalry is apparent from the first days of sibling relationships. Toddlers and preschoolers are very sensitive to the loss of maternal attention when a new baby arrives, and are often more confrontational, clingy, or deliberately naughty (Dunn & Kendrick, 1982). Although somewhat older siblings explicitly deny that rivalry motivates their conflicts (Prochanska & Prochanska, 1985), there are several lines of contemporary evidence that highlight the importance of parental favoritism. Parental differential treatment, especially if it is not well understood by the children, increases fighting and worsens the quality of their relationship (Kowal & Kramer, 1997). Consistent with these effects, siblings are fairly quick to report to parents on the transgressions of their brothers and sisters. Even children as young as 2 ½ tattle on their older siblings; by 4 years, tattling occurs as often in situations where the sibling's behavior has no direct negative consequences for the tattler (e.g., "He's chewing with his mouth open" or "She spilled her milk again") (Ross & Den Bak-Lammers, 1998). Tattling in such circumstances suggests that children wish only to keep parents informed about the wrongdoings of a wayward sibling, casting themselves as more righteous by comparison. Additionally, toddler and preschool-aged children reacted with apparent jealousy (i.e., distress and sadness) when parents directed attention exclusively to their brothers and sisters during the experimental situation, but importantly, reactions of anger or negative behavior were negligible (Miller, Volling, & McElwain, 2000). Jealousy was convincingly evoked, but the relation of jealousy to sibling aggression and conflict remains to be demonstrated.

An alternative, less psychodynamic view is that sibling conflicts are realistic – that brothers and sisters, who must share space and property and spend a great deal of time interacting with one another, naturally disagree because their goals and desires are not always compatible. One basis for this judgment is the concrete issues that divide young siblings – the possession or ownership of property is consistently the most common issue in sibling quarrels. Moreover, conflict as well as more positive interactions provide opportunities for children to learn to appreciate others' perspectives and to resolve differences. Although parents are still often urged to stay out of sibling conflicts so that children can learn to resolve their own differences (Brody & Stoneman, 1987), parents' intervention can also contribute to children's conflict management and resolution (Smith & Ross,

2007). However, what children can potentially learn from conflict depends on what they do in conflict.

Although only a minority of sibling conflicts involve forceful, hostile, or aggressive behaviors (Dunn & Munn, 1986a; Martin & Ross, 1995), children do sometimes fight aggressively; severe sibling aggression is associated with children's problematic behavior more generally. Children who frequently use aggression with their siblings also tend to have longer and more frequent fights and to resolve issues through adversarial opposition (Dunn & Munn, 1986a; Howe et al., 2002). Additionally, preschoolers who are frequently negative at home (e.g., arguing, complaining, teasing, provoking, being physically negative, yelling, etc., at a high rate) are particularly likely to initiate unprovoked coercive conflict episodes when their younger siblings behaved either positively or neutrally (Loeber & Tengs, 1986). Not only were their sibling conflicts more frequent, but also in families with an aggressive child, disputes were nearly twice as long. Similar differences were not found for mother–child interaction, suggesting that younger siblings were particularly targeted by children high in negative behavior. Thus, the sibling relationship provides some children with considerable experience in negative and aggressive interaction, and there is evidence that younger siblings, in particular, learn from this kind of experience. Longitudinal observations of 2- and 4-year-old siblings suggest that the aggressiveness of the older children is stable over a 2-year period, but not so the aggression shown by the younger children. Rather, younger siblings' aggression is positively associated with the earlier aggression they received from older brothers and sisters (Martin & Ross, 1995; Perlman, Garfinkel, & Turrel, 2007; see also Dunn & Munn, 1986a, for associations between older and younger siblings' hitting over a 6-month period).

On the more positive side, sibling conflict is also the occasion for the articulation and enforcement of rules, routines, and expectations that are central to harmonious family interaction (Dunn & Munn, 1985; Ross, Filyer, Lollis, Perlman, & Martin, 1994). This is because conflict often entails the violation of such rules, and, in resolving conflict issues, children invoke and justify their actions in relation to principles that will secure their fair and just treatment within the family (Dunn & Munn, 1987). Indeed, family rules may be developed in the context of repeated arguments about the breach of social and moral standards. Children who tattle on their siblings bring one another's rule violations to the attention of their parents (Ross & Den Bak-Lammers, 1998), and siblings become more important and mothers less important sources of social rules when younger siblings are preschoolers (Piotrowski, 1997). Moreover, although mother–child discussions focused primarily on conventional matters, such as tidiness and appropriate activities, children were equally likely to discuss conventional and moral rules, and particularly property rights and sharing, with one another. The children's own articulation of social and moral rules, both in conflicts with their siblings and in reports of violations, suggests that children participate in the enforcement of family rules and standards. Nowhere is that more apparent than in the violation and enforcement of property rights.

Property is the single most frequent, contentious, and long-lasting issue in sibling disputes (Dunn & Munn, 1985; Prochanska & Prochanska, 1985; Ross, 1996; Ross et al., 1994; Smith & Ross, 2007). Siblings fight over possessions long after such issues have been settled in their other relationships. Importantly, however, they tend to settle their disputes in line with well-established principles of property entitlement, assigning priority to owners and secondary rights to possessors of property (Ross, 1996). Moreover, children argue appropriately to support their rights in either case; even 2 ½- year-olds claim objects as "mine" more often as owners than as possessors. Parents, however, are far less consistent in the principles they endorse in their interventions into their children's disputes. They are as likely to favor possessors as owners, argue almost equivalently for either principle, and typically tell their children to share or to find another plaything. Apparently children are adopting rules of entitlement that are not commonly supported by what their parents say when property rights are breached. The children themselves seem to arrive at principled resolutions to their disputes that come from their own interactions, rather than from the teachings of their parents. Does this mean that parents should just stay out of their children's disputes?

The potential social benefits for children of learning to settle their own disputes are considerable (Dunn & Munn, 1985). In conflict, children express and defend their own positions and are exposed to perspectives that differ from their own. As a result, they learn how their own behavior affects antagonists and how to negotiate receptively with one another and to resolve or reconcile their differences through mutual concessions and compromise (Brody, Stoneman, McCoy, & Forehand, 1992; Herrera & Dunn, 1997; Howe et al., 2002). Compromises are desirable outcomes because both parties can achieve at least some of what they wanted at the outset of conflict; however, most sibling conflicts (indeed, most conflicts between any family members) are conducted with considerably more self-centered argumentation, emotional intensity, and hostility, and end without the resolution of issues of contention (Howe et al., 2002; Siddiqui & Ross, 1999; Tesla & Dunn, 1992; Vuchinich, 1987). The most common type of ending to sibling conflicts is stand-off (no resolution), followed by adversarial negotiations resulting in submission of one of the parties, and then compromise (Howe et al., 2002, 2003; Siddiqui & Ross, 1999). Observations of siblings (aged 2–7) consistently indicate that fewer than 12% of their disputes end in compromise (Howe et al., 2002; Siddiqui & Ross, 1999). Although reasoning increases over the age span, compromise does not, and reasoning is used increasingly to support one's own position rather than to give consideration to the other child's perspective (Perlman & Ross, 1997; Tesla & Dunn, 1992).

Perhaps sibling fights are not the most productive context in which to learn to manage conflicts. On the other hand, the lack of developmental progression in children's likelihood of compromising with others gives us pause; the issue may not be the ability to compromise but the motivation to do so in the heat of battle. Because individuals view conflicts from differing perspectives, it is often hard for them to understand their opponents' motivation and to appreciate the harmful impact of their own actions (Wilson, Smith, & Ross, 2003). Combatants typically presume that their own goals and actions are just, and may be more invested in fighting for what they believe they deserve than in resolving matters with their siblings. In short, conflict is often associated with a mind-set more conducive to destructive aims than to compromise.

Additionally, evidence suggests that young siblings are able to negotiate productively and to reach more positive resolutions if removed from the immediate context of ongoing conflict and they are asked to discuss and resolve their differences at a later point in time (Recchia & Howe, in press; Ross, Ross, Stein, & Trabasso, 2006). Siblings (between 3

½ and 12 years) are able to resolve issues of repeated conflicts in a majority of cases, with compromises occurring in 42–55% of conflict negotiations and agreeable win–loss outcomes 18–23% of the time (Recchia & Howe, 2009; Ross et al., 2006). Compromises are associated with negotiation strategies that include less opposition and more mutual planning concerning future behavior, so as to prevent or resolve the conflict issue. When older siblings like their younger counterparts, when siblings accept blame for their fights or describe feeling sad during conflict, or when fights include physical aggression, the likelihood of compromise is increased (Recchia & Howe, in press; Ross et al., 2006). Whereas compromise was not achieved in every negotiation, removing children from the immediate context of an ongoing fight makes it far more likely. Perhaps such experiences can actually teach children the conflict management skills that may motivate less contentious and more conciliatory resolutions of future disputes with siblings and others.

There are also good reasons that conflict would be a particularly potent source for learning to understand others. In conflict, children are confronted daily with what other people want, with their anger and sadness, and with beliefs that diverge from their own. In this way, others' internal states are made explicit. Moreover, the experience of having a sibling, perhaps particularly an older one, advances children's understanding of false beliefs – the understanding that other people have beliefs that differ from one's own (Carpendale & Lewis, 2006). However, to date, there is not strong evidence that conflict with siblings in itself advances children's social understanding. The frequency or intensity of conflict and children's internal state language, emotional understanding, or theory of mind are not related, either contemporaneously or across time. Rather, children who show greater social sensitivity to others in conflict also do so in other contexts. For example, children who use internal state talk in conflict also do so in other contexts such as pretense (Howe et al., 2002). Children who reason within sibling conflicts likewise display an understanding of others' emotional states. Thus, it may not be conflict per se, but rather the ability and experience of considering the perspectives of others within conflict, that promotes social understanding. Experimental evidence supports this view.

In several studies, parents were trained to mediate their children's disputes, with the results indicating that children more often discussed emotions and one another's perspectives, in comparison to children whose parents intervened as usual in their fights with siblings (Siddiqui & Ross, 2004; Smith & Ross, 2007). The changes in children's behavior during mediated conflicts had an impact on their social understanding. Siblings who had experience with parent mediation were better attuned to their siblings' perspectives on their disputes when interviewed about past conflicts than children who did not. Their independent accounts of what each of them wanted or felt more often agreed, and they better understood the motivational basis for one another's internal states. Moreover, children with mediation experience also advanced their own more abstract knowledge of the role of interpretation in conflict. They understood that antagonists would have divergent views of fault and blame, and that these differences related to their differing perspectives on their conflicts. Thus, the quality of children's conflict and conflict resolution needs to be considered in assessing what they know and learn about others in their disputes.

Siblings and Peers

There are at least two compelling but opposing explanations for expecting links between children's sibling and peer relationships. First, it is argued that if one key relationship does not meet children's needs, they may turn to other relationships as a means of compensating for this deficiency (Stocker, 1994). Thus, for example, hostile sibling relationships should be associated with positive peer relationships. Alternatively, various prominent developmental theories (e.g., social learning and attachment) suggest that children's interactions with familiar others will influence their patterns of behavior, social skills, and models of relationships. In turn, this development will be generalized to other types of relationships. This perspective suggests correspondence between the quality of children's sibling and peer interactions. Personality theorists would also suggest consistency in children's behavior across contexts, although it may be due to stable temperamental characteristics.

We have argued that sibling relationships provide opportunities for social and cognitive development. Thus, children without siblings should be at a disadvantage during peer interactions, as they are likely to have less experience interacting with other children. Consistent with this view, kindergarten-aged children with one or two siblings were rated by teachers as having better social skills with peers than children with no siblings (Downey & Condron, 2004). However, these advantages disappeared when children had more than three siblings, suggesting that the benefits of having siblings decline as family size increases. Further, this sibling effect does not extend to contexts in which one-child families are normative. Earlier research in China suggested associations between having siblings and positive peer relationships (Jiao, Ji, & Jing, 1986); however, since the institution of the one-child-per-family policy, these sibling advantages are no longer evident (Chen, Rubin, & Li, 1994).

Some studies find few associations between observations of sibling and peer interactions (Dunn, Slomkowski, Donelan, & Herrera, 1995; McElwain & Volling, 2005). However, others have provided support for compensation and/or correspondence between relationships, both concurrently and over time. A small body of work suggests that friendships may indeed compensate for low-quality sibling relationships. Observed competition and control between siblings have been linked to maternal reports of positive friendships in middle childhood (Stocker & Dunn, 1990), and relationship quality with same-sex siblings is inversely related to relationship quality with friends (Mendelson, Aboud, & Lanthier, 1994). Sibling relationships may also compensate for peer difficulties: Peer-reported social isolation is related to warm sibling relationships, and in fact, children who are isolated fare better when sibling relationship quality is high (East & Rook, 1992). Further, 5-year-olds' self-reports of negative relationships with friends are related to observed cooperation with their siblings at age 6 (Volling, Youngblade, & Belsky, 1997). Thus, some compensatory patterns are evident, though many studies also report other effects indicating correspondence between relationships, implying a relatively complex pattern of findings. For example, Lockwood, Kitzmann, and Cohen (2001) found that sibling conflict was associated with less peer-reported victimization and passive withdrawal, but more peer rejection. Thus, more research is needed to determine exactly which connections between peers and siblings will reflect compensatory patterns of association.

Supporting evidence for the correspondence between peer and sibling interactions indicates that sibling relationships high in warmth and closeness are related to peer reports of positive interactions and popularity with peers (Lockwood et al., 2001; Mendelson et al., 1994; Modry-Mandell et al., 2007), as well as self-rated relationship quality with friends (van Aken & Asendorpf, 1997). Further, less destructive sibling conflict is related to positive strategies in younger siblings' arguments with a close friend (Herrera & Dunn, 1997), more reciprocated friendships in the classroom (Lindsey, Colwell, Frabutt, & MacKinnon-Lewis, 2006) as well as less aggression with peers, but only when combined with rejecting parenting (Garcia, Shaw, Winslow, & Yaggi, 2000). In fact, other research suggests that older siblings' behavior may explain the links between parenting and younger siblings' teacher-rated social competence, especially in the context of positive, noncon-flictual sibling relationships (Brody & Murry, 2001). Further, parent-reported aggression was negatively associated with children's friendship quality – however, this was especially true when sibling relationship quality was low (McElwain & Volling, 2005). Indeed, sibling relationships have been shown to explain connections between temperament, parent–child relationships, and friendship quality (McCoy, Brody, & Stoneman, 1994). In sum, this literature suggests that there are small but unique positive associations between the quality of sibling and peer relationships, and further that sibling interactions may act as both moderators and mediators of connections between behavioral disposi-tions, parent–child relationships, and peer interactions.

It is worth noting that the above studies generally do not imply causal effects of sibling interactions on peer relationships; they simply reveal connections across relationship contexts. In fact, a few studies suggest that interactions with friends and peers may predict children's sibling relationships. Children's positive interactions with their friends before the birth of a sibling were associated with positive sibling relationships in early childhood (Kramer & Gottman, 1992) and even into adolescence (Kramer & Kowal, 2005). Further, after peer conflict mediation training at school, children's sibling relationships at home also improved (Gentry & Benenson, 1992). Thus, to date, there is accumulating evidence that sibling and peer relationships are indeed connected. However, the causal patterns underlying these corresponding and compensatory links between relationship quality, conflict, and social competence across peer and sibling contexts have yet to be unequivocally established. Indeed, the literature cited above reveals associations between sibling relationships and (a) peer relationships in general (e.g., social skills in the class-room) as well as (b) the nature of children's close friendships (e.g., friendship quality). However, whether sibling relationships show divergent or similar patterns of association with these two distinct types of peer relationships has not yet been determined.

Conclusion

Although there has been increased interest in the sibling relationship in recent years, there are many unanswered questions. For example, links between sibling relations and other important individuals in children's lives (e.g., parents or friends) warrant a more detailed examination. We know little about whether the positive outcomes associated with a warm and friendly relationship in the early years endure as children enter adolescence and move into adulthood. Also, little is known about the developmental outcomes associated with poor-quality sibling relationships over time and whether such relationships may eventually take on a more balanced and positive tone.

The sibling literature includes a number of limitations that also suggest avenues for future research. Most studies have been conducted on middle-class, urban, Caucasian, two-child, Canadian, American, and British families, and little is known about other siblings in these societies (e.g., African American, rural, or foster families), other demographic groups (e.g., low income), or siblings in other cultures (e.g., Asia, Europe, the Middle East, and Africa). We know almost nothing about sibling relations in more collectivistic cultures (e.g., Latin America) or in minority ethnic or linguistic groups in the West (e.g., South Asian and Hispanic families in the United States, or French-speaking populations in Canada). In addition, there are few studies examining sibling relationships beyond the dyad (e.g., families with three or more children). For example, one might ask about how a middle child alternates between a teaching and learning role when interacting with either an older or younger sibling. Another limitation is that in many studies, the variables of age gap between children and birth order are confounded with the siblings' chronological age, making it difficult to parse out the relative effects of each factor on the types and quality of sibling exchanges. Finally, the sibling relationships of children with a physical or intellectual disability have mainly been studied via parent or child reports (Orfus & Howe, 2008), and there is much room for observational research of these families.

In conclusion, it is apparent that siblings play an important role in one another's development in the early years. This relationship may be a training ground for learning to get along in the world, cooperating and sharing joyous experiences, expressing one's opinions, desires, and feelings, conveying one's knowledge and expertise, and standing up for one's beliefs and actions. In many ways, it is a safe context in which to develop social understanding. As an involuntary relationship, siblings have great leeway in which to learn these skills and test out actions, abilities, and motivations without the threat of losing their relationship (as opposed to friendships, where obnoxious behavior may signal the end of the relationship). In this sense, the sibling relationship is a natural laboratory for learning about the social world.

References

Adler, A. (1924). *The practice and theory of individual psychology.* Oxford: Harcourt, Brace.

Brody, G. H., & Murry, V. M. (2001). Sibling socialization of competence in rural, single-parent African American families. *Journal of Marriage & the Family, 63,* 996–1008.

Brody, G. H., & Stoneman, Z. (1987). Sibling conflict: Contributions of the siblings themselves, the parent-sibling relationship, and the broader family system. *Journal of Children in Contemporary Society, 19,* 39–43.

Brody, G. H., Stoneman, Z., McCoy, J. K., & Forehand, R. (1992). Contemporaneous and longitudinal association of sibling conflict with family relationship assessments and family discussions about sibling problems. *Child Development, 63,* 391–400.

Carpendale, J., & Lewis, C. (2006). *How children develop social understanding.* Malden, MA: Blackwell.

Chen, X., Rubin, K. H., & Li, B. (1994). Only children and sibling children in urban China: A re-examination. *International Journal of Behavioral Development, 17,* 413–421.

Cicirelli, V. O. (1972). The effect of sibling relationship on concept learning of young children taught by child-teachers. *Child Development, 43,* 282–287.

de Rosnay, M., & Hughes, C. (2006). Conversation and theory of mind: Do children talk their way to socio-cognitive understanding? *British Journal of Developmental Psychology, 24,* 7–37.

Downey, D. B., & Condron, D. J. (2004). Playing well with others in kindergarten: The benefit of siblings at home. *Journal of Marriage and Family, 66,* 333–350.

Dreikurs, R. (1964). *Children: The challenge.* New York: Hawthorne.

Dunn, J. (1983). Sibling relationships in early childhood. *Child Development, 54,* 787–811.

Dunn, J. (2002). Sibling relationships. In P. K. Smith & C. H. Hart (Eds.), *Blackwell handbook of childhood social development* (pp. 223–237). Malden, MA: Blackwell.

Dunn, J., & Dale, N. (1984). I a daddy: 2-year-old's collaboration in joint pretend with sibling and with mother. In I. Bretherton (Ed.), *Symbolic play: The development of social understanding* (pp. 131–158). New York: Academic Press.

Dunn, J., & Kendrick, C. (1982). Social behavior of young siblings in the family context: Differences between same-sex and different-sex dyads. *Annual Progress in Child Psychiatry & Child Development,* 166–181.

Dunn, J., & Munn, P. (1985). Becoming a family member: Family conflict and the development of social understanding in the second year. *Child Development, 56,* 480.

Dunn, J., & Munn, P. (1986a). Sibling quarrels and maternal intervention: Individual differences in understanding and aggression. *Journal of Child Psychology and Psychiatry, 27,* 583–595.

Dunn, J., & Munn, P. (1986b). Siblings and the development of prosocial behaviour. *International Journal of Behavioral Development, 9,* 265–284.

Dunn, J., & Munn, P. (1987). The development of justification in disputes with mother and sibling. *Developmental Psychology, 23,* 791–798.

Dunn, J., & Plomin, R. (1990). *Separate lives: Why siblings are so different.* New York: Basic Books.

Dunn, J., Slomkowski, C., & Beardsall, L. (1994). Sibling relationships from the preschool period through middle childhood and early adolescence. *Developmental Psychology, 30,* 315–324.

Dunn, J., Slomkowski, C., Donelan, N., & Herrera, C. (1995). Conflict, understanding, and relationships: Developments and differences in the preschool years. *Early Education and Development, 6,* 303–316.

East, P. L., & Rook, K. S. (1992). Compensatory patterns of support among children's peer relationships: A test using school friends, nonschool friends, and siblings. *Developmental Psychology, 28,* 163–172.

Garcia, M. M., Shaw, D. S., Winslow, E. B., & Yaggi, K. E. (2000). Destructive sibling conflict and the development of conduct problems in young boys. *Developmental Psychology, 36,* 44–53.

Gentry, D. B., & Benenson, W. A. (1992). School-age peer mediators transfer knowledge and skills to home setting. *Mediation Quarterly, 10,* 101–109.

Herrera, C., & Dunn, J. (1997). Early experiences with family conflict: Implications for arguments with a close friend. *Developmental Psychology, 33,* 869–881.

Hinde, R. A. (1979). *Towards understanding relationships*. London: Methuen.

Howe, N. (1991). Sibling-directed internal state language, perspective taking, and affective behavior. *Child Development, 62*, 1503–1512.

Howe, N., Brody, M., & Recchia, H. (2006). Effects of task difficulty on sibling teaching in middle childhood. *Infant & Child Development, 15*, 455–470.

Howe, N., Fiorentino, L. M., & Gariépy, N. (2003). Sibling conflict in middle childhood: Influence of maternal context and mother-sibling interaction over four years. *Merrill-Palmer Quarterly, 49*, 183–208.

Howe, N., Petrakos, H., & Rinaldi, C. M. (1998). "All the sheeps are dead. he murdered them": Sibling pretense, negotiation, internal state language, and relationship quality. *Child Development, 69*, 182–191.

Howe, N., Petrakos, H., Rinaldi, C. M., & LeFebvre, R. (2005). "This is a bad dog, you know …": Constructing shared meanings during sibling pretend play. *Child Development, 76*, 783–794.

Howe, N., & Recchia, H. (2004). Sibling relations and their impact on children's development. In *Encyclopedia on early childhood development*. Retrieved from http://www.enfant-encyclopedie.com/Pages/PDF/Howe-RecchiaANGxp.pdf

Howe, N., & Recchia, H. (2005). Playmates and teachers: Reciprocal and complementary interactions between siblings. *Journal of Family Psychology, 19*, 497–502.

Howe, N., & Recchia, H. (2008). Siblings and sibling rivalry. In M. Haith & J. Benson (Eds.), *Encyclopaedia of infant and early childhood development* (pp. 154–164). Oxford: Elsevier.

Howe, N., & Recchia, H. E. (in press). Individual differences in sibling teaching. *Early Education and Development*.

Howe, N., Rinaldi, C. M., Jennings, M., & Petrakos, H. (2002). "No! The lambs can stay out because they got cozies!": Constructive and destructive sibling conflict, pretend play, and social understanding. *Child Development, 73*, 1460–1473.

Hughes, C., & Dunn, J. (1998). Understanding mind and emotion: Longitudinal associations with mental-state talk between young friends. *Developmental Psychology, 34*, 1026–1037.

Jiao, S., Ji, G., & Jing, Q. (1986). Comparative study of behavioral qualities of only children and sibling children. *Child Development, 57*, 357–361.

Karos, L. K., Howe, N., & Aquan-Assee, J. (2007). Reciprocal and complementary sibling interactions, relationship quality and socio-emotional problem solving. *Infant and Child Development, 16*, 577–596.

Klein, P. S., Feldman, R., & Zarur, S. (2002). Mediation in a sibling context: The relations of older siblings' mediating behaviour and younger siblings' task performance. *Infant & Child Development, 11*, 321–333.

Kowal, A., & Kramer, L. (1997). Children's understanding of parental differential treatment. *Child Development, 68*, 113–126.

Kramer, L., & Gottman, J. M. (1992). Becoming a sibling: "With a little help from my friends." *Developmental Psychology, 28*, 685–699.

Kramer, L., & Kowal, A. K. (2005). Sibling relationship quality from birth to adolescence: The enduring contributions of friends. *Journal of Family Psychology, 19*, 503–511.

Laursen, B., Hartup, W. W., & Koplas, A. L. (1996). Towards understanding peer conflict. *Merrill-Palmer Quarterly, 42*, 76–102.

Lindsey, E. W., Colwell, M. J., Frabutt, J. M., & MacKinnon-Lewis, C. (2006). Family conflict in divorced and non-divorced families: Potential consequences for boys' friendship status and friendship quality. *Journal of Social and Personal Relationships, 23*, 45–63.

Lockwood, R. L., Kitzmann, K. M., & Cohen, R. (2001). The impact of sibling warmth and conflict on children's social competence with peers. *Child Study Journal, 31*, 47–69.

Loeber, R., & Tengs, T. (1986). The analysis of coercive chains between children, mothers, and siblings. *Journal of Family Violence, 1*, 51–70.

Martin, J. L., & Ross, H. S. (1995). The development of aggression within sibling conflict. *Journal of Early Education and Development, 6*, 335–358.

Maynard, A. E. (2004). Cultures of teaching in childhood: Formal schooling and Maya sibling teaching at home. *Cognitive Development, 19*, 517–535.

McCoy, J. K., Brody, G. H., & Stoneman, Z. (1994). A longitudinal analysis of sibling relationships as mediators of the link between family processes and youths' best friendships. *Family Relations, 43*, 400–408.

McElwain, N. L., & Volling, B. L. (2005). Preschool children's interactions with friends and older siblings: Relationship specificity and joint contributions to problem behavior. *Journal of Family Psychology, 19*, 486–496.

McGuire, S., McHale, S. M., & Updegraff, K. (1996). Children's perceptions of the sibling relationship in middle childhood: Connections within and between family relationships. *Personal Relationships, 3*, 229–239.

Mendelson, M. J., Aboud, F. E., & Lanthier, R. P. (1994). Kindergartners' relationships with siblings, peers, and friends. *Merrill-Palmer Quarterly, 40*, 416–435.

Miller, A. L., Volling, B. L., & McElwain, N. L. (2000). Sibling jealousy in a triadic context with mothers and fathers. *Social Development, 9*, 433–457.

Modry-Mandell, K. L., Gamble, W. C., & Taylor, A. R. (2007). Family emotional climate and sibling relationship quality: Influences on behavioral problems and adaptation in preschool-aged children. *Journal of Child and Family Studies, 16*, 61–73.

Orfus, M., & Howe, N. (2008). Stress appraisal and family influence in siblings of children with special needs. *Exceptionality Education Canada, 18*, 166–181.

Pepler, D. J., Abramovitch, R., & Corter, C. (1981). Sibling interaction in the home: A longitudinal study. *Child Development, 52*, 1344–1347.

Perez-Granados, D. R., & Callanan, M. A. (1997). Conversations with mothers and siblings: Young children's semantic and conceptual development. *Developmental Psychology, 33*, 120–134.

Perlman, M., Garfinkel, D. A., & Turrell, S. L. (2007). Parent and sibling influences on the quality of children's conflict behaviours across the preschool period. *Social Development, 16*, 619–641.

Perlman, M., & Ross, H. S. (1997). The benefits of parent intervention in their children's disputes: An examination of concurrent changes in children's fighting styles. *Child Development, 68*, 690–700.

Perlman, M., & Ross, H. S. (2005). If-then contingencies in children's sibling conflicts. *Merrill-Palmer Quarterly, 51*, 42–66.

Piotrowski, C. (1997). Rules of everyday family life: The development of social rules in mother-child and sibling relationships. *International Journal of Behavioral Development, 21*(3), 571–598.

Poris, M. P., & Volling, B. L. (2001, April). Am I my brother's teacher? The individual and family correlates of sibling teaching. Paper presented at the Biennial Meeting of the Society of Research in Child Development, Minneapolis, MN.

Prochanska, J. M., & Prochanska, J. O. (1985). Children's views of the causes and "cures" of sibling rivalry. *Child Welfare Journal, 64*, 427–433.

Recchia, H. E., & Howe, N. (2009). Associations between social understanding, sibling relationship quality, and siblings' conflict strategies and outcomes. *Child Development, 80*, 1564–1578.

Recchia, H. E., & Howe, N. (in press). When do siblings compromise? Associations with children's descriptions of conflict issues, culpability, and emotions. *Social Development.*

372 *Nina Howe et al.*

Recchia, H. E., Howe, N., & Alexander, S. (2009). "You didn't teach me, you showed me": Variations in children's approaches to sibling teaching. *Merrill-Palmer Quarterly, 55,* 55–78.

Rogoff, B. (1998). Cognition as a collaborative process. In W. Damon (Ed.), *Handbook of child psychology* (pp. 670–744). New York: Wiley.

Ross, H. S. (1996). Negotiating principles of entitlement in sibling property disputes. *Developmental Psychology, 32,* 90–101.

Ross, H. S., & Den Bak-Lammers, I. M. (1998). Consistency and change in children's tattling on their siblings: Children's perspectives on the moral rules and procedures of family life. *Social Development, 7,* 275–300.

Ross, H. S., Filyer, R. E., Lollis, S. P., Perlman, M., & Martin, J. L. (1994). Administering justice in the family. *Journal of Family Psychology, 8,* 254–273.

Ross, H., Ross, M., Stein, N., & Trabasso, T. (2006). How siblings resolve their conflicts: The importance of first offers, planning, and limited opposition. *Child Development, 77,* 1730–1745.

Siddiqui, A., & Ross, H. S. (1999). How do sibling conflicts end? *Early Education and Development, 10,* 315–332.

Siddiqui, A., & Ross, H. (2004). Mediation as a method of parent intervention in children's disputes. *Journal of Family Psychology, 18,* 147–159.

Smith, J., & Ross, H. (2007). Training parents to mediate sibling disputes affects children's negotiation and conflict understanding. *Child Development, 78*(3), 790–805.

Stocker, C. M. (1994). Children's perceptions of relationships with siblings, friends, and mothers: Compensatory processes and links with adjustment. *Journal of Child Psychology and Psychiatry, 35,* 1447–1459.

Stocker, C., & Dunn, J. (1990). Sibling relationships in childhood: Links with friendships and peer relationships. *British Journal of Developmental Psychology, 8,* 227–244.

Stoneman, Z., Brody, G. H., & MacKinnon, C. E. (1986). Same-sex and cross-sex siblings: Activity choices, roles, behavior, and gender stereotypes. *Sex Roles, 15,* 495–511.

Tesla, C., & Dunn, J. (1992). Getting along or getting your own way: The development of young children's use of argument in conflicts with mother and sibling. *Social Development, 1,* 107–121.

van Aken, M. A. G., & Asendorpf, J. B. (1997). Support by parents, classmates, friends and siblings in preadolescence: Covariation and compensation across relationships. *Journal of Social and Personal Relationships, 14,* 79–93.

Volling, B. L. (2003). Sibling relationships. In M. H. Bornstein, L. Davidson, C. L. M. Keyes, & K. A. Moore (Eds.), *Well-being: Positive development across the life course* (pp. 205–220). Mahwah, NJ: Erlbaum.

Volling, B. L., Youngblade, L. M., & Belsky, J. (1997). Young children's social relationships with siblings and friends. *American Journal of Orthopsychiatry, 67,* 102–111.

Vuchinich, S. (1987). Starting and stopping spontaneous family conflicts. *Journal of Marriage & Family, 49,* 591–601.

Wilson, A. E., Smith, M. D., & Ross, H. S. (2003). The nature and effects of young children's lies. *Social Development, 12,* 21–45.

Youngblade, L. M., & Dunn, J. (1995). Individual differences in young children's pretend play with mother and sibling: Links to relationships and understanding of other people's feelings and beliefs. *Child Development, 66,* 1472–1492.

Ziv, M., & Frye, D. (2004). Children's understanding of teaching: The role of knowledge and belief. *Cognitive Development, 19,* 457–477.

PART VI

Peer Group

Studies have emphasized the importance of competent peer group functioning and healthy interpersonal relationships. Alternatively, childhood difficulties with peers have been concurrently and longitudinally related to a host of psychosocial challenges.

Peer acceptance and rejection comprise an integral aspect of group functioning in childhood. Research in this area has a rich tradition of empirical inquiry that has illuminated many interpersonal processes that lend themselves to adaptive or maladaptive peer group functioning. Drawing from this research tradition, in Chapter 20 Shelley Hymel, Leanna Closson, Simona Caravita, and Tracy Vaillancourt discuss how the study of children's social status in the peer group has evolved. Specifically, research on children's sociometric status has moved from assessing interpersonal attraction to measuring peer group acceptance. More recently, our understanding has been enhanced by studies that distinguish sociometric status from perceived popularity. In the course of examining ways that sociometric studies have evolved, the authors address the strengths and limitations of various sociometric measurement techniques and the ethics of conducting sociometric assessments. Recent methodological issues in assessing the recently derived construct of perceived popularity and how it is distinguished from sociometric popularity are also overviewed. The authors also review recent studies that illustrate how sociometric and perceived popularity are differentially linked to social behavior, and consider how child age, gender, and culture play roles in these linkages.

In Chapter 21, Antonius Cillesen and Amy Bellmore pick up on a related theme as they discuss the complex construct of social competence. They review the research literature that supports varying conceptualizations of social competence. The theme of sociometric and perceived popularity is extended from Chapter 20 with a discussion of how these constructs play into different views of social competence. A dual-component model of social competence is developed in this chapter, and is illustrated by the types

The Wiley-Blackwell Handbook of Childhood Social Development, Second Edition, edited by Peter K. Smith and Craig H. Hart
© 2011 by Blackwell Publishing Ltd.

of behavioral and social cognitive skills that feed into each component. Competent play, peer group entry, and conflict resolution skills are highlighted in the behavioral skill domain. Studies that highlight ways that appropriate behavior depends on the accurate perception of the actions and intentions of peers are discussed in the social cognitive domain. The authors wind up the chapter with an overview of social skills observed in perceived popular, controversial, and bistrategic children, with an eye toward explaining how one form of social competence is distinguished from another form of social competence that is defined by sociometric popularity, acceptance, and preference by peers.

In Chapter 22, Susanne Denham, Heather Warren, Maria von Salisch, Oana Benga, Jui-Chih Chin, and Elena Geangu highlight the interdependency of emotional and social competence with a multicultural overview of the emotional processes that underlie peer group behavior. Throughout, cultural nuances are highlighted, illustrating how many aspects of emotional competence are culturally derived. The authors overview the basic components of emotional competence, outlining how children experience, regulate, and express emotions. They then describe the processes that underlie emotion understanding by discussing research that illuminates how affective messages are interpreted, while taking display rules and individuals' emotional styles into account. The etiology of emotional competence is also addressed. Parents, peers, and societal influences all play a role in the development of emotional competencies. They conclude by describing how emotions play out in friendships and peer relationships. Future directions for further examination are recommended.

Chapter 23 is centered on children who withdraw from peer group interaction. Ken Rubin, Robert Coplan, Julie Bowker, and Melissa Menzer overview a systematic line of theory and research that helps us not only better define social withdrawal but also understand how various forms of solitude carry with them different psychological meanings. Withdrawal is conceptualized and empirically validated as an umbrella construct for various forms of solitude, which play out across early and middle childhood. Biological factors and socialization influences that may play a role in children isolating themselves from peers are considered. The authors discuss how insecure attachment relationships and intrusive and overprotective parenting may serve to maintain and further exacerbate biologically based predispositions in ways that lead to maladaptive withdrawal from peers. Deficits reflected in the social cognitions, self-perceptions, rejection by peers, victimization, and lack of friendships of withdrawn children set the stage for the long-term negative consequences of social withdrawal that have been identified in longitudinal research. However, the authors provide a positive note by outlining some promising approaches for intervention and prevention. The chapter concludes with an informative look at cross-cultural perspectives on shyness and withdrawal. For an overview of friendship issues in early and middle childhood, see Hartup and Abecassis' chapter in the first edition of this handbook (Smith and Hart, 2002).

Reference

Hartup, W. W., & Abecassis, M. (2002). Friends and enemies. In P. K. Smith & C. H. Hart (Eds.), *Blackwell handbook of childhood social development* (pp. 285–306). Oxford: Blackwell Publishing.

CHAPTER TWENTY

Social Status Among Peers: From Sociometric Attraction to Peer Acceptance to Perceived Popularity

Shelley Hymel, Leanna M. Closson, Simona C. S. Caravita, and Tracy Vaillancourt

Research on children's peer relations and social development has relied heavily on sociometric methods to assess interpersonal relations within a group. Sociometric techniques first emerged in the 1930s and are generally credited to Jacob Moreno (1934), although many researchers contributed to the sociometric movement (for historical reviews, see Bukowski, 2000; Cillessen, 2009; Hymel, Vaillancourt, McDougall, & Renshaw, 2002; Renshaw, 1981). For Moreno, the focus of sociometric inquiry was the group or the larger social system within which the individual functioned, with interest in how various group structures lead to different interpersonal relationships. In the 75 years since Moreno's book was published, the majority of sociometric studies of children have focused not on group structures but on the individual and his or her status within the group. Far less research has emphasized the group itself (Bukowski & Cillessen, 1998), although interest in this area is growing (see Kindermann & Gest, 2009; Rubin, Bukowski, & Parker, 2006).

Most studies of children's peer relations have followed from early sociometric research by Koch (1933) and Northway (1944, 1946), who used sociometric evaluations to assess individual differences in social status among children. Sociometric status or "popularity" was considered an index of social effectiveness, and both Koch and Northway were interested in developing strategies for improving the acceptance of unpopular children. The belief that sociometric status reflects underlying social competence continued as a dominant perspective within the field through the 1980s and 1990s (Asher & Hymel, 1981;

The Wiley-Blackwell Handbook of Childhood Social Development, Second Edition, edited by Peter K. Smith and Craig H. Hart
© 2011 by Blackwell Publishing Ltd.

Cillessen, 2009; Ladd, 2005), and, with it, continued interest in helping children with low status develop the skills and competencies necessary for effective interpersonal relations (e.g., Asher & Coie, 1990; Coie & Cillessen, 1993). By the end of the 20th century, however, developmental psychologists began to distinguish peer acceptance or likeability from peer perceptions of "popularity" (e.g., Parkhurst & Hopmeyer, 1998), changing our view of children's social status within the school peer group. In this chapter, we consider how research on children's sociometric status has moved from tapping interpersonal attraction, to measuring peer group acceptance, and, most recently, to distinguishing sociometric status from perceived popularity, each contributing to our understanding of children's peer relations and social development.

From Attraction to Peer Acceptance

Moreno (1934) argued that two distinct dimensions of interpersonal judgment underlie the operation of groups – *attraction* (i.e., experiences that draw people together) and *repulsion* (i.e., experiences that push people apart). These forces were not envisioned as two ends of a single continuum; rather, the alternative to each was a third judgment – *indifference*. To understand (and assess) interpersonal relations within groups, Moreno believed that attraction, repulsion, and indifference must be considered in terms of *both* how one perceives others in the group *and* how one is perceived by others. Considering both perspectives, Moreno identified a number of dimensions that tap how individuals are situated within groups (see Bukowski, 2000).

To assess these dimensions, Moreno simply asked individuals how much they liked to associate with each of the other group members. The tradition of asking individuals to evaluate their attractions (liking) and repulsions (disliking) regarding group members remains today as the hallmark of the sociometric method. The use of peers as informants has several advantages, particularly for research with children (Hymel et al., 2002), including the "face validity" of providing an "insider" perspective on peer group relations rather than relying on the perceptions of adult "outsiders," and the benefit of integrating evaluations from multiple peers who have varied experiences with a child and who can consider low-frequency but significant interpersonal behaviors.

Despite the potential utility of considering multiple dimensions of individuals within groups, research on children's peer relations has focused primarily on *sociometric status* or how individuals are perceived by members of the group (see Hymel et al., 2002). This particular aspect of sociometric methodology has contributed greatly to our understanding of individuals within groups, albeit not always in the ways envisioned by Moreno (1934). Moreno's concepts of attraction and repulsion, respectively, led to the assessment of *peer acceptance* or the degree to which an individual is liked or preferred among peers, and *peer rejection* or the degree to which an individual is disliked by his or her peers.

Measuring Sociometric Acceptance and Rejection

Since the 1930s, sociometric research has been concerned with how best to assess an individual's peer acceptance or rejection within a group (e.g., Asher, Singleton, Tinsley,

& Hymel, 1979; Coie, Dodge, & Coppotelli, 1982; Terry & Coie, 1991; and see Bukowski, 2000; Cillessen, 2009; Hymel et al., 2002). One major and continuing debate concerns whether sociometric status is best assessed using nomination, rating scale, or paired-comparison techniques. Nomination approaches require participants to identify group members according to a specified sociometric criterion (e.g., "Who do you like to play with?"), rating methods require participants to rate group members according to specified sociometric criteria (e.g., "How much do you like to play with ____?"), and paired-comparison techniques require participants to evaluate all possible pairs of group members in terms of some specified criteria (e.g., "Which person would you rather play with?"). Regardless of the method used, sociometric evaluations from group members are typically combined to yield overall continuous indices of peer acceptance and rejection or to categorize individuals in terms of their sociometric status (see Cillessen, 2009; Hymel et al., 2002). Research has further shown that evaluations from 70–75% of group members are needed in order to obtain stable sociometric measures (Crick & Ladd, 1989), although a 60% participation rate may be sufficient with unlimited nominations (Wargo Aikins & Cillessen, 2007, as cited in Cillessen, 2009).

Over the years, peer nominations have become the most common approach used in developmental research, particularly the system developed by Coie et al. (1982). In this procedure, the sums of the positive and negative nominations received from peers are standardized and used as indices of *acceptance* and *rejection*, respectively, which in turn are combined to create summary scores of *social preference* (acceptance minus rejection) tapping relative likeability, and *social impact* (acceptance plus rejection) tapping visibility within the group. These continuous indices could also be used to categorize individuals into status groups: *accepted* or *popular* (high social preference, low rejection, and high acceptance), *rejected* (low social preference, high rejection, and low acceptance), *controversial* (high social impact, high acceptance, and high rejection) and *neglected* (low social impact, low rejection, and low acceptance), the latter category reflecting Moreno's (1934) concept of indifference.

Although paired-comparison and rating scale methods ensured equal consideration of all group members, thereby providing more refined measurement data, the greater administration time required made them less frequently used. Moreover, both were criticized for being unidimensional (Terry & Coie, 1991), either focusing solely on acceptance (paired comparisons) or placing acceptance and rejection along a single continuum (rating scales), and unable to distinguish "neglected" children within the group. However, research showed that children who are identified as *neglected* using nomination data are often viewed by peers as likeable (Newcomb, Bukowski, & Pattee, 1993) and receive peer ratings that span the entire scale, from disliked to liked (Hymel & Rubin, 1985; Maassen, van der Linden, & Akkermans, 1997; Rubin, Hymel, LeMare, & Rowden, 1989). Thus, it is as yet unclear whether the concept of interpersonal indifference, as conceptualized by Moreno, is actually being tapped with nomination measures. Moreover, Maassen, van der Linden, Goossens, and Bokhorst (2000) argued that attraction and repulsion (*sympathy–antipathy* in their terminology) *are unidimensional at the individual level*, although between the two is a neutral midpoint reflecting Moreno's construct of indifference. Using a 7-point scale, ranging from −3 (*extremely disliked*) to +3 (*extremely liked*) with a neutral midpoint of 0, Maassen and colleagues (2000) developed a rating approach that identifies the same status categories as nomination measures, but yields classifications that are more stable over a 1-year period.

Methodological Issues in Assessing Peer Acceptance and Rejection

Determining "best practices" in sociometric assessment remains a focus in sociometric research (see Cillessen, 2009; Hymel et al., 2002). Debates continue regarding whether the number of nominations allowed for a particular sociometric criterion should be limited or unlimited (Cillessen, 2009), although researchers today tend to rely on unlimited nominations (Poulin & Dishion, 2008), which yield sociometric scores with better distributional properties (Terry, 2000). Research also suggests that allowing participants to nominate peers of both sexes and from their entire grade (rather than classroom) improves the predictive validity of sociometric measures (Poulin & Dishion, 2008). Debates regarding the relative advantages of continuous sociometric scores versus categorical sociometric classifications have waned, with growing consensus that both are useful, albeit for different purposes and statistical analyses (Cillessen, 2009). Finally, in response to concerns raised by parents, teachers, and review boards, several researchers have addressed the ethics of sociometric testing. Briefly, the evidence suggests that, if administered carefully, with efforts to prevent negative consequences, sociometric assessments do not appear to pose significant risks for participants (see Hymel et al., 2002; Mayeux, Underwood, & Risser, 2007).

Perhaps one of the most important assessment issues within this literature concerns the dimensionality of acceptance and rejection. Initially, these two constructs were treated as unidimensional – opposite ends of one continuum. However, research in the 1960s and 1970s showed that they were only modestly (negatively) correlated or orthogonal and were associated with different behaviors (see Hymel et al., 2002), laying the foundation for classification schemes that treated acceptance and rejection as separate dimensions able to distinguish accepted, rejected, neglected, and controversial children (e.g., Coie et al., 1982; Gronlund, 1959; Maassen et al., 1997, 2000). Subsequently, Bukowski, Sippola, Hoza, and Newcomb (2000) showed that the relationship between acceptance and rejection is both linear (and negative) and curvilinear. Thus, children who are highly accepted are typically low in rejection, although poorly accepted children may vary in their level of rejection. Children who are highly rejected are usually low in acceptance, but children who are low in rejection may or may not be accepted. Recognition of this curvilinear relationship underscored the need for further research on the complex nature of children's status among peers and foreshadowed major shifts in research on social status that would unfold gradually over the next decade.

Many studies investigated the psychometric adequacy of sociometric measures, with particular interest in the stability of status over time. In a recent meta-analysis, Jiang and Cillessen (2005) found that continuous indices of status were highly stable over the short term (average test–retest reliability coefficients = .71 for acceptance, .70 for rejection, .82 for social preference, and .78 for liking ratings) and showed good stability over the long term (average coefficients of about .50 for both ratings and nominations). In contrast, in another meta-analysis, Cillessen, Bukowski, and Haselager (2000) found that sociometric status classifications were only somewhat stable over time (average coefficients <.40), with only about half of the students categorized as accepted or rejected retaining their status over one year, and neglected and controversial categories being even less stable. For both continuous and categorical sociometric data, stability indices increased with age and decreased with longer time intervals. The lower stability of status categories relative to continuous status indices is largely attributable to the statistical principle that information is lost when continuous data are dichotomized to yield categories (Cillessen & Mayeux, 2004a, 2004b). The modest stability of sociometric status indices may pose methodological problems for researchers, but it underscores the dynamic nature of sociometric status, as Moreno (1934) suggested, and offers hope to low-status children who want to improve their social standing.

Moreno (1934) suggested two broad types of sociometric criteria: emotional and reputational. Emotional criteria were personal, subjective evaluations, whereas reputational criteria tapped perceptions of an individual's behavior or reputation. In later sociometric literature, this became a distinction between sociometric measures of interpersonal attraction (liking and disliking) and peer assessments of behavior and reputation (Asher & Hymel, 1981; Gronlund, 1959). In fact, peer assessments of behavior were often used to examine the behavioral characteristics of accepted versus rejected children. In a large-scale meta-analysis of the correlates of sociometric status, Newcomb et al. (1993) were able to distinguish accepted and rejected children in four broad areas: aggression and withdrawal (greater among rejected children), and sociability and cognitive competence (greater among accepted children). The extensive literature on the correlates of sociometric status (see Hymel et al., 2002) provides rather solid evidence for the validity of these measures. Further discussion of the correlates of status follows later in this review.

Despite extensive methodological debates, research on children's sociometric status has flourished. The primary focus for several decades, however, was on the nature of peer rejection, or being disliked or unpopular within the group (e.g., see Asher & Coie, 1990; Bierman, 2004; Leary, 2001). Within the past decade, although interest in peer rejection continues, attention has shifted to the construct of peer acceptance or popularity (Cillessen & Mayeux, 2004b; Cillessen & Rose, 2005; Vaillancourt & Hymel, 2006).

From Peer Acceptance to Perceived Popularity

From the earliest sociometric research (e.g., Koch, 1933), high peer acceptance was considered synonymous with "popularity." Popular children were those who were liked or preferred by peers or who were most nominated as a friend. Initially, this seemed a reasonable assumption. After all, decades of research had shown that highly accepted or "popular" children were well-adjusted, socially competent, prosocial individuals who were well liked by definition (e.g., Newcomb et al., 1993). However, in 1998, Parkhurst and Hopmeyer pointed out that other research, primarily with adolescents, viewed high-status youth, not in terms of friendship or liking, but in terms of visibility, prestige, and social dominance (e.g., Eder, 1985; Eder & Kinney, 1995; Weisfeld, Bloch, & Ivers, 1983,

1984). Indeed, ethologists, anthropologists, and sociologists were uncovering a different characterization of popularity – one that hinged upon status being a product of social reputation and prominence within the group. In these studies, popular children were not always nice or well liked by peers; rather, they were described as cool, attractive, athletic, powerful, arrogant, exclusionary, and mean (Adler & Adler, 1998; Eder, 1985; Eder, Evans, & Parker, 1995; Merten, 1997).

What does it mean to be popular? By early adolescence, youth prioritize popularity over many other domains, including maintaining friendships, engaging in romantic relationships, showing compassion for low-status peers, conforming to behavioral norms, and athletic or academic achievement (LaFontana & Cillessen, 2009). Accordingly, it becomes important to investigate what popularity means to *youth* in order to better understand why they view popularity as a crucial achievement in their social lives. When developmental researchers directly asked children and youth what popularity means to them (Closson, 2009a; LaFontana & Cillessen, 2002; Xie, Li, Boucher, Hutchins, & Cairns, 2006), they found that physical attractiveness and social connectedness were key to defining popularity. Also, early adolescents described popularity in a manner that was more consistent with descriptions by anthropologists, sociologists, and ethologists rather than sociometric studies (Closson, 2009a), indicating that youth themselves understood the term *popular* to reflect social prominence (i.e., visibility and recognition) more than social preference (i.e., liking and acceptance).

In a first quantitative study of the issue, Parkhurst and Hopmeyer (1998) distinguished sociometric perceptions of likeability and peer perceptions of popularity, as measured by peer nominations for being *popular at school*. Among over 700 grade 7–8 students, only 31% of the students that peers viewed as *popular* were also categorized as *popular* on sociometric measures. Of the remaining students who were high on perceived popularity ($M + 1SD$), 19% were categorized as controversial, 2% as neglected, 8% as rejected, and 11% as average in status (with 29% unclassified in the Coie et al. [1982] system). In a study of 585 Canadian students in grades 6–10, Vaillancourt (2001) found that controversial students were viewed by peers as the *most* popular and powerful students, receiving mean popularity and power scores that were four times greater than those of sociometrically popular students.

Measurement of Perceived Popularity

Operational definitions of perceived popularity vary across studies. For instance, Gorman and colleagues (Gorman, Kim, & Schimmelbusch, 2002; Schwartz, Gorman, Nakamoto, & McKay, 2006) assessed perceived popularity by asking middle adolescents to rate a random subset of peers on a scale from *not at all popular* to *very popular*. Most frequently, however, perceived popularity has been measured using peer nominations of classmates or grade mates who are *most popular* and *least popular* (e.g., Closson, 2009a, 2009b; Lease, Kennedy, & Axelrod, 2002; Mayeux & Cillessen, 2008; Prinstein, 2007; Vaillancourt, 2001).

In some studies, *most popular* nominations are computed as an index of perceived popularity (e.g., Caravita, Di Blasio, & Salmivalli, 2009, 2010; Carlson & Rose, 2007;

Parkhurst & Hopmeyer, 1998; Vaillancourt & Hymel, 2006). Following the logic of social preference scores, some compute a difference of *most popular* minus *least popular* standardized nominations as a measure of perceived popularity (Cillessen & Mayeux, 2004a; Closson, 2009a, 2009b; Košir & Pečjak, 2005) or *perceived preference* (Kuppens, Grietens, Onghena, Michiels, & Subramanian, 2008; Lease et al., 2002). Most commonly, perceived popularity or preference is treated as a continuous variable, although some have used cutoff scores (typically ±0.5 or 1 SD) to classify youth into status categories (e.g., Closson, 2009a; Košir & Pečjak, 2005; Kuppens et al., 2008; LaFontana & Cillessen, 1999; Mayeux & Cillessen, 2008).

Methodological Issues in Assessing Perceived Popularity

Few studies have examined the psychometric properties of measures of perceived popularity. Cillessen and Mayeux (2004a) found perceived preference scores to be highly stable over 4 years (grades 5–9), with greater stability in older than younger grades and over shorter time intervals. Also, Prinstein (2007) demonstrated that a subsample of teacher-identified peer "experts" can be used to obtain stable assessments of perceived popularity similar to those obtained from the entire group. Considering the relative stability of sociometric versus perceived popularity (Wu, Hart, Draper, & Olsen, 2001), research to date shows greater stability for the latter, over both the short term (from fall grade 9 to spring grade 10; Schwartz et al., 2006), and the longer term (popular students from grades 5 to 12; Cillessen & Borch, 2006).

Some researchers (Estell, 2007; Farmer, Estell, Bishop, O'Neal, & Cairns, 2003; Rodkin & Berger, 2008; Rodkin, Farmer, Pearl, & Van Acker, 2000, 2006; Ryan & Shim, 2008; Xie et al., 2006) assessed perceived popularity using teacher evaluations on the Interpersonal Competence Scale (ICS-T; Cairns, Leung, Gest, & Cairns, 1995). The Popularity subscale of the ICS-T includes three items, each rated on a 7-point scale (e.g., from *not popular* to *very popular with boys/girls*, and from *lots of friends* to *no friends*), and has demonstrated good internal consistency ($\alpha = .70$ to .91) (Estell, 2007; Farmer et al., 2003; Rodkin & Berger, 2008; Rodkin et al., 2006; Ryan & Shim, 2008; Xie et al., 2006). Little is known about the correspondence between teacher and peer informants regarding perceived popularity. Although Rodkin and Berger found a similar pattern of relations across the teacher and peer reports of perceived popularity, suggesting some consistency across raters, Babad (2001) found that only 58% of teachers could accurately identify grade 4–9 students who peers perceived to be popular and only 50% of teachers could accurately identify students who were sociometrically popular.

With regard to the criteria used to assess perceived popularity, as an alternative to *most/ least popular* peer nominations, some researchers have considered student perceptions of who *others* view as preferred associates (Dijkstra, Lindenberg, & Veenstra, 2008) or as popular (e.g., Hawley, 2003; Hawley, Little, & Card, 2007, 2008). Some have assessed *perceived popularity* using self-perceptions (e.g., Barry & Wigfield, 2002; Leadbeater, Boone, Sangster, & Mathieson, 2006), although Mayeux and Cillessen (2008) found peer and self-perceptions of popularity to be positively but not highly correlated. Rodkin and

Berger (2008) assessed perceived popularity using a composite of popularity, coolness, and admiration. The overlap of these variations in criteria and measurement approaches remains a question for future research. As Košir and Pečjak (2005) have demonstrated, even *most popular* scores may be distinct from perceived preference scores as indices of perceived popularity, with different correlates, particularly during the elementary years. Thus, although the terminology may be the same across studies, what actually is being measured may vary. In subsequent sections, we consider research addressing the distinctiveness of sociometric popularity and perceived popularity, using the former term to refer to sociometric indices of peer acceptance, social preference, and/or likeability, and the latter term to refer to indices of reputational popularity, or peer evaluations of who is popular within the group.

Perceived Popularity Versus Sociometric Popularity: Distinct Constructs?

In establishing the distinctiveness of sociometric versus perceived popularity, Parkhurst and Hopmeyer (1998) reported moderate correlations between the two among middle school students ($r = .28$ to $.47$ across indices). Although this moderate relationship has generally been replicated in a number of studies (Košir & Pečjak, 2005; LaFontana & Cillessen, 2002; Lease et al., 2002; Prinstein & Cillessen, 2003; Rose, Swenson, & Waller, 2004; Schwartz et al., 2006 Vaillancourt & Hymel, 2006), the magnitude of the correlation varies across measures and across samples. For example, Caravita and colleagues (2009, 2010) reported modest to low and often nonsignificant correlations ($-.25$ to $.29$) between perceived and sociometric popularity from middle childhood through adolescence in Italy, and Babad (2001) found higher correlations between the two in an American sample ($r = .58$) than Israeli samples ($r = .42$ to $.47$). Even within a U.S. sample, the correlation was stronger among White students than among Black or Latino students (LaFontana & Cillessen, 2002). Other studies have demonstrated differential correlates of social status across ethnic and cultural groups (see Cillessen & Mayeux, 2004b). We do not yet fully understand the cultural and contextual factors that impact the relationship between sociometric and perceived popularity. Most studies to date have considered U.S. samples, with some evidence that, in this population, being seen as popular becomes a priority during early adolescence (LaFontana & Cillessen, 2009). Further research is needed to address how conceptions of "popularity" as well as their priority vary across cultures and groups.

The relationship between perceived and sociometric popularity does vary systematically with age and gender (Cillessen, 2009). Generally, the relationship between the two constructs declines with age from elementary to secondary school (e.g., Cillessen & Borch, 2006; Košir & Pečjak, 2005), although the nature of this decline differs for boys and girls. Specifically, longitudinal research (Cillessen, 2009; Cillessen & Borch, 2006; Cillessen & Mayeux, 2004a) indicates that the relationship between perceived and sociometric popularity is positive during the elementary years for both boys and girls, but as students move into middle and secondary school, girls are more likely to distinguish the two. For boys, the relationship between sociometric and perceived popularity declines but remains positive (i.e., from .77 to .63 from grades 5 to 9: Cillessen & Mayeux, 2004a; and to .30 in grade 12 among popular boys: Cillessen & Borch, 2006). Among girls, the correlation shifts from a positive relationship (.67) in grade 5, to no relationship (.04) in grade 9 (Cillessen & Mayeux, 2004a), to a negative relationship by the end of high school (–.49 in grade 12 among popular girls; Cillessen & Borch, 2006). As Cillessen and Borch noted, "[B]oys are able to maintain some compatibility between both popularity roles throughout adolescence, whereas for girls, being liked and being seen as popular are increasingly incompatible roles" (p. 957).

Sociometric and perceived popularity demonstrate differential links to social behavior (e.g., Babad, 2001; Parkhurst & Hopmeyer, 1998; Sandstrom & Cillessen, 2006), particularly during adolescence (Cillessen & Borch, 2006; Cillessen & Mayeux, 2004a; Košir & Pečjak, 2005; LaFontana & Cillessen, 2002; Schwartz et al., 2006; Vaillancourt & Hymel, 2006). For example, among middle childhood and adolescent students in Italy, Caravita and colleagues (2009, 2010) found that bullying was associated *negatively* with sociometric popularity (social preference) but *positively* with perceived popularity.

Theoretically, whereas Koch (1933) had proposed that sociometric popularity was an index of social competence, Parkhurst and Hopmeyer (1998) proposed that perceived popularity was essentially synonymous with social dominance. Support for the hypothesized link between perceived popularity and dominance comes primarily from studies of adolescence (e.g., Babad, 2001; Hawley, 2003; Parkhurst & Hopmeyer, 1998; Vaillancourt & Hymel, 2006). As one example, Vaillancourt and Hymel found that, for adolescents, perceived popularity was much more strongly related to peer perceptions of power ($r = .80$) than was sociometric popularity ($r = .25$). However, in a study of younger students (grades 4–6), Lease and colleagues (2002) found that indices of perceived and sociometric popularity were similarly correlated with social dominance (.62 and .57, respectively).

Consistent with proposed links between social competence and sociometric popularity (liking), LaFontana and Cillessen (2002) found that social preference was more strongly associated with prosocial behavior than was perceived popularity. However, both sociometrically popular and perceived popular students display positive social competencies, although it may be more accurate to characterize most students perceived to be popular as *bistrategic* (Cillessen & Rose, 2005; Closson, 2009b; Hawley, 2003; LaFontana & Cillessen, 2002), displaying a mix of positive and negative characteristics and behaviors (see Cillessen & Mayeux, 2004b). Accordingly, to understand the differential correlates of sociometric versus perceived popularity, it is helpful to examine subgroups of individuals who vary across status indices.

Parkhurst and Hopmeyer (1998) found that students who were high on both sociometric popularity *and* perceived popularity were characterized as kind, trustworthy, and nonsubmissive (not easy to push around), but not as aggressive or stuck-up. In contrast, students who were "likeable" but not "popular" were described by peers as kind and trustworthy but not submissive, aggressive, or stuck-up. Finally, students who were "popular" but not necessarily "likeable" were characterized as nonsubmissive, aggressive, stuck-up, and neither kind nor trustworthy.

Among grade 4–6 students, Lease et al. (2002) found that those perceived to be popular were viewed as socially dominant and socially visible (cool and athletic), prosocial, and bright (smart and socially skilled). Students who were considered popular but not well liked were seen as high in leadership, admiration, influence, and social control, whereas students who were liked but not considered popular were viewed as moderate in leadership, admiration, and influence. Also, among grade 4–8 students, LaFontana and Cillessen (2002) found that both sociometric and perceived popularity were associated with greater athletic and academic ability and prosocial behavior, and less social withdrawal. However, sociometric popularity was more strongly associated with academic ability and prosocial behavior than perceived popularity, whereas perceived popularity was more strongly correlated with athletic ability and sociability (less social withdrawal). Consistent with these findings, researchers have begun to distinguish subtypes of "popular" or high-status children and youth (e.g., Rodkin et al., 2000; and see Cillessen & Rose, 2005).

Popularity and Aggression

Perhaps most noteworthy are findings demonstrating that sociometric and perceived popularity are differentially linked to aggressive behavior. Both overt/physical aggression and especially relational aggression are positively related to perceived popularity but negatively related to sociometric popularity (Farmer & Rodkin, 1996; LaFontana & Cillessen, 2002; Rose et al., 2004; Schwartz et al., 2006; Vaillancourt & Hymel, 2006). Across grades, relational aggression is more strongly related to perceived popularity than overt aggression, especially among girls, both concurrently (Cillessen & Mayeux 2004a; Cillessen & Rose, 2005) and predictively (Rose et al., 2004). With age, the differential associations with relational aggression appear to get stronger, especially for girls, whereas the differential relations with overt/physical aggression gradually disappear (Cillessen & Mayeux, 2004a). As Cillessen (2009) noted, the two popularity constructs increasingly diverge as students move from elementary to secondary school (i.e., from middle childhood to adolescence), especially among girls. With age, the links between relational aggression and perceived popularity appear to grow more positive (but see Schwartz et al., 2006, for an exception), whereas the links between relational aggression and sociometric popularity tend to remain negative.

Based on a conceptual distinction made by LaFreniere and Charlesworth (1983) between implicit versus explicit social power, Vaillancourt and Hymel (2006) examined one mechanism that helps to explain the complex relationship between status and aggression. Aggression, as a form of explicit power, is forcefully expressed and elicits both fear and compliance or submission. As such, aggression should be negatively associated with social status. In contrast, implicit power is derived from others, based on recognition of status or competence. Vaillancourt and Hymel proposed that implicit power would be afforded to individuals by peers depending on whether or not they possessed *peer-valued characteristics* (PVCs; being attractive, athletic, funny, rich, etc.), and that such implicit power would moderate the relationship between aggression and social status (i.e., social preference, perceived popularity, and power). Among students in grades 6–10, Vaillancourt and Hymel found that, consistent with previous research (Cillessen & Mayeux, 2004a; Prinstein & Cillessen, 2003), students who were physically and relationally aggressive were generally disliked by their peers, although many were nevertheless viewed as both popular and powerful within the group. However, these relationships were moderated by possession of PVCs. Aggressive students with PVCs (especially girls) enjoyed higher levels of perceived popularity and power and less disliking than those who did not, although the magnitude of these relations varied by sex, type of aggression, and social status index. For example, relationally aggressive girls who possessed PVCs were seen as more popular than those who did not, and physically aggressive girls were less disliked when they possessed PVCs than when they did not. Vaillancourt and Hymel suggested that for many, the possession of PVCs serves as a buffer that affords aggressive students considerable status and power despite the fact that they are cruel. In other words, students can "get away with" aggression and still maintain status if they possess qualities that are revered by their peers.

Further research is needed to evaluate other psychological and group mechanisms that may influence the relationship between popularity and aggression. Considering prospective associations between forms of aggression as predictors and status as an outcome, relational aggression appears to be a more prominent predictor of perceived popularity, both influencing initial levels of popularity and moderating developmental trajectories of status through adolescence (Cillessen & Borch, 2006; Cillessen & Mayeux, 2004a; Rose et al., 2004), especially among girls. Of interest in future research is understanding the distinct ways in which different forms of aggression influence status over time, and how peer group sanctions, norms, and priorities contribute to these developmental shifts.

Cillessen and Mayeux (2004a) suggested that "physical aggression is increasingly less censured in the peer group, [and] relational aggression is increasingly reinforced" (p. 159). By adolescence, relational attacks are likely to be more tolerated and rewarded by peers as they attribute higher status to relationally aggressive peers. Thus, relational aggression provides popular youth with an effective instrument for achieving power within the group (Cillessen & Mayeux, 2004a; Vaillancourt, 2001; Vaillancourt & Hymel, 2006). Although both popular boys and girls engage in relational aggression, peer responses to such behavior may differ. Such behavior is more censured and associated with decreased likeability, especially for girls, perhaps resulting in more negative peer responses for girls than boys (Cillessen & Mayeux, 2004a). Also, Mayeux and colleagues (Mayeux, Sandstrom, & Cillessen, 2008) hypothesized that, relative to popular boys, popular girls may elicit more feelings of envy from less popular peers, resulting in decreases in their likeability.

Considering the Long Term

Researchers have long been interested in sociometric status given its role in current and future maladjustment. For decades, attention has been focused on children who were rejected by peers, owing in large part to retrospective and prospective studies that consistently showed rejected children to be at risk for internalizing problems (e.g., depression) and externalizing problems (e.g., aggression), and academic difficulties (e.g., truancy) in later years (see McDougall, Hymel, Vaillancourt, & Mercer, 2001; Prinstein, Rancourt, Guerry, & Brown, 2009). Three kinds of models have been considered in explaining how peer rejection contributes to maladjustment (Prinstein et al., 2009): (a) *incidental* models, which posit that underlying mechanisms, such as internal working models, serve as a common cause of both maladjustment and rejection; (b) *causal* models, which suggest that maladjustment is a direct outcome of poor status and negative peer experiences; and (c) *transactional* models, which posit that maladjustment stems from the dynamic interaction of peer experiences and individual characteristics. In one "transactional model" of the links between rejection and maladjustment, Parker and Asher (1987) suggested that rejection may result from deviant or aggressive behaviors that reflect preexistent social cognitive difficulties, such as tendencies to attribute hostile intent to peers. In turn, being rejected limits opportunities for positive interactions and experiences with peers, thereby depriving the child of opportunities for improving his or her social cognitive competencies. All three models provide convincing explanations for the relation between maladjustment and peer rejection, and all three find some confirmations in the literature (see Prinstein et al., 2009).

At the other end of the status hierarchy, peer acceptance or "popularity" was initially viewed as a reflection of social effectiveness or competence (e.g., Koch, 1933), presumably associated with positive long-term outcomes. However, as shown in this review, research on sociometric and perceived popularity has suggested a more complex view of social status, one that is also related to dominance and power. Nevertheless, as with peer rejection, research indicates that high perceived popularity can enhance one's risk of maladjustment in adolescence in three areas: externalization (i.e., aggression and disruptive behavior), engagement in risky behaviors, and academic difficulties (e.g., Cillessen & Mayeux, 2004a; Mayeux et al., 2008; Rose et al., 2004; Sandstrom & Cillessen, 2006; Schwartz et al., 2006).

Focusing on externalization, perceived popularity in late childhood predicts aggressive-disruptive behavior in adolescence (Cillessen & Mayeux, 2004a; Sandstrom & Cillessen, 2006), although effects vary across forms of aggression. Although findings regarding positive prospective effects of being highly popular on overt aggression (Cillessen & Mayeux, 2004a) have not been always confirmed (Prinstein & Cillessen, 2003; Rose et al., 2004), there is strong evidence that perceived popularity predicts relational aggression 6, 12, 17, and 36 months later (Cillessen & Mayeux, 2004a; Prinstein & Cillessen, 2003; Rose et al., 2004). This predictive relation is even more consistent than the reverse prospective association between aggression and later perceived popularity (Cillessen & Mayeux, 2004a), and emerges as early as preadolescence (grade 5; Rose et al., 2004). Even if being relationally aggressive implies a cost in likeability, popular youth may nevertheless engage in such behavior because they view it as an effective tool for maintaining power and dominance among peers (e.g., Cillessen & Mayeux, 2004a; Rose et al., 2004).

Beyond externalizing outcomes, perceived popularity in middle adolescence increases the probability of engaging in sexual behaviors and alcohol use 2 years later (Mayeux et al., 2008). Among aggressive youth, high perceived popularity predicts lower rates of school attendance and higher unexcused absences (Schwartz et al., 2006). In adolescence, risky behaviors are probably perceived as expressing maturity and, thus, may be useful strategies for maintaining a dominant position within the peer hierarchy (Mayeux & Cillessen, 2008). As well, fear of losing one's status among peers might prevent aggressive popular adolescents from reengaging in school (Schwartz et al., 2006). Taken together, authors converge in emphasizing the possible long-term, negative consequences of both peer rejection and high perceived popularity among children and adolescents. Far less attention has been directed to the fact that some youth are able to achieve high reputational status *and* maintain their likeability among peers. What are the developmental outcomes associated with this dual form of social status?

As well, most of the literature reviewed has been conducted with elementary school children (age 8 and above). Although the behaviors that distinguish sociometric status groups appear to be evident early on, even among preschoolers in different cultural settings (e.g., Nelson, Robinson, & Hart, 2005; Nelson, Robinson, Hart, Albano, & Marshall, in press), little is known about the emergence of status in early childhood. It is also unclear whether youth displaying different patterns of social status succeed or fail in adjustment as they move from adolescence into adulthood. Given that social development is a very gradual process, involving the development of social skills and an understanding of intergroup processes, it is important to recognize that children and adolescents are still acquiring interpersonal competencies throughout their time in school. Learning about power and dominance is an important but complex challenge across the elementary and secondary years. Longitudinal research is needed to determine whether various status subgroups are at risk for later maladjustment, or whether the interpersonal roles and strategies adopted during the school years serve as a critical training ground for later social competence in the world of adults.

Of more immediate concern is the fact that, even if high-status children are learning critical interpersonal skills, it is often at the expense of others. As educators increasingly recognize that social and emotional learning is an important focus in schools (e.g., www. casel.org; Hymel, Schonert-Reichl, & Miller, 2006), a major question for future research becomes whether children can acquire these social skills without causing harm to peers. Applying a transactional approach to explain the outcomes of various forms of status requires an examination of the interface between individual characteristics and group features and values (Vaillancourt & Hymel, 2006). However, group-level variables, such as aggressive behaviors of cliques or crowds (Kindermann & Gest, 2009) or the impact of group norms for aggression (Dijkstra et al., 2008), are still rarely examined as potential influences on developmental changes in status over time. As Moreno suggested long ago, multiple dimensions are needed to understand the individual within the group, and how group structures lead to different interpersonal relationships.

Acknowledgments

This paper was supported by the Social Sciences and Humanities Research Council of Canada (Knowledge Cluster and CURA grants), the Canadian Institutes of Health Research, and the Edith Lando Charitable Foundation.

References

Adler, P. A., & Adler, P. (1998). *Peer power: Preadolescent culture and identity*. New Brunswick, NJ: Rutgers University Press.

Asher, S., & Coie, J. (1990). *Peer rejection in childhood*. New York: Cambridge.

Asher, S., & Hymel, S. (1981). Children's social competence in peer relations: Sociometric and behavioral assessments. In J. Wine & M. Smye (Eds.), *Social competence* (pp. 125–157). New York: Guilford.

Asher, S., Singleton, L., Tinsley, B., & Hymel, S. (1979). A reliable sociometric measure for preschool children. *Developmental Psychology, 15*, 443–444.

Babad, E. (2001). On the conception and measurement of popularity: More facts and some straight conclusions. *Social Psychology of Education, 5*, 3–30.

Barry, C., & Wigfield, A. (2002). Self-perceptions of friendship-making ability and perceptions of friends' deviant behavior: Childhood to adolescence. *Journal of Early Adolescence, 22*(2), 143–172.

Bierman, K. (2004). *Peer rejection: Developmental processes and intervention strategies*. New York: Guilford.

Bukowski, W. (2000). *Recent advances in the measurement of acceptance and rejection in the peer system* (New Directions for Child and Adolescent Development No. 88). San Francisco: Jossey-Bass.

Bukowski, W. M., & Cillessen, A. H. N. (1998). *Sociometry then and now: Building on six decades of measuring children' experiences within the peer group* (New Directions for Child Development No. 80). San Francisco: Jossey-Bass.

Bukowski, W. M., Sippola, L., Hoza, B., & Newcomb, A. F. (2000). Pages from a sociometric notebook: An analysis of nomination and rating scale measures of acceptance, rejection and social preference. *New Directions for Child and Adolescent Development, 88*, 11–26.

Cairns, R., Leung, M., Gest, S., & Cairns, B. (1995). A brief method for assessing social development: Structure, reliability, stability, and developmental validity of the Interpersonal Competence Scale. *Behaviour Research and Therapy, 33*(6), 725–736.

Caravita, S. C. S., Di Blasio, P., & Salmivalli, C. (2009). Unique and interactive effects of empathy and social status on involvement in bullying. *Social Development, 18*, 140–163.

Caravita, S. C. S., Di Blasio, P., & Salmivalli, C. (2010). Early adolescents' participation in bullying: Is ToM involved? *Journal of Early Adolescence, 30*(1), 138–170.

Carlson, W., & Rose, A. (2007). The role of reciprocity in romantic relationships in middle childhood and early adolescence. *Merrill-Palmer Quarterly, 53*(2), 262–290.

Cillessen, A. H. N. (2009). Sociometric methods. In K. H. Rubin, W. M. Bukowski, & B. Laursen (Eds.), *Handbook of peer interactions, relationships and groups* (pp. 82–99). New York: Guilford.

Cillessen, A. H. N., & Borch, C. (2006). Developmental trajectories of adolescent popularity: A growth curve modeling analysis. *Journal of Adolescence, 29*, 935–959.

Cillessen, A. H. N., Bukowski, W., & Haselager, G. (2000). Stability of sociometric categories. *New Directions for Child and Adolescent Development, 88*, 75–93.

Cillessen, A. H. N., & Mayeux, L. (2004a). From censure to reinforcement: Developmental changes in the association between aggression and social status. *Child Development, 75*, 147–163.

Cillessen, A. H. N., & Mayeux, L. (2004b). Sociometric status and peer group behavior: Previous findings and current directions. In J. Kupersmidt & K. Dodge (Eds.), *Children's peer relations: From development to intervention*. Washington, DC: American Psychological Association.

Cillessen, A. H. N., & Rose, A. (2005). Understanding popularity in the peer system. *Current Directions in Psychological Science, 14*, 102–105.

Closson, L. M. (2009a). Status and gender differences in early adolescents' descriptions of popularity. *Social Development, 18*(2), 412–426.

Closson, L. M. (2009b). Aggressive and prosocial behaviors within early adolescent friendship cliques: What's status got to do with it? *Merrill-Palmer Quarterly, 55*(4), 406–435.

Coie, J. D., & Cillessen, A. H. N. (1993). Peer rejection: Origins and effects on children's development. *Current Directions in Psychological Science, 2*, 89–92.

Coie, J. D., Dodge, K., & Coppotelli, H. (1982). Dimensions and types of social status: A cross-age perspective. *Developmental Psychology, 18*, 557–570.

Crick, N., & Ladd, G. (1989). Nominator attrition: Does it affect the accuracy of children's sociometric classifications? *Merrill-Palmer Quarterly, 35*, 197–207.

Dijkstra, J., Lindenberg, S., & Veenstra, R. (2008). Beyond the class norm: Bullying behavior of popular adolescents and its relation to peer acceptance and rejection. *Journal of Abnormal Child Psychology, 36*, 1289–1299.

Eder, D. (1985). The cycle of popularity: Interpersonal relations among female adolescents. *Sociology of Education, 58*(3), 154–165.

Eder, D., Evans, C., & Parker, S. (1995). *School talk: Gender and adolescent culture*. New Brunswick, NJ: Rutgers University Press.

Eder, D., & Kinney, D. (1995). The effect of middle school extracurricular activities on adolescents' popularity and peer status. *Youth & Society, 26*, 298–324.

Estell, D. (2007). Aggression, social status, and affiliation in kindergarten children: A preliminary study. *Education and Treatment of Children, 30*(2), 53–72.

Farmer, T., Estell, D., Bishop, J., O'Neal, K., & Cairns, B. (2003). Rejected bullies or popular leaders? The social relations of aggressive subtypes or rural African American early adolescents. *Developmental Psychology, 39*(6), 992–1004.

Farmer, T., & Rodkin, P. (1996). Antisocial and prosocial correlates of classroom social positions: The social network centrality perspective. *Social Development, 5*, 174–188.

Gorman, A., Kim, J., & Schimmelbusch, A. (2002). The attributes adolescents associate with peer popularity and teacher preference. *Journal of School Psychology, 40*(2), 143–165.

Gronlund, N. (1959). *Sociometry in the classroom*. New York: Harper.

Hawley, P. (2003). Prosocial and coercive configurations of resource control in early adolescence: A case for the well-adapted Machiavellian. *Merrill-Palmer Quarterly, 49*(3), 279–309.

Hawley, P., Little, T., & Card, N. (2007). The allure of a mean friend: Relationship quality and processes of aggressive adolescents with prosocial skills. *International Journal of Behavioral Development, 31*(2), 170–180.

Hawley, P., Little, T., & Card, N. (2008). The myth of the alpha male: A new look at dominance-related beliefs and behaviors among adolescent males and females. *International Journal of Behavioral Development, 32*, 76–88.

Hymel, S., & Rubin, K. (1985). Children with peer relationship and social skills problems Conceptual, methodological and developmental issues. In G. J. Whitehurst (Ed.), *Annals of child development* (Vol. 2, pp. 251–297). Greenwich, CT: JAI.

Hymel, S., Schonert-Reichl, K., & Miller, L. (2006). Reading, 'riting, 'rithmetic and relationships: Considering the social side of education. *Exceptionality Education Canada, 16*(3), 149–192.

Hymel, S., Vaillancourt, T., McDougall, P., & Renshaw, P. (2002). Acceptance and rejection by the peer group. In P. Smith & C. Hart (Eds.), *Blackwell handbook of childhood social development* (pp. 265–284). London: Blackwell.

Jiang, X., & Cillessen, A. H. N. (2005). Stability of continuous measures of sociometric status: A meta-analysis. *Developmental Review, 25*, 1–25.

Kindermann, T., & Gest, S., (2009). Assessment of the peer group: Identifying naturally occurring social networks and capturing their effects. In K. Rubin, W. Bukowski, & B. Laursen (Eds.), *Handbook of peer interactions, relationships and groups* (pp. 100–117). New York: Guilford.

Koch, H. (1933). Popularity among preschool children: Some related factors and a technique for its measurement. *Child Development, 4*, 164–175.

Košir, K., & Pečjak, S. (2005). Sociometry as a method for investigating peer relationships: What does it actually measure? *Educational Research, 47*(1), 127–144.

Kuppens, S., Grietens, H., Onghena, P., Michiels, D., & Subramanian, S. (2008). Individual and classroom variables associated with relational aggression in elementary-school aged children: A multilevel analysis. *Journal of School Psychology, 46*, 639–660.

Ladd, G. (2005). *Children's peer relations and social competence: A century of progress.* New Haven, CT: Yale University Press.

LaFontana, K., & Cillessen, A. H. N. (1999). Children's interpersonal perceptions as a function of sociometric and peer-perceived popularity. *Journal of Genetic Psychology, 160*, 225–242.

LaFontana, K., & Cillessen, A. H. N. (2002). Children's perceptions of popular and unpopular peers: A multimethod assessment. *Developmental Psychology, 38*(5), 635–647.

LaFontana, K., & Cillessen, A. H. N. (2009). Developmental changes in the priority of perceived status in childhood and adolescence. *Social Development, 19*(1), 130–147.

LaFreniere, P., & Charlesworth, W. (1983). Dominance, attention, and affiliation in a preschool group: A nine-month longitudinal study. *Ethology and Sociobiology, 4*, 55–67.

Leadbeater, B., Boone, E., Sangster, N., & Mathieson, L. (2006). Sex differences in the personal costs and benefits of relational and physical aggression in high school. *Aggressive Behavior, 32*, 409–419.

Leary, M. (2001). *Interpersonal rejection.* New York: Oxford University Press.

Lease, A., Kennedy, C., & Axelrod, J. (2002). Children's social constructions of popularity. *Social Development, 11*(1), 87–109.

Maassen, G., van der Linden, J., & Akkermans, W. (1997). Nominations, ratings and dimensions of sociometric status. *International Journal of Behavioral Development, 21*, 179–199.

Maassen, G., van der Linden, J., Goossens, F., & Bokhorst, J. (2000). A rating-based approach to two-dimensional sociometric status determination. *New Directions for Child and Adolescent Development, 88*, 55–73.

Mayeux, L., & Cillessen, A. H. N. (2008). It's not just being popular, it's knowing it, too: The role of self-perceptions of status in the associations between peer status and aggression. *Social Development, 14*(4), 871–888.

Mayeux, L., Sandstrom, M., & Cillessen, A. H. N. (2008). Is being popular a risky proposition? *Journal of Research on Adolescence, 18*(1), 49–74.

Mayeux, L., Underwood, M., & Risser, S. (2007). Perspectives on the ethics of sociometric research with children: How children, peers, and teachers help to inform the debate. *Merrill-Palmer Quarterly, 53*(1), 53–78.

McDougall, P., Hymel, S., Vaillancourt, T., & Mercer, L. (2001). The consequences of early childhood rejection. In M. Leary (Ed.), *Interpersonal rejection* (pp. 213–247). New York: Oxford.

Merten, D. (1997). The meaning of meanness: Popularity, competition, and conflict among junior high school girls. *Sociology of Education, 70*, 175–191.

Moreno, J. L. (1934). *Who shall survive? A new approach to the problem of human interrelations.* Washington, DC: Nervous and Mental Disease Publishing.

Nelson, D. A., Robinson, C., & Hart, C. H. (2005). Relational and physical aggression of pre-school children: Peer status linkages across informants. *Early Education & Development, 16*, 116–139.

Nelson, D. A., Robinson, C., Hart, C. H., Albano, A. D., & Marshall, S. J. (in press). Italian preschoolers' peer status linkages with sociability and subtypes of aggression and victimization. *Social Development.*

Newcomb, A., Bukowski, W., & Pattee, L. (1993). Children's peer relations: A meta-analytic review of popular, rejected, neglected, controversial, and average sociometric status. *Psychological Bulletin, 113*, 99–128.

Northway, M. (1944). Outsiders: A study of the personality patterns of children least acceptable to their agemates. *Sociometry, 7*, 10–25.

Northway, M. (1946). Personality and sociometric status: A review of the Toronto studies. *Sociometry, 9*, 233–241.

Parker, J., & Asher, S. (1987). Friendship and friendship quality in middle-childhood: Links with peer group acceptance and feelings of loneliness and social dissatisfaction. *Developmental Psychology, 29*, 357–389.

Parkhurst, J., & Hopmeyer, A. (1998). Sociometric popularity and peer-perceived popularity: Two distinct dimensions of peer status. *Journal of Early Adolescence, 18*, 125–144.

Poulin, F., & Dishion, T. (2008). Methodological issues in the use of peer sociometric nominations with middle school youth. *Social Development, 17*(4), 908–921.

Prinstein, M. (2007). Assessment of adolescents' preference- and reputation-based peer status using sociometric experts. *Merrill-Palmer Quarterly, 53*(2), 243–261.

Prinstein, M., & Cillessen, A. H. N. (2003). Forms and functions of adolescent peer aggression associated with high levels of peer status. *Merrill-Palmer Quarterly, 49*(3), 310–342.

Prinstein, M., Rancourt, D., Guerry, J., & Browne, C. (2009). Peer reputations and psychological adjustment. In K. Rubin, W. Bukowski, & B. Laursen (Eds.), *Handbook of peer interactions, relationships, and groups* (pp. 548–567). New York: Guilford.

Renshaw, P. (1981). The roots of peer interaction research: A historical analysis of the 1930s. In S. Asher & J. Gottman (Eds.), *The development of children's friendships* (pp. 1–25). New York: Cambridge University Press.

Rodkin, P., & Berger, C. (2008). Who bullies whom? Social status asymmetries by victim gender. *International Journal of Behavioral Development, 32*(6), 473–485.

Rodkin, P., Farmer, T., Pearl, R., & Van Acker, R. (2000). Heterogeneity of popular boys: Antisocial and prosocial configurations. *Developmental Psychology, 36*, 14–24.

Rodkin, P., Farmer, T., Pearl, R., & Van Acker, R. (2006). They're cool: Social status and peer group supports for aggressive boys and girls. *Social Development, 15*, 175–204.

Rose, A. J., Swenson, L., & Waller, E. (2004). Overt and relational aggression and perceived popularity: Developmental differences in concurrent and prospective relations. *Developmental Psychology, 40*, 378–387.

Rubin, K. H., Bukowski, W., & Parker, J. (2006). Peer interactions, relationships and groups. In W. Damon & R. Lerner (Series Eds.) & N. Eisenberg (Vol. Ed.), *Handbook of child psychology: Vol. 3. Social, emotional and personality development* (6th ed., pp. 571–645). New York: Wiley.

Rubin, K., Hymel, S., LeMare, L., & Rowden, L. (1989). Children experiencing social difficulties: Sociometric neglect reconsidered. *Canadian Journal of Behavioral Science, 21*, 84–111.

Ryan, A., & Shim, S. (2008). An exploration of young adolescents' social achievement goals and social adjustment in middle school. *Journal of Educational Psychology, 100*, 672–668.

Sandstrom, M., & Cillessen, A. H. N. (2006). Likeable versus popular: Distinct implications for adolescent adjustment. *International Journal of Behavioral Development, 30*(4), 305–314.

Schwartz, D., Gorman, A., Nakamoto, J., & McKay, T. (2006). Popularity, social acceptance, and aggression in adolescent peer groups: Links with academic performance and school attendance. *Developmental Psychology, 42*(6), 1116–1127.

Terry, R. (2000). Recent advances in measurement theory and the use of sociometric techniques. In W. Damon (Series Ed.) and A. H. N. Cillessen & W. Bukowski (Vol. Eds.), *Recent advances in the measurement of acceptance and rejection in the peer system* (New Directions for Child and Adolescent Development No. 88, pp. 27–54). San Francisco: Jossey-Bass.

Terry, R., & Coie, J. (1991). A comparison of methods for defining sociometric status among children. *Developmental Psychology, 27*, 867–880.

Vaillancourt, T. (2001). *Competing for hegemony during adolescence: A link between aggression and social status* (Unpublished doctoral dissertation). University of British Columbia, Vancouver.

Vaillancourt, T., & Hymel, S. (2006). Aggression and social status: The moderating roles of sex and peer-valued characteristics. *Aggressive Behavior, 32*(4), 396–408.

Wargo Aikins, J., & Cillessen, A. H. N. (2007). *Stability and correlates of sociometric status in early adolescence*. Unpublished manuscript, Department of Psychology, University of Connecticut, Storrs, CT.

Weisfeld, G., Bloch, S., & Ivers, J. (1983). A factor-analytic study of peer-perceived dominance in adolescent boys. *Adolescence, 18*, 229–243.

Weisfeld, G., Bloch, S., & Ivers, J. (1984). Possible determinants of social dominance among adolescent girls. *Journal of Genetic Psychology, 144*, 115–129.

Wu, X., Hart, C., Draper, T., & Olsen, J. (2001). Peer and teacher sociometrics for preschool children: Cross-informant concordance, temporal stability, and reliability. *Merrill-Palmer Quarterly, 47*, 416–443.

Xie, H., Li, Y., Boucher, S., Hutchins, B., & Carins, B. (2006). What makes a girl (or a boy) popular (or unpopular)? African American children's perceptions and developmental differences. *Developmental Psychology, 42*(4), 599–612.

CHAPTER TWENTY-ONE

Social Skills and Social Competence in Interactions With Peers

Antonius H. N. Cillessen and Amy D. Bellmore

Role of Peer Relationships in Social Development

Children's relationships with their peers are an important aspect of their social development. The study of peer relations is a flourishing field in social development research. Researchers typically study peer relationships at three levels: individual, dyadic, and group. At the individual level are the social roles of individual children in the peer group, such as being popular, rejected, a bully, or a victim. At the dyadic level are relationships such as friendships or antipathies. At the group level are the larger social groups or cliques within which children organize themselves and interact with each other.

Two sides can be distinguished to research on peer relationships at each of these levels. On the one hand, researchers are concerned about the effects of peer relationships at each of these levels on children's development. Researchers ask what the consequences are of being rejected or popular on subsequent development and adjustment. Influential theories state that adequate peer relationships serve important functions for social and cognitive development (see, for a review, Hartup, 1992). Based on these views, rejection, exclusion, and victimization are expected to be detrimental for development, whereas popularity, inclusion, and cooperative relationships are expected to have multiple positive effects. A large body of research has shown evidence for these opposing developmental pathways (see Rubin, Bukowski, & Parker, 2006).

On the other hand, researchers are interested in the roots and causes of children's peer relationships. They also ask what the specific behaviors and social skills are that determine

The Wiley-Blackwell Handbook of Childhood Social Development, Second Edition, edited by Peter K. Smith and Craig H. Hart
© 2011 by Blackwell Publishing Ltd.

whether one child has successful peer relationships (is popular, has friends, and is included), whereas another does not. Which skills determine why one child is competent and successful in interactions with peers, with the added benefit of later positive consequences, whereas another is incompetent or unsuccessful? This chapter focuses on the behavioral and social cognitive skills that determine children's social competence with peers in early and middle childhood.

Conceptualizing Social Competence

The definition of *social competence* is a much debated and complex issue. General definitions refer to adequacy, effectiveness, or success in interactions with peers (see Rose-Krasnor, 1997). Beyond these somewhat abstract definitions, how has social competence been operationalized concretely in research? One common and frequently used operational definition of social competence is children's peer acceptance (Rose-Krasnor, 1997). Peer acceptance is measured by asking children who they like most and like least in the peer group. Children are then rank ordered according to their degree of likeability, acceptance, or preference in the peer group. It is then assumed that peer acceptance is caused by underlying social skills or social competence. Indeed, a high degree of peer acceptance correlates with many prosocial behaviors and skills, and a low degree of acceptance (e.g., rejection) with a lack of such skills (Rubin et al., 2006). This unidimensional view of social competence as represented by one dimension of peer acceptance was common and efficient for many years. Recent research on peer relationships, however, suggests that reality is a bit more complex. This research suggests that there is not one way to be socially competent with peers, but two. The formulation of two forms of social competence with peers was derived from recent research on popularity in the peer group.

Two forms of popularity

In the 1980s and 1990s, the majority of research on children's peer relations focused on children with problematic peer relations. From this research, much has been learned about the correlates, precursors, and consequences of peer rejection (see Asher & Coie, 1990). Recently, peer relations researchers have become increasingly interested in popularity, whereas understanding and preventing rejection remain concerns. One reason for the focus on popularity is that popular children are often seen as models of prosocial skills and behaviors, and thus that much about social competence could be learned from them. Reality, however, has turned out to be more complex. Not all popular children are uniformly prosocial (for a review, see Cillessen & Rose, 2005). Sometimes aggression, bullying, or manipulative behaviors are also correlated with popularity, for boys (Rodkin, Farmer, Pearl, & Van Acker, 2000) as well as girls (de Bruyn & Cillessen, 2006). These findings indicate that popularity is not a homogeneous construct.

The heterogeneity of popularity is captured well by the distinction between sociometric and perceived popularity (Parkhurst & Hopmeyer, 1998). *Sociometric popularity* is a measure of likeability or acceptance in the peer group, commonly assessed by asking children who they like most and like least in the peer group. *Perceived popularity* is a measure of social impact or visibility in the peer group, commonly assessed by asking children who they see as most popular and least popular (see also Chapter 20, this volume).

Sociometric and perceived popularity are unique dimensions of the peer group. Children who are seen as popular are not necessarily liked. The correlation between the two dimensions is moderate in elementary school and decreases further with development, especially for girls. Evidence for the discriminant validity of sociometric and perceived popularity also comes from their unique correlations with behavior. Sociometric popularity is consistently correlated with prosocial traits and behaviors, and perceived popularity with a mixture of prosocial and antisocial behaviors and outcomes (Cillessen & Rose, 2005; Mayeux, Sandstrom, & Cillessen, 2008).

Dual-component model of social competence

The heterogeneity of popularity can be placed in a broader perspective, theorizing that sociometric and perceived popularity reflect two different ways of being competent or successful in interactions with others. The first form of social competence refers to a child's abilities to be prosocial and cooperative, and to the social and cognitive skills to perceive others accurately, take their perspective, and read their emotions. Interpersonal perception accuracy, perspective taking, and emotion understanding and sharing enable a child to be prosocial, empathic, understanding, and supportive, and to respond to the needs of other children. Children who possess these skills behave in ways that make them well liked. They do not need force to assert or express themselves; hence, they are unlikely to use aggressive or dominant behaviors.

The second form of social competence refers to a child's abilities to be interpersonally effective and achieve goals in social situations, for either oneself or the group, in principle through playing by the rules, but if needed through convincing argumentation, coercion and forcefulness, strong self-assertions, or intelligent manipulation. A child who excels in this domain may not be the most interpersonally sensitive, but is a well-connected leader who can achieve goals in effective ways that may be seen as domineering, aggressive, or manipulative by some, but as assertive, socially savvy, and effective by others. Children who possess these skills behave in ways that make them visible, prestigious, and central in their peer group; hence, they are seen as popular but not necessarily well liked. They may use force to assert themselves; hence, certain forms of aggression or dominant behaviors are part of their behavioral repertoire.

In an application of this framework, de Bruyn, Cillessen, and Wissink (2010) hypothesized that both forms of social competence are protective against victimization. Children who are well liked provide few reasons to elicit bullying from peers. The perceived popular child is too dominant or well connected to become a victim. Therefore, equal negative associations were expected of sociometric and perceived popularity with victimization. These expectations were confirmed.

Contrasting associations were expected for bullying. Sociometric popularity, indicating the prosocial and interpersonally sensitive dimension of social competence, was expected to be negatively related to bullying. Perceived popularity, a marker of the interpersonally effective but not necessarily sensitive component of social competence, was expected to be positively related to bullying. Children who are primarily effective in achieving personal or group goals may sometimes resort to aggression and peer group manipulation to do so. These expectations were also confirmed. De Bruyn et al. (2010) indeed found negative associations of sociometric popularity with bullying, but positive associations of perceived popularity with bullying.

In this chapter, this dual-component model is used to examine social competence in early and middle childhood. The model refers to behavioral skills and social cognitive skills. Researchers have examined children's behavioral skills in critical situations, such as free playing with peers, entering a new peer group, and solving conflict. Such situations have been studied with experimental and naturalistic observations, as well as hypothetical vignettes. They are common for young children and excellent tests of their behavioral skills. In addition, social cognitive processes are important. They include, for example, children's social goal orientations and their perceptions of themselves and others. Thus, both behavioral and social cognitive skills will be reviewed for the two forms of social competence. Variations by culture, gender, and development will be discussed, as far as they have been investigated.

Social Skills of Sociometrically Popular, Accepted, and Preferred Children

Behavioral skills

Competent play with peers   Play is the context in which young children most frequently interact with their peers. Play behavior is most frequently observed in naturalistic settings such as preschool classrooms or child care settings during periods where children may freely choose their playmates and activities (e.g., Howes & Matheson, 1992). Within this context, researchers have attended to different aspects of play. For example, Howes (1988) assessed the complexity of social play (e.g., complementary and reciprocal play) and suggested that children's play forms follow a developmental sequence. Ladd, Price, and Hart (1988) attended to differences in the behavioral styles of preschool children's play (e.g., solitary) as well as structural characteristics (e.g., the average size of the group in which play occurs).

These measures of play behavior are related to concurrent and later indicators of a child's functioning with peers. Howes and Matheson (1992) found that preschool-aged children who engaged in more complex peer play were rated later by teachers as having less difficulty with their peers. Doyle and Connolly (1989) found that peer nominations of acceptance correlated positively with the frequency of social pretend play. Ladd et al. (1988) found that some play styles predict changes in peer acceptance over the course of a school year. Cooperative play of preschoolers in the fall of the school year predicted gains in peer acceptance by spring, whereas arguing during play in the fall predicted lower peer acceptance by the winter of the school year.

Cultural differences in play behavior have received attention. Fantuzzo, Coolahan, Mendez, McDermott, and Sutton-Smith (1998) argued that, given the contextual specificity of play, the associations between competent play and peer acceptance should be considered within cultural groups. They established the validity of an instrument to assess play competencies that differentiate children who have positive peer relationships from children who have poor peer relationships within a sample of African American Head Start children.

Farver, Kim, and Lee (1995) presented evidence that play complexity may be affected by culture-specific socialization practices. They found that Korean American preschool children participated in less social pretend play than their Anglo-American counterparts and suggested that this difference may be related to the more structured classroom setting of Korean American preschools or to the collectivistic orientation of Korean culture. This demonstrates the importance of assessing the associations between play behaviors and peer acceptance in settings that are suited for each group, if different cultural groups are considered.

Researchers have also established sex differences in the play behaviors that predict peer acceptance. Hart, DeWolf, and Burts (1993) found that lower peer preference was associated with solitary play for preschool girls but not for boys. In an observational study of preschoolers, Hart, DeWolf, Wozniak, and Burts (1992) found that prosocial behavior in play was related to peer acceptance for girls only. In addition to play styles, researchers have also examined sex differences in peer interaction contact. Ramsey (1995) found that older preschool children decreased their mixed-sex peer contacts over the course of a school year (from fall to spring), whereas younger preschool children increased their contacts. Playground behaviors and group composition (e.g., network intensivity versus extensivity, and network homogeneity versus diversity) also predict peer acceptance differentially for school-aged boys and girls (e.g., Ladd, 1983).

Children's play behaviors can be expected to be influenced by other contextual effects, such as the play environment and the composition of the play group. The effects of such contextual variables on the association between peer acceptance and play should be examined. Further, the stability of children's play behaviors from preschool to middle childhood should be studied. There is evidence that the quality of elementary school children's rough-and-tumble play is related to peer acceptance (Pellegrini, 1988), but no evidence shows that play behavior is stable from preschool to middle childhood. Thus, an avenue for future research is to examine age as a moderator of the relationship between play behaviors and peer acceptance.

Peer group entry   Adequately initiating social contact in a group is necessary to develop stable relationships. The behaviors that result in successful peer group entry are important indicators of social competence. Correspondingly, studies have examined which aspects of children's peer group entry behavior are related to their peer acceptance.

Following the protocol established by Putallaz and Gottman (1981), a target child's peer group entry behavior is usually assessed in a laboratory with experimenter-formed groups of children who play a game when the target child arrives. Some experimenters comprise the "host" group of children with whom the target "guest" child is acquainted (e.g., Zarbatany, Van Brunschot, Meadows, & Pepper, 1996). Others use host children who are unacquainted with the guest (e.g., Russell & Finnie, 1990) or hosts who are confederates of the experimenter (e.g., Wilson, 1999). Peer group entry behavior has also been observed outside of the laboratory in the classroom (Dodge, Coie, & Brakke, 1982) and playground (Putallaz & Wasserman, 1989).

Using these methods, researchers have established the association between peer acceptance and group entry behavior (cf. Putallaz & Wasserman, 1990). Unaccepted children are more likely to call attention to themselves, attempt to control the interaction, and take longer to enter the peer group than accepted children (Dodge, Schlundt, Schocken, & Delugach, 1983; Putallaz & Gottman, 1981). Such disruptive and self-centered strategies are ineffective; the children who use them are not accepted by the host children (Borja-Alvarez, Zarbatany, & Pepper, 1991; Putallaz & Gottman, 1981). Conversely, well-accepted children successfully become a part of the group by sharing in the group's interest and offering relevant statements to the ongoing interaction (Dodge et al., 1983; Putallaz & Wasserman, 1989).

Other factors influence children's group entry behaviors and their resulting success. Gelb and Jacobson (1988) examined social contextual factors and found that unaccepted children are less likely to behave aversively in noncompetitive peer group entry situations than in competitive peer group entry situations. Rabiner and Coie (1989) examined intrapersonal factors and found that when rejected children had positive expectations about an upcoming play session with unfamiliar peers, they were more likely to be accepted by these unfamiliar peers during a peer group entry situation than when their initial expectations were neutral.

The gender composition of the host group and the gender of the guest child also play a role. Playground observations showed that girls were less effective and rejected more often than boys during entry bids with peers (Putallaz & Wasserman, 1989). However, when only same-sex interactions were considered, girls were more effective and more likely to be accepted by their peers than boys. This may relate to the finding that girls are more likely to include newcomers than boys when they are the hosts in the peer entry paradigm (Zarbatany et al., 1996).

The findings reported above were for elementary school children. Hazen and Black (1989) found similar results for preschool children. Robinson, Anderson, Porter, Hart, and Wouden-Miller (2003) examined the behavioral shifts that preschoolers follow during peer group entry. Similar to school-aged children, preschoolers exhibited a sequential play pattern from onlooker behavior to parallel aware play to cooperative social play patterns.

Putallaz and Wasserman (1989) found that the group entry skills of first, third, and fifth grade children differed. Older children were more likely to remain with the peers they initially approached, whereas younger children were more likely to engage in entry bids with various groups of peers. This suggests that successful peer group entry behaviors vary by age, and that what is a successful and competent strategy at one age may not be the same at another.

Given the increasing ethnic diversity present within various populations around the world researchers have recently turned their attention to the impact of ethnicity and ethnic composition on the play behaviors that children demonstrate when they enter a new classroom. With an ethnically diverse sample attending classrooms that reflected a range of ethnic and linguistic diversity, Howes, Sanders, and Lee (2008) found that children who were among the only students with their ethnic background within their classroom settings and spoke a different language at home than the language used by most students within the classroom had the greatest difficulties in forming relationships with their classmates. In contrast, children in ethnically diverse classrooms showed increased complexity in the play behaviors they used with their new peers. Thus, as opposed to ethnicity per se being a determinant of peer interactions, the ethnic composition of the peer group may be the stronger influence on the success of children's peer entry behaviors.

In addition to these gender, age, and ethnicity differences, other social contextual variables influence children's peer group entry behavior. Previous research suggests that group size (Putallaz & Wasserman, 1989), group status composition (Gelb & Jacobson, 1988), and group psychological state (Zarbatany & Pepper, 1996) affect the guest's behavior and entry success. These studies highlight the interactional nature of the relationship between the target child and the hosts, and emphasize that children's social skills need to be considered in their social context.

Conflict resolution   Shantz (1987) defined *conflict* as a dyadic social exchange characterized by mutual opposition between two parties. Conflict management is necessary for the maintenance of relationships. Therefore, researchers have identified conflict resolution strategies as an important social skill for children. Indeed, research has shown that preschool and elementary school children's conflict resolution strategies are related to their peer acceptance.

The association between peer acceptance and conflict resolution strategies has been examined in various settings. Children's behavioral strategies in peer conflict situations (e.g., seeking an adult's help or using physical aggression) and their verbal strategies (e.g., discussing the situation or using verbal aggression) have been observed in field settings such as classroom free play (e.g., Hartup, Laursen, Stewart, & Eastenson, 1988) and in laboratory settings where the composition of dyads and the activities were manipulated (e.g., Hartup, French, Laursen, Johnston, & Ogawa, 1993). Observations of young children during free play have shown that low peer acceptance is correlated with more frequent participation in conflict episodes (Shantz, 1986). Verbal strategies are used far more frequently than physical force in conflict episodes (Eisenberg & Garvey, 1981). However, research in which observed behavior in conflict situations was related to peer acceptance is lacking.

The most widely used method to investigate peer acceptance and conflict resolution is to examine children's responses to hypothetical conflict situations. Typically, children are presented with a realistic conflict situation with a peer and asked to indicate how they would respond. Because every child is exposed to the same scenarios, this method allows researchers to make controlled comparisons. Rose and Asher (1999) used this method to assess the strategies that fourth- and fifth-grade children use in response to conflict with a friend. Children's use of hostile strategies (e.g., physical or verbal aggression) was negatively correlated with peer acceptance. Chung and Asher (1996) assessed fourth- through sixth-grade children's strategies in conflicts with a same-sex classmate and found that prosocial strategies (e.g., accommodation of the needs of both parties) were positively correlated with peer acceptance. They also found that gender moderated the association between peer acceptance and conflict strategies. Hostile strategies were negatively correlated with peer acceptance for girls, whereas adult-seeking strategies (requesting help from an adult) were negatively correlated with peer acceptance for boys.

Green and colleagues (Green, Cillessen, Rechis, Patterson, & Milligan, 2008) examined the prosocial assertive, passive, and coercive strategies that 6-year-olds proposed in response to two socially challenging situations: displacing another child in a game and obtaining a toy from another child. The scenarios also varied the gender composition of the story protagonists. Girls and boys responded similarly in their general suggestions of prosocial or assertive strategies, but girls were more likely to offer prosocial strategies with other girls than with boys. Teacher-rated competence and antisocial behavior interacted in predicting coercive responses by girls but not by boys. The results demonstrate that prosocial and antisocial behaviors need to be considered in interaction to fully understand the nature of social competence.

These gender differences correspond with the different social orientations expected of boys and girls. In response to both actual and hypothetical conflict, girls are more likely to select relationship-oriented strategies, whereas boys are more likely to select assertive, self-centered strategies (Chung & Asher, 1996; Hartup et al., 1993; Miller, Danaher, & Forbes, 1986; Rose & Asher, 1999). These differences are further qualified by the gender of the interaction partner. Miller et al.'s observational study of children's actual conflict behavior showed that boys used assertive strategies when interacting with boys and girls, whereas girls were more likely to use prosocial strategies with girls than with boys.

There is little information regarding developmental differences in children's conflict resolution strategies. Most studies of children's strategies have used elementary school–aged children, and within these studies, age differences typically have not been examined. An exception is a study by Mayeux and Cillessen (2003), who administered social cognitive interviews to kindergarten and first-grade boys in 2 consecutive years of a longitudinal study. Boys' responses were primarily prosocial, with a sizeable minority of avoidant and antisocial solutions. Older boys provided more effective solutions than younger boys, and stabilities were modest but significant for subcategories of both prosocial and antisocial responses. Boys who were accepted by their peers provided more prosocial and effective solutions than did boys of lower status, but no status differences emerged for antisocial responses. The data also suggested that young children view aggression as an acceptable means to solving peer conflict.

In addition to individual characteristics such as age, gender, and ethnicity, social contextual factors are expected to influence children's responses to conflict (Hartup & Laursen, 1993). Future research should examine how contextual variables such as relationship characteristics (e.g., friend versus nonfriend), characteristics of the setting (e.g., space, resources, and activities), and conflict type (e.g., object acquisition, peer provocation, and rights infraction) influence children's responses to conflict.

Conclusion   Children's behavior in various critical social tasks is related to their peer acceptance. The social tasks discussed are diagnostic to assess socially competent behavior. However, the critical social task approach has not provided much information about developmental changes in the association between behavior and peer acceptance. Although age differences can be identified indirectly by comparing studies with different age groups, few direct comparisons of developmental differences in relation to peer acceptance exist for the tasks reviewed here. Additionally, researchers have not consistently attended to gender differences. For example, although clear gender differences have been identified in conflict resolution strategies, they have not been examined for children's play styles. Given that the studies on peer group entry show interactions between gender of the actor and gender of the peer group, more research is needed on the situational specificity of skillful behaviors. In particular, researchers should conduct more detailed analyses of the interactions between characteristics of the actor and the dyadic or group partners and how they may vary by task.

Social and cognitive skills

Appropriate behavior may depend on accurate perception of the actions and intentions of peers. *Interpersonal perception* refers to one's understanding of self and of others in social interactions. Children's understanding of self and others in relationships is expected to influence their peer play, peer group entry, and conflict resolution strategies. Children's interpersonal perception skills are examined, both conceptually and empirically, and how they are related to social competence as measured by peer acceptance.

Interpersonal perceptions   Most early research on the development of interpersonal perception was directed toward establishing its normative development. For example, researchers addressed the types of perceptions that children form of themselves and others (see Dubin & Dubin, 1965, for a review). More recent research has focused on establishing individual differences in children's interpersonal perceptions and the factors related to them (see Berndt & Burgy, 1996, for a review). In this more recent trend, researchers have examined children's perceptions of their own and others' characteristics and competencies in the social, behavioral, cognitive, and physical domains, including their general peer sociability and liking by peers. In addition, researchers have examined children's assessments of how well liked they are by specific peers. A major question in this research has been the degree to which children's general and dyad-specific interpersonal perceptions are accurate.

An important distinction is made between perceptions of competencies and perceptions of liking. Accuracy of perceived competencies is usually measured by comparing children's ratings of themselves on some characteristic with another person's ratings of the same behavior. For example, children's self-ratings of disruptive behavior in school would be compared with teacher ratings of the same behavior. In some cases, children's self-perceptions are compared to the average perceptions of a peer group (classmates, grade mates, and clique members). Accuracy of liking perceptions, however, is usually assessed by comparing the sociometric nominations or ratings a target child expects to receive from others with others' actual nominations or ratings of the target child. This has been done at both the dyadic and group levels.

Perception accuracy   Research on the development of interpersonal perception accuracy has been guided by the assumption that children's social perception skills develop in accordance with general cognitive abilities. Based on Piaget's (1983) conclusion that young children's egocentric thinking prevents them from social perspective taking and being accurate perceivers of others, most studies of perception accuracy have excluded children under age 6. Consistent with Piaget's theory, interpersonal perception accuracy has been demonstrated in children age 6 and older (e.g., Malloy, Yarlas, Montvilo, & Sugarman, 1996). Further, perception accuracy increases throughout middle childhood and into early adolescence, although the improvement tends to be small (Ausubel, Schiff, & Gasser, 1952; DeJung & Gardner, 1962; Krantz & Burton, 1986; Malloy et al., 1996; Phillips, 1963).

Although perception accuracy does increase minimally throughout middle childhood, the notion that interpersonal perceptions will not be accurate until middle childhood is not supported. Smith and Delfosse (1980) found that preschool-aged children are able to correctly identify who their own friends are as well as who their classmates' friends are. Thus, the specific cognitive skills that underlie this ability might be established as early as 4 years of age.

Perceptions of competencies   The notion of interpersonal perception as a social skill has been propelled by demonstrations of individual differences in accuracy. The majority of studies on this topic have used peer acceptance as an indicator of social competence and have been conducted almost exclusively with elementary school–aged children. These studies have shown that low-accepted children are the least able to assess themselves or others accurately on various traits and behaviors, whereas accepted children are more accurate social perceivers.

Kurdek and Krile (1982) found that children in grades 3–8 who were seen as the most socially competent also reported the highest perceived social self-competence. This indicates that accepted children do have awareness of their peer acceptance. Patterson, Kupersmidt, and Griesler (1990) compared third- and fourth-grade children's social, academic, and behavioral self-perceptions with independent assessments of the same traits. They found that rejected children overestimated their social acceptance, accepted and average children underestimated their peer acceptance, and neglected children underestimated their behavioral competence. Cillessen and Bellmore (1999) also examined peer acceptance and social self-perceptions in the fourth grade. They found that rejected children's self-ratings showed the smallest amount of agreement with teacher ratings of conduct, peer sociability, and school adjustment.

Boivin and Bégin (1989) found two clusters of rejected children based on their self-perceptions: one group who underestimated the peer acceptance and competencies, and one group who overestimated them. Patterson et al. (1990) found that rejected children who overestimated their acceptance and competencies were likely to be aggressive. This pattern of self-perceptions complements other evidence for subgroups of rejected children, typically labeled *aggressive-rejected* and *withdrawn-rejected* (see Cillessen, van IJzendoorn, van Lieshout, & Hartup, 1992). It suggests that withdrawn-rejected children might underestimate themselves and be at risk for internalizing problems, whereas aggressive-rejected children may overestimate themselves and be at risk for externalizing problems. Findings by Hymel, Bowker, and Woody (1993) are consistent with this idea. They classified fourth and fifth graders into four groups (aggressive unpopular, withdrawn unpopular, aggressive-withdrawn unpopular, and average) and examined discrepancies between their self- and peer ratings in the academic, athletic, peer relations, and appearance domains. Average and withdrawn-unpopular children were the most accurate perceivers; both aggressive groups overestimated their competencies in all domains.

Few researchers have examined gender differences. The few studies that have indicate that the self- and other perceptions of competencies are somewhat more concordant for girls than for boys (Cillessen & Bellmore, 1999; Kurdek & Krile, 1982).

Perceptions of liking and disliking Studies on accuracy have also looked at children's perceptions of liking and disliking in the peer group. Krantz and Burton (1986) found that kindergarten through third grade children's own peer acceptance was correlated with greater accuracy in identifying the friendship preferences of their peers. MacDonald and Cohen (1995) examined dyadic accuracy scores of liking and disliking for first through sixth graders. Rejected children were the least accurate in their judgments of who liked them, and accepted children the least accurate in their judgments of who disliked them. Cillessen and Bellmore (1999) used the same method with fourth graders, but did not find an association with peer acceptance.

Zakriski and Coie (1996) compared the accuracy of perceived liking and disliking by peers in a sample of fourth-grade children who were classified as *aggressive-rejected, non-aggressive-rejected*, or *average*. The authors found that children who were both aggressive and rejected were the least accurate, and that aggressive-rejected children underestimated their rejection more than nonaggressive-rejected children did. Interestingly, this did not apply to perceptions of others but was limited to perceptions of self. This suggests that perception inaccuracy may serve a self-protective function for some children.

Again, relatively little is known about gender differences. Cillessen and Bellmore (1999) found that girls were more accurate than boys for perceptions of liking. MacDonald and Cohen (1995) found no sex differences in perception accuracy. A difference between these two studies is that Cillessen and Bellmore allowed cross-sex nominations in their sociometric procedure, whereas MacDonald and Cohen allowed only same-sex nominations. When gender effects due to the interaction between the gender of the perceiver and target were considered, Bellmore and Cillessen (2003) found that children were much more accurate perceivers of same-sex peers than other-sex peers, and this was equally true for both boys and girls.

Origins of interpersonal perception skill The association of perception accuracy with peer acceptance begs the question of how children arrive at their perceptions of self and others. Two processes may be at play. The first is congruent with the ideas of symbolic interactionists (Cooley, 1902), who claim that self-perceptions are internalized perceptions from others. According to symbolic interactionists, the accuracy of children's perceptions depends on the degree of their social interactions with others. Theorists agree that relations with others afford children the opportunity to acquire the skills they need to successful interact with them (Hartup, 1992). Thus, rejected children who are excluded from peer interaction may be inaccurate social perceivers because they lack opportunities to practice this skill.

The second process considers the social cognitions of the child as the antecedent to social interactions. Inaccurate self-perceptions are presumed to have negative consequences for social behavior and peer acceptance. This notion mirrors Dodge's model of social information processing, according to which perception deficits cause problematic social interactions (see Crick & Dodge, 1999).

These two processes are not mutually exclusive but may operate at the same time. The accuracy of children's social perceptions influences their peer interactions, but also depends on them. Future research should explore the directionality of the link between children's perceptions and their peer acceptance. Longitudinal studies will also help to determine the point in development at which an association between peer acceptance and perception accuracy emerges, and whether this association decreases with maturing social cognitive abilities.

Social Skills of Perceived Popular, Controversial, and Bistrategic Children

The traditional operational definition of *peer acceptance* has been challenged from at least three directions that have come together to reach a similar conclusion. One of these directions is research on bullying. Recent studies have shown that bullies are not always deficient aggressors who are rejected by their peers (e.g., Sutton, Smith, & Swettenham, 1999; Vaillancourt, Hymel, & McDougall, 2003). Instead, some bullies are high in status and well connected in the peer group. They may not be liked, but they are not unsuccessful. Their central position in the group may be derived from successful strategies to achieve and maintain a position of prominence in the peer group.

A second direction comes from research inspired by evolutionary or ethological approaches to social dominance and aggression (e.g., Hawley, Little, & Rodkin, 2007; Pellegrini & Long, 2002). Not surprising in this research tradition is the fact that some of the most dominant and successful members of a peer group use aggression. However, they do this often in combination with other, more prosocial strategies. The latter led Hawley (2002, 2003) to define a group of children labeled as *bistrategic*. This group is socially successful in that it has the highest degree of control over resources in the peer group, achieved through a combination of prosocial and aggressive behavioral strategies.

The third direction is research on popularity. Recent studies have shown that perceived popularity correlates with a mixture of prosocial and antisocial traits and behaviors, whereas sociometric popularity is primarily correlated with prosocial traits and behaviors. Noteworthy is the positive correlation of perceived popularity with relational aggression, a measure of indirect peer group manipulation (Cillessen & Mayeux, 2004; Rose, Swenson, & Waller, 2004).

The comparison is often made between perceived popularity and *controversial* peer status. Perceived popularity is a measure of social visibility and correlates positively with social impact (Cillessen, 2009). Because the controversial group scores high on social impact in traditional sociometric classification schemes (Parkhurst & Hopmeyer, 1998), the controversial group is examined here as well.

These directions converge to show a group of children who are socially successful in the peer group, but whose success is marked by an aggressive, manipulative, or domineering component. There is a form of success in the peer group that hinges on a combination of prosocial characteristics with aggressive and/or dominance-related behaviors. Prosocial behaviors alone lead to sociometric popularity, antisocial behaviors alone lead to peer rejection, but aggressive and/or manipulative behaviors in the context of a certain prosocial interaction style lead to visibility, dominance, influence, or power in the peer group that is expressed in perceived-popular, controversial, or bistrategic status. Evidence for this principle is examined in the same two areas considered above: behavioral skills and social cognitive skills.

Behavioral skills

There are positive correlations of perceived popularity with both prosocial and antisocial (aggressive) behaviors (see, for a review, Cillessen & Rose, 2005). For girls, the combination of perceived popularity and relational aggression is particularly pronounced (e.g., Cillessen & Mayeux, 2004; Rose et al., 2004). These findings are for middle childhood and early adolescent samples. Other studies have replicated them with younger children. For example, Green et al. (2008) found that the interaction between teacher-rated prosocial and antisocial behaviors predicted the highest levels of dominant behaviors in 6-year-old children, especially for girls.

Hawley (2002, 2003) distinguished two strategies that children may use to gain access to resources. Prosocial strategies work indirectly via positive behaviors such as reciprocity and cooperation. Coercive strategies work directly via agonistic behaviors such as taking, threatening, or manipulating others. These strategies can be used alone or in combination. Children who use both are called *bistrategic controllers*. These children score high not only on traditional measures of social skills, such as extroversion and attractiveness to peers, but also on aggression (Hawley, 2002, 2003). They are considered high in social dominance, because of their effectiveness in reaching their goals. These findings confirm that a high degree of social effectiveness or dominance is determined by prosocial and coercive strategies in concert.

Other studies specifically focused on relational aggression to establish dominance. Puckett, Wargo Aikins, and Cillessen (2008) found that adolescents who used relational aggression and were also prosocial or leaders were the most likely to be seen as popular. Relationally aggressive adolescents high in leadership, cooperation, and peer sociability were higher in perceived popularity than relationally aggressive students with low levels of these behaviors.

Again, other studies have replicated the role of relational aggression with younger children. Nelson, Robinson, and Hart (2005) examined the association between relational aggression and sociometric status in preschool-aged children. They found that the behavioral differences associated with sociometric status at older ages are already present in preschool. Specifically, relational aggression was associated with controversial status at this age already.

Together, these studies confirm that the combination of prosocial behaviors with manipulative or socially savvy behaviors that may be seen as aggressive predict a high degree of *social competence*, defined as being perceived as popular or bistrategically controlling. Children who are socially competent in this way, however, are not necessarily liked by their peers. These bistrategic children are controversial or perceived popular, depending on how status is measured.

Social cognitive skills

Less is known about the social cognitive skills of perceived popular, controversial, or bistrategically controlling youths than about their behavioral skills, as this is a relatively new but growing area of research. Studies have shown main effects of this type of social competence on social cognitive variables. Hawley (2002, 2003) found that bistrategic children score high on social perceptiveness. Caravita and Cillessen (2009) found a positive association between perceived popularity and agentic goals in middle childhood and early adolescence, whereas sociometric popularity was associated with communal goals. LaFontana and Cillessen (1999) found a correlation between perceived popularity and consensus with the rest of the classroom in judgments of liking and disliking in a sample of fourth through eighth graders.

However, as for behavioral skills, interactions are considered more important than main effects. This form of social competence is expected to be characterized by combinations of prosocial cognitions with agentic, dominance-related, or manipulative cognitions. Social success, defined as the ability to be influential or powerful in a peer group, is expected to depend on such combinations of variables (interactions) rather than on main effects.

LaFontana and Cillessen (2009) designed a measure to assess the degree to which youth prioritize being popular over other priorities of social life: maintaining a friendship, being altruistic, following rules, pursuing romance, or working toward achievements. They gave this measure to youths in every year of the 6- to 22-year-old age range. They found that the priority attached to popularity peaks in early adolescence. They also found a modest positive correlation between prioritizing popularity and actually being popular. This main effect was overshadowed by strong interactions of the same measure in a follow-up study. Cillessen, de Bruyn, and LaFontana (2009) examined how prioritizing popularity predicted peer nominations of behavior. They found that adolescents who both were perceived popular and highly prioritized popularity were more likely than others to be named for all aggressive and manipulative behavior items in the study, including bullying, picking fights, cheating, lying, and spreading rumors. Put differently, the combination of aggressive and manipulative behaviors with a high degree of prioritizing popularity was associated with the highest level of perceived popularity.

Puckett et al. (2008) also examined social cognitive variables as moderators of the perceived popularity–relational aggression link. Specifically, they looked at self-efficacy expectations – the belief of being effective in handling social situations with peers. Social self-efficacy significantly moderated the association between relational aggression and perceived popularity. Relational aggressors were most likely to gain high peer group status when they were also self-efficacious. Combining manipulative aggression with high expectations of one's own success in interactions with peers predicted the highest level of perceived popular status.

Finally, Mayeux and Cillessen (2008) looked at self-awareness. Moderators of the association between status and overt and relational aggression were tested in a 4-year longitudinal sample of high school students. Self-perceptions of popularity moderated the link between actual peer-perceived popularity and aggression. Adolescents who were both popular and aware of their popular status scored highest on aggression, and showed the greatest increases in aggression over time. This study highlighted the social cognitive elements of high status.

Together, these studies show that social cognitive skills are related to perceived popularity in important ways. However, the studies reviewed were with older rather than younger children. Research is needed on the social cognitive correlates of perceived popular, controversial, or bistrategic children in early and middle childhood.

Conclusion

In this chapter, two forms of social competence were examined: one defined by sociometric popularity, acceptance, and preference by peers, and the other by perceived popularity, controversial status, or being classified as bistrategic. The correlates of these two definitions of social competence were then examined in two domains of children's social skillfulness: behavioral skills and social cognitive skills.

As Rose-Krasnor (1997) indicated, defining social competence is a complex issue. Social competence cannot be conceptualized in terms of a single domain or a limited number of behaviors. The goal of this chapter was to expand the conceptualization of social competence by explicitly distinguishing two forms. Modest correlations between both dimensions indicate that they are not identical. Behaving in ways that lead to peer acceptance versus doing what it takes to meet one's goals are two different ways of being successful or competent in the peer system. The literature reviewed confirms the validity of this distinction. It would be possible to discuss whether social competence is more appropriately defined in one of both ways, but recognizing them both as unique forms or dimensions of social competence may be more fruitful.

Both constructs themselves are not without criticism. There are limitations to the definition of social competence as peer competence. Peer acceptance is a group-based construct that may not always adequately reflect a child's social skill. For example, peer acceptance may be a questionable index of social competence in deviant groups. In other circumstances, the ability to form friendships may be a better indicator of social skill than group acceptance.

Further discussion is also possible about the perceived popularity definition of social competence. It could be questioned whether the ability to successfully manipulate a group of peers is truly a sign of social competence. It is when judged by its effectiveness and the rewards and reinforcements it yields. Among adults, achievements signal success, even when the road toward it has been controversial. There is, however, another side to this. The combination of perceived popularity and relational aggression in adolescence may be a recipe for success in the social ecology of high school, but it predicts a mixed bag of successes and problems after high school (Sandstrom & Cillessen, 2010). Thus, although being popular, controversial, bistrategic, or agentic may be effective in the short run, there may be later costs. The exact mechanisms involved in the long-term consequences of perceived popularity still need to be determined.

The growing number of studies on perceived popular, bistrategic, or agentic status indicate that an exclusive focus on peer acceptance, and its prosocial traits and characteristics, is no longer sufficient; the body of knowledge on perceived popularity in young children is incomplete. Much work needs to be done to examine the predictors, correlates, and consequences of perceived popular, controversial, or bistrategic status in young children. In this effort, much can be learned from the detailed work on sociometric popularity. Sociometric popularity research has yielded a large number of detailed studies on behavioral and social cognitive processes. Research on perceived popularity has not yet reached this status. Much research is needed to examine perceived popularity in similar levels of detail as sociometric popularity has been studied. The phenomena and methods that have clarified the first definition of social competence need to be applied to the second.

More research is also needed on variation by development, gender, ethnicity, and cultural context. The characteristics of both forms of social competence may vary by each of these moderators. For example, although the distinction between sociometric and perceived popularity increases with development, "perceived popular" behavioral styles are already clearly present in preschool and early childhood. More research is needed on the developmental and contextual variations of both forms of social competence. In this effort, it will be important to pay attention to the increasingly diverse peer system when examining children's behavioral and social cognitive skills, and their unique associations with both forms of social competence.

References

Asher, S. R., & Coie, J. D. (1990). *Peer rejection in childhood*. Cambridge: Cambridge University Press.

Ausubel, D. P., Schiff, H. M., & Gasser, E. B. (1952). A preliminary study of developmental trends in sociempathy: Accuracy of perception of own and others' sociometric status. *Child Development, 23*, 111–128.

Bellmore, A. D., & Cillessen, A. H. N. (2003). Children's meta-perceptions and meta-accuracy of acceptance and rejection by same-sex and other-sex peers. *Personal Relationships, 10*, 217–234.

Berndt, T. J., & Burgy, L. (1996). The social self-concept. In B. A. Bracken (Ed.), *Handbook of self-concept: Developmental, social, and clinical considerations* (pp. 171–209). New York: Wiley.

Boivin, M., & Bégin, G. (1989). Peer status and self-perception among early elementary school children: The case of the rejected children. *Child Development, 60*, 591–596.

Borja-Alvarez, T., Zarbatany, L., & Pepper, S. (1991). Contributions of male and female guests and hosts to peer group entry. *Child Development, 62*, 1079–1090.

Caravita, S. C. S., & Cillessen, A. H. N. (2009). Agentic or communal? Effects of interpersonal goals on popularity and bullying in middle childhood and early adolescence. Unpublished manuscript, Department of Psychology, Catholic University of Milan.

Chung, T., & Asher, S. R. (1996). Children's goals and strategies in peer conflict situations. *Merrill-Palmer Quarterly, 42*, 125–147.

Cillessen, A. H. N. (2009). Sociometric methods. In K. H. Rubin, W. M. Bukowski, & B. Laursen (Eds.), *Handbook of peer interactions, relationships, and groups* (pp. 82–99). New York: Guilford Press.

Cillessen, A. H. N., & Bellmore, A. D. (1999). Accuracy of social self-perceptions and peer competence in middle childhood. *Merrill-Palmer Quarterly, 45*, 650–676.

Cillessen, A. H. N., de Bruyn, E. H., & LaFontana, K. M. (2009, April). Behavioral effects of prioritizing popularity. Paper presented at the biennial meeting of the Society for Research in Child Development, Denver, CO.

Cillessen, A. H. N., & Mayeux, L. (2004). From censure to reinforcement: Developmental changes in the association between aggression and social status. *Child Development, 75*, 147–163.

Cillessen, A. H. N., & Rose, A. J. (2005). Understanding popularity in the peer system. *Current Directions in Psychological Science, 14*, 102–105.

Cillessen, A. H. N., van IJzendoorn, H. W., van Lieshout, C. F. M., & Hartup, W. W. (1992). Heterogeneity among peer rejected boys: Subtypes and stabilities. *Child Development, 63*, 893–905.

Cooley, C. H. (1902). *Human nature and the social order*. New York: Scribner.

Crick, N. R., & Dodge, K. A. (1999). "Superiority" is in the eye of the beholder: A comment on Sutton, Smith, and Swettenham. *Social Development, 8*, 128–131.

de Bruyn, E. H., & Cillessen, A. H. N. (2006). Heterogeneity of girls' consensual popularity: Academic and interpersonal behavioral profiles. *Journal of Youth and Adolescence, 35*, 435–445.

de Bruyn, E. H., Cillessen, A. H. N., & Wissink, I. B. (2010). Associations of peer acceptance and perceived popularity with bullying and victimization in early adolescence. *Journal of Early Adolescence, 30*, 543–566.

DeJung, J. E., & Gardner, E. F. (1962). The accuracy of self-role perception: A developmental study. *Journal of Experimental Education, 31*, 27–41.

Dodge, K. A., Coie, J. D., & Brakke, N. P. (1982). Behavior patterns of socially rejected and neglected preadolescents: The roles of social approach and aggression. *Journal of Abnormal Child Psychology, 10*, 389–409.

Dodge, K. A., Schlundt, D. C., Schocken, I., & Delugach, J. D. (1983). Social competence in children's sociometric status: The role of peer group strategies. *Merrill-Palmer Quarterly, 29*, 309–336.

Doyle, A., & Connolly, J. (1989). Negotiation and enactment in social pretend play: Relations to social acceptance and social cognition. *Early Childhood Research Quarterly, 4*, 289–302.

Dubin, R., & Dubin, E. R. (1965). Children's social perceptions: A review of research. *Child Development, 36*, 809–838.

Eisenberg, A. R., & Garvey, C. (1981). Children's use of verbal strategies in resolving conflicts. *Discourse Processes, 4*, 149–170.

Fantuzzo, J., Coolahan, K., Mendez, J., McDermott, P., & Sutton-Smith, B. (1998). Contextually-relevant validation of peer play constructs with African American Head Start children: Penn Interactive Peer Play Scale. *Early Childhood Research Quarterly, 13*, 411–431.

Farver, J., Kim, Y. K., & Lee, Y. (1995). Cultural differences in Korean- and Anglo-American preschoolers' social interaction and play behaviors. *Child Development, 66,* 1088–1099.

Gelb, R., & Jacobson, J. L. (1988). Popular and unpopular children's interactions during cooperative and competitive peer group activities. *Journal of Abnormal Child Psychology, 16,* 247–261.

Green, V. A., Cillessen, A. H. N., Rechis, R., Patterson, M., & Milligan, J. (2008). Social problem solving and strategy use in young children. *Journal of Genetic Psychology, 169,* 92–112.

Hart, C. H., DeWolf, M., & Burts, D. C. (1993). Parental disciplinary strategies and preschoolers' play behavior in playground settings. In C. H. Hart (Ed.), *Children on playgrounds: Research perspectives and applications* (pp. 271–313). Albany: State University of New York Press.

Hart, C. H., DeWolf, M., Wozniak, P., & Burts, D. C. (1992). Maternal and paternal disciplinary styles: Relations with preschoolers' playground behavioral orientations and peer status. *Child Development, 63,* 879–892.

Hartup, W. W. (1992). Peer relations in early and middle childhood. In V. B. Van Hasselt & M. Hersen (Eds.), *Handbook of social development: A lifespan perspective* (pp. 257–281). New York: Plenum Press.

Hartup, W. W., French, D. C., Laursen, B., Johnston, M. K., & Ogawa, J. R. (1993). Conflict and friendship relations in middle childhood: Behavior in a closed-field situation. *Child Development, 64,* 445–454.

Hartup, W. W., & Laursen, B. (1993). Conflict and context in peer relations. In C. H. Hart (Ed.), *Children on playgrounds: Research perspectives and applications* (pp. 44–84). Albany: State University of New York Press.

Hartup, W. W., Laursen, B., Stewart, M. I., & Eastenson, A. (1988). Conflict and the friendship relations of young children. *Child Development, 59,* 1590–1600.

Hawley, P. H. (2002). Social dominance and prosocial and coercive strategies of resource control in preschoolers. *International Journal of Behavioral Development, 26,* 167–176.

Hawley, P. H. (2003). Prosocial and coercive configurations of resource control in early adolescence: A case for the well-adapted Machiavellian. *Merrill-Palmer Quarterly, 49,* 279–309.

Hawley, P. H., Little, T. D., & Rodkin, P. C. (2007). *Aggression and adaptation: The bright side to bad behavior.* Mahwah, NJ: Erlbaum.

Hazen, N. L., & Black, B. (1989). Preschool peer communication skills: The role of social status and interaction context. *Child Development, 60,* 867–876.

Howes, C. (1988). Peer interaction of young children. *Monographs of the Society for Research in Child Development, 53*(1, Serial No. 217).

Howes, C., & Matheson, C. C. (1992). Sequences in the development of competent play with peers: Social and social pretend play. *Developmental Psychology, 28,* 961–974.

Howes, C., Sanders, K., & Lee, L. (2008). Entering a new peer group in ethnically and linguistically diverse childcare classrooms. *Social Development, 17*(4), 922–940.

Hymel, S., Bowker, A., & Woody, E. (1993). Aggressive versus withdrawn unpopular children: Variations in peer and self-perceptions in multiple domains. *Child Development, 64,* 879–896.

Krantz, M., & Burton, C. (1986). The development of the social cognition of social status. *Journal of Genetic Psychology, 147,* 89–95.

Kurdek, L. A., & Krile, D. (1982). A developmental analysis of the relation between peer acceptance and both interpersonal understanding and perceived social self-competence. *Child Development, 53,* 1485–1491.

Ladd, G. W. (1983). Social networks of popular, average, and rejected children in school settings. *Merrill-Palmer Quarterly, 29,* 283–307.

Ladd, G. W., Price, J. M., & Hart, C. H. (1988). Predicting preschoolers' peer status from their playground behaviors. *Child Development, 59,* 986–992.

LaFontana, K. M., & Cillessen, A. H. N. (1999). Children's interpersonal perceptions as a function of sociometric and peer-perceived popularity. *Journal of Genetic Psychology, 160,* 225–242.

LaFontana, K. M., & Cillessen, A. H. N. (2009). Developmental changes in the priority of perceived status in childhood and adolescence. *Social Development, 19,* 130–147.

MacDonald, C. D., & Cohen, R. (1995). Children's awareness of which peers like them and which peers dislike them. *Social Development, 4,* 182–193.

Malloy, T. E., Yarlas, A. S., Montvilo, R. K., & Sugarman, D. B. (1996). Agreement and accuracy in children's interpersonal perceptions: A social relations analysis. *Journal of Personality and Social Psychology, 71,* 692–702.

Mayeux, L., & Cillessen, A. H. N. (2003). Development of social problem solving in early childhood: Stability, change, and associations with social competence. *Journal of Genetic Psychology, 164,* 153–173.

Mayeux, L., & Cillessen, A. H. N. (2008). It's not just being popular, it's knowing it, too: The role of self-perceptions of status in the associations between peer status and aggression. *Social Development, 17,* 881–888.

Mayeux, L., Sandstrom, M. J., & Cillessen, A. H. N. (2008). Is being popular a risky proposition? *Journal of Research on Adolescence, 18,* 49–74.

Miller, P. M., Danaher, D. L., & Forbes, D. (1986). Sex-related strategies for coping with interpersonal conflict in children aged five and seven. *Developmental Psychology, 22,* 534–548.

Nelson, D. A., Robinson, C. C., & Hart, C. H. (2005). Relational and physical aggression of preschool-age children: Peer status linkages across informants. *Early Education and Development, 16,* 115–139.

Parkhurst, J. T., & Hopmeyer, A. (1998). Sociometric popularity and peer perceived popularity: Two distinct dimensions of peer status. *Journal of Early Adolescence, 18,* 125–144.

Patterson, C. J., Kupersmidt, J. B., & Griesler, P. C. (1990). Children's perceptions of self and relationships with others as a function of sociometric status. *Child Development, 61,* 1335–1349.

Pellegrini, A. D. (1988). Elementary school children's rough-and-tumble play and social competence. *Developmental Psychology, 24,* 802–806.

Pellegrini, A. D., & Long, J. D. (2002). A longitudinal study of bullying, dominance, and victimization during the transition from primary school through secondary school. *British Journal of Developmental Psychology, 20,* 259–280.

Phillips, B. N. (1963). Age changes in accuracy of self-perceptions. *Child Development, 34,* 1041–1046.

Piaget, J. (1983). Piaget's theory. In P. H. Mussen (Series Ed.) & W. Kessen (Vol. Ed.), *Handbook of child psychology: Vol. 1. History, theory and methods* (4th ed., pp. 103–128). New York: Wiley.

Puckett, M. B., Wargo Aikins, J., & Cillessen, A. H. N. (2008). Moderators of the association between relational aggression and perceived popularity. *Aggressive Behavior, 34,* 563–576.

Putallaz, M., & Gottman, J. M. (1981). An interactional model of children's entry into peer groups. *Child Development, 52,* 986–994.

Putallaz, M., & Wasserman, A. (1989). Children's naturalistic entry behavior and sociometric status: A developmental perspective. *Developmental Psychology, 25,* 297–305.

Putallaz, M., & Wasserman, A. (1990). Children's entry behavior. In S. R. Asher & J. D. Coie (Eds.), *Peer rejection in childhood* (pp. 60–89). Cambridge: Cambridge University Press.

Rabiner, D., & Coie, J. D. (1989). Effect of expectancy inductions on rejected children's acceptance by unfamiliar peers. *Developmental Psychology, 23,* 450–457.

Ramsey, P. G. (1995). Changing social dynamics in early childhood classrooms. *Child Development, 66,* 764–773.

Robinson, C. C., Anderson, G. T., Porter, C. L., Hart, C. H., & Wouden-Miller, M. (2003). Sequential transition patterns of preschoolers' social interactions during child-initiated play: Is parallel-aware play a bidirectional bridge to other play states? *Early Childhood Research Quarterly*, *18*, 3–21.

Rodkin, P. C., Farmer, T. W., Pearl, R., & Van Acker, R. (2000). Heterogeneity of popular boys: Antisocial and prosocial configurations. *Developmental Psychology*, *36*, 14–24.

Rose, A. J., & Asher, S. R. (1999). Children's goals and strategies in response to conflicts within a friendship. *Developmental Psychology*, *35*, 69–79.

Rose, A. J., Swenson, L. P., & Waller, E. M. (2004). Overt and relational aggression and perceived popularity: Developmental differences in concurrent and prospective relations. *Developmental Psychology*, *40*, 378–387.

Rose-Krasnor, L. (1997). The nature of social competence: A theoretical review. *Social Development*, *6*, 111–135.

Rubin, K. H., Bukowski, W. M., & Parker, J. G. (2006). Peer interactions, relationships, and groups. In W. Damon & R. Lerner (Series Eds.) & N. Eisenberg (Vol. Ed.), *Handbook of child psychology: Vol. 3. Social, emotional, and personality development* (6th ed., pp. 571–645). Hoboken, NJ: Wiley.

Russell, A., & Finnie, V. (1990). Preschool children's social status and maternal instructions to assist group entry. *Developmental Psychology*, *26*, 603–611.

Sandstrom, M. J., & Cillessen, A. H. N. (2010). Life after high school: Adjustment of popular teens in emerging adulthood. *Merrill-Palmer Quarterly*, *56*.

Shantz, C. U. (1987). Conflicts between children. *Child Development*, *58*, 283–305.

Shantz, D. W. (1986). Conflict, aggression, and peer status: An observational study. *Child Development*, *57*, 1322–1332.

Smith, P. K., & Delfosse, P. (1980). Accuracy of reporting own and others' companions in young children. *British Journal of Social and Clinical Psychology*, *19*, 337–338.

Sutton, J., Smith, P. K., & Swettenham, J. (1999). Social cognition and bullying: Social inadequacy or skilled manipulation? *British Journal of Developmental Psychology*, *17*, 435–450.

Vaillancourt, T., Hymel, S., & McDougall, P. (2003). Bullying is power: Implications for school-based intervention strategies. *Journal of Applied School Psychology*, *19*, 157–176.

Wilson, B. J. (1999). Entry behavior and emotion regulation abilities of developmentally delayed boys. *Developmental Psychology*, *35*, 214–222.

Zakriski, A. L., & Coie, J. D. (1996). A comparison of aggressive-rejected and nonaggressive-rejected children's interpretations of self-directed and other-directed rejection. *Child Development*, *67*, 1048–1070.

Zarbatany, L., & Pepper, S. (1996). The role of the group in peer group entry. *Social Development*, *5*, 251–260.

Zarbatany, L., Van Brunschot, M., Meadows, K., & Pepper, S. (1996). Effects of friendship and gender on peer group entry. *Child Development*, *67*, 2287–2300.

CHAPTER TWENTY-TWO

Emotions and Social Development in Childhood

Susanne Denham, Heather Warren, Maria von Salisch, Oana Benga, Jui-Chih Chin, and Elena Geangu

> *Gary and Ron are practicing soccer moves on the playground. They have all their equipment – goal, shinpads, and regulation ball – and they're having fun together. Ron shows Gary how to head the ball into the goal, both shouting, "Hurray!" But then things get complicated, changing fast, as interaction often does. Ron, thinking twice about sharing his best technique, kicks the ball away from Gary on the next play. Then Huynh, who had been watching from the sidelines, asks Gary if he can join them. Simultaneously, Gary trips over a swiftly kicked ball and slumps to the ground. And just then, Jack, the class bully, approaches, laughing at Gary's discomfort, then angrily demanding they leave so that he and his buddies can use the field. Somehow, Gary deals with all of this. He hands the ball to Huynh, extends a hand to Ron, and calmly tells Jack, "It's our turn now."*

What do emotions have to do with social development? Our example abounds with instances where emotions help determine the flow and outcome of interaction. First, behaviors of others in one's social group often constitute antecedent conditions for children's emotions. When Ron became angry, it was because his goal of being the "best" was threatened. Huynh approached diffidently because he often had been "left out" from play. Second, when children exhibit emotion within dyads or groups, this emotional expressiveness also is important information for others involved. When Gary experienced delight at making a goal, he wanted to keep playing; others, like Huynh, wanted to join him. Jack is irritable and easily provoked by those he perceives to be "in his way." His

The Wiley-Blackwell Handbook of Childhood Social Development, Second Edition, edited by Peter K. Smith and Craig H. Hart
© 2011 by Blackwell Publishing Ltd.

classmates, observing his emotional behaviors, wisely leave the scene. Third, one child's expressions of emotion may form antecedent conditions for others' experience and expression of emotions. Playmates exiting from Jack's wrath may feel some combination of discomfort at his uncontrolled display, fear at his targeted nastiness, answering anger, and even spiteful delight if he *doesn't* get his way.

In concert with these views, theorists highlight the interdependency of emotional and social competence (Denham, 1998; Saarni, 1999). The interpersonal function of emotion is central to its expression and experience. Conversely, social interactions and relationships are guided, even defined, by emotional transactions (Halberstadt, Denham, & Dunsmore, 2001). Emotional and social competence are intimately intertwined, and become even more so with development.

Given these considerations, our *first goal* is to summarize varying social developmental tasks across childhood. Defining social issues of each age helps clarify the role of emotion within each period. Our *second goal* is to describe aspects of emotional competence important to social interaction and relationships with parents, peers, and friends, with an emphasis on cultural considerations. The social tasks and emotional competencies of each period of childhood are situated within social relationships and cultures; not only does culture set the parameters for emotional expressions, but also it influences the very meaning of emotions (Saarni, 1998). Our *third goal* is to evaluate existing research on contributions of emotional competence to social competence, using the framework of emotional competence changing across developmental epochs and within differing relationships. Finally, we suggest future directions.

Developmental Tasks of Social Competence

The nature of adaptive social functioning changes with development; what is useful for coordinating preschoolers' interactions may be less helpful later. These changes in children's social functioning are accompanied by parallel reorganizations of ways of dealing with emotional issues. Preschoolers' social tasks include managing emotional arousal within interaction while coordinating social play (Gottman & Mettetal, 1986). Processes inherent in succeeding at these tasks call for skills of emotional competence – arguments must be resolved so play can continue, and enjoying one another's company greases the cogs of sustained interaction. Emotion regulation is key; young children must learn to avoid disorganizing tantrums, and to think reflectively about distressing situations.

The goals, social processes, and emotional tasks central to social competence change radically as grade schoolers become aware of wider social networks than the dyad. Peer norms for social acceptance are complex and nuanced, with inclusion by peers and avoiding rejection or embarrassment paramount. Hence, socially competent responses to many salient social situations, such as group entry and provocation, are to be cool and unflappable. Social processes of gossip, social support, relationship talk, and self-disclosure serve this goal. Managing how and when to show emotion becomes crucial, as does knowing with whom to share emotion-laden experiences and ideas.

Elements of Emotional Competence

We focus on three basic components of emotional competence, crucial for success in these social developmental tasks: experiencing, expressing, and understanding emotion. Each component of emotional competence follows a partially independent developmental trajectory, which we now describe.

Experience of emotions

We refer to *experience of emotions* not only as awareness and recognition of one's own emotions, but also as effective regulation of one's emotional expression in the context of an ongoing social interaction. In Figure 22.1, we depict the process of emotional experience. First, there is arousal. Something happens – an environmental event (Gary fell down), one's own actions (Ron made a goal), others' actions (Jack came up to boss them), or even memories (Ron ruminated over giving up his "soccer secrets").

Sometimes this arousal, whether emanating from internal or external signals, is automatic – when Gary fell down, he didn't need contemplation to experience his pain and dismay. Emotion and attendant behavior ensued automatically (see the leftmost column of Figure 22.1). Sometimes emotional arousal needs to be understood, not just reacted to, because children create an increasingly complicated network of goals. Before Huynh

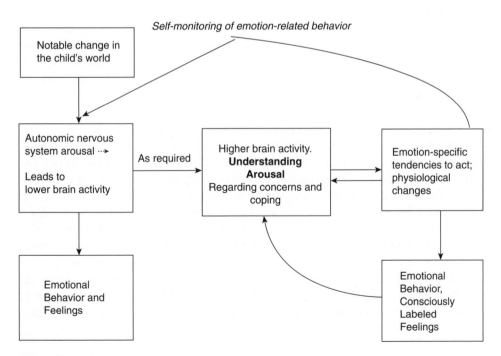

Figure 22.1 Emotional experience.

felt a specific emotion, or Gary noticed, Huynh attended to, comprehended, and interpreted the event: He engaged in appraisal processes (middle column, Figure 22.1). He
needed to attribute meaning to his arousal as he approached Gary. Do his "tummy but-
terflies" impact his goal of joining play? Does he acknowledge them as apprehension?
Interpretations of events' relations to ongoing goals lead not only to felt emotions but
also to actions and expressions associated with each specific emotion, and new changes
in arousal (rightmost column, Figure 22.1). Does Huynh try to "deal with" his jitters,
to present himself as a worthy teammate, by taking a deep breath and making an effort
to walk steadily? Do these attempts at regulation work, so that he really is calmer, and
his chances with Gary are better? Ability to access, manage, and communicate (or *not*
communicate) emotions is important to relationships' success.

To be emotionally competent, one must first recognize that an emotion is being
experienced – what emotional signal am I sending to others? How do my emotional
signals affect them? If Ron is not able to recognize his annoyance, and that it stems from
wanting to be "best," he risks cascading feelings and behaviors related to misplaced anger
– which, once enacted, are resistant to reorganization. One also must comprehend emotional experiences within the ongoing social context. Knowledge of feeling rules may
guide children in focusing on certain aspects of their emotional experiences. The glee that
Gary experiences at scoring a goal is more complicated than it appears. He may experience conglomerated delight, mild "macho" contempt, and fear when he almost didn't
make it; the feeling rule "When you win, you feel happy" may help him discern his
emotion, or decide which aspects to communicate to others. Further, it is noteworthy
that inner and outer emotional states may differ ("I know I'm scared of Jack, but I am
going to put on a calm face").

Next, regulation of emotional experience is necessary when the presence or absence of
emotional expression and experience interferes with goals – when emotions are distressing, positive but possibly overwhelming, or needing amplification for intra- or interpersonally strategic reasons. By preschool, such emotion regulation becomes both necessary,
due to the increasing complexity of children's emotionality and social world, and possible,
because of their increased comprehension and control of their emotionality.

"Doing something" about the experience of emotion need not be overt and active
(Figure 22.2). The experience of emotion may need to be diminished, modulated, or
even transformed; a child feeling anxious at preschool may smile to convince herself and
others that she is happy. Perceptual and cognitive coping steps are also possible; refocus-
ing attention is useful for regulating emotional experience – Huynh may focus on the
soccer ball rather than the boys whose social status makes him uncomfortable. Children
can reason about relinquishing goals, choosing substitute goals, or conceiving new, comforting attributions ("I didn't want to go to the pool anyway"). Children also *do* things
to cope with emotional experience – such as enacting a solution to the emotional situation, looking for support from adults, lashing out, or crying. Children learn to retain or
enhance relevant, helpful emotions; to attenuate relevant but not helpful ones; and to
dampen irrelevant emotions. These regulatory behaviors help them to maintain genuine
and satisfying relationships.

Experiencing and regulating emotion during the preschool period   Caregivers' support
allows preschoolers' regulatory strategies to be maximally effective. Parents assist with

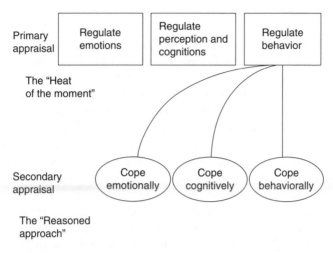

Figure 22.2   Model of emotion regulation.

cognitive coping strategies children will eventually use themselves (e.g., redeploying attention, or using emotion language to process causal associations between events and emotions). They also demonstrate behavioral coping strategies when they problem solve around emotional situations (e.g., a father avoids arranging an activity that will leave his son cranky).

As preschoolers become more autonomous and capable of cooperation, they collaborate with caregivers' regulation efforts and make independent regulation attempts, such as orientation of attention toward or away from a stimulus, self-distraction, or approaching or retreating from a situation. Next, they slowly see connections between these regulation efforts and changes in their feelings. Finally, they become more flexible in choosing contextually optimal means of coping. Behavioral disorganization resulting from strong emotion decreases dramatically.

Regulatory goals and strategies are value laden, even for preschoolers. Western societies value active emotion – or problem-focused regulatory strategies. In contrast, Chinese culture considers endurance a useful emotion regulation strategy (Lee & Yang, 1998). Even for young Chinese children, endurance serves the function of saving the "face" of others and preserving one's own "face"; Chin (2007) found that Taiwanese 5-year-olds nominated endurance second most frequently as a strategy to regulate sadness and fear.

Experiencing and regulating emotion during middle childhood   Age changes in emotion regulation occur due to socialization messages of others, as well as cognitive abilities to appraise the controllability of emotional experience, intentionally shift thoughts, or flexibly examine different aspects of situations (von Salisch, 2000a). Thus, grade schoolers increasingly use cognitive and problem-solving behavioral coping strategies to regulate emotion, and rely less on support seeking (von Salisch, 2008). Finally, older children endorse distancing from uncontrollable stressors. They are aware of the strategies at their command, and their cross-situational likelihood of success.

Expression of emotions

Another key element of emotional competence is expressiveness. Emotions must be expressed in keeping with the child's goals and the social context. Thus, emotional competence includes expressing emotions in a way that is advantageous for moment-to-moment interaction and relationships over time. First, an affective message should be contextually appropriate. Perhaps Ron is crankily ruminating that, because he gave Gary his best soccer moves, his status of best player is in jeopardy. Then, when Gary inadvertently pokes Ron on the way to the pencil sharpener, Ron may feel like sending an intensely angry message. But what affective message *should* be sent, for interaction to proceed smoothly? Second, children learn which expressions of emotion facilitate their goals in a given social context. Third, after determining a contextually appropriate affective message, children must also send it convincingly, in terms of method, intensity, and timing. Showing brief annoyance over a friend winning a game conveys a very different message than remaining angry for days. Fourth, one must adhere to prosocial and self-protective display rules in sending affective messages. Finally, unique characteristics of situations and interaction partners must be considered. Some situations, like a raucous street hockey game, and some people, like Great Aunt Martha, "pull for" particular modes of expressiveness.

Expressiveness during the preschool period   Preschoolers' emotional lives become quite complex. They are aware of the need to send affective messages, and can express vividly all the "basic" emotions. They also begin to show "social" emotions that require a sense of self and of others, including empathy, shame, guilt, and contempt. Preschoolers also begin to show blended emotions. After his best friend leaves angrily, saying, "You broke my truck – I'm not your friend anymore," Antonio expresses a multifaceted mixture of sadness, guilt, and anger.

Preschoolers also have rudimentary awareness that there are important contextual differences about what to send or not send (Zeman, Penza, Shipman, & Young, 1997). They begin to use, but not completely understand, display rules and "dissembling" emotions. Perhaps, despite feeling sad and guilty, Antonio may show his friend only his righteous anger. To look sad or act guilty would only make things worse.

Expressiveness during middle childhood   With time and experience, older children learn that goals are not always met by showing intense feelings. They often express emotions less directly and vividly than before; emotional expression depends on with whom, and in what situation, they are interacting; and display rules become important. For example, they regulate anger due to expected negative consequences (Zeman & Shipman, 1996). Along with the "cool rule" that mandates their more muted emotions within most settings (von Salisch, 2000a), older children's emotional messages can be more complex, with use of more blended signals and better differentiated expressions of social emotions.

Again, cultural beliefs may impact the developmental course of display rule usage and understanding. Although similar to Western children in understanding and endorsing self-protective display rules more readily than prosocial ones, understanding of prosocial rules begins earlier for some Asian children than for their Western counterparts (Chen

& Chin, 2007). The value of prosocial behavior in their cultural belief systems impacts their emotional development.

Understanding emotions

An initial appraisal that another individual is sending affective information is necessary – missing such information puts one at a disadvantage (e.g., if Gary misses muted expressions of annoyance on Ron's face, he may gloat about learning to head the soccer ball). Once perceived, the other's affective message must be interpreted accurately, taking into account operative display rules and individuals' emotional styles.

Understanding emotions during the preschool period   Preschoolers can name and recognize expressions for most basic emotions, and identify common emotion-eliciting situations. They can talk about emotions' causes and consequences. Young children also are acquiring the beginnings of even more sophisticated knowledge of emotion. They are becoming aware of equivocal emotions (e.g., some people feel sad when they fail, whereas others are angry) but are less able to reconcile any discrepancies between an emotion's outward expression and its eliciting situation. They are just beginning to understand emotion regulation, display rules, simultaneity, and ambivalence.

Children from different cultures seem to come to an understanding of basic emotions in a similar timeline. For example, U.S., Romanian, and Japanese preschool children are able to verbally label emotions by 3 or 4 years, and improve throughout preschool at identifying emotional expressions (Bassett, Warren, Mun, Graling, & Denham, 2008; Fujioka, 2008; Geangu, Ionescu, & Benga, 2008). Nonetheless, some cultural variations occur; Euro-American preschoolers acquire greater emotion knowledge than Chinese counterparts (Wang, 2004). Such results might be explained by cultural norms applied to emotion conversations. When Chinese parents and children converse about emotion-laden events, there seems to be little causal discussion of children's feeling states, and more focus on "teaching the child a lesson," or learning social norms (Wang & Fivush, 2005).

Understanding emotions during middle childhood   Intricate emotion knowledge blossoms as grade schoolers improve markedly in understanding that different events elicit different emotions in different people, and that enduring patterns of personality affect individuals' emotional reactions. They better understand nuances of emotions in self and others, including (a) display rules (Lin, 2003), (b) multiple emotions (Olthof, Meerum Terwogt, Van Eck, & Koops, 1987), (c) time course of emotions (Meerum Terwogt & Olthof, 1989), and (d) social emotions (Nunner-Winkler & Sodian, 1988).

Relationship-Specific Interconnectedness of Emotional and Social Competence

The utility of such emotional competence in relation to social competence often depends on the specific relationship in which it is embedded. In the following, we consider unique links between social and emotional competence in three relationships differing along dimensions of symmetry and closeness: parents (asymmetrical and close), peers (symmetrical and not close), and friends (symmetrical and close).

Emotional development in parent–child relationships

The asymmetry in the close relationship between parents and children is key for several reasons. Parents are children's primary attachment figures; secure attachment promotes preschoolers' positive expressiveness and understanding of emotions (DeMulder, Denham, Schmidt, & Mitchell, 2000; Laible & Thompson, 1998; Steele, Steele, Croft, & Fonagy, 1999).

Parents are also experienced adults who have advanced knowledge of emotions and strategies for regulating them. They can provide verbal labels for emotional experiences and displays and the antecedents and consequences of emotional experiences (von Salisch, 2008), thereby promoting children's emotional understanding and repertoire of regulatory strategies (Brown & Dunn, 1996; Denham, Zoller, & Couchoud, 1994; von Salisch, 2008).

Parents can also contribute negatively to children's emotional competence. When parents' reactions to, or admonitions about, emotions are misleading or idiosyncratic, children may develop distorted emotion understanding. Some parents also have difficulties with their own negative emotions. Angrier mothers tend to have less empathic, more defiant children. Witnessing interadult anger causes distress and sometimes anger in children, alleviated only when adults resolve their disagreement and show positive emotions (Shifflett-Simpson & Cummings, 1996).

Grade schoolers continue to look to parents to support their growing emotional competence. Many school-aged boys still share fears with their parents (Rimé, Dozier, Vandenplas, & Declercq, 1996). Most grade schoolers endorsed showing genuine emotions around their parents (Zeman & Shipman, 1996), but also expected that expressions of anger toward third parties would displease them. These findings may depend on the gender of the child and parent; elementary school boys expected fathers to react more negatively than mothers to their sadness (Zeman & Garber, 1996).

Parents, emotional development, and culture   Parents introduce their children to cultural rules about experiencing, expressing, and regulating emotions (Harkness & Super, 1995). In individualistic cultures, emotions are internal, personal reactions, with emotional expressions considered spontaneous manifestations of inner feelings; emotional experiences and expressions are therefore encouraged (Matsumoto, Yoo, & Fontaine, 2008). Even younger members of such individualistic cultures generally endorse expressing emotions, especially positive ones. Studying parents' beliefs and desires about children's emotional expressiveness in 48 nations, Diener and Lucas (2004) found that parents in individualistic cultures, and in those considering positive affect culturally appropriate, expected children to express more happiness.

In contrast, in collectivist societies, individual feelings are inseparable from feelings of the group – even the perception of emotional expressions incorporates social contextual information (Masuda et al., 2008). Control and suppression of emotions are valued and encouraged for the sake of group harmony. For example, Japanese and American parents often differ in their reactions to children's emotions (Ujiie, 1997); in keeping with their collectivistic cultural template of inhibitory self-regulation and acquisition of good manners, Japanese parents react most positively to children's suppression of emotion and demonstration of empathy (Zahn-Waxler, Friedman, Cole, Mizuta, & Hiruma, 1996).

Yet, even parental ethnotheories are dynamic; socioeconomic and political transitions may modulate a culture's shared ideas about socialization of emotion. Asian societies' modernization and openness to Western influences have been accompanied by a shift to more individualistic socialization goals (Chen, Cen, Li, & He, 2005; Lamm, Keller, Yovsi, & Chaudhary, 2008; Wang, 2008). Increased stress associated with sociopolitical trans-formations, such as in ex-communist countries, might affect socialization of emotions (Pinquart & Silbereisen, 2004; Uhlendorff, 2004). Further, subtle differences between social classes or subcultures of the same society may affect parents' personal goals and values for appraising, feeling, and displaying emotions.

In addition, more micro views of parental beliefs about emotions may complement cultural analyses based on more macrosocietal templates. Parents from different cultures may be both different *and* similar in their beliefs about socializing emotions – causes, means of expression, and intensity and frequency of their own emotions (Denham, Caal, Bassett, Benga, & Geangu, 2004). American-born, Hispanic-born, Japanese-born, and Romanian parents agreed broadly on antecedents of certain emotions, and appraised many situations similarly as antecedents of emotions. For example, both Hispanic-born parents, whose interdependent culture stresses the value of family (Fracasso & Busch-Rossnagel, 1992), and Romanian parents, who consider having children and a stable relationship as major reasons for happiness (Rughiniş, 2002), described loneliness and distance from family as major sources of their own sadness. They tended to differ on more advanced aspects of appraisal, such as control of and responsibility for emotion.

Experience and regulating of emotion and parent–child relationships   Parents use emotion language to support children's emotion regulation efforts. Preschoolers with access to more sophisticated maternal language about emotion coped more productively with their own emotions (Denham, Cook, & Zoller, 1992). Teachers and peers alike viewed these more affectively balanced children as more socially competent (Denham, McKinley, Couchoud, & Holt, 1990).

Parents' reactions to their children's negative emotions also have received attention. Concern over children's need for emotion regulation, if not punitive, fosters children's awareness of and attention to emotions (Denham, 1997). For example, parents' control of children's emotions and their own expressiveness during family discussions were associated with grade schoolers' emotion regulation and display rule usage (McDowell, Kim, O'Neil, & Parke, 2002; McDowell & Parke, 2005). In contrast, overly strict sanctions about emotional expressiveness may motivate children to hide – not regulate – emotions.

Parents' discussion of emotion can also contain both positive and negative elements. Dismissive utterances and reactions to children's emotions contributed to children's poorer emotion regulation, but instructive utterances buffered effects of dismissive ones (Lunkenheimer, Shields, & Cortina, 2007). Similarly, mothers of anxiety-disordered children, compared with mothers of nondiagnosed children, used fewer positive emotion words during emotion discussions, and discouraged children's emotion discussions more (Suveg, Zeman, Flannery-Schroeder, & Cassano, 2005).

Expression of emotion and parent–child relationships   Parental emotion may contribute to children's social competence, mediated by children's expressiveness during interaction with parents. For example, Isley, O'Neil, Clatfelter, and Parke (1999) have found that parents' positive affect during game playing was related to their children's social competence, as mediated by children's positive affect during the game; in contrast, parental negative affect made only a direct, negative contribution. Angry interchanges with parents can render children more aroused during interaction, and/or teach them a confrontational style, carrying over to peer aggression and avoidance (Carson & Parke, 1996; Denham & Grout, 1993). Parental affect is especially related to social competence for father–son shared negativity and maternal positive emotion.

Not unexpectedly, however, cross- and intracultural differences in parents' emotion-related beliefs influence their expressivity patterns. Romanian and Hispanic-born parents emphasize accessibility of their own emotional expressions to their children, emphasizing and amplifying some (e.g., happiness) but diminishing and hiding others (e.g., sadness). These parents seem open to show children their emotions, but Japanese parents stress not wanting to show most emotions around their children (Denham et al., 2004), supporting their goals of maximizing positive social interaction and sustaining interdependence and relationship harmony (Butler, Lee, & Gross, 2007). It can be inferred that Japanese parents' tendency to suppress emotions might have adaptive value, making sense within cultural context. Asian parents also use disapproval and shaming to train their children (Bowes, Chen, San, & Yuan, 2004; Fung, 1999), so that these emotion socialization strategies may not have the negative consequences seen in Western societies (Chin, 2008).

How do these cultural rules and beliefs contribute specifically to emotional expressiveness of children? In one study, distinct cultural patterns of emotional expressivity have also been found for United States, Nepalese Brahman, and Nepalese Tamang children. Children from all three cultural groups reported *experiencing* anger; in contrast, although American and Nepalese Tamang children consider it appropriate to *express* negative emotions they experience, such as anger, the Nepalese Brahman children were more likely not to (Cole, Bruschi, & Tamang, 2002). These differences stem from the children's societal structures, with respect for the caste system and social hierarchy for the Brahman communities; an egalitarian approach and selflessness for Tamang communities; and the value of self-expression and assertion for individual rights in U.S. society.

In another study, European American girls manifested more smiles, disgust-related expressions, and overall expressivity than Chinese American or Mainland Chinese girls (Camras, Chen, Bakeman, Norris, & Cain, 2006); yet, given that their adoptive culture encourages different aspects of facial emotional expressivity, Chinese American girls showed more disgust expressions than Mainland Chinese girls. These findings are complemented by Camras, Kolmodin, and Chen's (2008) findings that European American mothers report expressing more positive emotions than Chinese American or Mainland Chinese mothers.

Understanding of emotion and parent–child relationships   Parents' contributions to their preschool-aged children's understanding of emotion have been investigated with some interesting results. When mothers explained emotions, showed predominantly positive emotion, and were positively rather than negatively responsive to children's emotions, children evidenced greater emotion understanding (Denham, Zoller, & Couchoud, 1994; see also Dunn, Brown, & Beardsall, 1991). Presumably, children who experience mothers' positive emotion socialization are more willing to explore, and have greater access to, the world of emotions, which in turn enhances their social interactions and relationships (Dunn & Cutting, 1999; Dunn & Herrera, 1997).

Frequent emotion talk – more common in middle-class European American dyads – focused on antecedents of children's emotions and articulation of own feelings is an important contributor to emotion knowledge (Denham & Kochanoff, 2002; Fivush, 2001). Children themselves provide rich, coherent, organized recollections of events when talking about past negative emotions with parents (Benga, 2004; Hughes & Dunn, 1998).

Emerging research suggests that Japanese mothers also talk to their preschoolers about emotions (Clancy, 1999; Kojima, 2000; Sonoda & Muto, 1996). Their emotion language has similar functions as Americans' – to instruct toddlers and preschoolers about emotional meanings, to negotiate, and to explain the feelings of one sibling to another. What differs is the content of their conversations, which focus on aspects of emotion relevant for Japanese culture.

Parents' reactions to their children's emotions also impact children's emotion knowledge. Parental reactions to children's displays may be particularly useful in building emotion knowledge. Specifically, as might be expected, dismissive reactions to children's emotions (e.g., yelling, "Stop that crying!!") are powerful deterrents of self-reflection regarding emotions and, hence, barriers to emotion knowledge (Denham, Mitchell-Copeland, Strandberg, Auerbach, & Blair, 1997). Interestingly, Warren and Stifter (2008) have found mothers' supportive emotion socialization behaviors predicted young children's *self*-awareness of happiness; the converse was true for predicting children's self-awareness of sadness. Finally, McElwain, Halberstadt, and Volling's (2007) findings support an important corollary to the principle that parental supportiveness predicts greater emotion knowledge: When parents differ in their supportive reactions to children's emotions, children may need to engage in more effortful processing of emotional information, thus achieving greater awareness of emotions.

Emotional development in interaction with peers

Peers are expected to have pervasive influences on children's emotional development for two reasons. First, peers are in a better position to understand the emotional life of age mates than parents or children of other age groups (Dunn & Hughes, 1998). Age mates argue at similar sociocognitive and moral levels, face similar transitions and life events, and share roles in school (von Salisch, 2000c). Second, being with a group of like-minded peers may intensify children's emotional experiences, such as glee over teachers' faux pas or panic over crawling insects. Children create group cultures with unique norms and values, including shared appraisals of emotion-eliciting events, and explicit and implicit rules about expression and regulation of emotions.

Experiencing and regulating emotion and peer relations   From preschool through primary grades, children who improve or are consistently average or high in emotion regulation, show higher social competence than those whose regulation ability is consistently low or declining. Further, low-income preschoolers' emotional dysregulation is related to aggression, anxiety, and social skills in expected directions, even after covarying verbal ability, age, emotion knowledge, and negative emotion expression (Miller et al., 2006). Experience of emotions and their regulation also interact in contributing to social competence.

For grade schoolers, "letting it all hang out" is uniformly selected as the worst reaction to negative emotional experiences with peers (Saarni, 1997). They report cognitively distancing themselves from anger-provoking situations, redirecting attention to alleviate distress, avoiding confrontations altogether, or problem solving calmly (von Salisch, 2001). Although these "fronts" make children's expressions less genuine, they also have positive aspects, including saving face and "surviving" in a potentially hostile environment.

Expressiveness and peer relations   Preschoolers' expression of specific emotions also relates to their peer status and teachers' evaluations of their friendliness and aggression. Positive affect is important in initiating and regulating social exchanges, and for communication during socially directed acts; sharing positive affect may facilitate friendship formation. Happier, less angry preschoolers react more prosocially to peers' emotions, are better liked by peers, and are rated as friendlier and more cooperative by teachers (Denham et al., 1990). Conversely, preschoolers' negative affect is often associated with negative outcomes (Denham et al., 1990; Hart et al., 2000). Miller and colleagues (2005) found that negative emotion expression was related to preschoolers' aggression, even after covarying age, verbal ability, and other aspects of emotional competence.

The relation of emotional expressiveness to social competence often depends on context. Arsenio, Cooperman, and Lover (2000) examined preschoolers' emotions within and outside periods of conflict, in relation to aggression and social competence. Children's nonconflict anger, less frequent nonconflict happiness, and happiness during conflict were positively related to aggression and negatively related to sociometric status. Anger during conflict appears normative, but an irascible demeanor, or glee at another's discomfort, is incongruent with social competence. Relations between peer relations and sending or managing emotions effectively are moderated, as well, by gender (Dunsmore, Noguchi, Garner, Casey, & Bhullar, 2008).

To avoid peer rejection, grade schoolers adopt the "cool rule" (which makes it more difficult to code emotional expressions): They reduce expressions of anger, gloating, and envy in favor of polite negotiation. Rejected and accepted children's emotional profiles do, however, differ (Underwood, Hurley, Johanson, & Mosley, 1999). Older children also prefer to befriend peers who are "fun," ostensibly those who express positive emotions (Parker & Seal, 1996).

Some findings are also gender dependent with older children. Boys say they are unlikely to share fears, whereas girls report not displaying anger (Underwood, Coie, &

Herbsman, 1992). Other expectations about which emotions to show (or not show) around peers are culture dependent (Heyman, Fu, & Lee, 2008), perhaps mirroring cultural differences in parental practices (Ng, Pomerantz, & Lam, 2007): Chinese parents deemphasize school children's success and emphasize failure, whereas European American parents have opposite attitudes. Accordingly, Chinese children respond with fewer posi-tive emotions to success and more negative emotions to failure, whereas European American children show a reversed pattern.

Understanding emotions and peer relations   Children who strategically apply emotion knowledge more often succeed in peer interactions. Preschoolers' understanding of emotion is related to their peer likeability, reciprocated friendship, teacher-reported social competence, and prosocial reactions to others' emotions (Denham, 1986; Denham et al., 1990; Dunsmore et al., 2008; Geangu, 2003; Miller et al., 2005). Barth and Bastiani (1997) have uncovered a subtler relation: Preschoolers' mistaken perceptions of peers as angry are associated with negative social behavior.

Other discrete types of positive social behavior also are related to preschoolers' emotion knowledge. Preschoolers' emotion knowledge is related to use of reasoned argument, sibling caregiving, and lack of self-reported victimization and rejection, even across time (Dunn, Slomkowski, Donelan, & Herrera, 1995; Garner, Jones, & Miner, 1994; Miller et al., 2005). Older children's understanding of prosocial display rules is related to their observed and self-reported prosocial behavior and social competence (Garner, 1996; Jones, Abbey, & Cumberland, 1998).

Emotional development within friendships

Preadolescents' friendships become more intimate; friends' emotions are experienced "close up" (Krappmann, 1996). Observing another's emotions in such asymmetrical relationships may reinforce attention that facilitates learning. Friends' conformance to display rules, complex emotions, and emotional ambivalence may be especially instruc-tive. These theoretical speculations badly need empirical support. Caution is warranted, moreover, in assuming only beneficial aspects of friendships; reciprocal negative, as well as positive, effects can operate (von Salisch, 2000b).

Experiencing and regulating emotion within friendship   Friends are older children's "best bets" for sharing and managing emotional experience, especially feelings of vulnerability (e.g., "He's not worth crying over"; Rose & Asher, 1999b). Preadolescent friends also use distraction to minimize friends' ruminations over shame-, guilt-, or depression-inducing attributions. On the more negative side, grade schoolers who endorsed revenge goals and hostile strategies quarreled more in their best friendships (Rose & Asher, 1999a). In conflicts during a computer game, such friends expressed anger, contempt, and disgust, and self-reported more intense experiences of shame and guilt (von Salisch, 1999). Friends become able to regulate such anger by taking into account others' motives and the varying controllability of others' actions (Stadler, Janke, & Schmidt-Atzert, 1997). Von Salisch and Vogelgesang (2005), longitudinally examining ways that friends deal with anger, confirmed that negotiation, humor, and reconciliation were used more frequently during adolescence than childhood. Confrontation (or harming) and distancing strategies were used less often than in childhood.

Expressiveness within friendship   Preschoolers display positive affective reciprocity more frequently, and are more expressive overall, with friends than with siblings (Volling, Youngblade, & Belsky, 1997). Although preschoolers experience similarly intense anger with liked and disliked peers, their behavioral responses, especially boys', are more controlled with liked peers (Fabes, Eisenberg, Smith, & Murphy, 1996). Children also are more sympathetic to the hypothetical plight of a friend than a nonfriend, and more readily propose an intervention (Costin & Jones, 1992).

Understanding emotions and friendship   Preschoolers' understanding of causes and consequences of emotions already is differentiated by relationship (Dunn & Hughes, 1998). Understanding of emotions is related to 4-year-olds' positive interaction with friends – both child and friends' emotion knowledge contributes to cooperative shared pretend play and low frequency of conflict (Dunn & Cutting, 1999). Child–friend conversation about emotion also is related to cooperative interaction (Brown, Donelan-McCall, & Dunn, 1996). Finally, preschoolers' positive play within friendships predicts later understanding of mixed emotions (Maguire & Dunn, 1997), suggestive of a bidirectional relation.

Emotion talk goes on within preschool friendship groups (Kyratzis, 2001), but middle childhood is especially a time when friends use emotion talk about aspects of emotion understanding undergoing rapid development–display rules, and involving ambivalence and complex emotions (Gottman & Mettetal, 1986). Emotion-colored accounts are compared, contrasted, and validated as friends gossip, helping each other to sort out their shared and idiosyncratic feelings (e.g., "I hate it when he 'blows up,' don't you?"). Conversations within conflict are replete with emotion talk about regulating anger, sadness, envy, jealousy, and hurt feelings. Comforting, approving, or guiding reactions to friends' emotions (e.g., "Don't worry about the test," or "Stop crying – everybody's looking!") may be pivotal in learning about emotions, and conforming to group norms (Rose & Asher, 1999b). Research on emotion-related aspects of elementary school-aged friends' conversation and behaviors, especially relations with other aspects of their emotional competence, is sorely needed.

Where Do We Go From Here?

Much exciting work has been done to show ways in which emotional competence is an integral part of social competence. To expand upon this work, we must follow children's lives across time – what is the predictive power of emotional (in)competence? What happens to Gary, Ron, Huynh, and Jack? Only longitudinal study can spell out how emotional competence affects children's long-term adaptation, and settle issues about directions of causality. It also seems clear that we must do the following:

- Flesh out the dual roles of each relationship partner – such as parent, peer, and friend (and teachers, who were not discussed here, and for whom research is just beginning). Our foci were on parents' influence centered on socializing emotional competence, and the role of such competence within peer and friend relationships, but we need to know the converse, as well. *What does Huynh learn about expressing emotions from Gary, or from Jack? Conversely, how does Gary's shrewdness about emotions play out in the transformations of his relationship with his father, as he nears adolescence?*

- Examine these phenomena with minority or low–socioeconomic status children (however, see Garner, 1996; Garner et al., 1994), as well as children of other cultures. *If the boys had been playing stickball in an inner-city neighborhood, would they need the same or different emotional competencies? What if the four soccer players had been Nigerian? Or Chinese?*

- Make more headway in investigating children's "live" experience of emotions (e.g., Olthof & Engelberts-Vaske, 1997). *Was Jack really feeling so dominant in his bullying, or was that a "front"? What emotions does he experience and display in high school, and how do they affect his relationships?*

- Uncover possible moderating effects of gender; emotional competence may predict social competence differently for boys and girls. *What if the four children playing soccer had been girls?*

- Consider that emotional competence is not *always* beneficial for establishing and maintaining harmonious relationships. For example, attackers could use well-developed empathic sense to hone their attacks' malice (Sutton, Smith, & Swettenham, 1999). *Did Jack's perceptive reading of peers' weaknesses allow him to become an ever more powerful thug?*

Finally, we also must integrate inter- and intrapersonal aspects of emotional competence in our investigations; bidirectionality must be assumed. For example, intrapersonal representations, such as hostile attribution biases, may influence the expression of anger in interpersonal contexts; interpersonal practices, such as emotion talk in the family, can promote children's intrapersonal understanding of emotions. A transactional model that depicts reciprocal influences between intra- and interpersonal features of emotional competence, both concurrently and longitudinally, is necessary (von Salisch, 2008).

References

Arsenio, W. F., Cooperman, G., & Lover, A. (2000). Affective predictors of preschoolers' aggression and peer acceptance: Direct and indirect effects. *Developmental Psychology, 36*, 438–448.

Barth, J. M., & Bastiani, A. (1997). A longitudinal study of emotion recognition and preschool children's social behavior. *Merrill-Palmer Quarterly, 43*, 107–128.

Bassett, H. H., Warren, H., Mun, S. R., Graling, K., & Denham, S. (2008). Roles of preschoolers' demographic characteristics on development of emotion knowledge in a US sample. Paper presented at the 20th biennial meeting of the International Society for the Study of Behavioural Development, Würzburg, Germany.

Benga, O. (2004). *Dezvoltarea cogniţiei sociale la copii [Development of social cognition in children]*. Cluj-Napoca, Romania: Editura ASCR.

Bowes, J. M., Chen, M., San, L. Q., & Yuan, L. (2004). Reasoning and negotiation about child responsibility in urban Chinese families: Reports from mothers, father, and children. *International Journal of Behavioral Development, 28*, 48–58.

Brown, J. R., Donelan-McCall, N., & Dunn, J. (1996). Why talk about mental states? The significance of children's conversations with friends, siblings, and mothers. *Child Development, 67*, 836–849.

Brown, J. R., & Dunn, J. (1996). Continuities in emotion understanding from three to six years. *Child Development, 67*, 789–802.

Butler, E. A., Lee, T. L., & Gross, J. J. (2007). Emotion regulation and culture: Are the social consequences of emotion suppression culture-specific? *Emotion, 7*, 30–48.

Camras, L. A., Chen, Y., Bakeman, R., Norris, K., & Cain, T. R. (2006). Culture, ethnicity, and children's facial expressions: A study of European American, Mainland Chinese, Chinese American, and adopted Chinese Girls. *Emotion, 6*, 103–114.

Camras, L., Kolmodin, K., & Chen, Y. (2008). Mothers' self-reported emotional expression in Mainland Chinese, Chinese American, and European American families. *International Journal of Behavioral Development, 32*, 459–463.

Carson, J. L., & Parke, R. D. (1996). Reciprocal negative affect in parent-child interactions and children's peer competency. *Child Development, 67*, 2217–2226.

Chen, X., Cen, G., Li, D., & He, Y. (2005). Social functioning and adjustment in Chinese children: The imprint of historical time. *Child Development, 76*, 182–195.

Chen, Y. C., & Chin, J. C. (2007, March). Taiwanese children's understanding of hiding emotion. Paper presented at the biennial meeting of the Society for Research in Child Development, Boston.

Chin, J. C. (2007, March). Taiwanese children's perspectives on coping with negative emotions. Paper presented at the biennial meeting of the Society for Research in Child Development, Boston.

Chin, J. C. (2008, March). The relations of family emotional profiles and children's emotional competence. Paper presented at the annual meeting of the American Educational Research Association, New York.

Clancy, P. M. (1999). The socialization of affect in Japanese mother–child conversation. *Journal of Pragmatics, 31*, 1397–1421.

Cole, P. M., Bruschi, C. J., & Tamang, B. L. (2002). Cultural differences in children's emotional reactions to difficult situations. *Child Development, 73*, 983–996.

Costin, S. E., & Jones, D. C. (1992). Friendship as a facilitator of emotional responsiveness and prosocial interventions among young children. *Developmental Psychology, 28*, 941–947.

DeMulder, K. E., Denham, S. A., Schmidt, M., & Mitchell, J. (2000). Q-sort assessment of attachment security during the preschool years: Links from home to school. *Developmental Psychology, 36*, 274–282.

Denham, S. A. (1986). Social cognition, social behavior, and emotion in preschoolers: Contextual validation. *Child Development, 57*, 194–201.

Denham, S. A. (1997). "When I get have a bad dream, Mommy holds me": Preschoolers' conceptions of emotions, parental socialisation, and emotional competence. *International Journal of Behavioral Development, 20*(2), 301–319.

Denham, S. A. (1998). *Emotional development in young children*. New York: Guilford Press.

Denham, S., Caal, S., Bassett, H. H., Benga, O., & Geangu, E. (2004). Listening to parents: Cultural variations in the meaning of emotions and emotion socialization. *Cognitie, Creier, Comportament (Cognition, Brain, Behavior), 8*, 321–350.

Denham, S. A., Cook, M. C., & Zoller, D. (1992). "Baby looks very sad": Discussions about emotions between mother and preschooler. *British Journal of Developmental Psychology, 10,* 301–315.

Denham, S. A., & Grout, L. (1993). Socialization of emotion: Pathway to preschoolers' emotional and social competence. *Journal of Nonverbal Behavior, 17,* 205–227.

Denham, S. A., & Kochanoff, A. T. (2002). Parental contributions to preschoolers' understanding of emotion. *Marriage and Family Review, 34,* 311–345.

Denham, S. A., McKinley, M., Couchoud, E. A., & Holt, R. (1990). Emotional and behavioral predictors of peer status in young preschoolers. *Child Development, 61,* 1145–1152.

Denham, S. A., Mitchell-Copeland, J., Strandberg, K., Auerbach, S., & Blair, K. (1997). Parental contributions to preschoolers' emotional competence: Direct and indirect effects. *Motivation and Emotion, 21,* 65–86.

Denham, S. A., Zoller, D., & Couchoud, E. A. (1994). Socialization of preschoolers' emotion understanding. *Developmental Psychology, 30,* 928–936.

Diener, M., & Lucas, R. (2004). Desires for children's emotions across 48 countries: Associations with gender, emotional experience, norms for emotions, and characteristics of nations. *Journal of Cross-Cultural Psychology, 35,* 525–547.

Dunn, J., Brown, J., & Beardsall, L. (1991). Family talk about emotions, and children's later understanding of others' emotions. *Developmental Psychology, 27,* 448–455.

Dunn, J., & Cutting, A. L. (1999). Understanding others and individual differences in friendship interactions in young children. *Social Development, 8,* 201–219.

Dunn, J., & Herrera, C. (1997). Conflict resolution with friends, siblings, and mothers: A developmental perspective. *Aggressive Behavior, 23* (Special issue: Appeasement and reconciliation), 343–357.

Dunn, J., & Hughes, C. (1998). Young children's understanding of emotions within close relationships. *Cognition & Emotion, 12,* 171–190.

Dunn, J., Slomkowski, C., Donelan, N., & Herrera, C. (1995). Conflict, understanding, and relationships: Developments and differences in the preschool years. *Early Education and Development, 6,* 303–316.

Dunsmore, J. C., Noguchi, R. J. P., Garner, P. W., Casey, E. C., & Bhullar, N. (2008). Gender-specific linkages of affective social competence with peer relations in preschool children. *Early Education & Development, 19,* 211–237.

Fabes, R. A., Eisenberg, N., Smith, M. C., & Murphy, B. C. (1996). Getting angry at peers: Associations with like of the provocateur. *Child Development, 67,* 942–956.

Fivush, R. (2001). Owning experience: Developing subjective perspective in autobiographical narratives. In C. Moore & K. Skene (Eds.), *The self in time: Developmental issues* (pp. 35–52). Hillsdale, NJ: Erlbaum.

Fracasso, M., & Busch-Rossnagel, N. (1992). Parents and children of Hispanic origin. In M. Procidano & C. Fisher (Eds.), *Contemporary families: A handbook for school professionals* (pp. 83–98). New York: Teachers College Press.

Fujioka, K. (2008). Emotional competence in Japanese preschoolers: Gender differences and age differences. Paper presented at the 20th biennial meeting of the International Society for the Study of Behavioural Development, Würzburg, Germany.

Fung, H. (1999). Becoming a moral child: The socialization of shame among young Chinese children. *Ethos, 27,* 180–209.

Garner, P. W. (1996). The relations of emotional role taking, affect/moral attributions, and emotional display rule knowledge to low-income school-age children's social competence. *Journal of Applied Developmental Psychology, 17,* 19–36.

Garner, P. W., Jones, D. C., & Miner, J. L. (1994). Social competence among low-income pre-schoolers: Emotion socialization practices and social cognitive correlates. *Child Development, 65,* 622–637.

Geangu, E. (2003). *Aspecte cognitive ale empatiei [Cognitive aspects of empathy] (Master's of science dissertation).* Babeş-Bolyai University, Cluj-Napoca, Romania.

Geangu, E., Ionescu, T., & Benga, O. (2008). Development of emotion knowledge in Romanian preschoolers. Paper presented at the 20th biennial meeting of the International Society for the Study of Behavioural Development, Würzburg, Germany.

Gottman, J. M., & Mettetal, G. (1986). Speculations about social and affective development of friendship and acquaintanceship through adolescence. In J. M. Gottman & J. Parker (Eds.), *Conversations of friends: Speculations on affective development* (pp. 192–237). New York: Cambridge University Press.

Halberstadt, A., Denham, S. A., & Dunsmore, J. (2001). Affective social competence. *Social Development, 10,* 79–119.

Harkness, S., & Super, C. M. (1995). Culture and parenting. In M. H. Bornstein (Ed.), *Handbook of parenting: Vol. 2. Biology and ecology of parenting* (pp. 211–234). Hillsdale, NJ: Erlbaum.

Hart, C. H., Yang, C., Nelson, L. J., Robinson, C. C., Olsen, J. A., Nelson, D. A., et al. (2000). Peer acceptance in early childhood and subtypes of socially withdrawn behavior in China, Russia, and the United States. *International Journal of Behavioral Development, 24,* 73–81.

Heyman, G. D., Fu, G., & Lee, K. (2008). Reasoning about the disclosure of success and failure to friends among children in the United States and China. *Developmental Psychology, 44,* 908–918.

Hughes, C., & Dunn, J. (1998). Theory of mind and emotion understanding: Longitudinal associations with mental-state talk between friends. *Developmental Psychology, 34,* 1026–1037.

Isley, S. L., O'Neil, R., Clatfelter, D., & Parke, R. D. (1999). Parent and child expressed affect and children's social competence: Modeling direct and indirect pathways. *Developmental Psychology, 35,* 547–560.

Jones, D. C., Abbey, B., & Cumberland, A. (1998). The development of display rule knowledge: Linkages with family expressiveness and social competence. *Child Development, 69,* 1209–1222.

Kojima, Y. (2000). Maternal regulation of sibling interactions in the preschool years: Observational study of Japanese families. *Child Development, 71,* 1640–1647.

Krappmann, L. (1996). The development of diverse relationships in the social world of childhood. In A. E. Auhagen & M. von Salisch (Eds.), *The diversity of human relationships* (pp. 52–78). New York: Cambridge University Press.

Kyratzis, A. (2001). Emotion talk in preschool same-sex friendship groups: Fluidity over time and context. *Early Education & Development, 12,* 59–392.

Laible, D., & Thompson, R. A. (1998). Attachment and emotional understanding in preschool children. *Developmental Psychology, 34,* 1038–1045.

Lamm, B., Keller, H., Yovsi, R. D., & Chaudhary, N. (2008). Grandmaternal and maternal ethnotheories about early child care. *Journal of Family Psychology, 22*(1), 80–88.

Lee, M. L., & Yang, G. S. (1998). Endurance in Chinese people: Conceptual analysis and empirical study. *Indigenous Psychological Studies, 10,* 3–68.

Lin, C. Y. (2003). *Children's understanding of multiple emotions, ability of hiding emotion, and peer status (Unpublished master's thesis).* National Hualien Teachers' College, Taiwan.

Lunkenheimer, E., Shields, A., & Cortina, K. (2007). Parental emotion coaching and dismissing in family interaction. *Social Development, 16,* 232–248.

Maguire, M. C., & Dunn, J. (1997). Friendships in early childhood, and social understanding. *International Journal of Behavioral Development, 21,* 669–686.

Masuda, T., Ellsworth, P. C., Mesquita, B., Leu, J., Tanida, S., & van de Veerdonk, E. (2008). Placing the face in context: Cultural differences in the perception of facial emotion. *Journal of Personality and Social Psychology, 94,* 365–381.

Matsumoto, D., Yoo, S. H., & Fontaine, J. (2008). Mapping expressive differences around the world: The relationship between emotional display rules and individualism versus collectivism. *Journal of Cross-Cultural Psychology, 39*(1), 55–74.

McDowell, D. J., Kim, M., O'Neil, R., & Parke, R. D. (2002). Children's emotional regulation and social competence in middle childhood: The role of maternal and paternal interactive style. *Marriage & Family Review, 34,* 345–364.

McDowell, D. J., & Parke, R. D. (2005). Parental control and affect as predictors of children's display rule use and social competence with peers. *Social Development, 14,* 440–457.

McElwain, N. L., Halberstadt, A. G., & Volling, B. L. (2007). Mother- and father-reported reactions to children's negative emotions: Relations to young children's emotional understanding and friendship quality. *Child Development, 78,* 1407–1425.

Meerum Terwogt, M., & Olthof, T. (1989). Awareness and self-regulation of emotion in young children. In C. Saarni & P. Harris (Eds.), *Children's understanding of emotion* (pp. 209–237). New York: Cambridge University Press.

Miller, A. L., Fine, S. E., Gouley, K. K., Seifer, R., Dickstein, S., & Shields, A. (2006). Showing and telling about emotions: Interrelations between facets of emotional competence and associations with classroom adjustment in Head Start preschoolers. *Cognition & Emotion, 20,* 1170–1192.

Miller, A. L., Gouley, K. K., Seifer, R., Zakriski, A., Eguia, M., & Vergnani, M. (2005). Emotion knowledge skills in low-income elementary school children: Associations with social status and peer experiences. *Social Development, 14,* 637–651.

Ng, F. F., Pomerantz, E. M., & Lam, S. (2007). Chinese and European American parents' responses to children's success and failure: Implications for children's responses. *Developmental Psychology, 43,* 1239–1255.

Nunner-Winkler, G., & Sodian, B. (1988). Children's understanding of moral emotions. *Child Development, 59,* 1323–1338.

Olthof, T., & Engelberts-Vaske, A. (1997). Kindergarten-aged children's reactions to an emotionally charged naturalistic event: Relations between cognitions, self-reported emotions and emotional behaviour. *Journal of Child Psychology and Psychiatry, 38,* 449–456.

Olthof, T., Meerum Terwogt, M., Van Eck, O. V., & Koops, W. (1987). Children's knowledge of the integration of successive emotions. *Perceptual & Motor Skills, 65,* 407–414.

Parker, J. G., & Seal, J. (1996). Forming, losing, renewing and replacing friendships: Applying temporal parameters to the assessment of children's friendship experiences. *Child Development, 67,* 2248–2268.

Pinquart, M., & Silbereisen, R. K. (2004). Human development in times of social change: Theoretical considerations and research needs. *International Journal of Behavioral Development, 28,* 289–298.

Rimé, B., Dozier, S., Vandenplas, C., & Declercq, M. (1996). Social sharing of emotion in children. In N. Frijda (Ed.), *Proceedings of the 9th conference of the International Society for Research on Emotions, Toronto, Canada* (pp. 161–163). Storrs, CT: ISRE.

Rose, A., & Asher, S. (1999a). Children's goals and strategies in response to conflicts within a friendship. *Developmental Psychology, 35,* 69–79.

Rose, A., & Asher, S. (1999b, April). Seeking and giving social support within a friendship. Paper presented at the meeting of the Society for Research in Child Development, Albuquerque, NM.

Rughiniş, C. (2002). Valori europene in relatiile intime: Studiu comparativ. *Sociologie Romaneasca, 1/2,* 38–75.

Saarni, C. (1997). Coping with aversive feelings. *Motivation and Emotion, 21,* 45–63.

Saarni, C. (1998). Issues of cultural meaningfulness in emotional development. *Developmental Psychology, 34,* 647–652.

Saarni, C. (1999). *The development of emotional competence.* New York: Guilford Press.

Salisch, M. von. (1999). Kooperation und Konkurrenz unter gleichrangigen Partnern. In L. Krappmann, H-P. Kuhn, & H. Uhlendorff (Eds.), *Sozialisation zur Mitbürgerlichkeit.* Opladen, Germany: Leske & Budrich.

Salisch, M. von. (2000a). *Wenn Kinder sich ärgern. Emotionsregulierung in der Entwicklung.* Göttingen, Germany: Hogrefe Verlag.

Salisch, M. von. (2000b). The emotional side of sharing, social support, and conflict negotiation between siblings and between friends. In R. Mills & S. Duck (Eds.), *Developmental psychology of personal relationships* (pp. 49–70). Chichester, UK: Wiley.

Salisch, M. von. (2000c). Zum Einfluß von Gleichaltrigen (Peers) und Freunden auf die Persönlichkeitsentwicklung. In M. Amelang (Ed.), *Enzyklopädie der Psychologie, Differentielle Psychologie: Vol. 4. Determinanten individueller Differenzen* (pp. 345–405). Göttingen, Germany: Hogrefe.

Salisch, M. von. (2001). Children's emotional development: Challenges in their relationships to parents, peers, and friends. *International Journal of Behavioral Development, 25,* 310–319.

Salisch, M. von. (2008). Themes in the development of emotion regulation in childhood and adolescence and a transactional model. In S. Kronast, C. von Scheve, S. Ismer, S. Jung, & M. Vandekerckhove (Eds.), *Regulating emotions: Social necessity and biological inheritance* (pp. 146–167). Oxford: Blackwell.

Salisch, M. von, & Vogelgesang, J. (2005). Anger regulation among friends: Assessment and development from childhood to adolescence. *Journal of Social and Personal Relationships, 37,* 317–330.

Shifflett-Simpson, K., & Cummings, E. M. (1996). Mixed message resolution and children's responses to interadult conflict. *Child Development, 67,* 437–448.

Sonoda, N., & Muto, T. (1996). References to internal states in mother-child interactions: Effect of different settings and maternal individual differences. *Japanese Journal of Developmental Psychology, 7,* 159–169.

Stadler, C., Janke, W., & Schmidt-Atzert, L. (1997). Der Einfluß der Intentionsattribuierung auf aggressives Verhalten im Vorschulalter. *Zeitschrift für Entwicklungspsychologie und Pädagogische Psychologie, 29,* 43–61.

Steele, H., Steele, M., Croft, C., & Fonagy, P. (1999). Infant-mother attachment at one year predicts children's understanding of mixed emotions at six years. *Social Development, 7,* 161–178.

Sutton, J., Smith, P. K., & Swettenham, J. (1999). Social cognition and bullying: Social inadequacy or skilled manipulation? *British Journal of Developmental Psychology, 17,* 435–450.

Suveg, C., Zeman, J., Flannery-Schroeder, E., & Cassano, M. (2005). Emotion socialization in families of children with an anxiety disorder. *Journal of Abnormal Child Psychology, 33,* 145–155.

Uhlendorff, H. (2004). After the Wall: Parental attitudes to child rearing in East and West Germany. *International Journal of Behavioral Development, 28,* 71–82.

Ujiie, T. (1997). How do Japanese mothers treat children's negativism? *Journal of Applied Developmental Psychology, 18,* 467–483.

Underwood, M., Coie, J. D., & Herbsman, C. (1992). Display rules for anger and aggression in school age children. *Child Development, 63,* 366–380.

Underwood, M., Hurley, J., Johanson, C., & Mosley, C. (1999). An experimental, observational investigation of children's responses to peer provocation: Developmental and gender differences in middle childhood. *Child Development, 70,* 1428–1446.

Volling, B. L., Youngblade, L. M., & Belsky, J. (1997). Young children's social relationships with siblings and friends. *American Journal of Orthopsychiatry, 67*, 102–111.

Wang, Q. (2004). The emergence of cultural self-constructs: Autobiographical memory and self-description in European American and Chinese children. *Developmental Psychology, 40*, 3–15.

Wang, Q. (2008). Emotion knowledge and autobiographical memory across the preschool years: A cross-cultural longitudinal investigation. *Cognition, 108*, 117–135.

Wang, Q., & Fivush, R. (2005). Mother-child conversations of emotionally salient events: Exploring the functions of emotional reminiscing in European American and Chinese families. *Social Development, 14*, 473–495.

Warren, H. K., & Stifter, C. A. (2008). Maternal emotion-related socialization and preschoolers' developing emotion self-awareness. *Social Development, 17*, 239–258.

Zahn-Waxler, C., Friedman, R., Cole, P., Mizuta, I., & Hiruma, N. (1996). Japanese and United States preschool children's responses to conflict and distress. *Child Development, 67*, 2462–2477.

Zeman, J., & Garber, J. (1996). Display rules for anger, sadness, and pain: It depends on who is watching. *Child Development, 67*, 957–973.

Zeman, J., Penza, S., Shipman, K., & Young, G. (1997). Preschoolers as functionalists: The impact of social context on emotion regulation. *Child Study Journal, 27*, 41–67.

Zeman, J., & Shipman, K. (1996). Children's expression of negative affect: Reasons and methods. *Developmental Psychology, 32*, 842–849.

CHAPTER TWENTY-THREE

Social Withdrawal and Shyness

Kenneth H. Rubin, Robert J. Coplan, Julie C. Bowker, and Melissa Menzer

> There are days when solitude is a heady wine that intoxicates you with freedom, others when it is a bitter tonic, and still others when it is a poison that makes you beat your head against the wall.
>
> – Colette, *Earthly Paradise*

For centuries philosophers, writers, artists, and psychologists alike have offered opinions, hypotheses, and data pertaining to the phenomenon of solitude. For many writers, solitude is viewed romantically as a phenomenon that brings safety, quiet, and escape from the "madding crowd." Solitude is viewed as a source of inspiration, as a psychological venue for quiet reflection. For others, however, solitude brings with it loneliness and suffering.

The theoretical origins of developmental research on social withdrawal can be traced to the early writings of Piaget (1932) and Mead (1934) about the significance of social interaction for children's normal development. These researchers were among the first to stress that the peer group provided an important and unique context for children's social, social cognitive, and emotional development (Rubin, Bukowski, & Parker, 2006). Peer interaction also influences children's understanding of the rules and norms of their peer subcultures. It is this understanding of normative performance levels that engenders, in the child, an ability to evaluate her or his own competency against the perceived standards of the peer group. If peer interaction experiences do lead to the development of social competencies and the understanding of the self in relation to others, it seems reasonable to think about the developmental consequences for those children who, for

The Wiley-Blackwell Handbook of Childhood Social Development, Second Edition, edited by Peter K. Smith and Craig H. Hart
© 2011 by Blackwell Publishing Ltd.

whatever reason, refrain from engaging in social interaction and avoid the company of their peers.

Notwithstanding, for many years, researchers neglected the study of solitude and withdrawal from social company. In the past 25 years, however, a burgeoning literature has accumulated on the topic. In this chapter, we describe the origins, correlates, and consequences of this second vision of solitude – that which brings with it wariness in social company, fear of rejection, victimization, and loneliness. Thus, our focus is on the topic of *social withdrawal.*

Defining Social Withdrawal and Shyness

The early study of social withdrawal was hampered by the lack of both conceptual and definitional frameworks (Rubin & Asendorpf, 1993). The "lack of conceptual clarity" was contributed to by the frequent and interchangeable use of a variety of (not well-differentiated) terms (e.g., *shyness, withdrawal, reticence, inhibition,* and *isolation*). However, in more recent years there has been a more concerted effort to delineate a consistent typology of terms (Rubin, Coplan, & Bowker, 2009).

To begin with, *active isolation* is used to denote the process whereby some children play alone because their play partners do not wish to interact with them. In this case, the "cause" of the child's lack of social interaction is attributed to external factors (that is, the child is isolated *by* others), perhaps in response to social immaturity, behavioral undercontrol, or other unacceptable features characteristic of the child. The term *social withdrawal* is used to denote a child isolating him or herself *from* the peer group through the consistent (across situations and over time) display of solitary behavior in the presence of peers. In this regard, social withdrawal is seen to arise from internal factors, with the child opting, for some reason or another, not to interact with peers.

Thus, *social withdrawal* is an "umbrella term" (Rubin et al., 2009) encompassing at least two different "reasons" why children might choose to play alone. Most research has focused on children who refrain from social interaction because of their wariness and social fear. For example, *shy* children are wary and anxious when faced with social novelty and perceived social evaluation (Coplan, Prakash, O'Neil, & Armer, 2004). Asendorpf (1990) characterized shyness as reflecting two competing social motivations. In this regard, shy children desire social interaction, but their social *approach* motivations are inhibited by fear-induced social *avoidance* (Coplan et al., 2004). The motivational conflict is often manifested behaviorally through the display of reticent behavior, which includes watching other children without joining in and/or remaining unoccupied (that is, staring into space) in the presence of peers (Coplan, Rubin, Fox, Calkins, & Stewart, 1994).

Using different nomenclature, researchers have explored conceptually similar constructs related to wariness and anxiety in the face of novelty (e.g., *inhibition*; Kagan, 1997), social novelty and/or perceived social evaluation (e.g., *fearful* and *self-conscious shyness*; Cheek & Buss, 1981), and familiar peer contexts (e.g., *anxious solitude*; Gazelle & Ladd, 2003). Although there are "fine-grained" conceptual distinctions to be made between these different constructs, in this chapter we employ the term *shyness* to represent *all* forms of social wariness.

Much less is known about children who may refrain from social interaction because they prefer to play alone (for a recent review, see Coplan & Weeks, 2010). This "nonfearful" preference for solitary activities has been labeled *unsociability* (Asendorpf, 1993) or *social disinterest* (Coplan et al., 2004). Unsociable children are thought to lack a strong desire to play with others (low approach motivation), but are also not strongly averse to peer interaction (low avoidance motivation). Although unsociability has been assumed to be relatively benign in early childhood (Harrist, Zaia, Bates, Dodge, & Pettit, 1997), Coplan and colleagues (2004) recently reported that unsociability in preschool was associated with peer exclusion. These authors speculated that peers may come to feel "put off" by children who rarely invite others to play. It has also been argued that with increasing age, unsociability might become increasingly associated with peer difficulties and psychological ill-being because all forms of social withdrawal likely become increasingly viewed as atypical and deviant by peers (Rubin & Asendorpf, 1993).

Developmental Origins of Shyness and Social Withdrawal

Biological foundations

Where might social withdrawal come from? Some believe that it derives from a *biological disposition* to be emotionally primed to react to novelty with wariness and fear. Thus, the degree to which individuals vary with regard to reactivity, frequency, intensity, and latency of response in the expression of emotions may play a significant role in the early demonstration of shyness.

About 15 percent of infants display a high degree of negative affect and distress when presented with novel stimuli (Calkins, Fox, & Marshall, 1996; Kagan, Snidman, & Arcus, 1998). In toddlerhood, these infants often display fearful, cautious, and wary behaviors when presented with novel situations and adult strangers (Garcia-Coll, Kagan, & Reznick, 1984). Scholars suggest that this early-appearing shyness (also called *behavioral inhibition*) is a temperamental trait that emanates from a physiological "hard wiring" that evokes caution, wariness, and timidity in unfamiliar social and nonsocial situations (Kagan, 1997).

Extremely shy infants, toddlers, and preschoolers differ from their uninhibited counterparts in ways that imply variability in the threshold of excitability of the amygdala and its projections to the cortex, hypothalamus, sympathetic nervous system, corpus striatum, and central gray area. For example, researchers have found that shy children display greater right frontal EEG activation compared to noninhibited individuals during infancy and early childhood (Fox, Henderson, Marshall, Nichols, & Ghera, 2005). Another physiological entity that distinguishes wary from nonwary children is vagal tone, an index of the functional status or efficiency of the nervous system marking both general reactivity and the ability to regulate one's level of arousal. Shy children tend to demonstrate lower vagal tone in response to social stressors than nonshy children (Spangler & Schieche,

1998). Moreover, socially fearful children have shown elevated home *baseline* cortisol readings relative to nonwary children, suggesting that they are continually "primed" to react with wariness to novel or unsettling social situations (Schmidt, Fox, Schulkin, & Gold, 1999).

Last, in keeping with the notion that overexcitability in the amygdala can account for the demonstration (and stability) of shyness, recent functional magnetic resonance imaging (fMRI) research has demonstrated that adults identified as extremely shy at 2 years are more likely than typical, noninhibited (at 2 years) adults to demonstrate increased reactivity to the presentation of unfamiliar (as opposed to familiar) faces (Schwartz et al., 2003).

Parenting

Shyness is among the most stable of temperamental and personality characteristics (see Rapee & Coplan, 2010, for a recent review). However, it is hardly immutable. Many extremely shy infants and toddlers do not grow up to become withdrawn and socially anxious children (Degnan & Fox, 2007). The family environment constitutes one major influence on the stability and outcomes of temperamental shyness.

Attachment relationships   According to attachment theorists, children develop an internalized model of the self in relation to others from the quality of their early parenting experiences (Bowlby, 1973). Most children develop a *secure* parent–child relationship. The resultant internal working model allows the child to feel confident and self-assured, and to actively explore when introduced to novel social settings. However, some children develop an insecure-anxious attachment relationship, come to view the world as unpredictable and scary, and refrain from exploring their social environments (Sroufe, 1983).

There is some evidence linking insecure attachment with temperamental shyness. For example, infants who are dispositionally reactive to mildly stressful, novel social events are more likely to be classified as having an insecure-anxious attachment than their less reactive counterparts (Kochanska, 1998). Booth-LaForce and Oxford (2008) recently reported that toddlers with insecure attachment relationships were more likely than their securely attached counterparts to be rated as shy by teachers in elementary school. Thus, it is likely that the combination of insecure attachment and temperamental shyness represents the greatest risk for the development of later social withdrawal and anxiety (Rubin et al., 2009).

Parenting beliefs and behaviors   It is important to note that an insecure attachment relationship is itself predicted by maternal behavior. For example, mothers with insecure-anxious attachment relationships tend to be more controlling of and overinvolved with their children than mothers of securely attached babies (Erikson, Sroufe, & Egeland, 1985). It is this particular parenting style that appears to be quite significant in the lives of temperamentally shy infants and toddlers.

Given that temperamentally shy children may not adequately explore their environments, it has been suggested that their parents may develop the belief that the best (if not only) way to help their children understand their "worlds" is to either manipulate their child's behaviors in a power-assertive, highly directive fashion (e.g., telling the child how to act or what to do) or intervene and take over for the child the management of his or her interpersonal or impersonal dilemmas (see Hastings, Nuselovici, Rubin, & Cheah, 2010, for a recent review). The upside is that the child's difficulties will be solved. The downside is that for socially fearful children, the experience of parental overcontrol is likely to maintain or exacerbate, rather than ameliorate, their difficulties. In controlling what their children are exposed to and how such situations are handled, these parents may prevent their children from engaging in necessary, self-initiated coping techniques. Lacking practice in behavioral self-regulation, children who are poor physiological regulators may not learn to overcome their dispositional vulnerabilities. Further, such parenting experiences may prevent the development of a belief system of self-efficacy, and likely will perpetuate feelings of insecurity within and outside the family.

Given the above scenario, is there evidence that intrusively controlling parenting is an accompaniment and/or response to temperamental shyness? During the past decade, investigators have consistently reported linkages between maternal control and overprotectiveness and children's social withdrawal, anxiety, and shyness (Bayer, Sanson, & Hemphill, 2006; McShane & Hastings, 2009). For example, Rubin, Hastings, Stewart, Henderson, and Chen (1997) found that mothers of temperamentally shy toddlers were "oversolicitous," that is, they were observed to be highly affectionate and shielding of their toddlers when it was neither appropriate nor sensitive to do so.

It is also possible that children's shyness may also *cause* parental overprotection and overcontrol (e.g., Rubin, Nelson, Hastings, & Asendorpf, 1999). When some parents perceive their children to be socially anxious and vulnerable, they attempt to be supportive by manipulating, directing, and controlling their children's social behaviors. However, results from some recent studies suggest that these types of responses may only exacerbate the negative outcomes associated with temperamental shyness and behavioral inhibition. For example, shyness in preschoolers is more strongly predictive of social withdrawal in middle childhood if mothers are more controlling and oversolicitous (Degnan, Fox, Henderson, Rubin, & Nichols, 2008; Hane, Cheah, Rubin, & Fox, 2008). It has also been reported that withdrawn preschoolers with more oversolicitous mothers are, 3 years later, likely to be more shy and withdrawn than children with less solicitous mothers. Similarly, Coplan, Arbeau, and Armer (2008) reported that relations between shyness and indices of maladjustment were stronger among children with more anxious and overprotective mothers and weaker for children with more warm and supportive mothers. Interestingly, these parental effects have also been observed with assessments of the physiological substrates of behavioral inhibition. Hastings and colleagues (2008) found that children with lower vagal tone (less parasympathetic self-regulation) were more reticent and withdrawn with peers only if they had more overprotective mothers.

Summary   Although there is growing evidence that temperamental shyness has biological underpinnings, both temperament and parenting play critical roles in the development of shyness and social withdrawal in infancy and childhood. Mothers of shy children are more likely to endorse and practice intrusive, controlling, and overprotective parenting strategies. Such beliefs, behaviors, and responses are likely detrimental to the child's developing sense of autonomy and social efficacy, tend to increase the stability of shyness over time, and exacerbate the negative outcomes that may come to be associated with shyness.

Correlates and Outcomes of Shyness and Social Withdrawal

From early childhood through adolescence, and into adulthood, shyness and social withdrawal are concurrently and predictively associated with a wide range of socioe-motional difficulties (Rubin et al., 2009). In the following sections, we outline the correlates and outcomes of shyness and withdrawal, with a focus on implications for social development.

Social cognitions and social competence

Shy and withdrawn children demonstrate deficits in social competence and interpersonal problem-solving skills (Bohlin, Hagekull, & Andersson, 2005). For example, compared to their more sociable agemates, withdrawn children produce fewer alternative solutions and are more likely to suggest adult intervention in response to hypothetical social dilemmas (Rubin, Daniels-Beirness, & Bream, 1984). Moreover, when observing young withdrawn children during peer interaction, Rubin et al. (1984) reported that, as compared to the more sociable children, (a) the *goals* of socially withdrawn children's requests appeared less "costly" – for example, they were more likely to attempt to request attention from a playmate rather than attempt to obtain an object or elicit active behaviors from their playmates; (b) the *strategies* used by withdrawn children were less assertive and direct – specifically, their requests were less likely to be spoken in the imperative; and (c) the *outcomes* of withdrawn preschoolers' requests were more likely to result in failure despite the use of less costly and direct overtures.

These early experiences of social failure may give already fearful and insecure children good reason to further withdraw from their peers. For example, as a result of frequent interpersonal rejection by peers, withdrawn children may begin to attribute their social failures to internal causes (e.g., something is wrong with *me*) rather than attributing their social failures to other people or situations (Wichmann, Coplan, & Daniels, 2004). The combination of peer rejection and internal (dispositional) attributions for peer noncompliance could be construed as creating a negative feedback loop whereby an initially fearful, withdrawn child begins to believe that his or her social failures are personality based, and then these beliefs are reinforced by increasing failure of social initiatives or interactions (Rubin & Stewart, 1996). Ultimately, the consequence of such cognitions may be increased withdrawal from the social environment.

Self-perceptions and internalizing problems

The start of preschool, day care, or kindergarten represents an important and unique developmental milestone for young children (Hamre & Pianta, 2001). However, for young shy children, this experience may represent a particularly daunting challenge (Henderson & Fox, 1998). Coplan and Arbeau (2008) cited the presence of a large group of (initially unfamiliar) peers, increased demands for verbal participation, and a high child-to-staff ratio as factors that may exacerbate shy-withdrawn children's feelings of social fear and self-consciousness.

Perhaps as a result, even in early childhood, as compared to others, shy and withdrawn children report feeling less positively about themselves, are more lonely, and display more signs of anxiety and other internalizing problems (e.g., Coplan et al., 2008; Coplan, Closson, & Arbeau, 2007; Henderson, Marshall, Fox, & Rubin, 2004; Nelson et al., 2009). Unfortunately, this pattern appears to only worsen with age. In mid- to late child-hood, socially withdrawn children continue to develop negative self-perceptions of their social competencies and interpersonal relationships (e.g., Hymel, Bowker, & Woody, 1993; Nelson, Rubin, & Fox, 2005). Moreover, during this age period, shyness and withdrawal become increasingly associated with such internalizing problems as anxiety, loneliness, and depression (e.g., Bell-Dolan, Reaven, & Peterson, 1993; Findlay, Coplan, & Bowker, 2009; Gazelle & Rudolph, 2004; Weeks, Coplan, & Kingsbury, 2009).

Rejection and victimization

Even in early childhood, peers respond to shy behaviors with exclusion, rejection, and victimization (e.g., Chen, DeSouza, Chen, & Wang, 2006; Gazelle & Ladd, 2003; Hart et al., 2000; Perren & Alsaker, 2006). Moreover, with increased age, social withdrawal becomes increasingly concurrently and predictively associated with peer exclusion and rejection (e.g., Newcomb, Bukowski, & Pattee, 1993; Oh et al., 2008). Children begin to view social withdrawal and solitude as behaviors that contrast sharply with age-specific norms and expectations for social interaction and peer relationship involvement during early to middle childhood (Rubin, Wojslawowicz, Burgess, Rose-Krasnor, & Booth-LaForce, 2006; Younger, Gentile, & Burgess, 1993). Thus, withdrawn children become increasingly rejected and excluded during this age period because their behaviors are viewed by their peers as increasingly atypical and deviant. The increasing emphasis on peer interactions and relationships during late childhood and early adolescence may help to explain why the association between withdrawal and rejection becomes stronger during this developmental period (Rubin, Bukowski, et al., 2006). Of course, relatively poorer social skills undoubtedly also contribute to the lower likeability ratings of some withdrawn children.

Numerous studies have also indicated that many socially withdrawn children experience repeated and consistent victimization by peers during early and late childhood (e.g., Hanish & Guerra, 2004; Kochenderfer-Ladd, 2003). Because withdrawn young children are often unassertive and submissive with peers (Stewart & Rubin, 1995), researchers have argued that withdrawn children may experience victimization because they exude an "anxious vulnerability" and thus are viewed as "easy marks" who are unlikely to fight back or retaliate (Rubin, Wojslawowicz, et al., 2006).

However, it is important to note that some withdrawn children experience greater peer difficulties than others. For example, Gazelle (2008) found that socially withdrawn children who also displayed attention-seeking and/or aggressive behavior were at greater risk (relative to withdrawn children who do not display such behaviors) for such peer difficulties as rejection, exclusion, and victimization. It was hypothesized that such subtypes of socially withdrawn children may experience greater problems with their peers because they not only fail to display socially *desirable* behavior (e.g., approach, and sociable behavior) but also exhibit socially *undesirable* behavior.

Friendship

Withdrawn children are as likely as nonwithdrawn ones to have at least one mutual stable best friendship (e.g., Ladd & Burgess, 1999; Rubin, Wojslawowicz, et al., 2006). Despite apparent ease in forming *one* friendship, however, withdrawn children may have some difficulty forming *many* friendships (Pedersen, Vitaro, Barker, & Borge, 2007). In general, withdrawn children tend to befriend similarly withdrawn and victimized children, although these relationships do not appear to make for the "best" friendships. For example, Rubin, Wojslawowicz, et al. (2006) reported that socially withdrawn fifth-grade children and their mutual best friends both rated their best friendships as relatively poor in relationship quality. In another study, withdrawn children and their friends were observed to be less communicative than were nonwithdrawn children and their friends (Schneider, 1999).

Moreover, there is some evidence that having a socially withdrawn friend may actually be a risk factor for withdrawn children. In a longitudinal study that followed participants from the fifth to eighth grade, Oh and colleagues (2008) found that withdrawn children who had withdrawn friends were *more* likely to show initially high levels of withdrawal in the fifth grade and to become increasingly anxious-withdrawn over time. Results from this study suggest that the benefits of friendship involvement for socially withdrawn children are negative when the best friend is likewise withdrawn. But, we have yet to discover whether having a similarly withdrawn friend or a low-quality friendship contributes to the *psychological* difficulties of withdrawn children and young adolescents.

Long-term consequences of social withdrawal

There has been a handful of longitudinal studies exploring the longer term consequences of shyness and social withdrawal in childhood. For example, Rubin and colleagues reported that social withdrawal at 7 years of age predicted negative self-regard and loneliness at 9 and 10 years of age (Hymel, Rubin, Rowden, & LeMare, 1990; Rubin, 1993; Rubin, Hymel, & Mills, 1989) as well as loneliness, depression, and negative self-regard at 14 years (Rubin, Chen, McDougall, Bowker, & McKinnon, 1995). Prior, Smart, Sanson, and Oberklaid (2000) found that children rated as chronically shy from early childhood onward were at high risk for the development of anxiety. Relatedly, there is increasing evidence linking extreme shyness in early childhood to clinical anxiety disorders (particularly social phobia) during late childhood and adolescence (e.g., Schwartz, Snidman, & Kagan, 1999).

Finally, Asendorpf, Denissen, and van Aken (2008) found that, over a 19-year period, shy children remained consistently shyer than nonshy children. These researchers also reported that over the long run, shy males (but not females) entered romantic relationships later than nonshy males, a finding in keeping with that of Caspi, Elder, and Bem (1988). These findings suggest that the implications of shyness and withdrawal may vary for boys and girls. We explore this possibility in the following section.

Role of gender

Whereas there is little evidence that the prevalence or frequency of shyness and withdrawal in childhood differs for boys and girls (Rubin et al., 2009), some researchers have suggested that shyness is less socially acceptable for boys than for girls because it violates gender norms related to male social assertion and dominance (Rubin & Coplan, 2004). Evidence of the gender variability in the "social acceptability" of shyness can be extracted from how shy boy and girls are treated and responded to by significant others. For example, shyness in girls is more likely to be rewarded and accepted by parents, whereas shyness in boys is more likely to be discouraged and to result in more negative interactions (Radke-Yarrow, Richters, & Wilson, 1988; Stevenson-Hinde, 1989).

Gender differences are also evident in terms of peers' reactions to shy children. Even in early childhood, shyness and social withdrawal are more strongly associated with peer exclusion and rejection for boys than for girls (Coplan et al., 2008; Gazelle & Ladd, 2003). These findings may shed some light on the mechanism by which shy boys come to experience more negative outcomes later in life (e.g., Asendorpf et al., 2008). Results from a growing number of studies also suggest that shyness in boys is more strongly associated with socioemotional difficulties (e.g., loneliness, anxiety, and lower self-esteem) than shyness in girls (Coplan et al., 2007; Coplan & Weeks, 2009; Gest, 1997). There is evidence to suggest that shy children may be particularly vulnerable to the negative effects of peer exclusion (e.g., Gazelle & Ladd, 2003; Gazelle & Rudolph, 2004). If shy boys tend to experience greater peer exclusion from an earlier age, they may experience the cumulative negative effects of these experiences in later childhood and beyond.

Interventions for shyness and social withdrawal

In this section, we briefly review research related to early intervention and prevention. Despite the psychological and social risks associated with shyness and social withdrawal, there has been surprisingly little research into the development and evaluation of relevant intervention programs. Some previous interventions employed teachers and other adults to provide instruction and to prompt, praise, and reinforce social behaviors (e.g., Lindeman, Fox, & Redelheim, 1993; Storey, Smith & Strain, 1993). Other researchers have developed interventions that make extensive use of peers (Christopher, Hansen, & MacMillan, 1991). For example, Fantuzzo, Stovall, Schachtel, Goins, and Hall (1987) trained more sociable children to make competent social initiations to withdrawn peers as means of encouraging more positive social experiences.

Perhaps the most popular intervention strategy for socially withdrawn children has been *social skills training* (SST). Most SST programs involve training in verbal and nonverbal communication skills, and incorporate components of coaching, modeling, and social-problem-solving training. Some SST programs have demonstrated moderate short-term success in enhancing the social skills of withdrawn children (e.g., Sheridan, Kratochwill, & Elliott, 1990). However, other SST programs have produced inconsistent findings and treatment effects that fail to generalize from one setting to the next (Schneider, 1992).

Many intervention programs have suffered from methodological shortcomings, including single-subject or numerically small designs, a lack of control group, and a sole reliance on teacher referrals to identify withdrawn children (e.g., Lindeman et al., 1993; Sheridan et al., 1990). As well, ambiguity in the definitions of social withdrawal may result in the selection of a heterogeneous treatment group that could include socially wary, socially disinterested, and actively isolated children; therefore, the results of these studies are often inconsistent among participants.

Rubin and colleagues (2009) concluded that early intervention research for shy and socially withdrawn children clearly has a lot of "catching up" to do. They cited the need for larger scale studies with longer follow-up periods and careful designs, and suggested that social skills programs must be developed that are specifically designed for the particular needs of shy and withdrawn children. One promising area of recent research has included the more direct involvement of parents in the intervention process. For example, Rapee, Kennedy, Ingram, Edwards, and Sweeney (2005) found that as compared to controls, preschool-aged extremely shy children demonstrated a significantly greater decrease in anxiety after their parents received a targeted education and training program. This finding mirrors recent results from the clinical anxiety literature indicating that parental involvement also appears to improve treatment outcomes for school-aged anxious children (e.g., Spence, Donovan, & Brechman-Toussaint, 2000).

Summary From early childhood to adolescence, social withdrawal is associated with a host of negative incomes, particularly along the internalizing dimension. With increasing age, socially withdrawn children become increasingly rejected, victimized, and excluded by peers. These peer difficulties in turn likely lead to the development of negative self-perceptions of social relationships and skills. There is some evidence to suggest that shy boys are at greater risk for negative outcomes than shy-withdrawn girls. Yet, despite the growing evidence of shyness and social withdrawal as significant risk factors, there has been limited research in the area of early intervention and prevention.

Cross-Cultural Perspectives on Shyness and Social Withdrawal

Much of that discussed in this chapter has been ethnocentrically Western in thought and practice. Results from cross-cultural studies have suggested that across nations, social withdrawal may shape children's social experiences differently as well as similarly (Chen & French, 2008). Indeed, whereas the behavior of social withdrawal (the *form*) may appear similar across cultures, the psychological meaning (the *function*) of social withdrawal may vary substantially from culture to culture. For example, an emerging finding in the cross-cultural literature is that social withdrawal in Asian cultures (which tend to be more collectivist) appears to be more socially acceptable and associated with more positive outcomes than the same behavior in Western cultures (which tend to be more individualistic; e.g., Chen, Rubin, & Li, 1995). In the following sections, we review cross-cultural research related to social withdrawal and shyness.

Prevalence of shyness and social withdrawal

Some researchers have argued that temperamental shyness (i.e., inhibition) is more prevalent in East Asian countries compared to the United States, Canada, Western European countries, and Australia (Gartstein et al., 2006; Rubin, Hemphill, et al., 2006). For example, Rubin, Hemphill, et al. (2006) found that Chinese and Korean toddlers exhibited more inhibited behavior in Kagan's "Inhibition paradigm" (e.g., Kagan, Reznick, & Snidman, 1988) than Australian and Italian toddlers. Even in multicultural contexts, children of East Asian descent living in Canada have been found to be shyer than European Canadian children (Chen & Tse, 2008).

Interestingly, some researchers have explored cross-cultural differences in the genetic substrates of shyness and withdrawal. For example, at the genetic level, carrying the "short" allele of the serotonin transporter (5-HTT) polymorphism gene has been linked to high reactivity and shyness in children (Fox et al., 2005). It has been suggested that the short allele might be more prevalent in East Asian populations and the long allele more prevalent in European populations (Kim et al., 2005).

Parenting

Culture also influences parenting beliefs and behaviors (Bornstein, 1991). For example, Nelson et al. (2006) suggested that Chinese parents are more directive in their strategies to encourage their children to fit in with their peers and help their children learn socially acceptable behavior. Chinese mothers have also been found to be more accepting of their children's inhibited behavior than North American mothers (Chen et al., 1998). Yet, in more recent work, social withdrawal was reported to be negatively valued by Chinese mothers of preschool children (Cheah & Rubin, 2004).

It is important to note that the cultural meanings of inhibited versus socially withdrawn behavior may differ across studies. For example, reserved, inhibited behavior (Chen et al., 1998) may be interpreted as reflecting a cooperative, compliant demeanor, and thus may be viewed as acceptable behavior. Nonsocial and withdrawn behavior in social company (Cheah & Rubin, 2004) may be viewed as an uncooperative, unacceptable form of behavior. Moreover, in more recent research, there is also some evidence that parents of shy-withdrawn children in China are more intrusive, directive, overprotective, and coercive (Nelson et al., 2006).

Peer relationships

As previously noted, in Western and individualistic cultures within which such individual characteristics as independence, assertiveness, expressiveness, and competitiveness are valued and encouraged (e.g., Argentina, Canada, Greece, Italy, the Netherlands, and the United States), shyness and social withdrawal are generally linked to peer rejection and other negative outcomes (Casiglia, Lo Coco, & Zappulla, 1998; Cillessen, van IJzendoorn, van Lieshout, & Hartup, 1992; Rubin, Chen, & Hymel, 1993; Schaughency, Vannatta, Langhinrichsen, & Lally, 1992). In contrast, in a series of studies in the 1990s, Chen and colleagues demonstrated that shyness in collectivist China was more likely to be encouraged and accepted by peers, and positively associated with social competence, peer acceptance, and academic success (e.g., Chen et al., 1995; Chen, Rubin, Li, & Li, 1999). These findings might be explained by the fact that children in collectivist cultures, such as China, are more likely to encourage and be encouraged to display group harmony, behavioral and emotional control, and cooperation (Chen & French, 2008), and shyness may be viewed as nonthreatening and nondisruptive behavior.

More recent findings, however, suggest that socially withdrawn and wary Chinese children are rejected by the peer group, particularly in urban Chinese samples (Chang et al., 2005; Chen, Cen, Li, & He, 2005). Similar findings have been reported in a study of postcommunist Russian children (Hart et al., 2000). These more recent findings may reflect such historical changes as globalization and Westernization (Chen, Chung, & Hsiao, 2009).

It will be important for future researchers to consider cross-cultural differences beyond the dichotomization of culture into individualism or collectivism. For example, Prakash and Coplan (2007) reported that socially withdrawn children in India were more likely to be rejected by peers as compared to nonwithdrawn children. Although the cultural values of India are generally collectivistic, the authors argued that these values are influenced by additional factors such as a strong focus on family, social class, and caste. For example, whereas greater collectivistic ideals may be primarily espoused with regard to interactions with familiar others, in contexts outside of family interactions, more importance may be placed on living independently with individualistic intentions and personal goals. As such, shyness-withdrawal would not be considered a desirable trait outside of the context of family and caste.

Summary

Shyness and social withdrawal appear to be more prevalent, more positively valued, and associated with more positive outcomes in East Asian as compared to Western cultures. However, societal values change, and the findings of one historical era may not be replicated in subsequent eras. Thus, the focus of cross-cultural developmental work may need to tap into a variety of different domains, such as anthropology, sociology, political science, and history, in an attempt to understand the impact of societal change on cultural values, in particular reference to social withdrawal and children's social development.

Conclusion

The study of the developmental course of social withdrawal has garnered an enormous amount of attention in the past decade. A glance at the dates of the cited material in this review will attest to this fact. Much work has been directed toward establishing the developmental origins of social withdrawal and its related constructs, as well as examining the contemporaneous and predictive correlates at different points in childhood and adolescence. With regard to the latter, relatively few longitudinal studies exist; therefore, additional data are required to further examine the premise that social withdrawal represents a risk factor in childhood and adolescence.

Although we have suggested a number of etiological factors that conspire to produce a socially withdrawn profile in childhood, the supportive data derive from very few developmental laboratories. The extent to which biologically based, dispositional factors interact with parenting styles and parent–child relationships to predict the consistent display of socially withdrawn behavior in both familiar and unfamiliar peer contexts needs to be broadly established. Moreover, these phenomena need to be more broadly explored within a variety of cultural contexts.

In summary, the literature we have reviewed suggests that the quality of life for shy and socially withdrawn children is less than pleasant. Withdrawn children are socially deferent, anxious, lonely, rejected, and insecure in the company of peers. They fail to exhibit age-appropriate interpersonal problem-solving skills and tend to believe themselves to be deficient in social skills and relationships. The home lives of shy and withdrawn children are no more comforting: They tend to have insecure attachment relationships with their mothers, and they are recipients of overcontrolling, intrusive parenting. Taken together, these characteristics do not augur well for socially withdrawn children. As such, researchers would do well to be more active in developing ameliorative, if not preventive, interventions for these children.

References

Asendorpf, J. (1990). Beyond social withdrawal: Shyness, unsociability and peer avoidance. *Human Development, 33*, 250–259.

Asendorpf, J. (1993). Abnormal shyness in children. *Journal of Child Psychology and Psychiatry, 34*, 1069–1081.

Asendorpf, J. B., Denissen, J. J. A., & van Aken, M. A. G. (2008). Inhibited and aggressive preschool children at 23 years of age: Personality and social transitions into adulthood. *Developmental Psychology, 44*, 997–1011.

Bayer, J. K., Sanson, A. V., & Hemphill, S. S. (2006). Children's moods, fears, and worries: Development of an early childhood parent questionnaire. *Journal of Emotional and Behavioral Disorders, 14*, 41–49.

Bell-Dolan, D., Reaven, N. M., & Peterson, L. (1993). Depression and social functioning: A multidimensional study of the linkages. *Journal of Clinical Child Psychology, 22*, 306–315.

Bohlin, G., Hagekull, B., & Andersson, K. (2005). Behavioral inhibition as a precursor of peer social competence in early school age: The interplay with attachment and nonparental care. *Merrill-Palmer Quarterly, 51*, 1–19.

Booth-LaForce, C., & Oxford, M. L. (2008). Trajectories of social withdrawal from grades 1 to 6: Prediction from early parenting, attachment, and temperament. *Developmental Psychology, 44*, 1298–1313.

Bornstein, M. (Ed.). (1991). *Cultural approaches to parenting.* Hillsdale, NJ: Erlbaum.

Bowlby, J. (1973). *Attachment and loss: Separation, anxiety, and anger.* New York: Basic Books.

Calkins, S. D., Fox, N. A., & Marshall, T. R. (1996). Behavioral and physiological antecedents of inhibition in infancy. *Child Development, 67*, 523–540.

Casiglia, A. C., Lo Coco, A., & Zappulla, C. (1998). Aspects of social reputation and peer relationships in Italian children: A cross-cultural perspective. *Developmental Psychology, 34*, 723–730.

Caspi, A., Elder, G. H., Jr., & Bem, D. J. (1988). Moving away from the world: Life-course patterns of shy children. *Developmental Psychology, 24*, 824–831.

Chang, L., Lei, L., Li, K. K., Liu, H., Guo, B., Wang, Y., et al. (2005). Peer acceptance and self-perceptions of verbal and behavioural aggression and withdrawal. *International Journal of Behavioral Development, 29*, 49–57.

Cheah, C. L., & Rubin, K. H. (2004). European American and Mainland Chinese mothers' responses to aggression and social withdrawal in preschoolers. *International Journal of Behavioral Development, 28*, 83–94.

Cheek, J. M., & Buss, A. H. (1981). Shyness and sociability. *Journal of Personality and Social Psychology, 41*, 330–339.

Chen, X., Cen, G., Li, D., & He, Y. (2005). Social functioning and adjustment in Chinese children: The imprint of historical time. *Child Development, 76*, 182–195.

Chen, X., Chung, J., & Hsiao, C. (2009). Peer interactions, relationships and groups from a cross-cultural perspective. In K. H. Rubin, W. Bukowski, & B. Laursen (Eds.), *Handbook of peer interactions, relationships, and groups* (pp. 432–451). New York: Guilford Press.

Chen, X., DeSouza, A., Chen, H., & Wang, L. (2006). Reticent behavior and experiences in peer interactions in Canadian and Chinese children. *Developmental Psychology, 42*, 656–665.

Chen, X., & French, D. (2008). Children's social competence in cultural context. *Annual Review of Psychology, 59*, 591–616.

Chen, X., Hastings, P. D., Rubin, K. H., Chen, H., Cen, G., & Stewart, S. L. (1998). Child-rearing practices and BI in Chinese and Canadian toddlers: A cross-cultural study. *Developmental Psychology, 34*, 677–686.

Chen, X., Rubin, K. H., & Li, Z. (1995). Social functioning and adjustment in Chinese children: A longitudinal study. *Developmental Psychology, 31*, 531–539.

Chen, X., Rubin, K. H., Li, B., & Li, Z. (1999). Adolescent outcomes of social functioning in Chinese children. *International Journal of Behavioural Development, 23*, 199–223.

Chen, X., & Tse, H. C. (2008). Social functioning and adjustment in Canadian-born children with Chinese and European backgrounds. *Developmental Psychology, 44*, 1184–1189.

Christopher, J. S., Hansen, D. J., & MacMillan, V. M. (1991). Effectiveness of a peer-helper intervention to increase children's social interactions: Generalization, maintenance, and social validity. *Behavior Modification, 15*, 22–50.

Cillessen, A. H., van IJzendoorn, H. W., van Lieshout, C. F., & Hartup, W. W. (1992). Heterogeneity among peer-rejected boys: Subtypes and stabilities. *Child Development, 63*, 893–905.

Coplan, R. J., & Arbeau, K. A. (2008). The stresses of a brave new world: Shyness and adjustment in kindergarten. *Journal of Research in Childhood Education, 22*, 377–389.

Coplan, R. J., Arbeau, K. A., & Armer, M. (2008). Don't fret, be supportive! Maternal characteristics linking child shyness to psychosocial and school adjustment in kindergarten. *Journal of Abnormal Child Psychology, 36*, 359–371.

Coplan, R. J., Closson, L., & Arbeau, K. (2007). Gender differences in the behavioral associates of loneliness and social dissatisfaction in kindergarten. *Journal of Child Psychology and Psychiatry, 48*, 988–995.

Coplan, R. J., Prakash, K., O'Neil, K., & Armer, M. (2004). Do you "want" to play? Distinguishing between conflicted-shyness and social disinterest in early childhood. *Developmental Psychology*, *40*, 244–258.

Coplan, R. J., Rubin, K. H., Fox, N. A., Calkins, S. D., & Stewart, S. L. (1994). Being alone, playing alone, and acting alone: Distinguishing among reticence and passive and active solitude in young children. *Child Development*, *65*, 129–137.

Coplan, R. J., & Weeks, M. (2009). Shy and soft-spoken? Shyness, pragmatic language, and socio-emotional adjustment in early childhood. *Journal of Infant and Child Development*, *18*, 238–254.

Coplan, R. J., & Weeks, M. (2010). Unsociability in childhood. In K. H. Rubin & R. J. Coplan (Eds.), *The development of shyness and social withdrawal in childhood and adolescence* (pp. 64–83). New York: Guilford Press.

Degnan, K. A., & Fox, N. A. (2007). Behavioral inhibition and anxiety disorders: Multiple levels of a resilience process. *Development and Psychopathology*, *19*, 729–746.

Degnan, K. A., Fox, N. A., Henderson, H. A., Rubin, K. H., & Nichols, K. (2008). Predicting social wariness in middle childhood: The moderating roles of childcare history, maternal personality and maternal behavior. *Social Development*, *17*, 471–487.

Erikson, M. F., Sroufe, L. A., & Egeland, B. (1985). The relationship between quality of attachment and behavior problems in preschool in a high risk sample. In I. Bretherton & E. Waters (Eds.), Growing points of attachment theory and research. *Monographs of the Society for Research in Child Development*, *50*(1–2, Serial No. 209, pp. 233–256).

Fantuzzo, J. W., Stovall, A., Schachtel, D., Goins, C., & Hall, R. (1987). The effects of peer social initiations on the social behavior of withdrawn maltreated preschool children. *Journal of Behavior Therapy and Experimental Psychiatry*, *18*, 357–363.

Findlay, L. C., Coplan, R. J., & Bowker, A. (2009). Keeping it all inside: Shyness, internalizing coping strategies and socio-emotional adjustment in middle childhood. *International Journal of Behavioural Development*, *33*, 47–54.

Fox, N. A., Henderson, H. A., Marshall, P. J., Nichols, K. E., & Ghera, M. M. (2005). BI: linking biology and behavior within a developmental framework. *Annual Review of Psychology*, *56*, 235–262.

Garcia-Coll, C., Kagan, J., & Reznick, J. S. (1984). BI in young children. *Child Development*, *55*, 1005–1019.

Gartstein, M., Gonzalez, C., Carranza, J., Ahadi, S., Ye, R., Rothbart, M., et al. (2006). Studying cross-cultural differences in the development of infant temperament: People's Republic of China, the United States of America, and Spain. *Child Psychiatry & Human Development*, *37*, 145–161.

Gazelle, H. (2008). Behavioral profiles of anxious solitary children and heterogeneity in peer relations. *Developmental Psychology*, *44*, 1604–1624.

Gazelle, H., & Ladd, G. W. (2003). Anxious solitude and peer exclusion: A diathesis-stress model of internalizing trajectories in childhood. *Child Development*, *74*, 257–278.

Gazelle, H., & Rudolph, K. D. (2004). Moving toward and away from the world: Social approach and avoidance trajectories in anxious solitary youth. *Child Development*, *75*, 829–849.

Gest, S. D. (1997). Behavioral inhibition: Stability and association with adaptation from childhood to early adulthood. *Journal of Personality and Social Psychology*, *72*, 467–475.

Hamre, B. K., & Pianta, R. C. (2001). Early teacher-child relationships and the trajectory of children's school outcomes through eighth grade. *Child Development*, *72*, 625–638.

Hane, A. A., Cheah, C., Rubin, K. H., & Fox, N. A. (2008). The role of maternal behavior in the relation between shyness and social reticence in early childhood and social withdrawal in middle childhood. *Social Development*, *17*, 795–811.

Hanish, L. D., & Guerra, N. G. (2004). Aggressive victims, passive victims, and bullies: Developmental continuity or developmental change. *Merrill-Palmer Quarterly, 50,* 17–38.

Harrist, A. W., Zaia, A. F., Bates, J. E., Dodge, K. A., & Pettit, G. S. (1997). Subtypes of social withdrawal in early childhood: Sociometric status and social-cognitive differences across four years. *Child Development, 68,* 278–294.

Hart, C. H., Yang, C., Nelson, L. J., Robinson, C. C., Olsen, J. A., Nelson, D. A., et al. (2000). Peer acceptance in early childhood and subtypes of socially withdrawn behaviour in China, Russia, and the United States. *International Journal of Behavioural Development, 24,* 73–81.

Hastings, P., Nuselovici, J. N., Rubin, K. H., & Cheah, C. (2010). Shyness, parenting and parent-child relationships. In K. H. Rubin & R. J. Coplan (Eds.), *The development of shyness and social withdrawal in childhood and adolescence* (pp. 107–130). New York: Guilford Press.

Hastings, P. D., Sullivan, C., McShane, K. E., Coplan, R. J., Utendale, W. T., & Vyncke, J. D. (2008). Parental socialization, vagal regulation, and preschoolers' anxious difficulties: Direct mothers and moderated fathers. *Child Development, 79,* 45–64.

Henderson, H., & Fox, N. (1998). Inhibited and uninhibited children: Challenges in school settings. *School Psychology Review, 27,* 492–505.

Henderson, H. A., Marshall, P. J., Fox, N. A., & Rubin, K. H. (2004). Psychophysiological and behavioral evidence for varying forms and functions of nonsocial behavior in preschoolers. *Child Development, 75,* 251–263.

Hymel, S., Bowker, A., & Woody, E. (1993). Aggressive versus withdrawn unpopular children: Variations in peer and self-perceptions in multiple domains. *Child Development, 64,* 879–896.

Hymel, S., Rubin, K., Rowden L., & LeMare, L. (1990). Children's peer relationships: Longitudinal prediction of internalizing and externalizing problems from middle to late childhood. *Child Development, 61,* 2004–2021.

Kagan, J. (1997). Temperament and the reactions to the unfamiliarity. *Child Development, 68,* 139–143.

Kagan, J., Reznick, J. S., & Snidman, N. (1988). Biological bases of childhood shyness. *Science, 240,* 167–171.

Kagan, J., Snidman, N., & Arcus, D. (1998). Childhood derivatives of high and low reactivity in infancy. *Child Development, 69,* 1483–1493.

Kim, S., Kim, Y., Choi, N., Hong, H., Lee, H., & Kim, C. (2005). Serotonin transporter gene polymorphism and personality traits in a Korean population. *Neuropsychobiology, 51,* 243–247.

Kochanska, G. (1998). Mother-child relationship, child fearfulness, and emerging attachment: A short-term longitudinal study. *Developmental Psychology, 34,* 480–490.

Kochenderfer-Ladd, B. (2003). Identification of aggressive and asocial victims and the stability of their peer victimization. *Merrill-Palmer Quarterly, 49,* 401–425.

Ladd, G. W., & Burgess, K. B. (1999). Charting the relationship trajectories of aggressive, withdrawn, and aggressive/withdrawn children during early grade school. *Child Development, 70,* 910–929.

Lindeman, D. P., Fox, J. J., & Redelheim, P. S. (1993). Increasing and maintaining withdrawn preschoolers' peer interactions: Effects of double prompting and booster session procedures. *Behavior Disorders, 11,* 54–66.

McShane, K. E., & Hastings, P. D. (2009). The New Friends Vignettes: Measuring parental psychological control that confers risk for anxious adjustment in preschoolers. *International Journal of Behavioral Development, 33*(6), 481–495.

Mead, G. H. (1934). *Mind, self, and society.* Chicago: University of Chicago Press.

Nelson, L. J., Hart, C. H., Evans, C. A., Coplan, R. J., Olson Roper, S., & Robinson, C. C. (2009). Behavioral and relational correlates of low self-perceived competence in young children. *Early Childhood Research Quarterly, 24,* 350–361.

Nelson, L. J., Hart, C. H., Wu, B., Yang, C., Roper, S. O., & Jin, S. (2006). Relations between Chinese mothers' parenting practices and social withdrawal in early childhood. *International Journal of Behavioral Development, 30*, 261–271.

Nelson, L. J., Rubin, K. H., & Fox, N. A. (2005). Social and nonsocial behaviors and peer acceptance: A longitudinal model of the development of self-perceptions in children ages 4 to 7 years. *Early Education and Development, 20*, 185–200.

Newcomb, A., Bukowski, W., & Pattee, L. (1993). Children's peer relations: A meta-analytic review of popular, rejected, neglected, controversial, and average sociometric status. *Psychological Bulletin, 113*, 99–128.

Oh, W., Rubin, K., Bowker, J., Booth-LaForce, C., Rose-Krasnor, L., & Laursen, B. (2008). Trajectories of social withdrawal middle childhood to early adolescence. *Journal of Abnormal Child Psychology, 36*, 553–566.

Pedersen, S., Vitaro, F., Barker, E., & Borge, A. (2007). The timing of middle-childhood peer rejection and friendship: Linking early behavior to early-adolescent adjustment. *Child Development, 78*, 1037–1051.

Perren, S., & Alsaker, F. D. (2006). Social behavior and peer relationships of victims, bully-victims, and bullies in kindergarten. *Journal of Child Psychology and Psychiatry, 47*, 45–57.

Piaget, J. (1932). *The moral judgment of the child.* Glencoe, IL: Free Press.

Prakash, K., & Coplan, R. J. (2007). Socio-emotional characteristics and school adjustment of socially-withdrawn children in India. *International Journal of Behavioural Development, 31*, 123–132.

Prior, M., Smart, D., Sanson, A., & Oberklaid, F. (2000). Does shy-inhibited temperament in childhood lead to anxiety problems in adolescence? *Journal of the Academy of Child and Adolescent Psychiatry, 39*, 461–468.

Radke-Yarrow, M., Richters, J., & Wilson, W. E. (1988). Child development in a network of relationships. In R. A. Hinde & J. Stevenson-Hinde (Eds.), *Relationships within families: Mutual influences* (pp. 48–67). Oxford: Clarendon Press.

Rapee, R., & Coplan, R. J. (2010). Conceptual relations between behavioral inhibition and anxiety disorders in preschool children. *New Directions in Child Development, 2010*(127), 17–31.

Rapee, R., Kennedy, S., Ingram, M., Edwards, S., & Sweeney, L. (2005). Prevention and early intervention of anxiety disorders in inhibited preschool children. *Journal of Consulting and Clinical Psychology, 73*, 488–497.

Rubin, K. H. (1993). The Waterloo Longitudinal Project: Correlates and consequences of social withdrawal from childhood to adolescence. In K. H. Rubin & J. B. Asendorpf (Eds.), *Social withdrawal, inhibition, and shyness in childhood* (pp. 291–314). Hillsdale, NJ: Erlbaum.

Rubin, K. H., & Asendorpf, J. B. (1993). Social withdrawal, inhibition, and shyness in childhood: Conceptual and definitional issues. In K. H. Rubin & J. B. Asendorpf (Eds.), *Social withdrawal, inhibition, and shyness in childhood* (pp. 3–17). Hillsdale, NJ: Erlbaum.

Rubin, K. H., Bukowski, W. M., & Parker, J. G. (2006). Peer interactions, relationships and groups. In N. Eisenberg (Vol. Ed.), *The handbook of child psychology* (6th ed., pp. 571–645). New York: Wiley.

Rubin, K. H., Chen, X., and Hymel, S. (1993). Socioemotional characteristics of withdrawn and aggressive children. *Merrill-Palmer Quarterly, 39*, 518–534.

Rubin, K. H., Chen, X., McDougall, P., Bowker, A., & McKinnon, J. (1995). The Waterloo Longitudinal Project: Predicting adolescent internalizing and externalizing problems from early and mid-childhood. *Development and Psychopathology, 7*, 751–764.

Rubin, K. H., & Coplan, R. J. (2004). Paying attention to and not neglecting social withdrawal and social isolation. *Merrill-Palmer Quarterly, 50*, 506–534.

Rubin, K. H., Coplan, R. J., & Bowker, J. (2009). Social withdrawal in childhood. *Annual Review of Psychology, 60*, 11.1–11.31.

Rubin, K. H., Daniels-Beirness, T., & Bream, L. (1984). Social isolation and social problem solving: A longitudinal study. *Journal of Consulting and Clinical Psychology, 52*, 17–25.

Rubin, K. H., Hastings, P. D., Stewart, S. L., Henderson, H. A., & Chen, X. (1997). The consistency and concomitants of inhibition: Some of the children, all of the time. *Child Development, 68*, 467–483.

Rubin, K. H., Hemphill, S. A., Chen, X., Hastings, P., Sanson, A., Lo Coco, A., et al. (2006). A cross-cultural study of behavioral inhibition in toddlers: East-west-north-south. *International Journal of Behavioral Development, 30*, 219–226.

Rubin, K. H., Hymel, S., & Mills, R. S. (1989). Sociability and social withdrawal in childhood: Stability and outcomes. *Journal of Personality, 57*, 237–255.

Rubin, K. H., Nelson, L. J., Hastings, P., & Asendorpf, J. (1999). Transaction between parents' perceptions of their children's shyness and their parenting styles. *International Journal of Behavioral Development, 23*, 937–957.

Rubin, K., & Stewart, S. (1996). Social withdrawal. In E. J. Mash & R. A. Barkley (Eds.), *Child psychopathology* (pp. 277–307). New York: Guilford Press.

Rubin, K. H., Wojslawowicz, J. C., Burgess, K. B., Rose-Krasnor, L., & Booth-LaForce, C. L. (2006). The friendships of socially withdrawn and competent young adolescents. *Journal of Abnormal Child Psychology, 34*, 139–153.

Schaughency, E., Vannatta, K., Langhinrichsen, J., & Lally, C. (1992). Correlates of sociometric status in school children in Buenos Aires. *Journal of Abnormal Child Psychology, 20*, 317–326.

Schmidt, L. A., Fox, N. A., Schulkin, J., & Gold, P. W. (1999). Behavioral and psychophysiological correlates of self-presentation in temperamentally shy children. *Developmental Psychobiology, 35*, 119–135.

Schneider, B. H. (1992). Didactic methods for enhancing children's peer relations: A quantitative review. *Clinical Psychology Review, 12*, 363–382.

Schneider, B. H. (1999). A multi-method exploration of the friendships of children considered socially withdrawn by their peers. *Journal of Abnormal Psychology, 27*, 115–123.

Schwartz, C. E., Snidman, N., & Kagan, J. (1999). Adolescent social anxiety as an outcome of inhibited temperament in childhood. *Journal of the American Academy of Child and Adolescent Psychiatry, 38*, 1008–1015.

Schwartz, C., Wright, C., Shin, L., Kagan, J., Whalen, P., McMullin, K., et al. (2003). Differential amygdalar response to novel versus newly familiar neutral faces: A functional MRI probe developed for studying inhibited temperament. *Biological Psychiatry, 53*, 854–862.

Sheridan, S. M., Kratochwill, T. R., & Elliott, S. N. (1990). Behavioral consultation with parents and teachers: Delivering treatment for socially withdrawn children at home and school. *School Psychology Review, 19*, 33–52.

Spangler, G., & Schieche, M. (1998). Emotional and adrenocortical responses of infants to the strange situation: The differential function of emotional expression. *International Journal of Behavioral Development, 22*, 681–706.

Spence, S. H., Donovan, C., & Brechman-Toussaint, M. (2000). The treatment of childhood social phobia: The effectiveness of a social skills training-based, cognitive–behavioural intervention, with and without parental involvement. *Journal of Child Psychology and Psychiatry and Allied Disciplines, 41*, 713–726.

Sroufe, L. A. (1983). Infant-caregiver attachment and patterns of adaptation in preschool: The roots maladaptation and competence. In M. Perlmutter (Ed.), *Minnesota Symposium in Child Psychology* (Vol. 16). Hillsdale, NJ: Erlbaum.

Stevenson-Hinde, J. (1989). BI: Issues of context. In J. S. Reznick (Ed.), *Perspectives on BI* (pp. 125–138). Chicago: University of Chicago Press.

Stewart, S., & Rubin, K. (1995). The social problem-solving skills of anxious-withdrawn children. *Development and Psychopathology, 7*, 323–336.

Storey, K., Smith, D. J., & Strain, P. S. (1993). Use of classroom assistants and peer-mediated intervention to increase integration in preschool settings. *Exceptionality, 4*, 1–16.

Weeks, M., Coplan, R. J., & Kingsbury, A. (2009). The correlates and consequences of early appearing social anxiety in young children. *Journal of Anxiety Disorders, 23*, 965–972.

Wichmann, C., Coplan, R., & Daniels, T. (2004). The social cognitions of socially withdrawn children. *Social Development, 13*, 377–392.

Younger, A. J., Gentile, C., & Burgess, K. B. (1993). Children's perceptions of social withdrawal: Changes across age. In K. Rubin & J. Asendorpf (Eds.), *Social withdrawal, inhibition, and shyness in childhood* (pp. 215–235). Hillsdale, NJ: Erlbaum.

PART VII

Play, Cooperation, Competition, Aggression, and Bullying

The four chapters in this section survey different types of behavior, both positive and negative, but all common aspects of childhood. Thomas Power reviews the literature on children's social play in Chapter 24. The first edition of this handbook had separate chapters on rough-and-tumble play and pretend play. But play is broader than just these two types, and even social play can be locomotor (rather than rough-and-tumble, or pretend); and there are related topics such as videogame play, also covered in Powers's review. He explicitly updates the two chapters from the previous volume into a single integrated chapter, and extends it to a discussion of play partners, and to the relationship between dominance, conflict, and play.

In play, and also in peer interactions generally, cooperation and competition can be interwoven in complex ways. Barry Schneider, Joyce Benenson, Marta Fülöp, Mihaly Berkics, and Mónika Sándor discuss these intricacies in Chapter 25, starting with a consideration of different ways of defining these two terms. They consider the methodological issues involved in measuring cooperation and competition, and then the evidence regarding their development through childhood. There is a particularly strong section on cultural differences, as well as an overview of sex differences, both very important in this field. The final sections of the chapter develop the implications for learning and motivation, and for friendships and peer relations.

Sarah Coyne, David Nelson, and Marian Underwood also start their chapter, Chapter 26, on aggression by considering definitional issues and the distinctions between different types of aggression, especially physical and relational. They review the literature on age differences and gender differences (the evolutionary psychology approach to these gender differences is also discussed in Chapter 4). They then consider correlates and consequences of aggressive behavior, seen as primarily negative, while acknowledging some more recent literature that points to the adaptive value of aggression in certain circumstances. A substantial section of the chapter deals with causal influences leading to aggression: biological (cf. Chapter 2), parenting and family, the peer group, and the mass media. Finally, interventions to reduce aggression are considered.

In Chapter 27, Christina Salmivalli, Katlin Peets, and Ernest Hodges write about the topic of bullying. Bullying is a subset of aggressive behavior that is repeated and involves an imbalance of power against a relatively helpless victim. It is thus particularly vicious and can have very serious negative consequences. The authors discuss how bullying can be measured, and a variety of theoretical models that can help us understand why bullying occurs, mainly in school peer groups. They survey the empirical findings about bullying, not only on bullies and victims but also on bully-victims – those children who show characteristics of both bullies and victims. This chapter too ends with a mention of school-based interventions to reduce bullying; the KiVa project in Finland, with which the authors are involved, is a very promising example of this.

CHAPTER TWENTY-FOUR

Social Play

Thomas G. Power

Play, especially social play, is central to the lives of children the world over. Developmental theorists (e.g., Erikson, Freud, Piaget, and Vygotsky) have written about the importance of play, and play has been the focus of considerable research. In the late 1990s, I (Power, 2000) reviewed research on play since the early 1900s. This chapter summarizes what we have learned since then, and provides an update of the rough-and-tumble (Pellegrini, 2002) and pretend play (Göncü, Patt, & Kouba, 2002) chapters of the first edition of this handbook. The research cited here is representative of the studies conducted from 1998 to 2008.

Definitions and Types of Social Play

Play has been defined as a mode, as an observable set of behaviors, and as a context (Rubin, Fein, & Vandenberg, 1983). In the definitions used by Göncü et al. (2002), Pellegrini (2002), and Power (2000), play includes solitary play with objects (mastery play, generative play), play fighting, locomotor play, constructive play, sociodramatic play, language play, and games with rules (all except the first category represent social play). The most common elements across definitions were that play is pleasurable, intrinsically motivated, emotionally significant, and nonliteral, and differs from more serious forms of behavior in its timing, intensity, sequencing, predictability, social roles, and eliciting conditions. Play generally occurs in benign environments and rarely occurs in the face of uncertainty, fear, and discomfort. The types of play reviewed here are locomotor play, play fighting, and sociodramatic and social object play.

The Wiley-Blackwell Handbook of Childhood Social Development, Second Edition, edited by Peter K. Smith and Craig H. Hart
© 2011 by Blackwell Publishing Ltd.

Locomotor Play

Locomotor play involves large motor movements such as running, chasing, skipping, jumping, rolling, falling, and sliding. In one of the few time use studies of its kind, Bloch (1987) found that preschool children spent more time in "gross motor play" than any other type of play. Despite the time that children spend in such activities, little descriptive research has been conducted on locomotor play. This in unfortunate, because studies of the effects of physical activity (see below) suggest that locomotor play may have many benefits for children's physical, cognitive, and emotional well-being.

Both Power (2000) and Pellegrini (2002) noted the limited amount of research on locomotor play. A review of the research since 1998 revealed no new studies of locomotor play in children. However, research on children's physical activity has increased significantly. Because much (but obviously not all) physical activity in childhood occurs during locomotor play, research on physical activity may increase our understanding of the correlates and consequences of locomotor play.

In my review of the research on physical activity in childhood (Power, 2000), I found that physical activity shows the same inverted-U developmental course found for most forms of children's play (with activity level peaking sometime in the preschool years) and that boys show higher rates of physical activity than girls. Correlational studies indicated that low levels of physical activity (and high levels of inactivity – particularly television watching) were associated with children's obesity.

The review for this chapter located over 100 relevant, peer-reviewed journal articles on children's physical activity since 1998. This contrasts greatly with the Power (2000) review. This increase in research undoubtedly is the result of attention to (and funding to address) the problem of child obesity in the United States (Centers for Disease Control and Prevention, 2006).

In contrast to earlier studies, recent studies of physical activity use electronic technology (e.g., accelerometers and heart rate monitors) to monitor activity levels in children and to assess obesity and physical fitness. This research demonstrates that both low levels of vigorous physical activity and high levels of sedentary activities (e.g., watching television) are associated with obesity (e.g., Jago, Baranowski, Baranowski, Thompson, & Greaves, 2005; Janz et al., 2002). Furthermore, experimental interventions that increase the level of children's physical activity reduce children's age-adjusted Body Mass Index (see Connelly, Duaso, & Butler, 2007, for a review).

Physical activity may positively impact children's cognitive development and emotional health as well. Tomporowski, Davis, Miller, and Naglieri (2008) reviewed correlational and experimental research demonstrating that physical activity "facilitates children's executive function (i.e., processes required to select, organize, and properly initiate goal-directed actions)" (p. 111). Moreover, three Japanese studies (Uechi, Takenaka, & Oka, 2000; Uechi, Takenaka, Suzuki, & Oka, 2003; Wang, Sekine, Chen, Yamagami, & Kagamimori, 2008) show that physical activity was positively associated with children's social skills, positive appraisal of stressors, and reported quality of life, and negatively associated with emotional distress.

Factors associated with children's physical activity levels include individual factors such as enjoyment (Roemmich et al., 2008), self-efficacy (Annesi, 2006), and sports involvement (Saar & Jurimae, 2007); social factors such as peer involvement (e.g., Salvy et al., 2008), parental modeling (Zach & Netz, 2007), and parental support (e.g., Pugliese & Tinsley, 2007); and community factors such as availability of outdoor play spaces (Roemmich, Epstein, Raja, & Yin, 2007) and neighborhood safety (Carver, Timperio, & Crawford, 2008).

Conclusions

Given the physical, cognitive, and social emotional benefits of physical activity, it is important to understand which physical activities provide the greatest effects, and how these vary by child age and sex. Locomotor play, being a major activity of young children, provides numerous bouts of vigorous activity; however, little is known about the average length of these bouts, their intensity, or their frequency during the average play session. Although researchers have conducted assessments of the overall amount of physical activity over set time periods, such as 3 to 7 days (e.g., Sigmund, De Ste Croix, Miklankova, & Fromel, 2007), these studies tell us little about the specific activities, settings, and behaviors associated with high levels of physical activity. Moreover, given the diversity of motor behaviors during locomotor play, it would be valuable to understand its contribution to other aspects of physical development such as agility, balance, flexibility, muscular endurance, muscular strength, and anaerobic power.

Play Fighting

Play fighting involves physically active play that resembles fighting (e.g., wrestling, hitting, pushing, and shoving) but differs significantly from serious fighting in its tactics, intensity, and consequences. In their reviews, Pellegrini (2002) and Power (2000) described general characteristics of play fighting: its inverted-U shaped developmental trajectory; its increasing roughness with age; its sex differences, with higher frequency in boys and higher rates of withdrawal from play fighting in girls; the tendency to choose same-sex play-fighting partners; systematic differences between play fighting and serious fighting (e.g., intensity, duration, targets, role reversals, self-handicapping, and consequences); and its occurrence across a range of cultural settings. Both authors provided evidence for possible functions of this type of play; I suggested that it facilitates social bonding in young boys, and Pellegrini argued that it establishes and maintains dominance in older boys' social groups.

Since these reviews, a few new studies of play fighting have been published. These include a descriptive study by Scott and Panksepp (2003) and a study by Colwell and Lindsey (2005) showing that boys' rough-and-tumble play with same-sex peers was positively associated with peer liking, whereas rough-and-tumble play with opposite-sex peers was negatively related.

The remaining studies focused on adults' and children's perceptions of play fighting. In Tannock's (2008) interviews of early childhood educators and 5-year-olds, teachers understood the value of rough-and-tumble play (e.g., they believed it facilitated self-control, compassion, and boundaries), but were not sure how to best manage it in the classroom out of concerns about harm to the participants. Children did not believe that rough-and-tumble play was allowed in their classrooms, although most engaged in this behavior. In another interview study (Benenson, Carder, & Geib-Cole, 2008), 4- to 9-year-olds described how they played with their favorite toys and playmates. About half of the boys (and less than 10% of the girls) reported enjoying play with aggressive themes.

Two studies employed video playback methodology (i.e., videotaping children's play and having them watch and answer questions about their behavior). In the first (Reed & Brown, 2001), 6- to 9-year-old boys watched videotapes of their play fighting and answered a series of open-ended questions. The authors concluded that these boys used play fighting as a way to express care for one another. Examples included checking to see if other players were hurt during play-fighting episodes, delaying the play when someone *did* get hurt, prosocial behaviors observed during play fighting (e.g., handing another child his glasses that had fallen off), laughing and physical contact during play, reciprocal role taking in the play-fighting context, lack of injury during play fighting, and comments by the participants about how play fighting was fun.

Smith, Smees, and Pellegrini (2004) compared participants' and nonparticipants' perceptions of play- and serious-fighting episodes. In differentiating play fighting and serious fighting, participants had insights into what was going on in an episode, which outside observers, whether adult or child, often did not have. Participants gave more criteria to explain their judgments as to why an episode was playful or not; and they cited criteria that were likely to be useful and to which they had more privileged access – whether a hit or kick really hurt, and whether an apparently aggressive act was within a pretend or game framework previously agreed on by those involved.

Together, these results support the growing consensus that play fighting is a form of play, not aggression, and that children may benefit from such activities in multiple ways. By obtaining data on the participants' perspectives, rather than simply relying on the judgments of "impartial observers," these studies help further differentiate play fighting from serious aggression.

Violent videogames

In contrast to the literature on play fighting, research on violent videogames has increased significantly in the last 10 years. In Power (2000), I reviewed videogames in a section entitled "Symbolic Play-Fighting in Humans: The Case of War Play." Studies of war play (e.g., aggressive fantasy play) and violent videogames were considered. I concluded that boys engage in more war and videogame play than girls and that despite much debate on the pros and cons of war play, these debates were "fueled as much by political ideology as by developmental theory or empirical findings" (p. 186). The research was limited, and the published experiments had methodological shortcomings (one of the most common was not differentiating between serious and play fighting when examining "aggressive" outcomes). Although correlational studies revealed that children who played violent videogames showed higher levels of aggression, the direction of effects was unclear – did playing violent videogames increase aggression, or were aggressive children more likely to play violent videogames?

One recent study of war play was located. Dunn and Hughes (2001) found that "hard-to-manage" 4-year-olds (i.e., children showing high levels of hyperactive and conduct disorder symptoms) acted out more violent themes in pretend play than children in a comparison group. Within both groups, violent pretend was negatively associated with measures of verbal ability, theory of mind, and executive functioning. Within the hard-to-manage group, violent pretend play was associated positively with antisocial behavior, anger, refusal to help, and conflict in peer interactions, and negatively associated with cooperative pretend. Violent play was not associated with the peer interaction variables in the comparison group.

Regarding videogames, a consensus appears to be emerging that violent videogames contribute to aggression in children and adolescents. Most literature reviews since 2000 (including two meta-analyses) concluded that exposure to violent videogames increases aggressive behavior (Anderson & Bushman, 2001; Bensley & Van Eenwyk, 2001; Huesmann, 2007; Sherry, 2001; Swing & Anderson, 2007). These reviewers also argued that violent videogames increase physiological arousal, hostility, and aggressive thoughts, and decrease empathy and prosocial behavior. Violent videogames also portray and reinforce stereotypical gender roles (e.g., Dill & Thill, 2007).

Ferguson (2007a, 2007b) argued that publication bias has been a problem in videogame research and that after controlling for these biases, the effects of videogames on aggression become nonsignificant. Sherry (2001) found that the effects of videogames on aggression were smaller than the effects of television violence, and that violent sports games contributed less to aggression than did other violent games. Bensley and Van Eenwyk (2001) found greater effects of violent videogames for young children than for adolescents or adults. Finally, the strongest data are still correlational, and the experimental studies suffer from the methodological shortcoming cited above.

Whatever the possible negative effects of violent videogames, playing videogames can have positive effects as well. Orleans and Laney (2000) debunked the stereotype that videogames isolate children, showing that videogame play is often a social activity, especially for boys. Ferguson's (2007b) meta-analysis concludes that playing violent videogames is associated with higher levels of visual spatial skills, even after controlling for selection bias. And, finally, researchers have demonstrated how videogames may contribute to the development of attentional skills (e.g., Blumberg, 1998) and problem-solving strategies (e.g., VanDeventer & White, 2002).

Conclusions

Boys spend considerable time in play with aggressive themes. They clearly enjoy this form of play and see it as a way to have fun with their friends. However, given recent trends in the increasingly graphic nature of videogames over time, adults have raised concerns that such games may desensitize children to violence, decrease prosocial behavior and empathy, and contribute to aggressive thoughts and actions.

Researchers have begun to address these topics, providing evidence that violent video-games may have such effects – although the effect sizes are small and vary as a function of child age, game content, and other factors. One possibility is that the overall small effect sizes may be the result of videogame violence primarily affecting children already predisposed to aggression. Future research should investigate how child, peer, and family characteristics (e.g., temperament, physiological reactivity, empathy, and parent–child relationships) interact with videogame exposure in impacting desensitization, mood, physical arousal, and aggression. Because most research to date has been cross-sectional in nature, longitudinal studies are necessary to examine causal models. Although experimental studies have often "demonstrated" the causal effects of videogame violence on child and adolescent behavior, these experiments usually involve laboratory analogues measuring aggressive tendencies after only a brief period of videogame play. Because of questions about the validity of such tasks, it is difficult to draw strong conclusions about the long-term effects of videogames on the results of these short-term laboratory experiments alone. More long-term correlational and naturalistic intervention studies are necessary to further our understanding of this popular form of children's play.

Sociodramatic and Social Object Play

Sociodramatic and social object play involves two major forms of play identified by Smilansky (1968): social constructive play (e.g., block construction) and dramatic play (i.e., social play "in which participants transform the meanings of objects, identities, situations, and time"; Göncü et al., 2002, p. 419).

Play structure

In the Göncü et al. (2002) and Power (2000) reviews, the complexity of sociodramatic play was illustrated through studies of play roles (e.g., actor, director, and audience), metacommunicative strategies for moving in and out of the play frame, and symbolic transformations. Göncü et al. provided a discussion on the representation of affect in sociodramatic play (e.g., reproducing daily experiences, negotiating affect, and working through emotional experiences). I (Power, 2000) reviewed research by Connolly, Doyle, and associates that showed how sociodramatic play differed from other forms of social object play (more positive and negative affect, longer behavior sequences, more activity talk, more attempts to influence another's behavior, more shared play focus, etc.).

I also provided a review of work by Gottman and others on molecular analyses of the initiation, maintenance, and termination of play. Children who successfully *initiated* play engaged in synchronous play or made collaborative statements with a play partner; unsuccessful initiators tended to hover, wait, or use controlling statements. Children who successfully *maintained* play engaged in predicable patterns of behavior, developed with their play partners shared knowledge and goals, followed clear play rules, and successfully used metacommunicative statements to keep the play going.

Further studies of children's play elaborate on these conclusions. Curran (1999) examined the explicit and implicit rules that governed children's play; Trawick-Smith (1998) conducted a qualitative analysis of metacommunication during play; Walker (1999) examined the narrative features of sociodramatic play; and Robinson, Anderson, Porter, Hart, and Wouden-Miller (2003) examined the initiation of cooperative play through "parallel-aware" play.

Several European researchers compared how children's behavior during free play differed from behavior during teacher-structured activities (Fekonja, Umek, & Kranjc, 2005; Gmitrova & Gmitrov, 2003; Leseman, Rollenberg, & Rispens, 2001). All three studies showed that child behavior was more sophisticated during free play than during teacher-structured activities. During play, children showed more verbal interaction; multiword utterances, interrogative clauses, and negative clauses; regulatory speech; and intermediate- and high-level verbal and nonverbal distancing. These results are consistent with a large study of 70 preschool classes in Northern Ireland, where traditional (teacher-led) and enriched (play-based and child-centered) curricula were compared (Walsh et al., 2006). Children receiving the enriched curricula showed more intrinsic motivation, concentration, confidence, independence, higher order thinking skills, multiple-skill acquisition, well-being, social interaction, and self- and other respect than children receiving the traditional curriculum.

Developmental course

Both Göncü et al. (2002) and Power reviewed research on the developmental course of sociodramatic and social object play. I (Power, 2000) found that both social participation (Parten, 1932) and play complexity (Smilansky, 1968) increased during the preschool years, and the frequency of sociodramatic play appears to peak around age 6. The increased complexity of sociodramatic play was documented in other ways as well (e.g., the integration of multiple schemes, differentiated play scripts, and the number and complexity of play themes and transformations). Both Göncü et al. and Power reviewed studies showing that social coordination of play increases during the preschool years (e.g., planning, metacommunication, information getting and sharing, and verbal responsiveness). This coordination leads to increasingly coherent and longer play sequences with age. Surprisingly, only one more recent study of developmental differences was found – Mendez, McDermott, and Fantuzzo (2002) found that older African American preschoolers engaged in more cooperative, helpful behaviors during play than younger preschoolers, whereas younger preschoolers showed higher levels of play disruption.

Sex differences

I (Power, 2000) reviewed a large literature on sex differences in young children's sociodramatic and social object play. Although some sex differences in the *type* of play were identified (i.e., active, physical, outdoor, and fantasy play in boys; and constructive play in girls), more differences in preferred play *activities or themes* were found (e.g., boys: blocks, construction toys, transportation toys, riding toys, and balls; and girls: art, domestic play, dolls, and dancing). Moreover, adults and peers reinforce children for engaging in these activities. Boys and girls show behavioral differences in play style. Both Göncü et al. and Power described how boys and girls differ in establishing common ground during play. Girls are more likely to consider the behavior of the play partner (e.g., acknowledging others, using conversation facilitators, and requesting clarification); boys are more likely to focus on the self (e.g., verbal and nonverbal attention getting, showing off, asserting own desires, and protecting own self-interest).

Studies by Carpenter, Huston-Stein, and others (Carpenter & Huston-Stein, 1980; Huston, Carpenter, Alwater, & Johnson, 1986) suggest that many sex differences in play style may be a function of boys' and girls' activity preferences. I elaborated on this theory by showing how sex differences in play preferences could contribute to sex differences in independence, activity level, outside play, self-focus, cooperation, and more (see Power, 2000, p. 256, Table 8.7).

Few recent studies of sex differences in children's play were found. Harper and Huie (1998) replicated the sex differences in play preferences, with girls spending more time in art and doll play centers and boys spending more time in the sandbox, vehicle path, grass, and block play areas. Mendez et al. (2002) replicated the sex differences in play style, finding that older girls showed the highest level of cooperative, helpful behavior during play. Fabes, Martin, and Hanish (2003) found that boys' play was more active-forceful than the play of girls. Kyratzis (1999) examined the narrative structure and content of sociodramatic play, finding the protagonists constructed by girls valued "the qualities of lovingness, graciousness, and attractiveness," whereas boys' protagonists "suggested that they valued physical power" (p. 427).

Effects of sociodramatic and social object play on development

I (Power, 2000) reviewed numerous studies on the effects of play on children's development. The hypothesized effects fell into two general areas: cognitive stimulation and learning, and social development.

Cognitive stimulation and learning   In general, my review showed that children who spent more of their time playing at Smilansky's (1968) higher play levels scored higher on measures of cognitive development. Also, children who showed high levels of sociodramatic play scored high on standardized assessments of creativity. The problem with these correlational studies is that they provide no information on the direction of effects. Because play-coding systems tend to assign higher scores to more complex and/or creative play behaviors, these correlations might simply reflect the fact that more intelligent and/or creative children play in more intelligent and/or creative ways. To address the question of causality, numerous experimental studies were conducted – particularly in the 1970s and early 1980s with low-income children. These interventions were designed to stimulate children's competence by providing additional opportunities for high-level play, usually directed by adults. Although many studies reported significant effects of the interventions on children's cognitive functioning, Smith (1988) and others argued that experimenter bias and the use of inappropriate controls made it difficult to determine whether play or high levels of adult stimulation accounted for the effects. Studies in the mid-1980s with appropriate controls suggested that most of these effects were due to the level of adult stimulation, not play per se.

Many recent correlational studies (too many to be cited here) replicate the frequently found relations between sociodramatic play and measures of verbal competence (e.g., Lewis, Boucher, Lupton, & Watson, 2000), general cognitive and academic competence (e.g., Farmer-Dougan & Kaszuba, 1999), and divergent thinking (e.g., Farver, Kim, & Lee-Shin, 2000).

Only one new experimental study was located (Landazabal, 2005). In this study, 10- to 11-year-olds received an intensive play curriculum (weekly 2-hour sessions over the academic year) and were compared to a control group experiencing the normal school curriculum. At the end of the school year, experimental participants scored higher on verbal intelligence, the ability to form concepts or define words, and verbal associative thinking. Unfortunately, no process evaluation was conducted to compare levels of adult stimulation in the experimental and control groups, so given the literature in this area, it is not clear that it was play per se that accounted for these effects.

Social development   Correlational studies covered in my earlier review showed that the quality of children's play predicted peer acceptance and liking. For example, popular children showed more socially active, positive, cooperative, and responsive play interactions, whereas the play of rejected children was more domineering or disruptive. Neglected children often showed passivity during play. Similar play characteristics predicted children's friendships and social problem-solving skills. Sociodramatic play was often a significant correlate of perspective-taking abilities and empathy as well. Given the limitations of correlational studies, the results of the experimental studies are more enlightening. When using appropriate attention controls, there was strong evidence that play contributed to the development of children's perspective-taking abilities. Experimental evidence for other areas of social development was limited.

Although no new experimental studies could be found, numerous correlational studies (too many to be cited here) replicated the often found moderate relationships between quality of play and social competence (Farmer-Dougan & Kaszuba, 1999), peer acceptance (Colwell & Lindsey, 2005), empathy (Niec & Russ, 2002), and social perspective taking (Schwebel, Rosen, & Singer, 1999). Quality of play was also positively associated with children's emotion understanding and emotion regulation skills (e.g., Denham et al., 2001; Elias & Berk, 2002), areas that received little attention prior to my review. A study by Murphy, Laurie-Rose, Brinkman, and McNamara (2007) showed that quality of play was associated with sustained attention as well. This last finding is consistent with Panksepp's (2007) recent hypothesis (based on considerable animal and neuroscience research) that play may help facilitate the development of behavioral inhibition in young children, and that attention deficit/hyperactivity disorder (ADHD) symptoms might be reduced through facilitating frontal lobe maturation through intensive social play interventions.

Smith (2005, 2010) reviewed studies showing correlations between measures of pretend play and measures of theory of mind. The correlations were mostly positive, but often quite small once controlled for verbal ability or general intelligence. Smith argued that this variable pattern of quite modest correlations suggests that pretend play is facilitative of theory of mind, but that it is only one of a number of ways in which children can develop their theory-of-mind capabilities. This "equifinality" model can be taken more generally than just for theory of mind, and proposes that there are many routes to acquire developmental skills; play provides a useful and enjoyable way for children to acquire a range of skills, but it is not essential for this as other ways are also available.

Play Partners

Children usually play with same-sex playmates. I (Power, 2000) reviewed the research on gender segregation in children's play and found that it begins around 2 ½ years for girls and around 3 years for boys. By age 5, boys usually show more gender segregation than girls. Many theories have been proposed to account for this tendency – one of the most popular being that girls withdraw from mixed-sex play at an early age because boys are nonresponsive and disruptive play partners (Maccoby, 1998).

Research on the quality of same- versus mixed-sex interactions showed that children are usually more positive, responsive, and conciliatory in same-sex dyads, and that many sex differences in play behavior disappear when children are in mixed-sex dyads. Age of play partners also makes a difference, with children preferring same-sex, same-age partners. Partner familiarity and relatedness are important as well – children are more positive playing with friends, and more negative with siblings. Younger siblings fall into learner or managee roles during play, and older siblings fall into teaching or manager roles.

These findings have been extended in more recent research. Martin and Fabes (2001) found that gender segregation in preschool children was highly stable over two semesters and that children who played with same-sex partners at the first time point showed more sex-stereotyped play at the second time point. Munroe and Romney (2006) demonstrated that gender segregation occurs across a range of diverse, non-Western cultures, and that it increases from ages 3–5 to 7–9. Lewis and Phillipsen (1998) found that gender segregation increased during middle childhood as well. Pellegrini, Long, Roseth, Bohn, and Van Ryzin (2007) found that high-activity girls initially played with high-activity boys, but segregated among themselves over time.

Other studies have examined the effect of the identity of the play partner on behavior during play. Consistent with the tendency for sex differences in play style to be reduced in mixed-sex groups, Fabes et al. (2003) found that boys showed less active-forceful play when playing with groups of girls and that girls showed more active-forceful play when playing with groups of boys. Simpkins and Parke (2002) found that fourth to fifth graders showed more positive behavior, negative behavior, and play sophistication when interacting with friends versus unacquainted peers. McElwain and Volling (2005) found that preschool children showed greater play sophistication and conflict with friends than siblings.

Dominance and Conflict in Relation to Play

I (Power, 2000) reviewed research showing that the play of preschool children is influenced by dominance hierarchies – as early as 25 months of age. Dominance hierarchies based on aggressive threats and submission show the highest linearity and rigidity, but high levels are found for hierarchies based on nonagonistic social control as well. Once dominance hierarchies are established in children's groups, they usually reduce the level of conflict and aggression.

More recent studies of dominance have focused either on the strategies that children use to achieve dominance or on sex differences. In two studies of preschool children, Hawley (2002, 2003) found that both coercive and prosocial forms of social control were positively correlated with child dominance, and that dominance status was positively associated with peer liking. Prosocial and bistrategic controllers (i.e., children who frequently used both coercive and prosocial strategies during play) were liked most by their peers, but bistrategic controllers showed the highest resource control (i.e., dominance) (Hawley, 2003). In a qualitative study, Kyratzis, Marx, and Evelyn (2001) found that high-ranking boys asserted control through the use of commands, prohibitions, and threats during play, whereas high-ranking girls did so by assigning play roles, providing instructions, and bragging.

Most conflicts in children's play are over objects, play roles, and the correctness of play actions (Power, 2000). Conflicts during preschoolers' play tend to be short (usually <10 seconds) and usually have a clear winner and loser. Although about one third of preschoolers' conflicts lead to aggression, preschoolers also use nonaggressive strategies to deal with conflict (e.g., introducing added elements into the activity, appealing to rules, and making submissive gestures). With increasing age, conflicts are less about objects and more about play roles, rules, and the correctness of activities.

Two further studies demonstrated that conciliatory behaviors are often effective in resolving conflict (Ljunberg, Westlund, & Forsberg, 1999; Verbeek & de Waal, 2001). Ljunberg et al. demonstrated that such behaviors are usually general affiliative behaviors such as invitations to play, body contact, and verbal apologies. One of the most important predictors of conflict resolution identified by Vebeek and de Waal (2001) was the quality of preconflict interaction between the two parties, "illustrating participants' general concern with continuity and integrity of their social interactions with peers" (p. 5).

Chen, Fein, and Tam (2001) identified developmental changes in conflicts in their study of 2-, 3-, and 4-year-olds in preschool classrooms. With increasing age, children's conflicts were less about the distribution of resources and more about differences in opinion over play ideas. Child-generated resolutions increased with age, and "insistence" (i.e., the use of force or direct commands to resolve conflict versus the use of justifications or cooperation) decreased. O'Brien, Roy, Jacobs, Macaluso, and Peyton (1999) found that 3-year-old girls scored higher than boys on a measure of "conflict resolution competence" (a composite measure tapping positive resolution strategies and attempts to resume play after conflict). Verbeek and de Waal (2001) found that same-sex playmates were more likely to continuing playing with one another following conflicts than opposite-sex playmates.

Social Class and Cultural Differences in Play

Göncü et al. (2002) provided an excellent review of social pretend play in village and urban communities. The main differences concerned parental attitudes toward pretend play and parental involvement in pretend play (parents in urban communities had much more positive attitudes toward pretend play and pretended more with their children). They argued that the literature on social class differences in play was inconsistent.

I (Power, 2000) noted that children the world over engage in sociodramatic play, although few quantitative studies had been conducted. The literature suggested that play in non-Western village cultures tends to be less competitive and less likely to involve "fantastic transformations" (i.e., "character roles that the child will seldom … enact or encounter in later life"; Power, 2000, p. 272). Children in village communities almost always engage in play in mixed-age groups, with children of different ages playing different roles (e.g., toddlers on the periphery, mostly watching; young children following the lead of older children; and older children directing the play activities).

Several recent studies on social class differences and cultural differences were located. In three studies of social class differences (Dyer & Moneta, 2006; Gosso, Morais, & Otta, 2007; Schneider, Richard, Younger, & Freeman, 2000), children in lower-class settings spent less time in play and/or were less likely to show pretend or associate play. The cross-cultural research (Bock & Johnson, 2004; Edwards, 2000; Morelli, Rogoff, & Angelillo, 2003; Newman et al., 2007) showed how variations in play are due to such factors as adult expectations, environmental opportunities, and competing activities.

Conclusions

The last 10 years of research on social play provides little information beyond what was available at the time of the Göncü et al. (2002), Pellegrini (2002), and Power (2000) reviews. Few studies of developmental and sex differences have been published, few new play correlates have been identified (with the exception of emotion regulation and emotion understanding), and virtually no new experimental evidence is available. The major new findings were that (a) child behavior during play is more complex than behavior during teacher-led tasks; (b) early gender segregation predicts later sex-stereotyped play patterns; (c) a combination of coercive and prosocial control strategies is associated with both dominance and peer liking; and (d) during children's play conflicts, child-generated resolutions increase with age and insistence decreases.

The limited number of findings continues a trend since the mid-1980s, when research on children's play began to decline substantially. Apparently, only researchers in early childhood education continue to see children's play as an important topic of study in its own right. When other researchers study play, it is to address other questions – play is the context in which the phenomena can be observed. Examples include emotional regulation, emotion understanding, physical activity, aggression, prosocial behavior, dominance, peer relationships, sibling relationships, and conflict resolution. The only areas where there has been an increase in research on children's play has been in the study of videogames and the study of children's pretend play and theory of mind.

Future research needs to address the remaining questions about play (see Power, 2000), particularly the issue of the effects of play on development. Although the quality of play is correlated with a range of child outcomes, the direction-of-effects question still remains. The consensus among early childhood educators, for example, is that play is critical for the development of young children (National Association for the Education of Young Children, 1996). They likely are correct. However, without a strong empirical research base upon which to draw, it is difficult to design child care environments that maximize the positive impact of play.

The decline of research on children's play may have been in response to critiques of the experimental studies of the 1970s and 1980s (e.g., Rubin et al., 1983; Smith, 1988). Although these researchers provided clear guidelines for designing experimental studies that would answer the important causal questions, these papers inadvertently may have discouraged subsequent research. Given the wide range of experimental and quasi-experimental methodologies now available, as well as the increased interest among policy makers in the importance of early childhood, the time may be right to demonstrate once and for all the importance of play for children's development.

References

Anderson, C. A., & Bushman, B. J. (2001). Effects of violent video games on aggressive behavior, aggressive cognition, aggressive affect, physiological arousal, and prosocial behavior: A meta-analytic review of the scientific literature. *Psychological Science, 12*, 353–359.

Annesi, J. J. (2006). Relations of physical self-concept and self-efficacy with frequency of voluntary physical activity in preadolescents: Implications for after-school care programming. *Journal of Psychosomatic Research, 61*, 515–520.

Benenson, J. F., Carder, H. P., & Geib-Cole, S. J. (2008). The development of boys' preferential pleasure in physical aggression. *Aggressive Behavior, 34*, 154–166.

Bensley, L., & Van Eenwyk, J. (2001). Video games and real-life aggression: Review of the literature. *Journal of Adolescent Health, 29*, 244–257.

Bloch, M. N. (1987). The development of sex differences in young children's activity at home: The effect of social context. *Sex Roles, 16*, 279–301.

Blumberg, F. C. (1998). Developmental differences at play: Children's selective attention and performance in video games. *Journal of Applied Developmental Psychology, 19*, 615–624.

Bock, J., & Johnson, S. E. (2004). Subsistence ecology and play among the Okavango Delta peoples of Botswana. *Human Nature, 15*, 63–81.

Carpenter, J. C., & Huston-Stein, A. (1980). Activity structure and sex-typed behavior in preschool children. *Child Development, 51*, 862–872.

Carver, A., Timperio, A., & Crawford, D. (2008). Perceptions of neighborhood safety and physical activity among youth: The CLAN Study. *Journal of Physical Activity & Health, 5*, 430–444.

Centers for Disease Control and Prevention. (2006). Overweight and obesity. Retrieved from www.cdc.gov/nccdphp/dnpa/obesity/

Chen, D. W., Fein, G. G., & Tam, H. (2001). Peer conflicts of preschool children: Issues, resolution, incidence, and age-related patterns. *Early Education and Development, 12*, 523–544.

Colwell, M. J., & Lindsey, E. W. (2005). Preschool children's pretend and physical play and sex of play partner: Connections to peer competence. *Sex Roles, 52*, 497–509.

Connelly, J. B., Duaso, M. J., & Butler, G. (2007). A review of controlled trials of interventions to prevent childhood obesity and overweight: A realistic synthesis of the evidence. *Public Health, 121*, 510–517.

Curran, J. M. (1999). Constraints on pretend play: Explicit and implicit rules. *Journal of Research in Childhood Education, 14*, 47–55.

Denham, S., Mason, T., Caverly, S., Schmidt, M., Hackney, R., Caswell, C., et al. (2001). Preschoolers at play: Co-socialisers of emotional and social competence. *International Journal of Behavioral Development, 25*, 290–301.

Dill, K. E., & Thill, K. P. (2007). Video game characters and the socialization of gender roles: Young people's perceptions mirror sexist media depictions. *Sex Roles, 57*, 851–864.

Dunn, J., & Hughes, C. (2001). "I got some swords and you're dead!" Violent fantasy, antisocial behavior, friendship, and moral sensibility in young children. *Child Development, 72*, 491–505.

Dyer, S., & Moneta, G. B. (2006). Frequency of parallel, associative, and co-operative play in British children of different socioeconomic status. *Social Behavior and Personality, 34*, 587–592.

Edwards, C. P. (2000). Children's play in cross-cultural perspective: A new look at the Six Cultures study. *Cross-Cultural Research, 34*, 318–338.

Elias, C. L., & Berk, L. E. (2002). Self-regulation in young children: Is there a role for sociodramatic play? *Early Childhood Education Quarterly, 17*, 216–238.

Fabes, R. A., Martin, C. L., & Hanish, L. D. (2003). Young children's play qualities in same-, other-, and mixed-sex peer groups. *Child Development, 74*, 921–932.

Farmer-Dougan, V., & Kaszuba, T. (1999). Reliability and validity of play-based observations: Relationship between the PLAY behaviour observation system and standardised measures of cognitive and social skills. *Educational Psychology, 19*, 429–440.

Farver, J. A. M., Kim, Y. K., & Lee-Shin, Y. (2000). Within cultural differences: Examining individual differences in Korean American and European American preschoolers' social pretend play. *Journal of Cross-Cultural Psychology, 31*, 583–602.

Fekonja, U., Umek, L. M., & Kranjc, S. (2005). Free play and other daily preschool activities as a context for child's language development. *Studia Psychologica, 47*, 103–118.

Ferguson, C. J. (2007a). Evidence for publication bias in video game violence effects literature: A meta-analytic review. *Aggression and Violent Behavior, 12*, 470–482.

Ferguson, C. J. (2007b). The good, the bad, and the ugly: A meta-analytic review of positive and negative effects of violent video games. *Psychiatric Quarterly, 78*, 309–316.

Gmitrova, V., & Gmitrov, J. (2003). The impact of teacher-directed and child-directed pretend play on cognitive competence in kindergarten children. *Early Childhood Education Journal, 30*, 241–246.

Göncü, A., Patt, M. B., & Kouba, E. (2002). Understanding young children's pretend play in context. In P. K. Smith & C. H. Hart (Eds.), *Blackwell handbook of childhood social development* (pp. 418–437). Oxford: Blackwell.

Gosso, Y., Morais, M. L. S., & Otta, E. (2007). Pretend play in Brazilian children: A window into different cultural worlds. *Journal of Cross-Cultural Psychology, 38*, 539–558.

Harper, L. V., & Huie, K. S. (1998). Free play use of space by preschoolers from diverse backgrounds: Factors influencing activity choices. *Merrill-Palmer Quarterly, 44*, 423–446.

Hawley, P. H. (2002). Social dominance and prosocial and coercive strategies of resource control in preschoolers. *International Journal of Behavioral Development, 26*, 167–176.

Hawley, P. H. (2003). Strategies of control, aggression, and morality in preschoolers: An evolutionary perspective. *Journal of Experimental Child Psychology, 85*, 213–235.

Huesmann, L. R. (2007). The impact of electronic media violence: Scientific theory and research. *Journal of Adolescent Health*, *41*, S6–S13.

Huston, A. C., Carpenter, J. C., Alwater, J. B., & Johnson, L. M. (1986). Gender, adult structuring of activities, and social behavior in middle childhood. *Child Development*, *57*, 1200–1209.

Jago, R., Baranowski, T., Baranowski, J. C., Thompson, D., & Greaves, K. A. (2005). BMI from 3–6 years of age is predicted by TV viewing and physical activity, not diet. *International Journal of Obesity*, *29*, 557–564.

Janz, K. F., Levy, S. M., Burns, T. L., Torner, J. C., Willing, M. C., & Warren, J. J. (2002). Fatness, physical activity, and television viewing in children during the adiposity rebound period: The Iowa Bone Development Study. *Preventive Medicine*, *35*, 563–571.

Kyratzis, A. (1999). Narrative identity: Preschoolers' self-construction through narrative in same-sex friendship group dramatic play. *Narrative Inquiry*, *9*, 427–455.

Kyratzis, A., Marx, T., & Evelyn, R. (2001). Preschoolers' communicative competence: Register shift in the marking of power in different contexts of friendship group talk. *First Language*, *21*, 387–431.

Landazabal, M. G. (2005). Prosocial and creative play: Effects of a programme on the verbal and nonverbal intelligence of children aged 10–11 years. *International Journal of Psychology*, *40*, 176–188.

Leseman, P. P. M., Rollenberg, L., & Rispens, J. (2001). Playing and working in kindergarten: Cognitive co-construction in two educational situations. *Early Childhood Research Quarterly*, *16*, 363–384.

Lewis, T. E., & Phillipsen, L. C. (1998). Interactions on an elementary school playground: Variations by age, gender, race, group size, and playground area. *Child Study Journal*, *28*, 309–320.

Lewis, V., Boucher, J., Lupton, L., & Watson, S. (2000). Relationships between symbolic play, functional play, verbal and non-verbal ability in young children. *International Journal of Language and Communication Disorders*, *35*, 117–127.

Ljunberg, T., Westlund, K., & Forsberg, A. J. L. (1999). Conflict resolution in 5-year-old boys: Does postconflict affiliative behaviour have a reconciliatory role? *Animal Behavior*, *58*, 1007–1016.

Maccoby, E. E. (1998). *The two sexes: Growing up apart, coming together*. Cambridge, MA: Harvard University Press.

Martin, C. L., & Fabes, R. A. (2001). The stability and consequences of young children's same-sex peer interactions. *Developmental Psychology*, *37*, 431–446.

McElwain, N. L., & Volling, B. L. (2005). Preschool children's interactions with friends and older siblings: Relationship specificity and joint contributions to problem behavior. *Journal of Family Psychology*, *19*, 486–496.

Mendez, J. L., McDermott, P., & Fantuzzo, J. (2002). Identifying and promoting social competence in African American children: Developmental and contextual concerns. *Psychology in the Schools*, *39*, 111–123.

Morelli, G. A., Rogoff, B., & Angelillo, C. (2003). Cultural variation in young children's access to work or involvement in specialised child-focused activities. *International Journal of Behavioral Development*, *27*, 264–274.

Munroe, R. L., & Romney, A. K. (2006). Gender and age differences in same-sex aggregation and social behavior: A four-culture study. *Journal of Cross-Cultural Psychology*, *37*, 3–19.

Murphy, L. M. B., Laurie-Rose, C., Brinkman, T. M., & McNamara, K. A. (2007). Sustained attention and social competence in typically developing preschool-aged children. *Early Child Development and Care*, *177*, 133–149.

National Association for the Education of Young Children. (1996). Developmentally appropriate practice in early childhood programs serving children from birth through age 8. Retrieved from http://www.naeyc.org/about/positions.asp

Newman, J., Bidjerano, T., Ozdogru, A. A., Kao, C., Ozkose-Biyik, C., & Johnson, J. J. (2007). What do they usually do after school? A comparative analysis of fourth-grade children in Bulgaria, Taiwan, and the United States. *Journal of Early Adolescence, 27,* 431–456.

Niec, L. N., & Russ, S. W. (2002). Children's internal representations, empathy, and fantasy play: A validity study of the SCORS-Q. *Psychological Assessment, 14,* 331–338.

O'Brien, M., Roy, C., Jacobs, A., Macaluso, M., & Peyton, V. (1999). Conflict in the dyadic play of 3-year-old children. *Early Education and Development, 10,* 289–313.

Orleans, M., & Laney, M. C. (2000). Children's computer use in the home. *Social Science Computer Review, 18,* 56–72.

Panksepp, J. (2007). Can play diminish ADHD and facilitate the construction of the social brain? *Journal of the Canadian Academy of Child and Adolescent Psychiatry, 16,* 57–66.

Parten, M. B. (1932). Social participation among preschool children. *Journal of Abnormal and Social Psychology, 27,* 243–269.

Pellegrini, A. D. (2002). Rough-and-tumble play from childhood through adolescence: Development and possible functions. In P. K. Smith & C. H. Hart (Eds.), *Blackwell handbook of childhood social development* (pp. 438–453). Oxford: Blackwell.

Pellegrini, A. D., Long, J. D., Roseth, C. J., Bohn, C. M., & Van Ryzin, M. (2007). A short-term longitudinal study of preschoolers' (*Homo sapiens*) sex segregation: The role of physical activity, sex, and time. *Journal of Comparative Psychology, 121,* 282–289.

Power, T. G. (2000). *Play and exploration in children and animals.* Mahwah, NJ: Erlbaum.

Pugliese, J., & Tinsley, B. (2007). Parental socialization of child and adolescent physical activity: A meta-analysis. *Journal of Family Psychology, 21,* 331–343.

Reed, T., & Brown, M. (2001). The expression of care in the rough and tumble play of boys. *Journal of Research in Childhood Education, 15,* 104–116.

Robinson, C. C., Anderson, G. T., Porter, C. L., Hart, C. H., & Wouden-Miller, M. (2003). Sequential transition patterns of preschoolers' social interactions during child-initiated play: Is parallel-aware play a bidirectional bridge to other play states? *Early Childhood Research Quarterly, 18,* 3–21.

Roemmich, J. N., Barkley, J. E., Lobarinas, C. L., Foster, J. H., White, T. M., & Epstein, L. H. (2008). Association of liking and reinforcing value with children's physical activity. *Physiology & Behavior, 93,* 1011–1018.

Roemmich, J. N., Epstein, L. H., Raja, S., & Yin, L. (2007). The neighborhood and home environments: Disparate relationships with physical activity and sedentary behaviors in youth. *Annals of Behavioral Medicine, 33,* 29–38.

Rubin, K. H., Fein, G. G., & Vandenberg, B. (1983). Play. In P. H. Mussen & E. M. Hetherington (Eds.), *Handbook of child psychology* (Vol. 4, pp. 693–774). New York: Wiley.

Saar, M., & Jurimae, T. (2007). Sports participation outside school in total physical activity of children. *Perceptual and Motor Skills, 105,* 559–562.

Salvy, S., Bower, J. W., Roemmich, J. N., Romero, N., Kieffer, E., Paluch, R., et al. (2008). Peer influence on children's physical activity: An experience sampling study. *Journal of Pediatric Psychology, 33,* 39–49.

Schneider, B. H., Richard, J. F., Younger, A. J., & Freeman, P. (2000). A longitudinal exploration of the continuity of children's social participation and social withdrawal across socioeconomic status levels and social settings. *European Journal of Social Psychology, 30,* 497–519.

Schwebel, D. C., Rosen, C. S., & Singer, J. L. (1999). Preschoolers' pretend play and theory of mind: The role of jointly constructed pretence. *British Journal of Developmental Psychology, 17,* 333–348.

Scott, E., & Panksepp, J. (2003). Rough-and-tumble play in human children. *Aggressive Behavior, 29,* 539–551.

Sherry, J. L. (2001). The effects of violent video games on aggression: A meta-analysis. *Human Communication Research, 27*, 409–431.

Sigmund, E., De Ste Croix, M., Miklankova, L., & Fromel, K. (2007). Physical activity patterns of kindergarten children in comparison to teenagers and young adults. *European Journal of Public Health, 17*, 646–651.

Simpkins, S. D., & Parke, R. D. (2002). Do friends and nonfriends behave differently? A social relations analysis of children's behavior. *Merrill-Palmer Quarterly, 48*, 263–283.

Smilansky, S. (1968). *The effects of sociodramatic play on disadvantaged preschool children.* New York: Wiley.

Smith, P. K. (1988). Children's play and its role in early development: A reevaluation of the "play ethos." In A. D. Pellegrini (Ed.), *Psychological bases for early education* (pp. 207–226). Chichester, UK: Wiley.

Smith, P. K. (2005). Social and pretend play in children. In A. D. Pellegrini & P. K. Smith (Eds.), *The nature of play: Great apes and humans* (pp. 173–209). New York: Guilford Press.

Smith, P. K. (2010). *Understanding children's worlds: Children and play.* Chichester, UK: Wiley-Blackwell.

Smith, P. K., Smees, R., & Pellegrini, A. D. (2004). Play fighting and real fighting: Using video playback methodology with young children. *Aggressive Behavior, 30*, 164–173.

Swing, E. L., & Anderson, C. A. (2007). The unintended negative consequences of exposure to violent video games. *International Journal of Cognitive Technology, 12*, 3–13.

Tannock, M. T. (2008). Rough and tumble play: An investigation of the perceptions of educators and young children. *Early Childhood Education Journal, 35*, 357–361.

Tomporowski, P. D., Davis, C. L., Miller, P. H., & Naglieri, J. A. (2008). Exercise and children's intelligence, cognition, and academic achievement. *Educational Psychology Review, 20*, 111–131.

Trawick-Smith, J. (1998). A qualitative analysis of metaplay in the preschool years. *Early Childhood Research Quarterly, 13*, 433–452.

Uechi, H., Takenaka, K., & Oka, K. (2000). The relationship between physical activity and stress response of children. *Japanese Journal of Health Psychology, 13*, 1–8.

Uechi, H., Takenaka, K., Suzuki, H., & Oka, K. (2003). Effects of physical activity on social skill and cognitive appraisal of stressors in children. *Japanese Journal of Health Psychology, 16*, 11–20.

VanDeventer, S. S., & White, J. A. (2002). Expert behavior in children's video game play. *Simulation & Gaming, 33*, 28–48.

Verbeek, P., & de Waal, F. B. M. (2001). Peacemaking among preschool children. *Peace and Conflict, 7*, 5–28.

Walker, C. A. (1999). Playing a story: Narrative and writing-like features in scenes of dramatic play. *Reading Research and Instruction, 38*, 401–413.

Walsh, G., Sproule, L., McGuinness, C., Trew, K., Rafferty, H., & Sheehy, N. (2006). An appropriate curriculum for 4–5-year-old children in Northern Ireland: Comparing play-based and formal approaches. *Early Years, 26*, 201–221.

Wang, H., Sekine, M., Chen, X., Yamagami, T., & Kagamimori, S. (2008). Lifestyle at 3 years of age and quality of life (QOL) in first-year junior high school students in Japan: Results of the Toyama Birth Cohort Study. *Quality of Life Research, 17*, 257–265.

Zach, S., & Netz, Y. (2007). Like mother like child: Three generations' patterns of exercise behavior. *Families, Systems, & Health, 25*, 419–434.

CHAPTER TWENTY-FIVE

Cooperation and Competition

Barry H. Schneider, Joyce Benenson, Márta Fülöp, Mihaly Berkics, and Mónika Sándor

Definitions of Cooperation and Competition

In much of the social psychological and educational literature, competition is viewed as something harmful that can lead to negative consequences for children's psychosocial development, whereas cooperation is described as competent social behavior that entails many positive consequences (e.g., Foster, 1984). In spite of this common view, children from many cultures are continually encouraged to be competitive in various domains such as school and sports. Many individuals consider competition an important and healthy element in children's development (Roberts, 1992). One possible explanation of such contrasting positions is that there are as many different definitions of competition and cooperation as there are opinions regarding their effects on children. Another possibility, to be explained more fully later in this chapter, is that there are different forms of competition, some more healthy than others.

Competition and cooperation can refer to characteristics of social situations or to the psychological states of the participants in them (Van Avermaet, 1996). For example, a competitive or cooperative structure can be imposed on children playing with a ball. In one instance, there may be strict rules and one child may be required to try to achieve a specific outcome at the expense of another child, as in a tennis match. In another instance, children may be expected to work together to try to reach a common result, as in two children throwing a ball to one another during baseball practice with the aim of developing their throwing skills. The first situation would be described as a competitive situation, and the second as cooperative. However, the children involved in the activities may or

---

The Wiley-Blackwell Handbook of Childhood Social Development, Second Edition, edited by Peter K. Smith and Craig H. Hart

may not adopt the goals, attitudes, and behaviors that correspond to the apparent external demands of the situation. For example, one of the children in the baseball practice may try to throw the ball harder than his or her partner in an attempt to be perceived as a better player by the coach; even though the child was participating in an activity that should elicit cooperative behaviors, his or her goals and behaviors were competitive. To complicate things even further, most situations involving social interactions are not as clearly defined as competitive or cooperative, and many may in fact contain elements of competition and cooperation. Perhaps for these reasons, Smith (1996, p. 81) described competition and cooperation as "often interwoven in intricate ways in their behavioral expression."

Some definitions of competition and cooperation refer to the characteristics of social situations. For instance, Van Avermaet (1996) suggested that the extent to which the outcomes of a specific activity are the same for participants A and B vary, ranging from complete positive correspondence, which leads to cooperation (i.e., if participant A performs an action that produces a specific result, participant B will obtain the same result), to total negative correspondence, which leads to competition (i.e., if participant A performs an action that brings about a specific result, participant B loses the opportunity to obtain the same result). Most activities would be situated somewhere along a continuum between total competition and total cooperation.

Charlesworth (1996) proposed definitions of competition and cooperation based on resource allocation. He perceived competition as a strategy adopted to gain a limited resource in which several participants are interested, and cooperation as a collaborative effort with another to gain a shared resource. Cooperation is even described at times as one possible competitive tactic used to obtain valuable physical, social, or informational resources. According to this argument, the ability to combine cooperative and competitive behaviors is an important human social adaptation, because it employs culturally sanctioned cooperative behaviors that often benefit the self and others at the same time as it protects the individual from exploitation (LaFreniere & Charlesworth, 1987).

Examples of definitions of competition and cooperation that refer to the psychological state of the participants are ones that are based on the goals of the participants. There is competition when the goals are incompatible and mutually exclusive, and there is cooperation when the goals are compatible and interdependent (Butt, 1987). However, in some situations involving competition, the attainment of specific goals by one of the participants does not necessarily prevent the others from attaining some of these goals.

All of the definitions presented above are based on an undifferentiated concept of competition. This one-dimensional view may explain why some people perceive competition as either totally healthy or totally unhealthy. Ryckman, Libby, van den Borne, Gold, and Lindner (1997) differentiated two types of competitive attitudes: People who exhibit a *personal development* competitive attitude generally try to improve their skills regardless of the outcome, whereas those who manifest a *hypercompetitive* attitude usually possess a strong desire to achieve a specific outcome regardless of the necessary means required. Fülöp (2004) differentiated competitive processes according to their goals, functions, and the attributed role of the rival in the process. The goal of competition can be winning, outperforming the other, but also self-improvement, self-evaluation, or gaining mastery over something by competing. The function of competition therefore can be improvement, motivation, goal attainment, and also the "elimination" of the rival. Rivals can be conceived as motivators, comparative parties, opponents to win over, and enemies to be "destroyed." These different goals, functions, and roles of rivals determine qualitatively different competitive processes that can take a constructive or a destructive turn. These multidimensional models assume that some form of competition can exist in which the desire to outperform another person or obtain a greater share of resources than someone else is not the main goal.

Competition and Cooperation as Seen by Children

Complementing the contemplations of educators, psychologists, and philosophers, children themselves have their own ideas about competition and cooperation. Fülöp, Ross, Pergar Kuscer, and Razdevsek Pucko (2007) carried out focus group interviews with primary and secondary school children in England, Hungary, and Slovenia to determine their views of competition and cooperation. In all three countries, both primary and secondary school children found more enjoyment in the outcomes of competition (winning, and finding out who is best) than the process. The children described competition at times as exciting and fun, and suggested that competition allows someone to find out and demonstrate how good he or she is. They saw competition as motivating people to try. The primary school students dislike competition when there is cheating present and when there is too much pressure to win. In contrast, secondary school students stated that competition is not enjoyable if they are "not good enough" to compete or if they "will be embarrassed by others." Cooperation was seen in all three countries as enjoyable when participants help each other and discuss things but not enjoyable when the people involved are not friends, or if there is arguing, or if not all the team members make an effort.

Thorkildsen and White-McNulty (2002) studied the views of 6–14-year-old children about the fairness of individual and group contests in their schools. The participants saw some kinds of contests as fair. The older participants tempered this view with the proviso that competition is fair only if it leads to success by individuals who are the most skilled or who have worked the hardest, not those who are lucky.

Methodological Issues in the Study of Cooperation and Competition

Researchers have devised methodologies that either (a) manipulate the competitive or cooperative nature of specific situations in order to study their effects on children's behaviors, or (b) measure children's individual preferences for competitive or cooperative interaction. There are at least two commonly used methods to manipulate the competitive or cooperative nature of children's games or tasks. The first technique consists of using competitive, cooperative, or individualistic instructions when explaining the objective of a task. For example, Butler (1990) gave the following competitive instructions to half the participants in her study: "Try and make the best copy of this drawing. Try and make the best copy in your group. I shall collect your copies to judge who made the best copy"; and the following individualistic instructions to the other half: "Try to copy the drawing as closely as you can. I am collecting all the pictures that children copy with stickers" (p. 203).

Another strategy for controlling the competitive or cooperative nature of the activity consists of using cooperative, competitive, or individualistic reward structures in contrived situations. For example, Hom, Berger, Duncan, Miller, and Blevin (1994) informed children in the cooperative group that the amount of candy they would each receive depended on their team's performance, whereas children in the individualistic group were told that the reward was linked only to their own individual performances.

Children's preferences for cooperative or competitive interaction have been assessed mainly with dyadic games, forced-choice resource allocation measures, and questionnaires. Madsen (1971; see also Kagan & Madsen, 1971) pioneered the use of dyadic games and forced-choice resource allocation measures in their cross-cultural studies of children's competition and cooperation. The marble pull game is the earliest of these games (most of the others are structured according to the same general principles): A plastic cup is placed over a marble on a table, and two strings are attached, one to each side of the cup. If both children pull on their strings in opposite directions at the same time, the cup separates in two pieces, the marble is released, and no one collects it. If one child pulls toward his or her side and the other releases the string, the cup does not separate and the first child can capture the marble. The game is played over repetitive trials, and the marbles obtained by each child are later exchanged for prizes. The only way marbles can be obtained equally is if children cooperate by taking turns.

Charlesworth (1996) employed a task designed to elicit both cooperative and competitive strategies to obtain a resource. Four children entered a room with a movie viewer. In order to see the movie, one child had to push a button to turn on the screen and another child had to roll the film. A third child could watch the film via a hole, meaning that the fourth child became a bystander and had no task. Those children who could view the movie for the longest time (i.e., who were the "winners" in the situation) were those who cooperated the longest (pushed the button or rolled the film) and who also used assertiveness to get to the resource.

In contrast with the experimental tasks contrived by researchers, which have been the mainstay of traditional social psychology research, many contemporary researchers seek to assess competition and cooperation in the natural settings in which they occur. Some researchers assess children's competitive or cooperative preferences by self-report questionnaires (e.g., Engelhard & Monsaas, 1989), and by peer or teacher ratings of competitive and/or cooperative behaviors (e.g., Kerns & Barth, 1995; Tassi & Schneider, 1997). Although self-reports and ratings may offer greater insights into the day-to-day competitive and cooperative behaviors of children with their peers, they do not permit direct observation on the part of the researchers, who must rely on the accuracy of the informant. Tassi and Schneider argued that peer ratings, compared to self-reports, may provide more accurate data on children's competitive and cooperative behaviors.

All of those methodologies have assisted researchers in studying the relationships between competition and cooperation in children's behaviors and various relevant variables; all have their limitations. In interpreting any specific study, it is important to remember that the results reflect the researcher's choice of instrumentation to a considerable degree; different methods often yield drastically different results. It might be said that direct observation in a real-life setting is the *gold standard*. However, that is possible only in a minority of research settings.

The Developmental Unfolding of Competitive and Cooperative Behavior

According to Piaget (1950), cooperation emerges during the later stages of children's moral development, whereas Vygotsky (1978) maintained that cooperation appears earlier. Their theories have prompted developmental researchers to investigate preschoolers' peer interaction. Verba (1994) observed 1- to 4-year-old children who were engaged in spontaneous joint activity with objects during free play. Verba reported many examples of early cooperation and competition, such as "putting forward ideas that they tried to have their partner adopt, pooling their creative efforts in an atmosphere of good will, taking conflicting stands, and attempting to resolve disagreement" (p. 277). She concluded that young children (3 and 4 years old) are primarily egoistic across individualistic, cooperative, and competitive settings; they prefer to maximize their own short-term gain regardless of whether it is in their long-term self-interest. With increasing age, children learn competitive and cooperative choice rules that serve to maximize their long-term gains when used appropriately in relation to the setting. Learning to forgo one's own gain for a cooperative outcome in a setting where long-term individual gain is dependent upon maximizing joint gain begins only at 6–7 years old (McClintock, Moskowitz, & McClintock, 1977; Toda, Shinotsuka, McClintock, & Stech, 1978).

By 5 or 6 years, children fully understand the implications of their choices and can explain their decisions in a resource allocation task, and their verbal report is in harmony with their decision (Sándor, Fülöp, Berkics, & Xie, 2003). Sheridan and Williams (2006), using video observations, individual and group interviews, as well as children's drawings, revealed how 5-year-old children compete constructively and how they themselves express and conceive competition in different situations. Cooperation, and constructive forms of competition that motivate children to achieve better, stretch beyond their own expected abilities, and also make activities more exciting, can exist simultaneously. They found several examples of competition through cooperation, children competing to finish their own game and helping each other at the same time, for instance in a tower-building task, proving that constructive competition can be a dimension of children's collaboration as well as their individual activities.

Social comparison is an inherent feature of competition. Children younger than 7 to 9 years may not be able to adequately extract information from social comparison for the purpose of self-evaluation (Ruble, 1983). Children's sensitivity to such information may greatly influence their decisions to pursue competitive or cooperative interactions with their peers. In resource allocation tasks, this increase in competition is sometimes attributed to the development of mathematical abilities. Knight, Berning, Wilson, and Chao (1987) studied three different age groups: 3–5-year-olds, 6–8-year-olds, and 9–12-year-olds. Among younger children, individualistic resource distribution was the most frequently preferred option by both boys and girls. The proportion of competitive choices increased by age and was the most prevalent choice among the 9–12-year-olds.

Many studies show that the preference toward competitive choices in experimental situations increases with age (e.g., Kagan & Madsen, 1971; McClintock & Moskowitz, 1976; Strein, 1986). In real-life school settings, preference for competitive learning also increases with age (Graves & Graves, 1984; Owens & Barnes, 1982). Toda et al. (1978) examined Anglo-American, Japanese, Belgian, Greek, and Mexican American children using a game they devised. The age effect was stronger than any cultural effect. Whereas the younger samples of participants within the national groups displayed varying levels of competition, by early adolescence, all samples displayed relatively high levels of competitive choices.

Handel (1989) also found that cooperative behavior is more prevalent among older children than younger children. Comparing 5–7-, 8–10-, and 10–12-year-olds, he found that the older children were more willing to cooperate. This again suggests that competition should not be construed as the diametric opposite of cooperation. Shwalb and Shwalb (1985) argued that children do not become "more" or "less" competitive with age. Rather, the expression of such competitiveness changes in style with age as the activities prevalent at each school level change. These researchers differentiated three stages based upon types of competitive activities: general competitiveness in elementary school, competitiveness in academic and nonacademic fields in middle school, and individual versus group and intergroup competition in secondary school.

Cultural Differences

Beginning with the seminal fieldwork of the anthropologist Mead, researchers have focused their efforts on classifying cultures around the world as cooperative or competitive. Some researchers have also explored the features of cultures that give rise to both healthy and unhealthy forms of competition and to the social consequences of being competitive in different cultures.

The contemporary reader perusing Mead's (1937) pioneering compilation entitled *Cooperation and Competition Among Primitive Peoples* is likely to be astonished at how timely the research remains over 70 years later. Mead's volume contains not only reports of her own famous fieldwork in Samoa, New Guinea, and the Admiralty Islands in the late 1920s but also contributions from anthropologists who studied a dozen other cultures around the world. Her work was one of the earliest major interdisciplinary research endeavors, bringing together anthropology and psychology long before the term "interdisciplinary research" was coined (Mead, p. v). Underlying the research was the assumption that variation in the social structures of different cultures is linked with variation in individual personalities. Thus, both cultures and personalities could be considered competitive or cooperative. Mead used the distinction between hostile competition aimed at demonstrating one's own superiority and more benign forms related to personal development, similar to recent definitions discussed at the beginning of this chapter; but she soon discovered the limits of a sharp dichotomy between competition and cooperation, noting (p. 5) that people can cooperate in order to compete. She also discovered that friendly competition, as in sport, was sufficient to gratify personal "ego needs" in some societies, perhaps precluding the emergence of hostile forms of competition. Besides learning that cooperation and competition were thus not diametric opposites, Mead's observations led her to add a third category, *individualistic*, to refer to cultures where people strive to advance their own interests but not to outdo others.

Based on her contention that no social event or feature of a culture could be understood out of context, Mead's volume (1937) contains chapter-length ethnographies providing rich accounts of each culture studied. There is also a lengthy interpretive conclusion in which Mead compares and classifies the cultures. As sophisticated as her methods were, Mead was very cognizant of their limitations, the most important of which is that longitudinal follow-up was likely never to occur, leaving the depictions of each culture static and uninformed by the inevitable changes following increasing contact with the Western world.

Mead specified clear criteria for classifying the cultures observed as competitive, cooperative, or individualistic. The criteria included the goals toward which group activities are directed, the principal ends to which individuals devote their time, and the proportions of time and energy devoted to shared common goals, competitive goals, and individual goals. Nevertheless, she recognized that no society is a monolith, totally competitive or totally cooperative. For example, the Kwakiutl tribe of Vancouver Island, Canada, was generally the most competitive of the cultures studied. However, the fierce competition was played out within ranking tribal chiefs. Within each household, marked cooperation prevailed. Similarly, among the Manus of the Admiralty Islands, the marked competition among entrepreneurs was balanced by cooperation among members of the same clan. Without such internal cooperation, the entrepreneurs would not have the support and wealth needed to enter into competition.

Nevertheless, Mead was able to trace important distinctions between the competitive and cooperative societies. General wealth was not a very good discriminator. For example, in two parts of Canada, the scarcity of basic commodities made the Arctic Inuit highly cooperative but did not have the same effect on the Ojibwe in central Canada, who were markedly individualistic. The distinction between hunting, farming, and pastoral activity cut across the three categories of culture. More predictive was the flexibility of the power hierarchy: No culture characterized by a formally accepted, inflexible hierarchy of power was classified as competitive, probably because competition would not lead to any change in the status of an individual or subgroup. Where status is considered both very important and amenable to change, competition emerges as a means of achieving upward mobility or measuring one's potential ability to attain higher status.

Societies with a strong sense of common purpose, predictably, turned out to be quite cooperative. Cooperative societies were also stable ones, in which the same individuals were destined to associate with each other indefinitely, unlike nomadic groups such as the Arctic Inuit. In cooperative cultures, there are often many paths to recognition, whereas in competitive societies, one particular commodity, often in limited supply, or one particular skill leads to individual prestige. The more competitive cultures are characterized by strong individual needs to achieve and to amass property.

Mead assumed that competitive cultures socialize children to have "competitive characters." Another fascinating observation, unique even to this day in the competition literature, is that, in all the competitive cultures described in her anthology, children are rushed to become adults as quickly as possible. She attributed this to the anxiety about not training children sufficiently for the competition they will face later on. In cooperative cultures, children are given time to learn what they need to become cooperative citizens by maturation and experience. It would be interesting to see if this distinction would be confirmed in contemporary cross-cultural data.

From the field to the laboratory

A generation of social psychologists starting in the 1970s based their research on laboratory analogue situations such as the movie viewer discussed earlier or the Madsen Cooperation Board (Madsen, 1967). This methodology offers the advantage of allowing the systematic comparison of individuals from different cultures in situations that are identical down to the last detail; this is impossible in ethnographic fieldwork. The situations themselves can be varied systematically by the experimenter to test the hypotheses under study, for example to favor cooperative or competitive behavior. The major drawback of this method is that the individual is studied out of his or her social context in a contrived situation that may not elicit the participants' typical responses.

Emblematic of such cross-cultural studies are the comparisons of the responses of Anglo-American and Latin American children to the Cooperation Board. A great number of cross-cultural studies involving Anglo-American, Mexican, and/or Mexican American children were conducted by Kagan, Madsen, and their associates (e.g., Kagan & Knight, 1979). The methodology used in most of those studies consisted of a forced-choice experimenter-derived measure of resource allocation, such as the marble pull game described earlier; the participants were mostly between ages 5 and 12 years. Their studies have consistently reported more cooperative, and fewer competitive, behaviors among Mexican and Mexican American children than among their Anglo-American counterparts. Furthermore, Mexican children were found to be more cooperative and less competitive than Mexican American children (Kagan & Madsen, 1971). Thus, children from a collectivistic culture such as Mexico appear to value cooperation more highly than Anglo-American and even Mexican American children, both of whom are raised in an individualistic culture that generally values competition. This is further supported by the finding that third-generation Mexican American children showed a greater preference for competition than their second-generation peers (Kagan & Knight, 1979).

Parallel cross-cultural research comparing American and Chinese children is not as conclusive. Sparkes (1991) studied the cooperative and competitive behaviors of Chinese and American 3- to 5-year-old children. Pairs of same-culture children played an adaptation of Madsen's (1971) marble pull game. Pairs of Chinese children demonstrated more competitive behaviors than pairs of American children. This finding is unlike that of Domino (1992), who used a different methodology with older children. In his study, 10- to 12-year-old Chinese and American children's competitive and cooperative preferences were measured using a token allocation procedure. They could choose between various options in playing the game. In all options, some tokens were to be kept for oneself, but some were also to be given to the other child; the options differed in the relative proportions. In Domino's experiment, American children gave more competitive and fewer cooperative responses than Chinese children. These conflicting results may be an artifact of the different samples and dissimilar methods used or may reflect a cross-cultural developmental difference given the different ages of the children in both experiments. Nevertheless, the overwhelming trend in all cross-cultural studies indicates that Anglo-American children are more competitive than whatever other culture they are compared with.

Moving beyond classification

Attempts at classifying cultures are still very much underway, with many theorists favoring multiaxial classification schemes; competitiveness and cooperativeness can still be seen as comprising one of the many dimensions of culture that should be considered. Analogue tasks such as the marble pull game are no longer in widespread use, probably because of their contrived nature. A variety of methods including questionnaires, interviews, peer reports, and observations are currently favored by most researchers. Many contemporary researchers wish to go beyond the classification of cultures. There is a recent trend toward determining how individuals in different cultures view competition (e.g., the study by Fülöp et al., 2007, discussed earlier in this chapter). Hayward and Kemmelmeyer (2007) articulated interesting parallels between views of competition in different cultures and their guiding theories, for example Marxism, the Protestant ethic, and individualism.

There is also an emerging interest in studying the possible antecedents and consequences of cooperation and competition in different cultures. Grum, Lebaric, and Kolenc (2004) have focused on the complex relationship between competition and self-concept. Competition could be the result of individuals compensating for a low self-concept, but competition could also be a manifestation of the confidence that comes with a high self-concept. It is not inconceivable that competition is the cause of inflated or deflated self-concept, rather than the result. Distinguishing between hostile competition (hypercompetitiveness) and personal development competition may help unravel this. There are many ways in which cultural emphases on competition – and, indeed, on self-concept – could mediate the correlation between these variables. Data pertaining to children and adolescents may help clarify the many possible associations between these variables. More importantly, the range of cultures needs to be expanded: Competition may have a lot more to do with individual differences in self-concept in highly individualistic cultures than in very collectivistic societies where a large portion of self-concept is derived from membership in the collective group.

Sex Differences in Competition Within Children's Interpersonal Relationships

Evidence for the dominance of males over females in mixed-sex interactions occurs early in life, even in Western societies in which sex roles are more equal than in most other areas of the world. In one classic study, when mixed-sex pairs of unfamiliar 2-year-old children interacted in a laboratory, males intimidated females more than vice versa, causing females to withdraw (Jacklin & Maccoby, 1978). Likewise, in Charlesworth and LaFreniere's (1983) movie viewer study (see earlier in this chapter) in which groups of two male and two female 4–5-year-old children competed to view cartoons, males obtained almost four times as much viewing time as females. Not only did females attain less viewing time, but also they spent more than twice as much time as males not being involved at all. Additional studies with children in middle childhood and adolescence demonstrate that even females who are clearly superior to their male counterparts in a competition frequently subordinate their own interests so that males dominate (Cronin, 1986).

Several researchers suggest that the proximal mechanisms for males' domination of females consist of male competitors who display more overtly domineering forms of competitive behavior (Maccoby, 1990) coupled with females' greater physiological fear of competition (Campbell, 1999). Results with girls born with excess androgens demonstrate that these girls display more domineering behavior than their control sisters (Pasterski et al., 2007), suggesting that androgens increase overtly competitive behaviors. The degree of cultural bias favoring adult males over females also exerts a strong influence on the extent of males' dominance over females (Archer, 2006).

In same-sex interactions, males exhibit greater overt competition than do females for resources, territory, skillfulness at tasks, status, and power. Beginning in early childhood, male interactions consist of more direct physical challenges as well as rough-and-tumble play (Archer, 2006). These generate dominance hierarchies based on physical prowess that form an important part of a male's status and the basis for relationships through to adolescence (Savin-Williams, 1979; Strayer & Strayer, 1976). At all ages, males also engage in more overt verbal attempts to dominate others through boasts, commands, threats, name calling, and derisive jokes (Maccoby, 1990).

By middle childhood and increasingly in adolescence, males are more likely than females to engage in overt interference competition, frequently in the form of playing competitive sports, often against unfamiliar players (Maccoby, 1998), in which one individual must overtly prevent another individual from obtaining a desired outcome. Although some females do enjoy contact sports, many females find interference competition aversive and prefer to compete through more indirect or subtle means. Roy and Benenson (2002) demonstrated this effect with children in middle childhood, when they asked same-sex peers to play a game under two conditions: when only the first player to finish could win a prize, and when all players who finished won prizes. Whereas males chose to compete with each other in both contexts, female participants chose competitive tactics only in the zero-sum game condition. Likewise, Underwood, Scott, and Galperin (2004) showed that, in middle childhood and adolescence, when confronted by an unpleasant same-sex peer (a trained confederate), male peers directly challenged the confederate, whereas female peers did not. After the confederate had left, however, both male and female peers made disparaging remarks at similar rates.

By contrast, from early childhood onward, female interactions increasingly avoid direct physical provocation and consist of more polite speech and nonverbal communication, such as smiling and behaving modestly, which diminish retaliatory responses from potential competitors (Bjorkqvist, 1994). Denigrating an absent competitor's reputation, excluding a competitor using circuitous speech forms, and employing discreet nonverbal signals of disparagement aimed at a competitor (such as contemptuous facial expressions or bodily postures) constitute female forms of competition. These competitive forms limit retaliation because their intent takes longer to identify, and little recourse exists for the target as the competitor often is not even present. Competition between females increases in adolescence, when females begin to compete for male partners (Archer & Coyne, 2005). This makes sense as adult human females generally depend on males to obtain resources for themselves and their children, rather than competing for these resources themselves (Campbell, 2004). Further, given women's greater responsibility for the care of children, avoidance of physical danger and potential retaliation from competitors protects their ability to care for their children for extended periods (Campbell, 1999).

Sex differences in social structure additionally affect competitiveness. From middle childhood onward, males organize themselves into large, interconnected groups (Benenson, Apostoleris, & Parnass, 1998; Markovits, Benenson, & Dolenszky, 2001). Groups induce competitive behavior because fewer resources are available per individual within the group, and larger groups enhance competition with other groups (Benenson, Nicholson, Waite, Roy, & Simpson, 2001; Schopler & Insko, 1999). Focus on male out-groups forms a particular interest of human males, beginning in early childhood and continuing into adulthood (Sidanius, Sinclair, & Pratto, 2006). Nicolopoulou, Scales, and Weintraub (1994) demonstrated that in American preschools, almost all the boys spontaneously tell stories of heroes competing against aliens, enemy soldiers, out-groups within the community, and dangerous animals, whereas virtually none of the females tell such stories, preferring instead to recount stories of familial relationships.

Cooperative Versus Competitive Environments as Facilitators of Learning and Motivation

Stanne, Johnson, and Johnson (1999) conducted a meta-analysis of research on the circumstances in which cooperation and competition are useful. They found that the effect of cooperation and competition depended on the interdependence of the task and the way competition was structured. When an activity requires interdependence, cooperation is the most useful for performance. However, if interdependence is low and the competing parties cannot interfere with each other's performance, competition might be more advantageous. Therefore, the effect of cooperation and competition on performance is strongly influenced by the structure of the task. When competition is structured appropriately (not much emphasis on winning, an equal opportunity to win, clear rules, and an ability to gauge performance relative to one's opponent), it has the same effect on performance as cooperation.

Engagement in competition depends on the interaction of the individual and the situation. Previously, intrinsic and extrinsic motivation (Deci & Ryan, 1985) were conceived as polar opposites: Intrinsic motivation, just like cooperation, was regarded as solely positive, while extrinsic motivation was strongly connected to competition and seen as negative in the educational literature. However, studies from the early 1990s demonstrated that competition does not necessarily compromise intrinsic motivation. In fact, competitive contexts can increase the desire to do well and a sense of excitement and can promote intrinsic motivation (Epstein & Harackiewicz, 1992). Competition can have a positive effect because it provides an exciting challenge and increases the importance that an individual places on doing well. As a result, individuals may become more involved in the activity, thereby promoting intrinsic motivation. The positive feedback that is received at the conclusion of a competition can also increase intrinsic motivation (Tauer & Harackiewicz, 1999).

Despite this potential, there is little doubt that the traditional climate of most schools in Western countries leads to competition and not to cooperation. A meta-analysis by Roseth, Johnson, and Johnson (2008) indicates that both learning and social development would be furthered if cooperative goal structures predominated over competitive ones. These authors conducted a systematic review of 148 studies from at least 11 countries, involving over 17,000 adolescent participants. Their first conclusion was that achievement was higher in cooperative than in competitive settings. Children's relations with their peers were also better in the cooperative settings. Importantly, the correlations between achievement and positive relationships were also highest in the cooperative settings.

Competition, Friendships, and Peer Relationships

Peer relationships have often been seen as enhanced by cooperation and disrupted by competition. In Sherif, Harvey, White, Hood, and Sherif's (1961) extensive study, 11- and 12-year-old boys taking part in summer camps were divided into two groups and observed during intense, intergroup competitive and cooperative conditions. They observed strong negative interpersonal behaviors (e.g., verbal insults and destruction of property) between the two groups during the competitive conditions and reduction of those negative behaviors during subsequent cooperative conditions. However, the negative interpersonal behaviors were especially observed directly following the competitive conditions, during which time experimenters deliberately triggered hostile feelings by setting up situations that frustrated the groups. Nevertheless, their study was instrumental in showing that children's social behaviors can be influenced by competitive and cooperative situations.

In fact, some studies examining the associations between competition and sociometric status have suggested that competition is not always linked to discord and dislike. Defining competition as a multidimensional construct (see earlier), Tassi and Schneider (1997) measured 8-year-old children's competitive orientations using peer informant measures. Popular children scored significantly higher on personal development competition than children who were average in peer reputation. Lowest in personal development competition were children who were rejected by their peers. Conversely, rejected children scored significantly higher on hypercompetitiveness. Similar results were also obtained using teacher ratings of competition (Tassi, Schneider, & Richard, 2001). Thus, only hypercompetitiveness seems to lead to peer rejection. Similarly, Japanese adolescents report that competition can lead to closer relationships and higher cohesion in the group, as students sharing the same goal of self-improvement mutually develop each other by competing with each other (Fülöp, 2006).

Some data suggest that participating in cooperative activities can decrease the negative social behaviors manifested by rejected children during peer interaction. Gelb and Jacobson (1988) found that unpopular 9-year-old children were more likely than popular participants to break rules, disrupt play, and appeal to authority, but only during competitive play. During cooperative play, the unpopular children demonstrated fewer of those negative social behaviors and were more accepted by their peers. Popular children also used more socially oriented interventions (e.g., showing agreement or pleasure with one of the group members) when approaching the dyad at play. Differences between groups were much smaller during cooperative play.

These studies suggest that cooperation can have beneficial effects for peer acceptance. This has also been demonstrated elsewhere. Anderson (1985) found that 10- to 15-year-old learning-disabled boys identified a greater number of classmates whom they liked following participation in cooperative-learning activities than before the cooperative situation was set up. In a study by Smith, Boulton, and Cowie (1993), 8- and 9-year-old children participated for one year in either cooperative-learning groups in the classroom or traditional-teaching groups. Although no significant differences were observed in terms of changes in children's sociometric status, an increase in children's "liking" ratings of classmates was noted following participation in the cooperative-learning groups. Thus, participating in cooperative activities may not lead to immediate changes in children's peer status (i.e., a "rejected" child will probably not become "average" or "popular" following cooperation), but may have a more gradual effect on general acceptance among peers. One of the reasons that acceptance may be higher following cooperation is that children seem to manifest more prosocial behaviors, such as asking for and giving reciprocal help, when cooperating (Garaigordobil, Maganto, & Etxeberria, 1996) but more aggressive behaviors when competing (Bay-Hinitz, Peterson, & Quilitch, 1994).

Competition for resources between friends may have destructive consequences for the equity of the relationship, considered by many (e.g., Walster, Walster, & Berscheid, 1978) as an essential characteristic of friendship. Sullivan (1953) proposed that competition between friends may impede intimacy and lead to a breakup in the relationship.

Despite the consistent finding of greater cooperation and less competition between friends than between nonfriends, some competitive children may have many friends. In a study by Steinkamp (1990), preschool children perceived as highly competitive by their teachers were named as friends by their classmates more than low-competitive children. One possible explanation for this finding is that children may compete differently with friends than with nonfriends. There is some empirical evidence of this. For example, Fonzi, Schneider, Tani, and Tomada (1997) observed dyads of 8-year-old friends and nonfriends engaged in a car race competition with clear prestated rules. During the competition, dyads of friends showed greater positive affect and greater adherence to the rules than did dyads of nonfriends.

The implications of competition for friendship may depend strongly on both gender and culture. Schneider, Woodburn, del Pilar Soteras del Toro, and Udvari (2005) found that some forms of competition indeed enhanced the friendships of early adolescents. Their study was based on the position of Sullivan (1953) that hostile forms of competition between friends in early adolescence would generally destroy their friendship. Working with early adolescent samples in Canada, Costa Rica, and Cuba, they found that hypercompetitiveness was linked with conflict between friends, with termination of friendship, and, in general, with less closeness. However, simple enjoyment of competition with a friend and personal development competition were unrelated to friendship continuation. There were important gender and cultural differences in both the levels of competitive behavior and the mediators between competition and friendship continuation. In general, girls were less competitive with their friends than were boys. Path analysis revealed that both closeness and conflict mediated the link between hypercompetitiveness and the continuation of friendship; in other words, hypercompetitiveness led to increased conflict and greater affective distance, which in turn led to the termination of the relationships. Several dimensions of competition, including both personal development competition and hypercompetitiveness, were associated with greater companionship in the friendships of boys, especially in the Canadian sample, but were negative correlates of companionship between female friends.

Schneider, Dixon, and Udvari (2007) explored the implications of competition between friends in highly multicultural urban areas. They compared the interethnic and coethnic friendships of 390 junior high school students in multiethnic neighbourhoods of Montreal and Toronto. Friendship dyads were identified on the basis of reciprocal nomination as close friends. The quality of the friendships was measured by questionnaires completed by both members of each friendship dyad. Coethnic friendships were characterized by greater closeness, more conflict, and greater hypercompetitiveness than interethnic friendships. Coethnic friendships were more likely than interethnic friendships to survive during a 6-month interval. Interethnic friendships that survived after 6 months tended to increase in conflict and hypercompetitiveness. Regardless of sex, friendships characterized by conflict and lacking in overall positive quality were more likely than others to dissolve later in the school year. Regardless of ethnic composition, male friends who enjoyed competing with each other in nonhostile ways tended to maintain their relationships.

In view of such recent data and conceptual advances, contemporary thinking has shifted toward a more balanced approach in which the socially competent child is seen as one who can shift appropriately between competition and cooperation, rather than someone who always cooperates. Competence means knowing how to compete where the setting dictates it, but in a way that generates enjoyment, fun, enthusiasm, and interest among the others involved in the situation (Bukowski, 2003; Green & Rachis, 2006).

Ideas for New Research

In many of the earlier studies reviewed here, researchers investigated global and diametrical distinctions between competitive and cooperative behaviors. Throughout our exploration of developmental, gender, and cultural differences, we have highlighted studies in which more sophisticated, complex, multidimensional models of competition and cooperation have been tested. These studies have often illustrated the importance of balancing competitive and cooperative behaviors and of balancing competitive and cooperative goal structures in children's learning and social environments. If researchers recognize the complex nature of these constructs and their dynamic interplay, they can profitably proceed to explore the individual and social psychological factors that might influence children's competence in being both good cooperators and good competitors where and when either or both strategies are called for.

References

Anderson, M. A. (1985). Cooperative group tasks and their relationship to peer acceptance and cooperation. *Journal of Learning Disabilities, 18*, 83–86.

Archer, J. (2006). Cross-cultural differences in physical aggression between partners: A social-role analysis. *Personality and Social Psychology Review, 10*, 13–153.

Archer, J., & Coyne, S. M. (2005). An integrated review of indirect, relational, and social aggression. *Personality and Social Psychology Review, 9*, 212–230.

Bay-Hinitz, A. K., Peterson, R. F., & Quilitch, H. R. (1994). Cooperative games: A way to modify aggressive and cooperative behaviors in young children. *Journal of Applied Behavior Analysis, 27*, 435–446.

Benenson, J. F., Apostoleris, N. H., & Parnass, J. (1998). The organization of children's same-sex peer relationships. In W. M. Bukowski & A. H. Cillessen (Eds.), *Sociometry then and now: Building on six decades of measuring children's experiences with the peer group* (pp. 5–24). San Francisco: Jossey-Bass.

Benenson, J. F., Nicholson, C., Waite, R., Roy, R., & Simpson, A. (2001). The influence of group size on children's competitive behavior. *Child Development, 72*, 921–928.

Bjorkqvist, K. (1994). Sex differences in physical, verbal and indirect aggression: A review of recent research. *Sex Roles, 30*, 177–188.

Bukowski, W. M. (2003). What does it mean to say that aggressive children are competent or incompetent? *Merrill-Palmer Quarterly, 49*, 390–400.

Butler, R. (1990). The effects of mastery and competitive conditions on self-assessment at different ages. *Child Development, 61*, 201–210.

Butt, D. S. (1987). *Psychology of sport: The behavior, motivation, personality, and performance of athletes*. New York: Van Nostrand Reinhold.

Campbell, A. (1999). Staying alive: Evolution, culture, and women's intra-sexual aggression. *Behavioral and Brain Sciences, 22*, 203–252.

Campbell, A. (2004). Female competition: Causes, constraints, content, and contexts. *Journal of Sex Research, 41*, 16–26.

Charlesworth, W. R. (1996). Co-operation and competition: Contributions to an evolutionary and developmental model. *International Journal of Behavioral Development, 19*, 25–39.

Charlesworth, W. R., & LaFreniere, P. J. (1983). Dominance, friendship, and resource utilization in preschool children's groups. *Ethology and Sociobiology, 4*, 175–186.

Cronin, C. C. (1986). Female behavior in mixed-sex competition: A review of the literature. *Developmental Review, 6*, 278–299.

Deci, E. L., & Ryan, R. M. (1985). *Intrinsic motivation and self-determination in human behavior*. New York: Plenum Press.

Domino, G. (1992). Cooperation and competition in Chinese and American children. *Journal of Cross-Cultural Psychology, 23,* 456–467.

Engelhard, G., & Monsaas, J. A. (1989). Academic performance, gender, and the cooperative attitudes of third, fifth, and seventh graders. *Journal of Research & Development in Education, 22,* 13–17.

Epstein, J. A., & Harackiewicz, J. M. (1992). Winning is not enough: The effects of competition and achievement orientation on intrinsic interest. *Personality and Social Psychology Bulletin, 18,* 128–138.

Fonzi, A., Schneider, B. H., Tani, F., & Tomada, G. (1997). Predicting children's friendship status from their dyadic interaction in structured situations of potential conflict. *Child Development, 68,* 496–506.

Foster, W. K. (1984). Cooperation in the game and sport structure of children: One dimension of psychosocial development. *Education, 105,* 201–205.

Fülöp, M. (2004). Competition as a culturally constructed concept. In C. Baillie, E. Dunn, & Y. Zheng (Eds.), *Travelling facts: The social construction, distribution, and accumulation of knowledge* (pp. 124–148). Frankfurt: Campus Verlag.

Fülöp, M. (2006). Versengés a japán iskolában [Competition in the Japanese school]. In J. Gordon Györi (Ed.), *Az oktatás világa Kelet.Ázsiában: Japán és Szingapúr* [Education in East Asia: Japan and Singapore] (pp. 333–364). Budapest: Gondolat Könyvkiadó.

Fülöp, M., Ross, A., Pergar Kuscer, M., & Razdevsek Pucko, C. (2007). Competition and cooperation in schools: An English, Hungarian and Slovenian comparison. In F. Salili & R. Hoosain (Eds.), *Research in multicultural education and international perspective: Vol. 6. Culture, motivation and learning: A multicultural perspective* (pp. 235–284). Greenwich, CT: Information Age.

Garaigordobil, M., Maganto, C., & Etxeberria, J. (1996). Effects of a cooperative game program on socio-affective relations and group cooperation capacity. *European Journal of Psychological Assessment, 12,* 141–152.

Gelb, R., & Jacobson, J. L. (1988). Popular and unpopular children's interactions during cooperative and competitive peer group activities. *Journal of Abnormal Child Psychology, 16,* 247–261.

Graves, N. B., & Graves, T. D. (1984). Preferences for cooperative, competitive and individualistic learning. *Cooperative Learning, 5,* 19–20.

Green, V. A., & Rechis, R. (2006). Children's cooperative and competitive interactions in limited resource situations: A literature review. *Journal of Applied Developmental Psychology, 27,* 42–59.

Grum, D. K., Lebaric, N., & Kolenc, J. (2004). Relation between self-concept, motivation for education and academic achievement: A Slovenian case. *Studia Psychologica, 46,* 105–126.

Handel, S. J. (1989). Children's competitive behavior: A challenging alternative. *Current Psychology: Research and Reviews, 8,* 120–129.

Hayward, R. D., & Kemmelmeyer, M. (2007). How competition is viewed across cultures. *Cross-Cultural Research, 41,* 364–395.

Hom, H. L., Berger, M., Duncan, M. K., Miller, A., & Blevin, A. (1994). The effects of cooperative and individualistic reward on intrinsic motivation. *Journal of Genetic Psychology, 155,* 87–97.

Jacklin, C. N., & Maccoby, E. E. (1978). Social behavior at thirty-three months in same-sex and mixed-sex dyads. *Child Development, 49,* 557–569.

Kagan, S., & Knight, G. P. (1979). Cooperation-competition and self-esteem: A case of cultural relativism. *Journal of Cross-Cultural Psychology, 10,* 457–467.

Kagan, S., & Madsen, M. C. (1971). Cooperation and competition of Mexican, Mexican-American, and Anglo-American children of two ages under four instructional sets. *Developmental Psychology, 5*, 32–39.

Kerns, K. A., & Barth, J. M. (1995). Attachment and play: Convergence across components of parent-child relationships and their relations to peer-competence. *Journal of Social and Personal Relationships, 12*, 243–260.

Knight, G. P., Berning, A. L., Wilson, S. L., & Chao, C. G. (1987). The effects of information processing demands and social-situational factors on the social decision making of children. *Journal of Experimental Child Psychology, 42*, 244–259.

LaFreniere, P. J., & Charlesworth, W. R. (1987). Effects of friendship and dominance status on preschooler's resource utilization in a cooperative/competitive situation. *International Journal of Behavioral Development, 10*, 345–358.

Maccoby, E. E. (1990). Gender and relationships. *American Psychologist, 45*, 513–520.

Maccoby, E. E. (1998). *The two sexes: Growing up apart, coming together*. Cambridge, MA: Harvard University Press.

Madsen, M. C. (1967). Cooperative and competitive motivation of children in three Mexican sub-cultures. *Psychological Reports, 20*, 1307–1320.

Madsen, M. C. (1971). Developmental and cross-cultural differences in the cooperative and competitive behavior of young children. *Journal of Cross-Cultural Psychology, 2*, 365–371.

Markovits, H., Benenson, J., & Dolenszky, E. (2001). Evidence that children and adolescents have internal models of peer interactions that are gender differentiated. *Child Development, 72*, 879–886.

McClintock, C. G., & Moskowitz, J. M. (1976). Children's preferences for individualistic, competitive and cooperative outcomes. *Journal of Personality and Social Psychology, 34*, 543–555.

McClintock, C. G., Moskowitz, J. M., & McClintock, E. (1977). Variations in preferences for individualistic, competitive and cooperative outcomes as a function of age, game class and nursery school children. *Child Development, 48*, 1080–1085.

Mead, M. (Ed.). (1937). *Cooperation and competition among primitive peoples*. New York: McGraw-Hill.

Nicolopoulou, A., Scales, B., & Weintraub, J. (1994). Gender differences and symbolic imagination in the stories of four year olds. In A. H. Dyson & C. Genishi (Eds.), *The need for story: Cultural diversity in classroom and community* (pp. 102–123). Urbana, IL: National Council of Teachers of English.

Owens, L., & Barnes, J. (1982). The relationships between cooperative, competitive, and individualized learning preferences and student's perceptions of classroom learning atmosphere. *American Educational Research Journal, 19*, 182–200.

Pasterski, V., Hindmarsh, P., Geffner, M., Brook, C., Brain, C., & Hines, M. (2007). Increased aggression and activity level in 3- to 11-year-old girls with congenital adrenal hyperplasia (CAH). *Hormones and Behavior, 52*, 368–374.

Piaget, J. (1950). *Pensée biologique, pensée psychologique et pensée sociologique* [Biological thinking, psychological thinking and sociological thinking]. Paris: Presses Universitaires de France.

Roberts, G. C. (1992). Children in competition: A theoretical perspective and recommendations for practice. In A. Yiannakis & S. L. Greendorfer (Eds.), *Applied sociology of sport* (pp. 179–192). Champaign, IL: Human Kinetics Press.

Roseth, C. J., Johnson, D. W., & Johnson, R. T. (2008). Promoting early adolescents' achievement and peer relationships: the effects of cooperative, competitive, and individualistic goal structures. *Psychological Bulletin, 134*, 223–246.

Roy, R., & Benenson, J. F. (2002). Sex and contextual effects on children's use of interference competition. *Developmental Psychology, 38*, 306–312.

Ruble, D. N. (1983). The development of social comparison processes and their role in achievement-related self-socialization. In E. T. Higgins, D. N. Ruble, & W. W. Hartup (Eds.), *Social cognition and social development: A socio-cultural perspective* (pp. 134–157). New York: Cambridge University Press.

Ryckman, R. M., Libby, C. R., van den Borne, B., Gold, J. A., & Lindner, M. A. (1997). Values of hypercompetitive and personal development competitive individuals. *Journal of Personality Assessment, 69,* 271–283.

Sándor, M., Fülöp, M., Berkics, M., & Xie, X. (2003). A megosztó viselkedés kulturális és helyzeti meghatározói magyar és kínai óvodáskorú gyerekeknél [Cultural and situational determinants of sharing behaviour among Hungarian and Chinese preschool children]. *Pszichológia, 27,* 281–310.

Savin-Williams, R. C. (1979). Dominance hierarchies in groups of early adolescents. *Child Development, 50,* 923–935.

Schneider, B. H., Dixon, K., & Udvari, S. (2007). Closeness and competition in the inter-ethnic and co-ethnic friendships of early adolescents in Toronto and Montreal. *Journal of Early Adolescence, 27,* 115–138.

Schneider, B. H., Woodburn, S., del Pilar Soteras del Toro, M., & Udvari, S. J. (2005). Cultural and gender differences in the implications of competition for early adolescent friendship. *Merrill-Palmer Quarterly, 51,* 163–191.

Schopler, J., & Insko, C. A. (1999). The reduction of interindividual-intergroup discontinuity effect: The role of future consequences. In M. Foddy, M. Smithson, S. Schneider, & M. Hogg (Eds.), *Resolving social dilemmas: Dynamic, structural, and intergroup aspects* (pp. 281–293). Philadelphia: Psychology Press.

Sheridan, S., & Williams, P. (2006). Constructive competition in preschool. *Journal of Early Childhood Research, 4,* 291–310.

Sherif, M., Harvey, O. J., White, B. J., Hood, W. R., & Sherif, C. W. (1961). *Intergroup conflict and cooperation: The robber's cave experiment.* Norman: University of Oklahoma Institute of Group Relations.

Shwalb, D. W., & Shwalb, B. J. (1985). Japanese cooperative and competitive attitudes: Age and gender effects. *International Journal of Behavioral Development, 8,* 313–328.

Sidanius, J., Sinclair, S., & Pratto, F. (2006). Social dominance orientation, gender, and increasing educational exposure. *Journal of Applied Social Psychology, 36,* 1640–1653.

Smith, P. K. (1996). Strategies of co-operation: A commentary. *International Journal of Behavioral Development, 19,* 81–87.

Smith, P. K., Boulton, M. J., & Cowie, H. (1993). The impact of cooperative group work on ethnic relations in middle school. *School Psychology International, 14,* 21–42.

Sparkes, K. K. (1991). Cooperative and competitive behavior in dyadic game-playing: A comparison of Anglo-American and Chinese children. *Early Child Development and Care, 68,* 37–47.

Stanne, M., Johnson, D., & Johnson, R. (1999). Does competition enhance or inhibit motor performance: A meta-analysis. *Psychological Bulletin, 125,* 133–154.

Steinkamp, M. W. (1990). The social concomitants of competitive and impatient/aggressive components of the Type A behavior pattern in preschool children: Peer responses and teacher utterances in a naturalistic setting. *Journal of Personality and Social Psychology, 59,* 1287–1295.

Strayer, F. F., & Strayer, J. (1976). An ethological analysis of social agonism and dominance relations among preschool children. *Child Development, 47,* 980–989.

Strein, W. (1986). Sex and age differences in preschool children's cooperative behaviour: Partial support for the Knight/Kagan hypothesis. *Psychological Reports, 58,* 915–921.

Sullivan, H. S. (1953). *The interpersonal theory of psychiatry.* New York: Norton.

Tassi, F., & Schneider, B. H. (1997). Task-oriented versus other-referenced competition. *Journal of Applied Social Psychology, 27,* 1557–1580.

Tassi, F., Schneider, B. H., & Richard, J. F. (2001). Competitive behavior at school in relation to social competence and incompetence in middle childhood. *International Journal of Social Psychology, 14,* 165–184.

Tauer, J., & Harackiewicz, J. (1999). Winning isn't everything: Competition, achievement orientation, and intrinsic motivation. *Journal of Experimental Social Psychology, 35,* 209–238.

Thorkildsen, T. A., & White-McNulty, L. (2002). Developing conceptions of fair contest procedures and the understanding of skill and luck. *Journal of Educational Psychology, 94,* 316–326.

Toda, M., Shinotsuka, H., McClintock, C. G., & Stech, F. J. (1978). Development of competitive behavior as a function of culture, age, and social comparison. *Journal of Personality and Social Psychology, 36,* 825–839.

Underwood, M. K., Scott, B. L., & Galperin, M. B. (2004). An observational study of social exclusion under varied conditions: Gender and developmental differences. *Child Development, 75,* 1538–1555.

Van Avermaet, E. (1996). Cooperation and competition. In A. S. R. Manstead & M. Hewstone (Eds.), *The Blackwell encyclopedia of social psychology* (pp. 136–141). Cambridge, MA: Blackwell.

Verba, M. (1994). The beginnings of collaboration in peer interaction. *Human Development, 37,* 125–139.

Vygotsky, L. S. (1978). *Mind in society: The development of higher psychological processes.* Cambridge, MA: Harvard University Press.

Walster, E., Walster, G., & Berscheid, E. (1978). *Equity: Theory and research.* Boston: Allyn & Bacon.

CHAPTER TWENTY-SIX

Aggression in Children

Sarah M. Coyne, David A. Nelson, and Marion Underwood

Aggression unopposed becomes a contagious disease.

– Jimmy Carter

From the scuffs and skirmishes that can be found on nearly any school playground to the cruelty and anonymity of cyberbullying, aggression is one aspect of child development that cannot be ignored. The primary aim of this chapter is to examine the development of aggression in childhood. The chapter first begins with an overview of definitions. There are many different forms of aggression, and much controversy surrounding what terms to use. Therefore, an understanding of these issues is important before examining the actual development of aggressive behavior. Next, we will provide a developmental view of aggressive behavior and examine the stability of aggression over time. This is followed by an examination of sex differences in aggression, which shows that the stereotype of the "aggressive boy" and the "good girl" is incorrect. We then turn to the consequences of aggressive behavior to demonstrate that aggression hurts not only the victims of the behavior but also the aggressors themselves.

Many different factors contribute to the development of aggressive behavior, much of which are beyond the scope of this chapter. However, the next section of the chapter will examine several areas, namely, biology, parenting and family, the peer context, and the media, all of which have been shown to influence aggressive behavior in children. Understanding the causes and consequences of aggression is not enough; therefore, we will next examine several interventions that have been found to decrease childhood aggression. Finally, we will suggest future directions that may advance our understanding of aggressive behavior in children.

The Wiley-Blackwell Handbook of Childhood Social Development, Second Edition, edited by Peter K. Smith and Craig H. Hart
© 2011 by Blackwell Publishing Ltd.

Definitions of Aggression

What's in a name? That which we call a rose
By any other name would smell as sweet.

– William Shakespeare

Researchers have struggled to agree over how to define aggressive behavior. At a basic level, aggression is usually accepted as having two main qualities: (a) an intent to harm another individual who does not wish to be harmed, and (b) the victim perceives that he or she has been harmed (Harre & Lamb, 1983). In addition, researchers generally agree that it is important to examine both the form and the function of the aggression (see Murray-Close & Ostrov, 2009).

The *function of aggression* refers to the purpose for the harm. Indeed, there appear to be two very different reasons why a child might aggress against someone else (Dodge, 1991). Reactive aggression is typically motivated by anger or hostility and is often a direct response to some perceived threat (e.g., a child pushes another child who has just insulted him). Conversely, proactive aggression is motivated by a desire to achieve a specific goal (e.g., a child pushes another child off the swing in order to obtain the swing). Though some researchers feel that aggression should be examined on a continuum rather than using a categorical approach (Bushman & Anderson, 2001), other research has revealed that proactive and reactive aggression are differentially associated with child outcomes, such as social psychological adjustment (Ostrov & Crick, 2007).

The form that aggression takes is also important, but researchers appear to have particular trouble agreeing on the terminology for these subtypes (Underwood, Galen, & Paquette, 2001). Historically, researchers focused on overt, physical forms of aggression (e.g., hitting, kicking, and biting). Attention to this form of aggression is logical as it is easy to observe, the consequences have a noticeable and immediate impact for the victim, and it can have far-reaching societal implications. Such aggression can be either direct (e.g., punching someone in the face) or indirect (e.g., destroying someone's property). Verbal aggression, defined as using words to hurt another person, can also be direct (e.g., calling someone a mean name) or indirect (e.g., gossiping).

In addition, recent research has identified a type of aggression that is more manipulative and subtle, and can be enacted in a way that does not appear aggressive at all (e.g., spreading rumors or social exclusion). This form of aggression has been called three different names, depending on where the researchers put emphasis. The term *indirect aggression* highlights the circuitous nature of the aggression (Lagerspetz, Bjorkqvist, & Peltonen, 1988). Conversely, the term *relational aggression* focuses on the primary vehicle of harm, namely, relationships (Crick & Gropeter, 1995). Finally, the term *social aggression* highlights the social context (above and beyond relationships) where these types of behaviors thrive (Galen & Underwood, 1997; Underwood et al., 2001). Each of the terms adds something unique to our understanding of this form of aggression (Archer & Coyne, 2005). We will broadly use the term *relational aggression* in the current chapter, but will also delineate this type of behavior by the term used by the authors of each study. Similar to physical aggression, relational aggression can be direct (e.g., telling someone you will not be their friend unless they do what you say) or indirect (e.g., spreading a rumor behind someone's back) (see Nelson, Springer, Nelson, & Bean, 2008).

Physical and relational aggression have been found to vary by gender, follow a different developmental track, and often show different consequences. Accordingly, each subsequent section will be organized by physical and then relational aggression.

Developmental Trends in Aggression

> Growing up is never easy. You hold on to things that were. You wonder what's to come.
> — *The Wonder Years*

Just as different forms characterize aggressive behavior, the developmental trajectories of these forms appear to vary across early and middle childhood. In particular, physical aggression emerges and peaks early in life (around 30 months), long before sufficient verbal skills exist to engage in verbal forms of aggression (Côté, Vaillancourt, Barker, Nagin, & Tremblay, 2007). As children's language skills develop, however, verbal and relational aggression are expected to increase as physical aggression gradually subsides (Cairns, 1979).

This broad developmental characterization is qualified, however, by the observation that children tend to be fairly consistent over time in their manifest aggression (Vaillancourt, Brendgen, Boivin, & Tremblay, 2003). Moreover, relative to physical aggression, the stability of relational aggression has only infrequently been assessed and over shorter time frames (e.g., Côté et al., 2007; Zimmer-Gembeck, Geiger, & Crick, 2005). Yet there is sufficient evidence that both physical and relational forms of aggression tend to be moderately stable over time. Physical aggression may also be more stable than relational aggression (Vaillancourt et al., 2003). Stability suggests that aggression is a persistent trait in many individual children.

Recent research has attempted to better delineate developmental trajectories by assessing how children may be grouped according to differential patterns in their initial levels of aggression and its persistence. For example, when physical and indirect aggression are jointly considered from early to middle childhood, most children (~62%) show decreasing levels of physical aggression and little engagement in indirect aggression. In contrast, about 14% of children show only moderate desistance in physical aggression and rising engagement in indirect aggression. Another 14% engage in high levels of both direct and indirect aggression over time (Côté et al., 2007).

Relational aggression is somewhat unique in that there is substantial variability in how the behavior is manifest across development. In preschool children, relational aggression tends to be overt and unsophisticated, such as when a child directly tells peers that he will not invite them to a birthday party unless they do what is asked. A preschooler's whispering campaign against a peer also tends to happen directly in front of the peer, in immediate response to an issue that has arisen (see Nelson, Robinson, & Hart, 2005, for a recent review of related studies). By middle childhood, relationally aggressive strategies have become more complex as children increasingly take advantage of covert strategies in their bid to damage or manipulate the relationships of others. The overt strategies, such as social exclusion, may also be less direct, such as when a child pretends to not see another child (the target of exclusion). Accordingly, there appears to be a developmental trend toward the use of more indirect relationally aggressive strategies, at least within peer relationships.

Research also shows that gender is an important factor to consider in the course of aggression trajectories. For example, aggression in early childhood is a predictor of engagement in later antisocial behavior for boys but not for girls (Broidy et al., 2003). Another longitudinal study has shown that, from ages 5 to 11, the number of boys who engage in marked levels of physical aggression is stable over time (3.7%), whereas there is a significant decrease in the number of highly physically aggressive girls (from 2.3% to 0.5%; Lee, Baillargeon, Vermunt, Wu, & Tremblay, 2007). In contrast, girls are more likely to increase their use of indirect aggression as physical aggression fades (Côté et al., 2007).

Gender Differences in Aggression

> When guys compete it's overt. You know, ringing a bell with a sledge hammer, loogey chucking, the size of your engine, whatever. But when girls compete … it's art. And Alicia … is an artist.
> — *Drive Me Crazy* (Nicole talking about her best friend's aggressive behavior)

One of the most consistent and robust gender differences in the psychological literature is the finding that boys are more physically aggressive than girls. This result has been found in many different studies under many different conditions. Meta-analyses also confirm that boys use more physical aggression than girls during the preschool, early, and middle childhood ages (Archer, 2004; Card, Stucky, Sawalani, & Little, 2008). Additionally, this gender difference is evident across different socioeconomic groups and cultures (Baumrind, 1971). For example, Archer's meta-analysis found that boys were more physically aggressive than girls in a multitude of cultures, including the United States, India, Japan, Iran, China, Israel, Singapore, Slovenia, and Spain.

Boys are likely more physically aggressive than girls for a myriad of reasons. Apart from biological and size differences, boys are socialized differently than girls concerning aggression. The use of physical aggression by girls is highly discouraged by parents, teachers, and even peers (Crick, 1997). However, aggression by boys is less likely to be sanctioned by those in authority, particularly if the aggression is mild. Many boys are socialized to be "tough"; indeed, in some cultures, boys are sometimes taught that physical aggression is acceptable and even necessary when one's reputation is threatened (Cohen & Nisbett, 1997).

Stereotypically, boys are more aggressive than girls. However, this view has traditionally been built upon physical violence research. When we examine nonphysical forms of aggression, research reveals that girls can be just as aggressive as boys. Originally, girls were hypothesized to be more relationally aggressive than boys for a number of reasons. Girls are more likely than boys to invest and highly value relationships (Maccoby, 1998).

Accordingly, behavior that harms such a commodity would be a particularly effective means of aggression among females (see Crick et al., 1999). Other theories, based on sexual selection, argue that attacks on a girl's sexual behavior and social standing may be an effective way for girls to compete over boys (Artz, 2005). Additionally, relational aggression may offer girls a means to attack while escaping social sanctions regarding female overt aggression (Richardson & Green, 1999).

Though there are strong theoretical reasons why girls might be more relationally aggressive than boys, the evidence for such a gender difference is mixed. Some studies find that girls are more relationally aggressive than boys, some find no gender difference, and some find that boys are more relationally aggressive than girls (e.g. McNeilly-Choque, Hart, Robinson, Nelson, & Olsen, 1996; Ostrov, 2006; Shahim, 2008; Tomada & Schneider, 1997). Two meta-analyses suggest that any gender differences in relational aggression may be dependent on the way relational aggression is assessed and the age of the aggressor.

Archer's (2004) meta-analysis suggests that there are no gender differences in indirect (relational) aggression during early or middle childhood. However, girls may be slightly more relationally aggressive during later childhood and adolescence. Conversely, Card et al. (2008) found that though girls were slightly more indirectly (relationally) aggressive during preschool, early, and middle childhood, this effect was negligible ($d=-.06$).

Gender differences also appeared to depend on type of measurement, though this again differed by meta-analysis. Archer (2004) found that studies employing observational methods showed the largest gender difference, though this accounted for only a very small number of studies. Indeed, Card et al.'s (2008) later analysis found that observational methods did not yield a gender difference in indirect aggression. They did find that parent and teacher reports yielded a significant (though negligible) gender difference; however, these measures are generally less preferred than more objective assessments (Archer & Coyne, 2005).

As a whole, these analyses provide evidence for gender similarity in relational aggression as opposed to a strong gender difference. According to Card et al. (2008), the misperception that girls are more relationally aggressive than boys might be in part a reflection of popular media accounts focusing on gender differences. However, it is important to note that though girls might not use more relational aggression than boys, they are generally more likely to use relational aggression than physical forms (Archer & Coyne, 2005). Most importantly, despite the lack of gender differences found, this research shows the importance of focusing on both boys and girls in our examination of childhood aggression.

Consequences of Aggression in Childhood

> Aggression only moves in one direction – it creates more aggression.
>
> – Margaret Wheatley

Consequences of aggression, both physical and relational, accrue for both the perpetrator and the victim. To begin with, physical maltreatment is concurrently associated with significant adjustment difficulties such as internalizing problems (e.g., anxiety, depression, loneliness, and low self-esteem; Hodges & Perry, 1999; Olweus, 1978), school avoidance (Kochenderfer & Ladd, 1996), and school failure (Olweus, 1978). Victimized children are also likely to be rejected by peers (Perry, Kusel, & Perry, 1988) and to lack friends (Hodges, Malone, & Perry, 1997). Many of these problems endure well into adulthood, particularly because physical victimization is highly stable, with the same children receiving abuse over many years (Olweus, 1978). This stability can be attributed to a reciprocal effect, in that the victimized child's internalizing behaviors and lack of peer acceptance tend to elicit more victimization, which enables further declines in the child's emotional health and peer acceptance (Hodges & Perry, 1999).

Compared to research on physical victimization, research regarding relational, indirect, or social forms of victimization is sparse. Nonetheless, existing studies show widespread difficulties in those who chronically face such victimization, such as peer rejection and susceptibility to internalizing symptoms (depression, loneliness, social anxiety and avoidance, withdrawn behaviors, somatic complaints, and low self-esteem and self-concept; Baldry, 2004; Crick & Grotpeter, 1996; Paquette & Underwood, 1999). Girls are also more likely to be relationally victimized, whereas boys are more likely to be physically victimized (Crick & Bigbee, 1998).

Physical aggression also serves as a significant risk factor for concurrent and future maladjustment in the chronic perpetrator. Boys who engage in chronic childhood physical aggression are far more likely than peers to engage in serious and violent delinquency in adolescence (Nagin & Tremblay, 1999). Notably, this effect remains even when controlling for chronic levels of disruptive childhood behavior, which has long been considered a key predictor of adolescent and adult criminality. Physical aggression is a key predictor of peer rejection (Parker & Asher, 1987) as well as additional maladjustment like internalizing disorders and academic troubles (Conduct Problems Prevention Research Group [CPPRG], 2004).

Similarly, relational aggression is associated with a host of negative outcomes in preschool and middle childhood, such as peer rejection and victimization, internalizing problems, and externalizing difficulties (e.g., Crick, 1997; Crick & Grotpeter, 1995; McNeilly-Choque et al., 1996; Ostrov, 2008). Notably, many of these predictions remain when physical aggression is first taken into account.

The link between forms of aggression or victimization and maladjustment also appears to be moderated, to some degree, by gender of the perpetrator. In particular, evidence suggests that many maladjustment problems appear to be more severe for children who engage in gender nonnormative aggression (physically aggressive girls and relationally aggressive boys; Crick, 1997). Girls also appear to suffer most from relational victimization, whereas boys are most reactive to physical victimization (Crick & Nelson, 2002). This finding is consistent with the fact that girls are more likely to report emotional upset if targeted by a peer's relationally manipulative behavior (Nelson & Coyne, 2009).

Although aggression is generally presumed to be associated with negative outcomes for the perpetrator, recent research also shows that, as early as preschool, some aggressive children find significant social prominence. In particular, studies of sociometric status show that controversial and rejected children engage in the most aggression (Crick & Grotpeter, 1995; Nelson et al., 2005). However, controversial children, by definition, are not universally disliked and also engage in high levels of positive behavior. Accordingly, these children appear to selectively apply aggressive and positive behaviors and thereby avoid full-scale rejection (similar to Hawley's [2003] conceptualization of "bistrategic" controllers). Studies of perceived popularity, a measure of social prominence (the traditional definition of *popularity*), also show, from middle childhood onward, that perceived popular children are often very aggressive (Hoff, Reese-Weber, Schneider, & Stagg, 2009; LaFontana & Cillessen, 2002). Accordingly, some children may consider aggression to be useful in achieving social success. It is unlikely, however, that benefits outweigh the costs, particularly in the long term (Leadbeater, Boone, Sangster, & Mathieson, 2006).

Influences on Childhood Aggression: Biological Factors

> The tendency of aggression is an innate, independent, instinctual disposition in man. ...
> [I]t constitutes the most powerful obstacle to culture.
>
> – Sigmund Freud

Biological factors clearly influence individual differences in physical aggression. Childhood physical aggression is estimated to be 60% heritable (Moffitt, 2005). Genetic vulnerabilities may interact with children's life experiences to predict which children become physically violent. Children abused by their parents are more likely to develop aggressive behaviors if they have low levels of monoamine oxidase A (MAOA), due to a polymorphism on the MAOA gene, than abused children who do not have this polymorphism (Caspi et al., 2002). Genes may also affect the development of aggressive behavior by influencing structural features of the brain. The MAOA polymorphism is associated with reduced volume in the prefrontal cortex and in the amygdala, both of which have been found to be related to antisocial behavior (Raine, 2008). Genes likely also influence individual differences in aggression via temperament, those inherited character traits evidenced early in life (Buss & Plomin, 1984). Several temperamental qualities are associated with emerging aggression in childhood: fearlessness, low effortful control, and irritability (Lengua, West, & Sandler, 1998).

Early evidence also suggests that biological factors also relate to relational aggression. Genetic effects for relational aggression are likely weaker than for physical aggression; in one twin study, social aggression was found to be about 20% heritable (as compared to 50/50% heritability for physical aggression; Brendgen et al., 2005). Relations between temperamental characteristics and relational aggression have been understudied, but one investigation found that lower levels of inhibition predicted being higher on a composite of physical and relational aggression in the elementary grades (Park et al., 2005). Physiological reactivity may also relate to relational aggression. Preschoolers' stress reactivity as measured by rises in cortisol across the day in child care was positively related to relational aggression for both girls and boys (Dettling, Gunnar, & Donzella, 1999). Cardiac reactivity may relate to forms of aggressive conduct differently for girls and boys (Murray-Close & Crick, 2007). For girls only, heightened cardiac reactivity while discussing a relational provocation scenario was related to teacher ratings of relational aggression with peers. In studies with adults, experiencing social exclusion has been found to relate to physical pain, perhaps because responses to social rejection are governed by the same areas of the brain as physical pain (Eisenberger, Lieberman, & Williams, 2003).

Influences on Childhood Aggression: Parenting and Family

Don't worry that children never listen to you; worry that they are always watching you.
– Robert Fulghum

In considering the etiology of physical aggression, parenting and other family factors play a significant role in its development in young children (see Dodge, Coie, & Lynam, 2006, for a recent review). In particular, parental warmth is a key factor in how children are socialized, and a lack thereof is associated with child behavior problems, above and beyond potential biological influences (Caspi et al., 2002). Parental hostility impedes children's self-regulation skills, particularly emotion regulation, and thereby increases the likelihood of externalizing behavior (Eisenberg et al., 2003). Coercive home environments also serve as a training ground, with aggressive children learning through parent–child interactions that aversive behaviors are effective in handling the demands posed by others (Snyder, Reid, & Patterson, 2003). Studies also show a consistent connection between harsh forms of parenting (e.g., spanking) and children's aggressive behavior (Gershoff, 2002). Moreover, abusive parenting is a particularly robust predictor of significant adjustment problems in children (Dodge et al., 2006).

Parent characteristics often contribute to these interpersonal difficulties within the family. Maternal depression, for example, corresponds with less warmth and sensitivity and more punitive parenting (Romano, Tremblay, Boulerice, & Swisher, 2005). Conditions of poverty and lower education levels also tend to exacerbate parental weaknesses and, by extension, physical aggression in children (Côté, Vaillancourt, LeBlanc, Nagin, & Tremblay, 2006). Negative interactions may also exist in other familial contexts, such as the marital relationship. Parents who have serious marital difficulties in turn tend to have children who exhibit high levels of physical aggression during the early years of life (Tremblay et al., 2005).

Theoretical and conceptual models abound to explain the connection between childhood aggression and familial influences. In addition to Patterson's coercion theory, described above (Snyder et al., 2003), several other perspectives enlarge our understanding. Social learning theory (Bandura, 1973), in particular, describes how children may model aggression. Accordingly, parents who spank may expect more aggressive children. Alternatively, the cognitive-contextual framework (Grych & Fincham, 1990) purports that children may differentially experience distress in relation to marital conflict, depending on how the child interprets the conflict and chooses to cope (which may vary by gender and temperament of the child). Moreover, contextual variables tied to marital conflict, such as intensity, content, and whether it is resolved, also inform the child's understanding. Davies and Cummings (1994) alternatively suggested that a child's reaction to marital conflict is more emotional than cognitive. In their emotional security theory, a child's security is derived from the perceived strength of the parental dyad. If the dyad is threatened, emotional security is adversely affected and the child experiences debilitating distress and adjustment problems.

Relatively speaking, research regarding family dynamics and the development of relational, indirect, or social aggression is very sparse, particularly in regard to marital conflict. Extant research shows that marital conflict is predictive of both physical and relational aggression in boys (Hart, Nelson, Robinson, Olsen, & McNeilly-Choque, 1998). Similarly, mothers' negative marital conflict strategies (i.e., stonewalling, triangulation, and verbal and physical aggression) are connected to their daughters' social and physical aggression (Underwood, Beron, Gentsch, Galperin, & Risser, 2008). In contrast, parenting styles and practices have received greater attention. Early work with relational aggression, based on social learning theory, proposed that physical aggression would relate to physical discipline, whereas relational aggression would be modeled after parental psychological control (i.e., parenting practices in which parents seek to manipulate the parent–child relationship in seeking child conformance; Kuppens, Grietens, Onghena, & Michiels, 2009; Nelson, Hart, Yang, Olsen, & Jin, 2006). Some tactics of psychological control, such as love withdrawal, mirror relational aggression in peer relationships. Contrary to expectations, however, some studies find that both coercive and psychological control tend to predict both physical and relational aggression (e.g., Nelson et al., 2006).

In general, negative forms of parenting (e.g., hostility, criticism, intrusiveness, negative affect, and permissiveness) are related to relational aggression in children (see Nelson et al., 2006, and Sandstrom, 2007, for reviews of recent studies). Positive affect and responsiveness, in contrast, are linked to less relational aggression (e.g., Hart et al., 1998). Similar trends emerge in studies of parenting related to indirect aggression (Côté et al., 2007; Vaillancourt et al., 2007).

Influences on Childhood Aggression: The Peer Context

> The ugly reality is that peer pressure reaches its greatest intensity at just the age when kids tend to be most insensitive and cruel.
>
> – Walt Mueller

From the preschool years onward, peers likely exert powerful influence on individual children's physical aggression. Children segregate by gender by the second year of life (Serbin, Moller, Gulko, Powlishta, & Colbourne, 1994), and boys and girls may socialize each other in two different peer cultures (Maccoby, 1998). Time spent playing with same-gender peers in preschool relates to increases in gender-typical behaviors, which for boys means increases in active, rough play (Martin & Fabes, 2001). Even in preschool, young children play with peers who are similar in levels of physical aggression (Snyder, Horsch, & Childs, 1997). Moreover, when boys and girls who are emotionally dysregulated play frequently with other boys, aggressive behavior increases (Fabes, Shepard,

Guthrie, & Martin, 1997). Preschool girls generally desist in physical aggression because they know that girls are not supposed to fight (Giles & Heyman, 2005); they spend their time with other girls who also share this view, and when preschool girls do fight, their aggressive behaviors are less likely to influence peers (Fagot, Leinbach, & Hagan, 1986).

The peer context continues to influence individual differences in physical aggression during middle childhood. First and second graders in classrooms with higher proportions of physically aggressive peers increase in their physical aggression across time (Kellam, Ling, Merisca, Brown, & Ialongo, 1998). Highly aggressive peers tend to affiliate with one another (Espelage, Holt, & Henkel, 2003). Being a member of a peer group high on physical aggression predicts growth in physical aggression from late middle childhood through early adolescence, and peer socialization is stronger in high-status, visible groups (Ellis & Zarbatany, 2007; Espelage et al., 2003).

Relational aggression is also influenced by the peer context. Deploying relational aggression requires social connections and peer involvement, and is related to qualities of friendships and social groups. Children report that engaging in relational aggression is motivated by the goal of gaining higher status with the peer group, often at the expense of a relationship with a specific peer (Delveaux & Daniels, 2000). Several studies suggest that children with especially intense, close relationships may be at risk for relational aggression. Friendship jealousy explains a large amount of the variance in relational aggression as measured by peer nominations (Parker, Low, Walker, & Gamm, 2005). Highly relationally aggressive children report having close friendships that are higher on intimacy and exclusivity (Grotpeter & Crick, 1996), and growth in intimate self-disclosure predicts growth in relational aggression for girls only (Murray-Close, Ostrov, & Crick, 2007). Just as for physical aggression, having relationally aggressive friends predicts increases in one's use of relational aggression across time, particularly for girls (Werner & Crick, 1999). This is particularly the case if one is part of a group high in status and centrality (Ellis & Zarbatany, 2007). Moreover, highly socially aggressive adolescents are more likely to be central in their social networks in preadolescence, which likely augments their power to exclude and control others (Xie, Swift, Cairns, & Cairns, 2002).

Influences on Childhood Aggression: The Media

> Violence is one of the most fun things to watch.
>
> – Quentin Tarantino

Decades of research have revealed that exposure to violent media can influence the development of aggressive behavior in children (Anderson et al., 2003). Though some children's programs have an educational or prosocial theme (e.g., *Blue's Clues* and *Sesame Street*), others are saturated with violence. For example, as part of the National Television Study, Wilson et al. (2002) found that 99% of children's superhero programs contained violence, and a violent act was portrayed every 4 minutes. Additionally, much of this violence is shown as justified and rewarded, sending the message that violence is acceptable when the cause permits.

Viewing violence in the media can have both a short- and a long-term effect on children's aggression. In the short term, viewing violence can prime a child to behave aggressively in subsequent situations. For example, Josephson (1987) exposed boys to either a violent or a nonviolent movie before they played a game of hockey in the school gym. Boys who viewed the violent movie physically attacked (e.g., hit, pushed, and elbowed) other players significantly more than boys who viewed the nonviolent movie. Exposure to media violence in childhood can also have a substantial impact on the development of aggression in the long term. Huesmann, Moise, Podolski, and Eron (2003) found that young children who viewed a heavy diet of violence on television were more likely to be aggressive during childhood, during adolescence, and in adulthood, even after controlling for initial aggressiveness. Indeed, children are particularly vulnerable to media effects as they are still developing their attitudes and behaviors concerning aggression.

Other research has found that playing violent videogames can also influence the development of aggressive behavior, again in both the short and long term. Working with a sample of 7–11-year-olds, Anderson, Gentile, and Buckley (2007) found that violent videogame play was linked to both concurrent and future (5 months later) levels of physical and verbal aggression. Additionally, these results did not appear to be mediated by child sex, prior aggressiveness, or hostile attribution bias, thereby showing that all individuals can be influenced by playing violent videogames.

Most research has focused on physical forms of aggression, in terms of both exposure to violence in the media and the effect on subsequent aggressive behavior. However, children are also exposed to relational forms of aggression in the media. Linder and Gentile (2009) found that nearly 77% of television programs popular amongst fifth graders contained indirect (relational) aggression. Additionally, Coyne and Whitehead (2008) found that 100% of Disney movies showed some form of indirect aggression. However, both analyses found that, compared to physical aggression in children's programs, indirect aggression is generally portrayed in ways that would be less likely to facilitate imitation, for example by being shown as unjustified or by "bad" characters.

Nonetheless, evidence suggests that being exposed to relational aggression does have an impact on the development of aggression in children. Linder and Gentile (2009) found that exposure to *rewarded* relational aggression on television was associated with increased levels of relational aggression in 10–11-year-olds. Additionally, exposure to rewarded verbal aggression was associated with verbal aggression. These results highlight the importance of examining the contextual features of aggression in the media, as not all portrayals of aggression are likely to influence children in the same manner.

Experimental research with adults has also found evidence for a crossover effect of viewing relational aggression in the media: Depictions of relational aggression can also influence the development of physical aggression (Coyne et al., 2008). This crossover effect has not specifically been examined in children; therefore, it represents one useful avenue of future research. Additionally, all research in this area has focused on short-term effects. Though several longitudinal studies have been conducted on exposure to media violence, none have yet focused on the long-term effect of being exposed to relational aggression in the media. It is likely that exposure to both forms of aggression in the media have a real impact on the development of aggression in childhood and beyond.

Intervention

> When we can lay down our fear and anger and choose responses other than aggression, we create the conditions for bringing out the best in us humans.
>
> – Margaret Wheatley

Researchers and policy makers have made tremendous progress in developing interventions to reduce physical aggression. Discussing these in full is beyond the scope of this chapter, but effective approaches have included stimulant medication (to reduce attention problems, decrease impulsivity, and perhaps increase responsiveness to intervention; Frick, 2001), Parent Management Training (to teach parents to avoid coercive exchanges and to reinforce positive behavior; Patterson, 1982), classroom-based strategies such as the Good Behavior Game (Ialongo et al., 1999), the Providing Alternative Thinking Strategies (PATHS) curriculum (Greenberg & Kusche, 1993), and social-cognitive skills training (such as the Coping Power Program; Lochman & Wells, 2004). One large, comprehensive intervention, the Fast Track program, combined many of the above strategies to promote long-lasting decreases in aggression and antisocial behavior (CPPRG, 2004). A model program developed for youth already in the justice system, Multidimensional Treatment Foster Care (MTFC), reduces antisocial behavior by placing youth with foster parents trained not only to monitor their behavior closely and implement clear consequences for negative behaviors, but also to provide adult mentoring and reinforcement for positive change (Chamberlain, 2003).

All of these approaches have been demonstrated to be effective in reducing aggressive behavior. An analysis of the large Fast Track program found this intervention to be cost-effective for those at highest risk for chronic youth violence (Foster, Jones, & the CPPRG, 2006). Each chronically violent individual is estimated to cost society $1.6–2.3 million. Thus, a prevention program that costs $1,000 per high-risk child would be cost-effective, even if just one of 200 were saved from becoming chronically violent offenders (Dodge, 2008). Yet, policy makers and the public still have not embraced and invested in youth violence prevention, perhaps because we cling to metaphors for youth violence (e.g., the superpredator) that are not supported by research and that have failed to inspire creative, effective attempts at intervention (Dodge, 2008).

To move forward and make real progress in intervening to reduce aggressive behavior in youth, new metaphors may be needed (Dodge, 2008). On the basis of available evidence, Dodge (2008) suggested several promising new frames. One is approaching youth violence in a manner akin to preventive dentistry, with intervention at the community level (antiviolence public service messages in a manner akin to fluoride in the water), prevention at the family level (regular preventive care such as parents seeking assistance with parenting when needed), and daily practices at the individual level (learning and practicing nonaggressive solutions to solving social problems, similar to brushing and flossing). Another is reducing youth violence in the same way that we teach literacy, by making sure children are taught skills in emotional regulation as part of their regular education from the beginning of their school lives. As Dodge (2008) pointed out,

Although our society would not deny a child access to public education and then incarcerate him or her at age 18 for being illiterate, and we would not characterize illiteracy as a moral sin worthy of penance, we fail to see the folly in denying a child access to appropriate instruction and opportunities for self-regulation and then holding him or her responsible for incompetent behavior that results in a violent act in young adulthood. (p. 586)

Only a few intervention programs to reduce relational aggression have been developed or empirically tested (see Young, Boye, & Nelson, 2006, for a thorough discussion of this topic). Ostrov et al. (2009) implemented the Early Childhood Friendship Project, which utilized a variety of age-appropriate activities, including puppet shows and in vivo reinforcement periods to prevent relational aggression in preschool. After a 6-week period, relational aggression and victimization decreased, whereas prosocial behavior increased. In slightly older children, Harris and Bradley (2003) implemented a specific rule in a kindergarten class: "You can't say you can't play." This rule appeared to have a positive effect on the whole class, not just the children who are typically excluded. Another example is the Social Aggression Prevention Program (SAPP), a school-based group intervention consisting of discussion and role playing to increase awareness of social aggression, develop empathy, build positive leadership, and practice positive resolution of social conflicts with an emphasis on the group's responsibility for interrupting the behavior (Capella & Weinstein, 2006). This program randomly assigned fifth-grade girls to either the SAPP or a reading club. The girls who received the SAPP showed improvements in social problem solving, and there was a trend for a reduction in social aggression for those girls initially highest on this behavior. This type of school-based approach holds great promise for reducing relational aggression in the setting where students are often forced to be in close proximity to their tormentors. Strategies from this program, and from other intervention programs, could guide the addition of a relational aggression component to programs designed to reduce physical aggression, and could be helpful for therapeutic foster care programs that now seek to reduce relational aggression as well as other problematic behaviors (Leve, Chamberlain, & Reid, 2005).

Conclusion

Childhood aggression is a problem that will likely not go away anytime soon. As we look to the future, we must work together to discover what factors particularly influence the development of childhood aggression and how best to combat its devastating effects. As highlighted at the beginning of this chapter, Jimmy Carter described aggression as a "contagious disease." As we work together as researchers, parents, and practitioners, there may come a day when we might be able to halt this particular disease in its tracks.

References

Anderson, C. A., Berkowitz, L., Donnerstein, E., Huesmann, L. R., Johnson, J. D., Linz, D., et al. (2003). The influence of media violence on youth. *Psychological Science in the Public Interest, 4*, 81–110.

Anderson, C. A., Gentile, D. A., & Buckley, K. A. (2007). *Violent video game effects on children and adolescents: Theory, research, and public policy.* New York: Oxford University Press.

Archer, J. (2004). Sex differences in aggression in real-world settings: A meta-analytic review. *Review of General Psychology, 8,* 291–322.

Archer, J., & Coyne, S. M. (2005). An integrated review of indirect, relational, and social aggression. *Personality and Social Psychology Review, 9,* 212–230.

Artz, S. (2005). The development of aggressive behaviors among girls: Measurement issues, social functions, and differential trajectories. In D. J. Pepler, K. C. Madsen, C. Webster, & K. S. Levene (Eds.), *The development and treatment of girlhood aggression* (pp. 105–136). Mahwah, NJ: Erlbaum.

Baldry, A. C. (2004). The impact of direct and indirect bullying on the mental and physical health of Italian youngsters. *Aggressive Behavior, 30,* 343–355.

Bandura, A. (1973). *Aggression: A social learning theory analysis.* Englewood Cliffs, NJ: Prentice Hall.

Baumrind, D. (1971). Current patterns of parental authority. *Developmental Psychology, 4,* 1–103.

Brendgen, M., Dionne, G., Girard, A., Boivin, M., Vitaro, F., & Perusse, D. (2005). Examining genetic and environmental effects on social aggression: A study of six-year-old twins. *Child Development, 76,* 930–946.

Broidy, L. M., Nagin, D. S., Tremblay, R. E., Bates, J. E., Brame, B., Dodge, K. A., et al. (2003). Developmental trajectories of childhood disruptive behaviors and adolescent delinquency: A six-site, cross-national study. *Developmental Psychology, 39,* 222–245.

Bushman, B. J., & Anderson, C. A. (2001). Is it time to pull the plug on the hostile versus instrumental aggression dichotomy? *Psychology Review, 108,* 273–279.

Buss, A. H., & Plomin, R. (1984). *Temperament: Early developing personality traits.* Hillsdale, NJ: Erlbaum.

Cairns, R. B. (1979). *Social development: The origins and plasticity of interchanges.* San Francisco: Freeman.

Capella, E., & Weinstein, R (2006). The prevention of social aggression among girls. *Social Development, 15,* 434–459.

Card, N. A., Stucky, B. D., Sawalani, G. M., & Little, T. D. (2008). Direct and indirect aggression during childhood and adolescence: A meta-analytic review of gender differences, intercorrelations, and relations to maladjustment. *Child Development, 79,* 1185–1229.

Caspi, A., McClay, J., Moffitt, T. E., Mil, J., Martin, J., Craig, I. W., et al. (2002). Role of genotype in the cycle of violence in maltreated children. *Science, 297,* 851–854.

Chamberlain, P. (2003). *Treating chronic juvenile offenders: Advances made through the Oregon Multidimensional Treatment Foster Care Model.* Washington, DC: American Psychological Association.

Cohen, J., & Nisbett, R. E. (1997). Field experiments examining the culture of honor: The role of institutions in perpetuating norms about violence. *Personality and Social Psychology Bulletin, 23,* 1188–1199.

Conduct Problems Prevention Research Group (CPPRG). (2004). The effects of the Fast Track program on serious problem outcomes at the end of elementary school. *Journal Clinical Child and Adolescent Psychology, 33,* 650–661.

Côté, S. M., Vaillancourt, T., Barker, E. D., Nagin, D., & Tremblay, R. E. (2007). The joint development of physical and indirect aggression: Predictors of continuity and change during childhood. *Development and Psychopathology, 19,* 37–55.

Côté, S. M., Vaillancourt, T., LeBlanc, J. C., Nagin, D. S., & Tremblay, R. E. (2006). The development of physical aggression from toddlerhood to pre-adolescence: A nation-wide longitudinal study of Canadian children. *Journal of Abnormal Child Psychology, 34,* 71–85.

Coyne, S. M., Nelson, D. A., Lawton, F., Haslam, S., Rooney, L., Titterington, L., et al. (2008). The effects of viewing physical and relational aggression in the media: Evidence for a cross-over effect. *Journal of Experimental Social Psychology, 44*, 1551–1554.

Coyne, S. M., & Whitehead, E. (2008). Indirect aggression in animated Disney films. *Journal of Communication, 58*, 382–395.

Crick, N. R. (1997). Engagement in gender normative versus nonnormative forms of aggression: Links to social-psychological adjustment. *Developmental Psychology, 33*, 610–617.

Crick, N. R., & Bigbee, M. A. (1998). Relational and overt forms of peer victimization: A multiinformant approach. *Journal of Consulting and Clinical Psychology, 66*, 337–347.

Crick, N. R., & Grotpeter, J. K. (1995). Relational aggression, gender, and social-psychological adjustment. *Child Development, 66*, 710–722.

Crick, N. R., & Grotpeter, J. K. (1996). Children's treatment by peers: Victims of relational and overt aggression. *Development and Psychopathology, 8*, 367–380.

Crick, N. R., & Nelson D. A. (2002). Relational and physical victimization within friendships: Nobody told me there'd be friends like these. *Journal of Abnormal Child Psychology, 30*, 599–607.

Crick, N. R., Werner, N., Casas, J., O'Brien, K., Nelson, D., Grotpeter, J., et al. (1999). Childhood aggression and gender: A new look at an old problem. *Nebraska Symposium on Motivation, 45*, 75–141.

Davies, P. T., & Cummings, E. M. (1994). Marital conflict and child adjustment: An emotional security hypothesis. *Psychological Bulletin, 116*, 387–411.

Delveaux, K. D., & Daniels, T. (2000). Children's social cognitions: Physically and relationally aggression strategies and children's goals in peer conflict situations. *Merrill-Palmer Quarterly, 46*, 672–692.

Dettling, A. C., Gunnar, M. R., & Donzella, B. (1999). Cortisol levels of young children in full-day childcare centers: Relations with age and temperament. *Psychoneuroendocrinology, 24*, 519–536.

Dodge, K. A. (1991). The structure and function of reactive and proactive aggression. In D. J. Pepler & K. H. Rubin (Eds.), *The development and treatment of childhood aggression* (pp. 201–218). Hillsdale, NJ: Erlbaum.

Dodge, K. A. (2008). Framing public policy and prevention of chronic violence in American youths. *American Psychologist, 63*, 573–590.

Dodge, K. A., Coie, J. D., & Lynam, D. (2006). Aggression and antisocial behavior in youth. In N. Eisenberg, D. William, & R. M. Lerner (Eds.), *Handbook of child psychology: Vol. 3. Social, emotional, and personality development* (pp. 719–788). Hoboken, NJ: Wiley.

Eisenberg, N., Valiente, C., Morris, A. S., Fabes, R. A., Cumberland, A., Reiser, M., et al. (2003). Longitudinal relations among parental emotional expressivity, children's regulation, and quality of socioemotional functioning. *Developmental Psychology, 39*, 3–19.

Eisenberger, N. I., Lieberman, M. D., & Williams, K. D. (2003, October 10). Does rejection hurt? An fMRI study of social exclusion. *Science, 302*, 290–292.

Ellis, W. E., & Zarbatany, L. (2007). Peer group status as a moderator of group influence on children's deviant, aggressive, and prosocial behavior. *Child Development, 78*, 1240–1254.

Espelage, D. L., Holt, M. K., & Henkel, R. R. (2003). Examination of peer-group contextual effects on aggression during early adolescence. *Child Development, 74*, 205–220.

Fabes, R. A., Shepard, S. A., Guthrie, I. K., & Martin, C. L. (1997). Roles of temperamental arousal and gender-segregated play in young children's social adjustment. *Developmental Psychology, 33*, 693–702.

Fagot, B. I., Leinbach, M. D., & Hagan, R. (1986). Gender labeling and the adoption of sex-typed behaviors. *Developmental Psychology, 22*, 440–443.

Foster, E. M., Jones, D. E., & the Conduct Problems Prevention Research Group. (2006). Can a costly intervention be cost-effective? An analysis of violence prevention. *Archives of General Psychiatry, 63*, 1284–1291.

Frick, P. J. (2001). Effective interventions for children and adolescents with conduct disorder. *Canadian Journal of Psychiatry, 46*, 597–608.

Galen, B. R., & Underwood, M. K. (1997). A developmental investigation of social aggression among children. *Developmental Psychology, 33*, 589–600.

Gershoff, E. T. (2002). Parental corporal punishment and associated child behaviors and experiences: A meta-analytic and theoretical review. *Psychological Bulletin, 128*, 539–579.

Giles, J. W., & Heyman, G. D. (2005). Young children's beliefs about the relationship between gender and aggressive behavior. *Child Development, 76*, 107–121.

Greenberg, M. T., & Kusche, C. A. (1993). *Promoting social and emotional development in deaf children: The PATHS project*. Seattle: University of Washington Press.

Grotpeter, J. K., & Crick, N. R. (1996). Relational aggression, overt aggression, and friendship. *Child Development, 67*, 2328–2338.

Grych, J. H., & Fincham, F. D. (1990). Marital conflict and children's adjustment: A cognitive contextual framework. *Psychological Bulletin, 108*(2), 267–290.

Harre, R., & Lamb, R. (1983). *The encyclopedic dictionary of psychology*. Oxford: Basil Blackwell.

Harris, A. W., & Bradley, K. D. (2003). "You can't say you can't play": Intervening in the process of social exclusion in the kindergarten classroom. *Early Childhood Research Quarterly, 18*, 185–205.

Hart, C. H., Nelson, D. A., Robinson, C. C., Olsen, S. F., & McNeilly-Choque, M. K. (1998). Overt and relational aggression in Russian nursery-school-age children: Parenting style and marital linkages. *Developmental Psychology, 34*, 687–697.

Hawley, P. H. (2003). Strategies of control, aggression, and morality in preschoolers: An evolutionary perspective. *Journal of Experimental Child Psychology, 85*, 213–235.

Hodges, E. V. E., Malone, M. J., & Perry, D. G. (1997). Individual risk and social risk as interacting determinants of victimization in the peer group. *Developmental Psychology, 33*, 1032–1039.

Hodges, E. V. E., & Perry, D. G. (1999). Personal and interpersonal antecedents and consequences of victimization by peers. *Journal of Personality and Social Psychology, 76*, 677–685.

Hoff, K. E., Reese-Weber, M., Schneider, J. W., & Stagg, J. W. (2009). The association between high status positions and aggressive behavior in early adolescence. *Journal of School Psychology, 47*, 395–426.

Huesmann, L. R., Moise, J., Podolski, C., & Eron, L. (2003). Longitudinal relations between children's exposure to television violence and their later aggressive and violent behavior in young adulthood: 1977–1992. *Developmental Psychology, 39*, 201–221.

Ialongo, N. S., Werthamer, L., Kellam, S. G., Brown, C. H., Wang, S., & Lin, Y. (1999). Proximal impact of two first-grade preventive interventions on the early risk behaviors for later substance abuse, depression, and antisocial behavior. *American Journal of Community Psychology, 27*, 599–641.

Josephson, W. L. (1987). Television violence and children's aggression: Testing the priming, social script, and disinhibition predictions. *Journal of Personality and Social Psychology, 53*, 882–890.

Kellam, S. G., Ling, X., Merisca, R., Brown, C. H., & Ialongo, N. (1998). The effect of the level of aggression in the first grade classroom on the course and malleability of aggressive behavior into middle school. *Development and Psychopathology, 10*, 165–185.

Kochenderfer, B. J., & Ladd, G. W. (1996). Peer victimization: Cause or consequence of school maladjustment? *Child Development, 67*, 1305–1317.

Kuppens, S., Grietens, H., Onghena, P., & Michiels, D (2009). Associations between parental control and children's overt and relational aggression. *British Journal of Developmental Psychology, 27*, 607–623.

LaFontana, K. M., & Cillessen, A. H. N. (2002). Children's perceptions of popular and unpopular peers: A multimethod assessment. *Developmental Psychology, 38*, 635–647.

Lagerspetz, K., Björkqvist, K., & Peltonen, T. (1988). Is indirect aggression typical of females? Gender differences in aggressiveness in 11- to 12-year old children. *Aggressive Behavior, 14*, 403–414.

Leadbeater, B. J., Boone, E. M., Sangster, N. A., & Mathieson, L. C. (2006). Sex differences in the personal costs and benefits of relational and physical aggression in high school. *Aggressive Behavior, 32*, 409–419.

Lee, K., Baillargeon, R. H., Vermunt, J. K., Wu, H., & Tremblay, R. E. (2007). Age differences in the prevalence of physical aggression among 5-11-year-old Canadian boys and girls. *Aggressive Behavior, 33*, 26–37.

Lengua, L. L., West, S. G., & Sandler, I. N. (1998). Temperament as a predictor of symptomatology in children: Addressing contamination of measures. *Child Development, 69*, 164–181.

Leve, L. D., Chamberlain, P., & Reid, J. B. (2005). Intervention outcomes for girls referred from juvenile justice: Effects on delinquency. *Journal of Consulting and Clinical Psychology, 73*, 1181–1185.

Linder, J. R., & Gentile, D. A. (2009). Is the television rating system valid? Indirect, verbal, and physical aggression in programs viewed by fifth grade girls and associations with behavior. *Journal of Applied Developmental Psychology, 30*(3), 286–297.

Lochman, J. E., & Wells, K. C. (2004). The coping power program for preadolescent aggressive boys and their parents: Outcome effects at the 1-year follow-up. *Journal of Consulting and Clinical Psychology, 72*, 571–578.

Maccoby, E. E. (1998). *The two sexes: Growing up apart, coming together.* Cambridge, MA: Harvard University Press.

Martin, C. L., & Fabes, R. A. (2001). The stability and consequences of young children's same-sex peer interactions. *Developmental Psychology, 37*, 431–446.

McNeilly-Choque, M. K., Hart, C. H., Robinson, C. C., Nelson, L. J., & Olsen, S. F. (1996). Overt and relational aggression on the playground: Correspondence among different informants. *Journal of Research in Childhood Education, 11*, 47–67.

Moffitt, T. E. (2005). The new look at behavioral genetics in developmental psychopathology: Gene-environment interplay in antisocial behaviors. *Psychological Bulletin, 131*, 533–554.

Murray-Close, D., & Crick, N. R. (2007). Gender differences in the association between cardiovascular reactivity and aggressive conduct. *International Journal of Psychophysiology, 65*, 103–113.

Murray-Close, D., & Ostrov, J. M. (2009). A longitudinal study of forms and functions of aggressive behavior in early childhood. *Child Development, 80*, 828–842.

Murray-Close, D., Ostrov, J. M., & Crick, N. R. (2007). A short-term longitudinal study of growth in relational aggression during middle childhood: Associations with gender, friendship intimacy, and internalizing problems. *Development and Psychopathology, 19*, 187–203.

Nagin, D. S., & Tremblay, R. (1999). Trajectories of boys' physical aggression, opposition, and hyperactivity on the path to physically violent and nonviolent juvenile delinquency. *Child Development, 70*, 1181–1196.

Nelson, D. A., & Coyne, S. M. (2009). Children's intent attributions and feelings of distress: Associations with maternal and paternal parenting practices. *Journal of Abnormal Child Psychology, 37*, 223–237.

Nelson, D. A., Hart, C. H., Yang, C., Olsen, J. A., & Jin, S. (2006). Aversive parenting in China: Associations with child physical and relational aggression. *Child Development, 77*, 554–572.

Nelson, D. A., Robinson, C. C., & Hart, C. H. (2005). Relational and physical aggression of preschool-age children: Peer status linkages across informants. *Early Education and Development, 16*, 115–139.

508 *Sarah M. Coyne et al.*

Nelson, D. A., Springer, M. M., Nelson, L. J., & Bean, N. H. (2008). Normative beliefs regarding aggression in emerging adulthood. *Social Development*, *17*, 638–660.

Olweus, D. (1978). *Aggression in the schools: Bullies and whipping boys.* Washington, DC: Hemisphere.

Ostrov, J. M. (2006). Deception and subtypes of aggression during early childhood. *Journal of Experimental Child Psychology*, *93*, 322–336.

Ostrov, J. M. (2008). Forms of aggression and peer victimization during early childhood: A short-term longitudinal study. *Journal of Abnormal Child Psychology*, *36*, 311–322.

Ostrov, J. M., & Crick, N. R. (2007). Forms and functions of aggression during early childhood: A short-term longitudinal study. *School Psychology Review*, *36*, 22–43.

Ostrov, J. M., Massetti, G. M., Stauffacher, K., Godleski, S. A., Hart, K. C., Karch, K. M., et al. (2009). An intervention for relational and physical aggression in early childhood: A preliminary study. *Early Childhood Research Quarterly*, *24*, 15–28.

Paquette, J. A., & Underwood, M. K. (1999). Young adolescents' experiences of peer victimization: Gender differences in accounts of social and physical aggression. *Merrill-Palmer Quarterly*, *45*, 233–258.

Park, J. H., Essex, M. J., Zahn-Waxler, C., Armstrong, J. M., Klein, M. H., & Goldsmith, H. H. (2005). Relational and physical aggression in middle childhood: Early child and family risk factors. *Early Education and Development*, *16*, 233–256.

Parker, J. G., & Asher, S. R. (1987). Peer relations and later personal adjustment: Are low-accepted children at risk? *Psychological Bulletin*, *102*, 357–389.

Parker, J. G., Low, C. M., Walker, A. R., & Gamm, B. K. (2005). Friendship jealousy in young adolescents: Individual differences and links to sex, self-esteem, aggression, and social adjustment. *Developmental Psychology*, *41*, 235–250.

Patterson, G. R. (1982). *Coercive family process.* Eugene, OR: Castalia.

Perry, D. G., Kusel, S. J., & Perry, L. C. (1988). Victims of peer aggression. *Developmental Psychology*, *24*, 807–814.

Raine, A. (2008). From genes to brain to antisocial behavior. *Current Directions in Psychological Sciences*, *17*, 323–328.

Richardson, D. R.., & Green, L. (1999). Social sanction and threat explanations of gender effects on direct and indirect aggression. *Aggressive Behavior*, *25*, 425–434.

Romano, E., Tremblay, R. E., Boulerice, B., & Swisher, R. (2005). Multilevel correlates of childhood physical aggression and prosocial behavior. *Journal of Abnormal Child Psychology*, *33*, 565–578.

Sandstrom, M. J. (2007). A link between mothers' disciplinary strategies and children's relational aggression. *British Journal of Developmental Psychology*, *25*, 399–407.

Serbin, L. A., Moller, L. C., Gulko, J., Powlishta, K. K., & Colbourne, K. A. (1994). The emergence of gender segregation in toddler playgroups. In C. Leaper (Ed.), *Childhood gender segregation: Causes and consequences* (New Directions in Child Development Vol. 65, pp. 7–18). San Francisco: Jossey-Bass.

Shahim, S. (2008). Sex differences in relational aggression in preschool children in Iran. *Psychological Reports*, *102*, 235–238.

Snyder, J. J., Horsch, E., & Childs, J. (1997). Peer relationships of young children: Affiliative choices and the shaping of aggressive behavior. *Journal of Child Clinical Psychology*, *26*, 145–156.

Snyder, J. J., Reid, J. B., & Patterson, G. R. (2003). A social learning model of child and adolescent antisocial behavior. In B. B. Lahey, T. E. Moffitt, & A. Caspi (Eds.), *The causes of conduct disorder and juvenile delinquency* (pp. 27–48). New York: Guilford Press.

Tomada, G., & Schneider, B. H. (1997). Relational aggression, gender, and peer acceptance: Invariance across culture, stability over time, and concordance among informants. *Developmental Psychology*, *33*, 601–609.

Tremblay, R. E., Nagin, D. S., Séguin, J. R, Zoccolilo, M., Zelazo, P. D., Boivin, M., et al. (2005). Physical aggression during early childhood: Trajectories and predictors. *Canadian Child and Adolescent Psychiatry Review, 14,* 3–9.

Underwood, M. K., Beron, K. J., Gentsch, J. K., Galperin, M. B., & Risser, S. D. (2008). Family correlates of children's social and physical aggression with peers: Negative interparental conflict strategies and parenting styles. *International Journal of Behavioral Development, 32,* 549–562.

Underwood, M. K., Galen, B. R., & Paquette, J. A. (2001). Top ten methodological challenges for understanding gender and aggression: Why can't we all just get along? *Social Development, 10,* 248–267.

Vaillancourt, T., Brendgen, M., Boivin, M., & Tremblay, R. E. (2003). A longitudinal confirmatory factor analysis of indirect and physical aggression: Evidence of two factors over time? *Child Development, 74,* 1628–1638.

Werner, N. E., & Crick, N. R. (1999). Relational aggression and social-psychological adjustment in a college sample. *Journal of Abnormal Psychology, 108,* 615–623.

Wilson, B. J., Smith, S. L., Potter, W. J., Kunkel, D., Linz, D., Colvin, C. M., et al. (2002). Violence in children's television programming: Assessing the risks. *Journal of Communication, 52,* 3–35.

Xie, H., Swift, D. J., Cairns, B. D., & Cairns, R. B. (2002). Aggressive behaviors in social interaction and developmental adaptation: A narrative analyses of interpersonal conflicts during early adolescence. *Social Development, 11,* 205–224.

Young, E. L., Boye, A. E., & Nelson, D. A. (2006). Relational aggression: Understanding, identifying, and responding in schools. *Psychology in the Schools, 43,* 297–312.

Zimmer-Gembeck, M. J., Geiger, T. C., & Crick, N. R. (2005). Relational and physical aggression, prosocial behavior, and peer relations: Gender moderation and bidirectional associations. *Journal of Early Adolescence, 25,* 421–452.

CHAPTER TWENTY-SEVEN

Bullying

Christina Salmivalli, Kätlin Peets, and Ernest V. E. Hodges

Definition and Forms of Bullying

What is bullying?

Peer-to-peer bullying seems to be a universal phenomenon taking place in most school classes across different schools and cultures (Espelage & Swearer, 2004; Schwartz, Chang, & Farver, 2001; Smith et al., 1999). Being bullied was defined by Olweus (1991, p. 43; earlier version from 1978) as "being exposed, repeatedly and over time, to negative actions on the part of one or more other students." Although some researchers have phrased it a bit differently, there are at least three defining characteristics of bullying that seem to be universally accepted: (a) intent to harm, (b) repetition over time, and (c) power differential (i.e., the victim finds it difficult to defend him or herself against the perpetrator). Bullying is thus different from conflicts, quarrels, or fights between two individuals who are equal in terms of psychological or physical strength or social status.

Although all aggressive encounters taking place at school cannot be regarded as bullying, bullying clearly is a subtype of aggressive behavior. *Aggressive behavior* is often defined as behavior directed toward another individual that is carried out with the proximate (immediate) intent to cause harm. In addition, the perpetrator must believe that the behavior will harm the target and that the target is motivated to avoid the behavior (see Bushman & Anderson, 2001, p. 274). Although aggression is often measured in terms of its behavioral manifestation without taking into account the intent of the perpetrator, there is a widely recognized taxonomy based on the function of aggressive behavior. *Proactive aggression* is defined as goal-directed harmful behavior, and it is distinct from

---

The Wiley-Blackwell Handbook of Childhood Social Development, Second Edition, edited by Peter K. Smith and Craig H. Hart
© 2011 by Blackwell Publishing Ltd.

reactive aggression, which is a response to a perceived threat or social provocation (Dodge, 1991). As bullying is typically unprovoked and deliberate, it is considered a subtype of proactive aggression.

Another relevant construct is *victimization.* As victimization refers to being a recipient of any kind of aggressive attacks, it is usually measured without any reference to either repetition or power imbalance. Thus, *victimization* and *being bullied* do not necessarily represent identical constructs. The procedure used in studies on victimization might generate high scores to children who are involved in frequent, reciprocated, symmetrical aggressive encounters, such as fights between two individuals with equal power. The victimization score derived in this way would not necessarily be comparable with one from another study investigating victimization in the sense of being bullied. There is empirical evidence that the overlap between the *being bullied* and *victimization* constructs is only moderate (Schäfer, Werner, & Crick, 2002), the former being a more serious and more harmful phenomenon (Hunter, Boyle, & Warden, 2007).

Traditional and new forms of bullying

Similar to aggressive behavior in general, bullying takes many forms. Early studies on bullying focused on physical (such as hitting, pushing, or kicking) and verbal (such as verbal ridicule, insults, and threats) attacks. The early emphasis on these direct forms of bullying was associated with a strong research focus on boys. Since the late 1980s, research shifted from just examining physical and verbal aggression to studying more subtle forms of aggression. These involve circuitous, often socially manipulative behaviors such as spreading nasty rumors or lies about the target (indirect aggression; Lagerspetz, Björkqvist, & Peltonen, 1988), harming or threatening to harm the target's relationships (relational aggression; Crick & Grotpeter, 1995), or damaging the target's self-esteem or social status by social exclusion or portraying insulting facial expressions and gestures (social aggression; Underwood, Scott, Galperin, Bjornstad, & Sexton, 2004).

The original view of indirect, relational, and social aggression as "female aggression" was supported by studies showing that it was more common among females than among males (Björkqvist, Lagerspetz, & Kaukiainen, 1992; Crick & Grotpeter, 1995). This view has since been challenged, and findings from a recent meta-analysis confirm that gender differences in the use of indirect aggression are negligible (Card, Stucky, Sawalani, & Little, 2008). Even if females do not, after all, seem to be more indirectly aggressive, there is evidence that proportionally girls use indirect forms of aggression more often than direct forms (Salmivalli & Kaukiainen, 2004; Vaillancourt, 2005).

Recently, researchers have started to explore new forms of bullying such as electronic bullying (Raskauskas, 2007) or cyberbullying (Slonje & Smith, 2008). Cyberbullies deliver their harmful acts via electronic communication tools such as mobile phones or Internet web pages. They send hurtful text messages and e-mails to their victims, or they spread insulting material, such as stories, photos, or video clips portraying the victim in embarrassing situations, over the Internet. Although cyberbullying is less frequent than traditional forms of bullying, it has become more widespread with the development of new technologies.

Despite the fact that victimization involving physical violence receives the bulk of media attention, and cyberbullying represents a potential new threat to the well-being of children and youth, these are not the most common manifestations of bullying. Several studies have shown that *the majority of bullying consists of verbal attacks among girls as well as boys* (e.g., Rivers & Smith, 1994).

Assessment of Bullying and Victimization

Questionnaires are the most prevalent way to gather data about bullying and victimization. Usually, children themselves are utilized as informants. Often, children are first provided with a definition of bullying and are then asked to report how frequently they have bullied others or been bullied by others (Solberg & Olweus, 2003). The time span students are asked to think about is often limited to the past couple of months, but it depends on the purpose of the study. For instance, Nishina and Juvonen (2005) utilized daily diaries, asking sixth graders to report – on 4 randomly determined days during a 2-week period – whether they had experienced or witnessed bullying *today*.

In the case of peer reports, children nominate classmates or grade mates who bully others or are victimized by others (Perry, Kusel, & Perry, 1988). Utilizing adults (e.g., parents or teachers) as informants is more common among young children as they sometimes have difficulties responding to questionnaires themselves, but it is relatively rare in middle childhood and afterward.

In addition to assessing each child's tendency to bully others or to be bullied by others, dyadic questions ("Who do you bully/who bullies you"? or "Who bullies whom in your classroom?") have recently emerged in studies of bullying (Rodkin & Berger, 2008; Sijtsema, Veenstra, Lindenberg, & Salmivalli, 2009; Veenstra et al., 2007) as well as studies of aggressive behavior in general (Card & Hodges, 2007, 2010; Peets, Hodges, & Salmivalli, 2008). Dyadic data can shed light on which children form bully–victim dyads, how many perpetrators (or victims) a child has, and what characterizes these dyadic relationships. More importantly, such data open new possibilities for exploring short- and long-term dynamics between the bully and the victim, and in the bullying networks within whole classrooms.

Questionnaires are not the only method to gather data on bullying and victimization. Interviews are often necessary with younger children (Monks, Smith, & Swettenham, 2005), but they can be highly informative with older samples as well. Interviews can, of course, include self-reports, peer reports, as well as dyadic questions.

In addition, direct observations have been utilized in the assessment of bullying. Children's interactions in natural settings (e.g., playgrounds) have been observed and coded by means of videotapes and remote audio recorders (e.g., Pepler & Craig, 1995) as well as by trained observers (Frey et al., 2005). The potential biases influencing self-reports (socially desirable responding) and peer reports (peer reputations that are not based on the child's actual current behaviors) can be avoided with observational methods. On the other hand, observations are considered difficult and costly. Furthermore, aggressive attacks may be subtle and thus difficult to observe, especially in the case of indirect bullying such as rumor spreading or social exclusion.

The debate concerning the most reliable and valid method for the assessment of bullying and victimization has mainly concentrated on whether to use self-reports versus peer reports. There are arguments in favor of both methods. From middle childhood onward, peer reports are considered highly reliable (Ladd & Kochenderfer-Ladd, 2002), as they can be attained from very many classmates who have observed the behavior of the focal child in a wide range of situations. The composite scores based on reports from several peers include little error variance. A drawback is that peer reports disregard the subjective experience of victimization. However, the child's own perception of being victimized is especially associated with a number of intrapersonal problems that could be considered the most detrimental for the individual (Juvonen, Nishina, & Graham, 2001).

Although many studies still utilize a single method, using multiple informants and multiple methods has been called for in the bullying literature (e.g., Pellegrini, 2001). In a study by Ladd and Kochenderfer-Ladd (2002), combining victimization data from different informants (self, peers, parents, and teachers) yielded the best prediction of relational adjustment, such as rejection and loneliness, which speaks in favor of utilizing multiple informants.

Theories to Explain Bullying

Most theoretical accounts of bullying and victimization have focused on explaining individual differences in these behaviors and experiences by searching for possible sources of variance in genetics, attachment history, parenting practices, as well as social cognitive, emotional, and motivational factors. There have also been attempts to understand the function of bullying at the level of the peer group, and to describe how factors at multiple levels interact to influence bullying and victimization.

Can bullying be inherited?

Increasing use of genetically informed data sets in peer relations research has enabled estimating the heritability of peer difficulties, including bullying and victimization. Both have been found to have strong genetic components (Ball et al., 2008; Boivin, 2007; see also Chapter 2, this volume). Moreover, genetic vulnerabilities interact with environmental conditions, meaning that genetically driven dispositions for bullying or victimization are expressed only (or more strongly) in certain environments. For instance, Brendgen et al. (2008) found heritability estimates for physical aggression to be much larger for children with highly aggressive friends (75%) than for children with nonaggressive friends (35%).

Attachment theory

Attachment theory posits that within the relationship with the primary caregiver, the child creates a "working model of self and other(s)," which is later on generalized to other relationships (Bowlby, 1988), including relationships with peers. In this perspective, problematic peer relationships such as bullying others or being victimized could be hypothesized to be a function of insecure attachment history. There is evidence that especially avoidant attachment is related to aggression and preoccupied attachment to victimization (for a review, see Perry, Hodges, & Egan, 2001), whereas children with secure attachments are likely to avoid both aggressor and victim roles (Troy & Sroufe, 1987). These influences can be seen as mediated by social cognitions and behaviors that generalize from the child–caregiver relationship to peer relationships (Perry et al., 2001).

Parenting

As certain parenting practices are known to be associated with the risk for developing aggressive behavior, they have been used to explain the bullying type of aggression as well (for a review, see Curtner-Smith, Smith, & Porter, 2010). The hypothesized predictors of the proactive, bullying type of aggression include lack of parental monitoring, not being sanctioned (or even being rewarded) for the use of aggression, as well as observing aggressive models in the environment (Dodge, 1991). Many such effects are thought to be mediated via social cognitive processes. Children might learn in the home environment that aggression is an effective way to get what they want, and they continue using coercive strategies within the peer context.

Parental correlates of victimization seem to vary by child gender. Parenting styles that hinder the development of autonomy or encourage expressions of fear and anxiety have been assumed to increase victimization risk, especially among boys (Curtner-Smith et al., 2010; Perry et al., 2001). It might be adaptive to express insecurity to caregivers in order to get support, but such behaviors might be sanctioned by the male peer group (Finnegan, Hodges, & Perry, 1998). Among girls, on the other hand, it has been assumed that especially maternal disinterest and rejection are likely to make girls vulnerable to victimization by impeding the development of competency to connect to significant others – the major social competency among girls.

Social cognitive theories

According to social information processing and social cognitive learning theories, social behavior is affected by how children construe the social world around them. In the social information processing (SIP) model (Crick & Dodge, 1994), social behavior is seen as a consequence of several mental processes, such as encoding and interpreting cues, forming goals, accessing possible behavioral responses from memory, evaluating possible outcomes for the selected behavioral responses, and choosing the most effective one. Several studies have shown that aggression, particularly of the reactive type, is associated with a tendency to infer hostility from others in ambiguous situations, whereas proactive aggression is related to the preference of instrumental over relational goals, and to a positive evaluation of aggression (Crick & Dodge, 1996).

According to Bandura's (1986) social cognitive learning approach, self-efficacy beliefs (i.e., a belief in one's own capability to produce a given behavior) and outcome expectations are heavily influential in driving behavior. Children learn to aggress by observing other models successfully using aggressive strategies as a means to achieve desired goals. Studies show that aggressive, and especially proactively aggressive, children are more confident in their ability to aggress (Perry, Perry, & Rasmussen, 1986), and evaluate aggression more favorably in terms of its appropriateness (Erdley & Asher, 1998) and expected consequences (Perry et al., 1986). According to social cognitive learning theory, bullies are likely to attack children who are more likely to provide reinforcement for the bullies' behavior (e.g., showing signs of pain and suffering, and a lack of revenge seeking; Perry et al., 1986).

Goals underlying bullying

As bullying is proactive aggression, which is by definition instrumental or goal-directed behavior, a natural question to ask is "What motivates the bully?" It has been suggested that the reason for bullying behavior might be to establish, demonstrate, and maintain a high status or a dominant position in the peer group (Pellegrini & Long, 2002; Salmivalli, 2010; Salmivalli & Peets, 2009; Veenstra et al., 2007). Such a position, in turn, provides access to valuable resources such as a toy among young children or heterosexual relationships among adolescents. On the basis of this view, it could be predicted that the bully chooses (a) targets that are relatively powerless and submissive, and (b) situations where other peers are present to witness what happens. Both predictions are supported by empirical findings. Furthermore, studies suggest that bullying can be a successful strategy to meet the goals of status and dominance: It is related to dominance (Pellegrini & Long, 2002) and perceived popularity among peers (Caravita, DiBlasio, & Salmivalli, 2009).

What is the function of bullying for the group?

Some authors have attempted to explain bullying on the basis of its function for the whole peer group, such as a classroom. Bukowski and Sippola (2001) have argued that victimization is "a process by which an individual is forced out of a group because he or she is seen as a threat to the attainment of the group's goals" (p. 363). According to them, all groups have three main goals: cohesion, harmony, and evolution. The victimized individuals are seen as preventing movement toward novelty, and failing to contribute to group cohesion and harmony.

Scapegoating processes have been suggested to underlie bullying. According to Schuster (1999), there is always some tension and hostility in a group, and by bullying one or two innocent group members, this hostility is redirected at them. Victimization of one or two individuals is seen as beneficial for the other group members, because it reduces their risk of being attacked. Thus, every school class has one or two victims serving as scapegoats for the class. Empirical tests of the scapegoat hypothesis (Atria, Strohmeier, & Spiel,

2007; Mahdavi & Smith, 2007) have, however, provided little support for the idea that "every class needs a victim."

Garandeau and Cillessen (2006) suggested that victimization often results from the encounter between a skillful bully and a group that lacks cohesiveness. Bullying is used to provide the group members with a common goal and a sense of cohesion in groups that lack quality friendships and genuine cohesiveness. Juvonen and Galván (2010) also proposed that bullying can promote cohesiveness and conformity within the group. Groups might use bullying to define and maintain the group's norms. Through homophobic bullying, for instance, the group members define gay-like behavior as something *we* do not engage in. Similarly, in groups where less trendy individuals are being harassed, the group creates and enhances the norm of being trendy and good-looking. The group thus defines its identity by drawing boundaries between acceptable and unacceptable attributes and behaviors.

Social ecological or systemic models of bullying

According to the ecological systems perspective, bullying is a systemic problem that has causes at different levels of social reality. Reasons for bullying can be looked for not only in the individual characteristics of the bullies but also in the actions of peers, teachers, and other school personnel; the physical environment; as well as the family, community, and culture (Swearer & Doll, 2001). Many bullying intervention programs share this view and, accordingly, involve intervention components at various levels of social complexity: individuals and their families, school classes, and schools (see Smith, Pepler, & Rigby, 2004; Ttofi, Farrington, & Baldry, 2008). Empirical evidence of the truly influential factors on each of these levels is, however, only beginning to emerge.

Empirical Findings

Prevalence of bullying and victimization

Solberg and Olweus (2003) have argued that providing a definition of bullying and asking a single question regarding the frequency of being the target of bullying leads to valid prevalence estimates that are comparable across classrooms, schools, or countries. According to them, children who report being bullied at least 2–3 times per month should be categorized as victims. The prevalence of bullied children identified using that method varies considerably across countries, from 5% to over 30% in the World Health Organization's Health Behavior in School-Aged Children (HBSC) survey (see Craig & Harel, 2004). It should be noted that comparisons between countries are somewhat problematic, as the concept of *bullying* has different connotations in different languages and cultures (Smith, Cowie, Olafsson, & Liefooghe, 2002). In the HBSC survey, the average prevalence of victims across the 35 countries involved was 11%, whereas bullies represented another 11%. Children who report both bullying others and being bullied by others (i.e., bully-victims) were not identified in the HBSC study, but other studies have shown that by using a similar procedure, approximately 4–6% of the children can be classified as bully-victims (Haynie et al., 2001; Nansel et al., 2001).

Prevalence estimates are influenced by the assessment method (e.g., choice of informant). For instance, when utilizing peer reports, determining the cutoff score (the proportion of peers needed to nominate a child for classification as a *bully* or a *victim*) is difficult and somewhat arbitrary. Self-reports that include several items (tapping different forms of bullying), questions about the frequency, and a clearly defined time frame to consider provide prevalence estimates that are probably most comparable across classrooms, schools, and samples.

Even when bullying is assessed with similar methods, comparisons between different age groups might still be problematic, due to children's changing understanding of bullying (Smith & Monks, 2008). Several studies have shown that self-reported victimization decreases as a function of age. In a large body of nationally representative data from Finland (so-called KiVa data; see Salmivalli, Kärnä, & Poskiparta, 2010a), the prevalence of students who report being victimized "two to three times a month" or more often steadily decreases every year from 23% in the first grade to 8% in the eighth grade. Other studies utilizing self-reports have reported similar findings (Boulton & Underwood, 1992; Olweus, 1991). Interestingly, a similar trend is not necessarily present in peer-reported victimization, as indicated by the Finnish KiVa data (Kärnä, Voeten, Little, et al., in press) as well as a previous study (Salmivalli, 2002). It is thus an unresolved issue: whether victimization really decreases with age as some children succeed in escaping from the victim role (Smith, Shu, & Madsen, 2001), or whether changes in self-reports across age reflect differences in reporting or in thresholds for what is regarded as victimization.

The prevalence of children who bully others does not show a decreasing trend: Children do not just "grow out of it." In the national KiVa data, the frequency of students who self-report bullying others on a regular basis first goes down from 7.2% (grade 1) to 5.6% (grade 4), and then increases again to 7.5% in grade 8. Furthermore, as children get older, students who witness bullying are increasingly more likely to reinforce the bully and less likely to defend the victimized peers (Pöyhönen, Juvonen, & Salmivalli, 2010). This is in line with findings showing that both antibullying attitudes (Salmivalli & Voeten, 2004) and intentions to help the victims (Rigby & Johnson, 2006) decrease as a function of age, at least up to age 15.

Most studies on bullying and victimization have involved school-aged children as participants. Research conducted in preschools and kindergartens shows, however, that the same problems are evident in younger children (Kochenderfer & Ladd, 1996; Monks, Smith, & Swettenham, 2003; Monks et al., 2005). Although bullying behavior seems to be highly stable already among preschoolers, victimization is not (Monks et al., 2003). It is possible that many children are initially attacked by aggressive peers (who might be less selective at a very young age), and the victim role stabilizes during the school years.

Who are bullies, victims, and bully-victims?

Bullies   A glance at some recent titles in the area of bullying, such as "Bullying Is Power" (Vaillancourt, Hymel, & McDougall, 2003), or "It's Easy, It Works, and It Makes Me Feel Good" (Sutton, Smith, & Swettenham, 2001) reveals something about the shift in the way bullying is perceived. For a long time, researchers and practitioners regarded bullies as individuals who lacked social skills and had low self-esteem and low peer status, deficiencies in social information processing, and other adjustment problems. Although many of these factors are associated with aggression in general, or with reactive aggression, there is little empirical support for them being related to bullying specifically.

The view of bullies as socially incompetent was challenged by Sutton, Smith, and Swettenham (1999). They found that 7- to 10-year-old ringleader bullies scored relatively high in tasks designed to assess understanding of others' cognitions and emotions. Accordingly, Kaukiainen et al. (1999) argued that *social intelligence* (e.g., person perception and social flexibility) is a prerequisite for utilizing subtle, indirect forms of aggression such as manipulating others and turning them against the target. In their study, indirect aggression was positively associated with social intelligence after controlling for direct aggression. This is not to say that social intelligence is a prerequisite for bullying, but bullies with person perception and socially flexible skills might be more efficient in their bullying behavior. For instance, they might be better at choosing the "right" victims, or manipulating peers to join them (see Garandeau & Cillessen, 2006). Not all studies have confirmed the view of socially competent bullies. For instance, among 4- to 6-year-old preschoolers, bullies did *not* perform better than other children in social cognitive tasks (Monks et al., 2005). An accurate view of bullies would probably acknowledge their heterogeneity. There is ample evidence, for instance, that bullies and so-called bully-victims are distinct groups with different social cognitive and behavioral profiles.

Research has also shown that proactively aggressive children hold social cognitions that promote the use of aggression as a means to achieve one's goals. For instance, bullies feel confident about using aggression, expect positive outcomes for aggression (e.g., peer approval and tangible rewards), view aggression as an accepted way of behaving, and have an overall positive view regarding the use of aggression (Toblin, Schwartz, Hopmeyer-Gorman, & Abou-ezzeddine, 2005).

In addition, bullies value dominance (Björkqvist, Ekman, & Lagerspetz, 1982) and pursue highly agentic goals, such as being respected and admired by peers (Salmivalli, Ojanen, Haanpää, & Peets, 2005). Bullying seems to be an efficient way to achieve such goals. Even if bullies are not necessarily liked by many classmates, they are often perceived as popular, powerful, and "cool" among their classmates (Caravita et al., 2009; Juvonen & Galván, 2010). This is especially true of bullies who also possess peer-valued characteristics, such as physical attractiveness or a good sense of humor (Vaillancourt & Hymel, 2006). Moreover, bullies are often central members of their peer networks and have friends. They often establish and maintain friendships with other aggressive peers (Salmivalli, Huttunen, & Lagerspetz, 1997) with whom they share the same victims (Card & Hodges, 2006). Such relationships are highly conducive for the mutual reinforcement of coercive behavior.

Although aggression in general is related to peer rejection (especially among young children; see Asher & McDonald, 2008), some studies suggest that even at a very young age, bullies can be relatively popular among their peers. Alsaker and Nägele (2008, p. 238) used the "bus test" to evaluate the popularity of 5- to 8-year-old children according to their role in bullying incidents. Children were shown a picture of a bus on a cardboard and asked, "You are going on a bus trip. Which children from the kindergarten group do you want to take with you?" A child could choose up to six peers from among the photos of children in the group. Bullies received, on average, nominations from 40% of their group mates (which was similar to noninvolved children), whereas victims and those identified as bully-victims received nominations from 24% to 28% of their group mates.

Regarding familial correlates of bullying, Schwartz and colleagues (Schwartz, Dodge, Pettit, & Bates, 1997) provided evidence that bullies (the authors used the label "non-victimized aggressors") might learn to behave aggressively by observing adult conflict and aggression during their preschool years. Bullies also tend to perceive their parents as authoritarian, punitive, and less supportive (Baldry & Farrington, 2000), and they report less cohesiveness to their parents than other children (Bowers, Smith, & Binney, 1994). Rather than having a direct influence, these maladaptive parenting styles can promote the development of proactive aggression through social cognitive processes (e.g., Dodge, 1991). For instance, when children see that their parents get their way by using aggression, they may learn that aggression is an effective means to achieve desired outcomes. Moreover, parenting might, at least partly, influence certain goal orientations, such as valuing admiration and dominance, which in combination with aggression-encouraging cognitions and lack of empathy can result in bullying behavior.

Victims   Bullies do not target all of their classmates with the same probability, but tend to select victims who provide them with easy victories. By choosing victims who are submissive (Schwartz et al., 1998), insecure about themselves (Salmivalli & Isaacs, 2005), physically weak (Hodges & Perry, 1999), and rejected by the peer group (Hanish & Guerra, 2000; Hodges & Perry, 1999), bullies can repeatedly demonstrate their power to the rest of the group and thus renew their high-status position in the group without having to be afraid of confrontation.

In a meta-analytic review, Hawker and Boulton (2000) showed that victimization is associated with a number of psychosocial problems such as depression, loneliness, anxiety, and low social as well as general self-esteem. Card and Hodges (2008) reported numerous personal correlates of victimization such as physical weakness, internalizing and externalizing problems, low levels of prosocial behavior, suicidal ideation, negative self-concept, and low academic achievement. Victimization is also related to numerous interpersonal difficulties such as peer rejection, low peer acceptance, fewer friends, and negative friendship quality. Moreover, the presence of both personal and interpersonal vulnerabilities increases the risk of being victimized (Hodges, Boivin, Vitaro, & Bukowski, 1999; Hodges & Perry, 1999). Thus, a shy and anxious child who is also rejected by classmates or who has no friends serves as an ideal target for the bully, as the likelihood of retaliation from the peer group is very low. Such a situation creates an even larger power imbalance between the bully and the victim. Many of these risk factors can be understood in the light of the bullies' status goals. Children with inter- and intrapersonal difficulties and without any support from the peer group are likely to provide bullies with easy victories and thus increase the likelihood that bullies receive positive outcomes for their aggressive behavior, such as approval by peers.

Bully-victims   Children who have high scores on both bullying and victimization form a group called *bully-victims* (Bowers et al., 1994; Kumpulainen, Räsänen, & Puura, 2001; Salmivalli & Nieminen, 2002). Victims who attack other children have also been identified as *aggressive* or *provocative victims*. Whether these different types of aggressive victims represent overlapping categories or distinct groups is still unclear. However, there is initial evidence for the existence of three groups: (a) passive victims, (b) reactively aggressive victims, and (c) proactively and, to a lesser extent, reactively aggressive victims (Vermande et al., 2007). It might be that the second group represents the provocative victims, whereas the third group consists of children who have been labeled *bully-victims* in the literature.

Differences between aggressive or bully-victims and passive victims can at least partly be traced back to distinct socialization practices. Aggressive or bully-victims come from more punitive, hostile, and abusive families than passive victims (Schwartz et al., 1997). In addition, aggressive or bully-victims report high levels of parental neglect, overprotection (Bowers et al., 1994), and rejection (Veenstra et al., 2005), as well as low levels of parental monitoring and warmth (Bowers et al.,1994; Veenstra et al., 2005). In contrast, passive victims tend to enjoy a more positive home environment than bullies (aggressors) or aggressive or bully-victims (Bowers et al., 1994; Schwartz et al., 1997; Veenstra et al., 2005). However, studies have also indicated that passive victims, especially males, have parents characterized by preoccupied attachment (Finnegan, Hodges, & Perry, 1996) and overprotective parenting (Bowers et al., 1994).

The Contexts of Bullying: Dyadic Relationships and Peer Groups

The dyadic context of bullying

There is growing evidence that children's and adolescents' aggressive behavior is not randomly distributed across peers, but is delivered by and toward specific peers. For instance, Dodge and colleagues (Dodge, Price, Coie, & Christopoulos, 1990) observed playgroups of boys who were unacquainted with each other and found that 50% of all the aggressive acts took place in only 20% of the dyads. They classified the dyads as mutually aggressive when aggression was initiated equally by both members of the dyad, and asymmetric (i.e., a bully and a victim) when one of the boys was much more aggressive than the other. Twelve percent of all dyads were asymmetrically aggressive. These dyads were characterized by high levels of proactive aggression by the bully toward the victim, whereas reactive aggression was more common within symmetrically aggressive dyads (6% of all the dyads). Also, Card, Isaacs, and Hodges (2000) found that especially aggressive nonvictims (who could be considered bullies) were selective in their aggression, delivering their aggression mainly toward children who had a reputation of being victimized. Moreover, not only behaviors but also aggression-encouraging cognitions show target specificity (e.g., Peets, Hodges, Kikas, & Salmivalli, 2007). For instance, self-efficacy beliefs for aggression vary across different targets (Peets et al., 2008), which is likely to influence whom a particular bully selects as a victim.

The involvement of the group

Bullying incidents between two children do not occur in isolation from the larger social context. Peers have been found to be present in most bullying incidents (Hawkins, Pepler, & Craig, 2001). Salmivalli and colleagues (Salmivalli, Lagerspetz, Björkqvist, Österman, & Kaukiainen, 1996) investigated different *participant roles* that children may have in bullying situations (victims, bullies, assistants of bullies, reinforcers of bullies, outsiders, and defenders of the victim) and found that rather than supporting the victim, many children acted in ways that encouraged and maintained bullying. For instance, whereas some children reinforced the bullies' behavior by laughing or cheering, some children supported the bullying behavior by silently witnessing it. In addition, there is evidence that although most children have negative attitudes toward bullying, they seldom support the victim or intervene in bullying incidents (O'Connell, Pepler, & Craig, 1999).

It has been suggested (Juvonen & Galván, 2010) that two motives prevent children from taking sides with the victim. First, children want to improve their own social standing by appearing more like the person in power, and by distancing themselves from the low-status victim. As a consequence, victims tend to get even more rejected over time (Hodges & Perry, 1999). The second motive is self-protection. By siding with the bully, or at least appearing to accept his or her behavior, the child lowers his or her own risk of becoming the next victim (Juvonen & Galván, 2010). Siding with the bully can be adaptive, at least temporarily, for the other group members. In the long run, however, such behavior is likely to maintain bullying and compromise everyone's well-being.

Although individual characteristics, such as attitudes, self-efficacy, and empathy toward victims, can predict which participant role a child has in bullying situations (Caravita et al., 2009; Pöyhönen & Salmivalli, 2008; Salmivalli & Voeten, 2004), the classroom context seems to matter as well. For example, classrooms differ in their levels of reinforcing the bully or defending the victim (Salmivalli & Voeten, 2004). In a recent study, proportions of variance at the classroom level, so-called intraclass correlations, for reinforcing and defending were as high as .19 and .35, respectively (Kärnä, Voeten, Poskiparta, & Salmivalli, 2010). This means that as much as one third of the total variation in defending behavior, for instance, is due to classroom differences. Moreover, the behavior of onlookers does matter. Individual risk factors, such as anxiety and low self-esteem, are more likely to lead to victimization in classrooms where reinforcing is common, whereas the effect of these risk factors is minimized in classrooms with high levels of defending (Kärnä et al., 2010).

An important message from these studies is that in order to reduce victimization, we do not necessarily have to change the victims and make them "less vulnerable." Also, the behavior of the bullies might be almost impossible to change if the peer context is ignored. By influencing the behaviors of the classmates, we can reduce the rewards gained by the bullies and, consequently, lower their motivation to bully in the first place.

Interventions

Interventions against bullying have typically focused on individuals (discussions with specific students), classrooms (curriculum work, and class rules against bullying), or whole schools (developing whole-school policies, peer support schemes, or school tribunals). Also parental support and education have been suggested as ways to prevent bullying and victimization (Curtner-Smith et al., 2010). Among the different approaches, school-based antibullying programs targeting the various systemic levels simultaneously have been most systematically evaluated, with at least six meta-analyses on their effects published so far (Baldry & Farrington, 2007; Ferguson, Miguel, Kilburn, & Sanchez, 2007; Merrell, Gueldner, Ross, & Isava, 2008; Smith, Schneider, Smith, & Ananiadou, 2004; Ttofi et al., 2008; Vreeman & Carroll, 2007). Although average effects of interventions across studies are small, some encouraging findings have emerged. In a recent meta-analysis, Ttofi and colleagues analyzed 30 intervention studies conducted during 1983–2008 and concluded that nine of the programs were *clearly effective* in reducing bullying and victimization.

It seems that school-based programs that target multiple levels of influence (school, classroom, and individual students; Olweus, 1991) or include both universal and indicated actions to tackle bullying (e.g., Salmivalli et al., 2010a; Salmivalli, Kärnä, & Poskiparta, 2010b) can, at best, reduce bullying and victimization by 50% or more. As a recent example, the national KiVa program in Finland not only reduced victimization and bullying substantively but also contributed significantly to increases in antibullying attitudes, more constructive bystander behaviors (e.g., less reinforcing of the bully), as well as increases in school well-being, including perceived class climate and school motivation (Kärnä, Voeten, Little, et al., in press). Due to the huge variation in findings across intervention studies, the critical issues in future research are to find out which elements, or combinations of elements, are most crucial for the success of intervention efforts, under which circumstances the programs are effective, and how the effects unfold.

Acknowledgment

The writing of the present chapter was supported by an Academy of Finland grant (project 121091) to the first author.

References

Alsaker, F., & Nägele, C. (2008). Bullying in kindergarten and prevention. In D. Pepler & W. Craig (Eds.), *Understanding and addressing bullying: An international perspective* (PREVNet Series No. 1, pp. 230–248). Bloomington, IN: AuthorHouse.

Asher, S., & McDonald, K. (2008). The behavioural basis of acceptance, rejection, and perceived popularity. In K. Rubin, W. Bukowski, & B. Laursen (Eds.), *Handbook of peer interactions, relationships, and groups* (pp. 232–248). New York: Guilford Press.

Atria, M., Strohmeier, D., & Spiel, C. (2007). The relevance of the school class as social unit for the prevalence of bullying and victimization. *European Journal of Developmental Psychology*, *4*, 372–387.

Baldry, A. C., & Farrington, D. P. (2000). Bullies and delinquents: Personal characteristics and parental styles. *Journal of Community and Applied Social Psychology*, *10*, 17–31.

Baldry, A., & Farrington, D. (2007). Effectiveness of programs to prevent school bullying. *Victims & Offenders*, *2*, 183–204.

Ball, H. A., Arsenault, L., Taylor, A., Maughan, B., Caspi, A., & Moffitt, T. E. (2008). Genetic and environmental influences on victims, bullies and bully-victims in childhood. *Journal of Child Psychology and Psychiatry*, *49*, 104–112.

Bandura, A. (1986). *Social foundations of thought and action: A social cognitive theory*. Englewood Cliffs, NJ: Prentice Hall.

Björkqvist, K., Ekman, K., & Lagerspetz, K. (1982). Bullies and victims: Their ego picture, ideal ego picture and normative ego picture. *Scandinavian Journal of Psychology*, *23*, 307–313.

Björkqvist, K., Lagerspetz, K., & Kaukiainen, A. (1992). Do girls manipulate and boys fight? Developmental trends in regard to direct and indirect aggression. *Aggressive Behavior*, *18*, 117–127.

Boivin, M. (2007, June 8–10). Five easy pieces about the early development of peer relation difficulties. Paper presented at the Joint Effects Against Victimization conference, Kandersteg, Switzerland.

Boulton, M., & Underwood, K. (1992). Bully/victim problems among middle school children. *British Journal of Educational Psychology*, *62*, 73–87.

Bowers, L., Smith, P. K., & Binney, V. (1994). Perceived family relationships of bullies, victims and bully/victims in middle childhood. *Journal of Social and Personal Relationships*, *11*(2), 215–232.

Bowlby, J. (1988). *A secure base: parent-child attachment and healthy human development*. New York: Basic Books.

Brendgen, M., Vitaro, F., Boivin, M., Bukowski, W., Dionne, G., Tremblay, R., et al. (2008). Linkages between children's and their friends' social and physical aggression: Evidence for a gene-environment Interaction? *Child Development*, *79*, 13–29.

Bushman, B. J., & Anderson, C. A. (2001). Is it time to pull the plug on the hostile versus instrumental aggression dichotomy? *Psychological Review*, *108*, 273–279.

Caravita, S., DiBlasio, P., & Salmivalli, C. (2009). Unique and interactive effects of empathy and social status on involvement in bullying. *Social Development*, *18*, 140–163.

Card, N. A., & Hodges, E. V. E. (2006). Shared targets for aggression by early adolescent friends. *Developmental Psychology*, *42*, 1327–1338.

Card, N. A., & Hodges, E. V. E. (2007). Victimization within mutually antipathetic peer relationships. *Social Development*, *16*, 479–496.

Card, N. A., & Hodges, E.V.E. (2008). Peer victimization among schoolchildren: Correlations, causes, consequences, and considerations in assessment and intervention. *School Psychology Quarterly*, *23*, 451–461.

Card, N. A., & Hodges, E. V. E. (2010). It takes two to fight in school, too: A social relations model of the psychometric properties and relative variance of dyadic aggression and victimization in middle school. *Social Development*, *19*(3), 447–469.

Card, N. A., Isaacs, J., & Hodges, E. V. E. (2000, March). Dynamics of interpersonal aggression in the school context: Who aggresses against whom? Poster symposium conducted at the 8th biennial meeting of the Society for Research on Adolescence, Chicago.

Card, N. A., Stucky, B., Sawalani, G., & Little, T. (2008). Direct and indirect aggression during childhood and adolescence: A meta-analytic review of gender differences, intercorrelations, and relations to maladjustment. *Child Development*, *79*, 1185–1229.

Craig, W., & Harel, Y. (2004). Bullying, physical fighting, and victimization. In C. Currie, C. Roberts, A. Morgan, R. Smith, W. Settertobulte, O. Samdal, et al. (Eds.), *Young people's health in context: International report from the HBSC 2001/02 survey* (WHO Policy Series: Health Policy for Children and Adolescents No. 4, pp. 133–144). Copenhagen: World Health Organization Regional Office for Europe.

Crick, N. R., & Dodge, K. A. (1994). A review and reformulation of social information-processing mechanisms in children's social adjustment. *Psychological Bulletin, 115*, 74–101.

Crick, N. R., & Dodge, K. A. (1996). Social information-processing mechanisms on reactive and proactive aggression. *Child Development, 67*, 993–1002.

Crick, N., & Grotpeter, J. (1995). Relational aggression, gender, and social-psychological adjustment. *Child Development, 66*, 710–722.

Curtner-Smith, M., Smith, P. K., & Porter, M. (2010). Family-level intervention with bullies and victims. In E. Vernberg & B. Biggs (Eds.), *Preventing and treating bullying and victimization* (pp. 75–106). New York: Oxford University Press.

Dodge, K. (1991). The structure and function of reactive and proactive aggression. In D. Pepler & K. Rubin (Eds.), *The development and treatment of childhood aggression* (pp. 201–218). Hillsdale, NJ: Erlbaum.

Dodge, K. A., Price, J. M., Coie, J. D., & Christopoulos, C. (1990). On the development of aggressive dyadic relationships in boys' peer groups. *Human Development, 33*, 260–270.

Erdley, C. A., & Asher, S. R. (1998). Linkages between children's beliefs about the legitimacy of aggression and their behavior. *Social Development, 7*, 321–339.

Espelage, D., & Swearer, S. (2004). *Bullying in American schools: A social-ecological perspective on prevention and intervention.* Mahwah, NJ: Erlbaum.

Ferguson, C., Miguel, C., Kilburn, J., & Sanchez, P. (2007). The effectiveness of school-based anti-bullying programs: A meta-analytic review. *Criminal Justice Review, 32*, 401–414.

Finnegan, R. A., Hodges, E. V. E., & Perry, D. G. (1996). Preoccupied and avoidant coping during middle childhood. *Child Development, 67*, 1318–1328.

Finnegan, R. A., Hodges, E. V. E., & Perry, D. G. (1998). Victimization by peers: Associations with children's reports of mother-child interaction. *Journal of Personality and Social Psychology, 75*, 1076–1086.

Frey, K., Hirschstein, M., Snell, J., Van Schoiack Edstrom, L., MacKenzie, E., & Broderick, C. (2005). Reducing playground bullying and supporting beliefs: An experimental trial of the Steps to Respect program. *Developmental Psychology, 41*, 479–491.

Garandeau, C., & Cillessen, A. (2006). From indirect aggression to invisible aggression: A conceptual view on bullying and peer group manipulation. *Aggression and Violent Behavior, 11*, 641–654.

Hawkins, D., Pepler, D., & Craig, W. (2001). Naturalistic observations of peer interventions in bullying. *Social Development, 10*, 512–527.

Haynie, D., Nansel, T., Eitel, P., Crump, A., Saylor, K., Yu, K., et al. (2001). Bullies, victims, and bully-victims: Distinct groups of at-risk youth. *Journal of Early Adolescence, 21*, 29–49.

Hodges, E. V. E., Boivin, M., Vitaro, F., & Bukowski, W. M. (1999). The power of friendship: Protection against an escalating cycle of peer victimization. *Developmental Psychology, 35*, 94–101.

Hodges, E. V. E., & Perry, D. G. (1999). Personal and interpersonal antecedents and consequences of victimization by peers. *Journal of Personality and Social Psychology, 76*, 677–685.

Hunter, S., Boyle, J., & Warden, D. (2007). Perceptions and correlates of peer-victimization and bullying. *British Journal of Educational Psychology, 77*, 797–810.

Juvonen, J., & Galván, A. (2010). Peer contagion in involuntary social groups: Lessons from research on bullying. In M. Prinstein & K. Dodge (Eds.), *Understanding peer influence in children and adolescents* (pp. 225–244). New York: Guilford Press.

Juvonen, J., Nishina, A., & Graham, S. (2001). Self-views versus peer perceptions of victim status among early adolescents. In J. Juvonen & S. Graham (Eds.), *Peer harassment in school: The plight of the vulnerable and victimized* (pp. 105–124). New York: Guilford Press.

Kärnä, A., Voeten, M., Little, T., Poskiparta, E., Kaljonen, A., & Salmivalli, C. (in press). A large-scale evaluation of the KiVa anti-bullying program. *Child Development*.

Kärnä, A., Voeten, M., Poskiparta, E., & Salmivalli, C. (2010). Vulnerable children in varying classroom contexts: Bystanders' behaviors moderate the effects of risk factors on victimization. *Merrill-Palmer Quarterly, 56*, 261–282.

Kaukiainen, A., Björkqvist, K., Lagerspetz, K., Österman, K., Salmivalli, C., Rothberg, S., et al. (1999). The relationships between social intelligence, empathy, and three types of aggression. *Aggressive Behavior, 25*, 81–89.

Kochenderfer, B., & Ladd, G. (1996). Peer victimization: Manifestations and relations to school adjustment in kindergarten. *Journal of School Psychology, 34*, 267–283.

Kumpulainen, K., Räsänen, E., & Puura, K. (2001). Psychiatric disorders and the use of mental health services among children involved in bullying. *Aggressive Behavior, 27*, 102–110.

Ladd, G., & Kochenderfer-Ladd, B. (2002). Identifying victims of aggression from early to middle childhood: Analysis of cross-informant data for concordance, estimation of relational adjustment, prevalence of victimization, and characteristics of identified victims. *Psychological Assessment, 14*, 74–96.

Lagerspetz, K., Björkqvist, K., & Peltonen, T. (1988). Is indirect aggression typical of females? Gender differences in aggressiveness in 11- to 12-year-old children. *Aggressive Behavior, 14*, 403–414.

Mahdavi, J., & Smith, P. K. (2007). Individual risk factors or school dynamics? An investigation of the scapegoat hypothesis of victimization in school classes. *European Journal of Developmental Psychology, 4*, 353–371.

Merrell, K., Gueldner, B., Ross, S., & Isava, D. (2008). How effective are school bullying interventions? A meta-analysis of intervention research. *School Psychology Quarterly, 23*, 26–42.

Monks, C., Smith, P. K., & Swettenham, J. (2003). Aggressors, victims, and defenders in preschool: peer-, self-, and teacher reports. *Merrill-Palmer Quarterly, 49*, 453–469.

Monks, C., Smith, P. K., & Swettenham, J. (2005). Psychological correlates of peer victimization in preschool: social cognitive skills, executive function, and attachment profiles. *Aggressive Behavior, 31*, 571–588.

Nansel, T., Overpeck, M., Pilla, R., Ruan, W., Simon-Mortton, B., & Scheidt, P. (2001). Bullying behaviors among U.S. youth: Prevalence and association with psychosocial adjustment. *Journal of the American Medical Association, 285*, 2094–2100.

Nishina, A., & Juvonen, J. (2005). Daily reports of witnessing and experiencing peer harassment in middle school. *Child Development, 76*, 435–450.

O'Connell, P., Pepler, D., & Craig, W. (1999). Peer involvement in bullying: Insights and challenges for intervention. *Journal of Adolescence, 22*, 437–452.

Olweus, D. (1978). *Aggression in schools: Bullies and whipping boys.* Washington, DC: Hemisphere.

Olweus, D. (1991). Bully/victim problems among schoolchildren: Basic facts and effects of a school-based intervention program. In D. Pepler & K. Rubin (Eds.), *The development and treatment of childhood aggression* (pp. 411–448). Hillsdale, NJ: Erlbaum.

Peets, K., Hodges, E. V. E., Kikas, E., & Salmivalli, C. (2007). Hostile attributions and behavioral strategies in children: Does relationship type matter? *Developmental Psychology, 43*, 889–900.

Peets, K., Hodges, E. V. E., & Salmivalli, C. (2008). Affect-congruent social-cognitive evaluations and behaviors. *Child Development, 79*, 170–185.

Pellegrini, A. (2001). Sampling instances of victimization in middle school: A methodological comparison. In J. Juvonen & S. Graham (Eds.), *Peer harassment in school: The plight of the vulnerable and the victimized* (pp. 125–146). New York: Guilford Press.

Pellegrini, A. D., & Long, J. D. (2002). A longitudinal study of bullying, dominance, and victimization during the transition from primary school through secondary school. *British Journal of Developmental Psychology, 20*, 259–280.

Pepler, D., & Craig, W. (1995). A peek behind the fence: Naturalistic observations of aggressive children with remote audiovisual recording. *Developmental Psychology, 31*, 548–553.

Perry, D. G., Hodges, E. V. E., & Egan, S. K. (2001). Determinants of chronic victimization by peers: A review and a new model of family influence. In J. Juvonen & S. Graham (Eds.), *Peer harassment in school: The plight of the vulnerable and the victimized* (pp. 73–104). New York: Guilford Press.

Perry, D. G., Kusel, S., & Perry, L. (1988). Victims of peer aggression. *Developmental Psychology, 24*, 807–814.

Perry, D. G., Perry, L. C., & Rasmussen, P. (1986). Cognitive social learning mediators of aggression. *Child Development, 57*, 700–711.

Pöyhönen, V., Juvonen, J., & Salmivalli, C. (2010). What does it take to defend the victimized peer? The interplay between personal and social factors. *Merrill-Palmer Quarterly, 56*, 143–163.

Pöyhönen, V., & Salmivalli, C. (2008). New directions in research and practice addressing bullying: Focus on defending behavior. In D. Pepler & W. Craig (Eds.), *Understanding and addressing bullying: An international perspective* (PREVNet Series No. 1, pp. 26–43). Bloomington, IN: AuthorHouse.

Raskauskas, J. (2007). Involvement in traditional and electronic bullying among adolescents. *Developmental Psychology, 43*, 564–575.

Rigby, K., & Johnson, B. (2006). Expressed readiness of Australian schoolchildren to act as bystanders in support of children who are being bullied. *Educational Psychology, 26*, 425–440.

Rivers, I., & Smith, P. K. (1994). Types of bullying behaviour and their correlates. *Aggressive Behavior, 20*, 359–368.

Rodkin, P. C., & Berger, C. (2008). Who bullies whom? Social status asymmetries by victim gender. *International Journal of Behavioral Development, 32*, 473–485.

Salmivalli, C. (2002). Is there an age decline in victimization by peers at school? *Educational Research, 44*, 237–245.

Salmivalli, C. (2010). Bullying and the peer group: A review. *Aggression and Violent Behavior, 15*(2), 112–120.

Salmivalli, C., Huttunen, A., & Lagerspetz, K. (1997). Peer networks and bullying in schools. *Scandinavian Journal of Psychology, 38*, 305–312.

Salmivalli, C., & Isaacs, J. (2005). Prospective relations among victimization, rejection, friendlessness, and children's self- and peer-perceptions. *Child Development, 76*, 1161–1171.

Salmivalli, C., Kärnä, A., & Poskiparta, E. (2010a). From peer putdowns to peer support: A theoretical model and how it translated into a national anti-bullying program. In S. Jimerson, S. Swearer, & D. Espelage (Eds.), *Handbook of school bullying: An international perspective* (pp. 441–454). New York: Routledge.

Salmivalli, C., Kärnä, A., & Poskiparta, E. (2010b). Development, evaluation, and diffusion of a national anti-bullying program (KiVa). In B. Doll, W. Pfohl, & J. Yoon (Eds.), *Handbook of youth prevention science* (pp. 240–254). New York: Routledge.

Salmivalli, C., & Kaukiainen, A. (2004). "Female aggression" revisited: Variable- and person-centered approaches to studying gender differences in direct and indirect aggression. *Aggressive Behavior, 30*, 158–163.

Salmivalli, C., Lagerspetz, K., Björkqvist, K., Österman, K., & Kaukiainen, A. (1996). Bullying as a group process: Participant roles and their relations to social status within the group. *Aggressive Behavior, 22*, 1–15.

Salmivalli, C., & Nieminen, E. (2002). Proactive and reactive aggression in bullies, victims, and bully-victims. *Aggressive Behavior, 28*, 30–44.

Salmivalli, C., Ojanen, T., Haanpää, J., & Peets, K. (2005). "I'm O.K. but you're not" and other peer-relational schemas. Explaining individual differences in children's social goals. *Developmental Psychology, 41*, 363–375.

Salmivalli, C., & Peets, K. (2009). Bullies, victims, and bully-victim relationships. In K. Rubin, W. Bukowski, & B. Laursen (Eds.), *Handbook of peer interactions, relationships, and groups* (pp. 322–340). New York: Guilford Press.

Salmivalli, C., & Voeten, M. (2004). Connections between attitudes, group norms, and behaviors associated with bullying in schools. *International Journal of Behavioral Development, 28*, 246–258.

Schäfer, M., Werner, N. E., & Crick, N. R. (2002). A comparison of two approaches to the study of negative peer treatment: General victimization and bully/victim problems among German schoolchildren. *British Journal of Developmental Psychology, 20*, 281–306.

Schwartz, D., Chang, L., & Farver, J. (2001). Correlates of victimization in Chinese children's peer groups. *Developmental Psychology, 37*, 520–532.

Schwartz, D., Dodge, K., Hubbard, J., Cillessen, A., Lemerise, E., & Bateman, H. (1998). Social-cognitive and behavioral correlates of aggression and victimization in boys' play groups. *Journal of Abnormal Child Psychology, 26*, 431–440.

Schwartz, D., Dodge, K. A., Pettit, G. S., & Bates, J. E. (1997). The early socialization of aggressive victims of bullying. *Child Development, 68*, 665–675.

Sijtsema, J., Veenstra, R., Lindenberg, S., & Salmivalli, C. (2009). An empirical test of bullies' status goals: Assessing direct goals, aggression, and prestige. *Aggressive Behavior, 35*, 57–67.

Slonje, R., & Smith, P. K. (2008). Cyberbullying: Another main type of bullying? *Scandinavian Journal of Psychology, 49*, 147–154.

Smith, J. D., Schneider, B., Smith, P. K., & Ananiadou, K. (2004). The effectiveness of whole-school anti-bullying programs: A synthesis of evaluation research. *School Psychology Review, 33*, 548–561.

Smith, P. K., Cowie, H., Olafsson, R. F., & Liefooghe, A. (2002). Definitions of bullying: A comparison of terms used, and age and gender differences, in a fourteen-country international comparison. *Child Development, 73*, 1119–1133.

Smith, P. K., & Monks, C. (2008). Concepts of bullying: Developmental and cultural aspects. *International Journal of Adolescent Medicine and Health, 20*, 101–112.

Smith, P. K., Morita, J., Junger-Tas, D., Olweus, D., Catalano, R., & Slee, P. (1999). *The nature of school bullying: A cross-national perspective.* London: Routledge.

Smith, P. K., Pepler, D., & Rigby, K. (2004). *Bullying in schools: How successful can interventions be?* Cambridge: Cambridge University Press.

Smith, P. K., Shu, S., & Madsen, K. (2001). Characteristics of victims of school bullying. Developmental changes in coping strategies and skills. In J. Juvonen & S. Graham (Eds.), *Peer harassment in school: The plight of the vulnerable and the victimized* (pp. 332–351). New York: Guilford Press.

Solberg, M., & Olweus, D. (2003). Prevalence estimation of school bullying with the Olweus bully/victim questionnaire. *Aggressive Behavior, 29*, 239–268.

Sutton, J., Smith, P. K., & Swettenham, J. (1999). Social cognition and bullying: Social inadequacy or skilled manipulation? *British Journal of Developmental Psychology, 17*, 435–450.

Sutton, J., Smith, P. K., & Swettenham, J. (2001). "It's easy, it works, and it makes me feel good": A response to Arsenio and Lemerise. *Social Development, 10*, 74–78.

Swearer, S., & Doll, B. (2001). Bullying in schools: An ecological framework. *Journal of Emotional Abuse, 2*, 7–23.

Toblin, R., Schwartz, D., Hopmeyer-Gorman, A., & Abou-ezzeddine, T. (2005). Social-cognitive and behavioral attributes of aggressive victims of bullying. *Applied Developmental Psychology, 26*, 329–346.

Troy, M., & Sroufe, L. (1987). Victimization among preschoolers: The role of attachment relationship history. *Journal of the American Academy of Child and Adolescent Psychiatry, 26*, 166–172.

Ttofi, M., Farrington, D., & Baldry, A. (2008). *Effectiveness of programs to reduce school bullying: A systematic review* (Report prepared for the Swedish Council for Crime Prevention). Västerås, Sweden: Edita Norstedts Västerås.

Underwood, M., Scott, B., Galperin, M., Bjornstad, G., & Sexton, A. (2004). An observational study of social aggression under varied conditions: Gender and developmental differences. *Child Development, 75*, 1538–1555.

Vaillancourt, T. (2005). Indirect aggression among humans: Social construct or evolutionary adaptation? In R. Tremblay, W. Hartup, & J. Archer (Eds.), *Developmental origins of aggression* (pp. 158–177). New York: Guilford Press.

Vaillancourt, T., & Hymel, S. (2006). Aggression and social status: The moderating roles of sex and peer-valued characteristics. *Aggressive Behavior, 32*, 396–408.

Vaillancourt, T., Hymel, S., & McDougall, P. (2003). Bullying is power: Implications for school-based intervention strategies. *Journal of Applied School Psychology, 19*, 157–176.

Veenstra, R., Lindenberg, S., Oldehinkel, A. J., De Winter, A. F., Verhulst, F. C., & Ormel, J. (2005). Bullying and victimization in elementary schools: A comparison of bullies, victims, bully/victims, and uninvolved preadolescents. *Developmental Psychology, 41*, 672–682.

Veenstra, R., Lindenberg, S., Zijlstra, B. J. H., De Winter, A. F., Verhulst, F. C., & Ormel, J. (2007). The dyadic nature of bullying and victimization: Testing a dual perspective theory. *Child Development, 78*, 1843–1854.

Vermande, M., Aleva, L., Orobio de Castro, B., Olthof, T., Goossens, F., & van der Meulen, M. (2007, June 6). *Victims of bullying in school: Theoretical and empirical indications for the existence of three categories*. Presentation in ORD Dagen, Groningen, the Netherlands.

Vreeman, R., & Carroll, A. (2007). A systematic review of school-based interventions to prevent bullying. *Archives of Pediatrics and Adolescent Medicine, 161*, 78–88.

PART VIII

Cognition, Helping, and Moral Reasoning

Competence in social understanding and social skills are important for individual psychological well-being and peer group adjustment. Although the term *social cognition* implies an understanding of the social world, literature reviewed by Charlie Lewis and Jeremy Carpendale shows that the terminology reflects a far more complicated and diversified construct than what appears at first glance. In order to better understand and negotiate the social milieu, it is also important for children to develop altruistic and moral patterns of social behavior. The first three chapters in this section synthesize the literature in these areas and chart directions for promising new developments in our understanding of social cognition, altruism, and moral reasoning. The final chapter helps us step back and consider how societies are characterized by collections of different social, gender, occupational, political, ethnic, and religious groups. Children glean many of their values that can be translated into more or less altruistic and moral behaviors from these societal institutions that are connected to their immediate settings such as family, neighborhood, and school environments (cf. Bronfenbrenner & Morris, 2006).

To begin this section, in Chapter 28 Charlie Lewis and Jeremy Carpendale illustrate how vastly complex the study of social cognition is. Building upon their chapter from the 2002 edition of this handbook, the authors review more recent research and theory concerning children's social cognitive development. As a backdrop, they reflect upon how much of this work was initially focused on the point at which children master the idea that false beliefs are possible, which was initially accounted for by three theories. These theories came under review with the accumulating evidence of the role that social interaction and language appear to play in social cognitive development. The authors overview general assumptions agreed upon by all three theories that have been critiqued by another group of theories related to social understanding and language. Recently discovered linkages between children's understanding of the mind and other aspects of their social lives are emphasized in this chapter.

Joan Grusec, Paul Hastings, and Alisa Almas focus Chapter 29 on the development of prosocial behavior, which consists of helping, sharing, comforting, defending, and

The Wiley-Blackwell Handbook of Childhood Social Development, Second Edition, edited by Peter K. Smith and Craig H. Hart
© 2011 by Blackwell Publishing Ltd.

making restitution for antisocial behavior. The defining characteristic of prosocial behavior is that it is voluntary and intentional behavior that is enacted to benefit another, without being motivated by the hope of external reward or avoidance of punishment. The authors review how prosocial behavior develops, with insightful overviews of different developmental influences, including evolutionary aspects, genetic underpinnings, and socialization processes within the family. Recent research on maternal, paternal, and sibling influences on prosocial development is considered, as well as the roles that extra-familial influences play, including peers, teachers, media, and culture. The authors also consider recent research on neurophysiological and hormonal underpinnings of empathy and prosocial behavior. Of interest also is the section on relations between prosocial development and antisocial behavior, with recent findings suggesting that promoting early prosocial behavior might prevent or reduce later behavior problems. The chapter wraps up with a discussion of gender differences and ways that a supportive and nurturing parent–child relationship can promote prosocial development in children with weak innate propensities toward empathetic understandings.

Regarding moral development, Charles Helwig and Elliot Turiel begin Chapter 30 by briefly explaining how several disciplines, including philosophy, anthropology, psychology, and sociology, have each brought different perspectives to this area of inquiry. The theories of Piaget and Kohlberg are overviewed and then followed by more recent perspectives that separate the moral domain (issues of harm, fairness, and rights) from the social conventional domain (e.g., organizational rules for dress and conduct). Research indicates that very young children are able to distinguish these domains, but do so in increasingly complex ways over the course of early and middle childhood. How children's actions are actually influenced by their judgments in these domains has been a fruitful area of inquiry. The authors present convincing evidence that how children approach behavioral situations is related to domains of judgment, including those that involve exclusion based on race or gender. They also discuss how religious beliefs affect moral judgments as well as other issues concerning how children develop concepts of autonomy, rights, and democracy in the context of culture.

The discussion of cultural influences by Helwig and Turiel provides a meaningful transition to the final chapter in this section. In Chapter 31, Martyn Barrett and Eithne Buchanan-Barrow treat readers to a discussion of children's understanding of society. As noted earlier, the way children operate in society is based, in part, on their understanding of societal rules and conventions. The authors examine the most significant societal institutions that touch children beyond the family. How children come to understand the social organization of schools, economics, social class, politics, law, ethnic groups, and nationalities is carefully explained from a developmental perspective across the early and middle childhood years. In so doing, the authors draw heavily upon Piagetian perspectives when providing stage-based descriptions of children's understandings of societal phenomena.

Reference

Bronfenbrenner, U., & Morris, P. S. (2006). The bioecological model of human development. In R. M. Lerner (Ed.), *Handbook of child psychology: Vol. 1. Theoretical models of human development* (6th ed., pp. 297–342). Hoboken, NJ: Wiley.

CHAPTER TWENTY-EIGHT

Social Cognition

Charlie Lewis and Jeremy Carpendale

Social cognition refers to the skills we use to think about others and ourselves in psychological terms. It concerns the nature and complexity of our beliefs, intentions, emotions, and desires. The term originated in the study of naïve psychology (Heider, 1958) and covers a range of areas of scholarship, particularly in social psychology (Forgas, 1981). It has also had a continuing link with developmental psychology (Damon, 1978), in which the skills needed for children to become competent in engaging with others are highlighted. Children are embedded in social interaction, and they gradually come to understand human activity in psychological terms.

The importance of how young children come to engage successfully in their social worlds is reflected in the research attention devoted to this topic in developmental psychology. Over the last half century, this interest has been manifest in several different literatures. In the 1970s perspective taking, or role taking, was inspired by Piaget and Inhelder's (1948/1967) three-mountain task, designed to assess children's ability to construct others' differing visual perspectives. School-aged children's understanding of others' differing social perspectives dominated debate until the mid-1980s (e.g., Shantz, 1983). This literature was then eclipsed by what is now known as children's *theories of mind*, which is why this area of scholarship is the focus of wide attention within psychology as a whole. Flavell (1992) has pointed out the continuity between the Piagetian tradition and current approaches.

This chapter is concerned with how children develop social cognition. To cover this vast area of scholarship, we have had to be selective, focusing upon the dominant tradition in this area, which we identified above. In the 2002 edition of this book we narrowed the focus on *theory of mind* given an explosion of research in the 1980s and 1990s. We restricted our analysis to an evaluation of the major theories and some of their main

The Wiley-Blackwell Handbook of Childhood Social Development, Second Edition, edited by Peter K. Smith and Craig H. Hart
© 2011 by Blackwell Publishing Ltd.

criticisms. So extensive has this research tradition become that we have to narrow our analysis in this chapter to focus mainly upon the changes in the literature that have occurred since 2002. Given limited space, we have had to restrict the number of references; readers can download our previous contribution, which serves as a basis of this analysis (see Lewis, n.d.). The aim here will be to summarize a continuing and ever-changing debate and to predict the developments in this field that will occur in the coming years.

Our analysis is split into four main sections. The first introduces the main perspectives in the theory-of-mind literature over the past 20 years (for more extensive reviews, see Carpendale & Lewis, 2006; Doherty, 2008; Moore, 2006), adding what we feel are some important current shifts in each. The major lines of debate in the mainstream of this research have become the source of increasing theoretical analysis, and the rest of the chapter explores alternative evidence and theory. Section 2 explores the role of social processes in the development of social understanding. There are so many social correlates with cognitive tests of children's understanding that many researchers have conceded that we need to reestablish a social cognitive model of social understanding. In the third part, we highlight a recent debate in which authors have focused specifically upon the role of language in this developmental process. The fourth part presents recent theoretical perspectives that base social understanding on what in our original chapter we termed *social and relational aspects* of the child's everyday conduct.

Why Does Theory of Mind Remain a Central Construct in Social Cognition?

Interest in this research area has persisted because it homes in upon some key questions about the human condition, and these have continued to provide stimulating and changing impetus to this area of scholarship. Three are worthy of note here. First, the publication of Premack and Woodruff's (1978) article claiming that chimpanzees have a "theory of mind" stands as a landmark. This article not only stimulated much debate about what makes us human but also raised important questions about the abilities of the higher primates. The ensuing research tradition has continued to provide contradictory evidence. On the one hand, chimpanzees do not show a human form of social understanding: They are as likely to beg from an experimenter with her eyes covered than from an experimenter with her eyes open (Povinelli & Eddy, 1996). However, they do demonstrate a basic ability to orient to one another's perspective to compete for one of two rewards (Tomasello, Call, & Hare, 2003) and demonstrate altruism even when there is no reward for them (Warneken, Hare, Melis, Hanus, & Tomasello, 2007).

Second, Wimmer and Perner's (1983) false belief test became the staple method used in this area of research, following up on the suggestion of three philosophers commenting on Premack and Woodruff's (1978) target article. In their Unexpected Transfer test, a story character, Maxi, ends up with a false belief about the location of his chocolate because he was out of the room when his mother moved it from where he left it to a new location. Child participants who have watched these events unfold are then asked where

Maxi would look for his chocolate or where he would think it is. Although many 5-year-olds realize that Maxi would have an outdated belief and would look in the location where he left it, 3-year-olds tend to fail the test by stating that he would look in the new location. A second common false belief task is known as the Unexpected Contents task (Perner, Leekam, & Wimmer, 1987), in which children are presented with a well-known (e.g., candy) container and asked what they think it contains. Having said "candy," they are then shown that it contains something odd, like a pencil; the child is asked what they thought at first and what their friend would think is in the container. Again, 3-year-olds say that they thought their friend will say that there is a pencil inside, whereas 5-year-olds attribute their prior mental state and others with a false belief. Since then, hundreds of papers have replicated these findings (Wellman, Cross, & Watson, 2001). Yet there is continuing and growing concern that social cognition may not be reducible to an understanding of false beliefs alone (e.g., Astington, 2001), a point we return to later in the chapter.

Third, the publication of the first false belief task coincided with a dramatic increase in cognitive research of the nature of autism (Rutter, 1983). This interest inspired a series of studies finding that children with autism are likely to perform at or below chance on false belief tasks until their verbal age is considerably older than 5 years and/or their chronological age is above 11 (Baron-Cohen, Leslie, & Frith, 1985; Leslie & Frith, 1988). However, there are deep divisions about why such a shift occurs and a growing skepticism about what the term *theory of mind* captures with reference to autism (Rajendran & Mitchell, 2007), and this stems, in part, from a long-standing debate about what the nature of typical development consists of.

We next briefly rehearse the theoretical positions that have dominated our understanding of the development of social cognition.

Three (or four) dominant theoretical perspectives

From the first theoretical analyses of this new area of social cognition (Astington, Harris, & Olson, 1988), interpretations of the shift that occurs in false belief between 3 and 4 years of age have led the discussion. The term *theory of mind* is not just catchy but also captures the dominant account of development. This holds that our own and the child's understanding of mind are theory-like, in so far as we hold a consistent set of principles about the working of the mind; and, like all theories, this changes over time.

Wellman (1990) suggested that a theory must have *coherence* (i.e., it is not just a group of isolated facts); make *"ontological"* distinctions and commitments, like distinguishing mental processes from the physical world; and consist of a *causal-explanatory framework* about how our mental states fit together. According to Wellman and his followers, children grasp desires before beliefs and later more complex emotional states, and this process takes place from ages 2 to 6 (see Wellman, 2002, for a review).

The "theory theory" approach is really two theories. The alternative is that of Perner, who depicted the mind as a system of representations, in which the child starts with a *mentalistic theory of behavior*, where mental states simply reflect the World as it is. At about age 4, they develop a *representational theory of mind*, in which mental states are understood as serving a representational function that can be detached from the World and therefore can be false. Like Wellman, Perner (e.g., Perner, 1991, p. 11) used the metaphor of the child as a scientist, but he emphasizes the intellectual shift of being able to represent the same phenomenon in two different ways.

Opposition to the "child as theoretician" approach(es) came initially from Leslie (1987), who argued that an understanding of mind must be innately specified in a set of discrete mental modules. He argued that we have a specific propensity to understand mental states, called the *theory-of-mind mechanism* (ToMM). Our ability to employ this ToMM can be seen in early pretence play, but is constrained by a gradually developing information-processing device, which he calls the "Selection Processor" (Leslie, 1994). This perspective, usually termed the *Innate Module account*, thus differs from the theory view that the child has to construct an understanding of mental representations.

The second opposition group, led by Johnson (1988) and Harris (2000), suggests that understanding mental states simply involves a capacity for flexibility in one's imagination. Like Leslie, they argued that there are parallels between the 18-month-old's capacity for pretence and the capacity for the 4-year old to imagine another's beliefs. This approach is called *simulation theory*, and it has persisted because it offers a simple account of mental state understanding based on the ability to put oneself into the shoes of the protagonist and reason by analogy.

In our chapter in the first edition, we reported how the 1990s witnessed considerable theoretical debate between the three (or four) main perspectives. This appeared to reach a conclusion that all three factors might well be involved, particularly the combination of theory-like understanding and the imagination (e.g., Carruthers & Smith, 1996). The debate between theory theory and the innate module account has been less conciliatory, with the latter perspective refusing to concede that "theory-like" shifts occur when children pass false belief tests (e.g., Scholl & Leslie, 2001), and the former arguing that the amassed data show a shift that occurs at around age 4 that must be theory like (Wellman et al., 2001). We turn now to examine the development of these debates since 2002.

The reemergence of the main theories of social cognition

What has happened to the main theories? Each has been revitalized in recent years.

Theory theory   Perhaps the least changed has been Wellman's version of theory theory, where the main endeavor has been to consolidate the developmental trajectories of different mental states. In the 1990s his idea that children grasp desires before beliefs was thrown into question, when Chris Moore and his colleagues (1995) devised a "false desires" task in which a protagonist's need differed from the child's in a game. They found that 3-year-olds had as many problems with this task as with false belief. However, more recent research has reasserted the idea that children grasp discrepant desires before they understand false belief (Rakoczy, Warneken, & Tomasello, 2007). In a meta-analysis, Wellman and Liu (2004) confirmed that in 46 experimental manipulations across 16 published papers, children passed tests of desires before beliefs, then knowledge and ignorance, before, finally, false beliefs. They then developed a scale of graded tests in which they confirmed the above sequence and added a task of understanding that people could express one emotion while feeling a very different one, which came last in the sequence.

Although this pattern of findings has been replicated in a very different cultural setting, China (Wellman, Fang, Liu, Zhu, & Liu, 2006), it is hard to distinguish whether children's responses on this set of tests really demonstrate a theory-like progression from the 2-year-old's understanding of desire through to the 6-year-old's grasp of complex emotions. It could well be that the tests impose different general cognitive or linguistic demands on preschoolers and do not therefore reveal the unfolding of theory of mind. It is worth noting in passing that the latest theoretical contribution from a theory theory perspective dismisses the validity of the contribution of developmental psychology to our understanding of minds (Carruthers, 2009).

Representational theory theory Debate about the other "theory theory" has recently hinged upon the relationship between the child's ability to pass false belief tests and his or her performance on a range of more general cognitive skills under the banner of *executive function*. Such skills, including working memory, inhibitory control, and set shifting, involve the ability to impose controls on cognitive processes and choose between alternatives. The evidence suggests that false belief is closely related to these executive functions in Western (e.g., Carlson, Moses, & Breton, 2002; Hala, Hug, & Henderson, 2003; Hughes, 1998a), Asian (Sabbagh, Xu, Carlson, Moses, & Lee, 2006), and South American and African (Chasiotis, Kiessling, Winter, & Hofer, 2006) cultures. Both longitudinal (Hughes, 1998b) and microgenetic (Flynn, O'Malley, & Wood, 2004) studies suggest that executive skills predate social understanding. In particular, there is evidence for a link between inhibitory control (the ability to resist making a prepotent but wrong response, as in following the instruction in the game Simon Says) and mental state understanding (Carlson et al., 2002). The main interpretation of this finding is that executive skills are necessary for the emergence of social understanding.

However, our own work (Oh & Lewis, 2008) does not fully support this view, as Korean preschoolers are advanced in their executive skills, but neither do they show similar advances in their false belief reasoning, nor do our measures of such reasoning regress onto assessments of their executive skills. So, in Korean culture at least, it seems as if the link is neither necessary nor sufficient. But the evidence from training studies suggests that the two sets of skills may be functionally interdependent in Western children. Kloo and Perner (2003) trained children in either false belief understanding or the executive skill of set shifting: in the Dimensional Change Card Sort (DCCS) procedure (Frye, Zelazo, & Palfai, 1995), in which the child has to sort cards by one dimension (e.g., color) and then switch to sorting by another (e.g., shape). Training in one skill led to improved performance on the other. As a result, Perner has broadened his theory to suggest that false belief understanding is intertwined with the ability to grasp that events (Kloo & Perner, 2003) and experiences (Perner, Kloo, & Gornik, 2007) can be "redescribed" in ways in which they were not originally grasped.

Simulation A resurgence of interest in simulation has occurred as a result of the identification of the firing of single "mirror neuron" cells in specific areas of the brain, not only when a macaque monkey performs an act but also when it observes or hears specific gestures (Gallese, Fadiga, Fogassi, & Rizzolatti, 1996). Indeed, only part of an action, like watching someone reaching toward a hidden object, is sufficient to trigger these neurons (Umiltà et al., 2001). This work has led to a dramatic increase in attempts to show parallels in human neural processing. For example, Iacoboni et al. (2005) showed in an fMRI study that specific neural firing occurs when humans observe contextually relevant actions (like a tea set followed by someone reaching for a teacup) and are less in evidence when no such contextual cues are given (someone reaching for the same cup without the contextual cue). Such data have led to a speculation that neurons actually *represent* actions (Metzinger & Gallese, 2003) and provide a new version of simulation theory.

Even though the evidence for a range of mirror neuron skills in humans is mounting, the idea that simulation can be understood at the level of the neuron is still treated with caution by many in the field (Prinz, 2003). Much depends upon what we mean by the term *representation*, and we have argued that there must be a distinction between *information* and *knowledge* (Carpendale & Lewis, 2006). A shopping list is full of information but does not possess *knowledge* of where to buy each item: If psychology is about meaningful human conduct, it cannot be reduced to neurology. Recent simulation accounts make an attempt to relate different levels of experience from the "mirroring" of neurons to higher levels of agency (e.g., Hurley, 2008), but these do not reconcile the information–knowledge divide.

Innate module   This approach has witnessed a resurgence largely because Onishi and Baillargeon (2005) showed that 15-month-olds look longer at an agent's reach that is contrary to what would be expected from her previous actions – for example, to a yellow box after she has placed an object in the green one and the object has moved in her absence. They and others (Leslie, 2005; Surian, Caldi, & Sperber, 2007) interpret such data to suggest that toddlers already possess a "representational theory of mind." Theory theorists interpret these data in simple terms (Perner & Ruffman, 2005) – that the infant does not have a theory, but rather makes simple associations between the agent and the place where she put it. This would allow a more theoretical development 3 years later, as witnessed in passing true (!) "false belief."

In many respects these two accounts simply revisit the theory theory versus innate module accounts of the 1980s. In a critique, Stack and Lewis (2008) raised several cautions about both positions. We argued that results like those of Onishi and Baillargeon (2005) do not necessarily indicate that the child has an innate theory-of-mind skill or that the infant makes simple (nonmental) associations between agents and locations. Rather we suggested that these data can best be explained in terms of infants' experiences of agents' actions and orientations within shared versus nonshared environments. In our empirical work (Stack & Lewis, 2009), we have shown that when the experience is not shared (i.e., false belief), 10-month-olds look longer at an agent's intentional reaches to either location, as opposed to reaches toward the box with the back of the hand, which clearly could not lead to retrieving the object. We replicated the Onishi and Baillargeon effect with shared experience (i.e., true belief) in 10–18-month-olds, but only with intentional false belief reaches at 14 and 18 months. This suggests that we need a theoretical framework in which the infant gradually acquires a grasp of agency through shared interactions, and then generalizes them to nonshared interactions.

Social Understanding and Social Interaction

Although the research on children's social understanding initially focused on the average age of false belief understanding, such averages conceal important individual differences. Gender differences in false belief understanding are rarely found. When differences are found, girls have an advantage (Charman, Ruffman, & Clements, 2002; Hughes & Dunn, 1998), particularly in their understanding of emotions (Kuebli, Butler, & Fivush, 1995). However, what is of more interest are the range of social factors that are associated with children's advanced social understanding. Figure 28.1 shows just how many correlates are involved (a full account of these factors can be found in Carpendale & Lewis, 2006, Chap. 6). Our goal in presenting some of these correlates is not just to chart the course of cognitive changes over childhood but also, rather, to learn more about the processes that result in social cognitive development. In this section, we review evidence of four of the forms of social interaction listed in Figure 28.1 and tests like false belief.

One social factor linked to social cognitive development is that children with more siblings have been found to be advanced in false belief understanding (Lewis, Freeman, Kyriakidou, Maridaki-Kassotaki, & Berridge, 1996; Perner, Ruffman, & Leekam, 1994; Peterson, 2000). However, not all studies have replicated this "sibling effect" (e.g., Cutting & Dunn, 1999; Peterson & Slaughter, 2003), suggesting that it is the nature of the interaction, not just the presence of siblings, that is important. Related to this are

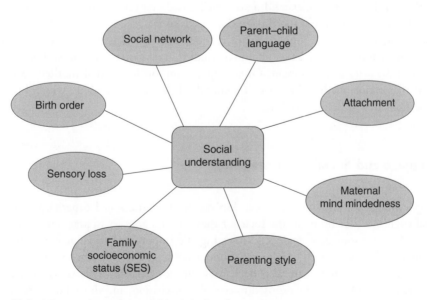

Figure 28.1 The social correlates of false belief understanding.

findings of the effect of social deprivation, showing that impoverished children (Holmes, Black, & Miller, 1996) and children who grow up in institutions tend to be delayed in false belief understanding (e.g., Tarullo, Bruce, & Gunnar, 2007).

A second factor found to relate to false belief performance concerns parents' styles of interaction (e.g., Hughes, Deater-Deckard, & Cutting, 1999; Pears & Moses, 2003; Ruffman, Perner, & Parkin, 1999). These suggest that in Western cultures, parents who steer a careful course between authoritarian and permissive interactions with their pre-schoolers (labeled *authoritative parents*) have children who perform better on such tasks. So too are parents who are more sensitive to social cues. For example, Sabbagh and Seamans (2008) reported that parents' skills in social competence were correlated with their children's level of social understanding, assessed with Wellman and Liu's (2004) series of tasks, discussed above. However, we must be cautious about the cultural specificity of data like these. For example, Vinden (2001) found that Korean American pre-schoolers' test performance was advanced when their parents were more authoritarian, not less as the Western data suggest.

Third, several studies have found that children with secure attachments are advanced in social understanding (Fonagy, Redfern, & Charman, 1997; Meins, 1997; Meins, Fernyhough, Russell, & Clark-Carter, 1998). This finding, however, has not always been replicated (Meins et al., 2002; Ontai & Thompson, 2008). Meins and her colleagues (1998, 2002) argued that what is important about security of attachment is appropriate responsiveness, which is facilitated by mothers' understanding of their children in psychological terms, or their "mindmindedness." This fourth factor is related to social cognitive development in longitudinal studies in which Meins found that how mothers describe their child at 5 months of age is a stronger predictor of false belief reasoning than attachment over 3 years later. Similarly, de Rosnay and colleagues (de Rosnay, Pons, Harris, & Morrell, 2004) found that mothers' description of their child in psychological terms is linked to the latter's understanding of belief-based emotions. Studies like this suggest that a full understanding of social cognition needs to take the social side of the equation as seriously as the more popular cognitive side, and also that factors like *attachment, conversation*, and *mindmindedness* should be studied in relation to each other. For example, instead of security of attachment, Ontai and Thompson found that mothers' conversational elaboration predicted their children's false belief understanding, which brings us to the final area to be reviewed here.

Language and Social Understanding

In reviewing studies of links between aspects of children's social experience and their social cognitive development, the focus of these studies appears to gravitate toward language. Another source of evidence indicating the importance of language is that deaf children tend to be delayed in false belief understanding, but only when their parents are not deaf. If their parents are also deaf, they are not delayed. This suggests that it is important for children to be exposed to complex discussion, and this tends to be lacking if their parents are not deaf and thus, usually not fluent in sign language (de Villiers &

de Villiers, 2000; Schick, de Villiers, de Villiers, & Hoffmeister, 2007; Woolfe, Want, & Siegal, 2002).

The importance of language is also indicated in the finding that the effect of having siblings is weaker for those children with strong linguistic abilities (Jenkins & Astington, 1996). Indeed, it has consistently been found that children's own linguistic ability tends to be correlated with their false belief performance (e.g., Astington & Baird, 2005; Cutting & Dunn, 1999; Hughes & Dunn, 1998). A meta-analysis of 104 studies confirms consistent moderate to strong correlations (Milligan, Astington, & Dack, 2007).

As well as children's own linguistic competence, the language they are exposed to is also related to their social cognitive development. Longitudinal studies indicate that mothers' use of psychological terms is linked to their children's social cognitive development (e.g., Moore, Furrow, Chiasson, & Patriquin, 1994). The possible causal directions underlying such correlations were further explored in Ruffman, Slade, and Crowe's (2002) longitudinal study. Although controlling for children's language and earlier social understanding, they found that mothers' use of psychological terms predicted children's later social understanding, but reverse correlations were not significant, suggesting that the language children are exposed to plays a causal role in social cognitive development. This general pattern of results has been extended to younger children beginning at 15 months (Taumoepeau & Ruffman, 2006, 2008), as well as older children up to 7 years of age (Adrián, Clemente, & Villanueva, 2007).

Although correlations are often found between parents' use of psychological terms and their children's social understanding, it is possible that a third factor is involved, or that such language is linked to other key factors. In one training study it was found that adding cognitive terms to children's stories read to them by parents did not facilitate the children's social cognitive development (Peskin & Astington, 2004), suggesting that simple exposure to psychological terms is not sufficient. Further cross-sectional (Ontai & Thompson, 2008; Slaughter, Peterson, & Mackintosh, 2007) and longitudinal (Racine, Carpendale, & Turnbull, 2006) research suggests that it is not just mentioning psychological terms but also, rather, explanatory, elaborative, causal, and contrastive talk that predicts social cognitive development. In this form of talk, mothers reflect on children's views, contrasting and providing further views about others' thoughts, feelings, desires, and intentions. Similar findings have been reported in the area of emotion understanding (Garner, Jones, Gaddy, & Rennie, 1997; Kuebli et al., 1995). Some of this elaborative conversation may involve psychological terms, but this is not necessarily required (Ontai & Thompson, 2008; Turnbull, Carpendale, & Racine, 2008). Talk about psychological events can involve the use of many words other than mental state terms like *think* and *know*, and false belief situations can even be discussed with words such as *see* and *look* (Turnbull et al., 2008). In fact, in a training study no difference was found between a condition using *see* and *look* compared with a condition using *think* and *know* (Lohmann & Tomasello, 2003).

Further evidence of the role of conversation about human activity in psychological terms comes from Ruffman et al.'s (1999) study of parents' self-reports regarding how they would respond to their child in various disciplinary situations. Parents who stated that they did or would talk to their child about the feelings of the other child involved had children who were advanced in false belief understanding. Peterson and Slaughter

(2003) developed a questionnaire for assessing parents' tendency to talk to their children in this way, and found that mothers who indicated that they discussed and elaborated on psychological aspects in their conversations with their children had children who were advanced in false belief understanding. Similarly, a longitudinal study by Dunn et al. (1991) found that family talk about causes of events and actions was linked to children's social cognitive development. This is also supported by training studies showing that discussion of situations involving false beliefs facilitates this development (e.g., Appleton & Reddy, 1996).

Comparing the roles of language and parent–child relationships in their effect on children's social cognitive development, in a longitudinal study, Ruffman, Slade, Devitt, and Crowe (2006) argued that it is mothers' use of mental state terms, not parental warmth, that predicts children's social cognitive development. However, they do acknowledge that this lack of results could be due to a restricted range of parental warmth – most parents in the study were high on the scale.

Instead of contrasting language and relationships, we could consider the question of whether they are really so separate. To see how they are intertwined, consider the notion of the *connectedness* of conversation. This is the extent to which the turns in conversation are linked to each other, in the sense that what a partner in conversation says is in response to the other (Dunn & Brophy, 2005). It can be considered an indicator of the quality of the conversation and the relationship, and may be related to the extent to which understanding can be achieved within that family dyad. Thus, it is not just being exposed to psychological terms but also understanding this talk. Children who are advanced in false belief understanding engage in such conversations with their friends (Dunn & Cutting, 1999). Connectedness of parent–child conversations at age 2 is linked to 4-year-olds' social understanding (Ensor & Hughes, 2008).

The link between children's linguistic ability and their social understanding suggests that children's language can then be viewed as a window on their level of social understanding (e.g., Bartsch & Wellman, 1995). Children's natural use of psychological language then becomes a useful tool for evaluating their levels of understanding. However, there are a number of points to keep in mind. Psychological terms are used in many different ways for different purposes; thus, it is important to categorize such uses (e.g., Bartsch & Wellman, 1995). Nelson (1996) has long pointed out that children begin using words at first without full adult meaning, and it may be within the context of conversations and interaction that children develop further understanding of such psychological words.

There are a number of ways to approach the correlations between language and social understanding. Regarding the possible causal directions, it could be that language causes social cognitive development, or social understanding influences language, or a third factor might be involved. There is evidence suggesting that it is early language ability that leads to later social cognitive development (Astington & Jenkins, 1999). This finding has been replicated (Milligan et al., 2007), and this was not just a particular aspect of language; rather, general language, semantics, vocabulary, syntax, as well as memory for complements were all significantly related to false belief understanding. The opposite effect, however, of early false belief understanding linked to later language ability has also been found, although this is a weaker effect (Milligan et al., 2007; Slade & Ruffman, 2005).

There is some difficulty in theorizing about the relations between language and social cognitive development because they are both such complex phenomena. For examples of how each has multiple levels and how they can be interconnected, consider the fact that early social cognitive development in infancy is necessary for infants to be able to achieve joint attention and to learn languages (e.g., Carpendale & Lewis, 2006). Alternatively, understanding pragmatic aspects of language depends on social understanding because it requires understanding others' intentions. This makes it difficult to make simple claims that one causes the other because both could be thought of as a broader competence in social interaction, although this entails a view of language as activity, differing from a Chomskian view of language as a cognitive skill.

A number of theories have been proposed to account for the relations between language and social cognitive development. According to Harris (2005), language is important because through conversation children are constantly faced with the fact that other people have differing beliefs, desires, and intentions. de Villiers and de Villiers (2000; and see de Villiers, 2005), in contrast, argued that it is the grammar of complementation, which provides a means for representing false beliefs, that is essential for this key aspect of social cognitive development. It has also been proposed that it is general syntax rather than complementation that is important (Astington & Jenkins, 1999), or general language ability (Ruffman et al., 2003). In a training study designed to address these issues, Lohmann and Tomasello (2003) found effects for Harris's claim about perspectives as well as de Villiers and de Villiers's (2000) account involving complementation, but the largest effect was for both combined. This debate continues (Perner, Zauner, & Sprung, 2005), but if what is important is children reaching understanding, then both of these factors should be expected to facilitate this. What unites the evidence of the roles that aspects of social interaction as well as language play in social cognitive development is that children need to reach an understanding of human activity and learn to talk about such action in psychological terms.

Recent Socially Based Accounts of Social Cognition

The data we have reviewed on the importance of social understanding and of language for social cognition call into question "traditional" (i.e., individualistic) accounts of social cognition based on the theory metaphor. Recently, alternative accounts have been proposed of typical (Carpendale & Lewis, 2004; Hutto, 2008; Leudar & Costall, 2009) and atypical (Hobson, 2002; Klin, Jones, Schultz, & Volkmar, 2003) development. Approaches to the development of social understanding are based on assumptions about the nature of mind and language. Furthermore, the generally shared view of the nature of the problem that children must solve in coming to understand others is based on a Cartesian view of mental states as underlying and causing outward behavior – such states are only privately accessible and are hidden from others. Thus, individuals can introspect upon their own inner states, but must make inferences about others (Russell, 1996; Ryle, 1949). This picture of the mind and thus the problem that children have to solve in acquiring social understanding tend to be assumed without question in the field and thus haves resulted in the common solutions suggested. That is, from this it follows that children may learn the meaning of psychological terms through mapping onto their own inner states. Others, however, have questioned the whole picture as the wrong way to set up the problem children face (e.g., Carpendale & Lewis, 2004; Leudar & Costall, 2009; Montgomery, 2004). Rather than thinking of mental states as underlying and causing behavior, intentions and beliefs can be talked about in terms of behavior. From this perspective, the underlying issue is how children learn the meaning of psychological words (Carpendale & Lewis, 2004).

In a related approach, Hutto (2008) argued that the practice of making sense of a person's actions in terms of beliefs and desires is primarily by means of narratives concerned with reasons based on engagement with others rather than from the third-person spectator stance assumed by theory theory. Relational approaches can be seen in the case of atypical development as contrasting with the view that autism is a deficit in a theory-of-mind module (Baron-Cohen et al., 1985). Instead, autism may emerge through differences in infants' tendency to identify with others (Hobson, 2002), or in the relative salience of social stimuli (Klin et al., 2003), or in emotional reactivity (Shanker, 2004). Small differences such as these could result in infants not engaging in the sort of social interaction in which they would have developed typical social understanding.

These more recent reassessments of the "theory-of-mind" construct are by no means new. For example, Chandler (e.g., 1988) characterized the focus on false belief acquisition as a "one miracle" view of development after which 4-year-olds' understanding was considered close to an adult's level. We are hopefully moving toward a more gradual view of development through many forms of increasingly complex understanding of the social world in the school age years such as an understanding of interpretation (e.g., Carpendale & Chandler, 1996; Lalonde & Chandler, 2002).

Conclusions

We have reviewed current research and theory concerning children's social cognitive development. Much of this work initially focused on the point at which children master the idea that false beliefs are possible, which was initially accounted for by three theories. These theories came under review with the accumulating evidence of the role that social interaction and language appear to play in this social cognitive development. However, because these are really research programs rather than theories, they cannot be disproved and instead tend to morph to fit the evidence. But the general assumptions agreed upon by all three theories have been critiqued by another group of theories related to social understanding and language.

Researchers have become more interested in the links between children's understanding of the mind and other aspects of their social lives. For example, advanced social understanding tends to be associated with advanced social skills, but there also can be disadvantages of advanced social understanding because such greater social awareness means that children are more aware of criticism from others such as teachers (for reviews, see Carpendale & Lewis, 2006; Cutting & Dunn, 2002). Wellman and Miller (2008) argued that focusing on an understanding of beliefs, desires, and intentions is incomplete because it overlooks an understanding of how human conduct is embedded in a social network of obligations and permissions. A broadened perspective would include this normative aspect of human life and, thus, a range of human skills including morality.

References

Adrián, J. E., Clemente, R. A., & Villanueva, L. (2007). Mothers' use of cognitive state verbs in picture-book reading and the development of children's understanding of mind: A longitudinal study. *Child Development, 78*, 1052–1067.

Appleton, M., & Reddy, V. (1996). Teaching three year-olds to pass false belief tests: A conversational approach. *Social Development, 5*, 275–291.

Astington, J. W. (2001). The future of theory-of-mind research: Understanding motivational states, the role of language, and real-world consequences. *Child Development, 72*, 685–687.

Astington, J. W., & Baird, J. A. (Eds.). (2005). *Why language matters for theory of mind*. New York: Oxford University Press.

Astington, J. W., Harris, P. L., & Olson, D. R. (Eds.). (1988). *Developing theories of mind*. New York: Cambridge University Press.

Astington, J. W., & Jenkins, J. M. (1999). A longitudinal study of the relations between language and theory-of-mind development. *Developmental Psychology, 35*, 1311–1320.

Baron-Cohen, S., Leslie, A. M., & Frith, U. (1985). Does the autistic child have a "theory of mind"? *Cognition, 21*, 37–46.

Bartsch, K., & Wellman, H. M. (1995). *Children talk about the mind*. Oxford: Oxford University Press.

Carlson, S. M., Moses, L. J., & Breton, C. (2002). How specific is the relation between executive function and theory of mind? Contribution of inhibitory control and working memory. *Infant and Child Development, 11*, 73–92.

Carpendale, J. I. M., & Chandler, M. J. (1996). On the distinction between false belief understanding and subscribing to an interpretive theory of mind. *Child Development, 67*, 1686–1706.

Carpendale, J. I. M., & Lewis, C. (2004). Constructing an understanding of mind: The development of children's social understanding within social interaction. *Behavioral and Brain Sciences, 27*, 79–96.

Carpendale, J. I. M., & Lewis, C. (2006). *How children develop social understanding*. Oxford: Blackwell.

Carruthers, P. (2009). How we know our own minds: the relationship between mindreading and metacognition. *Behavioral and Brain Sciences, 32*, 121–182.

Carruthers, P., & Smith, P. K. (Eds.). (1996). *Theories of theories of mind*. Cambridge: Cambridge University Press.

Chandler, M. J. (1988). Doubt and developing theories of mind. In J. W. Astington, P. L. Harris, & D. R. Olson (Eds.), *Developing theories of mind* (pp. 387–413). New York: Cambridge University Press.

Charman, T., Ruffman, T., & Clements, W. (2002). Is there a gender difference in false belief development? *Social Development, 11*, 1–10.

Chasiotis, A., Kiessling, F., Winter, V., & Hofer, J. (2006). Sensory motor inhibition as a prerequisite for theory of mind: A comparison of clinical and normal preschoolers differing in sensory motor abilities. *International Journal of Behavioral Development, 30*, 178–190.

Cutting, A. L., & Dunn, J. (1999). Theory of mind, emotion understanding, language, and family background: Individual differences and interrelations. *Child Development, 70*, 853–865.

Cutting, A. L., & Dunn, J. (2002). The cost of understanding other people: Social cognition predicts young children's sensitivity to criticism. *Journal of Child Psychology and Psychiatry, 43*, 849–860.

Damon, W. (Ed.). (1978). *Social cognition*. San Francisco: Jossey-Bass.

de Rosnay, M., Pons, F., Harris, P. L., & Morrell, J. M. B. (2004). A lag between understanding false belief and emotion attribution in young children: Relationships with linguistic ability and mothers' mental-state language. *British Journal of Developmental Psychology, 22*, 197–218.

de Villiers, J. G. (2005). Can language acquisition give children a point of view? In J. W. Astington & J. A. Baird (Eds.), *Why language matters for theory of mind* (pp. 186–219). New York: Oxford University Press.

de Villiers, J. G., & de Villiers, P. A. (2000). Linguistic determinism and the understanding of false beliefs. In P. Mitchell & K. J. Riggs (Eds.), *Children's reasoning and the mind* (pp. 191–228). Hove, UK: Psychology Press.

Doherty, M. J. (2008). *Theory of mind: How children understand others' thoughts and feelings*. Hove, UK: Psychology Press.

Dunn, J., & Brophy, M. (2005). Communication, relationships, and individual differences in children's understanding of mind. In J. W. Astington & J. A. Baird (Eds.), *Why language matters for theory of mind* (pp. 50–69). New York: Oxford University Press.

Dunn, J., Brown, J., & Beardsall, L. (1991). Family talk about feeling states and children's later understanding of others' emotions. *Developmental Psychology, 27*, 448–455.

Dunn, J., & Cutting, A. L. (1999). Understanding others, and individual differences in friendship interactions in young children. *Social Development, 8*, 201–219.

Ensor, R., & Hughes, C. (2008). Content or connectedness? Mother-child talk and early social understanding. *Child Development, 79*, 201–216.

Flavell, J. H. (1992). Perspectives on perspective taking. In H. Beilin & P. B. Pufall (Eds.), *Piaget's theory: Prospects and possibilities* (pp. 107–139). Hillsdale, NJ: Erlbaum.

Flynn, E., O'Malley, C., & Wood, D. (2004). A longitudinal, microgenetic study of the emergence of false belief understanding and inhibition skills. *Developmental Science, 7*, 103–115.

Fonagy, P., Redfern, S., & Charman, T. (1997). The relationship between belief-desire reasoning and a projective measure of attachment security (SAT). *British Journal of Developmental Psychology, 15*, 51–61.

Forgas, J. P. (Ed.). (1981). *Social cognition: Perspectives in everyday understanding*. London: Academic Press.

Frye, D., Zelazo, P. D., & Palfai, T. (1995). Theory of mind and rule-based reasoning. *Cognitive Development, 10*, 483–527.

Gallese, V., Fadiga, L., Fogassi, L., & Rizzolatti, G, (1996) Action recognition in the premotor cortex. *Brain, 119*, 593–609.

Garner, P., Jones, D., Gaddy, D., & Rennie, K. (1997). Low income mothers' conversations about emotion and their children's emotional competence. *Social Development, 6*, 125–142.

Hala, S., Hug, S., & Henderson, A. (2003). Executive function and false-belief understanding in preschool children: Two tasks are harder than one. *Journal of Cognition and Development, 4*, 275–298.

Harris, P. L. (2000). *The work of the imagination*. Oxford: Blackwell.

Harris, P. L. (2005). Conversation, pretense, and theory of mind. In J. W. Astington & J. A. Baird (Eds.), *Why language matters for theory of mind* (pp. 70–83). New York: Oxford University Press.

Heider, F. (1958). *The psychology of interpersonal relations*. New York: Wiley.

Hobson, R. P. (2002). *The cradle of thought*. London: Macmillan.

Holmes, H. A., Black, C., & Miller, S. A. (1996). A cross-task comparison of false-belief understanding in a Head Start population. *Journal of Experimental Child Psychology*, *63*, 263–285.

Hughes, C. (1998a). Executive function in preschoolers: Links with theory of mind and emotion and verbal ability. *British Journal of Developmental Psychology*, *16*, 233–253.

Hughes, C. (1998b). Finding your marbles: Does preschoolers' strategic behavior predict later understanding of mind? *Developmental Psychology*, *34*, 1326–1339.

Hughes, C., Deater-Deckard, K., & Cutting, A. L. (1999). "Speak roughly to your little boy"? Sex differences in the relations between parenting and preschoolers' understanding of mind. *Social Development*, *8*, 143–160.

Hughes, C., & Dunn, J. (1998). Understanding mind and emotions: Longitudinal associations with mental-state talk between young friends. *Developmental Psychology*, *34*, 1026–1037.

Hurley, S., (2008). The shared circuits model: How control, mirroring, and simulation can enable imitation, deliberation, and mindreading. *Behavioral and Brain Sciences*, *31*, 1–22.

Hutto, D. D. (2008). *Folk psychological narratives: The sociocultural basis of understanding reasons*. Cambridge, MA: MIT Press.

Iacoboni, M., Molnar-Szakacs, I., Gallese, V., Buccino, G., Mazziotta, J. C., & Rizzolatti, G. (2005). Grasping the intentions of others with one's own mirror neuron system. *PLoS Biology*, *3*, 529–535.

Jenkins, J. M., & Astington, J. W. (1996). Cognitive factors and family structure associated with theory of mind development in young children. *Developmental Psychology*, *32*, 70–78.

Johnson, C. N. (1988). Theory of mind and the structure of conscious experience. In J. W. Astington, P. L. Harris, & D. R. Olson (Eds.), *Developing theories of mind* (pp. 47–63). New York: Cambridge University Press.

Klin, A., Jones, W., Schultz, R., & Volkmar, F. (2003). The enactive mind, or from actions to cognition: Lessons from autism. *Philosophical Transactions of the Royal Society, London B*, *358*, 345–360.

Kloo, D., & Perner, J. (2003). Training transfer between card sorting and false belief understanding: Helping children apply conflicting descriptions. *Child Development*, *74*, 1823–1839.

Kuebli, J., Butler, S., & Fivush, R. (1995). Mother–child talk about past emotions: Relations of maternal language and child gender over time. *Cognition and Emotion*, *9*, 265–283.

Lalonde, C. E., & Chandler, M. J. (2002). Children's understanding of interpretation. *New Ideas in Psychology*, *20*, 163–198.

Leslie, A. M. (1987). Pretense and representation: The origins of "theory of mind." *Psychological Review*, *94*, 412–426.

Leslie, A. M. (1994). Pretending and believing: Issues in the theory of ToM. *Cognition*, *50*, 211–238.

Leslie, A. (2005). Developmental parallels in understanding minds and bodies. *Trends in Cognitive Science*, *9*, 459–462.

Leslie, A. M., & Frith, U. (1988). Autistic children's understanding of seeing, knowing and believing. *British Journal of Developmental Psychology*, *6*, 315–324.

Leudar, I., & Costall, A. (Eds.). (2009). *Against theory of mind*. Basingstoke: Palgrave Macmillan.

Lewis, C. (n.d.). Prof Charlie Lewis' homepage. Retrieved from http://www.psych.lancs.ac.uk/people/CharlieLewis.html

Lewis, C., Freeman, N. H., Kyriakidou, C., Maridaki-Kassotaki, K., & Berridge, D. M. (1996). Social influences on false belief access: Specific sibling influences or general apprenticeship? *Child Development*, *67*, 2930–2947.

Lohmann, H., & Tomasello, M. (2003). The role of language in the development of false belief understanding: A training study. *Child Development*, *74*, 1130–1144.

Meins, E. (1997). *Security of attachment and the social development of cognition*. Hove, UK: Psychology Press.

Meins, E., Fernyhough, C., Russell, J., & Clark-Carter, D. (1998). Security of attachment as a predictor of symbolic and mentalising abilities: A longitudinal study. *Social Development, 7*, 1–24.

Meins, E., Fernyhough, C., Wainwright, R., Das Gupta, M., Fradley, E., & Tuckey, M. (2002). Maternal mind-mindedness and attachment security as predictors of theory of mind understanding. *Child Development, 73*, 1715–1726.

Metzinger, T., & Gallese, V. (2003). The emergence of a shared action ontology: Building blocks for a theory. *Consciousness and Cognition, 12*, 549–571.

Milligan, K., Astington, J. W., & Dack, L. A. (2007). Language and theory of mind: Meta-analysis of the relations between language ability and false-belief understanding. *Child Development, 78*, 622–646.

Montgomery, D. E. (2004). Challenging theory-theory accounts of social understanding: Where is the social constructivist advantage? *Behavioral and Brain Sciences, 27*, 118–119.

Moore, C. (2006). *The development of commonsense psychology*. Mahwah, NJ: Erlbaum.

Moore, C., Furrow, D., Chiasson, L., & Patriquin, M. (1994). Developmental relationships between production and comprehension of mental terms. *First Language, 14*, 1–17.

Moore, C., Jarrold, C., Russell, J., Lumb, A., Sapp, F., & MacCallum, F. (1995). Conflicting desire and the child's theory of mind. *Cognitive Development, 10*, 467–482.

Nelson, K. (1996). *Language in cognitive development: The emergence of the mediated mind*. New York: Cambridge University Press.

Oh, S., & Lewis, C. (2008). Korean preschoolers' advanced inhibitory control and its relation to other executive skills and mental state understanding. *Child Development, 79*, 80–99.

Onishi, K., & Baillargeon, R. (2005). Do 15-month-old infants understand false beliefs? *Science, 308*, 255–258.

Ontai, L. L., & Thompson, R. A. (2008). Attachment, parent-child discourse and theory-of-mind development. *Social Development, 17*, 47–60

Pears, K. C., & Moses, L. J. (2003). Demographics, parenting, and theory of mind in preschool children. *Social Development, 12*, 1–20.

Perner, J. (1991). *Understanding the representational mind*. Cambridge, MA: MIT Press.

Perner, J., Kloo, D., & Gornik, E. (2007). Episodic memory development: Theory of mind is part of re-experiencing experienced events. *Infant and Child Development, 16*, 471–490.

Perner, J., Leekam, S. R., & Wimmer, H. (1987). 3-year-olds difficulty with false belief: The case for a conceptual deficit. *British Journal of Developmental Psychology, 5*, 125–137.

Perner, J., & Ruffman, T. (2005). Infants' insight into the mind: How deep? *Science, 308*, 214–216.

Perner, J., Ruffman, T., & Leekam, S. R. (1994). Theory of mind is contagious: You catch it from your sibs. *Child Development, 65*, 1228–1238.

Perner, J., Zauner, P., & Sprung, M. (2005). What does "that" have to do with point of view? Conflicting desires and "want" in German. In J. W. Astington & J. A. Baird (Eds.), *Why language matters for theory of mind* (pp. 220–244). New York: Oxford University Press.

Peskin, J., & Astington, J. W. (2004). The effects of adding metacognitive language to story texts. *Cognitive Development, 19*, 253–273.

Peterson, C. C. (2000). Kindred spirits: Influences of siblings' perspectives on theory of mind. *Cognitive Development, 15*, 435–455.

Peterson, C., & Slaughter, V. (2003). Opening windows into the mind: Mothers' preferences for mental state explanations and children's theory of mind. *Cognitive Development, 18*, 399–429.

Piaget, J., & Inhelder, B. (1967). *The child's conception of space*. New York: Norton. (Original work published in 1948)

Povinelli, D. J., & Eddy, T. J. (1996). *What young chimpanzees know about seeing. Monographs of the Society for Research in Child Development, 61*(2, Serial No. 247).

Premack, D., & Woodruff, G. (1978). Does the chimpanzee have a theory of mind? *Behavioral and Brain Sciences, 4*, 515–526.

Prinz, W. (2003). Neurons don't represent. *Consciousness and Cognition, 12*, 572–573.

Rajendran, G., & Mitchell, P. (2007). Cognitive theories of autism. *Developmental Review, 27*, 224–260.

Rakoczy, H., Warneken, F., & Tomasello, M. (2007). "This way!" "No! That way!" 3-year olds know that two people can have mutually incompatible desires. *Cognitive Development, 22*, 47–68.

Ruffman, T., Perner, J., & Parkin, L. (1999). How parenting style affects false belief understanding. *Social Development, 8*, 395–411.

Ruffman, T., Slade, L., & Crowe, E. (2002). The relation between children's and mothers' mental state language and theory-of-mind understanding. *Child Development, 73*, 734–751.

Ruffman, T., Slade, L., Devitt, K., & Crowe, E. (2006). What mothers say and what they do: The relation between parenting, theory of mind, language and conflict/cooperation. *British Journal of Developmental Psychology, 24*, 105–124.

Rutter, M. (1983). Cognitive deficits in the pathogenesis of autism. *Journal of Child Psychology & Psychiatry, 24*, 513–531.

Ryle, G. (1949). *The concept of mind*. Middlesex, UK: Penguin.

Sabbagh, M. A., & Seamans, E. L. (2008). Intergenerational transmission of theory-of-mind. *Developmental Science, 11*, 354–360.

Sabbagh, M., Xu, F., Carlson, S. M., Moses, L. J., & Lee, K. (2006). The development of executive functioning and theory of mind: A comparison of Chinese and U.S. preschoolers. *Psychological Science, 17*, 74–81.

Schick, B., de Villiers, P., de Villiers, J., & Hoffmeister, R. (2007). Language and theory of mind: A study of deaf children. *Child Development, 78*, 376–396.

Scholl, B. J., & Leslie, A. M. (2001). Minds, modules, and meta-analysis. *Child Development, 72*, 696–701.

Shanker, S. G. (2004). Autism and the dynamic developmental model of emotions. *Philosophy, Psychiatry & Psychology, 11*, 219–233.

Shantz, C. V. (1983). Social cognition. In J. H. Flavell & E. M. Markman (Eds.), *Handbook of child psychology: Cognitive development* (pp. 495–555). New York: John Wiley.

Slade, L., & Ruffman, T. (2005). How language does (and does not) relate to theory-of-mind: A longitudinal study of syntax, semantics, working memory and false belief. *British Journal of Developmental Psychology, 23*, 117–141.

Slaughter, V., Peterson, C. C., & Mackintosh, E. (2007). Mind what mother says: Narrative input and theory of mind in typical children and those on the autism spectrum. *Child Development, 78*, 839–858.

Stack, J., & Lewis, C. (2008). Steering towards a developmental account of infant social understanding. *Human Development, 51*, 229–234.

Stack, J., & Lewis, C. (2009, April). A developmental account of infant false-belief reasoning: The role of intentional actions in shared and non-shared settings. Poster presented at Society for Research in Child Development.

Surian, L., Caldi, S., & Sperber, D. (2007). Attribution of beliefs by 13-month-old infants. *Psychological Science, 18*, 580–586.

Tarullo, A. R., Bruce, J., & Gunnar, M. R. (2007). False belief and emotion understanding in post-institutionalized children. *Social Development, 16*, 57–78.

Taumoepeau, M., & Ruffman, T. (2006). Mother and infant talk about mental states relates to desire language and emotion understanding. *Child Development*, *77*, 465–481.

Taumoepeau, M., & Ruffman, T. (2008). Stepping stones to others' minds: Maternal talk relates to child mental state language and emotion understanding at 15, 24, and 33 months. *Child Development*, *79*, 284–302.

Tomasello, M., Call, J., & Hare, B. (2003). Chimpanzees understand psychological states: The question is which ones and to what extent. *Trends in Cognitive Science*, *7*, 153–156.

Turnbull, W., Carpendale, J. I. M., & Racine, R. P. (2008). Relations between mother-child talk and 3- to 5-year-old children's understanding of belief: Beyond mental state terms to talk about the mind. *Merrill-Palmer Quarterly*, *54*, 367–385.

Umiltà, M. A., Kohler, E., Gallese, V., Fogassi, L., Fadiga, L., Keysers, C., et al. (2001). "I know what you are doing": A neurophysiological study. *Neuron*, *32*, 91–101.

Vinden, P. G. (2001). Parenting attitudes and children's understanding of mind: A comparison of Korean American and Anglo-American families. *Cognitive Development*, *16*, 793–809.

Warneken, F., Hare, B., Melis, A. P., Hanus, D., & Tomasello, M. (2007). Spontaneous altruism by chimpanzees and young children. *PLOS Biology*, *5*, 1414–1420.

Wellman, H. M. (1990). *The child's theory of mind*. Cambridge, MA: MIT Press.

Wellman, H. M. (2002). Understanding the psychological world: Developing a theory of mind. In U. Goswami (Ed.), *The Blackwell handbook of cognitive development* (pp 167–187). Oxford: Blackwell.

Wellman, H. M., Cross, D., & Watson, J. (2001). Meta-analysis of theory of mind development: The truth about false belief. *Child Development*, *72*, 655–684.

Wellman, H. M., Fang, F. X., Liu, D., Zhu, L. Q., & Liu, G. H. (2006). Scaling of theory-of-mind understandings in Chinese children. *Psychological Science*, *17*, 1075–1081.

Wellman, H. M., & Liu, D. (2004). Scaling of theory of mind tasks. *Child Development*, *75*, 523–541.

Wellman, H. M., & Miller, J. G. (2008). Including deontic reasoning as fundamental to theory of mind. *Human Development*, *51*, 105–135.

Wimmer, H., & Perner, J. (1983). Beliefs about beliefs: Representation and constraining function of wrong beliefs in young children's understanding of deception. *Cognition*, *13*, 103–128.

Woolfe, T., Want, S. C., & Siegal, M. (2002). Signposts to development: Theory of mind in deaf children. *Child Development*, *73*, 768–778.

CHAPTER TWENTY-NINE

Prosocial Behavior

Joan E. Grusec, Paul Hastings, and Alisa Almas

Aggression and other forms of antisocial behavior have captured the attention of developmental researchers to a far greater extent than prosocial behaviors such as helping, comforting, sharing, defending, and making restitution for antisocial behavior. Yet the ability to feel empathy for the distress of others and to care for them is surely an equally if not more admirable feature of human behavior than simply refraining from harming others. At the same time, it is a more complex form of behavior. Thus, conditions under which people should assist others, particularly when that assistance involves personal sacrifice, are ambiguous, at least in Western European cultures. Although children who help others have more positive relationships and interactions with their peers (Eisenberg, Fabes, & Spinrad, 2006) and people who were prosocial as children are less likely to be antisocial as adults (Hamalaimen & Pulkiinen, 1995), prosocial behavior may make excessive demands on the resources of the giver as well as occasionally be viewed negatively by the recipient. Accordingly, studies indicate that prosocial behavior is often not praised by parents or teachers (Caplan & Hay, 1989; Grusec, 1991) and that parents frequently do not welcome it in young children (Rheingold, 1982).

Not all acts that benefit others, of course, have a personal cost. Helping others leads to feelings of mastery and opportunities for social interaction, even when that help is not likely to be reciprocated. What characterizes prosocial behavior is that it is voluntary and intentional behavior that benefits another. It is not done in response to direction or request, and it appears to be motivated by some form of internal direction rather than by hope of external reward or fear of punishment.

In this chapter we survey a number of features of empathy and prosocial behavior in children. We begin with an overview of the development of prosocial behavior. Then we consider its evolutionary and genetic underpinnings as well as its developmental

The Wiley-Blackwell Handbook of Childhood Social Development, Second Edition, edited by Peter K. Smith and Craig H. Hart
© 2011 by Blackwell Publishing Ltd.

progression. We next turn to the various ways in which it is socialized as well as to differences in cultural demands for and expressions of concern for others. Next we review recent work on the neurological and hormonal influences underlying prosocial behavior. Finally, we discuss the relation between prosocial and antisocial behavior.

The Development of Prosocial Behavior

The behavioral precursors of empathy and prosocial behavior emerge in the middle of the first year of life, when infants display a primitive form of empathy by crying when they hear others crying. As children develop a concept of person permanence, role-taking abilities, and a sense of personal identity during the second year of life, they begin to display concern for others, including comforting and helpfulness (Rheingold, 1982; Zahn-Waxler, Radke-Yarrow, Wagner, & Chapman, 1992). They also display a beginning awareness of rules and standards of behavior (Emde, Biringen, Clyman, & Oppenheim, 1991) as well as the ability to regulate their own behavior (Kopp, 1982). Continuing increases in sociocognitive functioning, including the ability to understand the emotions of others, to evaluate situations in terms of moral standards, and to plan, as well as increasing knowledge and skills relevant to prosocial behavior, also contribute to the developmental process. Balancing all these forces for increases in prosocial behavior are norms concerning the appropriateness of its expression. Help is not always appropriate under all circumstances because it can threaten the recipient's self-esteem (Fischer, Nadler, & Witcher-Alagna, 1982), induce internal attributions for failure (Gross, Wallston, & Piliavin, 1979), and lead to feelings of indebtedness (Greenberg & Shapiro, 1971), particularly if the help does not involve family members (Clark, 1983). Under these sorts of circumstances, then, displays of empathic concern may be inappropriate. All these complexities interact to blur a picture of consistent changes in prosocial behavior over time.

Reviews of the literature on age changes in prosocial behavior reveal, not surprisingly given the situation described above, a somewhat confused picture. However, an extensive meta-analysis suggests that prosocial behavior does increase throughout childhood, although the magnitude of effect sizes does depend on a number of variables including the form that prosocial behavior takes, the way in which data are collected (e.g., observation or self-report), and the target of behavior (Eisenberg et al., 2006).

Evolutionary Aspects

The human abilities to apprehend and share another's emotional state, to feel sympathy and compassion, and to engage in helpful acts that benefit others are rooted in the evolutionary history of social mammalian species. Although strict interpretations of the "selfish gene" theory would hold that animals should never act in ways that potentially give greater advantage to another creature's ability to procreate, many sociobiologists have proposed mechanisms by which cooperative actions increase the likelihood of survival (McAndrew, 2002). Because mammals have a relatively prolonged infancy and consequent dependence, they need parental nurturance in order to guarantee survival. The offspring's survival increases the likelihood of shared genes being passed on to another generation. Helpful behaviors directed to nonkin members of one's social group would increase the likelihood of receiving assistance at a future time of need and thereby also increase the chance of survival. In small social groups, which have characterized most of human evolutionary history, prosocial acts increase the cohesion and survival of the social group. Computational modeling has shown that groups that include members with the genetic propensity toward helping others experience greater population growth over generations than do groups lacking a genetic basis toward prosocial behavior (Sober & Wilson, 1998). Thus, human engagement in prosocial behavior increased the evolutionary fitness of the species, thereby preserving this pattern of behavior.

Familial and social groups were also the contexts within which evolutionary forces acted on mammalian neurophysiology and human neuropsychology, the substrates of prosocial behavior (Tucker, Luu, & Derryberry, 2005). The integration of affective motivators of behavior and cognitive skills of perspective taking, anticipation, and planning allowed parents to perceive and respond to their infants' cues of hunger, pain, and distress, thereby meeting infants' needs and nurturing infants' developing caregiving behavioral system. Emotional contagion, empathy, and sympathy, the proximal affective motivators of parental nurturance (de Waal, 2008), can also be elicited when distress or need is perceived in nonfamilial others, leading to prosocial behaviors toward peers or strangers. In enduring social groups, gratitude for assistance (McCullough, Kimeldorf, & Cohen, 2008) and forgiveness for transgressions (Gold & Davis, 2005) have also been proposed as emotional motivators of prosocial behavior that serves to maintain group harmony.

Evolutionary forces have preserved the capacity for prosocial behavior within humans, and genetic variation has ensured that some humans are more prone toward prosocial behavior than others. In accord with epigenetic theory, whether such genes are activated and the extent to which their behavioral phenotype is evidenced will depend upon the eliciting cues of environmental stimulation. We turn then to a discussion of the roles of genetics and of environmental experiences on the development of prosocial behavior.

Genetic Underpinnings of Prosocial Behavior

Studies of the genetic underpinnings of prosocial behavior have focused on two areas: the extent to which prosocial behavior is genetically mediated and, more recently, the identification of genes specifically involved in its expression. With respect to the first, studies indicate that genetic heritability, shared environmental influences such as parental socialization and the home context, and the unshared environment (individuals' unique experiences, and measurement error) all contribute to individual differences in children's empathy and prosocial behavior. Cross-sectional and longitudinal twin studies (Knafo & Plomin, 2006; Vierikko, Pulkkinen, & Rose, 2006; Zahn-Waxler, Schiro, Robinson, Emde, & Schmitz, 2001) have repeatedly shown that heritability contributes less to prosocial behavior in toddlers and young children (0–30%) than does the shared environment. However, by adolescence, measures of prosocial behavior are principally attributable to genetic factors (30–80%), and by adulthood the contribution is even more considerable (Rushton, Fulker, Neale, Nias, & Eysenck, 1986).

There are several possible explanations for this change over time. First, later emerging cognitive competencies that influence prosocial behavior, such as perspective taking, are also genetically based and might exert greater increases on prosocial behavior over time (Plomin, DeFries, McClearn, & McGuffin, 2001). Second, prosocial behavior is likely to be polygenic, and some of the many contributing genes might only become active with later maturation (Knafo & Plomin, 2006). Finally, different procedures typically are used to measure prosocial behavior in children than in youth or adults, and these methodological differences might affect heritability estimates. Most studies of young children's prosocial behavior have utilized observational or other-report (mother, teacher, and peer) measures of prosocial behavior, whereas most studies of adults have used self-report questionnaires. Self-reports are notoriously susceptible to biased response patterns and social desirability; these might be heritable tendencies that could exaggerate the apparent genetic basis of adult empathy and prosocial behavior.

The search for specific genes linked to prosocial behavior has just begun. Polymorphisms of the dopamine D4 receptor gene have been linked to adult reports of prosocial behavior (Bachner-Melman et al., 2005). Variants of the arginine vasopressin 1a receptor gene, which has been linked to affiliation and social bonding in lower animals, also predict adults' self-reported and observed prosocial behavior (Knafo et al., 2008). However, given that at least 25 genes have been associated with adults' self-reported cooperativeness (Comings et al., 2000), the polygenic nature of prosocial behavior will require that researchers move beyond single-candidate gene studies. Adding to the challenge is the necessity of identifying interactions between different kinds of genes as well as between genes and the environment, and the need for developmental research on the timing of activation of genes associated with prosocial behavior.

The Socialization of Prosocial Behavior in the Family

Children are differentially oriented to prosocial behavior by virtue of their evolutionary and genetic predispositions. But manifestation of these predispositions is guided by and interacts with their socialization experiences. There are several ways in which parents and other agents of socialization assist children to adopt a caring and helpful orientation toward others, by way of both the values they endorse and the behaviors they exhibit. A major focus is on the role of empathy, as is evident from the evolutionary perspective described above. But a reading of the research literature suggests that parents who not only facilitate their children's ability to feel empathy for the distress of others but also discipline appropriately, teach them about the feelings of others, model prosocial behavior, and develop a relationship of cooperation and mutual compliance are likely to produce prosocial children. It may be, however, that the specific nature of prosocial behavior acquired as well as the reasons for its occurrence as a function of these various approaches differ. In other words, there is no single learning mechanism for the acquisition of concern for others. Instead, it can be argued that socialization occurs in a variety of domains, with each domain involving a different aspect of the relationship between parent and child as well as different mechanisms of change (Bugental, 2000; Grusec & Davidov, 2010). We address each of those domains in turn.

Encouraging empathic and sympathetic feelings (protection domain)

Empathy (responding to another's distress with a similar emotion) and sympathy (responding to another person's distress with feelings of sadness or concern) are vicarious affective responses that can be experienced in the face of another person's emotion and that are facilitated in the protection domain. They are powerful motivators of assistance to others because they are unpleasant emotional states that can be reduced if the distress of the other is reduced. An important distinction between empathy and personal distress is that personal distress is less effective as a motivator of prosocial behavior because it motivates escape from the upsetting situation, rather than assistance. Empathy, however, is an emotion centered on the other rather than the self, and, accordingly, its unpleasantness can be reduced only by reducing the other's distress (Batson, 1991). A number of studies (see Eisenberg et al., 2006, for one review) have compared children who exhibit empathy and sympathy in reaction to another's distress with those who show personal distress as indicated by self and by facial and physiological indices (e.g., facial expressions of concerned attention and heart rate deceleration in the former, and facial expressions of anxiety and distress and heart rate acceleration in the latter). When given the opportunity to help others but given the possibility of escape from the emotion-inducing situation, these studies generally show that children who experience empathy are more prosocial than those who experience personal distress. The question with respect to parenting, then, is how children can be socialized so as not to experience overwhelming personal distress when observing distress in others.

Considerable evidence supports the view that children whose parents are sensitively responsive to their distress develop neurobiological systems that are involved in the adaptive regulation of negative emotion (Gunnar, 2000) as well as greater competence at regulating their own distress (Cassidy, 1994). Moreover, these children are more likely to engage in sympathetic and prosocial behavior (Eisenberg et al., 2006), with the ability to regulate self-distress the mediator or link between responsive parenting and empathy (Davidov & Grusec, 2006). Children whose parents restrict their expression of negative emotion and who emphasize the importance of controlling expressions of sadness and anxiety tend to be high in personal distress (Eisenberg et al., 1991). Note that the comfort offered by parents must be appropriate and, moreover, that what is appropriately comforting for one child may not be appropriately comforting for another. Thus such variables as developmental status and temperament do have an impact on how children perceive parental actions and respond to them (e.g., Buck, 1991).

Reinforcement and punishment of prosocial behavior (control domain)

When parents comfort and reassure their children, they are assuming the role of protectors of their children's physical and psychological safety. But parents play other roles as well. An important one is that of an authority figure who manages the prosocial actions of children by taking advantage of having greater control over resources, including reinforcement and punishment. The evidence suggests that material rewards do not promote prosocial behavior once they are no longer available, no doubt because they make it too easy for children to see that their actions have been extrinsically rather than intrinsically or autonomously motivated (Lepper, 1983). Fabes, Fultz, Eisenberg, May-Plumlee, and Christopher (1989), for example, found that being rewarded with a toy for helpful behavior enhanced such behavior in the immediate situation. However, it undermined later helping when rewards were no longer available, although only for children whose mothers felt positive about the use of rewards in general. As well, Fabes et al. reported that mothers who felt more positive about the use of rewards reported that their children were generally less prosocial. Some forms of reinforcement such as social approval are more subtle and, accordingly, are less likely to lead children to make extrinsic attributions for their actions (Smith, Gelfand, Harmann, & Partlow, 1979). Attributing prosocial behavior to a positive dispositional characteristic (e.g., "I see you shared because you're the kind of person who likes to help others") seems particularly effective in facilitating prosocial behavior beyond the setting in which the reinforcement is administered: This finding holds only with older children who are able to think in terms of people having characteristics that affect their behavior across a variety of situations (Grusec & Redler, 1980).

Interestingly enough, although punishment plays a part in the parental control process, punishment or threats of punishment for failures to be prosocial are rarely used, at least by Anglo-European mothers (Grusec, 1991), presumably a reflection of the ambivalence surrounding the display of prosocial behavior. Indeed, lying, stealing, and physical aggression are far more clear-cut in terms of their undesirability than is failure to help or show concern (which may, for example, threaten the self-esteem of the recipient or make unreasonable demands on the donor). What does appear to be linked to the successful socialization of prosocial behavior is the use of reasoning (Hoffman, 1970). Reasoning appears in many different forms, including that which emphasizes the empathic distress of another. We suggest that one of the major features of reasoning is the opportunity it provides for parents to teach or guide their children in how to be empathic and prosocial.

Learning how to be empathic and prosocial (guided learning domain)

Parents talk to their children about social and emotional issues, and this talk is an important contributor to children's socialization in yet another domain, that of guided learning (see Denham, Bassett, & Wyatt, 2007). Thus preschoolers who display high levels of empathy-related responsiveness and prosocial behavior tend to have parents who frequently discuss the causes of their emotions. Garner (2003) reported that when mothers tried to explain emotions when talking with their toddlers, the toddlers made more attempts to understand the emotional states of others, and when mothers gave directions to their toddlers to label emotions, the toddlers were more likely to express emotional concern for others. When this teaching is carefully matched to the abilities of the child, the child and parent-teacher are especially likely to arrive at a shared understanding of the task (e.g., Puntambekar & Hübscher, 2005).

Modeling prosocial behavior (group identification domain)

Modeling and routine practices are an important venue through which prosocial behavior is acquired. For example, children who routinely perform household work that involves benefits to other members of the family are more likely to show concern for others than those who do work only in response to parental requests or do work that benefits only themselves (Grusec, Goodnow, & Cohen, 1997). In experimental situations, children match their behavior to that of adults who help others or who donate rewards to others (e.g., Rice & Grusec, 1975). Highly involved civil rights activists report that their parents were nurturant and strongly involved in humanitarian activity, whereas activists who were less involved and committed reported that their parents preached about the importance of prosocial values but often did not practice what they preached (Rosenhan, 1969). Correlational studies of the sort we have described above that link parental comforting to empathy and prosocial outcomes are no doubt also examples of the role of modeling in the socialization of prosocial behavior, where children learn how to comfort others by having been comforted themselves.

Mutual reciprocity (reciprocity domain)

Children whose parents comply with their reasonable requests are more likely to be compliant themselves (Parpal & Maccoby, 1985). In this case, parent and child operate as equals who are involved in an exchange relationship, one that probably involves both specific exchanges of favors ("tit for tat") as well as nonconditional mutuality, with the latter more frequent within the family. Although researchers have not looked specifically at mutual reciprocity and comforting or concern for others, it makes good sense that acts of reciprocated helpfulness could be the norm in families where such exchange experiences have been nurtured. Moreover, attitudes to assisting others that are developed in the family could well be generalized to others beyond the family.

The Socialization of Prosocial Behavior Outside the Family

The mother–child relationship has been the primary context for research on child development, and research on prosocial behavior provides no exception. Nevertheless, the roles of other family members as well as peers, teachers, and the larger community in the development of concern for others have received attention.

Other family members

Fathers   Research on the role of fathers in the development of prosocial behavior has yielded inconsistent results. Similar to mothers, fathers' parenting characteristics have been found to be positively related to children's prosocial behavior (e.g., Davidov & Grusec, 2006; Dekovic & Janssens, 1992), although other studies show the influence of fathers to be weaker than that of mothers (e.g., Hastings, McShane, Parker, & Ladha, 2007) or nonexistent (Hastings, Rubin, & DeRose, 2005). Fathers may well have a lesser influence on their children's concern for others than do mothers because of more varied levels of involvement they have with them. Grusec et al. (1997), for example, found that fathers were less aware than mothers of their children's prosocial behavior at home.

Siblings   Relationships with siblings provide a unique context for children to learn about social interactions, including prosocial behavior, because they are different from both parent–child relationships and those with peers. Children spend more time in play situations that require sharing with siblings than with parents, and have more opportunities to provide help to siblings than to parents. One thing that makes sibling relationships distinct from those with peers is the fact that, of course, siblings differ in age, whereas peers most often do not. Thus, older siblings have the opportunity to help and care for younger siblings. Indeed, cultures in which children are assigned caregiving roles have higher rates of prosocial behaviors (Whiting & Whiting, 1975). Researchers have found evidence, even at very young ages, of prosocial behavior amongst siblings (Abramovitch, Corter, & Pepler, 1980; Dunn & Munn, 1986), although having a sibling does not seem to affect prosocial actions to peers, at least in young children (Demetriou & Hay, 2004).

Influences outside of the family

Peers   Peers have equal status with each other and therefore must learn to share with and accommodate one another. Thus peer interactions provide many opportunities for learning prosocial skills. Accordingly, researchers have reported that children and adolescents learn from their friends as well as model each others' behavior. Haselager and colleagues (Haselager, Hartup, van Lieshout, & Riksen-Walraven, 1998), for example, found that children were more similar to a friend than an acquaintance on peer-reported helping and cooperative behavior. Children with friends who were rated as more prosocial than themselves were more helpful and considerate 2 years later, whereas children with friends who were rated as less prosocial showed declines in these same behaviors (Wentzel, Barry, & Caldwell, 2004). It has also been shown that children who help and share with classmates are more popular (Warden & Mackinnon, 2003), and those who are altruistic have a greater number of friends (McGuire & Weisz, 1982). It seems that acting in prosocial ways may elicit positive reactions from peers and also facilitate the formation of friendships that, in turn, continue to influence prosocial behavior.

Teachers   Researchers examining the influence of teachers have drawn parallels between the mother–child and teacher–child relationships by showing that, similarly to the former, those latter relationships characterized as close and less conflictual are associated with higher rates of prosocial behavior (Birch & Ladd, 1998; Palermo, Hanish, Martin, Fabes, & Reiser, 2007). As well, Wentzel (2002) found that teachers who were less nurturing and encouraging had students who received lower ratings of sharing, helping, and "being nice" by classmates. The way teachers respond to children's behavior is important, with some early work showing that when teachers asked students to be helpful or to share and then provided positive feedback (e.g., smiling and praise) for these behaviors, children were more likely to exhibit prosocial behavior in the classroom (Eisenberg, Cameron, Tryon, & Dodez, 1981). More recently, in an experimental study, teachers were trained to encourage and reward prosocial behavior at school as part of a schoolwide violence prevention program in grades kindergarten to 5 (the PeaceBuilders Program; Embry, Flannery, Vazsonyi, Powell, & Atha, 1996; Flannery et al., 2003). The results showed increases in students' reports of their own prosocial behavior one year after the program was implemented.

Volunteering   Participation in community activities and volunteering has also been associated with prosocial behavior during childhood and adolescence. Thus, students who participated in extracurricular activities (these included a wide variety of activities ranging from sports through civic involvement) were more likely to exhibit prosocial behaviors in the community (e.g., volunteering) as young adults (Zaff, Moore, Papillo, & Williams, 2003). As well, Pratt and colleagues (Pratt, Hunsberger, Pancer, & Alisat, 2003) found that youth who reported being involved in helping activities reported a stronger commitment to being kind and caring 2 years later. The consequences of volunteer activities have also been examined within the school system, where structured programs have been created to encourage students to engage in these types of activities. Switzer and colleagues (Switzer, Simmons, Dew, Regalski, & Wang, 1995) found that, among children who participated in a mandatory volunteering program, boys reported greater community involvement and girls reported more positive self-perceptions once the program was over.

Television, videogames, and the Internet   Children and adolescents spend a considerable amount of time watching television, playing videogames, and surfing the Internet. Studies have shown that viewing educational television programming does not impact prosocial behavior during early childhood (Ostrov, Gentile, & Crick, 2006), although this may be due to the fact that educational programming was not uniformly prosocial in content. Anderson, Huston, Schmitt, Linebarger, and Wright (2001) did find that watching educational programming was related to greater participation in service activities during adolescence. The few studies that have been conducted on videogame playing show that playing games with aggressive content has a negative effect on prosocial behavior (e.g., Chambers & Ascione, 1987), and studies have shown that children's preferences for aggressive videogames, but not videogame playing in general, are related to lower prosocial ratings by classmates (van Schie & Wiegman, 1997; Wiegman & van Schie, 1998). Surprisingly little research has been done examining the effects of Internet usage on prosocial behavior, despite the fact that the Internet provides easy access to volunteer opportunities (Amichai-Hamburger, 2008).

Prosocial Behavior in the Cultural Context

The study of how prosocial behavior is manifested in different cultural contexts broadens considerably our understanding of concern for others. Whiting and Whiting (1975), for example, conducted one of the classic cultural studies of prosocial behavior by observing children between the ages of 3 and 11 years in six different settings – Kenya, Mexico, the Philippines, Okinawa, India, and the United States. They found that children from Kenya, Mexico, and the Philippines were more likely to offer help or support and make responsible suggestions to others than those from Okinawa, India, and the United States, and they attributed the differences to the greater assignment of responsibility to the former, particularly responsibility for the care of younger children. This work is a good example of how the way in which a culture is organized can contribute to the opportunities available for the learning of prosocial behavior. Thus, in cultures such as Kenya, Mexico, and the Philippines, in which women's workload and contribution to the family economy are greater, more responsibility is delegated to children and they therefore have more opportunity to engage in prosocial activities.

In addition to providing different opportunities for its learning, cultures also differ in the value they place on different forms of prosocial behavior. A value dimension that has attracted particular attention is that of individualism and collectivism (Markus & Kitayama, 1991). In individualist cultures (primarily North American and Western European ones), self-assertion, self-expression, and self-actualization are prized. In collectivist cultures (loosely linked to Asian, African, and Latin American countries), propriety, fitting in, and harmonious family relationships are more strongly appreciated. These differences in values appear to influence the forms of prosocial behavior favored in each type of culture. In individualist cultures, unsolicited or spontaneous prosocial behavior is viewed more positively than reciprocal or solicited prosocial behavior, whereas in collectivist cultures, they are valued equally or the latter is valued even more (Miller & Bersoff, 1994): This is a difference that presumably reflects a more positive attitude toward interdependence and compliance with social roles in the latter context and autonomy and feelings of self-generation in the former context. Similarly, differences in values can affect the expression of concern for others. For example, in some collectivist cultures where deference for authority is emphasized, individuals may be reluctant to help those who are older when such behavior would cause those older individuals to lose face (Trommsdorff, Friedlmeier, & Mayer, 2007).

Differences in values are also reflected in reasons given for prosocial action. Although American and Hindu children do not make different attributions for their prosocial behavior, American adults are more likely to attribute it to personal dispositions and Hindu adults to the social context (Miller, 1984), a finding that fits again with the differential emphasis on self-expression and propriety. Clary and Snyder (1999) noted that there are a variety of reasons for why people volunteer to help others and that a large proportion of them are individualistic in nature in the sense of promoting the individual. For example, helping may be undertaken to further personal growth, to advance one's own career, or because of deeply held values and convictions. Accordingly, Kemmelmeier, Jambor, and Letner (2006) found that volunteerism and charitable giving across the United States were higher in those states ranked higher on individualism. Presumably volunteerism and charitable giving reflect concern for strangers that may have a base in a more abstract valuing of community. More personal and family-oriented concern could well be a feature of collectivist values.

Neurological and Hormonal Processes in Prosocial Behavior

Evolutionary forces, genetic predispositions, and cultural experience combine and interact to produce prosocial behavioral outcomes. Psychologists in the last several years have become increasingly interested in the neural and hormonal changes that accompany these outcomes. Thus empathy, like all emotions, involves a neural representation of the salience of an evoking stimulus for the self, and this neural representation serves to regulate behavioral responses to that stimulus. Accordingly, researchers who study affect are turning their attention toward understanding the neurophysiological underpinnings of the human capacity for empathy (Braten, 2007). Their work informs our understanding of both normative prosocial development, as the maturation of neural systems may facilitate positive engagement with others, and such developmental problems as autism spectrum disorders, which appear to involve deficits in empathy. Recently, neuroscientists have focused on the possible involvement of mirror neurons in empathy, that is, of neurons that are activated in the same way when individuals see a goal-oriented action, including facial expressions of emotion, performed by another as when they perform the action themselves (Iacoboni & Dapretto, 2006). Given that empathy entails perceiving and, to some extent, sharing the emotional states of others, mirror neurons have therefore been posited as the neurophysiological mechanism for one important motivation to behave in prosocial ways.

Iacoboni and Dapretto (2006) proposed that humans have mirror neurons active in a network of frontal cortical regions that form a mirror neuron system (MNS). This MNS has been found to be activated when children and adults observe or imitate pictures of facial expressions (Killgore & Yurgelun-Todd, 2007; Pfeifer, Iacoboni, Mazziotta, & Dapretto, 2005, as reported in Iacoboni & Dapretto, 2006; Schulte-Ruther, Markowitsch, Fink, & Piefke, 2007). More strikingly, stronger MNS activation has been correlated with greater empathic concern on questionnaire measures (Pfeifer et al., 2005; Schulte-Ruther et al., 2007). Parts of the MNS also have been found to be uniquely activated when viewing others in pain, but not when experiencing pain oneself (Ochsner et al., 2008). Thus, there is accumulating evidence that mirror neurons are involved in attention to and engagement with the emotions and distress of others, and that mirror neurons begin serving this function at least as early as childhood.

Of course, activation of specific brain regions, in and of itself, cannot produce complex behaviors like helping or comforting; numerous neural and hormonal processes are necessary to convey that activation into action. Psychophysiologists have therefore begun to identify hormonal regulators of prosocial behaviors, with the greatest amount of evidence implicating sex and reproductive hormones in the development of empathy and nurturance. Increased parental responsiveness to infants is linked with higher levels of estradiol in women and prolactin in both men and women, whereas lower levels of testosterone are associated with being more nurturant, empathic, and prosocial in both men and women (Hastings, Zahn-Waxler, & McShane, 2006). Similarly, higher in utero testosterone levels in the second trimester have been found to predict lower mother-reported empathy in school-aged boys, and less accurate identification of facial emotion in boys and girls (Chapman et al., 2006). Thus, the development of greater prosocial tendencies might be supported by female sex hormones but undermined by male sex hormones, perhaps contributing to the frequently noted sex difference of greater empathy in girls and women than in boys and men.

Beyond Prosocial Behavior

Understanding the development of prosocial behavior is important in its own right, yet its understanding also has implications for other areas of interest. Most notably, there has been a strong interest in the relations between prosocial development and antisocial behavior. Not surprisingly, people who are highly empathic, compassionate, and altruistic typically are not highly hostile or aggressive. Surprising, however, is the fact that this inverse relation between prosocial and antisocial tendencies is not a developmental constant (Eisenberg & Miller, 1988). Toddlers who engage in relatively more prosocial behavior actually tend to be more aggressive (Gill & Calkins, 2003), suggesting both patterns of behavior might be connected to a common temperamental characteristic such as sociability or activity level. By preschool and kindergarten, prosocial and aggressive behavior are not correlated (Ostrov, 2008), such that preschoolers are as likely to show similar or dissimilar levels of caring and hurtful behaviors. By elementary school, the negative relation is generally found. The importance of the preschool period is evident, however, from findings that preschoolers who are highly prosocial are less likely to be aggressive in later years, and, in parallel fashion, those who are highly aggressive are less likely to be prosocial in later years (Hastings, Zahn-Waxler, Usher, Robinson, & Bridges, 2000). The extent to which dispositional or socialization forces contribute to this complex pattern of growth and change is not clear, but one possibility emerging from these findings is that efforts to preserve or promote early prosocial inclinations might be an effective way to prevent or reduce later problematic development.

Adding to the complexity of the picture, recent studies have shown that the negative relation between prosocial and aggressive behavior is either weaker, or more complicated, in girls than in boys (Pursell, Laursen, Rubin, Booth-LaForce, & Rose-Krasnor, 2008; Vaillancourt, Miller, Fagbemi, Côté, & Tremblay, 2007; Zahn-Waxler et al., 2008). Zahn-Waxler (Zahn-Waxler, Crick, Shirtcliff, & Woods, 2006) has argued that biological, parental, and cultural contributions to early sex differences lead young girls to be highly focused on social relationships and the emotional needs of others. This results in not only a heightened sense of responsibility but also strong experiences of guilt in girls who are aggressive, generating confusion and distress for the girls and apparently contradictory patterns of positive and aversive behaviors. Accordingly, Vaillancourt and colleagues (2007) found that, for girls only, being more prosocial at 2 years predicted a developmental trajectory of increasing indirect or relational aggression from 4 to 10 years, independent of girls' early physically aggressive behaviors (which also predicted this trajectory). Zahn-Waxler and colleagues (2008) found that, compared to all boys and to girls with fewer problems, girls with more disruptive behavior problems at 10 years included more prosocial content in the way they talked about the resolution of hypothetical social dilemmas at both 5 and 7 years. These studies might suggest that empathy and interpersonal responsibility are relatively preserved in aggressive girls and might serve as avenues for intervention, or that prosocial inclinations have lost their inhibitory function in aggressive girls, possibilities that require future investigation.

Another emerging perspective is that there might be a subgroup of youths with serious, stable conduct problems who are relatively lacking in concern for others from a very early age. This "callous-unemotional" characteristic (Frick & White, 2008) involves a lack of empathy and guilt, and is hypothesized to be the developmental precursor of psychopathy. Behavioral genetics research has indicated that children's conduct problems are more attributable to hereditary factors when they are highly callous-unemotional, whereas the shared environment (e.g., parental socialization) contributes to conduct problems only in children who are not callous-unemotional (Viding, Blair, Moffitt, & Plomin, 2005). However, this should not be pessimistically interpreted as suggesting that some children are "born bad," destined to become delinquent youths or criminal adults regardless of reparative efforts. In fact, an intervention study demonstrated that training parents to positively reinforce prosocial behaviors in callous-unemotional young boys with conduct problems led to improvements in the boys' behavior (Hawes & Dadds, 2005). Thus, as is evident in typically developing children, a positive and supportive parent–child relationship serves to promote prosocial development even in children with a relatively weak innate drive to share and respond to the emotions of others.

Conclusion

Developmental psychologists are more and more focused on the complex interplay between evolutionary processes, genetic predispositions, cultural experiences, and neurological and hormonal events. This survey shows how each of these approaches contributes to one very important aspect of children's social development – their growing concern for the welfare of others. Changes in empathy play an important role in this development, although, as we have noted, other processes operate as well. Exploration of these processes and of the complex nature of feeling and showing concern for others should remain an important priority for students of human nature.

References

Abramovitch, R., Corter, C., & Pepler, D. J. (1980). Observations of mixed-sex sibling dyads. *Child Development, 51*, 1268–1271.

Amichai-Hamburger, Y. (2008). Potential and promise of online volunteering. *Computers in Human Behavior, 24*, 544–562.

Anderson, D. R., Huston, A. C., Schmitt, K. L., Linebarger, D. L., & Wright, J. C. (2001). Early childhood television viewing and adolescent behavior. *Monographs of the Society for Research in Child Development, 66*, 90–99.

Bachner-Melman, R., Gritsenko, I., Nemanov, L., Zohar, A. H., Dina, C., & Ebstein, R. P. (2005). Dopaminergic polymorphisms associated with self-report measures of human altruism. *Molecular Psychiatry, 10*, 333–335.

Batson, C. D. (1991). *The altruism question: Towards a social-psychological answer*. Hillsdale, NJ: Erlbaum.

Birch, S. H., & Ladd, G. W. (1998). Children's interpersonal behaviors and the teacher-child relationship. *Developmental Psychology, 34*, 934–946.

Braten, S. (Ed.). (2007). *On being moved: From mirror neurons to empathy* (Advances in consciousness research). Amsterdam: John Benjamins.

Buck, R. (1991). Temperament, social skills, and the communication of emotions: A developmental-interactionist view. In D. G. Gilbert & J. J. Connolly (Eds.), *Personality, social skills, and psychopathology: An individual differences approach* (Perspectives on individual differences, pp. 85–105). New York: Wiley.

Bugental, D. B. (2000). Acquisition of the algorithms of social life: A domain-based approach. *Psychological Bulletin, 26*, 187–209.

Caplan, M. Z., & Hay, D. (1989). Preschoolers' responses to peers' distress and beliefs about bystander intervention. *Journal of Child Psychology and Psychiatry, 30*, 231–242.

Cassidy, J. (1994). Emotion regulation: Influences of attachment relationships. *Monographs of the Society for Research in Child Development, 59*, 228–283.

Chambers, J. H., & Ascione, F. R. (1987). The effects of prosocial and aggressive videogames on children's donating and helping. *Journal of Genetic Psychology, 148*, 499–505.

Chapman, E., Baron-Cohen, S., Auyeung, B., Knickmeyer, R., Taylor, K., & Hackett, G. (2006). Fetal testosterone and empathy: Evidence from the Empathy Quotient (EQ) and the Reading the Mind in the Eyes test. *Social Neuroscience, 1*, 135–148.

Clark, M. S. (1983). Some implications of close social bonds for help seeking. In B. M. DePaulo, A. Nadler, & J. D. Fisher (Eds.), *New directions in helping: Vol. 2. Help seeking* (pp. 205–233). New York: Academic Press.

Clary, E. G., & Snyder, M. (1999). The motivations to volunteer: Theoretical and practical considerations. *Current Directions in Psychological Science, 8*, 156–159.

Comings, D. E., Gade-Andavolu, R., Gonzalez, N., Wu, S., Muhleman, D., Blake, H., et al. (2000). A multivariate analysis of 59 candidate genes in personality traits: The temperament and character inventory. *Clinical Genetics, 58*, 375–385.

Davidov, M., & Grusec, J. E. (2006). Untangling the links of parental responsiveness to distress and warmth to child outcomes. *Child Development, 77*, 44–58.

de Waal, F. B. M. (2008). Putting the altruism back into altruism: The evolution of empathy. *Annual Review of Psychology, 59*, 279–300.

Dekovic, M., & Janssens, J. M. (1992). Parents' child-rearing style and child's sociometric status. *Developmental Psychology, 28*, 925–932.

Demetriou, H., & Hay, D. F. (2004). Toddlers' reactions to the distress of familiar peers: The importance of context. *Infancy, 6*, 299–318.

Denham, S. A., Bassett, H. H., & Wyatt, T. (2007). The socialization of emotional competence. In J. E. Grusec & P. D. Hastings (Eds.), *Handbook of socialization* (pp. 614–637). New York: Guilford Press.

Dunn, J., & Munn, P. (1986) Siblings and the development of prosocial behaviour. *International Journal of Behavioral Development, 9*, 265–284.

Eisenberg, N., Cameron, E., Tryon, K., & Dodez, R. (1981). Socialization of prosocial behavior in the preschool classroom. *Developmental Psychology, 17*, 773–782.

Eisenberg, N., Fabes, R. A., Schaller, M., Miller, P., Gustavo, C., Shea, C., et al. (1991). Personality and socialization correlates of vicarious emotional responding. *Journal of Personality and Social Psychology, 61,* 459–470.

Eisenberg, N., Fabes, R. A., & Spinrad, T. L. (2006). Prosocial development. In N. Eisenberg (Vol. Ed.), *Handbook of child psychology: Vol. 3. Social, emotional, and personality development* (pp. 646–718). Hoboken, NJ: Wiley.

Eisenberg, N., & Miller, P. A. (1988). The relation of empathy to prosocial and related behaviors. *Psychological Bulletin, 101*(1), 91–119.

Embry, D. D., Flannery, D. J., Vazsonyi, A. T., Powell, K. E., & Atha, H. (1996). PeaceBuilders: A theoretically driven, school-based model for early violence prevention. *American Journal of Preventive Medicine, 12*(Suppl.), 91–100.

Emde, R. N., Biringen, Z., Clyman, R. B., & Oppenheim, D. (1991). The moral self of infancy: Affective core and procedural knowledge. *Developmental Review, 11,* 251–270.

Fabes, R. A., Fultz, J., Eisenberg, N., May-Plumlee, T., & Christopher, F. S. (1989). Effects of rewards on children's prosocial motivation: A socialization study. *Developmental Psychology, 25,* 509–515.

Fischer, J. D., Nadler, A., & Witcher-Alagna, S. (1982). Recipient reactions to aid. *Psychological Bulletin, 91,* 27–54.

Flannery, D. J, Vazsonyi, A. T., Liau, A. K., Guo, S., Powell, K. E., Atha, H., et al. (2003). Initial behavior outcomes for the PeaceBuilders universal school-based violence prevention program. *Developmental Psychology, 39,* 292–308.

Frick, P. J., & White, S. F. (2008). The importance of callous-unemotional traits for developmental models of aggressive and antisocial behavior. *Journal of Child Psychology and Psychiatry, 49,* 359–375.

Garner, P. W. (2003). Child and family correlates of toddlers' emotional and behavioral responses to a mishap. *Infant Mental Health Journal, 24,* 580–592.

Gill, K. L., & Calkins, S. D. (2003). Behavioral and physiological indicators of empathic responding in 2-year-old children. *Development and Psychopathology, 15,* 55–71.

Gold, G. J., & Davis, J. R. (2005). Psychological determinants of forgiveness: An evolutionary perspective. *Humboldt Journal of Social Relations, 29,* 111–134.

Greenberg, M. S., & Shapiro, S. P. (1971). Indebtedness: An adverse aspect of asking for and receiving help. *Sociometry, 34,* 290–301.

Gross, A. E., Wallston, B. S., & Piliavin, I. M., (1979). Reactance, attribution, equity, and the help recipient. *Journal of Applied Psychology, 9,* 297–313.

Grusec, J. E. (1991). Socializing concern for others in the home. *Developmental Psychology, 27,* 338–342.

Grusec, J. E., & Davidov, M. (2010). Integrating different perspectives on socialization theory and research: A domain-specific approach. *Child Development, 81*(3), 687–709.

Grusec, J. E., Goodnow, J. J., & Cohen, L. (1997). Household work and the development of children's concern for others. *Developmental Psychology, 32,* 999–1007.

Grusec, J. E., & Redler, E. (1980). Attribution, reinforcement, and altruism: A developmental analysis. *Developmental Psychology, 16,* 525–534.

Gunnar, M. R. (2000). Early adversity and the development of stress reactivity and regulation. In C. A. Nelson (Ed.), *The effects of early adversity on neurobehavioral development* (Minnesota Symposia on Child Psychology, Vol. 31, pp. 163–200). Mahwah, NJ: Erlbaum.

Hamalaimen, M., & Pulkiinen, L. (1995). Aggressive and non-prosocial behavior as precursors of criminality. *Studies on Crime and Crime Prevention, 4,* 6–21.

Haselager, G. J. T., Hartup, W. W., van Lieshout, C. F. M., & Riksen-Walraven, J. M. A. (1998). Similarities between friends and nonfriends in middle childhood. *Child Development, 69,* 1198–1208.

Hastings, P. D., McShane, K. E., Parker, R., & Ladha, F. (2007). Ready to make nice: Parental socialization of young sons' and daughters' prosocial behaviors with peers. *Journal of Genetic Psychology, 168,* 177–200.

Hastings, P. D., Rubin, K. H., & DeRose, L. (2005). Links among gender, inhibition, and parental socialization in the development of prosocial behaviour. *Merrill-Palmer Quarterly, 51,* 467–493.

Hastings, P. D., Zahn-Waxler, C., & McShane, K. E. (2006). We are, by nature, moral creatures: Biological bases of concern for others. In M. Killen & J. Smetana (Eds.), *Handbook of moral development* (pp. 483–516). Mahwah, NJ: Erlbaum.

Hastings, P. D., Zahn-Waxler, C., Robinson, J., Usher, B., & Bridges, D. (2000). The development of concern for others in children with behavior problems. *Developmental Psychology, 36,* 531–546.

Hawes, D. J., & Dadds, M. R. (2005). The treatment of conduct problems in children with callous-unemotional traits. *Journal of Consulting and Clinical Psychology, 73,* 737–741.

Hoffman, M. L. (1970). Moral development. In P. H. Mussen (Ed.), *Carmichael's manual of child psychology* (Vol. 2, pp. 261–360). New York: Wiley.

Iacoboni, M., & Dapretto, M. (2006). The mirror neuron system and the consequences of its dysfunction. *Nature Reviews Neuroscience, 7,* 942–951.

Kemmelmeier, M., Jambor, E. E., & Letner, J. (2006). Individualism and good works: Cultural variations in giving and receiving across the United States. *Journal of Cross-Cultural Psychology, 37,* 327–344.

Killgore, W. D. S., & Yurgelun-Todd, D. A. (2007). Unconscious processing of facial affect in children and adolescents. *Social Neuroscience, 2,* 28–47.

Knafo, A., Israel, S., Darvasi, A., Bachner-Melman, R., Uzefovsky, F., Cohen, L., et al. (2008). Individual differences in allocation of funds in the dictator game associated with length of the arginine vasopressin 1a receptor RS3 promoter region and correlation between RS3 length and hippocampal mRNA. *Genes, Brain & Behavior, 7,* 266–275.

Knafo, A., & Plomin, R. (2006). Prosocial behavior from early to middle childhood: Genetic and environmental influences. *Developmental Psychology, 42,* 771–786.

Kopp, C. B. (1982). Antecedents of self-regulation: A developmental view. *Developmental Psychology, 18,* 199–214.

Lepper, M. (1983). Social control processes, attributions of motivation, and the internalization of social values. In E. T. Higgins, D. N. Ruble, & W. W. Hartup (Eds.), *Social cognition and social development: A sociocultural perspective* (pp. 294–330). New York: Cambridge University Press.

Markus, H. R., & Kitayama, S. (1991). Culture and the self: Implications for cognition, emotion, and motivation. *Psychological Review, 98,* 224–253.

McAndrew, F. T. (2002). New evolutionary perspectives on altruism: Multilevel-selection and costly-signaling theories. *Current Directions in Psychological Science, 11,* 79–82.

McCullough, M. E., Kimeldorf, M. B., & Cohen, A. D. (2008). An adaptation for altruism? The social causes, social effects, and social evolution of gratitude. *Current Directions in Psychological Science, 17,* 281–285.

McGuire, K. D., & Weisz, J. R. (1982). Social cognition and behavior correlates of preadolescent chumship. *Child Development, 53,* 1478–1484.

Miller, J. G. (1984). Culture and the development of everyday social explanation. *Journal of Personality and Social Psychology, 46,* 961–978.

Miller, J. G. E., & Bersoff, D. M. (1994). Culture and moral judgment: How are conflicts between justice and interpersonal responsibilities resolved? *Journal of Personality and Social Psychology, 62,* 541–554.

Ochsner, K. N., Zaki, J., Hanelin, J., Ludlow, D. H., Knierim, K., Ramachandran, T., et al. (2008). Common and distinct neural systems supporting the perception of pain in self and other. *Social Cognitive and Affective Neuroscience, 3*, 144–160.

Ostrov, J. M. (2008). Forms of aggression and peer victimization during early childhood: A short-term longitudinal study. *Journal of Abnormal Child Psychology, 36*, 311–322.

Ostrov, J. M., Gentile, D. A., & Crick, N. R. (2006). Media exposure, aggression, and prosocial behavior during early childhood: A longitudinal study. *Social Development, 15*, 612–627.

Palermo, F., Hanish, L. D., Martin, C. L., Fabes, R. A., & Reiser, M. (2007). Preschoolers' academic readiness: What role does the teacher–child relationship play? *Early Childhood Research Quarterly, 22*, 407–422.

Parpal, M., & Maccoby, E. E. (1985). Maternal responsiveness and subsequent child compliance. *Child Development, 56*, 1326–1334.

Plomin, R., DeFries, J. C., McClearn, G. E., & McGuffin, P. (2001). *Behavioral genetics* (4th ed.). New York: Worth.

Pratt, M. W., Hunsberger, B., Pancer, M. S., & Alisat, S. (2003). A longitudinal analysis of personal values and socialization: Correlates of a moral self-ideal in late adolescence. *Social Development, 12*, 563–585.

Puntambekar, S., & Hübscher, R. (2005). Tools for scaffolding students in a complex learning environment: What have we gained and what have we missed? *Educational Psychologist, 40*, 1–12.

Pursell, G. R., Laursen, B., Rubin, K. H., Booth-LaForce, C., & Rose-Krasnor, L. (2008). Gender differences in patterns of association between prosocial behavior, personality, and externalizing problems. *Journal of Research in Personality, 42*, 472–481.

Rheingold, H. (1982). Little children's participation in the work of adults: A nascent prosocial behavior. *Child Development, 53*, 114–125.

Rice, M., & Grusec, J. E. (1975). Saying and doing: Effects on observer performance. *Journal of Personality and Social Psychology, 32*, 584–593.

Rosenhan, D. (1969). Some origins of concern for others. In P. H. Mussen, J. Langer, & M. Covington (Eds.), *Trends and issues in developmental psychology*. New York: Holt, Rinehart and Winston.

Rushton, J. P., Fulker, D. W., Neale, M. C., Nias, D. K. B., & Eysenck, H. J. (1986). Altruism and aggression: The heritability of individual differences. *Journal of Personality and Social Psychology, 50*, 1192–1198.

Schulte-Rüther, M., Markowitsch, H. J., Fink, G. R., & Piefke, M. (2007). Mirror neuron and theory of mind mechanisms involved in face-to-face interactions. *Journal of Cognitive Neuroscience, 19*, 1354–1372.

Smith, C. L., Gelfand, D. M., Harmann, D. P., & Partlow, M. E. (1979). Children's causal attributions regarding helping. *Child Development, 50*, 203–210.

Sober, E., & Wilson, D. S. (1998). *Unto others: The evolution and psychology of unselfish behavior*. Cambridge, MA: Harvard University Press.

Switzer, G. E., Simmons, R. G., Dew, M. A., Regalski, J. M., & Wang, C. H. (1995). The effect of a school-based helper program on adolescent self-image, attitudes and behavior. *Journal of Early Adolescence, 15*, 429–455.

Trommsdorff, G., Friedlmeier, W., & Mayer, B. (2007). Sympathy, distress, and prosocial behaviour of preschool children in four cultures. *International Journal of Behavioural Development, 31*, 284–293.

Tucker, D. M., Luu, P., & Derryberry, D. (2005). Love hurts: The evolution of empathic concern through the encephalization of nociceptive capacity. *Development and Psychopathology, 17*, 699–713.

Vaillancourt, T., Miller, J. L., Fagbemi, J., Côté, S., & Tremblay, R. E. (2007). Trajectories and predictors of indirect aggression: Results from a nationally representative longitudinal study of Canadian children aged 2–10. *Aggressive Behavior, 33*, 314–326.

van Schie, E. G. M., & Wiegman, O. (1997). Children and videogames: Leisure activities, aggression, social integration, and school performance. *Journal of Applied Social Psychology, 27*, 1175–1194.

Viding, E., Blair, R. J. R., Moffitt, T. E., & Plomin, R. (2005). Evidence for substantial genetic risk for psychopathy in 7-year-olds. *Journal of Child Psychology and Psychiatry, 46*, 592–597.

Vierikko, E., Pulkkinen, L., & Rose, R. J. (2006). Genetic and environmental factors in girls' and boys' socioemotional behavior. In L. Pulkkinen, J. Kaprio, & R. J. Rose (Eds.), *Socioemotional development and health from adolescence to adulthood* (pp. 176–196). New York: Cambridge University Press.

Warden, D., & Mackinnon, S. (2003). Prosocial children, bullies and victims: An investigation of their sociometric status, empathy and social problem-solving strategies. *British Journal of Developmental Psychology, 21*, 367–385.

Wentzel, K. R. (2002). Are effective teachers like good parents? Teaching styles and student adjustment in early adolescence. *Child Development, 73*, 287–301.

Wentzel, K. R., Barry, C. M., & Caldwell, K. A. (2004). Friendships in middle school: Influences on motivation and school adjustment. *Journal of Educational Psychology, 96*, 195–203.

Whiting, B. B., & Whiting, J. W. M. (1975). *Children of six cultures: A psycho-cultural analysis.* Cambridge, MA: Harvard University Press.

Wiegman, O., & van Schie, E. G. M. (1998). Video game playing and its relations with aggressive and prosocial behaviour. *British Journal of Social Psychology, 37*, 367–378.

Zaff, J. F., Moore, K. A., Papillo, A. R., & Williams, S. (2003). Implication of extracurricular activity participation during adolescence on positive outcomes. *Journal of Adolescent Research, 18*, 599–630.

Zahn-Waxler, C., Crick, N. R., Shirtcliff, E. A., & Woods, K. E. (2006). The origins and development of psychopathology in females and males. In D. Cicchetti & D. J. Cohen (Eds.), *Developmental psychopathology: Vol. 1. Theory and method* (2nd ed., pp. 76–138). Hoboken, NJ: Wiley.

Zahn-Waxler, C., Park, J-H., Usher, B., Belouad, F., Cole, P., & Gruber, R. (2008). Young children's representations of conflict and distress: A longitudinal study of boys and girls with disruptive behavior problems. *Development and Psychopathology, 20*, 99–119.

Zahn-Waxler, C., Radke-Yarrow, M., Wagner, E., & Chapman, M. (1992). Development of concern for others. *Developmental Psychology, 28*, 126–136.

Zahn-Waxler, C., Schiro, K., Robinson, J. L., Emde, R. N., & Schmitz, S. (2001). Empathy and prosocial patterns in young MZ and DZ twins. In R. N. Emde & J. K. Hewitt (Eds.), *Infancy to early childhood: Genetic and environmental influences on developmental change* (pp. 141–162). New York: Oxford University Press.

CHAPTER THIRTY

Children's Social and Moral Reasoning

Charles C. Helwig and Elliot Turiel

Introduction

The study of morality has been approached from different perspectives within several disciplines, including philosophy, anthropology, sociology, and psychology. In psychology, proponents of the major theoretical approaches have attempted to explain the acquisition or development of morality. Behavioristic and social-learning theorists have proposed that moral development entails a process of acquiring behaviors (Skinner, 1971) or internalizing the standards and values of society so that they are maintained without the necessity of external surveillance (Aronfreed, 1968). Psychoanalytic theorists, too, have presumed that morality comes from the incorporation of societal standards (Freud, 1930). In the psychoanalytic account the process of moral development, as well as the maintenance of morality, is full of conflict and tension for individuals. This is because in acquiring society's moral standards, the individual must control strongly felt instinctual drives and needs (through the formation of what Freud referred to as a *superego*). The emotion of guilt operates so as to maintain control over instincts. Recently, there has been a turn to biologically based explanations of moral acquisition in which moral reactions and decisions are seen to be due to hard-wired brain processes (Hauser, 2006).

An alternative view on moral development, in keeping with a long line of philosophical analyses from Aristotle to Kant and to modern versions (e.g., those of Dworkin, 1977, and Rawls, 1971), is that it involves the construction of judgments about welfare, justice, and rights through children's social interactions. Extensive study of children's moral judgments dates back to the research of Piaget (1932), which was later extended by Kohlberg (1981). They were instrumental in drawing attention to the importance of

The Wiley-Blackwell Handbook of Childhood Social Development, Second Edition, edited by Peter K. Smith and Craig H. Hart
© 2011 by Blackwell Publishing Ltd.

processes of judgment in the moral realm. The research of Piaget and Kohlberg went far in demonstrating that children do not solely accommodate to societal standards or comply with rules and parental or other social expectations. Rather, children attempt to understand social relationships, and in the process construct judgments about right and wrong, about how people should act toward each other.

There is substantial evidence demonstrating that children form systematic judgments about right and wrong, in the moral sense, that are central to their actions, social interactions, and development. Piaget and Kohlberg also described sequences for the development of moral judgments in which concepts of justice and rights are not constructed until late childhood or adolescence. Research on a variety of aspects of children's social and moral judgments conducted over the past two decades has shown, however, that young children begin to develop moral judgments, distinct from other types or domains of social judgments. After a brief overview of the characterizations by Piaget and Kohlberg, we consider research on how children form moral judgments that differ from their judgments about the domains of societal convention and personal jurisdiction. We also consider issues raised by this "domain" approach for development and culture.

The Development of Social and Moral Judgments

The moral thinking of young children was described by Piaget and Kohlberg as oriented toward punishment, respect for authority, and the maintenance of existing social rules and laws. Piaget (1932) described moral development as moving from heteronomy, or a strong respect for adult authority and rules, to an autonomous morality in later childhood in which rules are understood as social constructions formulated in social relations of cooperation among peers. According to Piaget, young children view social rules as fixed and unalterable, and conceptualize moral obligation in terms of strict adherence to the rules or commands of adult authorities. A morality based on adult constraint gives way to a morality based on mutual respect, or cooperation. This progression is facilitated by the older child's cognitive development from egocentrism to perspectivism, and by a corresponding shift in the child's social relations from one-way relations of adult constraint to reciprocal relations of mutual respect among peers.

Similarly, Kohlberg (1981) characterized children's moral reasoning in terms of a punishment and obedience orientation. Kohlberg believed that Piaget mischaracterized the thinking of the young child as reflecting a reverence for rules; Kohlberg, rather, saw young children's moral thinking as expressing an expedient concern with obedience to authority as connected to punishment avoidance. Nonetheless, Kohlberg likewise saw the young child as prone to take the perspective of authority in moral judgments and to exhibit a focus on the concrete consequences of moral acts and disobedience. Based on analyses of children's reasoning about moral dilemmas, Kohlberg described moral development as moving through a series of stages, in which morality is defined first in terms of punishment or obedience to authority, through a conventional level in which individuals take the perspective of the legal system and uphold existing laws; in adulthood, a principled level may be reached where individuals develop truly moral principles of justice and rights (attained only by a minority of adults).

These propositions yield a portrait of young children's moral reasoning as oriented toward authority and characterized by rigid adherence to and respect for existing social rules, norms, and customs. A substantially different picture of children's moral judgments has emerged from research that examined whether children make distinctions between different kinds of social rules and acts. It is a portrait in which children distinguish among social rules in accordance with different domains of social reasoning, and in which they possess conceptions of autonomy, rights, and democracy which sometimes lead them to take a critical perspective on the dictates of authorities and existing social systems. Even young children possess moral concepts that are independent of authority or existing social sanctions or rules, and their moral judgments are sensitive to both the content of social rules and the context of their application.

Researchers working within what has come to be known as the *domain approach* have proposed that children's thinking is organized from an early age into the domains of morality and social convention (Turiel, 1983). The *moral domain* pertains to issues of harm, fairness, and rights. The *social conventional domain* is composed of behavioral uniformities that serve to coordinate social interactions in social systems (e.g., the organizational rules of the classroom, or uniformities involving matters like dress, etiquette, or titles). Research with children of different ages has shown that they discriminate between moral and social conventional events and reason about them differently (see Turiel, 2006, for a review). Two types of assessments have been employed in the research on domain distinctions. The first, termed *criterion judgments*, pertains to the criteria used in making judgments of acts or rules associated with each domain. Criterion judgments include judgments of the generalizability, universality, rule contingency, and alterability of prohibitions regarding the act. Judgments of moral transgressions (e.g., hitting and stealing) have been found to be generalizable (i.e., wrong across social contexts) and non–rule contingent (i.e., wrong even if there were no rule against it), and rules that pertain to moral acts are seen as unalterable. In contrast, social conventional transgressions (e.g., calling a teacher by his or her first name, or eating with one's fingers) are seen as relative to the social context, contingent on the existence of an explicit social rule, and rules regarding social conventions are seen as alterable by authority or social consensus. For example, children judge it acceptable to call a teacher by his or her first name in a school in which there was no rule or social uniformity prohibiting it, and existing rules prohibiting the behavior were seen as alterable if the relevant authorities approved. In contrast, hitting is judged as wrong even if a teacher permitted it, and rules about hitting were not seen as alterable by the commands of those holding authority.

The second type of assessment is children's reasons or justifications for the judgments they make. Reasoning in the moral domain is characterized by references to issues of harm, fairness, and rights. Reasoning in the social conventional domain is characterized by references to rules, authority, social customs, and the coordination of social behavior. The different reasons given by children for moral and social conventional transgressions correspond to their criterion judgments and help account for their differential judgments of generalizability and rule contingency. Because moral events entail acts with intrinsic consequences of harm or unfairness, children's judgments of these acts are independent of social conventional aspects of the social system, such as authority or the presence of explicit social rules. In contrast, social conventions derive their meaning from being embedded within an existing social system with prescribed rules and roles, social hierarchies, or shared symbolic meanings that may be specific to the group. Accordingly, the meaning of a social convention may change along with social agreement or the commands of recognized authorities, and conventions may vary across social systems and across time and place. It has been proposed that different social interactions are associated with each of the domains, by which children construct different types of social judgments (Turiel, 2006). For example, when faced with a moral transgression (e.g., one child pushes another off a swing), children may consider the direct consequences of the act, and arrive at the conclusion that the act is wrong (Turiel, 1983). However, when observing a violation of social convention (e.g., a child calls a teacher by her first name) with no intrinsic consequences of harm or unfairness, children must infer the wrongness of the behavior from features extrinsic to the event. If others (e.g., adult authorities) react to the event as a rule transgression or as part of authority jurisdiction, children will see the act as a violation of social convention.

A large number of studies have yielded evidence that children distinguish morality from convention on these dimensions (see Turiel, 2006, for a review). As a means of conveying how young children make this distinction, we present an example of responses given by a 5-year-old boy. The boy's responses come from a study (Weston & Turiel, 1980) in which children from 5 to 11 years of age were presented with hypothetical stories of preschools in which certain actions are permitted. In one story, children are allowed to be without clothes on warm days (a conventional issue). In a second story, children are allowed to hit each other (a moral issue). Prior to the presentation of these hypothetical stories, the children had judged both acts as wrong. The first interview excerpt begins with the boy's responses to the question of whether it is all right for a school to allow hitting and the second with his responses as to whether it is all right to allow children to remove their clothes (the excerpts come from Turiel, 1983):

> No, it is not okay. (WHY NOT?) Because this is like making other people unhappy. You can hurt them that way. It hurts other people, hurting is not good. (MARK GOES TO PARK SCHOOL. TODAY IN SCHOOL HE WANTS TO SWING BUT HE FINDS THAT ALL THE SWINGS ARE BEING USED BY OTHER CHILDREN. SO HE DECIDES TO HIT ONE OF THE CHILDREN AND TAKE THE SWING. IS IT OKAY FOR MARK TO DO THAT?) No. Because he is hurting someone else. …
>
> Yes, because that is the rule. (WHY CAN THEY HAVE THAT RULE?) If that's what the boss wants to do, he can do that. (HOW COME?) Because he's the boss, he is in charge of the school. (BOB GOES TO GROVE SCHOOL. THIS IS A WARM DAY AT GROVE SCHOOL. HE HAS BEEN RUNNING IN THE PLAY AREA OUTSIDE AND HE IS HOT SO HE DECIDES TO TAKE OFF HIS CLOTHES. IS IT OKAY FOR BOB TO DO THAT?) Yes, if he wants to he can because it's the rule. (p. 62)

For this child, all rules are not alike, and the type of act involved is evaluated in relation to the jurisdiction of the person in authority. With regard to removing one's clothes, the justification of the act and the school policy are based on rules and authority. Although the principal is the "boss and in charge" of the school, it matters in one case but not in the other. This boy's responses provide an example of the general findings of the study (Weston & Turiel, 1980). The majority of children at all ages responded in similar fashion, distinguishing between moral and conventional issues regarding rules and authority.

Research on very young children's ability to distinguish morality and social convention suggests that judgments of these events undergo important development during the pre-school years. A set of studies have examined criterion judgments with children from 2 to 5 years (e.g., Smetana, 1981; Smetana & Braeges, 1990). Children appear to reliably distinguish basic or prototypical moral and social conventional events by about 4 or 5 years, although not at 2 years. Between these ages, children distinguish the events on some criteria, but not others. For example, during the third year, children apply judgments of generalizability to distinguish moral events from social conventions (with moral events more likely to be judged wrong across social contexts than social conventions). By the end of the third year, they also judge moral transgressions to be independent of rules or authority (Smetana & Braeges, 1990).

Children also have been found to distinguish morality from authority and legal rules, and to adopt a critical perspective on authority, especially when it conflicts with the demands of morality (Damon, 1977; Laupa, Turiel, & Cowan, 1995). For example, Damon found that young children do not accept as legitimate parental commands to engage in acts that violate moral rules, such as commands to steal or to cause harm to another person. Other research explored children's judgments and reasoning about the attributes that give legitimacy to authority, and how children account for the type of act commanded (see Laupa et al., 1995). When reasoning about acts entailing theft or physical harm to persons, 4–6-year-old children give priority to the act itself, rather than the status of the person in a position of authority. For example, commands for children to stop fighting were seen as legitimate whether or not they came from adults or children holding positions of authority. Children also judged commands from a peer (with or without a position of authority in a school) to stop fighting as more legitimate than conflicting commands from an adult authority, such as a teacher. However, with regard to other acts, such as turn taking or interpretations of game rules, children give priority to adults in positions of authority over children or other adults who are not in positions of authority. Children's judgments of obedience in these cases are based on the attributes possessed by authorities, such as their social position in a school or their superior knowledge and experience. Children's reasoning about authority is not based on unilateral respect or an unexamined acceptance of authority injunctions; rather, even young children make subtle discriminations taking into account the type of command given and the attributes lending legitimacy to individuals in authority. Children also take a critical perspective on rules and laws when they conflict with the demands of morality (Helwig & Jasiobedzka, 2001). In that study, children 6 years of age and older judged laws that discriminate against individuals on the basis of age, income, or appearance to be wrong and their violation to be permissible.

The Development of Social Thought and Action

Most of the studies considered thus far examined children's judgments regarding different aspects of morality and social convention. This leaves open the question of whether children's actions are related to, or influenced by, their judgments. Within the perspective presented, it is proposed that thought and action are closely related to each other (Piaget, 1932). This does not mean that we can simply predict what people will do from what they say they would do. There are many reasons people may not be able to predict their own actions, including that they cannot necessarily foresee the variety of issues that may come up in particular contexts (Ross & Nisbett, 1991). The propositions instead are that people's judgments influence how they approach situations calling for actions, and actions, in turn, influence the development of their judgments. One feature of this proposition is that children's social interactions influence the development of judgments. A second is that children's judgments are important in how they frame events they experience, and that the different domains of judgments have a bearing on this process.

A number of studies examined children's (ages 2–3 years to late childhood) social interactions around moral and conventional events in a variety of contexts such as the home, the school, and the playground. The research shows that children's social interactions are differentiated according to domains of reasoning (e.g., Nucci & Turiel, 1978; Wainryb, Brehl, & Matwin, 2005). The results of these studies are consistent with the proposition that children's domain distinctions are based on early social experiences. The development of morality involves constructions of judgments about welfare, justice, and rights through multiple social relationships and experiences. Young children participate in a variety of events that involve, as examples, people harming or helping each other, sharing or failing to share, excluding or including others, and treating people equally or unequally. Children's observations and reflections about such events are important sources of the formation and changes in moral judgments.

A study by Wainryb et al. (2005) that examined children's narratives about events involving harm they had experienced as either perpetrators or victims revealed how they think about exchanges with others, the feelings evoked, and the effects of acts on self and others. For example, in talking about their experiences as victims, two preschoolers (one a boy and the other a girl) recalled their physical and emotional hurt:

> I remember one thing about um someone, um a friend hurting me. I, it was just a little bit. He was a friend, his name was William, he hit me with his hammer in the middle of the head and it really hurt. It was plastic.

> My friend Sydney ... when I came inside her house, she said she really didn't want to play with me and she um she hit me and um and I felt bad and so I asked her mom ... if I could go home and she said yes. (Wainryb et al., 2005, p. 54)

By the first grade, children expressed feelings and thoughts about the nature of relationships and mutual expectations. An example comes from a first-grade girl who discussed a time she felt slighted by her best friend, who referred to another girl as her best friend:

> And I kind of thought to myself that was kind of making me feel bad. So I wonder if I can go over there and tell her that I that that kind of hurt my feelings. ... She is a best friend of mine and I just can't get it out of my mind because she, because whenever I walked home from her house at night time she would always give me a hug and I would always do that

and we would and I would never want to leave her house. Then at the birthday. ... I'm wondering if she's really her um best friend. (Wainryb et al., 2005, p. 56)

These types of concerns and reflections on social relationships, which were expressed by children of various ages, indicate that there is a correspondence between their judgments in moral and social domains and how they approach behavioral situations.

Most of the observational studies have found that young children do not respond as frequently to conventional violations as to moral transgressions. However, adults do respond to violations of social conventions, and their communications generally focus on issues of disorder, the importance of maintaining rules, and obedience to authority, rather than on harmful consequences or the perspectives of others. The criterion judgments and justifications evident in studies using hypothetical situations are also used in children's thinking about situations they experience. In one study (Turiel, 2008), elementary school–aged children and adolescents were found to reason about actual moral events that they had experienced as wrong even if no rule existed, whereas a minority judged that the conventional acts would be wrong under those circumstances. Similarly, a majority judged that evaluations of moral acts were not based on authority expectations, whereas a majority did so for the conventional acts. Children used domain-appropriate justifications in both instances. These findings suggest that the types of events that children experience, as well as the communications they receive or generate during social interactions, are distinguished in ways predicted by the domains of social reasoning.

Reasoning About Exclusion Based on Gender and Race

Children's attempts to relate the moral and social conventional components of social situations are relevant for socially important experiences that children have in their daily lives, including those involving exclusion based on gender or race. Recent work has explored the conditions under which children believe that it may be acceptable to exclude a child from a group activity, and the impact of gender and racial stereotypes as well as beliefs about social organizational functioning on these judgments. Research (e.g., Theimer, Killen, & Stangor, 2001) has found that although children become aware of gender and racial stereotypes in early childhood, they nevertheless apply moral concepts of fairness and equality to critically evaluate many instances of exclusion based on gender and race. For example, preschool children use beliefs about fairness to negatively evaluate straightforward instances of exclusion based on gender stereotypes (e.g., that it would be unfair for a group of girls who play with dolls to exclude a boy from playing with them, or for a group of boys who play with trucks to exclude a girl). However, in situations in which a group has to decide on whether to choose a boy or a girl to play with if there is space for only one more child, preschoolers will tend to prefer the child who fits the gender stereotype and appeal to stereotypical beliefs in their reasoning.

Studies with older children and adolescents (e.g., Killen & Stangor, 2001), however, indicate that moral considerations tend to take priority over stereotypical considerations in similar kinds of forced choice situations, such as where two candidates of equal ability are being considered for membership in a group (e.g., a girl or a boy for a ballet or baseball club, or a White or Black child for a basketball team or a math club). Older children tended to believe that the child who does not fit the stereotype should be chosen, for reasons of equal opportunity and access, that is, in order to give the nonstereotypical child a chance. The priority given to moral considerations in these situations probably reflects older children's greater awareness of existing patterns of exclusion and discrimination in society at large. However, when the nonstereotypical child was portrayed as having less ability than the stereotypical child (thereby placing equal opportunity into conflict with group functioning), older children and adolescents were more likely than younger children to advocate choosing the stereotypical child over the nonstereotypical child. Thus, social conventional considerations of group functioning appear to be given greater weight with age than moral considerations of equal opportunity when these issues conflict.

Children also distinguish between different situations when evaluating the acceptability of race-based exclusion. For example, deciding not to be friends with someone because of his or her ethnicity is more likely to be seen as acceptable and up to personal choice than is excluding someone from a club or denying him or her access to school (Killen, Lee-Kim, McGlothlin, & Stangor, 2002). Reasoning about ethnic exclusion appears to be influenced by students' experiences and the characteristics of their school environments. Students from schools that are more racially heterogeneous and that provide more opportunities for children from different backgrounds to interact in academic and extra-curricular activities are more likely to view race-based exclusion in choosing one's friends or in other situations as wrong and unfair (Crystal, Killen, & Ruck, 2008). These findings call to mind Piaget's (1932) ideas about the role of egalitarian peer interactions and reciprocity in facilitating the development of more advanced conceptions of justice. Taken together, the findings from studies of racial and gender exclusion indicate that moral concerns with fairness, justice, and equality are present from an early age and are used by children to critically evaluate racial and gender discrimination in many situations. However, how children coordinate and balance concerns with group functioning, personal choice, and moral considerations of equal opportunity in reasoning about issues involving race and gender is influenced by factors such as age and children's experience with ethnic diversity in close interpersonal relationships.

The Development of Concepts of Autonomy, Rights, and Democracy

The development of children's autonomy is an area that has received much attention in recent research. Piaget (1932) described autonomy mainly as a feature that emerges when children transcend heteronomy and begin to make moral judgments that are independent of authority and existing social rules. As previously noted, however, even young children have been found to distinguish morality from authority and social convention and to identify a moral domain composed of issues of rights, welfare, and fairness. The turn away from describing moral development in terms of a general shift from heteronomy to autonomy has led researchers to refocus their attention on children's reasoning about their own autonomy throughout the age span. Researchers have also taken up the question of how early emerging concepts of autonomy relate to, and inform, more sophisticated moral concepts of individual rights and freedoms.

Research has shown that young children identify a domain of personal issues, distinct from the moral and social conventional domains, composed of matters considered to be up to the individual's personal choice and beyond the bounds of legitimate regulation by parents, teachers, and other authorities. For example, American elementary school children judged issues such as choices about friends, appearance (clothing, hairstyle), and preferences for leisure activities as up to the child to decide (Nucci, 1981). Children of 7 years of age in Nucci's (1981) study stated that there should not be a rule governing these matters and that they should be up to individual choice. More recent research (Nucci & Smetana, 1996) suggests that the personal domain emerges during the preschool years. Preschoolers have been found to make similar judgments about age-appropriate personal issues. Observations of parent–child interactions show that children are much more likely to challenge parental authority over personal issues than moral or conventional issues. Nucci (1996) provides the following example of a conflict between a parent and a child over what a child is going to wear on the last day of nursery school:

Mother:	Evan, it's your last day of nursery school. Why don't you wear your nursery school sweatshirt?
Child:	I don't want to wear that one.
Mother:	This is the last day of nursery school, that's why we wear it. You want to wear that one?
Child:	Another one.
Mother:	Are you going to get it or should I?
Child:	I will. First I got to get a shirt.
Mother:	[Goes to the child's dresser and starts picking out shirts.] This one? This one? Do you know which one you have in mind? You have to decide, because we have to do car pool. Here, this is a new one.
Child:	No, it's too big.
Mother:	Oh Evan, just wear one, and when you get home, you can pick whatever you want, and I won't even help you. [Child puts on shirt.]

The example illustrates a conflict between the parent's assertion of a dress convention (wearing the nursery school sweatshirt on the last day of school) and the child's assertion that it is a matter of personal choice. The example illustrates, first, that the child challenges adult rules when they are perceived to infringe upon the child's sense of autonomy. Second, the adult responds by recognizing the child's agency and autonomy and through negotiation and compromise. Although the child ultimately complies in the immediate instance, the interaction concludes with the mother offering the child autonomy about what to wear after school is over. Nucci (1996) proposed that these kinds of conflicts and negotiations are central to the formation of a sense of autonomy and self, a process that begins very early in life and continues throughout childhood and into adolescence. The negotiations and discussions in these conflicts appear to be important in aiding the child's gradual construction of independence and self-efficacy within an expanding personal domain.

Basic concepts of personal autonomy and individual choice are likely to serve as a foundation for more abstract notions of individual freedom, such as in concepts of civil liberties like freedom of speech and religion (Helwig, 1995). Freedom of speech and religion are important individual and political rights, often associated with modern democratic political systems. Until very recently, it was assumed that concepts of civil liberties and democracy do not develop until adolescence (Gallatin, 1985). This conclusion was based on previous research showing that young children are unable to define terms such as *democracy*, or that they often subordinate individual rights and freedoms to other concerns in certain situations (e.g., in times of war, or when rights conflict with other important social goals). However, research examining children's reasoning about rights and democracy shows that these concepts have emerged by the early elementary school years. For example, research investigating children's and adolescents' reasoning about freedom of speech and religion (Helwig, 1995, 1997, 1998) found that by 6 years of age, children judge restrictions of these rights by governments or other authorities as wrong and illegitimate. Moreover, children, adolescents, and adults view freedom of speech and religion as moral rights that should be upheld in all countries.

Developmental changes have been found in children's reasoning regarding the basis of these rights (i.e., why people should have them). Younger children (6–8-year-olds) link these rights mainly to concerns with ensuring personal autonomy and individual self-expression. However, older children and adolescents also recognize broader societal, cultural, and democratic aspects to these rights. For example, with age, freedom of speech increasingly was seen as serving interpersonal or societal purposes, such as fostering communication or facilitating the discovery of important innovations that might help to improve society, or as allowing for minorities to express themselves through protest or other democratic means in order to rectify social injustices. Freedom of religion was seen by older children not only as serving individual autonomy and personal expression, but also as ensuring that group and cultural traditions may be preserved and respected.

Developmental differences are also evident in how children apply these concepts. Older children and adolescents apply civil liberties to a broader set of issues and are generally more likely to give priority to civil liberties when they are in conflict with other social concepts. For example, older children and adolescents are more likely than young children to maintain that it would be acceptable for individuals to violate unjust laws restricting civil liberties (Helwig, 1995, 1998). Children also, with age, increasingly make distinctions between beliefs, speech, and behavior when reasoning about issues that may have moral implications (e.g., Wainryb, Shaw, & Maianu, 1998). For example, although 6-year-olds believed that it would be acceptable for a father to hold the belief that boys deserved greater rights and privileges than girls, they did not believe that it would be acceptable for him to advocate for this position at a public meeting, unlike older children (10-year-olds), who endorsed the fathers' freedom of speech. Despite their varying tolerance for such speech, however, children at all ages did not believe it would be acceptable for a father to discriminate against his daughter based on his beliefs.

In early childhood, children also begin to understand another fundamental aspect of democracy – the idea of democratic participation – as reflected in decision-making procedures like majority rule (voting) or consensus that enable people to contribute equally to decisions that affect them. Regarding their own participation in decisions, with age, children increasingly draw distinctions between when and where democratic decision making may be appropriate (Helwig & Kim, 1999). For example, by late elementary school, children saw democratic procedures such as consensus (where everyone must agree on a decision) or majority rule as more appropriate in the peer group than in more hierarchically structured settings such as the school or family, where unilateral decision making by adult authorities was seen as more acceptable. Nevertheless, even within the school or the family, children drew distinctions among different decisions in which these procedures might be applied. For example, consensus or voting was seen as an appropriate way for a school class to make decisions about where to go on a field trip, but not for decisions about the curriculum. Children reasoned that teachers had more knowledge about curriculum matters than children, and that children would be tempted to compromise their education by choosing "easy" subjects. In contrast, a field trip was seen more as a recreational activity, and thus within the bounds of children's personal choice.

Emerging democratic notions of participation and fairness are extended into the political sphere during the elementary school years. Children see democratic governments (e.g., a direct or representative democracy) as more fair than nondemocratic forms of government, such as an oligarchy in which the most wealthy rule or a meritocracy in which the most knowledgeable govern (Helwig, 1998). In justifying their preferences for democratic government, children appeal to democratic principles of voice (everyone has a say) or accountability (i.e., the government should be accountable to the people themselves). As with civil liberties, children's views of democratic government undergo developmental changes. Elementary school–aged children tend to have limited understandings of the concept of political representation (Sinatra, Beck, & McKeown, 1992), and so they tend to prefer governments based on direct democracy, in which everyone votes on issues of policy, to representative democracies in which the people elect representatives to govern in their interest (Helwig, 1998). Despite these and other limitations in children's political understandings that may be overcome later in adolescence, the newer research reveals that the basic foundations of important political concepts such as civil liberties and democracy are fairly well established by middle childhood.

Theory of Mind and Reasoning About Social and Moral Norms

An area of research receiving attention is the relation between children's developing psychological knowledge, or theory of mind, and their judgments about social obligations (e.g., Wellman & Miller, 2008). Research on theory of mind has shown that, between 2 and 5 years of age, children develop an understanding of others as intentional beings motivated by beliefs and desires that, in some situations, may conflict with those of other people. At the same time that children are developing the capacity to conceive of people as psychological agents who act according to their desires, beliefs, and intentions, they also begin to recognize that their behavior occurs in a rich social context permeated by different types of social norms and obligations. Recent research examined how children integrate and coordinate their developing knowledge of individuals as psychological agents with their emerging knowledge of the social obligations that constrain what may or may not be permitted in different circumstances.

Lagattuta (2005) presented children between the ages of 4 and 8 years with situations in which a character's desire (e.g., wanting to eat a cookie) was pitted against a parental prohibition (e.g., "You should not eat cookies right before dinner"). Children were asked to predict the agent's behavior (whether the character would transgress or not) and how the character would feel if they either fulfilled the desire or abided by the rule. Younger children tended to predict that the agent would fulfill the desire and break the rule, whereas older children (7–8 years) judged that the agent would follow the rule or norm. Moreover, younger children tended to predict that agents who transgressed would feel positive emotions "because they got what they wanted," whereas older children tended to predict that agents who showed willpower and resisted their desires would feel positive emotions "because they listened to their mother and followed the rule." Older children predicted that agents who fulfilled their personal desires under these circumstances would actually feel negative or mixed emotions about doing so, and they referred to the rule as a source of these negative emotions. Thus, for older children, social norms become more integrated into psychological agency and enable the prediction of individuals' behavior and their emotional responses in situations of temptation and transgression.

How children reason about decisions and emotions is influenced by the domain of the rule in question. Lagattuta, Nucci, and Bosacki (2010) presented 4- to 8-year-olds with situations in which rules prohibited actions in the moral (e.g., hitting and stealing) and personal domains (e.g., clothing, activity, and friendship choice). Although children increasingly predicted with age that agents would follow rules in the moral domain and that compliance there would result in positive emotions, children of all ages rarely predicted that a person would comply and feel good in situations in which rules infringed on the personal, especially when the personal issue was seen as central to the person's identity. Thus, psychological autonomy is important for understanding how individuals may resist and negatively react to attempts by authorities to impose rules in the personal domain.

Culture and Social Development

The research we have reviewed demonstrates that starting at a young age, children form different domains of social judgment. Children make moral judgments based on issues of harm, fairness, and rights, and differentiate morality from social conventions, punishment, and explicit rules. Children do not go through a period of rigid adherence to social rules and unilateral respect for adult authority, but often adopt a critical perspective in evaluating and judging the legitimacy of rules and authority. Children also develop notions of autonomy and personal freedom that place limits on the types of social regulations that are seen as legitimate.

Most of the research discussed thus far was conducted in North America – in Western cultures. It may be, therefore, that the types of judgments found in this research reflect a particular cultural orientation. Our view is that the development of judgments about morality and social conventions stems not from a particular cultural orientation but from children's experiences with others and their ways of making sense of those experiences. It has been argued by some, however, that broad cultural orientations, such as individualism and collectivism, structure views about self and morality (Greenfield, Keller, Fuligni, & Maynard, 2003; Shweder, Mahapatra, & Miller, 1987; Triandis, 1996). Western cultures are oriented to the idea of persons as autonomous agents who are free to belong or not to social groups, and therefore their morality emphasizes individual choice, personal autonomy, and rights. In contrast, collectivist cultures, such as those in Asia, South America, and Africa, emphasize duties, social harmony, obedience to authority, and hierarchy. Accordingly, in these cultures, the person is seen as part of a social network of interdependence into which persons are increasingly socialized, leading morality to be defined in terms of duties rather than rights and concerned primarily with maintenance of the social order. Shweder et al. (1987) proposed that the idea of conventionality is exclusively associated with Western cultures in which social obligations and duties are defined by social contract and consent. In contrast, in collectivist cultures such as India, social obligations are seen as part of the natural order and thus distinct from individual choice or arbitrary social conventions.

Shweder et al. (1987) based this conclusion on a study they conducted in which children and adults from the United States along with Orthodox Hindus from India were given practices to evaluate that included moral issues of harm and unfairness versus items usually associated in the West with social conventions or personal choice (e.g., matters of diet or dress). It was found that although a number of the moral items were judged in similar ways by Indians and Americans, some of the "conventional" items, such as violations of prohibitions against a widow eating fish or wearing bright clothing, or a son eating chicken and getting a haircut the day after his father's death, were judged differently by the two groups. These items were judged by Indians as serious transgressions and it was thought that the practices were not alterable, whereas Americans largely viewed them as acceptable and up to personal choice.

The conclusions drawn by Shweder et al. (1987) about these findings – that what Americans might treat as conventional are treated by Indians as moral – fail to account for a significant aspect of what goes into people's application of their moral judgments. We are referring to their assumptions about reality. As shown by a reanalysis of the items (Turiel, Killen, & Helwig, 1987), assumptions about the "reality" of an afterlife and the effects of earthly actions on unobservable entities – such as the soul of a deceased husband, father, or ancestors – entered into their moral judgments. As an example, it is believed that if a son were to get a haircut and eat chicken the day after his father's death, the father would fail to receive salvation. Although the beliefs about reality varied across cultures (Americans did not believe these practices to result in these kinds of consequences), the moral concern with avoiding inflicting harmful consequences on others appears to be shared. The events interpreted by Shweder et al. (1987) as inherently conventional appear to have been transformed into moral events (having harmful consequences for others) by virtue of the specific beliefs brought to them by Indians. This example shows the importance of considering such beliefs (termed *informational* or *factual assumptions* in subsequent research on this topic; see Wainryb, 1991) in studying the application of moral judgments.

Other research has confirmed that the moral and social conventional domains are distinguished in India and other cultures. For example, Miller and Bersoff (1992) found that children and adults in India reasoned about school dress codes as social conventions, seeing them as alterable and relative across social contexts, whereas theft was reasoned about as a moral event in the same manner as in the West. It has been found that children and adults in several cultures distinguish morality and social convention, including Indonesia, Nigeria, Korea, Zambia, and Brazil (see Turiel, 2006, for a review).

Subsequent research, conducted in a variety of cultures usually described as collectivistic, has documented that children and adults in these cultures also distinguish a domain of personal issues that should be free from social interference. Preschool and older children in societies as diverse as Colombia (Ardilla-Rey & Killen, 2001), Hong Kong (Yau & Smetana, 2003), and Japan (Yamada, 2009) identify similar sorts of issues (e.g., choice of friends and recreational activities) as up to personal choice, and they criticize authorities' attempts to regulate these actions.

Studies with older children and adolescents from non-Western cultures have found, as in studies in the West, that the scope of the personal expands throughout childhood and adolescence, although the ages at which certain issues are claimed by children as personal sometimes vary across different environments. A study by Nucci, Camino, and Sapiro (1996) with middle- and lower-class children and mothers in cities and rural regions of Brazil showed that children across social classes and regions differentiated among personal, moral, and social conventional issues in the same way as found in North America. However, there were social class differences in the ages at which personal issues were identified, with middle-class children claiming some areas of personal discretion at earlier ages than lower-class children. Similarly, mothers of lower-class children and mothers from rural regions were less likely to grant personal decision-making autonomy to young children. However, by adolescence, these differences disappeared. Both mothers and children granted personal decision-making autonomy to adolescents over similar issues, and gave reasons of autonomy, choice, and the development of uniqueness and identity in justifying their judgments (see also Lahat, Helwig, Yang, Tan, & Liu, 2009, for similar developmental patterns in a study examining reasoning about freedom of speech and religion with adolescents from urban and rural China).

Other research has documented the existence of cultural variations in the scope of the personal domain accorded to different classes of persons. For instance, in many traditional cultures, males are conventionally accorded greater entitlements to personal choice and freedom than females. Nevertheless, many individuals from these societies, especially those in subordinate positions such as females, have been found to judge as unfair many cultural practices that restrict the personal freedoms or rights of girls or women (see, e.g., Conry-Murray, 2009, for Benin, Africa; Neff, 2001, for India; and Wainryb & Turiel, 1994, for an Arab Druze society in Israel). Findings of diversity within cultures in judgments of personal freedoms and rights are difficult to reconcile with homogeneous, global classifications of collectivist cultures in terms of purely duty-based moralities. Instead, these findings point to the complex ways in which individuals in non-Western cultural settings apply different domains of social judgments to evaluate cultural practices.

Conclusion

The findings of the extensive body of research reviewed lead to a picture of children's social and moral development as entailing the construction of distinct domains of judgment through their social interactions. Children distinguish between different types of social rules and construct domains of moral, social conventional, and personal concepts. Children take into account the consequences of actions on others and construct concepts of harm, fairness, and rights which they use to evaluate individual actions, social rules, and social systems. Neither young children's social judgments nor their social relations can be characterized in unitary terms as reflecting heteronomy or unilateral constraint. Rather, children's social judgments are heterogeneous and differentiated by domain, and their social interactions are characterized by relations of both cooperation and conflict, with peers and authority figures, throughout development. Accounting for the different kinds of social interactions that children experience, and the concepts they construct from these experiences, is an important task for an understanding of children's social and moral judgments and behavior.

Acknowledgment

Preparation of this chapter was supported by a research grant from the Social Sciences and Humanities Research Council of Canada to Charles C. Helwig.

References

Ardilla-Rey, A., & Killen, M. (2001). Middle-class Colombian children's evaluations of personal, moral, and social conventional interactions in the classroom. *International Journal of Behavioral Development, 25*, 246–255.

Aronfreed, J. (1968). *Conduct and conscience: The socialization of internalized control over behavior.* New York: Academic Press.

Conry-Murray, C. (2009). Adolescent and young adult reasoning about gender and fairness in traditional practices in Benin, West Africa. *Social Development, 18*, 427–446.

Crystal, D. S., Killen, M., & Ruck, M. (2008). It is who you know that counts: Intergroup contact and judgments about race-based exclusion. *British Journal of Developmental Psychology, 26*, 51–70.

Damon, W. (1977). *The social world of the child.* San Francisco: Jossey-Bass.

Dworkin, R. (1977). *Taking rights seriously.* Cambridge, MA: Harvard University Press.

Freud, S. (1930). *Civilization and its discontents.* London: Hogarth Press.

Gallatin, J. (1985). *Democracy's children: The development of political thinking in adolescents.* Ann Arbor, MI: Quod.

Greenfield, P. M., Keller, H., Fuligni, A., & Maynard, A. (2003). Cultural pathways through universal development. *Annual Review of Psychology, 54*, 461–490.

Hauser, M. (2006). *Moral minds.* New York: HarperCollins.

Helwig, C. C. (1995). Adolescents' and young adults' conceptions of civil liberties: Freedom of speech and religion. *Child Development, 66,* 152–166.

Helwig, C. C. (1997). The role of agent and social context in judgments of freedom of speech and religion. *Child Development, 68,* 484–495.

Helwig, C. C. (1998). Children's conceptions of fair government and freedom of speech. *Child Development, 69,* 518–531.

Helwig, C. C., & Jasiobedzka, U. (2001). The relation between law and morality: Children's reasoning about socially beneficial and unjust laws. *Child Development, 72,* 1382–1393.

Helwig, C. C., & Kim, S. (1999). Children's evaluations of decision making procedures in peer, family, and school contexts. *Child Development, 70,* 502–512.

Killen, M., Lee-Kim, J., McGlothlin, H., & Stangor, C. (2002). How children and adolescents evaluate gender and racial exclusion. *Monographs of the Society for Research in Child Development, 67*(4, Serial No. 271).

Killen, M., & Stangor, C. (2001). Children's social reasoning about inclusion and exclusion in gender and race peer group contexts. *Child Development, 72,* 174–186.

Kohlberg, L. (1981). *Essays on moral development: Vol. 1. The philosophy of moral development.* San Francisco: Harper & Row.

Lagattuta, K. H. (2005). When you shouldn't do what you want to do: Young children's understanding of desires, rules, and emotions. *Child Development, 76,* 713–733.

Lagattuta, K. H., Nucci, L. P., & Bosacki, S. (2010). Bridging theory of mind and the personal domain: Children's reasoning about resistance to parental control. *Child Development, 81*(2), 616–635.

Lahat, A., Helwig, C. C., Yang, S., Tan, D., & Liu, C. (2009). Mainland Chinese adolescents' judgments and reasoning about self-determination and nurturance rights. *Social Development, 18,* 690–710.

Laupa, M., Turiel, E., & Cowan, P. (1995). Obedience to authority in children and adults. In M. Killen & D. Hart (Eds.), *Morality in everyday life: Developmental perspectives* (pp. 131–165). Cambridge: Cambridge University Press.

Miller, J. G., & Bersoff, D. M. (1992). Culture and moral judgment: How are conflicts between justice and interpersonal responsibilities resolved? *Journal of Personality & Social Psychology, 62,* 541–554.

Neff, K. (2001). Judgments of personal autonomy and interpersonal responsibility in the context of Indian spousal relationships: An examination of young people's reasoning in Mysore, India. *British Journal of Developmental Psychology, 19,* 233–257.

Nucci, L. P. (1981). The development of personal concepts: A domain distinct from moral or social concepts. *Child Development, 52,* 114–121.

Nucci, L. P. (1996). Morality and the personal sphere of action. In E. Reed, E. Turiel, & T. Brown (Eds.), *Values and knowledge* (pp. 41–60). Hillsdale, NJ: Erlbaum.

Nucci, L. P., Camino, C., & Sapiro, C. (1996). Social class effects on northeastern Brazilian children's conceptions of areas of personal choice and social regulation. *Child Development, 67*(3), 1223–1242.

Nucci, L. P., & Smetana, J. G. (1996). Mothers' concept of young children's areas of personal freedom. *Child Development, 67*(4), 1870–1886.

Nucci, L. P., & Turiel, E. (1978). Social interactions and the development of social concepts in preschool children. *Child Development, 49,* 400–407.

Piaget, J. (1932). *The moral judgment of the child.* London: Routledge and Kegan Paul.

Rawls, J. (1971). *A theory of justice.* Cambridge, MA: Harvard University Press.

Ross, L., & Nisbett, R. M. (1991). *The person and the situation: Perspectives on social psychology.* Philadelphia: Temple University Press.

Shweder, R. A., Mahapatra, M., & Miller, J. G. (1987). Culture and moral development. In J. Kagan & S. Lamb (Eds.), *The emergence of morality in young children* (pp. 1–83). Chicago: University of Chicago Press.

Sinatra, G., Beck, I., & McKeown, M. (1992). A longitudinal characterization of young students' knowledge of their country's government. *American Educational Research Journal, 29*, 633–661.

Skinner, B. F. (1971). *Beyond freedom and dignity.* New York: Knopf.

Smetana, J. G. (1981). Preschool children's conceptions of moral and social rules. *Child Development, 52*, 1333–1336.

Smetana, J. G., & Braeges, J. L. (1990). The development of toddler's moral and conventional judgments. *Merrill-Palmer Quarterly, 36*, 329–346.

Theimer, C. E., Killen, M., & Stangor, C. (2001). Preschool children's evaluations of exclusion in gender-stereotypic contexts. *Developmental Psychology, 37*, 1–10.

Triandis, H. C. (1996). The psychological measurement of cultural syndromes. *American Psychologist, 51*(4), 407–415.

Turiel, E. (1983). *The development of social knowledge: Morality and convention.* Cambridge: Cambridge University Press.

Turiel, E. (2006). The development of morality. In W. Damon, R. M. Lerner, & N. Eisenberg (Eds.), *Handbook of child psychology: Vol. 3. Social, emotional, and personality development* (6th ed., pp. 789–857). Hoboken, NJ: Wiley.

Turiel, E. (2008). Thought about actions in social domains: Morality, social conventions and social interactions. *Cognitive Development, 23*, 136–154.

Turiel, E., Killen, M., & Helwig, C. C. (1987). Morality: Its structure, functions and vagaries. In J. Kagan & S. Lamb (Eds.), *The emergence of morality in young children* (pp. 155–244). Chicago: University of Chicago Press.

Wainryb, C. (1991). Understanding differences in moral judgments: The role of informational assumptions. *Child Development, 62*, 840–851.

Wainryb, C., Brehl, B., & Matwin, S. (2005). Being hurt and hurting others: Children's narrative accounts and moral judgments of their own interpersonal conflicts. *Monographs of the Society for Research in Child Development, 70*(3), 1–114.

Wainryb, C., Shaw, L., & Maianu, C. (1998). Tolerance and intolerance: Children's and adolescents' judgments of dissenting beliefs, speech, persons, and conduct. *Child Development, 69*, 1541–1555.

Wainryb, C., & Turiel, E. (1994). Dominance, subordination, and concepts of personal entitlements in cultural contexts. *Child Development, 65*, 1701–1722.

Wellman, H., & Miller, J. G. (2008). Including deontic reasoning as fundamental to theory of mind. *Human Development, 51*, 105–135.

Weston, D. R., & Turiel, E. (1980). Act-rule relations: Children's concepts of social rules. *Developmental Psychology, 16*, 417–424.

Yamada, H. (2009). Japanese children's reasoning about conflicts with parents. *Social Development, 18*, 962–977.

Yau, J., & Smetana, J. G. (2003). Conceptions of moral, social-conventional, and personal events among Chinese preschoolers in Hong Kong. *Child Development, 74*, 1–12.

CHAPTER THIRTY-ONE

Children's Understanding of Society

Martyn Barrett and Eithne Buchanan-Barrow

This chapter describes the research that has been conducted into the development of children's understanding of the economic and political institutions and systems that characterize the societies in which they live, and the development of children's understanding of four large-scale social groupings that characterize most societies: social class, race, ethnicity, and nation.

Children's Understanding of Economics

Money and economic transactions are omnipresent in the societies within which children live. People carry money around in their purses, children are given pocket money by their parents, people use their money to buy goods in shops, and adults have jobs that consume many hours of their lives in order to earn money. Children's understanding of these phenomena has been subject to intense research in recent years.

Children's understanding of money

Understanding the nature of money is fundamental to all aspects of socioeconomic understanding. Berti and Bombi (1988) examined 3- to 11-year-old children's understanding of money using Piagetian interviewing. They found that 3- to 4-year-old children have little understanding of the nature of money or the origins of money. Ignorant

The Wiley-Blackwell Handbook of Childhood Social Development, Second Edition, edited by Peter K. Smith and Craig H. Hart
© 2011 by Blackwell Publishing Ltd.

of the link between work and money, very young children believe money is simply obtained from purses. Between 5 and 7 years, children begin to puzzle out connections, as their opportunities to observe the monetary transactions in everyday life increase. Their explanations now include such sources of money as the bank, shops, and work. By about 7 years, children grasp the essential connection with work, and tend to believe that work is the only source of money. Finally, by about 10–11 years, children understand both inherited wealth and money obtained through crime.

More recent research has focused on the role played by social context in children's thinking about money, thus emphasizing differences in understanding as a function of context rather than general developmental trends. For example, South African children (aged 7–14 years) have been found to exhibit differences in their understanding of the origin of money according to their rural, urban, or semiurban location (Bonn & Webley, 2000).

Children's understanding of banking

Variations in children's economic understanding also occur in their comprehension of banking transactions. Examinations of children's thinking about interest payments on deposits and loans show that the thinking of Scottish (Jahoda, 1981) and New Zealand (Ng, 1985) children lags behind that of Hong Kong children by about 2 years (Wong, 1989). Although there are similar stages in their developing thinking about banking, Hong Kong children display a comprehension of interest as early as 9 years, as opposed to around 11 years for the other two samples. On the other hand, Japanese (Takahashi & Hatano, 1994) and Black South African (Bonn & Webley, 2000) children show the least mature understanding. Children's development in this domain must be subject to complex influences; whereas Black South African children have little exposure to banks, this is not the case for Japanese children, who are growing up in a sophisticated economic system and might be expected to display more mature thinking.

Further evidence of the complexities of development in this area comes from a study of the economic thinking of children from 10 countries (Leiser, Sevon, & Levy, 1990). Differences in the sophistication of the children's thinking about banks did not always reflect the economic standing of their country. For example, whereas the children of Finland were in the most mature group, the children from the neighboring country of Norway displayed some of the least advanced thinking. Evidently, the development of an understanding of the concepts of banking and interest may be influenced by factors other than the prominence of the banking sector.

Children's naïve theory of economics

Whereas understanding the roles played by money and banks is challenging for young children, the essential economic transactions involved in the exchange of goods are even more inaccessible to their understanding. In order to have a fully integrated economic understanding, children not only need to grasp such basic concepts as prices, supply, demand, and profits but also need to have knowledge of the complex interactions and causal relationships between them.

Some research has examined individual aspects of the exchange of goods, such as price or profit. Examinations of price or value have revealed that whereas very young children price items with reference to their physical attributes, with increasing age children focus first on the function and finally on the work and/or materials involved in the manufacture (10–12 years) (Berti & Bombi, 1988; Fox & Kehret-Ward, 1990). The concept of profit begins to be properly understood by 11 years, with children recognizing that shopkeepers must charge their customers more than they paid to their suppliers in order to make a living and pay their employees (Berti & Bombi, 1988). Factors related to the child's understanding include the level of education attained by the child's mother, and her efforts to instruct her child about economic activities (such as shopping, banks, etc.; Nakhaie, 1993). There is further evidence from cross-cultural studies to suggest that personal experiences may be involved. Comparing data from Scottish (Jahoda, 1979), English (Furth, 1980), Dutch (Jahoda, 1982), and Zimbabwean children, Jahoda (1983) found a lag in European children in their grasp of the principles of trading, although the stages in the development of their thinking were similar. Using a role-playing situation, Jahoda found that Zimbabwean children display an understanding of profit at around 9, 2 years before European children. Zimbabwean children's more extensive and relevant experience of trading in their everyday lives (at that time) may bring about this earlier acquisition of the concept of profit, indicating that cultural context influences the development of economic understanding.

Thompson and Siegler (2000) conducted a more detailed study of children's understanding of such core economic concepts as supply, demand, price, and profits, together with their underlying causal relationships. They proposed that children's thinking is underpinned by informal, domain-specific, "naïve" theories that they use to explain and predict economic phenomena. Using vignettes about lemonade stands, thus describing economic activities familiar to even young children, they looked at children's understanding of the causal relations between supply, demand, price, and volume of sales of lemonade. They also investigated whether children used any of four major, unobservable, but essential economic concepts in their deliberations: profit seeking, competition among sellers, acquisition of desired goods, and economizing. Although the youngest children recognized only people's desire for goods, there was a major shift around the age of 7–8 years, with an emerging understanding of both the causal relations and unobservable constructs. Thompson and Siegler argued that, by this age, children are constructing a naïve theory of economics. This research would indicate that children hold a qualitatively different informal theory of economics from middle childhood onward (Webley, 2005).

Children's understanding of social class

Children are aware of inequalities of wealth at an early age (Jahoda, 1959; Leahy, 1981) but initially at a superficial level. When asked to describe rich or poor people, Jahoda found that 6-year-old children perceive outward differences, mentioning variations in housing, clothing, and lifestyle. Leahy also reported that children aged 6–11 years tended to emphasize "peripheral" characteristics (possessions, appearances, and behavior) as opposed to life chances or class differences. Around 6–7 years, children begin to explain inequalities according to jobs, without reference to income, but by 8 years, children become aware of the link between social differences and income, and relate the differences in wealth to earnings from work (Berti & Bombi, 1988; Jahoda, 1959). Leahy (1981) also found that there was an increase, with age, in references to the role played by earnings in inequalities of wealth.

Cross-cultural research has revealed variations in children's thinking about social class according to nationality (Leiser et al., 1990). A comparison of Algerian and French children (Roland-Levy, 1990) found that the most prevalent explanation for both poverty and wealth in Algerian children was the personal characteristics of the individual, whereas for French children poverty was seen as a consequence of the socioeconomic system. Furthermore, whereas the French children believed that fate played more of a role in being rich than being poor, Algerian children were more likely to attribute being poor to fate. A study of the thinking of Black children in South Africa (Bonn, Earle, Lea, & Webley, 1999) also found differences according to location. Rural children were more likely to say that unemployment was an important cause of poverty and inequality than children from a semiurban location. Additionally, rural children had a more fatalistic view of poverty, attributing it to God almost as much as to unemployment. However, Bonn et al. found that age was still a more important factor than social niche. Although children's social environment may have affected their thinking about such concepts as wealth, poverty, inequality, and unemployment, their capacity to formulate causal links between these concepts was more likely to be associated with age than with location.

Evidently, there are culturally based explanations for income inequalities. As most research in this area has been conducted from a Piagetian perspective, cognitive developmental level is often seen as being more strongly related to social class understanding, with cultural context playing a more peripheral role by affecting the rate of acquisition. But there are findings that suggest that social influences may have a bigger role in children's acquisition of concepts of inequalities of income (Emler & Dickinson, 1985, 2005). Emler and Dickinson (1985) found differences associated with socioeconomic class, but notably none with age, in Scottish children's perceptions of wage differentials. For all the occupations under consideration, middle-class children reported higher overall estimates of income and a greater spread, with a much wider division between manual and nonmanual occupations, than working-class children. Furthermore, the explanations offered by the children for wage differentials varied according to socioeconomic class, with middle-class children expressing greater support for income inequality than working-class children. Overall, Dickinson and Emler (1996) argued that, as children from different socioeconomic backgrounds are developing in very different social worlds, they develop varying beliefs about the extent, the causes, and the justifications for economic inequalities in society.

However, a replication of Emler and Dickinson's study with West German children (Burgard, Cheyne, & Jahoda, 1989) failed to find substantial class differences in the children's thinking, while conversely finding differences associated with age. It may be that there is a greater awareness of class differences amongst Scottish children than amongst German children. Or it may be that when class differences are found, they partly reflect the greater availability of relevant information to middle-class children, thus allowing them to report a more accurate, rather than a more biased, understanding (Jahoda, 1981).

Children as economic actors

Research into children's understanding of economics has been mainly focused on their comprehension of the adult economic world. However, some research has examined children's own economic activities, through spending of pocket money or their own part-time earnings or through an examination of the playground economy.

Research has examined children's behavior as consumers, investigating their own purchasing and saving strategies. Children aged 6–10 years, tested on their skills as consumers, had some understanding of the need to judge prices in terms of the value of the item (Pliner, Freedman, Abramovitch, & Darke, 1996). Other studies have examined children's behavior in play economies using tokens; although very young children have little concept of the value of saving, between 6–12 years, children do develop more complex strategies (Sonuga-Barke & Webley, 1993; Webley, Levine, & Lewis, 1991). By about 9 years, children understand that saving can be used for future expenditure and that savings and expenditure are not separate activities. The 12-year-olds displayed an even better grasp of the flows of funds over the course of the study; not only did they save more, but also they used a greater range of strategies to achieve their goals (Webley et al., 1991). Further research by Webley and colleagues (Otto, Schots, Westerman, & Webley, 2006) used a board game in order to explore children's use of saving strategies when the future is uncertain, as an essential part of adult saving behavior. With age, children developed increasingly sophisticated, though not necessarily more successful, strategies to deal with unexpected difficulties. To sum up, even young children acknowledge the desirability of saving, even if lacking in strategies, and by middle childhood most children comprehend the value of saving and become increasingly skillful in undertaking it (Webley, 2005).

Finally, children also undertake economic behaviors totally separate from the adult world through the playground economy. The autonomous economic world of the child involves mainly swapping and trading possessions and may make an essential and revealing contribution to their wider economic understanding (Webley, 2005). Research suggests that children develop complex swapping economies, where marbles are used as a type of currency (Webley, 1996).

Conclusion

Much research into children's economic socialization has been conducted from a Piagetian perspective, proposing that children's thinking develops according to a universal series of stages that themselves are grounded in the Piagetian stages of cognitive development (Berti & Bombi, 1988). This approach has drawn criticism because its emphasis on the universality of stages has resulted in the underrating of social and cultural differences (Emler & Dickinson, 1985, 2005). The evidence actually suggests that the development of economic thinking proceeds through the child drawing upon both personal economic experience (e.g., dealing with pocket money, and experience in trading) and socially provided information (which may be available, for example, from discourse with parents). As both economic experience and the social provision of information vary according to sociocultural context, it is perhaps inevitable that the child's understanding of economic institutions and phenomena will exhibit sociocultural variation.

Children's Political Understanding

Whereas children's economic understanding has been extensively researched, children's understanding of politics has been a neglected topic in recent years. This may be partly due to the difficulty in finding a productive research perspective. Extensive research in the 1960s and 1970s from within a political socialization perspective failed to elucidate developmental mechanisms and processes. Subsequent research from a Piagetian perspective again drew criticism for its emphasis on universality at the expense of contextual variation. There are indications that a more productive line of research may be possible using the naïve theory approach as a conceptual framework.

Content of children's political understanding

Some studies have examined children's political thinking by probing their knowledge of specific political institutions and events through open-ended interviewing. Connell (1971) investigated the political understanding of children and adolescents from a Piagetian perspective. Under the age of 7 years, children revealed *intuitive thinking*, in which political and nonpolitical issues were undifferentiated. From 7 to 10 years, children demonstrated *primitive realism*, with some awareness of areas of political interest. Over the age of 10 years, *the construction of political order*, children began to show a clearer sense of the tasks of government and to see political power as hierarchically and institutionally structured. However, even the older children still lacked much specific understanding. Moore, Lare, and Wagner (1985), also using a Piagetian approach, found similar increases in the content of children's thinking from kindergarten to the fourth grade, but with girls less knowledgeable than boys. Although these studies produced a wealth of detail about young children's knowledge of specific political institutions and events, they revealed little of the meanings underlying the children's responses, nor much about the influences involved in their formation.

Children's political concepts

In order to examine more fundamental aspects of children's political cognition, Berti (1988) investigated their understanding of a hypothetical island society, focusing on such concepts as power, conflict, laws, and community. Using open-ended interviewing, Berti found that the children's responses were grouped into four main areas: (a) collective needs, (b) conflicts, (c) political organization, and (d) laws. The youngest children (under 8) were generally oblivious of conflicts, of the need for organization, or of the function of laws. Children aged 8–9 years, after some prompting, mentioned *chiefs* who would govern by some sort of *orders*. Children aged 10–11 years demonstrated a major advance on the younger children, referring spontaneously to collective needs and political organization. By about 12–13 years, children volunteered that the whole community was responsible for lawmaking in some sense.

Children's reasoning about rights, such as freedom of speech and religion, and democratic systems has been examined by Helwig (1997, 1998). He found that concepts of rights emerge in early childhood, with a majority of 6-year-old children affirming such basic freedoms. Offered a choice of various forms of government, children rejected non-democratic governmental systems in favor of democratic ones, often with reference to the importance of people having a voice in decisions. Further research found that children (aged 6–10) recognized that individuals might be justified in violating unjust laws (Helwig & Jasiobedzka, 2001). Overall, even young children appear capable of understanding basic democratic principles.

Children's understanding of the state

A sequence of studies by Berti and colleagues (Berti, 2005; see also Barrett, 2007) examined children's understanding of such concepts as *state*, *democracy*, *law*, and *dominion*, together with a series of public offices, governmental processes, and political events, through open-ended interviewing. Whereas children aged 8–9 had little understanding, there was a major shift around the age of 10 years, with children that age being capable of more overt political explanation. They were more likely to mention governmental machinery, laws, and political authority. They were aware of the hierarchical power structure and the territorial integrity of the nation-state. Berti concluded from these studies that they collectively indicate the emergence of a political domain and that children by this age have acquired a naïve theory of politics.

Children's understanding of community

The child's first contact with a major societal institution is that with the school. Schools have hierarchical power–authority relations, rules, and a strong sense of community. Therefore, they offer an important early experience of a micropolitical society and may contribute to children's understanding of citizenship (Buchanan-Barrow, 2005). Buchanan-Barrow and Barrett (1996, 1998) examined the thinking of 5- to 11-year-old primary school children about the school, probing their understanding of rules, community, self-system interaction, and power, and the links between them. Children's thinking began with a simple focus on the role of the headteacher, and even the youngest children understood their importance in the school system. Then, around 7–8 years of age, the children began to acknowledge the teachers as the next layer down in the power hierarchy. The oldest children suggested that parents have influence in school matters, and also claimed an important role for children. Thus, the oldest children understood the school as a community, in which all members, from head teacher to pupils, had a part to play. Furthermore, the children's developing understanding of each system concept was linked to others, contributing to their overall comprehension of the system of the school.

Conclusion

The shift in recent years from the focus on children's political knowledge to investigations of their political concepts (Berti, 1988, 2005; Buchanan-Barrow & Barrett, 1996, 1998) has opened up the possibility of a more fruitful perspective for examining children's political cognition, that of the naïve theory approach (Wellman & Gelman, 1998). The pattern of acquisition of political concepts revealed in these studies supports the view that children construct a naïve theory of politics, as they attempt to make sense of systems of power. Children's thinking begins with a simple focus on the role of a powerful individual, a *chief, prime minister,* or *headteacher,* exercising absolute power from the highest point in the system. With age, children develop an understanding of the hierarchies of power, becoming cognizant of lower levels in the system and spreading the decision-making processes to include other politicians or teachers. Finally, as older children acquire a sense of the whole community, their thinking displays a basic grasp of a consent to government, as they propose that all members of a community should be involved in its organization and decision making.

Children's Understanding of Ethnic and Racial Groups

Nowadays, the societies within which children live are rarely homogeneous in terms of their ethnic and racial composition. Ethnic and racial groups identify themselves, and are identified by others, through numerous characteristics, including country of origin, religion, culture, language, skin color, and so on. Here, the term *ethnic groups* is used to refer to cultural communities based on myths of common ancestry, shared historical memories, and common cultural traditions and practices (Hutchinson & Smith, 1996), whereas the term *racial groups* is used to refer to socially constructed pseudobiological categories that nevertheless impact seriously on the lives of ethnic minority individuals through racist practices and racial discrimination (Banton, 1977; Hirschfeld, 2005). The task facing the child in mastering these systems of ethnic and racial categorizations is considerable. Three principal aspects of the developmental process have been studied: the development of racial awareness, the development of racial and ethnic self-identification, and the development of racial and ethnic attitudes.

The development of racial awareness

One method commonly used to study children's racial awareness is to show the child pictures or dolls representing people from different racial groups, and to ask the child to point to, for example, the White person, the Black person, and so on. This method reveals that even some 3-year-olds can identify the race of Black and White pictures or dolls; among 4–5-year-olds, 75% of children make accurate Black–White distinctions; and among 6–7-year-olds, the figure is usually 90% or higher (Clark & Clark, 1947; Williams & Morland, 1976). These figures are typically obtained when the targets are White and Black, and are exhibited by both White and Black children. Other studies have found that White and Chinese American children acquire the ability to identify Chinese people between 5 and 7 years (Fox & Jordan, 1973), whereas White and Native American children's ability to identify Native American people continues to develop up to 9 years (Rosenthal, 1974).

One problem with these studies is that they only show that children can identify people from different racial categories when asked to do so by an experimenter; they do not show whether children spontaneously use these categories in their own social judgments. Consequently, other methods have been used to see whether children do spontaneously employ racial categories. For example, Davey (1983) presented 7- to 10-year-olds with pictures of people who differed according to their age, gender, race, and clothing (which was used to flag social class), and asked the children to group them. He found that race was used spontaneously more frequently than any of the other criteria to sort the pictures into sets. This finding suggests that racial categories are indeed salient to children during middle childhood.

The development of racial and ethnic self-identification

Early studies examined racial self-identification by showing children pictures or dolls representing people from different racial groups, and asking the child to point to the one that most closely resembles him or her. These studies found that, from 3–4 years onward, White children identified with the White person or doll 75% of the time, rising to almost 100% by 6–7 years (Aboud, 1977; Williams & Morland, 1976). A more complicated picture was found with Black children growing up in Western societies in these older studies, with some children identifying with the Black doll or picture from about 3–4 years but others identifying with the White doll or picture and only switching their identifications to the Black doll or picture by 7 years (see Aboud, 1988, for a detailed review). More recent studies using other methods such as ethnography and identification scales show that this pattern of minority identifications has now changed, with racial and ethnic minority children unambiguously identifying with their own racial and ethnic group from an early age (e.g., Connolly, 1998; Davis, Leman, & Barrett, 2007).

The development of racial and ethnic attitudes

Early studies also examined children's racial attitudes by using pictures or dolls and asking the children which one they liked the best or least. As far as White children were concerned, they were found to display a consistent preference for the White pictures or dolls from the age of 3–4 years onward, a preference that often grew in strength between 4 and 7 years (Aboud, 1980; Asher & Allen, 1969).

Once again, a more complicated picture arose in the case of Black children. In some of the studies conducted before the end of the 1960s, it was found that many young Black children in Western societies preferred White dolls or pictures over Black ones (Asher & Allen, 1969; Clark & Clark, 1947). Furthermore, this preference for the racial outgroup peaked at about 6–7 years, before declining and turning into a pro-Black bias instead. Nevertheless, even in these early studies, not all young Black children exhibited this outgroup preference (Aboud, 1988; Banks, 1976). However, the picture has changed dramatically since the late 1960s. The positive bias toward the White outgroup has disappeared in 4- to 7-year-old Black children in more recent years, with these children now showing an ingroup bias that is equivalent to that shown by White children (Aboud, 1980; Hraba & Grant, 1970; Vaughan, 1978). Some commentators (e.g., Brown, 1995) have argued that this shift was due to the emergence of Black consciousness political movements during the 1960s that helped foster greater ingroup pride among Black people (including children).

As far as attitudes toward racial and ethnic outgroups are concerned, some authors (e.g., Aboud, 1988) have proposed that between 4 and 7 years, negative prejudice against outgroups increases, with a peak occurring at about 7 years, and that after this age, prejudice against outgroups declines. This finding has been obtained using tasks in which children are asked to assign positive and negative traits to particular target groups. However, in more recent years it has become clear that there is actually considerable variability in the development of attitudes toward ethnic and racial outgroups, and that the same child may display different levels of prejudice, and indeed different developmental patterns, depending on the specific ethnic or racial outgroup concerned (Barrett & Davis, 2008; Black-Gutman & Hickson, 1996; Dunham, Baron, & Banaji, 2006). Because the overt expression of prejudice is usually discouraged by adults, more recent researchers have begun to use measures of implicit attitudes in order to avoid social desirability effects biasing the findings (e.g., Davis et al., 2007; Dunham et al., 2006). For example, Dunham et al. used the Implicit Association Test (IAT) in which reaction times for associating positive and negative traits with particular racial groups are measured. They found that White American children's implicit attitudes to Japanese people became more positive between 6 and 10 years of age, but that their implicit (comparatively negative) attitudes to Black people did not show any changes at all across this same age range. In other words, different developmental profiles were shown depending on the particular outgroup concerned.

Studies into the sources of children's racial and ethnic attitudes have revealed that these attitudes are related to many factors, including parental discourse about racial and ethnic issues (Branch & Newcombe, 1986; Carlson & Iovini, 1985; Spencer, 1983), teachers' discourse and practices within the classroom in relationship to race and ethnicity (Kinket & Verkuyten, 1999; Schiffauer, Baumann, Kastoryano, & Vertovec, 2004; Verkuyten, 2002), the contents of the school curriculum (Kinket & Verkuyten, 1999; McGregor, 1993; Pfeifer, Brown, & Juvonen, 2007), representations of racial and ethnic others in the books that children use in school (Litcher & Johnson, 1969), and the stories that children read at school about cultural others (Cameron, Rutland, Brown, & Douch, 2006). Representations of racial and ethnic groups in the mass media also impact on children's racial and ethnic attitudes (Bogatz & Ball, 1971; Gorn, Goldberg, & Kanungo,

1976; Graves, 1999), as does children's own direct personal contact with members of other racial and ethnic groups under appropriate conditions (Dovidio, Glick, & Rudman, 2005; Pettigrew & Tropp, 2006).

Children's racial and ethnic attitudes are affected not only by these various environmental and experiential factors, but also by children's own cognitive abilities, including their conservation skills, their ability to classify people in multiple ways rather than in just a single way, and their ability to understand that different people holding different opinions can both be correct when considered from their own point of view (Aboud, 2003; Bigler & Liben, 1993; Black-Gutman & Hickson, 1996). Aboud (1988; see also Aboud & Amato, 2001) has argued that the development of these cognitive abilities is responsible for the reduction in prejudice that takes place during middle childhood. However, this argument fails to accommodate the fact that prejudice against racial and ethnic outgroups does *not* always reduce during middle childhood at the time when these cognitive skills are acquired (Davis et al., 2007; Dunham et al., 2006). Hence, it is clear that the influence of these cognitive factors can be overridden by other factors, depending on the outgroups concerned.

Conclusion

Children's understanding of and attitudes toward racial and ethnic groups show considerable change between 3 and 12 years. Although some authors have argued that these changes are linked primarily to the development of children's cognitive skills (e.g., Aboud, 1988; Aboud & Amato, 2001), others have instead argued that these changes are linked to a wide range of environmental factors in addition to cognitive skills, including the way in which specific outgroups are represented in the child's environment (e.g., in the mass media, in the school curriculum, and in school textbooks) and how these outgroups are regarded by those adults with whom the child regularly interacts (especially parents and teachers) (e.g., Barrett, 2009; Barrett & Davis, 2008).

Children's Understanding of Nations and National Groups

In addition to social class, race, and ethnicity, the societies within which children live today are also structured in terms of nation. This section describes the research that has been conducted into children's knowledge of, and attitudes to, nations and national groups.

Children's knowledge of their own country and national group

Studies investigating children's knowledge in this area have shown that, before 5 years, children often have little knowledge of their own country or national group. From about

5 or 6 years, most children are able to provide the name of their own country and spontaneously classify themselves as members of their own national group (Barrett, 2007). Knowledge of emblems such as the national flag, national anthem, national landscapes, and national historical figures also develops from about 5 years onward (Barrett, 2005a, 2007; Jahoda, 1963b). However, the emotional significance that is attached to these kinds of emblem varies considerably within individual countries depending on children's ethnicity (Barrett, 2007; Moodie, 1980).

Children's geographical knowledge of their own country also develops through middle childhood, but this knowledge is very error-prone until at least early adolescence (Barrett, 1996; Jahoda, 1963a). Initially, children learn about their own immediate locale and some of the larger cities in their country; subsequently, they learn about other places located between these initial landmarks, gradually filling in the gaps in their mental maps (Gould & White, 1986). Interestingly, knowledge of national geography is related to levels of performance on Piagetian class inclusion tasks (Wilberg, 2002), suggesting that such knowledge may be at least partially dependent on children's more general level of cognitive development.

In a study of the attributes that 5- to 11-year-old children ascribe to the members of their own national group, Barrett, Wilson, and Lyons (2003) found that the younger children were more likely than the older ones to ascribe only positive attributes to their own national group, with older children being more likely to assign a mixture of both positive and negative attributes to the group. Thus, as the children got older, the degree of stereotyping lessened and they came to attribute greater variability to the ingroup.

Children's feelings about their own country and national group

Several studies have investigated how children feel about their own country and national group. Some have found that children exhibit a systematic preference for their own country and for members of their own national group from at least 5–6 years (e.g., Barrett et al., 2003; Bennett, Lyons, Sani, & Barrett, 1998; Lambert & Klineberg, 1967), whereas other studies have found that children do not develop a systematic preference for their own country or national group until 7 years or even later (e.g., Middleton, Tajfel, & Johnson, 1970; Piaget & Weil, 1951). In addition, those children who are members of negatively evaluated national groups may not develop a systematic preference for their own group at all (Tajfel, Jahoda, Nemeth, Rim, & Johnson, 1972). Thus, there is substantial variability in development here.

In addition, although children do usually classify themselves as members of their national group at the age of 5–6 years, there is a great deal of variability in how strongly children identify with their national group. Variations occur depending on where children live within their country (with national identification sometimes being stronger among children who live in the capital city), children's ethnicity, the use of national languages within the family home, and children's language of schooling (Barrett, 2005b, 2007).

Children's knowledge of other countries and national groups

Children's ability to name other countries is also very poor before about 5 years. Knowledge about other countries begins to develop shortly thereafter, although even at 10 or 11 years, some children still have very poor geographical knowledge of other countries (Barrett & Farroni, 1996; Bourchier, Barrett, & Lyons, 2002). There are significant variations in children's geographical knowledge of other countries depending on their social class, ethnicity, and geographical location (Barrett, 2007). These variations are unsurprising, because children's knowledge of other countries is acquired primarily from foreign travel, schooling, and the mass media (Axia, Bremner, Deluca, & Andreason, 1998; Holloway & Valentine, 2000; Wiegand, 1991), all of which also vary according to social class, ethnicity, and geographical location.

Between 5 and 11 years, children also acquire stereotypes of the people who live in other countries (Barrett, 2007; Barrett & Short, 1992; Lambert & Klineberg, 1967; Piaget & Weil, 1951). The amount of individual variation that is acknowledged to exist around these national stereotypes increases between 5 and 11 years (Barrett et al., 2003). Thus, older children are more willing than younger children to admit that there is much variability amongst the people who belong to different national groups (not just their own ingroup). Knowledge about people in other countries is, once again, largely acquired from foreign travel, schooling, and the mass media (see Barrett, 2007, for a detailed review).

Children's attitudes to, and feelings about, other countries and national groups

Children sometimes acquire strong feelings about particular groups of foreign people before they have acquired any concrete knowledge about those groups (Barrett & Short, 1992; Johnson, Middleton, & Tajfel, 1970). In addition, children can feel very positively indeed about some national outgroups – indeed, outgroup denigration is a comparatively rare phenomenon (Barrett, 2007). However, those countries that have been the traditional enemies of the child's own country in the past are usually liked significantly less than all other countries (Barrett, 2007; Lambert & Klineberg, 1967).

That said, there is a great deal of variability in the development of attitudes toward other national groups, depending on children's own national group and the specific outgroup that is involved. In factor analyses of cross-national comparative data collected from 6- to 15-year-old children growing up in 12 different national contexts, Barrett (2007) found that even the underlying structures of children's national attitudes varied according to the specific pattern of international relationships within which their own national group was embedded.

Conclusion

The overall picture that emerges is that there is considerable learning about nations and national groups from 5 years onward. However, there are significant variations in children's development depending on a wide array of different factors, including children's country, ethnicity, social class, geographical location, education, level of cognitive development, use of national languages, foreign travel, and exposure to information in the mass media about other countries. Addressing these various phenomena, as well as the phenomena that children exhibit while learning about race and ethnicity, Barrett (2007, 2009; Barrett & Davis, 2008) has articulated an integrated model of the development of children's national, ethnic, and racial understanding that explicitly incorporates attention to all of these different factors.

Conclusions

This chapter has reviewed the research literature on children's understanding of society. A substantial proportion of the early research that has been reviewed was Piagetian in orientation, relying on open-ended interviewing to gather data; proposing that children's development is dependent on changes to underlying domain-general cognitive skills, often with the tacit (and sometimes explicit) assumption that the development patterns that can be observed are universal; and proposing that influences from the child's socio-cultural context are minimal and can only either accelerate or decelerate the rate at which the child progresses through the postulated developmental sequence.

There has been a major shift in recent years in terms of how researchers conceptualize children's development in this area (Barrett & Buchanan-Barrow, 2005; Hatano & Takahashi, 2005). It has now become clear that the child does not always have firsthand personal experience of the phenomena or institutions in societal domains (e.g., of profit generation in shops and banks, of political power and decision making, and of people living in other countries), and so the child's own personal experience cannot always function as the source of the child's knowledge. Instead, contemporary researchers widely recognize that children are heavily reliant on indirect and socially mediated sources of information for learning about many societal phenomena, with the mass media (especially television), parent, teacher, and peer discourse and the school curriculum being the most important sources of information. It is for this reason that children's understanding in many different societal domains exhibits variation as a function of the specific sociocultural context in which they grow up.

Children's own cognitive skills and motivations determine how they use the various information sources that are potentially available to them. The uptake of information from environmental sources is affected by the child's attentional, cognitive representational, and memory processes; by the child's perceptual set and motivational state; by the salience of the available information for the child; and by the child's own affective preferences (Barrett, 2007). Children are highly active agents in the processing of information provided by the environment, not passive recipients of that information. For further progress to be made in this field, it is vital that researchers do not ignore any of the required levels of analysis: the societal and sociocultural contexts within which children grow up, the specific social influences that operate within those contexts, children's cognitive capacities and skills, and children's own motivational processes.

References

Aboud, F. (1977). Interest in ethnic information: A cross-cultural developmental study. *Canadian Journal of Behavioural Science, 9*, 134–146.

Aboud, F. (1980). A test of ethnocentrism with young children. *Canadian Journal of Behavioural Science, 12*, 195–209.

Aboud, F. (1988). *Children and prejudice.* Oxford: Blackwell.

Aboud, F. E. (2003). The formation of in-group favouritism and out-group prejudice in young children: Are they distinct attitudes? *Developmental Psychology, 39*, 48–60.

Aboud, F. E., & Amato, M. (2001). Developmental and socialization influences on intergroup bias. In R. Brown & S. L. Gaertner (Eds.), *Blackwell handbook of social psychology: Intergroup processes* (pp. 65–85). Oxford: Blackwell.

Asher, S. R., & Allen, V. L. (1969). Racial preference and social comparison processes. *Journal of Social Issues, 25*, 157–166.

Axia, G., Bremner, J. G., Deluca, P., & Andreasen, G. (1998). Children drawing Europe: The effects of nationality, age and teaching. *British Journal of Developmental Psychology, 16*, 423–437.

Banks, W. C. (1976). White preference in Blacks: A paradigm in search of a phenomenon. *Psychological Bulletin, 83*, 1179–1186.

Banton, M. (1977). *The idea of race.* London: Tavistock.

Barrett, M. (1996). English children's acquisition of a European identity. In G. Breakwell & E. Lyons (Eds.), *Changing European identities: Social psychological analyses of social change* (pp. 349–369). Oxford: Butterworth-Heinemann.

Barrett, M. (2005a). Children's understanding of, and feelings about, countries and national groups. In M. Barrett & E. Buchanan-Barrow (Eds.), *Children's understanding of society* (pp. 251–285). Hove, UK: Psychology Press.

Barrett, M. (2005b). National identities in children and young people. In S. Ding & K. Littleton (Eds.), *Children's personal and social development* (pp. 181–220). Milton Keynes, UK: Open University/Blackwell.

Barrett, M. (2007). *Children's knowledge, beliefs and feelings about nations and national groups.* Hove, UK: Psychology Press.

Barrett, M. (2009). The development of children's intergroup attitudes. In A. Hu & M. Byram (Eds.), *Interkulturelle Kompetenz und Fremdsprachliches Lernen: Modelle, Empirie, Evaluation* [Intercultural competence and foreign language learning: Models, empiricism, assessment] (pp. 69–86). Tübingen, Germany: Gunter Narr Verlag.

Barrett, M., & Buchanan-Barrow, E. (2005). Emergent themes in the study of children's understanding of society. In M. Barrett & E. Buchanan-Barrow (Eds.), *Children's understanding of society* (pp. 1–16). Hove, UK: Psychology Press.

Barrett, M., & Davis, S. C. (2008). Applying social identity and self-categorization theories to children's racial, ethnic, national and state identifications and attitudes. In S. M. Quintana & C. McKown (Eds.), *Handbook of race, racism and the developing child* (pp. 72–110). Hoboken, NJ: Wiley.

Barrett, M., & Farroni, T. (1996). English and Italian children's knowledge of European geography. *British Journal of Developmental Psychology, 14*, 257–273.

Barrett, M., & Short, J. (1992). Images of European people in a group of 5–10 year old English school children. *British Journal of Developmental Psychology, 10*, 339–363.

Barrett, M., Wilson, H., & Lyons, E. (2003). The development of national in-group bias: English children's attributions of characteristics to English, American and German people. *British Journal of Developmental Psychology, 21*, 193–220.

Bennett, M., Lyons, E., Sani, F., & Barrett, M. (1998). Children's subjective identification with the group and ingroup favoritism. *Developmental Psychology, 34*, 902–909.

Berti, A. E. (1988). The development of political understanding in children between 6–15 years old. *Human Relations, 41*, 437–446.

Berti, A. E. (2005). Children's understanding of politics. In M. Barrett & E. Buchanan-Barrow (Eds.), *Children's understanding of society* (pp. 69–103). Hove, UK: Psychology Press.

Berti, A., & Bombi, A. (1988). *The child's construction of economics*. Cambridge: Cambridge University Press.

Bigler, R. S., & Liben, L. (1993). A cognitive-developmental approach to racial stereotyping and reconstructive memory in Euro-American children. *Child Development, 64*, 1507–1519.

Black-Gutman, D., & Hickson, F. (1996). The relationship between racial attitudes and social-cognitive development in children: An Australian study. *Developmental Psychology, 32*, 448–456.

Bogatz, G. A., & Ball, S. (Eds.). (1971). *The second year of Sesame Street: A continuing evaluation.* Princeton, NJ: Educational Testing Service.

Bonn, M., Earle, D., Lea, S., & Webley, P. (1999). South African children's views of wealth, poverty, inequality and unemployment. *Journal of Economic Psychology, 20*, 593–612.

Bonn, M., & Webley, P. (2000). South African children's understanding of money and banking. *British Journal of Developmental Psychology, 18*, 269–278.

Bourchier, A., Barrett, M., & Lyons, E. (2002). The predictors of children's geographical knowledge of other countries. *Journal of Environmental Psychology, 22*, 79–94.

Branch, C. W., & Newcombe, N. (1986). Racial attitude development among young Black children as a function of parental attitudes: A longitudinal and cross-sectional study. *Child Development, 57*, 712–721.

Brown, R. (1995). *Prejudice: Its social psychology*. Oxford: Blackwell.

Buchanan-Barrow, E. (2005). Children's understanding of the school. In M. Barrett & E. Buchanan-Barrow (Eds.), *Children's understanding of society* (pp. 17–41). Hove, UK: Psychology Press.

Buchanan-Barrow, E., & Barrett, M. (1996). Primary school children's understanding of the school. *British Journal of Educational Psychology, 66*, 33–46.

Buchanan-Barrow, E., & Barrett, M. (1998). Individual differences in children's understanding of the school. *Social Development, 7*, 250–268.

Burgard, P., Cheyne, W. M., & Jahoda, G. (1989). Children's representations of economic inequality: A replication. *British Journal of Developmental Psychology, 7*, 275–287.

Cameron, L., Rutland, A., Brown, R., & Douch, R. (2006). Changing children's intergroup attitudes toward refugees: Testing different models of extended contact. *Child Development, 77*, 1208–1219.

Carlson, J. M., & Iovini, J. (1985). The transmission of racial attitudes from fathers to sons: A study of Blacks and Whites. *Adolescence, 20*, 233–237.

Clark, K. B., & Clark, M. P. (1947). Racial identification and preference in Negro children. In T. M. Newcomb & E. L. Hartley (Eds.), *Readings in social psychology* (pp. 169–178). New York: Holt.

Connell, R. W. (1971). *The child's construction of politics*. Carlton, VIC: Melbourne University Press.

Connolly, P. (1998). *Racism, gender identities and young children: Social relations in a multi-ethnic inner-city primary school*. London: Routledge.

Davey, A. (1983). *Learning to be prejudiced*. London: Edward Arnold.

Davis, S. C., Leman, P. J., & Barrett, M. (2007). Children's implicit and explicit ethnic group attitudes, ethnic group identification, and self-esteem. *International Journal of Behavioral Development, 31*, 514–525.

Dickinson, J., & Emler, N. (1996). Developing ideas about distribution of wealth. In P. Lunt & A. Furnham (Eds.), *Economic socialization: The economic beliefs and behaviours of young people* (pp. 47–68). Cheltenham: Edward Elgar.

Dovidio, J. F., Glick, P., & Rudman, L. A. (Eds.). (2005). *On the nature of prejudice: Fifty years after Allport.* Oxford: Blackwell.

Dunham, Y., Baron, A. S., & Banaji, M. R. (2006). From American city to Japanese village: A cross-cultural investigation of implicit race attitudes. *Child Development, 77,* 1268–1281.

Emler, N., & Dickinson, J. (1985). Children's representation of economic inequalities: The effects of social class. *British Journal of Developmental Psychology, 3,* 191–198.

Emler, N., & Dickinson, J. (2005). Children's understanding of social class and occupational groupings. In M. Barrett & E. Buchanan-Barrow (Eds.), *Children's understanding of society* (pp. 169–197). Hove, UK: Psychology Press.

Fox, D. J., & Jordan, V. D. (1973). Racial preference and identification of Black, American Chinese, and White children. *Genetic Psychology Monographs, 88,* 229–286.

Fox, K. F. A., & Kehret-Ward, T. (1990). Naïve theories of price: A developmental model. *Psychology and Marketing, 7,* 311–329.

Furth, H. (1980). *The world of grown-ups: Children's conceptions of society.* New York: Elsevier.

Gorn, G. J., Goldberg, M. E., & Kanungo, R. N. (1976). The role of educational television in changing the intergroup attitudes of children. *Child Development, 47,* 277–280.

Gould, P., & White, R. (1986). *Mental maps* (2nd ed.). Boston: Allen & Unwin.

Graves, S. B. (1999). Television and prejudice reduction: When does television as a vicarious experience make a difference? *Journal of Social Issues, 55,* 707–725.

Hatano, G., & Takahashi, K. (2005). The development of societal cognition: a commentary. In M. Barrett & E. Buchanan-Barrow (Eds.), *Children's understanding of society* (pp. 287–303). Hove, UK: Psychology Press.

Helwig, C. (1997). The role of agent and social context in judgments of freedom of speech and religion. *Child Development, 68,* 484–495.

Helwig, C. (1998). Children's conceptions of fair government and freedom of speech. *Child Development, 69,* 518–531.

Helwig, C., & Jasiobedzka, U. (2001). The relation between law and morality: Children's reasoning about socially beneficial and unjust laws. *Child Development, 72,* 1382–1393.

Hirschfeld, L. A. (2005). Children's understanding of racial groups. In M. Barrett & E. Buchanan-Barrow (Eds.), *Children's understanding of society* (pp. 199–221). Hove, UK: Psychology Press.

Holloway, S. L., & Valentine, G. (2000). Corked hats and Coronation Street: British and New Zealand children's imaginative geographies of the other. *Childhood, 7,* 335–357.

Hraba, J., & Grant, G. (1970). Black is beautiful: A re-examination of racial preference and identification. *Journal of Personality and Social Psychology, 16,* 398–402.

Hutchinson, J., & Smith, A. D. (1996). Introduction. In J. Hutchinson & A. D. Smith (Eds.), *Ethnicity* (pp. 1–14). Oxford: Oxford University Press.

Jahoda, G. (1959). Development of the perception of social differences in children from 6 to 10. *British Journal of Psychology, 50,* 159–177.

Jahoda, G. (1963a). The development of children's ideas about country and nationality, Part I: The conceptual framework. *British Journal of Educational Psychology, 33,* 47–60.

Jahoda, G. (1963b). The development of children's ideas about country and nationality, Part II: National symbols and themes. *British Journal of Educational Psychology, 33,* 143–153.

Jahoda, G. (1979). The construction of economic reality by some Glaswegian children. *European Journal of Social Psychology, 9,* 115–127.

Jahoda, G. (1981). The development of thinking about economic institutions: The bank. *Cahiers de Psychologie Cognitive, 1,* 55–73.

Jahoda, G. (1982). The development of ideas about an economic institution: A cross-national replication. *British Journal of Social Psychology, 21,* 337–338.

Jahoda, G. (1983). European "lag" in the development of an economic concept: A study in Zimbabwe. *British Journal of Developmental Psychology, 1,* 113–120.

Johnson, N., Middleton, M., & Tajfel, H. (1970). The relationship between children's preferences for and knowledge about other nations. *British Journal of Social and Clinical Psychology, 9,* 232–240.

Kinket, B., & Verkuyten, M. (1999). Intergroup evaluations and social context: A multilevel approach. *European Journal of Social Psychology, 29,* 219–237.

Lambert, W. E., & Klineberg, O. (1967). *Children's views of foreign peoples: A cross-national study.* New York: Appleton-Century-Crofts.

Leahy, R. L. (1981). Development of the conception of economic inequality: I. Descriptions and comparisons of rich and poor people. *Child Development, 52,* 523–532.

Leiser, D., Sevon, G., & Levy, D. (1990). Children's economic socialization: Summarizing the cross-cultural comparison of ten countries. *Journal of Economic Psychology, 11,* 591–614.

Litcher, J. H., & Johnson, D. W. (1969). Changes in attitudes toward Negroes of White elementary school students after use of multiethnic readers. *Journal of Educational Psychology, 60,* 148–152.

McGregor, J. (1993). Effectiveness of role-playing and antiracist teaching in reducing student prejudice. *Journal of Educational Research, 86,* 215–226.

Middleton, M., Tajfel, H., & Johnson, N. (1970). Cognitive and affective aspects of children's national attitudes. *British Journal of Social and Clinical Psychology, 9,* 122–134.

Moodie, M. A. (1980). The development of national identity in white South African schoolchildren. *Journal of Social Psychology, 111,* 169–180.

Moore, S. W., Lare, J., & Wagner, K. A. (1985). *The child's political world: A longitudinal perspective.* New York: Praeger.

Nakhaie, M. R. (1993). Knowledge of profit and interest among children in Canada. *Journal of Economic Psychology, 14,* 147–160.

Ng, S. (1985). Children's ideas about the bank: A New Zealand replication. *European Journal of Social Psychology, 15,* 121–123.

Otto, A. M. C., Schots, P. A. M., Westerman, J. A. J., & Webley, P. (2006). Children's use of saving strategies: An experimental approach. *Journal of Economic Psychology, 27,* 57–72.

Pettigrew, T. F., & Tropp, L. R. (2006). A meta-analytic test of intergroup contact theory. *Journal of Personality and Social Psychology, 90,* 751–783.

Pfeifer, J. H., Brown, C. S., & Juvonen, J. (2007). Teaching tolerance in schools: Lessons learned since *Brown v. Board of Education* about the development and reduction of children's prejudice (Social Policy Report Vol. 21, No. 2). Ann Arbor, MI: Society for Research in Child Development.

Piaget, J., & Weil, A. M. (1951). The development in children of the idea of the homeland and of relations to other countries. *International Social Science Journal, 3,* 561–578.

Pliner, P., Freedman, J., Abramovitch, R., & Darke, P. (1996). Children as consumers: In the laboratory and beyond. In P. Lunt & A. Furnham (Eds.), *Economic socialization: The economic beliefs and behaviours of young people* (pp. 35–46). Cheltenham, UK: Edward Elgar.

Roland-Levy, C. (1990). A cross-national comparison of Algerian and French children's economic socialization. *Journal of Economic Psychology, 11,* 567–581.

Rosenthal, B. G. (1974). Development of self-identification in relation to attitudes towards the self in the Chippewa Indians. *Genetic Psychology Monographs, 90,* 43–141.

Schiffauer, W., Baumann, G., Kastoryano, R., & Vertovec, S. (Eds.). (2004). *Civil enculturation: Nation-state, school and ethnic difference in the Netherlands, Britain, Germany and France.* New York: Berghahn.

Sonuga-Barke, E. J. S., & Webley, P. (1993). *Children's saving: A study in the development of economic behaviour.* Hove, UK: Erlbaum.

Spencer, M. B. (1983). Children's cultural values and parental rearing strategies. *Developmental Review, 3*, 351–370.

Tajfel, H., Jahoda, G., Nemeth, C., Rim, Y., & Johnson, N. (1972). The devaluation by children of their own national and ethnic group: Two case studies. *British Journal of Social and Clinical Psychology, 11*, 235–243.

Takahashi, K., & Hatano, G. (1994). Understanding of the banking business in Japan: Is economic prosperity accompanied by economic literacy? *Journal of Developmental Psychology, 12*, 585–590.

Thompson, D. R., & Siegler, R. S. (2000). Buy low, sell high: The development of an informal theory of economics. *Child Development, 71*, 660–677.

Vaughan, G. M. (1978). Social change and intergroup preferences in New Zealand. *European Journal of Social Psychology, 8*, 297–314.

Verkuyten, M. (2002). Ethnic attitudes among minority and majority children: The role of ethnic identification, peer group victimization and parents. *Social Development, 11*, 558–570.

Webley, P. (1996). Playing the market: The autonomous economic world of children. In P. Lunt & A. Furnham (Eds.), *Economic socialization: The economic beliefs and behaviours of young people* (pp. 149–161). Cheltenham, UK: Edward Elgar.

Webley, P. (2005). Children's understanding of economics. In M. Barrett & E. Buchanan-Barrow (Eds.), *Children's understanding of society* (pp. 43–67). Hove, UK: Psychology Press.

Webley, P., Levine, M., & Lewis, A. (1991). A study in economic psychology: Children's saving in a play economy. *Human Relations, 44*, 127–146.

Wellman, H. M., & Gelman, S. A. (1998). Knowledge acquisition in foundational domains. In W. Damon (Ed.), *Handbook of child psychology: Vol. 2. Cognition, perception and language* (pp. 523–573). New York: Wiley.

Wiegand, P. (1991). The "known world" of primary school children. *Geography, 76*, 143–149.

Wilberg, S. (2002). Preschoolers' cognitive representations of their homeland. *British Journal of Developmental Psychology, 20*, 157–169.

Williams, J. E., & Morland, J. K. (1976). *Race, color, and the young child.* Chapel Hill: University of North Carolina Press.

Wong, M. (1989). Children's acquisition of economic knowledge: Understanding banking in Hong Kong and USA. In J. Valsiner (Ed.), *Child development in cultural context* (pp. 225–246). Norwood: NJ: Ablex.

PART IX

Intervening in Social Development

Many child development researchers are concerned to see that our increased knowledge of developmental processes can be put to practical use. There are many areas where children, and those concerned with children, can benefit from the dissemination of knowledge, and from practical interventions designed to enhance childhood well-being and reduce maladaptive behaviors or undesirable outcomes. Examples of this have been mentioned, for example, in Chapter 26 on aggression and Chapter 27 on bullying.

Mary Ellen Voegler-Lee and Janis Kupersmidt start in Chapter 32 by emphasizing the importance of social and emotional development in children, and then discuss programs and school curricula designed to enhance this. The vital issue of "training the trainers" (often teachers) is also reviewed in detail, as is the involvement of parents. Finally, some critical factors relevant to the success of such programs are discussed.

Children with disabilities are, by definition, likely to face some challenges in development, and may need more help than nondisabled children in certain areas. In Chapter 33, Karen Diamond, Hsin-Hui Huang, and Elizabeth Steed discuss the concept of disability, and the social and cultural contexts in which it is viewed. They give a thorough account of the main different types of disabilities and how they impact social development. They then consider the kinds of interventions employed – classroom wide, peer mediated, and teacher mediated – and some of the issues in carrying these out.

In the Western world, most (but not all) children have at least their basic needs met in terms of nutrition, housing, and basic health. But in many countries of the world, these cannot be taken for granted. In developing countries, there are additional challenges for children, and those caring for children, to face. Programs and interventions to help such children can partly draw on the knowledge base that is primarily from the Western experience, and also need to be aware of context-specific needs and the indigenous psychology or local knowledge. Suman Verma and Rajani Konantambigi, based in India,

The Wiley-Blackwell Handbook of Childhood Social Development, Second Edition, edited by Peter K. Smith and Craig H. Hart
© 2011 by Blackwell Publishing Ltd.

write about these issues in Chapter 34, particularly in the context of developing social skills and competence. They give details of a number of exemplars of such approaches. They consider the methodological issues involved, and conclude with a "call to action" in this area. Although the majority of readers of this handbook are unlikely to come from developing countries, the majority of the world's children live in them; and it is vital to develop our knowledge bases and our intervention programs to help all the world's children, and not just those in the countries we are most familiar with.

CHAPTER THIRTY-TWO

Intervening in Childhood Social Development

Mary Ellen Voegler-Lee and Janis B. Kupersmidt

The purpose of this chapter is to provide a survey of interventions designed to promote the social and emotional development of children from preschool age through age 11. First, we will define social and emotional development. Then, we will discuss the importance of social and emotional development in reference to children's overall functioning and adjustment. Next, we will discuss three common approaches to intervening in regard to children's social and emotional development and the reported efficacy of universal programs designed to promote functioning in these areas. Finally, we will explore factors that have emerged as moderators of child outcomes and discuss directions for future work.

What Is Social-Emotional Development?

Social-emotional interventions are designed to foster the development of skills that are considered essential for children's social and emotional development. At the preschool and elementary school levels, social and emotional competence includes the ability to effectively express and regulate emotions, establish positive relationships with peers and adults, and solve interpersonal problems (Hemmeter, Ostrosky, & Fox, 2006). The Collaborative for Academic, Social, and Emotional Learning (CASEL, 2003) provides a framework of five core competencies of social and emotional learning (SEL): (a) self-awareness, (b) social awareness, (c) self-management, (d) relationship skills, and (e) responsible decision making. Although the core competencies themselves do not vary, the specific skills that comprise them differ across developmental stages.

The Wiley-Blackwell Handbook of Childhood Social Development, Second Edition, edited by Peter K. Smith and Craig H. Hart
© 2011 by Blackwell Publishing Ltd.

Self-awareness in preschoolers includes recognizing one's own basic emotions, such as being happy, sad, and angry. For elementary-aged children, self-awareness also includes the ability to accurately label one's emotions and understand that feelings can vary in intensity. *Social awareness* in preschool children involves understanding others' thoughts and feelings and demonstrating empathy, whereas elementary school children not only recognize similarities and differences among people but also learn to recognize verbal and physical cues that identify how others feel. For preschoolers, *self-management* includes the development and utilization of emotion regulation skills to manage their emotions. For elementary school children, self-management skills extend to the ability to understand the steps involved in establishing and working toward goals. *Relationship skills* consist of those skills necessary to build positive relationships with both peers and adults. At the preschool level this includes skills such as cooperation and sharing. Elementary-aged children are expected to be able to identify and implement strategies for establishing and maintaining friendships. *Responsible decision making* for preschoolers includes the skills for solving common social problems such as waiting for something or having something taken away. For elementary-aged children, decision making requires the skills to recognize problematic interpersonal situations and to generate and enact positive solutions to resolve the problem(s).

Why Is Social-Emotional Development Important?

Children who exhibit positive social-emotional development are those who get along well with their peers as well as with adults. They are cooperative, resolve conflict amicably, have competent social problem-solving skills, and have good communication skills. Social and emotional skills are important in their own right, but in addition, they are associated with children's academic adjustment both concurrently (Arnold et al., 1999; McLelland, Morrison, & Holmes, 2000; Wentzel & Asher, 1995) and longitudinally (Alexander, Entwistle, & Dauber, 1993; Ladd, Kochendorfer, & Coleman, 1997).

Consistent with these findings, outcome studies of programs that instruct children in social-emotional skill development find that these children are more connected to teachers and school, more engaged in learning, more motivated to learn, better behaved, less likely to engage in problem behavior, and better able to perform on achievement tests and obtain higher grades (Zins, Weissberg, Wang, & Walberg, 2004). In contrast, children with poor social-emotional skills are at heightened risk for a range of negative adjustment problems including aggression, delinquency, substance abuse, and school failure (Kupersmidt & Coie, 1990; Kupersmidt & DeRosier, 2004).

Why Is Early Social-Emotional Learning Important?

Early intervention or education in social and emotional development during the preschool years is important for several reasons. First, preschool is a time of rapid growth and development in both of these domains of functioning. Many new social and emotional skills are first being developed, tried, and tested outside the home with both peers and teachers, often in a classroom context. For example, during the preschool years, children develop skills for engaging in positive social interactions (Odom et al., 1999). Children who might never have had to share or take turns are now faced with interacting with peers who also want to have their needs and desires met. Preschool children have the opportunity to practice these and other social skills that will lay the foundation for more complex social interactions that will be encountered with peers and teachers later in elementary school.

The preschool period is not only a time to teach and practice social skills, but also a time to engage in early intervention to prevent the escalation of emerging behavior problems. For example, Head Start and community child care teachers reported that about one quarter of the children in their preschool classes exhibited aggressive or disruptive behavior at least once a week (Kupersmidt, Bryant, & Willoughby, 2000). Similarly, in a nationally representative study of kindergarten teachers, 20% reported that at least half of their students had problems with social skills and a full 30% reported that at least half of the children had difficulty working in a group and following directions in addition to having academic problems (Rimm-Kaufman, Pianta, & Cox, 2000). Thus, if exposure to intervention or educational programs coincides with initial developmental processes, then preschool children will have the opportunity to learn adaptive social skills at the outset rather than have the need for more intensive and serious remediation efforts later in elementary school.

Second, not only is growth rapid and powerful during preschool, but if children are successfully prepared for the transition to kindergarten, then they are at less risk for problems academically, socially, and behaviorally in early elementary school. Social and emotional skills problems are stable over time and across settings. For example, patterns of problem behavior established as early as 2 or 3 years of age are likely to persist over time and be associated with later behavioral problems (Bates, Bayles, Bennett, Ridge, & Brown, 1991; Campbell, 1995). As a result, young aggressive children are at increased risk for later school failure, delinquency, and poor peer relationships (Moffitt, 1993; Tremblay, Masse, Pagani, & Vitaro, 1996).

As children enter the early elementary years, behavioral and social demands increase as interactions with peers and adults require more nuanced social skills. For children with existing social and emotional deficits, then, the associated negative outcomes are likely to be exacerbated if intervention does not take place. Furthermore, it has been suggested that social, emotional, and behavior problems are less malleable if intervention occurs after age 8 (Eron, 1990), perhaps indicating a critical period for intervention. For these reasons, curricula or intervention programs for children in the preschool and early school years are a critical component of universal prevention programming.

What are the Characteristics of Effective Intervention Programs?

Numerous programs have been developed to provide social-emotional learning to children. Several of the most effective social and emotional curricula and programs for preschool and elementary-aged children will be discussed in the following sections. The selection of these interventions as model programs was guided by several factors.

First, the intervention programs we chose have been empirically validated in one or more randomized controlled trials (RCTs). Numerous intervention programs target children's social and emotional learning. Although many of these programs show promise in positively impacting children's social and emotional development, relatively few of these have undergone the rigorous evaluation of their efficacy and/or effectiveness that an RCT provides.

Second, we included only intervention programs that are implemented in school settings. School-based programs are considered one of the most promising avenues for promoting children's social and emotional functioning because the school is the setting that serves the greatest number of children. Even at the preschool level, enrollment in child care, public prekindergarten, and programs such as Head Start continues to increase dramatically, such that as many as 67% of young children are served in these settings (Innes, Denton, & West, 2001).

Third, in order to present an overview of the basic characteristics of effective intervention programs, we focused on intervention programs that are *universal* in nature and scope. Universal programs are those that target and educate all children and are typically preventive in nature. They aim to establish environments and skills that prevent the onset of social, emotional, and behavioral problems for all students. Because of their intended audience and target skills, these programs emphasize the acquisition of the

Table 32.1   Characteristics of effective school-based, universal intervention programs

	Grades	Core components	Curriculum materials	Method of instruction
Al's Pals: Kids Making Healthy Choices (Geller, 1999) www.wingspanworks.com	PreK–3	Conflict resolution Resilience Substance abuse prevention	Guided creative play Puppets Original music Role plays Posters	46 lessons 10–15 minutes per lesson 2 lessons per week 9 booster lessons (grades 2–3)
I Can Problem Solve (ICPS) (Shure, 1992a, 1992b, 1992c) www.researchpress.com	PreK–5	Pre-problem-solving vocabulary Feeling word concepts How to think of solutions to problems and consequences to actions	Puppets Stories Games Role play	59–83 lessons 20–30-minute lessons 3–5 lessons per week

basic components of social and emotion skill development. In contrast are interventions that are *selected* and those that are *targeted*. Selected interventions aim to support children who are at risk for problematic outcomes, such as children in low-income families or children with disabilities. Such interventions are also primarily preventive, but their focus is on a circumscribed student population. Targeted programs are those that intervene with children who have already demonstrated problem behaviors or skill deficits. (See Hemmeter et al., 2006, for a brief review of effective selected and targeted interventions.)

Table 32.1 presents an overview of several preschool and elementary school curricula and intervention programs and the social and emotional outcomes associated with each. Although there is variation among the characteristics and components of the programs, each program has proven effective in positively impacting children's social and emotional functioning.

How Do We Teach Social and Emotional Skills to Children?

Although intervention programs differ in their methods, duration, and other characteristics, a commonality across programs is the focus on a core set of skills that are recognized as the building blocks of SEL. Lane and colleagues found that teachers rated cooperation

Teacher training	Duration of intervention	Consultation resources	Parenting component	Outcomes
2 day on-site workshop Booster and advanced training available	23 weeks	On-site follow-up support available	Home activities to practice skills Parent letters and message pads 13-module parent program	Improved social skills, problem-solving skills, and social interaction skills Increased positive coping behaviors Decreased negative coping behaviors Decreased social withdrawal Reduced antisocial aggressive behaviors
1–3-day workshop (optional)	4–6 months	On-site follow-up support available	Parent workshops Parent workbook	Increased problem-solving skills Increased peer acceptance Improved academic achievement Reduced problem behaviors (impulsivity and inhibition)

(Continued)

Table 32.1   *Continued*

	Grades	Core components	Curriculum materials	Method of instruction
The Incredible Years: Dina Dinosaur Classroom Curriculum (Webster-Stratton & Reid, 2003) www.incredibleyears.com	PreK–K; 1–2	Learning school rules School success Emotional literacy and empathy Interpersonal problem solving Anger management Social skills Communication skills	Videotaped vignettes Life-sized puppets Picture cue cards Games Refrigerator magnets 4 problem-solving books	30 lessons 300+ small-group activities 20–30-minute lessons 2–3 lessons per week
PATHS (Kusche & Greenberg, 1994) www.preventionscience.com	K–6	Self-control Feelings and relationships Interpersonal problem solving	Puppets Photo cards Feelings face cards Turtle stamp Posters Display charts	30–45 lessons 100+ activities
PATHS-Preschool (Domitrovich, Greenberg, Kusche, & Cortes, 2004) www.preventionscience.com	PreK	Basic feelings Self-control Sharing, caring, and friendship Basic problem solving Intermediate feelings Advanced feelings	Puppets Feelings photos Feelings face cards Posters Turtle magnets Turtle stamp 5 storybooks	44 lessons across 9 units
Second Step Violence Prevention Curriculum (Committee for Children, 2002) www.cfchildren.org	PreK–K; 1–5	Empathy training Emotion management Problem solving	Puppets Photo cards Posters Hearts	8–28 lessons 15–20 minutes per lesson 1–2 lessons per week

Teacher training	Duration of intervention	Consultation resources	Parenting component	Outcomes
28 hours over 4 monthly sessions	6 months	Certification program available	Parent letters Weekly homework Invitations to visit the classroom	Greater social competence Greater emotional self-regulation Fewer conduct problems
2-day on-site workshop	9 months	On-site follow-up support available	Parent handbook with letters and activities Teacher manual for involving parents	Increased social competence Improved cognitive skills Decreased aggressive behavior
2–3-day on-site workshop	9 months	On-site follow-up support available	Parent letters and activities	Higher emotion knowledge skills Teacher rated and peer rated as more socially competent Less socially withdrawn
1 day on-site workshop (optional) *or* 20-hour training for trainers	9 months	On-site follow-up support available	6-session parent workshop	PreK–K: Increased emotion knowledge Decreased problem behaviors School-aged: Decreased physical aggression Increased prosocial behaviors More collaborative-negotiating strategies in girls

skills as most critical to school success for preschool children (Lane, Stanton-Chapman, Jamison, & Phillips, 2007), whereas elementary teachers rated not only cooperation skills but also self-control skills as essential (Lane, Givner, & Pierson, 2004). Parents, on the other hand, rated cooperation, self-control, and assertion skills as all being important to children's school success in both preschool and elementary school. Notably, these studies illustrate that in addition to developmental variations in how optimal adaptation is conceptualized, expectations for children's social and emotional functioning also differ across informants, in this case between teachers as compared to parents. These findings highlight the importance of recognizing differences in expectations for children's behavior and designing and/or adapting interventions to meet the needs of those children participating in them.

This chapter addresses three modalities for intervention with children's social-emotional learning: direct instruction to students, typically delivered by the classroom teacher; teacher training; and parent education.

How Do Curricula Provide Direct Instruction to Children?

Direct instruction to children in the development and practice of social and emotional skills is typically provided using universal SEL programs delivered by regular education teachers to whole classrooms of students during the school day. In a meta-analysis of 213 school-based, universal programs, Durlak and colleagues (Durlak, Weissberg, Dymnicki, Taylor, & Schellinger, submitted) found that such programs were highly effective in increasing children's social and emotional skills and behaviors.

The social-emotional skills-based curricula have in common the use of a combination of pedagogical strategies for introducing and practicing skills with children. The most successful programs tend to be those that follow SAFE principles: a *s*equenced approach, *a*ctive learning, a *f*ocus on providing time for skill development, and *e*xplicit goals (Durlak et al., submitted). Strategies for providing direct instruction of social-emotional skills include teacher-led group discussions, teacher modeling of new skills, role playing or practice by the children, and providing opportunities for transfer of learning throughout the school day. The curricula themselves vary in duration, ranging from several months to an entire academic year. With preschool children, the curricula are typically taught in short 20–30-minute lessons that may be repeated several times a week; with school-aged children, lessons may last for as much as one to two hours a week. Intervention materials differ across programs but generally include puppets or stuffed animals; oversized cards with black-and-white or color photographs depicting children displaying "feelings faces" as well as social scenes between pairs or groups of children; posters with icons or graphical reminders; cards, lists, pamphlets, or teacher manuals with directions for conducting activities; and picture or easy-reader story books. Curriculum lessons are typically presented in groups, either small or large, during the school day and include direct instruction of skills, role plays, reading story books and discussion of stories, and teacher-led group discussions. Several evidence-based programs are commercially available and include in-person teacher-training workshops as well as ready-to-use comprehensive kits (e.g., Dina Dinosaur Classroom Curriculum: Webster-Stratton & Reid, 2003; Fast Track: Conduct Problems Prevention Research Group, 1999; Promoting Alternative Thinking Strategies [PATHS]: Kusche & Greenberg, 1994; PATHS Preschool: Domitrovitch, Greenberg, Kusche, & Cortes, 2004; and Second Step Violence Prevention Curriculum: Committee for Children, 2002).

Direct instruction programs target the acquisition of specific skills associated with social and emotional competence. The development of these skills typically follows a set sequence, such that the development of one set of skills is a prerequisite to learning subsequent skills. Programs also tend to be recursive such that skills are revisited and reviewed, and build cumulatively upon one another. The Second Step Violence Prevention Curriculum (Committee for Children, 2002) and PATHS (Kusche & Greenberg, 1994) are two examples of interventions that facilitate skill development by targeting a sequential set of core skill areas: empathy, emotion management, and problem solving. These curricula instruct children in emotion management skills as a necessary precursor to effective problem solving. Others, such as the I Can Problem Solve (ICPS) program (Shure, 1992a, 1992b, 1992c), teach problem solving prior to emotion management, based on the theory that it's easier to regulate one's emotions once a problem has been resolved. In either case, a core set of competencies is consistently addressed in the goals and activities included in such universal programs.

The first training component targets the acquisition of *emotion knowledge and empathy skills*. In order for young children to negotiate the demands of their social and emotional worlds, they must first be able to recognize their own feelings as well as the feelings of others. Children learn to identify basic emotions and their accompanying physical characteristics (e.g., facial emotional expressions, nonverbal behavior, and display rules for emotions). They are exposed to a vocabulary of feeling words that cover a broad range of emotions so that they can correctly label their own feelings in different situations. Children also learn features of emotions such as the fact that they can vary in intensity and can change across time and/or contexts. Once children achieve this level of understanding, they are taught empathy skills, which extend their understanding of their own emotions to understanding of and sensitivity toward others' feelings.

Children next learn how to *regulate emotions* in social situations. They are taught to recognize when their emotions reach an intense level and to then use emotion management skills to decrease the intensity of the emotions. Children learn techniques such as belly breathing, counting, and self-talk and are provided numerous opportunities to practice these skills both in structured lessons and in informal situations throughout the school day. Some curricula include posters and other visual aids to assist children in recalling the calming down techniques so that these strategies can be utilized when needed.

Children require self-regulation skills in order to calm themselves so that they can engage in the next set of skills, namely, *social problem solving*. Problem solving involves being able to identify the presence of a problem and then generate one or more effective solutions to resolve it. Children with social skill deficits and/or behavior problems often have difficulty in accurately assessing interpersonal situations. In addition, they tend to generate few, if any, prosocial responses to problem situations. Direct training of social and emotional skills involves assisting children in identifying environmental cues, exploring possible solutions, and choosing and enacting an appropriate solution. Children are taught these skills and given opportunities to practice through role plays so that they will be equipped to use these skills when real-life interpersonal problems arise.

A key component to direct child instruction is ensuring that students be exposed to frequent opportunities for the transfer of learning of their new skills. The most effective teachers are those who not only teach the skills to children but also find numerous situations to practice these skills in real classroom situations. It is this reinforcement of new skills over many months and many situations that solidifies the skills that students develop.

Recent research suggests that the implementation of this type of universal approach to social-emotional skills development can result in changing the overall climate of the classroom by enhancing children's self-control and reducing disruptions, which makes the classroom more conducive to learning (Conduct Problems Prevention Research Group, 1999). Given the mass delivery and broad reach of these universal programs to all students in a classroom or school, these programs tend to be relatively low cost and time effective. Although one meta-analysis of curricula suggested that most curricula have low- to moderate-effect sizes (less than .3) and result in only modest, short-term impacts on children's social and emotional behavior (Quinn, Kavali, Mathur, Rutherford, & Forness, 1999), a recent meta-analysis of universal, school-based programs for school-aged children reported a much larger impact, namely, an effect size of .57 for social and emotional learning outcomes (Durlak et al., submitted). Moreover, although the average effect size was smaller at 6-month follow-up (i.e., .26), it remained significant. Although the latter meta-analysis included students from kindergarten through 12th grade and did not separate outcomes by grade level, approximately half the sample was elementary aged, suggesting that these positive results provide evidence of the effectiveness of social-emotional programs with young children. These findings also suggest that early intervention efforts might need to be supplemented, over time, by developmentally appropriate booster lessons and opportunities for practice in order to sustain the social-emotional gains made in early preventive intervention programs.

How Do We Train Teachers to Facilitate Children's Social and Emotional Development?

The teacher's role in facilitating children's social and emotional functioning is multifaceted. As such, teacher training in the promotion of social-emotional development addresses several distinct objectives. First, for teachers who participate in the implementation of a direct instruction program for children (described above), training typically focuses on providing education in the theory and practice of carrying out the intervention program in the classroom setting. Table 32.1 provides information regarding the training requirements for several effective social-emotional programs. Workshops provide teachers with an understanding of the conceptual basis for the curriculum and its components, as well as opportunities for hands-on learning and practice with the curriculum lessons, activities, and materials.

A second type of training targets teachers' professional development, including their behaviors, knowledge, beliefs, and attitudes. Teachers' behavior in the classroom – toward both children and other adults – serves as an important model for children's own behavior toward peers and adults. Children are keen observers of each other and of their teacher. From this perspective, the assessment and training of teachers to exhibit high levels of social and emotional functioning comprise a fundamental prerequisite of any curriculum-based program. In addition, teachers are faced with an increasing array of challenging behaviors exhibited by young children and need education, skills, and access to helpful resources to effectively handle these challenging behaviors in the classroom (Kupersmidt et al., 2000). When teachers work in school contexts that do not provide training, resources, and/or support, they often experience stress and disengagement on the job, which, in turn, contributes to high staff turnover as well as negative child outcomes (Hale-Jinks, Knopf, & Kemple, 2006). The provision of teacher training is included in most conceptual models of social-emotional interventions with children in school settings, because changes in teacher's attitudes, knowledge, and behaviors are commonly hypothesized to be the mediators of change in children's behavior.

Both types of teacher training are typically conducted in the form of workshops or courses. This format provides direct training on specific content areas. In addition, many training programs offer workshops or didactic training of teachers as well as access to a trained classroom consultant who provides mentoring or coaching to assist the teacher in planning and/or implementing new curricula or ideas in the classroom setting. For some programs, the consultation occurs on site and provides hands-on assistance with the implementation of new curriculum materials or activities, or interpersonal or pedagogical approaches. Other programs offer follow-up support by phone or online, which allows teachers or school administrators to check in as needed to facilitate the implementation of the intervention.

Two types of consultative models have been developed in the early education field, with one focusing on building teachers' general skills in promoting social and emotional development in their students, and a second providing a more clinical approach designed to help teachers modify the problematic behaviors of individual children (e.g., First Step to Success: Walker et al., 1998). Because this chapter focuses on universal programs, we will not discuss the more clinical approaches directly. In a recent review, Brennan and her colleagues (Brennan, Bradley, Allen, & Perry, 2008) located only two studies using whole-class consultation in a randomized controlled group design. In both of these studies, teachers were randomly assigned to intervention or wait-list control groups, and all teachers in the intervention group received a mental health consultant (MHC; Gilliam, 2007; Raver et al., 2008). Notably, Raver and her colleagues (2008) reported differences between teachers who received a mental health consultant and control teachers on key mediator variables that addressed teacher outcomes, including the classroom climate, teacher sensitivity, and management of disruptive behavior. The literature review located 24 additional studies that did not utilize a randomized design; however, the findings were fairly consistent in providing support for the hypothesis that mental health consultation helps improve teachers' perceptions of self-efficacy and their ability to more effectively promote children's social and emotional development and manage children's problematic behaviors (Brennan et al., 2008). A note of caution emerged from this review in that there were mixed findings regarding the relationship between mental health consultation and overall classroom quality as assessed on the ECERS. Improvement was noted for some classrooms, but some had no change, and some even had a reduction in scores after consultation. The authors suggested the need for future research to explore these complex but promising findings.

What Content Is Commonly Included in Teacher Training?

The social and emotional climate that teachers provide sets the stage for children's exploration of and engagement in social behaviors. In addition, teachers are responsible for directly instructing children in acquiring social and emotional skills. Fox and colleagues conceptualized these components as multitiered, with four central components: building positive relationships with children, families, and colleagues; designing supportive and engaging environments; teaching social and emotional skills; and developing individualized interventions for children with the most challenging behavior (Fox, Dunlap, Hemmeter, Joseph, & Strain, 2003). Intervention curricula such as the Incredible Years Teacher Classroom Management Program (Webster-Stratton, Reid, & Hammond, 2001) focus on these core areas in their teacher training curricula.

Building positive relationships with children is one of the fundamental components of social and emotional interventions (e.g., Hemmeter et al., 2006; Webster-Stratton et al., 2001). The presence of a warm, trusting relationship with a teacher provides the springboard for positive interactions with peers in the classroom setting. In addition, before children will respond to preventive strategies or behavioral interventions, they must first be able to trust that they are in an environment that provides a caring, sensitive, and positive emotional climate. Numerous studies highlight the finding that high-quality early childhood environments – which include high-quality teacher–child interactions – have been associated with more positive social outcomes and fewer behavior problems in young children (e.g., Burchinal, Peisner-Feinberg, Pianta, & Howes, 2002).

Training teachers about building positive relationships involves educating them about the importance of praise, attention, and encouragement for young children (Webster-Stratton et al., 2001). Teachers learn to distinguish between praise that is ineffective because it is too general and vague, and praise that is effective because it labels the specific positive behavior and thus tells the child exactly what behavior is expected. Training often includes engaging teachers in role play activities to enable them to practice using effective praise statements. This aspect of training can be particularly helpful for teachers who believe that excessive praise is unnecessary and even detrimental to children's development of self-efficacy and confidence.

In addition to a focus on effective praise, training in relationship building also highlights the positive impact of attention and encouragement. Teachers are taught the difference between negative attention and positive attention, a critical concept in both preventing and intervening with challenging behaviors. *Negative attention* refers to attention that is given to someone in an effort to stop the negative behavior he or she is engaged in, akin to the "squeaky wheel getting the grease." Because negative behaviors are typically the ones that garner more attention, and because children at preschool and elementary ages frequently seek attention from their adult caregivers, negative attention provides the unintended result of increasing rather than decreasing the undesired behavior. Positive attention, in contrast, is that which is given in response to desired behaviors. Teachers learn to "catch kids being good" by attending to situations and interactions in which children are demonstrating such positive behaviors as sharing and problem solving. Positive attention results in increasing these prosocial, desired behaviors, not only in the child receiving the attention but also in peers who observe the positive teacher–child interaction and seek the same attention for themselves. Social-emotional training provides teachers with the tools for promoting desired behaviors by focusing positive attention on children and ignoring minor negative behaviors.

A second component of teacher training is the use of *proactive teaching strategies*. These strategies enable teachers to prevent the occurrence of most challenging behaviors by establishing an environment that promotes positive behaviors. One of the key elements of proactive teaching is appropriate and effective room arrangement. Teachers learn how the organization and content of their classrooms send "messages" to children (Creative Curriculum: Dodge, Colker, & Heroman, 2002). Wide-open spaces in the classroom, for example, encourage such undesired behaviors as running, whereas defined, circum-scribed spaces inherently prevent such behavior. Disorganized, cluttered spaces discourage children from respecting materials and using them appropriately. Quiet activity areas placed in close proximity to more active areas limit children's ability to benefit from such activities as listening to music and reading. These principles are particularly important in the preschool environment, in which children use many parts of the classroom through-out the day, but they are also relevant in early elementary classrooms in terms of helping teachers become aware of the ways in which they use their classroom space and how these impact children's behavior.

A third central component of teacher training focuses on the role of *behavior observa-tion and intervention* when challenging behaviors emerge. Although more intensive inter-ventions exist to address such behaviors at the individual level, classroom teachers can be trained to manage many inappropriate and challenging behaviors without the aid of outside consultants. First, the teacher must be able to observe and document character-istics of the problem behavior, including the settings and situations that tend to trigger the behavior, the features of the behavior such as its intensity and duration, and the consequences of the behavior for the child. Teacher training emphasizes the importance of observing behavior for all students rather than just those for whom there is a problem. In this way, teachers can learn a great deal about normative behavior across students and can also provide baseline information for individual students when a challenging behavior occurs.

Once teachers have learned to observe and document the characteristics of problem behaviors, they can then utilize specific strategies for decreasing the behaviors in the classroom setting. Even teachers with large class sizes can learn efficient and effective ways to alter problem behaviors with such strategies as establishing simple behavior plans. These plans detail the undesired behavior they wish to change, the desired behavior they wish to see, opportunities for providing praise and attention for positive behaviors (rather than negative attention for the undesired behavior), and individualized rewards for the desired behaviors. Although more severe and/or persistent behaviors might require assistance from mental health or educational specialists, there is a host of less severe inappropriate behaviors that can be managed effectively by teachers themselves. Empowering and motivating teachers to do so is a key element of intervention training.

Webster-Stratton and colleagues examined the effectiveness of teacher training, finding that teachers who participated in the Incredible Years Teacher Classroom Management Program demonstrated more positive classroom management strategies (decreased critical behaviors) and a more positive classroom climate (Webster-Stratton, Reid, & Stoolmiller, 2008). The effect sizes for these outcomes were moderate to high, ranging from $-.387$ for critical behaviors to 1.03 for positive classroom climate.

How Do Social and Emotional Interventions Involve Parents?

As a complement to training teachers in the use of strategies to promote children's social and emotional development, a number of intervention programs include a parent education component to extend children's social-emotional learning to the home environment. Webster-Stratton and colleagues (Webster-Stratton, Reid, & Hammond, 2004) found that when families receive training on social-emotional skill development in addition to the child's exposure to social-emotional curricula in school, the positive effects on children were significantly greater than with the use of the school-based curriculum alone. The primary aims of parent training are to assist families in "identifying the skills and supports the child needs to engage in daily routines in home and community settings, and engaging families as active participants in their children's education" (Hemmeter et al., 2006).

The format of parent training varies across programs. Some programs include direct parent contact in the school setting, such as monthly parent education workshops that focus on specific topic areas (e.g., Second Step: Committee for Children, 2002). Other interventions are home based, with teachers or interventionists providing education in the family home (e.g., First Step for Success: Walker et al., 1998). Less direct interventions involve parents by sending home educational materials (e.g., newsletters, activity sheets, and books) that encourage parents to engage their children in positive activities related to social and emotional skill development (e.g., Al's Pals: Geller, 1999; and PATHS Preschool: Domitrovich, Greenberg, Kusche, & Cortes, 2004).

The components of parent training share many commonalities with the components of teacher training. Just as teachers are taught to use praise effectively and consistently with students, parents also learn the best ways to praise their children. Materials such as refrigerator magnets and posters often are given to parents to serve as visual reminders of the correct ways to praise children and suggestions for behaviors to praise. In addition to learning techniques for praising their children, parents are educated in the importance of praise for children's social and emotional development and the power of praise in teaching young children what behaviors are expected and valued at home and in the community.

A second aim of many parent-training programs is the enhancement of children's communication skills. Given the strong association between communication deficits and social and behavior problems (Cantwell & Baker, 1980), facilitating communication in the home environment augments the emphasis on communication in the school setting. One of the most effective techniques for improving children's language and communication skills at home is the use of dialogic reading. This approach to reading teaches parents to encourage a dialogue with children while reading to them. Research has demonstrated very positive outcomes for parent–child dialogic reading (Arnold, Lonigan, Whitehurst, & Epstein, 1994).

A third component of parent training focuses on the use of effective and appropriate discipline strategies. Children of parents who use harsh or coercive, authoritarian styles of discipline have been found to exhibit problematic social behaviors, whereas children raised with a firm yet warm style of parenting demonstrate better self-control and self-reliance as well as higher academic achievement (Baumrind, 1967). These findings serve as the basis for educating parents on the use of more appropriate, less harsh ways of interacting with their children, particularly in response to children's inappropriate behaviors. Parents learn to identify minor inappropriate behaviors that can be ignored, and to appropriately reward the behaviors that they want to see. Some curricula include the use of such resources as behavior charts and sticker sheets to provide visual cues to both parents and children of the child's progression toward positive social and emotional behaviors. Parents might also learn ways to support their children's efforts at self-regulation by practicing alongside their children such emotion management skills as belly breathing and counting.

School-based interventions often include a parent component in order to help families effectively support their children's social and emotional development. Although parents and teachers might have different expectations for children's behavior and, therefore, somewhat divergent goals in terms of social and emotional skill development, it is the implementation of consistent and developmentally appropriate practices – rather than the specific content of the practices – that results in positive social and emotional outcomes (Lane et al., 2007).

Research on the effectiveness of parent education as a component of universal intervention programs suggests that involving parents in the intervention process contributes significantly to positive child outcomes. For example, the I Can Problem Solve program (Shure & Spivack, 1978) resulted in the generalization of social problem-solving skills to the home setting as a function of parent participation. Likewise, parent training as part of the Incredible Years program (Webster-Stratton et al., 2001) yielded significantly fewer conduct problems in children in the treatment group compared to children who received no treatment.

What Factors Contribute to Successful Outcomes in Implementation of These Programs?

The success of even the best intervention programs relies on the interplay of a number of environmental and individual factors. Although a program might be comprehensive and empirically validated, the setting and participants involved in its implementation play a major role in determining the effectiveness of the intervention.

Environmental Factors

Perhaps the most essential precondition for a successful intervention effort is the presence of a supportive school environment in which to implement it. Interventions by their nature require that participants adopt a new or different way of doing things. Even in situations in which an intervention is clearly needed, it will have limited success unless the system as a whole is conducive to change. School administrators must be supportive, committed, and available to teachers to assist them in learning and implementing the intervention. In addition, systemic support must be evident in terms of the provision of adequate resources – including materials, time, classroom coverage, and mentoring – to enable the intervention to be implemented as intended. Teachers who report concern about the availability of program support are less likely to implement an intervention. In contrast, teachers who view their school environment in a positive light – such as good leadership by the director and collegiality among staff – tend to be more open and willing to implement a program (Baker, Kupersmidt, Voegler-Lee, Arnold, & Willoughby, 2010).

A second critical factor is the fit of the intervention goals with the needs of the individual school or system. The best-designed program will provide little benefit if it focuses on something that the school and its staff do not need or want. Schoolwide coordination of intervention efforts as well as the integration of intervention components with existing school activities set the stage for successful outcomes (CASEL, 2003).

Staff participation is a third key element. The most successful programs are those that include staff at all levels: administrators, teachers, teacher assistants, and all those who play a regular role in the students' school lives. Adoption of an intervention should reflect a commitment to the professional development of school personnel. Participation in the intervention should provide teachers and staff with the skills they need to feel more competent in facilitating children's social and emotional development as well as in addressing challenging student behaviors (Hemmeter et al., 2006). In addition, supports must be in place to provide staff with assistance in managing children with more severe behavioral issues.

Finally, the introduction of an intervention program requires that administrators provide oversight, supervision, and monitoring of its implementation. This includes high-quality training at the outset as well as ongoing training and support in later years of implementation to ensure the continued quality of the program (Hemmeter et al., 2006).

Teacher Factors

As the primary agents of change in universal, school-based intervention programs, teachers play perhaps the most central role in determining whether the program has a successful outcome. Several teacher characteristics come into play to determine, at least in part, the success of an intervention.

Teacher motivation is a key element to a successful intervention outcome. If teachers are not motivated to put forth their best effort, it is unlikely that they will achieve success with their students. A number of factors can influence a teacher's motivation, particularly in the case of teachers who are being asked to adopt and implement a classroom-wide curriculum or intervention program (Moriarty, Edmonds, Blatchford, & Martin, 2001). A teacher's individual beliefs and attitudes about social and emotional development, developmentally appropriate practice, and approaches to challenging behavior can all impact how motivated he or she will be to engage in an intervention and implement it well (Hemmeter et al., 2006). In addition, motivation can be affected by such external factors as the availability of program resources and the extent of administrative support (described above).

Teachers' sense of efficacy also plays a role in the success of interventions. Not only must a teacher be motivated to successfully implement a program, but also the teacher must believe that he or she can do so effectively (Abrami, Poulsen, & Chambers, 2004). Teachers' self-efficacy includes both personal efficacy (the perceived ability to personally effect desired outcomes) and general teaching efficacy (the ability to do so in the face of such obstacles as the child's problematic home environment) (Hoy & Woolfolk, 1993).

A third critical factor involves the quality and quantity of the teacher's implementation of the intervention. An intent-to-treat (ITT) approach to evaluating effectiveness is based on the assumption that participants implement intervention programs as designed, conducting all lessons fully, in the correct sequence, and with fidelity to the content of the program. Yet ITT outcomes often indicate that successful outcomes require fidelity to the implementation in both quantity and quality (Fixsen, Naoom, Blasé, Friedman, & Wallace, 2005). The quantity of implementation is reflected in what is often termed the *dosage* of implementation – specifically, the number of lessons implemented. The quality of a teacher's implementation reflects his or her *fidelity* to the program – how well his or her implementation adheres to the program's design, and how competently the teacher implements its components. Thus, a teacher might implement all of the program's components, but if he or she does so without a high degree of competence, then the intervention's success will likely be compromised. In their meta-analysis of universal SEL programs, Durlak and colleagues (submitted) found that implementation fidelity was a key moderator of overall program effectiveness.

Child Factors

Children's language and communication ability appears to play a role in the extent to which they benefit from an intervention. Although effective teachers are able to provide adaptations to children with limited communication skills, in general these children tend to demonstrate poorer social and emotional outcomes, including higher levels of behavior problems (Hart, Fujiki, Brinton, & Hart, 2004; Lundervold, Heimann, & Manger, 2008). This is likely due in part to one or more factors. First, children with language challenges are less adept at receiving and processing information presented in group settings, the format in which most social-emotional curricula are taught. Second, children who have difficulty expressing themselves verbally will be less effective at practicing the social-emotional skills being taught. For example, they might be able to accurately identify their own feelings but be unable to communicate them appropriately; have difficulty expressing negative emotions appropriately and, in turn, have difficulty managing them; and/or be unable to successfully negotiate the steps required for effective interpersonal problem solving. Children with average or better language skills, on the other hand, are more likely to experience more positive outcomes.

A second consideration is the behavioral functioning of the child prior to the intervention. A child who is able to attend to and sit still for group instruction, participate positively in activities, and engage appropriately with peers and adults is likely to demonstrate improvements in social and emotional outcomes as a function of participating in an intervention. For children who lack these skills, however, the benefits might be minimal at best. Unfortunately, it is this group of children for whom intervention is most important, but their social and behavioral challenges are likely to preclude the level of positive engagement needed to experience emotional and behavioral gains from a universal intervention program (Joseph & Strain, 2003).

A child's family background can also impact how much he or she will benefit from an intervention. Children from low-income families tend to be at higher risk for a host of negative outcomes, including school failure and behavioral problems (Webster-Stratton & Hammond, 1998). These outcomes are associated with such factors as harsh and/or inconsistent parental discipline, lack of parental warmth, and negative parental affect. Although their risk is high, these children tend to benefit more from interventions aimed at improving behavioral functioning. Consistent with these findings, the Chicago School Readiness Project (Raver et al., 2009) reported decreased internalizing and externalizing behaviors in children attending Head Start programs. These findings demonstrate the significance and success of providing appropriate intervention opportunities for children in high-risk groups.

Summary and Future Directions

As the link between social-emotional development and children's short- and long-term outcomes has become increasingly recognized, high-quality SEL programs have continued to emerge to provide teachers, parents, and children with tools for maximizing the development of social and emotional competence. The results are in, and they are exciting: programs that are well designed, well supported, and well implemented do, in fact, increase children's social and emotional skills and decrease their problematic behaviors, at both the preschool and elementary school levels (CASEL, 2003; Durlak et al., submitted). Children who participate in these programs demonstrate better social problem-solving skills, an increase in positive coping strategies, increased self-regulation, and reduced withdrawn and aggressive behaviors.

Now that we know it can be done, how do we ensure that it can be done for every child, with every teacher, and in every educational setting? These are the questions that remain, and that researchers and practitioners continue to strive to answer. Studies that have examined child-, teacher-, and system-level moderators have illuminated many of the factors associated with positive outcomes. These moderating variables provide important information regarding what works, and under what conditions. The great challenge before us, then, is how to produce successful outcomes when the conditions are not ideal. How do we encourage system administrators to adopt an effective program and provide the adequate resources and support to see it implemented in its entirety? How do we motivate teachers to change their beliefs and practices to provide an optimal climate for SEL, and to then implement with fidelity a new and often time-consuming program? How do we adapt programs to effectively provide SEL to those children who are traditionally least likely to benefit?

The proliferation of effective programs and the ongoing study of what makes them successful hold out the promise that we will someday be able to provide positive SEL opportunities for all children. Intervening in this critical area of development will not only improve children's functioning in the short term but also lay the foundation for lifelong success, an outcome that all children deserve.

Acknowledgments

This chapter was supported by grant R01HD046126 (Kupersmidt), cofunded by the National Institute of Child Health and Human Development (NICHD), the Administration for Children and Families (ACF), the Office of the Assistant Secretary for Planning and Evaluation (ASPE), and the Office of Special Education and Rehabilitative Services (OSERS) in the U.S. Department of Education.

References

Abrami, P. C., Poulsen, C., & Chambers, B. (2004). Teacher motivation to implement an educational innovation: Factors differentiating users and non-users of cooperative learning. *Educational Psychology, 24*, 201–216.

Alexander, K. L., Entwisle, D. R., & Dauber, S. L. (1993). First grade classroom behavior: Its short and long-term consequences for school performance. *Child Development, 64*, 801–814.

Arnold, D. H., Lonigan, C. J., Whitehurst, G. J., & Epstein, J. N. (1994). Accelerating language development through picture book reading: Replication and extension to a videotape training format. *Journal of Educational Psychology, 86*, 235–243.

Arnold, D. H., Ortiz, C., Curry, J. C., Stowe, R. M., Goldstein, N. E., Fisher, P. H., et al. (1999). Promoting academic success and preventing disruptive behavior disorders through community partnership. *Journal of Community Psychology, 5*, 589–598.

Baker, C. N., Kupersmidt, J. B., Voegler-Lee, M. E., Arnold, D. H., & Willoughby, M. T. (2010). Predicting teacher participation in a classroom-based, integrated preventive intervention for preschoolers. *Early Childhood Research Quarterly, 25*(3), 270–283.

Bates, J. E., Bayles, K., Bennett, D. S., Ridge, B., & Brown, M. M. (1991). Origins of externalizing behavior problems at eight years of age. In D. J. Pepler & K. H. Rubin (Eds.), *The development and treatment of childhood aggression*. Hillsdale, NJ: Erlbaum.

Baumrind, D. (1967). Child care practices anteceding three patterns of preschool behavior. *Genetic Psychology Monographs, 75*, 43–88.

Brennan, E. M., Bradley, J. R., Allen, M. D., & Perry, D. (2008). The evidence base for mental health consultation in early childhood settings: Research synthesis addressing staff and program outcomes. *Early Education and Development, 19*(6), 982–1022.

Burchinal, M. R., Peisner-Feinberg, E., Pianta, R., & Howes, C. (2002). Development of academic skills from preschool through second grade: Family and classroom predictors of developmental trajectories. *Journal of School Psychology, 40,* 415–436.

Campbell, S. B. (1995). Behavior problems in preschool children: A review of recent research. *Journal of Child Psychology and Psychiatry, 36,* 113–149.

Cantwell, D. P., & Baker, L. (1980). Psychiatric and behavioral characteristics of children with communication disorders. *Journal of Pediatric Psychology, 5,* 161–178.

Collaborative for Academic, Social, and Emotional Learning (CASEL). (2003). *Safe and sound: An educational leader's guide to evidence-based social and emotional learning (SEL) programs.* Chicago: Author.

Committee for Children. (2002). *Second Step Violence Prevention Curriculum* (3rd ed.). Seattle, WA: Author.

Conduct Problems Prevention Research Group. (1999). Initial impact of the Fast Track Prevention Trial for Conduct Problems: II. Classroom effects. *Journal of Consulting and Clinical Psychology, 67,* 648–657.

Dodge, D. T., Colker, L. J., & Heroman, C. (2002). *Creative Curriculum for Preschool* (4th ed.). Washington, DC: Teaching Strategies.

Domitrovich, C. E., Greenberg, M. T., Kusche, C. A., & Cortes, R. (2004). *The PATHS Preschool Curriculum.* Deerfield, MA: Channing Bete.

Durlak, J. A., Weissberg, R. P., Dymnicki, A. B., Taylor, R. D., & Schellinger, K. B. (Submitted). The impact of enhancing students' social and emotional learning: A meta-analysis of school-based universal interventions.

Eron, L. D. (1990). Understanding aggression. *Bulletin of the International Society for Research on Aggression, 12,* 5–9.

Fixsen, D. L., Naoom, S. F., Blasé, K. A., Friedman, R. M., & Wallace, F. (2005). *Implementation research: A synthesis of the literature* (FMHI Publication No. 231). Tampa: University of South Florida, Louis de la Parte Florida Mental Health Institute, National Implementation Research Network.

Fox, L., Dunlap, G., Hemmeter, M. L., Joseph, G. E., & Strain, P. S. (2003). The Teaching Pyramid: A model for supporting social competence and preventing challenging behavior in young children. *Young Children, 58,* 48–52.

Geller, S. (1999). *Al's Pals: Kids making healthy choices.* Richmond, VA: Wingspan.

Gilliam, W. S. (2007, May). Early Childhood Consultation Partnership: Results of a random-controlled evaluation: Final report and executive summary. New Haven, CT: Yale University, Child Study Center.

Hale-Jinks, C., Knopf, H., & Kemple, K. (2006). Tackling teacher turnover in child care: Under-standing causes and consequences, identifying solutions. *Childhood Education, 82,* 219–226.

Hart, K. I., Fujiki, M., Brinton, B., & Hart, C. H. (2004). The relationship between social behavior and severity of language impairment. *Journal of Speech, Language, and Hearing Research, 47,* 647–662.

Hemmeter, M. L., Ostrosky, M., & Fox, L. (2006). Social and emotional foundations for early learning: A conceptual model for intervention. *School Psychology Review, 35,* 583–601.

Hoy, W. K., & Woolfolk, A. E. (1993). Teachers' sense of efficacy and the organizational health of schools. *Elementary School Journal, 93,* 355–372.

Innes, F. K., Denton, K. L., & West, J. (2001, April). *Child care factors and kindergarten outcomes: Findings from a national study of children.* Paper presented at the biennial meeting of the Society for Research in Child Development, Minneapolis, MN.

Joseph, G. E., & Strain, P. S. (2003). Comprehensive evidence-based social-emotional curricula for young children: An analysis of efficacious adoption potential. *Topics in Early Childhood Special Education, 23*, 65–76.

Kupersmidt, J. B., Bryant, D., & Willoughby, M. (2000). Prevalence of aggressive behaviors among preschoolers in Head Start and community child care programs. *Behavioral Disorders, 26*(1), 42–52.

Kupersmidt, J. B., & Coie, J. D. (1990). Preadolescent peer status, aggression, and school adjustment as predictors of externalizing problems in adolescence. *Child Development, 61*, 1350–1362.

Kupersmidt, J. B., & DeRosier, M. E. (2004). An integrative mediational model of the relation between peer problems and negative outcomes. In J. B. Kupersmidt & K. A. Dodge (Eds.), *Children's peer relations: From development to intervention* (pp. 119–138). Washington, DC: American Psychological Association.

Kusche, C. A., & Greenberg, M. T. (1994). *The PATHS Curriculum.* Seattle, WA: Developmental Research and Programs.

Ladd, G. W., Kochenderfer, B. J., & Coleman, C. (1997). Classroom peer acceptance, friendship and victimization: Distinct relational systems that contribute uniquely to children's school adjustment. *Child Development, 68*, 1181–1197.

Lane, K. L., Givner, C. C., & Pierson, M. R. (2004). Teacher expectations of student behavior: Social skills necessary for success in elementary school classrooms. *Journal of Special Education, 38*, 104–110.

Lane, K. L., Stanton-Chapman, T., Jamison, K. R., & Phillips, A. (2007). Teacher and parent expectations of preschoolers' behavior: Social skills necessary for success. *Topics in Early Childhood Special Education, 27*, 86–97.

Lundervold, A. J., Heimann, M., & Manger, T. (2008). Behaviour–emotional characteristics of primary-school children rated as having language problems. *British Journal of Educational Psychology, 78*, 567–580.

McLelland, M. M., Morrison, F. J., & Holmes, D. L. (2000). Children at risk for early academic problems: The role of learning-related social skills. *Early Childhood Research Quarterly, 15*, 307–329.

Moffitt, T. E. (1993). Adolescence-limited and life-course-persistent antisocial behavior: A developmental taxonomy. *Psychological Review, 100*, 674–701.

Moriarty, V., Edmonds, S., Blatchford, P., & Martin, C. (2001). Teaching young children: Perceived satisfaction and stress. *Educational Research, 43*, 33–46.

Odom, S. L., McConnell, S. R., McEvoy, M. A., Peterson, C., Ostrosky, M., Chandler, L. K., et al. (1999). Relative effects of interventions supporting the social competence of young children with disabilities. *Topics in Early Childhood Education, 19*, 75–91.

Quinn, M. M., Kavali, K. A., Mathur, S. R., Rutherford, R. B., & Forness, S. R. (1999). A meta-analysis of social skills interventions for students with emotional and behavioral disorders. *Journal of Emotional and Behavioral Disorders, 7*, 54–64.

Raver, C. C., Jones, S. M., Li-Grining, C., Metzger, M., Smallwood, K., & Sardin, L. (2008). Improving preschool classroom processes: Preliminary findings from a randomized trial implemented in Head Start settings. *Early Childhood Research Quarterly, 23*, 10–26.

Raver, C. C., Jones, S. M., Li-Grining, C., Zhai, F., Metzger, M. W., & Solomon. B. (2009). Targeting children's behavior problems in preschool classrooms: A cluster-randomized controlled trial. *Journal of Consulting and Clinical Psychology, 77*, 302–316.

Rimm-Kaufman, S. E., Pianta, R. C., & Cox, M. J. (2000). Teachers' judgments of problems in the transition to kindergarten. *Early Childhood Research Quarterly, 15*, 147–166.

Shure, M. B. (1992a). *I Can Problem Solve (ICPS): An interpersonal cognitive problem solving program [Preschool].* Champaign, IL: Research Press.

Shure, M. B. (1992b). *I Can Problem Solve (ICPS): An interpersonal cognitive problem solving program [Kindergarten/primary grades]*. Champaign, IL: Research Press.

Shure, M. B. (1992c). *I Can Problem Solve (ICPS): An interpersonal cognitive problem solving program [Intermediate elementary grades]*. Champaign, IL: Research Press.

Shure, M. B., & Spivack, G. (1978). *Problem solving techniques in child rearing*. San Francisco: Jossey-Bass.

Tremblay, R. E., Masse, L. C., Pagani, L., & Vitaro, F. (1996). From childhood physical aggression to adolescent maladjustment: The Montreal prevention experiment. In R. D. Peters & R. J. McMahon (Eds.), *Preventing childhood disorders, substance abuse, and delinquency*. Thousand Oaks, CA: Sage.

Walker, H. M., Kavanagh, K., Stiller, B., Golly, A., Severson, H. H., & Feil, E. (1998). First Step to Success: An early intervention approach for preventing school antisocial behavior. *Journal of Emotional and Behavioral Disorders, 6*, 66–80.

Webster-Stratton, C., & Hammond, M. (1998). Conduct problems and level of social competence in Head Start children: Prevalence, pervasiveness and associated risk factors. *Clinical Child Psychology and Family Psychology Review, 1*, 101–124.

Webster-Stratton, C., & Reid, M. J. (2003). Treating conduct problems and strengthening social-emotional competence in young children (ages 4–8 years): The Dina Dinosaur treatment program. *Journal of Emotional and Behavioral Disorders, 11*, 130–143.

Webster-Stratton, C., Reid, M. J., & Hammond, M. (2001). Preventing conduct problems, promoting social competence: A parent and teacher training partnership in Head Start. *Journal of Clinical Child Psychology, 30*, 283–302.

Webster-Stratton, C., Reid. M. J., & Hammond, M. (2004). Treating children with early-onset conduct problems: Intervention outcomes for parent, child, and teacher training. *Journal of Clinical Child and Adolescent Psychology, 33*, 105–124.

Webster-Stratton, C., Reid, M. J., & Stoolmiller, M. (2008). Preventing conduct problems and improving school readiness: Evaluation of the Incredible Years Teacher and Child Training Programs in high-risk schools. *Journal of Child Psychology and Psychiatry, 49*(5), 471–488.

Wentzel, K. R., & Asher, S. R. (1995). The academic lives of neglected, rejected, popular, and controversial children. *Child Development, 66*, 754–763.

Zins, J., Weissberg, R., Wang, M. C., & Walberg, H. J. (2004). *Building academic success on social and emotional learning (SEL): What does the research say?* New York: Teachers College Press.

CHAPTER THIRTY-THREE

The Development of Social Competence in Children With Disabilities

Karen E. Diamond, Hsin-Hui Huang, and Elizabeth A. Steed

Definitions of disability, and implications of specific disabilities, vary across communities and cultures (Klingner, Blanchett, & Harry, 2007). In Western and Asian societies, definitions of disability typically include physical and mental impairments that interfere with major life activities (such as caring for oneself) and entitle individuals to state-supported social services, including education and employment. A substantial majority of people with disabilities live in low-income countries in which there are few resources to support individuals with disabilities and limited resources for prevention and intervention (World Health Organization [WHO], 2004). For these reasons alone, understanding the development of socially competent behaviors by children with disabilities requires attention to social and cultural influences as well as to characteristics of children and families.

Culture influences the meanings that individuals construct for disabilities. Parents' understandings of their child's disability and their aspirations for their child reflect cultural perspectives that are enacted in behaviors within the family and in opportunities for participation in various social contexts. In the United States, families' ideas about a child's disability are shaped by their race, social class, and cultural and ethnic heritage, as well as by access to programs and services in their local communities (Klingner et al., 2007). In Asian societies, Buddhist and Hindu concepts of "retribution" or "karma" may shape individuals' beliefs that disabilities are an effect of wicked actions in the last incarnation (Kim, 2001), leading to feelings of overwhelming sadness and guilt about a child's disability (cf. Tsau & Chuang, 2007).

In many Western countries, there has been an increasing emphasis on providing normalized life experiences for children with disabilities, whereas there has been less attention

The Wiley-Blackwell Handbook of Childhood Social Development, Second Edition, edited by Peter K. Smith and Craig H. Hart
© 2011 by Blackwell Publishing Ltd.

to full inclusion in low-income countries (WHO, 2008). In a recent report, the proportion of elementary school–aged children with disabilities enrolled in regular education
classes in the United States ranged between 30% and 70%, with variations related to
state policies (U.S. Department of Education, 2007). Bochner and Pieterse (1996)
reported that at least half of children with Down syndrome born in the 1970s in New
South Wales, Australia, received education in primary schools designed for typically
developing children, whereas almost all children with Down syndrome born during the
same time period in South Wales, Great Britain, were enrolled in self-contained special
education schools. Research in both the United States and Japan suggests that attitudes
toward individuals with disabilities may limit opportunities for full participation in the
community (Klingner et al., 2007; Ozawa & Yaeda, 2007).

If children are to successfully participate in community activities, developing appropriate social behaviors is an important challenge. Peer relationship problems have been
reported for children with milder as well as more significant mental, physical, sensory,
and behavioral disabilities (Erwin, 1993; Guralnick, Connor, Hammond, Gottman, &
Kinnish, 1996; Staub, Schwartz, Gallucci, & Peck, 1994). Problems with social relationships become especially evident as children's activities become less structured.

Cultural norms and values affect meanings of social behaviors. Independent living is
an important value in Western societies, and interpersonal relationships are typically
viewed as a personal decision in Western cultures (Eisenberg, Pidada, & Liew, 2001).
Compared with Western cultures, individuals in non-Western cultures characterized as
group oriented or collectivistic may value group benefits and compliance with social order
over personal needs and individual rights (Ho, Chen, & Chao, 1991; Kagitçibasi, 1997).
In these contexts, self-control and regulation may be particularly important socialization
goals (Eisenberg et al., 2001); social interactions and pretend play that require social
initiative are less common among children in non-Western cultures (Edwards, 2000).
Understanding how collectivist values affect the social development of children with disabilities is difficult, however, because most of the research on social relationships and
interpersonal cooperation between children with disabilities and their typically developing
peers has taken place in individualistic Western countries.

The contexts in which social interactions occur may influence the quality of the interaction. Guralnick and his colleagues (1996) found that preschool children with mild
disabilities displayed more frequent social interaction and higher levels of social play when
they played with typically developing children. Bronson and her colleagues (Bronson,
Hauser-Cram, & Warfield, 1997) found that preschool children with disabilities were
more independent and engaged in more and higher levels of peer interaction when they
were enrolled in classrooms that were most similar (e.g., class size and activity choices)
to classrooms designed for children without disabilities. Similar results have been reported
for older children and for children with more severe disabilities (Fryxell & Kennedy,
1995).

Bronfenbrenner's bioecological *process–person–context–time* model provides a framework for understanding the social competence of children with disabilities by integrating
broader contextual factors with characteristics of individuals and interactions between
individuals and others (Bronfenbrenner & Morris, 2006). As an example, recent work
on bullying and teasing of school-aged children with learning disabilities suggests that

both individual child characteristics, especially social and communicative competence, and characteristics of school and neighborhood environments are related to the likelihood that a child will be the target of name calling, teasing, and bullying by peers (Mishna, 2003; Norwich & Kelly, 2004; see also Chapter 27, this volume). This bioecological model provides a framework for considering simultaneous influences of distal (culture) and proximal (home, school, and peer group) contexts, developmental processes, and individual child characteristics on the development of children's social competence. This model highlights the importance of stability and consistency in experiences and reflects our understanding that the "processes affecting development vary systematically as a joint function of the characteristics of the developing person, [and] the environment – both immediate and more remote – in which the processes are taking place" (Bronfenbrenner, 1999, p. 5).

Developmental Perspectives on Peer-Related Social Competence for Children With Disabilities

The extent to which children with disabilities live independently as adults depends to a considerable extent on their ability to engage in appropriate social interactions. Major outcomes of competent social behaviors include children's use of appropriate and effective strategies for achieving specific social goals and developing and maintaining relations with peers (Rubin, Bukowski, & Parker, 2006). Social information processing foundation processes, including emotion regulation, shared understanding, and joint attention, along with higher order processes determine the social strategies that a child uses in an interaction. If any of these processes is adversely affected by characteristics of the individual (e.g., cognitive deficits) or of the immediate context (e.g., environmental factors that make emotion regulation more difficult), less competent social strategies may result.

Additionally, processes within the social environment contribute to the development of socially competent behavior. Peers provide support for children developing social competence when they initiate, respond to, and persist in interactions (Sigman & Ruskin, 1999). Teachers provide support when they arrange the physical environment to allow interactions to occur and use child-directed learning strategies in their teaching (Staub et al., 1994). Parents of children with and without disabilities play an important role in fostering children's peer social networks by arranging play opportunities outside of the school classroom. Finally, the attitudes of others, including peers and adults, play a role in maintaining opportunities for social interactions (Diamond & Innes, 2001).

What does this suggest about the social development of children with disabilities? First, disabilities associated with deficits in cognitive processes (such as mental retardation) or emotion regulation (e.g., autism) affect social information processing and increase the likelihood that a child will have significant difficulties in peer interaction. In addition, processes within proximal contexts mediate the influence of cognitive and emotion regulation deficits on the development of socially competent behaviors. These contextual factors include a broad range of consistent social networks and support from adults in helping children develop and use appropriate social interaction strategies. Finally, disabilities that do not affect cognition or emotion regulation (e.g., physical disabilities or blindness) are likely to have different, lesser impacts on children's development of age-appropriate social relationships.

Research in inclusive settings has demonstrated substantial variability in peer social acceptance of young children with disabilities. Odom and colleagues (2006) found that a substantial proportion of children who had disabilities "that were less likely to affect social problem solving and emotional regulation" (p. 820) were more likely to be well accepted by their peers. Siperstein and Leffert (1997) reported similar results for older children with mental retardation. Dyadic friendships reflect different processes and afford different benefits than peer acceptance (Buhs, Ladd, & Herald, 2006). Although somewhat fewer studies have examined dyadic friendships, preschool- and elementary-aged children with disabilities who participate in programs with their typically developing peers are reported to have mutual friends (Buysse, Goldman, & Skinner, 2002; Juvonen & Bear, 1992).

The sections that follow focus on individual (person) and contextual characteristics related to the social development of children with disabilities.

Children with mild mental retardation or learning disabilities

In the United States, children with learning problems and low levels of school achievement without other obvious disabilities are typically identified as having either a learning disability or mild mental retardation. Gresham and MacMillan (1997) suggested that research on the social skills of children with these mild disabilities should be aggregated because these are not clinically different groups, and we adopt this approach.

Young children with mild mental retardation are typically less preferred playmates and more likely to be targets of bullying and teasing than same-age peers (Guralnick et al., 1996; Mishna, 2003). Peer interaction difficulties are associated with deficits in communication skills (a higher order process) and difficulties using appropriate interaction strategies (i.e., deficits in social information processing) that may or may not be related to deficits in communication and cognition. The importance of communication skills for social interaction is supported in many studies in which typically developing children were more successful in their social bids than were children with communication disorders (Hartas & Donahue, 1997).

Difficulties in interpersonal understanding (Kravetz, Faust, Lipshitz, & Shalhav, 1999) and in generating alternative solutions to social problems (Hartas & Donahue, 1997) contribute to social behavior problems in preadolescent and adolescent children with learning disabilities. Leffert and Siperstein (1996) found that 10–13-year-old children with mild mental retardation were similar to typically developing peers in accurately interpreting hostile intentions in peer conflict situations and varying their choice of social strategy based on situational context. Unlike typically developing children, however, children with mental retardation interpreted benign intention cues with significantly less accuracy than they encoded them. Both hostile and benign intention cues were associated with negative outcomes. Leffert and Siperstein suggested that children's difficulties with interpreting benign cues were related to underlying cognitive difficulties with reconciling situations in which there was a conflict between intention (benign) and outcome (negative). Bauminger, Edelsztein, and Morash (2005) found that 9–13-year-olds with learning disabilities experience significant difficulties in social information processing, including understanding complex and mixed emotions. These studies suggest that deficits in social understanding are related to difficulties in peer interaction, with these deficits appearing as early as preschool.

Although many children with mild cognitive disabilities display deficits in peer interaction, the developmental processes that underlie peer-related social competence may be substantially similar to those described for children without disabilities. Guralnick and Hammond (1999) found similar sequential play patterns for typically developing preschool children and children with disabilities regardless of the setting in which children were observed (an inclusive class with typically developing peers or a self-contained special education class). Siperstein and Leffert (1997) found that children with mental retardation who displayed sociable behaviors gained greater acceptance from their peers without disabilities in inclusive settings, whereas children who displayed sensitive-isolated behaviors were more likely to be rejected.

Research on the social development of children with learning disabilities and mild mental retardation points to the important relationship between communication skills and social initiations with peers. Context also plays an important role in children's social competence: In a recent study, Norwich and Kelly (2004) reported that students with learning disabilities who were enrolled in mainstream schools reported significantly less bullying and teasing than did peers with learning disabilities enrolled in special education schools.

Deficits in foundation processes (specifically, a mutual understanding of roles, rules, and expectations governing social behavior) and in social cognitive processes (especially interpreting social cues) may account for delays in the social development of children with mild cognitive disabilities (Guralnick, Hammond, Connor, & Neville, 2006). Although there is evidence that children with mild mental retardation and learning disabilities are less popular than their typically developing peers, research suggests that contextual factors contribute to children's social experiences.

Children with Down syndrome

As a group, children with Down syndrome show greater expressive than receptive language delays, especially as they advance in mental age. Cognitive performance is also delayed, with IQ scores often diminishing (and mental age scores increasing) as children grow older (Rynders & Horrobin, 1990). Using the model of social competence described earlier, deficits in cognitive and language abilities (higher order variables) should be associated with difficulties in many social cognitive processes, including encoding and accurately interpreting cues, and generating and enacting social strategies. Sigman and Ruskin (1999) have reported, however, that delays in language skills were not associated with comparable delays in nonverbal communication or play skills for children with Down syndrome. In addition, they found that preschool children with Down syndrome were responsive to adults' displays of emotion, and regularly initiated social interactions with adults. The frequency of early social interactions with adults was associated with peer involvement in later childhood. Classroom and playground observations suggested that peers accepted more than 70% of the social play initiations of children with Down syndrome, and children with Down syndrome accepted a significant majority (73%) of peer play initiations. Although children with Down syndrome have significantly delayed cognitive abilities and expressive language skills, nonverbal abilities, including joint attention and social responsiveness, may buffer the effects of cognitive and language delays on social competence.

Many children with Down syndrome are reported to have best friends, including friends who are typically developing (Sigman & Ruskin, 1999). Begley (1999) found that 8–16-year-old children with Down syndrome in Great Britain had positive perceptions of their acceptance by peers, with children in mainstream schools reporting more positive self-perceptions than children enrolled in self-contained special education schools. Bochner and Pieterse (1996) reported that slightly more than one third of the teenagers with Down syndrome they studied in New South Wales participated in inclusive social activities with typically developing peers (e.g., Girl Guides), and approximately half participated in a club or activity designed specifically for adolescents with disabilities (e.g., Special Olympics). In a study of friendships of adolescents with Down syndrome in Leeds, UK, Cuckle and Wilson (2002) found that childhood friendships with typically developing peers were difficult to maintain, in part because peers were allowed more independence. Across studies, reports are consistent in describing teenagers with Down syndrome as spending much of their social lives with their families.

Children and adolescents with Down syndrome have cognitive and communication delays that are typically associated with deficits in many of the social information processing components underlying socially competent behaviors. They may be especially adept at emotion regulation, generally appear socially interested and responsive, and show relatively few negative behaviors. Thus, motivation to participate in social interactions, along with a "more sociable style" (Kasari & Hodapp, 1996, p. 6), may partially mitigate the effects of cognitive and communication deficits on social competence.

Children with severe mental retardation and multiple disabilities

When children with severe disabilities are enrolled in self-contained special education classrooms with peers who also have severe disabilities, opportunities for peer interactions are limited by the nature of each child's disability. There is evidence, however, that significant social benefits accrue to children with severe disabilities from their planned participation in general education settings with classmates without disabilities (Fryxell & Kennedy, 1995). Hanline (1993) found that preschool children with severe disabilities had numerous opportunities for peer social interactions in an inclusive summer program. Kennedy, Shukla, and Fryxell (1997) reported that elementary and middle school students with severe disabilities, enrolled in general education classes, had more social contacts with typically developing peers, received and provided higher levels of social support, and had larger and more durable friendship networks than students in self-contained special education classrooms. Hughes and colleagues (1999) reported different results when they observed social behaviors, however. In a 3-month study in a high school lunchroom, they observed few social interactions between typically developing students and their classmates with moderate to severe mental retardation. Hughes et al. suggested that, because these children with disabilities received education in self-contained special education classrooms, a lack of shared classroom experiences may have played an important role in limiting interactions. These results highlight the importance of context in providing opportunities for consistent social interactions with peers.

For children with severe disabilities, some competencies appear more important than others in the development of peer interactions. Responsiveness to others and motivation to engage in interactions are positively associated with the development of social relationships for children with severe disabilities, whereas limitations in physical mobility, often associated with severe mental retardation, reduce opportunities to participate in activities with peers (Grenot-Scheyer, 1994). Interactions between children with severe disabilities and typically developing peers are usually not symmetrical: The peer often directs the interaction, whereas the child with a severe disability is a more passive recipient.

Not surprisingly, the significant deficits in cognition and communication that are found in individuals with severe disabilities are related to deficits in many of the social cognitive processes that underlie socially competent behavior. Children with severe disabilities who are more responsive to peers' initiations and motivated to engage in social interactions demonstrate higher levels of social competence, and may have more social strategy capabilities than are often identified. Many children and adolescents with severe disabilities participate in social relationships with peers, and opportunities to participate in age-appropriate contexts with peers are related to more competent social interactions.

Children with autism spectrum disorders (ASDs)

Children with ASDs show consistent, pervasive impairments in social interactions and communication that are manifested in the first 3 years of life (Sigman & Ruskin, 1999). Current estimates suggest that autism affects 1 in 150 births in the United States, with the rate of ASDs ranging from 0.5% to 1.0% of the school-aged population in Western countries (Kadesjö, Gillberg, & Hagberg, 1999; Sponheim & Skjeldal, 1998). Defining features of ASDs include social and communicative deficits and repeated stereotyped behaviors; mental retardation is present in approximately 75% of individuals with autism, with the frequency of stereotyped behaviors increasing with more severe retardation (Volkmar & Lord, 1998).

Descriptions of social development of children with ASDs point to deficits in basic interpersonal skills during infancy, including failure to make eye contact, to use gaze to regulate interaction, and to engage in early social games, such as peek-a-boo (Volkmar, 1993). Initiating social interactions and responding to others' initiations occur infrequently (Strain, Schwartz, & Bovey, 2008). Although social skills change as children develop, social responsivity remains problematic.

Deficits in emotion regulation and infrequent use of age-appropriate gestures and verbalizations are common. Yirmiya, Kasari, Sigman, and Mundy (1989) found that children with ASDs showed significantly more facial expressions of negative affect than did children of the same mental age who had mental retardation or were typically developing.

They suggested that the effect on the interactive partner may have been significant because the negative expressions were so unexpected. Similarly, Strain and Schwartz (2001) suggested that, because of confusing and unexpected behaviors, peers may find it difficult to determine the behavioral intents of a child with ASDs.

Social deficits in children with ASDs may be associated with specific deficits related to theory-of-mind skills, especially deficits in shared attention and understanding of others' intentions and desires (Phillips, Baron-Cohen, & Rutter, 1998). Children with ASDs appear to have most difficulty with tasks that require nonverbal joint attention. Children's joint attention bids may provide a measure of motivation to communicate (Mundy & Crowson, 1997), with impairments in joint attention resulting from a more basic failure to attend to social stimuli (Dawson, Meltzoff, Osterling, Rinaldi, & Brown, 1998). Problems with understanding others' social intentions and responding to social intention cues may be related to difficulties in social communication for young children with ASDs (Parish-Morris, Hennon, Hirsh-Pasek, Golinkoff, & Tager-Flusberg, 2007).

Because autism is associated with significant impairments in social interaction, school-aged children with autism are often educated in self-contained special education classrooms that provide few opportunities for social interaction. However, typically developing peers may play important roles in facilitating social interactions for children with ASDs. O'Neill and Lord (in Lord, 1993) reported that children with ASDs who had normally developing siblings were more likely to produce spontaneous peer-directed language in their classrooms, whereas Tsao and Odom (2006) found that a sibling-mediated intervention led to positive changes in joint attention and social behavior for children with ASDs. Children with ASDs who have regular opportunities to interact with typically developing peers make significant gains in social skills, including increases in frequency of initiations and decreases in stereotyped behaviors (Roeyers, 1996). In observations of school-aged children in classrooms and on the school playground, Sigman and Ruskin (1999) found that children with ASDs were as likely as children with other disabilities to receive initiations but were much less likely than others to accept social bids or to initiate interactions with peers.

In sum, research suggests that deficits in paying attention to faces, participating in joint attention, orienting to social stimuli, and understanding others' intentions are early characteristics of children with ASDs. Thus, in the model of social competence discussed earlier in this chapter, children with ASDs show deficits in foundation processes, including both emotion regulation and social understanding, which are critical for the development of socially competent behavior.

Children with physical disabilities

When a physical disability limits a child's opportunities to participate in activities with peers and the child requires assistance from others for locomotion, the child may be at risk for peer relationship difficulties because of social isolation, independent of a child's social competence (Harper & McCluskey, 2002). Neurocognitive deficits associated with physical disabilities also may increase a child's risk for peer relationship difficulties. For example, in studies examining the social adjustment of a cohort of children with hemiplegia enrolled in mainstream primary schools in London, Yude and Goodman (1999) found that 9–11-year-old children were less popular, were more likely to be rejected, had fewer friends, and were more often victimized than were their classmates without disabilities. The most powerful predictors of peer relationship problems were teachers' reports of conduct problems and/or hyperactivity, together with low IQ, measured soon after school entry (age 6 or 7). Yude and Goodman suggested that at least some of the peer relationship problems faced by children with hemiplegia may be related to significant neurological deficits that affect learning and behavior. Zurmohle and colleagues (1998) found that children who attended an "IQ-appropriate" school for children with disabilities had a higher rate of social adjustment problems than those who were enrolled in mainstream schools. These studies suggest that both child-specific factors (including mobility as well as learning and behavior problems) and contextual factors, including accessibility, are related to the social development and adjustment of children with physical disabilities.

Children with visual impairments

Whereas vision impairments that are severe enough to interfere significantly with children's daily activities are relatively rare, significant vision impairments are associated with social relationship difficulties. In the model of social competence described earlier, the ability to encode and interpret social cues is a critical component of socially competent behavior. Encoding and interpreting social cues include the ability to observe and interpret others' behaviors (Rosenblum, 1997). Self-monitoring also requires encoding and interpreting both verbal and nonverbal responses to one's own behaviors (Erwin, 1993). Children who have significant visual impairments may experience social relationship difficulties because they are unaware of subtle social cues that provide information about others' feelings. Shared understandings of play activities, social rules, and social conventions are components of socially competent behavior that can be affected by a child's inability to observe social interactions and play (McAlpine & Moore, 1995).

Children and adolescents with visual impairments often have lower rates of social interaction with peers, have more frequent interactions with adults, and engage in solitary activities more often than do same-age peers without disabilities (Skellenger, Rosenblum, & Jager, 1997). Children with some useful vision (i.e., children who were visual learners) typically engaged in significantly more interaction with peers than did children who were blind (i.e., tactile learners), although rates of interaction were lower than for children without disabilities.

Visual impairments may make it difficult for a child to participate in some activities with peers. Many sports require visual skills such as throwing or hitting a ball. Young children with visual impairments have reported that their inability to participate in activities such as these interferes with the development of social relationships with sighted peers, and peers often think it takes an extra effort to be friends (MacCuspie, in Rosenblum, 1997) with a child who has impaired vision.

In sum, children and adolescents with visual impairments are more isolated from peers, have more frequent contacts with adults, and participate in more solitary activity than do their sighted peers. Functional vision that is sufficient for making eye contact and recognizing nonverbal social cues appears to be associated with higher rates of interactions with peers. Children with visual impairments whose vision is not sufficient for recognizing nonverbal behaviors typically have deficits in encoding social cues, as well as in monitoring their own behaviors and interpreting others' responses to them, that interfere with socially competent behavior.

Social Skills Interventions for Children With Disabilities

There is substantial evidence of the importance of links between distal (culture) and proximal (such as school and peer group) contexts, individual child characteristics, and social cognitive processes that support children's developing social competence. Understanding social development leads to the identification of effective interventions that support increased social competence across different contexts (Odom, 2000). Many evidence-based strategies exist to improve the social skills of children with disabilities, with many interventions addressing proximal contexts and developmental processes.

Classroom-wide interventions

Classroom-wide social skills interventions involve low-cost prevention strategies including classroom organization (e.g., classroom layout and schedule), instructional materials, and teaching strategies that may be used with large groups of children. Social skills are promoted when teachers use instructional materials that focus on social relationships and friendships. Some classroom materials and activities (e.g., sand and blocks) are associated with more sophisticated social interactions between young children with disabilities and their peers (Ivory & McCollum, 1999). Teachers may use explicit strategies directed at the classroom as a whole to support children's peer interactions, including positive reinforcement for engaging in targeted social skills (Stormont, Smith, & Lewis, 2007), group contingencies that encourage positive interactions (Kohler, Strain, Hoyson, & Davis, 1995), classroom rules that are reinforced throughout the day (Benedict, Horner, & Squires, 2007), and providing choices (McCormick, Jolivette, & Ridgely, 2003) to support children's social competence. In a study with children at risk for emotional or behavioral disorders, those who received classroom-wide sharing and problem-solving interventions demonstrated improved adaptive and social behavior compared to children who did not (Serna, Nielsen, Lambros, & Forness, 2000).

Peer-mediated interventions

Peer-mediated interventions involve typically developing children who, while interacting with peers with disabilities, model appropriate behavior and provide feedback to peers (Brown, Odom, McConnell, & Rathel, 2008). Peer-mediated interventions may be more effective than teacher-mediated interventions in promoting children's socially competent behaviors (Carter, Cushing, Clark, & Kennedy, 2005), particularly for children who are motivated to interact with peers.

One application of peer-mediated interventions involves the use of play scripts. Children with disabilities and typically developing peers are taught to use a play script with the intent of increasing social interactions during play. Robertson and Weismer (1999) found that children with and without disabilities increased their verbal and social interactions while using play scripts with specific roles including gestural, motor, and verbal responses for each child to use during play.

Peer-mediated interventions may also involve technology, such as video feedback or video- or computer-based instruction to model and teach social skills to children with disabilities using typical peer exemplars (Chung et al., 2007). This shows promise as an effective intervention strategy, because reliable modeling of social skills by peers may be repeated as necessary and extraneous environmental variables typical of live social interactions may be reduced. Finally, recent research on interventions with high school students suggests that peer support interventions may be especially successful in promoting access to the general curriculum and increasing social interactions of students with severe disabilities (Carter et al., 2005).

Teacher-mediated interventions

Some children with significant social skills deficits may require more explicit and individualized instruction of social skills in addition to or in lieu of peer-mediated interventions (Brown, Odom, & Conroy, 2001). Teacher-mediated interventions have been used to effectively teach social skills across a wide range of disabilities, including children with developmental delays (LeBlanc & Matson, 1995) and ASDs (e.g., Feng, Lo, Tsai, & Cartledge, 2008). Such interventions involve systematic, planned procedures to teach skills, along with sufficient opportunities to practice across environments. Teaching strategies often include the use of positive reinforcement, modeling, rehearsal, and feedback (Grisham-Brown, Hemmeter, & Pretti-Frontczak, 2005).

Teachers may utilize a range of naturalistic interventions to teach a particular social skill within the context of everyday classroom routines (Pretti-Frontczak & Bricker, 2004). In one application of incidental teaching, three preschool boys with autism were taught to use social phrases such as "All right" and "You know what?" with peers (McGee & Daly, 2007). After the teaching sessions and a prompt-fading procedure, the boys were observed to utilize the phrases in untrained settings, including free play. In another study, teachers embedded preschool children's social goals into classroom routines and children increased their use of selected social goals and socially competent behaviors (Macy & Bricker, 2007). A benefit of naturalistic interventions that occur during everyday classroom routines is the increased probability that children's newly learned skills will generalize to untrained settings, people, and materials.

Self-monitoring strategies may be added to explicit social skills instruction to transfer the management of the intervention from the teacher to the child (O'Reilly et al., 2005). Self-monitoring strategies involve teaching the child to identify target and nontarget behaviors and to self-record and/or self-reinforce behaviors. Morrison, Kamps, Garcia, and Parker (2001) taught four students with autism to self-monitor their social skills, including requesting, commenting on, and sharing materials while playing games with typically developing peers. Peers were taught to monitor the social skills of students with autism. The self-monitoring and peer-monitoring procedures were equally effective in increasing the initiations and social interactions of students with autism during game-playing sessions. Self-monitoring strategies demonstrate promise in facilitating the maintenance of desired social skills, because children with disabilities monitor their behavior in the absence of prompting from an adult.

Interventions to decrease challenging behaviors

Positive behavior support (PBS) is designed to increase children's prosocial behaviors and reduce challenging behaviors in educational settings (Sugai & Horner, 2001). PBS addresses the ecological context of challenging behavior, emphasizes consistent positive practices (e.g., the use of reinforcement and teaching replacement behaviors), and invests in systems-level features such as establishing teams, ensuring adequate funding, and utilizing data collection to monitor and evaluate PBS efforts (Blonigan et al., 2008). The PBS model includes three levels: (a) primary, universal, classroom-wide interventions; (b) targeted interventions for some children; and (c) intensive and individualized interventions for children who engage in severe and/or chronic challenging behavior. The third level of intervention begins with a functional behavior assessment (FBA) to determine the relationship between a child's challenging behavior and environmental variables that precede and follow the behavior. When the environmental variables that precede and follow the challenging behavior are determined, an intervention plan is developed that addresses the function or motivating purpose of the challenging behavior (e.g., access to a preferred item). Interventions that address the function of the behavior are more effective than those that do not (Newcomer & Lewis, 2004).

Interventions based on an FBA include making changes to antecedent conditions and consequences that follow the challenging behavior, and teaching replacement behaviors (Gettinger & Stoiber, 2006). Changes to antecedent conditions include physical changes, such as a change to the classroom layout or furniture, or instructional modifications, such as using an alternative method of communication (Dooley, Wilczenski, & Torem, 2001). Teaching replacement behaviors involves teaching a child to replace a challenging behavior with a socially appropriate behavior that meets the child's communicative and/or social needs. For example, a child who screams and throws materials to receive teacher assistance in high-demand situations may be taught to ask for help with words, signs, or augmentative communication. Asking for help meets the child's needs (in this case, assistance with the difficult task) in a socially appropriate way with replacement behaviors that serve the same function as the challenging behavior and efficiently meet the child's needs (Crone & Horner, 2003).

Issues in intervention

Several issues may affect the use of social skills interventions for children with disabilities. First, many social skills interventions fail to promote generalization of social skills outside of the immediate context in which they were taught (Landrum & Lloyd, 1992). Embedding social skills instruction in everyday routines, choosing socially valid social skills, and utilizing peer-mediated interventions are strategies for generalizing newly learned skills to novel environments and behaviors (Maag, 2005).

A second issue is the limited implementation of research-based interventions in natural environments such as inclusive and general education classrooms. There are several hypotheses to explain the gap between research and practice, including an absence of professional expertise to implement complex interventions (Kaiser, 2007) and teachers' reluctance to implement individualized interventions in classrooms (Diamond, Hong, & Baroody, 2008). Duda, Dunlap, Fox, Lentini, and Clarke (2004) documented preschool teachers' failure to implement certain aspects of children's intervention plans to reduce challenging behaviors. Teachers implemented strategies related to structural changes to the classroom more often than strategies involving individualized interactions with children, supporting the idea that teachers may be reluctant to adopt interventions that are individualized for one child. More research is needed to better understand teachers' rationale for choosing to adopt or not adopt social skills interventions.

Future Directions

Future directions in the area of social skills interventions for children with disabilities include the use of conceptual models, such as positive behavior support, to frame the delivery of effective, research-based interventions that may be implemented within existing systems of service delivery. PBS has a growing research base to support its use in preschool and school settings (Benedict et al., 2007; Crone & Horner, 2003) and children's homes (Dishion et al., 2008), and it has the potential to address issues of cultural diversity across contexts (Carr, 2007). More research must be conducted to understand how a model such as PBS may be implemented in rural areas and low-income countries in which there may be limited resources for prevention and intervention.

More frequent interactions, and higher levels of social skills, have been reported for preschool, elementary school, and high school students with disabilities when they participate in activities that include peers without disabilities. Greater social benefits may result when the environment is most similar to that of typically developing children and includes appropriate social skills interventions. Although children with disabilities are likely to have delayed social skills, the development of these skills can be enhanced for many children when they participate in activities with typically developing peers, and are supported in their interactions by parents and teachers. Research is only beginning to examine the roles of adults and peers in facilitating children's socially competent behaviors, and there has been little attention to the effects of more distal cultural processes on the social development of children with disabilities. Our knowledge of how to design and implement culturally sensitive adaptations of effective social skills interventions is limited.

Models of social competence, such as those proposed by Dodge and his colleagues (Dodge, Pettit, McClaskey, & Brown, 1986) and Guralnick (1999), provide a beginning point to understand the ways in which disability interferes with children's participation in social settings. Research that examines specific cognitive processes, such as the work on joint attention and theory-of-mind skills in children with ASDs or role understanding in children with mild mental retardation, offers beginning steps toward understanding the ways in which child-specific competencies affect social relationships. Understanding how proximal social contexts and more distal societal values and cultural expectations interact to support children's social development is an important focus of future research. Finally, there is evidence that typically developing children may reap benefits from interactions with peers with disabilities. Research that examines the ways in which these interactions foster the development of socially desirable characteristics (such as altruism) in children without disabilities provides an important focus for future research.

Acknowledgment

Support for the first author comes, in part, from the Agricultural Research Programs at Purdue University.

References

Bauminger, N., Edelsztein, H. S., & Morash, J. (2005). Social information processing and emotional understanding in children with LD. *Journal of Learning Disabilities, 38*, 45–61.

Begley, A. (1999). The self-perceptions of pupils with Down syndrome in relation to their academic competence, physical competence and social acceptance. *International Journal of Disability, Development and Education, 46*, 515–529.

Benedict, E. A., Horner, R. H., & Squires, J. (2007). Assessment and implementation of positive behavior support in preschools. *Topics in Early Childhood Special Education, 27*, 174–192.

Blonigan, B. A., Harbaugh, W. T., Singell, L. D., Horner, R. H., Irvin, L. K., & Smolkowski, K. S. (2008). Application of economic analysis to school-wide positive behavior support (SWPBS) programs. *Journal of Positive Behavior Interventions, 10*, 5–19.

Bochner, S., & Pieterse, M. (1996). Teenagers with Down syndrome in a time of changing policies and practices: Progress of students who were born between 1971 and 1978. *International Journal of Disability, Development and Education, 43*, 75–95.

Bronfenbrenner, U. (1999). Environments in developmental perspective: Theoretical and operational models. In S. L. Friedman & T. D. Wachs (Eds.), *Measuring environment across the life span: Emerging methods and concepts* (pp. 3–30). Washington, DC: American Psychological Association.

Bronfenbrenner, U., & Morris, S. (2006). The bioecological model of human development. In W. Damon & R. M. Lerner (Eds.), *Handbook of child psychology: Vol. 1. Theoretical models of human development* (6th ed., pp. 793–823). New York: Wiley.

Bronson, M. B., Hauser-Cram, P., & Warfield, M. E. (1997). Classrooms matter: Relations between the classroom environment and the social and mastery behavior of five-year-old children with disabilities. *Journal of Applied Developmental Psychology, 18*, 331–348.

Brown, W. H., Odom, S. L., & Conroy, M. A. (2001). An intervention hierarchy for promoting young children's peer interactions in natural environments. *Topics in Early Childhood Special Education, 21*, 162–175.

Brown, W. H., Odom, S. L., McConnell, S. R., & Rathel, J. M. (2008). Peer interaction interventions for preschool children with developmental difficulties. In W. H. Brown, S. L. Odom, & S. R. McConnell (Eds.), *Social competence of young children: Risk, disability, and intervention* (pp. 141–163). Baltimore: Paul H. Brookes.

Buhs, E. S., Ladd, G. W., & Herald, S. L. (2006). Peer exclusion and victimization: Processes that mediate the relation between peer group rejection and children's classroom engagement and achievement? *Journal of Educational Psychology, 98,* 1–13.

Buysse, V., Goldman, B. D., & Skinner, M. (2002). Setting effects on friendship formation among young children with and without disabilities. *Exceptional Children, 68,* 503–517.

Carr, E. G. (2007). The expanding vision of positive behavior support: Research perspectives on happiness, helpfulness, hopefulness. *Journal of Positive Behavior Interventions, 9,* 3–14.

Carter, E. W., Cushing, L. S., Clark, N. M., & Kennedy, C. H. (2005). Effects of peer support interventions on students' access to the general curriculum and social interactions. *Research and Practice for Persons with Severe Disabilities, 30,* 15–25.

Chung, K. M., Reavis, S., Mosconi, M., Drewry, J., Matthews, T., & Tasse, M. J. (2007). Peer-mediated social skills training program for young children with high-functioning autism. *Research in Developmental Disabilities, 4,* 423–436.

Crone, D. A., & Horner, R. H. (2003). *Building positive behavior support systems in schools.* New York: Guilford Press.

Cuckle, P., & Wilson, J. (2002). Social relationships and friendships among young people with Down's syndrome in secondary schools. *British Journal of Special Education, 29,* 66–71.

Dawson, G., Meltzoff, A. N., Osterling, J., Rinaldi, J., & Brown, E. (1998). Children with autism fail to orient to naturally occurring social stimuli. *Journal of Autism and Developmental Disorders, 28,* 479–485.

Diamond, K. E., Hong, S., & Baroody, A. E. (2008). Promoting young children's social competence in early childhood programs. In W. H. Brown, S. L. Odom, & S. R. McConnell (Eds.), *Social competence of young children: Risk, disability, and intervention* (pp. 165–184). Baltimore: Paul H. Brookes.

Diamond, K. E., & Innes, F. K. (2001). The origins of young children's attitudes toward peers with disabilities. In M. J. Guralnick (Ed.), *Early childhood inclusion: Focus on change* (pp. 159–178). Baltimore: Paul H. Brookes.

Dishion, T. J., Shaw, D., Connell A., Gardner, F., Weaver, C., & Wilson, M. (2008). The family check-up with high-risk indigent families: Preventing problem behavior by increasing parents' positive behavior support in early childhood. *Child Development, 79,* 1395–1414.

Dodge, K. A., Pettit, G. S., McClaskey, C. L., & Brown, M. M. (1986). Social competence in children. *Monographs of the Society for Research in Child Development, 44*(2, Serial No. 213).

Dooley, P., Wilczenski, F. L., & Torem, C. (2001). Using an activity schedule to smooth school transitions. *Journal of Positive Behavior Interventions, 3,* 57–61.

Duda, M. A., Dunlap, G., Fox, L., Lentini, R., & Clarke, S. (2004). An experimental evaluation of positive behavior support in a community preschool program. *Topics in Early Childhood Special Education, 24,* 143–155.

Edwards, C. P. (2000). Children's play in cross-cultural perspective: A new look at the Six Culture Study. *Cross-Cultural Research, 34,* 318–338.

Eisenberg, N., Pidada, S., & Liew, J. (2001). The relations of regulation and negative emotionality to Indonesian children's social functioning. *Child Development, 72,* 1747–1763.

Erwin, E. J. (1993). Social participation of young children with visual impairments in specialized and integrated environments. *Journal of Visual Impairment and Blindness, 87,* 138–142.

Feng, H., Lo, Y., Tsai, S., & Cartledge, G. (2008). The effects of theory-of-mind and social skill training on the social competence of a sixth-grade student with autism. *Journal of Positive Behavior Interventions, 10,* 228–242.

Fryxell, D., & Kennedy, C. H. (1995). Placement along the continuum of services and its impact on students' social relationships. *Journal of the Association for Persons With Severe Handicaps, 20,* 259–269.

Gettinger, M., & Stoiber, K. C. (2006). Functional assessment, collaboration, and evidence-based treatment: Analysis of a team approach for addressing challenging behaviors in young children. *Journal of School Psychology, 44,* 231–252.

Grenot-Scheyer, M. (1994). The nature of interactions between students with severe disability and their friends and acquaintances without disabilities. *Journal of the Association for Persons With Severe Handicaps, 19,* 253–262.

Gresham, F. M., & MacMillan, D. L. (1997). Social competence and affective characteristics of students with mild disabilities. *Review of Educational Research, 67,* 377–415.

Grisham-Brown, J., Hemmeter, M. L., & Prett-Frontczak, K. (2005). *Blended practices for teaching young children in inclusive settings.* Baltimore: Paul H. Brookes.

Guralnick, M. J. (1999). Family and child influences on the peer-related social competence of young children with developmental delays. *Mental Retardation and Developmental Disabilities Research Reviews, 5,* 21–29.

Guralnick, M. J., Connor, R. T., Hammond, M. A., Gottman, J. M., & Kinnish, K. (1996). The peer relations of preschool children with communication disorders. *Child Development, 67,* 471–489.

Guralnick, M. J., & Hammond, M. A. (1999). Sequential analysis of the social play of young children with mild developmental delays. *Journal of Early Intervention, 22,* 243–256.

Guralnick, M. J., Hammond, M. A., Connor, R. T., & Neville, B. (2006). Stability, change, and correlates of the peer relationships of young children with mild developmental delays. *Child Development, 77,* 312–324.

Hanline, M. F. (1993). Inclusion of preschoolers with profound disabilities: An analysis of children's interactions. *Journal of the Association for People with Severe Handicaps, 18,* 28–35.

Harper, L. V., & McCluskey, K .S. (2002). Caregiver and peer responses to children with language and motor disabilities in inclusive preschool programs. *Early Childhood Research Quarterly, 17,* 148–166.

Hartas, D., & Donahue, M. L. (1997). Conversational and social problem-solving skills in adolescents with learning disabilities. *Learning Disabilities Research and Practice, 12,* 213–220.

Ho, D. Y. F., Chen, S. C., & Chao, C. Y. (1991). Quan xi qu xiang: Wei zhong quo she hui xin li fang fa lun qiu da an [Relationship-oriented: Answers for methodology of Chinese social psychology]. In K. S. Yang & K. K. Hwang (Eds.), *Zhong guo ren di xin li yu xing wei (1989) [Chinese psychology and behaviors (1989)]* (pp. 49–66). Taipei: Laureate.

Hughes, C., Rodi, M. S., Lorden, S. W., Pitkin, S. E., Derer, K. R., Hwang, B., et al. (1999). Social interactions of high school students with mental retardation and their general education peers. *American Journal on Mental Retardation, 104,* 533–544.

Ivory, J. J., & McCollum, J. A. (1999). Effects of social and isolate toys on social play in an inclusive setting. *Journal of Special Education, 13,* 328–343.

Juvonen, J., & Bear, G. (1992). Social adjustment of children with and without learning disabilities in integrated classrooms. *Journal of Educational Psychology, 84,* 322–330.

Kadesjö, B., Gillberg, C., & Hagberg, B. (1999). Autism and Asperger syndrome in 7-year-old children: A population study. *Journal of Autism and Developmental Disorders, 29,* 327–331.

Kagitçibasi, C. (1997). Individualism and collectivism. In J. W. Berry, M. H. Segall, & C. Kagitçibasi (Eds.), *Handbook of cross-cultural psychology 3: Social behavior and applications* (2nd ed., pp. 1–49). Needham Heights, MA: Allyn & Bacon.

Kaiser, A. P. (2007). Addressing challenging behavior: Systematic problems, systematic solutions. *Journal of Early Intervention, 29,* 114–118.

Kasari, C., & Hodapp, R. M. (1996). Is Down syndrome different? Evidence from social and family studies. *Down Syndrome Quarterly*, *1*, 1–8.

Kennedy, C. H., Shukla, S., & Fryxell, D. (1997). Comparing the effects of educational placement on the social relationships of intermediate school students with severe disabilities. *Exceptional Children*, *64*, 31–47.

Kim, M. G. (2001). San yan gu shi zhong fo jiao si wang si wei tan suo: chao yue yin guo lun hui hou di nie pan shi jie [Exploring the Buddhist concepts of death from the fiction of San Yan: The Nirvana beyond karma]. *Chung-Hwa Buddhist Studies*, *5*, 441–463.

Klingner, J. K., Blanchett, W. J., & Harry, H. (2007). Race, culture and developmental disabilities. In S. L. Odom, R. H. Horner, M. E. Snell, & J. Blacher (Eds.), *Handbook of developmental disabilities* (pp. 55–76). New York: Guilford Press.

Kohler, F. W., Strain, P. S., Hoyson, M., & Davis, L. (1995). Using a group-oriented contingency to increase social interactions between children with autism and their peers: A preliminary analysis of corollary supportive behaviors. *Behavior Modification*, *19*, 10–32.

Kravetz, S., Faust, M., Lipshitz, S., & Shalhav, S. (1999). LD, interpersonal understanding and social behavior in the classroom. *Journal of Learning Disabilities*, *32*, 248–255.

Landrum, T. J., & Lloyd, J. W. (1992). Generalization in social behavior research with children and youth who have emotional or behavioral disorders. *Behavior Modification*, *16*, 593–616.

LeBlanc, L. A., & Matson, J. L. (1995). A social skills training program for preschoolers with developmental delays. *Behavior Modification*, *19*, 234–246.

Leffert, J. S., & Siperstein, G. N. (1996). Assessment of social-cognitive processes in children with mental retardation. *American Journal on Mental Retardation*, *100*, 441–455.

Lord, C. (1993). The complexity of social behavior in autism. In S. Baron-Cohen, H. Tager-Flusberg, & D. Cohen (Eds.), *Understanding other minds: Perspectives from autism* (pp. 292–316). New York: Oxford University Press.

Maag, J. W. (2005). Social skills training for youth with emotional and behavioral disorders and learning disabilities: Problems, conclusions, and suggestions. *Exceptionality*, *13*, 155–172.

MacCuspie, P. A. (1990). *The social acceptance and interaction of integrated visually impaired children*. Unpublished doctoral dissertation, Dalhousie University, Halifax, Nova Scotia, Canada.

Macy, M. G., & Bricker, D. D. (2007). Embedding individualized social goals in routine activities in inclusive early childhood classrooms. *Early Child Development and Care*, *177*, 107–120.

McAlpine, L. M., & Moore, C. L. (1995). The development of social understanding in children with visual impairments. *Journal of Visual Impairment and Blindness*, *89*, 349–358.

McCormick, K. M., Jolivette, K., & Ridgely, R. (2003). Choice making as an intervention strategy for young children. *Young Exceptional Children*, *6*, 3–10.

McGee, G. G., & Daly, T. (2007). Teaching of age-appropriate phrases to children with autism. *Research & Practice for Persons with Severe Disabilities*, *32*, 112–123.

Mishna, F. (2003). Learning disabilities and bullying: Double jeopardy. *Journal of Learning Disabilities*, *36*, 336–347.

Morrison, L., Kamps, D., Garcia, J., & Parker, D. (2001). Peer mediation and monitoring strategies to improve initiations and social skills for students with autism. *Journal of Positive Behavior Interventions*, *3*, 237–250.

Mundy, P., & Crowson, M. (1997). Joint attention and early social communication: Implications for research on intervention with autism. *Journal of Autism and Developmental Disorders*, *27*, 653–676.

Newcomer, L. L., & Lewis, T. (2004). Functional behavioral assessment: An investigation of assessment reliability and effectiveness of function-based interventions. *Journal of Emotional Behavioral Disorders*, *12*, 168–181.

Norwich, B., & Kelly, N. (2004). Pupils' views on inclusion: moderate learning difficulties and bullying in mainstream and special schools. *British Educational Research Journal, 30*, 43–65.

Odom, S. L. (2000). Preschool inclusion: What we know and where we go from here. *Topics in Early Childhood Special Education, 20*, 20–27.

Odom, S. L., Zercher, C., Li, S., Marquart, J. M., Sandall, S., & Brown, W. H. (2006). Social acceptance and rejection of preschool children with disabilities: A mixed-method analysis. *Journal of Educational Psychology, 98*, 807–823.

O'Neill, P. J., & Lord, C. (1982). Functional and semantic characteristics of child-directed speech of autistic children. In D. Park (Ed.), *Proceedings from the international meeting for the National Society for Autistic Children*. Washington, DC: National Society for Autistic Children.

O'Reilly, M. F., O'Halloran, M., Sigafoos, J., Lancioni, G. E., Green, V., Edrishinha, C., et al. (2005). Evaluation of video feedback and self-management to decrease schoolyard aggression and increase pro-social behaviour in two students with behavioural disorders. *Educational Psychology, 25*, 199–206.

Ozawa, A., & Yaeda, J. (2007). Employer attitudes toward employing persons with psychiatric disability in Japan. *Journal of Vocational Rehabilitation, 26*, 105–113.

Parish-Morris, J., Hennon, E. A., Hirsh-Pasek, K., Golinkoff, R. M., & Tager-Flusberg, H. (2007). Children with autism illuminate the role of social intention in word learning. *Child Development, 78*, 1265–1287.

Phillips, W., Baron-Cohen, S., & Rutter, M. (1998). Understanding intention in normal development and autism. *British Journal of Developmental Psychology, 16*, 337–348.

Pretti-Frontczak, K., & Bricker, D. (2004). *An activity-based approach to early intervention* (3rd ed.). Baltimore: Paul H. Brookes.

Robertson, S., & Weismer, S. E. (1999). The influence of peer models on the play scripts of children with specific language impairment. *Journal of Speech, Language and Hearing Research, 41*, 1444–1458.

Roeyers, H. (1996). The influence of nonhandicapped peers on the social interactions of children with a pervasive developmental disorder. *Journal of Autism and Developmental Disorders, 26*, 303–320.

Rosenblum, L. P. (1997). Adolescents with visual impairments who have best friends: A pilot study. *Journal of Visual Impairment and Blindness, 91*, 224–235.

Rubin, K. H., Bukowski, W., & Parker, J. G. (2006). Peer interactions, relationships, and groups. In N. Eisenberg (Ed.), *Handbook of child psychology: Social, emotional, and personality development* (pp. 571–645). New York: Wiley.

Rynders, J. E., & Horrobin, J. M. (1990). Always trainable? Never educable? Updating educational expectations concerning children with Down syndrome. *American Journal on Mental Retardation, 95*, 77–83.

Serna, L., Nielsen, E., Lambros, K., & Forness, S. (2000). Primary prevention with children at risk for emotional or behavioral disorders: Data on a universal intervention for Head Start classrooms. *Behavioral Disorders, 26*, 70–84.

Sigman, M., & Ruskin, E. (1999). Continuity and change in the social competence of children with autism, Down syndrome, and developmental delay. *Monographs of the Society for Research in Child Development, 64*(1, Serial No. 256).

Siperstein, G. N., & Leffert, J. S. (1997). Comparison of socially accepted and rejected children with mental retardation. *American Journal on Mental Retardation, 101*, 339–351.

Skellenger, A. C., Rosenblum, L. P., & Jager, B. K. (1997). Behaviors of preschoolers with visual impairments in indoor play settings. *Journal of Visual Impairment and Blindness, 91*, 519–530.

Sponheim, E., & Skjeldal, O. (1998). Autism and related disorders: Epidemiological findings in a Norwegian study using ICD-10 diagnostic criteria. *Journal of Autism and Developmental Disorders, 28*, 217–227.

Staub, D., Schwartz, I. S., Gallucci, C., & Peck, C. A. (1994). Four portraits of friendship at an inclusive school. *Journal of the Association for Persons With Severe Handicaps, 19*, 314–326.

Stormont, M. A., Smith, S. C., & Lewis, T. J. (2007). Teacher implementation of precorrection and praise statements in Head Start classrooms as a component of a program-wide system of positive behavior support. *Journal of Behavioral Education, 16*, 280–290.

Strain, P. S., & Schwartz, I. S. (2001). ABA and the development of meaning social relations for young children with autism. *Focus on Autism and Other Developmental Disabilities, 16*, 120–128.

Strain, P. S., Schwartz, I. S., & Bovey, E. H. (2008). Social competence interventions for young children with autism. In W. H. Brown, S. L. Odom, & S. R. McConnell (Eds.), *Social competence of young children: Risk, disability, and intervention* (pp. 253–272). Baltimore: Paul H. Brookes.

Sugai, G., & Horner, R. H. (2001). Features of effective behavior support at the district level. *Beyond Behavior, 11*, 16–19.

Tsao, L., & Odom, S. L. (2006). Sibling-mediated social interaction intervention for young children with autism. *Topics in Early Childhood Special Education, 26*, 106–123.

Tsau, C. C., & Chuang, Y. L. (2007). The study on parents' psychological adaptation of parenting young children with autism. *Bulletin of Eastern-Taiwan Special Education, 9*, 109–123.

U.S. Department of Education. (2007). *27th Annual (2005) Report to Congress on the Implementation of the Individuals with Disabilities Education Act*. Washington, DC: Author. Retrieved from http://www.edpubs.ed.gov

Volkmar, F. R. (1993). Social development in autism. In S. Baron-Cohen, H. Tager-Flusberg, & D. Cohen (Eds.), *Understanding other minds: Perspectives from autism* (pp. 40–55). New York: Oxford University Press.

Volkmar, F. R., & Lord, C. (1998). Diagnosis and definition of autism and other pervasive developmental disorders. In F. Volkmar (Ed.), *Autism and pervasive developmental disorders* (pp. 1–25). New York: Cambridge University Press.

World Health Organization (WHO). (2004). The global burden of disease: 2004 update. Retrieved from http://www.who.int/healthinfo/global_burden_disease/2004_report_update/en/index.html

World Health Organization (WHO). (2008). Disability, including prevention, management and rehabilitation. Retrieved from http://www.who.int/topics/disabilities/en/

Yirmiya, N., Kasari, C., Sigman, M., & Mundy, P. (1989) Facial expressions of affect in autistic, mentally retarded and normal children. *Journal of Child Psychology and Psychiatry, 30*, 725–735.

Yude, C., & Goodman, R. (1999). Peer problems of 9- to 11-year-old children with hemiplegia in mainstream schools. Can these be predicted? *Developmental Medicine and Child Neurology, 41*, 4–8.

Zurmohle, U. M., Homann, T., Schroeter, C., Rothgerger, H., Hommel, G., & Ermert, J. A. (1998). Psychosocial adjustment of children with spina bifida. *Journal of Child Neurology, 13*, 64–70.

CHAPTER THIRTY-FOUR

Interventions for Development of Social Skills Among Children in Developing Countries

Suman Verma and Rajani Konantambigi

The State of the World's Children (UNICEF, 2009b) calls for concerted social interventions and strong, cohesive partnerships to improve child survival and health care for mothers, newborns, and children across developing countries. According to the report, Africa and Asia present the greatest challenge to the survival and health of children. Poverty and related health hazards, nutrition, and associated social factors prevent close to 200 million children under 5 years old in the developing countries from attaining their developmental potential (Grantham-McGregor et al., 2007). Other challenges to the effective social development of children in these countries include the quality and accessibility of education, access to basic amenities, child abuse and violence, and long-standing resistance to the idea of a child's right to participation. Many social, cultural, religious, and other factors that affect the success of interventions on behalf of children are also similar in developing countries.

As the 2015 deadline for the Millennium Development Goals draws closer, the challenge for improving the state of children worldwide is looming large. In collaboration with nodal United Nations organizations, developing countries are combining efforts to plan and implement child-sensitive social protection interventions to improve comprehensive child well-being measured by survival, health, education, protection, and development outcomes (UNICEF, 2009a). For the purposes of this chapter, we use the UN categorization of developing countries using the Human Development Index. A compound indicator of economic development, the index attempts to get away from purely monetary measurements by combining per capita GNP with life expectancy and literacy in a weighted average (United Nations Development Programme, 2003). There are several

The Wiley-Blackwell Handbook of Childhood Social Development, Second Edition, edited by Peter K. Smith and Craig H. Hart
© 2011 by Blackwell Publishing Ltd.

common experiential themes emerging from the larger sociocultural milieu that shape the contours of childhood experiences in the developing world.

We began writing this chapter to compile existing work on childhood social development in developing countries across the globe. We took a broad approach in order to understand the different aspects of social development being studied with children in the age group of 3 to 11 years. Our goals were humble and straightforward: to compile material essential for understanding and contextualizing the theories, methods, and findings of the research being carried out in childhood across developing countries. Our search focused on specific areas in social development such as social cognition, socialization and family, peer relations, play, social participation, social competencies, and interventions for social skills development.

We initially restricted ourselves to published work, only to be discouraged by the lack of relevant materials. Even the expert help provided by the library staff at the Center for Advanced Study in the Behavioral Sciences at Stanford University did not prove very helpful. We then began making personal requests to colleagues and department heads around the globe to share materials in the said area and specified age group. In this fast-track life space, as expected, very few responded, leaving us to make sense of the limited body of work that focused on school effectiveness and school adjustment, ethnotheories on parenting, play interactions, child abuse, social deviance, peer group dynamics, victimization, bullying, and social interventions. It was difficult to cull out themes from the few studies we had under each section. Finally, we decided to analyze and present work across developing countries on the nature of interventions that enhance the psychosocial competence among children. The purpose of this chapter is thus a narrower one, namely, to document the implementation of social skills development programs for children in developing countries, to share the process and outcome evaluation, and to identify conceptual and methodological issues in program efficacy along with implications for research and practice.

Definition and Scope

Social skills refer to abilities that promote adaptive behavior and facilitate adjustment and effective coping with daily life demands (World Health Organization [WHO], 1994). Social competence is a concept that is an integral part of life skills training programs. As a construct, it is widely applied and is considered an important factor associated with areas such as mental illness, conduct disorders and behavioral problems in children, problems in academic adjustment and achievement, and social anxiety, as well as areas that relate to sexual behavior, delinquency, and substance abuse (Hamburg, 1990; Khan, 1998; Malhotra, 2003). The underlying assumption is that these skills are essential for the promotion of psychosocial well-being in children. These skills include emotion regulation, self-awareness, relationship building, conflict resolution, communication, social decision making, pressure resistance, coping with stress, self-esteem development, and critical thinking.

The basic premise of skill development interventions is that children are disconnected from real-life issues in school settings that rely almost exclusively on academic achievement with little regard to personal and social development, including healthy values, social perspectives, self-worth, and awareness about alternative behaviors (Bierman, 1986; Chalmers & Townsend, 1990). Development of personal and social skills helps children translate that knowledge into behavior that puts them in advantageous positions to make healthy and responsible choices in different settings throughout life. These skills foster social competence and a sense of individual empowerment (UNICEF, 2002; WHO, 2004).

Key areas of social competence training among children are (a) social transactions, or the ability to maintain satisfying personal relationships and to resolve interpersonal conflicts in a socially acceptable way; (b) the ability to manage socially conflicting situations; and (c) the ability to handle stress and anxiety (Hamburg, 1990, p. 19). Successful social skills programs have shown improvements in participants' self-control, social awareness, group interaction participation, and interpersonal decision making, thus laying the groundwork for the role of socially competent, responsible, and productive citizens (Jenkins, 1995). For children to successfully and comfortably enter the adult community with its diverse social roles, they must possess critical-thinking and problem-solving skills (Elias, 1994), as well as coping resources and personal and social abilities. The most direct and effective interventions are done in supportive learning environments (WHO, 1994).

Conceptual Framework and Core Elements

Tracing the historical roots of psychological skills training, Goldstein (1981) commented that until the early 1970s, there were three major psychological approaches designed to alter the behavior of unhappy, ineffective, and disturbed individuals – psychodynamic/psychoanalytic, humanistic/nondirective, and behavior modification. These approaches assumed that the desired behavior was inherent in the individual, and could be extracted. But as psychological skills training grew in popularity in the early 1970s, there was a shift in this kind of thinking. The skill trainer now took an educational approach, actively teaching desirable behaviors with particular attention to prevention.

The conceptual basis for the planning and implementation of life skills programs for children recognizes the essential role that life skills play in the development of nonacademic integrative and sequential logical-thinking skills. Abstract reasoning is taught through interactive learning methods and an emphasis on lateral thinking. Programs also highlight nonacademic cognitive development as meaningful linkages with future life demands. Broadly, the programs serve to augment the overall learning experiences for children, provide knowledge and information, and counter past negative reinforcement with positive achievement motivation. They also aim to foster work habits, work ethics, and a positive attitude toward society and the future.

The social skills training interventions are greatly influenced by the cognitive behavioral model of Bandura in the aspects of self-efficacy and theoretical concepts provided by social learning theory (modeling, behavioral rehearsal, and social reinforcement), which offers assessment and intervention procedures for many kinds of problem behaviors (Bandura, 1986). The theory points to the salience of observation, imitation, and practice as the fundamentals of learning. The components of attention, retention, enactment of behavior, and motivation form the core elements of many skill-training programs. The emphasis is also on the use of influential models: rewards for socially desirable behaviors, negotiable tasks presented in successive approximations, and directed practice. Intervention grounded in social learning theory has been demonstrably effective in its application across a variety of adolescent problem behaviors and has shown promising results in influencing youth's risk reduction behavior (Bandura, 1995; Schinke, Moncher, & Holden, 1989), development of social competence skills (Bierman, 1986; Chalmers & Townsend, 1990; Misener, 1995), and cognitive skills training (Botvin, 1989; Elias, 1992; Ross, 1981).

Other fields including clinical and counseling psychology, social work, and education have also sought to address the causes of behavior problems and skill competencies. Causes may include social incompetence or the pursuit of socially unacceptable goals (Beyth-Marom, Fischhoff, Jacobs, & Furby, 1989). Jessor and Jessor's (1977) problem behavior theory takes a cognitive psychosocial approach to mitigate socially undesirable behavior, integrating training in social skills, thinking skills, and decision-making skills to improve personal and interpersonal functioning. The field of instructional psychology advances cognitive competence by developing thinking skills with the goal of identifying and correcting cognitive deficiencies through education and training (Beyth-Marom et al., 1989).

Programs to Enhance Competence in Social Skills: An Overview

This section provides an overview of various social skills programs in developing countries in terms of the core elements and skills-targeted intervention procedures, and treatment and outcome evaluation criteria. Although the review covers programs for children in the age group of 3–11 years, it is important to note that some of these programs overlap with the adolescent age group (12–18 years).

The review of some of the best examples of effective social skills development is based on evidence from quasi-experimental studies, program reports, and review articles, and, where relevant, evidence is taken from qualitative studies. We examine interventions in developing countries that deal with enhancing skills for education, health, and social competence as prevention for childhood problem behaviors. These programs can be categorized as school based, community based, and those specifically targeted at at-risk children, in both school and nonschool settings. We begin by highlighting some exemplary social skills programs in the developing countries, followed by a brief summary of the key elements of these programs.

Some Exemplars of Social Skill Development Programs in Developing Countries

In the developing countries, there are a number of noteworthy initiatives that nodal agencies, government policies, and nongovernment agencies (NGOs) carried out with an objective to enhance the physical and psychosocial competence in children. In various low-income countries, life skills programs have been initiated through the interagency collaboration Focusing Resources on Effective School Health (FRESH) launched by UNESCO, UNICEF, WHO, and the World Bank. It is a collective agency recognition and response to the growing need to improve holistic approaches and multiple strategies to promote health and well-being through schools. A major force behind this support for the enhancement of life skills education in schools is the United Nations Convention on the Rights of the Child, which makes clear statements about the role of education systems in support of the healthy psychosocial development of children (Articles 19 and 28).

Effective health programs contribute to the development of child-friendly schools, and thus to the promotion of education for all. A basic rights-based approach to learning is adopted wherein children are fundamentally entitled to quality education. One of the key components of these programs is skills-based education that focuses upon the development of knowledge, attitudes, values, and core life skills needed to make and act on the most appropriate and positive health-related decisions. The notion of health in this context extends beyond physical health to psychosocial and environmental health issues. Changes in social and behavioral factors have given greater prominence to such health-related issues as HIV/AIDS, injuries, violence, and substance use (O'Donoghue, 1995). The development of specific skills, such as dealing with peer pressure, is also central to effective skills-based health education and positive psychosocial environments. The assumption is that when children develop such skills, they are more likely to adopt and sustain a healthy lifestyle during schooling and for the rest of their lives.

Recognizing the importance of these skills, the 164 nations committed to Education for All have included life skills as an essential learning outcome for all children and adolescents. Life skills education is offered as part of the formal curriculum at both the primary and secondary school levels in at least 70 developing countries (UNESCO, n.d.). WHO (1994) has prepared a document to guide professionals in the development of life skills programs in schools. It also issues a *Skill for Life* newsletter about life skills teaching programs and new life skills initiatives from around the world. In an effort to offer guidance on implementing life skills–based education, UNICEF has created a special website that showcases promising examples of life skills–based education around the world, catalogs studies that have evaluated skills-based programs, and provides practical tools and materials related to program implementation (UNICEF, 2008).

Heckert and Baldo (1998) reviewed case studies in school life skills education programs that meet the UN'S best practices guidelines for relevance, effectiveness, efficiency, ethical soundness, sustainability, and replicability from India, Hong Kong, Zimbabwe, Uganda, Kenya, South Africa, Brazil, and the Caribbean. The life skills approach offers the best promise for strengthening schoolchildren's skills to develop healthy behaviors before risk taking commences. Reporting on the school-based initiative to strengthen health education, Buczkiewicz and Carnegie (2001) reviewed the life skills education approach in schools of Uganda. The focus is on the development of effective communication, assertiveness, and social decision making that are crucial to putting knowledge into practice. The program adopts a participatory, active-learning approach, which poses a challenge to Ugandan schools with the low teacher-to-pupil ratio. The report explores how the schools are meeting this challenge and the role of NGOs, the mass media, and other health organizations.

In India, mental health institutes in collaboration with NGOs across the country are actively involved in program implementation, the development of resource materials, and teacher training for life skills education in both schools and local communities (Verma, 2006). There is evidence that providing skill learning to students can influence positive mental health outcomes. Studies report improved competence and self-worth with a decrease in emotional and behavioral problems (Dogra & Veeraghavan, 1994; Goyal, 2005; Malhotra & Kohli, 2005). These studies focus on a wide range of generic risk factors and mental health problems, such as academic failure, aggression, and bullying, and have demonstrated increased individual competence and resilience and reductions in depressive symptoms.

Jabeen and Karkara (2005) from the Save the Children Sweden Regional Program for South and Central Asia reviewed community-based programs for early childhood development (ECD) in Bangladesh and India that empower caregivers to create enabling environments that support and promote the cognitive, emotional, and social development of children to 6 years of age. The programs identify parents as a strategic group for implementing the Convention on the Rights of the Child and point out that the state parties have specific obligations toward parents in their role of primary caregivers. Emphasis is on supporting and strengthening the parental role in awareness around child participation, gender sensitization, and violence against children. The programs are aimed at (a) helping children realize their full potential and providing access to health, nutrition, education, water, and sanitation; (b) serving the best interests of children in national, social, family, and personal situations (empowerment); (c) ensuring safety and security at home and in the public space (protection against abuse, exploitation, and violence); and (d) establishing and protecting children's rights (social inclusion, decent work, and livelihood).

Engle et al. (2007) assessed and evaluated interventions in developing countries to reduce the effects of social, environmental, and infectious risks on young children with special focus on cognitive and socioemotional outcomes. These early child development programs that target socially disadvantaged children are designed to improve the survival, growth, and development of children; prevent occurrence of risks; and reduce the negative effects of risks. The programs provide for a mixed strategy – some work with children by providing services to improve their health and nutrition, whereas others work with parents to enhance their parenting skills and resources, using techniques of home visits, information sharing, and focused group discussions. The programs reviewed in the developing countries for disadvantaged children below 6 years of age were those that were initiated after 1990 and fulfilled the criteria of (a) randomized controlled trial or matched comparison group; (b) program evaluation outcome; and (c) assessment of child development parameters. The 20 intervention studies that met the criteria were short listed and categorized into center-based early learning, parenting or parent–child, and comprehensive programs, including health and nutrition interventions.

The *center-based program* evaluations from Argentina, Guinea, Cape Verde, Bangladesh, Burma, Nepal, Vietnam, and Colombia reported substantial gains in both cognitive and social skills among children such as sociability, self-confidence, willingness to talk to adults, and motivation. Some of these studies had longitudinal data that recorded improvements in school enrollments, retention, and academic performance. The *parenting and parent–child programs* from Jamaica, Bolivia, and Bangladesh resulted in improved parenting practices, improved skills in play interactions with children, and positive effects on children's socioemotional development. The *comprehensive programs* from India, Peru, Bolivia, Uganda, and the Philippines illustrate different models for early child development. The evaluation outcome presents a mixed picture with modest positive effects on measures of child development when compared to the control group, higher scores on indices of school performance, and benefits in cognitive and psychosocial development, irrespective of age.

The authors highlighted some of the salient features associated with program effectiveness and success across the countries, such as (a) integrated programs that provide for holistic child development with effective partnerships between government and civil society; (b) early direct child exposure with adequate quality, intensity, and duration; (c) the involvement of parents, families, and teachers in promoting child development outcomes; (d) providing a culturally sensitive, stimulating environment for children that fosters self-learning experiences; and (e) including a systematic approach of monitoring, evaluation, resource development, and capacity building of the program implementers.

An exemplar of another early childhood education program is the Child-to Child for School Readiness program initiated by UNICEF in developing countries. This approach works on strengthening readiness for school and is based on the belief that apart from their primary caregivers, young children below school age are most influenced by other children. Child-to-Child enables older children already in school to provide much needed support to younger children before they enroll in school in order to help them develop early learning competencies, a positive attitude toward school, and the readiness to start school at the right age. The program provides games and learning activities for children in primary school (grades 2 to 5) that can also be used for younger siblings and children younger than 4 years old. An informal child development awareness program is conducted in each participating school for students, teachers, and heads, and a formal program is undertaken with the upper primary school children, which includes sessions and a community survey taken by the children with help from teachers and/or community members. It also involves a structured program of weekly activities for the older children to help children in school enrollments in the next session (UNICEF, 2007).

Galli Galli Sim Sim is an innovative program launched in the urban slums and rural areas of India by Sesame Workshop India (a subsidiary of Sesame Workshop, New York) to expand early education opportunities to all preschoolers. Taking a multilevel, multimedia approach, the program creates high-quality on-air and off-air experiences that educate caregivers in childhood development while encouraging an activity-based method of learning basic literacy, academic, and life skills for children. A key component of Sesame Workshop India's initiative is to supplement the television show with its outreach program and bring Galli Galli Sim Sim to places where access to television is limited. This program is being carried out in preschool centers and in the streets on vegetable carts equipped with televisions, DVD players, generators, and themed educational materials for caregivers and children. Funded by the Michael and Susan Dell Foundation, this outreach program is designed to work on mass and local levels through mobile community viewing. The culturally relevant educational modules and the research methodology are widely used in a number of developing countries to provide skills-based quality education to children (Sesame Workshop India, 2006).

Programs in social skills development are increasingly being directed toward high-risk children from rural and urban areas who are considered at risk for adverse outcomes. Barker and Fontes (1996) reviewed 23 program models in the Latin American and Caribbean regions that target at-risk children and youth. These children are from disadvantaged backgrounds and are at risk of dropping out of school, compromising their health because of environmental, familial, and social factors. Other at-risk groups are already school dropouts, working or loitering in the streets, involved in gang activities, or homeless, or have severed all ties with their families, communities, and social institutions. A great many of these children come from social environments that are disorganized, lacking dependable family, school, and community resources. Therefore, unlike mainstream children, these children lack familiarity with the most basic skills, strategies, and knowledge that are required for successful living and succeeding in the mainstream.

Programs tailored for these children involve culturally sensitive strategies with structured, problem-focused sessions to build a knowledge base. They involve peer teaching, cooperative learning, and participation in civic activities in the community. The program goals are (a) to help children develop positive social behaviors, such as self-discipline, self-awareness, responsibility, good judgment, and the ability to get along with others; and (b) to help them develop strong commitments to their families, schools, peers, and communities, including a commitment to lead healthy lives. These programs are run by collaborative efforts of the government and NGOs in different countries in the said region with some aid from the World Bank in both school and nonschool settings. Specific skill training targets areas in educational attainment, reproductive health, sex education, and substance use. Using the Child Rights approach, the focus is on child participation and empowerment. The sessions, using interactive teaching modules, combine individual and group counseling with meeting the personal and social needs of subjects. Given the nature of a group that is constantly mobile or not easily accessible, only a few organizations have carried out thorough impact evaluations of their programs, and even fewer have information on cost-effectiveness and cost–benefit analysis.

Basic Concepts and Skills Targeted in the Programs

A review of the current programs in the above section suggests that the programs essentially rely on procedures derived from social learning theory (e.g. modeling, behavioral rehearsal, and performance feedback) and education's contemporary pedagogic principles and procedures (e.g. instruction, simulation games, and structured discussions). According to Schinke, Gordon, and Weston (1990), labeling and stigmatization can be avoided by employing a model that uses learning theory to explain problem behaviors and at the same time encourage proactive behaviors. Learning theory gives the subject control, creating expectation and confidence in the individual's ability to change, while simultaneously emphasizing that negative behaviors can be unlearned and replaced by positive ones. In addition, cognitive behavioral approaches reject causal explanations based on intrapsychic processes and instead focus on overt, measurable behaviors, making these types of interventions ideal for controlled research and hypothesis testing.

There is a wide range of skills targeted in these programs. Some teach specific life skills such as decision making, resisting peer pressure, building self-awareness, and dealing with emotions, whereas others teach generic skills useful for social adjustment. A number of social skills programs have focused on health issues such as HIV/AIDS prevention, sex education and reproductive health (Barker and Fontes, 1996; O'Donoghue, 1995), and substance abuse and use (Buczkiewicz & Carnegie, 2001; Malhotra, 2003). There are other programs designed to improve peer and family relationships to help children cope with stress, aggression, and conduct disorders (Dogra & Veeraghavan, 1994; Goyal, 2005; Malhotra & Kohli, 2005). Most social skills programs are designed with the greater goal of improving social behaviors in general.

Some recent research has focused on attempts to create "relevant" interventions by engaging the target subject in the development of the program or making the program culturally relevant (Attig & Hopkins, 2006; Chabbott, 2004). Thus the basic concepts in the social skills model are that positive behavior elicits an imitative response, leading to corrective feedback and opportunities to practice the new skills.

Intervention Format and Procedures

Interventions have adopted a variety of methods to teach different skills to children. Advances in social skills interventions have led to procedures that enhance not only specific skill acquisition but also the generalization and maintenance of an effective interpersonal repertoire (Miske, 2003). These interventions have successfully treated or partially treated children and adolescents with behavior problems (Goyal, 2005; Malhotra & Kohli, 2005). Most programs favor nonaversive methods such as modeling, coaching, and reinforcement to improve behavior. Programs can also be integrated into existing classroom or home environments, maximizing opportunities for treatment generalization. These programs are appropriate for both individuals and groups, and because they mainly focus on increasing prosocial behaviors, all students stand to benefit from participating. The programs begin by teaching broad strategies for social interaction, encompassing a range of specific behaviors across a variety of situations. The goal is to facilitate the generalization of skill-training concepts across various naturalistic settings (UNICEF, 2002). Older children, in comparison to their younger counterparts, are at an advantage to develop abstract representations of various social strategies that foster generalizations across settings and develop self-monitoring skills that enhance skill acquisition (Attig & Hopkins, 2006).

Goyal (2005) provided training in social skills instruction, modeling, role play, and performance appraisal to reduce behavior disorders among schoolchildren. The activity-based sessions focused on the development of social competence, self-evaluation skills, and appropriate emotional expression.

Evaluation Outcome

Process and outcome evaluation of treatments is an important program component to demonstrate the impact and effectiveness of the intervention. The evaluation component in the reviewed programs presents a mixed picture. Those conducted in school settings with a pre-post experimental design have clear-cut evaluation criteria and have been able to show the impact of the intervention (Dogra & Veeraghavan, 1994; Engle et al., 2007; Goyal, 2005; Malhotra & Kohli, 2005). However, programs that are community based or those conducted with disadvantaged groups of children do not have a strong evaluation component. Instead, the success of these programs is documented by the change in behavior of the subjects, the reduction in problem behaviors, and secondary sources of information such as teachers, parents, or peers. In early childhood education programs, school enrollment and school adjustment are considered important indicators of the efficacy of the program.

To summarize, social skills development interventions seek to improve skill competence in a wide variety of social and personal domains. They employ personal, situational, and context-specific scenarios to bring about the desired change in behavior. These programs recognize that existing skill deficits can be treated through training and counseling to ultimately improve skill competence and foster adjustment and well-being in children. The structures of the programs vary, as does the role of the trainer or mentor: from peers to parents to community members. Interactive activities provide participative environments to facilitate skill transfer to real-life settings. Evaluation methods include self-reports, feedback from peers and parents, and sociometric measurements. The overall recommendation is to strengthen the evaluation component in many existing programs to improve the efficacy and viability of the program, with an eye toward replicability in other settings.

Methodological Issues

An important aspect for consideration in any intervention study is methodological issues such as appropriate research design, timing, duration, comparison groups at baseline, sample attrition, procedures, validity checks, fidelity of program implementation, process and outcome evaluation, transfer of skill learning, sustainability, and maintenance effects. Some of these issues are discussed in this section.

Timing

Skill learning is an active process of acquisition, processing, and the structuring of experiences. However, the issue of how early skill learning should be provided is still widely debated. Considerable evidence suggests that early adolescence is the right time for preventive interventions. Targeting subjects at a younger age, before negative patterns of behavior, habits, and interaction have become established, may prove more successful (Dryfoos, 1990; WHO, 1994). Ideally, the necessary skills for healthy development would be taught continually by teachers and parents in developmentally appropriate ways throughout middle childhood and early adolescence (Schorr, Both, & Copple, 1991). Given that this does not always happen, researchers still need to identify the best times and stages for various kinds of intervention (Petersen, 1993). This leads to the related question of what is developmentally appropriate. If the ultimate goal of social skills training is not just to increase competence in specific skills but also to foster holistic psychosocial competence, programs must to be planned according to the developmental changes occurring at specific ages. Relatively few skills training programs reviewed in the earlier section have incorporated developmental considerations into their design; even fewer have directly compared the effects of various intervention techniques on subjects representing different developmental levels. Further, long-term developmental changes may require multiple interventions, such as those placed at "transition" periods of development (Bierman & Montminy, 1993). A developmental perspective should be integrated into the process of program planning to help address the crucial issue of optimal timing for social skills training.

Duration

A review of social skills programs suggests that the duration of programs varies from 2 weeks to 5 or 6 months, sometimes with follow-up programs in the following years. Short-term programs seem to have an impact on information acquisition, whereas long-term programs are more likely to bring about changes in behavior and are most effective (WHO, 1994). However, one limitation of social skills programs is the paucity of studies with long-term follow-up data. Botvin, Baker, Dusenbury, Botvin, and Diaz (1995) suggested several reasons for the failure of past studies to demonstrate long-term effects in prevention programs. These are (a) inadequate length of the intervention, (b) a lack of booster sessions as a part of the program's long-term planning, (c) implementation of intervention with insufficient fidelity to the intervention model, and (d) a lack of clear-cut assumptions of the intervention (Botvin et al., 1995, p. 1107). In the case of early childhood development programs for disadvantaged sections, the most effective interventions are those with a comprehensive coverage including children and families with optimum duration and quality, those that integrate health and nutrition components, and those that provide direct services to children including an active parenting and skill-building dimension (Engle et al., 2007).

Skill transfer and maintenance enhancement

Skill training programs must demonstrate successful generalization to the natural environment in order to be considered valid and effective. In order for social skills programs to be successful, trainee effectiveness and satisfaction must be proven (a) over an extended period of time, and (b) in a variety of contexts. According to Goldstein (1981), a program will actively seek to incorporate specific procedures in the training process to achieve both these goals.

Another unresolved issue is transfer enhancement. The likelihood of transfer is higher when there is greater similarity in the physical and interpersonal stimuli in the structured learning setting, as well as in the home assignment, community, or other setting where the skill is applied. Stokes and Osnes (1989) have identified various "generalization facilitators" that enhance generalization beyond the specific aspects of an intervention. These include (a) teaching behaviors that are likely to be maintained by naturally occurring contingencies, (b) training across stimuli (e.g., persons and settings) common to the natural environment, (c) fading response contingencies to approximate naturally occurring consequences, (d) reinforcing skill application to new situations, and (e) including peers in training (p. 352). Apart from these facilitators, offering intervention booster sessions at regular intervals enhances maintenance and generalization of skills (Elliott & Gresham, 1993).

Implications for Research and Practice

This review provides implications for research, program planning, and dissemination. The issues outlined in the last section explicitly point to relevant problems that are yet to be resolved and are thus a call to action.

Research

- Additional research is needed to better understand the extent to which the psychosocial competence approach can effectuate skill development in varied groups of children. Additional empirical evidence is needed to identify potential differences in the efficacy of this type of skill development approach with different sections of the child population. The goal is to determine the extent to which modifications and/or tailoring may be necessary to maximize the impact on the broadest possible range of participants, or, alternatively, specific populations.
- The nature of an individual's developmental transition from childhood to adolescence is conditioned both by the opportunities available and by the skills that he or she has accumulated. Given the increasing incidence of childhood problems across developing countries, there is a significant need for research on developmental trajectories in children who exhibit behavioral and conduct disorders. Such research can provide meaningful feedback for designing preventive interventions to avert and/or treat negative developmental trajectories and reducing risk behavior among children.

Advancement in the field of social skills training has led to an increase in the number and quality of intervention procedures and measures designed to assess skill development in subjects. Further action research around the effects of various approaches, program models, curriculum content, and competency motivation on skill enhancement of different age groups across various cultural settings will contribute to wider applicability and dissemination of social skills training.

Practice

- There is an urgent need to extend action on social skills training to schools and communities that caters to the needs of children with different abilities and special needs from various socioeconomic strata of the society, in both urban and rural settings. Disadvantaged children are most in need of such training to help them function successfully in mainstream society.
- Single-skill-targeted, single-problem-focused interventions are limited in their potential benefits (Petersen, Kennedy, & Sullivan, 1991). Further childhood problems are triggered by various personal, social, and environmental influences (WHO, 1994). A successful program will recognize that integration between personal and contextual variables focusing on generic skills with a multimethod approach will be more effective in promoting self-efficacy beliefs and well-being in children.
- Attention is needed for issues relating to the large-scale dissemination of effective skill development approaches in developing countries by nodal agencies and NGOs in a manner that preserves the scientific rigor as well as the cultural ethos and indigenous resources available in program development and implementation. Developmental psychologists have expressed concern about the lack of appropriate use of theoretical and local knowledge of mediating risk and protective factors in developing culturally sensitive program models in different social and interpersonal contexts (Nsamenang, 2008; Super & Harkness, 2008). Dawes and Donald (2000) suggested four guiding principles for interventions aimed at children at the community level: (a) combine cultural sensitivity and understanding of developmental pathways, (b) build on and promote protective factors, (c) undertake at multiple levels, and (d) promote community participation. Thus, in program implementation, developers need to recognize culture as a key determinant of developmental outcome (Nsamenang, 2008).
- Lack of longitudinal studies around the development, maintenance, and generalization of skill is a cause of concern. Such work requires resources and interagency collaboration such as school, home, and community. This issue of follow-up needs to be addressed by nodal agencies that fund the programs, researchers, and program implementers and developers.

Concluding Comments

There is a paucity of accessible published work on social development in children aged 3 to 11 years across the developing world. Although the contribution of various nodal UN agencies and NGOs is laudable in widespread implementation of social skill development programs for children, there are both strengths and weaknesses in their implementation that need to be addressed. Programs primarily target children in early childhood or from 10 years of age through adolescence. Special attention to the middle childhood years as a target population is needed, given the growing incidence of early problem behaviors among children. There have been few systematic evaluations of programs, which makes it difficult to assess the efficacy of the program for wider implementation. The low priority given to education at the national level across developing countries is evident from the poor fund allocation. There is an urgent need to reorganize funding to educational institutions to promote action research and to develop and disseminate innovative programs to foster mental health and well-being in our future generation.

The experiences of several developing countries, explored in the *The State of the World's Children* (UNICEF, 2009b) report, prove that rapid progress is possible when sound strategies, political commitment, adequate resources, and collaborative efforts are applied in support of the health and well-being of children. Children in developing countries that experience weak institutional policy, poor governance, political instability, and weak rule of law require particular attention. Often these states lack the institutional capacity and adequate resources to deliver basic social and infrastructure services to children, thus exposing them to biological and psychosocial risks that compromise their health and development.

The study of the social development of children in the developing world is mapped by the realities of childhood that is embedded and enfolded in conventional family values, the sociocultural ethos, and choices of a combination of environmental factors that result in a variety of childhoods marked by cultural diversities, social constraints, and geographical boundaries. Social developmentalists need to recognize that childhood as a variable of social analysis can never be entirely separated from other variables such as social class, gender, caste, or ethnicity. Researchers in developing countries have primarily been restricted in their orientation within national boundaries. The need of the hour demands that they explore opportunities to discuss and engage in ideas with interdisciplinary collaborations to develop indigenous frameworks for the study of childhood from a social perspective with inclusion of socioemotional outcomes into a culture of equality and reciprocity.

Acknowledgments

Suman Verma was a fellow at the Center for Advanced Study in the Behavioral Sciences (CASBS) at Stanford University at the onset of work on this chapter (2007–2008). We are grateful to the assistance in literature searches provided by Tricia Soto and Kelly Gordon from CASBS, Stanford University, and Nandini Ravi from Tata Institute of Social Sciences, Mumbai. We are also grateful to all the colleagues across countries who shared relevant work, with a special mention to Anne Petersen, Bame Nsamenang, and Silvia Koller.

References

Attig, G., & Hopkins, J. (2006). *Assessing child-friendly schools: A guide for program managers in East Asia and the Pacific.* Bangkok: UNICEF East Asia and Pacific Regional Office.

Bandura, A. (1986). *The social foundations of thought and action: A social cognitive theory.* Englewood Cliffs, NJ: Prentice Hall.

Bandura, A. (1995). Exercise of personal and collective efficacy in changing societies. In A. Bandura (Ed.), *Self-efficacy in changing societies* (pp. 1–45). Cambridge: Cambridge University Press.

Barker, G., & Fontes, M. (1996). *Review and analysis of international experience with programs targeted on at-risk youth* (LASHC Paper Series No. 5). Washington, DC: World Bank Human and Social Development Group, Latin America and the Caribbean Region.

Beyth-Marom, R., Fischhoff, B., Jacobs, M., & Furby, L. (1989). *Teaching decision making to adolescents: A critical review.* New York: Carnegie Corporation.

Bierman, K. L. (1986). Process of change during social skills training with preadolescents and its relation to treatment outcome. *Child Development, 57,* 230–240.

Bierman, K. L., & Montminy, H. P. (1993). Developmental issues in social-skills assessment and intervention with children and adolescents. *Behaviour Modification, 17,* 229–255.

Botvin, G. J. (1989). *Life skills training: Promoting health and personal development: Teacher's manual.* Ithaca, NY: Cornell University Medical College.

Botvin, G. J., Baker, E., Dusenbury, L., Botvin, E. M., & Diaz, T. (1995). Long-term follow-up results of a randomized drug abuse prevention trial in a white middle-class population. *Journal of the American Medical Association, 273,* 1106–1112.

Buczkiewicz, M., & Carnegie, R. (2001). The Ugandan life skills initiative. *Health Education, 101,* 15–22.

Chabbott, C. (2004). *UNICEF's child-friendly schools framework: A desk review.* New York: UNICEF.

Chalmers, J. B., & Townsend, M. A. R. (1990). The effects of training in social perspective taking on socially maladjusted girls. *Child Development, 61,* 178–190.

Dawes, A., & Donald, D. (2000). Improving children's chances: Developmental theory and effective interventions in community contexts. In D. Donald, A. Dawes, & J. Louw (Eds.), *Addressing childhood adversity* (pp. 1–25). Cape Town: David Philip.

Dogra, A., & Veeraraghavan, V. (1994). A study of psychological intervention of children with aggressive conduct disorder. *Indian Journal of Clinical Psychology, 21,* 28–32.

Dryfoos, J. G. (1990). *Adolescents at risk: Prevalence and prevention.* New York: Oxford University Press.

Elias, M. J. (1992). *Social decision-making and life skills development: Guidelines for middle school education.* Frederick, MD: Aspen.

Elias, M. (1994). SPS enters the computer age: Problem solving software. *Problem Solving Connection, 8,* 1–3.

Elliott, S. N., & Gresham, F. M. (1993). Social skills interventions for children. *Behaviour Modification, 17,* 287–313.

Engle, P. L., Black, M. M., Behrman, J. R., Cabral de Mello, M., Gertler, P. J., Kapiriri, L., et al. (2007). Strategies to avoid the loss of developmental potential in more than 200 million children in the developing world. *Lancet, 369,* 229–242.

Goldstein, A. P. (1981). *Psychological skill training.* New York: Pergamon Press.

Goyal, V. (2005). *Impact of life skill training on psychosocial competence of early and middle adolescents* (Ph.D. thesis). Panjab University, Chandigarh, India.

Grantham-McGregor, S., Cheung, Y., Cueto, S., Glewwe, P., Richter, L., & Strupp, B. (2007). Developmental potential in the first 5 years for children in developing countries. *Lancet, 369,* 60–70.

Hamburg, B. A. (1990). *Life skills training: Preventive interventions for young adolescents.* New York: Carnegie Council on Adolescent Development.

Heckert, K., & Baldo, M. (1998). Best practices in school AIDS/life skills education: Selected case studies (Abstract No. 13499). *International Conference on AIDS Meeting Abstracts, 12,* 185.

Jabeen, F., & Karkara, R. (2005). *Government support to parenting in Bangladesh and India. Kathmandu.* Stockholm: Save the Children Sweden.

Jenkins, K. B. (1995). The effect of a structured social skills curriculum on the self-esteem, the attitude and the social skills proficiency of seventh grade students. *Dissertation Abstracts International, 56,* 1644.

Jessor, R., & Jessor, S. L. (1977). *Problem behaviour and psychosocial development: A longitudinal study of youth.* New York: Academic Press.

Khan, A. A. (1998, November 18–19). Family life education programmes for adolescents: Case presentations. Paper presented at the National Institute for Public Cooperation and Child Development's (NIPCCD) national convention of family life education: Emerging challenges, New Delhi.

Malhotra, S. (2003). Protecting adolescents from high risk situations: Alcohol, drugs, STI/HIV/AIDS. In Bhagbanprakash (Ed.), *Adolescence and life skills* (pp. 226–243). New Delhi: Tata McGraw-Hill.

Malhotra, S., & Kohli, A. (2005). School mental health programme: Chandigarh experience. In S. Malhotra, P. Sharan, N. Gupta, A. Malhotra, & S. Gill (Eds.), *Mental disorders in children and adolescents: Need and strategies for intervention* (pp. 245–267). Delhi: CBS Publishers.

Misener, D. B. (1995). An evaluation of a secondary prevention social skills training program for children. *Dissertation Abstracts International, 55,* 3750.

Miske, S. (2003). *Proud pioneers: Improving teaching and learning in Malawi through continuous assessment.* Washington, DC: American Institute of Research.

Nsamenang, A. B. (2008). Culture and human development. *International Journal of Psychology, 43,* 73–77.

O'Donoghue, J. (1995). *Zimbabwe's AIDS action programme for schools.* Zimbabwe: UNICEF-Harare.

Petersen, A. C. (1993). Creating adolescents: The role of context and process in developmental trajectories. *Journal of Research on Adolescence, 3,* 1–18.

Petersen, A. C., Kennedy, R. E., & Sullivan, P. (1991). Coping with adolescence. In M. E. Colten & S. Gore (Eds.), *Adolescent stress: Causes and consequences* (pp. 93–110). New York: Aldine de Gruyter.

Ross, J. A. (1981). Improving adolescent decision-making skills. *Curriculum Inquiry, 11,* 279–295.

Schinke, S. P., Gordon, A. N., & Weston, R. E. (1990). Self-instruction to prevent HIV infection among African-American and Hispanic adolescents. *Journal of Consulting and Clinical Psychology, 58,* 432–436.

Schinke, S. P., Moncher, M. S., & Holden, G. W. (1989). Preventing HIV infection among black and Hispanic adolescents. *Journal of Social Work and Human Sexuality, 8,* 63–73.

Schorr, L. B., Both, B., & Copple, C. (Eds.). (1991). *Effective services for children: Report of a workshop.* Washington, DC: National Academy Press.

Sesame Workshop India. (2006). [Home page]. Retrieved from http://www.sesameworkshopindia.org

Stokes, T. F., & Osnes, P. J. (1989). An operant pursuit of generalization. *Behaviour Therapy, 20,* 337–355.

Super, C. M., & Harkness, S. (2008). Globalization and its discontents: Challenges to developmental theory and practice in Africa. *International Journal of Psychology, 43,* 107–113.

UNESCO. (N.d.). EFA flagship initiatives. Retrieved from http://www.unesco.org/education/efa/know_sharing/flagship_initiative

UNICEF. (2002). Child- and learning-friendly environment in primary schools: The school cluster approach – Ethiopia. Addis Ababa, Ethiopia: Author. Retrieved from http://www.unicef.org/evaluation/files/ethiopia2002schoolclusterapproach.doc

UNICEF. (2007). Communication Strategy for the Child-to-Child for School Readiness. Retrieved from http://www.unicef.org/evaluation/files/communication_strategy.doc

UNICEF. (2008). Basic education and gender equality. Retrieved from http://www.unicef.org/girlseducation/index_focus_lifeskills.html

UNICEF. (2009a). Policy brief. Retrieved from http://www.uniteforchildren.org

UNICEF. (2009b). The state of the world's children. Retrieved from http://www.unicef.org/sowc09/report/report.php

United Nations Development Programme. (2003). *Human development report 2003*. Retrieved from http://hdr.undp.org/en/reports/global/hdr2003/chapters/

Verma, S. (2006). Life skills for psychosocial competence in youth: Intervention initiatives in India. *ISSBD Newsletter, 30*, 7–10.

World Health Organization (WHO). (1994). *Training workshops for the development and implementation of life skills programmes*. Geneva: Division of Mental Health, World Health Organization.

World Health Organization (WHO). (2004). *Promoting mental health: Concepts, emerging evidence, practice*. Geneva: Author.

Author Index

Aalborg, A.E. 239
Abbey, B. 425
Aber, J. 313
Abou-ezzeddine, T. 518
Aboud, F. 169, 300, 302–5, 310–11, 366, 592–4
Abraham, M.M. 321, 327
Abrami, P.C. 621
Abramovitch, R. 361, 556, 588
Abrams, D. 306
Achenbach, T.M. 33
Adams, E.E. 337, 340, 347–8
Adams, F. 37
Adams, J. 215–16
Adamsons, K. 343
Adcock, R.A. 58
Adler, P. 119, 134, 380
Adolph, K.E. 7
Adrian, J.E. 539
Agatson, P.W. 188
Aguiar, A. 46
Ahadi, S. 233, 253, 444
Ahnert, L. 253
Ainsworth, M.D.S. 11, 266, 319–23
Akkermans, W. 377–8
Aksan, N. 10, 14, 230, 234, 240, 337, 340, 347–8
Albano, A.D. 387
Alegria, M. 163

Alexander, G.E. 55
Alexander, G.M. 282
Alexander, K.L. 606
Alexander, S. 359
Alexandra, B.S. 347
Alisat, S. 557
Allen, J. 271
Allen, L. 313
Allen, M.D. 615
Allen, V.L. 592–3
Allman, J.M. 75
Alpert, R. 8
Alsaker, F. 188, 519
Altman, I. 214
Alva, S. 170
Alvarez, A.N. 171
Alwater, J.B. 462
Amato, M. 594
Amichai-Hamburger, Y. 557
Amin, N. 215
Ammaniti, M. 323, 325
Ananiadou, K. 522
Anderson, A.K. 45
Anderson, C.A. 459, 492, 500–1, 510
Anderson, D.R. 557
Anderson, G.T. 398, 461
Anderson, K.J. 291
Anderson, M.A. 484
Andersson, K. 439

Andreasen, G. 596
Angelillo, C. 102–4, 466
Anker, A.L. 153
Annesi, J.J. 457
Apostoleris, N.H. 482
Aquan-Assee, J. 361
Arbeau, K.A. 232, 438, 440
Archer, J. 481, 482, 492, 494, 495
Ardilla-Rey, A. 580
Ariel, S. 146
Ariès, P. 82, 92–3
Armer, M. 149, 235–6, 253, 438, 440
Armony, J.L. 45
Armstrong, J.M. 193–4, 497
Arnett, J.J. 3, 101
Arnold, D.H. 12, 606, 619–20
Arnold, E.H. 12
Arnold, M.B. 47
Aronfreed, J. 567
Arsenault, L. 33, 35–8, 273–4
Arsenio, W.F. 424
Arsiwalla, D.D. 340, 343–4, 347
Artz, S. 495
Asai, M. 152
Asbury, K. 40
Ascione, F.R. 557
Asencio, M. 164–5
Asendorpf, J.B. 142, 149, 435–6, 438, 442

The Wiley-Blackwell Handbook of Childhood Social Development, Second Edition, edited by Peter K. Smith and Craig H. Hart
© 2011 by Blackwell Publishing Ltd

Chiu, C. 174
Cho, G.E. 152
Chodorow, N. 124
Choi, N. 444
Chou, J. 167
Chow, T.W. 55, 57
Christopher, F.S. 554
Christopher, J.S. 442
Christopoulos, C. 520
Chuang, Y.L. 627
Chung, H. 167
Chung, J. 143, 154, 445
Chung, K.M. 637
Chung, O.B. 344
Chung, T. 399–400
Churchill, W.S. 207
Cicirelli, V.O. 359
Cillessen, A.H.N. 196, 375–87, 394–6, 400, 402–8, 445, 497, 516, 518
Clancy, P.M. 423
Clark, C. 213
Clark, K.B. 301, 592–3
Clark, M.K. 301
Clark, M.P. 592–3
Clark, M.S. 550
Clark, N.M. 636–7
Clark-Carter, D. 538
Clarke, S. 639
Clary, E.G. 558
Clatfelter, D. 422
Clausen, J. 119
Clausen, J.A. 9, 14
Clemente, R.A. 539
Clements, R. 210
Clements, W. 537
Clements, W.A. 72
Clifford, R.M. 247, 250
Closson, L.M. 232, 380–1, 383, 440
Clyman, R.B. 550
Coates, B. 8
Cohen, A.D. 551
Cohen, D. 100
Cohen, J. 494
Cohen, L. 552, 555
Cohen, R. 367, 403
Cohen-Kettenis, P.T. 287
Cohn, D. 273
Cohn, J.F. 11, 14
Coie, J.D. 14, 182–4, 187, 192, 196–8, 376–80, 394, 398, 403, 424–5, 498, 520, 606
Colbourne, K.A. 499
Colburne, K. 282
Colby, A. 103
Cole, A. 325
Cole, M. 101
Cole, P. 51, 235, 421
Cole, P.M. 145, 148, 422

Coleman, C. 182, 186–7, 191, 606
Colker, L.J. 617
Collaer, M.L. 281
Colletti, C.J.M. 343, 347
Collins, M.L. 265, 270
Collins, P.F. 47, 55–6
Collins, W.A. 9, 12, 14–15, 73, 273, 328, 337, 340–1, 344, 347
Coltrane, S. 169
Colunga, E. 46
Colvin, C.M. 500
Colwell, M.J. 346–7, 457, 463
Comings, D.E. 552
Compas, B. 10
Condron, D.J. 366
Conger, R.D. 339, 344–5, 349
Connell, R.W. 588
Connelly, J.B. 456, 460
Connolly, J. 396
Connolly, P. 592
Connor, J.J. 343
Connor, R.T. 628, 630–1
Conroy, M.A. 637
Conry-Murray, C. 580
Contreras, H. 164
Contreras, J.M. 325–8
Conway, G.S. 288–9
Conzen, K.N. 173
Cook, K.V. 290
Cook, M.C. 421
Cook, W.L. 340, 343–4
Coolahan, K. 397
Cooley, C.H. 5, 403
Cooper, C.R. 153
Cooper, S. 234
Cooper Marcus, C. 214
Cooperman, G. 424
Coplan, R.J. 149, 184–5, 231, 232, 234–5, 253, 342, 344, 346–7, 435–6, 437–40, 442–3, 445
Copple, C. 656
Coppotelli, H. 14, 377
Corbishley, P. 209, 214
Corby, B.C. 325
Corley, R.P. 34, 35
Correa-Chavez, M. 104
Corsaro, W.A. 103–5, 126, 128–9, 143, 154
Corter, C. 361, 556
Cortes, R. 610, 618
Cortina, K. 421
Cosmides, L. 64, 65
Costa, R.M. 56
Costall, A. 541, 542
Costin, S.E. 426
Cote, S. 273–4
Coté, S.M. 493–4, 498–9, 560
Couchoud, E.A. 420, 421, 423–5
Council of Economic Advisors 162

Cowan, C.P. 344
Cowan, N. 50
Cowan, P. 571
Cowan, P.A. 344
Cowie, H. 484, 516
Cox, M.J. 231, 337, 339, 343, 607
Coyne, S.M. 482, 492, 495–6, 501
Craig, I.W. 35, 497
Craig, W. 516, 521
Craig, W.M. 200, 512
Cravens, H. 3
Crawford, D. 457
Crawford, L. 275
Crick, N.R. 75, 267, 377, 404, 492–7, 500, 511, 514, 557
Criss, M.M. 271–3, 343
Crnic, K. 349
Crockenberg, S. 257
Croft, C. 420
Crombie, G. 284
Crone, D.A. 638–9
Crook, C. 282
Crosnoe, R. 172
Cross, D. 71, 533
Cross, W. 169
Crouter, A. 275
Crowe, E. 72, 539, 540
Crowhurst Lennard, S.H. 210–11, 213, 215
Crowson, M. 634
Crump, A. 517
Cryer, D. 247, 250
Crystal, D.S. 309, 574
Cuckle, P. 632
Cueto, S. 646
Cumberland, A. 330, 425, 498
Cummings, E.M. 325, 339, 345, 347–9, 420, 498–9
Cummings, J.L. 55, 57
Cummins, D.D. 72, 74
Cunningham, W. 301
Curran, J.M. 460
Curry, J.C. 606
Curtner-Smith, M. 514, 522
Cushing, L.S. 636–7
Cutting, A.L. 423, 426, 537–40, 543
Cyphers, L. 283
Cyr, C. 325

Dack, L.A. 539–41
Dadds, M.R. 238, 561
Dahinten, V.S. 349
Daigle, L.E. 36
Dale, N. 360
Daly, K. 343
Daly, M. 65, 74–6
Daly, T. 637
Damasio, H. 46
Damast, A. 265

Subject Index

The Wiley-Blackwell Handbook of Childhood Social Development, Second Edition, edited by Peter K. Smith and Craig H. Hart
© 2011 by Blackwell Publishing Ltd

Laura Spelman Rockfeller Memorial 7
learning disability and social competence development
    630–1
  severe conditions 632–3
learning mechanisms 655–6
  early studies 7–8
  interaction of genetic and environmental factors 66–7
  reward anticipation and feedback systems 54–7
  and synaptic plasticity 58
"life chances" (Weber) 120
life skills education programs, in developing countries
    650–1
likeability studies 380
  see also group acceptance; popularity
linkage studies 32
locomotor play 456–7
longitudinal studies 14–15

marital conflict, and attachment theory 326
maternal caregiving 342
  and attachment theory 325
  insensitive 35
media influences, violence and aggression 458–9, 500–1
metaparenting 341
Michael and Susan Dell Foundation 652–3
migration
  cultural implications and brokering 111–12, 168–9,
    170
  demographic changes and population growth (US)
    162–3
  implications for cultural values 111–12
  implications for family structures 163–6
  language acquisition 167–8
  language brokering 170
  loss of homeland/caregivers 166–7
  new cultural norms 168–9
  research directions and limitations 172–5
  racial prejudice and discrimination 170–1
  social development challenges 166–72
  socialization impact of early childcare programs 246–59
  socioeconomic difficulties 171–2
  see also ethnicity
mirror neuron systems (MNS) 559
mobile phone use, bullying 511
models of child/environment relationships 192–7
  additive models 192–3
  mediator models 194–5
  moderator models 193–4
  provisions and prospects 195–7
  research directions and applications 197–9
models of cultural and developmental interfaces in
    childcare 247–8
models of emotion regulation 416–17
models of parent–child relationships 338–41
  bidirectionality models 340
  child effects model 340
  domains 341
  gender related models 341
  metaparenting model 341

social relations model 340
  style vs. process model 340–1
  systems-based 338–9
models of social competence 395–6
money matters, children's understanding of 584–6
monoamine oxidase A (MAOA) gene studies 34–5, 497
moral behavior
  early studies 7
  see also social and moral reasoning
mother–child relations
  and attachment theory 267
  involvement in play 268–9
motivation and desire 47–9, 51–2, 58–60
  basic neurobiology 53–8
  feedback action loops 48, 49, 54, 56–8
  motivation–action interface 54–5
motor cortex, and concept formation 55
Multidimensional Treatment Foster Care (MTFC) 502

name calling 251
NAS *see* nucleus accumbens (NAS)
national identity and nationalism 594–7
National Institute of Child Health and Human
    Development Early Child Care Research Network
    (NICHD ECCRN) 247, 252, 254, 257, 269, 324
natural selection 65
nature–nurture debate 66
  see also behavioral genetics; gene–environment
    interactions
neighborhood risk
  and later delinquency 275
  and life stressors 274–5
neurobiology
  of antisocial behavior, influence of genes 34
  of concept formations 53–7
  of prosocial behaviors 559–60
NGOs *see* nongovernment agencies (NGOs)
nongovernment agencies (NGOs), and social skills
    development programs 649–53
nucleus accumbens (NAS) 54–5, 56–7

object boundaries 46
observational studies, early methodologies 13–14
OFC *see* orbitofrontal cortex (OFC)
One Boy's Day (Barker and Wright) 212–13
ontogenetic adaptations 69
operant learning 8
opportunity education 108–9
orbitofrontal cortex (OFC) 55
organizations, as social structures 121

Parent Management Training programs 502
parent–child attachments 266–7, 319–31
  definitions and patterns 319–20
  factors that promote differences in attachments 324–7
  influence on social development 327–9
  measurement challenges 322–3
  normative changes in early and middle childhood
    320–2